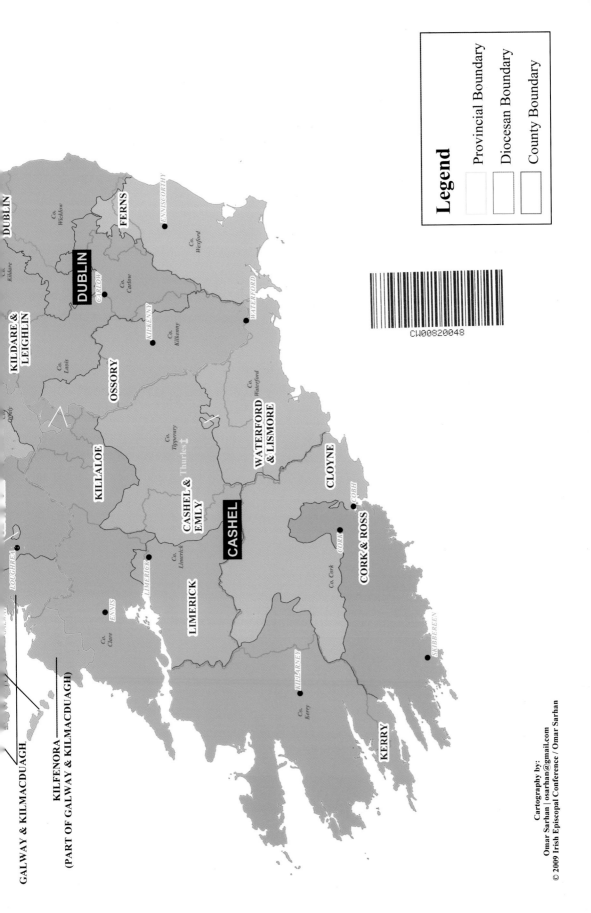

Legend

- Provincial Boundary
- Diocesan Boundary
- County Boundary

DUBLIN

Co. Wicklow

FERNS

ENNISCORTHY

Co. Wexford

Co. Kildare

DUBLIN

CARLOW

Co. Carlow

KILDARE & LEIGHLIN

WATERFORD

KILKENNY

Co. Laois

OSSORY

Co. Kilkenny

Co. Offaly

Co. Waterford

WATERFORD & LISMORE

Co. Tipperary

Thurles

KILLALOE

CASHEL & EMLY

CLOYNE

CASHEL

COBH

LOUGHREA

Co. Limerick

CORK

CORK & ROSS

LIMERICK

ENNIS

Co. Clare

Co. Cork

LIMERICK

SKIBBEREEN

KILLARNEY

GALWAY & KILMACDUAGH

Co. Kerry

KILFENORA
(PART OF GALWAY & KILMACDUAGH)

KERRY

CW00820048

Cartography by:
Omar Sarhan | osarhan@gmail.com
© 2009 Irish Episcopal Conference / Omar Sarhan

Redemptorist Communications
    St. Joseph's Monastery
    St. Alphonsus Road
    Dundalk   A91 F3FC

00-353 42 933 4042   Deirbhíle/Ann

Sacred Heart Messenger
    Account 7817   Accounts desk. Frances 087 654 04 08

00-353-1 6767 491

Glencairn Eucharist Bread   Ref. NIOMAGH
    St. Mary's Abbey
    Glencairn - Lismore
    Co. Waterford

00-353-58 561 68

IRISH CATHOLIC DIRECTORY 2023

FRANCIS
BISHOP OF ROME
Vicar of Jesus Christ

Successor of the Prince of the Apostles, Supreme Pontiff of the Universal Church, Primate of Italy, Archbishop and Metropolitan of the Roman Province, Sovereign of the State of the Vatican City.

Servant of the Servants of God, Jorge Mario Bergoglio, born in Buenos Aires, Argentina, on 17 December 1936; ordained priest on 13 December 1969. From 1973 to 1979 he was Argentina's Provincial superior of the Society of Jesus. He was ordained Auxiliary Bishop of Buenos Aires on 27 June 1992; became Archbishop of Buenos Aires in 1998 and created cardinal on 21 February 2001. He was elected pope on 13 March 2013 and inaugurated on 19 March 2013.

IRISH CATHOLIC DIRECTORY 2023

PUBLISHED BY AUTHORITY
FOR THE HIERARCHY OF IRELAND

THE OFFICIAL DIRECTORY OF THE IRISH CATHOLIC CHURCH

This publication
has been supported
by the generous
sponsorship
of

VERITAS

Published for the Hierarchy by
Veritas Publications
7–8 Lower Abbey Street
Dublin 1
Ireland
publications@veritas.ie
www.veritas.ie

The publishers are not responsible for any
errors or omissions.

ISBN 978 1 80097 049 6

Cover design: Colette Dower, Veritas Publications
Design & Typesetting: Colette Dower, Veritas Publications
Printed in Ireland by W & G Baird, Antrim

*Veritas books are printed on paper made from the wood pulp of managed forests.
For every tree felled, at least one tree is planted, thereby renewing natural resources.*

PREFACE

This is the thirty-third edition of the *Irish Catholic Directory*. Information for this edition was collected between August 2022 and November 2022. In general, all information comes from the organisation or community concerned.

Veritas has made every effort to ensure the accuracy and completeness of the information in the *Directory*. However, this information can only be as good as that supplied to us.

We would like to express our gratitude to all the bishops, diocesan secretaries, priests, brothers, sisters and lay people who have over the years supplied information, answered queries, chased details and checked proofs.

We are also indebted to the advertisers and sponsors, without whose support this publication would not be possible.

Finally, it may be appropriate to remind readers that the *Directory* is simply an orderly listing of personnel in the Church and related organisations. Our task is to make this listing as easy to use as possible. The *Directory* is not a statement of Church policy, nor an expression of precedence, and should not be taken as such.

CONTENTS

ALL IRELAND STD DIALLING .

All STD numbers in this Directory are listed with both the number and the local area code.

Callers from the Irish Republic to Northern Ireland simply **need to dial 048 followed by the 8-digit local number.**

2022 REVIEW OF PASTORAL ACTIVITIES
OF IRISH EPISCOPAL CONFERENCE
(for more information see www.catholicbishops.ie)

JANUARY

In his New Year's Message for 2022, Primate of All Ireland Archbishop Eamon Martin of Armagh spoke of his hope for young people as future leaders, stating that 'Governments should see the funding of education and training of our young people not as an expenditure, but as an investment.'

In his World Day of Peace homily, Primate of Ireland Archbishop Dermot Farrell of Dublin spoke of the ongoing global struggle against Covid-19. He said, 'It is our faith, our living faith, that links us to the millions of people who cannot receive a vaccine.'

On 9 January, Archbishop Francis Duffy was installed as Archbishop of Tuam. During his homily, Archbishop Duffy preached, 'I come here knowing very few and so I really look forward to getting to know the priests, religious and parishioners as I move around and meet a great variety of people.' At the installation, Archbishop Michael Neary, Archbishop Emeritus of Tuam, said, 'I thank you that over fifty years as a priest, thirty years as a Bishop and twenty-seven years as your Archbishop you have prayed for me, befriended me, supported and encouraged me.'

On 14 January, in the Diocese of Ardagh & Clonmacnois, and arising from the vacancy caused by the appointment of Archbishop Duffy as Archbishop of Tuam, the College of Consultors elected Father Tom Healy, Parish Priest of Edgeworthstown, Co Longford, as Diocesan Administrator of Ardagh & Clonmacnoise.

On 18 January, the Funeral Mass of teacher Ms Ashling Murphy took place in Mount Bolus, Co Offaly. This terrible murder shocked everyone on the island, and beyond. Speaking at the Mass, Bishop Tom Deenihan of Meath said, 'A depraved act of violence which deprived a kind, talented, loved and admired young woman of her life has since united the country in grief and support.'

On 24 January, Archbishop Eamon Martin welcomed the World Communications Day message of Pope Francis on the theme of 'Listening with the ear of the heart'. He said, 'Communion, in fact, is not the result of strategies and programmes, but is built in mutual listening between brothers and sisters.'

On 27 January, Bishop Denis Nulty, Bishop of Kildare & Leighlin, and Bishop Pat Storey, Church of Ireland Bishop of Meath & Kildare, welcomed the Government announcement of an additional bank holiday to take place around Saint Brigid's Day.

On 28 January, Bishop Donal McKeown of Derry celebrated the 50th anniversary Mass of Remembrance for the victims of Bloody Sunday in Saint Mary's Church, Creggan. During his homily, Bishop McKeown said, 'It takes a wise heart to look at the rubble of what has been shattered in the past and to make it into a foundation for the future.'

FEBRUARY

On 5 February, Archbishop Farrell celebrated Mass for the Day of Consecrated Life 2022 at the Redemptoristine Monastery, Iona Road, Dublin. During his homily, he said, 'Today, I thank God for the wisdom and experience, the generosity and prayer, of the women and men whom the Lord has called to consecrate their lives in love of Him and in the service of their sisters and brothers.'

On 7 February, Bishop Michael Router, Auxiliary Bishop of Armagh, welcomed Pope Francis' message for World Day of the Sick. Bishop Router said, 'Pope Francis tells us that "Mercy is God's name par excellence". It is not something fleeting or sentimental but ever-present and active, combining strength and tenderness.'

On 11 February, it was announced that Pope Francis accepted the retirement request of Bishop Brendan Kelly as Bishop of Galway, Kilmacduagh & Apostolic Administrator of Kilfenora, and appointed Bishop Michael Duignan, Bishop of Clonfert, to minister simultaneously as Bishop of Galway, Kilmacduagh & Apostolic Administrator of Kilfenora *in persona episcopi*. Paying tribute to Bishop Kelly on his retirement, Archbishop Eamon Martin said, 'The Bishops' Conference has benefited greatly from Bishop Kelly's wisdom and expertise in the field of education, liturgy, and especially as one of our key advisors on the Irish language.'

On 12 February, Archbishop Martin laid the foundation stone for the Redemptoris Mater Seminary extension in Dundalk. Speaking at the ceremony, Archbishop Martin said 'I am hopeful that our young men who are being formed here in Dundalk will be able to bring that missionary spirit into their priesthood within the Archdiocese and beyond.'

On 14 February, Bishop Nulty celebrated Mass at the Shrine of Saint Valentine in Whitefriar Street, Dublin, for the Blessing of the Rings ceremony for a number of soon-to-be-married engaged couples. During the ceremony, Bishop Nulty said, 'May the heart of Saint Valentine pulsate for all loving couples.'

On 20 February, Archbishop Farrell celebrated the Ordination Mass for Father Joseph Keegan. During his homily, the Archbishop said, 'The ordination of a priest is one of the high points in the life of a Diocese.'

On 24 February, the Bishops' Council for Justice and Peace prayed for Ukraine following the Russian invasion which took place that day. Chair of the CJP, Bishop Alan McGuckian SJ stated, 'This is the first invasion in Europe since 1945. Indeed, until a few weeks ago it seemed unthinkable that any country would be invaded by another. It makes us realise how much we take peace for granted.'

Ahead of Temperance Sunday on 27 February, the Irish Bishops' Drugs Initiative launched the first episode of the 'Leave Your Mark Podcast' series on addiction, featuring 2002 All-Ireland winner Oisín McConville and 2021 All-Ireland winner Conn Kilpatrick. IBDI vice-chair Bishop Router said, 'This series will help to

highlight the problems that exist and how those who have struggled with addiction have overcome their challenges.'

MARCH

On 1 March, Archbishop Martin echoed the call of Pope Francis for prayer and fasting on Ash Wednesday for peace in Ukraine. He said, 'Our Lenten journey this year begins as we watch the distressing and frightening scenes from Ukraine. Our hearts and prayers go out to the people of Ukraine. We can never take peace for granted.'

On 9 March, the Spring 2022 General Meeting of the Irish Catholic Bishops' Conference in Maynooth discussed: Praying for peace in Ukraine; Synodal Pathway; New Lay Ministries of Lector, Acolyte and Catechist; Return to full public worship; Trócaire's Lenten appeal; Safeguarding; Reconfiguration of patronage at primary-school level; Lent and preparation for Holy Week and Easter; and International Women's Day.

On 11 March, Archbishop Martin commented on the Sir Anthony Hart report on historical institutional abuse. He said, 'The courage, perseverance and determination of survivors has helped bring to light the truth about what happened in the past and ensure that lessons are learned so that these awful things are prevented from happening again.'

On 17 March, Bishop Paul Dempsey of Achonry delivered a message of support for Irish Emigrants. He said, 'On Saint Patrick's Day we remember all Irish people who had to leave home to find a new life in a different land.'

On 25 March, Archbishop Farrell preached the homily during a prayer service for peace in Ukraine, and dedication of Russia and Ukraine to the Immaculate Heart of Mary, in the Church of the Sacred Heart, Donnybrook. He said, 'We make this solemn act of consecration of humanity, and especially of Russia and Ukraine to the Immaculate Heart of Mary, so that she, the Queen of Peace, may inspire us all to be instruments of peace for the world.'

On 28 March, Bishop Nulty paid tribute to the late Bishop James Moriarty RIP. He said, 'All of us will remember Bishop Jim as a kind and humble pastor as we hold his family and many friends in our prayers these days.' Bishop Moriarty's Funeral Mass took place on 30 March in the Cathedral of the Assumption, Carlow, Diocese of Kildare & Leighlin.

APRIL

On 5 April, Bishop McGuckian launched the new Pastoral Plan for the Diocese of Raphoe, which will run until 2024. He said, 'Our Plan proposes a renewal of faith formation across the ages with an emphasis on children and young adults.'

On 10 April, Archbishop Martin celebrated the Mass for the Disappeared in Saint Patrick's Cathedral, Armagh. During the homily the Archbishop said, 'I appeal again to the conscience of anyone who can help with these cases so that the agonising wait of their families can be shortened, and those who remain hidden can at last have a Christian burial.'

On 13 April, the Irish Church Leaders' Group, which consists of Archbishop Eamon Martin, Church of Ireland Archbishop John McDowell of Armagh, The Right Reverend Dr David Bruce, The Reverend Dr Sahr Yambasu, and The Right Reverend Andrew Forster, issued a joint Easter message. They said, 'We stand united as Church Leaders in Ireland, with a message of support for the people of Ukraine. As we did when faced with conflict here in our own land, we call for people to pray for peace, to reach out to support the injured and bereaved, and to do all that they can to help and support the victims of unnecessary suffering.'

The same day, Bishop Fintan Monahan of Killaloe celebrated the Chrism Mass in the Cathedral of Saints Peter and Paul, Ennis, during which he announced the commissioning of 24 new lay ministers for the diocese. During his homily, the Bishop said, 'What we are doing, in offering ourselves for ministry in response to a call is not bringing ourselves – but Jesus Christ to those to whom we minister.'

On 14 April, the Archbishops of Armagh and Dublin thanked parishioners for their extraordinary generosity in raising €3.25m in support of the Ukrainian crisis.

On 16 April, Bishop Kevin Doran of Elphin celebrated the Easter Vigil Mass in the Cathedral of the Immaculate Conception, Sligo. During his homily, the Bishop of Elphin said, 'People sometimes speak about Christianity as if it were simply a moral code. It is much more than that. It is a relationship.'

On 22 April, Bishop Brendan Leahy of Limerick presented John Paul II Awards to 50 young people across the diocese. He said, 'The work these young people have been doing in their local areas is tremendous and brings such richness to their parishes, their local communities and to themselves.'

On 24 April, Bishop Monahan celebrated the Ordination Mass of Father Antun Pasalic in the Cathedral of Saint Peter and Paul, Ennis. He said, 'Antun, we all rejoice with you and your family today as you begin a life of commitment to the gospel of Christ.'

On 28 April, the Catholic Bishops of Northern Ireland issued a pastoral reflection, Make Your Voices Heard, on the upcoming NI Assembly Elections on 5 May, addressing: Importance of voting; Poverty in society; Rights and dignity of unborn children; Effectively responding to refugees fleeing war in Ukraine; Committing to safeguarding creation and sustaining our environment; Respect for religious freedom and faith in the public square including for Catholic and other faith-based schools; and political stability serving the common good.

On 30 April, the Funeral Mass of Canon Pat McHugh RIP took place in Saint Mary's Church, Pettigo, Co Donegal. In his homily, Bishop Larry Duffy of Clogher said, 'Last Autumn I was so grateful to Father Pat for taking on Director of the Synodal Pathway. He had a vision and plans for Clogher going forward. God had other plans and now we pray for his guidance in heaven.'

MAY

On 1 May, the Installation Mass for Bishop Michael Duignan of Clonfert as Bishop of Galway, Kilmacduagh & Apostolic Administrator of Kilfenora, took place in the Cathedral of Our Lady Assumed into Heaven and Saint Nicholas, Galway. During the Mass, the retiring Bishop Brendan Kelly thanked the people of the diocese, 'From my first day as a priest to today you have been my mentors, my teachers. You have revealed the face of God to me, the compassion of Jesus Christ.' During his homily at the Mass, Bishop Duignan said, 'I thank you, the priests and people of the Diocese of Galway, Kilmacduagh & Kilfenora for your generous welcome. I thank you for receiving me and accepting me as a travelling companion on the journey of life.'

On 4 May, Bishop Ger Nash of Ferns celebrated the Annual 1916 Commemoration Requiem Mass in Dublin at the Church of the Sacred Heart – the church for the Defence Forces – the site of burial of the executed leaders of 1916. During his homily he said, 'In the words of today's Gospel, the 1916 leaders were the grain of wheat which produced a great harvest.'

On 6 May, Bishop Alphonsus Cullinan of Waterford & Lismore welcomed Pope Francis' message for Vocations Sunday, and said, 'I encourage the faithful to read the Holy Father's message and to pray for vocations, synodality and harmony in our Church.'

On 10 May, Bishop Nulty welcomed Pope Francis' message for the World Day for Grandparents and the Elderly. He said, 'I warmly welcome Pope Francis' message encouraging the elderly to persevere in hope and to embrace their great power to transform the world through prayer and a revolution of tenderness.'

On Vocations Sunday, 8 May, Bishop William Crean of Cloyne celebrated Mass in Knock Shrine in the Archdiocese of Tuam. During his homily he said, 'If we dismiss our past as a source of shame and embarrassment only, we risk depriving a new generation of connection with deep wells of spirituality.'

On 20 May, the Council for Life launched a nine-day Novena of Prayer for Life. Bishop Doran said, 'I hope the Pray for Life Novena will help people to celebrate and protect the gift of life and to be more conscious of the practical support that they can offer to women for whom pregnancy is experienced as a crisis.'

On 22 May, ahead of *Laudato Si'* week, Bishop Martin Hayes of Kilmore encouraged parishes to get involved in *Laudato Si'* initiatives and said, 'We cannot afford to be slow learners on the vital issue of sustaining creation.'

On 24 May, Archbishop Martin welcomed Pope Francis' World Communications Day message on the theme of listening. He said, 'The Holy Father is inviting all of us to reflect on how listening – which is both sincere and deep – can have a profound and positive effect on every part of our lives, in our interaction with others, and on how we pray.'

On 31 May, the Shrine of Our Lady of Clonfert was formally recognised as a Diocesan Marian Shrine. Bishop Duignan said, 'We look forward to the development of the Shrine as a fount of rich spiritual sustenance for future generations.'

JUNE
On 3 June, Archbishop Martin issued a statement stating Pentecost Sunday would mark a Day of Prayer in thanksgiving of the diocesan phase of the Universal Synod. 'This diocesan phase of the Synodal Pathway represents the largest consultation ever to take place in the Catholic Church.'

On 3 June, Bishop Monahan prayed for safety on our roads over the June holiday weekend ahead of the blessing of the roads ceremony.

On 15 June, the Summer General Meeting of the Irish Catholic Bishops Conference concluded in Maynooth. The main topics for discussion were: National Pre-Synodal Assembly to take place in Athlone this Saturday, 18 June; Bishops' appreciation for €4.3m collected for the people of Ukraine and discuss plight of refugees in Ireland; Child safeguarding; Northern Ireland; 10th World Meeting of Families in Rome; World Day for Grandparents and the Elderly; and Trócaire – one person to die from hunger every 48 seconds in the Horn of Africa.

On 18 June, the National Pre-Synodal Pathway Assembly took place in Athlone which concluded with a prayer walk at the sixth century monastic site of Clonmacnoise. During the Assembly, chair of the Steering Committee of the Synodal Pathway, Dr Nicola Brady, said, 'Our pre-synodal Assembly represents an important moment in the life of the Church. As a Church we take great encouragement from the number of people who have taken part in this listening process so far, and we are deeply grateful to all those who gave generously of their time to make this possible.'

On 22 June, the 10th World Meeting of Families took place in Rome on the theme 'Family love: a vocation and a path to holiness.' The delegation from Ireland that attended included family members as well as the President of the Bishops' Conference, Archbishop Martin, and the chair of the Council for Marriage and the Family, Bishop Nulty.

On 21 June, Archbishop Neary delivered a homily at the Pilgrimage

of Eucharistic Adorers in Knock stating, 'On this Corpus Christi weekend I welcome all present in the Basilica in Knock today, those who join us on line and especially all who are celebrating the National Pilgrimage of Eucharistic Adorers.'

JULY
In his homily during Mass at Saint Saviour's Church, Dublin, ahead of the 2022 Rally for Life, Archbishop Martin spoke on the pro-life mission saying, 'We will continue to seek dialogue about how a respectful and life-supporting environment can be created for every person in Ireland, at every stage and in every state of life.'

On 18 July, Bishop Nulty, chair of the Bishops' Council for Marriage and the Family, invited parishes to reach out to grandparents and the elderly on this the second World Day for Grandparents and the Elderly, which was celebrated around the world Sunday 24 July.

In his homily at the annual Mass and investiture of the Equestrian Order of the Holy Sepulchre of Jerusalem in Saint Patrick's College Chapel, Maynooth, Archbishop Martin spoke on the synthesis document for the Church's Synodal Pathway in Ireland prepared as a contribution to the next Synod of Bishops in Rome in October 2023.

On 23 July, Archbishop Kieran O'Reilly SMA of Cashel & Emly, published a pastoral letter to the people of the Archdiocese on the renewal and the future of Church life in Cashel & Emly.

On 28 July, Bishop Monahan prayed for safety on our roads over the August holiday weekend and for the protection of all road users during Mass which he celebrated on the summit of Croagh Patrick as part of the annual national Reek Sunday pilgrimage.

On 31 July, Bishop Noël Treanor of Down & Connor ordained Father John O'Laverty to the priesthood.

The same day, Archbishop Duffy celebrated Reek Sunday Mass in Saint Mary's Church, Westport, Co Mayo, as part of the Croagh Patrick pilgrimage.

AUGUST
On 2 August, Bishop Fintan Gavin of Cork & Ross published the pastoral letter: Transforming parishes in Cork & Ross into mission-centred faith communities.

Allianz ⓘ

On 21 August, the Knock National Novena returned to its traditional format for the first time since the Covid-19 pandemic. Bishops welcomed the publication of the National Synthesis document for the Irish Synodal Pathway. Among the speakers at the Knock Novena were Dr Nicola Brady, Archbishop Duffy, Bishop Doran and Bishop Router who also concelebrated Mass.

On 20 August, Archbishop Martin paid tribute to Bishop Séamus Freeman RIP, Bishop Emeritus of Ossory. He said, 'Bishop Freeman was a committed member of the Episcopal Conference for nine years, bringing to our discussions many insights from his previous experience as a religious in the Pallotine Order and as a parish priest.'

On 23 August, Ms Julieann Moran was appointed as the new General Secretary of the Synodal Pathway in Ireland.

On 25 August, Bishop Duffy preached a homily during Mass in the Basilica of Our Lady, Queen of Ireland, Knock, as part of the Clogher Pilgrimage to Knock.

The same day, the leaders of the four main churches in Ireland released a statement calling for cost of living crisis action. The Church Leaders' Group said, 'We want to join our voices with many others, calling for more practical support to be delivered urgently through direct government initiatives in both jurisdictions and also via grassroots charity and community partnerships.'

On 28 August, Archbishop Martin celebrated Mass in Saint Patrick's Cathedral, Armagh, to mark the beginning of the Season of Creation 2022, which ran from September 1 until 4 October. During his homily, the Archbishop said, 'God is calling us today, more than ever, to be caring stewards of creation, to protect and nourish our planet and its resources, and not to selfishly waste them or ruthlessly and excessively exploit and destroy them.'

SEPTEMBER
On 2 September, the Funeral Mass of Joseph Sebastian and Reuven Simon was celebrated in Saint Mary's Church, Ardmore Parish, Diocese of Derry, at which Bishop McKeown of Derry stated, 'These two boys were a huge gift to all of us in their life. Today we hand them back, so reluctantly, to the strong hands of the God who made them in love.'

On 8 September, Her Majesty Queen Elizabeth II passed away. Archbishop Martin paid tribute to the late Queen, 'I pray that Queen Elizabeth's faith in the Risen Lord will be of comfort to many people, and especially to her grieving family at this sad time.'

On 14 September, the Catholic Bishops joined in a Day of Prayer for Ukraine which took place throughout Europe. Bishop Kenneth Nowakowski, Apostolic visitator for Ukrainians Resident in Ireland and Northern Ireland, published a message for Peace in Ukraine.

On 18 September, the Catholic and Church of Ireland communities of Cavan came together in a prayer ritual as Bishop Hayes and Canon Mark Lidwell facilitated a Season of Creation ceremony in the Cathedral of Saint Patrick and Saint Felim, Cavan.

On 19 September, Bishop Gavin celebrated the Ordination Mass in Cork & Ross of Father Ronan Sheehan, the current youngest priest in Ireland.

On 22 September, Archbishop Farrell delivered a homily during Mass at Dublin City University's Saint Patrick's Campus for the opening of the Academic Year.

On 27 September, the Northern Catholic Bishops published a statement on the current economic crisis for the Feast of Saint Vincent de Paul. Bishops said, 'For the poorest in our society, this is an emergency, not a crisis. We call on everyone, from public representatives to parishioners in our parishes, to come together in a spirit of solidarity and active concern for those who are in need among us at this time.'

On 28 September, it was announced that ten seminarians had begun their 2022-2023 academic programme and priestly formation for Irish dioceses and that there are 56 seminarians currently studying for the priesthood for dioceses.

On 30 September, Pope Francis appointed Ms Teresa Devlin, chief executive of the National Board for Safeguarding Children in the Catholic Church in Ireland, to the Pontifical Commission for the Protection of Minors.

OCTOBER
On Day for Life Sunday, 2 October, Bishop Doran celebrated Mass in the Cathedral of the Immaculate Conception, Sligo. During his homily he said, 'It is important that we don't forget the lessons of the recent pandemic, when older people, especially those in nursing homes, were exposed to greater risk, because they were not adequately factored into public policy.'

On 4 October, Irish bishops welcomed Pope Francis' message to world leaders ahead of COP27 urging more ambition to tackle the climate crisis. Bishops said, 'No one in Ireland should suffer from fuel poverty this Winter.'

On 5 October, the Autumn 2022 General Meeting of the Bishops' Conference concluded in Maynooth. The main talking points at the meeting were: Cost of living crisis; support for refugees from Ukraine and asylum seekers; Safeguarding; Travellers' mental health and concern about unused exchequer resources; Synodal Pathway; World Mission Sunday on 23 October; Hunger crisis in the Horn and East Africa; 60th anniversary of the Second Vatican Ecumenical Council (1962–1965); and reflecting on the Centenary of the Legion of Mary.

On 8 October, Bishop McGuckian visited the site of the Creeslough tragedy to pray with the heartbroken families of the victims. He said, 'Yesterday was the darkest day in Donegal. It was with utter disbelief that I heard the news of the devastating explosion at a filling station in Creeslough. I am deeply saddened at the loss of life and at the extent of injuries caused.'

On World Mission Sunday, 23 October, Mass was celebrated and broadcast from RTÉ's Donnybrook studios in Dublin.

On 24 October, Bishops criticised the Northern Ireland abortion regulations. They said, 'The abortion regulations introduced by Westminster, against the will of the majority of people here, are predicated on the assumption that the unborn child in the womb has no right to love, care and protection from society, unless the child is wanted.'

The same day, Archbishop Martin celebrated the Mass of Thanksgiving at Saint Mary's Drumcar, Dunleer, Co Louth, Archdiocese of Armagh, on the occasion of Saint John of God's leaving Drumcar after 76 years. During his homily he said, 'For generations the people of Ireland were almost entirely dependent and were very grateful for the provision of health services by Catholic religious congregations like the Saint John of God brothers.'

On 25 October, Bishop Gavin announced the death of Archbishop Patrick Coveney RIP. Since his retirement as Apostolic Nuncio to Greece in 2009, Archbishop Coveney resided in Crosshaven Parish in the Diocese of Cork & Ross.

On 27 October, the leaders of the four main Churches in Ireland met with the Secretary of State for Northern Ireland, Rt Hon Chris Heaton-Harris MP. The Church Leaders' Group stressed 'the need for urgent action to be taken in light of the fact that the people of Northern Ireland are experiencing the worst cost of living crisis in generations'.

On 28 October, Pope Francis appointed Father Niall Coll of the Diocese of Raphoe as the new Bishop for the Diocese of Ossory. Welcoming the announcement, Bishop Nulty, Apostolic Administrator of the Diocese of Ossory, said, 'I, along with the people, priests and religious of Ossory, very warmly welcome this announcement and assure Father Niall of our support, our prayers and our encouragement.'

NOVEMBER
On 3 November, the Council for Life made a submission to the Oireachtas Committee in respect of the 'Review of the Termination of Pregnancy Act 2018', in which the Council criticised the legislation 'on the grounds that the Act, in its intention and its consequences, is in total conflict with the common good.'

On 6 November, Bishop Hayes, Liaison Bishop to the Irish Prison Service, issued a statement to mark Prisoners' Sunday. He said, 'On this Prisoners' Sunday, as we pray for all prisoners, we remember their families, all prison staff and prison chaplains, whose work is vital but unheralded within prison services throughout the world.'

On 12 November, Archbishop Martin spoke to the graduate class of 2022 in theology and philosophy in his role as Chancellor of Saint Patrick's Pontifical University, Maynooth. He said, 'There is a crying need for atonement, inner healing and hope in the aftermath of the abuse scandals.'

On 20 November, Bishop Deenihan celebrated Mass for the opening of the cause for sainthood of the Servant of God, Father William Doyle SJ. During his homily, the Bishop of Meath said, 'That heroic desire of Father Doyle to serve and promote God's Kingdom found ultimate expression on the battlefield when he was ministering as an army chaplain.'

On 26 November, Pope Francis appointed Bishop Noël Treanor as Apostolic Nuncio to the European Union. Speaking on his new appointment, Bishop Treanor said, 'I have accepted this appointment and, with God's grace, I will seek to carry out this mission which has been entrusted to me.'

On 26 November, Bishop Deenihan celebrated Mass in Saint Catherine's Church, Oristown, Co Meath, for the First Sunday of Advent and for the Families of the Disappeared. During his homily, he said, 'I appeal for information on the Disappeared to be given to the Commission or to my office.'

On 27 November, Archbishop Martin paid tribute to Bishop Martin Drennan RIP. He said, 'A quiet person by nature, Bishop Drennan was a deeply spiritual, devoted and generous priest and bishop, who was widely respected for his piety, humility, intelligence and strength of character.'

Also today, to mark the First Sunday of Advent, Archbishop Eamon Martin launched the online digital and interactive Advent Calendar. Now it its ninth year, this popular prayer resources is accessible on www.catholicbishops.ie.

DECEMBER
On 7 December, the Winter 2022 General Meeting of the Irish Catholic Bishops' Conference concluded in Maynooth. Together with the plight of immigrants and emigrants, the work of the Bishops' Alcohol and Drug Initiative, and army chaplaincy, other topics discussed by Bishops included: Supporting the people of Ukraine; Cost of living crisis; Political uncertainty in Northern Ireland; 50th anniversary of the Ballymascanlon talks; Vocations; Lay Ministry of Catechist; Safeguarding; Synodal Pathway; COP27; Hunger crisis in the Horn of Africa; Advent 2022; and Catholic Schools Week 2023.

Archbishop Martin criticised the decision by the UK Supreme Court to introduce so called 'buffer zones' close to abortion facilities. On 9 December he said, 'the way has now been paved by the UK Supreme Court to impose exclusion zones outside centres in Northern Ireland that provide or facilitate abortions. This is tantamount to enforcing a ban on pro-life activities, including prayer and respectful witness, outside such settings. Buffer zones will further silence the voice of the innocent unborn. Given that the law already prevents harassment and intimidation, I believe the new legislation represents a disproportionate response with potentially wide implications for freedom of religion and speech.'

On 16 December, Bishop McGuckian paid tribute to Irish Defence Force member Private Seán Rooney RIP, who was killed in action while on UN peacekeeping duty in Lebanon. Bishop McGuckian said, 'Seán's passing in these circumstances is a terrible blow to his immediate family and the communities of Newtowncunningham and Dundalk; it is especially difficult as we approach Christmas.'

Bishops around Ireland lead liturgies to celebrated the Feast of the Nativity on 25 December.

On 31 December the death was announced in Rome of Pope Emeritus Benedict XVI. Archbishop Martin and Archbishop Farrell attended the Funeral Mass in the Vatican on 5 January 2023 and representing the Bishops' Conference and the faithful of Ireland. Archbishop Martin said, 'at this time of mourning in the Catholic Church throughout the world, we remember his gentle soul in prayer, asking God, in His great mercy, to forgive his sins and human failings, while rewarding his generous service and complete dedication to the Gospel and to the Church. On behalf of the Irish Bishops' Conference, and the faithful across Ireland, I extend sympathy to Pope Francis, to the family members and carers of the Pope Emeritus, and to all those in his native Germany and around the globe who loved him and will mourn his loss.'

As part of the Church's response in Ireland to the death, Masses were offered for the repose of the soul of Pope Emeritus Benedict XVI, Archbishop Martin hosted a press conference in Armagh and books of condolence were opened in cathedrals around the country. In addition an online book was opened on catholicbishops.ie as well as on the Bishops' digital platforms of Facebook, Twitter and Instagram.

For more information please see www.catholicbishops.ie. See also 'Irish Catholic Bishops' Conference' on Facebook and follow on Twitter @CatholicBishops.

THE ROMAN CURIA

SECRETARIAT OF STATE

Palazzo Apostolico Vaticano,
Città del Vaticano 00120
Tel 66988-3913

Secretary of State:
Cardinal Pietro Parolin

Relations with States
Secretary:
Archbishop Paul Richard Gallagher
Undersecretary:
Mgr Mirosław Stanisław Wachowski

General Affairs
Substitute: Archbishop Edgar Peña Parra
Assessor: Mgr Roberto Campisi
Secretary for Pontifical Representations:
Archbishop Luciano Russo
Head of Protocol: Mgr Joseph Murphy

CONGREGATIONS

Congregation for the Doctrine of the Faith
Prefect: Archbishop Luis Francisco
Ladaria Ferrer (SJ)
Secretary: Archbishop Giacomo Morandi
Piazza del S. Uffizio 11, 00193 Roma
Tel 66988-3357/3413

Congregation for Divine Worship and the Discipline of the Sacraments
Prefect: Archbishop Arthur Roche
Secretary:
Archbishop Vittorio Francesco Viola
Palazzo delle Congregazioni,
Piazza Pio XII, 10, 00193 Roma
Tel 66988-4316/4318

Congregation for the Causes of Saints
Prefect: Bishop Marcello Semeraro
Secretary: Archbishop Fabio Fabene
Palazzo delle Congregazioni,
Piazza Pio XII, 10, 00193 Roma
Tel 66988-4247

Congregation for Bishops
Prefect: Cardinal Marc Ouellet (PSS)
Secretary:
Archbishop Ilson de Jesus Montanari
Palazzo della Congregazioni,
Piazza Pio XII, 10, 00193 Roma
Tel 66988-4217

Congregation for Clergy
Prefect:
Archbishop Lazzaro You Heung-sik
Secretary: Archbishop Andrés Gabriel
Ferrada Moreira
Palazzo delle Congregazioni,
Piazza Pio XII, 3, 00193 Roma
Tel 66988-4151

Congregation for the Institutes of Consecrated Life and for Societies of Apostolic Life
Prefect: Cardinal João Bráz de Aviz
Secretary: Archbishop José Rodríguez
Carballo (OFM)
Palazzo della Congregazioni,
Piazza Pio XII, 3, 00193 Roma
Tel 66988-4128

TRIBUNALS

Apostolic Penitentiary
Major Penitentiary:
Cardinal Mauro Piacenza
Regent: Mgr Krzysztof Józef Nykiel
Palazzo della Cancelleria,
Piazza della Cancelleria, 1, 00186 Roma
Tel 66988-7526/7523

Supreme Tribunal of the Apostolic Signatura
Prefect: Cardinal Dominique François
Joseph Mamberti
Secretary: Bishop Andrea Ripa
Palazzo della Cancelleria,
Piazza della Cancelleria, 1, 00186 Roma
Tel 66988-7520

Tribunal of the Roman Rota
Dean: Mgr Alejandro Arellano Cedillo
Palazzo della Cancelleria,
Piazza della Cancelleria, 1, 00186 Roma
Tel 66988-7502

DICASTERIES

Dicastery for Evangelisation
Prefect: Pope Francis
Pro-Prefect for the Section of New Evangelisation:
Archbishop Salvatore Fisichella (Rino)
Pro-Prefect for the Section of Evangelisation:
Cardinal Luis Antonio Gokim Tagle
Secretary for the Section of Evangelisation:
Archbishop Protase Rugambwa

Dicastery for the Eastern Churches
Prefect: Archbishop Claudio Gugerotti
Secretary:
Archbishop Giorgio Demetrio Gallaro
Palazzo del Bramante,
Via della Conciliazione, 34, 00193 Roma
Tel 66988-4282

Dicastery for Laity, Family and Life
Prefect: Cardinal Kevin Joseph Farrell
Secretary: Dr Gleison De Paula Souza
Piazza San Callisto 16,
00153 Roma, Italy
Tel 66986-9300/66987-9823

Dicastery for Culture and Education
Prefect: Cardinal José Tolentino Calaça
de Mendonça
Secretary: Mgr Giovanni Cesare Pagazzi

Discastery for Promoting Integral Human Development
President:
Cardinal Michael Czerny
Secretary: Sr Alessandra Smerilli
Piazza San Callisto 16,
00153 Roma, Italy
Tel 066989-2711

Dicastery for Communication
Prefect: Dr Paulo Ruffini
Secretary: Mgr Lucio Adrián Ruiz
Palazzo Pio, Piassa Pia, 3,
00193 Roma, Italy
Tel 66988-1800

Allianz ⑪

PONTIFICAL COUNCILS

Pontifical Council for Promoting Christian Unity
President: Cardinal Kurt Koch
Secretary: Bishop Brian Farrell (LC)
Via dell'Erba, 1, 00193 Roma
Tel 66988-3072/4271

Pontifical Council for Legislative Texts
President:
Archbishop Filippo Iannone
Secretary:
Bishop Juan Ignacio Arrieta Ochoa de Chinchetru
Palazzo delle Congregazioni, Piazza Pio XII, 10, 00193 Roma
Tel 66988-4008

Pontifical Council for Inter-Religious Dialogue
President: Cardinal Miguel Ángel Ayuso Guixot (MCCJ)
Secretary: Mgr Indunil Janakaratne Kodithuwakku Kankanamalage
Via dell'Erba, 1, 00193 Roma
Tel 66988-4321

OFFICES

Apostolic Camera
Chamberlain of the Holy Roman Church:
Cardinal Kevin Joseph Farrell
Vice-Chamberlain:
Archbishop Ilson de Jesus Montanari
Palazzo Apostolico,
00120 Vatican City State
Tel 66988-3554/2139

Administration of the Patrimony of the Apostolic See
President: Bishop Nunzio Galantino
Secretary: Dr Fabio Gasperini
Palazzo Apostolico,
00120 Vatican City State
Tel 66989-3403

Secretariat for the Economy
Prefect:
Fr Juan Antonio Guerrero Alves (SJ)
Secretary General:
Dr Maximino Caballero Ledo
Palazzo Pio, Piazza Pia, 3,
00193 Roma, Italy
Tel 066988-1098

Council for the Economy
Coordinator: Cardinal Reinhard Marx
Palazzo Apostolico, 00120,
Vatican City State
Tel 66988-1771

Office of the Auditor General
Auditor General:
Dr Alessandro Cassinis Righini

OTHER INSTITUTES OF THE ROMAN CURIA

Prefecture of the Papal Household
Prefect: Archbishop Georg Gänswein
Regent: Mgr Leonardo Sapienza (RCI)
00120 Vatican City State
Tel 66988-3114

Office for the Liturgical Celebrations of the Supreme Pontiff
Master of Papal Liturgical Celebrations:
Mgr Diego Giovanni Ravelli
Palazzo Apostolico, 00120,
Vatican City State
Tel 66988-3253

Press Office of the Holy See
Director: Mr Matteo Bruni
Deputy Director: Dr Cristiane Murray
Via della Conciliazione, 54,
00193 Roma, Italy
Tel 0669-8921

PONTIFICAL COMMISSIONS

Pontifical Commission for Latin America
President: Cardinal Marc Ouellet (PSS)
Secretary: Prof. Rodrigo Guerra López
00120 Vatican City State
Tel 66988-3131/3500

Pontifical Commission for Sacred Archaeology
President: Mgr Pasquale Iacobone
Secretary: Dr Raffaella Giuliani
Via Napoleone III, 1, 00185 Roma
Tel 6446-5610

Pontifical Biblical Commission
President:
Cardinal Luis Francisco Ladaria Ferrer (SJ)
Secretary:
Sr Nuria Calduck-Benages (MHSFN)
Technical Secretary:
Fr Alessandro Belano (FDP)
Palazzo della Congr. per la Dottrina della Fede, Piazza del S. Uffizio, 11, 00193 Roma
Tel 66988-4682

INSTITUTIONS CONNECTED WITH HOLY SEE

L'Osservatore Romano
Director Manager: Prof. Andrea Monda
00120 Vatican City State
Tel 66988-3461

Vatican Apostolic Archive
Archivist:
Archbishop Angelo Vincenzo Zani
Prefect: Bishop Sergio Pagano (B)
00120 Vatican City State
Tel 66988-3314

Vatican Apostolic Library
Librarian:
Archbishop Angelo Vincenzo Zani
Prefect: Mgr Cesare Pasini
Cortile del Belvedere,
00120 Vatican City State
Tel 66987-9411

APOSTOLIC NUNCIATURE

Address: Apostolic Nunciature in Ireland, 183 Navan Road, Dublin D07 CT98
Tel 01-8380577
Email na.ireland@diplomat.va

Papal Nuncio: Vacant

Chargé d'Affaires, a.i: Very Rev Mgr Julien Kaboré

THE IRISH EPISCOPATE

THE HIERARCHY

Archbishops

Most Rev Eamon Martin DD
Archbishop of Armagh
Primate of All Ireland
and Apostolic Administrator, Diocese of Dromore
Ara Coeli, Armagh BT61 7QY
Tel 028-37522045 Fax 028-37526182
Email admin@aracoeli.com

Most Rev Dermot Farrell DD
Archbishop of Dublin and Primate of Ireland
Archbishop's House,
Drumcondra, Dublin 9
Tel 01-8373732 Fax 01-8369796

Most Rev Kieran O'Reilly (SMA) DD
Archbishop of Cashel and Emly
Archbishop's House, Thurles,
Co Tipperary
Tel 0504-21512 Fax 0504-22680
Email office@cashel-emly.ie

Most Rev Francis Duffy DD
Archbishop of Tuam
Archbishop's House, Tuam, Co Galway
Tel 093-24166 Fax 093-28070
Email admin@tuamarchdiocese.org

Retired Archbishops

His Eminence Seán Cardinal Brady DCL, DD
Retired Archbishop of Armagh
Ara Coeli, Armagh BT61 7QY

Most Rev Dermot Clifford DD
Retired Archbishop of Cashel and Emly
Archbishop's House, Thurles,
Co Tipperary

Most Rev Diarmuid Martin DD
Retired Archbishop of Dublin and Primate of Ireland
Archbishop's House,
Drumcondra, Dublin 9
Tel 01-8373732 Fax 01-8369796

Most Rev Michael Neary DD
Retired Archbishop of Tuam
Archbishop's House, Tuam, Co Galway
Tel 093-24166 Fax 093-28070
Email admin@tuamarchdiocese.org

Bishops

Most Rev Raymond A. Browne DD
Bishop of Kerry
Bishop's House, Killarney, Co Kerry
Tel 064-6631168 Fax 064-6631364
Email admin@dioceseofkerry.ie

Most Rev Niall Coll DD
Bishop of Ossory
Blessed Felix House, Tilbury Place,
Kilkenny R95 DXC9
Tel 056-7762448
Email bishop@ossory.ie

Most Rev William Crean DD
Bishop of Cloyne
Cloyne Diocesan Centre,
Cobh, Co Cork
Tel 021-4811430 Fax 021-4811026
Email info@cloynediocese.ie

Most Rev Alphonsus Cullinan DD
Bishop of Waterford and Lismore
Bishop's House, John's Hill, Waterford
Tel 051-874463 Fax 051-852703
Email info@waterfordlismore.ie

Most Rev Thomas Deenihan DD
Bishop of Meath
Bishop's House, Dublin Road,
Mullingar, Co Westmeath
Tel 044-9348841/9342038
Fax 044-9343020
Email bishop@dioceseofmeath.ie

Most Rev Paul Dempsey DD
Bishop of Achonry
Bishop's House, Ballaghaderreen,
Co Roscommon
Tel 094-986 0034
Email bishop@achonrydiocese.org

Most Rev Kevin Doran DD
Bishop of Elphin
St Mary's, Sligo
Tel 071-9162670/9162769 Fax 071-9162414
Email office@elphindiocese.ie

Most Rev Larry Duffy DD
Bishop of Clogher
Bishop's House, Monaghan
Tel 047-81019 Fax 047-84773
Email diocesanoffice@clogherdiocese.ie

Most Rev Michael Duignan DD
Bishop of Clonfert
St Brendan's, Coorheen, Loughrea,
Co Galway
Tel 091-841560 Fax 091-841818
Email office@clonfertdiocese.ie

Most Rev Michael Duignan DD
Bishop of Galway
Diocesan Office,
The Cathedral, Galway
Tel 091-563566 Fax 091-568333
Email info@galwaydiocese.ie

Most Rev John Fleming DD, DCL
Bishop of Killala
Bishop's House, Ballina, Co Mayo
Tel 096-21518 Fax 096-70344
Email bishop@killaladiocese.org

Most Rev Fintan Gavin DD
Bishop of Cork and Ross
Diocesan Office, Bishop's House,
Redemption Road, Cork
Tel 021-4301717 Fax 021-4301557
Email secretary@corkandross.org

Most Rev Martin Hayes DD
Bishop of Kilmore
Bishop's House, Cullies, Co Cavan
Tel 049-4331496 Fax 049-4361796
Email admin@kilmorediocese.ie

Most Rev Brendan Leahy DD
Bishop of Limerick
Limerick Diocesan Centre, St Munchin's,
Corbally, Limerick
Tel 061-350000
Email office@ldo.ie

Most Rev Alan McGuckian (SJ) DD
Bishop of Raphoe
Ard Adhamhnáin, Letterkenny,
Co Donegal
Tel 074-9121208 Fax 074-9124872
Email diocesanoffice@raphoediocese.ie

Most Rev Donal McKeown DD
Bishop of Derry
Bishop's House, St Eugene's Cathedral
Francis Street, Derry BT48 9AP
Tel 028-71262302 Fax 028-71371960
Email office@derrydiocese.org

Most Rev Fintan Monahan DD
Bishop of Killaloe
Westbourne, Ennis, Co Clare
Tel 065-6828638 Fax 065-6842538
Email office@killaloediocese.ie

Most Rev Ger Nash DD
Bishop of Ferns
Bishop's House,
Summerhill, Wexford
Tel 053-9122177 Fax 053-9123436
Email adm@ferns.ie

Most Rev Denis Nulty DD
Bishop of Kildare and Leighlin
Bishop's House, Carlow
Tel 059-9176725 Fax 059-9176850
Email bishop@kandle.ie

Most Rev Michael Router DD
Titular Bishop of Lugmad and
Auxiliary Bishop in Armagh
Annaskeagh, Mount Pleasant,
Dundalk, Co Louth

Retired Bishops

Most Rev Philip Boyce (OCD) DD
Retired Bishop of Raphoe
Columba House, Windyhall,
Letterkenny, Co Donegal

Most Rev Denis Brennan DD
Retired Bishop of Ferns
Bishop's House, Summerhill, Wexford

Most Rev John Buckley DD
Retired Bishop of Cork and Ross
Diocesan Office, Bishop's House,
Redemption Road, Cork

Most Rev Brendan Comiskey DD
Retired Bishop of Ferns
PO Box 40, Summerhill, Wexford

Most Rev Martin Drennan DD
Retired Bishop of Galway
Mount St Mary's, Taylor's Hill, Galway

Most Rev Joseph Duffy DD
Retired Bishop of Clogher
Bishop's House, Monaghan, Co Monaghan

Most Rev Anthony Farquhar DD
Retired Titular Bishop of Ermiana and
Retired Auxiliary Bishop in Down and
Connor
24 Fruithill Park, Belfast BT11 8GE

Most Rev Raymond Field DD
Retired Titular Bishop of Ard Mor and
Auxiliary Bishop in Dublin
3 Castleknock Road,
Blanchardstown, Dublin 15

Most Rev Brendan Kelly DD
Retired Bishop of Galway
Diocesan Office,
The Cathedral, Galway

Most Rev John Kirby DD
Retired Bishop of Clonfert
St Brendan's, Coorheen, Loughrea,
Co Galway

Most Rev William Lee DD, DCL
Retired Bishop of Waterford and Lismore
Bishop's House, John's Hill, Waterford

Most Rev John McAreavey DD, DCL
Retired Bishop of Dromore
Bishop's House, 44 Armagh Road,
Newry, Co Down BT35 6PN

Most Rev Liam MacDaid DD
Retired Bishop of Clogher
Bishop's House, Monaghan

Most Rev John Magee DD
Retired Bishop of Cloyne
'Cormeen', Convent Hill,
Mitchelstown, Co Cork

Most Rev William Murphy DD
Retired Bishop of Kerry
Bishop's House, Killarney, Co Kerry

Most Rev Donal Murray DD
Retired Bishop of Limerick
Limerick Diocesan Centre, St Munchin's,
Corbally, Limerick

Most Rev Colm O'Reilly DD
Retired Bishop of Ardagh and
Clonmacnois
St Michael's, Longford, Co Longford

Most Rev Leo O'Reilly DD
Retired Bishop of Kilmore
Bishop's House, Cullies, Co Cavan

Most Rev Eamonn Walsh DD, VG
Retired Titular Bishop of Elmham and
Auxiliary Bishop in Dublin
Naomh Brid, Blessington Road,
Tallaght, Dublin 24

Most Rev Patrick J. Walsh DD
Retired Bishop of Down and Connor
6 Waterloo Park North,
Belfast BT15 5HW

Most Rev William Walsh DD
Retired Bishop of Killaloe
Westbourne, Ennis, Co Clare

Most Rev Michael Smith DD, DCL
Retired Bishop of Meath
Bishop's House, Dublin Road,
Mullingar, Co Westmeath

MITRED ABBOTS

Rt Rev Dom Brendan Coffey (OSB),
Abbot
Glenstal Abbey, Murroe, Co Limerick
Tel 061-386103

Rt Rev Dom Michael Ryan (OCSO), Abbot
Bolton Abbey, Moone, Athy, Co Kildare
Tel 059-8624102

Rt Rev Dom Celsus Kelly (OCSO), Abbot
Our Lady of Bethlehem Abbey,
11 Ballymena Road, Portglenone,
Ballymena, Co Antrim BT44 8BL
Tel 028-25821211 Fax 028-25822310

Rt Rev Dom Brendan Freeman (OCSO),
Superior
Mellifont Abbey, Collon, Co Louth
Tel 041-9826103

Br Malachy Thompson (OCSO), Prior
Mount Saint Joseph, Roscrea,
Co Tipperary
Tel 0505-25600

Rt Rev Dom Mark Ephrem Nolan (OSB),
Abbot
Holy Cross Monastery, 119 Kilbroney Road,
Rostrevor, Co Down BT34 3BN
Tel 028-41739979

THE IRISH EPISCOPAL CONFERENCE

President
His Grace Most Rev Eamon Martin
Vice President
His Grace Most Rev Dermot Farrell
Episcopal Secretary
His Grace Most Rev Francis Duffy
Finance Secretary
Most Rev Ger Nash
Executive Secretary
Mgr Joseph McGuinness
Columba Centre, Maynooth, Co Kildare
Tel 01-5053000 Fax 01-6292360
Email ex.sec@iecon.ie
Communications Director
Mr Martin Long
Columba Centre, Maynooth, Co Kildare
Tel 01-5053000 Fax 01-6016401
Email mlong@catholicbishops.ie
*Executive Administrator of the
Commissions & Agencies of the Episcopal
Conference:* Mgr Joseph McGuinness
Columba Centre, Maynooth, Co Kildare
Tel 01-5053000 Fax 01-6016401
Email ex.sec@iecon.ie

Standing Committee
His Grace Most Rev Eamon Martin; His
Grace Most Rev Dermot Farrell; His Grace
Most Rev Kieran O'Reilly; His Grace Most
Rev Francis Duffy; Most Rev Brendan
Leahy; Most Rev William Crean; Most Rev
Denis Nulty; Most Rev Fintan Gavin; Most
Rev Thomas Deenihan and Most Rev Paul
Dempsey

THE FIVE EPISCOPAL COMMISSIONS OF THE IRISH EPISCOPAL CONFERENCE

*An Episcopal Commission advises or
makes proposals/recommendations to the
Standing Committee and Plenary
Assembly of the Irish Episcopal
Conference. Councils and Agencies assist
the Episcopal Commissions, and the
Episcopal Conference itself, in attaining
their objectives. An Advisory Group/Body/
Committee to a Council of the Irish
Episcopal Conference advises the
relevant Council.*

**Episcopal Commission for Catholic
Education and Formation**
Chaired by Most Rev Brendan Leahy DD

Episcopal Commission for Pastoral Care
Chaired by Most Rev Denis Nulty DD

**Episcopal Commission for Planning,
Communications and Resources**
*Chaired by His Grace Most Rev Dermot
Farrell DD*

**Episcopal Commission for Social Issues
and International Affairs**
Chair: Vacant

**Episcopal Commission for Worship,
Pastoral Renewal and Faith Development**
Chaired by Most Rev Fintan Gavin DD

Allianz ⑪

The Councils and Agencies of the Irish Episcopal Conference are clustered in five Departments corresponding to the five Episcopal Commissions. Details of several bodies which are linked to the Episcopal Conference are placed in square brackets and provided for your information.

COMMISSION FOR CATHOLIC EDUCATION AND FORMATION

Executive Secretary to the Episcopal Commission/Department
Rev Paul Connell PhD
Tel 01-5053014
Email education@iecon.ie

COUNCIL FOR CATECHETICS OF THE IRISH EPISCOPAL CONFERENCE

Members of the Council
Most Rev Brendan Leahy DD (Chair)
Most Rev William Crean DD, Mr Eoin Walshe, Dr Gerry O'Connell, Dr Cora O'Farrell, Mrs Hilda Campbell, Rev Dr Edward McGee, Sr Antoinette Dilworth (RSJ), Dr Aiveen Mullaly, Mrs Kate Liffey, Dr Daniel O'Connell, Dr Amalee Meehan, Rev Dr Billy Swan and Rev Paul Connell PhD (Council for Education of the IEC) and Dr Alexander O'Hara KM (Executive Secretary and National Director for Catechetics)
Contact details: Dr Alexander O'Hara KM Columba Centre, Maynooth, Co Kildare
Tel 086-0588786
Email alex.ohara@iecon.ie

COUNCIL FOR DOCTRINE OF THE IRISH EPISCOPAL CONFERENCE

Members of the Council
Most Rev Kevin Doran DD;
Most Rev Brendan Leahy DD;
Most Revd Fintan Gavin DD
The Council for Doctrine works with the Theological Committee and the Bioethics Consultative Group (see Commission for Pastoral Care under Council for Life) on matters relating to faith and morals.
Columba Centre, Maynooth, Co Kildare
Tel 01-5053000

COUNCIL FOR ECUMENISM AND DIALOGUE OF THE IRISH EPISCOPAL CONFERENCE

Members of the Council
Most Rev Larry Duffy DD (Chair);
Most Rev Brendan Leahy DD

Advisory Committee on Ecumenism
Secretary: Dr Gary Carville
Columba Centre, Maynooth, Co Kildare
Tel 01-5053000
Email gary.carville@iecon.ie

Advises the Episcopal Conference on ecumenical affairs in Ireland and maintains contact with the Dicastery for Promoting Christian Unity, Rome. The committee has a membership of approximately 35, including the episcopal members, a representative from each diocese, and people chosen for their competence and experience in the ecumenical field.

COUNCIL FOR EDUCATION OF THE IRISH EPISCOPAL CONFERENCE [WITH NORTHERN IRELAND COUNCIL FOR CATHOLIC EDUCATION (NICCE)]

The Council for Education articulates policy and vision for Catholic Education in Ireland, north and south, on behalf of the Episcopal Conference. It has responsibility for the forward planning necessary to ensure the best provision for Catholic Education in the country. It liaises with other Catholic Education Offices, the Department of Education and Skills and the Department of Education, Northern Ireland. The Council advises the Conference on all government legislation as applied to education. It responds to and acts as spokesperson for the Episcopal Conference on issues related to the work of education. It seeks also to develop long-term strategies in education for the Episcopal Conference

Members of the Council for Education
Most Rev Thomas Deenihan DD (Chair)
Most Rev Donal McKeown DD
Most Rev Francis Duffy DD
Rt Rev Mgr Dan O'Connor, Sr Evelyn Byrne, Mr Seamus Mulconry, Mr John Curtis, Dr Marie Griffin, Mr Fintan Murphy

Executive Secretary
Rev Paul Connell PhD
Council for Education of the IEC, Columba Centre, Maynooth, Co Kildare
Tel +353-1-5053014
Email education@iecon.ie
Administrative Assistant
Ms Cora Hennelly
Tel +353-1-5053027
Email chennelly@iecon.ie

Northern Ireland Commission for Catholic Education (NICCE)
Until 2005, there was no central body seeking to offer leadership across the Catholic education sector in NI. The 'Maintained' schools (nursery, primary and non-selective post-primary) were managed by CCMS (a statutory body) while the Voluntary Grammar schools had a considerable degree of independence. The Northern Ireland Commission for Catholic Education (NICCE) was set up in 2005 by the Trustees in order to provide co-ordination of the Catholic sector in a time of rapid change. Today, there are 460 Maintained Schools and 29 Voluntary Grammar Schools.

Current Directors of the Northern Ireland Commission for Catholic Education (NICCE)
Most Rev Donal McKeown DD (Chair), Most Rev Eamon Martin DD, Sr Eithne Woulfe (SSL) (Vice-Chair), Mr Dermot McGovern (ERST NI), Monsignor Peter O'Reilly, Dean Kevin Donaghy, Sr Maureen O'Dee (Sister of St Clare), Rev Feidhlimidh Magennis, Rev Timothy Bartlett, Rev Gerard Fox and Sr Brighde Vallely
In attendance
Rev Paul Connell

Secretary
Mr Fintan Murphy
Northern Ireland Commission for Catholic Education (NICCE)
St Mary's College, Belfast BT12 6FE
Tel 028-90268368
Email f.murphy@csts.stmarys-belfast.ac.uk
Website info@catholiceducation-ni.org

The Catholic Education Services Committee (CESC)
The CESC is an education committee established by the Irish Episcopal Conference (IEC) and the Association of Leaders of Missionaries and Religious of Ireland (AMRI). Formally consisting of six Bishops and six Religious nominated by AMRI, it was reconstituted in 2019.

The membership now consists of six Bishops, four Religious nominated by AMRI, two representatives of the six educational Trusts that have Public Juridic Person status (PJPs), and a representative of third level Catholic Education. As such, it is now representative of the entire Catholic Education sector.

CESC aims to support a vibrant Catholic education sector in response to changing social, economic and political conditions in Ireland. It promotes the Catholic education sector nationally and assists providers and practitioners in encouraging people to choose Catholic education at all stages of lifelong learning. The development of a co-ordinated and strategic approach to education across the entire Catholic sector in Ireland is a priority for CESC.

Members of the Catholic Education Services Committee (CESC)
Most Rev Thomas Deenihan DD (Chair), Most Rev Francis Duffy DD, Most Rev Donal McKeown DD, Most Rev Dermot Farrell DD, Most Rev Kieran O'Reilly DD, Fr Leonard Moloney (SJ), Fr John Hennebry (OSA), Sr Ella McGuinness (RSM), Mr T.J. Coakley, Mr Noel Merrick.
In attendance Dr Marie Griffin (Chair CEP).

Executive Secretary: Rev Paul Connell
Catholic Education Service
Columba Centre, Maynooth, Co Kildare
Tel +353-1-5053014
Email education@iecon.ie

Catholic Education Service Trust (CEST)

The Catholic Education Service is a charity created by Deed of Trust. The Trustees of CEST are four Catholic Bishops who are Ordinaries of Catholic dioceses in Ireland and each representing one of the four ecclesiastical provinces of Ireland (Most Rev Thomas Deenihan DD, Most Rev Dermot Farrell DD, Most Rev Kieran O'Reilly DD, Most Rev Francis Duffy DD) and two Religious appointed by AMRI, Rev Leonard Moloney (SJ) and Rev John Hennebry (OSA). The Trustees of the CEST are ex officio members of Catholic Education Service Committee (CESC).

Catholic Education Partnership (CEP)

In November 2020, a new structure for the management and trusteeship of Catholic Post-Primary Education came into being. As part of this new structure, two new companies have been established: the Association of Patrons and Trustees of Catholic Schools (APTCS) (see below), and the Catholic Education Partnership (CEP). The CEP replaces the Catholic Schools Partnership (CSP) and will continue its work of providing support for all the partners in Catholic education at first, second and third level in the Republic of Ireland. The CEP going forward will be closely aligned with the Secretariat of Secondary Schools (SSS) which provides support for Boards of Management and Principals in Catholic Post Primary Schools. In addition, it will also be closely aligned with the APTCS which provides support and advice for Patrons and Trustees of Catholic Schools. The activities of the CEP will be supported and funded by CEST.

The Directors of the CEP Company are: Most Rev Leo O'Reilly DD, Dr Marie Griffin (Chair), Fr Gareth Byrne, Ms Mary Bergin, Dr John McCafferty, Dr Andrew McGrady, Ms Deirdre Matthews, Dr Amalie Meehan, Mr Jonathan Tiernan, Mr Paul Meany, Ms Cathy Burke, Ms Angela Mitchell and Sr Eithne Woulfe (SSL).

Chair: Dr Marie Griffin
CEO: Mr Alan Hynes
Company Secretary: Fr Paul Connell
Columba Centre, Maynooth, Co Kildare
Tel 01-5053100
Email ceo@catholiceducation.ie
Website www.catholiceducation.ie

Association of Patrons and Trustees of Catholic Schools (APTCS)

The Association of Patrons and Trustees of Catholic Schools (APTCS) came into being in November 2020. The APTCS is the representative body for the 'Catholic Trustee Voice' in Irish education at primary and post-primary level.

Its membership includes members of the Irish Episcopal Conference, representatives of various religious congregations, representatives of the PJP trusts, as well as the trustees of a number of other Catholic schools.

The Directors of APTCS are:
Mr Paul Meany (Chair), Mr Michael Sexton, Ms Sheila McManamly (Company Secretary), Sr Ann O'Donoghue, Ms Maeve Mahon, Ms Deirdre Matthews, Mr John Barry, Mr Declan Lawlor, Fr Paul Connell, Mr Gerry Bennett, Mr Edmund Corrigan.

Contact details:
Association of Patrons and Trustees of Catholic Schools (APTCS)
Chairperson: Mr Paul Meany
CEO: Dr Eilis Humphreys
New House, St Patrick's College, Maynooth, Co Kildare
Tel 01-5053164
Email ceo@aptcs.ie

Secretariat of Secondary Schools (SSS)

General Secretary: Ms Deirdre Matthews
Secretariat of Secondary Schools, Emmet House, Dundrum Road, Milltown, Dublin 14
Tel +353-1-2838255 Fax +353-1-2695461
Email info@jmb.ie
Website www.jmb.ie

The Secretariat of Secondary Schools is the company which governs the Association of Management of Catholic Secondary Schools (AMCSS). The AMCSS promotes, advises and supports Catholic Voluntary Secondary Schools in Ireland. Founded in the 1960s, it adopted its present structure in 1987. Its membership includes a principal and chairperson of a Board of Management from each of its ten constituent regions. It also includes a representative of the Irish Episcopal Conference and a representative of AMRI (Association of Leaders of Missionaries and Religious of Ireland). The Council cooperates and maintains links with other national and international groups interested in Catholic education. Its Secretariat provides a wide range of educational services and advice to its members. When the Council joins with representatives of the Protestant Voluntary Secondary Schools the Irish School Heads (ISA) it forms the Council of the Joint Managerial Body (JMB). The JMB is recognised by the Department of Education & Skills as the negotiating body for Voluntary Secondary Schools.

Catholic Primary School Management Association (CPSMA)

Chair: Ms Anne Fay
General Secretary: Mr Seamus Mulconry
New House, St Patrick's College, Maynooth, Co Kildare
Tel +353-1-6292462/1850-407200
Fax +353-1-6292654
Email info@cpsma.ie
Website www.cpsma.ie

CPSMA represents the boards of management of all Catholic primary schools. Its standing committee has close links with the Episcopal Commission for Education.

COMMISSION FOR PASTORAL CARE

Executive Secretary to the Episcopal Commission/Department
Ms Sandra Garry
Tel 01-5053000
Email sandra.garry@iecon.ie

COUNCIL FOR MARRIAGE AND THE FAMILY OF THE IRISH EPISCOPAL CONFERENCE

Members of the Council for Marriage and Family of the Irish Episcopal Conference
Most Rev Denis Nulty DD (Chair)
Most Rev Dermot Farrell DD
Mr Gerry Mangan, Mrs Breda McDonald, Very Rev Michael McGinnity, Ms Patricia Conway, Mrs Anne O'Leary, Mr Mark O'Leary, Rev Mr John Taaffe, Mrs Maire Printer, Rev Mr Gabriel Corcoran, Mrs Finola Bruton, Mrs Gemma Rowley, Mr Francis Cousins, Mrs Catherine Wiley, Mrs Rose Curtin, Mr Mike Curtin, Mrs Sallyann Huss and Mr Torbjorn Huss and Mr Tony Shanahan
Columba Centre, Maynooth, Co Kildare
Tel 01-5053000 Fax 01-6016401
Email columbacentre@iecon.ie

The purpose of the Council for Marriage and the Family is to assist the Bishops in their mission, specifically as it relates to marriage, families and family life.

COUNCIL FOR LIFE

Members of the Council
Most Rev Kevin Doran (Chair)
Columba Centre, Maynooth, Co Kildare
Tel 01-5053000

Consultative Group on Bioethics and Life

Most Rev Kevin Doran (Chair)
Secretary: Rev Michael Shortall
St Patrick's College, Maynooth, Co Kildare
Tel 01-7086165

Allianz ⓘ

ACCORD

Accord Catholic Marriage Care Service comprises three autonomous companies limited by guarantee: Accord NI, chaired by Archbishop Eamon Martin; Accord Dublin, chaired by Archbishop Dermot Farrell; and Accord Catholic Marriage Care Service CLG, chaired by Mr Gordon Nicholl. Accord has over fifty centres located throughout the 26 dioceses of Ireland. Its ministry is primarily concerned with supporting the Sacrament of Marriage by helping couples as they prepare for sacramental marriage and offering support to them in times of difficulty. Accord's aim is to promote a better understanding of Christian marriage and to help couples initiate, sustain and enrich their commitment to one another and to family life. Accord's core services include Marriage Preparation and Counselling (marriage and relationships) and Schools' Programmes in Relationships and Sexuality Education.

Accord Catholic Marriage Care Service CLG
President: Most Rev Denis Nulty DD
Vice President
Most Rev Michael Router DD
Chairperson
Mr Matt Walsh
Executive Director
Mr Tony Shanahan
Central Office: Columba Centre, Maynooth, Co Kildare
Tel 01-5053112 Fax 01-6016410
Email info@accord.ie
www.accord.ie

ACCORD Dublin Catholic Marriage Care Service CLG
Chairperson
Most Rev Dermot Farrell DD
Diocesan Director: Ms Jennifer Griffin
Holy Cross Diocesan Centre, Clonliffe Road, Dublin DO3 P2E7
Tel 01-4784400
Emails
marriagepreparation@accorddublin.ie *or* schoolsprogramme@accorddublin.ie *or* admin@accorddublin.ie
www.accord.ie and www.accorddublin.ie

Accord Northern Ireland Catholic Marriage Care Service CLG
Chairperson: Most Rev Eamon Martin DD
Regional Director: Ms Deirdre O'Rawe
Cana House, St Mary's Church, Chapel Lane, Belfast BT11HH
Tel 028-90233002
Email info@accordni.com
www.accord.ie and www.accord-ni.co.uk

COUNCILS FOR EMIGRANTS AND IMMIGRANTS OF THE IRISH EPISCOPAL CONFERENCE

EMIGRANTS (IECE)
The Irish Episcopal Council for Emigrants (IECE) seeks to respond to the needs of Irish emigrants prior to and following departure. It is particularly committed to addressing the needs of our most vulnerable emigrants, especially the elderly Irish emigrant community, the undocumented in the United States and Irish prisoners overseas. Working in conjunction with the host Church, our apostolates and sister organisations, the IECE seeks to respond to the needs of the Irish as an emigrant community.

Members of the Council for Emigrants
Most Rev Paul Dempsey DD *(Chair)*
Rev Gerry French, Ms Joanna Joyce, Sr Liz Murphy (RSM)
Acting Director of IECE: Vacant
Emigrant Officer: Brian Hanley
Administrator: Ms Bernadette Martin
Columba Centre, Maynooth, Co Kildare
Tel 01-5053155 Fax 01-6292363
Email bernie.martin@iecon.ie
emigrants@iecon.ie
Website www.catholicbishops.ie

Irish Council for Prisoners Overseas is an outreach of IECE
The Irish Council for Prisoners Overseas (ICPO) works on behalf of Irish prisoners overseas and their families. Established in 1985, the ICPO promotes social justice and human dignity for Irish people in prisons overseas and for their families. ICPO provides information, support and advocacy to Irish prisoners wherever they are: it makes no distinction in terms of religious faith, the nature of the prison conviction or of a prisoner's status. Casework, family support work, prison visits and policy work comprise core components of this work.

Coordinator: Mr Brian Hanley,
Administrator: Ms Bernadette Martin
Ms Ciara Kirrane, Mr Ian Hanna, Ms Catherine Kenny and Ms Orla Dick
Volunteers Maynooth: Ms Eileen Boyle, Ms Joan O'Cléirigh, Sr Anne Sheehy and Ms Betty Wilson
Staff London: Rev Gerry McFlynn, Ms Elizabeth Power, Ms Breda Power, Mr Declan Ganly and Ms Sally Murphy
Volunteer London: Sr Moira Keane
Maynooth Office: Columba Centre, Box No 13484, Maynooth, Co Kildare, Republic of Ireland
Tel 01-5053156 Fax 01-6292363
Email icpo@iecon.ie
Website www.catholicbishops.ie
www.icpo.ie
London Office: PO Box 75693, London NW1W 7ZT
Tel 0044-2074824148
Fax 0044-2074824815

[The Irish Chaplaincy
Director: Mr Eddie Gilmore
Tel 0044-207-4825528
Fax 0044-207-4824815
Email prisoners@irishchaplaincy.org.uk
Website www.irishchaplaincy.org.uk]

IMMIGRANTS (IECI)
The Irish Episcopal Council for Immigrants (IECI) develops and fosters initiatives for the pastoral care of immigrants among the dioceses and parishes of Ireland. It identifies immigrant communities within a local setting, recognises their needs and develops pastoral outreach strategies to engage with, support and integrate immigrant communities into dioceses and local parishes.

Most Rev Michael Duignan DD *(Chair)*
Columba Centre, Maynooth, Co Kildare
Tel 01-5053022
Email gary.carville@iecon.ie

COUNCIL FOR HEALTHCARE

Membership
Most Rev Michael Router DD *(Chair)*;
Most Rev Ray Browne DD;
Fr John Kelly, Sr Helena O'Donoghue RSM, Professor Bernard Walsh, Fr Pierce Cormac, Dr Keith Holmes, Sr Dervilla O'Donnell (MMM), Dr Aoife McGrath

Secretary: Sr Pat O'Donovan (RSM)
c/o Columba Centre, Maynooth, Co Kildare
Tel 01-5310055
Email pat.odonovan@iecon.ie
www.catholicbishops.ie/healthcare

IRISH BISHOPS' DRUGS INITIATIVE

Chair: Ms Patricia Conway
Vice Chair: Most Rev Michael Router DD
National Coordinator: Mr Darren Butler
Committee Members
Mr David Conway, Ms Elizabeth Murray and Ms Elizabeth Cullinane
Columba Centre, Maynooth, Co Kildare
Tel 01-5053044/087-7901461
Email ibdi@iecon.ie

The Irish Bishops' Drugs Initiative was established in 1997 as a Church response to the growing problem of drug/alcohol misuse in Ireland. Its vision is to enable parishes to use a pastoral response in partnership with other service providers to respond to the primary and secondary prevention of drug/alcohol harms in parish communities.

OUTREACH TO PRISONERS

Irish Prison Chaplains Team
Episcopal Liaison
Most Rev Martin Hayes DD
National Coordinator of Prison Chaplains
Vacant

There are at present twenty full-time and five part-time chaplains working in Irish prisons. The vision of the chaplaincy is one that affirms the dignity of the person and seeks to be a voice for those deprived of their freedom. It is a vision that urges us to take a prophetic stance on issues of social justice and to continue the exploration of Restorative Justice as a valid alternative to imprisonment.

COMMISSION FOR PLANNING, COMMUNICATIONS AND RESOURCES

Executive Secretary to the Episcopal Commission/Department
Mr Paul Corcoran
Tel 01-5053000
Email paul.corcoran@iecon.ie

COUNCIL FOR COMMUNICATIONS OF THE IRISH EPISCOPAL CONFERENCE

Members of the Council
Archbishop Eamon Martin *(Chair)*
Archbishop Kieran O'Reilly SMA *(ex officio)*
Bishop Alphonsus Cullinan
Mgr Joseph McGuinness
Fr Paul Clayton-Lea *(Intercom)*
Mr Tony Moroney *(Director, Veritas)*
Ms Denise Murphy *(Secretary)*
Fr Bill Kemmy *(iCatholic)*
Ms Petra Conroy *(Council for Life)*
Mr Martin Long *(CCO)*
Veritas Company,
7-8 Lower Abbey Street, Dublin 1
Tel 01-8788177 Fax 01-8786507

Catholic Communications Office
Director: Mr Martin Long
Communications Officer: Mr Oisín Walsh
Email owalsh@catholicbishops.ie
Communications Executive
Ms Lisa Sheridan
Email info@catholicbishops.ie
Editor of Intercom: Fr Paul Clayton-Lea
Assistant to Editor of Intercom
Mr Oisín Walsh
Columba Centre, Maynooth, Co Kildare
Tel 01-5053000 Fax 01-6016401
Email info@catholicbishops.ie
www.catholicbishops.ie
Twitter: @CatholicBishops
Facebook: Irish Catholic Bishops' Conference
Instagram: CatholicBishops
YouTube: Irish Catholic Bishops' Conference
Audioboo:
www.audioboo.fm/IrishCatholicBishops

Veritas Communications
President: Bishop Brendan Leahy
Chair: Mr Chris Queenan
Deputy Chair: Mr Frank Murphy
Director: Mr Tony Moroney

Veritas advises the Episcopal Commission on Communications on matters related to communications. It has the following divisions:

Veritas Company DAC
7-8 Lower Abbey Street, Dublin D01 W2C2
Tel 01-8788177
Email sales@veritas.ie

Unit 309, Blanchardstown Centre,
Dublin D15 N447
Tel 01-8864030
Email blanchardstownshop@veritas.ie

Carey's Lane, Cork T12 AW26
Tel 021-4251255
Email corkshop@veritas.ie

20 Shipquay Street,
Derry BT48 6DW
Tel 028-71266888 Fax 028-71365120
Email derryshop@veritas.ie

12-14 Upper Main Street, Letterkenny,
Co Donegal F92 HR9W
Tel 074-9124814
Email letterkennyshop@veritas.ie

122 O'Connell Street, Limerick V94 TF79
Tel 061-511075
Email limerickshop@veritas.ie

40-41 The Mall, Newry,
Co Down BT34 1AN
Tel 028-30250321
Email newryshop@veritas.ie

Belgard Square E, Tallaght,
Dublin D24 XV52
Tel 01-885 3737
Email tallaghtshop@veritas.ie

Veritas Warehouse
Unit 8, Orion Business Centre,
Northwest Business Park, Ballycoolin,
Dublin D15 VX62, Ireland
Tel 01-8829680
Email warehouse@veritas.ie

Veritas Publications
7-8 Lower Abbey Street, Dublin 1
Tel 01-8788177 Fax 01-8786507
Publishers of general religious books, liturgical texts in Irish and English, and catechetical texts.
Director: Mr Tony Moroney
Managing Editor: Ms Síne Quinn

Intercom Magazine
Catholic Communications Office,
Columba Centre, Maynooth, Co Kildare
Tel 01-5053000 Fax 01-6016401
Editor: Rev Paul Clayton-Lea
Assistant to Editor: Mr Oisín Walsh
Email intercom@catholicbishops.ie
Subscriptions: Veritas
Tel 01-8788177 Fax 01-8786507
Email intercomsubscriptions@veritas.ie
Twitter @IntercomJournal

COUNCIL FOR RESEARCH AND DEVELOPMENT OF THE IRISH EPISCOPAL CONFERENCE

Members of the Council
Most Rev Kieran O'Reilly (SMA) DD *(Chair)*
Prof Darach Turley; Ms Louise McCann; Ms Ann Morash; Dr Brian Conway

Council for Research and Development
Social Researcher: Vacant
Tel 01-5053000 Fax 01-6016401

The Council co-ordinates and assists in research projects approved or requested by the Episcopal Conference, its Agencies and Commissions.

COUNCIL FOR FINANCE AND GENERAL PURPOSES OF THE IRISH EPISCOPAL CONFERENCE

Episcopal Members of the Council
Most Rev Ger Nash DD *(Chair)*
Most Rev John Fleming DD
Most Rev Michael Duignan DD
Finance Manager: Mr Paul Corcoran
Columba Centre, Maynooth, Co Kildare
Tel 01-5053000 Fax 01-6292360
Email finance@iecon.ie

The Finance and General Purposes Council is composed of three Episcopal members and seven lay persons.

COMMISSION FOR SOCIAL ISSUES AND INTERNATIONAL AFFAIRS

Executive Secretary to the Episcopal Commission/Department
Dr Gary Carville
Tel 01-5053000
Email gary.carville@iecon.ie

COUNCIL FOR EUROPEAN AFFAIRS OF THE IRISH EPISCOPAL CONFERENCE

Members of the Council on European Affairs
Chair: Vacant
Most Rev Kieran O'Reilly DD

COMECE
19 Square de Meeûs, 1050 Bruxelles,
Belgium
Tel 32-(0)-22350510 Fax 0032-2-2303334
Email comece@comece.eu
Website www.comece.org

COMECE is a Commission of the Episcopal Conferences of the member countries of the European Union, with an office in Brussels.

General Secretary
Fr Manuel Enrique Barrios Prieto
The *Irish Episcopal Conference* representative and a *Vice-President of COMECE* is vacant.

Allianz (⭑)

COUNCIL FOR JUSTICE AND PEACE OF THE IRISH EPISCOPAL CONFERENCE

Members of the Council
Most Rev Alan McGuckian (SJ) DD *(Chair)*
Most Rev Kevin Doran DD
Most Rev Martin Hayes DD

Research Co-ordinator
Dr Gary Carville
Columba Centre, Maynooth,
Co Kildare
Tel 01-5053000 Fax 01-6016401
Email cjp@iecon.ie

The Council's role is to assist the Church in responding to the challenges facing it in the areas of human rights, social justice in Ireland and internationally, peace, including peace education, and world development. Its main activities are in research, education and information. The Council is also represented on the Social Affairs Commission of COMECE at EU level and participates in the work of Justice and Peace Europe.

COUNCIL FOR THE MISSIONS OF THE IRISH EPISCOPAL CONFERENCE

Episcopal Members of the Council
Most Rev Kieran O'Reilly DD *(Chair)*
Most Rev Larry Duffy DD

Missio Ireland (Pontifical Mission Societies)
National Director
Fr Michael Kelly (SPS)
64 Lower Rathmines Road,
Dublin 6
Tel 01-4972035
Email director@wmi.ie

Co-ordinates the activities of national missionary bodies and acts as a forum for discussion on matters related to national mission policy.

TRÓCAIRE

The Catholic Agency for World Development
Company Members (Members are from the Irish Episcopal Conference)
His Grace Most Rev Eamon Martin DD *(Chair)*
His Grace Most Rev Dermot Farrell DD
His Grace Most Rev Kieran O'Reilly (SMA) DD
His Grace Most Rev Francis Duffy DD
Most Rev William Crean DD
Most Rev Alan McGuckian (SJ) DD

Company Directors (Board members)
Bishop William Crean DD *(Chair)*
Bishop Fintan Monahan DD
Rosemary McCreery *(Deputy Chair)*
Annette Honan
Margaret Rugadya
David Donoghue
Emma Murray
Karen Dillon
Matt Walsh
Sandra Lawler
Sr Carmel Flynn
Gerry Culligan
Melissa Bosch

Chief Executive Officer
Caoimhe de Barra
Director of International
Sorcha Fennell
Director of Global Programmes
Finola Finnan
Director of Fundraising and Marketing
Gwen Dempsey
Director of Public Engagement
John Smith
Director of Corporate Services
Dearbhla Fitzsimons
Head of Communications
Miriam Donohoe
Mobile: +353 (0) 87-2393914
Maynooth, Co Kildare W23 NX63
Tel 01-6293333 Fax 01-6290661
Email info@trocaire.ie
Website http://www.trocaire.org

Offices and Resource Centres:
50 King Street, Belfast BT1 6AD
9 Cook Street, Cork T12 F583

Trócaire, the Catholic Agency for World Development, was established by the Irish bishops in 1973 to express the Church's concern for the needs and problems of the people of the developing nations. Trócaire's long-term development projects and emergency relief programmes in Africa, Asia, Latin America and the Middle East tackle the injustice of global poverty. In Ireland, through its education programmes and campaigning, Trócaire works to raise awareness about development issues and the principles of social justice involved.

COMMISSION FOR WORSHIP, PASTORAL RENEWAL AND FAITH DEVELOPMENT

Executive Secretary to the Episcopal Commission/Department
Rev Neil Xavier O'Donoghue PhD
Tel 01-5053000
Email liturgy@iecon.ie

COUNCIL FOR PASTORAL RENEWAL AND ADULT FAITH DEVELOPMENT OF THE IRISH EPISCOPAL CONFERENCE

Members of the Council
Most Rev Donal McKeown DD *(Chair)*
Most Rev Fintan Gavin DD
Mgr La Flynn
Ms Eileen Kelly
Ms Rosemary Lavelle
Ms Maureen Kelly
Sr Karen Kent
Ms Teresa Geraghty
Mr Seamus McDonald
Ms Anne Murray
Rev Frank McGuinness
Dom Richard Purcell
Rev Dr Gareth Byrne

Executive Staff of the Council
Project Officer: Vacant
Columba Centre,
Maynooth, Co Kildare
Tel 01-5053025

The Council supports ongoing dialogue between the groups and agencies represented by its members. The fruits of these dialogues are brought to the Episcopal Commission for Worship, Pastoral Renewal and Faith Development, from where recommendations are presented to the Episcopal Conference.

On behalf of the Conference, the Council fosters a shared vision as well as pastoral priorities and strategies at national level. Areas for research, reflection and supportive action by the Council include evangelisation, adult faith development, parish development, lay discipleship and ministry, and the young Church.

National Committee of Diocesan Youth Directors (NCDYD)
Most Rev Donal McKeown DD *(Chair)*
St Eugene's Cathedral
Francis Street,
Derry BT48 9AP
Tel 028-71262302 Fax 028-71371960
Email office@derrydiocese.org

COUNCIL FOR LITURGY OF THE IRISH EPISCOPAL CONFERENCE

Episcopal Members of the Council for Liturgy
Most Rev Francis Duffy DD *(Chair)*
Most Rev Fintan Monahan DD
Secretary
Rev Neil Xavier O'Donoghue PhD
Columba Centre, Maynooth, Co Kildare
Email liturgy@iecon.ie

National Centre for Liturgy
St Patrick's College, Maynooth, Co Kildare
Tel 01-7083478

The National Centre, relocated at
Maynooth in 1996, offers programmes
in liturgical formation and provides an
advisory service on liturgical matters.
Since 2020, the Centre is a constitutive
part of the Maynooth Centre for
Mission and Ministries, located within
the Faculty of Theology of the
Pontifical University.

Advisory Committee on Church Music
Chair: Rev Columba McCann OSB
Secretary: Sr Moira Bergin
National Centre for Liturgy,
St Patrick's College, Maynooth, Co Kildare
Tel 01-7083478
Email moira.bergin@spcm.ie

Advisory Committee on Sacred Art and Architecture
Chair: Mr Brian Quinn
National Centre for Liturgy,
St Patrick's College, Maynooth, Co Kildare
Tel 01-7083478

An Coiste Comhairleach um an Liotúirge nGaeilge
Cathaoirleach
An Dr Marie Whelton
Rúnaí: An Dr Micheál Ó Cearúil
Páirc Ghort na mBláth,
Portobello, An Cuarbhóthar Theas,
Baile Átha Cliath 8
Fón 086-0874814
R-phost cearbhallmp@gmail.com

Schola Cantorum
Director: Mr Gerard Lillis
St Finian's College, Mullingar,
Co Westmeath
Tel 044-9342906/086-2528029
Email schola@stfinianscollege.ie
Website www.scholacantorum.ie

Established by the hierarchy in 1970 to
provide specialised training in music for
boys and girls within the framework of
their general post-primary education.

Scholarships are awarded to students of
good general and musical ability.

COUNCIL FOR VOCATIONS OF THE IRISH EPISCOPAL CONFERENCE

Members of the Council
Most Rev Alphonsus Cullinan DD *(Chair)*
Most Rev Larry Duffy DD
National Co-ordinator for Vocations
Rev William Purcell
Administrator: Rev Eric Cooney (Deacon)
Tel 01-5053118
Email eric.cooney@vocations.ie
Website www.vocations.ie
Twitter twitter.@nvocations

COUNCIL FOR RELIGIOUS OF THE IRISH EPISCOPAL CONFERENCE

Member of the Council for Religious of the IEC
Most Rev Eamon Martin DD

COUNCIL FOR CLERGY OF THE IRISH EPISCOPAL CONFERENCE

Episcopal Members of the Council
Most Rev Ray Browne DD *(Chair)*
Most Rev Fintan Monahan DD
Most Rev Denis Nulty DD

National Training Authority for the Permanent Diaconate
Most Rev Raymond Browne DD *(Chair)*
Columba Centre, Maynooth, Co Kildare
Tel 01-5053000 Fax 01-6016401

COIMIRCE [NATIONAL BOARD FOR SAFEGUARDING CHILDREN IN THE CATHOLIC CHURCH IN IRELAND

Chair
Mr Justice Garrett Sheehan
Chief Executive Officer
Ms Teresa Devlin
Director of Training and Support
Mr Niall Moore
Part-time Director of Safeguarding
Mr Peter Kieran
Administrator: Ms Imelda Ashe
Administrator: Ms Ann Cunningham
National Board for Safeguarding
Children in the Catholic Church in
Ireland
New House, St Patrick's College,
Maynooth, Co Kildare
Tel 01-5053124 Fax 01-5053026
Email admin@safeguarding.ie

The National Board for Safeguarding
Children in the Catholic Church in
Ireland was established in 2008 in order
to provide best practice advice and to
monitor the safeguarding of children in
the Catholic Church.

Over recent years there has been an
increasing recognition of the existence
of child abuse and growing acceptance
of the potential risks to children from
others working in positions of trust.
Greater attention, therefore, has been
paid to how church organisations ensure
that the children with whom they are in
contact are kept safe from harm.]

ARCHDIOCESES AND DIOCESES OF IRELAND

Ireland is divided into four provinces: Armagh, Dublin, Cashel and Tuam, named from metropolitan sees. The areas covered by each province and diocese are described at the beginning of the entry for each diocese; a map of the ecclesiastical areas is printed on the front endpaper of this directory.

For ease of reference, the four archdioceses appear at the beginning of this section in the traditional order, but the individual dioceses appear in full alphabetical order regardless of province. Thus Achonry, from the Province of Tuam, starts the section, followed by Ardagh and Clonmacnois from the Province of Ardagh and so on.

The provinces and their suffragan sees are as follows:

Province of Armagh
Metropolitan See: Armagh
Suffragan Sees: Dioceses of Ardagh & Clonmacnois, Clogher, Derry, Down & Connor, Dromore, Kilmore, Meath, Raphoe.

The Archbishop of Armagh is Primate of All Ireland.

Province of Dublin
Metropolitan See: Dublin
Suffragan Sees: Dioceses of Ferns, Kildare & Leighlin, Ossory.

The Archbishop of Dublin is Primate of Ireland.

Province of Cashel
Metropolitan See: Cashel
Suffragan Sees: Dioceses of Cloyne, Cork & Ross, Kerry, Killaloe, Limerick, Waterford & Lismore.

Province of Tuam
Metropolitan See: Tuam
Suffragan Sees: Dioceses of Achonry, Clonfert, Elphin, Galway & Kilmacduagh with Kilfenora*, Killala.

*Kilfenora is in the Province of Cashel, but the Bishop of Galway and Kilmacduagh is its Apostolic Administrator.

ARCHDIOCESE OF ARMAGH

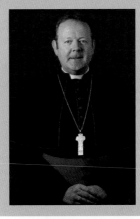

Most Rev Eamon Martin DD
Archbishop of Armagh;
Primate of All Ireland;
born 30 October 1961;
ordained priest 28 June 1987;
ordained Coadjutor Archbishop
21 April 2013; succeeded as
Archbishop of Armagh
8 September 2014.

Residence: Ara Coeli,
Cathedral Road,
Armagh BT61 7QY
Tel 028-37522045
Fax 028-37526182
Email admin@aracoeli.com
www.armagharchdiocese.org

PATRONS OF THE ARCHDIOCESE
ST MALACHY, 3 NOVEMBER; ST PATRICK, 17 MARCH;
ST OLIVER PLUNKETT, 1 JULY

SUFFRAGFEN SEES: ARDAGH AND CLONMACNOIS, CLOGHER, DERRY,
DOWN AND CONNOR, DROMORE, KILMORE, MEATH, RAPHOE

INCLUDES ALMOST ALL OF COUNTIES ARMAGH AND LOUTH
APPROX HALF OF COUNTY TYRONE
AND PARTS OF COUNTIES DERRY AND MEATH

ST PATRICK'S CATHEDRAL, ARMAGH

The building and decoration of the new St Patrick's Cathedral lasted from St Patrick's Day 1840, when the foundation stone was laid, until its solemn consecration in 1904. The Cathedral had been opened and dedicated in 1873. However, there were occasional intermissions of the work, and one of the longest gaps occurred because of the Great Famine. Primate Crolly, who had initiated the building, became a victim of famine cholera, and, at his own wish, his body was laid to rest under the sanctuary of the unfinished cathedral.

For five years the low outline of the bare walls remained, but with the translation of Dr Paul Cullen to the See of Dublin, work was resumed under Primate Dixon. On Easter Monday 1854, tarpaulins and canvas covers were drawn from wall to wall to allow Mass to be celebrated in the unfinished building.

During the Famine cessation the original architect, Thomas J. Duff, died. The architect to take over from Duff's original perpendicular Gothic design was J. J. McCarthy, destined to become one of the famous architects of the nineteenth century. In his anxiety to achieve a greater degree of classical purity, McCarthy drew up a continuation design in the old fourteenth-century Decorated Gothic. While critics may debate the wisdom of such a radical change when the building had reached a relatively advanced stage, the effect was undoubtedly to create an overall impression of massive grandeur.

The final impetus to complete the building came when Dr McGettigan was appointed (1870) to Armagh, and the solemn dedication took place in 1873.

Cardinal Logue, following Primate McGettigan's death, was to achieve the splendid interior decoration and the addition of the Synod Hall. He travelled to Rome and Carrara in search of precious marble for the reredos, pulpit and altar, and it was he also who achieved the decoration of the interior with mosaic. Under him, stained-glass windows were commissioned from Meyer in Germany. Cardinal Vanutelli represented Pope Pius X at the solemn consecration in 1904. A grand carillon was installed in 1924.

Vatican II's decree on Sacred Liturgy stressed the participation of the laity and hence greater visibility had to be afforded to the congregation. For this reason all the architects who submitted designs based their plans on the removal of the 1904 marble screens, which hindered visibility of the sanctuary from the sides. By raising, enlarging and opening the sanctuary area, the cathedral has, to a large extent, been restored to its original form.

With the removal of the rood screen, a new crucifix had to be placed at the sanctuary, and a specially commissioned 'Cross of Life' by Imogen Stuart was affixed to the right of the sanctuary.

The rededication took place in 1982, and a portion of St Malachy's relics from France, together with a relic of St Oliver Plunkett, was placed in the new altar. And so, the mortal remains of two of Armagh's most celebrated *comharbaí Phádraig* were carried back to the scene of their labours in more troubled times.

The most recent restoration project was completed in 2003 at a cost of £7.5 million, the majority of which was generously funded by parishioners and friends throughout the diocese and beyond.

A unique, but now also an historical feature of the primatial cathedral, are the five Cardinals' Hats. They are no longer conferred on new Cardinals. They were hung here and went deliberately untended so that their decay would represent the end of all earthly glory. The most recently hung (and last to be presented) is that of Cardinal Conway. Beside it are Cardinal Logue's and Cardinal O'Donnell's, while on the opposite side are the hats of Cardinals D'Alton and MacRory.

Allianz (il)

His Eminence Cardinal Seán Brady DCL, DD
Archbishop Emeritus of Armagh; born 1939; ordained priest 22 February 1964; ordained Coadjutor Archbishop 19 February 1995; installed Archbishop of Armagh 3 November 1996; created Cardinal 24 November 2007. Residence: Parochial House, 86 Maydown Road, Tullysaran, Benburb, Co Tyrone BT71 7LN

Most Rev Michael Router DD
Titular Bishop of Lugmad; Auxiliary Bishop of Armagh; born 15 April 1965; ordained priest 25 June 1989; ordained Bishop 21 July 2019 Residence: Annaskeagh, Ravensdale, Dundalk, Co Louth A91 KP64

CHAPTER

Dean: Very Rev Kevin Donaghy PP, VG
Archdeacon: Rt Rev James Carroll
Canons: Rt Rev Mgr Colum Curry PP, VG
Very Rev Eugene Sweeney PP, VG
Very Rev Patrick McDonnell PE
Rt Rev Christopher O'Byrne PE
Rt Rev Raymond Murray PE
Very Rev James Clyne PE, AP
Very Rev Michael Crawley PE
Very Rev Benedict Fee PP, EV
Very Rev Peter Murphy PP
Very Rev Michael C. Toner PP

ADMINISTRATION

Diocesan Secretary
Rev Mr Paul Mallon Deacon

Vicars General
Rt Rev Mgr Colum Curry PP, VG
Very Rev Eugene Sweeney PP, VG
Very Rev Dean Kevin Donaghy PP, VG

Episcopal Vicars
Rt Rev Mgr James Carroll PP, EV
Very Rev Canon Benedict Fee PP, EV
Very Rev Malachy Conlon PP, EV
Very Rev Gerard Campbell PP, EV

Vicars Forane
St John's: Fr Martin McArdle PP
An Ciorcal: Fr Brian Slater CC
The Martyrs: Fr David Moore PP
Cardinal MacRory: Fr Cathal Deveney PP
St Colman's: Canon Benedict Fee PP, EV
Tír Uí Néill: Dean Kevin Donaghy PP, VG
St John Paul II: Fr Michael Woods PP
St Patrick's: Fr John McKeever PP
Cardinal Ó Fiaich: Vacant
Killeavy: Fr Liam McKinney PP
St Brigid's: Fr Emlyn McGinn PP
Peninsula: Fr Malachy Conlon PP, EV
Dún Dealgan: Fr Mark O'Hagan PP
Our Lady Queen of Peace: Fr Gerard Campbell PP, EV
St Cillian's: Canon Peter Murphy PP
St Colmcille's: Fr Patrick Rushe PP
St Oliver's: Canon Eugene Sweeney PP, VG

Chancellor
Very Rev Canon Michael C. Toner PP

Assistant Chancellor
Very Rev John McKeever PP

Diocesan Curia
Mr Tiarnán O'Neill
Financial Administrator
Email toneill@aracoeli.com
Ara Coeli, Cathedral Road,
Armagh BT61 7QY
Tel 028-37522045 Fax 028-37526182

Diocesan Safeguarding Office
Director and Designated Officer
Mr Aidan Gordon
Email safeguardingdirector@ archdioceseofarmagh.com
Tel 028-37525592
Training coordinator and Designated Officer: Mrs Eleanor Kelly
Email ekelly@archdioceseofarmagh.com
Tel 07584-323138
Administrative Staff: Mr Pierce Fox
Email pfox@archdioceseofarmagh.com
Archdiocese of Armagh,
Cathedral Road,
Armagh BT61 7QY
Tel 028-37525592

CATECHETICS EDUCATION

Catholic Primary School Managers' Association
Secretary: Mrs Niamh Black
c/o Parochial House, Top Rath,
Carlingford, Co Louth
Tel 042-9376105
Email armaghedu@gmail.com

Council for Catholic Maintained Schools
Linenhill House, 23 Linenhall Street,
Lisburn BT28 1FJ
Tel 028-92013014

Diocesan Advisers for Religious Education
Primary Schools
Sr Anne Lyng (RSM)
Diocesan Pastoral Office,
Holy Family Parochial House,
Hoey's Lane, Dundalk,
Co Louth A91 K761
Tel 042-9351316
Email annepastoralcentre@gmail.com
Post-Primary Schools
Rev Declan O'Loughlin
Parochial House, 30 Newline,
Killeavy, Newry, Co Down BT35 8TA
Tel 028-30889609
Email decoloughlin@yahoo.co.uk

PASTORAL

ACCORD
Drogheda Chairperson
Ms Eileen Mulcahy
Verona, Cross Lane,
Drogheda, Co Louth
Tel 041-9843860
Email droghedaaccord@gmail.com

Armagh Chairperson
Ms Deirdre O'Rawe
Drumcree Pastoral Centre,
Garvaghy Road, Craigavon
Armagh BT62 1EB
Tel 079-808988399

Dundalk Chairperson
Very Rev Mark O'Hagan PP, VF
St Patrick's, Roden Place,
Dundalk, Co Louth
Tel 042-9331731
Email accorddundalk@eircom.net

Apostolic Work Society
Diocesan President: Ms Jean Hanratty
13 College Street, Armagh BT61 9BT
Tel 028-37522781

Armagh Diocesan Pastoral Office
Diocesan Pastoral Workers
Sr Anne Lyng (RSM)
Email annepastoralcentre@gmail.com
Mrs Sharon Dunne
Email dunnesharon.pastoralcentre@gmail.com
Administrative Staff: Ms Milanda Kelly
Email milanda@parishandfamily.ie
Armagh Diocesan Pastoral Office,
Holy Family Parochial House,
Hoey's Lane, Dundalk, Co Louth A91 K76
Tel 042-9351316

Armagh Diocesan Pastoral Council
Chairperson: Patricia McGrane
Secretary: Milanda Kelly
Email milanda@parishandfamily.ie

Charismatic Renewal
Rt Rev Mgr Colum Curry PP, VG

Communications
Diocesan Officer: Mr Martin Long
Catholic Communications Office,
Irish Bishops' Conference,
Columba Centre, Maynooth, Co Kildare
Tel 01-5053010
Email martinlong@catholicbishops.ie

Council of Priests
Chairman: Very Rev Malachy Conlon PP

Ecumenism
Very Rev Pádraig Murphy PE
Very Rev Seán Dooley PP

Knock Pilgrimage
Director
Very Rev Canon Benedict Fee PP, EV

egion of Mary
rmagh Curia President
Ms Margaret McManus
3 Newry Road, Armagh BT60 1ES
el 077-99867714
roghada Curia President
Ms Elizabeth Maloney
el 086-3658358
undalk Curia President
Ms Katrina Loughran
el 087-9903154

iturgy Commission
hair: Vacant

MFM Community Radio
en Archdeacon James Carroll PP, EV

ourdes Pilgrimage
irector: Very Rev Mark O'Hagan PP

Marriage Tribunal
(See Marriage Tribunals section.)

ermanent Diaconate
irector: Rev Brian White CC
Circular Road, Dungannon,
o Tyrone BT71 6BE
mail roadbowler@hotmail.com

ioneer Total Abstinence Association
iocesan Director: Ms Mary Livingstone
el 028-37551458

ontifical Mission Societies
iocesan Director
t Rev Mgr Colum Curry PE, AP, VG

PRED
o-ordinator: Miss Caoímhe McNeill
4 Annaboe Road, Kilmore,
o Armagh BT61 8NP
mail caoimhemcneill@gmail.com

avellers
o-ordinator: Vacant

ocations Commission
ocations Director
ev Barry Matthews CC

outh Commission (ADYC)
hairperson
ery Rev Thomas McHugh Adm
mail thomasmch@gmail.com
outh Coordinator (Northern)
anet Forbes
el 079-68738486
mail jforbes@aracoeli.com
outh Coordinator (Co Louth)
ob O'Hara
el 086-8636296
mail rohara@aracoeli.com
rchdiocese of Armagh, Cathedral Road,
rmagh BT61 7QY
el 028-37523084
mail armaghyouth@yahoo.co.uk

PARISHES

Mensal parishes are listed first. Other parishes follow alphabetically. Historical names are given in parentheses. Church titulars are in italics.

ARMAGH
St Patrick's Cathedral, St Malachy, Irish Street, *St Colmcille's,* Knockaconey
Immaculate Conception, Tullysaran
Email armaghparishoffice@gmail.com
Very Rev Peter McAnenly Adm
Email pmcanenly21@gmail.com
Rev Barry Matthews CC
Email barrymatthews@gmail.com
Rev Emmanuel Fasakin (MSP) CC
Email emmafash725@yahoo.com
Rev Mr Paul Mallon, Permanent Deacon
Email pjmallon@gmail.com
Rev Mr Eunan McCreesh, Permanent Deacon
Email eunan.mccreesh@googlemail.com
Parochial House, 42 Abbey Street, Armagh BT61 7DZ
Tel 028-37522802 Fax 028-37522245
Parish Office: Cathedral Gate Lodge, 41a Cathedral Road, Armagh BT61 7QX
Tel 028-37522813

DUNDALK, ST PATRICK'S
St Patrick's, Roden Place
St Nicholas', Church Street
www.stpatricksparishdundalk.org
Email stpatricksparishdundalk@gmail.com
Very Rev Mark O'Hagan PP, VF
Email ohagan.mark2@gmail.com
Rev Maciej Zacharek CC
Email zacharekmaciej8@gmail.com
Rev Stephen Wilson CC
Email swilson2205@gmail.com
Rev Peter Hassan CC
Email pethaz@hotmail.com
St Patrick's Presbytery, Roden Place, Dundalk, Co Louth A91 K2P4
Tel 042-9334648 Fax 042-9336355

DUNDALK, HOLY REDEEMER
Holy Redeemer, Ard Easmuinn
www.redeemerparish.ie
Email holyredeemerdundalk@gmail.com
Very Rev Mark O'Hagan Adm
Email ohagan.mark2@gmail.com
Rev Maciej Zacharek CC
Email zacharekmaciej8@gmail.com
Rev Stephen Wilson CC
Email swilson2205@gmail.com
Rev Peter Hassan CC
Email pethaz@hotmail.com
Parochial House, Ard Easmuinn, Dundalk, Co Louth A91 W8Y1
Tel 042-9334259

DUNDALK, ST JOSEPH'S
St Joseph's
Email dundalkoffice@redemptorists.ie
Very Rev Noel Kehoe (CSsR) Adm
Email nkehoe@cssr.ie
Rev Ryan Holovlasky (CSsR) CC
Email ryanh@cssr.ie
St Joseph's, St Alphonsus Road, Dundalk, Co Louth A91 F3FC
Tel 042-9334042 Fax 042-9330893

DUNDALK, HOLY FAMILY
Holy Family
Email theholyfamily@eircom.net
Very Rev Derek Ryan (CSsR) Adm
Email dryan@cssr.ie
Rev Richard Delahunty (CSsR) CC
Email richard.delahu@yahoo.ie
Holy Family Parish, Hoey's Lane, Muirhevnamor, Dundalk, Co Louth A91 K761
Tel 042-9336301 Fax 042-9336350

DROGHEDA
St Peter's, West Street
Our Lady of Lourdes, Hardman's Gardens
www.saintpetersdrogheda.ie
Email stpetersadmin1@eircom.net
Very Rev Canon Eugene Sweeney PP, VF, VG
Email esweeney64@btconnect.com
Rev Mr David Durrigan, Permanent Deacon
Email ddurrigan@gmx.com
Rev Mr John Taaffe, Permanent Deacon
Email johntaaffe1@gmail.com
Parochial House, 9 Fair Street, Drogheda, Co Louth A92 T6WY
Tel 041-9838537 Fax 041-9841351
Rev Desmond Branigan CC
Email desmond.brannigan@gmail.com
Rev Piotr Wojtala CC
Email pedrowojtala@gmail.com
Our Lady of Lourdes Presbytery, Hardman's Gardens, Drogheda, Co Louth A92 PXF3
Tel 041-9831899
Very Rev Aidan Murphy PE, AP
Email amrev@icloud.com
St Peter's Presbytery, 10 Fair Street, Drogheda, Co Louth A92 NX3T
Tel 041-9838239

DUNGANNON (DRUMGLASS, KILLYMAN AND TULLYNISKIN)
St Patrick's, Dungannon, *St Malachy's* Edendork, *St Brigid's,* Killyman, *Sacred Heart,* Clonmore
www.parishofdungannon.com
Very Rev Kevin Donaghy PP, VF, VG
4 Circular Road, Dungannon, Co Tyrone BT71 6BE
Tel 028-87722775
Email kdonaghy55@gmail.com
Rev Brian White CC
Email roadbowler@hotmail.com
Very Rev Eamonn McCamley
Email ep2018@btinternet.com
Rev Jibin James CC
Email jibinjamesp@gmail.com
Rev Mr Andrew Hegarty, Permanent Deacon
Email andythegarty@gmail.com
Rev Mr Tony Hughes, Permanent Deacon
Email tonyhughes24@hotmail.com
Parochial House, 6 Circular Road, Dungannon, Co Tyrone BT71 6BE
Tel 028-87722631
Parish Office: 4 Killyman Road, Dungannon, Co Tyrone BT71 6DH
Tel/Fax 028-87726893
Email info@parishofdungannon.com

ARDBOE
Blessed Sacrament, Mullinahoe
Immaculate Conception, Moortown
Very Rev Gerard Tremer PP
Parochial House, 19 Ardboe Road,
Moortown, Cookstown,
Co Tyrone BT80 0HT
Tel 028-86737236
Email ardboepp@outlook.com
Parish Office: 1 Mullanahoe Road,
Ardboe, Dungannon,
Co Tyrone BT71 5AT
Tel 028-86736997
Email ardboeparochial@btinternet.com

ARDEE & COLLON
Nativity of Our Lady, Ardee
St Catherine's, Ballapousta
Mary Immaculate, Collon
Website www.ardeeparish.com
Email ardee.collon@gmail.com
Very Rev Canon Peter Murphy PP, VF
Parochial House, Moorehall,
Ardee, Co Louth A92 PXF3
Tel 041-6850920 Fax 041-6850922
Rev Stefano Colleluori CC
Parochial House, Ardee Street,
Collon, Co Louth A92 F2P7
Tel 041-9826106
Email stefanocoll93@gmail.com

AUGHNACLOY (AGHALOO)
St Mary's, Aughnacloy, St Brigid's, Killens,
St Joseph's, Caledon
Email parishofaghaloo@gmail.com
Very Rev Cathal Deveney PP, VF
Parochial House, 19 Caledon Road,
Aughnacloy, Co Tyrone BT69 6HX
Tel 028-85557212
Email cdeveney@icloud.com
Rev Dermot McCaul (SMA) *(Priest in Residence)*
Parochial House, 56 Minterburn Road,
Lairakeann, Caledon,
Co Tyrone BT68 4XH
Tel 028-37568288
Email mccaulda@hotmail.com

BALLINDERRY
St Patrick's
Very Rev Peter Donnelly PP
Parochial House,
130 Ballinderry Bridge Road, Coagh,
Cookstown, Co Tyrone BT80 0AY
Tel 028-79418244
Email ballinderryparish@outlook.com

BALLYGAWLEY (ERRIGAL KIERAN)
St Matthew's, Garvaghy, St Mary's,
Dunmoyle, Immaculate Conception,
Ballygawley, St Malachy's, Ballymacilroy
Very Rev Michael O'Dwyer PP
Parochial House, 31 Church Street,
Ballygawley, Co Tyrone BT70 2HA
Tel 028-85567096
Email errigalciaran99@gmail.com

BERAGH
Immaculate Conception, Beragh,
St Malachy's, Seskinore,
St Patrick's, Drumduff
Very Rev Seán McCartan PP
Parochial House, Beragh, Omagh,
Co Tyrone BT79 OSY
Tel 028-80758206
Email seancmccartan@gmail.com
Email beraghparochial@btinternet.com

BESSBROOK (KILLEAVY LOWER)
SS Peter and Paul, Bessbrook,
St Malachy, Camlough,
Sacred Heart, Lislea,
Immaculate Conception, Lissummon Road,
Newry, Good Shepherd, Cloughreagh
Very Rev Aidan Dunne PP
Parochial House, 11 Chapel Road,
Bessbrook, Newry, Co Down BT35 7AU
Tel 028-30830206
Email fadunne@gmail.com
Rev Seán Larkin PE, AP
Parochial House, 9 Chapel Road,
Bessbrook, Newry, Co Down BT35 7AU
Tel 028-30830272
Email larkseanj@aol.com
Rev Mr Philip Carder, Deacon
c/o Parochial House, 11 Chapel Road,
Bessbrook, Newry, Co Down BT35 7AU
Tel 028-30830206 Fax 028-30838154
Email philipcarder34@gmail.com

CARLINGFORD AND CLOGHERNY
St Michael's, Carlingford
St Lawrence's, Omeath
www.carlinnparish.com
Very Rev Magnus Ogbonna (MSP) PP
Parochial House, Chapel Hill,
Carlingford, Co Louth A91 FX76
Tel 042-9373111
Email doziemsp@yahoo.com
Rev Christopher McElwee (IC) CC
Parochial House, Omeath,
Co Louth A91 HK76
Tel 042-9375198

CLOGHERHEAD
St Michael's, Clogherhead,
SS Peter and Paul, Walshestown
www.clogherhead.com
Very Rev Martin McVeigh PP
Parochial House, Clogherhead,
Drogheda, Co Louth A92 K97O
Tel 041-9822224
Email clogherheadparish@gmail.com

CLOGHOGUE (KILLEAVY UPPER)
Sacred Heart, Cloghogue, St Joseph's,
Meigh, St Michael's, Killean
Very Rev Richard Naughton PP
Mountain Lodge, 132 Dublin Road,
Newry, Co Down BT35 8QT
Tel 028-30262174 Fax 028-30262174
Very Rev Canon S. James Clyne PE, AP
24 Chapel Road, Killeavy, Newry,
Co Down BT35 8JY
Tel 028-30848222
Email clynesj@gmail.com

CLONOE
St Patrick's, Clonoe, St Columcille's,
Kingsland, St Brigid's, Brockagh
Email clonoeparish@gmail.com
Very Rev Canon Benedict Fee PP, EV, VF
Teac na h'Ard Croise, 3 Cloghog Road,
Clonoe, Coalisland, Co Tyrone BT71 5EH
Tel 028-87749184
Email frbennyfee@hotmail.com
Rev John McCallion CC
Parochial House, 140 Mountjoy Road,
Brocagh, Dungannon,
Co Tyrone BT71 5DY
Tel 028-87738381
Email jmccallion384@gmail.com

COAGH
Our Lady's, Coagh
SS Joseph and Malachy, Drummullan
Very Rev Laurence Boyle PP
Email lorcanboyle@gmail.com
Parochial House, 1 Convent Road,
Cookstown, Co Tyrone BT80 8QA
Tel 028-86763370
Rev Francis Coll CC
Parochial House, Hanover Square,
Coagh, Cookstown, Co Tyrone BT80 0EF
Tel 028-86737212
Email gabrielfcoll@gmail.com

COALISLAND
Holy Family, Coalisland
St Mary & St Joseph, Coalisland,
St Mary's, Stewartstown
Email coalislandparish@yahoo.co.uk
Very Rev Eugene O'Neill PP
Parochial House, 31 Brackaville Road,
Coalisland, Co Tyrone BT71 4NH
Tel 028-87740221 Fax 028-87746449
Email freoneill@btinternet.com
Rev Mr Malachy McElmeel, Permanent Deacon
c/o Parochial House, 31 Brackaville Road,
Coalisland, Co Tyrone BT71 4NH
Tel 028-87740221 Fax 028-87746449
Email malachy.motability@gmail.com

COOKSTOWN (DESERTCREIGHT AND DERRYLORAN)
Holy Trinity, Cookstown, Sacred Heart,
Tullydonnell, St John's, Slatequarry,
St Laurán's, Cookstown
Very Rev Laurence Boyle PP
Email lorcanboyle@gmail.com
Rev Mr Eamon Quinn, Permanent Deacon
Email eamonquinn1@outlook.com
Parochial House, 1 Convent Road,
Cookstown, Co Tyrone BT80 8QA
Parish email cookstownparish@gmail.com
Tel 028-86763370
Rev Brian Slater CC, VF
Email brianslater60@hotmail.com
Parochial House, 3 Convent Road,
Cookstown, Co Tyrone BT80 8QA
Tel 028-86763490

COOLEY

St James's, Grange
Our Lady, Star of the Sea, Boher
St Anne's, Mullaghbuoy
Very Rev Malachy Conlon PP, VF, EV
Chapel Rath, Carlingford, Co Louth A91 XW24
Tel 042-9376105 Fax 042-9376075
Email malachycooley@gmail.com

CROSSMAGLEN (CREGGAN UPPER)

St Patrick's, Crossmaglen,
St Brigid's, Glassdrummond,
Sacred Heart, Shelagh
Email uppercreggan@gmail.com
Very Rev Dermot Maloney PP
Parochial House, 9 Newry Road,
Crossmaglen, Newry,
Co Down BT35 9HH
Tel 028-30861208 Fax 028-30860163
Email maloney750@btinternet.com
Rev Mr Paul Casey, Permanent Deacon
c/o Parochial House, 9 Newry Road,
Crossmaglen, Newry, Co Down BT35 9HH
Tel 028-30861208
Email paulcasey2121@gmail.com

CULLYHANNA (CREGGAN LOWER)

St Patrick's, Cullyhanna
St Michael's, Newtownhamilton
St Oliver Plunkett's, Dorsey
Email lowercregganparish@hotmail.com
Very Rev Canon Michael C. Toner PP
Parochial House, Tullynavall Road,
Cullyhanna, Newry, Co Down BT35 OPZ
Tel 028-30861235

DARVER AND DROMISKIN

St Peter's, Dromiskin, St Michael's, Darver
Very Rev Gerard Campbell Adm
c/o Parochial House, Knockbridge,
Dundalk, Co Louth A91 NA03
Tel 042-6827418
Very Rev Patrick McEnroe PE, AP
Darver, Readypenny, Dundalk,
Co Louth A91 YC60
Tel 042-9379147
Email patmmcenroe@gmail.com

DONAGHMORE

St Patrick's, Donaghmore
St John's, Galbally
Very Rev Gerard McAleer PP
Parochial House, 63 Castlecaulfield Road,
Donaghmore, Dungannon,
Co Tyrone BT70 3HF
Tel 028-87761327
Email gerard0826@icloud.com
Very Rev Patrick Breslan PE, AP
Parochial House, 55 Dermanaught Road,
Galbally, Dungannon,
Co Tyrone BT70 2NR
Tel 028-87758277

DROMINTEE

St Patrick's, Dromintee
Sacred Heart, Jonesboro
Email drominteeparish@btinternet.com
Very Rev Seamus White PP
Email seamuswhite@ymail.com
Rev Mr George Kingsnorth, Permanent
Deacon
Email deacongeorgekingsnorth@gmail.com
Parochial House, 40 The Village,
Jonesboro, Newry,
Co Down BT35 8HP
Tel 028-30849345

DUNLEER

St Brigid's, Dunleer,
St Finians', Dromin,
St Kevin's, Philipstown
www.dunleerparish.ie
Very Rev G. Michael Murtagh PP
Parochial House, Old Chapel Lane,
Dunleer, Co Louth A92 W29X
Tel 041-6851278
Email gmichaelmurtagh@gmail.com

EGLISH

St Patrick's
Email parishofeglish@gmail.com
Very Rev Thomas McHugh Adm
Email thomasmch@gmail.com
Very Rev John Heagney PE, AP
Email heagneyjh@aol.com
124 Eglish Road, Dungannon,
Co Tyrone BT70 1LB
Tel 028-37549661

FAUGHART

St Brigid's, Kilcurry,
Most Holy Rosary, Brid-a-Crinn,
St Joseph's, Castletown
Email info@faughartparish.ie
Very Rev Vinod Kurian (IC) PP
Email thennattil@hotmail.com
Rev Oliver Stansfield (IC) CC
Email ostansfield@gmail.com
Rev Mr George Kingsnorth, Permanent
Deacon
Email deacongeorgekingsnorth@gmail.com
Parochial House, Kilcurry,
Dundalk, Co Louth, A91 E8N8
Tel 042-9334410/9333235

HAGGARDSTOWN AND BLACKROCK

St Fursey's Haggardstown
St Oliver Plunkett's, Blackrock
Very Rev Pádraig Keenan PP
Parochial House, Chapel Road,
Haggardstown, Dundalk,
Co Louth A91 X0PR
Tel 042-9321621
Email pkballygoley@hotmail.com
Rev Mr Dermot Clarke, Permanent
Deacon
c/o Parochial House, Chapel Road,
Haggardstown, Dundalk,
Co Louth A91 X0PR
Tel 042-9321621
Email dkclarke@eircom.net

KEADY (DERRYNOOSE)

St Patrick's, Keady, St Joseph's,
Derrynoose, St Joseph's, Madden
Email info@keadyparish.net
Very Rev John McKeever PP, VF
Assistant Chancellor of the Diocese
Email john_mckeever@yahoo.com
Rev Mr Martin Barlow,
Permanent Deacon
Email martin@thebarlows.biz
Parochial House, 35 St Patrick Street,
Keady, Co Armagh BT60 3TQ
Tel 028-37531246 Fax 028-37530850
Rev Aidan McCann CC
Parochial House, 34 Madden Row,
Keady, Co Armagh, BT60 3RW
Tel 028-37531242
Email aidmccann@gmail.com

KILDRESS

St Joseph's, Killeenan
St Mary's, Dunamore
Very Rev Patrick Hughes PP
Parochial House, 10 Cloughfin Road,
Kildress, Cookstown,
Co Tyrone BT80 9JB
Tel 028-86751206
Email
patrickhughes309@btinternet.com

KILKERLEY

Immaculate Conception
Very Rev Gerard Campbell PP, VF, EV
Parochial House, Knockbridge,
Dundalk, Co Louth A91 NA03
Tel 042-9374125
Email gerrycampbell65@gmail.com
Very Rev Brian MacRaois PE, AP
The Holly Tree, Grange,
Knockbridge, Dundalk,
Co Louth A91 VK18
Tel 042-6827409

KILLCLUNEY

St Patrick's, Baile Mhic an Aba,
St Michael's, Cladaí Móra,
St Mary's, Grainseach Mhór
Email cillchluanaparish@gmail.com
Very Rev Gregory Carvill PP
Parochial House,
194 Newtown Hamilton Road,
Ballymacnab, Armagh BT60 2QS
Tel 028-37531641
Email carvillgreg@gmail.com

KILLEESHIL

Assumption, Killeeshil, St Patrick's,
Aughnagar, St Joseph's, Ackenduff
Email killeeshilparish@yahoo.co.uk
Very Rev Patrick Hannigan PP
Parochial House,
65 Tullyallen Road,
Dungannon, Co Tyrone BT70 3AF
Tel 028-87761211 Fax 028-87769211
Email pathannigan494@gmail.com

KILMORE
Immaculate Conception, Mullavilly,
St Patrick's, Stonebridge
Email parishofkilmore@gmail.com
www.parishofkilmore.com
Very Rev Michael Sheehan Adm
c/o Parochial House, 15 Moy Road,
Portadown, Co Armagh BT62 1QL
Rev Paul Murphy CC
Parochial House, 114 Battlehill Road,
Richhill, Co Armagh BT61 8QJ
Tel 028-38871661
Email pmurph12@tcd.ie

KILSARAN
St Mary's, Kilsaran
St Nicholas, Stabannon
Email
kilsaranandstabannonparish@gmail.com
Very Rev Anselm Emechebe (MSP) PP
Parochial House, Kilsaran,
Castlebellingham, Dundalk,
Co Louth A91 A256
Tel 042-9372255 Fax 042-9372255
Email aemechebe@yahoo.com

KNOCKBRIDGE
St Mary's, Knockbridge
www.ourladyqueenofpeacepa.org
Very Rev Gerard Campbell PP, VF, EV
Email gerrycampbell65@gmail.com
Rev Mr Martin Cunningham, Permanent
Deacon
Email mtcunningham@gmail.com
Parochial House, Knockbridge,
Dundalk, Co Louth A91 NA03
Tel 042-9374125

LISSAN
St Michael's
Very Rev Patrick Hughes Adm
Parochial House, 10 Cloughfin Road,
Kildress, Cookstown, Co Tyrone BT80 9JB
Tel 028-86751206
Email patrickhughes309@btinternet.com
Rt Rev Mgr Colum Curry PE, AP, VG
Parochial House, 2 Tullynure Road,
Cookstown, Co Tyrone BT80 9XH
Tel 028-86769921
Email columcurry@yahoo.com

LORDSHIP (AND BALLYMASCANLON)
St Mary's, Ravensdale
St Mary's, Lordship
Our Lady of the Wayside, Jenkinstown
www.lordship-ballymascanlon.org
Very Rev Stephen Duffy PP
Parochial House, Ravensdale,
Dundalk, Co Louth A91 V523
Tel 042-9371327
Email duffyst@hotmail.co.uk

LOUGHGALL
Our Lady of Peace, Maghery
St Peter's, Collegeland
St Patrick's, Loughgall
St John's, Tartaraghan
Email loughgallsecretary@gmail.com
Very Rev Garrett Campbell PP
Parochial House, 17 Eagralougher Road,
Loughgall, Co Armagh BT61 8LA
Tel 028-38891231 Fax 028-38891827
Email loughgallpp@gmail.com

LOUTH
Our Lady of Immaculate Conception,
Louth
Our Lady of the Snows, Stonetown
Very Rev Gerard Campbell Adm
c/o Parochial House, Knockbridge,
Co Louth A91 NA03
Tel 042 9374125
Email gerrycampbell65@gmail.com
Rev Sijo John CC
Parochial House, Louth Village,
Dundalk, Co Louth A91 XE42
Tel 042-9374285
Email svenkitta@gmail.com

MAGHERAFELT AND ARDTREA NORTH
Assumption, Magherafelt
St John's, Milltown
St Patrick's Castledawson
Email office@magherafeltparish.org
www.magherafeltparish.org
Very Rev John Gates PP
Parochial House, 30 King Street,
Magherafelt, Co Derry BT45 6AS
Tel 028-79632439
Email jgatesbrack@gmail.com
Rev Juan Jesus Gonzalez-Borrallo CC
Parochial House, 12 Aughrim Road,
Magherafelt, Co Derry BT45 6AY
Tel 077-36955013
Email borrallo.juanjesus@gmail.com
Rev Mr Kevin Duffy, Permanent Deacon
Parochial House, 30 King Street,
Magherafelt, Co Derry BT45 6AS
Tel 028-79632439
Email deacon.kevin@yahoo.co.uk

MELL
St Joseph's
Very Rev John McAlinden PP
Parochial House, Slane Road, Mell,
Drogheda, Co Louth A92 WAC4
Tel 041-9838278
Email frjohnmcalinden@gmail.com

MELLIFONT
Our Lady of the Assumption, Tullyallen
Very Rev Seán Dooley PP
Parochial House, Tullyallen,
Drogheda, Co Louth A92 H243
Tel 041-9838520
Email seandooleyfriesian@btconnect.com

MIDDLE KILLEAVY (NEWRY)
St Mary's, Dromalane,
St Malachy's, Carnagat
www.middlekilleavy.com
Email assumptionnewry@gmail.com
Very Rev Liam McKinney PP, VF
'Glenshee', 9 Dublin Road,
Newry, Co Down BT35 8DA
Tel 028-30262376
Tel Parish Office 028-30252459
Email ltpmckinney@yahoo.com
Rev Damien Quigley CC
27 Woodhill, Monaghan Row, Newry,
Co Down BT35 8DP
Tel 028-30269032
Email quigleydamien@gmail.com

MIDDLETOWN (TYNAN)
St John's, Middletown
St Joseph's, Tynan
Very Rev Seán Moore PP
Parochial House,
290 Monaghan Road,
Middletown, Co Armagh BT60 4HS
Tel 028-37568406
middletowntynanparish@hotmail.co.uk

MONASTERBOICE
Immaculate Conception, Tenure,
Nativity of Our Lady, Fieldstown
Email
monasterboiceparish2018@gmail.com
Very Rev Patrick Rushe PP, VF
Parochial House, Monasterboice,
Drogheda, Co Louth A92 RT66
Tel 086-8807470
Email patrickrushe@me.com

MONEYMORE (ARDTREA)
SS John and Trea, Moneymore
St Patrick, Loup
Very Rev Martin McArdle PP, VF
Parochial House, 10 Springhill Road,
Moneymore, Magherafelt,
Co Derry BT45 7NG
Tel 028-86748242
Email ardtrea@btconnect.com

MOY (CLONFEACLE)
St John the Baptist, Moy
St Jarlath's, Clonfeacle
www.clonfeacleparish.com
Very Rev Thomas McHugh Adm
75 Clonfeacle Road,
Blackwatertown, Dungannon,
Co Tyrone BT71 7HP
Tel 028-87511215
Email thomasmch@gmail.com

MULLAGHBAWN (FORKHILL)
St Mary's, Mullaghbawn
Our Lady, Queen of Peace, Aughanduff
St Oliver Plunkett, Forkhill
Very Rev Emlyn McGinn PP, VF
Parochial House, 9a Forkhill Road,
Mullaghbawn, Newry,
Co Down BT35 9RA
Tel 028-30888286
Email emlynmcginn@yahoo.com

NEWBRIDGE
St James, Newbridge
Very Rev John Fox PP
Parochial House, 153 Aughrim Road,
Toomebridge, Antrim BT41 3SH
Tel 028-79468277
Email newbridgechurch@gmail.com

Allianz (ⅲ)

OMEROY
ssumption, Pomeroy,
maculate Conception, Altmore
ww.pomeroyparish.homestead.com
ery Rev David Moore PP, VF
rochial House,
Cavanakeeran Road,
omeroy, Dungannon,
Tyrone BT70 2RD
l 028-87757867
nail d.moore2323@outlook.com

ORTADOWN (DRUMCREE)
John the Baptist's, Garvaghy Road
Patrick's, William Street
ww.drumcreeparish.com
nail parishofdrumcree@gmail.com
ery Rev Michael Sheehan PP
rochial House, 15 Moy Road,
ortadown, Co Armagh BT62 1QL
l 028-38350610
nail frmichaelsheehan@gmail.com
ery Rev Peter Clarke PE, AP
rochial House,
Moy Road, Portadown,
Armagh BT62 1QL
l 028-38332218
nail petergerardclarke@gmail.com

LLANSTOWN
Malachy's, Reaghstown,
Medoc's, Clonkeen,
Peter and Paul, Tallanstown
ery Rev Paul Montague PP
rochial House, Reaghstown,
dee, Co Louth A92 KW68
l 041-6855117
nail tallanstownparish@hotmail.com

ANDRAGEE (BALLYMORE AND ULLAGHBRACK)
James's, Tandragee
Patrick's, Ballyargan
Joseph's, Poyntzpass
James's, Markethill
ery Rev Michael Woods PP, VF
rochial House, 10 Acton Road,
yntzpass, Newry,
Down BT35 6TB
l 028-38318471
nail admin@parish57.com
nail mjw@mick58.com

RMONFECHIN
maculate Conception, Termonfechin
e Assumption, Sandpit
nail termonfechinparish@gmail.com
ery Rev Paul Byrne PP
nail pauldbyrne2012@gmail.com
v Mr Patrick Butterly, Permanent
acon
nail 157pat@gmail.com
rochial House, Termonfeckin,
ogheda, Co Louth A92 W4O3
l 041-9822121

TERMONMAGUIRC (CARRICKMORE, LOUGHMACRORY & CREGGAN)
St Colmcille's, Carrickmore
St Oliver Plunkett, Creggan
St Mary's, Loughmacrory
Rev Sean O'Neill PP
Parochial House, 1 Rockstown Road,
Carrickmore, Omagh, Co Tyrone BT79 9BE
Tel 028-80761207
Email termonmaguircparish@gmail.com
Very Rev Thomas Mallon PE, AP
Parochial House,
170 Loughmacrory Road,
Loughmacrory, Omagh,
Co Tyrone BT79 9LG
Tel 028-80761230 Fax 028-80761131
Email mallon393@gmail.com

TOGHER
St Columcille, Togher
St Finnian, Dillonstown
St Borchill, Dysart
St Mary's, Drumcar
Rt Rev Mgr James Carroll PP, EV
Parochial House, Big Strand Road,
Clogherhead, Drogheda,
Co Louth A92 T938
Tel 041-9889335
Email jcarlpp73@gmail.com
Very Rev Thomas Daly PE, AP
Parochial House, Boicetown, Togher,
Drogheda, Co Louth A92 C597
Tel 041-6852110
Email macurta6@icloud.com

WHITECROSS (LOUGHILLY)
St Teresa's, Tullyherron
St Malachy's, Ballymoyer
St Brigid's, Carrickananney
St Laurence O'Toole, Belleeks
Parish Email info@parishofloughgilly.com
Very Rev Malachy Murphy PP
Parochial House, 25 Priestbush Road,
Whitecross, Co Armagh BT60 2TP
Tel 028-37507214
Email malomurphy@gmail.com

INSTITUTIONS AND CHAPLAINCY SERVICES

Community School
Ardee, Co Louth
Mr Seán Moran
Tel 041-6853313

Our Lady of Lourdes Hospital
Drogheda, Co Louth
Sr Dervilla O'Donnell MMM
Our Lady of Lourdes Hospital,
Drogheda, Co Louth
Tel 041-9837601
Email odonnelldervilla@gmail.com

St Paul's High School
Bessbrook, Co Armagh
Email drominteeparish@btinternet.com
Very Rev Séamus White PP
Parochial House,
40 The Village, Jonesboro,
Newry, Co Down BT35 8HP
Tel 028-3084945 (H) 028-30830309 (S)
Email seamuswhite@ymail.com

The following hospitals are served by parochial clergy:

Armagh Community Hospital
Armagh
Tel 028-37522802 (Chaplain)

Daisy Hill Hospital
Newry, Co Down
Tel 028-30835000 (Chaplain)

Longstone Special Care Hospital
Armagh
Tel 028-37522802 (Chaplain)

Louth County Hospital
Dundalk, Co Louth
Tel 042-9334648 (Chaplain)

Mid-Ulster Hospital
Magherafelt, Co Derry
Tel 028-79632351

St Brigid's Hospital
Ardee, Co Louth
Tel 041-6850920 (Chaplain)

St Joseph's Hospital
Ardee, Co Louth
Tel 041-6853313 (Chaplain)

St Oliver Plunkett's Hospital
Dundalk, Co Louth
Tel 042-9334259 (Chaplain)

South Tyrone Hospital
Dungannon, Co Tyrone
Tel 028-87722631 (Chaplain)

PRIESTS OF THE DIOCESE ELSEWHERE

Rev John Connolly
c/o Ara Coeli, Armagh BT61 7QY
Rev Patrick Coyle
c/o Ara Coeli, Armagh BT61 7QY
Rev Rory Coyle
c/o Ara Coeli, Armagh BT61 7QY
Email rory_coyle@hotmail.com
Rev Seamus Dobbin
c/o Ara Coeli, Armagh BT61 7QY
Rev Dominic Mallon
13 Richview Heights, Keady,
Co Armagh BT60 3SW
Rev Ryan McAleer
Sint-Michielsstraat 4/3101,
3000 Leuven, Belgium
Email ryan.mcaleer@kuleuven.be

Very Rev Seán McEvoy
St Moninna's Hermitage,
207 Dublin Road, Newry,
Co Down BT35 8RL
Tel 028-30849424
Very Rev John McGoldrick
St Richard's, 3010 S 18th Street,
Philadelphia, PA 19145, USA
Tel 001-215-9291326
Email minterburn@hotmail.com
Rev Callum Young
On loan to Dromore Diocese

RETIRED PRIESTS

Very Rev John Bradley PE
8 Killymeal Road, Dungannon,
Co Tyrone BT71 6DP
Tel 028-87722183
Very Rev Oliver Brennan PE
Parochial House, Dillonstown,
Dunleer, Co Louth A92 HH24
Email olivervbrennan@eircom.net
Very Rev Fergus Breslan PE
Parochial House, 17 Carnmore Drive,
Newry, Co Down BT35 8SB
Tel 028-30269047
Email fr.fergusbreslan@btinternet.com
Very Rev Laurence Caraher PE
The Ravel, School Lane, Tullyallen,
Drogheda, Co Louth
Tel 041-9834293
Email frcaraher@gmail.com
Very Rev Paul Clayton-Lea PE
Woodside, Strand Road, Termonfechin,
Drogheda, Co Louth A92 W7W6
Tel 041-9822631
Email claytonleapaul@gmail.com
Rev Desmond Corrigan
17 Chapel Street, Poyntzpass, Newry,
Co Down BT35 6SY
Tel 028-38318217
Very Rev Canon Michael Crawley PE
Parochial House,
89 Derrynoose Road,
Derrynoose, Co Armagh BT60 3EZ
Tel 028-37531222
Email
michaelcrawley89@btinternet.com
Very Rev Kevin Cullen PE
Parochial House, 9a Newry Road,
Crossmaglen, Newry,
Co Down BT35 9HH
Tel 028-30868698

Very Rev John Hughes PE
30 Jockey Lane, Moy,
Dungannonn, Co Tyrone BT71 7SR
Tel 028-87784240
Email revhughes135@btinternet
Very Rev Peter Kerr PE
42 Innishatieve Road, Carrickmore,
Omagh, Co Tyrone BT79 9HS
Tel 028-80761837
Very Rev Patrick J. McCrory PE
Parochial House, Sixemilecross,
Omagh, Co Tyrone BT79 9NF
Tel 028-80758344
Email pjmccrory@icloud.com
Very Rev Gerard McGinnity PE
4 Rowan Road, Armagh BT60 3DR
Very Rev Patrick McGuckin PE
79 Reclain Road,
Galbally, Dungannon,
Co Tyrone BT70 2PQ
Tel 028-87759692
Email frpmcguckin@hotmail.com
Very Rev Seán McGuigan PE
65 Iniscarn Road, Desertmartin,
Magherafelt, Co Derry BT45 5NG
Email seanmcguigan65@gmail.com
Rev Thomas McNulty
Goretti Cottage, Acre Road,
Carlingford, Co Louth A91 PW95
Tel 042-9376577
Email tommymcnulty37@gmail.com
Very Rev Pádraig Murphy PE
Parochial House, Jenkinstown,
Dundalk, Co Louth A91 CC79
Tel 042-9371328
Email pplordship@outlook.com
Rt Rev Mgr Raymond Murray PE
60 Glen Mhacaha, Cathedral Road,
Armagh BT61 8AF
Tel 028-37510821
Email raylmurray@outlook.com
Rt Rev Mgr Christopher O'Byrne PE
3 Grange Court, Magherafelt,
Co Derry BT45 5RU
Tel 028-79631791
Email cobyrne@magherafeltparish.org
Very Rev Owen O'Donnell PE
Parochial House, Dunamore,
Cookstown, Co Tyrone
Tel 028-86751216
Email o.odonnell37@gmail.com
Very Rev Seán J. Quinn PE
c/o The Diamond, Pomeroy,
Dungannon, Co Tyrone BT70 2QX
Email sjqdill@gmail.com
Very Rev Séamus Rice PE
4 Ballymacnab Road,
Armagh BT60 2QS
Tel 028-37531620
Email seamusrice@live.co.uk

RELIGIOUS ORDERS AND CONGREGATIONS

PRIESTS

AUGUSTINIANS
St Augustine's Priory, Shop Street,
Drogheda, Co Louth
Tel 041-9838409 Fax 041-9831847
Prior: Rev Colm O'Mahony (OSA)
Email focal@eircom.net

CISTERCIANS
Mellifont Abbey, Collon, Co Louth
Tel 041-9826103 Fax 041-9826713
Email info@mellifontabbey.ie
Superior: Rev Brendan Freeman
Email brbrendan@newmelleray.org

DOMINICANS
St Malachy's Priory, Dundalk, Co Louth
Tel 042-9334179/9333714
Fax 042-9329751
Superior: Rev David Barrins (OP)

JESUITS
Iona, 211 Churchill Park,
Portadown, Co Armagh BT62 1EU
Tel 028-38330366 Fax 028-38338334
Superior: Rev Brendan MacPartlin (SJ)
Email iona@jesuit.ie

MARISTS
Cerdon, Marist Fathers,
St Mary's Road, Dundalk, Co Louth
Tel 042-9334019
Superior: Rev James O'Connell (SM)

St Mary's College, Dundalk, Co Louth
Tel 042-9339984
Principal: Mr Alan Craven

REDEMPTORISTS
St Joseph's, St Alphonsus Road,
Dundalk, Co Louth
Tel 042-9334042/9334762
Fax 042-9330893
Superior: Rev Noel Kehoe (CSsR) PP
Vicar-Superior
Rev Richard Delahunty (CSsR)
Rev Dan Baragry (CSsR) *(Provincial)*

(See also under parishes – Dundalk,
St Joseph's)

ROSMINIANS
See under parishes – Carlingford &
Clogherny and Faughart

SERVITES
Servite Priory, Benburb,
Co Tyrone BT71 7JZ
Tel 028-37548241
Retreat, conference and youth centre
Prior: Rev Bernard Thorne (OSM)

BROTHERS

E LA SALLE BROTHERS
e La Salle College, Dundalk, Co Louth
I 042-9331179 Fax 042-9330870
incipal: Ms Patricia O'Leary

IINT JOHN OF GOD NORTH EAST
RVICES
Mary's, Drumcar, Dunleer, Co Louth
I 041-6851211 Fax 041-6851529
hail admin.northeast@sjog.ie
terim Regional Director: Paula Hand
Mary's School, Drumcar, Co Louth
I 041-6851211
hool Principal: Mr Kevin Toale
sidential, day and community services
r children and adults with varying
grees of intellectual disability.

SISTERS

iRMELITE SISTERS
ach Bríd,
, Coopers Cross, Annagassan Road,
stlebellinghim, Co Louth
I 042-6821550

iNGREGATION OF THE SISTERS OF
iERCY
ll Street, Dundalk, Co Louth A91 C2C4
I 042-9334200
mmunity: 6

le End, Avenue Road,
indalk, Co Louth A91 X6A0
I 042-9330410
mmunity: 3

thany, 34 Point Road,
indalk, Co Louth A91 W0C9
I 042-9331602

Cypress Gardens,
y Estate, Dundalk,
Louth A91 P0A2
I 042-9329315

Fairhill Road, Cookstown,
Tyrone BT80 8AG
I 028-86763363
mmunity: 5

ters of Mercy, 10 Killymeal Road,
ingannon, Co Tyrone BT71 6DP
I 028-87722623

ters of Mercy,
Church View, Bessbrook,
wry, Co Down BT35 78T
I 028-30837140

115 Oaklawns,
Dundalk, Co Louth A91 K6W7
Tel 042-9334569

No. 8 Central Avenue,
Cookstown, Co Tyrone BT80 8AJ
Tel 028-86764861

Sisters of Mercy, Hale Street,
Ardee, Co Louth A92 NY36
Tel 041-6842001
Community: 7

39 Moorehall Lodge,
Moorehall Village, Ardee, Co Louth
Tel 041-6871406

21 The Village,
Moorehall Lodge, Ardee, Co Louth
Tel 041-6850165

DOMINICAN CONTEMPLATIVE NUNS
Monastery of St Catherine of Siena,
The Twenties, Drogheda,
Co Louth A92 KR84
Tel 041-9838524
Email sienamonastery@gmail.com
www.dominicannuns.ie
Prioress: Sr M. Breda Carroll (OP)
Community: 17

FRANCISCAN MISSIONARY SISTERS FOR
AFRICA
Franciscan Convent, Mount Oliver,
Dundalk, Co Louth (Motherhouse)
Tel 042-9371123 Fax 042-9371159
Email mtofmsa20@gmail.com
Team Leadership
Contact Person
Sr Kathleen Moran (FMSA)
Community: 34

MEDICAL MISSIONARIES OF MARY
Motherhouse, Beechgrove,
Hardman's Gardens,
Drogheda, Co Louth A92 XKX0
Tel 041-9837512
Email beechgroveadmin@mmm37.org
Leader: Sr Catherine Young

MMM Nursing Facility
Áras Mhuire, Beechgrove,
Hardman's Gardens,
Drogheda, Co Louth A92 HN29
Nursing Tel 041-9842222
Admin Tel 041-9845762
Administration
businessmanager@arasmhuire.com
Pastoral Dept
pastoralcare@arasmhuire.com

Greenbank, Mell, Drogheda,
Co Louth A92 X54F
Tel 041-9831028
Email mmmgreenbankmell@gmail.com
Community: 4

Area Office, No 13 Ashleigh Heights,
Drogheda, Co Louth A92 RTF4
Tel 041-9830779
Email arealeader@mmmeuarea.ie

No 14 Ashleigh Heights,
Drogheda, Co Louth A92 E6CV
Community: 2

MMM Communications Department,
Beechgrove Hardman's Gardens,
Drogheda, Co Louth A92 XKX0
Email mmmcomm37@gmail.com

MISSIONARIES OF CHARITY
19A Cathedral Road, Armagh BT61 7QX
Tel 04837-528654
Superior: Sr M. Vincy Joseph (MC)
Community: 4
Hostel for men

PRESENTATION SISTERS
Greenhills, Drogheda,
Co Louth A92 FY800
Tel 041-9831420
Community: 4
School ministry and pastoral

103 Thomas Street, Portadown,
Co Armagh BT62 3AH
Tel 028-38332220
Community: 2
Cross community work and pastoral
ministry

28 Garvaghy Park,
Portadown, Co Armagh BT62 1HB
Tel 028-38335964
Community: 2
Pastoral ministry

SACRED HEART SOCIETY
6 Convent Road, Armagh BT60 4BJ
Tel 028-37522046 Fax 028-37518764
Education, pastoral work and youth
work. Provincial Administration.

ST LOUIS SISTERS
Dún Lughaidh, Dundalk, Co Louth
Tel 042-9335786
Community: 8

Sacred Heart Community,
6 Convent Road, Armagh BT60 4BG
Community: 1

EDUCATIONAL INSTITUTIONS

**Redemptoris Mater Archdiocesan
Missionary Seminary**
De La Salle Terrace, Castletown,
Dundalk, Co Louth A91 C5D6
Tel 042-9336584
Rector: Rev Giuseppe Pollio
Email gpollio24@gmail.com
Director of Studies
Rev Maciej Zacharek CC

Coláiste Rís
Chapel Street, Dundalk, Co Louth
Tel 042-9334336 Fax 042-9338380
Principal: Ms Noilin Ní Dhulaíng

St Patrick's Academy
37 Killymeal Road, Dungannon,
Co Tyrone BT71 6DS
Tel 028-87722668
Fax 028-87722745
Principal: Mr Colin Holmes

St Patrick's Grammar School
Cathedral Road, Armagh BT61 7QZ
Tel 028-37522018 Fax 028-37525930
Principal: Mr Dominic Clarke

St Joseph's Convent Grammar School
58 Castlecaulfied, Donaghmore,
Co Tyrone BT70 3HE
Tel 028-87761227
Principal: Mrs Geraldine Donnelly

CHARITABLE AND OTHER SOCIETIES

Aras Mhuire
14 Irish Street, Dungannon,
Co Tyrone BT70 1DB
Tel 028-87726852
Oratory and bookshop

Avila Nursing Home
Convent of Mercy, Convent Hill,
Bessbrook, Co Armagh BT35 7AW
Tel 028-30838969

Cuan Mhuire
200 Dublin Road,
Newry, Co Down BT35 8RL
Tel 028-30849010
Alcohol counselling

Family of God Community
The Oratory, Carroll's Village,
Dundalk, Co Louth
Tel 042-9339888

St John of God Community Services CLC
North East Services,
St Mary's, Drumcar, Co Louth
Tel 041-6862600

SOS Prayer
The Oratory, Carroll's Village,
Dundalk, Co Louth
Tel 042-9339888

Shop online at www.veritas.ie

The Veritas website features a wide range of resources to meet the needs of parishes, educators, families and individuals.

Visit www.veritas.ie to see how we can help you today.

 VERITAS

For Books and Gifts with a Difference · www.veritas.ie

36

Allianz (ⁱⁱⁱ)

RADIO MARIA
IRELAND
Sanctifying the Airwaves!

MARY FITZPATRICK
hosts

The Immaculate Heart of Mary

Prayer Meeting

WED @ 1PM
only on
RADIO MARIA

OLLIE CLARKE
presents

The Lunchtime SHOW

FRI @ 1PM
only on
RADIO MARIA

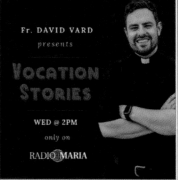

Fr. DAVID VARD
presents

VOCATION STORIES

WED @ 2PM
only on
RADIO MARIA

THOMAS ROCHE
presents

CEOL AGUS CRAIC

SAT @ 1PM
only on
RADIO MARIA

Fr. EAMONN McCARTHY
presents

CHATECHESIS

TUE - SAT @ 11.15AM
only on
RADIO MARIA

PATRICIA KEANE
presents

HEALTH & FAITH MATTERS

TUES @ 2.30PM
only on
RADIO MARIA

MARY STENSON
presents

ALL THINGS LEGION

TUE @ 6.10PM
only on
RADIO MARIA

Fr. JOHN McCARTHY
presents

THE RADIO MARIA BOOK CLUB

THURS @ 4PM
only on
RADIO MARIA

TARA McDERMOTT
presents

Total Beauty

FRI @ 6.10PM
only on
RADIO MARIA

SAORVIEW
TV Channel 210
Freeview

Download Mobile App
'Radio Maria Ireland'

Online Website
www.radiomaria.ie

Radio Feed
via Telephone
Dial: 01-437-3277

IT'S NOT JUST A WARZONE

FOR SAMI, IT'S HOME

Photo: Trócaire

PLEASE GIVE NOW
ROI 1800 408 408 NI 0800 912 1200
TROCAIRE.ORG

ROI Charity Regulatory Authority No. 20204842
NI Charity Commission for NI No. NIC103321

1973 50 YEARS 2023

Trócaire
TOGETHER FOR A JUST WORLD

Becoming Human,
BECOMING DIVINE
The Christian Life According to
Blessed Columba Marmion

Columba McCann OSB

ISBN 978 1 80097 044 1
PRICE €10.99/£9.99

In this fascinating book commemorating the centenary of Blessed Columba Marmion's death in 1923, Columba McCann OSB explores Marmion's spiritual teachings and highlights key moments in his life that influenced his writing – from his early childhood in Dublin to his later years as a Benedictine and as abbot of Maredsous Abbey in Belgium.

This wonderful introduction to the inspirational Benedictine's life and work examines his influential writing and highlights how his spiritual teaching is relevant today. In a clear and accessible style it emphasises the breadth and confidence of Marmion's teaching, which puts the reader in touch with the deep spiritual sources of Christian life and at the same time suggests a certain serene freedom as to how each person draws from those sources.

Columba McCann OSB is a monk of Glenstal Abbey, Murroe, Co. Limerick. He has studied at the Pontifical Liturgical Institute in Rome, and lectured in liturgical studies in Holy Cross College and the National Centre for Liturgy. He is a former chairman of the Dublin Diocesan Liturgical Commission.

ARCHDIOCESE OF DUBLIN

PATRONS OF THE ARCHDIOCESE
ST KEVIN, 3 JUNE; ST LAURENCE O'TOOLE, 14 NOVEMBER

SUFFRAGEN SEES: KILDARE AND LEIGHLIN, FERNS, OSSORY

NCLUDES CITY AND COUNTY OF DUBLIN, NEARLY ALL OF COUNTY WICKLOW
AND PORTIONS OF COUNTIES CARLOW, KILDARE, LAOIS AND WEXFORD

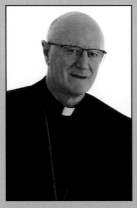

Most Rev Dermot Farrell DD
Born 1954 in Co Westmeath;
ordained priest 7 June 1980;
appointed as Bishop of Ossory
by Pope Francis 3 January 2018;
ordained bishop in
St Mary's Cathedral, Kilkenny,
11 March 2018;
appointed by Pope Francis as
Archbishop of Dublin
29 December 2020

Residence: Archbishop's House,
Drumcondra, Dublin D09 H4C2
Tel 01-8373732

ST MARYS PRO-CATHEDRAL, DUBLIN

ough Catholic Dublin has not
ssessed a cathedral since the
formation, for almost two hundred
ars now St Mary's Pro-Cathedral has
rved as the Mother Church of the
ıblin arch-diocese. In that time it has
on a special place in the hearts of the
ıblin people, to whom it is known
fectionately as 'The Pro'.

e Pro-Cathedral was born of the
ion of Archbishop John Thomas Troy
d brought to fruition thanks to the
stinting labours of its second
ministrator, Archdeacon John
milton. The parish of Saint Mary's,
addling the Liffey, was established in
07 and a chapel dedicated to St Mary
as opened in 1729. In 1797
chbishop Troy successfully petitioned
e Holy See to allow him take St Mary's
his *mensal* parish. He thereupon set
out raising funds to build a
ignified, spacious church' in a central
cation in the parish.

e site chosen was a building on
arlborough Street, opposite Tyrone
ouse. Formerly the town house of the
rl of Annesley, it was purchased for
,100 and a deposit was paid in 1803.
owever, it was not until 1814 that
signs were publicly invited for the
w church. A design of uncertain
uthorship, marked only with the letter
, for a church in the form of a
ecian Doric temple, was chosen as
e winner. The only substantial
teration to the design was the
ection of a dome.

e foundation stone was laid by
chbishop Troy in 1815. On the feast
St Laurence O'Toole in 1825,
chbishop Murray celebrated High
ass, to mark the dedication of the
urch to the 'Conception of the Virgin
ary', to a packed congregation, which
cluded Daniel O'Connell. After the
dication, the interior embellishment
the church continued. Highlights
cluded the alto relief representation of
e Ascension by John Smyth; the high

altar carved by Peter Turnerelli, and the
marble statues of Archbishops Murray
and Cullen by Thomas Farrell. Stained-
glass windows, depicting Our Lady
flanked by St Laurence O'Toole and St
Kevin, were installed behind the

sanctuary in 1886. The high point of
liturgical embellishment was the
generous benefaction by Edward
Martyn, who endowed the Palestrina
choir for male voices in 1902.

Most Rev Diarmuid Martin DD
Archbishop Emeritus of Dublin
c/o Archbishop's House, Drumcondra,
Dublin D09 H4C2

Most Rev Eamonn Walsh DD
Auxiliary Bishop Emeritus;
Residence: Naomh Brid,
Blessington Road, Tallaght, Dublin 24
Tel/Fax 01-4598032

Most Rev Raymond Field DD
Auxiliary Bishop Emeritus;
Marymount Care Centre,
Westmanstown, Lucan, Co Dublin

Vicars General
Very Rev Gareth Byrne VG
Very Rev Ciaran O'Carroll VG
Very Rev Donal Roche VG
Archbishop's House, Dublin 9
Tel 01-8379253

CHAPTER

Dean
Most Rev Eamonn Walsh
Precentor
Very Rev John Canon Flaherty Co-PP
Chancellor
Very Rev Patrick Canon Fagan PE
Treasurer
Vacant
Archdeacon of Dublin
Ven Archdeacon Peadar Murney
Archdeacon of Glendalough:
Ven Archdeacon Kevin Lyon CC

Prebendaries
Cullen
Very Rev Martin Canon Cosgrove,
(Moderator)
St Mary's Presbytery, Willbrook Road,
Rathfarnham, Dublin 14
Kilmactalway
Very Rev James Canon Fingleton
279 Howth Road, Raheny, Dublin 5
Swords
Very Rev Patrick Canon Boyle Adm
8 Slademore Close, Ard Na Greine,
Ayrfield, Dublin 13
Tel 086-1011405
Yago
Very Rev Damian Canon O'Reilly
Chaplain, St Vincent's University Hospital,
Elm Park, Dublin 4
St Audoen's
Very Rev John Canon McNamara PP
Apt 2, The Presbytery, Dublin Street,
Balbriggan, Co Dublin
Clonmethan
Very Rev Walter Canon Harris PE
The Four Ferns, Brighton Road,
Foxrock, Co Dublin
Wicklow
Very Rev Liam Canon Belton (Moderator)
Presbytery No 1, St John the Evangelist
Parish, Ballinteer Avenue,
Dublin 16 PY54
Timothan
Very Rev Francis Canon McEvoy Adm
Parochial House, Moyglare Road,
Maynooth, Co Kildare

Malahidert
Very Rev Patrick Canon Shiel
74 Mount Drinan Avenue,
Kinsealy Downs, Swords, Co Dublin
Castleknock
Very Rev Dr Martin Canon Hogan CC
Parochial House, 4 The Lawn,
Finglas, Dublin 11
Tel 01-8341000
Tipper
Rev John Canon Piert *(Team Assistant)*
Our Lady's Manor, Bulloch Harbour,
Dalkey, Co Dublin
Tassagard
Very Rev Padraig Canon Ó Cochlain
(Moderator)
Parochial house, Arcklow, Co Wicklow
Dunlavin
Very Rev Dr Liam Canon Rigney PP
Parochial House, 1 Stanhope Place,
Athy, Co Kildare
Maynooth
Very Rev Sean Canon Smith CC
The Presbytery, Newtownmountkennedy,
Co Wicklow
Howth
Very Rev John Canon Killeen CC
20 Abbey Court, Abbey Road, Blackrock,
Co Dublin
Rathmichael
Very Rev John Canon Delany *(Moderator)*
Parochial House, St Mary's,
Sandyford Village, Dublin 18
Monmahenock
Very Rev Dr J. Anthony Canon Gaughan PE
56 Newtownpark Avenue,
Blackrock, Co Dublin
Stagonilly
Very Rev Michael Canon Hurley PC
85 Tymon Crescent, Old Bawn,
Tallaght, Dublin D24 FK0W
Tipperkevin, 1a pars
Very Rev John Canon Fitzgibbon PE
The Presbytery, Chapel Road,
Lusk, Co Dublin
Tipperkevin, 2a pars
Very Rev Anthony Canon Reilly PP
Parochial House, Palmerstown, Dublin 20
Donaghmore, 1a pars
Very Rev Paul Canon O'Driscoll, PP
Parish of the Travelling People
St Laurence House, 6 New Cabra Road,
Phibsborough, Dublin 7
Donaghmore, 2a pars
Very Rev Derek Canon Farrell *(Moderator)*
Parochial House, Garristown, Co Dublin

Deaneries and Vicars Forane
Bray: Very Rev Aquinas Duffy VF
19 Woodlands, Road, Johnstown,
Glenageary, Co Dublin
Tel 01-5672374
Dun Laoghaire
Very Rev Paul Tyrrell PP
St Michael's Parochial House,
4 Eblana Avenue, Dun Laoghaire,
Co Dublin
Tel 01-2804969
Wicklow
Very Rev Derek Doyle *(Moderator)* VF
Parochial House, Rathdrum, Co Wicklow
Tel 0404-46229

Donnybrook: Very Rev Fergus O'Connor
(Opus Dei) PP, VF
31 Herbert Avenue,
Merrion Road, Dublin 4
Tel 01-2692001
South City Centre
Very Rev Seán Forde (OCarm) PP, VF
Our Lady of Mount Carmel Parish,
Whitefriar Street Church,
56 Aungier Street, Dublin 2
North City Centre
Appointment pending
Cullenswood
Very Rev Paul Taylor Adm, VF
49 Rathgar Road, Dublin 6
South Dublin
Very Rev Philip Bradley Adm, VF
Parochial House, 83 Terenure Road East
Dublin 6
Tel 01-4905520
Tallaght
Very Rev William O'Shaughnessy
(Moderator), VF
70 Maplewood Road, Tallaght, Dublin 24
Tel 01-4590746
Blessington
Very Rev John Gilligan *(Moderator)*,VF
St Mary's Prochial House, Saggart,
Co Dublin
Tel 087-4103239
Fingal North
Very Rev John Canon McNamara PP
Apt 2, The Presbytery, Dublin Street,
Balbriggan, Co Dublin
Tel 01-8020185
Blanchardstown
Very Rev Damian McNeice PP, VF
6 Beechpark Lawn,
Castleknock, Dublin 15
Tel 01-6408595
Maynooth
Very Rev Kieran Coghlan, Moderator, VF
St Cecilia's, New Road, Clondalkin,
Dublin 22
Tel: 01-4592665
Fingal South-East
Vacant
Fingal South-West
Very Rev Frank Reburn Co-PP, VF
137 Ballymun Road, Dublin 11
Tel 01-8376341
Howth
Very Rev Martin Noone *(Moderator)*, VF
7 Seabury Drive, Malahide,
Co Dublin K36 YN67
Tel 01-8451902

College of Consultors
Very Rev Gareth Byrne, VG, Moderator
of the Diocesan Curia
Very Rev Ciaran O'Carroll PP, VG
Very Rev Donal Roche PP, VG
Very Rev Paul Coyle, Chancellor
Very Rev Andrew O'Sullivan PP, Chair of
the Council of Priests
Very Rev Joseph Mullan, Moderator,
Vice-Chair of the Council of Priests
Very Rev Philip Curran PP
Very Rev Gerry Kane PP

ADMINISTRATION

Moderator of the Curia
Very Rev Gareth Byrne VG
Office of the Moderator,
Dublin Diocesan Offices,
20-23 Arran Quay, Dublin D07 XK85
Tel 01-8087500

Chancellor
Very Rev Paul Coyle
The Chancellery, Archbishop's House,
Drumcondra, Dublin D09 H4C2
Tel 01-8087500 Fax 8571650

Ecclesiastical Censor
Rt Rev Mgr John Dolan
The Chancellery, Archbishop's House,
Drumcondra, Dublin D09 H4C2
Tel 01-8087500

Episcopal Vicar for Clergy
Rt Rev Mgr Eoin Thynne
Archbishop's House, Drumcondra,
Dublin D09 H4C2
Tel 01-8087500

Episcopal Vicar for Religious and Extern Priests
Rt Rev Mgr John Dolan
Archbishop's House, Drumcondra,
Dublin D09 H4C2
Tel 01-8087500

Diocesan Archivist
Ms Noelle Dowling
204-206 Clonliffe Road, Dublin D03 PD86
Tel 01-8087500

Financial Administrator/Head of Operations
Ms Íde Finnegan
20-23 Arran Quay, Dublin D07 XK85
Tel 01-8087500 Fax 01-8368393

Archbishop's PA
Ms Mary Irwin
Archbishop's House, Drumcondra,
Dublin D09 H4C2
Tel 01-8087500

Office for Mission and Ministry
Director: Ms Patricia Carroll
St Paul's Church, 19 Arran Quay,
Dublin D07 KX66
Tel 01-8087500

Child Safeguarding and Protection Service
Dublin Diocesan Offices,
20-23 Arran Quay, Dublin D07 XK85
Tel 01-8360314
Email cps@dublindiocese.ie
Website www.cps.dublindiocese.ie
Director: Mr Andrew Fagan
Priest Delegate: Rev Richard Shannon

Child Safeguarding and Protection Training Co-ordinator
Mr Garry Kehoe
Email garry.kehoe@dublindiocese.ie

Communications Officer
Mr Peter Henry
Tel 01-8087500 Fax 01-8360793
Email communications@dublindiocese.ie
Website www.dublindiocese.ie

Education Secretariat
Episcopal Vicar for Education
Very Rev Mgr Dan O'Connor
51 Home Farm Road, Drumcondra,
Dublin D09 W5W4
Tel 01-8087500 Fax 01-8368393
Email dan.oconnor@dublindiocese.ie
Senior Education Specialist
Mr Declan Lawlor
Email declan.lawlor@dublindiocese.ie

DIOCESAN COMMITTEES

Clerical Fund Society
Archbishop's House, Drumcondra,
Dublin D09 H4C2
Tel 01-8379253
President: The Archbishop of Dublin
Chairperson: Very Rev Gareth Byrne VG
Secretary: Ms Keava Lyons

Commission on Parish Boundaries
c/o Archbishop's House,
Drumcondra, Dublin D09 H4C2
Tel 01-8379253
Chairperson
Rev Deacon Dermot McCarthy

Common Fund Executive Committee
Archbishop's House, Drumcondra,
Dublin D09 H4C2
Tel 01-8379253
Chairperson: Very Rev Paul Taylor
Secretary: Ms Íde Finnegan

Finance Committee
Archbishop's House, Drumcondra,
Dublin D09 H4C2
Tel 01-8379253
Chairperson: Mr Michael Duffy
Secretary: Ms Ide Finnegan

CATECHETICS EDUCATION

Diocesan Advisers for Religious Education in Primary Schools
51 Home Farm Road, Drumcondra,
Dublin D09 W5W4
Tel 01-8379253 Fax 01-8368393
Sr Maureen Matthews,
Sr Anne Neylon DC
All at the Education Secretariat

Diocesan Advisors for Religious Education in Post-Primary Schools
Sr Bernadette Carron DC,
Sr Concepta Foley RSM

LITURGY

Commission for Sacred Art and Architecture & Historic Churches
Chairperson: Edward O'Shea

PASTORAL

ACCORD
Ms Jennifer Griffin (Dublin Director)
168 Pembroke Road, Dublin D04 WR86
Tel 01-4784400
Email admin@dublin.accord.ie

CROSSCARE
Social Support Agency for the Archdiocese of Dublin
Chairperson: Ms Evelyn Cregan
Director: Mr Conor Hickey
2 St Mary's Place North, Dublin D07 Y768
Tel 01-8360011

Council of Priests
President: Most Rev Dermot Farrell DD
Chairperson
Very Rev Andrew O'Sullivan PP

Dublin Roman Catholic Diocesan Hospital Chaplains Association
Chairperson of Committee:
Rev John Kelly
Chaplain, Tallaght Hospital
Tel 01-4142482
Email john.kelly@tuh.ie

Ecumenism
Chairperson and Secretary
Very Rev Kieran McDermott Adm

Knock Diocesan Pilgrimage
Director: Deacon Gerard Reilly

Legion of Mary
Diocesan Chaplain: Vacant

Lourdes Diocesan Pilgrimage
Director: Very Rev Martin Noone
Lourdes Pilgrimage Office,
51 Home Farm Road, Drumcondra,
Dublin D09 W5W4
Tel 01-8376820

Marriage Tribunal
(See Marriage Tribunals section)

National Chaplaincy for Deaf People
Chaplain
Very Rev Patrick Canon Boyle Adm
Tel 086-1011415
Website www.ncdp.ie

Permanent Diaconate
Diocesan Director of Permanent Diaconate: Very Rev John Gilligan
Diocesan Director of Diaconal Formation:
Deacon Noel Ryan
20-23 Arran Quay, Dublin D07 XK85
Tel 01-8087531

Missio Ireland
Diocesan Director: Rev John Greene
The Parochial House, St Kevin's Parish,
Laragh, Glendalough, Co Wicklow
Tel 044-45140

Travellers
Ministry to the Travelling People (Dublin Diocese)
Very Rev Paul Canon O'Driscoll PP
Office: St Laurence House,
6 New Cabra Road, Phibsboro, Dublin 7
Tel 01-8388874/087-2573857
Fax 01-8388901
Email partravs@iol.ie

Vocations
Director: Very Rev Seamus McEntee
c/o Dublin Diocesan Offices,
20-23 Arran Quay, Dublin D07 XK85
Tel 01-8379253

PARISHES

Mensal parishes are listed first. Other parishes follow alphabetically. Church titulars are in italics.

PRO-CATHEDRAL
St Mary's (Immaculate Conception)
Marlborough Street, Dublin 1
Very Rev Kieran McDermott Adm
Rt Rev Mgr Lorcan O'Brien TA
Rev Brendan Staunton (SJ) PC
Rev Deacon Thomas Groves
Pro-Cathedral House,
83 Marlborough Street, Dublin 1
Tel 01-8745441
Email procath@dublindiocese.ie
Website www.procathedral.ie

WESTLAND ROW
St Andrew's, Westland Row, Dublin 2
Very Rev Enda Cunningham Adm
47 Westland Row, Dublin 2
Tel 01-8368746
Rev Egidijus Arnasius, Chaplain to Lithuanian Community
48 Westland Row
Tel 01-6761030/087-7477554
Email arnasius@gmail.com
Rev Anthony Hou
Chaplain to the Chinese Community
Rev Deacon Dermot McCarthy
Parish Office: Tel 01-6761270 Fax 01-6763544
Email westlandrow@dublindiocese.ie
Website www.saintandrewsparish.ie

CITY QUAY
Immaculate Heart of Mary, Dublin 2
Very Rev Pearse Walsh Adm
The Presbytery, City Quay, Dublin 2
Parish Office: Tel 01-6773073
Website jocityquayparish@gmail.com

SEAN MCDERMOTT STREET
Our Lady of Lourdes,
Sean McDermott Street, Dublin 1
Very Rev Michael Casey (SDB) Adm
Tel 01-8363358
Rev Hugh O'Donnell (SDB) CC
40/41 Sean McDermott Street,
Dublin 1, D01 H7P6
Rev Eugen Timpu, Chaplain to Romanian Community
Parish Office: Tel 01-8551259/086-8382631
Email seanmcdermott@dublindiocese.ie

ARDLEA
St John Vianney, Ardlea Road,
Artane, Dublin 5
Very Rev Michel Simo Temgo (SCJ) PP
Rev Marian Szalwa (SCJ) PC
Parochial House, St John Vianney,
Ardlea Road, Dublin 5
Tel 01-8474173
Parish Office: Tel 01-8474123
Email ardleaparish@yahoo.com

ARKLOW
(Grouped with the parish of Castletown)
SS Mary and Peter, Arklow, Co Wicklow
Chapel of Ease: St David's, Johnstown,
Co Wicklow
Very Rev Padraig Canon Ó Cochlain
(Moderator)
Parochial House, Arklow, Co Wicklow
Tel/Fax 0402-32294
Email mfc53@indigo.ie
Very Rev David Brough Co-PP (parishes of Arklow, Castletown, Aughrim & Avoca)
2 St Mary's Terrace, Arklow, Co Wicklow
Tel 0402-32196
Parish Office: Tel/Fax 0402-31716
Email office@arklowparish.ie
www.arklowparish.ie

ARTANE
Our Lady of Mercy, Brookwood Grove,
Dublin 5
Very Rev Peter O'Reilly Adm
16 Brookwood Grove, Artane, Dublin 5
Rev Brian Durnin CC
12 Brookwood Grove, Artane, Dublin 5
Tel 01-8187996
Parish Office
Tel 01-8314297 Fax 01-8314054
Email ourladyofmercy.church@gmail.com

ASHFORD
Church of the Most Holy Rosary, Co Wicklow
Very Rev Eamonn Crosson Adm
Parochial House, Ashford, Co Wicklow
Tel/Fax 0404-40540
Rev Deacon Jeremy Seligman

ATHY
St Michael's, Co Kildare
Very Rev Liam Canon Rigney PP
Parochial House, 1 Stanhope Place,
Athy, Co Kildare
Tel 059-8631781
Rev Timothy Hannon CC
3 Stanhope Place, Athy
Tel 059-8631698
Rev Francis McCarthy CC
Parochial House, Crookstown, Co Kildare
Tel 087-6078143
Ms Natasha Geoghegan, Parish Pastoral Worker
Mr Conor McCann, Parish Pastoral Worker
c/o Parish Office
Email natasha.curran@dublindiocese.ie
Parish Office: Tel 059-8638391
Email athyparishrc@eircom.net
Website www.stmichaelsathy.net

AUGHRIM
The Most Sacred Heart, Co Wicklow
Very Rev Diarmuid Byrne TA
Parochial House, Arklow, Co Wicklow
Tel 0402-32294

AUGHRIM STREET
The Holy Family, Dublin 7
Very Rev Patrick Madden Adm
Parochial House,
34 Aughrim Street, Dublin 7
Tel 01-8386571
Rev Coriolan Muresan CC
Presbytery No 2,
St Joseph's Road, Dublin 7
Rev Deacon Victor Garvin

AVOCA
SS Mary and Patrick, Co Wicklow
Very Rev Padraig Canon Ó Cochlain
(Moderator)
Parochial House, Arklow, Co Wicklow
Tel 0402-32294
Very Rev Michael Murphy Co-PP
Parochial House, Avoca, Co Wicklow
Parish Offices: Avoca Tel 0402-35156
Email avpar@eircom.net
Templerainey Tel 0402-31943
Email stjoseph@eircom.net

AYRFIELD
St Paul's, Dublin 13
Very Rev Gerard Corcoran *(Moderator)*
Very Rev Gerard Deegan Co-PP
28 Glentworth Park, Ayrfield, Dublin 13
Tel 01-8674007
Very Rev Mgr Paul Callan TA
Ms Kirsten Mahon, Faith Development Worker
Parish Office: Tel 01-8160984
Email parishofficeayrfield@eircom.net
Website www.stpaulsparishayrfield.com

BALALLY
(Grouped with Sandyford)
Church of the Ascension of The Lord,
Dublin 16
Very Rev John Canon Delany *(Moderator)*
Parochial House, St Mary's,
Sandyford, Dublin 18
Tel 01-2956317
Very Rev Jim Caffrey Co-PP
The Presbytery, Hawthorns Road, Dublin 18
Rt Rev Mgr Dermot A. Lane DD, PC
162 Sandyford Road, Dublin 16
Tel 01-2956165
Email dalane@eircom.net
Parish Office: Tel 01-2954296
Email parishofbalally@eircom.net
Website www.balallyparish.ie

BALBRIGGAN
SS Peter and Paul, Balbriggan, Co Dublin
Very Rev John Canon McNamara PP, VF
Apt 2, The Presbytery,
Parish of SS Peter & Paul, Dublin Road,
Balbriggan, Co Dublin
Tel 01-8020185
Rev Donal Toal (SMA), CC
Apt 1, Parochial House,
Balbriggan, Co Dublin
Tel 01-8412116
Rev Anthony Gill (SMA)
Apt 1, Parochial House,
Balbriggan, Co Dublin
Tel 087-369533
Ms Siobhán Gormally, Parish Pastoral Worker
Parish Office: Tel 01-8412116 Fax 01-6904834
Email balbrigganparishoffice@gmail.com

Allianz (ⅱ)

BALDOYLE
(Grouped with Howth/Sutton)
SS Peter and Paul, Dublin 13
Very Rev Cyril Mangan *(Moderator)*
Very Rev Peter O'Connor Co-PP
The Presbytery, Baldoyle, Dublin 13
Tel 01-8322060
Rev Gerard Tanham PC
Presbytery No. 1,
Thormanby Road, Howth
Tel 01-8167599
Parish Office: Tel 01-8324313
Email info@baldoyleparish.ie
Website www.baldoyleparish.ie

BALLINTEER
Ballinteer parish is now under the Team Ministry of Dundrum/Ballinteer/Meadowbrook
St John the Evangelist, Ballinteer Avenue, Dublin 16
Very Rev Liam Canon Belton *(Moderator)*
Presbytery No 1, Ballinteer Avenue,
Dublin 16
Tel 01-4944448
Email rmfb@eircom.net
Rev Deacon Noel Ryan
Parish Office: Tel 01-4994203
Email
parishoffice@ballinteer.dublindiocese.ie
Website www.ballinteer.dublindiocese.ie

BALLYBODEN
Our Lady of Good Counsel, Dublin 16
Very Rev John Hughes (OSA) PP
Tel 01-4944966
Rev Dick Lyng (OSA) CC
St Augustine's, Taylor's Lane,
Ballyboden, Dublin 16
Parish Office: Tel 01-4944966
Website www.ballybodenparish.com

BALLYBRACK-KILLINEY
SS Alphonsus and Columba, Co Dublin
Very Rev Tom Dalzell *(Moderator)*
Parochial House, Church Avenue,
Killiney, Co Dublin
Tel 01-2826404
Rt Rev Mgr Enda Lloyd Co-PP
10 The Oaks, Loughlinstown Drive,
Dun Laoghaire, Co Dublin
Tel 01-2826895
Parish Offices:
St Alphonsus & Columba. Tel 01-2820788
St Stephens Tel 01-2854512
Church of the Apostles Tel 01-2024804
Website www.ballybrack-killiney-parish.org

BALLYFERMOT
Our Lady of the Assumption, Dublin 10
Very Rev Adrian Egan (CSsR) PP &
Coordinator
Rev Seamus Devitt (CSsR) CC
197 Kylemore Road,
Ballyfermot, Dublin 10
Parish Office: Tel 01-6264691
Community: Tel 01-5356977

BALLYFERMOT UPPER
St Matthew, Blackditch Road, Dublin 10
Very Rev Piaras MacLochlainn Adm
No 2, 148D Presbytery, Blackditch Road,
Dublin 10
Tel 01-6265119
Rev Simon Mundisye PC
Presbytery, Blackditch Road,
Ballyfermot, Dublin 10
Tel 01-6265695
Parish Office:
Tel 01-6265695 Fax 01-6230654
Website www.stmatthewsballyfermot.com

BALLYGALL
(Grouped with Iona Road, Drumcondra, Glasnevin and Ballymun Road)
Our Mother of Divine Grace, Ballygall Road East, Dublin 11
Very Rev Joseph Ryan *(Moderator)*
41 Cremore Heights, St Canice's Road,
Glasnevin, Dublin 11
Tel 01-8573776
Very Rev Harry Gaynor Co-PP
112 Ballygall Road East,
Glasnevin, Dublin 11
Tel 01-8342248
Rev Paul St John (SVD) PC
4 Claremount Drive, Ballygall, Dublin 11
Tel 01-8087553
Very Rev Gareth Byrne TA
Parish Office: Tel 01-8369291
Email omdgballygallchurch@eircom.net
Website www.ballygallparish.ie

BALLYMORE EUSTACE
Immaculate Conception, Naas, Co Kildare
Very Rev Joe Connolly Adm
Parochial House, Ballymore Eustace,
Naas, Co Kildare
Tel 045-864114
Rev James Prendiville CC
The Presbytery, Hollywood (via Naas),
Co Wicklow
Tel 045-864206
Parish Office: Tel 045-864114
Email hwparishoffice@gmail.com

BALLYMUN, ST PAPPIN'S
Holy Spirit, Silloge Road, Dublin 11
Tel 01-8620586
St Joseph's, Dane Road, Balcurris, Ballymun. Tel 01-8423865/8165700
Email stpappinspastoralcentre@gmail.com
Church of the Virgin Mary, Shangan Road, Dublin 9. Tel 01-8421551
Email vmballymun@live.ie
Parish Tel 01-8620586
Email stpappinspastoralcentre@gmail.com
Website www.stpappinsparish.com
Very Rev Declan Blake *(Moderator)*
Presbytery No. 2,
Shangan Road, Dublin 9
Tel 01-8421486
Rev Kevin Moore CC
30 Willow Park Crescent, Dublin 11
Tel 01-8423865
Rev Rajesh Joseph CC
Presbytery No 2, Shangan Road,
Ballymun, Dublin 9
Tel 01-8421551

BALLYMUN ROAD
(Grouped with Iona Road, Drumcondra, Glasnevin and Ballygall)
Our Lady of Victories, Ballymun Road, Dublin 9
Very Rev Joseph Ryan *(Moderator)*
Very Rev Frank Reburn Co-PP, VF
137 Ballymun Road, Dublin 11
Tel 01-8376341
Rev Patrick Sweeney TA
13 Home Farm Road, Drumcondra,
Dublin 9
Tel 01-8377402
Very Rev Gareth Byrne TA

BALLYROAN
Ballyroan Parish is now under the Team Ministry of Rathfarnham/Churchtown/Ballyroan
Church of the Holy Spirit, Marian Road, Dublin 14
Very Rev Michael Murtagh Co-PP
69 Anne Devlin Park, Ballyroan, Dublin 14
Tel 01-4950444
Rev Deacon Frank Browne
Parish Office: Tel 01-4947303
Email ballyroanparish@gmail.com
Website www.ballyroanparish.ie

BAWNOGUE
Clondalkin/Rowlagh/Neilstown/Deansrath/Bawnogue Grouping
Church of the Transfiguration, Bawnogue, Clondalkin, Dublin 22
Very Rev Kieran Coghlan *(Moderator)*, VF
Very Rev Brian McKittrick Co-PP
Rev Brian Starken (CSSp) Co-PP
Presbytery, Bawnogue, Clondalkin,
Dublin 22
Tel 01-4519810
Ms Saule Cameron, Parish Pastoral Worker
Rev Deacon Derek Leonard
www.bawnogueparish.com

BAYSIDE
Church of the Resurrection, Bayside, Dublin 13
Very Rev Peter Finnerty PP
Parochial House, Bayside Square North,
Sutton, Dublin 13
Tel 01-8323150
Rev Joe Kelly CC
5 Bayside Square East, Sutton, Dublin 13
Tel 01-8322305
Email gradyjoe1@eircom.net
Rev Christopher Sheridan CC
7 Bayside Square East, Sutton, Dublin 13
Tel 01-8322964
Parish Office: Tel 01-8323083
Email baysidercchurch@eircom.net
Website www.baysideparish.ie

BEAUMONT
(Grouped with the parishes of Larkhill, Whitehall, Santry & Kilmore Road West)
Church of Nativity of Our Lord, Dublin 5
Very Rev Robert Smyth Adm
Presbytery, Montrose Park,
Beaumont, Dublin 5
Tel 01-8710013
Rev Dominic Kwikiriza CC
Presbytery 1, Montrose Park,
Beaumont, Dublin 5
Tel 01-8477740
Parish Office: Tel 01-8477740

BEECHWOOD AVENUE
Church of the Holy Name, Dublin 6
Very Rev Paul Taylor Adm
43 Upper Beechwood Avenue, Ranelagh,
Dublin D06 X3F4
Parish Office: Tel 01-4967449
Email info@beechwoodparish.com
Website info@beechwoodparish.com

BERKELEY ROAD
St Joseph's, Dublin 7
Very Rev Paul Churchill PP
The Presbytery, Berkeley Road, Dublin 7
Tel 01-8306336
Rev Deacon Declan Barry
Parish Office: Tel 01-8302071

BLACKROCK
St John the Baptist, Blackrock, Co Dublin
Very Rev Peter O'Connor Adm
24 Barclay Court, Blackrock, Co Dublin
Tel 01-2832302
Very Rev Edward Conway PC
1 Maretimo Gardens West, Blackrock,
Co Dublin
Tel 01-2882248
Email eddieconway@indigo.ie
Parish Office: Tel 01-2882104
Email saintjohnthebaptist@eircom.net

BLAKESTOWN
*Blakestown Parish is now under the Team
Ministry of Blakestown/Hartstown/
Huntstown/Mountview
St Mary of the Servants, Dublin 15*
Very Rev Joseph Coyne *(Moderator)*
36 Ashfield Lawn, Huntstown,
Dublin 15
Tel 01-8216447
Very Rev George Adzato (SVD) Co-PP
Rev Justin Purba (SVD) CC
c/o St Philip the Apostle Church,
No. 2 Presbytery, Mountview Road,
Clonsilla, Dublin 15
Parish Office: Tel 01-8210874
Email
blakestownparish@dublindiocese.ie

BLANCHARDSTOWN
St Brigid's
Very Rev Michael Carey PP
Parochial House,
Blanchardstown, Dublin 15
Tel 01-8213660
Rev Deacon Jim Adams
Rev Deacon Michael O'Connor
Ms Mairin Keegan, Parish Pastoral
Worker

BLESSINGTON
*(Grouped with the parish of Valleymount)
Church of Our Lady*
Very Rev Richard Behan PP
The Presbytery, Main Street,
Blessington, Co Wicklow
Tel 045-865442
Our Lady of Mercy, Crosschapel
Archdeacon Kevin Lyon CC
Parochial House, Crosschapel,
Blessington, Co Wicklow
Tel 045-865215
Email lyonk@indigo.ie

St Brigid's Church, Manor Kilbride
Rev Padraic McDermott (CSSp) CC
The Presbytery, Manor Kilbride,
Blessington, Co Wicklow
Tel 01-4582154
Rev Deacon Gerard Malone
Ms Aine Egan, Parish Pastoral Worker
Parish Office: Tel/Fax 045-865327
Email office@blessington.info
Website www.blessington.info

BLUEBELL
*Bluebell Parish is now under the Team
Ministry of Inchicore (Mary Immaculate
& St Michael's) & Bluebell
Our Lady of the Wayside, Dublin 12*
Very Rev Martin Moran (OMI) *(Moderator)*
Very Rev Anthony Clancy (OMI) Co-PP
Oblate Fathers House of Retreat,
Inchicore, Dublin 8
Tel 01-4541117
Parish Office: Tel 01-4501040
Website www.oblateparishesindublin.ie

BOHERNABREENA
St Anne's, Dublin 24
Very Rev James Daly PP
The Parochial House, St Anne's Church,
Bohernabreena, Tallaght, Dublin 24
Rev Michael Canon Hurley PC
85 Tymon Crescent,
Oldbawn, Dublin 24
Tel/Fax 01-4627080
Rev Hilary Etomike CC
Rev Hector Mwale PC
Rev Deacon Padraic O'Sullivan
c/o Parish Office
Parish Office: Tel 01-4626893
Email stannes.bohernabreena@gmail.com

BONNYBROOK
St Joseph's, Bonnybrook, Dublin 17
Very Rev Joseph Jones *(Moderator)*
122 Greencastle Road, Dublin 17
Tel 01-8487657
Parish Office: Tel 01-8485262

BOOTERSTOWN
Church of the Assumption
Rt Rev Mgr Ciaran O'Carroll PP
Rev Anastasius Ezenwata PC
Parochial House,
Parish of the Assumption, Booterstown
Parish Office: Tel/Fax 01-2831593
Email info@booterstownparish.ie
Website www.booterstownparish.ie

BRACKENSTOWN
*Swords/River Valley/Brackenstown
Grouping/St Cronan's*
Very Rev Desmond Doyle *(Moderator)*
Very Rev Richard Sheehy Co-PP, EV
Parochial House, Brackenstown Road,
Swords, Co Dublin
Tel 01-8401661
Rev Joseph Hao PC
Parochial House, Brackenstown Road,
Swords, Co Dublin
Tel 01-8408926
Rev Deacon Declan Colgan
Parish Office: Tel 01-8401188
Email brackenstownparish@gmail.com
www.brackenstown.dublindiocese.ie

BRAY (BALLYWALTRIM)
*(Bray grouping: Holy Redeemer/Our Lao
Queen of Peace/St Fergal's/St Peter's
Little Bray/Enniskerry)
St Fergal's, Bray, Co Wicklow*
Very Rev Michael O'Kelly *(Moderator)*
Very Rev Jimmy McPartland Co-PP
St Fergal's, Killarney Road,
Bray, Co Wicklow
Tel 01-2768191
Rev Niall Mackey TA
Rev Owen Lynch TA
Parish Office: Tel 01-2860980
Fax 01-2768196
Email info@stfergalsbray.ie
Website www.stfergalsbray.ie

BRAY (HOLY REDEEMER)
*(Bray grouping: Holy Redeemer/Our Lad
Queen of Peace/St Fergal's/St Peter's
Little Bray/Enniskerry)
Holy Redeemer, Main Street,
Bray, Co Wicklow*
Very Rev Michael O'Kelly *(Moderator)*
Cluain Mhuire, Killarney Road,
Bray, Co Wicklow
Tel 01-2116639
Rev Cosmos Iyans PC
Holy Redeemer Parish, Main Street,
Bray, Co Wicklow
Rev Niall Mackey TA
Rev Owen Lynch TA
Parish Office: Tel 01-2868413
Email office@holyredeemerbray.ie
Website www.holyredeemerbray.ie

BRAY, PUTLAND ROAD
*(Bray grouping: Holy Redeemer/Our Lad
Queen of Peace/St Fergal's/St Peter's
Little Bray/Enniskerry)
Our Lady Queen of Peace*
Rev Owen Lynch TA
Rev Niall Mackey TA
Sacristy: 01-2867303
Email secretary@queenofpeace.ie
Parish Office: Tel 01-2745497
Villa Pacis – Parish Centre: 01-2760045
Email villafas1@hotmail.com

BRAY, ST PETER'S
*(Bray grouping: Holy Redeemer/Our Lady
Queen of Peace/St Fergal's/St Peter's
Little Bray/Enniskerry)
St Peter's, Little Bray, Co Wicklow*
For clergy: See Bray (Ballywaltrim)
Email stpeterslittlebray1@gmail.com

BROOKFIELD
*St Aidan's, Brookfield Road
(Springfield, Jobstown, Brookfield
Grouping)*
Very Rev William O'Shaughnessy
(Moderator)
Rev Colin Rothery CC
Rev Martin Hughes TA
447 The Oaks, Belgard Heights,
Tallaght, Dublin 24
Tel 01-4519399
Rev Michael Shortall TA
Rev Deacon Victor Okafor
Ms Christina Malone (PPW)

Allianz ⑪

CABINTEELY
St Brigid's, Dublin 18
Very Rev Aquinas Duffy *(Acting Moderator)*
9 Woodlands Road, Johnstown,
Glenageary, Co Dublin
Tel 01-5672374
Rev Arthur O'Neill *(Team Assistant)*
3 Willow Court, Druid Valley,
Cabinteely, Dublin 18
Tel 087-2597520
Rev Thomas O'Keeffe
10 Glen Avenue, The Park, Cabinteely
Tel 01-2853643

CABRA
*Cabra Parish is now under the Team
Ministry of Cabra/Cabra West/Phibsboro
Christ the King, Dublin 7*
Very Rev Paul Thornton PP, EV
24 New Cabra Road, Dublin 7
Tel 01-8385244
Rev Thomas F. O'Shaughnessy *(Assistant
Priest)*
3 Annamoe Road, Dublin 7
Tel 01-8385626
Rev Joe Keegan CC
The Presbytery, 1 Dunmanus Court,
Kilkiernan Road, Cabra West,
Dublin D07 C8K1
Rev Deacon Damien Murphy
c/o Parish Office
Parish Office: Tel 01-8680804
Email parishoffice@cabraparish.ie

CABRA WEST
*Cabra West Parish is now under the Team
Ministry of Cabra/Cabra West/Phibsboro
Church of the Most Precious Blood, Dublin 7*
Very Rev Paul Thornton PP, EV
24 New Cabra Road, Dublin 7
Tel 01-8385244
Rev Joe Keegan CC
The Presbytery, 1 Dunmanus Court,
Kilkiernan Road, Cabra West,
Dublin D07 C8K1
Rev John Joe Spring PC
Presbytery No. 2, 2 Dunmanus Road,
Cabra West, Dublin D07 Y6TI
Tel 01-8384418
Rev Deacon Damien Murphy
Parish Office: Tel 01-8384418

CASTLEDERMOT
The Assumption, Castledermot, Co Kildare
Very Rev Tom Kennedy PP
Parochial House, Castledermot, Co Kildare
Tel 059-9144164
Parish Office: Tel/Fax 059-9144888

CASTLEKNOCK
*Laurel Lodge/Carpenterstown/
Castleknock Grouping
Our Lady Mother of the Church
Castleknock, Dublin 15*
Very Rev Damian McNeice PP, VF
Beechpark Lawn,
Castleknock, Dublin 15
Tel 01-6408595
Rev Denis O'Connor (CSsR) CC
2 Auburn Drive, Dublin 15
Tel 01-8214003
Rev Brendan Quinlan CC
The Presbytery, Church Grounds,
Laurel Lodge, Castleknock, Dublin 15
Tel 01-8208144

CASTLETOWN
*(Grouped with the parish of Arklow)
St Patrick's, Castletown, Co Wexford*
Very Rev Padraig Canon Ó Cochlain
(Moderator)
Parochial House, Arklow, Co Wicklow
Tel 0402-32294
Email mfc53@indigo.ie

CELBRIDGE
St Patrick's, Celbridge, Co Kildare
Very Rev Joe McDonald PP, VF
Parochial House, Celbridge, Co Kildare
Tel 01-6275874
Rev Peter Nwigwe PC
12 Coarsemoor Park, Straffan, Co Kildare
Tel 01-6012303
Rev Jacob Shanet PC
c/o 12 Coarsemoor Park,
Straffan, Co Kildare
Rev Jonathan Nwanko PC
c/o 12 Coursemoore Park,
Straffan, Co Kildare
Rev Deacon John Graham
Parish Office: Tel 01-6288827
Email celbridgeparishoffice@gmail.com

CHAPELIZOD
Nativity of the BVM, Chapelizod, Dublin 20
Very Rev Sean Mundow Adm
The Presbytery, Chapelizod, Dublin 20
Tel 01-6264645/087-8195073

CHERRY ORCHARD
*Most Holy Sacrament
Parish Team*
Very Rev Michael Murtagh (CSsR) PP
103 Cherry Orchard Avenue, Dublin 10
Tel 01-6267930

CHURCHTOWN
*Churchtown Parish is now under the
Team Ministry of Rathfarnham/
Churchtown/Ballyroan
The Good Shepherd*
Very Rev Martin Canon Cosgrove
(Moderator)
Rev Deacon Frank Browne
Parish Office: Tel 01-2984642
Email info@goodshepherdchurchtown.ie
Website
www.goodshepherdchurchtown.ie

CLOGHER ROAD
*Clogher Parish is now under the Team
Ministry of Crumlin/Mourne Road/
Clogher Road
St Bernadette's*
Very Rev Anthony O'Shaughnessy
(Moderator)
Very Rev Brian Lawless Co-PP
54 Clogher Road, Dublin 12
Tel 01-4536988
Parish Office: Tel 01-4733109
Sacristy: Tel 01-4535099
Email clogherroadparish@eircom.net
Website www.clogherroad.ie

CLONDALKIN
*Clondalkin/Rowlagh/Neilstown/
Deansrath/Bawnogue Grouping
Immaculate Conception, Dublin 22*
Website
www.clondalkin.dublindiocese.ie
Very Rev Kieran Coghlan *(Moderator)*, VF
St Cecilia's, New Road, Clondalkin,
Dublin 22
Tel 01-4592665
Rev Brian McKittrick Co-PP
St Columba Parish House, New Road,
Clondalkin, Dublin 22
Tel 01-4640441
Rev Seamus McEntee, Chaplain DCU
St Mary's, New Road, Clondalkin,
Dublin 22
Rev Deacon Don Devaney
Rev Deacon Derek Leonard
Ms Saule Cameron, Parish Pastoral
Worker

Clonburris, Our Lady Queen of the Apostles
Rev Shan O'Cuiv *(Team Assistant)*
c/o The Presbytery, Clonburris,
Clondalkin, Dublin 22
Tel 01-4573440
Parish Office: Tel 01-4640706

Knockmitten
Rev Desmond Byrne (CSSp) *(Team
Assistant)*
45 Woodford Drive, Monastery Road,
Clondalkin, Dublin 22
Tel 01-4592323
Parish Office: Tel 01-4640706

CLONSKEAGH
*(Grouped with Mount Merrion and
Kilmacud–Stillorgan)
Immaculate Virgin Mary of the Miraculous
Medal, Bird Avenue, Dublin 14*
Very Rev Joe Mullan Adm
79 The Rise, Mount Merrion, Co Dublin
Tel 01-2889879
Rev Fergus O'Donoghue (SJ) PC
Gonzaga College, Sandford Road,
Dublin 6
Tel 01-4972943
Rev Donie O'Connor (MHM) CC
In residence: Very Rev Maurice O'Shea PE
Parish Office: Tel/Fax 01-2837948
Email parishoffice@clonskeagh.org
Website www.clonskeaghparish.ie

CLONTARF, ST ANTHONY'S
St Anthony, Clontarf, Dublin 3
Very Rev John O'Brien *(Moderator)*
186 Clontarf Road, Dublin 3
Tel 01-8338575
Very Rev Larry White Co-PP
119 Stiles Road, Clontarf, Dublin 3
Tel 01-8333394/086-4143888
Rev Peter F. Byrne TA
Rev John Callanan (SJ) TA
Parish Office: Tel 01-8333459
saintanthonysclontarf@dublindiocese.ie
Website www.stanthonysclontarf.ie

CLONTARF, ST JOHN'S
St John the Baptist, Clontarf Road,
Dublin 3
Very Rev John O'Brien *(Moderator)*
186 Clontarf Road, Dublin 3
Tel 01-8338575
Rev Peter F. Byrne TA
Rev John Callanan (SJ) TA
Parish Office: Tel 01-8334606
Email sjtbclontarf@eircom.net
Website stjohnsclontarf.dublindiocese.ie

CONFEY
St Charles Borromeo, Leixlip, Co Kildare
Very Rev Gregory O'Brien PP
Parochial House, Old Hill,
Leixlip, Co Kildare
73 Newtown Park, Leixlip, Co Kildare
Tel 01-6244637
Rev Peter Clancy CC
75 Newtown Park, Leixlip, Co Kildare
Tel 01-6243533
Rev Aloysius Zuribo CC
Presbytery No. 1, 4 Old Hill,
Leixlip, Co Kildare
Tel 01-6243718
Parish Office: Tel/Fax 01-6247410
Email confeyparish@gmail.com

COOLOCK
St Brendan's, Coolock Village, Dublin 5
Very Rev Edwin McCallion (SM) PP
Rev John Harrington (SM) TA
Rev Paddy Stanley (SM) PC
Rev Francis Corry (SM) PC
The Presbytery, Coolock Village, Dublin 5
Tel 01-8477133
Parish Office: Tel 01-8480102/01-8484799
Parish Mobile: 087-2269887
Email malachy@stbrendanscoolock.org
Website www.stbrendanscoolock.org

CORDUFF
St Patrick's, Corduff, Blanchardstown,
Dublin 15
Very Rev John O'Connor (SAC) PP
Parochial House, Corduff
Blanchardstown, Dublin 15
Tel 01-8213596
Rev John Regan (SAC) CC
The Presbytery, Corduff,
Blanchardstown, Dublin 15
Tel 01-8215930

CRUMLIN
Crumlin Parish is now under the Team
Ministry of Crumlin/Mourne Road/
Clogher Road
St Agnes
Very Rev Anthony O'Shaughnessy
(Moderator)
41 St Agnes' Road, Crumlin, Dublin 12
Tel 01-5611500
Very Rev Mgr John F. Deasy TA
55 St Agnes' Road, Crumlin, Dublin 12
Tel 01-4550955
Rev Thomas Clowe (SDB) *(Team Assistant)*
45 St Teresa's Road, Crumlin,
Dublin D12 XK52
Rev Deacon Jimmy Fennell
Parish Office: Tel 01-4555383
Fax 01-4652500
Email info@crumlinparish.ie
Website www.crumlinparish.ie

DALKEY
Assumption of BVM
Very Rev Liam Lacey PP
No 1 Presbytery, Castle Street,
Dalkey, Co Dublin
Tel 01-2857773
Rev Declan Gallagher CC
No 3 Presbytery, Castle Street,
Dalkey, Co Dublin
Tel 01-2859212
Parish Office: Tel 01-2859418
Email office@dalkeyparish.org
Website www.dalkeyparish.org

DARNDALE-BELCAMP
Our Lady Immaculate, Dublin 17
Very Rev Eduardo Nunez Yepez (OMI) PP
The Presbytery, Darndale, Dublin 17
Tel 086-7954706
Rev Michael O'Connor (OMI) CC
The Presbytery, Darndale, Dublin 17
Parish Office: Tel 01-8474547
Email parish@darndaleparish.ie
Website www.darndalebelcamp.ie

DEANSRATH
Clondalkin/Rowlagh/Neilstown/
Deansrath/Bawnogue Grouping
Very Rev Kieran Coghlan *(Moderator)*, VF
Very Rev Brian McKittrick Co-PP
Very Rev Rodrigues Da Silva (CSSp) Co-PP
St Ronan's Presbytery, Deansrath,
Clondalkin, Dublin 22
Tel 01-4570380
Rev Deacon Derek Leonard
Ms Saule Cameron, Parish Pastoral Worker
Email stronansdeansrath@hotmail.com

DOLLYMOUNT
St Gabriel's, St Gabriel's Road, Dublin 3
Very Rev John O'Brien *(Moderator)*
186 Clontarf Road, Dublin 3
Tel 01-8338575
Very Rev Patrick McManus CC
34 Dollymount Grove, Clontarf, Dublin 3
Tel 01-8057692/087-2371089
Email frpatmcmanus@eircom.net
Rev Peter F. Byrne TA
Rev Richard Shannon TA
Parish Office: Tel 01-8333602
Email info@stgabrielsparish.ie

DOLPHIN'S BARN/RIALTO
(Grouped with the parish of Rialto)
Our Lady of Dolours, Dublin 8
Very Rev Fergal MacDonagh Adm
18 St Anthony's Road, Rialto, Dublin 8
Tel 01-4534469
Rev Roy George PC
Parish Office: Tel 01-4547271
Email dolphinsbarn@dublindiocese.ie

DOMINICK STREET
St Saviour's, Dublin 1
Very Rev Joseph Dineen (OP) PP
Tel 01-8897610
Rev Cezary Binkiewicz (OP) CC
St Saviour's,
Upper Dorset Street, Dublin 1
Parish Office: Tel 01-8897610
Email stsaviours@eircom.net
Website www.saintsavioursdublin.ie

DONABATE
St Patrick's
Very Rev Patrick Reilly (OPraem) PP
13 Seaview Park, Portrane, Co Dublin
Tel 01-8436099
Rev Augustine Fokchet PC
St Mary's, Donabate, Co Dublin
Tel 01-8434604
Parish Office: Tel/Fax 01-8434574 (9.30-
12.00 noon)
Email stpatricksrcdonabate@gmail.com
Website www.donabateparish.ie

DONAGHMEDE-CLONGRIFFIN-
BALGRIFFIN
Church of the Holy Trinity
Very Rev Gerard Corcoran *(Moderator)*
12 Grangemore Grove, Donaghmede,
Dublin D13 A264
Tel 01-8474652
Very Rev Mgr Paul Callan TA
Ms Kirsten Mahon, Faith Development
Worker
Parish Office: Tel 01-8479822
Email info@holytrinity.ie
Website www.holytrinityparish.ie

DONNYBROOK
Church of the Sacred Heart, Dublin 4
Rt Rev Mgr Ciaran O'Carroll PP, VG
Presbytery No. 1, Sacred Heart Parish,
Stillorgan Road, Donnybrook,
Dublin D04 E8C7
Tel 01-2693926
Rev Patrick Sheary (SJ) CC
Jesuit House, Milltown Park,
Sandford Road, Dublin 6
Tel 01-2698411
Rev Kieran O'Mahony (OSA) PC
Presbytery No. 2, Stillorgan Road,
Dublin 4
Rev John Boyers PC
16 'Wilfield', Sandymount Avenue,
Ballsbridge, Dublin 4
Tel 087-1557887
Parish Office: Tel 01-2693903
Email secretary@donnybrookparish.ie
Website www.donnybrookparish.ie

DONNYCARNEY
Our Lady of Consolation, Dublin 5
Very Rev Michael O'Grady PP, VF
1 Maypark, Malahide Road, Dublin 5
Tel 01-8313033
Parish Office: Tel 01-8316016 (9 am-12 pm
Rev Vasyl Kornitsky PC
Chaplain to Ukrainian Community
3 Maypark, Malahide Road, Dublin 5
Tel 01-5164752
Email info@donnycarneyparish.ie
Website www.donnycarneyparish.ie

DONORE AVENUE
St Teresa of the Child Jesus, Dublin 8
Very Rev David Corrigan (SM) PP
Rev John O'Gara (SM) PC
Rev John Hannan (SM) PC
The Presbytery, 78A Donore Avenue,
Dublin 8
Tel 01-4542425
Email donoreavenue@dublindiocese.ie

RUMCONDRA

(Grouped with Iona Road, Glasnevin,
allymun Road and Ballygall)
orpus Christi, Home Farm Road, Dublin 9
ery Rev Joseph Ryan *(Moderator)*
t Rev Mgr Martin O'Shea Co-PP
3 Clare Road, Drumcondra, Dublin 9
el 01-8378552
ery Rev Gareth Byrne TA
arish Office: Tel 01-8360085
mail corpuschristi@eircom.net
Vebsite
www.drumcondra.dublindiocese.ie

UBLIN AIRPORT *see* SWORDS

UNDRUM

(Grouped with Meadowbrook and
allinteer)
oly Cross, Dublin 14
ery Rev Liam Canon Belton *(Moderator)*
ery Rev John Bracken Co-PP
mmaus, Main Street, Dundrum,
ublin 14
el 01-2983494
ev Deacon Gabriel Corcoran
el 01-4240613
arish Office: Tel 01-2983494
mail parishofficedundrum@eircom
Vebsite www.holycrossdundrum.org

UN LAOGHAIRE

t Michael's, Co Dublin
ery Rev Paul Tyrrell PP, VF
t Michael's Parochial House,
Eblana Avenue, Dun Laoghaire,
o Dublin
el 01-2801505
ev Martin Daly CC
Renvyle', Corrig Avenue,
un Laoghaire, Co Dublin
el 01-2802100
ev Ciaran Enright CC
arish Office: Tel 01-2804969
mail stmichdl2@eircom.net
Vebsite www.dunlaoghaireparish.ie

UNLAVIN

t Nicholas of Myra, Dunlavin, Co Wicklow
ev Douglas Malone Adm
he Presbytery, Dunlavin,
o Wicklow
el 045-401227
ev Eamonn McCarthy CC
he Presbytery, Donard,
o Wicklow
el 045-404614
arish Office: Tel 045-401871
mail parish10@eircom.net
Vebsite www.dunlavinparish.ie

ADESTOWN

he Immaculate Conception,
Iaas, Co Kildare
ery Rev Micheál Comer Adm
he Presbytery, Eadestown,
Iaas, Co Kildare
el 045-862187
mail eadestownparish@gmail.com

EAST WALL-NORTH STRAND

St Joseph's, Church Road, Dublin 3
Very Rev John Ennis PP
Parochial House, 78 St Mary's Road,
East Wall, Dublin 3
Tel 01-8742320
Rev Deacon Paul F. Kelly
Parish Office: Tel 01-8560980
Email stjosephsparish1941@gmail.com

EDENMORE

(Grouped with the parish of Grange Park)
St Monica's, Dublin 5
Very Rev Patrick Canon Boyle Adm
Rev Ronnie Dunne CC
c/o Parish Office
Tel 086-4513904
Rev Anthony Power CC
35 Grange Park Avenue
Tel 01-8480244
Very Rev Mgr Paul Callan TA
Ms Kirsten Mahon, Faith Development
Worker
Parish Office: Tel 01-8471497
Email info@stbenedicts-stmonicas.ie

ENNISKERRY/KILMACANOGUE

*(Bray grouping: Holy Redeemer/Our Lady
Queen of Peace/St Fergal's/St Peter's
Little Bray/Enniskerry)*
*Immaculate Heart of Mary, Enniskerry,
Co Wicklow*
Very Rev Michael O'Kelly *(Moderator)*
Parochial House, Enniskerry,
Co Wicklow
Tel 01-2863506/087-2660821
Very Rev Bernard Kennedy Co-PP
Parochial House, Enniskerry,
Co Wicklow
Rev Hyacinth Nwakuna (CSSp) CC
The Presbytery,
Kilmacanogue, Co Wicklow
Tel 01-2760030
Parish Office Enniskerry: Tel 01-2760030
(10 am-1 pm, Mon-Fri)
Email stmarys@enniskerryparish.ie
Parish Office Kilmacanogue
Tel 01-2021882 (10 am-1 pm, Mon-Fri)
Email stmochonogs@enniskerryparish.ie

ESKER-DODDSBORO-ADAMSTOWN

*Esker-Doddsboro-Adamstown Parish is
now under the Team Ministry of Lucan/
Esker-Doddsboro-Adamstown/Lucan South
St Patrick's*
Very Rev Philip Curran PP
Rev John Hassett CC
127 Castlegate Way,
Adamstown, Co Dublin
Tel 01-6812088
Email hassettorama@gmail.com
Parish Office: Tel 01-6281018
Email stpatrickschurchlucan@gmail.com
Website www.stpatrickslucan.ie

FAIRVIEW

Church of the Visitation of BVM, Dublin 3
Very Rev Maximilian McKeown (OFM
Conv) PP
Rev Marius Tomulesei (OFM Conv) CC
Rev Aidan Walsh (OFM Conv) CC
Friary of the Visitation,
Fairview Strand, Dublin 3
Tel 01-8376000 Fax 01-8376021
Parish Office: Tel 01-8376000

FINGLAS

St Canice's, Dublin 11
Very Rev Richard Hyland PP
5 The Lawn, Finglas, Dublin 11
Tel 01-8341894
Rev Michael Shiels CC
Tel 01-8341051
The Presbytery 1, St Canice's,
Finglas, Dublin 11
Very Rev Martin Canon Hogan CC
Rev Éamonn Cahill TA
Rev Seamus Ahearne (OSA) TA
Mr Christopher Okereke, PPW
Parish Office: Tel 01-8343110
Email info@stcanicesfinglas.com
Website www.stcanicesfinglas.com

FINGLAS WEST

Church of the Annunciation, Dublin 11
Very Rev Richard Hyland PP
5 The Lawn, Finglas West, Dublin 11
Tel 01-8341000
Very Rev Martin Canon Hogan CC
Rev Éamonn Cahill TA
Rev Seamus Ahearne (OSA) TA
Mr Christopher Okereke, PPW

FIRHOUSE

Our Lady of Mount Carmel, Dublin 24
Very Rev Peter Reilly Adm
Presbytery 1, Ballycullen Avenue,
Firhouse, Dublin 24
Tel 01-4599855
Parish Office: Tel 01-4524702
Email olmcfirhouseparish@gmail.com

FOXROCK

Our Lady of Perpetual Succour
Very Rev Gerard Kane PP
Parochial House, Foxrock, Dublin 18
Tel 01-2893229
Parish Office: Tel 01-2893492/01-2898879
Email secretary@foxrockparish.ie
Website www.foxrockparish.ie

FRANCIS STREET

*(Grouped with James' Street and Meath
Street)*
St Nicholas of Myra, Dublin 8
Very Rev Martin Dolan Adm
The Presbytery, Francis Street, Dublin 8
Tel 01-4544861/086-4035318
Parish Office: Tel 01-5157512
Email rita@francisstreetparish.ie
Website www.francisstreetparish.ie

GARDINER STREET
St Francis Xavier, Dublin 1
Very Rev Niall Leahy (SJ) PP
The Presbytery, Upper Gardiner Street,
Dublin 1
Tel 01-8363411
Email sfx@jesuit.ie
Website www.gardinerstparish.ie

GARRISTOWN
(Grouped with Rolestown and The Naul)
Church of the Assumption, Co Dublin
Very Rev Derek Canon Farrell *(Moderator)*
Parochial House, Main Street,
Garristown, Co Dublin A42 PF64
Tel 01-8354138
Parish Office: 01-8354138

GLASNEVIN
(Grouped with Iona Road, Drumcondra,
Ballymun Road and Ballygall)
Our Lady of Dolours, Dublin 9
Very Rev Joseph Ryan *(Moderator)*
Very Rev Paul Coyle Co-PP
159 Botanic Road, Glasnevin, Dublin 9
Rev Kieran Dunne CC
50 Cremore Road, Glasnevin, Dublin 9
Tel 01-8373455
Very Rev Gareth Byrne TA
Parish Office: Tel 01-8379445

GLASTHULE
St Joseph's, Glasthule, Co Dublin
Very Rev William Farrell CC
Parochial House, St Joseph's,
Glasthule, Co Dublin
Tel 01-2801226
Rev Denis Kennedy (CSSp) CC
c/o St Joseph's Pastoral Centre,
Glasthule, Co Dublin
Rev Ciaran Enright CC
Parish Office: Tel 01-6638604/5
Sacristy: 01-2800182
Email stjosephsglasthule@gmail.com
Website www.glasthuleparish.com

GLENDALOUGH
(Grouped with Rathdrum and Roundwood)
St Kevin's, Co Wicklow
Very Rev Derek Doyle *(Moderator)*
Rev John Greene CC
The Parochial House, St Kevin's Parish,
Laragh, Glendalough, Co Wicklow
Tel 044-45140
Rev Deacon Jeremy Seligman
Parish Office: Tel 0404-45777
Email glendaloughparish@gmail.com
Website www.glendalough.dublindiocese.ie

GRANGE PARK
(Grouped with the parish of Edenmore)
St Benedict's, Grange Park View, Dublin 5
Very Rev Patrick Canon Boyle Adm
Rev Ronald Dunne CC
c/o Parish Office
Tel 086-4513904
Rev Tony Power CC
35 Grange Park Avenue
Tel 01-84802441/086-3905205
Very Rev Mgr Paul Callan TA
Ms Kirsten Mahon, Faith Development
Worker
Email info@benedicts-stmonicas.ie

GREENHILLS
Church of the Holy Spirit, Dublin 12
Very Rev Michael Kilkenny (CSSp)
(Moderator)
Rev Isaac Antwi-Boasiako (CSSp) CC
55 Fernhill Road, Greenhills, Dublin 12
Tel 01-4504040
Parish Office: Tel 01-4509191
Fax 01-4605287
Email greenhillsparish@eircom.net
Website holyspiritparishgreehills.ie

GREYSTONES
Church of the Holy Rosary, Co Wicklow
Very Rev John Daly PP
Parochial House, La Touche Road,
Greystones, Co Wicklow
Tel 01-2874278
Rev Denis Quinn CC
The Presbytery, Kimberley Road,
Greystones, Co Wicklow
Tel 01-2877025
Rev Gerard Tyrrell CC
The Presbytery, Blacklion,
Greystones, Co Wicklow
Tel 01-2819658
Parish Office: Tel 01-2860704
Email office@greystonesparish.com

HADDINGTON ROAD
St Mary's, Dublin 4
Very Rev Fachtna McCarthy Adm
Parochial House, St Mary's,
Haddington Road, Dublin 4
Tel 01-6600075/087-3936327
Rev Pat Claffey (SVD) CC
The Presbytery,
Haddington Road, Dublin 4
Tel 085-7123675
Rev Josip Levakovic CC & Chaplain to the
Croatian Community
The Presbytery, Haddington Road,
Dublin 4
Tel 01-6600075
Rev Deacon Greg Pepper
Email info@stmaryshaddingtonroad.ie
Website stmaryshaddingtonroad.ie

HALSTON STREET AND ARRAN QUAY
St Michan's, Halston Street, Dublin 7
Very Rev Richard Hendrick (OFM Cap) PP
Capuchin Friary, Church Street,
Dublin 7
Tel 01-8730599 Fax 01-8730250
Email halstonst@gmail.com

HAROLD'S CROSS
Our Lady of the Rosary, Dublin 6W
Very Rev Alex Conlon PP
Rev William King, Parish Chaplain,
protem
213B Harold's Cross Road, Dublin 6W
Tel 01-4972816
Parish Office: Tel 01-4965055
Email enquiries@hxparish.ie
Website www.hxparish.ie

HARRINGTON STREET
St Kevin's, Dublin 8
Very Rev Gerard Deighan Adm
Parochial House, Harrington Street,
Dublin 8
Tel 01-4751506

Rev William Richardson PC
Rev Michael G. Nevin *(priest in residence)*
The Presbytery, Harrington Street,
Dublin 8
Tel 01-4789093

HARTSTOWN
Hartstown Parish is now under the Team
Ministry of Blakestown/Hartstown/
Huntstown/Mountview
St Ciaran's, Dublin 15
Very Rev Joseph Coyne *(Moderator)*
St Ciaran's, 36 Ashfield Lawn,
Huntstown, Dublin 15
Tel 01-8216447
Rev Deacon Noel McHugh
Parish Office: Tel 01-8249651/01-8204777
Website www.st-ciarans-parish.ie

HOWTH
(Grouped with Balcoyle and Sutton)
Church of the Assumption,
Howth, Co Dublin
Very Rev Cyril Mangan *(Moderator)*
Rev Gerard Tanham PC
Presbytery No 1, Thormanby Road,
Howth, Co Dublin
Tel 01-8232193
Rev Bernard Zong PC
Tel 01-8397398
Email assumptionhowth@eircom.net
Sacristy: Tel 01-8397398
Email assumptionhowth@eircom.net

HUNTSTOWN
Hartstown Parish is now under the Team
Ministry of Blakestown/Hartstown/
Huntstown/Mountview
Sacred Heart of Jesus, Dublin 15
Very Rev Joseph Coyne *(Moderator)*
36 Ashfield Lawn, Huntstown, Dublin 15
Tel 01-8216447
Very Rev George Adzato (SVD) Co-PP
Rev Justin Purba (SVD) CC
No 2 Presbytery, Mountview Road,
Clonsilla, Dublin 15

INCHICORE, MARY IMMACULATE
Inchicore/Bluebell Grouping
Mary Immaculate, Tyrconnell Road,
Dublin 8
Very Rev Martin Moran (OMI)
(Moderator)
Very Rev Paul Horrocks (OMI) Co-PP
Oblate Fathers, House of Retreat,
Inchicore, Dublin 8
Tel 01-4541117
Website www.oblateparishesinchicore.ie

INCHICORE, ST MICHAEL'S
Inchicore/Bluebell Grouping
St Michael's, Emmet Road, Dublin 8
Very Rev Martin Moran (OMI)
(Moderator)
Very Rev Dominick Domagala (OMI) Co-PP
Website www.stmichaelsinchicore.ie

NA ROAD
(Grouped with Drumcondra, Glasnevin,
Ballymun Road and Ballygall)
St Columba's, Dublin 9
Very Rev Joseph Ryan (Moderator)
Very Rev Patrick Jones TA
Iona Road, Dublin 9
Tel 01-8308257
Very Rev Gareth Byrne TA
Email ionaroadparish@gmail.com
Website www.ionaroadparish.ie

JAMES'S STREET
(Grouped with Meath Street and Francis
Street)
St James's Church, Dublin 8
Very Rev Eugene Taaffe PP
The Presbytery,
James's Street, Dublin 8
Tel 01-4531143
Rev John Damascene Akaolisa PC
St Catherine's, Meath Street, Dublin 8
Tel 01-4543356
Parish Office: Tel 01-4531143
Email jamesstreet@dublindiocese.ie

JOBSTOWN
(Springfield, Jobstown and Bookfield
Grouping)
St Thomas the Apostle
Very Rev William O'Shaughnessy
(Moderator)
The Presbytery, Jobstown, Tallaght,
Dublin 24
Tel 01-4610971
Email jobstownparish@gmail.com
Rev Colin Rothery CC
Rev Michael Shortall TA
Rev Deacon Derek Leonard
Rev Deacon Victor Okafor
Ms Christina Malone, Parish Pastoral
Worker
c/o Parish Office

JOHNSTOWN-KILLINEY
Our Lady of Good Counsel, Killiney,
Co Dublin
Very Rev John Sinnott Co-PP
5 Auburn Road, Killiney, Co Dublin
Tel 01-2856660/087-8122651
Parish Office: Tel 01-2351416
Email johnstownparish@gmail.com
Website www.johnstownparish.org

KILBARRACK-FOXFIELD
St John the Evangelist, Greendale Road,
Kilbarrack, Dublin 5
Very Rev Peter Finnerty PP
Rev Cathal Price (retired)
4 Foxfield St John, Dublin 5
Tel 01-8323683
Parish Office: Tel 01-8390433
Email info@kilbarrackfoxfieldparish.ie
Website www.kilbarrackfoxfieldparish.ie

KILBRIDE AND BARNDARRIG
St Mary's, Barndarrig, Co Wicklow
Very Rev Donal Roche PP, VG
Rev Timothy Murphy PC
St Mary's Barndarrig, Co Wicklow

KILCULLEN
Sacred Heart and St Brigid, Kilcullen
Very Rev Gary Darby PP
Parochial House, Kilcullen, Co Kildare
Tel 045-481230
Email mclm@eircom.net
Rev Martin Harte CC
Presbytery, Kilcullen, Co Kildare
Tel 045-481222
Parish Office: Tel 045-480727
Email kilcullenparish@eircom.net
Website www.kilcullenparish.net

KILLESTER
St Brigid's, Howth Road, Dublin 5
Very Rev Joe Whelan Adm
126 Furry Park Road, Dublin 5
Tel 01-8333793
Parish Office: Tel 01-8332974
Website www.killester.dublindiocese.ie

KILLINARDEN
Church of the Sacred Heart, Killinarden,
Tallaght, Dublin 24
Very Rev Fintan O'Driscoll (MSC) PP
Rev Con O'Connell (MSC) CC
The Presbytery, Killinarden, Tallaght,
Dublin D24 R521
Tel 01-4522251
Email
sacredheartparishkillinarden@gmail.com
Website
www.sacredheartparishkillinarden.com

KILL-O'-THE-GRANGE
Holy Family, Kill Avenue,
Dun Laoghaire, Co Dublin
Very Rev Michael O'Connor Adm
Presbytery No 2, Church Grounds,
Kill Avenue, Dun Laoghaire, Co Dublin
Tel 01-2140863
Very Rev John Canon Killeen CC
20 Abbey Court, Monkstown, Co Dublin
Tel 01-2802533
Rev Deacon John O'Neill
Parish Office: Tel 01-2845299

KILMACANOGUE see ENNISKERRY

KILMACUD-STILLORGAN
St Laurence, Co Dublin
(Grouped Mount Merrion and
Clonskeagh)
Very Rev Joseph Mullan (Moderator)
(Kilmacud & Mount Merrion)
79 The Rise, Mount Merrion, Co Dublin
Tel 01-2889879
Rev Paddy O'Byrne CC
Presbytery No. 2, Church Grounds
Tel 01-2882257
Very Rev Brian O'Reilly (Team Assistant)
Rev Donie O'Connor (MHM) CC
6 Allen Park Road, Stillorgan,
Co Dublin A94 X261
Tel 089-9796447
Parish Office: Tel 01-2884009
Email kilmacudparish@eircom.net
Website www.kilmacudparish.com

KILMORE ROAD WEST
St Luke the Evangelist, Dublin 5
Very Rev Joseph Jones (Moderator)
Very Rev Padraig O'Sullivan Co-PP
St Luke's, Kilbarron Road,
Kilmore West, Dublin 5
Rev Roland Ntambang PC
Parish Office: Tel 01-8488149

KILNAMANAGH-CASTLEVIEW
St Kevin's, Dublin 24
Very Rev Frank Drescher Adm
Presbytery No 1, Treepark Road,
Kilnamanagh, Dublin 24
Tel 01-4523805
Rev Fergus McGlynn (retired)
43 Chestnut Grove, Ballymount Road,
Dublin 24
Parish Office: Tel 01-4515570

KILQUADE
St Patrick's, Kilquade, Co Wicklow
Very Rev John Daly PP
Parochial House, La Touche Road,
Greystones, Co Wicklow
Tel/Fax 01-2874278
Rev Eamonn Clarke
The Presbytery, Kilcoole, Co Wicklow
Tel 01-2876207
Very Rev Sean Canon Smith CC
The Presbytery,
Newtownmountkennedy, Co Wicklow
Tel 01-2819253
Parish Office: Tel 01-2819658
Email kilquadeparish@eircom.net
Website www.kilquadeparish.com

KIMMAGE MANOR
Church of the Holy Spirit, Kimmage Manor,
Whitehall Road, Dublin 12
Very Rev Michael Kilkenny (CSSp)
(Moderator)
Rev Isaac Antwi-Boasiako (CSSp) CC
Rev John Mahon (CSSp) CC
Tel 01-4064377
Parish Office: Tel 01-4064377
Email kimmagemanorparish@gmail.com
Website www.kimmagemanorparish.com

KINSEALY
(Grouped with the parishes of Malahide,
Yellow Walls & Portmarnock)
St Nicholas of Myra, Malahide Road,
Co Dublin
Very Rev Martin Noone (Moderator), VF
Very Rev Conleth Meehan Co-PP
21 Wheatfield Grove,
Portmarnock, Co Dublin
Tel 01-8461561
Parish Office: Tel 01-8460028

KNOCKLYON
St Colmcille, Idrone Avenue, Dublin 16
Very Rev Eamonn Donnelly (SVD) Adm
Rev Cyril Ma Ming (SVD) CC
Presbytery, Idrone Avenue, Knocklyon,
Dublin 16
Tel 01-4941204
Rev Deacon Michael Giblin
Email knocklyonparish@gmail.com
Website www.knocklyonparish.ie

LARKHILL-WHITEHALL-SANTRY
(Grouped with the parishes of Kilmore Road West & Beaumont)
Holy Child, Thatch Road, Dublin 9
Very Rev Paul Kenny *(Moderator)*
149 Swords Road, Dublin 9
Tel 01-8375274
Very Rev John Jones PC
151 Swords Road, Whitehall, Dublin 9
Tel 01-8374887
Email jj362972@gmail.com
Rev Thomas Kearney PC
137 Shantalla Road,
Whitehall, Dublin 9
Tel 01-8420260
Parish Office: Tel 01-8375274
Email whitehall@dublindiocese.ie
Website www.whitehall@dublindiocese.ie

LAUREL LODGE-CARPENTERSTOWN
St Thomas the Apostle, Laurel Lodge/
Carpenterstown, Dublin 15
Very Rev Damian McNeice PP, VF
Rev Brendan Quinlan CC
Presbytery, Church Grounds,
Laurel Lodge, Castleknock, Dublin 15
Tel 01-8208144
Rev Dan Joe O'Mahony (OFM Cap) TA
The Oratory, Blanchardstown Dublin 15
Tel 01-8200915/086-8090633
Email danjoe2006@gmail.com
Parish Office: Tel 01-8208112
Website www.laurellodgeparish.ie

LEIXLIP
Our Lady's Nativity, Co Kildare
Very Rev Gregory O'Brien PP
Parochial House, Old Hill, Leixlip,
Co Kildare
Tel 01-6245597
Rev Aloysius Zuribo CC
No 1 Presbytery, 4 Old Hill,
Leixlip, Co Kildare
Tel 01-6243718
Rev Michael Chimalenji PC
Presbytery No 2, 6 Old Hill, Leixlip,
Co Kildare
Parish Office:
Tel 01-6243673/01-6245159
Email leixlip.parish@oln.ie
Website www.oln.ie

LITTLE BRAY see BRAY, ST PETER'S

LOUGHLINSTOWN
(Grouped with Ballybrack-Killiney)
St Columbanus, Dun Laoghaire
Very Rev Tom Dalzell *(Moderator)*
Parochial House, Church Avenue,
Killiney, Co Dublin
Tel 01-2826404
Rt Rev Mgr Enda Lloyd Co-PP
10 The Oaks, Loughlinstown Drive,
Dun Laoghaire, Co Dublin
Tel 01-2826895
Email loughlinstownparish@eircom.net
Website www.loughlinstownparish.ie
Parish Office: Tel 01-2824085

LUCAN
Lucan Parish is now under the Team Ministry of Lucan/Esker-Dodsboro-Adamstown/Lucan South
St Mary's, Lucan, Co Dublin
Very Rev Philip Curran PP
231 Beech Park, Lucan, Co Dublin
Tel 01-2533804
Rev Ubaldo Muhindo CC
14 Roselawn, Lucan, Co Dublin
Tel 01-5037528
Parish Office: Tel 01-6217041
Email
parishoffice@stmarysparishlucan.ie
Website www.stmarysparishlucan.ie

LUCAN SOUTH
Lucan South Parish is now under the Team Ministry of Lucan/Esker-Dodsboro-Adamstown/Lucan South
Church of Divine Mercy, Balgaddy
Very Rev Aidan Kieran PP
Parochial House, Foxdene Avenue,
Balgaddy, Lucan South,
Co Dublin K78 DD89
Rev Pius Faruna PC
Rev Samuel Akubuenyi PC
Parish Office: Tel 01-4572900
Email churchdivinemercy@eircom.net
Website www.lucansouthparish.net

LUSK
St MacCullin's, Lusk, Co Dublin
Very Rev George Begley Adm
Parochial House, Chapel Road,
Lusk, Co Dublin
Tel 01-8949229
Parish Office: Tel 01-8438421
Email luskparish@eircom.net
Website www.luskparish.ie

MALAHIDE
(Grouped with the parishes of Yellow Walls, Kinsealy & Portmarnock)
St Sylvester's, Malahide, Co Dublin
Very Rev Martin Noone *(Moderator)*, VF
Very Rev Kevin Doherty Co-PP
Apartment No. 1, St Sylvester's Church,
Malahide, Co Dublin
Rev Deacon Gerard Reilly
c/o Parish Office
Parish Office: Tel 01-8451244
Email stsylvesters@malahideparish.ie
Website www.malahideparish.ie

MARINO
St Vincent de Paul, Griffith Avenue, Dublin 9
Very Rev Thomas Noone PP
69 Griffith Avenue, Dublin 9
Tel 01-8332864
Rev Christian Ameh PC
c/o The Sacristy, St Vincent de Paul Church,
Griffith Avenue, Dublin 9
Tel 01-8339756
Parish Office: Tel 01-8332772/087-2506786
Email info@marinoparish.ie
Website www.marinoparish.ie

MARLEY GRANGE
The Divine Word, 25/27 Hermitage Down, Rathfarnham, Dublin 16
Very Rev Liam Tracey (OSM) PP
Rev Jim Mulherin (OSM) CC
25–27 Hermitage Downs,
Marley Grange, Rathfarnham, Dublin 16
Tel 01-4944295
Parish Office: Tel 01-4944295 Fax 01-494104
Email divine_word@ireland.com
Website www.marleygrangeparish.ie

MAYNOOTH
St Mary's, Maynooth, Co Kildare
Very Rev Frank Canon McEvoy Adm
Parochial House, Moyglare Road
Tel 01-6286220
Rev Paul Kelly CC
The Presbytery, 18 Straffan Way,
Maynooth, Co Kildare
Tel 087-2463876
Rev Gerhard Osthues (SVD) PC
c/o Parish Office, Maynooth, Co Kildare
Parish Office: Tel 01-6293018
Email maynoothparishoffice@gmail.com
www.maynoothparish.dublindiocese.ie

MEADOWBROOK
(Grouped with Dundrum and Ballinteer)
St Attracta's Oratory, Dublin 16
Very Rev Liam Canon Belton *(Moderator*
Presbytery 1,
St John the Evangelist Parish,
Ballinteer Avenue, Dublin 16
Rev Martins Ebuka TA
Rev Moses Daniel Murtala TA
75 Ludford Road, Ballinteer, Dublin 16
Parish Office: Tel 01-2980471
Email info@meadowbrookparish.ie
www.meadowbrookparish.ie

MEATH STREET
(Grouped with James' Street and Francis Street)
St Catherine of Alexandria, Dublin 8
Very Rev Eugene Taffe PP
Rev John Damascene Akaolisa PC
St Catherine's Presbytery, Meath Street,
Dublin 8
Parish Office
Tel 01-4543356 Fax 01-4738303
Email meathst@hotmail.com
Website www.meathstreetparish.ie

MERRION ROAD
Our Lady Queen of Peace, Dublin 4
Very Rev Fergus O'Connor (Opus Dei) PP, VF
Email fc.oconnor@gmail.com
Rev James Hurley (Opus Dei) CC
Email jpatrickhurley@gmail.com
31 Herbert Ave., Merrion Road, Dublin 4
Tel 01-2692001
Parish Office: Tel 01-2691825
Email info@merrionroadchurch.ie
Website www.merrionroadchurch.ie

MILLTOWN

SS Columbanus and Gall, Dublin 6
Rt Rev Mgr Peter Briscoe Adm
7 Ramleh Park, Milltown, Dublin 6
Tel 01-2196600
Rev Alan Mowbray (SJ) PC
Gonzaga Jesuit Community,
Sandford Road, Dublin 6
Tel 01-4972943
Parish Office: Tel 01-2680041
Parish Centre: Tel 01-2196740
Email milltownparishcentre@gmail.com
Website www.milltownparish.ie

MONKSTOWN

St Patrick's, Carrickbrennan Road
Very Rev Kevin Rowan PP
Parochial House, Carrickbrennan Road,
Monkstown, Co Dublin
Tel 01-2802130
Rev Deacon Eric Cooney
Parish Office: Tel 01-2807854
Email secretary@monkstownparish.ie
Website www.monkstownparish.ie

MOONE

Church of the Blessed Trinity
Very Rev Liam Canon Rigney PP
Parochial House, 1 Stanhope Place,
Athy, Co Kildare
Tel 059-8631781
Parish Office: Tel 059-8623154
Email stlaurenceschurch@gmail.com
Wesbite www.narraghmoreparish.org

MOUNT ARGUS

*St Paul of the Cross, Harold's Cross,
Dublin 6W*
Very Rev Paul Francis Spencer (CP) PP
Rev Patrick Fitzgerald (CP) CC
St Paul's Retreat,
Mount Argus, Dublin 6W
Email secretary@mountargusparish.ie
Website www.mountargusparish.ie
Parish Office: Tel 01-4992000

MOUNT MERRION

St Therese, Mount Merrion, Co Dublin
Very Rev Joseph Mullan *(Moderator)*
79 The Rise, Mount Merrion, Co Dublin
Tel 01-2889879
Rev Patrick J. O'Byrne CC
188 Lower Kilmacud Road, Kilmacud,
Co Dublin
Tel 01-2981955
Rev Brian O'Reilly *(Team Assistant)*
Rev Donie O'Connor (MHM) CC
5 Allen Park Road, Stillorgan,
Co Dublin A94 X261
Tel 089-9796447
Parish Office: Tel 01-2881271
Email
parishoffice@mountmerrionparish.ie
Website www.mountmerrionparish.ie

MOUNTVIEW

*Mountview Road Parish is now under the
Team Ministry of Blakestown/Hartstown/
Huntstown/Mountview*
*St Philip the Apostle, Blanchardstown,
Dublin 15*
Very Rev Joseph Coyne *(Moderator)*
Very Rev George Adzato (SVD) Co-PP
Very Rev Justin Purba (SVD) PC
No. 2 The Presbytery, Mountview,
Clonsilla, Dublin 15
Tel 01-8216380
Email mountview@dublindiocese.ie
Website www.stphilipsmountview.ie

MOURNE ROAD

*Mourne Road Parish is now under the
Team Ministry of Crumlin/Mourne Road/
Clogher Road*
Our Lady of Good Counsel, Dublin 12
Very Rev Anthony O'Shaughnessy
(Moderator)
Very Rev David Brannigan Co-PP
89 Sperrin Road, Drimnagh, Dublin 12
Tel 01-4652418
Email copp@mourneroad.ie
Rev Dan An Nguyen Co-PP
Parochial House, Sperrin Road, Dublin 12
Parish Office: Tel 01-4556105
Email office@mourneparish.ie
Website www.mourneroad.ie

MULHUDDART

Rt Rev Mgr Eoin Thynne Adm
24 The Court, Mulhuddart Wood,
Mulhuddart, Dublin 15
Rev Adrian F. Crowley CC
4 Summerfield Lawn, Clonsilla Road,
Blanchardstown, Dublin 15
Parish Office: Tel 01-8205480
Email mulhudoffice@gmail.com

NARRAGHMORE

(Grouped with the parish of Moone)
SS Mary and Laurence, Co Kildare
Very Rev Liam Canon Rigney PP
Parochial House, Crookstown,
Athy, Co Kildare
Email stlaurencechurch@gmail.com
Website www.narraghmoreparish.org

NAUL

*The Naul Parish is now under the Team
Ministry Rolestown/Garristown/The Naul*
St Canice's, Damastown, Co Dublin
The Nativity of BVM, Naul
The Assumption of BVM, Ballyboughal
Very Rev Derek Canon Farrell *(Moderator)*
Parochial House, Main Street,
Garristown, Co Dublin A42 PF64
Tel 01-8412932
Rev Deacon Declan Colgan

NAVAN ROAD

Our Lady Help of Christians, Dublin 7
Very Rev Liam Ó Cuív PP
Parochial House, 211 Navan Road,
Dublin 7
Tel 01-8681436
Rev Patrick O'Byrne CC
194 Navan Road, Dublin 7
Tel 01-8383313
Rev Deacon Eamonn Murray
c/o Parish Office
Parish Office: Tel 01-8380265
Email info@navanroadparish.ie
Website www.navanroadparish.com

NEILSTOWN

*St Peter the Apostle, Dublin 22
(Clondalkin/Rowlagh/Neilstown/
Deansrath/Bawnogue Grouping)*
Very Rev Kieran Coghlan *(Moderator)*, VF
Very Rev Hugh Kavanagh Co-PP
The Presbytery, Neilstown,
Clondalkin, Dublin 22
Tel 01-6263920
Very Rev Brian McKittrick Co-PP
Rev Cherian Thazamhon CC
30 Wheatfield Close,
Clondalkin, Dublin 22
(Also Chaplain to Syro-Malakara
Community)
Rev Deacon Derek Leonard
Ms Saule Cameron, Parish Pastoral Worker
Parish Office:
Tel 01-4573546/085-7199087

NEWCASTLE

*(Grouped with the parishes of Saggart,
Rathcoole & Brittas)*
St Finian's, Co Dublin
Very Rev John Gilligan *(Moderator)*, VF
St Mary's Parochial House,
Saggart, Co Dublin
Tel 087-4103239
Rev David Fleming CC
87 Beechwood Lawns,
Rathcoole, Co Dublin
Tel 01-4587187
Rev Patrick Murphy Amos CC
No 1 The Glebe, Peamount Road,
Newcastle Lyons, Co Dublin
Tel 086-0108420
Rev Deacon Paul Ferris,
c/o Parish Office, Saggart, Co Dublin

NEWTOWNPARK

*The Guardian Angels, Blackrock,
Co Dublin*
Very Rev Gerry Kane PP
64 Newtownpark Avenue,
Blackrock, Co Dublin
Tel 01-2784860
Rev William Fortune PC
32 Newtownpark Avenue,
Blackrock, Co Dublin
Tel 01-2100337
Parish Office: Tel 01-2832988
Email parishoffice@newtownparkparish.ie
Website www.newtownparkparish.com

NORTH WALL-SEVILLE PLACE
St Laurence O'Toole's (North Wall),
Dublin 1
Very Rev Robert Colclough Adm
Parochial House,
49 Seville Place, Dublin 1
Tel 01-2865457
Parish Office: Tel 01-8744236

NORTH WILLIAM STREET
St Agatha's, Dublin 1
Very Rev Brendan Kealy Adm
Parochial House,
46 North William Street, Dublin 1
Tel 01-8556474
Parish Office: Tel 01-8554078
Email office@stagathasparish.ie
Website www.stagathasparish.ie

OLD BAWN (*see* TALLAGHT, OLDBAWN)

PALMERSTOWN
St Philomena's, Dublin 20
Very Rev Anthony Canon Reilly PP
Parochial House, Palmerstown, Dublin 20
Tel 01-6266254 Fax 01-6266255
Email reillya48@gmail.com
Parish Office: Tel 01-6260900/01-6266241
Email stphilomenasparish48@gmail.com
Website www.palmerstownparish.com

PHIBSBOROUGH
(Grouped with Cabra and Cabra West)
St Peter's, Dublin D07 FW29
Very Rev Eamon Devlin (CM) PP
Email pp@stpetersphibsboro.ie
St Peter's, Phibsboro, Dublin D07 FW29
Tel 01-8389708/8102566
Rev Deacon Damian Murphy
Email info@stpetersphibsboro.ie
Website www.stpetersphibsboro.ie

PORTERSTOWN-CLONSILLA
St Mochta's, Porterstown, Dublin 15
Very Rev Michael Carey Adm
Rev Paul Ward TA
St Mochta's, Porterstown, Dublin 15
Tel 01-8213218 Fax 01-8213516
Rev Deacon Timothy Murphy
c/o Parish Office
Website www.stmochtasparish.ie

PORTMARNOCK
(Grouped with the parishes of Malahide,
Yellow Walls & Kinsealy)
St Anne's, Portmarnock, Co Dublin
Very Rev Martin Noone *(Moderator)*, VF
Very Rev John Canon Flaherty Co-PP
St Anne's, Strand Road,
Portmarnock, Co Dublin
Tel/Fax 01-8461081
Rev Deacon Gerard Reilly
Parish Office
Tel 01-8461561 Fax 01-8169802
Email stannes@portmarnockparish.ie
Website www.portmarnockparish.ie

PRIORSWOOD
St Francis of Assisi, Dublin 17
Very Rev Martin Bennett (OFMCap) PP
Rev Bill Ryan (OFMCap) PC
Clonshaugh Drive, Priorswood, Dublin 17
Parish Office: Tel 01-8474469
Fax 01-8487296
Email priorswoodparish@yahoo.ie
Website www.priorswoodparish.ie

RAHENY
Our Lady Mother of Divine Grace,
Howth Road, Dublin 5
Very Rev Michael Cullen Adm
5 St Assam's Road West, Raheny, Dublin 5
Tel 01-8313806
Rev Paul Dunne CC
24 Watermill Road, Raheny, Dublin 5
Tel 01-8313232
Parish Office: Tel 01-8313232
Email info@rahenyparish.ie

RATHDRUM
SS Mary and Michael, Co Wicklow
Very Rev Derek Doyle *(Moderator)*
Parochial House, Rathdrum, Co Wicklow
Tel 0404-46229
Rev John Greene CC

RATHFARNHAM
(Grouped with Churchtown and
Ballyroan)
The Annunciation, Dublin 14
Very Rev Martin Canon Cosgrove
(Moderator)
St Mary's Presbytery, Willbrook Road,
Rathfarnham, Dublin 14
Tel 01-4954554
Rev Michael Coady Co-PP
St Mary's Presbytery, Willbrook Road,
Rathfarnham, Dublin 14
Tel 01-4932390
Rev Deacon Frank Browne
Parish Office:
Tel 01-4958695
Email
parishoffice@rathfarnhamparish.com

RATHGAR
Church of the Three Patrons,
Rathgar Road, Dublin 6
Very Rev Andrew O'Sullivan PP
52 Lower Rathmines Road,
Dublin D06 AK19
Rev David Larkin (SPS) CC
c/o Parish Office
Parish Office: Tel 01-4972215
Email office@rathgarparish.ie
Website www.rathgarparish.ie

RATHMINES
Mary Immaculate, Refuge of Sinners,
Rathmines, Dublin 6
Very Rev Andrew O'Sullivan PP
52 Lower Rathmines Road, Dublin 6
Tel 01-4969049
Parish Office: Tel 01-4971531
Email secretary@rathminesparish.com
Website www.rathminesparish.ie

RIALTO/DOLPHIN'S BARN
(Grouped with the parish of Dolphin's Barn
Our Lady of the Holy Rosary of Fatima,
Rialto, Dublin 8
Very Rev Fergal MacDonagh Adm
18 St Anthony's Road, Rialto, Dublin 8
Tel 01-4534469
Rev Roy George PC
500 South Circular Road, Rialto, Dublin 8
Parish Office: Tel 01-4539020
Website www.rialtoparish.com
Syromalabar Chaplaincy,
St Thomas Pastoral Centre, 19 Saint
Anthony's Road, Rialto, Dublin D08 E8P.
Chaplains
Rev Clement Padathiparambil,
Rev Roy George, Rev Joseph Mathew,
Rev Ceban Sebastian

RINGSEND
St Patrick's, Dublin 4
Very Rev Ivan Tonge PP
St Patrick's, 2 Cambridge Road, Dublin 4
Tel 087-2726868
Rt Rev Mgr Daniel O'Connor PC
St Mary's, Irishtown Road, Dublin 4
Parish Office: Tel 01-6697429
Email
stpatrickschurchringsend@gmail.com
Website
www.stpatrickschurchringsend.com

RIVERMOUNT
St Oliver Plunkett, St Helena's Drive,
Dublin 11
Very Rev Richard Hyland PP
Very Rev Martin Canon Hogan CC
Rev Seamus Ahearne (OSA) TA
Rev Éamonn Cahill TA
Mr Christopher Okereke, Parish Pastoral
Worker

RIVER VALLEY
Swords/River Valley/Brackenstown
Grouping
St Finian's, Swords, Co Dublin
Very Rev Desmond G. Doyle *(Moderator,*
Tel 01-8447283
Parish Office: Tel 01-8409043
Website www.rivervalley.dublindiocese.i◆

ROLESTOWN-OLDTOWN
Rolestown parish is now under the Team
Ministry of Rolestown Garristown/The Na◆
St Brigid's, Rolestown, Co Dublin
Very Rev Derek Canon Farrell *(Moderator*
Very Rev John F. Keegan Co-PP
Rolestown, Swords, Co Dublin
Tel 01-8401514
Email parishrolestown@gmail.com

ROUNDWOOD
St Laurence O'Toole, Co Wicklow
Very Rev Derek Doyle *(Moderator)*
Rev John Greene CC
Rev Deacon Jeremy Seligman
Parish Office: Tel 01-2818384 (mornings)
Email roundwoodparish@gmail.com

OWLAGH AND QUARRYVALE
Iondalkin/Rowlagh/Neilstown/
eansrath/Bawnogue Grouping
nmaculate Heart of Mary, Clondalkin,
ublin 22
ery Rev Kieran Coghlan *(Moderator)*, VF
ery Rev Hugh Kavanagh Co-PP
ery Rev Brian McKittrick Co-PP
ev Cherian Thazhamon CC
0 Wheatfield Close,
Iondalkin, Dublin 22
ev Deacon Derek Leonard
1s Saule Cameron, Parish Pastoral
Vorker
arish Office: Tel/Fax 01-6261010
mail
owlaghquarryvaleparish@gmail.com
Vebsite
ww.rowlaghandquarryvaleparish.com

USH
t Maur's, Rush, Co Dublin
ery Rev Kevin Bartley Adm
he Presbytery, Chapel Green,
ush, Co Dublin
el 01-8437208
ev Clinton Nkem CC
Ceol Na Mara, Lower Main Street,
ush, Co Dublin
el 01-8949464
mail rushparish@dublindiocese.ie
Vebsite www.rushparish.dublindiocese.ie

AGGART/RATHCOOLE/BRITTAS
Grouped with the parish of Newcastle)
Iativity of the BVM, Co Dublin
ery Rev John Gilligan *(Moderator)*, VF
t Mary's Parochial House,
aggart, Co Dublin
el 087-4103239
ev David Fleming CC
7 Beechwood Lawns,
athcoole, Co Dublin
el 01-4587187
ev Patrick Murphy Amos, CC
Io 1 the Glebe, Peamount Road,
Iewcastle Lyons, Co Dublin
ev Michael McGowan PC
St Patrick's Crescent,
athcoole, Co Dublin
el 01-4589210
ev Deacon Paul Ferris
arish Office, Saggart, Co Dublin
mail saggartparish@gmail.com
el 086-0108420

ALLYNOGGIN
Our Lady of Victories, Co Dublin
ery Rev Padraig Gleeson Adm
ev Michael Simpson CC
t Kevin's Presbytery, Pearse Street,
allynoggin, Co Dublin
el 01-2854667 Fax 01-2847024
arish Office: Tel 01-2854667
mail sallynogginparish@gmail.com

SANDYFORD
St Mary's, Dublin 18
Very Rev John Canon Delany *(Moderator)*
Parochial House, St Mary's,
Sandyford Village, Dublin 18
Tel 045-2956317
Very Rev Paul Ludden Co-PP
c/o St Mary's, Sandyford, Dublin 18
Rev Aaron Vinduska (LC) PC
The Presbytery, St Mary's,
Sandyford, Dublin 18
Tel 01-2958933
Parish Office: Tel 01-2956414
Email office@sandyfordparish.org
Website www.sandyfordparish.org

SANDYMOUNT
St Mary's Star of the Sea, Dublin 4
Very Rev John McDonagh PP
'Stella Maris', 15 Oswald Road,
Sandymount, Dublin 4
Tel 01-6684265
Rev Cormac McIlraith PC
10 Cranfield Place,
Sandymount, Dublin 4
Tel 01-6686845
Parish Office: Tel 01-6683316
Fax 01-6683894
Email sandymountparish@eircom.net

SHANKILL
St Anne's, Co Dublin
Very Rev Derry Murphy (SAC) PP
St Benin's Parish, Dublin Road,
Shankill, Co Dublin
Tel 01-2824425
Rev Michael O'Dwyer (SAC) CC
Rev Jamie Twohig (SAC) CC
St Benin's, Dublin Road
Tel 01-2824425
Parish Office: Tel 01-2822277
Email st.annes_parishoffice@yahoo.ie

SKERRIES
St Patrick's, Co Dublin
Very Rev Melvyn Mullins PP
42 Strand Street, Skerries,
Co Dublin
Tel 01-8491250
Parish Office: Tel 01-8492145
Email stpatrickschurchskerries@gmail.com

SPRINGFIELD
St Mark's, Maplewood Road,
Tallaght, Dublin 24
Very Rev William O'Shaughnessy
(Moderator), VF
70 Maplewood Road,
Tallaght, Dublin 24
Tel 01-4590746
Rev Colin Rothery CC
Rev Martin Hughes TA
Rev Michael Shortall TA
Rev Deacon Victor Okafor
Ms Christina Malone, Parish Pastoral
Worker
Parish Office: Tel 01-4620777
Email saintmarksparishchurch@gmail.com
Website www.stmarksspringfield.com

SRULEEN
Sacred Heart, St John's Drive, Clondalkin,
Dublin 22
Very Rev Vincent Fallon (SSCC) PP
Rev Michael Ruddy (SSCC) PC
Parish Office: Tel 01-4570032
Website www.sruleenparish.ie

SUTTON
Sutton/Howth/Baldoyle Grouping
St Fintan's, Greenfield Road, Dublin 13
Very Rev Cyril Mangan *(Moderator)*
8 Greenfield Road, Sutton, Dublin 13
Tel 01-8322396
Rev Gerry Tanham PC
Rev Gabriel Flynn TA
Apt 1, The Presbytery, Greenfield Road,
Sutton, Dublin 13
Parish Office: Tel 01-8392001
Email office@stfintansparish.ie
Website www.stfintansparish.ie

SWORDS
Swords/River Valley/Brackenstown
Grouping
St Colmcille's, Co Dublin
(Dublin Airport Church, Our Lady Queen
of Heaven is in this parish)
Very Rev Desmond Doyle *(Moderator)*
Chaplain's Residence,
Dublin Airport, Co Dublin
Very Rev John Collins Co-PP
18 Aspen Road, Kinsealy Court, Swords,
Co Dublin
Tel 01-8405948
Parish Office: Tel 01-8407277
Email stcolmcilleschurch@gmail.com
Website www.swords-parish.com

TALLAGHT, DODDER
St Dominic's, Dublin 24
Very Rev Laurence Collins (OP) Adm
Rev Timothy Mulcahy (OP) CC
Presbytery, St Dominic's Road, Tallaght,
Dublin 24
Tel 01-4510620 Fax 01-4623223
Parish Office: Tel 01-4510620
Fax 01-4623223
Website www.stdominicsparishtallaght.ie

TALLAGHT, OLDBAWN
St Martin de Porres, Dublin 24
Very Rev James Daly PP
Parochial House,
Bohernabreena, Dublin 24
Very Rev Michael Canon Hurley PC
The Presbytery, St Martin's, Aylesbury,
Dublin 24
Tel 01-4627080
Rev Hilary Etomike CC
Rev Hector Mwale PC
Rev Deacon Padraic O'Sullivan
Parish Office: Tel/Fax 01-4510160
Email stmartinsparish2020@gmail.com

TALLAGHT, ST MARY'S
St Mary's, Tallaght Village, Dublin 24
Very Rev Donal Roche (OP) Adm
Rev Robert Regula (OP) CC
St Mary's Priory, Tallaght, Dublin 24
Tel 01-4048100 Fax 01-4596784

TALLAGHT, TYMON NORTH
St Aengus's, Castletymon Road,
Dublin 24
Very Rev Benedict Moran (OP) PP
Dominican Community,
St Aengus's, Balrothery, Tallaght, Dublin 24
Tel 01-4513757
Email ben.moran25@gmail.com
Rev Pat Lucey (OP) CC
The Presbytery, St Aengus's,
Balrothery, Tallaght, Dublin 24
Tel 01-4528161
Parish Office
Tel 01-4513757 Fax 01-4624038
Email staenguschurch@eircom.net.
Website www.staengusparishtallaght.ie

TEMPLEOGUE
St Pius X, College Drive, Dublin 6W
Very Rev Gerard Moore PP
23 Wainsfort Park,
Terenure, Dublin 6W
Tel 01-4900218
Rev Deacon Gerard Larkin
Parish Office
Tel 01-4905284/087-9672258
Email info@stpiusx.ie
Website www.stpiusx.ie

TERENURE
St Joseph's, Dublin 6
Very Rev Philip Bradley Adm, VF
Parochial House,
83 Terenure Road East, Dublin 6
Tel 01-4905520
Parish Office: 01-4921755
Email stjosephterenure@gmail.com

TRAVELLING PEOPLE
Chapel of Ease, St Oliver's Park,
Clondalkin, Dublin 22
Very Rev Paul O'Driscoll PP
6 New Cabra Road, Phibsborough,
Dublin 7
Parish Office: St Laurence House,
6 New Cabra Road, Phibsborough,
Dublin 7
Tel 01-8388874 Fax 01-8388901
Email into@ptrav.ie. www.ptrav.ie
Recommended Websites:
www.exchangehouse.ie
www.paveepoint.ie
www.stpetersphibsborough.com

UNIVERSITY CHURCH
Our Lady, Seat of Wisdom,
St Stephen's Green, Dublin 2
Very Rev Enda Cunningham Adm
University Church is in the charge of the
Congregation of Holy Cross, Notre Dame
Rev Gary Chamberland (CSC)
c/o Parish Office
Parish Office: Tel 01-4759674

VALLEYMOUNT
(Grouped with the parish of Blessington)
St Joseph's, Valleymount
Our Lady of Mount Carmel, Lacken
Very Rev Richard Behan PP
The Presbytery, Main Street,
Blessington, Co Wicklow
Tel 045-865442

WALKINSTOWN
Assumption of the BVM, Dublin 12
Very Rev Paul Glennon PP
162 Walkinstown Road,
Dublin D12 Y0F1
Tel 01-4501372
Rev John Jacob CC
12 Walkinstown Road, Dublin 12
Tel 01-4502541
Parish Sacristy: Tel 01-4502649

WHITEFRIAR STREET
Our Lady of Mount Carmel,
Whitefriar Street, Dublin 2
Very Rev Seán Ford (OCarm) PP, VF
Carmelite Priory,
56 Aungier Street, Dublin 2
Tel 01-4758821
Email hello@whitefriarstreetchurch.ie

WICKLOW
St Patrick's, Wicklow, Co Wicklow
Very Rev Donal Roche PP, VG
The Abbey, Wicklow, Co Wicklow
Tel 0404-671961 Fax 0404-69971
Rev Patrick O'Rourke CC
The Presbytery, St Patrick's Road,
Wicklow Town, Co Wicklow
Parish Office: Tel 0404-61699
Email parishofficewicklow@gmail.com

WILLINGTON
St Jude the Apostle, Orwell Park,
Dublin 6W
Very Rev Brendan Madden PP
2 Rossmore Road,
Templeogue, Dublin 6W
Tel 01-4508432
Parish Office: Tel 01-4600127
Email judesparishoffice@eircom.net

YELLOW WALLS, MALAHIDE
(Grouped with the parishes of Malahide,
Kinsealy & Portmarnock)
Sacred Heart Church, Eastuary Road,
Malahide, Co Dublin
Very Rev Martin Noone *(Moderator)*, VF
7 Seabury Drive, Malahide,
Co Dublin K36 YN67
Tel 01-8451902
Rev Deacon Gerard Reilly
yellowwallsparish@gmail.com
Website www.yellowwallsparish.ie

INSTITUTIONS AND THEIR CHAPLAINS

COLLEGES

Dublin City University
Chaplains: Rev Seamus McEntee
InterFaith Centre, Dublin 9
Tel 01-7005268 Fax 01-7005663
Rev Paul Hampson
Ms Anne O'Farrell
DCU St Patrick's Campus
Drumcondra Road Upper, Dublin 9
Tel 01-8842000

DCU Mater Dei Centre for Catholic Education
DCU St Patrick's Campus
Drumcondra Road Upper, Dublin 9
Director: Dr Cora O'Farrell
Tel 01-7009171

Institute of Technology
Tallaght, Dublin 24
Tel 01-4042000

Marino Institute of Education
Griffith Avenue, Dublin D09 R232
Chaplain: Dr Lily Barry
Tel 01-8055111
Email lily.barry@mie.ie

National College of Art and Design
100 Thomas Street, Dublin 8
Chaplain: Vacant

National University of Ireland, Maynooth (NUIM)
Tel 01-7086000
Chaplaincy Service,
NUI Maynooth, Co Kildare
Tel 01-7083588
Chaplain: Ciaran Coughlan
Tel 01-7083588
Email chaplaincy@nuim.ie

Trinity College, Dublin 2
Rev Peter Sexton (SJ)
Rev Alan O'Sullivan (OP)
House 27 Trinity College, Dublin 2
Tel 01-8961260

Technological University Dublin
Co-ordinator, Pastoral Care and Chaplaincy Service
Appointment pending
Room 254, TU Dublin – Bolton Street,
Dublin D01 K822

Technological University Dublin, Bolton Street
Appointment pending
Room 254, TU Dublin – Bolton Street,
Dublin D01 K822

echnological University Dublin, Tallaght
r Bernadette Purcell (PBVM)
oom 010, TU Dublin – Tallaght Campus,
ublin D24 FKT9
el 01-2207671
mail bernadette.purcell@tudublin.ie

echnological University Dublin, lanchardstown
oom C114, TU Dublin – Blanchardstown Campus, Dublin D24 FKT9
el 01-2207201

echnological University Dublin, rangegorman
r Ultan Naughton (SSCC)
oom RD-117, Rathdown House,
U Dublin, Grangegorman,
ublin D07 H6K8
el 01-2207078
mail ultan.naughton@tudublin.ie

echnological University Dublin, rangegorman
ev Joseph Loftus (CM)
oom RD-117, Rathdown House,
U Dublin – Grangegorman,
ublin D07 H6K8
el 01-2207079
mail joseph.loftus@tudublin.ie

echnological University Dublin, Aungier treet
Andrew Somerville (C of I) and Becky Heaslip (C of I)
oom 4070, TU Dublin – Aungier Street,
ublin D02 HW71
el 01-2207086
Email andrew.somerville@tudublin.ie

echnological University Dublin, Grangegorman
ev Rob Jones (C of I)
oom RD-117, Rathdown House,
TU Dublin – Grangegorman,
ublin D07 H6K8
el 01-2205230
Email rob.jones@tudublin.ie

Technological University Dublin
Suzanne Greene, Administrative Assistant to the Pastoral Care and Chaplaincy Service
Room RD-116, Rathdown House,
TU Dublin – Grangegorman,
Dublin D07 H6K8
Tel 01-2207076
Email suzanne.greene@tudublin.ie

University College, Dublin
Chaplains' Room, UCD, Belfield, Dublin 4
Tel 01-7168317
Rev Brendan Ludlow
Head Chaplain: Rev Eamonn Bourke
Chaplains' Residence:
St Stephen's, UCD, Belfield, Dublin 4
Tel 01-7161971

DEFENCE FORCES

Head Chaplain
Rev Paschal Hanrahan
Tel 087-3128209
Administrative Secretary: Sgt Liam Bellew
Tel 01-8042638
Defence Forces Headquarters,
McKee Barracks, Blackhorse Avenue,
Dublin 7

McKee Barracks
Dublin 7
Tel 086-2256794
Rev Damian Farnon

Cathal Brugha Barracks
Rathmines, Dublin 6
Tel 01-8046484

Casement Aerodrome
Baldonnel, Co Dublin
Tel 01-4037536
Rev Bernard McCay-Morrissey (OP)

International Military Pilgrimage to Lourdes
(Pelerinage Militaire Internationale)
Director: Rev Paschal Hanrahan
Tel 087-3128209

HOSPITALS

Beaumont Hospital
Beaumont Road, Dublin 9
Tel 01-8377755
Direct Line: 01-8092815/8093229
Rev Eoin Hughes Tel 01-8477573
Rev Suresh Babu Chintagunta (OSCam)
Ms Rosaleen Butterly
Mr Michael Ward
Ms Orla McMahon,
Mr Cathal O'Sullivan
Mr Prakash Varkey

Beaumont Convalescent Home
Tel 8379186
Beaumont Parish

Blackrock Clinic
Blackrock, Co Dublin
Tel 01-2832222
Most Rev Eamonn Walsh, Auxiliary Bishop Emeritus of Dublin

Blackrock Hospice
Sweetman's Avenue, Blackrock,
Co Dublin
Tel 01-2064000
Sr Ann Purcell (RSC)
Tel 01-2064024 – direct line

Bloomfield
Donnybrook, Dublin 4
Tel 01-4950021
Carmelite Fathers, Avila,
Morehampton Road, Dublin 4
Tel 01-6683091

Bon Secours Hospital
Glasnevin, Dublin 9
Tel 01-8065300
Director of Pastoral Care and Mission
Mr Alan Burke
Rev Christopher Twomey (OFM Cap),
Ms Ann Martin
Ms Eileen Kavanagh
Ms Julie Long
Ms Belinda Walsh

Cappagh National Orthopaedic Hospital
Cappagh, Dublin 11
Tel 01-8341211
Congregation of the Holy Spirit and Finglas West Parish

Central Mental Hospital
Dundrum
Tel 01-2989266
Ms Mary Monaghan

Cherry Orchard Hospital
Ballyfermot
Tel 01-6264702
Rev Patrick Cully (CSSp) (on behalf of the Holy Spirit Congregation)

Children's Health Ireland at Crumlin (Our Lady's Children's Hospital)
Crumlin, Dublin 12
Tel 01-4096100
Ms June O'Toole
Ms Deirdre Gallagher
Ms Mary Young

Children's Health Ireland at Temple Street
Temple Street
Tel 01-8784200
Ms Carmel Battigan,
Ms Rachel Cooney
Ms Eden Dela Cruz

Clonskeagh Hospital
Vergemount, Dublin 6
Tel 01-2697877
Rev Jude Lynch (CSSp) (on behalf of the Holy Spirit Congregation)

Connolly Hospital
Blanchardstown, Dublin 15
Tel 01-8213844
Office (direct line) 01-6465168
Rev Anthony O'Riordan (SVD)
Ms Alison Mannion
Ms Jenny Cuypers

Coombe Women and Infants University Hospital
Dolphin's Barn, Dublin 8
Tel 01-4085200
Ms Josette Devitt Vassallo

Eye and Ear Hospital (Royal Victoria)
Adelaide Road, Dublin 2
Tel 01-6644600
Jesuit Community, Lower Leeson Street

Hermitage Medical Clinic
Old Lucan Road, Lucan, Co Dublin
Tel 01-6459000
Rev Tomy George Paradiyil (OSCam)

Leopardstown Park Hospital
Tel 01-2955055
Very Rev John Canon Delaney
(Moderator), Sandyford and Balally

Mater Misericordiae University Hospital
Eccles Street, Dublin 7
Tel 01-8301122/8032000
Direct line 01-8032239/8032411
Rev Vincent Xavier Kakkadampallil
(OSCam),
Rev Prince Mathew (OSCam),
Rev Suneesh Mathew (OSCam)
Rev Damian Casey (OFM)
Ms Margaret Sleator

Mater Private Hospital
Dublin 7
Tel 01-8858888
Rev Peter Murphy

National Maternity Hospital
Holles Street, Dublin 2
Tel 01-6373100
Very Rev Enda Cunningham Adm
Ms Helen Miley
Ms Angela Neville-Egan

National Rehabilitation Hospital
Rochestown Avenue,
Dun Laoghaire, Co Dublin
Tel 01-2355000
Rev Michael Kennedy (CSSp)

Newcastle Hospital
Tel 01-2819001
Very Rev Sean Canon Smith CC
The Presbytery, Newtownmountkennedy,
Co Wicklow
Tel 01-2819253

Orthopaedic Hospital
Castle Avenue, Clontarf
Tel 01-8332521
Appointment pending

Our Lady's Hospice and Care Services
Harold's Cross
Tel 01-4068700
Ms Maria O'Keeffe
Ms Shauna Sweeney

Peamount Hospital
Newcastle, Co Dublin
Tel 01-6010300
Vacant

Phoenix Care Centre
Grangegorman, North Circular Road,
Dublin 7
Tel 01-8276500
Vacant

Rotunda Hospital
Parnell Street, Dublin 1
Tel 01-8730700
Ms Anne Charlton

Royal Hospital Donnybrook
Morehampton Road, Dublin 4
Tel 01-4972844
Appointment Pending

St Bricin's Military Hospital
Infirmary Road, Dublin 8
Tel 01-6776112

St Columcille's Hospital
Loughlinstown, Co Dublin
Tel 01-2825800
Mr Jack Michael Byrne

**St Francis Hospice, Raheny/
Blanchardstown**
Tel 01-8327535 (Raheny)
Tel 01-8294000 (Blanchardstown)
Rev Desmond McNaboe (OFMCap),
Capuchin Friary, Raheny, Dublin 5
Tel 01-8313886
Rev Owen O'Sullivan (OFMCap)
Blanchardstown
Ms Mary Bergin
Sr Maire Brady
Ms Lucy Higgins
Mr Mark Davis

St Ita's, Portrane
Tel 01-8436337
Very Rev Patrick Reilly (OPraem) PP

St James's Hospital
James's Street, Dublin 8
Tel 01-4103000
Direct Line 01-4103659
Rev Brian Gough, Rev Jayan Joseph
Chamakalayil (MI), Ms Eithne O'Reilly

St John of God Hospital
Stillorgan, Co Dublin
Tel 01-2771400
Rev Hugh Gillan (OH)
Mr Damian Murray

St Joseph's Hospital
Clonsilla
Tel 01-8217177
Vacant

St Joseph's Hospital
Springdale Road, Raheny, Dublin 5
Tel 01-8478433
Vacant

St Loman's Hospital
Ballyowen, Palmerstown, Dublin 20
Tel 01-6264077
Vacant

St Luke's Hospital
Highfield Road, Rathgar, Dublin 6
Tel 01-4065000
Fr Michael Commane (OP)

St Mary's Hospital
Phoenix Park, Dublin 20
Tel 01-6250300
Rev Samson Mann (CSSp)

St Michael's Hospital
Lower George's Street, Dun Laoghaire
Tel 01-2806901
Ms Anita Delaney

St Patrick's Hospital
James Street, Dublin 8
Tel 01-2493200
Augustinian Fathers, John's Lane

St Paul's (Autistic Children)
Beaumont
Tel 01-8377673
Beaumont Parish

St Vincent's Hospital
Athy, Co Kildare
Tel 059-8643000
Very Rev Liam Rigney PP
Tel 059-8646022

St Vincent's University Hospital
Elm Park, Dublin 4
Tel 01-2214000
Direct Line 01-2214325
Rev Liam Cuffe
Very Rev Damian Canon O'Reilly
Ms Caoimhe Hurley
Deacon Matthew Murphy

St Vincent's Private Hospital
Tel 01-2638000
Sr Mary Helen Anthonythasan

St Vincent's, Fairview
Tel 01-8375101
Sr Angela Burke

Stewart's Hospital, Palmerstown
Tel 01-6264444
Rev Samson Mann (CSSp)

St Colman's, Rathdrum
Tel 0404-46109
Very Rev Derek Doyle
Tel 0404-46229

Tallaght Hospital
Tel 01-4142000
Roman Catholic Bleep: 2725
Director of Pastoral Care: Rev John Kelly
22 Nugent Road, Churchtown,
Dublin 14
Tel 01-4142482
Email john.kelly@tuh.ie
Pastoral Care Team:
Rev Manus Ferry (MSC)
Mr Gabriel Ogunjobi
Sr Gabrielle Murphy
Ms Amy Guinan
Ms Anne Marie Leahy
Tel 01-4142485

PRIESTS ELSEWHERE IN THE DIOCESE

Very Rev Laurence Behan
On Leave
Rev John Dunphy
On sabbatical
Rev Brian Edwards
c/o Archbishop's House, Drumcondra,
Dublin D09 H4C2
Very Rev Patrick McKinley
On Sabbatical
Rev Finbarr Neylon
On Sabbatical
Rev Alan Hilliard
On Sabbatical
Rev Patrick Desmond
Apostolic Nunciature
The Lodge, Mount Sackville,
Chapelizod, Dublin 20
Tel 01-8214004

PRIESTS WORKING OUTSIDE THE DIOCESE

Rev Ian Evans
c/o Archbishop's House, Drumcondra,
Dublin D09 H4C2
Rt Rev Mgr John Kennedy (Dicastery for
the Doctrine of the Faith)
Via del Mascherino 12,
00193 Roma, Italy
Rev Brendan Purcell
St Mary's Cathedral House,
St Mary's Road, Sydney NSW 2000,
Australia
Most Rev Paul Tighe
Bishop of Drivastrum
Adjunct Secretary of the Pontifical
Council for Social Communications,
Vatican City

RETIRED PRIESTS

Rev Kilian Brennan
Apartment 3 Seascape,
166 Contarf Road, Dublin 3
Rev Noel Campbell
Ballysmuttan, Manor Kilbride,
Blessington, Co Wicklow
Rev John Carey
Sacred Heart Residence,
Sybil Hill Road, Raheny, Dublin 5
Rev Aidan Carroll
Hillcrest Manor,
Templeogue, Dublin 6W
Rev Denis Carroll
Marymount Care Centre,
Westmanstown, Lucan, Co Dublin
Very Rev Seamus Cassidy
Davis, Kilmainham Wood,
Kells, Co Meath
Rev Eamonn Clarke
The Presbytery, Beechwood Park,
Kilcoole, Co Wicklow

Rev Michael Collins,
2 Traverslea Woods,
Glenageary Road Lower,
Dun Laoghaire, Co Dublin
Rev Seamus Connell
56 Foxfield St John,
Kilbarrack, Dublin 5
Rev Edward Corry
Presbytery No. 2, Treepark Road,
Kilnamanagh, Dublin 24
Rev Thomas Coughlan
Our Lady's Manor, Bulloch Harbour,
Dalkey, Co Dublin
Rev Michael V. Dempsey
The Presbytery, Kilmede,
Narraghmore, Co Kildare
Rev Patrick Devitt
17 Prospect Lawn, The Park,
Cabinteely, Dublin 18
Very Rev Francis Dooley
Our Lady's Manor, Bulloch Harbour,
Dalkey, Co Dublin
Rev Cornelius Dowling
Our Lady's Manor, Bulloch Harbour,
Dalkey, Co Dublin
Email dowcpb@eircom.net
Rev Edward Downes
Sacred Heart Residence,
Sybil Hill Road, Raheny, Dublin 5
Very Rev Patrick Canon Fagan
Our Lady's Manor, Bulloch Harbour,
Dalkey, Co Dublin
Rev John Ferris
14 The Coral, The Grange,
Stillorgan, Co Dublin
Most Rev Raymond Field
Auxiliary Bishop Emeritus,
Marymount Care Centre,
Westmanstown, Lucan, Co Dublin
Very Rev James Canon Fingleton
279 Howth Road, Raheny, Dublin 5
Very Rev John Canon Fitzgibbon PE
The Presbytery, Chapel Road,
Lusk, Co Dublin
Very Rev Denis Foley
c/o Archbishop's House, Dublin 9
Rev John Galvin
60 Lower Mount Pleasant Avenue,
Rathmines, Dublin 6
Very Rev J. Anthony Canon Gaughan PE
56 Newtownpark Avenue, Blackrock,
Co Dublin
Rev Patrick Gleeson
14 Deerpark Road, Mount Merrion,
Co Dublin A94 Y0C1
Very Rev Edward Griffin
15 Connawood, Bray, Co Wicklow
Very Rev Walter Canon Harris
The Four Ferns, Brighton Road,
Foxrock, Co Dublin
Rev Peter Kilroy
64 Cherbury Court,
Booterstown, Co Dublin

Very Rev William King
156b Rathgar Road, Dublin 6
Very Rev Paul Lavelle
123 Foxfield Grove,
Kilbarrack, Dublin 5
Rev Denis Laverty
47 Silken Vale, Maynooth, Co Kildare
Very Rev Dermot Leycock
64 Newtownpark Avenue,
Blackrock, Co Dublin
Very Rev Patrick Littleton
2 Maypark, Donnycarney, Dublin 5
Very Rev Patrick J. Mangan
Dun Mhuire, 44 Upper Beechwood Avenue,
Ranelagh, Dublin 6
Tel 01-4975180/087-9857264
Most Rev Diarmuid Martin
Archbishop Emeritus
c/o Archbishop's House
Very Rev Val Martin
'Logatryna', Dunlavin, Co Wicklow
Very Rev Eugene McCarney
Middletown House, Nursing Home,
Middletown, Courtown,
Co Wexford Y25 P6H7
Rev Peter McCarron
Email petermccarron@eircom.net
Rev Dermod McCarthy
26 Brackens Bush Road,
Killiney, Co Dublin
Rev Padraig McCarthy
14 Blackthorn Court,
Sandyford, Dublin 16
Very Rev Niall McDermott
The Presbytery, 91 Grange Road,
Baldoyle, Dublin 13
Rev Fergus McGlynn
43 Chestnut Grove,
Ballymount Road, Dublin 24
Rev Thomas McGowan
Beechtree Nursing Home, Murragh,
Oldtown, Co Dublin
Rev Patrick Monahan
Earlsfort, 291A Old Greenfield,
Maynooth, Co Kildare
Rev John F. Moran
192 Navan Road, Dublin 7
Rev Patrick Moran
1 Seapark, Mount Prospect Avenue,
Dublin 3
Very Rev Benedict Mulligan PE
The Fern, Dean Grange Terrace,
Deansgrange, Dublin A94 TN25
Very Rev Peadar Canon Murney
25 Thomastown Road,
Dun Laoghaire, Co Dublin
Tel 01-2856660
Rev Eoin Murphy
25 The Haven, Glasnevin, Dublin 9

Very Rev Tim Murphy
Gorey, Co Wexford
Very Rev Liam Murtagh
33 Grace Park Road,
Drumcondra, Dublin 9
Tel 087-2408416
Rev Sean Noone
The Presbytery, Pollathomas, Co Mayo
Very Rev Martin O'Farrell
Acorn Nursing Home,
Cashel, Co Tipperary
Very Rev Thomas O'Keeffe
20 Glen Avenue, The Park, Cabinteely,
Dublin 18
Rev Sean O'Rourke
15 Seaview Park, Shankill, Co Dublin
Very Rev Maurice O'Shea PE
64 White Oaks,
Clonskeagh, Dublin 14
Rev Colm O'Siochru
Our Lady's Manor, Bulloch Castle,
Dalkey, Co Dublin
Rev Brian O'Sullivan
The Cottage, Glengara Park,
Glenageary, Dun Laoghaire, Co Dublin
Rev Sean O'Toole
Our Lady's Manor, Bulloch Harbour,
Dalkey, Co Dublin
Email seanotoole@eircom.net
Rev John Canon Piert *(Team Assistant)*
Our Lady's Manor, Bulloch Harbour,
Dalkey, Co Dublin
Rev Cathal Price
54 Foxfield St John, Dublin 5
Rev Sean Quigley
Tara Wintrop Nursing Home,
Nevinstown Lane, Pinnockhill,
Swords, Co Dublin
Very Rev Leo Quinlan
The Fern Dean Nursing Home,
Grange Terrace, Deansgrange,
Dublin A94 TN25
Rev Henry Regan
Presbytery No. 1, Church Grounds,
Kill Avenue, Dun Laoghaire, Co Dublin
Very Rev Seamus Ryan
Milbrea Nursing Home,
Newport, Co Tipperary
Rev Anthony Scully
Presbytery No. 4, Dunmanus Road,
Cabra, Dublin 7
Very Rev Canon Patrick Shiel
74 Mount Drinan Avenue, Kinsealy
Downs, Swords, Co Dublin
Rev Derek Smyth
No 2 Kill Lane, Foxrock, Dublin 18
Rt Rev Mgr Alex Stenson
5 Calderwood Avenue, Drumcondra,
Dublin 9

Very Rev John Stokes
Sacred Heart Residence,
Sybill Hill Road, Raheny, Dublin 5
Rev John M. Ward
1 Chestnut Grove, Ballymount Road,
Dublin 24
Rt Rev Mgr John Wilson
St Mary's, 97 Ballymun Road, Dublin 9
Tel 01-8375440

PERSONAL PRELATURE

OPUS DEI
Harvieston, 22 Cunningham Road,
Dalkey, Co Dublin A96 CX59
Tel 01-2859877
Rev Patrick Gorevan
Rev Donncha Ó hAodha
Rev Francis Planell

30 Knapton Road,
Dun Laoghaire, Co Dublin A96 XA46
Tel 01-2804353
Rev Daniel Cummings
Rev Thomas McGovern

Cleraun Study Centre,
90 Fosters Avenue, Mount Merrion,
Co Dublin A94 VX73
Tel 01-2881734
Rev Brendan O'Connor
Rev Philip Griffin
Rev Walter Macken

Ely University Centre
10 Hume Street, Dublin D02 VY39
Tel 01-6767420
Rev Gavan Jennings
Rev Thomas Dowd

RELIGIOUS ORDERS AND CONGREGATIONS

PRIESTS

AUGUSTINIANS
St Augustine's, Taylor's Lane,
Ballyboden, Dublin 16
Tel 01-4241000 Fax 01-4939915
Email www.augustinians.ie
Provincial: Rev John Hennebry (OSA)
Prior & CC: Rev Francis Aherne (OSA)

St John's Priory, Thomas Street, Dublin 8
Tel 01-6770393/0415/0601
Fax 01-6713102 (Mission Office)/6770423
(House)
Prior: Rev Padraig A. Daly (OSA)

(See also under parishes – Ballyboden,
Meath Street and Rivermount)

BLESSED SACRAMENT CONGREGATION
Blessed Sacrament Chapel,
20 Bachelors Walk,
Dublin D01 NW14
Tel 01-8724597 Fax 01-8724724
Email sssdublin@eircom.net
Web www.blessedsacramentuki.org
Superior: Rev James Campbell (SSS)

CAMILLIANS
St Camillus, South Hill Avenue,
Blackrock, Co Dublin
Tel 01-2882873 Fax 01-2833380
Superior: Rev Denis Sandham

St Camillus,
11 St Vincent Street North, Dublin 7
Tel 01-8300365 (Residence)
Tel 01-8301122 (Mater Hospital)

CAPUCHINS
Provincial Office
12 Halston Street, Dublin D07 Y2T5
Tel 01-8733205 Fax 01-8730294
Email capcurirl@eircom.net
Provincial Minister
Very Rev Seán Kelly (OFMCap)
Guardian: Rev Brian Shortall (OFMCap)

Capuchin Friary, St Mary of the Angels,
137-142 Church Street,
Dublin D07 HA22
Tel (Parish) 01-8730925
Tel (Friary) 01-8730599/Fax 01-8730250
Guardian
Rev Kevin Kiernan (OFMCap)

Capuchin Friary (Immaculate Heart of
Mary), Station Road, Raheny,
Dublin D05 T9E4
Tel 01-8313886/8312805
Guardian: Rev Seán Donohue (OFMCap)

(See also under parishes – Halston Street
and Priorswood)

CARMELITES (OCARM)
Provincial Office, Gort Muire,
Ballinteer, Dublin D16 EI67
Tel 01-2984014 Fax 01-2987221
Provincial
Very Rev Michael Troy (OCarm)

Whitefriar Street Church,
56 Aungier Street,
Dublin D02 R598
Tel 01-4758821 Fax 01-4758825
Email whitefriars@eircom.net
Prior: Rev Simon Nolan (OCarm)
Bursar: Rev Martin Baxter (OCarm)
Parish Priest
Rev Seán MacGiollarnáth (OCarm)

Allianz (ⅲ)

renure College,
renure, Dublin D6W DK72
el 01-4904621 Fax 01-4902403
mail admin@terenurecollege.ie
ior/Bursar
ev Éanna Ó hÓbain (OCarm)
incipal (Senior School)
ev Éanna Ó hÓbáin (OCarm)

ee also under parishes – Whitefriar
reet)

ARMELITES (OCD)
vila, Bloomfield Avenue,
orehampton Road, Dublin 4
el 01-6430200 Fax 01-6430281
mail avila@ocd.ie
ior: Rev Liam Finnerty (OCD)
ovincial: Rev John Grennan (OCD)
mail jtgrennan@hotmail.com
ebsite www.ocd.ie

Teresa's, Clarendon Street, Dublin 2
el 01-6718466/6718127
ior: Rev Jim Noonan (OCD)

STERCIANS
olton Abbey, Moone, Co Kildare
el 059-8624102/087-9366723
mail boltonabbeymoone@gmail.com
ebsite www.boltonabbey.ie
bbot
: Rev Dom Michael Ryan (OCSO)

OMBONI MISSIONARIES
Clontarf Road, Dublin 3
el/Fax 01-8330051
mail combonimission@eircom.net
uperior
ev Ruben Padilla Rocha (MCCJ)

ONGREGATION OF THE PRIESTS OF THE
ACRED HEART OF JESUS
airfield,
Inchicore Road, Dublin 8
el 01-4538655
mail scjdublin@eircom.net
ouse of Formation
uperior and Formation Director:
ev John Kelly (SCJ)

ee also under parishes – Ardlea)

ONGREGATION OF THE SACRED
EARTS OF JESUS AND MARY (SACRED
EARTS COMMUNITY)
oudrin House,
Northbrook Road, Dublin D06 W294
el 01-6604898
mail ssccdublin@sacredhearts.ie
ebsite www.sacredhearts.ie
elegation Superior
ery Rev Michael Ruddy (SSCC)

cred Heart Presbytery, St John's Drive,
ondalkin, Dublin D22 W1W6
el 01-4570032

ee also under parishes – Sruleen)

DIVINE WORD MISSIONARIES
1 & 3 Pembroke Road,
Ballsbridge, Dublin 4
Rector: Rev Liam Dunne (SVD)
Email pembroke@svdireland.com
Provincial: Rev Timothy Lehane (SVD)
Email provincial@svdireland.com

133 North Circular Road,
Dublin 7
Tel 01-8386743
Praeses: Rev Anthony O'Riordan (SVD)

Maynooth, Co Kildare
Tel 01-6286391/2 Fax 01-6289184
Rector: Rev Finbarr Tracey (SVD)
Email secretary@svdireland.com

Church of St Philip the Apostle,
Mountview, Dublin 15
Tel 01-9216447
Parish Priest: Rev George Adzato (SVD)

(See also under parishes – Blakestown)

DOMINICANS
Provincial Office, St Mary's,
Tallaght, Dublin D24 X585
Tel 01-4048118
Email provincial@dominicans.ie
Provincial: Very Rev John Harris (OP)

St Mary's Priory, Tallaght, Dublin 24
Tel 01-4048100
Parish 01-4048188
Prior: Very Rev Donal Roche (OP) PP

St Saviour's,
Upper Dorset Street, Dublin 1
Tel 01-8897610 Fax 01-8734003
Email stsaviours@eircom.net
Prior: Very Rev Joseph Dineen (OP) PP

(See also under parishes – Dominick
Street and three of the Tallaght parishes)

FRANCISCANS (OFM)
Provincial Office, Franciscan Friary,
4 Merchant's Quay, Dublin D08 XY19
Tel 01-6742500 Fax 01-6742549
Email info@franciscans.ie
Provincial: Rev Aidan McGrath
Email provincial@franciscans.ie

Adam and Eve's, Merchants' Quay,
Dublin D08 XY19
Tel 01-6771128 Fax 01-6771000
Guardian: Br Niall O'Connell (OFM)

Franciscan House of Studies,
Dún Mhuire, Seafield Road,
Killiney, Co Dublin
Tel 01-2826760 Fax 01-2826993
Email dmkilliney@eircom.net
Guardian: Br Stephen O'Kane (OFM)

(See also under parishes – Merchants
Quay)

FRANCISCANS: ORDER OF FRIARS MINOR
Conventual (Greyfriars) (OFMConv)
The Friary of the Visitation of the BVM,
Fairview Strand,
Fairview, Dublin 3
Tel 01-8376000 (office)
Tel 01-4825821 (priest)
Guardian: Rev Aidan Walsh (OFM Conv)

(See also under parishes – Fairview)

HOLY SPIRIT CONGREGATION
Holy Spirit Provincialate,
Temple Park,
Richmond Avenue South, Dublin 6
Tel 01-4977230/4975127 Fax 01-4975399
Email communications@spiritanplt.ie
Provincial Leadership Team
Rev Martin Kelly (CSSp) *(Provincial)*
Rev Peter Conaty (CSSp)
Rev Patrick Moran (CSSp)
Rev Colm Reidy (CSSp)
Rev David Conway (CSSp) *(Provincial*
Bursar)
Rev Michael Kilkenny (CSSp) *(Provincial*
Secretary)

Spiritan Education Trust,
Kimmage Manor, Dublin 12
Tel 01-4997610
www.spiritaneducation.ie
Mr Patrick Kitterick *(Chair)*

Heritage and Archives Centre,
Kimmage Manor, Dublin 12
Manager: Rev Brendan Cogavin (CSSp)
Email heritage@spiritan.ie

Holy Spirit Missionary College,
Kimmage Manor,
Whitehall Road, Dublin D12 P5YP
Tel 01-4064300
Email kimmagereception@spiritan.ie
Community Leader
Rev Eddie O'Farrell (CSSp)

Spiritan House,
213 North Circular Road,
Dublin D07 KH9C
Community Leader
Rev Edward Flynn (CSSp)

SPIRASI, Spiritan Asylum Services
Initiative, 213 North Circular Road,
Dublin D07 KH9C
Tel 01-8389664
Executive Director: Mr Rory Halpin

Blackrock College,
Blackrock, Co Dublin
Tel 01-2888681 Fax 01-2834267
Email info@blackrockcollege.com
Community Leader
Rev Cormac Ó Brolcháin (CSSp)
Principal: Alan MacGinty

Allianz (ⅱ)

Willow Park
Tel 01-2881651 Fax 01-2783353
Email admin@willowparkschool.ie
Principal Senior School: Mr Alan Rogan
Principal Junior School
Mr James Docherty

St Mary's College, Rathmines, Dublin 6
Tel 01-4995760 Fax 01-4972621
Junior School Tel 01-4995721
Email junsec@stmarys.ie
Senior School Tel 4995700 Fax 01-4972574
Email sensec@stmarys.ie
Community Leader
Rev Patrick Moran (CSSp)
Principal Secondary School
Mr Denis Murphy
Principal Junior School
Ms Judith Keane

St Michael's College,
Ailesbury Road, Dublin 4
Tel 01-2189400 Fax 01-2698862
Email admin@stmc.ie
Principal: Mr Tim Kelleher
Principal Junior School: Ms Lorna Heslin

Duquesne University,
Duquesne in Dublin,
St Michael's College,
1 Ailesbury Road, Ballsbridge, Dublin 4
Tel/Fax 01-2080940
www.duq.edu/ireland
Resident Director: Ms Nora McBurney
Email nora.mcburney@gmail.com

Templeogue College,
Templeville Road, Dublin 6W
Principal: Ms Niamh Quinn
Tel 01-4905788
Email info@templeoguecollege.ie

(See also under parishes – Bawnogue/
Deansrath, Greenhills/Kimmage)

JESUITS
Irish Jesuit Provincialate
Milltown Park, Milltown Road, Dublin 6
Tel 01-4987333 Fax 01-4987334
Email curia@jesuit.ie
Provincial: Rev Leonard Moloney (SJ)
Assistant Provincial
Rev Shane Daly (SJ)

Jesuit Centre for Faith and Justice
54/57 Upper Gardiner Street,
Dublin 1
Tel 01-8556814
Email info@jcfj.ie
www.jcfj.ie
Director: Mr Kevin Hargaden

Jesuit Communication Centre
Irish Jesuit Provincialate,
Milltown Park,
Milltown Road, Dublin 6
Tel 01-4987347/01-4987348
Director: Ms Pat Coyle
Email coylep@jesuit.ie

Jesuit Curia Community,
Loyola House, Milltown Park,
Milltown Road, Dublin 6
Tel 01-2180276
Email loyola@jesuit.ie
Superior: Rev Terry Howard (SJ)

Belvedere College SJ, Dublin 1
Tel 01-8586600 Fax 01-8744374
Rector: Rev Patrick Greene (SJ)
Secondary day school
Headmaster: Mr Gerard Foley

Gardiner Street Primary School,
Belvedere Court, Dublin 1
Tel 01-8722894
Principal: Ms Eileen O'Doherty

Milltown Park,
Milltown Road, Dublin 6
Tel 01-2698411/2698113
Fax 01-2600371
Email milltown@jesuit.ie
Rector: Rev Tom Casey (SJ)

25 Croftwood Park,
Cherry Orchard, Dublin 10
Tel 01-6267413

Gonzaga College SJ,
Sandford Road, Dublin 6
Community Tel 01-4972943
Email gonzaga@s-j.ie
(College) Tel 01-4972931
Fax 01-4967769
Email (College) office@gonzaga.ie
Email (Community) gonzaga@jesuit.ie
Rector: Rev John O'Keeffe (SJ)
Headmaster: Mr Damon McCaul

Manresa House,
426 Clontarf Road,
Dollymount, Dublin 3
Tel 01-8331352
Rector: Rev William Reynolds (SJ)

St Ignatius House of Writers,
35 Lower Leeson Street, Dublin 2
Tel 01-6761248 Fax 01-7758598
Superior: Rev Jim Culliton (SJ)
Vice-Superior: Rev Michael Kirwan (SJ)

(See also under parishes – Gardiner
Street)

LEGIONARIES OF CHRIST
Leopardstown Road, Foxrock, Dublin 18
Tel 01-2955902
Email ireland@legionaries.org
Superior: Rev Joseph Fazio (LC)

Creidim Centre,
Leopardstown Road,
Dublin D18 FF64
Tel 01-2955902
Email faithandfamilycentre@arcol.org
School Retreats: Email team@clonlost.ie
School retreats, Communion and
Confirmation retreats, Children and
Adult Catechesis Programmes, Marriage
Enrichment days, Spiritual retreats,
Courses on the Faith, Spiritual Direction
Director: Rev Aaron Vinduska
Email avinduska@legionaries.org

Dublin Oak Academy
Kilcroney, Bray, Co Wicklow
Tel 01-2863290 Fax 01-2865315
Email secretary@dublinoakacademy.com
Director: Rev Oscar Sanchez (LC)
Chaplain: Rev Joseph Fazio (LC)

Woodlands Academy
Wingfield House,
Bray, Co Wicklow
Tel 01-2866323 Fax 01-2864918
Chaplain: Rev Vincent McMahon (LC)

MARIANISTS
Marianist Community,
13 Coundon Court, Killiney,
Co Dublin A96 K0T9
Tel 01-2858301
Director: Br Gerard McAuley (SM)

St Laurence College,
Loughlinstown, Dublin 18
Tel 01-2826930
Principal: Mr Shane Fitzgerald

MARIST FATHERS
Marist Fathers Chanel,
Finance & Administrative Office,
Coolock Village Dublin D05 KU62
Admnistrator
Rev Declan Marmion (SM)
Tel 01-2698100/086-2597905
Email dmarmion50@gmail.com

Catholic University School,
89 Lower Leeson Street, Dublin 2
Tel 01-6762586
Headmaster: Mr Clive Martin

Chanel College,
Coolock, Dublin 5
Tel 01-8480896/8480655
Superior: Rev Edwin McCallion (SM)
Headmaster: Mr Dara Gill

(See also under parishes – Coolock and
Donore Avenue)

MILL HILL MISSIONARIES

St Joseph's House,
50 Orwell Park, Rathgar,
Dublin D06 C535
Tel 01-4127700 Fax 01-4127781
Email josephmhm@eircom.net
Regional Superior
Rev Philip O'Halloran (MHM)
Tel 089-4385320
Email millhillregional.irl@gmail.com
Rector: Rev Philip O'Halloran (MHM)
Vice Rector: Rev Patrick Molloy (MHM)
Bursar: Rev Maurice McGill (MHM)
Email millhill@iol.ie

MISSIONARIES OF AFRICA

Community House, Cypress Grove Road,
Templeogue, Dublin D6W YV12
Tel 01-4055263/4063966
Email pep.irl.del@mafr.org
Community Superior
Rev Michael P. O'Sullivan (M.Afr)
Bursar
Rev Diarmuid Sheehan (M.Afr)
Promotion Director
Rev Neil Loughrey (M.Afr)
Email m.africaprom@yahoo.com

MISSIONARIES OF THE SACRED HEART

Provincialate,
65 Terenure Road West,
Dublin D6W P295
Tel 01-4906622
Email office@mscmissions.ie
Provincial Leader
Rev Carl Tranter (MSC)

Woodview House,
Mount Merrion Avenue, Blackrock,
Co Dublin A94 DW95
Tel 01-2881644
Leader: Rev Manus Ferry (MSC)

(See also under parishes – Killinarden)

OBLATES OF MARY IMMACULATE

Provincial Residence,
Oblates of Mary Immaculate House of
Retreat, Tyrconnell Road,
Inchicore, Dublin 8
Email provincialoffice@oblates.ie
Provincial: Very Rev Oliver Barry (OMI)

Oblate House of Retreat,
Inchicore, Dublin 8
Tel 01-4534408/4541805 Fax 01-4543466
Superior: Rev William Fitzpatrick (OMI)

170 Merrion Road,
Ballsbridge, Dublin 4
Tel 01-2693658 Fax 01-2600597

Oblate Scholasticate, St Anne's,
Goldenbridge Walk, Inchicore, Dublin 8
Tel 01-4540841/4542955 Fax 01-4731903

(See also under parishes – Bluebell,
Darndale and the two Inchicore parishes)

PALLOTTINES

Provincial House, 'Homestead',
Sandyford Road, Dundrum, Dublin 16
Tel 01-2956180
Provincial
Very Rev Liam McClarey (SAC)
Rector: Rev Michael Irwin (SAC)
Email motherofdivinelove@gmail.com

(See also under parishes – Corduff and
Shankill)

PASSIONISTS

St Paul's Retreat,
Mount Argus, Dublin 6W
Tel 01-4992000 Fax 01-4992001
Email passionistsmtargus@eircom.net
Provincial: Rev James Sweeney (CP)

(See also under parish – Mount Argus)

REDEMPTORISTS

Dún Mhuire
461/463 Griffith Avenue,
Dublin D09 X651
Tel 01-5180196 Fax 01-8369655

(See also under parishes – Ballyfermot
and Cherry Orchard)

ROSMINIANS

Clonturk House, Ormond Road,
Drumcondra, Dublin 9, D09 F821
Tel 01-6877014
Provincial: Rev Joseph O'Reilly (IC)
Rector: Rev Matt Gaffney (IC)

SACRED HEART FATHERS
Congregation of the Priests of the
Sacred Heart of Jesus
Fairfield, 66 Inchicore Road, Dublin 8
Tel 01-4538655
Email scjdublin@eircom.net
Provincial: Rev John Kelly (SCJ)

St John Vianney, Ardlea Road, Dublin 5
Tel 01-8474123/8474173
Email jvianney@indigo.ie
Rev Hugh Hanley (SCJ) (Moderator)

(See also under parishes – Ardlea)

ST COLUMBANS MISSIONARY SOCIETY

House of Studies
St Columban's,
67-68 Castle Dawson, Rathcoffey Road,
Maynooth, Co Kildare
Tel 01-8286036
Contact Person
Rev Hugh MacMahon (SSC)
Email hugh.macmahonssc@columban.ie

ST PATRICK'S MISSIONARY SOCIETY

21 Leeson Park, Dublin 6
Tel 01-4977897 Fax 01-4962812
House Leader: Rev David Larkin (SPS)

SALESIANS

Provincialate: Salesian House,
45 St Teresa's Road, Crumlin,
Dublin 12, D12 XK52
Tel 01-4555787
Email (secretary) office@salesians.ie
Provincial
Very Rev Eunan McDonnell (SDB)
Email provincial@salesiansireland.ie
Provincial Secretary
Rev Lukasz Nawrat (SDB)
Novitiate: Tel 01-4555605
Rector: Rev Martin McCormack (SDB)

Salesian College, Maynooth Road,
Celbridge, Co Kildare, W23 W0XK
Tel 01-6275058/6275060 Fax 01-6272208
Rector: Rev Patrick Hennessey (SDB)
Secondary School Tel 01-6272166/6272200

Rinaldi House,
40-41 Seán McDermott Street,
Dublin D01 H7P6
Rector: Rev Michael Casey (SDB) Adm

(See also under parishes – Crumlin and
Seán McDermott Street)

SERVITES

Servite Priory, St Peregrine,
36 Grangewood Estate, Rathfarnham,
Dublin 16
Tel 01-4936755
Prior: Rev Jimmy M. Kelly (OSM)

Prior Provincial
Rev Colm M. McGlynn (OSM)
Email colmmcglynn154@hotmail.com

St Peregrine Ministry – Director
Rev Timothy M. Flynn (OSM)

Church of the Divine Word,
Marley Grange, 25-27 Hermitage Downs,
Rathfarnham, Dublin 16
Tel 01-4944295/4941064
Prior: Rev Liam Tracey (OSM) PP

(See also under parish – Marley Grange)

SOCIETY OF AFRICAN MISSIONS
SMA House, 81 Ranelagh Road,
Ranelagh, Dublin D06 WT10
Tel 01-4968162/3 Fax 01-4968164
www.sma.dublin@sma.ie
Superior
Rev Joseph Egan (SMA)

SOCIETY OF ST PAUL
St Paul's House, Moyglare Road,
Maynooth, Co Kildare W23 NX34
Tel 01-6285933 Fax 01-6289330
Email book@stpauls.ie
Rev Alexander Anandam (SSP)
Rev Sebastian Kanayammakunnel (SSP)
Rev Thomas Devasia Perumparambil (SSP)
Rev Bangcaya Jose Jereus (SSP)

St Paul Book Centre
Moyglare Road, Maynooth,
Co Kildare W23 NX34
Email sspireland@gmail.com
www.stpauls.ie

St Paul's Books and Mass Leaflets
Moyglare Road, Maynooth,
Co Kildare W23 NX34
Email sales@stpauls.ie

SONS OF DIVINE PROVIDENCE
Sarsfield House, Sarsfield Road,
Ballyfermot, Dublin 10
Tel 01-6266233/6266193
Email don-orion@clubi.ie
Rev John Perrotta (FDP)
Email jperrotta16@yahoo.ie

VINCENTIANS
Provincial Office: Sybil Hill, Raheny,
Dublin D05 AE38
Tel 01-8510842 Fax 01-8510846
Email cmdublin@vincentians.ie
Provincial: Very Rev Paschal Scallon (CM)

St Joseph's, 44 Stillorgan Park,
Blackrock, Co Dublin A94 PC62
Tel 01-2886961
Superior: Very Rev Colm McAdam (CM)

St Vincent's Castleknock College,
Castleknock, Dublin D15 PD95
Tel 01-8213051
Superior: Very Rev Paschal Scallon (CM)

St Paul's, Raheny, Dublin D05 AE38
Email rmccm@eircom.net
Tel 01-8318113 (Community)
Fax 01-8316387
Superior: Very Rev Stepen Monaghan (CM)

(See also under parishes – Phibsboro)

BROTHERS

CHRISTIAN BROTHERS
Province Centre, Marino,
Griffith Avenue, Dublin 9
Tel 01-8073300 Fax 01-8073366
Email cbprov@edmundrice.eu
Province Leader: Br David Gibson
Community Leader: Br Denis Gleeson
Community: 9

St Helen's, York Road,
Dun Laoghaire, Co Dublin
Tel 01-2801214/2841656
Fax 01-2841657
Community Leader: Br Pat Madigan
Community: 8

Christian Brothers' House,
Woodbrook, Bray, Co Wicklow
Tel 01-2821510
Community Leader: Vacant
Community: 4

Christian Brothers' House,
10 Rosmeen Gardens, Dun Laoghaire,
Co Dublin
Tel 01-2844639
Community Leader: Br Pat Payne
Community: 7

Christian Brothers' Residence,
St David's Park, Artane, Dublin 5
Tel 01-8317833
Community Leader: Br Colm Griffey
Community: 4

Oratory of the Resurrection,
Artane, Dublin 5
Tel 01-8317833

St Patrick's, Baldoyle, Dublin 13
Tel 01-8391287
Retirement home for brothers
Community Leader: Br Ferdi Foley
Community: 18

Christian Brothers' Monastery,
St Declan's, Nephin Road, Dublin 7
Tel 01-8389560
Community Leader: Br Pat Bowler
Community: 6

Clareville, 89A Finglas Road,
Finglas, Dublin 11
Tel 01-8309811
Community Leader: Br Tom Connolly
Community: 6

Marino Institute of Education,
Griffith Avenue, Dublin 9
Tel 01-8057700 Fax 01-8335290
President: Teresa O'Doherty

Christian Brothers,
St Joseph's Community,
Marino Institute of Education,
Griffith Avenue, Marino,
Dublin 9
Tel 01-8057790
Community Leader: Br Michael Murray
Community: 6

Edmund Rice House,
North Richmond Street, Dublin 1
Tel 01-8556258 Fax 01-8555243
Community Leader: Br Brendan Prior
Community: 12

Mainistir Aodhain,
Collins Avenue West,
Whitehall, Dublin 9
Tel 01-8379953
Community Leader: Br Des Young
Community: 6

Christian Brothers,
8 Croftwood Grove, Cherry Orchard,
Ballyfermot, Dublin 10
Community: 2
Tel 01-6208920

DE LA SALLE BROTHERS
Provincialate,
121 Howth Road,
Dublin D03 XN15
Tel 01-8331815 Fax 01-8339130
Email province@iol.ie
Superior: Br Patrick Collier
Assistant Provincial: Br Ben Hanlon
Community: 3

Beneavin College,
Beneavin Road, Finglas East,
Dublin D11 NH7E
Tel 01-8341410
Principal: Dr Aideen Cassidy

Ard Scoil La Salle,
Raheny Road, Dublin D05 Y132
Tel 01-8480055 Fax 01-8480082
Principal: Mr Colin Mythen

Benildus House,
160A Upper Kilmacud Road,
Dublin D14 N778
Tel 01-2981110
Superior: Br Patrick Kelliher
Community: 4

Benildus Pastoral Centre,
160A Upper Kilmacud Road,
Dublin D14 N778
Tel 01-2694195 Fax 01-2694168
Director: Mr Eugene Smyth

Benildus College,
pper Kilmacud Road,
ublin A94 X886
l 01-2986539 Fax 01-2962710
incipal: Mrs Mary Brohan

John's Monastery,
Fanu Road, Dublin D10 X735
l 01-6260867
perior: Br Lawrence Cahill
mmunity: 6
condary School
incipal: Ms Ann Marie Leonard
l/Fax 01-6264943

ANCISCAN BROTHERS
Laurleen Estate,
illorgan, Co Dublin
mail franciscanbrs@eircom.net
ntact person: Br Peter Roddy
l 087-9970760
mmunity: 1

ARIST BROTHERS
arian College, Lansdowne Road,
allsbridge, Dublin 4
l 01-6683740
perior: Br Sebastian Davis
mmunity: 4
condary School

oyle Park College,
ondalkin, Dublin 22
l 01-4577683
perior: Br Nicholas Smith
mmunity: 4
condary School

ATRICIAN BROTHERS
Cardiffcastle Road,
nglas West, Dublin 11
l 01-8342811
perior: Br Dermot Dunne (FSP)
mail dermotmdunne@eircom.net
mmunity: 2

RESENTATION BROTHERS
esentation Novitiate,
asthule, Co Dublin
l 01-2842228
ntact: Br Barry Nool (FPM)
mmunity: 5

AINT JOHN OF GOD BROTHERS
Patrick's Community,
illorgan, Co Dublin A94 E244
l 01-2771431 Fax 01-2782938
ior: Br Ronan Lennon (OH)
mmunity: 9

cena Community,
Orwell Road, Rathgar,
ublin D06 W1C0
ior: Br Finnian Gallagher (OH)
mmunity: 2

SAINT JOHN OF GOD HOSPITAL
Stillorgan, Co Dublin A94 7H92
Tel 01-2771400 Fax 01-2881034
Chief Executive: Ms Emma Balmaine
Private psychiatric hospital

St Joseph's Centre,
Crinken Lane, Shankill,
Co Dublin D18 TY00
Tel 01-2823000 Fax 01-2823119
Email stjosephs@sjog.ie
Director of Nursing: Ms Norma Sheehan
Residential and day service for people
with dementia

**SAINT JOHN OF GOD COMMUNITY
SERVICES CLG**
Cluain Mhuire,
Community Mental Health Services,
Newtownpark Avenue,
Blackrock, Co Dublin A94 HX01
Tel 01-2172100 Fax 01-2833886
Email cms@sjog.ie
Regional Director: Mr Kevin Madigan

Saint John of God Lucena Clinic Services,
59 Orwell Road, Rathgar,
Dublin D06 4X93
Tel 01-4923596 Fax 01-4923823
Email admin.lucena@sjog.ie
Regional Director: Mr Kevin Madigan
St Peter's School,
59 Orwell Road, Rathgar,
Dublin D06 X594
Tel 01-4923596 Fax 01-4907768
School Principal: Ms Helen Heneghan
Child and adolescent psychiatric services

Saint John of God Menni Services,
Block A, Gleann na hEorna,
Springfield, Tallaght,
Dublin D24 AD62
Tel 01-4686400 Fax 01-4686499
Email admin.menni@sjog.ie
Regional Director
Ms Eliza Doyle
St John of God School,
Islandbridge, Dublin 8
Tel 01-6741534 Fax 01-6741501
School Principal: Ms Marie Ryan
Incorporating day services, residential
services (Tel 01-4731474), enterprises (Tel
01-4569320) and community services

Saint John of God Liffey Services,
St Raphael's, Celbridge,
Co Kildare W23 F2P5
Tel 01-6288161 Fax 01-6273614
Email admin.kildare@sjog.ie
Regional Director
Ms Eliza Doyle
St Raphael's School, Church Road,
Celbridge, Co Kildare W23 F2P5
Tel 01-6288161 Fax 01-6012468
School Principal: Mrs Kathy Waldron
Residential, day centre and community
services for children and adults with
varying degrees of intellectual disability

Saint John of God,
Carmona Services, Dunmore House,
111 Upper Glenageary Road,
Dun Laoghaire, Co Dublin A96 E223
Tel 01-2852900 Fax 01-2851713
Email admin.carmona@sjog.ie
Regional Director
Mr Desmond North
St John of God School,
Glenageary Road, Glenageary,
Co Dublin A96 EV66
Tel 01-2852900 Fax 01-2851713
School Principal: Marie Burke
Incorporating residential, day, enterprise
and community services for people with
intellectual disability.

STEP, 30 Carmanhall Road,
Sandyford Industrial Estate,
Dublin D18 P7X0
Tel 01-2952379 Fax 01-2952371
Email step@sjog.ie
Regional Director
Mr Desmond North
Training centre and supported
employment

City Gate, 30 Carmanhall Road,
Sandyford Industrial Estate,
Dublin D18 P7X0
Tel 01-2952379 Fax 01-2952371
Email citygate@sjog.ie
Regional Director
Mr Desmond North
Housing Service

St Augustine's School,
Obelisk Park, Carysfort Avenue,
Blackrock, Co Dublin A94 X8K7
Tel 01-2881771 Fax 01-2834117
Email staugustines@sjog.ie
Regional Director
Mr Desmond North
Principal: Mr David O'Brien
Special National School

Suzanne House,
6 Main Road, Tallaght,
Dublin D24 CC60
Tel 01-4521966 Fax 01-4525504
Director: Ms Eliza Doyle
Email eliza.doyle@sjog.ie
Respite service for children with terminal
illness and/or complex nursing needs

SISTERS

BLESSED SACRAMENT SISTERS
91 Seabury Crescent,
Malahide, Co Dublin K36 EY72
Tel 01-8451878
Email annamay@live.ie
Community: 2

BON SECOURS SISTERS (PARIS)
Sisters of Bon Secours,
9 Abbeyvale, 215 Botanic Avenue,
Drumcondra, Dublin 9
Tel 01-8373209
Community: 1
Hospital Ministry

Sisters of Bon Secours,
119 Esker Lawns, Lucan, Co Dublin
Tel 01-6217158
Community: 1
Parish Ministry

BRIGIDINE SISTERS
106 The Edges 1, Beacon South Quarter,
Sandyford, Dublin D18 WY00
Congregational Leadership Team
Sr Catherine O'Connor
Email coconnorcsb07@gmail.com

5 Sycamore Drive,
Dundrum, Dublin 16
Tel 01-2988130
Contact: Sr Theresa Kilmurray
Community: 1
Administration

7 Sycamore Drive, Dublin 16
Tel 01-2966449
Community: 1
Contact: Sr Loretto Ryan
Community Work

15 Gortmore Drive, Rivermount,
Finglas, Dublin 11
Tel 01-8642440
Contact: Sr Imelda Barry
Community: 1
Parish

94 Moyville,
Ballyboden, Dublin 16
Tel 01-7941596
Contact: Sr Anna Hennessy
Community: 1
Education and Parish Ministry

163 Park Drive Avenue, Castleknock,
Dublin 15
Tel 01-8200482
Contact: Sr Kay Mulhall
Community: 1
Retired

18 Maryville Apartments,
Sybil Hill Road, Raheny, Dublin 5
Contact: Sr Elizabeth Cleary
Spiritual Direction

12 Margaret Holme,
Claremont Road,
Sandymount, Dublin 4
Contact: Mairead Brophy

CARMELITES
Carmelite Monastery of the Immaculate
Conception, Roebuck,
Dublin D14 T1H9
Tel 01-2884732
Altar Breads
Email altarbreads@roebuckcarmel.com
www.roebuckcarmel.com
Email carmel@roebuckcarmel.com
Prioress: Sr Teresa Whelan
Community: 9
Contemplatives; altar breads supplied

Star of the Sea Carmelite Monastery,
Seapark, Malahide,
Dublin K36 P586
Tel 01-8454259/087-9643953
Prioress: Sr Rosalie Burke
Email rmebodc@gmail.com
Community: 7
Contemplatives, honey (in season)
www.malahidecarmelites.ie
Contemplative Community

Carmelite Monastery of St Joseph,
Upper Kilmacud Road, Stillorgan,
Blackrock, Co Dublin A94 YY33
Tel 01-2886089
Email contact@kilmacudcarmel.ie
www.kilmacudcarmel.ie
Prioress: Sr Mary Brigeen Wilson
Community: 10
Contemplatives, altar breads supplied

CARMELITE SISTERS FOR THE AGED AND INFIRM
Our Lady's Manor, Bulloch Castle,
Dalkey, Co Dublin
Tel 01-2806993 Fax 01-2844802
Email ourladysmanor1@eircom.net
Superior
Sr Mary Therese Healy (OCarm)
Email smtjhealy57@gmail.com
Administrator
Sr Bernadette Murphy (OCarm)
Community: 6

CHARITY OF NEVERS SISTERS
76 Cherrywood,
Loughlinstown Drive,
Dun Laoghaire, Co Dublin
Contact person: Sr Rosaleen Cullen
Tel 01-4585654/086-8411466
Email rosaleencullen@upcmail.ie

Flat 12 Verschoyle Court,
Dublin 12
Email noradowney60@gmail.com

CHARITY OF ST PAUL THE APOSTLE SISTERS
40 Rockfield Avenue
Perrystown, Dublin D12 N6K5
Tel 01-4556741
Email marylyons2010@gmail.com
Contact: Sr Mary Lyons
Community: 3
Education and parish

51 Orwell Park Rise, Dublin D6W H678
Tel 01-4908856
Contact: Sr Clare Hartley
Email norahartl@yahoo.co.uk
Community: 2
Parish and education

CLARISSAN MISSIONARY SISTERS OF THE BLESSED SACRAMENT
Our Lady of Guadalupe Residence for
Students, 28 Waltersland Road,
Stillorgan, Co Dublin
Tel 01-2886600
Email
info@ourladyofguadaluperesidence.com
www.ourlady ofguadaluperesidence.com
www.misionerasclarisas.org
Superior: Sr Elisa Padilla
Tel 087-0510783
Community: 5

CONGREGATION OF THE SISTERS OF MERCY
'Rachamim', 13/14 Moyle Park,
Convent Road, Clondalkin,
Dublin D22 HR94
Tel 01-4673737 Fax 01-4673749
Email mercy@csm.ie
Website www.sistersofmercy.ie
Congregational Leader
Sr Marie Louise White

Mercy International Centre
64A Lower Baggot Street,
Dublin D02 HD68
Tel 01-6618061
Email director@mercyinternational.ie
Director: Sr Berneice Loch
Heritage tours, school tours, conference
facilities and pilgrimages to the tomb of
Ven. Catherine McAuley
Website www.mercyworld.org

South Central Province

*The Sisters of Mercy minister throughout
the diocese in pastoral and social work,
community development, counselling,
spirituality, education and health care,
answering current needs.*

1 & 2 Church Crescent,
Athy, Co Kildare R14 KX43
Tel 059-8631361
Community: 7

Allianz (ⅰ)

01 Rockfield Green,
Maynooth, Co Kildare W23 A4P9
Tel 01-6291992
Community: 2

St Anne's, Booterstown,
Co Dublin A94 NW53
Tel 01-2882140
Province Archives
Community: 12

22A Camron Court,
Cork Street, Dublin D08 R3K8
Tel 01-4530498
Community: 2

t Brendan's Drive,
Coolock, Dublin D05 K7F1
Tel 01-8486420
Community: 10

Sisters of Mercy, Convent of Mercy,
Eblana Avenue, Dun Laoghaire,
Co Dublin A96 X657
Tel 01-2360686 Fax 01-2805470
Community: 21

23-26 The Paddocks,
Kilmainham, Dublin D08 N260
Tel 01-4021727
Community: 5

31 Mackintosh Park,
Dun Laoghaire, Co Dublin A96 VIF2
Tel-2851707
Community: 1

3 Emmet Crescent,
nchicore, Dublin D08 X6X9
Community: 3

Mater Misericordiae, Eccles Street,
Dublin D07 R2WY
Tel 01-8824550 Fax 01-8309070
Community: 18

Leo Street, Dublin D07 V0Y9
Tel 01-8858593
Community: 2

Stella Maris, Convent Lane,
Rush, Co Dublin K56 W965
Tel/Fax 01-8437347
Community: 2

4 Coolatree Close,
Beaumont, Dublin D09 DK29
Tel 01-8377023
Community: 3

3 Kenilworth Park, Harolds Cross,
Dublin D6W E654
Tel 01-4452905
Community: 3

5 Kenilworth Park, Harolds Cross,
Dublin D6W HY57
Tel 01-4929414
Community: 1

90/91 The Park,
Beaumont Woods, Dublin D09 E921
Tel 01-8570741
Community: 2

McAuley House,
Beaumont, Dublin D09 AP9D
Tel 01-8379186 Fax 01-8373503
Community: numbers vary

83/85 Silloge Park,
Ballymun, Dublin D11 AW86
Tel 01-8547611
Community: 1

40 Gilford Road,
Sandymount, Dublin D04 XR61
Tel 01-2601081
Community: 3

Sisters of Mercy,
14 Walnut Avenue, Courtlands,
Drumcondra, Dublin D09 X5A4
Tel 01-8377602
Community: 3

Sisters of Mercy,
1/2 Charlemont, Griffith Avenue,
Dublin D09 W7X6
Tel 01-8571246
Community: 5

Sisters of Mercy,
25 Cork Street, Dublin D08 RY86
Tel 01-4535262
Community: 4

11 Grangemore Road,
Donaghmede,
Dublin D13 H2H9
Tel 01-8482242
Community: 1

Knockfin, Glendalough,
Co Wicklow A98 FH58
Tel 0404-45791
Community: 1

CROSS AND PASSION CONGREGATION
Cross and Passion Sisters,
3-5 Carberry Road, Glandore Road,
Dublin 9
Tel 01-8377256
Community: 5
Pastoral ministry

Cross and Passion Convent
22 Griffith Avenue,
Marino, Dublin 9
Tel 01-8336077
Community: 17
Care of elderly

Cross and Passion Convent,
41 Alderwood Green, Springfield,
Tallaght, Dublin 24
Tel 01-4511850
Community: 3
Pastoral ministry, school chaplaincy,
retreat work

Cross and Passion Convent,
13 Clare Road,
Drumcondra, Dublin 9
Tel 01-8375511
Community: 3
Community development, pastoral
ministry

DAUGHTERS OF CHARITY OF ST VINCENT DE PAUL
St Catherine's Provincial House,
Dunardagh, Blackrock,
Co Dublin
Tel 01-2882669/2882896
Local Superior: Sr Marie Fox
Community: 20
Provincial administration and retreats

'Avignon', Daughters of Charity,,
Navan Road, Dublin 7
Tel 01-8684017
Superior: Sr Geraldine Henry
Community: 6
Mission development, hospice
administration, parish work

77 Kilbarron Park,
Kilmore West, Dublin 5
Tel 01-8470648
Superior: Sr Mary Connaire
Community: 5
Social ministry, pastoral ministry, parish
ministry

3 St Assam's Drive,
Raheny, Dublin 5
Tel 01-8312859
Superior: Sr Maire Brady
Community: 3
House of residence for sisters involved in
St Francis Hospice and child and family
services and parish ministry

St Louise's, Drumfinn Road,
Ballyfermot, Dublin 10
Tel 01-6264921
Superior: Sr Margaret O'Donovan
Community: 6
Education and parish work

St Joseph's, Sisters Residence,
Clonsilla, Co Dublin
Tel 01-8217177
Superior: Sr Bernadette Carron
Community: 6
Work for social justice, diocesan adviser,
special schools, Boards of Management

10 Henrietta Street, Dublin 1
Tel 01-8583063
Superior: Sr Sheila Ryan
Community: 21
House of residence for sisters, catechesis,
Virgo Potens Office, pastoral work

Daughters of Charity Community
Services,
8/9 Henrietta Street, Dublin 1
Education and Community Services
Tel 01-8874100 Fax 01-8723486

109 Mount Prospect Avenue,
Clontarf, Dublin 3
Tel 01-8338508
Superior: Sr Mary O'Toole
Community: 20
House for sisters needing care and
retired

7 Belvedere Road,
Dublin 1
Tel 01-8556719
Superior: Sr Margaret Cashman
Community: 3 and 3 sisters in Nursing
Homes attached to this community
House of residence, pastoral care and
parish work

166 Navan Road, Dublin 7
Tel 01-8383801
Superior: Sr Zoe Killeen
Community: 3
House of residence for sisters involved in
pastoral work, fundraising for people
with intellectual disability

St Louise's, 16 Dalymount,
Phibsboro, Dublin 7
Tel 01-8680308
Superior: Sr Claire McKiernan
Community: 4
House of residence for sisters involved
in work with pastoral ministry, homeless
people, care of older sisters,
co-ordinator Vincentian family

25 Killarney Street, Dublin 1
Tel 01-8366487
Superior: Sr Angela Burke
Community: 3
House of residence for sisters involved in
work with refugees, pastoral care,
Society of St Vincent de Paul

Labouré House,
Dunardagh, Temple Hill,
Blackrock, Co Dublin
Tel 01-2833933
Superior: Sr Brenda Hunter
Community: 13
House of residence for sisters, pastoral
care

DAUGHTERS OF THE CROSS OF LIÈGE
Beech Park Convent,
Beechwood Court,
Stillorgan, Co Dublin
Tel 01-2887401/2887315 Fax 01-2881499
Email beechpark1833@gmail.com
Superior: Sr Kathleen McKenna
Community: 8

DAUGHTERS OF THE HEART OF MARY
St Joseph's, 1 Crosthwaite Grove,
Crosthwaite Park South,
Dun Laoghaire, Co Dublin
Superior: Sr Mary Brogan
Tel 01-2801204
Email heartofmary3@gmail.com
St Joseph's Primary School
Principal's Office: Tel 01-2803504

32 Brackenbush Road,
Killiney, Co Dublin
Tel 01-2750917

DAUGHTERS OF THE HOLY SPIRIT
9 Walnut Park,
Drumcondra, Dublin 9
Tel 01-8371825
Community: 2
Contact person: Sr Ita Durnin
Email itadhs@yahoo.co.uk
Pastoral ministry

DAUGHTERS OF MARY AND JOSEPH
65 Iona Road, Glasnevin,
Dublin D09 Y7F4
Tel 01-8305640
Community: 4
Pastoral

37 Bancroft Road,
Tallaght, Dublin 24
Tel 01-4515321
Community: 3
Pastoral

55 Rowan Hamilton Court,
Dublin 7
Tel 01-8380525
Contact person: Sr Peggy McArdle
Community: 1
Community Development

109 Botanic Avenue,
Dublin 9
Community: 1

10 Moynihan Court,
Main Road, Tallaght, Dublin 24
Community: 1

2 Moynihan Court,
Main Road, Tallaght, Dublin 24
Tel 01-4627923
Community: 1

DAUGHTERS OF OUR LADY OF THE SACRED HEART
Provincial House,
14 Rossmore Avenue,
Templeogue, Dublin 6W
Tel 01-4903200 Tel/Fax 01-4903113
Email olshprov@eircom.net
Provincial: Sr Mairéad Kelleher
Community: 4

DAUGHTERS OF WISDOM
20 Grace Park Meadows,
Drumcondra,
Dublin D09 X2X5
Tel 01-8316508
Contact: Sr Gráinne Hilton
Community: 2

DISCIPLES OF THE DIVINE MASTER
Divine Master Centre,
Newtownpark Avenue, White's Cross,
Blackrock, Co Dublin A94 V2N8
Tel 01-2114949 *(community)*
01-2886414 *(Liturgical Centre)*
Contact: Sr Brid Geraghty
Email dublin@ppdm.org
Community: 7
Contemplative-apostolic Congregation.
Chapel of Adoration with daily
Adoration, open to public. Prayer,
support and intercession for priests.
Website: www.pddm.ie
Liturgical Centre-distributor and
producer of liturgical vestments/altar
linens, high-quality liturgical art,
religious gifts. Promotion of liturgical
formation. Bethany House available for
private retreats. Daily prayer and
support groups.
Website: www.liturgicalcentre.ie

DOMINICAN SISTERS
Mary Bellew House,
Dominican Campus,
Cabra, Dublin D07 Y2E7
Tel 01-8299700 Fax 01-8299799
Email domgen@dominicansisters.com
Community: 5
Administration

St Mary's, Rectory Green,
Riverston Abbey, Cabra,
Dublin D07 X5F3
Tel 01-8683041
Email riverstonabbey@gmail.com
Community: 8
Varied ministries

St Mary's, Cabra,
Dublin D07 AF8P
Tel 01-8380567 Fax 01-8682050
Email dominicancabra@gmail.com
Prioress: Sr Margaret Purcell (OP)
Community: 16
Varied ministries

Dominican Convent,
Sion Hill, Blackrock,
Co Dublin A94 X5N3
Tel 01-2886832/3
Email sionhillconvent@gmail.com
Prioress: Sr Darina Hosey (OP)
Community: 15
Varied ministries
Dominican College Sion Hill
Tel 01-2886791

Dominican Sisters,
St Mary's, 47 Mount Merrion Avenue,
Blackrock, Co Dublin A94 Y94D
Tel 01-2888551
Email 47mtmerrion@gmail.com
Community: 3
Varied ministries

Dominican Convent,
Convent Road,
Dun Laoghaire,
Co Dublin A96 TP02
Tel 01-2801379 Fax 01-2302209
Email domdunlg@gmail.com
Community: 6
Primary School. Tel 01-2809011
Education, varied ministries

Dominican Convent,
204 Griffith Avenue, Dublin 9
Tel 01-8379550
Email dsisters204@yahoo.ie
Prioress: Sr Catherine Gibson (OP)
Secondary School. Tel 01-8376080
Community: 11
Varied ministries

Veritas House,
Muckross Park,
Marlborough Road,
Donnybrook, Dublin D04 P9Y9
Community: 7

Dominican Sisters,
St Catherine's,
2 Heather View Road, Aylesbury,
Tallaght, Dublin D24 EAW8
Tel 01-4523462 Fax 01-4625636
Email domabury2@gmail.com
Community: 2
Varied ministries

Dominican Sisters,
1 Avonbeg Road, Tallaght,
Dublin D24 RKH3
Tel 01-4514627
Email ruthpilkington@yahoo.co.uk
Community: 2
Pastoral

Dominican Sisters,
2 Croftwood Crescent,
Cherry Orchard, Ballyfermot,
Dublin D10 XE61
Tel 01-6231127
Email cherrydoms5@gmail.com
Community: 2
Varied ministries

Dominican Sisters,
93 Nephin Road,
Cabra, Dublin D07 V0F5
Tel 01-8682054
Email domsis9395@gmail.com
Community: 4
Varied ministries

Dominican Sisters,
Santa Sabina House, Cabra,
Dublin D07 WK25
Tel 01-8682666 Fax 01-8682667
Email
santasabina@dominicansisters.com
Community: 27 Nursing Home

Dominican Sisters,
St Mary's Convent,
Wicklow A67 YX26
Tel 0404-67328
Email dcw1870@gmail.com
Community: 6
Ecological centre, varied ministries

Dominican Sisters,
62 Ashington Avenue, Navan Road,
Dublin D07 E1X7
Tel 01-8386304
Community: 2
Varied ministries

Dominican Sisters,
5 Westfield Road, Dublin 6W CD93
Tel 01-5164932
Email dominicanhive@gmail.com
Varied ministries

FRANCISCAN MISSIONARIES OF THE DIVINE MOTHERHOOD
Arus Mhuire, 185 Swords Road,
Whitehall, Dublin D09 YW40
Tel 01-8572876
Community: 2

St Francis Convent,
3/4 Fonthill Abbey, Ballyboden Road,
Rathfarnham, Dublin 14
Tel 01-4932537 Fax 01-4954846
Community: 5

FRANCISCAN MISSIONARIES OF MARY
Assisi, 36 Grange Abbey Drive,
Donaghmede, Dublin 13
Tel 01-8470591
Superior: Sr Mary Dunne
Community: 4
Social, pastoral work

97 St Lawrence Road,
Clontarf, Dublin 3
Tel 01-8332683/8332181
Email fmmclontarf@yahoo.co.uk
Superior: Sr Ann Condon
Community: 4
Pastoral, hospitality for missionary sisters

St Joseph's Convent, Old Road,
Hayestown, Rush, Co Dublin
Tel 01-8439308
Superior: Sr Mary Dornan
Community: 20
Care of elderly sisters

FMM, 4 Muckross Drive,
Perrystown, Dublin 12
Tel 01-4562028
Community: 3
Youth ministry, hospital chaplaincy

FRANCISCAN MISSIONARIES OF ST JOSEPH
St Joseph's, 16 Innismore,
Crumlin Village, Dublin 12
Tel 01-4563445
Regional Leader
Sr Mary Butler
Community Leader
Sr Margaret Lonergan
Community: 3

FRANCISCAN MISSIONARY SISTERS FOR AFRICA
Generalate,
Central Team, 34A Gilford Road,
Sandymount, Dublin 4
Tel 01-2838376 Fax 01-2602049
Email generalate@fmsa.net
Leader: Sr Jeanette Watters (FMSA)
Community: 4

34 Gilford Road,
Sandymount, Dublin 4
Tel 01-2691923
Contact person
Sr Avril Reynolds (FMSA)
Email avrilmreynnolds@gmail.com
Community: 4

142 Raheny Road,
Raheny, Dublin 5
Tel 01-8480852
Email fmsaraheny142@iol.ie
Contact person
Sr Bridgette Cormack (FMSA)
Email bcormack@fmsa.net
Community: 1

FRANCISCAN SISTERS OF THE IMMACULATE CONCEPTION

Franciscan Sisters, 97/99 Riverside Park, Clonshaugh, Dublin 17
Tel 01-8771778
Contact person: Sr Immaculata Owhotemu
Community: 2
Administration, pastoral ministry, nursing

SISTERS OF ST FRANCIS OF PHILADELPHIA

3 St Andrew Fairway, Lucan, Co Dublin
Contact: Sr Nora McCarthy,
Sr Carmel Earls, Sr Kathleen Kelly

CONGREGATION OF OUR LADY OF CHARITY OF THE GOOD SHEPHERD

Province Administration
63 Lower Sean McDermott Street,
Dublin D01 NX93
Tel 01-8711109
Email province.office@rgs.ie
www.goodshepherdsisters.ie
Province Leader: Sr Cait O'Leary

65 Taney Crescent,
Goatstown, Dublin D14 FY62
Tel 01-2960235
Email rgstaney@gmail.com
Community: 2

Beechlawn Complex, High Park,
Grace Park Road, Drumcondra,
Dublin D09 YK82
Nursing Home Tel 01-8369622
Community: 13

Apt 6, Woodview House,
Mount Merrion Avenue,
Blackrock, Co Dublin A94 DW95
Community: 1

HANDMAIDS OF THE SACRED HEART OF JESUS

St Raphaela's, Upper Kilmacud Road,
Stillorgan, Co Dublin A94 TP38
Tel 01-2889963 Fax 01-2889536
Superior: Sr Irene Guia
Email iguiaci@gmail.com
Community: 11
Primary School. Tel 01-2886878
Secondary School. Tel 01-2888730
Students' residence. Tel 01-2887159
Fax 01-2889536

HOLY CHILD JESUS, SOCIETY OF THE

1 Stable Lane, Off Harcourt Street,
Dublin D02 HX83
Tel 01-4754053

21 Grange Park Avenue,
Raheny, Dublin D05 AY65
Tel 01-8488961

HOLY FAITH SISTERS

Generalate, Aylward House,
Glasnevin, Dublin D11 YEF1
Tel 01-8371426
Email admin@hfaith.ie
Congregational Leader
Sr Rosaleen Cunniffe

Regional House,
25 Clare Road,
Drumcondra, Dublin D09 TY76
Tel 01-8572100
Email regional@hfsi.ie
Regional Leader: Sr Evelyn Greene

183 Clontarf Road,
Dublin D03 P3X5
Tel 01-8338331
Community: 6
Varied Apostolates

Star of the Sea,
182 Clontarf Road, Dublin D03 KD63
Tel 01-8338352
Community: 4
Varied Apostolates

The Coombe, Dublin 8
Tel 01-4540244
Email coomconvent@eircom.net
Community: 7
Varied Apostolates

11 Drumcairn Green,
Fettercairn, Tallaght,
Dublin D24 E5X9
Tel 01-4513951
Community: 2
Parish work

12 Finglaswood Road,
Dublin D11 EAX9
Tel 01-8641551
Community: 2
Varied Apostolates

15 Forestwood Avenue,
Ballymun, Dublin D09 EY92
Tel 01-8623482
Community: 1
Varied Apostolates

St Joseph the Artisan Parish,
124 Greencastle Road, Bonnybrook,
Coolock, Dublin D17 Y157
Community 2
Varied Apostolates

13 Wellmount Parade,
Dublin D11 WDE7
Tel 01-8640874
Community: 1
Administration

14 Wellmount Parade,
Dublin D11 F1C8
Tel 01-8645153
Community: 1
Music ministry

Holy Faith Sisters,
144 Cappagh Road, Finglas,
Dublin D11 T3F1
Tel 01-8643205
Community: 1
Varied Apostolates

Glasnevin, Dublin D11 HN8F
Tel 01-8373427/8377967
Community: 23
Varied Apostolates

Margaret Aylward Centre for Faith and Dialogue,
Holy Faith Convent,
Glasnevin, Dublin D11 TC21
Tel 01-7979364/087-6649862
Director: Ms Dympna Mallon

Marian House Nursing Home
Tel 01-8376165
Email administration@marianhouse.net

Greystones,
Co Wicklow A63 YX40
Tel 01-2874081
Community: 3
Varied Apostolates

Credo, 1 Fairways Grove,
Griffith Road, Dublin D11 E2N6
Tel 01-8348015
Community: 1
Parish ministry

2 Fairways Grove,
Griffith Road, Dublin D11 E2N6
Tel 01-8533772
Community: 1
Holy Faith community service

Haddington Place, Dublin D04 K312
Tel 01-6681124
Community: 6
Varied Apostolates

18 Church Street,
Skerries, Co Dublin K34 X981
Tel 01-8491203
Community: 3
Varied Apostolates

4 Main Road,
allaght, Dublin D24 T2KE
el 01-4515904
Community: 2
aith development

1 Aylward Green,
inglas, Dublin D11 AV67
el 01-8646401
Community: 1
Varied Apostolates

78-180 Clontarf Road,
Dublin 3
Community: 9
Varied Apostolates

oseph's Cottage,
ippure East, Manor Kilbride,
Co Wicklow W91 AY74
el 01-4582923
Community: 1
Varied Apostolates

t Anne's Presbytery,
Kilcarrig Avenue, Fettercairn,
allaght, Dublin D24 EN25
el 01-4141916
Community: 2
Varied Apostolates

osedale Bungalow,
athdown Road, Greystones,
Co Wicklow A63 V968
Community: 1
pirituality

0 Seamount, Priory Drive,
den Gate, Delgany,
Co Wicklow A63 RC80
el 01-2812838
Community 1
pirituality

ISTERS OF THE HOLY FAMILY OF BORDEAUX
5 Griffith Downs,
Dromcondra, Dublin 9
el 01-5477709
Contact : Sr Claire McGrath (Councillor
or Ireland)
mail clairemcgrath.hfb@gmail.com

Holy Family of Bordeaux Sisters,
rishtown, Clane, Co Kildare
el 01-6288459
Contact: Sr Bernadette Deegan
Community: 5
Parish work, chaplaincy, adult religious
education, literacy and pastoral work

INFANT JESUS SISTERS
Provincial House,
56 St Lawrence Road,
Clontarf, Dublin D03 Y5F2
Tel 01-8338930
Provincial: Sr Marie Pitcher
Email mariepitcher1@gmail.com
Tel 086-8054249

140 Carrickhill Rise, Portmarnock,
Co Dublin D13 CP74
Tel 01-8461647
Pastoral ministry

16 Ard na Meala, Ballymun,
Dublin D11 P9O2
Tel 01-8426534
Pastoral ministry, youth ministry, social
work

7 Ard na Meala, Ballymun,
Dublin D11 YW50
Pastoral ministry

54 Knowth Court, Poppintree,
Ballymun, Dublin D11 PF51
Pastoral ministry

2 Carrig Close, Poppintree,
Ballymun, Dublin D11 T635
Pastoral ministry

1 Eccles Court, Dublin D07 V9K5
Tel 01-8309004
Pastoral ministry

JESUS AND MARY, CONGREGATION OF
Provincialate, 'Errew House',
110 Goatstown Road, Dublin 14
Provincial Offices: Tel 01-2993130
Direct line: Tel 01-2969150
Bursar's Office: Tel 01-2993140
Provincial Superior: Sr Marie O'Halloran
Tel 01-2969150
Email marieohalloran68@gmail.com
Tel 01-2966059
Community: 5

'Errew House',
Our Lady's Grove Community,
110 Goatstown Road, Dublin 14
Community: 5
Convent. Tel 01-2966104
Our Lady's Grove Primary School
Principal: Ms Anne Kernan
Pupils: 480
Jesus & Mary College Secondary School
Principal: Mr Colm Dooley
Tel 01-2951913. Pupils: 360

'Errew House',
110 Goatstown Road, Dublin 14
Tel 01-2993665
Community: 3

LA RETRAITE SISTERS
77 Grove Park, Rathmines,
Dublin D06 C583
Tel 01-4911771
Contact: Sr Barbara Stafford
Email barbarastaffordrlr@gmail.com

LA SAINTE UNION DES SACRES COEURS
Teallach Mhuire, 41 Broadway Road,
Blanchardstown, Dublin 15
Tel 01-8214459
Leadership work base – Ireland
Hospitality

9 Tandy's Hill, Lucan, Co Dublin
Tel 01-6218863
Community: 1
Parish work

126 Malahide Road,
Clontarf, Dublin 3
Tel 01-8332778
Community: 3
Pastoral work, literacy

14 Glenshane Grove,
Brookfield, Tallaght, Dublin 24
Tel 01-4527684
Community: 2
Teaching, pastoral work, travellers,
counselling

7 Summerfield Close,
Clonsilla Road, Dublin 15
Community: 1
Counselling, education

8 Myross Mews, 181 Strand Road,
Sandymount, Dublin 4
Community: 1
Pastoral

LITTLE COMPANY OF MARY
Provincialate, Cnoc Mhuire,
29 Woodpark, Ballinteer Avenue,
Dublin 16
Tel 01-2987040
Province Leader: Sr Mary Flanagan

40 Braemor Park,
Churchtown, Dublin 14
Tel 01-4991357/4991358/4904795/
4904692
Community: 16

14 Heather Lawn,
Marlay Wood, Dublin 16
Tel 01-4942324
Community: 1

16 Heather Lawn,
Marlay Wood, Dublin 16
Tel 01-4947205
Community: 1

Little Company of Mary,
45 Priory Way, Whitehall Road,
Dublin 12
Tel 01-4907763
Community: 1

Little Company of Mary,
62 West Priory, Navan Road, Dublin 7
Tel 01-8682312
Community: 1

LITTLE SISTERS OF THE ASSUMPTION
Administration Office,
42 Rathfarnham Road,
Terenure, Dublin 6W
Tel 01-4909850 Fax 01-4925740
Email pernet42r@gmail.com
Co-ordinator: Sr Mary O'Sullivan
Sisters work in family care and with local
community development groups

12 Convent Lawns,
Ballyfermot, Dublin 10
Tel 01-6230898
Email conventlawns12@gmail.com

8 Owendore Crescent,
Rathfarnham, Dublin 14
Tel 01-4931147
Email lasair@hotmail.com

Patrickswell Place,
Finglas, Dublin 11
Tel 01-8342592
Email fagefinglas@yahoo.co.uk

Mount Argus,
Assumption Convent,
Mount Argus Road, Dublin 6W
Tel 01-4977038
Email mountarguslsa15@gmail.com

41 Liscarne Court,
Rowlagh,
Clondalkin, Dublin 22
Tel 01-6263077
Email rowlaghlsa@gmail.com

14 Forestwood Avenue,
Santry Avenue, Dublin 9
Email lsaballymun@gmail.com

308 St James Road,
Greenhills, Dublin 12
Tel 01-4089982
Email lsaghills@gmail.com

Apts 196, 198, 199,
Block F Seven Oaks,
Ballyfermot, Dublin 10
Tel 01-6300389
Email sevenoaks.lsa@gmail.com

36 Oileáin na Crannóige,
Poppintree, Ballymun,
Dubin D11 T2WY

LITTLE SISTERS OF THE POOR
Sacred Heart Residence,
Sybil Hill Road, Raheny,
Dublin D05 XK58
Tel 01-8332308
Provincial: Sr Anthony Francis (London)
Superior: Sr Jacinta
Email msraheny@lspireland.com
Community: 13
Nursing home for the elderly

Holy Family Residence,
Roebuck Road, Dublin 14
Tel 01-2832455
Superior: Sr Miriam
Email ms.holyfamily@lspireland.com
Community: 14
Nursing home for the elderly

St Brigid's Novitiate,
Roebuck Road, Dublin 14
Tel 01-2832536
Email ms.stbrigids@lspireland.com

LORETO (IBVM)
Provincialate, Loreto House,
Beaufort, Dublin 14
Tel 01-4933827
Email provadmin@loreto.ie
Provincial: Sr Carmel Swords

Abbey House,
Loreto Terrace, Grange Road,
Rathfarnham, Dublin 14
Tel 01-4932807
Shared Community Leader
Sr Moira MacManus
Community: 27
Primary School, Secondary Day School,
pastoral work

Loreto College and Junior School,
53 St Stephen's Green, Dublin 2
Tel 01-6618179/6618181

Loreto Community,
Nos 3, 6, 8, 9 Fort Ostman,
Old County Road,
Crumlin, Dublin 12
Community: 3
Loreto Secondary School. Tel 01-4542380
Senior Primary School. Tel 01-4541669
Junior Primary School. Tel 01-4541746
Loreto Centre, Old County Road,
Crumlin Road
Tel 01-4541078
Community: 1
Personal and community development

Nos 29/30 The Courtyard
Vevay Crescent
Community: 2

Loreto Abbey,
Dalkey, Co Dublin
Tel 01-2804331/2804416
Leader: Sr Brede Quirke
Community: 10
Primary and secondary schools;
pastoral work

Teach Muire, Leslie Avenue,
Dalkey, Co Dublin
Tel 01-2800495
Leader: Sr Brede Quirke
Community: 3
Educational and pastoral work

Loreto Community,
Balbriggan, Co Dublin
Tel 01-8412796
Team Leader: Sr Mary Jo Corcoran
Community: 12
Secondary school; pastoral work

Loreto Education Trust,
Foxrock, Dublin 18
Tel 01-2899956
Education and offices

Loreto,
13 Carrigmore Place, City West,
Saggart, Co Dublin
Tel/Fax 01-4589918
Also, 15 Carrigmore Place, City West,
Saggart, Co Dublin
Tel 01-4580780

Loreto, 22 Brookdale Drive,
River Valley, Swords,
Co Dublin
Community: 5
Tel 01-8405982
Secondary School, River Valley, Swords
Social and pastoral work

oreto,
Greenville Road, Blackrock,
Co Dublin
Tel 01-2843171
Leader: Sr Brede Quirke
Community: 1
Education, social and pastoral work

Loreto, 20 Herberton Park,
Rialto, Dublin 8
Tel 01-4535048
Email lorialto@hotmail.com
Community: 3
Social and pastoral work

65 Sundrive Road,
Dublin 12
Tel 01-4541509
Community: 3
Education and pastoral work

7/8/9/10 Stonepark Orchard,
Stonepark Abbey
Tel 01-4952110/4952111/
4951444/495017
Community: 7
Education and pastoral work

175, 176, 178, 184, 185 Prior's Gate,
Greenhills Road, Tallaght, Dublin 24

9, 11, 50, 52 New Bancrost Hall,
Tallaght Main Street, Dublin 24

10 Loreto, Crescent, Rathfarnham,
Dublin 14

21, 30, 33 The Croft,
Parc na Silla Avenue, Loughlinstown,
Dublin 18

MARIE AUXILIATRICE SISTERS
Florence Street,
Portobello, Dublin 8
Tel 01-4537622
Contact Person: Sr Margaret McDermott
Email
margaret.mcdermott54@gmail.com
Community: 4
Spiritual direction, social outreach,
counselling

Marie Auxiliatrice Sisters
30 Upper Glenageary Road,
Dun Laoghaire, Co Dublin
Tel 01-2857389
Contact Person: Sr Mary O'Dea
Email maryodea6@gmail.com
Community: 4
Spiritual direction, social outreach,
education

MARIST SISTERS
Provincialate, 51 Kenilworth Square,
Rathgar, Dublin 6
Tel 01-4972196
Email secirlmarists@gmail.com
Leader – Ireland: Sr Miriam McManus
Community: 2

10 Cambridge Terrace,
Dartmouth Square, Dublin 6
Tel 01-6605332
Email maristcam22@gmail.com
Community: 4
Justice, education, social work

Sundrive Road,
Crumlin, Dublin 12
Tel 01-4540778
Email maristsundrive@gmail.com
Community Leader: Sr Ann Wrynn
Community: 10
Primary school
Social work, youth work, adult
education, Marist laity

21 Dunlin House,
Red Court Oak, Seafield Road East,
Clontarf, Dublin 3

MEDICAL MISSIONARIES OF MARY
Congregational Centre,
Rosemount, Rosemount Terrace,
Booterstown, Blackrock,
Co Dublin A94 AH63
Tel 01-2882722
Email rcsmmm37@gmail.com

3 Danieli Road, Artane,
Dublin D05 KV91
Tel 01-8316469
Community: 1

Réalt na Mara,
11 Rosemount Terrace,
Booterstown, Co Dublin A94 A7P8
Tel 01-2887180
Email mmmrealtnamara@gmail.com
Community: 3

26 Malahide Road,
Artane, Dublin D05 WK53
Tel 01-8310427
Email mmmartane@gmail.com
Community: 2

33 Templeville Drive
Templeogue, Dublin D6W VR62
Tel 01-4991803
Email mmm.templeogue@upcmail.ie
Community: 1

1 The Grange, Laurel Place,
Terenure Road West, Dublin D6W YI90
Tel 01-4925263
Email mmmterenure@gmail.com
Community: 4

2A St Margaret's Avenue,
Raheny, Dublin D05 E0P6
Tel 01-8324221
Email mmmraheny@mmm37.org
Community: 4

MISSIONARIES OF CHARITY
223 South Circular Road, Dublin 8
Tel 01-4540163
Superior: Sr M. Perpetua (MC)
Community 4
Hostel For men

MISSIONARY FRANCISCAN SISTERS OF THE IMMACULATE CONCEPTION
Assisi House, Navan Road, Dublin 7
Tel 01-8682216
Community: 3
Contact: Sr Philomena Conroy

MISSIONARY SISTERS OF THE HOLY ROSARY
Generalate, 23 Cross Avenue,
Blackrock, Co Dublin
Tel 01-2881708/9 Fax 01-2836308
Email mshrgen@indigo.ie
Superior General: Sr Franca Onyibor
Community: 8

Regional Administration,
41 Westpark, Artane, Dublin 5
Tel 01-8510010 Fax 01-8187494
Email mshrreg@eircom.net
Regional Superior: Sr Paula Molloy
Community: 4

Holy Rosary Convent,
Brookville, Westpark, Artane, Dublin 5
Tel 01-8510002
Superior: Sr Maura Garry
House for sisters on leave from mission.
Pastoral, health care
Community: 40

Holy Rosary Convent,
48 Temple Road, Dartry, Dublin 6
Tel 01-4971918/4971094
Superiors: Sr Conchita McDonnell and
Sr Colette McCann
Pastoral, education, care of the elderly
Community: 22

Holy Rosary Sisters,
Glankeen, 9 Richmond Avenue South,
Dartry, Dublin 6
Tel 01-4977277
Pastoral, health care, care of elderly
Community: 7

Holy Rosary Sisters,
2 Grange Abbey Cresent, Baldoyle,
Dublin 13
Tel 01-8476219
Pastoral, health care, education
Community: 3

Holy Rosary Sisters,
72 Grange Park, Baldoyle, Dublin 13
Tel 01-8390291
Regional admin., counselling
Community: 1

MISSIONARY SISTERS OF ST COLUMBAN
St Columban's Convent,
Magheramore, Wicklow
Tel 0404-67348
Email mhreception@mssc.ie
Community Leaders: Sr Anne Ryan/
Sr Margaret Murphy
Community: 55
Motherhouse, congregational nursing
home for sick and retired members

St Agnes Road,
Crumlin, Dublin 12
Tel 01-4555435
Community: 4
Mission awareness

Apt C14, Killarney Court,
Killarney Street, Dublin 1
Tel 01-6577339
Community: 1
Parish ministry, work with migrants

Columban Sisters,
Parish House No. 1,
Holy Spirit Parish, Silloge,
Ballymun, Dublin 11
Tel 01-8423696
Community: 3

Columban Sisters,
5/6 Grange Crescent, off Pottery Road,
Dun Laoghaire, Co Dublin
Tel 01-2853961
Community: 3

Contact Person for above five houses
Sr Nora Wiseman
Columban Sisters,
5/6 Grange Crescent, off Pottery Road,
Dun Laoghaire, Co Dublin
Tel 01-2853961

MISSIONARY SISTERS OF ST PETER CLAVER
81 Bushy Park Road,
Terenure, Dublin D06 V6Y9
Tel 01-4909360
Community: 4
Email missiondublin@stpeterclaver.ie
Dedicated to the Service of the
Missionary Church

MISSIONARY SISTERS SERVANTS OF THE HOLY SPIRIT
143 Philipsburgh Avenue,
Fairview, Dublin D03 HF80
Tel 01-8369383
Email sspsfairview1@gmail.com
Community Leader: Sr Joan Quirke
Community: 5

CONGREGATION OF OUR LADY OF THE MISSIONS
Notre Dame Convent,
Upper Churchtown Road,
Leading to Sweetmount Avenue,
Dublin D14 N8E8
Tel 01-2983306
Community Leader
Sr Elizabeth Hartigan
Tel 0044-(0)-833798969
Email hartiganliz8@gmail.com
Community: 7
Retired sisters

Congregation of Our Lady of the
Missions
5 Griffeen Glen Park,
Griffeen Valley, Lucan South,
Co Dublin K78 XP70
Tel 01-6219088
Community: 2
Retired sister

OUR LADY OF THE CENACLE
Contact: Helen Grealy
Email helenbgrealy@gmail.com

POOR CLARES
St Damian's,
3A Simmonscourt Road,
Ballsbridge, Dublin D04 P8A0
Fax 01-6685464
Email pccdamians@mac.com
Website www.pccdamians.ie
Abbess/Contact: Sr Mary Brigid Haran
Community: 8
Contemplatives
Rosary and Evening Prayer on Sundays at
4 pm
First Fridays, Evening Prayer and
Benediction at 4.30 pm

POOR SERVANTS OF THE MOTHER OF GOD
St Mary's Convent, Manor House,
Raheny, Dublin 5
Tel/Fax 01-8317626

St Mary's Convent, Manor House,
Raheny, Dublin 5
Tel 01-8313652 Fax 01-8313299
Community: 10
Education, pastoral ministry

Maryfield Convent, Chapelizod,
Dublin 20
Tel 01-6264684/6265402
Fax 01-6233673
Community: 17
Home for elderly

216 Tonlegee Road,
Dublin 5
Tel 01-8478566
Community: 3
Care of the elderly, pastoral ministry

Croí Mhuire,
120 Lucan Road,
Chapelizod, Dublin 20
Fax/Tel 01-6233734
Community: 2
Elderly and pastoral work

39 Glenayle Road, Dublin 5
Tel 01-8770700
Community: 2
Pastoral Ministry

CONGREGATION OF THE SISTERS OF NAZARETH
Nazareth House,
Malahide Road, Dublin 3
Tel 01-8338205
Superior: Sr Bernadette O'Gorman
Email
superior.dublin@sistersofnazareth.com
Community: 12
Regional Superior: Sr Patricia Enright
Email regional.ie@nazarethcare.com
Tel 01-8338205
Home for elderly. Beds: 120

PRESENTATION SISTERS
Mission House,
Lucan, Co Dublin K78 A6Y5
Tel 01-6280305
Community: 1
Home for missionaries on leave
Mission Office Tel/Fax 01-6282467
Email lucan@pbvm.org

North-East Province:
George's Hill, Dublin D07 AE39
Tel 01-8746914
Community: 8
School, safeguarding, adult education,
marriage tribunal, postulator for cause
of Nano Nagle and pastoral ministry

2/3 Castlebridge Estate,
Maynooth, Co Kildare W23 D6X4
Tel 01-6289952
Community: 5
Pastoral ministry and province finance

Allianz (ⅲ)

5 Anley Court, Esker Lane, Lucan,
Dublin K78 ND89
el 01-6289952
ommunity: 1

5 Anley Court, Esker Lane, Lucan,
Dublin K78 ED80
ommunity: 1
ovince leadership and administration

7 Castlegate Way,
damstown, Lucan,
Dublin K78 Y598
ommunity: 1

Fortlawn Drive, Mountview,
anchardstown, Dublin D15 YW7Y
l 01-8119430
ommunity: 3
hool, prison and pastoral work

Wainsfort Drive,
renure, Dublin D6W XE40
l 01-4929588
ommunity: 2
ovince leadership and administration

ovincialate of NE Province at:
orn Centre Warrenmount,
ackpitts, Dublin D08 W2X8
l 01-4166010 Fax 01-4165787
nail secretary@presprone.com

esentation Sisters,
ondalkin, Dublin D22 NF67
l 01-4592656
ommunity: 9
hool, parish and pastoral work

esentation Sisters,
arrenmount, Dublin D08 H92R
l 01-4113831
ommunity: 14
esentation Primary. Tel 01-4539547
ommunity counselling, education and
ayer ministry and Provincial Leadership

Oliver Bond House,
ublin D08 X2K7
01-6776702
ommunity: 1
ommunity and pastoral work

Brigid's New Road,
ondalkin, Dublin D22 V406
01-4643319
ommunity: 1
son ministry

O'Curry Road, Dublin D08 K1H7
01-4542806
ommunity: 3
ucation and pastoral work

2 The Weavers,
Meath Place, Dublin D08 DF30
Community: 1
Spirituality

27 Mayfield Park,
Watery Lane, Dublin D22 DA21
Tel 01-4037316
Community: 1
Education and pastoral work

105 Tyrconnell Place,
Inchicore, Dublin D08 DA0P
Community: 1
Chaplaincy 3rd Level

9A Kilmahuddrick Walk,
Clondalkin, Dublin D22 RX39
Tel 01-4576441
Community: 2
Parish and pastoral work

9B Kilmahuddrick Walk,
Clondalkin, Dublin D22 RX39
Community: 1

REDEMPTORISTINES
Monastery of St Alphonsus,
St Alphonsus Road, Dublin D09 HN53
Tel 01-8305723 Fax 01-8309129
Superior: Sr Gabrielle & Sr Lucy
Community: 14
Contemplatives

RELIGIOUS OF CHRISTIAN EDUCATION
Generalate Office,
3 Bushy Park House,
Templeogue Road, Dublin 6W
Tel 01-4909912
Congregational Leader: Sr Cara Nagle
Email cara.nagle@gmail.com

Community Residence,
4/5 Bushy Park House,
Templeogue Road, Dublin 6W
Tel 01-4905516

Our Lady's School,
Templeogue Road, Dublin 6W
Secondary School. Tel 01-4903241
Principal: Ms Marguerite Gorby

RELIGIOUS OF SACRED HEART OF MARY
13/14 Huntstown Wood,
Huntstown, Dublin D15 XT9X
Tel 01-8223566
Community: 2
Spiritual direction, pastoral ministry,
education

70 Upper Drumcondra Road, Dublin 9
Tel 01-8379898
Community: 3 plus 1 attached
Pastoral ministry, prison, refugees

72 Upper Drumcondra Road, Dublin 9
Tel 01-8368331
Community: 1 plus 1 attached
Spiritual direction, ministry in local area

RELIGIOUS SISTERS OF CHARITY
Generalate, Caritas,
15 Gilford Road, Sandymount,
Dublin 4
Tel 01-2697833/2697935

Mary Aikenhead Heritage Centre,
Our Lady's Mount, Harold's Cross,
Dublin 6W
Tel 01-4910041

Office of the Cause,
Sisters of Charity, St Mary's,
Merrion Road, Dublin 4
Tel 086-4680427

Overseas and Development Office,
Sisters of Charity, 15 Gilford Road,
Sandymount, Dublin 4
Tel 01-2605788

Provincialate, Provincial House,
Our Lady's Mount, Harold's Cross,
Dublin D6W W934
Tel 01-4973177

Marmion House, St Mary's,
185 Merrion Road, Dublin D04 P2T8
Tel 01-2027223
Various Apostolic Ministries

St Anne's, 29 Thornville Drive,
Kilbarrack East, Dublin D05 C3V5
Tel 01-8321112/8321114
Various Apostolic Ministries

Stanhope Street Convent,
Manor Street, Dublin D07 T1K2
Tel 01-6779183
Various Apostolic Ministries

Stanhope Lodge,
Stanhope Green, Dublin D07 DH72
Tel 01-6704016
Various Apostolic Ministries

St Monica's,
28/38 Belvedere Place,
Dublin D01 EY21
Tel (Community) 01-8552317
Various Apostolic Ministries

Naomh Bríd Community,
28/38 Belvedere Place,
Dublin D01 EY21
Tel 01-8557647
Various Apostolic Ministries

Our Lady of the Nativity,
Lakelands, Sandymount,
Dublin D04 KP40
Tel 01-2692076/2603362
Various Apostolic Ministries

St Mary's, Donnybrook,
Dublin D04 P7D0
Tel 01-2600315/2600818
Various Apostolic Ministries

Mary Aikenhead House, St Mary's,
Donnybrook, Dublin 4
Tel 01-2693258
Various Apostolic Ministries

Sisters of Charity,
Our Lady's Mount, Harold's Cross,
Dublin D6W W281
Ard Mhuire Community
Tel 01-4961488
Maranatha Community D6W HN76
Tel 01-4961423
Shandon community
Tel 01-4982614

4 Telford House, St Mary's,
Merrion Road, Dublin D04 F9V3
Tel 01-2605495
Various Apostolic Ministries

Stella Maris Convent,
Baily, Co Dublin D13 YK71
Tel 01-8322228 Fax 01-8063469
Various Apostolic Ministries

Our Lady Queen of Ireland,
Walkinstown, Dublin 12
Tel 01-4503491
Various Apostolic Ministries

Sisters of Charity,
St Laurence Place East,
Seville Place, Dublin D01 E5Y9
Tel 01-8744179
Various Apostolic Ministries

Sisters of Charity,
1 Temple Street, Dublin D01 XD99
Tel 01-8745778/8745779

26 Park Avenue,
Sandymount, Dublin 4
Tel 01-2604659
Various Apostolic Ministries

28 Park Avenue,
Sandymount, Dublin 4
Tel 01-2604654
Various Apostolic Ministries

Providence,
St Mary's, Merrion Road,
Dublin D04 H1F2
Tel 01-2693450
Various Apostolic Ministries

Shalom,
St Mary's, Merrion Road,
Dublin D04 A5V0
Tel 01-2602775
Various Apostolic Ministries

SACRED HEART SOCIETY
Provincial Office,
76 Home Farm Road,
Drumcondra, Dublin D09 R903
Tel 01-8375412 Fax 01-8375542
Canonical Leader: Sr Dairne McHenry
Email d.mchenry@rscjirs.org
Executive Officer: Orla O'Hanlon
Email executive@rscjirs.org
Provincial Secretary: Helen Mulholland
Email provsec@rscjirs.org

37 Church Road,
East Wall, Dublin D03 CP26
Tel 01-2602533
Provincial Administration, Voluntary
work

1 Dunlin House, Redcourt Oaks,
Seafield Road East, Clontarf,
Dublin D03 TX47
Tel 01-8540450
Educational trusteeships and voluntary
work

29 Gilford Pines, Gilford Road,
Sandymount, Dublin D04 DX67
Tel 01-2304094
Historical research

Cedar House Nursing Home,
35 Mount Anville Park,
Dublin D14 F240
Tel 01-2831024/5 Fax 01-2831348
Email cedarhousejim@gmail.com

36 Mount Anville Park,
Dublin D14 X314
Tel 01-2880739
Pastoral ministry and Cedar House

37 Mount Anville Park,
Dublin D14 NX03
38 Mount Anville Park,
Dublin D14 AC98
Tel 01-2880708
Work in parish and community service

96 Mount Anville Wood,
Dublin D14 DD30
Tel 01-2880786
Work in Mount Anville School, spiritual
ministry

201 Lower Kilmacud Road,
Blackrock, Co Dublin A94 FC90
Tel 01-2834832 Fax 01-2104825
Spiritual and parish ministry

Schools
Mount Anville Primary School,
Lower Kilmacud Road
Tel 01-2831138 Fax 01-2836395

Mount Anville Secondary School
Mount Anville House
Tel 01-2885313/4 Fax 01-2832373

Mount Anville Junior and Montessori
School, Mount Anville House
Tel 01-2885313/4 Fax 01-2832373

SACRED HEARTS OF JESUS AND MARY (PICPUS) SISTERS
Delegation House,
11 Northbrook Road,
Ranelagh, Dublin D06 Y962
Tel 01-4974831 (Community)
Community: 4
Contact: Sr Aileen Kennedy (SSCC)
Email aileenkennedyssc@hotmail.com

Aymer House, 11 Northbrook Lane,
Ranelagh, Dublin 6
Tel 01-4975614
Community: 5

SALESIAN SISTERS OF ST JOHN BOSCO
Provincialate,
203 Lower Kilmacud Road,
Stillorgan, Co Dublin
Tel 01-2985188
Provincial Superior: Sr Bridget O'Conne
Convent Tel 01-2985908
Superior: Sr Brid Shanahan
Community: 4
Parish ministry, provincial administratic

38–40 Morehampton Road,
Donnybrook, Dublin 4
Tel 01-6684643
Community: 5
Mission promotion, Hospital ministry,
facilitators' training course for youth
retreats, provincial administration

91-95 Ashwood Road, Bawnoge,
Clondalkin, Dublin 22
Tel 01-4571792
Contact person: Sr Annette Murtagh
Community: 5
Teaching and related activities

36 Glenties Park,
Finglas South, Dublin 11
Tel 01-8345777
Superior: Sr Elizabeth Lawler
Community: 3
Youth and parish work, mission
promotion

Hazelwood Crescent,
eenpark, Clondalkin,
blin 22
01-4123928
ntact person: Sr Catherine Kelly
mmunity: 4
hool chaplaincy, Adult Education

STERS OF OUR LADY OF APOSTLES
b Shellbourne Road,
llsbridge, Dublin D04 T021
01-6685796
ail olasrsdublin@gmail.com
mmunity: 6

STERS OF ST CLARE
Clare's Convent,
01-4995100
Harold's Cross Road, Dublin 6W
ntact: Sr Anne Kelly
ail annedkelly@yahoo.com
mmunity: 12
mary School

ters of St Clare, 10 Maple Green,
urel Lodge, Dublin 15
01-8213967
mmunity: 3

TERS OF ST JOHN OF GOD
St David's Wood,
alahide Road,
tane, Dublin 5
: 01 8329798

TERS OF ST JOSEPH OF CHAMBERY
Joseph's Convent,
ringdale Road,
heny, Dublin 5
01-8774985
erior: Sr Marian Connor (CSJ)
ail marianconnor91@gmail.com
gional Superior
Joan Margaret Kelly (CSJ)
ail joanmkelyl1@yahoo.fr
mmunity: 7
re of the sick and pastoral activity

TERS OF ST JOSEPH OF CLUNY
ount Sackville Convent,
apelizod, Dublin 20
01-8213134
ail provirlgb@sjc.ie
ebsite www.sjc.ie
ovincial Superior: Sr Maeve Guinan
01-8213134
erior: Sr Ignatius Davis
01-8213134
mmunity: 32
mary school; secondary day school;
rsing home

St Joseph of Cluny Convent,
Ballinclea Road, Killiney, Co Dublin
Tel 01-2851038
Superior: Sr Mary Shiels
Community: 4
Secondary schools

Parslickstown Drive,
Mulhuddart, Dublin 15
Tel 01-8217339
Superior: Sr Rowena Galvin
Community: 3
Pastoral ministry

ST JOSEPH OF THE SACRED HEART SISTERS
St Joseph's Convent,
6 Farmleigh Avenue,
Stillorgan, Co Dublin
Tel 01-2781228
Email farmleigh2017@gmail.com
Sr Eileen Kirby

Sisters of St Joseph of the Sacred Heart,
25 Nutley Square,
Donnybrook, Dublin 4
Tel 01-2602306
Sr Mary Kirrane

Sisters of St Joseph,
11 The Courtyard, Vevay Crescent,
Bray, Co Wicklow
Tel 01-2761288
Sr Briege Buckley

Sisters of St Joseph,
3 Carrigalea, Queens Park,
Monkstown, Co Dublin
Sr Clare Ahern

ST LOUIS SISTERS
St Louis Generalate,
3 Beech Court, Ballinclea Road,
Killiney, Dublin
Tel 01-2350304/2350309 Fax 01-2350345
Institute Leader: Sr Patricia Ojo

St Louis Convent,
Charleville Road, Dublin 6
Tel 01-4975467
Community: 15

7 Grosvenor Road,
Rathgar, Dublin 6
Tel 01-4965485
Community: 6
Varied apostolates

130 Beaufort Downs,
Rathfarnham, Dublin 16
Tel 01-4934194
Community: 2
Varied apostolates

17 Kilclare Crescent, Jobstown,
Tallaght, Dublin 24
Tel 01-4526344
Community: 1
Education

49 Moynihan Court,
Main Road, Tallaght Village,
Dublin 24
Tel 01-4628386
Community: 5
Varied apostolates

St Genevieve's Community
1 Charleville Road, Rathmines,
Dublin 6
Tel 01-4914752
Email stgenevievessl@gmail.com
Community: 7

ST PAUL DE CHARTRES SISTERS
6-8 Garville Avenue,
Rathgar, Dublin 6
Tel 01-4972366
Email fabiolapak@gmail.com
Regional Superior: Sr Fabiola Pak
Community: 3
Pastoral care service in Orwell Queen of
Peace and Orwell Healthcare

URSULINES
Provincialate, 17 Trimleston Drive,
Booterstown, Co Dublin
Tel 01-2693503
Provincial: Sr Anne Harte Barry
Community: 2

Ursuline Sisters,
3 Cedermount, St Brigid's Church Road,
Stillorgan, Co Dublin
Community: 1
Pastoral ministry

St Ursula's, Sandyford, Dublin 18
Tel 01-2956881
Community: 3
Pastoral ministry

URSULINES OF JESUS
26 The Drive, Seatown Park,
Swords, Co Dublin
Tel 01-8404323
Email ujswords@eircom.net
Contact Person: Sr Mary McLoughney
Email marymcloughney45@gmail.com
Community: 3
Parish ministry, volunteer with Spirasi
Befriending service.

EDUCATIONAL INSTITUTIONS

Colaiste Mhuire Marino
President: Teresa O'Doherty
Chaplain: Ms Lily Barry

Marino Institute of Education
Griffith Avenue, Dublin 9
Tel 01-8057700

St Patrick's College
Maynooth, Co Kildare
Tel 01-7083958 Fax 01-7083959
President: Very Rev Michael Mullaney DD
(See Seminaries and Houses of Study section)

EDUCATIONAL TRUSTS

Association of Patrons and Trustees of Catholic Schools (APTCS)
Columba House, Maynooth, Co Kildare
Tel 087-0509227
Email ceo@aptcs.ie
CEO: Dr Eilis Humphreys

The Edmund Rice Schools Trust
Meadow Vale, Clonkeen Road,
Blackrock, Co Dublin
Tel 01-2897511 Fax 01-2897540
Email reception@erst.ie
CEO: Gerry Bennett

LE CHÉILE SCHOOLS TRUST
Le Chéile Education Centre,
Bushy Park House, Templeogue Road,
Dublin D6W EH51
Tel 01-5380104
Email admin@lecheiletrust.ie
www.lecheiletrust.ie
CEO: Marie Therese Kilmartin
Tel 087-2759345
Ethos Development Leadership Officer
Claire Kilroy

CEIST
Ceist Education Office, Dublin Road,
Kildare Town, Co Kildare
Tel 01-6510350 Fax 01-6510180
Email info@ceist.ie
CEO: Gerry McGuill
Tel 01-6510350

Spiritan Education Trust
Des Places House, Kimmage Manor,
Whitehall Road, Kimmage, Dublin 12
Tel 01-4997610
Email reception@desplaces.ie

Loreto Education Trust
Springfield Park, Foxrock, Loreto
Education Centre
Tel 01-2899956
Director: Vacant
Email info@loretoeducationcentre.ie

CHARITABLE AND OTHER SOCIETIES

Travellers Family Care

Derralossary House
Roundwood, Co Wicklow
Tel 01-2818355
Residential home for girls
Ballyowen Meadows
Tel 01-6235735
Exchange House Youth Service
61 Great Strand Street, Dublin 1
Tel 01-4546488
Training and employment programme and youth work

Hostels

Don Bosco House
57 Lower Drumcondra Road, Dublin 9
Tel 01-8360696
Salesian hostel for homeless boys.
Priest in Charge: Rev V. Collier (SDB)
Homeless Girls' Hostel
Sherrard House,
19 Upper Sherrard Street, Dublin 1
Tel 01-8743742

Iveagh Hostel
Bride Road, Dublin 8
Tel 01-4540182

Morning Star Hostel
Morning Star Avenue,
Brunswick Street, Dublin 7
Tel 01-8723401

Regina Coeli Hostel
Morning Star Avenue,
Brunswick Street, Dublin 7
Tel 01-8723142

St Vincent de Paul Night Shelter
Back Lane, Dublin 8
Tel 01-4542181

Housing

Catholic Housing Aid Society (CHAS)
Fr Scully House,
Middle Gardiner Street, Dublin 1
Tel 01-8741020
Flats for the aged

Threshold
21 Stoneybatter, Dublin 7
Tel 01-6353600/6786090
Website www.threshold.ie

Other

Cuan Mhuire
Athy, Co Kildare
Tel 059-8631493 Fax 059-8638765
Rehabilitation centre for alcoholics and those with allied problems

Our Lady's Choral Society
(The Archdiocesan Choir)
Director: Rev Paul Ward
Hon Secretary: Tom Gaynor

Society of St Vincent de Paul
Dublin Office,
91-92 Sean McDermott Street, Dublin 1
Tel 01-8550022 Fax 01-8559168

Fear not.
I am with you.

DIVINE MASTER CENTRE

Dedicated as a place of hospitality and welcome
Retreat spaces to rest and encounter the Eucharistic Jesus in the spirit of Bethany

LITURGICAL CENTRE

For liturgical and religious items for homes, churches, chapels, and prayer spaces.
Gifts and handmade cards for religious and other special occasions.

Ministry of prayer, support and service to priests and those called to serve others in the Church.

ATHLONE
8 Castle Street, Athlone
Co. Westmeath
T: 09064 92278

DUBLIN
Newtownpark Avenue
White's Cross, Blackrock
Co. Dublin A94 V670
T: 01 2886414 • E: dublin@pddm.org
www.pddm.ie

Parish Resource for First Holy Communion

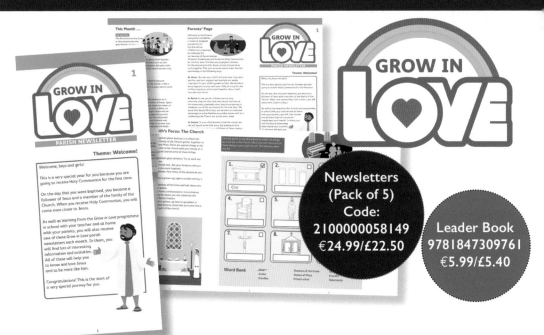

GROW IN LOVE

Newsletters
(Pack of 5)
Code:
2100000058149
€24.99/£22.50

Leader Book
9781847309761
€5.99/£5.40

IN THE PARISH
Connecting Home, School and Parish Communities

The Grow in Love in the Parish programme aims to help parents and guardians to link in with what their child is learning at school during First Communion year. It also links in with the Liturgical Year and builds awareness among the parish community about the preparation for First Communion.

There are three main elements:

1.   A series of liturgically based initiatives
These initiatives, which take place during Sunday Mass, help families with young children to be more involved in the celebration of the Eucharist, both in the year of sacramental preparation and beyond, and to be more connected to their parish community.

2.   A series of newsletters
The newsletters are designed to run in parallel with the school-based Grow in Love programme, and

to reinforce the concepts therein. It is envisaged that they would be distributed on a monthly basis to families. Ideally, this should be done in a parish context – for example, at a monthly Family Mass. However, when that's not possible they can be sent to families directly from the Parish.

3.   Speaking notes
Each month, speaking notes are offered for the priest, together with a sample Prayer of the Faithful. The speaking notes draw attention to the key features of the newsletter for that particular month, and the Prayer of the Faithful picks up on the theme for that month.

We hope these newsletters will be a source of information and inspiration to parents/guardians, and will serve to strengthen the engagement of children and their families in the life of the Church.

For further information email: growinlove@veritas.ie

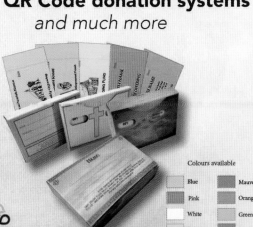

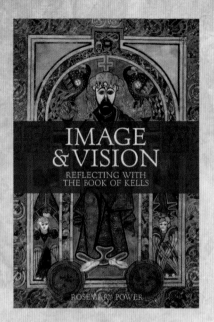

Image & Vision

Reflecting with the Book of Kells

Rosemary Power

978 1 80097 008 3

€24.99/£22.50

About the book

The Book of Kells was originally prepared as a devotional and liturgical work. *Image & Vision: Reflecting with the Book of Kells* explores the intricate relationship between the text, image and vision, and the scriptural texts that underpin them.

Concentrating on twelve of the magnificent illuminations in the Book of Kells, this beautiful book provides clear and accessible guidelines on ways to reflect and meditate on these illuminations and the scripture as a whole. The book contains original research, especially on some of the lesser-known illuminations, and is filled with fascinating analysis of this ancient and sacred work.

In *Image & Vision: Reflecting with the Book of Kells*, Rosemary Power shows how we can use the beauty, humour and insight of this ancient devotional work today to deepen our understanding of scripture and society.

About the author

Rosemary Power gives illustrated talks on the imagery of the Book of Kells, for audiences of all ages and backgrounds. An established writer, her previous publications include *The Celtic Quest* (Columba Press, 2010) and *The Story of Iona: Columban and Medieval Sites and Spirituality* (Canterbury Press, 2013).

ARCHDIOCESE OF CASHEL AND EMLY

PATRON OF THE ARCHDIOCESE
ST AILBE, 12 SEPTEMBER

SUFFRAGEN SEES: CLOYNE, CORK AND ROSS, KERRY, KILLALOE,
LIMERICK, WATERFORD AND LISMORE

INCLUDES MOST OF COUNTY TIPPERARY AND PARTS OF COUNTY LIMERICK

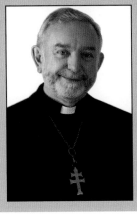

Most Rev Kieran O'Reilly (SMA) DD
Archbishop of Cashel and Emly
born 1952; ordained priest 17
June 1978; ordained Bishop of
Killaloe 29 August 2010;
Appointed Archbishop of Cashel
and Emly 22 November 2014

Residence: Archbishop's House,
Thurles, Co Tipperary E41 NY92
Tel 0504-21512
Email office@cashel-emly.ie
Website www.cashel-emly.ie

The Metropolitan Archdiocese of Cashel and Emly in mid-western Ireland is in the province of Munster. The then separate dioceses of Cashel and Emly were established in 1111 by the Synod of Rathbreasail. Cashel diocese was promoted to the status of a Metropolitan province in 1152 at the Synod of Kells. Emly diocese was formally joined to Cashel in 1718.

CATHEDRAL OF THE ASSUMPTION, THURLES

The Cathedral of the Assumption stands on the site of earlier chapels. The first church on this site was part of the Carmelite Priory, which dates from the early fourteenth century.

Some time before 1730 George Mathew, Catholic proprietor of the Thurles Estate, built a chapel for the Catholics of Thurles beside the ruins of the Carmelite Priory. It was known as the Mathew Chapel. In 1810 Archbishop Bray consecrated the new 'Big Chapel', which was more spacious and ornate than its humble predecessor.

Soon after his appointment as archbishop in 1857, Dr Patrick Leahy revealed his plan to replace the Big Chapel with 'a cathedral worthy of the archdiocese'. Building commenced in 1865, and the impressive Romanesque cathedral, with its façade modelled on that of Pisa, was consecrated by Archbishop Croke on 21 June 1879. The architect was J. J. McCarthy. Barry McMullen was the main builder, and J. C. Ashlin

was responsible for the enclosing walls, railing and much of the finished work.

The cathedral has many beautiful features, including an impressive rose window, a free-standing baptistry and a magnificent altar. The prize possession of the cathedral is its exquisite tabernacle, the work of Giacomo dello Porta (1537–1602), a pupil of Michelangelo. This tabernacle, which belonged to the Gesú (Jesuit) Church in Rome, was purchased

by Archbishop Leahy and transported to Thurles.

The cathedral was extensively renovated and the sanctuary sympathetically remodelled on the occasion of its first centenary in 1979.

The most recent extensive conservation and renewal of the Cathedral, during 2001–2003, has restored the building to its original splendour.

Most Rev Dermot Clifford PhD, DD
Archbishop Emeritus of Cashel and Emly;
born 1939; ordained priest 22 February
1964; ordained Coadjutor Archbishop
9 March 1986; installed Archbishop of
Cashel and Emly 12 September 1988;
acted as Apostolic Administrator of
Cloyne, March 2009–January 2013;
Retired 22 November 2014
Residence: The Green, Holycross,
Thurles, Co Tipperary
Tel 0504-43802

CHAPTER

Dean
Rt Rev Mgr Christy O'Dwyer
Archdeacon
Venerable Eugene Everard
Chancellor: Vacant
Precentor: Vacant
Treasurer: Vacant
Penitentiary
Very Rev Canon Conor Ryan, Hospital
Theologian
Very Rev Canon Liam McNamara,
Prebendaries
Newchapel
Very Rev Canon Thomas J. Ryan, Murroe
Lattin: Vacant
Killennellick: Vacant

ADMINISTRATION

College of Consultors
Rt Rev Mgr Christy O'Dwyer AP, VG
Venerable Archdeacon Eugene Everard
PP, VG
Very Rev Nicholas J. Irwin PP
Rev Dr Michael Mullaney CC
Very Rev Joe Egan PP
Very Rev Thomas Fogerty PP

Vicars General
Rt Rev Mgr Christy O'Dwyer AP, VG
Venerable Archdeacon Eugene Everard
PP, VG

Vicars Forane
Very Rev Canon Conor Ryan
Very Rev James O'Donnell
Very Rev Canon Thomas F. Breen
Very Rev Canon John O'Neill

Diocesan Finance Committee
Archbishop Kieran O'Reilly
Rt Rev Mgr Christy O'Dwyer
Venerable Archdeacon Eugene Everard
Very Rev Nicholas J. Irwin
Very Rev Thomas Fogarty
Mr Owen Smyth
Mrs Mary Fitzgibbon
Ms Kathleen Burke

Finance Project Manager
Ms Arlene Moore
Archbishop's House, Thurles
Tel 0504-21512

Finance Office
Ms Martha Fitzpatrick
Tel 0504-21512

Diocesan Archivist
Rt Rev Mgr Christy O'Dwyer AP, VG
Moyne, Thurles, Co Tipperary
Tel 0504-34959

Diocesan Secretary/Chancellor
Very Rev Nicholas J. Irwin PP
Archbishop's House,
Thurles, Co Tipperary
Tel 0504-21512

CATECHETICS EDUCATION

Adult Religious Education
Very Rev Thomas Dunne PP
Parochial House, Liscreagh,
Murroe, Co Limerick V94 E8CP
Tel 083-4854776

Catechetics
Director: Very Rev Pat Coffey PP
Golden, Co Tipperary
Tel 062-72146
Assistant Director
Very Rev Michael Kennedy PP
The Parochial House,
Lattin, Co Tipperary
Tel 087-4147229

**Boards of Management of Primary
Schools**
Education Secretary
Very Rev John O'Keeffe PP
Birdhill, Killaloe, Co Tipperary
Tel 061-379172/087-2421678

St Senan's Education Office
Diocesan Centre,
St Munchin's, Corbally, Limerick
Tel 061-347777

PASTORAL

ACCORD
Accord House, Cathedral Street,
Thurles, Co Tipperary
Tel 0504-22279
Diocesan Director
Very Rev Tomás O'Connell PP
Tel 087-6482544

Adoption Society
Director: Rev Celsus Tierney PP
Holy Cross Abbey, Holy Cross,
Thurles, Co Tipperary
Tel 0504-43118

Communications
Very Rev Joseph Tynan PP
Parochial House, Kilteely, Co Limerick
Tel 061-384213/087-2225445
Email joetynan3@gmail.com

Director of Safeguarding
Ms Cleo Yeats
Tel 087-3553024
Email safeguarding@cashel-emly.ie

Ecumenism
Archbishop's House,
Thurles, Co Tipperary
Tel 0504-21512

Emigrant Commission
Vacant

Marriage Tribunal
(See Marriage Tribunals section.)

Pastoral Planning and Development
Diocesan Director
Ms Katherine Dullaghan
Assistant: Ms Sadie Moloney
Email pastoral.office@cashel-emly.ie

Pilgrimages
Director: Very Rev James Donnelly PP
Doon, Co Limerick
Tel 061-380165

Pioneer Total Abstinence Association
Diocesan Director
Vacant

Travellers
Chaplain
Very Rev Daniel O'Gorman PP
The Parochial House,
Mullinahone, Co Tipperary
Tel 052-9153152

Trócaire
Diocesan Director
Very Rev Dominic Meehan PP
(Loughmore)
Church Avenue,
Templemore, Co Tipperary
Tel 0504-31492

Vocations
Director: Rev Joseph Walsh CC
Thurles, Co Tipperary
Tel 0504-22229
Email vocations@cashel-emly,ie

Missio Ireland
Diocesan Director
Very Rev Celsus Tierney PP
The Parochial House, Holycross,
Thurles, Co Tipperary
Tel 0504-43124

PARISHES

Mensal parishes are listed first. Other parishes follow alphabetically. Church titulars are in italic.

THURLES, CATHEDRAL OF THE ASSUMPTION

Very Rev James Purcell PP
Rev Joseph Walsh CC
Cathedral Presbytery, Thurles,
Co Tipperary
Tel 0504-22229/22779

THURLES, SS JOSEPH AND BRIGID

Rev Vincent Stapleton CC
Bóthar na Naomh Presbytery,
Thurles, Co Tipperary
Tel 0504-22042/22688

ANACARTY

St Brigid's, Anacarty
Immaculate Conception, Donohill
Very Rev James Kennedy PP
Anacarty, Co Tipperary
Tel 062-71104

BALLINA

Our Lady and St Lua, Ballina,
Mary, Mother of the Church, Boher
Very Rev Thomas Lanigan-Ryan PP
Ballina, Killaloe, Co Clare
Tel 061-376178
Very Rev Edmond V. O'Rahelly AP
Main Street, Ballina, Co Clare
Tel 087-2262636

BALLINAHINCH

St Joseph's, Ballinahinch,
Sacred Heart, Killoscully
Very Rev James O'Donoghue PP
Ballinahinch, Birdhill, Limerick
Tel 061-781510

BALLINGARRY

Assumption
Very Rev Gerard Quirke PP
Ballingarry, Thurles, Co Tipperary
Tel 052-9154115

BALLYBRICKEN

St Ailbe's, Ballybricken,
Immaculate Heart of Mary, Bohermore
Very Rev James Walton PP
Ballybricken, Grange, Kilmallock,
Co Limerick
Tel 061-351158

BALLYLANDERS

Assumption of BVM
Very Rev Thomas O. Breen PP
Ballylanders, Kilmallock,
Co Limerick
Tel 062-46705

BANSHA AND KILMOYLER

Annunciation, Our Lady of the
Assumption, Kilmoyler
Very Rev Michael Hickey PP
Bansha, Co Tipperary
Tel 062-54132

BOHERLAHAN AND DUALLA

Immaculate Conception, Boherlahan
Our Lady of Fatima, Dualla
Very Rev Joseph Egan PP
Boherlahan, Cashel, Co Tipperary
Tel 0504-41114

BORRISOLEIGH

Sacred Heart, Borrisoleigh
Very Rev Gerard Hennessy PP
Parochial House, Borrisoleigh, Thurles,
Co Tipperary
Tel 0504-51935

CAHERCONLISH

Our Lady, Mother of the Church
Arch. O'Hurley Mem., Caherline
Very Rev Roy Donovan PP
Caherconlish, Co Limerick
Tel 061-450730
Very Rev Patrick Currivan AP
Caherconlish, Co Limerick
Tel 061-351248

CAPPAMORE

St Michael's
Very Rev Richard Browne PP
Cappamore, Co Limerick
Tel 061-381288

CAPPAWHITE

Our Lady of Fatima
Very Rev Tadhg Furlong PP
Cappawhite, Co Tipperary
Tel 062-75427

CASHEL

St John the Baptist, Cashel
St Thomas the Apostle, Rosegreen
Very Rev Enda Brady PP
Bohereenglas, Cashel, Co Tipperary
Tel 062-61127
Rt Rev Mgr James Ryan AP
Bohermore, Cashel, Co Tipperary
Tel 062-61353
Very Rev Pat Burns AP
Bohermore, Cashel, Co Tipperary
Tel 087-2036763

CLERIHAN

St Michael's
Very Rev Peter Brennan PP
Parochial House, Clerihan,
Clonmel, Co Tipperary
Tel 087-2362603

CLONOULTY

Church of St John the Baptist, Clonoulty
Church of Jesus Christ Our Saviour,
Rossmore
Very Rev Thomas Hearne PP
Parochial House, Clonoulty,
Cashel, Co Tipperary
Tel 052-7462810
Very Rev Matthew McGrath AP
Tel 0504-42494

DOON

St Patrick's
Very Rev James Donnelly PP
Doon, Co Limerick
Tel 061-380165

DRANGAN

Immaculate Conception, Visitation,
Cloneen
Very Rev Anthony Lambe PP
Drangan, Thurles, Co Tipperary
Tel 052-9152103

DROM AND INCH

St Mary's, Drom,
St Laurence O'Toole, Inch
Very Rev Martin Murphy PP
Drom, Thurles, Co Tipperary
Tel 0504-51196
Very Rev Thomas Egan *(priest in residence)*
Inch, Bouladuff, Thurles,
Clonmel, Co Tipperary
Tel 086-8199678

EMLY

St Ailbe's
Very Rev Bernie Moloney PP
Emly, Co Tipperary
Tel 062-57111
Very Rev Seamus Rochford AP
Emly, Co Tipperary
Tel 062-57103

FETHARD

Holy Trinity, Fethard
Sacred Heart, Killusty
Very Rev Liam Everard PP
Parochial House, Fethard, Co Tipperary
Tel 052-6131178
Very Rev Canon Thomas F. Breen AP
Fethard, Co Tipperary
Tel 052-6131680

GALBALLY

Christ the King, Galbally
Sacred Heart, Lisvernane
Very Rev Canon John O'Neill PP, VF
Lisvernane, Aherlow,
Co Tipperary
Tel 062-56155
Very Rev Canon Denis Talbot AP
Millbrae Lodge, Newport, Co Tipperary

GOLDEN
Blessed Sacrament, Golden
St Patrick's, Kilfeade
Very Rev Patrick Coffey PP
Golden, Co Tipperary
Tel 062-72146

GORTNAHOE
Sacred Heart, Gortnahoe
SS Patrick & Oliver, Glengoole
Very Rev Nicholas J. Irwin PP
Parochial House, Gortnahoe,
Thurles, Co Tipperary
Tel 056-8834855

HOLY CROSS
Holy Cross Abbey, Holy Cross
St Cataldus, Ballycahill
Very Rev Celsus Tierney PP
Parochial House, Holy Cross Abbey,
Thurles, Co Tipperary
Tel 0504-43124
Rev Michael Mullaney CC
Ballycahill, Thurles, Co Tipperary
Tel 0504-26080

HOSPITAL
St John the Baptist, Hospital
Sacred Heart, Herbertstown
Very Rev Sean Fennelly PP
Barrysfarm, Hospital,
Co Limerick V35 YF53
Tel 061-383565
Very Rev Canon Conor Ryan AP, VF
Castlefarm, Hospital,
Co Limerick V35 X257
Tel 061-383108

KILBEHENNY
St Joseph's, Kilbehenny,
St Patrick's, Anglesboro
Very Rev Richard Kelly PP
Kilbehenny, Mitchelstown, Co Cork
Tel 025-24040

KILCOMMON
St Patrick's, Kilcommon
St Joseph's, Hollyford
Our Lady of the Visitation, Rearcross
Very Rev Daniel Woods PP
Kilcommon, Thurles, Co Limerick
Tel 062-78103
Very Rev Patrick O'Gorman AP
Golden, Co Tipperary
Tel 087-6347773

KILLENAULE
St Mary's, Killenaule
St Joseph the Worker, Moyglass
Very Rev James O'Donnell PP
Killenaule, Co Tipperary
Tel 052-9156244

KILTEELY
SS Patrick & Brigid, Kilteely
St Bridget's, Dromkeen
Very Rev Joseph Tynan PP
Kilteely, Co Limerick
Tel 061-384213

KNOCKAINEY
Our Lady, Knockainey
St Patrick's, Patrickswell
Very Rev Edward Cleary PP
Knockainey, Hospital, Co Limerick
Tel 061-584873

KNOCKAVILLA
Assumption, Knockavilla
St Bridget's, Donaskeigh
Very Rev James Egan PP
Knockavilla, Dundrum, Co Tipperary
Tel 062-71157

KNOCKLONG
St Joseph's, Knocklong
St Patrick's, Glenbrohane
Very Rev Joe Tynan Adm
Kilteely, Co Limerick
Tel 061-384213

LATTIN AND CULLEN
Assumption, Lattin
St Patrick's, Cullen
Very Rev Michael Kennedy PP
Lattin, Co Tipperary
Tel 087-4147229
Very Rev John Egan AP
Cullen, Co Tipperary
Tel 086-8871961

LOUGHMORE
Nativity of Our Lady, Loughmore
St John the Baptist, Castleiney
Very Rev Dominic Meehan PP
Church Avenue,
Templemore, Co Tipperary
Very Rev Mgr Maurice Dooley AP
Loughmore, Templemore, Co Tipperary
Tel 0504-31375

MOYCARKEY
St Peter's, Moycarkey
St James's, Two-Mile-Borris
Our Lady & St Kevin, Littleton
Very Rev Thomas Fogarty PP
Ballydavid, Littleton,
Thurles, Co Tipperary
Tel 0504-44317
Very Rev George Bourke AP
Moycarkey, Thurles, Co Tipperary
Tel 0504-44227

MULLINAHONE
St Michael's
Very Rev Daniel O'Gorman PP
Mullinahone, Co Tipperary
Tel 052-9153152

MURROE AND BOHER
Holy Rosary, Murroe
St Patrick's, Boher
Very Rev Thomas Dunne PP
Parochal House, Liscreagh,
Murroe, Co Limerick V94 E8CP
Tel 083-4854776
Very Rev Canon Thomas J. Ryan AP
Bohergar, Brittas, Co Limerick
Tel 061-352223

NEW INN
Our Lady Queen, New Inn,
St Bartholomew's, Knockgrafton
Very Rev Robert Fletcher PP
New Inn, Cashel, Co Tipperary
Tel 087-4147229

NEWPORT
Most Holy Redeemer, Newport
Our Lady of the Wayside, Birdhill
Our Lady of Lourdes, Toor
Very Rev John O'Keeffe PP
Birdhill, Killaloe, Co Tipperary
Tel 061-379172
Very Rev Joseph Delaney AP
Clonbealy, Newport, Co Tipperary
Tel 061-378126

PALLASGREEN
St John the Baptist, Pallasgreen
St Brigid's, Templebraden
Very Rev Tomás O'Connell PP
Pallasgreen, Co Limerick
Tel 061-384114

SOLOHEAD
Sacred Heart, Oola
Very Rev John Morris PP
Solohead, Co Limerick
Tel 062-47614

TEMPLEMORE
Sacred Heart, Templemore
St Anne's, Clonmore
St James's, Killea
Very Rev Conor Hayes PP
Templemore, Co Tipperary
Tel 0504-31684
Rev Francis Mudungwe, CC
Church Avenue,
Templemore, Co Tipperary
Tel 0504-35772
Rt Rev Mgr Jim Costigan *(priest in residence)*
Richmond Road,
Templemore, Co Tipperary
Tel 0504-35772

TEMPLETUOHY
Sacred Heart, Templetuohy
St Mary's, Moyne
Very Rev Patrick Murphy PP
Templetuohy, Thurles, Co Tipperary
Tel 0504-53114
Rt Rev Mgr Christy O'Dwyer AP, VG
Moyne, Thurles, Co Tipperary
Tel 0504-34959

TIPPERARY
St Michael's
Ven Archdeacon Eugene Everard PP, VG
St Michael's Street, Tipperary Town
Tel 062-51536
Very Rev John Beaty AP
St Michael's Street, Tipperary Town
Tel 062-80475
Very Rev Canon Liam McNamara AP
Tipperary Town
Tel 062-82664

Allianz ⓘ

PPERCHURCH
cred Heart, Upperchurch
Mary's, Drombane
ery Rev Anthony Ryan PP
pperchurch, Thurles, Co Tipperary
el 0504-54492
ery Rev Donal Cunningham AP
pperchurch, Thurles, Co Tipperary
el 0504-54181

INSTITUTIONS AND THEIR CHAPLAINS

ashel Community School
el 062-61167
r Tony Nolan

t John the Baptist Community School, ospital
el 061-383283
ery Rev Sean Fennelly
arrysfarm, Hospital, Co Limerick
el 061-383565
mail info@johnthebaptist.ie

olaiste Mhuire Co-Ed, Thurles
el 0504-22055
ev Joe Walsh

IIC (St Patrick's Campus)
hurles, Co Tipperary
ev Joe Walsh
el 0504-22055

ocational School, Tipperary Town
el 062-51242
ery Rev John Beatty AP

PRIESTS OF THE DIOCESE ELSEWHERE

ev John Littleton
he Priory Institute,
allaght Village, Dublin 24
el 01-4048100
ev Francis McCarthy CC
arochial House, Crookstown, Co Kildare

RETIRED PRIESTS

ery Rev Padraig Corbett
astleiney, Co Tipperary
ev Daniel J. Ryan
o Archbishop's House,
hurles, Co Tipperary

RELIGIOUS ORDERS AND CONGREGATIONS

PRIESTS

AUGUSTINIANS
The Abbey, Fethard, Co Tipperary
Tel 052-31273
Bursar: Rev Gerard Horan (OSA)

BENEDICTINES
Glenstal Abbey,
Murroe, Co Limerick V94 A725
Tel 061-621000 Fax 061-386328
Email monks@glenstal.org
Abbot
Rt Rev Dom Brendan Coffey (OSB)

HOLY SPIRIT CONGREGATION
St Joseph's, Rockwell,
Cashel, Co Tipperary
Tel 062-61444 Fax 062-61661
Email info@rockwellcollege.ie
www.rockwell-college.ie
Principal: Ms Audrey O'Byrne
Secondary Residential and Day School;
Agricultural College

PALLOTTINES
Pallottine College,
Thurles, Co Tipperary
Tel 0504-21202
Rector
Very Rev George Ranahan (SAC)
Vice-Rector: Br Stephen Buckley (SAC)

SISTERS

CONGREGATION OF THE SISTERS OF MERCY
The Sisters of Mercy minister throughout the diocese in pastoral and social work, community development, counselling, spirituality, education and health care, answering current needs.

Sisters of Mercy, 5 Slieve Chormac,
Áras na Rí, Old Road,
Cashel, Co Tipperary E25 Y276
Tel 062-64574
Community: 2

1 Church Street,
Templemore, Co Tipperary E41 YE36
Tel 0504-32019
Community: 2

Sisters of Mercy,
1 Parkview Drive, Thurles,
Co Tipperary E41 V440
Tel 0504-21137
Community: 3

Convent of Mercy,
Tipperary Town E34 FF68
Tel 062-51218 Fax 062-52277
Community: 13

Convent of Mercy,
Knockanrawley,
Tipperary Town E34 YR02
Tel 062-51120
Community: 3

Sisters of Mercy, Clonbealy,
Newport, Co Tipperary V94 H67R
Tel 061-378072
Community: 2

PRESENTATION SISTERS
Presentation Sisters,
Thurles, Co Tipperary E41 AC82
Tel 0504-21250
Community: 22
Education, parish and pastoral area

Presentation Sisters, Hospital,
Co Limerick V35 NP23
Tel 061-383141
Community: 7
Pastoral and prayer ministry

Presentation Sisters,
14 Assumption Terrace, Ballingarry,
Thurles, Co Tipperary E41 P893
Tel 052-9154118
Community: 1
Community work

Presentation Sisters,
16/17 Greenane Drive,
Tipperary E34 KP93
Tel 062-80577
Community: 2
PHN and community/pastoral work

URSULINES
Ursuline Convent,
Thurles, Co Tipperary
Tel 0504-21561
Email srberchmans@uct.ie
Community: 10
Scoil Aingeal Naofa Primary School
Tel 0504-22561 Fax 0504-20763
Email scoilangela@unison.ie
Secondary School
Tel 0504-22147 Fax 0504-22737
Email sec.uct@oceanfree.net
Website www.uct.ie

CHARITABLE AND OTHER SOCIETIES

Community Social Services Centres
Rossa Street, Thurles, Co Tipperary
Tel 0504-22169

St Michael's Street, Tipperary Town
Tel 062-51622

Cashel, Co Tipperary
Tel 062-61395

ARCHDIOCESE OF TUAM

PATRON OF THE ARCHDIOCESE
ST JARLATH, 6 JUNE

SUFFRAGEN SEES: ACHONRY, CLONFERT, ELPHIN, KILLALA,
UNITED DIOCESES OF GALWAY AND KILMACDUAGH

INCLUDES HALF OF COUNTY MAYO, HALF OF COUNTY GALWAY
AND PART OF COUNTY ROSCOMMON

Most Rev Francis Duffy DD
Archbishop of Tuam;
born 21 April 1958;
ordained priest 20 June 1982;
ordained Bishop of Ardagh and
Clonmacnois 6 October 2013;
appointed Archbishop of Tuam
10 November 2021; installed as
Archbishop of Tuam 9 January
2022

Residence: Archbishop's House,
Tuam, Co Galway H54 HP57
Tel 093-24166
Email
admin@tuamarchdiocese.org
Twitter Tuamarchdiocese
Facebook Tuam Archdiocese

CATHEDRAL OF THE ASSUMPTION, TUAM

The Cathedral of the Assumption is the metropolitan cathedral of the Western Province.

Archbishop Oliver Kelly (1815–34) laid the foundation stone on 30 April 1827 – before Catholic Emancipation. The cathedral was dedicated on 18 August 1836 by Archbishop John MacHale (1834–81). It cost £14,204.

The cathedral is English-decorated Gothic in style, is cruciform in shape and has a three-stage West Tower. It was designed by architect Dominick Madden. Nineteen windows light the cathedral. It has seating capacity for 1,100 people.

Among the cathedral's notable features are its superbly cut Galway and Mayo limestone, its plaster-vaulted ceiling with heads and bosses, and its cantilevered oak organ loft. Its huge Oriel window has eighty-two compartments, is forty-two feet high and eighteen feet wide; it is the work of Michael O'Connor and was made in Dublin in 1832. Four large windows from the Harry Clarke studio also grace the cathedral. It has a very fine Compton organ with 1,200 pipes, a unique set of early nineteenth-century Stations of the Cross, recently restored, and a seventeenth-century painting of the Assumption by Carlo Maratta.

The sanctuary, as shown below, was completely redesigned by Wejchert Architects in 2020. The altar is of Carrara marble with the reredos combining granite uprights with free-standing oak hardwood screens. The sanctuary floor is of Portuguese granite. The tabernacle and plinth as well as the sanctuary lamp are all retained from the previous sanctuary. Local craftsman Tom O'Dowd designed and executed the ambo. Archbishop Neary dedicated the new Altar on the Feast of the Assumption 2021 in the presence of the Apostolic Nuncio to Ireland, His Excellency Jude Thaddeus Okolo.

Allianz (ii)

Most Rev Michael Neary DD
Retired Archbishop of Tuam;
born 15 April 1946;
ordained priest 20 June 1971; ordained
bishop 13 September 1992; installed
Archbishop of Tuam 5 March 1995.
Retired 9 January 2022.
Residence: Blackfort, Castlebar, Co Mayo

CHAPTER

Dean
Rt Rev Mgr Dermot Moloney PE

Prebendaries
Very Rev Conal Canon Eustace PP, VF
The Parochial House, Castlebar, Co Mayo
Very Rev James Canon Ronayne PP, VF,
Clifden
Very Rev Brendan Canon Kilcoyne PP, VF,
Athenry
Very Rev James Canon Quinn AP
Augheen, Claremorris
Very Rev James Canon Walsh AP
Kilmeena, Westport
Very Rev Stephen Canon Farragher PP,
PG, Ballyhaunis
Very Rev Martin Canon O'Connor,
Ballindine

Honorary Canons
Very Rev Eamon Canon Concannon PE,
Knock
Very Rev John Canon Cosgrove PE,
Castlebar
Very Rev Austin Canon Fergus AP,
Mayo Abbey
Very Rev John D. Canon Flannery PE,
Milltown
Very Rev Anthony Canon King PE,
Westport
Very Rev John Canon Garvey PE,
Ballinrobe
Very Rev Martin Canon Gleeson PE, Tuam
Very Rev Des Canon Grogan PE,
Partry, Claremorris
Very Rev Michael Canon Goaley PE,
Corrandulla, Co Galway
Very Rev Joseph Canon Moloney PE,
Tuam
Very Rev Patrick Canon Mooney,
Glenamaddy
Very Rev Martin Canon Newell PE, Claran
Very Rev Joseph Canon O'Brien PE,
Curloughmore, Co Galway
Very Rev Kieran Canon Waldron PE,
Ballyhaunis
Very Rev Des Canon Walsh PE,
Claremorris, Co Mayo
Very Rev John Canon Walsh PP,
Knock, Co Mayo
Very Rev Enda Canon Howley,
College Road, Galway
Very Rev Patrick Canon Mullins, Tuam
Rt Rev John O'Boyle, Galway
Very Rev Joseph Canon Feeney AP,
Ballinlough
Very Rev Pádraig Standún PE, Cill
Chiaráin

ADMINISTRATION

Vicars General
Very Rev Stephen Farragher
Very Rev Tod Nolan

Chancellor
Sr Mary Lyons RSM, JCD
Archbishop's House, Tuam
Tel 093-24166
Email chancellortuam@gmail.com

Data Protection Officer
Mr Malachaí Duddy BL
Email dpo@elphindiocese.ie

Vicars Forane
Very Rev Conal Canon Eustace VF
Very Rev Martin O'Connor VF
Very Rev Brendan Canon Kilcoyne VF
Very Rev James Canon Ronayne VF
Very Rev Michael Molloy VF
Very Rev Charles McDonnell VF
Very Rev Fergal Cunnane VF
Very Rev John Kenny VF

Diocesan Secretary
Rev Francis Mitchell
Archbishop's House, Tuam, Co Galway
Tel 093-24166
Email admin@tuamarchdiocese.org

Council of Priests
Chairperson: Very Rev Tod Nolan VG
Secretary: Rev Shane Costello
Treasurer: Rev Denis Carney

Communications
Catholic Communications Office
Tel 01-5053017
Email info@catholicbishops.ie

Finance
Ms Catherine Dolan
Diocesan Accountant,
Diocesan Resource Centre,
Bishop Street, Tuam
Tel 093-52284
Email finance@tuamdiocese.org

Archives
Archivist/Historian
Very Rev Kieran Canon Waldron PE
Ballyhaunis
Tel 094-9630246
Email pkwaldron36@gmail.com

CATECHETICS EDUCATION

Post-Primary Education
Director
Sr Margaret Buckley
Email secondaryre@tuamarchdiocese.org
Sisters of the Christian Retreat
Diocesan Resource Centre,
Bishop Street, Tuam, Co Galway
Tel 093-52284

Primary Catechetics
Director: Mr John McDonagh
Diocesan Resource Centre,
Bishop Street, Tuam, Co Galway
Tel 093-52284
Email
primarycatechetics@tuamarchdiocese.org

Primary Education
Secretary
Mrs Rosaleen Crowe-O'Neill
Diocesan Resource Centre,
Bishop Street, Tuam, Co Galway
Tel 093-52284
Email education@tuamarchdiocese.org

CPSMA – Diocesan Committee
Chairperson: Mr Frank Burns
Garrafrauns, Dunmore

Safeguarding Office
Director: Maureen Walsh
Diocesan Resource Office
Tel 093-52284
Email
safeguarding@tuamarchdiocese.org
Delegates: Rev Francis Mitchell
Archbishop's House, Tuam,
Co Galway H54 HP57
Tel 093-24166 *or*
DLP Official Number 087-4070206
Mrs Mary Trench
Robeen, Hollymount, Co Mayo
Email marytrench@gmail.com
Tel 087-9331679

Diocesan Safeguarding Committee
Chairperson: Ms Maureen Walsh
Designated Liaison Person:
Rev Francis Mitchell
Designated Liaison Person:
Ms Mary Trench

PASTORAL

ACCORD
Diocesan Directors
Rev Conal Eustace PP
Castlebar, Co Mayo Tel 094-9021844
Email eustaceconal@gmail.com
Rev James Ronayne PP
Clifden, Co Galway Tel 095-21251
Email clifdenparish@gmail.com

Catholic Grandparents Association
Contact: Ms Catherine Wiley
Tel 085-8704722
Email info@
catholicgrandparentsassociation.org
www.catholicgrandparentsassociation.org

Diocesan Pastoral Council
Chairperson: Vacant – Pending election
Secretary: Vacant – Pending election

Ecumenism
Contact: Rev Francis Mitchell
Diocesan Office, Tuam, Co Galway
Tel 093-24166
Email admin@tuamarchdiocese.org

Emigrants
Director: Very Rev Gerard Burns PP
The Parochial House,
Clonbur, Co Galway
Email gerburns1956@gmail.com

Family Ministry
www.thefamilycentre.com
Director: Máire Uí Dhomhnaill
The Family Centre, Castle Street,
Castlebar, Co Mayo
Tel 094-9025900
Email info@thefamilycentre.com

GMIT, Castlebar
Castlebar Presbytery Priests
Tel 094-9021844
Mr Daniel Caldwell
Tel 094-9043150

Immigrants
Very Rev Stephen Farragher PP, VG
Ballyhaunis, Co Mayo
Tel 094-9630006
Email stephenfarragher@gmail.com

John Paul II Awards
Coordinator: Mr John McDonagh
Contact: Diocesan Resource Centre,
Tuam
Tel 093-52284
Email youth@tuamarchdiocese.org

L'Arche
National Chaplain
Very Rev Fergal Cunnane PP
Dunmore, Co Galway
Tel 093-38124

Marriage Tribunal
(See Marriage Tribunals section.)

Pilgrimage Director
Mr John McLoughlin
3 Trinity Court, Tuam, Co Galway
Tel 087-7627910
Email latinjohnb@gmail.com

Pioneer Total Abstinence Association
Director: Very Rev Seán Cunningham PP
Parochial House,
Corrandulla, Co Galway
Tel 091-791125
Rev John O'Gorman PP
Lackagh, Turloughmore, Co Galway
Tel 091-797114

Polish Chaplain
Rev Krzysztof Sikora (SVD) PP
The Parochial House,
Roundstone, Co Galway
Tel 095-37123
Email roundstoneparish@gmail.com

Pontifical Mission Societies
Diocesan Director
Very Rev Chris Brennan
Parochial House,
Islandeady, Co Mayo
Tel 087-1962674

Travellers
Chaplain: Very Rev Pat Farragher Adm
Tuam, Co Galway
Tel 093-24250
Email tuamparishoffice@gmail.com

Trócaire
Very Rev Michael Molloy PP
Moore, Ballydangan,
Athlone, Co Roscommon
Tel 090-9673539
Email stmarysmoore@gmail.com

Vocations Committee
Contact: Rev Francis Mitchell
Archbishop's House,
Tuam, Co Galway
Tel 093-24166
Email admin@tuamarchdiocese.org

Youth
Director of Youth Ministry
Vacant
Diocesan Resource Centre, Bishop Street,
Tuam, Co Galway
Tel 093-52284
Email youth@tuamarchdiocese.org

Youth – Diocesan Youth Council
Chairperson: Mr John McDonagh
Secretary: Sr Margaret Buckley
Diocesan Resource Office
Tel 093-52284

PARISHES

Mensal parishes are listed first. Other parishes follow alphabetically. Historica names are in parentheses.

TUAM (CATHEDRAL OF THE ASSUMPTION)
www.tuamparish.com
Email tuamparishoffice@gmail.com
Very Rev Pat Farragher Adm
Rev Seán Flynn CC
Tuam, Co Galway
Tel 093-24250

WESTPORT (AUGHAVAL)
www.westportparish.ie
Email office@westportparish.ie
Very Rev Charlie McDonnell Adm
Westport, Co Mayo
Tel 098-28871

ABBEYKNOCKMOY
Very Rev Ronnie Boyle PP
Parochial House, Chapel Field,
Abbeyknockmoy, Tuam, Co Galway
Tel 093-43510

ACHILL
Email achillparish@gmail.com
Very Rev John Murray PP
Achill Sound, Achill, Co Mayo
Tel 098-45288
Rev Nelson Joseph CC
Achill Sound, Achill, Co Mayo
Tel 098-45109

AGHAMORE
Rev Jerald David Adm
Aghamore, Ballyhaunis, Co Mayo
Tel 094-9367024

ARAN ISLANDS
Very Rev Máirtín Ó Conaire PP
Kilronan, Aran Islands, Co Galway
Tel 099-61221
Email aranislesparish@gmail.com

ATHENRY
www.athenryparish.ie
Very Rev Brendan Canon Kilcoyne PP, VF
Tel 091-844076
Email athenryparish@gmail.com
Rev Benny McHale CC
Tel 091-844169

AUGHAGOWER
Very Rev Britus Kadavunkal Francis Adm
Aughagower, Westport, Co Mayo
Tel 098-25057

BALLA AND MANULLA
Very Rev Denis Carney PP
Balla, Co Mayo
Tel 094-9365025
Email stcronansballa@eircom.net

Allianz ⓘ

ALLINDINE (KILVINE)
Very Rev Martin Canon O'Connor PP, VF
allindine, Co Mayo
el 094-9364423
mail kilvineparish@gmail.com

ALLINLOUGH (KILTULLAGH)
Very Rev Stephen Canon Farragher PP, VG
Very Rev Joseph Canon Feeney AP
mail frjoefeeney@gmail.com
arochial House, Ballinlough,
o Roscommon F45 R208
el 094-9640155

ALLINROBE
Very Rev Michael Gormally PP
allinrobe, Co Mayo
el 094-9541085/9541784
mail stmarysbrobe@gmail.com

ALLYHAUNIS (ANNAGH)
Very Rev Stephen Canon Farragher PP, VG
allyhaunis, Co Mayo
el 094-9630006
mail stephenfarragher@gmail.com

EKAN
ww.bekan-parish.ie
very Rev Brendan McGuinness PP
ekan, Claremorris, Co Mayo
el 094-9380203
mail brendanmcguinness@eircom.net

URRISCARRA AND BALLINTUBBER
www.ballintubberabbey.ie
mail info@ballintubberabbey.ie
Very Rev Michael Farragher PP
arnacon, Claremorris, Co Mayo
el 094-9360205

**AHERLISTRANE (DONAGHPATRICK AND
ILCOONA)**
very Rev Dixy Faber Adm
arochial House, Kilcoona,
eadford, Co Galway
el 089-9428637

ARNA (MOYRUS)
Very Rev Shane Sullivan PP
arna, Co Galway
el 095-32232

ARRAROE (KILEEN)
Very Rev Hugh Loftus PP
arraroe, Co Galway
el 091-595452
mail paroisteanchillin@gmail.com

**ASTLEBAR (AGLISH, BALLYHEANE AND
REAGHWY)**
mail
astlebarparishsecretary@gmail.com
Very Rev Conal Canon Eustace PP, VF
el 094-9021274
ev Jose Raju CC
ev Shane Costello CC
el 094-9021844
astlebar, Co Mayo

Parish Co-ordinator: Mrs Mary Connell
The Monastery, Castlebar, Co Mayo
Tel 094-9028473

CLARE ISLAND/INISHTURK
Pastoral Care
Ver Rev John Kenny PP and priests of
Westport Deanery
Tel 098-28871

CLAREMORRIS (KILCOLMAN)
Email stcolmansparishchurch@gmail.com
Very Rev Peter Gannon PP
The Presbytery, Claremorris, Co Mayo
Tel 094-9362477

CLIFDEN (OMEY AND BALLINDOON)
Very Rev James Canon Ronayne PP, VF
Clifden, Co Galway
Tel 095-21251
Email clifdenparish@gmail.com
Rev George Izidor CC
Ballyconneely, Clifden, Co Galway
Tel 095-21251

CLONBUR (ROSS)
Very Rev Gerry Burns PP
The Parochial House,
Clonbur, via Claremorris, Co Galway
Tel 094-9546304
Email gerburns1956@gmail.com

CONG, CROSS AND THE NEALE
Very Rev Declan Carroll PP
Cong, Co Mayo
Tel 094-9546030
Email congcrossneale@gmail.com

CORRANDULLA (ANNAGHDOWN)
Very Rev Seán Cunningham PP
Corrandulla, Co Galway
Tel 091-791125
Email newsletter@carrandullachurch.com
Rev Oliver McNamara CC
Annaghdown, Co Galway
Tel 091-791142

CROSSBOYNE AND TAUGHEEN
Email crossboyneparish@gmail.com
For Administration
Very Rev Martin Canon O'Connor PP, VF
Ballindine
For Pastoral Services
Very Rev James Canon Quinn AP
Taugheen, Claremorris, Co Mayo
Tel 094-9362500
Email frjquinn@gmail.com

CUMMER (KILMOYLAN AND CUMMER)
Very Rev Ciarán Blake PP
Cummer, Tuam, Co Galway
Tel 093-41427
Email belclare.corofin@gmail.com

DUNMORE
Email newsletter@dunmoreparish.ie
Very Rev Fergal Cunnane PP, VF
Dunmore, Co Galway
Tel 093-38124

GLENAMADDY (BOYOUNAGH)
www.glenamaddychurch.ie
Email glenamaddychurch@gmail.com
Very Rev Eugene O'Boyle PP
Glenamaddy, Co Galway
Tel 094-9659962

HEADFORD (KILLURSA AND KILLOWER)
Email info@headfordchurch.com
Very Rev Raymond Flaherty PP
Headford, Co Galway
Tel 093-35448

INISHBOFIN
Email office@ballinakillparish.com
Very Rev Anthaiah Pudota Adm
Letterfrack, Co Galway
Tel 095-41053

ISLANDEADY
www.islandeady.ie
Very Rev Chris Brennan (SMA) Adm
Islandeady, Castlebar, Co Mayo
Tel 094-9024125
Email parishig2017@gmail.com

KEELOGUES
Very Rev Peter Suttle (CSSp) Adm
Parochial House, Parke,
Castlebar, Co Mayo
Tel 094-9031314

KILCONLY AND KILBANNON
Email kilconlykilbannon@gmail.com
Very Rev Frank Conlisk (SPS) Adm
Parochial House, Milltown,
Tuam, Co Galway
Tel 089-2064773

KILKERRIN AND CLONBERNE
Email
kilkerrinclonberneparish@gmail.com
Very Rev Thomas Commins PP
Kilkerrin, Ballinasloe, Co Galway
Tel 094-9659212

KILLERERIN
Email kilererinparish@gmail.com
Very Rev Jarlath Heraty PP
Killererin, Barnderg, Tuam, Co Galway
Tel 093-49222

KILMAINE
Very Rev Michael Gormally PP
Parochial House, Ballinrobe, Co Mayo
Tel 094-9541085
Email stmarysbrobe@gmail.com

KILMEEN
Very Rev Iomar Daniels PP
Killoran, Ballinasloe, Co Galway
Tel 091-841758
Email idaniels@garbally.ie

KILMEENA
For Pastoral Services
Very Rev James Walsh AP
Kilmeena, Westport, Co Mayo
Tel 098-41270
For Administration
Very Rev Charlie McDonnell, Westport

KNOCK
Very Rev Richard Gibbons PP
The Presbytery, Knock Shrine,
Knock, Co Mayo
Tel 094-9388100
Email frgibbons@knock-shrine.ie

LACKAGH
email lackaghparish@gmail.com
Very Rev John O'Gorman PP
Turloughmore, Co Galway
Tel 091-797114

LEENANE (KILBRIDE)
Very Rev Kieran Burke PP
Leenane, Co Galway
Tel 095-42251
Email rathfran@gmail.com

LETTERFRACK (BALLINAKILL)
Email office@ballinakillparish.com
Very Rev Anthaiah Pudota Adm
The Parochial House, Letterfrack,
Connemara, Co Galway
Tel 095-41053

LOUISBURGH (KILGEEVER)
Email louisburghparish@icloud.com
Very Rev Martin Long PP
Louisburgh, Co Mayo
Tel 098-66198

MAYO ABBEY (MAYO AND ROSSLEA)
For Pastoral Services
Very Rev Austin Canon Fergus AP
Mayo Abbey, Claremorris, Co Mayo
Tel 094-9365086
For Administration
Very Rev Denis Carney PP
Balla
Email stcronansballa@eircom.net

MENLOUGH (KILLASCOBE)
Email killascobeparish@gmail.com
Very Rev Karl Burns PP
Mountbellew, Ballinasloe, Co Galway
Tel 090-9679235

MILLTOWN (ADDERGOLE AND LISKEEVEY)
Email milltownkilconly@gmail.com
Very Rev Frank Conlisk (SPS) Adm
Parochial House, Milltown,
Tuam, Co Galway
Tel 089-2064773

MOORE
Very Rev Michael Molloy PP, VF
Ballydangan, Athlone, Co Roscommon
Tel 090-9673539
Email stmarysmoore@gmail.com

MOYLOUGH AND MOUNTBELLEW
Very Rev Karl Burns PP
Mountbellew, Ballinasloe, Co Galway
Tel 090-9679235
Email karlburns07@gmail.com

NEWPORT (BURRISHOOLE)
Email burrishooleparish@gmail.com
Very Rev Tod Nolan PP, VG
Newport, Co Mayo
Tel 098-41123

PARKE (TURLOUGH)
Very Rev Peter Suttle (CSSp), Adm
Parochial House, Parke,
Castlebar, Co Mayo
Tel 094-9031314

PARTRY (BALLYOVEY)
Very Rev John Kenny PP, VF
Partry, Claremorris, Co Mayo
Tel 094-9543013
Email frjohnkenny@yahoo.ie

ROBEEN
Very Rev Michael Murphy PP
Robeen, Hollymount, Co Mayo
Tel 094-9540026
Email michaelmurphypp@gmail.com

ROUNDFORT (KILCOMMON)
Very Rev Michael Murphy PP
Roundfort, Hollymount, Co Mayo
Tel 094-9540934
Email michaelmurphypp@gmail.com

ROUNDSTONE
Email roundstoneparish@gmail.com
Very Rev Krzystof Sikora (SVD) PP
Roundstone, Co Galway
Tel 095-37123

SPIDDAL/KNOCK
Very Rev Hughie Loftus PP
Carraroe, Co Galway
Tel 091-595452

WILLIAMSTOWN (TEMPLETOHER)
For Administration & Pastoral Services
Very Rev Eugene O'Boyle PP
Parochial House,
Williamstown, Co Galway
Tel 094-9659962

PRIESTS OF THE DIOCESE ELSEWHERE

Rev Éamon Conway
University of Nortre Dame, Australia
Rev Thomas Gallagher
Cloughmore, Achill, Co Mayo
Very Rev Gerard Needham
Louisburgh, Co Mayo
Very Rev James O'Grady
Headford, Co Galway
Rev Gerard Quirke
Priestly Society of St Peter
Rev Bernard, Shaughnessy
The Parochial House, Coolarne,
Athenry, Co Galway
Rev Michael Whelan
c/o Archbishop's House

RETIRED PRIESTS

Very Rev Pádraig Audley PE
Leitir Mealláin, Co na Gaillimhe
Rev James Buggy
Castlebar, Co Mayo
Very Rev Éamonn Canon Concannon PE
Ballyhowley, Knock, Co Mayo
Very Rev John Canon Cosgrove PE
Claremorris, Co Mayo
Very Rev Séamus Cunnane PE
Grove House, Tuam, Co Galway
Very Rev Patrick Donnellan PE
25 Drisín, Knocknacarra, Galway
Very Rev Frank Fahey
Ballintubber, Claremorris, Co Mayo
Very Rev John D., Canon Flannery PE
Cartron, Milltown, Co Galway
Very Rev John Canon Garvey PE
Clonbur Road, Ballinrobe, Co Mayo
Very Rev Patrick Gill
Louisburgh, Co Mayo
Very Rev Martin Canon Gleeson PE
Tuam, Co Galway
Very Rev Michael Canon Goaley PE
Corrandulla, Co Galway
Very Rev Des Canon Grogan PE
Partry, Claremorris, Co Mayo
Very Rev Enda Canon Howley
College Road, Galway
Very Rev Anthony King PE
Westport, Co Mayo
Rt Rev Mgr Dermot Moloney PE
5 Gold Cave Crescent,
Tuam, Co Galway
Very Rev Joseph Canon Moloney PE
Grove House, Tuam, Co Galway
Very Rev Patrick Mooney
Glenamaddy, Co Galway
Very Rev Patrick Canon Mullins PE
Tuam, Co Galway
Rev Anthony Neville
Moycullen, Co Galway
Very Rev Martin Canon Newell PE
Claran, Ower PO, Co Galway
Rt Rev John O'Boyle
Dalysfort Road, Salthill, Galway
Very Rev Joseph Canon O'Brien
Lakcaghmore, Turloughmore, Co Galway
Rev Éamon Ó Conghaile
Ard Thiar, Carna, Co na Gaillimhe
Rev Michael O'Malley
c/o Archbishop's House,
Tuam, Co Galway
Very Rev Pádraig Canon Standún
Cill Chiaráin
Very Rev Kieran Waldron PE
Devlis, Ballyhaunis, Co Mayo
Very Rev Desmond Canon Walsh PE
Claremorris, Co Mayo
Very Rev John Walsh
Knock, Co Mayo

RELIGIOUS ORDERS AND CONGREGATIONS

PRIESTS

APUCHIN FRANCISCANS
resence in Knock Shrine,
nock, Co Mayo
uardian
r John Wright
icar
ev Maitiu O Clerichin

1ILL HILL MISSIONARIES
t James Apartments
nock Shrine, Knock, Co Mayo
ev Denis Hartnett (MHM)
ev Gerald Doyle (MHM)

**T PATRICK'S MISSIONARY SOCIETY
(ILTEGAN FATHERS)**
1ain Street, Knock, Co Mayo
el 094-9388661
ouse Leader
ev Gary Howley (SPS)

BROTHERS

LEXIAN BOTHERS
egional Residence
hurchfield, Knock, Co Mayo
el 094-9376996
mail cellerbruders@gmail.com
ommunity Leader
r Dermot O'Leary (CFA)
egional Leader: Br Barry Butler (CFA)
ommunity: 3

E LA SALLE BROTHERS
t Gerald's College,
astlebar, Co Mayo
el 094-9021383 Fax 094-9026157
eadmaster: Mr Sean Burke

RANCISCAN BROTHERS
ranciscan Brothers Generalate
ewtown, Mountbellew, Co Galway
el 090-9679295 Fax 090-9679687
mail franciscanbrs@eircom.net
1inister General: Br Tony Dolan

orrandulla, Co Galway
el 091-791127
ocal Minister: Br Alan Farrell
ommunity: 4

ifden, Co Galway
el 095-21195
ocal Minister: Br James Mungovan
ommunity: 3

ranciscan Brothers, Newtown,
1ountbellew, Co Galway
el 090-9679906
ontact Person: Br William Martyn
ommunity: 5

SISTERS

BENEDICTINE NUNS
Kylemore Abbey, Kylemore,
Connemara, Co Galway H91 VR90
Tel 095-52011
Email info@kylemoreabbey.ie
Abbess: Sr Máire Hickey (OSB)
Email patricia@kylemoreabbey.ie
Community: 10
Daily Liturgy: Morning Prayer – 7.15 am
weekdays; 8.30 am Sundays and Feasts.
Mass or Midday Prayer – 12.15 pm
weekdays; 11.30 am Sundays and Feasts.
Vespers – 6.00 pm in the Monastic Church.
Mondays 5.00 pm. Visitors welcome.
Visitor Destination, Abbey, Gothic
Church, Craft Shop, Restaurant, Pottery
Studio, Monastic Church and 6-acre
Victorian Walled Garden open to visitors.
Soap and chocolate manufacturing by
the Benedictine Community.
Global Centre Catholic University of
Notre Dame, Indiana
Website www.kylemoreabbey.com

CARMELITES
Carmelite Monastery,
Tranquilla, Knock,
Claremorris,
Co Mayo F12 AH64
Email tranquilla.knock@gmail.com
Prioress: Sr Claire
Community: 19
Hidden life of prayer in the service of the
Church

CHRISTIAN RETREAT SISTERS
'The Demesne',
Mountbellew, Ballinasloe,
Co Galway H53 RH61
Tel 090-9679311
Contact: Sr Assumpta Collins
Community: 2

Holy Rosary College Coeducational
Secondary School
Tel 090-9679222
Pupils: 733
Catechetical and pastoral ministry

CONGREGATION OF THE SISTERS OF MERCY
Sisters of Mercy, The Glebe,
Tuam, Co Galway H54 CC43
Tel 093-25045
Community: 2

Teach Mhuire, The Lawn,
Castlebar, Co Mayo F23 YV12
Tel 094-9022141 Fax 094-9025266
Community: 2

Ard Bhride, The Lawn,
Castlebar, Co Mayo F23 W571
Tel 094-9286410 Fax 094-9286404
Community: 25

Pontoon Road,
Castlebar, Co Mayo F23 YX85
Tel 094-9025463 Fax 094-9026695
Community: 3

Chapel Street,
Castlebar, Co Mayo F23 FK52
Tel 094-9021734
Community: 1

6 Riverdale Court,
Castlebar, Co Mayo F23 VW98
Tel/Fax 094-9023622
Community: 2

Manor Court, Westport Road,
Castlebar, Co Mayo
Community: 4

1 Clareville,
Claremorris, Co Mayo F12 T622
Tel 094-9372654
Community: 1

Sisters of Mercy,
16, 28, 38, 39 St Jarlath's Court,
The Glebe, Tuam, Co Galway
Community: 4

7 Spencer Manor,
Castlebar, Co Mayo F23 XT21
Tel 094-9035240
Community: 1

7 Liosdubh Court, Newport Road,
Castlebar, Co Mayo F23 AX08
Tel 094-9035240

5 Manor Quarter,
Knock,Co Mayo F12 Y735
Community: 1

52 Carrowmore, Meadows,
Knock, Co Mayo F12 PH22
Community: 1

31 Carrowmore, Meadows,
Knock, Co Mayo F12 F596
Community: 1

50 An Sruthán, Turlough Road,
Castlebar, Co Mayo F23 DX80
Community: 1

Fern Hill (11, 14, 15, 16),
Knockranny, Westport, Co Mayo
Community: 4

35 Gilmartin Road,
Tuam, Co Galway H54 XV38
Community: 1

New Street,
Ballinrobe, Co Mayo F31 NP94
Community: 1

Sisters of Mercy, Church View, Dalton
Street, Claremorris, Co Mayo
Tel 094-9373757
Community: 4

DAUGHTERS OF CHARITY OF ST VINCENT DE PAUL
St Louise's, Carramore, Claremorris,
Knock, Co Mayo F12 WC61
Tel 094-9376828
Superior: Sr Carmel Ryan
Community: 4
Evangelisation, pastoral care, prayer
guidance

FRANCISCAN SISTERS OF LITTLEHAMPTON
Eden, Knock, Claremorris,
Co Mayo FT12 YC83
Leader: Sr Anastasia McGonagle
Email mcgonagle.anastasia@gmail.com
Sr Benignus Kearney
Registered charity 232931
Community: 2

LA SAINTE UNION DES SACRES COEURS
57 Carrowmore Meadows,
Kiltimagh Road, Knock, Co Mayo
Community: 1
Pastoral

13 Glencarra, Kiltimagh Road,
Knock, Co Mayo
Community: 1
Pastoral

13 Carrowmore Drive, Knock, Co Mayo
Community: 1
Pastoral

POOR SERVANTS OF THE MOTHER OF GOD
SMG Sisters, Main Street,
Knock, Co Mayo
Community: 3
Pastoral Ministry

PRESENTATION SISTERS
Presentation Convent,
St Joseph's, Tuam,
Co Galway H54 AY55
Tel 093-24111 Fax 093-25584
Community: 21
Community and pastoral ministry

Presentation Convent,
Athenry, Co Galway H65 P623
Tel 091-844077
Community: 11
School and pastoral ministry

SACRED HEART SISTERS OF JESUS AND MARY
Fatima House, Carramore North,
Knock, Co Mayo F12 FK49
Tel 094-9388719
Community: 4

SISTERS OF OUR LADY OF APOSTLES
52 Elm Park, Claremorris,
Co Mayo F12 T0A9
Tel 094-9373569
Community: 1

ST JOSEPH OF THE SACRED HEART SISTERS
14 Glencara, Kiltimagh Road,
Knock, Co Mayo
Sr Elizabeth McGoldrick

ST LOUIS SISTERS
17 Manor Quarter, Cavanagh Road,
Knock, Co Mayo
Community: 4
Prayer ministry

Brook Lodge, Ballyhaunis Road,
Knock, Co Mayo
Community: 2
Kiltimagh Community School: 730

EDUCATIONAL INSTITUTIONS

St Colman's College
Claremorris, Co Mayo
Tel 094-9371442
Principal: Roy Hession
Chaplain: Very Rev Peter Gannon PP
Claremorris

St Jarlath's College
Tuam, Co Galway
Tel 093-24342
www.jarlaths.ie
President: Mr John Kelly
Tel 093-24248
Email presidentsjc@jarlaths.ie
Chaplain: Rev Francis Mitchell
Email admin@tuamarchdiocese.org
Tel 093-24166

CHARITABLE AND OTHER SOCIETIES

ACCORD
Tuam Parish Centre, Dublin Road,
Tuam, Co Galway
Tel 094-9022214
Contact: Very Rev Conal Canon Eustace

Society of St Vincent de Paul
Conferences at: Castlebar, Tuam,
Athenry, Westport, Dunmore,
Claremorris, Ballyhaunis, Ballinrobe,
Ballinlough, Headford, Monivea.

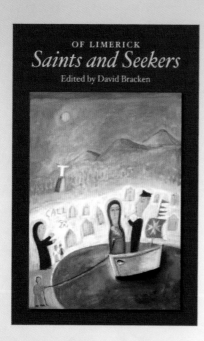

Of Limerick Saints and Seekers

David Bracken (ed.)

978 1 80097 031 1
€24.99/£22.50

About the book

Journey through a millennium and a half of Limerick history with scholars and scribes, poets and preachers, martyrs and missionaries, and founders of churches and religious communities. *Of Limerick Saints and Seekers* is an impressive collection of stories of the lives of extraordinary people from a variety of faith traditions and perspectives, from well-known saints to unknown and unsung religious and lay people.

Drawing from early Ireland to the present day – including figures such as St Íte, foster mother of the saints; Gille, Limerick's first bishop; the medieval Askeaton Madonna; Terence Albert O'Brien, bishop of Emly; Sikh scholar Max Arthur MacAuliffe and Sr Mary Clare Whitty, Anglican nun, martyred in Korea – with contributions from academics, archaeologists, archivists, poets, pastors and theologians and an introduction from Bishop Brendan Leahy, this fascinating collection remembers the lives of these remarkable individuals.

About the editor

David Bracken, Limerick diocesan archivist, is rooted in the heart of Limerick City where he lives with his wife and five children. He edited *The End of All Things Earthly: Faith Profiles of the 1916 Leaders* (Veritas, 2016).

Abbey Street, Blanchardstown Centre and Tallaght, Dublin
Cork • Derry • Letterkenny • Limerick • Newry

✳ VERITAS

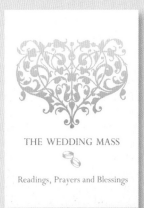
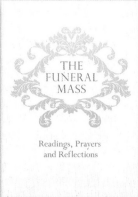
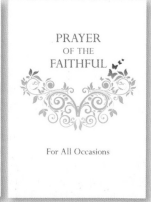
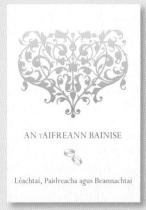

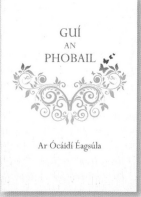

DIOCESE OF ACHONRY

PATRONS OF THE DIOCESE
ST NATHY, 9 AUGUST; AT ATTRACTA, 11 AUGUST

INCLUDES PARTS OF COUNTIES MAYO, ROSCOMMON AND SLIGO

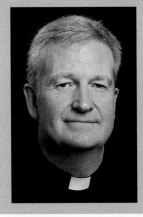

Most Rev Paul Dempsey DD
Bishop of Achonry;
born 20 April 1971;
ordained priest 6 July 1997;
ordained Bishop of Achonry
30 August 2020

Residence: Bishop's House,
Convent Road, Ballaghaderreen,
Co Roscommon F45 H004
Tel 094-9860034
Email
bishop@achonrydiocese.org
Website www.achonrydiocese.org

CATHEDRAL OF THE ANNUNCIATION AND ST NATHY, BALLAGHADERREEN

The building of the cathedral was begun in 1855 by Bishop Durcan. The architects were Messrs Hadfield & Goldie of Sheffield, while the Clerk of Works was Mr Charles Barker. It was completed in 1860.

The style is simple Gothic, known as Early English, of the Gothic Revival. The original intention was to have the roof fan-vaulted in wood and plaster, but it was abandoned owing to cost, and was finished in open timbers. The plan for a spire also had to be abandoned. This, however, was built in 1905 by Bishop Lyster, and a carillon of bells was installed.

The organ was built with continental pipes by Chestnutt of Waterford in 1925. The sanctuary was reconstructed to conform to the liturgical reforms of Vatican II in 1972. The baptistry in the left-hand Side Chapel was donated by Lydia Viscountess Dillon in memory of Charles Henry Viscount Dillon who died on 18 November 1865. The Apostles' Creed is carved on the baptistry lid.

There are commemorative plaques to former bishops of Achonry in the left-hand side Chapel: Bishops McNicholas, Durcan, Lyster and Morrisroe.

The window in the Lady Chapel has the inscription: 'This window to the Glory of God and Honour of the Blessed Virgin Mary was erected by united subscription of the Bishop, Clergy and 19 inhabitants of the Parish and neighbourhood to commemorate their respect and esteem for Charles Strickland and his wife Maria of Loughglynn and their zealous assistance in the erection of the Cathedral Church in 1860.' Charles Strickland was agent for Lord Dillon and was associated with the building of the neighbouring town of Charlestown and its church.

ADMINISTRATION

Vicar General
Very Rev Dermot Meehan
Parochial House, Swinford, Co Mayo
Tel 094-9251790

College of Consultors
Very Rev Dermot Meehan
Very Rev Vincent Sherlock
Very Rev Michael Quinn
Very Rev Gerard Davey
Rev Martin Henry
Very Rev Thomas Towey
Very Rev Padraig Costello

Finance Committee
Chairman: Pending

Vicars Forane
Very Rev Dermot Meehan PP, VG
Swinford
Very Rev James McDonagh PP, VF
Ballymote
Very Rev Padraig Costello PP, VF
Foxford

Church Building Advisory Commission
Rt Rev Mgr Thomas Johnston Adm
Charlestown, Co Mayo
Very Rev Joseph Caulfield PP
Gurteen, Co Sligo
Mr John Halligan
Charlestown, Co Mayo

Diocesan Secretary and Communications Officer
Very Rev Vincent Sherlock PP
Parochial House, Tubbercurry,
Co Sligo F91 HN34
Tel 071-9185049
Email vsherlock@achonrydiocese.org

Chancellor
Very Rev Vincent Sherlock PP
Parochial House, Tubbercurry,
Co Sligo F91 HN34
Tel 071-9185049
Email vsherlock@achonrydiocese.org

Episcopal Vicar for Pastoral Renewal and Development
Dr Eugene Duffy
Convent Road, Ballaghaderreen,
Co Roscommon
Tel 087-9621410

CATECHETICS
EDUCATION

Primary Education
Secretary: Rev Martin Henry
St Nathy's College,
Ballaghaderreen, Co Roscommon
Tel 094-9861728
Email mhenry@achonrydiocese.org

Religious Education in Schools
Diocesan Religious Adviser
Primary: Sr Mary Richardson
Marist Convent, Tubbercurry, Co Sligo
Tel 071-9185018
Email eskerglas@gmail.com
Ms Marian Maloney
Drum, Knock, Co Mayo
Tel 087-2112555
Email marianmaloney@eircom.net
Post-Primary: Rev Gerry Davey Adm
Carracastle, Ballaghaderreen, Co Mayo
Tel 094-9254301

LITURGY

Chairperson
Very Rev Dermot Meehan PP, VG
Swinford, Co Mayo
Tel 094-9251790
Secretary
Very Rev Thomas Towey PP
Ballisodare, Co Sligo
Tel 071-9167467

PASTORAL

ACCORD
Director
Very Rev Joseph Caulfield PP
Gurteen, Co Sligo
Tel 071-9182551

Council of Priests
Chairman
Very Rev Michael Quinn
Secretary
Very Rev Gerard Davey

Ecumenism
Director: Very Rev John Durkan PP
Killasser, Swinford, Co Mayo
Tel 094-9024761

Emigrants
Director
Very Rev Vincent Sherlock PP
Parochial House, Tubbercurry,
Co Sligo F91 HN34
Tel 071-9185049
Email vsherlock@achonrydiocese.org

Marriage Tribunal
(See Marriage Tribunals section)

Pastoral Centre
Rt Rev Mgr Thomas Johnston Adm
St Nathy's Pastoral Centre,
Charlestown, Co Mayo
Tel 094-9254315

Pilgrimage Director
Very Rev John Maloney Adm
Attymass, Ballina, Co Mayo
Tel 096-29990

Pioneer Total Abstinence Association
Spiritual Director
Very Rev Joseph Gavigan PP
Parochial House, Kilmovee,
Ballaghaderreen, Co Roscommon
Tel 094-9649137

Pontifical Mission Society
Diocesan Director
Very Rev Peter Gallagher PP
Lavagh, Ballymote, Co Sligo
Tel 071-9184002

Travellers
Chaplain
Pending appointment

Trócaire
Very Rev Gerard Davey Adm
Carracastle,
Ballaghaderreen,
Co Mayo F45 W822
Tel 094-9254301

Vocations
Director: Very Rev Paul Kivlehan Adm
Ballaghaderreen, Co Roscommon
Tel 094-9860011

Youth
Very Rev Paul Kivlehan Adm
Ballaghaderreen, Co Roscommon
Tel 094-9860011

PARISHES

The mensal parish is listed first. Other parishes follow alphabetically. Historical names are in parentheses. Church titulars are in italics.

BALLAGHADERREEN (CASTLEMORE AND KILCOLMAN)
Cathedral of The Annunciation & St Nathy
St Aidan, Monasteraden
SS John the Baptist & Colman,
Derrinacartha
Sacred Heart, Brusna
Very Rev Paul Kivlehan Adm
The Presbytery, Ballaghaderreen,
Co Roscommon
Tel 094-9860011 Fax 094-9860350

ACHONRY
SS Nathy and Brigid, Achonry, Ballymote
Sacred Heart, Mullinabreena, Ballymote
Very Rev Peter Gallagher PP
Lavagh, Ballymote, Co Sligo
Tel 071-9184002

ATTYMASS
St Joseph's
Very Rev John Maloney Adm
Attymass, Ballina, Co Mayo
Tel 096-29990

BALLISODARE
St Brigid
Very Rev Thomas Towey PP
Ballisodare, Co Sligo
Tel 071-9167467

BALLYMOTE (EMLEFAD AND KILMORGAN)
Immaculate Conception, Ballymote
St Joseph's, Doo
Very Rev James McDonagh PP, VF
Ballymote, Co Sligo
Tel 071-9191790

BOHOLA
Immaculate Conception & St Joseph
Very Rev Stephen O'Mahony PP
Bohola, Claremorris, Co Mayo
Tel 094-9384115

BONNICONLON (KILGARVAN)
Immaculate Heart of Mary
Very Rev John Geelan PP
Parochial House, Bonniconlon,
Ballina, Co Mayo
Tel 096-45016

BUNNINADDEN (KILSHALVEY, KILTURRA AND CLOONOGHILL)
Sacred Heart, Bunninadden
Immaculate Heart of Mary, Killavil
Very Rev Michael Reilly PP
Bunninadden,
Ballymote, Co Sligo
Tel 071-9183232
Fax 071-9189167

CARRACASTLE
St James', Carracastle
St Joseph's, Rooskey
Very Rev Gerard Davey Adm
Carracastle, Ballaghaderreen,
Co Mayo
Tel 094-9254301

CHARLESTOWN (KILBEAGH)
St James', Charlestown
St Patrick's, Bushfield
Rt Rev Mgr Thomas Johnston Adm
Charlestown, Co Mayo
Tel 094-9254315

COLLOONEY (KILVARNET)
Assumption, Collooney
SS Fechin & Lassara, Ballinacarrow
Very Rev Martin Convey PhD, PP
Tel 071-9167235
Very Rev James Canon Finan CC
Tel 071-9167109
Collooney, Co Sligo

COOLANEY (KILLORAN)
Church of the Sacred Heart & St Joseph,
Coolaney
Very Rev Patrick Holleran PP
Coolaney, Co Sligo
Tel 071-9167745

CURRY
Immaculate Conception, Curry
St Patrick's, Moylough
Very Rev Leo Henry PP
Curry, Ballymote, Co Sligo
Tel 087-6306938

FOXFORD (TOOMORE)
St Michael's, Foxford
Assumption, Toomore
Attymachugh
Very Rev Padraig Costello PP, VF
Foxford, Co Mayo
Tel 094-9256131

GURTEEN (KILFREE AND KILLARAGHT)
St Patrick's, Gurteen
St Joseph's, Cloonloo
St Attracta's, Killaraght
Very Rev Joseph Caulfield PP
Gurteen, Ballymote, Co Sligo
Tel 071-9182551 Fax 071-9182762

KEASH (DRUMRAT)
St Kevin, Keash
Our Lady of the Rosary, Culfadda
Very Rev Gabriel Murphy PP
Keash, Ballymote, Co Sligo
Tel 086-3429686

KILLASSER
All Saints, Killasser
St Thomas', Callow
Very Rev John Durkan PP
Killasser, Swinford, Co Mayo
Tel 094-9024761

KILMOVEE
Immaculate Conception, Kilmovee
St Joseph's, Urlaur
St Celsus, Kilkelly
St Patrick's, Glann
Very Rev Joseph Gavigan PP
Parochial House, Kilmovee,
Ballaghaderreen, Co Mayo
Tel 094-9649137

KILTIMAGH (KILLEDAN)
Holy Family, Souls in Purgatory &
St Aidan
Very Rev Michael Quinn PP
Tel 094-9381198
Rev Patrick Lynch *(priest in residence)*
Tel 094-9381492
Kiltimagh, Co Mayo

STRAIDE (TEMPLEMORE)
SS Peter & Paul
Very Rev Stephen O'Mahony Adm
Straide, Foxford, Co Mayo
Tel 094-9031029

SWINFORD (KILCONDUFF AND MEELICK)
Our Lady Help of Christians, Swinford
St Luke's, Meelick
St Joseph's, Midfield
Very Rev Dermot Meehan PP, VG
Swinford, Co Mayo
Tel 094-9251790
Rev Victor Akongwale CC
Curate's House, Carrowbeg,
Swinford, Co Mayo F12 FK81
Tel 094-9252895

TOURLESTRANE (KILMACTIGUE)
St Attracta's, Tourlestrane
Our Lady of the Rosary, Kilmactigue
Sacred Heart, Loch Talt
Very Rev John Glynn PP
Tourlestrane, Ballymote, Co Sligo
Tel 071-9181105

TUBBERCURRY (CLOONACOOL)
St John the Evangelist, Tubbercurry
St Michael's, Cloonacool
Very Rev Vincent Sherlock PP
Parochial House, Tubbercurry,
Co Sligo F91 HN34
Tel 071-9185049
Email vsherlock@achonrydiocese.org

PRIESTS OF THE DIOCESE IN OTHER MINISTRIES

Rev Seamus Collery
St Attracta's Community School,
Tubbercurry, Co Sligo
Tel 071-9120814
Dr Eugene Duffy
Convent Road, Ballaghaderreen,
Co Roscommon
Tel 087-9621410
Rev Martin Henry
St Nathy's College,
Ballaghadereen, Co Roscommon
Tel 094-9861728
Rev Tomás Surlis DD
St Patrick's College, Maynooth,
Co Kildare
Tel 01-7084700

RETIRED PRIESTS

Very Rev Farrell Cawley PE
Ballinacarrow, Co Sligo
Tel 086-0864347
Rt Rev Mgr John Doherty PE
(priest in residence)
Charlestown, Co Mayo
Tel 094-9255793
Very Rev Martin Jennings PE
4 St Mary's House, Shantalla, Galway
Tel 087-9476115
Very Rev Pat Lynch PE
(Priest in residence)
Kiltimagh, Co Mayo
Tel 094-9381492

Very Rev Tom Mulligan PE
Árd Aoibhinn, Madogue,
Swinford, Co Mayo
Tel 083-8997039
Very Rev Dan O'Mahony PE
Magheraboy, Kilmovee,
Ballaghaderreen, Co Mayo
Te 087-2401625
Very Rev Patrick Peyton PE
Carrownanty, Ballymore, Co Sligo
Tel 071-9328537

RELIGIOUS ORDERS AND CONGREGATIONS

SISTERS

CONGREGATION OF THE SISTERS OF MERCY
Convent of Mercy,
Collooney, Co Sligo F91 Y386
Tel/Fax 071-9167153
Community: 3

21 Dun na Rí, Rathscanlon,
Swinford, Co Mayo F12 VK74
Community: 1

An Cheathrú Mhór, Cill Lasrach,
Swinford, Co Mayo
Community: 1

Belgarrow, Sisters of Mercy,
Foxford, Co Mayo F26 PW74
Tel 094-9256573
Community: 2

Apt B5, Cormullen,
Foxford, Co Mayo F26 K721
Community: 1

7 Brabazon Heights,
Swinford, Co Mayo F12 X456
Community: 1

Apt A7, Cormullen,
Foxford, Co Mayo F26 H9E4
Community: 1

48 Marren Park,
Ballymote, Co Sligo F56 VF63
Community: 1

MARIST SISTERS
Marist Convent,
Tubbercurry, Co Sligo
Tel 071-9185018
Email ms3tub@gmail.com
Community Leader: Sr Kathleen Gilligan
Community: 15
Parish ministry, Marist laity

Marist Convent,
Charlestown, Co Mayo
Tel 094-9254133
Email maristch@eircom.net
Community: 2
Parish ministry, Marist laity

SISTERS OF ST JOSEPH OF THE APPARITION
St Joseph's Convent,
Dun Bríd, Ballymote, Co Sligo
Tel 071-9183973
Email stjsligo@eircom.net
Contact: Sr Teresa Cooney
Community: 6
Members: 775
Missionary Congregation

ST JOSEPH OF THE SACRED HEART SISTERS
Sisters of St Joseph of Sacred Heart,
Killasser, Swinford, Co Mayo
Tel 094-9251265
Sr Margaret Maloney

EDUCATIONAL INSTITUTIONS

St Nathy's College
Ballaghaderreen,
Co Roscommon
Tel 094-9860010 Fax 094-9860891
Email info@stnathys.com
Principal: Rev Martin Henry
Chaplain: Appointment pending

St Joseph Secondary School
Foxford, Co Mayo
Tel 094-9256145 Fax 094-9256126
Email info@stjosephsfoxford.ie
Principal: Eileen O'Brien
Chaplain: Very Rev Padraig Costello PP

CHARITABLE AND OTHER SOCIETIES

Hope House
Foxford, Co Mayo
Tel 094-9256888 Fax 094-9256865
Counsellors: Sr Attracta Canny,
Sr Dolores Duggan
Treatment centre for addiction problems

Fr Patrick Peyton Centre
Attymass, Co Mayo
Tel 096-45374 Fax 096-45376
Chaplain: Fr Steve Gibson CSC

Society of St Vincent de Paul
Contact: Mr John McDonnell
Tel 087-9227552

DIOCESE OF ARDAGH AND CLONMACNOIS

PATRON OF THE DIOCESE
ST MEL, 7 FEBRUARY

INCLUDES NEARLY ALL OF COUNTY LONGFORD,
THE GREATER PART OF COUNTY LEITRIM
AND PARTS OF COUNTIES CAVAN, OFFALY, ROSCOMMON,
SLIGO AND WESTMEATH

SEDE VACANTE

Diocesan Administrator
Rev Thomas Healy

St Michael's,
Ballinalee Road,
Longford N39 Y4X5
Tel 043-3346432
Fax 043-3346833
Email info@ardaghdiocese.org

ST MEL'S CATHEDRAL, LONGFORD

On 19 May 1840, Bishop William O'Higgins laid the foundation stone of a new cathedral for the Diocese of Ardagh and Clonmacnois. The foundation stone was taken from the original Cathedral of St Mel at Ardagh. The preacher at that ceremony was the Archbishop of Tuam, Archbishop John MacHale. Four other bishops, one hundred and twenty priests and an estimated forty thousand people were present.

The architect of the cathedral was Mr John Benjamin Keane. The magnificent portico was not included in the original design. This was the work of another architect, Mr George Ashlin, and was not erected until 1883. Without any doubt Bishop O'Higgins influenced the original design, which reflected some of his own life experience, having been educated in Paris, Rome and having lived for a time in Vienna. The cathedral owes something in its design to the Madeleine in Paris, and the Pantheon and the Basilica of St John Lateran in Rome. Certainly something of the Lateran is to be seen in the attempt that was made to incorporate the bishop's house at the rear of the sanctuary.

Raising the money necessary to build the cathedral was an enormous challenge in poverty-stricken Ireland in the 1840s. Bishop O'Higgins travelled the length and breadth of the diocese and his appeals for help went well beyond the diocesan boundaries. He received great help, especially from the Dioceses of Elphin, Tuam and Meath, and contributions came from as far away as Belfast. A priest of the diocese toured North America and Canada to raise funds there.

By 1846 the walls, pillars and entire masonry were completed and the roof was the next stage in the building programme. Then the potato blight came and the Great Hunger. Work had to be suspended. Bishop O'Higgins would never see the great cathedral completed. He died in 1853.

Bishop John Kilduff, successor of Bishop O'Higgins, resumed work on the cathedral. It was opened for worship in September 1856. Though the work was not complete, it was a time of great rejoicing. Present on that special day were Archbishop Dixon of Armagh and Archbishop Cullen of Dublin, and fourteen other bishops.

It was Bishop Bartholomew Woodlock who commissioned the erection of the impressive portico, with its huge Ionic columns. He was still bishop of the diocese in 1893 when the cathedral was consecrated on 19 May.

Since 1893 much additional work has been done. Bishop Hoare, successor of Bishop Woodlock, added a pipe organ and bell chimes. Later still, two beautiful stained-glass windows, the work of the Harry Clarke Studios in Dublin, were installed in the transepts. In the 1970s a major restyling of the sanctuary was undertaken.

On Christmas Morning 2009 St Mel's Cathedral was badly damaged by fire. A major restoration project was immediately undertaken. St Mel's Cathedral was rededicated on Sunday, 17 May 2015.

Most Rev Colm O'Reilly DD
Retired Bishop of Ardagh and
Clonmacnois; born 11 January 1935;
ordained priest 19 June 1960;
ordained Bishop of Ardagh and
Clonmacnois 10 April 1983;
retired 6 October 2013
Residence: Deanscurragh, Longford
Tel 043-3347831

DIOCESAN TRUSTEES

Rev Liam Murray (Secretary)
Mgr Bernard Noonan
Rev Michael Bannon
Rev Thomas Healy
Rev Bernard Hogan
Rev Peter Burke
Rev Liam Murray
Rev Pat Murphy
Rev Gerard O'Brien

ADMINISTRATION

Vicar General
Vacant

Diocesan Chancellor
Rev Michael Bannon PP
Gowna, Co Cavan
Tel 043-6683120

College of Consultors
Vacant

Vicars Forane
Vacant

Financial Administrator
Rev Liam Murray PP
Diocesan Office,
St Michael's, Longford
Tel 043-3346432

Finance Committee
Chairman: Rev Thomas Healy
Members
Mgr Bernard Noonan
Mr Frank Gearty
Rev Liam Murray
Mr Brian Loughran
Mr Tom Mulligan

Diocesan Archivist
Rev Tom Murray PP
Parochial House, Ballinalee, Co Longford
Tel 043-3323110

Diocesan Secretary
Rev Liam Murray
Diocesan Office, St Michael's,
Longford
Tel 043-3346432
Email diocesansec@ardaghdiocese.org

CATECHETICS EDUCATION

**Pastoral Renewal and Faith
Development**
Rev James MacKiernan Adm
Diocesan Office, St Michael's,
Longford
Tel 043-3346432

Religious Education in Schools
Diocesan Advisers
Primary: Mr Colm Harte
Mrs Margaret Kelly
Post-Primary: Fr Turlough Baxter
Diocesan Office,
St Michael's, Longford
Tel 043-3346432

Education Secretary (Primary)
Secretary: Mrs Eileen Ward
Diocesan Office,
St Michael's, Longford
Tel 043-3346432

LITURGY

Church Music
Director: Rev Turlough Baxter Adm
Parochial House, Killashee,
Co Longford
Tel 043-3345546

Liturgy Commission
Secretary: Rev Turlough Baxter Adm
Parochial House, Killashee,
Co Longford
Tel 043-3345546

Sacred Art and Architecture Commission
Secretary: Rev Sean Casey PP
Killoe, Co Longford
Tel 043-3323119

PASTORAL

ACCORD
Director: Rev Patrick Murphy Adm
St Mary's, Athlone, Co Westmeath
Tel 090-6472088

Communications
Diocesan Communications Officer
Rev Tom Cox Adm
Shannonbridge, Athlone, Co Offaly
Tel 090-9674125

Council of Priests
Chairman: Vacant
Secretary: Vacant

Ecumenism
Rev Tony Gilhooly
The Presbytery, Longford
Tel 043-3346465

Marriage Tribunal
(See Marriage Tribunals section.)

Pilgrimage (Lourdes)
Director
Mgr Bernard Noonan PP
Moate, Co Westmeath
Tel 090-6481180

Pioneer Total Abstinence Association
Diocesan Director
Rev Michael Campbell PP
Abbeylara, Co Longford
Tel 043-6686270

Pontifical Mission Societies
Diocesan Director
Rev P.J. Hughes
Parochial House, Mullahoran,
Kilcogy, Co Cavan
Tel 043-6683141

**Safeguarding Children Diocesan
Committee**
Mr Sean Leydon
Ms Maria Beirne
Mr Liam Faughnan
Rev Liam Murray
Rev Michael Bannon
Rev Thomas Healy
Ms Philomena Lynch
Ms Evelyn Breen (Choir)

Trócaire
Diocesan Director
Rev Bernard Hogan PP
Drumlish, Co Longford
Tel 043-3324132

Vocations
Director: Rev Seamus O'Rourke CC
Curate's Residence, Dublin Road,
Carrick-on-Shannon, Co Leitrim
Tel 071-9620054

PARISHES

Mensal parishes are listed first. Other
parishes follow alphabetically. Historical
names are given in parentheses. Church
titulars are in italics.

**LONGFORD (TEMPLEMICHAEL,
BALLYMACORMACK)**
*St Mel's Cathedral; St Anne's, Curry;
St Michael's, Shroid*
Rev James MacKiernan Adm
Rev Michael McGrath CC
Rev Tony Gilhooly CC
Rev Joseph Ukut (MSP) CC
The Presbytery, Longford
Tel 043-3346465

THLONE
Mary's, Athlone
ur Lady Queen of Peace, Coosan
ev Patrick Murphy Adm
ev Padraig Kelliher CC
ev John Eze (MSP) CC
Mary's, Athlone, Co Westmeath
el 090-6472088

BBEYLARA
Bernard's, Abbeylara
Mary's, Carra
ev Michael Campbell PP
arra, Granard, Co Longford
el 043-6686270

NNADUFF
maculate Conception, Annaduff
maculate Conception, Drumsna
ev John Wall PP
nnaduff, Carrick-on-Shannon,
Leitrim
l 071-9624093

RDAGH AND MOYDOW
Brigid's, Ardagh; Our Lady's, Moydow
ev Vincent Connaughton PP
rdagh, Co Longford
l 043-6675006

UGHAVAS AND CLOONE
Joseph's, Aughavas
Stephen's, Rossan
Mary's, Cloone
ev Peter Tiernan PP
loone, Co Leitrim
l 071-9636016

ALLINAHOWN, BOHER AND PULLOUGH (EMANAGHAN)
Colmcille's, Ballinahown
Manchain's, Ballycumber
Mary's, Pullough
ev Brendan O'Sullivan PP
allinahown, Athlone, Co Westmeath
l 090-6430124
ev Reji Kurian *(in residence)*
oher, Ballycumber, Co Offaly
l 057-9336119

ALLYMAHON (SHRULE)
Matthew's, Ballymahon
ev Liam Murray PP
allymahon, Co Longford
l 090-6432253

ORNACOOLA
Michael's, Bornacoola
Joseph's, Clonturk
ev Gerard O'Brien PP
ornacoola, Carrick-on-Shannon,
Leitrim
l 071-9638229

ARRICKEDMOND AND ABBEYSHRULE
aghshiney, Taghshinod & Abbeyshrule)
acred Heart, Carrickedmond
ur Lady of Lourdes, Abbeyshrule
ev Charles Healy PP
arrickedmond, Colehill, Co Longford
l 044-9357442

CARRICK-FINEA (DRUMLUMMAN SOUTH AND BALLYMACHUGH)
St Mary's, Carrick
St Mary's, Ballynarry
Rev Gerard Brady PP
Carrick, Finea, Mullingar,
Co Westmeath
Tel 043-6681129

CARRICK-ON-SHANNON (KILTOGHERT)
St Mary of the Assumption
Carrick-on-Shannon
Sacred Heart, Jamestown
St Patrick's, Gowel
St Joseph's, Leitrim
Rev Francis Garvey PP
Carrick-on-Shannon, Co Leitrim
Tel 071-9620118
Rev Seamus O'Rourke CC
Tel 071-9620054
Rev Mark Bennett CC
Tel 071-9620347
St Mary's, Carrick-on-Shannon,
Co Leitrim

CLOGHAN AND BANAGHER (GALLEN AND REYNAGH)
St Mary's, Cloghan
St Rynagh's Banagher
Rev Pat Kiernan PP
Banagher, Co Offaly
Tel 057-9151338

CLONBRONEY
St James, Clonbroney
Holy Trinity, Ballinalee
Rev Tom Murray PP
Ballinalee, Co Longford
Tel 043-3323110

CLOONE (CLOONE-CONMAICNE)
St Mary's, Cloone
See Aughavas & Cloone

COLMCILLE
St Colmcille's, Aughnacliffe
St Joseph's, Purth
Rev Seamus McKeon PP
Aughnacliffe, Co Longford
Tel 043-6684118

DROMARD
St Mary's, Legga; St Mary's, Moyne
Rev Patrick Lennon PP
Dromard, Moyne, Co Longford
Tel 049-4335248

DRUMLISH
St Mary's, Drumlish
St Patrick's, Ballinamuck
Rev Bernard Hogan PP
Drumlish, Co Longford
Tel 043-3324132

DRUMSHANBO (MURHAUN)
St Patrick's, Drumshanbo
Rev Francis Murray PP
Drumshanbo, Co Leitrim
Tel 071-9641010

EDGEWORTHSTOWN (MOSTRIM)
St Mary of the Immaculate Conception
Rev Thomas Healy PP
St Mary's, Edgeworthstown,
Co Longford
Tel 043-6671046

FENAGH
St Mary's, Foxfield
See Mohill Parish

FERBANE HIGH STREET AND BOORA (TISARAN AND FUITHRE)
Immaculate Conception, Ferbane
SS Patrick and Saran, Belmont
St Oliver Plunkett, Boora
Rev Peter Burke PP
Tel 090-6454380
Rev Michael Morris (SPS) CC
Tel 090-6454309
Ferbane, Co Offaly

GORTLETTERAGH
St Mary's, Gortletteragh
St Thomas', Fairglass
St Joseph's, Cornageetha
Rev John Quinn PP
Gortletteragh,
Carrick-on-Shannon, Co Leitrim
Tel 071-9631074

GRANARD
St Mary's
Rev Simon Cadam PP
St Mary's, Granard, Co Longford
Tel 043-6686550

KEADUE, ARIGNA AND BALLYFARNON (KILRONAN)
Nativity of the Blessed Virgin, Keadue
Immaculate Conception, Arigna
St Patrick's, Ballyfarnon
Rev Cathal Faughnan PP
Keadue, Boyle, Co Roscommon
Tel 071-9647212

KILCOMMOC (KENAGH)
St Dominic's
Rev Thomas Barden PP
Kenagh, Co Longford
Tel 043-3322127

KILLASHEE
St Patrick's, Killashee
St Brendan's, Clondra
Rev Turlough Baxter Adm
Parochial House, Killashee,
Co Longford
Tel 043-3345546

KILLENUMMERY AND BALLINTOGHER (KILLENUMMERY AND KILLERY)
St Mary's, Killenummery
St Michael's, Killavoggy
St Teresa's, Ballintogher
Rev Patsy McDermott PP
Killenummery, Dromahair,
via Sligo, Co Leitrim
Tel 071-9164125

KILLOE
St Mary's, Ennybegs
St Oliver Plunkett's, Cullyfad
Rev Sean Casey PP
Ennybegs, Longford
Tel 043-3323119

KILTUBRID
St Brigid's, Drumcong
St Joseph's, Rantogue
Rev Tomás Flynn PP
Drumcong, Carrick-on-Shannon,
Co Leitrim
Tel 071-9642021

LANESBORO (RATHCLINE)
St Mary's, Lanesboro
Rev Merlyn Kenny PP/Rev Turlough
Baxter PP
Lanesboro, Co Longford
Tel 043-3321166

LEGAN AND BALLYCLOGHAN (KILGLASS AND RATHREAGH)
Nativity of the Blessed Virgin Mary,
Lenamore
St Ann's, Ballycloghan
Rev Charles Healy PP
Carrickedmond, Co Longford
Tel 044-9357442

LOUGH GOWNA AND MULLINALAGHTA (SCRABBY AND COLMCILLE EAST)
Holy Family, Lough Gowna
St Columba's, Mullinalaghta
Rev Michael Bannon PP
Gowna, Co Cavan
Tel 043-6683120

MOATE AND MOUNT TEMPLE (KILCLEAGH AND BALLYLOUGHLOE)
St Patrick's, Moate; St Ciaran's, Castledaly
Corpus Christi, Mount Temple
Mgr Bernard Noonan PP, VG
Tel 090-6481180
Rev Liam Farrell CC
Tel 090-6481189
Moate, Co Westmeath
Rev Joe McGrath CC
Mount Temple, Moate, Co Westmeath
Tel 090-6481239

MOHILL (MOHILL-MANACHAIN)
St Patrick's, Mohill
St Joseph's, Gorvagh
St Mary's, Eslin Bridge
St Mary's, Foxfield
Rev Nigel Charles PP
Tel 071-9631024
Rev Sean Burke CC
Tel 071-9631097
Mohill, Co Leitrim

MULLAHORAN AND LOUGHDUFF (DRUMLUMMAN NORTH)
Our Lady of Lourdes, Mullahoran
St Joseph's, Loughduff
Rev P.J. Hughes PP
Mullahoran, Kilcogy via Longford,
Co Cavan
Tel 043-6683141

NEWTOWNCASHEL (CASHEL)
The Blessed Virgin
Rev Merlyn Kenny PP
Newtowncashel, Co Longford
Tel 043-3325112

NEWTOWNFORBES (CLONGUISH)
St Mary's
Rev Ciaran McGovern PP
Newtownforbes, Co Longford
Tel 043-3346805

RATHOWEN (RATHASPIC, RUSSAGH & STREETE)
St Mary's, Rathowen
Rev Pierre Pepper Adm
Parochial House,
Boherquill, Lismacaffrey,
Mullingar, Co Westmeath
Tel 043-6685847

SHANNONBRIDGE (CLONMACNOIS)
St Ciaran's, Shannonbridge
St Ciaran's, Clonfanlough
Rev Tom Cox Adm
Shannonbridge, Athlone, Co Offaly
Tel 090-9674125

STREETE AND RATHOWEN
St Mary's
See Rathown (Rathaspic and Rossagh)
Rev Pierre Pepper Adm
Parochial House,
Boherquill, Lismacaffrey,
Mullingar, Co Westmeath
Tel 043-6685847

PRIESTS OF THE DIOCESE ELSEWHERE

Rev Colman Carrigy
Clonee, Killoe, Co Longford
Rev Liam Cuffe
Chaplaincy, St Vincent's Hospital,
Dublin 4
Rev Aidan Ryan
Lake Road, Moate, Co Westmeath
Rev Declan Shannon
Chaplain, Custume Barracks,
Athlone, Co Westmeath
Rev Christy Stapleton
St Michael's, Longford
Rev Hugh Turbitt
St Michael's, Longford

RETIRED PRIESTS

Rev Peter Beglan PE
The Presbytery,
Edgeworthstown, Co Longford
Rev Peter Brady PE
Lenamore, Co Longford
Rev Brian Brennan PE
Hollybrook, Drumanure,
Abbeyshrule, Co Longford
Tel 044-9357521
Rev Eamonn Corkery PE
Aughnacliffe, Co Longford N39 T2P1

Rev Owen Devaney PE
Treanlawn, Killoe, Co Longford N39 T9F
Mgr Patrick Earley PE
Parochial House,
Rathowen, Co Westmeath
Tel 043-6676044
Rev PJ Fitzpatrick
6 St Ciaran Park, Tullamore Road,
Shannonbridge, Co Offaly
Rev Francis O'Hanlon PE
St James' Apartment, Knock, Co Mayo
Rev Michael Reilly
Park Place, Colehill, Co Longford
Rev Michael Scanlon PE
Parochial House, Cloghan, Co Offaly

RELIGIOUS ORDERS AND CONGREGATIONS

PRIESTS

FRANCISCANS
Franciscan Friary,
Athlone, Co Westmeath
Tel 090-6472095 Fax 090-6424713
Email athlonefriary@eircom.net
Guardian: Rev Gabriel Kinahan (OFM)
Vicar: Rev Seamus Donohue (OFM)

MARIST FATHERS (SOCIETY OF MARY)
Rev Tim Kenny (SM)
Innis Ree Nursing Home,
Ballyleague, Lanesboro, Co Longford

BROTHERS

MARIST BROTHERS
Champagnat House, Athlone,
Co Westmeath
Tel 090-6476032
Superior: Br P.J. McGowan
Community: 3

Marist College,
Athlone, Co Westmeath
Tel 090-6474491
Secondary pupils: 510

SISTERS

CONGREGATION OF THE SISTERS OF MERCY
Sisters of Mercy,
Shalom, Edgeworthstown,
Co Longford N39 TW44
Tel 043-71852 Fax 043-72989

Upper Main Street,
Ballymahon, Co Longford N39 XTD1
Tel 090-6432532
Community: 3

7 Mill Street,
Drumlish, Co Longford N39 X500
Tel 043-29585
Community: 1

sters of Mercy, 61 Cnoc na Greine,
ranard, Co Longford N39 XD57
el 043-6686563
ommunity: 1

annagh Grove,
ohill, Co Leitrim N41 X067
el 071-9631064
ommunity: 2

Midara Gardens,
ngford N39 W8C2
l/Fax 043-3346702
ommunity: 1

sters of Mercy,
e Lodge,
rumshanbo, Co Leitrim N41 CF64
el 071-9641308
ommunity: 2

Cara Court,
rrick-on-Shannon,
Leitrim N41 HP08
071-9622582
ommunity: 1

Cluain Doire,
ewtownforbes,
Longford N39 AN25
ommunity: 1

7 Mostrim Oaks,
dgeworthstown,
Longford N39 KN12
ommunity: 1

or 1, Boderg House,
arbour Road, Tarmonbarry,
Roscommon N39 YE63
l 043-3326027
ommunity: 1

Oaklands Grove,
aklands, Ballinalee Road,
ngford N39 X4T1
ommunity: 1

St Mary's Terrace, Dublin Road,
ngford N39 C6C4
ommunity: 1

8 Mostrim Oaks,
geworthstown,
Longford N39 RH67
ommunity: 1

Convent of Mercy, St Joseph's Road,
Longford N39 C4E4
Community: 22

Sisters of Mercy,
8 St Patrick's Terrace,
Major Well Road, Longford N39 P6Y9
Community: 1

Sisters of Mercy,
10 St Patrick's Terrace,
Longford N39 R9Y7
Community: 1

Rose Cottage,
Ardagh Road, Feraghfad,
Longford N39 P9D3
Community: 1

Sisters of Mercy,
St Joseph's Way, Dublin Road,
Longford N39 C4E4
Community: 6

7 Ard Michael, Ballinalee Road,
Longford N39 T6T3
Community: 1

LA SAINTE UNION DES SACRES COEURS
11 Retreat Park, Athlone,
Co Westmeath
Community: 2
Pastoral

Secondary School (day)
Pupils: 650
Principal: Mr Noel Casey
Tel 090-6474777/6475524
Fax 090-6476356
Email bower@iol.ie

Banagher, Co Offaly
Tel 0509-51319
Email lsu1@eircom.net
Community: 7
Teaching, Parish care of the Sick
and Frail Elderly

11 Sonas Care Home,
Cloghanboy, Ballymahon Road,
Athlone, Co Westmeath
Community: 3

MARIST SISTERS
Marist Convent
Carrick-on-Shannon, Co Leitrim
Tel 071-9620010
Email carrickmarist@gmail.com
Co-ordinator: Sr Elizabeth Gilmartin
Community: 9

7 Summerhill Grove,
Carrick-on-Shannon, Co Leitrim
Tel 071-9621396
Community: 2

CONGREGATION OF OUR LADY OF THE MISSIONS SISTERS
Ratharney, Abbeyshrule,
Co Longford N39 RX29
Tel 044-9357827
Community: 2 retired sisters
Parish ministry

POOR CLARES
Poor Clare Monastery of Perpetual
Adoration, Drumshanbo,
Co Leitrim
Abbess: Mother Jemma Hayag
Community: 6
Contemplatives
Perpetual adoration of the Blessed
Sacrament
Fax 071-9640789

ST JOSEPH OF CLUNY SISTERS
St Joseph's Convent,
Main Street, Ferbane, Co Offaly
Tel 090-6454324
Email stjf@eircom.net
Superior: Sr Benedict Behan
Community: 3
Pastoral Ministry

EDUCATIONAL INSTITUTIONS

St Mel's College, Longford
Tel 043-3346469
Principal: Mr Malachy Flanagan

Athlone Institute of Technology
Athlone, Co Westmeath
Chaplain: Rev Seamus Casey
Tel 090-6424400
Res: 11 Auburn Heights, Athlone,
Co Westmeath
Tel 090-6478318

DIOCESE OF CLOGHER

PATRON OF THE DIOCESE
ST MACARTAN, 24 MARCH

INCLUDES COUNTY MONAGHAN, MOST OF COUNTY FERMANAGH
AND PORTIONS OF COUNTIES TYRONE, DONEGAL, LOUTH AND CAVAN

Most Rev Lawrence Duffy D
Bishop of Clogher;
born 27 November 1951;
ordained priest 13 June 1976
ordained Bishop of Clogher 10
February 2019

Residence: Bishop's House,
Monaghan H18 PN35
Tel 047-81019
Email diocesanoffice
@clogherdiocese.ie
Website www.clogherdiocese.

ST MACARTAN'S CATHEDRAL, MONAGHAN

On Sunday, 3 January 1858, at a meeting of the Catholic inhabitants of the parish and vicinity of Monaghan, with the Bishop of Clogher, Dr Charles MacNally, presiding, it was formally resolved that a new Catholic church at Monaghan was urgently required. An eight-acre site was purchased by the bishop from Humphrey Jones of Clontibret for £800, and an architect, James Joseph McCarthy of Dublin, was employed to draw a design.

The style is French Gothic of the fourteenth century. In June 1861 the foundation stone was laid, and the work got underway the following year. Dr MacNally died in 1864, and work resumed under his successor, Dr James Donnelly, in 1865. The architect died in 1882 and was succeeded by William Hague, a Cavan man, who was responsible for the design of the spire and the gate-lodge. The work was completed in 1892, and the cathedral was solemnly dedicated on 21 August of that year.

Under the direction of Bishop Joseph Duffy, a radical rearrangement and refurbishing of the interior of the cathedral was begun in 1982 to meet the requirements of the revised liturgy. The artist responsible for the general scheme was Michael Biggs of Dublin, in consultation with local architect Gerald MacCann. The altar is carved from a single piece of granite from south County Dublin. The sanctuary steps are in solid Travertine marble. The sanctuary crucifix is by Richard Enda King; the cross is of Irish oak and the figure of Christ is cast in bronze. The Lady Chapel has a bronze Pietà by Nell Murphy, and the lettering of the Magnificat is by Michael Biggs.

The tabernacle, made of silver-plated sheet bronze and mounted on a granite pillar, has the form of a tent and was designed and made by Richard Enda King. In the chapel of the Holy Oils the aumbry was designed by Michael Biggs, while the miniature bronze gates were executed by Martin Leonard. The five great tapestries on the east walls of the cathedral are a striking feature of the renovation; they were designed by Frances Biggs and woven by Terry Dunne, both of Dublin.

Allianz (li)

ost Rev Liam S. MacDaid DD
tired Bishop of Clogher;
rn 19 July 1945; ordained priest 15
ne 1969; ordained Bishop of Clogher
July 2010; retired 1 October 2016
sidence: Drumhirk, Dublin Road,
naghan H18 YE30
047-82208

ost Rev Joseph Duffy DD
hop Emeritus
rn 3 February 1934; ordained priest 22
ne 1958; ordained Bishop of Clogher 2
ptember 1979; retired 25 July 2010
sidence: Doire na gCraobh, Monaghan
047-62725

CHAPTER

an: Rt Rev Mgr Peter O'Reilly
chdeacon
Rev Mgr Shane McCaughey
embers
Rev Mgr Joseph McGuinness
ry Rev Ramon Munster
ry Rev Patrick MacEntee
ry Rev Michael Daly
ry Rev Owen J. McEneaney
ry Rev Patrick McGinn
ry Rev Jimmy McPhillips
ry Rev Noel McGahan
ry Rev Martin Treanor
ry Rev Kevin Duffy

ADMINISTRATION

ars General
Rev Mgr Peter O'Reilly
Rev Mgr Shane McCaughey

ancellor
ry Rev John Chester
ocesan Office, Bishop's House,
naghan H18 PN35
047-81019
ail diocesanoffice@clogherdiocese.ie
ohn@clogherdiocese.ie

uncil of Administration
hop Lawrence Duffy
hop Liam S. MacDaid
hop Joseph Duffy
Rev Mgr Peter O'Reilly
Rev Mgr Joseph McGuinness
Rev Mgr Shane McCaughey

ance Committee
mbers: Bishop Lawrence Duffy
Rev Mgr Joseph McGuinness,
Rev Mgr Shane McCaughey,
Rev Mgr Peter O'Reilly
Michael Duffy, Mr Cormac Meehan,
Martin McVicar, Mr Fintan Timoney,
Caitriona Lonergan,
Tom McGrade, Ms Deborah McArdle
ocesan Office Administrator
Mary McCrystal
ancial Administrator
Aileen Hughes
hop's House, Monaghan H18 PN35
047-81019
ail diocesanoffice@clogherdiocese.ie

Diocesan Secretary
Rt Rev Mgr Shane McCaughey
Diocesan Office, Bishop's House,
Monaghan H18 PN35
Tel 047-81019
Email diocesanoffice@clogherdiocese.ie
frshane@clogherdiocese.ie

Diocesan Office Administrator
Ms Mary McCrystal
Diocesan Office, Bishop's House,
Monaghan H18 PN35
Tel 047-81019
Email diocesanoffice@clogherdiocese.ie
mary@clogherdiocese.ie

Diocesan Archivist
Dr Gary Carville
Diocesan Office, Bishop's House,
Monaghan H18 PN35
Tel 047-81019
Email gary@clogherdiocese.ie

Communications
Director of Communications
Dr Gary Carville. Tel 087-1767226
Diocesan Office, Bishop's House,
Monaghan H18 PN35
Tel 047-81019
Email gary@clogherdiocese.ie

CATECHETICS EDUCATION

Adult Faith Development
Diocesan Adviser
Very Rev Canon Macartan McQuaid
Mullanarockan, Tydavnet,
Co Monaghan H18 YV20
Tel 087-2454705
Email macqua743@gmail.com

**Catholic Primary School Managers'
Association (RI)**
Diocesan Council Secretary
Very Rev Canon Michael Daly PP
Broomfield, Castleblayney,
Co Monaghan A75 A344
Tel 042-9743617
Email dalyml@sky.com

Religious Education
Diocesan Advisers
Primary
Very Rev John Flanagan PP
Ballyoisin Emyvale,
Monaghan H18 F207
Tel 047-87152
Email truaghp@gmail.com
Post-Primary (NI)
Mrs Eileen Gallagher
St Michael's College,
Enniskillen, Co Fermanagh BT74 6DE
(Friday 9.00am-5.00pm)
Tel 028-66328210
Email eccgallagher@yahoo.co.uk
Post-Primary (ROI)
Vacant

LITURGY

Diocesan Liturgy Commission
Chairman
Rev Deacon Martin Donnelly
St Michael's Parish Centre,
28 Church Street, Enniskillen,
Co Fermanagh BT74 7EJ
Tel 028-66322075
Email deacon@st-michaels.net
Secretary: Dr Gary Carville,
Tel 047-81019/087-1767226
Email gary@clogherdiocese.ie

PASTORAL

ACCORD
Diocesan Directors
Very Rev John Chester PP
Roslea, Co Fermanagh BT92 7QY
Tel 028-67751227
Email parishofroslea@gmail.com
Rt Rev Mgr Peter O'Reilly PP, VG
1 Darling Street, Enniskillen,
Co Fermanagh BT74 7DP
Tel 028-66322075
Email pp@st-michaels.net

Council of Priests
Chairman
Very Rev Canon Michael Daly
Broomfield, Castleblayney,
Co Monaghan A75 A344
Tel 042-9743617
Email dalyml@sky.com
Secretary: Rev Owen Gorman
Shantonagh, Castleblayney,
Co Monaghan A75 NN12
Tel 042-9745015
Email fr.owengorman@gmail.com

Ecumenism
Director
Rt Rev Mgr Peter O'Reilly PP, VG
1 Darling Street, Enniskillen,
Co Fermanagh BT74 7DP
Tel 028-663226275
Email pp@st-michaels.net

Emigrants
Director: Vacant

Lourdes Pilgrimage
Director: Mr Brian Armitage
6 Drumhaw Avenue, Lisnaskea,
Co Fermanagh BT92 0LY
Tel 028-67721964
Secretary: Mr Jonn Heuston
Gave, Mackagh, Crom Road,
Lisnaskea, Co Fermanagh
Tel 028-67724320
Email john.cdp@btconnect.com
Spiritual Director
Very Rev Canon Noel McGahan PP
Clogher, Co Tyrone BT76 0TQ
Tel 028-85549604

Marriage Tribunal
Clogher Office of Armagh Regional
Marriage Tribunal
Mr Kevin Slowey
Ros Erne House, 8 Darling Street,
Enniskillen, Co Fermanagh BT74 7DP
Tel 028-66327222
Email tribunalcloghermt@gmail.com

Pioneer Total Abstinence Association
Director: Rev Sean Mulligan CC
Parochial House, 25 Lisdergan Road,
Fintona, Co Tyrone BT78 2NR
Tel 028-82841907

Pontifical Mission Societies
Diocesan Director: Very Rev Brian Early PE
St Dympna's, Tydavnet,
Co Monaghan H18 Y190
Tel 047-79434
Email pbbearly64@gmail.com

Safeguarding
Director/Co-ordinator: Ms Martha Smyth
Ros Erne House, 8 Darling Street,
Enniskillen, Co Fermanagh BT74 7EW
Tel 0044-7775507445
Email
safeguardingdirector@clogherdiocese.ie
Designated Liaison Persons
Ms Martha Smyth
Ros Erne House, 8 Darling Street,
Enniskillen, Co Fermanagh BT74 7EW
Tel 0044-7775507445
Email
safeguardingdirector@clogherdiocese.ie
Mr Brendan Kelly
Safeguarding Office,
St Macartan's College, Mullaghmurphy
Monaghan H18 YX03
Tel 087-3874742
Email dlp1@clogherdiocese.ie
Ms Anne Molloy
Dunene Avenue, Kesh Road, Irvinestown,
Co Fermanagh
Tel 078-79413855
Email amolloy164@live.co.uk
Vetting Officer: Ms Geraldine McKenna
Safeguarding Office,
St Macartan's College,
Monaghan H18 YX03
Tel 087-3874742
Email vetting@clogherdiocese.ie

Suicide Awareness and Prevention
Resource Person
Very Rev Cathal Deery PP
15 Knockmore Road, Drumary,
Derrygonnelly,
Co Fermanagh BT93 6GA
Tel 028-68641207
Email cdeery1966@gmail.com

Synodality Contact Person
Ms Linda Walsh Fitzgerald
Diocesan Office, Bishop's House,
Monaghan H18 PN35
Tel 047-81019
Email diocesanoffice@clogherdiocese.ie
synod@clogherdiocese.ie

Travellers
Chaplain: Rev Michael Jordan CC
Parochial House, Killanny,
Carrickmacross, Co Monaghan A81 PX31
Tel 042-9378105
Email michaelgjordan@aol.com

Vocations (Priesthood)
Director and Chairman of Vocations
Rev Raymond Donnelly CC
4 Darling Street, Enniskillen,
Co Fermanagh BT74 7DP
Tel 028-66322075
Email parishcentre@st-michaels.net

Vocations (Permanent Diaconate)
Director
Rev Deacon Martin Donnelly
28 Church Street, Enniskillen,
Co Fermanagh BT74 7EJ
Tel 028-66322075
Email deacon@st-michaels.net

Youth Ministry Co-ordinator
Chairperson: Rev Leo Creelman CC
St Joseph's Presbytery, Park Street,
Monaghan H18 C588
Tel 047-81220
Co-ordinator: Mr James McLoughlin
Office: Clogher don Óige,
St Macartan's College,
Monaghan H18 YX03
Tel 047-72784
Email james@clogherdiocese.org
Website www.clogherdonoige.com

PARISHES

The mensal parish is listed first. Other
parishes follow alphabetically. In each
case the postal name is given first,
except where inappropriate, and the
official name in parentheses. Church
titulars are in italics.

MONAGHAN
St Macartan's Cathedral, St Joseph's,
St Michael's
Email
parishoffice@stjosephsmonaghan.com
Very Rev Canon Patrick McGinn Adm
Rev Leo Creelman CC
St Joseph's Presbytery, Park Street,
Monaghan H18 C588
Tel 047-81220 Fax 047-84004

AUGHNAMULLEN EAST
Sacred Heart, Lough Egish
St Mary's, Carrickatee
Very Rev Adrian Walshe PP
Parochial House, Beech Corner,
Castleblayney, Co Monaghan A75 KR96
Tel 042-9740027
Rev Owen Gorman (OCDS) CC
(Priest in residence)
Shantonagh, Castleblayney,
Co Monaghan A75 NN12
Tel 042-9745015
Email parishaughnamulleneast@yahoo.com

BALLYBAY (TULLYCORBET)
St Patrick's, Ballybay
Holy Rosary, Tullycorbet
Our Lady of Knock, Ballintra
Very Rev Canon Owen J. McEneaney PP
Rev Kieran Danfulani CC
Parochial House, St Patrick's, Ballybay,
Co Monaghan A75 K299
Tel/Fax 042-9741032
Email contact@tullycorbetparish.com

BELLEEK-GARRISON (INIS MUIGHE SAMI
Our Lady, Queen of Peace, Garrison
St John the Baptist, Toura
St Joseph's, Cashelnadrea
St Patrick's, Belleek
St Michael's, Mulleek
Very Rev Tiernach Beggan PP
6 Boa Island, Belleek, Enniskillen,
Co Fermanagh BT93 3AE
Tel 028-68658229
Email belleekgarrison@btinternet.com

BROOKEBORO (AGHAVEA-AGHINTAINE
St Mary's, Brookeboro
St Joseph's, Coonian
St Mary's, Fivemiletown
Very Rev Brendan Gallagher PP
146 Ballagh Road, Fivemiletown,
Co Tyrone, BT75 0QP
Tel 028-89521291
Email aghaveaaughintaine@gmail.com
Very Rev Canon Laurence Dawson PE
25 Teiges Hill, Brookeborough,
Co Fermanagh BT94 4EZ
Tel 028-89531770
Email dawson829@btinternet.com

BUNDORAN (MAGH ENE)
Our Lady, Star of the Sea, Bundoran
St Joseph's, The Rock, Ballyshannon
Very Rev Canon Ramon Munster PP
Parochial House, Church Road,
Bundoran, Co Donegal F94 AK80
Tel 071-9841290 Fax 071-9841596
Email ppbundoran@gmail.com
Very Rev Canon Michael McGourty PE
(Priest in residence)
Lisnarick Road, Irvinestown, Co Fermanag
Email mmcgourtylive@co.uk

CARRICKMACROSS (MACHAIRE ROIS)
St Joseph's, Carrickmacross
St Michael's, Corduff
St John the Evangelist, Raferagh
Rt Rev Mgr Shane McCaughey PP, VG
St Joseph's Carrickmacross,
Co Monaghan A81 F688
Tel 042-9664367
Email
stjosephscarrickmacross@outlook.com
Rev Kevin Connolly CC
St Joseph's, Carrickmacross,
Co Monaghan A81 WP68
Tel 083-0025311/042-9661231

...STLEBLAYNEY (MUCKNO)
Mary's, Castleblayney
Patrick's, Oram
ry Rev Adrian Walshe PP
ach na Sagart, Castleblayney,
 Monaghan A75 KR96
 042-9740027
v Stephen Duffy CC
ach na Sagart, Castleblayney,
 Monaghan A75 PF98
 042-9740637
ail info@mucknoparish.ie

...EENISH (ARNEY)
Mary's, Arney
Patrick's, Holywell
Joseph's, Mullaghdun
ry Rev Séamus Quinn PP
lcoo East, Belcoo,
 Fermanagh BT93 5FL
l/Fax 028-66386225
ail ocoinne@gmail.com
ry Rev Canon John Finnegan PE
ney, Enniskillen,
 Fermanagh BT92 2AB
 028-66348217
ail cleenishparish@gmail.com

...OGHER
Patrick's, St Macartan's
ry Rev Canon Noel McGahan PP
 Augher Road, Clogher,
 Tyrone BT76 0AD
 028-85549604
ail noelmcgahan@gmail.com
ry Rev Canon Laurence Dawson PE
 Teiges Hill, Brookeborough,
 Fermanagh BT94 4EZ
 028-89531770
ail dawson829@btinternet.com

...ONES
cred Heart, Clones
Macartan's, Aghadrumsee
Alphonsus, Connons
ry Rev James Moore PP
rochial House, Clonkeencole,
ones, Co Monaghan H23 V895
 047-51048
ail info@clonesparish.ie
 Rev Mgr Richard Mohan PE
 Lacky Road, Drumswords, Roslea,
 Fermanagh BT92 7NQ
 028-67751374

...ONTIBRET
Michael's, Annyalla
Mary's, Clontibret
 Saints, Doohamlet
ry Rev Adrian Walshe PP
ach na Sagart, Castleblayney,
 Monaghan A75 KR96
 042-9740027
ail clontibretparish@gmail.com
ry Rev Paudge McDonnell PE
rochial House, Annyalla, Castleblayney,
 Monaghan A75 PX20
 042-9740121

Very Rev Canon Philip Connolly PE
Parochial House, Doohamlet,
Castleblayney, Co Monaghan A75 PX09
Tel 042-9741239
Email fr.p.connolly@gmail.com

CORCAGHAN (KILMORE AND DRUMSNATT)
St Michael's, Corcaghan
St Mary's, Threemilehouse
Email
parishofkilmoredrumsnatt@gmail.com
Very Rev Canon Patrick McGinn PP
St Joseph's Presbytery, Park Street,
Co Monaghan H18 C588
Tel 047-81220
Very Rev Canon Macartan McQuaid
Mullanarockan, Tydavnet,
Co Monaghan H18 YU20
Tel 087-2454705
Very Rev Thomas Coffey PE
Parochial House, Corcaghan,
Co Monaghan H18 H673
Tel 042-9744806

DERRYGONNELLY (BOTHA)
St Patrick's, Derrygonnelly
Sacred Heart, Boho
Immaculate Conception, Monea
Tel 028-68641889
Email office@bothaparish.com
Very Rev Cathal Deery PP
15 Knockmore Road,
Drumary, Derrygonnelly,
Co Fermanagh BT93 6GA
Tel 028-68641207
Email fr.cathal@bothaparish.com
cdeery1966@gmail.com

DONAGH
St Mary's, Glennan
St Patrick's, Corracrin
Very Rev Hubert Martin PP
Parochial House, Glennan, Glaslough,
Co Monaghan H18 FV10
Tel 047-88120
Email donaghparishoffice@gmail.com

DONAGHMOYNE
St Lastra's, Donaghmoyne
St Patrick's, Broomfield
St Mary's, Lisdoonan
Very Rev Canon Michael Daly PP
Broomfield, Castleblayney,
Co Monaghan A75 A344
Tel 042-9743617
Email dalyml@sky.com

DROMORE
St Davog's
Very Rev Canon Patrick MacEntee PP
35A Esker Road, Dromore,
Co Tyrone BT78 3LE
Tel 028-82898641
Email p.macentee1@gmail.com
Very Rev Denis Dolan PE
Shanmullagh, Dromore,
Co Tyrone BT78 3DZ
Tel 028-82898641

EDERNEY (CÚL MÁINE)
St Joseph's, Ederney
St Patrick's, Montiagh
Very Rev Frank McManus PP
19 Ardvarney Road, Ederney,
Enniskillen, Co Fermanagh BT93 0EG
Tel 028-68631315
Email culmaine@gmail.com

ENNISKILLEN
St Michael's, Enniskillen
St Mary's, Lisbellaw
Rt Rev Mgr Peter O'Reilly PP, VG
1 Darling Street, Enniskillen,
Co Fermanagh BT74 7DP
Tel 028-66322075
Email pp@st-michaels.net
Rev Raymond Donnelly CC
4 Darling Street, Enniskillen,
Co Fermanagh BT74 7DP
Tel 028-66322075 Fax 028-66322248
Email parishcentre@st-michaels.net
Rev Martin Donnelly *(Permanent Deacon)*
2 The Everglades,
Enniskillen, Co Fermanagh BT74 6FE
Email deacon@st-michaels.net
Rev Paul Flynn *(Permanent Deacon)*
Petros, Drumcave, Co Cavan H12 T228
Email paulwilliamflynn98@gmail.com

ERRIGAL TRUAGH
Holy Family, Ballyoisin
St Patrick's, Clara
Sacred Heart, Carrickroe
Very Rev John Flanagan PP
Ballyoisin, Emyvale,
Co Monaghan H18 F207
Tel/Fax 047-87152
Email truaghp@gmail.com

ESKRA
St Patrick's
Very Rev Canon Noel McGahan PP
25 Augher Road, Clogher,
Co Tyrone BT76 0AD
Tel 028-85549604
Email noelmcgahan@gmail.com
Very Rev Terence Connolly PE
178 Newtownsaville Road,
Omagh, Co Tyrone BT78 2RJ
Tel 028-82841306

FINTONA (DONACAVEY)
St Laurence's
Very Rev Canon Patrick MacEntee PP
35A Esker Road, Dromore,
Co Tyrone BT78 3LE
Tel 028-82898641
Email p.macentee1@gmail.com
Rev Sean Mulligan CC
Parochial House, 25 Lisdergan Road,
Fintona, Co Tyrone BT78 2NR
Tel 028-82841907
Email pastoralcentrefintona@gmail.com

INNISKEEN
Mary, Mother of Mercy
Very Rev Martin Canon Treanor PP
Parochial House, Inniskeen, Dundalk,
Co Louth A91 WN32
Tel 042-9378105
Email inniskeenchurch@gmail.com
Rev Noel Conlon *(in residence)*
Inniskeen, Dundalk, Co Louth
Tel 042-9378678

IRVINESTOWN (DEVENISH)
Sacred Heart, Irvinestown
St Molaise, Whitehill
Very Rev Kevin Canon Duffy PP
42 Church Street, Burfits Hill,
Irvinestown, Co Fermanagh BT94 1EN
Tel 028-68621856
Email devenishparish19@outlook.com

KILLANNY
St Enda's
Very Rev Martin Canon Treanor PP
Parochial House, Inniskeen, Dundalk,
Co Louth A91 WN32
Tel 042-9378105
Email killannyparish@hotmail.com
Rev Michael Jordan CC *(priest in residence)*
Parochial House, Killanny,
Carrickmacross, Co Monaghan A81 PX31
Tel 042-9661452
email michaelgjordan@aol.com

KILLEEVAN (CURRIN, KILLEEVAN AND AGHABOG)
St Livinus', Killeevan, St Mary's, Ture
Immaculate Conception, Scotshouse
St Mary's, Latnamard
Ver Rev James Moore PP
Parochial House, Clonkeencole, Clones,
Co Monaghan H23 V895
Tel 047-51048
Email frjimmoore@gmail.com
Very Rev Peter Corrigan PE
Shanco, Newbliss,
Co Monaghan H18 K303
Tel 047-54011
Email pocorragin@yahoo.com
Rev John F. McKenna CC
Scotshouse, Clones,
Co Monaghan H23 YT10
Tel 047-56016
Email jmckenna420@live.ie

LATTON (AUGHNAMULLEN WEST)
St Mary's, Latton, St Patrick's, Bawn
Very Rev Canon Owen J. McEneaney PP
Parochial House, St Patrick's, Ballybay,
Co Monaghan A754 K299
Tel 042-9741032
Email contact@tullycorbetparish.com
Very Rev Thomas Quigley PE
Parochial House, Latton, Castleblayney,
Co Monaghan A75 E953
Tel 042-9742212
Email
aughnamullenwestparish@gmail.com

LISNASKEA (AGHALURCHER)
Holy Cross, Lisnaskea
St Mary's, Maguiresbridge
Email fermanaghparishes@gmail.com
Very Rev Canon Jimmy McPhillips PP
10 Knocks Road, Lisnaskea,
Co Fermanagh BT92 0GA
Tel 028-67721342
Email jimmymcp1@gmail.com

MAGHERACLOONE
St Patrick's (The Rock Chapel), Carrickasedge
SS Peter and Paul, Drumgossatt
Rt Rev Mgr Shane McCaughey PP, VG
St Joseph's, Carrickmacross,
Co Monaghan A81 F688
Tel 042-9664367
Rev Philip Crowe (CSSp) CC
Drumgossatt, Carrickmacross, Co Monaghan
Tel 042-9661388
Email magheraclooneparish@gmail.com

NEWTOWNBUTLER (GALLOON)
St Mary's, Newtownbutler
St Patrick's, Donagh, Lisnaskea
Very Rev Canon Jimmy McPhillips PP
10 Knocks Road, Lisnaskea,
Co Fermanagh BT92 0GA
Email jimmymcp1@gmail.com
Very Rev Michael King PE
21 Wattlebridge Road, Drumquilla,
Newtownbutler, Co Fermanagh BT92 8JP
Tel 028-67738229
Email galloonparish@gmail.com
Rev Kevin Malcolmson CC
3 Landbrock Road, Drumquilla,
Newtownbutler, Co Fermanagh BT92 8JJ
Tel 028-67738244
Email frkevinm@gmail.com

PETTIGO
St Mary's, Pettigo
St Joseph's, Lettercran
Rt Rev Mgr Laurence Flynn Adm
Priest's House, Main Street,
Pettigo, Co Donegal F94 FYN7
Tel 071-9861666
Lough Derg (See Charitable Societies)
Tel/Fax 071-9861518
Email pettigoparish@loughderg.org

ROCKCORRY (EMATRIS)
Holy Trinity, St Mary's, Corrawacan
Very Rev Canon Owen J. McEneaney PP
Parochial House, St Patrick's,
Ballybay, Co Monaghan A75 K299
Tel 042-9741032
Email contact@tullycorbetparish.ie
Rev Jerry White (SSCC) CC
Sacred Hearts Community, Tanagh,
Cootehill, Co Cavan H16 CA22
Tel 049-5552188

ROSLEA
St Tierney's, Roslea
St Mary's, Magherarney
Very Rev John Chester PP
4a Monaghan Road, Roslea, Enniskillen
Co Fermanagh BT92 7QY
Tel 028-67751227
Rt Rev Mgr Vincent Connolly PE
Magherarney, Smithborough,
Co Monaghan H18 H297
Tel 047-57011
Email parishofroslea@gmail.com

TEMPO (POBAL)
Immaculate Conception, Tempo
St Joseph's, Cradien
Rt Rev Mgr Peter O'Reilly PP, VG
1 Darling Street, Enniskillen,
Co Fermanagh BT74 7DP
Tel 028-66322075
Email pp@st-michaels.net
Very Rev John Halton PE
26 Cullion Road, Tempo, Enniskillen,
Co Fermanagh BT94 3LY
Tel 028-89541344
Email johnhalton19@btinternet.com

TRILLICK (KILSKEERY)
St Macartan's, Trillick
St Mary's, Coa
Very Rev Pádraig McKenna PP
Parochial House, Millbank,
Trillick, Co Tyrone
Tel 028-89561982
Email parishoffice@kilskerryparish.co.u
Very Rev Canon John McKenna PE
Email john.mckenna35@btinternet.com
Trillick, Omagh, Co Tyrone BT78 3RD
Tel 028-89561350

TYDAVNET
St Dympna's, Tydavnet
St Mary's, Urbleshanny
St Joseph's, Knockatallon
Email tydavnetparishoffice@gmail.com
Very Rev Stephen Joyce PP
Parochial House, Stracrunnion,
Scotstown, Co Monaghan H18 X620
Tel 047-89204
Email stephen.joyce@icloud.com
Very Rev Brian Early PE
Parochial House, St Dympna's,
Tydavnet, Co Monaghan H18 Y190
Tel 047-79434
Email pbbearly64@gmail.com

TYHOLLAND
St Patrick's
Very Rev Canon Paddy McGinn Adm
St Joseph's Presbytery, Park Street,
Monaghan H18 C588
Tel 047-81220
Email
parishoffice@stjosephsmonaghan.com

INSTITUTIONS AND THEIR CHAPLAINS

ughters of Our Lady of the Sacred rt Convent
ybay, Co Monaghan A75 K193
042-9741141

ner Army Camp
lyshannon, Co Donegal F94 C985
Jeremiah (Jerry) Carroll CF
ail jerryzulu@gmail.com
071-9842294

naghan General Hospital
sts of Monaghan parish
047-81220 Fax 047-84004

Davnet's Hospital, Monaghan
sts of Monaghan parish
047-81220 Fax 047-84004

Mary's Hospital
tleblayney, Co Monaghan
sts of Castleblayney parish
042-9740027

th West Acute Hospital, Enniskillen
sts of Enniskillen Parish
028-66322075 Fax 028-66322248

PRIESTS OF THE DIOCESE ELSEWHERE

Dr Patrick Connolly
ology Department,
y Immaculate College,
th Circular Road,
erick V94 VN26
061-204575 Fax 061-313632
ail patrick.connolly@mic.ul.ie
ev Mgr Joseph McGuinness
cutive Secretary to the Irish
scopal Conference
umba Centre, Maynooth,
Kildare W23 P6D3
01-5053000
Alan Ward
Drumlin Heights, Enniskillen,
ermanagh BT74 7NR

dy Leave/contact addresses
Benedict Hughes
plaincy Centre, NUI Galway,
versity Road, Galway H91 TK33
091-495055
il ben.hughes@nuigalway.ie

RETIRED PRIESTS

st Rev Liam S. MacDaid DD
op Emeritus
mhirk, Dublin Road,
naghan H18 YE30
047-82208
st Rev Joseph Duffy DD
op Emeritus
re na gCraobh, Monaghan
047-62725

Very Rev Canon Patrick Marron
St Anne's Nursing Home, Clones Road,
Ballybay, Co Monaghan A75 K193
Very Rev Lorcan Lynch
St Anne's Nursing Home,
Clones Road, Ballybay,
Co Monaghan A75 K193
Very Rev Canon Brian McCluskey PE
Apt 2, 2 Danesfort Park North,
Stranhillis Road, Belfast BT9 5RB
Tel 028-90683544
Rev Brendan McCague
Castleross Nursing Home,
Castleross Village, Carrickmacross,
Co Monaghan A81 X242
Rt Rev Mgr Gerard McSorley
St Anne's Nursing Home, Clones Road,
Ballybay, Co Monaghan A75 K193
Very Rev Canon Joseph Mullin PE
c/o 10 Knocks Road, Lisnaskea,
Co Fermanagh BT92 0JA
Rev Séan Nolan PE
Gate Lodge, St Maccartan's Cathedral,
Dublin Road, Monaghan H18 TR79
Rev Joseph McVeigh PE
Tattygar House, 4 Tattygar, Lisbellaw,
Co Fermanagh BT94 5SQ

RELIGIOUS ORDERS AND CONGREGATIONS

PRIESTS

CONGREGATION OF THE SACRED HEARTS OF JESUS AND MARY (SACRED HEARTS COMMUNITY)
Cootehill, Co Cavan H16 CA22
Tel 049-5552188
Rev Jerry White
Email jerrysscc@gmail.com

(See also under Rockcorry parish)

PASSIONISTS
St Gabriel's Retreat, The Graan,
Enniskillen, Co Fermanagh BT7 45PB
Tel 028-66322272 Fax 028-66325201
Superior: Rev Charles Cross (CP)
Email charlescrosscp@gmail.com

SISTERS

CONGREGATION OF THE SISTERS OF MERCY
Northern Province, Provincial House,
74 Main Street, Clogher,
Co Tyrone BT76 0AA
Tel 028-85548127 Fax 028-85549459
Provincial Leader: Sr Rose Marie Conlan

11 Castlehill Gardens, Augher,
Co Tyrone BT77 0HA
Tel 028-85548157

St Brigid's, 2 Ballagh Road, Clogher,
Co Tyrone BT76 0HE
Tel 028-85548015

Convent of Mercy, 6 Belmore Street,
Enniskillen, Co Fermanagh
Tel 028-66322561
Community: 14

6 Gorminish Park, Garrison,
Co Fermanagh BT93 4GP
Tel 028-68659742

No. 16 The Grange,
Presentation Walk, Monaghan
Tel 047-84569

Buíochas,
29 The Commons, Bellanaleck,
Enniskillen, Co Fermanagh BT92 2BD
Tel 028-66349722

St Faber's, 8 Castlecourt, Monea,
Co Fermanagh BT93 7AR
Tel 028-66341197

73 Scaffog Avenue, Sligo Road,
Enniskillen, Co Fermanagh BT74 7JJ
Tel 028-66327474

7 Friar's Park, Drumlyon, Enniskillen,
Co Fermanagh BT74 5NR
Tel 028-66320224

No 19 The Sidings,
Breandrum, Enniskillen,
Co Fermanagh BT74 6GZ
Tel 028-66326836

27 Ashbourne Manor, Charterhill,
Enniskillen, Co Fermanagh BT74 4BB
Tel 028-66426904

The Lodge, Glor na Mara, West End,
Bundoran, Co Donegal F94 NY72
Tel 071-9841818

Glor na Mara, West End,
Bundoran, Co Donegal F94 NY72
Tel 071-9833899

2 Marina View,
Dinglei Coush, Bundoran,
Co Donegal F94 WSR6
Tel 071-9829832

Ennis View,
4A Hollyhill Road, Enniskillen,
Co Fermanagh BT74 6DD

9 Roscarrig, 119 Sligo Road, Enniskillen,
Co Fermanagh BT74 7AZ

DAUGHTERS OF OUR LADY OF THE SACRED HEART
Ballybay, Co Monaghan
Tel 042-9741068
Email olshballybay@eircom.net
Superior: Sr Mary Mallin
Community: 6
St Joseph's Nursing Home
Superior: Sr Kathleen McQuillan
Tel 042-9741141. Beds: 31
Community: 5

PRESENTATION SISTERS
14 Laragh Lee, Ballycassidy,
Ballinamallard, Enniskillen,
Co Fermanagh BT94 2JA
Community: 1

ST LOUIS SISTERS
St Louis Convent, Louisville, Monaghan
Community: 17
Varied apostolates

Rowan Tree Court,
24 Mullach Glas Close, Monaghan
Tel 047-38685
Community: 1

Iona House, Farney Street
Carrickmacross, Co Monaghan
Tel 042-9663326
Community: 5
Varied apostolates

4 Lakeview, Monaghan
Tel 047-84719
Community: 1

Drummond Radraic,
Dundalk Road, Carrickmacross,
Co Monaghan
Tel 042-9661827
Community: 1

2 The Grange,
Monaghan Town

EDUCATIONAL INSTITUTIONS

St Macartan's College
Monaghan, Co Monaghan H18 X704
Tel 047-81642/83365/83367
Fax 047-83341
Email admin@stmacartanscollege.ie
President
Rt Rev Mgr Shane McCaughey BD
Principal
Mr David McCague

St Michael's College
Enniskillen, Co Fermanagh BT74 6DE
Tel 028-66322935
Fax 028-66325128
Email office@saintmichaels.org.uk
Principal: Mr Mark Henry

CHARITABLE AND OTHER SOCIETIES

ACCORD
St Macartan's College,
Monaghan H18 YX03
Tel 047-83359
(10am-1pm Mon-Fri)

Ros Erne House,
8 Darling Street, Enniskillen,
Co Fermanagh BT74 7EW
Tel 028-66325696
(9am-5pm Mon-Fri)

Lough Derg, St Patrick's Purgatory
Pettigo, Co Donegal F94 K725
Tel 071-9861518 Fax 071-9861525
Email info@loughderg.org
Prior: Rt Rev Mgr Laurence Flynn
Pilgrimage season, 1 June-15 August.
No advance booking or notice required
Pilgrims arrive daily before 3 pm, having
fasted from midnight, and remain on the
island for two complete days of prayer
and penance.
One-day retreats before and after main
pilgrimage season.
School retreats also offered.
Tel for details and reservations.

DIOCESE OF CLONFERT

PATRON OF THE DIOCESE
ST BRENDAN, 16 MAY

INCLUDES PORTIONS OF COUNTIES GALWAY, OFFALY AND ROSCOMMON

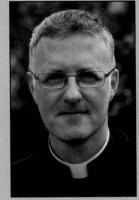

Most Rev Michael Duignan SThD
Bishop of Clonfert;
born 15 July 1970
ordained priest 17 July 1994
ordained Bishop of Clonfert
13 October 2019

Residence: Coorheen,
Loughrea, Co Galway
H62 TD82
Tel 091-841560
Email office@clonfertdiocese.ie

ST BRENDAN'S CATHEDRAL, LOUGHREA

Brendan's Cathedral stands at the
estern extremity of the Diocese of
onfert on the main highway from
ublin to Galway. The foundation stone
f the cathedral was laid on 10 October
397, and the fabric was completed in
902. Plans were drawn by the Dublin
chitect William Byrne for a building in
e neo-Gothic style, having a nave and
aspidal sanctuary, lean-to aisles and
allow transepts, with a graceful spire
the western end. Its dimensions were
etermined by the needs of the parish of
ughrea. While not impressive, its
roportions are good, and despite a
eparture from the original plan by
urtailment of the sanctuary, the overall
ffect is pleasing. The simplicity of the
terior, however, hardly prepares the
sitor for the riches within.

was due to two fortuitous
rcumstances that St Brendan's became
veritable treasure house of the Celtic
evival in sculpture, stained glass,
oodcarving, metalwork and textiles.

he first circumstance was that the
uilding of a Catholic cathedral was
elayed for various reasons until close to
e turn of the last century. The Irish
terary Renaissance was by then well
dvanced. When the building was
ompleted in 1902, the Arts and Crafts
ovement was having effect.

he second circumstance was that of
dward Martyn's birth at the home of his
aternal grandfather, James Smyth, in
e parish of Loughrea. Martyn was an
scetic man and devoted his time and
ortune to the development of every
hase of the Irish revival, the Gaelic
eague, Sinn Féin, the Irish Literary
heatre, Irish music, church music and
urch art. With innate business acumen,
e insured by personal donation and the
nancial support of the Smyth family
hat the new cathedral would reflect his
iews. The bishop, Dr John Healy, who
as sensitive to the prevailing trend,
ccepted the challenge and assigned the
roject to the supervision of a young

curate in the parish, Fr Jeremiah
O'Donovan, who was himself actively
engaged in propaganda for Revival.

John Hughes was the foremost sculptor
in the country at the time, and Bishop
Healy commissioned him to do the
modelling and carving. His work is found
in the bronze figure of Christ on the
reredos of the high altar and in the
magnificent marble statue of the Virgin
and Child. Michael Shortall, a student of
Hughes in the Metropolitan School of
Art, did the carvings on the corbels and
executed the statue of St Brendan on the
wall of the tower. His connection with
the cathedral continued over twenty
years, and he was responsible for
carvings of incidents from the life and
voyage of St Brendan carved on the
capitals of the pillars.

The Yeats sisters, Lily and Elizabeth,
along with their friend Evelyn Gleeson,
set up the Dun Emer guild. They
embroidered twenty-four banners of
Irish saints for use in the cathedral. Jack
B. Yeats and his wife Mary designed

these banners. With an economy of
detail and richness of colour, they almost
achieve the effect of stained glass. Mass
vestments, embroidered with silk on
poplin, also came from the same studio.

More than anything else, St Brendan's is
famous for its stained glass. Martyn was
particularly concerned about the quality
of stained glass then available in Ireland.
He was eager to set up an Irish stained-
glass industry. He succeeded in having
Alfred E. Childe appointed to the
Metropolitan School of Art, and he later
persuaded Sarah Purser to open a co-
operative studio, where young artists
could be trained in the technique of
stained glass. This new studio, An Túr
Gloinne, opened in January 1903, with
Childe as manager, and so began the
work of the Loughrea stained-glass
windows. Over the next forty years,
Childe, Purser and Michael Healy
executed almost all the stained-glass
windows in the cathedral, and it is these
windows that have given St Brendan's its
place in the Irish Artistic Revival.

Allianz ⑪

Most Rev John Kirby DD
Retired Bishop of Clonfert;
born October 1938; ordained priest 23
June 1963; ordained Bishop of Clonfert 9
April 1988
Residence: Cappataggle, Ballinasloe,
Co Galway H53 X206
Tel 091-843017

ADMINISTRATION

Vicar General
Rt Rev Mgr Cathal Geraghty PP, VG
Cathedral of St Brendan, Barrack Street,
Loughrea, Co Galway H62 YE09
Tel 091-841212

Chancellor
Very Rev Michael Byrnes PP, JV
Parochial House, Dunkellin Tec,
Portumna, Co Galway H53 F584
Tel 090-9741092

Diocesan Secretary
Ms Marcella Fallon
Coorheen, Loughrea, Co Galway H62 TD82
Tel 091-841560
Email office@clonfertdiocese.ie

Diocesan Communications Officer
Rt Rev Mgr Cathal Geraghty PP, VG
Cathedral of St Brendan, Barrack Street,
Loughrea, Co Galway H62 YE09
Tel 091-841212

College of Consultors
Mgr Cathal Geraghty PP, Vicar General
Very Rev Michael Byrnes PP JV,
Chancellor
Very Rev Niall Foley PP, VF
Very Rev Iomar Daniels PP, EV
Very Rev John Garvey PP
Very Rev Ciarán Kitching PP

Diocesan Council of Priests
Mgr Cathal Geraghty PP, Vicar General
Very Rev Michael Byrnes PP, JV,
Chancellor
Very Rev Niall Foley PP,
Very Rev Seamus Bohan PP
Very Rev Iomar Daniels PP, EV
Very Rev Declan Mc Inerney PP
Very Rev Benny Flanagan PE
Very Rev John Garvey PP
Very Rev Ciarán Kitching PP
Very Rev Mícheál Mc Laifeartaigh (OCD)

Diocesan Finance Committe
Most Rev Michael Duignan SThD,DD
Rt Rev Mgr Cathal Geraghty PP
Very Rev Martin McNamara PP
Mr Gerard McInerney
Mr Terry Doyle
Mr Patrick McDonagh
Mr Sean O'Dwyer
Ms Marcella Fallon
Rev Declan McInerney

Clergy Wellbeing Committee
Chairperson: Very Rev Ciarán Kitching PP
Parochial House, Killimor, Ballinasloe,
Co Galway H53 R8C4
Tel 090-9676151

**Master of Ceremonies and Chairperson
of the Diocesan Liturgical Committee**
Very Rev Michael Byrnes PP, JV
Parochial House, Dunkellin Tec,
Portumna, Co Galway H53 F584
Tel 090-9741092

CATECHETICS AND EDUCATION

Diocesan Education Secretariat
Chairperson
Rt Rev Mgr Cathal Geraghty PP, VG
Cathedral of St Brendan, Barrack Street,
Loughrea, Co Galway H62 YE09
Tel 091-841212

**Catholic Primary School Managers'
Association**
Secretary: Mr Eamon Lally
Gortnahorna, Clontuskert,
Ballinasloe, Co Galway
Tel 090-9643250

Sacramental Preparation
Chairperson of the Diocesan Committee
for Preparation and Celebration of the
Sacraments of Initiation
Very Rev Kieran O'Rourke PP
Parochial House, Looscaun, Woodford,
Co Galway H62 AK18
Tel 090-9749100

Life-Long Religious Education
Very Rev John Garvey PP
Parochial House, Ballinasloe,
Co Galway H53 EC98
Tel 090-9643916

PASTORAL

**Diocesan Committee for Parish
Restructuring and Renewal**
Chairperson: Rev Iomar Daniels PP, EV
Parochial House, Leitrim,
Loughrea, Co Galway H62 RP40
Tel 091-841758

Co-ordinator for Safeguarding Children
Ms Isabella Mulkern
Coorheen, Loughrea, Co Galway H62 TD82
Tel 091-841560

**Co-ordinator for Safeguarding of
Vulnerable Persons**
Ms Isabella Mulkern
Coorheen, Loughrea, Co Galway H62 TD82
Tel 091-841560

Youth Ministry
Chairperson of the Dicoesan Committee
for Ministry to Young People
Very Rev Declan McInerney PP
Parochial House, Eyrecourt, Ballinasloe,
Co Galway H53 KX85
Tel 090-9675113

Marriage and Family Life
Chairperson of the Diocesan Committee
for Marriage, Family Life and Life-Long
Religious Education and Directory of
ACCORD: Very Rev John Garvey PP
Parochial House, Ballinasloe,
Co Galway H53 EC98
Tel 090-9643916

Vocations
Director of Vocations and Chairperson o
the Diocesan Committee for Vocations:
Rev Aidan Costello CC
Cathedral of St Brendan, Barrack Street,
Loughrea, Co Galway H62 YE09

Pilgrimages
Director: Very Rev Pat Conroy PP
Parochial House, Ballinakill, Loughrea,
Co Galway H62 AW68
Tel 090-9745021

Trócaire and Pontifical Mission Societie
Director: Very Rev Brendan Lawless PP
Carrabane, Athenry, Co Galway H65 EP0
Tel 091-841103

Ecumenism and Interreligious Dialogue
Chairperson of the Diocesan Committee
for Ecumenism and Interreligious
Dialogue: Very Rev Raymond Sweeney P
Parochial House, Ballymacward,
Ballainasloe, Co Galway H53 P2W0
Tel 090-9687614

Charitable Outreach
Chairperson of the Diocesan Committee
for Charitable Outreach
Very Rev Seamus Bohan PP
Parochial House, Tynagh,
Loughrea, Co Galway H62 DH32
Tel 090-9745113

Legion of Mary
Director: Very Rev Patrick Conroy PP
Parochial House, Ballinakill, Loughrea,
Co Galway H62 AW68
Tel 090-9745021

PARISHES

Mensal parishes are listed first. Other
parishes follow alphabetically. Historical
names are given in parentheses. Church
titulars are in italics.

LOUGHREA, ST BRENDAN'S CATHEDRAL
Rt Rev Mgr Cathal Geraghty PP
Rev Aidan Costello CC
Rev Michael Ifiora CC and pastoral area
Rev Anthony Nzinang CC
The Presbytery, Loughrea,
Co Galway H62 YE09
Tel 091-841212

**BALLINASLOE, CREAGH AND
KILCLOONEY**
St Michael's, Ballinasloe
Our Lady of Lourdes, Creagh
Very Rev John Garvey PP
Rev Bernard Costello Adm
Very Rev Colm Allman
Rev Charles Nyameh CC and pastoral
area
St Michael's Presbytery, Ballinasloe,
Co Galway H53 EC98
Tel 090-9643916

AUGHRIM AND KILCONNELL
St Catherine's, Aughrim
Sacred Heart, Kilconnell
Very Rev Gerard Geraghty PP
Aughrim, Ballinasloe,
Co Galway H53 PY13
Tel 090-9673724

BALLINAKILL AND DERRYBRIEN
St Joseph's, Ballinakill
St Patrick's, Derrybrien
Very Rev Pat Conroy PP
Ballinakill, Loughrea,
Co Galway H62 AW68
Tel 090-9745021

BALLYMACWARD AND GURTEEN (BALLYMACWARD AND CLONKEENKERRIL)
SS Peter and Paul
St Michael's
Very Rev Raymond Sweeney PP
Ballymacward, Ballinasloe,
Co Galway H53 P2W0
Tel 090-9687614

CAPPATAGLE AND KILRICKLE (KILLALAGHTAN AND KILRICKLE)
St Michael's, Cappatagle
Our Lady of Lourdes, Kilrickle
Most Rev John Kirby PP
Cappataggle, Ballinasloe,
Co Galway H53 X206
Tel 091-843017

CLONTUSKERT
St Augustine's
Very Rev Michael Finneran PP, VF
Clontuskert, Ballinasloe,
Co Galway H53 CV99
Tel 090-9642256

CLOSTOKEN AND KILCONIERAN (KILCONICKNY, KILCONIERAN AND LICKERRIG)
Holy Family, Immaculate Conception
Very Rev Brendan Lawless PP
Carrabane, Athenry,
Co Galway H65 EP04
Tel 091-841103

DUNIRY AND ABBEY (DUNIRY AND KILNELEHAN)
Holy Family
Assumption
Very Rev Seamus Bohan, Moderator
Tynagh, Loughrea,
Co Galway H62 DH32
Tel 090-9745113

EYRECOURT, CLONFERT AND MEELICK (CLONFERT, DONANAGHTA AND MEELICK)
St Brendan's, St Francis
Very Rev Declan McInerney PP
Eyrecourt, Ballinasloe,
Co Galway H53 KX85
Tel 090-9675113

FAHY AND QUANSBORO (FAHY AND KILQUAIN)
Consoler of the Afficted, Christ the King
Very Rev Michael Byrnes, Moderator
Dunkellin Terrace, Portumna,
Co Galway H53 F584

FOHENAGH AND KILLURE (FOHENAGH AND KILGERRILL)
St Patrick's
St Teresa's
Very Rev Christy McCormack PP
Fohenagh, Ahascragh,
Ballinasloe, Co Galway H53 KO37
Tel 090-9688623

KILLIMOR AND TIRANASCRAGH (KILLIMORBOLOGUE AND TIRANASCRAGH)
St Joseph's
Immaculate Conception
Very Rev Ciaran Kitching PP
Killimor, Ballinasloe,
Co Galway H53 R8C4
Tel 090-9676151

KILNADEEMA AND AILLE (KILNADEEMA AND KILTESKILL)
St Dympna's, St Mary's, Aille, Loughrea
Rt Rev Mgr Cathal Geraghty, Moderator
Cathedral of St Brendan, Barrack Street,
Loughrea, Co Galway H62 YE09
Tel 091-841212

KILTULLAGH, KILLIMORDALY AND CLOONCAGH
SS Peter & Paul, Kiltulla,
St Mary's, Cloncagh,
St Iomar's, Killimordaly
Rt Rev Mgr Cathal Geraghty Adm
The Presbytery, Loughrea,
Co Galway H62 YE09
Tel 091-841212

LAWRENCETOWN AND KILTORMER (KILTORMER AND OGHILL)
St Mary's, St Patrick's
Very Rev Bernard Costello, Moderator
13 Garbally Oaks, Ballinasloe,
Co Galway H53 KW27
Tel 087-2396208

LEITRIM AND BALLYDUGGAN (KILCOOLEY AND LEITRIM)
St Andrew's, St Jarlath's, Ballyduggan
Very Rev Iomar Daniels PP
St Andrew's Church, Leitrim,
Loughrea, Co Galway H62 RP40
Tel 091-841758

LUSMAGH
St Cronan's
Very Rev Michael Kennedy PP
Lusmagh, Banagher, Co Offaly R42 WP40
Tel 0509-51358

MULLAGH AND KILLORAN (ABBEYGORMICAN AND KILLORAN)
St Brendan's
Our Lady of the Assumption
Very Rev Niall Foley PP
Mullagh, Loughrea,
Co Galway H62 AR27
Tel 091-843119

NEW INN AND BULLAUN (BULLAUN, GRANGE AND KILLAAN)
St Killian's, New Inn
St Patrick's, Bullaun
Very Rev Pat Kenny PP
St Killian Church, New Inn,
Ballinasloe, Co Galway H53 P6C0
Tel 090-9675819

PORTUMNA (KILMALINOGUE AND LICKMOLASSEY)
St Brigid's, SS Peter & Paul, Ascension
Very Rev Michael Byrnes PP, JV
Dunkellin Terrace,
Portumna, Co Galway H53 F584
Tel 090-9741092

TAGHMACONNELL
St Ronan's
Very Rev Sean Neylon PP
Taghmaconnell,
Ballinasloe, Co Galway H53 RT28
Tel 090-9683929

TYNAGH AND KILLEEN
St Lawrence's, Sacred Heart
Very Rev Seamus Bohan PP
Tynagh, Loughrea,
Co Galway H62 DH32
Tel 090-9745113

WOODFORD AND LOOSCAUN
St John the Baptist, St Brendan's
Very Rev Kieran O'Rourke PP
Looscaun, Woodford,
Co Galway H62 AK18
Tel 090-9749100

INSTITUTIONS AND THEIR CHAPLAINS

Emmanuel House of Providence
Clonfert, Ballinasloe, Co Galway
Director: Mr Eddie Stones
Chaplain and Episcopal Delegate
Very Rev Michael Kennedy
Tel 057-9151552

Diocesan Family Life Centre (Ballinasloe)
Brackernagh, Ballinasloe, Co Galway
Chairperson Management Board
Very Rev John Garvey PP
St Michael's, Ballinasloe,
Co Galway H53 EC98
Tel 090-9643916

Portiuncula Hospital
Ballinasloe, Co Galway
Tel 090-9648200
Rev Bernard Costello

St Brendan's
Community Nursing Unit
Loughrea, Co Galway
Tel 091-871200
Rt Rev Mgr Cathal Geraghty PP
Tel 091-841212
Rev Aidan Costello
Tel 091-841212

RETIRED PRIESTS

Rev Joe Clarke
Foxhall, Gurlymadden,
Loughrea, Co Galway
Rev Sean Egan
Kilrickle Loughrea, Co Galway H62 PO27
Rev Benny Flanagan
14 Kilgarve Gardens, Creagh,
Ballinasloe, Co Galway
Rev Martin McNamara
Kiltullagh, Athenry,
Co Galway H65 DYM0
Rev Cathal Stanley
Dominic Street, Portumna,
Co Galway H53 EC66
Tel 090-9759182
Rev Sean Slattery
18 The Orchard, Limerick V94 F97N
Rev John Naughton
Clonfert Avenue, Portumna,
Co Galway H53 WC82

RELIGIOUS ORDERS AND CONGREGATIONS

PRIESTS

CARMELITES (OCD)
The Abbey,
Loughrea, Co Galway
Tel 091-841209 Fax 091-842343
Prior
Rev Michéal MacLaifeartaigh (OCD)

REDEMPTORISTS
St Patrick's, Esker,
Athenry, Co Galway
Tel 091-844007
Outside office hours 086-8440619
Fax 091-845698
Superior: Rev Brendan Callanan (CSsR)
Vicar Superior: Rev Patrick O'Keeffe (CSsR)

SISTERS

CONGREGATION OF THE SISTERS OF MERCY
Sisters of Mercy, Lake Road,
Loughrea, Co Galway H62 D592
Tel/Fax 091-847715
Community: 4

Mount Pleasant,
Ballinasloe, Co Galway H53 XP74
Tel 090-9631695
Community: 2

7 Woodview, The Pines,
Ballinasloe, Co Galway H53 H319
Tel 090-9644055
Community: 1

17 Hawthorn Crescent,
Ballinasloe, Co Galway H53 XR86
Tel 090-9644171
Community: 2

An Gairdín,
Portumna, Co Galway H53 E891
Tel 090-9741689
Community: 2

St Brendan's Convent of Mercy,
Eyrecourt, Co Galway H53 V0Y7
Tel 090-9675123
Community: 1

Sisters of Mercy, Bark Hill,
Woodford, Co Galway H62 WN40
Community: 1

5 College Crescent,
The Pines, Ballinasloe,
Co Galway H53 AX82
Community: 1

75 Danesfort Drive, Caheronaun,
Loughrea, Co Galway H62 PR86
Community: 1

Kilgarve, Creagh,
Ballinasloe, Co Galway H53 F2H0
Community: 2

Sisters of Mercy, 1 Church Street,
Ballinasloe, Co Galway
Community: 1

FRANCISCAN MISSIONARIES OF THE DIVINE MOTHERHOOD
Franciscan Convent, Garbally Drive,
Ballinasloe, Co Galway H53 RF84
Tel 090-9642314/9648548
Community: 26

La Verna, Brackernagh,
Ballinasloe, Co Galway H53 EV97
Tel 090-9643679
Community: 1

St Clare's, Brackernagh,
Ballinasloe, Co Galway H53 E642
Tel 090-9643986 Fax 090-9631757
Community: 2

San Damiano, Ard Mhuire, Ballinasloe,
Co Galway H53 HN28
Community: 3

Assisi, 7 Ard Muire, Ballinasloe,
Co Galway H53 YY18
Community: 2

EDUCATIONAL INSTITUTIONS

St Joseph's College
Garbally Park, Ballinasloe, Co Galway
Tel 090-9642504/9642254
President
Very Rev Colm Allman BA, HDE
Principal
Mr Paul Walsh MA, HDE

Portumna Community School
Portumna, Co Galway
Tel 090-9741053
Principal: Mr Shane McClearn
Chaplain: Ms Brid Dunne

St Raphael's College
Convent of Mercy,
Loughrea, Co Galway
Tel 091-841062
Chaplain: Rev Michael Ifiora CC

Mercy College
Woodford, Co Galway
Tel 090-9749076
Chaplain: Very Rev Kieran O'Rourke PP

Ardscoil Mhuire
Mackney, Ballinasloe, Co Galway
Chaplain: Very Rev John Garvey PP

St Brigid's College
Loughrea, Co Galway
Tel 091-841919
Chaplain: Rev Tony Nzinang CC

St Killian's College
New Inn Ballinasloe
Chaplain: Very Rev Pat Kenny PP

DIOCESE OF CLOYNE

PATRON OF THE DIOCESE
ST COLMAN, 24 NOVEMBER

COVERS MOST OF COUNTY CORK

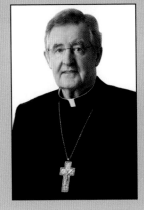

Most Rev William Crean DD
Bishop of Cloyne;
born 16 December 1951;
ordained priest 20 June 1976;
ordained Bishop of Cloyne
27 January 2013

Residence: Cloyne Diocesan
Centre, Cobh, Co Cork
Tel 021-4811430
Email info@cloynediocese.ie
website: www.cloynediocese.ie

ST COLMAN'S CATHEDRAL, COBH

Colman's Cathedral, overlooking Cobh, enshrines within its walls the traditions of thirteen centuries of the Diocese of Cloyne.

Built in the form of a Latin cross, its exterior is of Dalkey granite, with dressings of Mallow limestone. The style of architecture is French Gothic. The architects were Pugin (the Younger), Ashlin and Coleman.

The cathedral took forty-seven years to build (1868–1915). The total cost was £235,000. Of this, £90,000 was raised by the people of Cobh, with the remainder coming from the diocese and from collections in America and Australia.

The spire was completed in 1915 and the famous carillon and the clock were installed in 1916. The carillon – the largest in Britain and Ireland – has forty-nine bells and is tuned to the accuracy of a single vibration. This unusual instrument covers a range of four octaves and is played from a console located in the belfry, consisting of a keyboard and pedalboard. Inside, the cathedral has all the hallmarks of Gothic grandeur: the massive marble pillars, the beautiful arches, the capitals with their delicate carving of foliage, the shamrock design on the Bath Stone, and mellow, delicate lighting.

The carved panels over the nave arches give a history of the Church in Ireland from the time of St Patrick. The stained-glass windows in the northern aisle depict the parables of Christ, while those in the southern aisle depict the miracles of Christ. Overhead, in the clerestory, are forty-six windows, each having the patron of one of the forty-six parishes of the diocese. The high altar and its surround was designed by Ashlin. The pulpit is of Austrian oak. Towards the rear of the cathedral is the magnificent rose window, which depicts St John's vision of the throne of God. The organ was built by Telford and Telford, and has a total of 2,468 pipes.

Most Rev John Magee DD
Retired Bishop of Cloyne;
born 24 September 1936;
ordained priest 17 March 1962;
ordained Bishop of Cloyne 17 March 1987;
retired 24 March 2010
Residence: 'Carnmeen', Convent Hill,
Mitchelstown, Co Cork
Tel 025-41887

CHAPTER

Dean: Rt Rev Mgr Eamonn Goold PE
Midleton
Archdeacon: Vacant
Chancellor: Very Rev Seán Cotter PE
Charleville
Prebendaries
Aghulter: Vacant
Ballyhea: Rt Rev Mgr Denis O'Callaghan
PE, Mallow
Cahirulton: Vacant
Coole: Vacant
Cooline: Very Rev Patrick Twomey PE
Kildorrery
Glanworth: Very Rev Colman O'Donovan
PE, Inniscarra
Inniscarra: Rt Rev Mgr James O'Brien PP,
Ballyhea
Kilmaclenine: Rt Rev Mgr James
O'Donnell AP, Macroom
Killenemer: Very Rev Michael Fitzgerald
PE, Mitchelstown
Subulter: Very Rev John Terry PE
Kanturk
Brigown: Very Rev Mgr Denis Reidy PE,
Carrigtwohill
Kilmacdonogh: Vacant
Donoughmore: Very Rev Donal Roberts
PP, VF, Macroom
Laken: Vacant
Honorary Canons
Very Rev Thomas Browne PE, Youghal
Very Rev Donal Leahy PE, Kilworth
Very Rev Denis Kelleher PE, Aghada
Very Rev David Herlihy PE, Youghal
Very Rev Donal O'Mahony PP,
Charleville
Rt Rev Mgr Anthony O'Brien PP, VG,
Mallow
Very Rev Michael Leamy PP, VF,
Mitchelstown
Rt Rev Mgr Jim Killeen PP, VG,
Midleton
Very Rev Tobias Bluitt PP, VF, Kanturk
Very Rev William Bermingham PP,
Youghal

ADMINISTRATION

College of Consultors
Secretary: Very Rev Gerard Condon PP
Ballygriffin, Killavullen, Co Cork
Tel 022-46578

Vicars General
Rt Rev Mgr Anthony O'Brien PP, VG
Mallow, Co Cork
Tel 022-20391
Rt Rev Mgr Jim Killeen PP, VG
Midleton, Co Cork
Tel 021-4631750

Episcopal Vicar for the Gaeltacht
Vacant

Financial Administrator
Rt Rev Mgr Eamonn Goold PE
Midleton
Tel 021-4633659
Accountants: Messrs Deloitte & Touche
6 Lapp's Quay, Cork

Diocesan Administration
Diocesan Secretary for Primary Education
Mr Dan Leo
Tel 086-8162370
*Diocesan Education Commission
Chairperson*
Rt Rev Mgr Jim Killeen PP, VG
Midleton, Co Cork
Diocesan Secretary for Canonical Affairs
Very Rev William O'Donovan PP
Conna, Co Cork
Tel 058-59138

Religious Education
Co-ordinator of Mission and Ministry:
Very Rev Gerard Condon PP
Ballygriffin, Killavullen, Co Cork
Tel 022-46578
Sr Emmanuel Leonard
5 Ashgrove, Cluain Ard, Cobh, Co Cork
Tel 021-4815305
Primary Schools
Mr Anthony Kenneally
c/o Cloyne Diocesan Centre,
Cobh, Co Cork

Diocesan Secretary
Rev James Moore
Cloyne Diocesan Centre, Cobh, Co Cork
Tel 021-4811430

Administrative Secretary
Mrs Eileen Greaney
Cloyne Diocesan Centre, Cobh, Co Cork
Tel 021-4811430
Email info@cloynediocese.ie

Curator of the Diocesan Archives
Rt Rev Mgr Jim Killeen PP, VG
Midleton, Co Cork
Tel 021-4631750
Archivist: Ms Máiréad Foley
Cloyne Diocesan Centre, Cobh, Co Cork
Tel 021-4811430

LITURGY

Diocesan Master of Ceremonies
Rev Andrew Carvill
Mallow, Co Cork
Tel 022-51606

Church Music
Director: Very Rev Gerard Coleman PP
Castlelyons, Co Cork
Tel 025-36372

PASTORAL

**Accord Catholic Marriage Care Service
CLG**
Diocesan Director
Very Rev Canon Michael Leamy PP, VF
Mitchelstown, Co Cork
Tel 025-41765

Communications
Diocesan Director
Rev James Moore
Cloyne Diocesan Centre,
Cobh, Co Cork
Tel 021-4811430

Diocesan Youth Services
Chairman: Richard Dempsey
Director: Vacant
Mallow Community Youth Centre,
New Road, Mallow, Co Cork
Tel 022-53526

Ecumenism
Secretary: Vacant

Immigrant Apostolate
Diocesan Director
Rev Andrew Carvill CC
Mallow, Co Cork
Tel 022-51606

Marriage Tribunal
(See also Marriage Tribunals section)
Cork Regional Marriage Tribunal:
Officialis:
Very Rev Richard Keane VJ

Perpetual Eucharistic Adoration
Diocesan Directors
Rev John Keane CC
Ballyvongane, Coachford, Co Cork
Tel 089-7078770
Rev Patrick O'Donoghue CC
Mitchelstown, Co Cork
Tel 025-84077

Pilgrimage Director
Very Rev Canon Tobias Bluitt PP, VF
Kanturk, Co Cork
Tel 29-50192
Assistant Director
Very Rev Canon Donal O'Mahony PP
Charleville, Co Cork
Tel 063-81319

Pioneer Total Abstinence Association
Diocesan Director
Very Rev Chris Donlon PP
Ladysbridge, Co Cork
Tel 021-4667173

ntifical Mission Societies
ocesan Director
ry Rev Micheál Leader PP
llyclough, Mallow, Co Cork
l 022-27650

ayer Groups
)-ordinator
v John Keane CC
llyvongane, Coachford, Co Cork
l 089-7078770

afeguarding
esignated Liaison Person (DLP)
ry Rev Patrick Winkle
oyne Diocesan Office,
bh, Co Cork
l 086-0368999
mail dlp@cloynediocese.ie

eputy Designated Liaison Person
r Ger Crowley
l 086-0368999

oyne Diocese Safeguarding Office
allow Community Youth Centre,
ew Road, Mallow, Co Cork
l 022-21009
mail safeguardingchildrenoffice@
oynediocese.ie
ww.safeguardingchildrencloyne.ie

*oyne Diocese Safeguarding Committee
DSC)*
hairperson: Mr Willie Keane
ontact through the Safeguarding Office

*afeguarding Training Coordinator and
arda Vetting Authorised Liaison Person*
s Rosarie O'Riordan

avellers
haplain: Vacant

ócaire
ry Rev Eugene Baker
uttevant, Co Cork
l 086-8031876

icar for Religious
ry Rev Canon Sean Cotter PE
ove Lane, Charleville, Co Cork

ocations
irector: Very Rev Brian Boyle Adm
avenswood, Fermoy, Co Cork
l 085-2553787
ssistant Director: Rev Damien Lynch CC
Bellevue Circle, Mallow, Co Cork
l 022-53909

PARISHES

*ensal parishes are listed first. Other
arishes follow alphabetically. Historical
ames are given in parentheses.*

COBH, ST COLMAN'S CATHEDRAL
Sacred Heart, Rushbrooke
Sacred Heart, Ballymore
Very Rev Tom McDermott Adm
Cobh, Co Cork
Tel 021-4815934
Very Rev Liam Kelleher PE
Cobh, Co Cork
Tel 087-8516984
Rev James Moore *(in residence)*
Rushbrooke, Cobh, Co Cork
Tel 086-8694744
Very Rev Aquin Casey CC
Cobh, Co Cork
Tel 021-4908657
Rev Paul Bennett CC
Cobh, Co Cork
Tel 021-4908317

FERMOY
St Patrick's
Very Rev Brian Boyle Adm
Ravenswood, Fermoy, Co Cork
Tel 085-2553787
Rev Eamon Roche CC
Monument Hill, Fermoy, Co Cork
Tel 086-9972539
Rev Patrick Corkery
Parochial House, The Square,
Kilworth, Co Cork
Tel 087-9601558

AGHABULLOGUE
St John's, Aghabullogue
St Patrick's, Coachford
St Olan's, Rylane
Very Rev Peadar Murphy PP
Aghabullogue, Co Cork
Tel 021-7334035

AGHADA
St Erasmus, Aghada
Church of the Mother of God, Saleen
St Mary's, Ballinrostig
Very Rev Daniel Murphy PP
Church Road, Aghada, Co Cork
Tel 086-0224682

AGHINAGH
*St John the Baptist, Bealnamorrive,
Rusheen, Ballinagree*
Very Rev Joseph O'Mahony Adm
Sandyhill, Macroom, Co Cork
Tel 026-41092

BALLYCLOUGH
St John the Baptist, Ballyclough, Kilbrin
Very Rev Mícheál Leader PP
Ballyclough, Mallow, Co Cork
Tel 022-27650

BALLYHEA
St Mary's
Rt Rev Mgr James O'Brien PP
Ballyhea, Co Cork
Tel 063-81470

BALLYMACODA AND LADYSBRIDGE
St Mary's, Ladysbridge
St Peter in Chains, Ballymacoda
Very Rev Chris Donlon PP
Ladysbridge, Co Cork
Tel 021-4667173

BALLYVOURNEY
St Gobnait, Ballyvourney
Séipéal Ghobnatan, Cúil Aodha
Very Rev John McCarthy PP
Tel 086-8212101

BANTEER (CLONMEEN)
St Fursey's, Banteer
St Nicholas', Kilcorney
St Joseph's, Lyre
Very Rev William Winter PP
Banteer, Co Cork
Tel 029-56010

BLARNEY
Immaculate Conception, Blarney
St Patrick's, Whitechurch
St Mary's, Waterloo
Very Rev Michael Fitzgerald PP
Blarney, Co Cork
Tel 021-4385105
Rev Gabriel Burke CC
5 Lavallin Drive, Whitechurch, Co Cork
Tel 021-4200184

BUTTEVANT
St Mary's, Buttevant
St Mary's, Lisgriffin
Very Rev Eugene Baker PP
Buttevant, Co Cork
Tel 086-8031876

CARRIGTWOHILL
St Mary's
Very Rev Patrick Winkle PP
Carrigtwohill, Co Cork
Tel 021-4882439

CASTLELYONS
St Nicholas', Castlelyons
St Mary's, Coolagown
Very Rev Gerard Coleman PP
Tel/Fax 025-36372
Rev Marek Pecak *(in residence)*
Tel 087-1410470
Castlelyons, Fermoy, Co Cork

CASTLEMAGNER
St Mary's
Very Rev Canon Tobias Bluitt Adm
Kanturk, Co Cork
Tel 029-50192

CASTLETOWNROCHE
*Immaculate Conception,
Castletownroche*
Nativity of Our Lady, Ballyhooly
Very Rev Robin Morrissey PP
Castletownroche, Co Cork
Tel 087-6727925
Very Rev Donal Broderick PE
Ballyhooly, Co Cork
Tel 025-39148

CHARLEVILLE
Holy Cross
Very Rev Canon Donal O'Mahony PP
Tel/Fax 063-81319
Rev Anthony Sheehan AP
Tel 063-32320
Charleville, Co Cork

CHURCHTOWN (LISCARROLL)
St Nicholas', Churchtown
St Joseph's, Liscarroll
Very Rev Eugene Baker Adm
Buttevant, Co Cork
Tel 086-8031876

CILL NA MARTRA
St Lachtaín's, Kilnamartyra
Renaniree Church
Very Rev John McCarthy Adm
Ballyvourney, Co Cork
Tel 085-8783823

CLONDROHID
St Abina's, Clondrohid
St John the Baptist, Carriganimma
Very Rev James Greene Adm
Clondrohid, Macroom, Co Cork
Tel 085-8471249

CLOYNE
St Colman's, Cloyne
Star of the Sea, Ballycotton
Immaculate Conception, Shanagarry
St Colmcille's, Churchtown South
Very Rev Patrick Linehan PP
Cloyne, Midleton, Co Cork
Tel 021-4652597
Very Rev Michael Dorgan PE, CC
Ballycotton, Co Cork
Tel 083-8230854

CONNA
St Catherine's, Conna
St Catherine's, Ballynoe
St Mary's, Glengoura
Very Rev William O'Donovan PP
Conna, Mallow, Co Cork
Tel 058-59138

DONERAILE
The Nativity of the Blessed Virgin Mary,
Doneraile
Christ the King, Shanballymore
St Joseph the Worker, Hazelwood
Very Rev Aidan Crowley PP
Tel 086-0434911
Doneraile, Co Cork

DONOUGHMORE
St Lachteen's, Stuake
St Joseph's, Fornaught
Very Rev Jeremiah O'Riordan PP
Donoughmore, Co Cork
Tel 021-7337023

GLANTANE
St Peter the Apostle, Dromahane
St John the Evangelist, Glantane
St Columba, Bweeng
Very Rev Gerard Coleman PP
Dromahane, Mallow, Co Cork
Tel 087-9580420

GLANWORTH AND BALLINDANGAN
Holy Cross, Glanworth
Immaculate Conception, Ballindangan
Holy Family, Curraghagulla
Very Rev Michael Corkery PP
Glanworth, Co Cork
Tel 025-38123
Very Rev Dan Gould PE
Ballindangan, Mitchelstown, Co Cork

GRENAGH
St Lachteen's, Grenagh
St Joseph's, Courtbrack
Very Rev Micheál Ó Loingsigh PP
Grenagh, Co Cork
Tel 021-4886128

IMOGEELA (CASTLEMARTYR)
Sacred Heart, Mogeely
St Joseph's, Castlemartyr
St Peter's, Dungourney
St Lawrence's, Clonmult
Very Rev Francis O'Neill PP
Castlemartyr, Co Cork
Tel 021-4667133
Rev Finbarr O'Flynn CC
Dungourney, Co Cork
Tel 021-4668406

INNISCARRA
St Senan's, Cloghroe
St Mary's, Berrings
St Joseph's, Matehy
Very Rev Patrick Buckley PP
4 Upper Woodlands, Cloghroe, Co Cork
Tel 021-4385311
Rev Patrick McCarthy CC
Berrings, Co Cork
Tel 086-3831621

KANTURK
Immaculate Conception, Kanturk
St Joseph's, Lismire
Very Rev Canon Tobias Bluitt PP, VF
Tel 029-50192
Rev John Magner CC
Tel 029-50061
Kanturk, Co Cork

KILDORRERY
St Bartholomew's, Kildorrery
St Molaga's, Sraharla
Very Rev Eamonn Kelleher PP
Kildorrery, Co Cork
Tel 022-40703

KILLAVULLEN
St Nicholas', Kilavullen
St Crannacht's, Anakissa
Very Rev Gerard Condon PP
Ballygriffin, Killavullen, Co Cork
Tel 022-46578
Very Rev Richard Hegarty PE
Killavullen, Co Cork
Tel 022-26125

KILLEAGH
St John the Baptist, Killeagh
St Patrick's, Inch
Very Rev Tim Hazelwood PP
Killeagh, Co Cork
Tel 024-95133

KILWORTH
St Martin's, Kilworth
Immaculate Conception, Araglin
Very Rev Brian Boyle Adm
Fermoy, Co Cork
Tel 085-2553787
Rev Patrick Corkery *(priest in residence)*
Kilworth, Co Cork
Tel 087-9601558

LISGOOLD
St John the Baptist, Lisgoold
Sacred Heart, Leamlara
Very Rev Denis O'Hanlon PP
Lisgoold, Co Cork
Tel 021-4642363

MACROOM
St Colman's, Macroom
St John the Baptist, Caum
Very Rev Canon Donal Roberts PP, VF
Tel 026-21068
Rt Rev Mgr James O'Donnell AP
Tel 026-41042
Very Rev Joseph O'Mahony Adm
Tel 026-41092
Macroom, Co Cork
Rev John Keane CC
Ballyvongane, Coachford, Co Cork
Tel 089-7078770

MALLOW
St Mary's, Mallow
Resurrection, Mallow
Rt Rev Mgr Anthony O'Brien PP, VG
Tel 022-20391
Rev Thomas Lane CC
2 Bellevue Circle, Mallow, Co Cork
Tel 087-0660615
Rev Damien Lynch CC
4 Bellevue Circle, Mallow, Co Cork
Tel 022-53909
Rev Andrew Carvill CC
Tel 022-51606

MIDLETON
Holy Rosary, Midleton
St Colman's, Ballintotas
Rt Rev Mgr Jim Killeen PP, VG
Tel 021-4631750
Very Rev John Ryan PE, CC
Tel 086-2697503
Rev Mark Hehir CC
Tel 021-4621670
Rt Rev Mgr Eamonn Goold PE
Tel 021-4633659
Midleton, Co Cork

MILFORD
Assumption of BVM, Milford
St Michael's, Freemount
St Berchert's, Tullylease
Very Rev Peter O'Farrell PP
Milford, Charleville, Co Cork
Tel 063-80038

Allianz (ⅱ)

MITCHELSTOWN
Our Lady Conceived Without Sin, Mitchelstown
Holy Family, Ballygiblin, Killacluig
Very Rev Canon Michael Leamy PP, VF
Tel 025-41765
Rev Patrick O'Donoghue CC
Tel 025-84077
Mitchelstown, Co Cork

MOURNE ABBEY
St Michael the Archangel, Analeentha
St John the Baptist, Burnfort
Rt Rev Mgr Anthony O'Brien Adm
Mallow, Co Cork
Tel 022-20391

NEWMARKET
Immaculate Conception, Newmarket
Holy Spirit, Taur
Very Rev Francis Manning PP
Newmarket, Co Cork
Tel 029-60999

NEWTOWNSHANDRUM
St Joseph's, Shandrum
St Peter & Paul's, Dromina
Very Rev Anthony Wickham PP
Newtownshandrum,
Charleville, Co Cork
Tel 063-70836

RATHCORMAC
Immaculate Conception, Rathcormac
St Bartholomew's, Bartlemy
Very Rev Joseph O'Keeffe PP
Main Street, Rathcormac, Co Cork
Tel 025-37371
Very Rev Cornelius O'Donnell PE
Rathcormac, Fermoy, Co Cork
Tel 025-36286

ROCKCHAPEL AND MEELIN
St Joseph's, Meelin
St Peter's, Rockchapel
Very Rev Denis Stritch PP
Meelin, Newmarket, Co Cork
Tel 029-68007

YOUGHAL
St Mary's, Our Lady of Lourdes, Holy Family, Youghal; St Ita's, Gortroe
Very Rev Canon William Bermingham PP
Tel 083-8687196
Rev Brendan Mallon CC
Tel 024-92456
Rev Gerard Cremin CC
Tel 024-92270
Youghal, Co Cork
Very Rev Canon Tom Browne PE
South Abbey, Youghal, Co Cork
Tel 024-93199

PRIESTS OF THE DIOCESE ELSEWHERE

Rev Seán Corkery
Director of Formation,
St Patrick's College,
Maynooth, Co Kildare
Tel 086-2420240

Rev Daniel McCarthy CF
Office of the Chaplain,
James Stephens Barracks, Kilkenny City
Rev Eamonn McCarthy
Radio Maria Ireland,
Unit 8, St Anthony's Business Park,
Ballymount Road, Dublin 22
Tel 085-8585308
Very Rev Mgr Joseph Murphy
Head of Protocol, Secretariat of State,
00120 Vatican City
Tel 0039-0669883193
Rev P. J. O'Driscoll CF
29th Commando Regiment, RA,
The Royal Citadel, Plymouth,
Devon PL1 2PD, England
Tel 0044-7816-135137

RETIRED PRIESTS

Rev Eamonn Barry
Gortacrue, Midleton, Co Cork
Tel 086-8157952
Very Rev Donal Broderick PE
Ballyhooly, Co Cork
Tel 025-39148
Very Rev Richard P. Browne PE
Nadrid, Coachford, Co Cork
Tel 021-7334059
Very Rev Canon Thomas Browne PE
Southabbey, Youghal, Co Cork
Tel 024-93199
Very Rev Donal Coakley
Buttevant, Co Cork
Very Rev John Cogan PE
Killeen, Vicarstown, Co Cork
Tel 021-4385535
Very Rev Canon Seán Cotter PE
Love Lane, Charleville, Co Cork
Tel 063-89778
Very Rev Mortimer Downing PE
Stuake, Donoughmore, Co Cork
Very Rev Canon Michael Fitzgerald PE
Garrycahera, Ballynoe,
Mallow, Co Cork
Rt Rev Mgr Eamonn Goold PE
Midleton, Co Cork
Tel 021-4633659
Very Rev Daniel Gould PE
Ballinadangan, Co Cork
Tel 025-85563
Dr Patrick Hannon
Emeritus Professor of Theology,
St Patrick's College, Maynooth,
Co Kildare
Tel 01-6285222
Very Rev Martin Heffernan PE, PhD
Skahardgannon, Doneraile, Co Cork
Tel 022-24570
Very Rev Richard Hegarty PE
Killavullen, Co Cork
Tel 022-26125
Very Rev Canon David Herlihy PE
Freemount, Charleville, Co Cork
Very Rev Canon Denis Kelleher PE
Inegrega, Midleton, Co Cork

Very Rev Liam Kelleher PE
4 Cathedral Terrace, Cobh, Co Cork
Tel 087-8516984
Very Rev Canon Dónal Leahy PE
Jamesbrook, Midleton, Co Cork
Very Rev Michael Madden PE
c/o Cloyne Diocesan Centre,
Cobh, Co Cork
Rev Kevin Mulcahy
Ballymacoda, Co Cork
Tel 024-98110
Rt Rev Mgr Denis O'Callaghan PE
Mallow, Co Cork
Tel 022-21112
Very Rev Peadar O'Callaghan PE
Teach an tSagairt, Main Street,
Carrigtwohill, Co Cork
Very Rev Cornelius O'Donnell PE
Rathcormac, Fermoy, Co Cork
Tel 025-36286
Very Rev Canon Colman O'Donovan PE
1 Youghal Road, Midleton, Co Cork
Tel 021-4621617
Very Rev Stephen O'Mahony PE
Liscarroll, Mallow, Co Cork
Tel 022-48128
Very Rev David O'Riordan PE
Midleton, Co Cork
Tel 086-3590047
Very Rev Mgr Denis Reidy PE
4 Carrig Downs, Carrigtwohill, Co Cork
Very Rev Patrick Scanlan PE
Castlemagner, Co Cork
Very Rev Canon John Terry PE
Terriville, Ballylanders,
Cloyne, Co Cork
Tel 087-2584091
Very Rev Canon Patrick Twomey PE
Bellevue, Mallow, Co Cork
Tel 022-55632
Rev Denis Vaughan
45 The Oaks, Maryborough Ridge,
Douglas, Cork

RELIGIOUS ORDERS AND CONGREGATIONS

SISTERS

ADORERS OF THE SACRED HEART OF JESUS OF MONTMARTRE, OSB
St Benedict's Priory,
The Mount, Cobh, Co Cork
Tel 021-4811354
Prioress: Mother M. Catherine
Community: 7
Contemplative Benedictines
Residential retreats
Contact person: Guest Mistress
Email cobhtyburnconvent@gmail.com

BON SECOURS SISTERS (PARIS)
38 Norwood Park, Cobh, Co Cork
Tel 021-4815350
Co-ordinator: Sr Paschal Barry
Community: 4
Pastoral Ministry, Care of Elderly

St Martin's Carrignafoy,
Cobh, Co Cork
Community: 1

CONGREGATION OF THE SISTERS OF MERCY
'Trócaire', 6 Castleowen,
Blarney, Co Cork
Tel 021-4381745

Friaryville, Buttevant, Co Cork
Tel 022-23014

Charleville, Co Cork
Tel 063-81276

Dan Corkery Place,
Macroom, Co Cork
Tel 026-42673

Holy Spirit Convent,
Bank Place, Mallow, Co Cork
Tel 022-21780

Convent of Mercy, Bathview,
Mallow, Co Cork
Tel 022-21395

3 Beechwood Grove,
Cluain Ard, Cobh, Co Cork
Tel 021-4815062

5 Ashgrove, Cluain Ard,
Cobh, Co Cork
Tel 021-4815305

41 Ivy Gardens, Mallow, Co Cork
Tel 022-58036

17 Bromley Court,
Midleton, Co Cork

Mercy House, Church Street,
Kanturk, Co Cork

Convent Bungalow,
Bathview, Mallow, Co Cork

INFANT JESUS SISTERS
Bellevue, Mallow,
Co Cork P51 X658
Tel 022-43085
Retired sisters

12 Glenanaar Row,
Mallow, Co Cork P51 TK8N

Main Street, Ballyclough,
Mallow, Co Cork P51 AN8K

11a Upper Duhallow Park,
Mallow, Co Cork P51 A4O9

LITTLE COMPANY OF MARY
Little Company of Mary, 'Lima',
College Road, Fermoy,
Co Cork
Tel 025-40627
Community: 1

MISSIONARIES OF CHARITY
St Helen's Convent,
Blarney, Co Cork
Tel 021-4382041
Superior: Sr Vianita (MC)
Community: 6
Residential Treatment Centre

CONGREGATION OF THE SISTERS OF NAZARETH
Nazareth House, Mallow, Co Cork
Tel 022-64180
Superior: Sr Brigid Comerford
Email
superior.mallow@nazarethcare.com
Community: 10
Home for elderly. Beds: 120

PRESENTATION SISTERS
Presentation Convent, Midleton, Co Cork
Tel 021-4631892
Email presmidleton@gmail.com
Team Leadership
Community: 6
Primary School Tel 021-4631593
St Mary's Secondary School
Tel 021-4631973

82 Brookdale,
Midleton, Co Cork P25 HV59
Community: 1

'Srahaun', 20 Barry's Court,
Duntahane, Fermoy, Co Cork P61 YD76
Tel 025-31248
Email fermoypresentation@gmail.com
Community: 3

Presentation Lodge, College Road,
Fermoy, Co Cork
Tel 025-49928
Community: 1

Presentation Convent,
Front Strand, Youghal, Co Cork
Tel 024-93039
Local Leader: Sr Placida Barry
Email placidapres@gmail.com
Community: 4

Presentation Sisters, 'Darchno',
Castleredmond, Midleton, Co Cork
Tel 021-4631912
Community: 1

Presentation Primary School,
Mitchelstown, Co Cork
Tel 025-24264
Presentation Secondary School
Mitchelstown, Co Cork
Tel 025-24394

Nano Nagle Birthplace,
Presentation Sisters,
Ballygriffin, Mallow, Co Cork P51 CV91
Tel 022-26411 Fax 022-26953
Email secretary@nanonaglebirthplace.ie
Community: 3
Website www.nanonaglebirthplace.ie

20 Church View,
Charleville, Co Cork
Email kathleenstoranpbvm@gmail.com
Community: 1

31 Churchview,
Charleville, Co Cork
Tel 087-6894549
Email counihanmary@gmail.com
Community: 1

ST JOSEPH OF THE SACRED HEART SISTERS
Sisters of St Joseph of Sacred Heart,
Penola, 25B Harrison Place,
Charleville, Co Cork
Sr Maura Murphy

Cullinagh, Fermoy, Co Cork
Tel 089-2210409
Sr Christina Scannell
Email christine.scannell@sosj.org.au

EDUCATIONAL INSTITUTIONS

St Colman's College (Diocesan College)
Fermoy, Co Cork
Tel 025-31622 Fax 025-31634
Email stcolmansfermoy@eircom.net

Patrician Academy
Mallow, Co Cork
Tel 022-21884

Scoil Mhuire gan Smál
Blarney, Co Cork
Tel 021-4385331

De La Salle College
Macroom, Co Cork
Tel 026-41832

CHARITABLE AND OTHER SOCIETIES

St Mary's District Hospital
Youghal, Co Cork

County Hospital
Mallow, Co Cork

Society of St Vincent de Paul
Conferences at: Ballyvourney,
Castlemartyr, Cobh, Fermoy, Doneraile,
Kanturk, Macroom, Mallow, Midleton,
Mitchelstown, Youghal, Carrigtwohill,
Lisgoold, Aghada, Charleville

SAINT KIERAN'S COLLEGE
KILKENNY
www.stkieranscollege.ie

FOUNDED 1782

ST KIERAN'S IS A CATHOLIC DIOCESAN COLLEGE UNDER THE PATRONAGE OF THE BISHOP OF OSSORY

Its objectives are the advancement of Catholic religion and education by providing a well-rounded academic education for second level students and supporting faith formation in the Diocese of Ossory as a pastoral centre and home for many diocesan initiatives.

■ **SECONDARY SCHOOL** which promotes real excellence in education and formation to 800 pupils, with a wide range of sporting, co-curricular and extra-curricular activities.

■ **ASPAL** the home for Ireland's leading digital learning platform for all involved in ministry and the faith life of our parishes and dioceses. A collaboration of Ossory Adult Faith Development, St Patrick's Pontifical University, supported by The Benefact Trust.

■ **MYFAITH** the home for this innovative online parish based programme of preparation for the Sacraments of First Holy Communion and Confirmation. Supporting children and their families on this important journey.

■ **CENTRE FOR RETREAT AND THEOLOGICAL REFLECTION** which offers parish evenings and weekend retreats and on-going formation courses for clergy and laity.

■ **PASTORAL AND FAITH DEVELOPMENT** which supports parishes, various groups and people of our Diocese to deepen their understanding of faith, through reflection, lectures and various other initiatives.

■ **THE HOME FOR LIGHTHOUSE STUDIOS, THE KILKENNY RESEARCH & INNOVATION CENTRE** and so much more.

Further information: The President, St Kieran's College, Kilkenny. Tel: +353 (0)56 7721086 Email: president@stkieranscollege.ie

EXCLUSIVE TO VERITAS

15% OFF*

SCULPTURE BY
TIMOTHY P. SCHMALZ

HOMELESS JESUS, AS SEEN AT CHRIST CHURCH CATHEDRAL, DUBLIN

Christ Washing Peter's Feet

When I Was Hungry & Thirsty

Homeless Jesus

Cross of Life

Timothy P. Schmalz is one of the greatest Christian sculptors of our day, with pieces on display across the world.

Pope Francis has blessed and endorsed many of Timothy's works, including the iconic *Homeless Jesus*, which is installed at Dublin's Christ Church Cathedral

Veritas is delighted to offer **exclusive access** to beautiful reproductions of Timothy's work at a **special price**. Each replica is detailed by hand to the exacting standards of this modern-day master sculptor.

Timothy's sculptures are elegant devotional pieces that would make a **unique gift** for a loved one.

SCAN HERE

Find out more at
www.veritas.ie

 VERITAS

***WHEN YOU ORDER ONLINE OR VISIT US IN-STORE (PRICES FROM €139)**

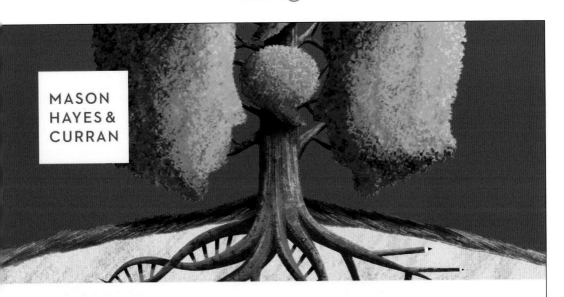

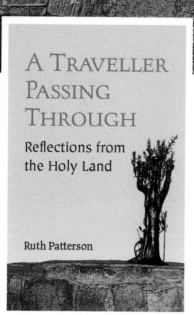

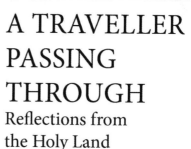

A TRAVELLER PASSING THROUGH

Reflections from
the Holy Land

Ruth Patterson

ISBN **978 1 80097 016 8**
PRICE **€12.99/£11.70**

In *A Traveller Passing Through* Ruth Patterson invites us to accompany her in our imaginations to places in the Holy Land that have significance in the life of Jesus. Her beautiful reflections take the reader on a pilgrimage to these places and beyond to the experiences and encounters they inspire, opening the door to a deeper appreciation of our own brokenness and belovedness, and to the gift of exploring the mystery and wonder of the spiritual journey.

Ruth Patterson is a Presbyterian minister and the director of Restoration Ministries, a nondenominational, Christian organisation committed to peace and reconciliation. In 2003 she was awarded an OBE for her efforts in reconciliation. Her previous publications include *The Gaze of Love* (2016) and *Looking Back to Tomorrow: A Spirituality for Between the Times* (2009).

'In the midst of the familiar, to unlearn what we are confident we know, and to make room for what we don't know yet: that is the invitation extended by Dr Ruth Patterson in this book.' **Rev. Dr Katherine P. Meyer**

'*A Traveller Passing Through* is more about an inner journey by a pilgrim to sacred places, recalling people and events in the Holy Land, and then interpreting them in a creative, refreshing and prophetic way as good news to our modern world. The transforming word of God, which is challenging, is incarnated in the human story calling for growth in inner freedom and to awaken a vision that sees beyond the ordinary to welcome and live the deeper gifts of unity and peace that the Lord desires for us.' **Fr Michael Drennan**

DIOCESE OF CORK AND ROSS

PATRON OF THE DIOCESE OF CORK
ST FINBARR, 25 SEPTEMBER

PATRON OF THE DIOCESE OF ROSS
ST FACHTNA, 14 AUGUST

INCLUDES CORK CITY AND PART OF COUNTY CORK

Most Rev Fintan Gavin DD
Bishop of Cork and Ross;
born 1966;
ordained priest 1991;
ordained Bishop of Cork & Ross
30 June 2019

Residence:
Cork and Ross Offices,
Redemption Road, Cork
Tel 021-4301717
Fax 021-4301557

CATHEDRAL OF ST MARY AND ST ANNE, CORK

The first cathedral on the site of the present Cathedral of St Mary and St Anne was the vision of Bishop Francis Moylan, who was Bishop of Cork from 1786 to 1815. The foundation stone was laid in 1799 and the cathedral was opened in 1808 as the parish church of the single parish then on the northside of the city – hence its local, popular name: the North Chapel. But in June 1820, the heat of the political climate struck the North Chapel when it was maliciously burned during the night.

Bishop John Murphy, one of the famous brewing family, wasted no time in calling a meeting to help restore the cathedral. The people of Cork generously rallied to the call.

The task of rebuilding was given to architect George Pain, who later designed Blackrock Castle, the court house and St Patrick's Church. The interior of the present-day cathedral, including the ornate ceiling, owes much to his creative gifts.

The next major alteration to the cathedral was undertaken in the 1870s when Canon Foley set about building the tower and the great Western Door – now the main door of the cathedral. The tower is higher than that of its more famous neighbour: St Anne's Church, Shandon, home of the much-played bells.

Almost a hundred years later, after the Second Vatican Council, Cornelius Lucey, then Bishop of Cork and Ross, added a further major extension at the other end of the cathedral. This included a completely new sanctuary and a smaller tower, and added capacity to the church, which served an area with a rapidly increasing population.

In 1994, major problems were discovered in the roof and other fabric of the building, which led to the closing of the cathedral for major refurbishment. The Bishop, Michael Murphy, decided it was time to renovate the interior of the

cathedral too. The task was entrusted to architect Richard Hurley, whose plan for the new interior saw a greater unity being achieved between the sanctuary and the rest of the floor area, and the new altar occupying the central place of

prominence. The reordering and renovation was completed in 1996 at a cost of £2.5m and Bishop Murphy presided over its rededication – his last public function before he died a week later.

Most Rev John Buckley DD
Retired Bishop of Cork & Ross; born 1939; ordained priest 1965; ordained Titular Bishop of Leptis Magna 29 April 1984 and installed 6 February 1998
Residence: Cork and Ross Offices, Redemption Road, Cork
Tel 021-4301717 Fax 021-4301557

CHAPTER

Dean: Very Rev Noel O'Sullivan
Precentor: Very Rev Canon Jim O'Donovan
Treasurer: Very Rev Canon Ted O'Sullivan
Chancellor:
Very Rev Canon John O'Donovan
Prebendaries
Kilbritain
Very Rev Canon Bertie O'Mahony
Desertmore
Very Rev Canon Martin Keohane
Kilnaglory: Very Rev Canon Dan Crowley
Holy Trinity
Very Rev Canon Martin O'Driscoll
Kilbrogan
Rt Rev Mgr Kevin O'Callaghan
Caherlag: Very Rev Canon John Kingston
Kilanully: Very Rev Canon George Murphy
Killaspugmullane
Very Rev Canon Michael Murphy
Liscleary: Very Rev Canon Robert Brophy
St Michael
Very Rev Canon Bernard Donovan
Inniskenny
Very Rev Canon John Paul Hegarty
Drimoleague: Vacant

Honorary Canons
Very Rev Canon Thomas Kelleher
Very Rev Canon John K. O'Mahony
Archdeacon Kerry Murphy O'Connor
Very Rev Canon Tadhg Ó Mathuna
Very Rev Canon Liam O'Regan
Very Rev Canon Michael Riordan
Very Rev Canon Richard Hurley

ADMINISTRATION

Vicars General
Rt Rev Mgr Tom Hayes PP, VG
Parochial House, Clonakilty, Co Cork
Tel 023-8833165
Rt Rev Mgr Aidan O'Driscoll PP, VG
Cork road, Carrigaline, Co Cork
Tel 021-4371684

Diocesan Secretary
Rev Michael Keohane
Cork & Ross Offices,
Redemption Road, Cork
Tel 021-4301717
Email secretary@corkandross.org

PASTORAL

Catechetics
Primary: Seamus Ó Dálaigh
Email diocesanadvisors@corkandross.org
Second-level: Mr Paul Kelly
Cork and Ross Offices,
Redemption Road, Cork
Tel 021-4301717
Email postprimary@corkandross.org

Child Protection
Diocesan Director: Ms Cleo Yates
Diocesan Offices,
Redemption Road, Cork
Tel 021-4301717
Email safeguarding@corkandross.org

Marriage Counselling
ACCORD, 5 Main Street,
Bantry, Co Cork
Tel 027-50272

Diocesan Education Office
Cork and Ross Offices,
Redemption Road, Cork
Tel 021-4301717 Fax 021-4301557
Diocesan Education Secretary
Rev Michael Keohane
Secretary: Ms Regina O'Sullivan
Email education@corkandross.org

Immigrants
Cois Tine, SMA Justice Office,
African Mission, Wilton, Cork
Tel 021-4933475
Email coistine@sma.ie
Diocesan Chaplain to Polish Community
c/o St Augustine's,
Washington Street, Cork
Tel 021-4275390

Marriage Tribunal
(See Marriage Tribunals section)

Office of Mission and Ministry
Cathedral Presbytery, Roman Street, Cork
Email missionandministry@corkandross.org
Co-ordinator of Liturgy
Rev Christopher Fitzgerald
Email liturgy@corkandross.org

Pilgrimages
Director
Very Rev Canon James O'Donovan AP
The Presbytery, St Finbarr's West,
The Lough, Cork
Tel 087-2553021

Pontifical Mission Society
Rev Pat Fogarty Co-PP
The Presbytery, Glanmire, Co Cork
Tel 021-4820654

PARISHES

FAMILY OF PARISHES OF BANTRY, CAHERAGH, GOLEEN, MUINTIR BHÁIRE AND SCHULL
Very Rev Myles McSweeney Co-PP
Meenvane, Schull
Tel 028-28171

Very Rev Canon Martin O'Driscoll Co-PP
The Presbytery, Bantry, Co Cork
Tel 027-50096

Rev Michael Anthony Buckley CC
The Presbytery, Goleen, Co Cork
Tel 028-35188

Rev Ben Hodnett CC
The Presbytery, Bantry, Co Cork
Tel 027-50193

Rev John C. O'Donovan AP
The Presbytery, Dromore,
Bantry, Co Cork
Tel 028-31126
Moderator
Very Rev Myles McSweeney Co-PP

FAMILY OF PARISHES OF AUGHADOWN CASTLEHAVEN, KILMACABEA, RATH AN THE ISLANDS AND SKIBBEREEN
Very Rev Bernard Cotter Co-PP
Parish House, Union Hall,
Skibbereen, Co Cork P81 C433
Tel 028-34940

Very Rev John Heinhold (SPS) Co-PP
The Presbytery, Skibbereen, Co Cork
Tel 028-22878/22877
Parish Office: Tel 028-22828

Very Rev Terence O'Brien (MSC) Co-PP
Parochial House, Leap, Co Cork
Tel 028-33177

Rev Evin O'Brien CC
The Presbytery, Skibbereen, Co Cork
Tel 028-22878/22877
Moderator
Very Rev John Heinhold Co-PP

FAMILY OF PARISHES OF ARDFIELD/RATHBARRY, BARRYROE, CLONAKILTY, KILMEEN/CASTLEVENTRY, ROSSCARBERY AND TIMOLEAGUE
Very Rev Tom Hayes Co-PP, VG
The Presbytery, Clonakilty, Co Cork
Tel 023-8833165
Parish Office: Tel 023-8834441

Very Rev Canon John Kingston Co-PP
Parochial House, Timoleague, Co Cork
Tel 023-8839114

Very Rev John McCarthy Co-PP
Rosscarbery, Co Cork
Tel 023-8848168

Very Rev David O'Connell Co-PP
Lislevane, Bandon, Co Cork
Tel 023-8846171

Rev Fergus Tuohy (SMA) CC
The Presbytery, Clonakilty, Co Cork
Tel 023-8834441
Parish Office: Tel 023-8834441

Very Rev Timothy Collins AP
The Presbytery, O'Rahilly Street,
Clonakilty, Co Cork
Parish Office: Tel 023-8834441

Moderator: Very Rev Tom Hayes Co-PP

FAMILY OF PARISHES OF DRIMOLEAGUE, DUNMANWAY, KILMICHAEL AND UIBH LAOIRE

Very Rev Liam Crowley Co-PP
Drimoleague, Co Cork
Tel 028-31133

Very Rev Pat O'Donovan Co-PP
The Presbytery, Dunmanway, Co Cork
Tel 023-8845000
Parish Office: Tel 023-8856610

Very Rev Anthony O'Mahony Co-PP
Parochial House, Inchigeela,
Macroom, Co Cork
Tel 026-49838/087-2691432
Parish Office: Tel 087-1446958

Rev Rafal Zielonka CC
The Presbytery, Dunmanway, Co Cork
Tel 023-8845000
Parish Office: Tel 023-8856610

Moderator
Very Rev Pat O'Donovan Co-PP

FAMILY OF PARISHES OF BANDON, ENNISKEANE, INNISHANNON, KILLBRITTAIN, KILMURRY AND MURRAGH/TEMPLEMARTIN

Very Rev Jerry Cremin Co-PP
Parochial House, Kilbrittain, Co Cork
Tel 023-8849637

Very Rev Finbarr Crowley Co-PP
Innishannon, Co Cork
Tel 021-4775348
Parish Office: Tel 021-4776794

Very Rev Canon Bernard Donovan Co-PP
Cloughdubh, Crookstown, Co Cork
Tel 021-7336054

Very Rev Michael Kelleher Co-PP
Parochial House, Enniskeane, Co Cork
Tel 023-8847769
Parish Office:
parishoffice@enniskeaneparish.ie

Very Rev John Newman Co PP
The Presbytery, Bandon, Co Cork
Tel 023-8854666
Parish Office: Tel 023-8841666

Rev Bartlomiej Dziedzic CC
The Presbytery, Bandon, Co Cork
Tel 023-8865067
Parish Office: Tel 023-8841666

Canon Bertie O'Mahony AP
The Presbytery, Bandon, Co Cork
Parish Office: Tel 023-8841666

Moderator
Very Rev John Newman Co-PP

FAMILY OF PARISHES OF BALLINHASSIG, CLONTEAD, COURCEYS AND KINSALE

Very Rev Michael O'Mahony Co-PP
Ballinspittle, Co Cork
Tel 021-4778055

Very Rev Dr Daniel Pyburn Co-PP
Barrett's Hill, Ballinhassig, Co Cork
Tel 021-4885104
Parish Office: Tel 021-4805062

Very Rev Michael Regan Co-PP
Unit 1B, Riverside Grove,
Riverstick, Co Cork
Email clonteadbabhub@gmail.com

Very Rev Robert Young Co-PP
The Presbytery, Kinsale, Co Cork
Tel 021-4774019
Parish Office: Tel 021-4773821

Moderator
Very Rev Robert Young Co-PP

FAMILY OF PARISHES OF CARRIGALINE, CROSSHAVEN, HARBOUR PARISHES AND TRACTON ABBEY

Very Rev James McSweeney Co-PP
Cork Road, Carrigaline, Co Cork
Tel 021-4371860
Parish Office: Tel 021-4371109

Very Rev Chris O'Donovan Co-PP
New Parochial House,
Monkstown, Co Cork
Tel 021-4863267

Rt Rev Mgr Aidan O'Driscoll Co-PP, VG
Tel 021-4371684
Cork Road, Carrigaline, Co Cork
Parish Office: Tel 021-4371109

Very Rev Patrick Stevenson Co-PP
The Presbytery, Crosshaven, Co Cork
Tel 021-4831218

Rev Aidan Cremin CC
Cork Road, Carrigaline, Co Cork
Tel 021-4372229/4371860
Parish Office: Tel 021-4371109

Moderator
Rt Rev Mgr Aidan O'Driscoll Co-PP, VG

FAMILY OF PARISHES OF SOUTH PARISH, ST PATRICK'S AND SS PETER AND PAUL'S

Very Rev Eoin Whooley PP
South Presbytery, Dunbar Street, Cork
Tel 085-1471147

Rev Jilson Kokkandathil CC
South Presbytery, Dunbar Street, Cork

Rev Marius O'Reilly CC
35 Paul Street, Cork
Tel 021-4276573

Moderator
Very Rev. Eoin Whooley PP

FAMILY OF PARISHES OF CLOGHEEN/KERRY PIKE, FARRANREE, GURRANABRAHER AND KNOCKNAHEENY

Very Rev Cian O'Sullivan Co-PP
The Presbytery, Knocknaheeny, Cork
Parish Office: Tel 021-4392459

Very Rev Sean O'Sullivan Co-PP
The Presbytery, Farranree, Cork
Tel 021-4393815/4210111
Parish Office: Tel 021-4932230

Very Rev Tomás Walsh (SMA) Co-PP
Ascension Presbytery,
Gurranabraher, Cork
Tel 021-4303655
Parish Office: Tel 021-4303655

Rev Aidan Vaughan (OFMCap) CC
Ascension Presbytery,
Gurranabraher, Cork
Tel 021-4303655
Parish Office: Tel 021-4303655

Moderator
Very Rev Sean O'Sullivan Co-PP

FAMILY OF PARISHES OF CARRIGNAVAR, GLANMIRE, GLOUNTHAUNE AND WATERGRASSHILL

Very Rev Christopher Fitzgerald Co-PP
Parochial House,
Watergrasshill, Co Cork
Tel 021-4889103
Parish Office: Tel 021-4513671

Very Rev Pat Fogarty Co-PP
Glanmire, Co Cork
Tel 021-4866307
Parish Office: Tel 021-4820654

Very Rev Canon Martin Keohane Co-PP
Parish House,
Carraig na bhFear, Co Cork
Tel 021-4884119

Very Rev Damian O'Mahony Co-PP
Glounthaune, Co Cork
Tel 021-4232881
Parish Office: Tel 021-4353366

Rev Pat Nugent CC
Springhill, Glanmire, Co Cork
Tel 021-4866306/086-1689292
Parish Office: Tel 021-4820654

Moderator
Very Rev Christopher Fitzgerald Co-PP

FAMILY OF PARISHES OF BALLYPHEHANE, THE LOUGH AND TOGHER

Very Rev Greg Howard Co-PP
The Presbytery, Ballyphehane, Cork
Tel 021-4965560

Very Rev Canon John Paul Hegarty Co-PP
The Lough Presbytery,
St Finbarr's West, Cork
Tel 021-4322633

Very Rev John Walsh Co-PP
The Presbytery, Togher, Cork
Tel 021-4316700
Parish Office: 021-4318899

Very Rev Canon Jim O'Donovan AP
St Finbarr's Presbytery, The Lough, Cork

Moderator
Very Rev Greg Howard Co-PP

FAMILY OF PARISHES OF BALLINORA, BALLINCOLLIG AND OVENS

Very Rev Liam Ó hÍcí Co-PP
Ovens, Co Cork
Tel 021-4871180

Very Rev Alan O'Leary Co-PP
Parochial House,
Ballincollig, Co Cork
Parish Office: Tel 021-4871206

Rev Kamil Bachara CC
64 Westcourt, Ballincollig, Co Cork
Parish Office: Tel 021-4871206

Rev Ronan Sheehan CC
The Bungalow, St Mary & St John,
Ballincollig, Co Cork
Tel 021-4877161

Rev John Collins AP
Parochial House
Ballinora, Waterfall, near Cork
Tel 021-4872792

Moderator
Very Rev Alan O'Leary Co-PP

FAMILY OF PARISHES OF BALLINEASPAIG, CURAHEEN ROAD, SACRED HEART WESTERN ROAD AND SMA WILTON

BALLINEASPAIG
Very Rev Donal Cotter Adm
Ballineaspaig, Cork
Tel/Fax 021-4346818
Parish Office: Tel 021-4344452

CURRAHEEN ROAD
Very Rev Canon Robert Brophy PP
The Presbytery,
Curraheen Road, Cork
Tel 021-4343535

SACRED HEART
Very Rev Con Doherty (MSC) PP
Rev Des Farren (MSC) CC
Sacred Heart Parish,
Western Road, Cork
Tel 021-4804120 Fax 021-4543823
Parish Office: Tel 021-4346711

WILTON, ST JOSEPH'S
Very Rev Michael O'Leary (SMA) PP
St Joseph's, Wilton, Cork T12 E436
Tel 021-4341362 Fax 021-4343940
Parish Office:
stjosephschurchwilton@yahoo.com

FAMILY OF PARISHES OF BALLINLOUGH, BLACKROCK, BLACKROCK ROAD AND MAHON

BALLINLOUGH
Rt Rev Mgr Gearóid Dullea PP
The Presbytery, Ballinlough, Cork
Tel 021-4292296
Parish Office: Tel 021-4294332
Very Rev Canon Michael Murphy AP
Willow Lawn, Ballinlough, Cork

BLACKROCK
Very Rev Colin Doocey Adm
1 The Presbytery,
Holy Cross Church, Mahon, Co Cork
Tel 021-2414624
Rev Michael Keohane AP
1 The Presbytery, Blackrock, Cork
Tel 021-4301717

ST JOSEPH'S (BLACKROCK ROAD)
Very Rev Gus O'Driscoll (SMA) *(Father-in-Charge)*
Rev Jerome Sassou (SMA) CC
St Joseph's, Blackrock Road,
Cork T12 X281
Tel 021-4292871
Parish Office: Tel 021-4616327
Email parish.blackrock@sma.ie

MAHON
Very Rev Colin Doocey PP
1 The Presbytery,
Holy Cross Church, Mahon, Cork
Tel 021-2414624
Parish Office: Tel 021-4357040

FAMILY OF PARISHES OF DOUGLAS, FRANKFIELD AND TURNER'S CROSS

DOUGLAS
Very Rev Canon Ted O'Sullivan PP
Parochial House, Douglas, Cork
Tel 021-4891265
Parish Office: Tel 021-4894128
St Patrick's, Rochestown:
Rev Pat O'Mahony (SMA) CC
St Patrick's Presbytery,
Rochestown Road, Cork
Tel 021-4892363
Parish Office: Tel 021-4896797

FRANKFIELD-GRANGE
Very Rev Kevin O'Regan PP
The Presbytery, Frankfield, Cork
Tel 021-4361711
Parish Office: Tel 021-4897379

TURNER'S CROSS
Very Rev Dean Noel O'Sullivan Adm
The Presbytery, Turner's Cross, Cork

FAMILY OF PARISHES OF BLACKPOOL/ THE GLEN/BALLYVOLANE, ST JOSEPH'S MAYFIELD, ST VINCENT'S, UPPER MAYFIELD AND THE CATHEDRAL

BLACKPOOL/THE GLEN/BALLYVOLANE
Very Rev John O'Donovan PP
Cathedral Presbytery,
Roman Street, Cork
Tel 021-4501022
Rev Seán Crowley CC
Cathedral Presbytery,
Roman Street, Cork
Tel 021-4304325
Parish Office: Tel 021-4300518

ST JOSEPH'S (MAYFIELD)
Very Rev Chriostóir MacDonald PP
Murmont Lawn, Mayfield, Cork
Tel 021-4501861
Parish Office: Tel 021-4503531

UPPER MAYFIELD
Very Rev Dr Charles Kiely PP
The Presbytery, Our Lady Crowned,
Upper Mayfield, Cork
Tel 021-4503116
Parish Office: Tel 021-4551276

CATHEDRAL OF ST MARY & ST ANNE
Very Rev Canon John O'Donovan Adm
Tel 021-4501022
Rev Seán Crowley CC
Cathedral Presbytery, Cork
Tel 021-4304325 Fax 021-4304204
Parish Office: Tel 021-4304325

ST VINCENT'S, SUNDAY'S WELL
Administered by Cathedral Parish
Tel 021-4304325
Email cathedral@corkandross.org

INSTITUTIONS AND THEIR CHAPLAINS

THIRD LEVEL COLLEGES

Cork Institute of Technology
Chaplaincy Office: 021-4326225
Chaplain: Rev Dr David McAuliffe
Tel 021-4346244
Co-ordinator of Pastoral Care
Ms Edel Dullea
Tel 021-4326778

University College, Cork
Chaplaincy Office: Iona, College Road, Cork
Tel 021-4902459
Chaplain: Rev Gerard Dunne (OP)
Tel 021-4902704

HOSPITALS

Bandon District Hospital
Bandon, Co Cork
Tel 023-8841403
Chaplain: Parish clergy, Bandon

Bantry Hospital
Bantry, Co Cork
Tel 027-50133
Chaplain: Parish clergy, Bantry

Bon Secours Hospital
College Road, Cork
Tel 021-4542807
Chaplain: Rev Jack Twomey (OFMCap)
Tel 021-4546682

Cork South Infirmary
Victoria Hospital Ltd
Old Blackrock Road, Cork
Tel 021-4926100
Chaplain: Rev Michael Forde
Tel 021-4926100

Cork University Hospital
Wilton, Cork
Tel 021-4546400
Chaplains: Rev Pierce Cormac
Tel 021-4546400
Rev Thomas Lyons
Tel 021-4546400/4922391
Rev Kieran O'Driscoll
Tel 021-4546400
Rev Joyel John Michael (IC)
Tel 021-4546400

Marymount Hospice
Curraheen, Co Cork
Tel 021-4501201
Chaplain: Rev Declan Mansfield

Mercy Urgent Care Centre
Baker's Road, Cork
Tel 021-4303264
Chaplains: Parish clergy, Gurranabraher
Tel 021-4303655

Mercy University Hospital
Grenville Place, Cork
Tel 021-4271971
Chaplain: Rev Pat McCarthy

Mount Carmel Hospital
Clonakilty, Co Cork
Tel 023-8833205
Chaplain: Parish Clergy

Sacred Heart Hospital
Kinsale, Co Cork
Tel 021-4772202
Chaplain: Parish clergy, Kinsale

St Anthony's Hospital
Dunmanway, Co Cork
Tel 023-8845102
Chaplain: Parish clergy, Dunmanway

St Finbarr's Hospital
Douglas Road, Cork
Tel 021-4966555
Chaplain: Rev Michael Forde
Tel 021-4926100

St Gabriel's Hospital
Schull, Co Cork
Tel 028-28120
Chaplain: Parish clergy, Schull

St Joseph's Hospital
Mount Desert, Lee Road, Cork
Tel 021-4541765

St Stephen's Hospital
Glanmire, Co Cork
Tel 021-4821411
Chaplain: Rev Gerry Thornton (MSC)

Skibbereen Community Hospital
Skibbereen, Co Cork
Tel 028-21677
Chaplain: Parish Clergy

PORT

Port Chaplaincy
Rev Desmond Campion (SDB)
Tel 021-4378046

PRISONS

Cork Prison
Chaplain: Rev Ray Riordan
Tel 021-2388000

PRIESTS OF THE DIOCESE ELSEWHERE

Rev Dr Pádraig Corkery
St Patrick's College,
Maynooth, Co Kildare
Tel 01-7083639
Rev Joseph O'Leary
1-38-16 Ekoda, Nakanoku, Tokyo,
16J0022 Japan
Rev Ted Sheehan CF
Chaplain, Collins Barracks, Dublin

RETIRED PRIESTS

Rev Michael O'Driscoll
Bushmount, Clonakilty, Co Cork
Tel 023-33991
Rev. Tom Clancy PE
Woodlawn, Model Farm Road, Cork
Rev Pat Walsh
Priests House, Ahiohill,
Enniskeane, Co Cork
Very Rev Tom Riordan
Willow Lawn, Ballinlough, Cork
Very Rev Canon Thomas Kelleher
Kinsale, Co Cork
Very Rev Timothy O'Sullivan
Mount Desert, Lee Road, Cork
Very Rev Canon Michael Riordan
Mount Desert, Lee Road, Cork
An tÁth Seosaimh Ó Cochláin
c/o Cork & Ross Diocesan Office
Very Rev Denis Cashman
Ballincollig, Co Cork
Rev James Tobin
St Patrick's Presbytery,
Lower Road, Cork
Archdeacon Kerry Murphy O'Connor
The Bungalow, Turner's Cross, Cork
Rev Paul O'Donoghue
c/o Cork & Ross Diocesan Office
Very Rev Canon Tadhg Ó Mathúna PE
2 The Presbytery, Blackrock, Cork

Very Rev Canon Richard Hurley
c/o Cork & Ross Diocesan Office
Very Rev Canon Dan Crowley PE
Woodlawn, Model Farm Road, Cork
Very Rev Patrick J. McCarthy PE
The Presbytery, O'Rahilly Street,
Clonakilty, Co Cork
Very Rev Canon Liam O'Regan PE
Cramer's Court Nursing Home,
Ballindeenisk, Kinsale, Co Cork
Rev John K. O'Mahony
Mount Desert, Lee Road, Cork
Rev Billy O'Sullivan PE
The Presbytery, The Lough, Cork
Rt Rev Mgr Kevin O'Callaghan PE
The Presbytery, Lissarda, Co Cork
Rev Charlie Nyhan
c/o Cork & Ross Diocesan Office
Rev Donal Cahill
Lisheen, Skibbereen, Co Cork
Very Rev Canon George Murphy PE
Minane Bridge, Co Cork
Very Rev. Patrick Hickey PE
The Presbytery, Newcestown,
Bandon, Co Cork

PERSONAL PRELATURE

OPUS DEI
Dunmahon Study Centre
Model Farm Road, Cork T12 KHC1
Tel 021-2029112
www.dunmahon.ie
Rev Brian McCarthy

RELIGIOUS ORDERS AND CONGREGATIONS

PRIESTS

AUGUSTINIANS
St Augustine's Priory,
Washington Street, Cork
Tel 021-4275398/4270410 Fax 021-4275381
Prior: Rev John Lyng (OSA)
Bursar: Rev Tom Sexton (OSA)

CAPUCHINS
Holy Trinity,
Fr Mathew Quay, Cork T12 PK24
Tel 021-4270827 Fax 021-4270829
Guardian
Br Declan O'Callaghan (OFMCap)
Vicar: Rev Eddie Dowley (OFMCap)

St Francis Capuchin Franciscan College,
Rochestown, Co Cork T12 TK82
Principal: Mrs Marie Ring
Tel 021-4891417 Fax 021-4361254

CARMELITES (OCARM)
Carmelite Friary, Kinsale,
Co Cork P17 WR88
Tel 021-4772138
Email kinsale@irishcarmelites.com
Prior: Rev James Eivers (OCarm)

DOMINICANS
St Mary's, Pope Quay, Cork
Tel 021-4502267
Prior: Very Rev Maurice Colgan (OP)

St Dominic's Retreat House,
Montenotte, Cork
Tel 021-4502520 Fax 021-4502712
Prior: Very Rev Bernard Treacy (OP)

FRANCISCANS
Franciscan Friary, Liberty Street, Cork
Tel 021-4270302 Fax 021-4271841
Guardian: Rev Patrick Younge (OFM)

MISSIONARIES OF THE SACRED HEART
MSC Mission Support Centre,
PO Box 23, Western Road,
Cork T12 WT72
Tel 021-4545704/4543988
Fax 021-4343587
Director: Rev John Fitzgerald (MSC)
Email info@mscmissions.ie
www.mscmissions.ie

Western Road,
Cork, T12 TN80
Tel 021-4804120 Fax 021-4543823
Leader: Very Rev John Finn (MSC)
Parish Priest
Rev Con Doherty (MSC) PP

Carrignavor, Co Cork
Tel 021-4884404

(See also Kilmacabea Parish)

REDEMPTORISTS
Scala, Castle Mahon House,
Castle Road, Blackrock, Cork
Tel 021-4358800 Fax 021-4359696
Co-ordinator: Rev Brian Nolan (CSsR)

ROSMINIANS
Rosmini House, Dunkereen,
Innishannon, Cork, T12 N9DH
Tel 021-4776268/4776923
Fax 021-4776268
Rector: Rev Polachan Thettayil (IC)

ST COLUMBAN'S MISSIONARY SOCIETY
No. 2 Presbytery, Our Lady Crowned
Church, Mayfield Upper, Cork
Tel 021-4508610
Rev Patrick O'Herlihy (SSC)

ST PATRICK'S MISSIONARY SOCIETY
Kiltegan House, 11 Douglas Road, Cork
Tel 021-4969371
House Leader: Rev James Kelleher (SPS)

SOCIETY OF AFRICAN MISSIONS
St Joseph's Provincial House, Feltrim,
Blackrock Road, Cork T12 N6C8
Tel 021-4292871 Fax 021-4292873
Email provincial@sma.ie
www.sma.ie
Provincial: Rev Malachy Flanagan (SMA)

SMA House, African Missions,
Blackrock Road, Cork T12 TD54
Superior
Rev Patrick O'Rourke (SMA)
Vice Superior
Rev Aidan J. McCrystal (SMA)

SMA House, Wilton, Cork T12 KR23
Tel 021-4541069/4541884
Fax 021-4541069
Superior: Rev Noel O'Leary (SMA)
Vice-Superior: Rev Colum O'Shea (SMA)

Justice Office,
SMA House, Wilton, Cork T12 KR23
Email justice@sma.ie
Mr Gerry Forde

(See also under parishes – St Joseph's
(Blackrock Road))

BROTHERS

BROTHERS OF CHARITY
Our Lady of Good Counsel, Lota,
Glanmire, Co Cork
Tel 021-4556200
Chaplain: Fr Paul Thettayil (IC)

CHRISTIAN BROTHERS
Sunday's Well Life Centre,
6 Winter's Hill, Sunday's Well, Cork
Tel 021-4304391
Email corklifecentre@gmail.com
Director: Don O'Leary

PRESENTATION BROTHERS
4 Lynbrook, Glasheen Road, Cork
Tel 021-4679007
Community: 2

Mardyke House, Cork
Tel 021-4272239
Community: 2
Contact: Br John Hunt (FPM)

Maiville, Turner's Cross, Cork
Tel 021-4272649
Community: 16
Contact: Br Bede Minehane (FPM)

Mount St Joseph, Blarney Street, Cork
Tel 021-4392160
Community: 5
Contact: Br Kevin Mascerenhas (FPM)

SISTERS

BON SECOURS SISTERS (PARIS)
Bon Secours Convent,
College Road, Cork
Tel 021-4542416 Fax 021-4542533
Co-ordinator: Sr Martha Leamy
Email marthaleamy@gmail.com
Community: 6

Cnoc Mhuire, Fernhurst,
College Road, Cork
Tel 021-4345410 Fax 021-4345491
Co-ordinator: Sr Baptist Libby
Community: 29
Pastoral, community and hospital
ministry

Casa Maria, Fernhurst,
College Road, Cork
Tel 021-4345411
Community: 2
Pastoral and vocation ministry

20 Old Quarry,
Coolroe, Ballincollig, Co Cork
Tel 021-4810622
Community: 1

St Enda's, College Road, Cork
Tel 021-4542750
Community: 2

CONGREGATION OF THE SISTERS OF MERCY
Provincial Offices, Bishop Street, Cork
Tel 021-4975380 Fax 021-4915220
Email provincialoffice@mercysouth.ie
Provincial: Sr Eileen O'Flynn

13 Kempton Park,
Ballyvolane, Cork
Tel 021-4551375

14 Kempton Park,
Ballyvolane, Cork

27 Ronayn's Court,
Rochestown Road, Cork

19 Sheraton Court,
Glasheen Road, Cork

2 Woodbrook Grove,
Bishopstown, Cork
Tel 021-4342286

1 St Columba's,
Bishopstown Avenue West,
Model Farm Road, Cork

St Columba's,
shopstown Avenue West,
odel Farm Road, Cork

St Columba's,
shopstown Avenue West,
odel Farm Road, Cork

St Columba's,
shopstown Avenue West,
odel Farm Road, Cork

St Columba's,
shopstown Avenue West,
odel Farm Road, Cork

St Columba's,
shopstown Avenue West,
odel Farm Road, Cork

St Columba's,
shopstown Avenue West,
odel Farm Road, Cork

St Columba's,
shopstown Avenue West,
odel Farm Road, Cork

) St Columba's,
shopstown Avenue West,
odel Farm Road, Cork

St Columba's,
shopstown Avenue West,
odel Farm Road, Cork

Parkview, Church Hill,
ssage West, Co Cork

Parkview, Church Hill,
ssage West, Co Cork

Marie's Bungalow, Convent Place,
osses Green, Cork

Marie's of the Isle,
arman Crawford Street, Cork
l 021-4316029

Sheares Street, Cork
l 021-4248755

Sharman Crawford Street, Cork

Kinloch Court, Bishopstown Avenue,
odel Farm Road, Cork

Ard na Rí, Closes Green,
rranree, Cork

Sandymount Drive,
asheen Road, Cork
l 021-4541613

uan na Trócaire, 23 Benvoirlich Estate,
shopstown, Cork
l 021-4343371

Sunville, 36 Laburnum Drive,
Model Farm Road, Cork

Convent of Mercy, Winter's Hill, Kinsale,
Co Cork
Tel 021-4772165

Avila, Ard na Gaoithe Mór,
Bantry, Co Cork
Tel 027-50035

The Bungalow, Balindeasig,
Belgooly, Co Cork
Tel 021-4887954

Casa Maria Seskin,
Bantry, Co Cork
Tel 027-51198

Arus Muire,
Scartagh, Clonakilty, Co Cork
Tel 023-8833391

Apt 1, Arus Muire,
Scartagh, Clonakilty, Co Cork

Apt 2, Arus Muire,
Scartagh, Clonakilty, Co Cork

Apt 3, Arus Muire,
Scartagh, Clonakilty, Co Cork

Apt 4, Arus Muire,
Scartagh, Clonakilty, Co Cork

Studio 26, Arus Muire,
Scartagh, Clonakilty, Co Cork

2 The Drive, Priory Court,
Watergrasshill, Co Cork
Tel 021-4513949

Studio 25 Arus Muire,
McCurtain Hill, Scartagh,
Clonakilty, Co Cork

Mercy House, Tullineasky West.
Clonakilty, Co Cork
Tel 023-8848116

DAUGHTERS OF CHARITY OF ST VINCENT DE PAUL
St Louise's, Hollyhill House,
Harbour View Road,
Knocknaheeny, Cork
Tel 021-4392762
Superior: Sr Marguerite Buckley
Community: 4
Parish and social work, pastoral care of
asylum seekers

FRANCISCAN MISSIONARIES OF ST JOSEPH
Convent of St Francis,
Blackrock Road, Cork
Tel 021-4317059
Community Leader: Sr Mary Coyne
Community: 12

CONGREGATION OF OUR LADY OF CHARITY OF THE GOOD SHEPHERD
Baile an Aoire,
Leycester's Lane, Montenotte,
Cork T23 WO85
Tel 021-4551200
Email rgscorklocalleader@gmail.com
Community: 7

17 Killiney Heights, Knockaheeny,
Cork T23 E3H1
Tel 021-4302660
Email jane.murphy100@gmail.com
Community: 2

INFANT JESUS SISTERS
19 Cherry Walk, Muskerry Estate,
Ballincollig, Co Cork P31 FN51
Tel 021-4873599
Pastoral ministry

LITTLE SISTERS OF THE ASSUMPTION
32 St Francis Gardens,
Thomas Davis Street,
Blackpool, Cork
Tel 021-4391407
Email isasfg33@gmail.com

2–3 College View,
Old Youghal Road, Cork
Tel 021-2357070
Email lsacollegev@gmail.com

SISTERS OF MARIE REPARATRICE
6 Knockrea Lawn,
Ballinlough Road, Cork T12 KV8P
Tel 087-9860536
7 Knockrea Lawn,
Ballinlough Road, Cork T12 H4FN
Tel 021-2357070
Email scoughlansmr@gmail.com
Contact: Sr Stephanie Coughlan
Community: 3

MISSIONARY SISTERS OF THE HOLY ROSARY
7 The Circle, Broadale,
Douglas, Cork
Tel 021-4362424
Healthcare, work with refugees
Community: 2

OUR LADY OF THE CENACLE
19 St Francis' Gardens, Blackpool, Cork
Tel 087-2891545
Email peggycronin.8@gmail.com
Contact: Sr Peggy Cronin
Ministry: Retreats and Spiritual Direction

POOR CLARES
Poor Clare Colettine Monastery,
College Road, Cork
Abbess: Sr Miriam Buckley
Community: 7
Contemplatives
Mass: Daily (Monday–Friday) 7.30 a.m.;
(Saturday and Sunday) 10 a.m.
Public chapel open daily
(Sunday–Saturday) 7.00 a.m.–5.30 p.m.
Exposition of the Blessed Sacrament all
day
Rosary: 5.00 p.m. daily

PRESENTATION SISTERS
Presentation Provincial Office,
Nano Nagle Place, Douglas Street,
Cork T12 X70A
Tel 021-4975190
Email presprovsw@gmail.com
Provincial Leader: Sr Grace McKernan

Presentation Community,
Nano Nagle Place, Douglas Street,
Cork T12 X70A
Tel 021-4193586
Email sistersnanonagleplace@pbvm.org
Community: 3

South Presentation Convent,
Douglas Street, Cork T12 P7FE
Tel 021-4975042
Email southpres1@gmail.com
Local Leader: Sr Patricia O'Shea
Community: 9

Presentation Convent,
Ballyphehane, Cork
Tel 021-4321606
Email presballyork@gmail.com
Team Leadership
Community: 6
Primary School. Tel 021-4315724
Secondary School. Tel 021-4961765

18 The Orchards, Montenotte, Cork
Tel 021-4501456
Community: 2

North Presentation Convent,
Gerald Griffin Street, Cork
Tel 021-4302878
Email northpres.convent@gmail.com
Local Leader: Sr Angela Ryan
Community: 11
Primary School Tel 021-4307132
An Gleann Primary School
Tel 021-4504877

Regina Coeli Convent, Farranree, Cork
Tel 021-4302770
Email presfarranree@gmail.com
Team Leadership
Community: 5
Aiséirí Chríost Primary School
Tel 021-4301383
Secondary School
Tel 021-4303330

126 Deerpark,
Friar's Walk, Cork T12 VY7X
Tel 021-4323321
Community: 2

Presentation Convent,
Bandon, Co Cork
Tel 023-8841476
Email bandonpresentation1@gmail.com
Non-resident Leader: Sr Jo McCarthy
Community: 8
Primary School. Tel 023-8841809
Secondary School. Tel 023-8841814

'Ruah', 33 Kingsbridge,
South Douglas Road, Cork T12 WR66
Tel 021-4809008
Community: 1

40 Woodhaven, Bishopstown,
Cork T12 Y386
Tel 086-8246087
Email 40woodhaven@gmail.com
Community: 1

Ardán Mhuire, Togher Road, Cork
Tel 021-4961471
Community: 2

7 Churchfield Terrace West,
Gurranabraher, Cork
Tel 021-4306640
Community: 3

7 Old Waterpark,
Carrigaline, Co Cork
Tel 021-4372718
Community: 1

Dóchas, 21 Ashdene,
South Douglas Road, Cork
Tel 021-4897597
Email presdochas@gmail.com
Community: 1

44 Castlemeadows,
Mahon, Cork
Tel 021-4515944
Community: 2

44 Ashbrook Heights, Lehenaghmore,
Togher, Cork
Tel 021-4320006
Community: 1

78 Grange Way, Douglas, Cork
Tel 021-4899704
Community: 1

5 Abbey View, Nano Nagle Walk,
Douglas Street, Cork
Tel 021-4322097
Community: 1

18 Convent View, Nano Nagle Walk,
Douglas Street, Cork
Tel 021-4915380
Community: 1

Apt 15, Ard na Rí, Closes Green,
Farranree, Cork
Community: 1

Apt 31, Ard na Rí, Closes Green,
Farranree, Cork
Tel 021-4564733
Community: 1

Apt 37, Ard na Rí, Closes Green,
Farranree, Cork
Tel 021-4309262
Community: 1

Apt 39, Ard na Rí, Closes Green,
Farranree, Cork
Tel 021-4308784
Community: 1

35 Lios na Greine,
South Douglas Road, Cork
Community: 1

84 Earlwood Estate,
The Lough, Cork
Tel 087-7662245
Email maryfquinn@hotmail.com
Community: 2

RELIGIOUS SISTERS OF CHARITY
St Anthony's Convent,
Vincent's Avenue,
St Mary's Road, Cork T23 XVW8
Tel 021-4308162

SACRED HEARTS OF JESUS AND MARY
Sacred Heart Convent, Blackrock,
Cork T12 W200
Tel 021-4936200
Community Leader
Sr Annie Mary Nally
Email amnally@sacredheartsjm.org
Community: 23

SISTERS OF OUR LADY OF APOSTLES
Ardfoyle Convent,
Ballintemple, Cork T12 Y304
Tel 021-4291851 Fax 021-4291105
Email prov@ardfoyle.com
Provincial: Sr Kathleen McGarvey
Sister-in-Charge: Sr Katherine Donovan
Community: 35

Allianz (ⅲ)

URSULINES

rsuline Convent, Blackrock, Cork
021-4358663 Fax 021-4356077
mail osucork@gmail.com
mmunity: 6
imary School
021-4358476 Fax 021-4359073
condary School
021-4358012 Fax 021-4358012

Meadowgrove, Blackrock, Cork
021-4357249
Máire O'Donohoe
mail mariefod55@gmail.com
mmunity: 1
storal Ministry

Fort Hill, Moneygurney,
uglas, Cork
021-4617091
mail
zabethbradley010.eb@gmail.com
mmunity: 1
storal Ministry

EDUCATIONAL INSTITUTIONS

Christ the King Secondary School
South Douglas Road, Cork
Tel 021-4961448 Fax 021-4314563

Christian Brothers College, Cork
Tel 021-4501653 Fax 021-4504113

Coláiste Chríost Rí, Cork
Tel 021-4274904 Fax 021-4964784

Coláiste an Spioraid Naoimh
Bishopstown, Cork
Tel 021-4543790 Fax 021-4543625

Coláiste Phobail Bheanntraí
Bantry, Co Cork
Tel 027-56434

Coláiste Éamann Rís
St Patrick's Road, Cork
Tel 021-4962025 Fax 021-4311792

Edmund Rice College
Carragline, Co Cork
Tel 021-4373785

Mercy Sisters Secondary School
Roscarbery, Co Cork
Tel 023-8848114 Fax 023-8848520

Mount Mercy College
Model Farm Road, Cork
Tel 021-4542366 Fax 021-4542709

North Monastery,
Our Lady's Mount, Cork
Tel 021-4301318 Fax 021-4309891

Presentation College, Cork
Tel 021-4272743 Fax 021-4273147

Presentation Convent
Bandon, Co Cork
Tel 023-8841814 Fax 023-8841385

Presentation Convent Secondary School
Crosshaven, Co Cork
Tel/Fax 021-4831604

Presentation Secondary School
Ballyphehane, Cork
Tel 021-4961765/4961767
Fax 021-4312864

Regina Coeli Convent Secondary School
Farranree, Cork
Tel 021-4303330 Fax 021-4303411

Sacred Heart College
Carrig na bhFear, Co Cork
Tel 021-4884104 Fax 021-4884442

Sacred Heart Secondary School
Clonakilty, Co Cork
Tel 023-8833737 Fax 023-8833908

St Aloysius School, Cork
Tel 021-4316017 Fax 021-4316007

St Angela's College, Cork
Tel 021-4500059 Fax 021-4504515

St Francis Capuchin College,
Rochestown, Co Cork
Tel 021-4891417 Fax 021-4361254

St Vincent's Secondary School, Cork
Tel 021-4307730 Fax 021-4307252

Skibbereen Community School
Gortnaclohy, Skibbereen, Co Cork
Tel 028-51272

Ursuline Convent Secondary School
Blackrock, Cork
Tel/Fax 021-435801

DIOCESE OF DERRY

PATRONS OF THE DIOCESE
ST EUGENE, 23 AUGUST; ST COLUMBA, 9 JUNE

INCLUDES ALMOST ALL OF COUNTY DERRY,
PARTS OF COUNTIES DONEGAL AND TYRONE
AND A VERY SMALL AREA ACROSS THE RIVER BANN IN COUNTY ANTRIM

Most Rev Donal McKeown D
Bishop of Derry
Born 12 April 1950; ordained
priest 3 July 1977; appointed
Auxiliary Bishop of Down and
Connor 21 February 2001;
ordained Bishop 29 April 2001
appointed Bishop of Derry 25
February 2014; installed 6 Apri
2014

Office Address:
Diocesan Offices,
St Eugene's Cathedral,
Francis Street, Derry BT48 9AP
Tel 028-71262302
Fax 028-71371960
Email office@derrydiocese.org

ST EUGENE'S CATHEDRAL, DERRY

In the 1830s, following the Catholic Emancipation Act of 1829, the Catholic community of Derry was able to contemplate building a cathedral. In the summer of 1838, a number of Catholics of the city met with the then Bishop of Derry, Peter McLaughlin, to consider such a project. Over the next thirteen years a weekly collection was made in the city and eventually, on 26 July 1851, the foundation stone was laid by Bishop Francis Kelly.

The construction of the cathedral was sporadic as the funds became available over twenty-five years, and owing to the difficulty in raising money, it was agreed to postpone the building of the tower, belfry and spire until a later date. Due to the lack of funds in the diocese, the windows were initially all of plain glass, and it was only in later years that the stained glass was installed.

J. J. McCarthy (1817–1882) was the architect commissioned to design St Eugene's Cathedral. He was one of the most outstanding church architects in Ireland in his time and he designed many churches and convents all over the country, including St Patrick's Cathedral, Armagh, St Macartan's Cathedral, Monaghan and the Cathedral of the Assumption, Thurles.

The actual construction work took twenty-two years to complete, at a cost of £40,000. It was not until 1873 that the building was brought to a stage where it could be dedicated and used for liturgical celebrations. The cathedral was dedicated by Bishop Francis Kelly on 4 May 1873.

In 1899 it was decided to add a spire to the tower, which was estimated to cost £15,000. The spire was completed on 19 June 1903, and on 27 June the eight-foot-high granite cross was put in position by Fathers John Doherty and Lawrence Hegarty. The full complement of stained-glass windows was achieved in the Spring and Autumn of 1896 at a cost of £2,270. The ten bells of the cathedral first rang out on Christmas Eve, 1902.

St Eugene's was solemnly consecrated on 21 April 1936, the seventh cathedral in Ireland to be consecrated, and the event is celebrated annually on 21 April.

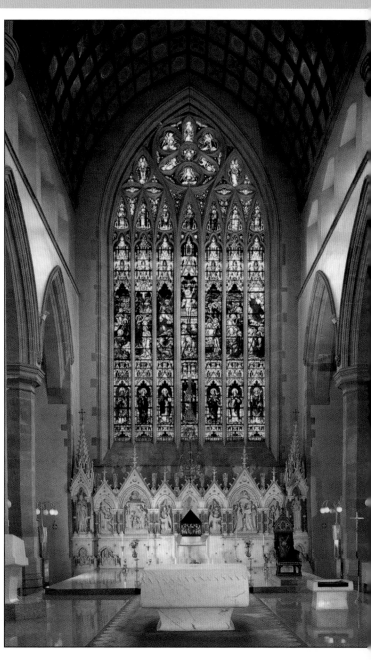

ADMINISTRATION

icars General
ev Paul McCafferty VG
ry Rev Michael Canny PP, VG

ancellor
ry Rev Francis Bradley PP

icars Forane
erry City Deanery
ry Rev David O'Kane PP, VF
Derry Deanery
ry Rev Peter Madden PP, VF
Tyrone Deanery
ry Rev Kevin McElhennon PP, VF
ishowen Deanery
ry Rev Brian Brady PP, VF

erry Diocesan Trust
Columb's Diocesan Trust is Trustee of
e Derry Diocesan Trust) *Directors:*
ost Rev Donal McKeown DD *(Chairperson)*
v Paul McCafferty
v Michael McCaughey PP
ry Rev Michael Canny PP
r Shaun McElhinney
r Sean O'Kane
r Ciaran Hampson
s Fiona Schlindwein
s Aine Gallagher
s Brenda Morris
cretary: Teresa McMenamin

iocesan Office
shop: Most Rev Donal McKeown DD
v Paul McCafferty VG
dministrative & Financial Secretary
s Teresa McMenamin
ecutive Director, Derry Diocesan Trust
r Kevin McCauley
ocesan Trust Support Officer
rs Oonagh Robinson
ocesan Offices,
Eugene's Cathedral,
ancis Street, Derry BT48 9AP
l 028-71262302 Fax 028-71371960
nail office@derrydiocese.org

iocesan Notaries
ry Rev Kevin McElhennon PP, VF
v Colum Clerkin PEm
v Eamonn Graham PP
s Teresa McMenamin

CATECHETICS EDUCATION

atholic Primary School Managers'
sociation
ntact: Rev Peter Devlin PP
rochial House,
alin, Co Donegal
l 074-9142022

Catechetical Centre
Derry Diocesan Catechetical Centre,
The Gate Lodge, 2 Francis Street,
Derry BT48 9DS
Tel 028-71264087 Fax 028-71269090
Email ddcc@derrydiocese.org
Director: Rev Paul Farren
Adviser: Miss Thérèse Ferry
Youth Co-ordinator: Ms Lizzie Rea
Secretary: Anne Marie Hickey

PASTORAL

ACCORD
Derry Centre
Diocesan Pastoral Centre,
164 Bishop Street, Derry BT48 6UJ
Tel 028-71362475 Fax 028-71260970

Omagh Centre
Mount St Columba Pastoral Centre,
48 Brook Street, Omagh,
Co Tyrone BT78 5HD
Tel 028-82242439

Maghera Centre
Pastoral Centre,
159 Glen Road, Maghera
Tel 028-79642983

Inishowen Centre
Pastoral Centre
Church Road, Carndonagh, Co Donegal
Tel 074-9374103

Chaplain to the Deaf
Rev Thomas Canning CC
143 Melmount Road, Sion Mills,
Strabane, Co Tyrone BT82 9EX
Tel 028-81658264

Charismatic Renewal
Director: Rev Seamus Kelly PP
19 Chapel Road, Dungiven,
Co Derry BT47 4RT

Columba Community
Director: Marguerite Hamilton
St Anthony's, Dundrean,
Burnfoot, Co Donegal
Tel 074-9368370
Email sarce@eircom.net
Columba House,
11 Queen Street, Derry BT48 7E6
Tel 028-71262407

Communications
Media Liaison Person:
Very Rev Michael Canny PP, VG
32 Chapel Road, Derry BT47 2BB
Tel 028-71342303
Email michaelcanny1958@gmail.com

Ecumenism
Director: Rev Eamon McDevitt PP
78 Lisnaragh Road, Dunamanagh,
Strabane, Co Tyrone BT82 0QN
Tel 028-71398212

Library/Museum
Curators: Rev John R. Walsh CC
Rev Brian McGoldrick PEm

Marriage Tribunal
(See Marriage Tribunals section)

Migrants and Asylum Seekers
Rev Pat O'Hagan PP
Parochial House, 25 Ballynease Road,
Bellaghy, Co Derry BT45 8JS
Tel 028-79386259

NEST – New Existence for Survivors of Trauma
Ministry to adult victims of abuse of all kinds.
Centre: Pastoral Centre,
Maghera BT46 5JN
Tel 028-79642983
Email nest.int@btconnect.com

Pastoral Centres
Diocesan Pastoral Centre
164 Bishop Street, Derry BT48 6UJ
Tel 028-71362475 Fax 028-71260970
Director: Rev Micheál McGavigan Adm

Inishowen Pastoral Centre
Carndonagh, Co Donegal
Tel 074-9374103
Director: Rev Con McLaughlin PP

Maghera Pastoral Centre
159 Glen Road, Maghera, Co Derry
Tel 028-79642983
Director: Rev Patrick Doherty PP

Omagh Pastoral Centre
Mount St Columba Pastoral Centre,
48 Brooke Street, Omagh,
Co Tyrone BT78 5HD
Tel 028-82242439
Director: Rev Eugene Hasson PP

Pilgrimages
Lourdes Pilgrimages:
Mr Charles Glenn
Diocesan Pastoral Centre, 164 Bishop
Street, Derry BT48 6HJ
Tel 028-71260293
Email derrypilgrim@outlook.com
Other Pilgrimages:
Rev Gerard Sweeney PP
Tel 028-71882274
Eail leckpatrick.rc@talktalk.net

Pioneer Total Abstinence Association
Spiritual Director
Rev Thomas Canning CC
143 Melmount Road, Sion Mills,
Strabane, Co Tyrone BT82 9EX
Tel 028-81658264

Travellers
Chaplain: Rev Brian Donnelly PP
20 Derbrough Road, Plumbridge,
Co Tyrone BT79 8EF

Trócaire
Diocesan Representative:
Rev Edward Gallagher PP
Parochial House, Moville, Co Donegal
Tel 074-9382057

Vocations
Director: Rev Pat O'Hagan PP
Tel 0770-3444280
Email pgoh2111@gmail.com

PARISHES

*Mensal parishes are listed first, followed
by other Derry city parishes. Other
parishes follow alphabetically. Historical
names are in parentheses. Church titulars
are in italics.*

DERRY CITY
Templemore (St Eugene's)
Rev Paul Farren Adm
Rev Roni Zacharias CC
Parochial House, St Eugene's Cathedral,
Derry BT48 9AP
Tel 028-71262894/71365712
Fax 028-71377494
Email steugenes@btconnect.com

Templemore (St Columba's)
Rev Gerard Mongan Adm
St Columba's Presbytery,
6 Victoria Place, Derry BT48 6TJ
Tel 028-71262301
Email longtowerparish@aol.com

THE THREE PATRONS
Rev Michael M. Caughey PP
St Patrick's, Buncrana Road,
Pennyburn, Derry BT48 7QL
Tel 028-71262360
Rev Sean O'Donnell CC
St Brigid's, Carnhill,
Derry BT48 9QE
Tel 028-71263152

ST MARY'S, CREGGAN
Rev Daniel McFaul PP
Rev Ignacy Sanuita CC
Parochial House, St Mary's, Creggan,
Derry BT48 9QE
Tel 028-71263152
Email stmaryscreggan@derrydiocese.org

OUR LADY OF LOURDES, STEELSTOWN
Rev John McDevitt PP
The Presbytery, 11 Steelstown Road,
Derry BT48 8EU
Tel 028-71351718 F
ax 028-71357810
Email steelstownparish@derrydiocese.org

HOLY FAMILY, BALLYMAGROARTY
Rev Joseph Gormley PP
1 Aileach Road, Ballymagroarty,
Derry BT48 0AZ
Tel 028-71267070
Email office@holyfamilyparish.com
Rev Kevin Mulhern (SMA) CC
c/o 1 Aileach Road, Ballymagroarty,
Derry BT48 0AZ

AGHYARAN (TERMONAMONGAN)
St Patrick's
Rev Paul Fraser PP
16 Castlefin Road,
Castleder, Co Tyrone BT81 7BT
Tel 028-81670728
Email aghyaranparish@derrydiocese.org

ARDMORE
St Mary's
Rev James McGrory PP
Parochial House, 49 Ardmore Road,
Derry BT47 3QP
Tel 028-71349490
Email ardmoreparish@btinternet.com

BALLINASCREEN (DRAPERSTOWN)
St Columba's
Very Rev Peter Madden PP, VF
40 Derrynoid Road, Draperstown,
Magherafelt, Co Derry BT45 7DN
Tel 028-79628376
Email ballinascreenparish@gmail.com
Rev Dermot McGirr CC
50 Tobermore Road, Desertmartin,
Magherafelt, Co Derry BT45 5LE
Tel 028-79632196

BANAGHER
St Joseph's, Fincairn
Rev Micheál McGavigan Adm
42 Glenedra Road, Feeny,
Co Derry BT47 4TW
Tel 028-77781223

BELLAGHY (BALLYSCULLION)
St Mary's
Rev Pat O'Hagan PP
25 Ballynease Road, Bellaghy,
Magherafelt, Co Derry BT45 8JS
Tel 028-79386259
Email info@bellaghyparish.com

BUNCRANA (DESERTEGNEY AND LOWER FAHAN)
St Mary's, Cockhill
Very Rev Francis Bradley PP
Cockhill, Buncrana, Co Donegal
Tel 074-9363455
Rev John Walsh CC
Parochial House, Buncrana, Co Donegal
Tel 074-9361393 Fax 074-9361637
Rev Patrick Baker CC
Castlequarter, Fahan, Co Donegal F93 H9Y3
Parish Office: Tel 074-9361253
Fax 074-9361637
Email buncranaparish@eircom.net

CARNDONAGH (DONAGH)
Sacred Heart
Rev Con McLaughlin PP
Barrack Hill, Carndonagh,
Lifford, Co Donegal
Tel 074-9374104

CASTLEDERG (ARDSTRAW WEST AND CASTLEDERG)
St Patrick's
Rev Paul Fraser PP
16 Castlefin Road, Castlederg,
Co Tyrone BT81 7BT
Tel 028-81671393
Email castledergparish@derrydiocese.or

CLAUDY (CUMBER UPPER AND LEARMOUNT)
St Patrick's
Very Rev David O'Kane PP
9 Church Street, Claudy,
Co Derry BT47 4AA
Tel 028-71337727 Fax 028-71338236

CLONMANY
St Mary's
Very Rev Brian Brady PP, VF
Parochial House,
Ardnascanlon, Ballyliffin, Co Donegal
Tel 074-9376264
Rev Karl Haan CC
Parochial House, Culdaff, Co Donegal
Tel 074-9379107

COLERAINE (DUNBOE, MACOSQUIN AN AGHADOWEY)
St John's
Rev Neil Farren PP
Chapelfield, 59 Laurel Hill,
Coleraine, Co Derry BT51 3AY
Tel 028-70343130
Rev Gerald Hasson CC
Aghadowey, Coleraine

CULDAFF
St Mary's, Bocan
Very Rev Brian Brady PP, VF
Parochial House, Ardnascanlon,
Ballyliffin, Co Donegal
Tel 074-9376264
Rev Karl Haan CC
Parochial House, Culdaff,
Co Donegal
Tel 074-9379107
Email culdaffnotes@gmail.com

CULMORE
Assumption
Rev John McDevitt Adm
11 Steelstown Road,
Derry BT48 8EU
Tel 028-71351718
Email culmoreparish@derrydiocese.org
Website www.culmore.com

ESERTMARTIN (DESERTMARTIN AND LCRONAGHAN)
Mary's, Coolcalm
ry Rev Peter Madden PP, VF
Derrynoid Road, Draperstown,
agherafelt, Co Derry BT45 7DN
l 028-79628376
v Dermot Mcgirr CC
Tobermore Road, Desertmartin,
agherafelt, Co Derry BT45 5LE
l 028-79632196

ONEYLOOP (URNEY AND CASTLEFINN)
Columba's
v Ciaran Hegarty *(Down & Connor ocese)* Adm
oneyloop, Castlefin, Lifford, Co Donegal
l 074-9146183
v Oliver Crilly *(priest in residence)*
rochial House, Castlefin,
fford, Co Donegal
l 074-9146251

RUMQUIN (LANGFIELD)
Patrick's
v Eugene Hasson Adm
Brook Street,
nagh, Co Tyrone BT78 5HD
l 028-82243011
v Peter O'Kane CC
Brook Street,
nagh, Co Tyrone BT78 5HD
028-82242092

UNAMANAGH (DONAGHEADY)
Patrick's
v Eamon McDevitt PP
Lisnaragh Road, Dunamanagh,
abane, Co Tyrone BT82 0QN
028-71398212

UNGIVEN
Patrick's
v Seamus Kelly PP
Chapel Road, Dungiven,
Derry BT47 4RT
028-77741219 Fax 028-77742633
ail dunpar@icloud.com
v Joseph Varghese CC
tation Road, Dungiven,
Derry BT47 4LN
028-77741256 Fax 028-77742953

HAN (BURT, INCH AND FAHAN)
Mura's
ry Rev Francis Bradley PP
ckhill, Buncrana, Co Donegal
v Patrick Baker CC
rochial House, Fahan,
ford, Co Donegal
074-9360151
v Fintan Diggin CC
rochial House, Burt,
ford, Co Donegal
074-9368155

FAUGHANVALE (FAUGHANVALE AND LOWER CUMBER)
Star of the Sea
Rev Noel McDermott PP
91 Ervey Road, Eglinton,
Co Derry BT47 3AU
Tel 028-71810235

GARVAGH (ERRIGAL)
St Mary's, Ballerin
Rev Brendan Crowley PP
78 Ballerin Road, Garvagh,
Co Derry BT51 5EQ
Tel 028-29558251
Email errigalparish@gmail.com
Rev Christopher McDermott CC
4 Garvagh Road, Kilrea,
Co Derry BT51 5QP
Tel 028-29540343
Email
christopher.mcdermott@derrydiocese.org

GORTIN (BADONEY LOWER)
St Patrick's
Very Rev Brian Donnelly PP
Parochial House, Plumbridge,
Co Tyrone BT79 8EF
Tel 028-81648283
Rev Roland Colhoun CC
41 Moyle Road, Newtownstewart,
Co Tyrone BT78 4AP
Tel 028-81661445
Email gortinparish@derrydiocese.org

GREENCASTLE
St Patrick's
see Gortin (Baldoney Lower)

GREENLOUGH (TAMLAGHT O'CRILLY)
St Mary's
Rev Pat O'Hagan Adm
25 Ballynease Road, Bellaghy,
Magherafelt, Co Derry BT45 8JS
Tel 028-79386259

ISKAHEEN (ISKAHEEN AND UPPER MOVILLE)
St Mary's
Rev John Farren PP
Muff, Co Donegal
Tel 074-9384037 Fax 074-9384029
Email farrenjohn@eircom.net
Rev Anthony Mailey CC
Parochial House
Quigley's Point, Co Donegal
Tel 074-9383008

KILLYCLOGHER (CAPPAGH)
St Mary's
Very Rev Kevin McElhennon PP, VF
14 Killyclogher Road, Omagh,
Co Tyrone BT79 0AX
Tel 028-82243375
Email info@cappaghparish.com
Rev Declan McGeehan CC
5 Strathroy Road, Omagh,
Co Tyrone BT79 7DW
Tel 028-82251055
Email declan.mcgeehan@derrydiocese.org

KILLYGORDON (DONAGHMORE)
St Patrick's
Rev Patrick Arkinson PP
Sessiaghoneill, Ballybofey,
Co Donegal
Tel 074-9131149

KILREA (KILREA AND DESERTOGHILL)
St Mary's, Drumagarner
Very Rev Brendan Crowley PP
78 Ballerin Road, Garvagh,
Co Derry BT51 5EQ
Tel 028-29558251
Rev Christopher McDermott CC
4 Garvagh Road, Kilrea,
Co Derry BT51 5QP
Tel 028-29540343
Email
christopher.mcdermott@derrydiocese.org

LAVEY (TERMONEENY AND PART OF MAGHERA)
St Mary's
Rev Eamon Graham PP
65 Mayogall Road, Knockloughrim,
Magherafelt, Co Derry BT45 8PG
Tel 028-79642458

LECKPATRICK (LECKPATRICK AND PART OF DONAGHEADY)
St Mary's, Cloughcor
Rev Gerard Sweeney PP
Parochial House, 447 Victoria Road,
Ballymagorry, Strabane,
Co Tyrone BT82 0AT
Tel 028-718802274 Fax 028-71884353
Email leckpatrick.rc@talktalk.net

LIFFORD (CLONLEIGH)
St Patrick's, Murlog
Rev Colm O'Doherty PP
6 Orchard Park, Murlog,
Lifford, Co Donegal
Tel 074-9142022
Parish Office: St Patrick's Church,
Murlog, Lifford, Co Donegal
Tel 074-9142001
Email clonleighparish@derrydiocese.org

LIMAVADY (DRUMACHOSE, TAMLAGHT, FINLAGAN AND PART OF AGHANLOO)
St Mary's, Irish Green Street
Rt Rev Mgr Bryan McCanny PP
119 Irish Green Street, Limavady,
Co Derry BT49 9AB
Tel 028-77765649
Fax 028-77765290
Email parishoflimavady@btinternet.com
Rev Dermott Harkin CC
20 Loughermore Road,
Ballykelly, Co Derry BT49 9PD
Tel 028-77762721

MAGHERA
St Patrick's, Glen
Very Rev Patrick Doherty PP
Rev Kieran O'Doherty *(priest in residence)*
159 Glen Road, Maghera,
Co Derry BT46 5JN
Tel 028-79642496 Fax 028-79644593
Email accordmaghera@btconnect.com
Parish Office: 159A Glen Road,
Maghera, Co Derry BT46 5JN
Tel 028-79642983

MAGILLIGAN
St Aidan's
Rev Francis O'Hagan PP
71 Duncrun Road, Bellarena,
Limavady, Co Derry BT49 0JD
Tel 028-77750226
Email frohagan@aol.com

MALIN (CLONCA)
St Patrick's, Aghaclay
Rev Peter Devlin PP
Malin, Co Donegal
Tel 074-9370615
Email pnd4680@eircom.net
Rev Charles Logue CC
Malin Head, Co Donegal
Tel 074-9370134

MELMOUNT (MOURNE)
St Mary's, Melmount, Strabane
Rev Michael Doherty PP
39 Melmount Road, Strabane,
Co Tyrone BT82 9EF
Tel 028-71882648
Rev Thomas Canning CC
143 Melmount Road, Sion Mills,
Strabane, Co Tyrone BT82 9EX
Tel 028-81658264
Rev Malachy Gallagher CC
44 Barrack Street, Strabane,
Co Tyrone BT82 8HD
Email
malachy.gallagher@derrydiocese.org
Parish Office: Melmount Parish Centre,
Melmount Road, Strabane,
Co Tyrone BT82 9EF
Tel 028-71383777 Fax 028-71886469
Email melparish@aol.com

MOVILLE (MOVILLE LOWER)
St Mary's, Ballybrack
Rev Edward Gallagher PP
Parochial House, Moville, Co Donegal
Tel 074-9382057

NEWTOWNSTEWART (ARDSTRAW EAST)
St Eugene's, Glenock
Very Rev Brian Donnelly PP
Parochial House, Plumbridge,
Omagh, Co Tyrone BT79 8EF
Tel 028-81648283
Email bpdey@aol.co.uk
Rev Roland Colhoun CC
41 Moyle Road, Newtownstewart,
Co Tyrone BT78 4AP
Tel 028-81661445
Email ardstraweast@derrydiocese.org

OMAGH (DRUMRAGH)
St Mary's, Drumragh
Rev Eugene Hasson PP
52 Brook Street, Omagh,
Co Tyrone BT78 5HE
Tel 028-82243011 Fax 028-82252149
Email info@drumraghparish.com
Rev Peter O'Kane CC
48 Brook Street, Omagh,
Co Tyrone BT78 5HE
Tel 028-82242092
Parish Office: 48 Brook Street,
Omagh, Co Tyrone BT78 5HE
Tel 028-82442092

PLUMBRIDGE (BADONEY UPPER)
Sacred Heart
Very Rev Brian Donnelly PP
Parochial House, Plumbridge,
Omagh, Co Tyrone BT79 8EF
Tel 028-81648283
Email bpdey@aol.co.uk
Rev Roland Colhoun CC
41 Moyle Road, Newtownstewart,
Co Tyrone BT78 4AP
Tel 028-81661445
Email ardstraweast@derrydiocese.org

SION MILLS
St Theresa's
Rev Michael Doherty PP
39 Melmount Road, Strabane,
Co Tyrone BT82 9EF
Tel 028-71882648
Email frmdoc@aol.com
Rev Thomas Canning CC
143 Melmount Road, Sion Mills,
Strabane, Co Tyrone BT82 9EX
Tel 028-81658264
Rev Malachy Gallagher CC
44 Barrack Street, Strabane,
Co Tyrone BT82 8HD
Email
malachy.gallagher@derrydiocese.org

STRABANE (CAMUS)
Immaculate Conception
Rev Declan Boland PP
44 Barrack Street, Strabane,
Co Tyrone BT82 8HD
Tel 028-71883293 Fax 028-71882615
Email declan@strabaneparish.com

STRATHFOYLE (STRATHFOYLE, ENAGH LOUGH)
St Oliver Plunkett
Served by the Parish of Glendermott
Parochial House, Parkmore Drive,
Strathfoyle, Co Derry BT47 1XA
Tel 028-71342303

SWATRAGH
St John the Baptist
Rev Charles Keaney PP
34 Moneysharvin Road,
Swatragh, Maghera, Co Derry BT46 5PY
Tel 028-79401236
Email charleskeaney@derrydiocese.org

WATERSIDE (GLENDERMOTT)
St Columb's
Very Rev Michael Canny PP, VG
Rev Patrick Lagan CC
Rev Joshi Parokkaran CC
Parochial House, 32 Chapel Road,
Waterside, Derry BT47 2BB
Tel 028-71342303
Email secretary@watersideparish.net
Website www.watersideparish.org

INSTITUTIONS AND THEIR CHAPLAINS

**Altnagelvin Hospital, Derry
Waterside General Hospital**
Rev Daniel McFaul PP
Parochial House,
Creggan, Derry BT48 9QE
Tel 028-71263152
Very Rev Michael Canny PP, VG
Parochial House, 32 Chapel Road,
Waterside, Derry BT47 2BB
Tel 028-71342303
Rev Sean O'Donnell
St Brigid's Presbytery, Carnhill,
Derry BT48 8HJ
Tel 028-71351261

Community Hospital, Lifford
Rev Colm O'Doherty PP
6 Orchard Park, Lifford, Co Donegal
Tel 074-9142001

District Hospital, Carndonagh
Rev Con McLaughlin PP
Parochial House, Carndonagh
Tel 074-9174104

Gransha Hospital, Derry
Rev Daniel McFaul PP
Parochial House,
Creggan, Derry BT48 9QE
Tel 028-71263152
Rev Sean O'Donnell CC
St Brigid's, Cornhill,
Derry BT48 9QE
Tel 028-71263152

Magilligan Prison
Point Road, Magilligan,
Limavady BT49 0LR, Co Derry
Rev Francis O'Hagan PP
Tel 028-77763311

Nazareth House
Fahan, Co Donegal
Rev Francis Bradley PP
Tel 074-9360151

Tyrone County Hospital, Omagh
Very Rev Kevin McElhennon PP, VF

Tyrone and Fermanagh Hospital, Omagh
Very Rev Kevin McElhennon PP, VF

PRIESTS OF THE DIOCESE ELSEWHERE

v Manus Bradley
90 Croissant Oscar,
ossard, Quebec J4Y 2JB
00-1450-8127858

Rev Mgr Brendan Devlin MA, DD
Patrick's College,
aynooth, Co Kildare
01-6285222

v Christopher Ferguson
Sabbatical, c/o Diocesan Offices

v James Devine
Sabbatical, c/o Diocesan Offices

RETIRED PRIESTS

gr Joseph Donnelly PEm
v John Farrell PEm
v George McLaughlin PEm
v Peter McLaughlin PEm
v Michael Keaveny PEm
v Michael Collins PEm
v John Doherty PEm
v Patrick Crilly PEm
v Brian McGoldrick PEm
v James McGonagle PEm
v Liam Donnelly PEm
v Seamus O'Connell PEm
v Brendan Doherty PEm
v Eugene Boland PEm
v John Gilmore PEm
v Edward Kilpatrick PEm
v Neil McGoldrick PEm
v Art O'Reilly PEm
v Kevin Mullan PEm
v Michael Porter PEm
gr Andrew Dolan PEm
v Colum Clerkin PEm
v John Forbes PEm
v John Downey PEm

RELIGIOUS ORDERS AND CONGREGATIONS

PRIESTS

RMELITES (OCD)
Joseph's Retreat House,
rmonbacca, Derry BT48 9XE
028-71262512 Fax 028-71373589
or: Rev Stephen Quinn (OCD)
mmunity: 3

ANCISCAN FRIARS OF THE RENEWAL
FR)
Columba Friary,
rview Road, Derry BT48 8NU
028-71419980 Fax 028-71417652
ail derryfranciscans@gmail.com
cal Servant (Superior)
v Francesco Gavazzi (CFR)

LVATORIANS
aomh Mhuire', Upper Slavery,
ncrana, Co Donegal
074-9322264
ntact: Rev Malachy McBride (SDS)

SISTERS

CONGREGATION OF THE SISTERS OF MERCY

St Catherine's,
123 Culmore Road, Derry BT48 8JF
Tel 028-71352209

22 Newtownkennedy Street,
Strabane, Co Tyrone BT82 8HT
Tel 028-71882269
Community: 10

8A Sheelin Park, Ballymagroarty,
Derry BT48 0PD
Tel 028-71260398
Community: 2

6 Ballycolman Road, Melmount,
Strabane, Co Tyrone BT82 9PH
Tel 028-71885913

60 Steelstown Village,
Derry BT48 8JA
Tel 028-71352300

North Gate Lodge,
125 Culmore Road, Derry BT48 8JF
Tel 028-71350014

19 Towncastle Road,
Strabane, Co Tyrone BT82 0AH
Tel 028-71419891

3 Milestone Way, Fintona Road,
Tattyreagh, Omagh,
Co Tyrone BT78 2LY
Sr Mary Daly RSM
Sr Maura Twohig PBVM

32 Berkeley Heights, Killyclogher,
Omagh, Co Tyrone BT79 7PR

44 Ballynagard Crescent,
Culmore, Derry BT48 8JR
Tel 028-71355776

16 Papworth Avenue,
Derry BT48 8PT
Tel 028-71358827

27 Rockfield, Derry BT48 8AU
Tel 028-71350361

7 Culmore Park,
Culmore Road, Derry BT48 7AN

Flat 20, Abbey House,
Little Diamond, Derry BT48 9EJ

Flat 6, Abbey House,
Little Diamond, Derry BT48 9EJ

CONGREGATION OF OUR LADY OF CHARITY OF THE GOOD SHEPHERD

38 Dungiven Road, Waterside,
Derry BT47 6BW
Tel 028-71342429
Email rgsderry@hotmail.com
Leader: Sr Myriam McLaughlin
Community: 6

LORETO (IBVM)

Convent Grammar, Omagh BT78 1DL
Tel 028-82243633
Primary School,
Brookmount Road, Omagh
Tel 028-82243551

Loreto Community, 1 Osborne Park,
Coleraine, Co Derry BT51 3LU
Tel 028-70344426
Leader: Sr Mary Jo Corcoran
Community: 7
Loreto College, Coleraine BT51 3JZ
Tel 028-70343611

Loreto Sisters, 30 Buskin Way, Coleraine,
Co Derry BT51 3BD
Tel 028-70358065
Community: 2
Educational and pastoral work

CONGREGATION OF THE SISTERS OF NAZARETH

Nazareth House, Fahan,
Lifford, Co Donegal
Tel 074-9331987
Superior: Sr Margaret Gibbons
Email
srmargaret.gibbons@sistersofnazareth.com
Community: 7
Home for aged. Beds: 48

Nazareth House Primary School
Principal: Mr Antoin Moran
Tel 028-71280212
Pupils: 253

EDUCATIONAL INSTITUTIONS

Christian Brothers Grammar School,
Kevlin Road, Omagh BT78 1LD
Tel 028-82243567 Fax 028-82240656
Principal: Mr Fonsie McConnell

CHARITABLE SOCIETIES

Society of St Vincent de Paul
4 Elagh Business Park, Buncrana Road,
Derry BT48 8QH
Tel 028-71265489

DIOCESE OF
DOWN AND CONNOR

PATRONS OF THE DIOCESE
ST MALACHY, 3 NOVEMBER; ST MACNISSI, 4 SEPTEMBER

INCLUDES COUNTY ANTRIM, THE GREATER PART OF COUNTY DOWN
AND PART OF COUNTY DERRY

SEDE VACANTE

Residence: Lisbreen,
73 Somerton Road,
Belfast, Co Antrim BT15 4DE
Tel 028-90776185
Fax 028-90779377
Email
dcoffice@downandconnor.org

HISTORY OF THE DIOCESE

St Patrick does not provide many geographical details in his Confession about his sojourn in Ireland, yet a later tradition associated his work as a slave with Slemish in Co Antrim, his return as a missionary with Saul in Co Down and his burial place with Downpatrick.

In the course of his evangelisation of Ireland St Patrick ordained bishops to minister to local communities. Among those bishops was Mac Nissi, who, following his baptism by St Patrick, founded the church of Connor. However, by the sixth century, after Christianity had been well established, the monastic system was becoming the dominant form of ecclesiastical life. About 555 St Comgall founded a monastery at Bangor that was destined to become one of the most famous in Ireland. Monasteries were also founded in France, Switzerland and Italy, and these became influential centres for the conversion of many peoples. Other monasteries founded in the early centuries of Christianity in Down and Connor include those at Moville, Nendrum, Inch, Drumbo, Antrim and Comber. Some of these later adopted the Benedictine or Augustinian Rule.

The Norsemen cast greedy eyes on Irish monasteries, especially those near the coast, which could be easily attacked and plundered for silver and gold. Bangor fell victim to one such raid in 823, when many monks were killed and the shrine of St Comgall was destroyed. The loss of life and damage to buildings helped weaken the discipline and commitment of the monks. When St Malachy, the great reformer, became Abbot of Bangor in 1123, he found much of the abbey in ruins and the Rule being poorly observed.

In 1111, at the Synod of Rathbreasail, Ireland was at last given the diocesan territorial system that had been common in the western Church. Among the dioceses created were Connor for the Kingdom of Dalriada and Down for the Kingdom of Uladh. Though separate, these Sees were united under St Malachy in 1124. He continued to reside at Bangor and pursue his reforms, but was driven from the monastery and forced to take refuge at Lismore. In 1129 he was appointed Archbishop of Armagh

but because of local opposition, was not able to take control of the See until five years later. In 1137 he resigned and returned to the Diocese of Down, which was again separate from Connor. Invited by his fellow bishops to travel to Rome to obtain the pallia for the archbishops of Armagh and Cashel, Malachy set off in 1139 and visited St Bernard at Clairvaux. Though unsuccessful in his quest, he was appointed papal legate for Ireland. He left some monks at Clairvaux to be trained in the Cistercian way of life and they established the first Cistercian monastery at Mellifont in 1142. A second journey to Rome in 1148 to seek the pallia was cut short by his death on 2 November in the arms of St Bernard. The great Cistercian abbot later wrote Malachy's life story, which ensured that his fame spread widely on the Continent. Malachy was canonised in 1190.

In 1177 the Anglo-Norman adventurer, John de Courcy, carved out the Lordship of Ulster for himself and set up his base at Dunlethglaisse which he renamed Downpatrick. He took a keen interest in ecclesiastical affairs and brought Anglo-Norman Benedictine monks to the cathedral at Downpatrick. His wife founded the Cistercian Monastery at Greyabbey in the Ards Peninsula and he brought other Orders, such as the Premonstratensian and the Augustinian Canons to his territories.

In 1192 the Diocese of Dromore was cut off from Down to make provision for the native Irish, as the part that retained the name Down was by then regarded as Anglo-Norman. The Dioceses of Down and Connor continued to be administered separately until the fifteenth century. In 1439 Pope Eugene IV decided that, after the death of John Sely, the Bishop of Down, the two Sees should be united, and, although Sely was deprived of office three years later for misbehaviour, the Archbishop of Armagh resisted the union of the two dioceses for several years and it did not take place until 1453. In the 1220s the newly founded mendicant Orders, the Dominicans and Franciscans, established houses in the diocese. By the sixteenth century the Third Order of Franciscans had numerous friaries.

Robert Blyth, an English Benedictine, was Bishop of Down and Connor when Henry VIII demanded recognition as

supreme Head of the Church. Blyth surrendered in 1539 and received a substantial pension. The Pope then deprived him of office and appointed in his place Eugene Magennis. Magennis also accepted the royal supremacy but later retracted his submission and was able to retain his See under Mary Tudor. The Franciscan pluralist, Miler McGrath, who succeeded in 1565 and accepted the royal supremacy in 1567, was deposed by Pope Gregory XIII in 1580 but had already been appointed Archbishop of Cashel by Queen Elizabeth. Two years later the Donegal Franciscan, Conor O'Devany, became bishop and after a lengthy episcopate of nearly thirty years was cruelly martyred in Dublin in 1612. (In 1992 he was one of the seventeen Irish martyrs beatified by Pope John Paul II)

During the upheavals of the seventeenth century and the harsh penal legislation of the early eighteenth century, the diocese was left vacant for long periods. After the death of Bishop Daniel Mackey in 1673 no appointment was made until Terence O'Donnelly became vicar apostolic in 1711. When O'Donnelly's successor, James O'Sheil, died in 1724 the See remained vacant until 1727. After the death of Bishop John Armstrong in 1739 all subsequent vacancies never lasted more than a year.

In 1825 William Crolly, who had been parish priest of Belfast for thirteen years, became bishop. Several of his predecessors had lived in or near Downpatrick but he chose to remain in the growing town which he rightly foresaw would become the largest in the diocese. Not only was Belfast geographically more central and convenient but its Catholic population soon dwarfed that of Downpatrick and of all other parishes in the diocese. By 1900 Catholics numbered 85,000 and represented just under a quarter of the city's population. The number of priests serving in it had greatly increased and religious orders of men and women had been brought in to care for the spiritual, educational and social needs of the people.

The continued increase in the number of Catholics in and around Belfast accounts for the position Down and Connor holds as the second largest diocese in Ireland, with a population of approximately 350,000.

st Rev Anthony Farquhar DD
ular Bishop of Ermiana; Former
xiliary Bishop of Down and Connor;
lained priest 13 March 1965; ordained
hop 15 May 1983
sidence: 24 Fruithill Park,
lfast BT11 8GE Tel 028-90624252

st Rev Patrick J. Walsh DD
tired Bishop of Down and Connor;
lained priest 25 February 1956;
lained Titular Bishop of Ros Cré 15
y 1983; installed Bishop of Down and
nnor 28 April 1991
sidence: Nazareth House Care Village,
Ravenhill Road, Belfast BT6 0BW
0044-77-32104366

CHAPTER

an: Vacant
y Rev Brian Daly PP
y Rev Sean Emerson PP
y Rev Robert Fleck PP
y Rev John Forsythe PP
y Rev Sean Gilmore PP
y Rev Joseph Gunn PP
y Rev Colm McBride PP
y Rev Denis McKinley PP
y Rev Patrick McWilliams PP
y Rev John Murray PP
y Rev Edward O'Donnell PP
y Rev Hugh J. O'Hagan PP

norary Canons
y Rev Brendan Beagon PE
Rev Mgr Sean Connolly PE
y Rev Noel Conway PE
y Rev Aidan Kerr PE
y Rev Austin McGirr PE
y Rev Patrick McKenna PE
y Rev Brendan Murray PE
y Rev Sean Rogan PE
y Rev Daniel Shyte PE

ADMINISTRATION

ncellor
y Rev Eugene O'Hagan
reen, 75 Somerton Road,
fast BT15 4DE
028-90776185 Fax 028-90779377
ail chancellor@downandconnor.org

ars General
y Rev Eugene O'Hagan VG
Somerton Road, Belfast BT15 4DE
028-90776185

y Rev John Murray PP, VG
ochial House, 54 St Patrick's Avenue,
wnpatrick, Co Down BT30 6DN
028-44612443

cesan Commission for Religious
irperson: Rev Willie McGettrick (CSsR)
e-Chair: Sr Nuala Kelly DC
ail mar_illac@yahoo.co.uk

cesan Safeguarding Office
Cliftonville Road, Belfast BT14 6LA
ing Diocesan Director and
cesan Liaison Person
Philip O'Hara

*Training and Parish Development
Officer:* Ms Susan Gordon
*Safeguarding Champion for
Safeguarding Adults:* Mr Philip O'Hara
Office Tel 028-90492798
Emergency Tel 07534992124
Safeguarding Secretary
Ms Marion Adams
*Vetting & Barring Co-ordinator for the
Northern Dioceses:* Mr Andrew Thomson
Vetting Supervisor (part-time)
Mrs Lorraine Moreland
Assistant Vetting Officer (Part-time)
Denise Rooney
Safeguarding Support Officers for Parish
Safeguarding Committees can be
contacted through the Safeguarding
Office
Tel 028-90492798

Episcopal Vicar for Safeguarding
Very Rev Peter Owens

Safeguarding Tel 028-90492798
Safeguarding Email office@soddc.org
Vetting Tel 028-90492783
Vetting Email vetting@soddc.org
Designated Liaison Person
Emergency Tel 07534-992124

Consultors
Very Rev Eugene O'Hagan VG
Very Rev Patrick Delargy VG
Very Rev Sean Emerson
Very Rev Aidan Kerr
Very Rev Austin McGirr
Very Rev Thomas McGlynn
Very Rev Feargal McGrady
Very Rev Peter Owens

**Episcopal Vicar for Clergy (Permanent
Deacons)**
Very Rev Michael Sheehan PP
Tel 028-90812238

**Episcopal Vicar for Diocesan Forward
Planning**
Very Rev Timothy Bartlett
Tel 028-90320482

Council of Priests
Chairman: Pending appointment
Secretary: Pending appointment

**Judicial Vicar for Diocese of Down and
Connor**
Very Rev Joseph Rooney JCL
120 Cliftonville Road, Belfast BT14 6LA
Tel 028-90491990 Fax 028-90491440

Diocesan Trust Board
Chairman: Most Rev Noel Treanor
Secretary: Mr Gareth Hughes
Trustees: Very Rev Eugene O'Hagan VG
Very Rev Martin Graham
Mr Joseph Higgins
Mr Gerard McGinn
Ms Orlaigh O'Neill
Ms Brenda Heenan
Mr Michael Scullion
Ms Rose Kelly
Mr Nicholas McKenna

Diocesan Director of Civil Administration
Mr Gareth Hughes
75 Somerton Road, Belfast BT15 4DE
Email g.hughes@downandconnor.org
Tel 028-90776185

DIOCESAN OFFICES
Finance Section
Ms Ann McColgan
Email ann@downandconnor.org
Mr Raymond Noade
Email raymond@downandconnor.org

Property Section
Property Liaison Officer
Mrs Martina Crilly
Email property@downandconnor.org

HR Section
Ms Marie Toner
Email m.toner@downandconnor.org
Ms Mary Harrison
Email m.harrison@downandconnor.org

Media Liaison Officer
Very Rev Edward McGee
120 Cliftonville Road, Belfast BT14 6LA
Tel 078-11144268
Email dcpress@downandconnor.org

Diocesan Archivist
Very Rev Thomas McGlynn PP
St Malachy's Presbytery,
24 Alfred Street, Belfast BT2 8EN
Tel 028-90321713
Email t.mcglynn@downandconnor.org

Diocesan Secretary
Very Rev Gerard Fox
Lisbreen, 75 Somerton Road,
Belfast BT15 4DE
Tel 028-90776185 Fax 028-90779377
Email g.fox@downandconnor.org

CATECHETICS AND EDUCATION

Episcopal Vicar for Education
Very Rev Gerard Fox
75 Somerton Road, Belfast BT15 4DE
Tel 028-90776185
Email education@downandconnor.org

**Down & Connor Catholic Schools
Support Service**
Director: Rev Colin Grant
120 Cliftonville Road, Belfast BT14 6LA
Tel 028-90491886 Fax 028-90491440
Email
dctrusteeservice@downandconnor.org

Council for Catholic Maintained Schools
Linen Hill House, 23 Linenhall Street,
Lisburn BT28 1FJ
Tel 028-92013014
Email info@ccmsschools.com

Diocesan Living Church Office
Director: Ms Paula McKeown
*Pastoral Renewal and Faith Development
Workers:* Aisling Steen, Grace McCann
Support Officer/PA: Claire Carmichael
SPRED Co-ordinator: Ms Louise McQuillan
120 Cliftonville Road, Belfast BT14 6LA
Tel 028-90690920
Email livingchurch@downandconnor.org

LITURGY

Diocesan Commission on Liturgy
Chairman: Mr Malachy McKeever
Tel 075-98346011
Email liturgy@downandconnor.org

PASTORAL

ACCORD (NI) Catholic Marriage Care Service
Regional Office
Administration Officer: Ms Brenda Russell
68 Berry Street, Belfast BT1 1JF
Tel 028-90233002
Email info@accordni.com
www.accordni.com

Belfast
68 Berry Street, Belfast BT1 1JF
Tel 028-90339944

Ballymena
All Saints Parish Centre, 9 Cushendall Road,
Ballymena, Co Antrim
Tel 028-38334781

Downpatrick
Passionist Retreat Centre,
16A Downpatrick Road, Crossgar,
Co Down BT30 9EQ
Tel 028-90233002
Email downpatrick@accordni.com

Judicial Vicariate of Down & Connor
Very Rev Joseph G. Rooney, Judicial Vicar
120 Cliftonville Road,
Belfast BT14 6LA
Tel 028-90491990
Email
judicialvicariate@downandconnor.org

Down & Connor Office of the Armagh Inter-Diocesan Marriage Tribunal
120 Cliftonville Road,
Belfast BT14 6LA
Tel 028-90491990
Email
marriagetribunal@downandconnor.org
Judicial Vicar
Very Rev Joseph Rooney JCL
Associate Judge
Rev Vincent P. Cushnahan JCL
Tribunal/Chancery Administrators
Mrs Deirdre Rafferty
Mrs Maeve Laverty

Diocesan Ecumenical Commission
Secretary: Rev Colin Grant
Aquinas Grammar School,
518 Ravenhill Road, Belfast BT6 0BY
Tel 028-90643939

Pioneer Total Abstinence Association
Diocesan Director
Very Rev Raymond McCullagh PP
143 Andersonstown Road,
Belfast BT11 9BW
Tel 028-90615702/90603951

Pontifical Mission Societies
Diocesan Director
Very Rev Conor McGrath
191 Upper Newtownards Road,
Belfast BT4 3JB
Tel 028-90654157

Diocesan Vocations Commission
Director: Very Rev Conor McGrath
191 Upper Newtownards Road,
Belfast BT4 3JB
Tel 028-90654157

Diocesan Commission on Family Ministry
Secretary: Very Rev Michael McGinnity
Parochial House, 4 Broughshane Road,
Ballymena BT43 7DX
Email m.mcginnity@downandconnor.org

Diocesan Social Affairs Commission
Director: Rev Timothy Bartlett
St Mary's, Marquis Street, Belfast BT1 1JJ
Tel 028-90320482

PARISHES

Cathedral is listed first. Other parishes follow alphabetically, city parishes first. Historical names are in parentheses.

THE CATHEDRAL (ST PETER'S)
Very Rev Martin Graham Adm
Rev Brian Watters CC
Rev Aidan McCaughan *(priest in residence)*
Deacon Martin Whyte
St Peter's Cathedral Presbytery,
St Peter's Square, Belfast BT12 4BU
Tel 028-90327573

CITY PARISHES

CHRIST THE REDEEMER, LAGMORE
Very Rev Colin Crossey PP
81 Lagmore Grove, Dunmurry,
Belfast BT17 0TD
Tel 028-90309011

CORPUS CHRISTI
Very Rev Patrick McCafferty PP
Corpus Christi Presbytery,
4-6 Springhill Grove, Belfast BT12 7SL
Tel 028-90246857

DERRIAGHY
Very Rev Brian McCann Adm
Deacon Kevin Webb
111 Queensway,
Lambeg, Lisburn BT27 4QS
Tel 028-92662896

GREENCASTLE
Very Rev David Delargy PP
824 Shore Road, Newtownabbey,
Co Antrim BT36 7DG
Tel 028-90370845

HANNAHSTOWN
Very Rev Patrick Devlin PP
Parochial House, 23 Hannahstown Hill,
Belfast BT17 0LT
Tel 028-90614567

HOLY CROSS
Very Rev John Craven (CP) PP
Rev Frank Trias (CP) CC
Rev Gareth Thomas (CP) CC
Holy Cross Retreat, 432 Crumlin Road,
Ardoyne, Belfast BT14 7GE
Tel 028-90748231/2

HOLY FAMILY
Very Rev Michael Spence PP
Rev Robert Sloan CC
Deacon Brendan Dowd
Holy Family Presbytery,
Newington Avenue, Belfast BT15 2HP
Tel 028-90743119

HOLY ROSARY
Very Rev Brendan Hickland PP
503 Ormeau Road, Belfast BT7 3GR
Tel 028-90642446
Rev Paddy Keown *(Permanent Deacon)*

HOLY TRINITY
Very Rev Brendan Mulhall Adm
Holy Trinity Presbytery,
26 Norglen Gardens, Belfast BT11 8EL
Tel 028-90590985/6

THE NATIVITY
Very Rev Brian McCann Adm
The Presbytery, Bell Steel Road,
Poleglass, Belfast BT17 0PB
Tel 028-90625739

OUR LADY QUEEN OF PEACE, KILWEE
Very Rev Rory Sheehan PP
Netherley Lodge,
130 Upper Dunmurry Lane,
Belfast BT17 0EW
Tel 028-90616300

SACRED HEART
Very Rev Kieran Creagh (CP) Adm
Deacon Joseph Baxter
Rev Manuelito Milo *(Chaplain, Belfast City Hospital)*
Sacred Heart Presbytery,
1 Glenview Street, Belfast BT14 7DP
Tel 028-90351851

ST AGNES'
Very Rev Raymond McCullagh PP
Deacon Gregory McGuigan
143 Andersonstown Road,
Belfast BT11 9BW
Tel 028-90615702/90603951

ANNE'S
Very Rev Peter O'Hare PP
Deacon Patrick McNeill
Anne's Parochial House,
...ngsway, Finaghy, Belfast BT10 0NE
...l 028-90610112

ANTHONY'S
Very Rev Henry McCann PP
Anthony's Presbytery,
...Willowfield Crescent, Belfast BT6 8HP
...l 028-90458158

BERNADETTE'S
Very Rev Brendan Hickland Adm
...ev Paul Morely CC
...Willowbank Park, Belfast BT6 0LL
...l 028-90793023

BRIGID'S
Very Rev Edward O'Donnell PP
Deacon Brett Lockhart
...Derryvolgie Avenue, Belfast BT9 6FP
...l 028-90665409

COLMCILLE'S
Very Rev Conor McGrath
...1 Upper Newtownards Road,
...lfast BT4 3JB
...l 028-90654157

GERARD'S
Redemptorist Fathers
Very Rev Patrick O'Keeffe (CSsR) PP
...ev Denis Luddy (CSsR) CC
...2 Antrim Road, Newtownabbey,
...o Antrim BT36 7PG
...l 028-90774833/4

JOHN'S
Very Rev Martin Magill PP
...0 Falls Road, Belfast BT12 6EN
...l 028-90321511
...ery Rev Anthony McLaverty (priest in
...sidence)
...18 Donegall Road, Belfast BT12 6DY
...l 028-90314112

LUKE'S
Very Rev Brian McCann PP, VF
...t Luke's Presbytery, Twinbrook Road,
...unmurry, Co Antrim BT17 0RP
...l 028-90619459
...ev John Downey (Permanent Deacon)

MALACHY'S
Very Rev Thomas McGlynn PP
...t Malachy's Presbytery,
...4 Alfred Street, Belfast BT2 8EN
...l 028-90321713

MARY'S
Very Rev Timothy Bartlett PP, EV
Very Rev Paul Armstrong, PE
...ev Brian Watters, Assistant Priest
...t Mary's, Marquis Street,
...elfast BT1 1JJ
...l 028-90320482

ST MARY'S ON THE HILL
Very Rev Pat Sheehan PP, VF
Elmfield, 165 Antrim Road, Glengormley,
Newtownabbey, Co Antrim BT36 7QR
Tel 028-90832979
Very Rev Aidan Kerr PE
142 Carnmoney Road, Newtownabbey,
Co Antrim BT36 6JU
Tel 028-90832488
Very Rev Brendan Beagon CC
1 Christine Road, Newtownabbey,
Co Antrim BT36 6TG
Tel 028-90841507
Rev Kieran Hunt (Permanent Deacon)

ST MATTHEW'S
Very Rev Peter Carlin PP
St Matthew's Presbytery, Bryson Street,
Newtownards Road, Belfast BT5 4ES
Tel 028-90457626

ST MICHAEL'S
Very Rev Ciaran Feeney PP
200 Finaghy Road North, Belfast BT11 9EG
Tel 028-90617519

ST OLIVER PLUNKETT
Very Rev Aidan Brankin PP
27 Glenveagh Drive, Belfast BT11 9HX
Tel 028-90618180

ST PATRICK'S
Very Rev Eugene O'Neill PP, VF
Rev Anthony Mc Aleese CC
St Patrick's Presbytery,
199 Donegall Street, Belfast BT1 2FL
Tel 028-90324597

ST PAUL'S
Very Rev Anthony Devlin PP, VF
St Paul's Presbytery, 125 Falls Road,
Belfast BT12 6AB
Tel 028-90325034
Rev Eddie Craemer (CSsR) CC
Clonard Monastery, Clonard Gardens,
Belfast BT13 2RL
Rev Renson Joseph CC

ST TERESA'S
Very Rev Gabriel Lyons PP
St Teresa's Presbytery, Glen Road,
Belfast BT11 8BL
Tel 028-90612855

ST VINCENT DE PAUL
Very Rev Vincent Cushnahan PP
St Vincent de Paul Presbytery,
169 Ligoniel Road, Belfast BT14 8DP
Tel 028-90713401

WHITEABBEY (ST JAMES'S)
Very Rev David Delargy PP
824 Shore Road,
Newtownabbey BT36 7DG

WHITEHOUSE
Very Rev David Delargy PP
824 Shore Road,
Newtownabbey BT36 7DG

COUNTRY PARISHES

AGHAGALLON AND BALLINDERRY
Very Rev Declan Mulligan PP
Parochial House, 5 Aghalee Road,
Aghagallon, Craigavon,
Co Armagh BT67 0AR
Tel 028-92651214

AHOGHILL
Very Rev Hugh J O'Hagan PP
Parochial House, 31 Ballynafie Road,
Ahoghill BT42 1LF
Tel 028-25871351

ANTRIM
Very Rev Sean Emerson PP, VF
Parochial House, 3 Oriel Road,
Antrim BT41 4HP
Tel 028-94428016
Rev James O'Reilly CC
St Joseph's Presbytery,
56 Greystone Road, Antrim BT41 1JZ
Tel 028-94429103
Rev Jain Matthew Mannathukaran CC
5 Oriel Road, Antrim BT41 4HP
Tel 028-94428086

ARMOY
Very Rev Robert Butler Adm (pro tem)
Parochial House, Armoy,
Ballymoney, Co Antrim BT53 8RL
Tel 028-20751205

BALLINTOY
Very Rev Brian Daly Adm
15 Moyle Road, Ballycastle,
Co Antrim BT54 6LB
Tel 028-20762223

BALLYCASTLE (RAMOAN)
Very Rev Brian Daly PP
Parochial House, 15 Moyle Road,
Ballycastle, Co Antrim BT54 6LB
Tel 028-20762223
Rev Barney McCahery (CSsR) CC
74a Moyle Road,
Ballycastle BT54 6LG
Tel 028-20762202
Very Rev Raymond Fulton PE
4 Gortanclochair Park,
Ballycastle, Co Antrim BT54 6N1

BALLYCLARE AND BALLYGOWAN
Very Rev Joseph Rooney Adm, JCL
Parochial House, 69 Doagh Road,
Ballyclare, Co Antrim BT39 9BG
Tel 028-93342226

BALLYGALGET
Very Rev Feargal McGrady PP
Parochial House, 60 Windmill Hill,
Portaferry, Co Down BT22 1RH
Tel 028-42771212

BALLYMENA (KIRKINRIOLA)
Very Rev Michael McGinnity PP, VF
4 Broughshane Road, Ballymena,
Co Antrim BT43 7DX
Tel 028-25643828
Rev Joe David
Parochial House, 4 Boughshane Road,
Ballymena BT43 7DX

BALLYMONEY AND DERRYKEIGHAN
Very Rev Damian McCaughan PP
81 Castle Street, Ballymoney,
Co Antrim BT53 6JT
Tel 028-27662003

BANGOR
Very Rev Joseph Gunn PP, VF
St Comgall's Presbytery,
27 Brunswick Road, Bangor,
Co Down BT20 3DS
Tel 028-91465522

CARNLOUGH
Very Rev Anthony Fitzsimons PP
51 Bay Road, Carnlough,
Ballymena, Co Antrim BT44 0HJ
Tel 028-28885220

CARRICKFERGUS
Very Rev Peter Owens PP
Parochial House,
8 Minorca Place, Carrickfergus,
Co Antrim BT38 8AU
Tel 028-93363269

CASTLEWELLAN (KILMEGAN)
Very Rev Denis McKinlay PP, VF
41 Lower Square,
Castlewellan BT31 9DN
Tel 028-43770377
Rev Mark Lenaghan *(Permanent Deacon)*

COLERAINE
Very Rev Kevin McGuckien Adm
Rev Nideesh Varghese CC
72 Nursery Avenue, Coleraine,
Co Derry BT52 1LR
Tel 028-70343156

CROSSGAR (KILMORE)
Very Rev Brendan Smyth PP
Parochial House,
10 Downpatrick Street, Crossgar,
Downpatrick, Co Down BT30 9EA
Tel 028-44830229

CULFEIGHTRIN
Very Rev Con Boyle PP
87 Cushendall Road, Ballyvoy,
Ballycastle, Co Antrim BT54 6QY
Tel 028-20762248

CUSHENDALL
Very Rev Kieran Whiteford PP
Parochial House, 28 Chapel Road,
Cushendall, Ballymena BT44 0RS
Tel 028-21771240

CUSHENDUN
Very Rev Kieran Whiteford PP
Parochial House, 28 Chapel Road,
Cushendall, Ballymena,
Co Antrim BT44 0RS
Tel 028-21771240
Very Rev James O'Kane PE, CC
21 Knocknacarry Avenue,
Cushenden, Co Antrim BT44 0NX
Tel 028-21761269

DOWNPATRICK
Very Rev John Murray PP, VF
Very Rev Maurice Henry PE
Parochial House, 54 St Patrick's Avenue,
Downpatrick, Co Down BT30 6DN
Tel 028-44612443
Very Rev Liam Toland CC
29 Killough Road, Downpatrick,
Co Down BT30 6PX
Tel 028-44612443
Very Rev Canon Noel Conway *(priest in residence)*
23 Rathkeltair Road, Downpatrick,
Co Down BT30 6NL
Tel 028-44614777
Rev Jackie Breen *(Permanent Deacon)*

DRUMAROAD AND CLANVARAGHAN
Very Rev Ciaran Dallat Adm
Parochial House, 15 Drumaroad Hill,
Castlewellan, Co Down BT31 9PD
Tel 028-44811474

DRUMBO AND CARRYDUFF
Very Rev Michael Sheehan PP
Parochial House, 546 Saintfield Road,
Carryduff, Belfast BT8 8EU
Tel 028-90812238
Very Rev Canon Sean Rogan PE
546 Saintfield Road, Carryduff,
Belfast BT8 8EU
Tel 028-90812238

DUNDRUM AND TYRELLA
Very Rev Robert Fleck PP
Parochial House, Dundrum,
Newcastle, Co Down BT33 0LU
Tel 028-43751212

DUNEANE
Very Rev Patrick McWilliams PP
103 Roguery Road, Moneyglass,
Toomebridge, Co Antrim BT41 3PT
Tel 028-79650225

DUNLOY AND CLOUGHMILLS
Very Rev Darren Brennan PP
Parochial House, 14 Presbytery Lane,
Dunloy, Co Antrim BT44 9DZ
Tel 028-27657223

DUNSFORD AND ARDGLASS
Very Rev Gerard McCloskey PP
Parochial House, Ardglass,
Co Down BT30 7TU
Tel 028-44841208

GLENARIFFE
Very Rev David White PP
Parochial House, 182 Garron Road,
Glenariffe, Co Antrim BT44 0RA
Tel 028-21771249

GLENARM (TICKMACREEVAN)
Very Rev Anthony Fitzsimons PP
51 Bay Road, Carnlough,
Co Antrim BT44 0HJ
Tel 028-28885220

GLENAVY AND KILLEAD
Very Rev Colm McBride PP, VF
Parochial House, 59 Chapel Road,
Glenavy, Crumlin, Co Antrim BT29 4LY
Tel 028-94422262

GLENRAVEL AND THE BRAID (SKERRY)
Very Rev Paul Strain PP
119A Glenravel Road, Martinstown,
Ballymena, Co Antrim BT43 6QL
Tel 028-21758217

HOLYWOOD
Very Rev Stephen McBrearty PP
2A My Lady's Mile, Holywood,
Co Down BT18 9EW
Tel 028-90422167

KILCLIEF AND STRANGFORD
Very Rev John McManus PP
Parochial House, Strangford,
Co Down BT30 7NL
Tel 028-44881206

KILCOO
Very Rev Denis McKinlay PP, VF
41 Lower Square, Castlewellan BT31 9DN
Tel 028-43770377

KILKEEL (UPPER MOURNE)
Very Rev Sean Dillon PP
Parochial House, Greencastle Road,
Kilkeel, Co Down BT34 4DE
Tel 028-41762242
Very Rev Sean Cahill PE
Curates' Residence, Massforth,
152 Newry Road, Kilkeel,
Co Down BT34 4ET
Tel 028-41762257

KILLOUGH (BRIGHT)
Very Rev Peter O'Kane PP
16 Rossglass Road, Killough,
Co Down BT30 7QQ
Tel 028-44841221

KILLYLEAGH
Very Rev Brendan Smyth PP
4 Irish Street, Killyleagh,
Co Down BT30 9QS
Tel 028-44828211

KIRCUBBIN (ARDKEEN)
Very Rev Anthony Alexander PP
46 Blackstaff Road, Ballycranbeg,
Kircubbin, Newtownards,
Co Down BT22 1AG
Tel 028-42738294

Allianz (ili)

ARNE
Very Rev Francis O'Brien PP
Parochial House, 51 Victoria Road, Larne,
Co Antrim BT40 1LY
Tel 028-28273230/28273053
Rev Ricky Looney (Permanent Deacon)

LISBURN (BLARIS)
Very Rev Dermot McCaughan PP
St Patrick's Presbytery,
39 Chapel Hill, Lisburn,
Co Antrim BT28 1EP
Tel 028-92662341
Rev Eamon Magorrian CC
Tel 028-92660206
Parochial House, 27 Chapel Hill, Lisburn,
Co Antrim BT28 1EP

LOUGHGUILE
Very Rev Patrick Mulholland PP
Parochial House, 44 Lough Road,
Loughguile, Ballymena,
Co Antrim BT44 9JN
Tel 028-27641206

LOUGHINISLAND
Very Rev Ciaran Dallat PP
Parochial House, Loughinisland,
Downpatrick, Co Down BT30 8QH
Tel 028-44811661

LOWER MOURNE
Very Rev Sean Gilmore PP
Parochial House,
84 Glassdrumman Road, Annalong,
Newry, Co Down BT34 4QN
Tel 028-43768208

NEWCASTLE (MAGHERA)
Very Rev James Crudden PP
4 Downs Road, Newcastle,
Co Down BT33 0AG
Tel 028-43722401

NEWTOWNARDS
Very Rev Martin O'Hagan PP, VF
Deacon James McAllister
1 North Street, Newtownards,
Co Down BT23 4JD
Tel 028-91812137

PORTAFERRY (BALLYPHILIP)
Very Rev Feargal McGrady PP
Parochial House, 60 Windmill Hill,
Portaferry, Co Down BT22 1RH
Tel 028-42728234

PORTGLENONE
Very Rev Anthony Curran PP
St Mary's Presbytery, 12 Ballymena Road,
Portglenone, Co Antrim BT44 8BL
Tel 028-25821218

PORTRUSH
Very Rev Kevin McGuckien Adm
Parochial House, 4 The Crescent,
Portstewart, Co Derry BT55 7AB
Tel 028-70832534

Rev Mgr Patrick Delargy (priest in
residenced)
Parochial House, 111 Causeway Street,
Portrush, Co Antrim BT56 8JE
Tel 028-70823388

PORTSTEWART
Very Rev Kevin McGuckien PP, VF
Deacon Terence Butcher
Parochial House, 4 The Crescent,
Portstewart, Co Derry BT55 7AB
Tel 028-70832534

RANDALSTOWN
Very Rev John Forsythe PP
Parochial House, 1 Craigstown Road,
Randalstown, Co Antrim BT41 2AF
Tel 028-94472640

RASHARKIN
Very Rev Luke McWilliams PP
Parochial House, 9 Gortahor Road,
Rasharkin, Ballymena,
Co Antrim BT44 8SB
Tel 028-29571212

SAINTFIELD AND CARRICKMANNON
Very Rev Anthony McHugh PP
Parochial House,
33 Crossgar Road, Saintfield,
Ballynahinch, Co Down BT24 7JE
Tel 028-97510237

SAUL AND BALLEE
Very Rev Paul Alexander PP
10 St Patrick's Road, Saul,
Downpatrick, Co Down BT30 7JG
Tel 028-44612525
Rev Jackie Breen (Permanent Deacon)

INSTITUTIONS AND THEIR CHAPLAINS

HOSPITALS

Antrim Area Hospital
Tel 028-94424000
Rev James O'Reilly CC

Belfast City Hospital
Tel 028-90329241
Rev Manuelito Milo
St Paul's Presbytery,
125 Falls Road, Belfast BT12 6AB
Tel 028-90325034
Tel 028-90638621 (chaplain's office)

Causeway Hospital
Tel 028-70327032
Very Rev Damian McCaughan

Mater Hospital, Belfast
Tel 028-90741211
Rev Anthony McAleese
St Patrick's Presbytery,
199 Donegall Street, Belfast BT1 2FL
Tel 028-90324597

Musgrave Park Hospital, Belfast
Tel 028-90902000
Rev Adrian Eastwood (CM)
99 Cliftonville Road,
Belfast BT14 6JQ
Tel 028-90751771

Royal Victoria Hospital, Belfast
Tel 028-95040503
Very Rev Darach Mac Giolla Catháin
111 Queensway, Lambeg,
Lisburn, BT27 4QS
Tel 028-90606980

Ulster Hospital, Dundonald
Tel 028-90654157
Very Rev Conor McGrath PP
Very Rev Martin O'Hagan PP
Very Rev Henry McCann PP

PENAL INSTITUTIONS

Maghaberry Prison
Old Road, Ballinderry Upper,
Lisburn,
Co Antrim BT28 2TP
Tel 028-92614825
Prison General Office: 028-92611888

Hydebank Wood College and Women's Prison
Hydebank Wood, Hospital Road,
Belfast BT8 8NA
Co-ordinating Lead Chaplain of Catholic
Pastoral Team
Very Rev Stephen McBrearty
Tel 028-90253666
Rev Ciaran Dallat
Rev Frank Brady (SJ)
Sr Oonagh Hanrahan
Deacon Joseph Baxter
Deacon James McAllister

PRIESTS OF THE DIOCESE ELSEWHERE

Rev Andrew Black
Canadian Pontifical College,
Via Crescenzio 75, 00193 Roma, Italy
Very Rev Paul Byrne
3 Fortwilliam Demesne, Belfast BT15 4FD
Rev Ciarán Hegarty CC
Doneyloop, Castlefin,
Lifford, Co Donegal
Tel 074-9146183
Rev Martin Henry
Rev Oliver Treanor
Very Rev Hugh Kennedy
75 Somerton Road, Belfast BT15 4DE
Rev Gerard McFlynn
18 Maresfield Gardens, London NW3 5SX
Rev John O'Laverty
Venerable English College,
via di Monserrato, 45, Roma 00186, Italy

RETIRED PRIESTS

Very Rev Paul Armstrong
5 Balmoral Mews, Belfast BT9 6NM
Rt Rev Mgr Sean Connolly VG
7 Tullyview, Loughguile,
Co Antrim BT44 9JY
Rev Mgr Patrick Delargy
111 Causeway Street, Portrush BT56 8JE
Very Rev Peter Donnelly
c/o Diocesan Office
Email p.donnelly@downandconnor.org
Very Rev Raymond Fulton PE
4 Gortanclochair Park,
Ballycastle BT54 6NU
Very Rev Padraic Gallinagh
'Polperro', 8 Beverley Close,
Newtownards BT23 7FN
Very Rev Maurice Henry PE
Parochial House, 54 St Patrick's Avenue,
Downpatrick, Co Down BT30 6DN
Tel 028-44612443
Very Rev John Hutton
Nazareth House Care Village,
516 Ravenhill Road, Belfast BT6 0BW
Very Rev Aidan Keenan
c/o Diocesan Office
Very Rev Martin Kelly
93 Ballylenaghan Park, Belfast BT8 6WR
Very Rev Sean McCartney
25 Alt-Min Avenue, Belfast BT8 6NJ
Rev Michael McConville
Nazareth House Care Village,
516 Ravenhill Road, Belfast BT6 0BW
Very Rev Laurence McElhill
43B Glen Road, Belfast BT11 8BL
Very Rev Austin McGirr
Ranamona, Annagry, Co Donegal F94 CY99
Very Rev Dermott McKay
53 Ballinlea Road, Ballycastle
Very Rev Patrick McKenna
19 Broughshane Road,
Ballymena BT43 7DX
Rev Gordon McKinstry
12 The Meadows, Randalstown,
Co Antrim BT41 2JB
Very Rev Anthony McLaverty
518 Donegall Road, Belfast BT12 6DY
Very Rev Brendan McMullan
26 Willowbank Park, Belfast BT6 0LL
Tel 028-90794440
Very Rev Kevin McMullan
Nazareth House Care Village,
516 Ravenhill Road, Belfast BT6 0BW
Very Rev Albert McNally
6 Hillside Avenue, Dunloy BT44 9DQ
Very Rev Vincent Maguire
26 Rodney Street, Portrush,
Co Antrim BT56 8LB
Very Rev John Moley
24 Mallard Road, Downpatrick,
Co Down BT30 6DY
Very Rev John Murray
c/o 75 Somerton Road, Belfast BT15 4DE
Very Rev Michael Murray
c/o 75 Somerton Road, Belfast BT15 4DE

Very Rev Patrick Neeson
Parochial House, Drumardan Road,
Ballygalget BT22 1NE
Rev John O'Connor
c/o Lisbreen, 75 Somerton Road,
Belfast BT15 4DE
Very Rev Jim Sheppard
c/o 32 Dromlin Drive, Lurgan BT66 8PG
Very Rev Daniel Whyte
53 Marlo Park, Bangor,
Co Down BT19 6NL
Tel 078-12184624

PERSONAL PRELATURE

OPUS DEI
Dunraven,
104 Malone Road, Belfast BT9 5HP
Tel 028-90506947
Email dunraven104bt9@gmail.com
Rev Brendan O'Connor

RELIGIOUS ORDERS AND CONGREGATIONS

PRIESTS

CISTERCIANS
Our Lady of Bethlehem Abbey,
11 Ballymena Road, Portglenone,
Ballymena, Co Antrim BT44 8BL
Tel 028-25821211
Email cinfo@bethabbey.com
Website www.bethlehemabbey.com
Abbot/Superior
Rt Rev Dom Celsus Kelly (OCSO)

JESUITS
Peter Faber House,
28 Brookvale Avenue, Belfast BT14 6BW
Tel 028-90757615 Fax 028-90747615
Email peter_faber@lineone.net
Superior: Rev Tom Layden (SJ)

PASSIONISTS
Holy Cross Retreat, Ardoyne,
Crumlin Road, Belfast BT14 7GE
Tel 028-90748231 Fax 028-90740340
Superior: Rev John Friel (CP)

Passionist Retreat Centre,
16A Downpatrick Road,
Crossgar, Downpatrick,
Co Down BT30 9EQ
Tel 028-44830242 Fax 028-44831382
Superior: Rev Thomas Scanlon (CP)

REDEMPTORISTS
Clonard Monastery,
1 Clonard Gardens,
Belfast BT13 2RL
Tel 028-90445950 Fax 028-90445988
Superior: Rev Peter Burns (CSsR)

St Gerard's Parish,
722 Antrim Road, Newtownabbey,
Co Antrim BT36 7PG
Tel 028-90774833 Fax 028-90770923
PP: Rev Kevin Browne (CSsR)

VINCENTIANS
99 Cliftonville Road, Belfast BT14 6JQ
Tel 028-90751771 Fax 028-90740547
Superior
Very Rev Adrian Eastwood (CM)

BROTHERS

CHRISTIAN BROTHERS
An Dúnán, 210 Glen Road,
Belfast BT11 8BW
Tel 028-90611343
Community Leader
Br Brian Monaghan
Community: 5

The Open Doors Learning Centre,
Barrack Street, Belfast BT12 4AH
Tel 028-90325867 Fax 028-90241013
Coordinator: Cormac McArt
Email opendoorsbelfast@yahoo.co.uk

Education and Outreach Centre,
Westcourt Centre,
Barrack Street, Belfast BT12 4AH
Tel 028-90323009
Project Manager: Cormac McArt
Email westcourtcentre@btconnect.com

DE LA SALLE BROTHERS
De La Salle College,
Edenmore Drive, Belfast BT11 8LT
Tel 028-90508800
Principal: Ms Claire Whyte

De La Salle Brothers, Glanaulin,
141 Glen Road, Belfast BT11 8BP
Tel 028-90614848
Superior: Br Ailbe Mangan
Community: 3

La Salle Pastoral Retreat Centre,
Glanaulin, 141 Glen Road,
Belfast BT11 8BP
Tel 028-90501932 Tax 028-90501932
Director: Ms Margaret McClory

La Salle House, 4 Stream Street,
Downpatrick, Co Down BT30 6DD
Tel 028-44612996
Superior: Br Mark Jordan
Community: 3

St Patrick's Grammar School,
Downpatrick, Co Down BT30 6NJ
Tel 028-44619722
Principal: Mr Joseph McCann

Secondary School, Struell Road,
Downpatrick, Co Down BT30 6JR
Tel 028-44612520
Principal: Mr Ciaran Maguire

Allianz (ⅲ)

SISTERS

CONGREGATION OF THE SISTERS OF MERCY
Convent of Mercy, Beechmount,
Rd Na Va Road, Belfast BT12 6FF
Tel 028-90319496
Community: 5

Mercy Convent,
Whiteabbey, 453 Shore Road,
Newtownabbey, Co Antrim BT37 9SE
Tel 028-90863128

Convent of Mercy,
52 Limestone Road, Belfast BT15 3AR
Tel 028-90749259

Sisters of Mercy
6 Crumlin Road, Belfast BT14 7GL
Tel 028-90717112

Fortwilliam Fold,
Fortwilliam Park, Belfast BT15 4AN
Tel 028-90371268

Camberwell Court,
Limestone Road, Belfast BT15 3BH
Tel 028-90286584

8 Crumlin Road,
Belfast BT14 7GL
Tel 028-90715478

Ashgrove Lodge, Glengormley,
Newtownabbey, Co Antrim BT36 6WY
Tel 028-90843890

Camberwell Court,
Limestone Road, Belfast BT15 3BH
Tel 028-90290213

Camberwell Court,
Limestone Road, Belfast BT15 3BH
Tel 028-90748830

Camberwell Court,
Limestone Road, Belfast BT15 38H
Tel 028-90507842

Springhill Park, Downpatrick,
Co Down BT30 6QR
Tel 028-44615645

CROSS AND PASSION CONGREGATION
St Teresa's Convent,
Glen Road, ΩBelfast BT11 8BH
Tel 028-90613955
Community: 4
Pastoral care, ecumenical work,
bereavement counselling

Villa Pacis, 78A Glen Road,
Belfast BT11 8BH
Tel 028-90621766
Community: 13
Care of sick and elderly

Drumalis Retreat Centre,
47 Glenarm Road, Larne,
Co Antrim BT40 1DT
Tel 028-28276455/28272196
Email drumalis@btconnect.com
Community: 2

5c Easton Avenue, Cliftonville road,
Belfast BT14 6LL
Tel 028-90749507
Community: 2
Retreat work, Vietnam project,
counselling and facilitation

DAUGHTERS OF CHARITY OF ST VINCENT DE PAUL
23 Glen Road,
Belfast BT11 8BA
Tel 028-90203052
and
Apt 6, 2 Glenhill Park,
Belfast BT11 8GB
Tel 028-90628483
Superior: Sr Claire Sweeney
Community: 5
Parish and pastoral work and education
and work with De Paul Trust – homeless

DOMINICAN SISTERS
St Catherine's, 133 Falls Road,
Belfast BT12 6AD
Tel 028-90327056
Email opfalls133@gmail.com
Prioress: Sr Geraldine Maris Smyth (OP)
Community: 11
Varied ministries
St Dominic's Grammar School
Tel 028-90320081

Dominican Convent,
28 Fortwilliam Park, Belfast BT15 4AP
Tel 028-90370008
Email ionahouseop@gmail.com
Community: 7
Varied ministries
Dominican College Forthwilliam
Tel 028-90370298

FAMILY OF ADORATION
63 Falls Road, Belfast BT12 4PD
Tel 01232-325668
Email adorationsisters@utv.net
A contemplative community with
mission of adoration, making of altar
breads and Holy Shop

CONGREGATION OF OUR LADY OF CHARITY OF THE GOOD SHEPHERD
Lys Marie, 19 Rossmore Drive,
Belfast BT7 3LA
Tel 028-90641346
Email 25rossmoredrive@gmail.com
Community: 8

Congregation of Our Lady of Charity of
the Good Shepherd (Contemplative
Sisters)
Lys Marie, 19 Rossmore Drive,
Belfast BT7 3LA
Tel 028-90641346
Email lysmariesisters@yahoo.com
Community: 5

49 Knockbreda Park, Belfast BT6 0HD
Tel 028-90582391
Community: 1

MISSIONARY SISTERS OF THE HOLY CROSS
86 Glen Road, Belfast BT11 8BH
Tel 028-90614631
Email holycrossbelfast@gmail.com
Superior: Sr Patricia Kelly
Email patkelly8686@gmail.com
Community: 3

POOR SERVANTS OF THE MOTHER OF GOD
15 Martin's Lane, Carnagat,
Newry, Co Down BT35 8PJ
Tel 028-30268512
Contacts: Sr Margaret O'Sullivan (SMG),
Sr Marie Slacke (SMG)
Comunity: 2
Pastoral

CONGREGATION OF THE SISTERS OF NAZARETH
Nazareth House Care Village,
516 Ravenhill Road, Belfast BT6 0BX
Tel 028-90690604/666
Superior: Sr Bridget Broderick
Email
superior.belfastuk@sistersofnazareth.com
Community: 7
Home for the elderly. Beds: 88

Bethlehem Nursery School,
514 Ravenhill Road,
Belfast BT6 0BW
Tel 028-90640406
Pupils: 52
St Michael's Primary,
516 Ravenhill Road, Belfast BT6 0BW
Tel 028-90491529. Pupils: 410

RELIGIOUS OF SACRED HEART OF MARY
100 Hillsborough Road, Lisburn,
Co Antrim BT28 1JU
Tel 01846-678501
Community: 1
Ministry in local area

28 Upper Green, Dunmurry,
Belfast BT17 0EL
Tel 01232-600792
Community 3
Ministry in local area and education

Sacred Heart of Mary Grammar School
for Boys and Girls,
Rathmore, Finaghy,
Belfast BT10 0LF
Pupils: 1,350
Tel 01232-610115
Email
userid.rathmore@schools.class-ni.org.uk

ST CLARE SISTERS
St Clare's Convent, 43 Rosetta Park,
Belfast BT6 0DL
Tel 028-90694108
Community: 2

ST LOUIS SISTERS
14 Carndale Meadows,
Carniny Road,
Ballymena BT43 5NX
Tel 028-25651683
Community: 1

7 Riverdale Park Avenue,
Belfast BT11 9BP
Tel 028-90209074
Community: 1

22 Riverdale Park North,
Belfast BT11 9DL
Tel 028-90619375
Community: 1

Apartment 2 Hollycroft,
1-3 Inver Avenue,
Belfast BT15 5DG
Tel 028-90721037
Community: 1

49 Bracken Avenue,
Castlewellan Road,
Newcastle, Co Down BT33 0HG
Tel 028-43726282
Community: 1

1 River Mill, New Street,
Randalstown BT41 3FT

THIRD LEVEL INSTITUTIONS AND THEIR CHAPLAINS

St Mary's University College
A College of Queen's University Belfast
191 Falls Road, Belfast 12 6FE
Tel 028-90327678
Principal
Professor Peter Finn BA MSSc KSG
Priest Lecturers
Rev Feidhlimidh Magennis MA, BD, LSS
(Dromore)
Rev Edward McGee BSc, MA, DD
Rev Paul Fleming BA, BD, STL, PhD

Queen's University of Belfast
Chaplain: Rev Dominic McGrattan
Catholic Chaplaincy,
28 Elmwood Avenue,
Belfast BT9 6AY
Tel 028-90669739
Email qubcc@downandconnor.org
Facebook page The Catholic Chaplaincy
at QUB

Ulster University
Coleraine Campus
Chaplain: Vacant
The Chaplaincy Office, L101,
University of Ulster, Coleraine
Tel 028-70124652

Jordanstown and Belfast Campuses
Chaplain: Rev Gerry Clarke (SJ)
Belfast Jesuit Centre,
193-195 Donegall Street, Belfast

EDUCATION TRUSTS

ST MACNISSI'S EDUCATIONAL TRUST
75 Somerton Road, Belfast BT15 4DE
Email education@downandconnor.org

EDMUND RICE SCHOOLS TRUST (NI)
Westcourt Centre
8-30 Barrack Street, Belfast BT12 4AH
Chief Executive: Mr Kevin Burke
Tel 028-90333205
Email erstni@live.com

CHARITABLE AND OTHER SOCIETIES

Apostolic Work Society
Xavier House, 156 Cliftonpark Avenue,
Belfast BT14 6DT
Tel 028-90351912
Email apostolic.work@btinternet.com
Office hours:
Monday-Wednesday 9.00 am-2.30 pm
Society for lay women
President: Ms Mary McGrath

**Down and Connor Pioneer Association -
DCPA**
1st Floor, The McCoy Buildings,
68 Berry Street, Belfast BT1 7FJ
Tel 028-90894070
Email dandcpioneers@gmail.com
Spiritual Director
Rev Raymond McCullagh

Knights of Columbanus
Provincial Grand Knight Area 2
Charlie Clarke
67 Ballynahinch Road
Carryduff, Belfast, BT8 8DL
Tel 078-50203835
Email pgkarea2@outlook.com
Provincial Secretary Area 2
Con McLaughlin
2 Glenview Crescent
Newtownabbey BT37 0TW
Tel 077-75523937
Email provsecarea2@gmail.com

Legion of Mary
14 Cliftonville Road, Belfast BT14 6JX
Tel 028-90746626

Morning Star House
2-12 Divis Street, Belfast
Tel 028-90333500

Regina Coeli Hostel
8-10 Lake Glen Avenue, Belfast BT11 8FE
Tel 028-90612473
Night shelter for destitute and homeless
women. Under the care of the Legion of
Mary

Society of St Vincent de Paul
196-200 Antrim Road, Belfast BT15 2AJ
Tel 028-90351561
Regional Administrator
Ms Pauline Brown

St Joseph's Centre for the Deaf
321 Grosvenor Road, Belfast BT12 4LP
Tel 028-90713401
The Centre provides a wide range of
facilities for the deaf.
Co-ordinator: Very Rev Patrick Devlin
Northern Diocesan Lay Chaplain:
Ms Denise Flack
Tel 078-77643961

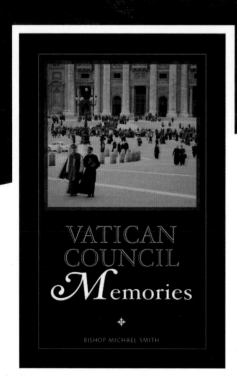

VATICAN COUNCIL eMemories

BISHOP MICHAEL SMITH

ISBN **978 1 80097 011 3**
PRICE **€19.99/£17.99**

Pope John XXIII's announcement on 25 January 1959, just three months after his election as pope, of his intention to convoke an ecumenical council came as a great surprise to all. The Second Vatican Council officially opened on 11 October 1962, welcoming more than two thousand bishops from across the world to Rome for what would become one of the most influential events in the history of the Catholic Church.

In *Vatican Council Memories*, Bishop Michael Smith revisits his experiences as a young student of the Pontifical Irish College in Rome invited to join a small group tasked with creating the official record of the events of the Council. This book offers readers a unique insight into the Council's many remarkable moments, decisions and debates, highlighting the significant figures, including the many Irish participants, who helped shape this historic event.

Bishop Michael Smith is bishop emeritus of Meath and a native of Oldcastle in County Meath. Following an education at the Pontifical Irish College, Rome, he was ordained a priest in 1963. He served in the cathedral parish of Mullingar and as chaplain to St Loman's Hospital. He was ordained auxiliary bishop of Meath in 1984 and coadjutor bishop in 1988.

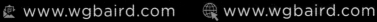

Providing Professional Ethical Advice

L&P specialises in providing ethical investment management and stewardship services to religious congregations, charities and non-profit organisations, trusts and endowments.

With over 30 years' experience, we work with many organisations worldwide. Our team of dedicated professionals specialises in the following areas:

CONSULTANCY
- Resource Assessment
- Strategic Planning
- Trust & Charity Law

STEWARDSHIP
- Accounting & Finance
- Business Management
- Corporate Governance
- Communication & Training

ETHICAL INVESTMENT MANAGEMENT

L&P forms part of the Cantor Fitzgerald Group, a leading global financial services firm with offices in 25 countries.

With a proud history of stockbroking and servicing our clients and financial advisors in Ireland since 1995, Cantor Fitzgerald Ireland provides a full suite of investment services and is committed to the highest level of service.

75 St Stephen's Green, Dublin 2, Ireland
Tel: + 353 1 633 3826
Email: L&P@cantor.com

L&P **CANTOR** *Fitzgerald*

www.cantorfitzgerald.ie/LPgroup

Commercial Acumen with an Ethical Foundation

Cantor Fitzgerald Ireland is regulated by the Central Bank of Ireland and is a member firm of the Irish Stock Exchange and the London Stock Exchange.
L&P Trustee Services Ltd is authorised as a Trust & Company Service Provider.

DIOCESE OF DROMORE

PATRONS OF THE DIOCESE
ST PATRICK, 17 MARCH; ST COLMAN, 7 JUNE

INCLUDES PORTIONS OF COUNTIES ANTRIM, ARMAGH AND DOWN

SEDE VACANTE

Apostolic Administrator
Most Rev Eamon Martin DD

Residence:
Bishop's House,
44 Armagh Road,
Newry, Co Down BT35 6PN
Tel 028-30262444
Fax 028-30260496
Email
bishop@dromorediocese.org
Website dromorediocese.org

ST PATRICK AND ST COLMAN'S CATHEDRAL, NEWRY

ewry cathedral was founded 1825, at the centre of a owing and prosperous town. symbolised, in many ways, e increasing confidence of the cal Catholic population of the ay, especially the newly merging Catholic middle class.

e cathedral was designed by omas J. Duff, a prominent chitect in the northern part of eland at the turn of the ntury. The building was dicated in May 1829 by the en Irish Primate, Dr Curtis. It as believed to be the first ajor dedication ceremony in eland following the granting Catholic Emancipation.

riginally, the cathedral was arsely furnished, and it ceived its first significant terior decoration in 1851. The ilding was developed nsiderably between 1888 and 391. During these years, its vo transepts were added and handsome bell tower erected. om 1904 to 1909, Bishop enry O'Neill oversaw a further ajor phase of building. The ain body of the church was tended in length by some rty feet and a new sanctuary as added. Much of the ternal fabric of the cathedral, we know it today, belongs to is period. Rich interior mosaic coration was undertaken, de chapels were constructed d the cathedral's tubular gan was installed. The thedral was solemnly nsecrated in July 1925 – a ntury after its foundation! It enjoys e joint patronage of Ss Patrick and lman.

terior renovation was necessary in the ake of the Second Vatican Council. This work of extending and refurbishing the sanctuary area was undertaken by Bishop Francis Gerard Brooks from 1989 to 1990. It included the construction of the present marble altar, the rebuilding of the reredos of the former high altar, now in three parts, and the relocation of the bishop's chair to the front of the sanctuary. This work of renovation has earned widespread praise in the field of contemporary ecclesiastical architecture.

Most Rev John McAreavey DD
Retired Bishop of Dromore; born 1949;
ordained priest 10 June 1973; ordained
Bishop of Dromore 19 September 1999;
resigned 1 March 2018
Residence: Bishop's House,
44 Armagh Road, Newry,
Co Down BT35 6PN

CHAPTER

Prebendaries
Saint Colman and Lann: Vacant
Drumeragh: Vacant
Lanronan: Vacant
Aghaderg
Very Rev Canon Liam Stevenson PP, VF
Shankill
Clondallon: Vacant
Newry
Kilmycon: Vacant
Downaclone
Very Rev Canon Gerald Powell VF
Tullylish
Retired Members, Honorary Canons:
Very Rev Francis Boyle
Rt Rev Mgr Arthur Byrne
Very Rev Michael Hackett
Rt Rev Mgr A. Hamill
Very Rev Canon John Kearney
Very Rev Canon Frank Kearney

ADMINISTRATION

Vicar General
Vacant

Chancellor/Diocesan Secretary
Very Rev Canon Gerald Powell
c/o Bishop's House, 44 Armagh Road,
Newry, Co Down BT35 6PN

Council of Priests
Chairman
Vacant

Dromore Diocesan Trust
Diocese of Dromore Trustee is the
Trustee for the Dromore Diocesan Trust
Most Rev Eamon Martin *(Chairperson)*
Very Rev Feidhlimidh Magennis,
Rt Rev Mgr Hugh Connolly
Mr Michael Gillen,
Mr Brendan Jackson,
Mrs Nuala McKeagney
Mr Tony McCusker
Mrs Oonagh Murtagh

Finance Council
Administrator and Secretary
Very Rev Feidhllimidh Magennis
St Mary's University College, Belfast
Finance and Compliance Officer
c/o Diocesan Office, Bishop's House,
44 Armagh Road, Newry,
Co Down BT35 6PN
Tel 028-30262444
Email finance@dromorediocese.org

Members of Diocesan Finance Council
Chairman: Most Rev Eamon Martin DD
Minute Secretary: Agatha Larkin
Very Rev Charlie Byrne
Mr Michael Gillen
Mr Gerry Gray
Mr John Heenan
Mr David Finan

Bishop's Secretary
Miss Agatha Larkin
Bishop's House, Newry, Co Down
Tel 028-30262444
Email agatha@dromorediocese.org

CATECHETICS EDUCATION

Diocesan Advisers for Religious Education
Primary Schools: Mrs Joan Aldridge and
Mr Gerard McBrien
c/o Diocesan Office, Bishop's House,
44 Armagh Road, Newry,
Co Down BT35 6PN
Tel 028-30262444
Post-Primary Schools: Mrs Susan Morgan
c/o Diocesan Office, Bishop's House,
44 Armagh Road, Newry,
Co Down BT35 6PN
Tel 028-30262444

Diocesan Education Committee
Chairman: Vacant

PASTORAL

ACCORD
Director: Vacant
c/o Diocesan Office, 44 Armagh Road,
Newry, Co Down BT35 6PN
Tel 028-30262444

Adult Faith Development
Deacon Kevin Devine
c/o 70 North Street, Lurgan,
Co Armagh BT67 9AH
Tel 028-38323161
Eail afmcmahon@hotmail.co.uk

Chaplaincy to Deaf People
Contact: Fr Colum Wright
c/o Diocesan Office, Bishop's House,
44 Armagh Road, Newry,
Co Down BT35 6PN
Email colum.wright@btinternet.com

Communications
Press Officer
Rev Feidhlimidh Magennis
c/o Bishop's House, Newry, Co Down

Dromore Clerical Provident Society
c/o Bishop's House,
44 Armagh Road, Newry,
Co Down BT35 6PN
Tel 028-30262444

Ecumenism
Director: Deacon Frank Rice
c/o Parochial House, Maypole Hill,
Dromore, Co Down BT25 1BQ
Email ricefa@aol.com

Emigrant Services
Director: c/o Diocesan Office,
44 Armagh Road, Newry,
Co Down BT35 6PN
Tel 028-30262444

Immigrant Services
c/o Diocesan Office, 44 Armagh Road,
Newry, Co Down BT35 6PN
Tel 028-30262444

Knock Diocesan Pilgrimage
Director: c/o Diocesan Office,
44 Armagh Road, Newry,
Co Down BT35 6PN
Tel 028-30262444

Lourdes Diocesan Pilgrimage
Director: Very Rev Brian Fitzpatrick
c/o Diocesan Office, 44 Armagh Road,
Newry, Co Down BT35 6PN
Tel 028-30262444

Marriage Tribunal
Armagh Regional Marriage Tribunal,
Diocesan Office, 44 Armagh Road,
Newry, Co Down BT35 6PN
Tel 028-30269836

Permanent Diaconate
Director: Deacon Kevin Devine
c/o Parochial House, 70 North Street,
Lurgan,Co Armagh BT67 9AH
Email kevinbdevine@btinternet.com

Pioneer Total Abstinence Association
Diocesan Director
c/o Diocesan Office, 44 Armagh Road,
Newry, Co Down BT35 6PN
Tel 028-30262444

Pontifical Mission Societies and
Dromore/Lodwar Mission Project
Diocesan Director: c/o Diocesan Office,
44 Armagh Road, Newry,
Co Down BT35 6PN

Safeguarding Children
Diocesan Offices, 44 Armagh Road,
Newry, Co Down BT35 6PN
Designated person and Director
Mrs Joan Aldridge
Email safeguarding@dromorediocese.or
Chair, Safeguarding Committee
Mrs Bridget McConville

Special Needs Committee – Reachout
Mrs Anne Loughlin
22 Dallan Hill, Warrenpoint
Tel 077-34330336

Vocations
Director: Very Rev Brian Fitzpatrick
The Presbytery, 11 Tullygally Road,
Legahory, Craigavon, BT65 5BL

Youth
Chair Youth Commission: Vacant
Director: Mrs Frances Fox
Pastoral Centre, The Mall, Newry
Tel 028-30833898
Email dromoreyd@btconnect.com

Allianz ⑪

outh Ministry
rs Frances Fox
storal Centre, The Mall, Newry
l 028-30833898
nail dromoreyd@btconnect.com

PARISHES

ensal parishes are listed first. Other
arishes follow alphabetically. Hostorical
ames are given in parenthesis).

EWRY
ry Rev Canon Francis Brown Adm
v Alphonsus Chukwunenye (MSP)
v Callum Young
v Wojciech Stachyra (SCHr)
athedral Presbytery, 38 Hill Street,
ewry BT34 1AT
l 028-30262586 Fax 028-30267505
nail office@newrycathedralparish.org

LONALLON, ST PETER'S (WARRENPOINT)
ry Rev Brendan Kearns PP
rochial House, Great George's Street,
arrenpoint, Co Down BT34 3NF
l 028-41754684 Fax 028-41754685
rish Office: Tel 028-41759981
x 028-41759980
nail
arrenpointparish@dromorediocese.org

GHADERG
ry Rev Conor McConville PP
Monteith Road, Annaclone,
anbridge, Co Down BT32 5AQ
l 028-40671201
nail
hadergparish@dromorediocese.org

NNACLONE
ry Rev Conor McConville PP
Monteith Road, Annaclone,
anbridge, Co Down BT32 5AQ
l 028-40671201
nail
naacloneparish@dromorediocese.org

LONALLON, ST MARY'S (BURREN)
ry Rev Brendan Kearns PP
rochial House, Great George's Street,
arrenpoint, Co Down BT34 3NF
l 028-41754684 Fax 028-41754685
nail burrenparish@dromorediocese.org

LONALLON, ST PATRICK'S (MAYOBRIDGE)
t Rev Mgr Hugh Connolly PP
5 Chapel Hill, Mayobridge,
ewry, Co Down BT34 2EX
l 028-30850089
rish Office: Tel 028-30850270
nail
ayobridgeparish@dromorediocese.org

LONDUFF (HILLTOWN)
ry Rev Charles Byrne PP
1 Newry Road, Rathfriland,
o Down BT34 5AP
l 028-40630306
nail
onduffparish@dromorediocese.org

DONAGHMORE
Rev John Brown (SMA)
2 Moneymore Road, Glenn, Newry,
Co Down BT34 1RN
Parish Office: Tel 028-30821549
Email
donaghmoreparish@dromorediocese.org

DROMORE
Very Rev Feidhlimidh Magennis PP
Maypole Hill, Dromore,
Co Down BT35 1BQ
Rev Frank Rice, Permanent Deacon
c/o Maypole Hill, Dromore,
Co Down BT35 1BQ
Parish Office: Tel 028-92692218
Email
dromoreparish@dromorediocese.org

DRUMGATH (RATHFRILAND)
Very Rev Charles Byrne PP
91 Newry Road, Rathfriland,
Co Down BT34 5AP
Tel 028-40630306
Parish Office: Tel 028-30850270
Email
drumgathparish@dromorediocese.org

DRUMGOOLAND
Very Rev Peter C. McNeill PP
58 Ballydrumman Road,
Castlewellan, Co Down BT31 9UG
Tel 028-40650207 Fax 028-40650205
Email
dromaradgooland@dromorediocese.org

DROMARA
Very Rev Peter C. McNeill PP
58 Ballydrumman Road,
Castlewellan, Co Down BT31 9UG
Email dromaradgooland@aol.co.uk
Tel 028-40650207 Fax 028-40650205
Email
drumaradgooland@dromorediocese.org

KILBRONEY (ROSTREVOR)
Very Rev Demond Mooney PP
44 Church Street, Rostrevor,
Co Down BT34 3BB
Tel 028-41738277 Fax 028-41738315
Parish Office: Tel 028-41739495
Email
kilbroneyparish@dromorediocese.org

MAGHERADROLL (BALLYNAHINCH)
Very Rev Brian Brown PP
Church Street, Ballynahinch,
Co Down BT24 8LP
Tel/Fax 028-97562410
Email
magheradrollparish@dromorediocese.org
Parish Office: 028-97565429

MAGHERALIN
Very Rev Feidhlimidh Magennis PP
25 Bottier Road, Moira, Craigavon,
Co Armagh BT67 0PE
Tel 028-92611347
Parish Office: 028-92617435
Email
magheralinparish@dromorediocese.org

MOYRAVERTY (CRAIGAVON)
Very Rev Brian Fitzpatrick PP
The Presbytery, 11 Tullygally Road,
Legahory, Craigavon BT65 5BL
Tel 028-38341901
Very Rev Michael Maginn
The Presbytery, Tullygally Road,
Legahory, Craigavon BT65 5BL
Tel 028-38311872
Rev Colum Murphy CC
The Presbytery, Tullygally Road,
Legahory, Craigavon BT65 5BL
Rev Gerry Heaney, Permanent Deacon
c/o The Presbytery, Tullygally Road,
Legahory, Craigavon BT65 5BL
Parish Office: Moyraverty,
10 Tullygally Road
Tel 028-38343013
Email
moyravertyparish@dromorediocese.org

SAVAL
Very Rev Canon Francis Brown PP
Cathedral Presbytery,
38 Hill Street, Newry BT34 1AT
Tel 028-30256372
Email savalparish@dromorediocese.org

SEAGOE (DERRYMACASH)
Very Rev Brian Fitzpatrick PP
The Presbytery, 11 Tullygally Road,
Legahory, Craigavon BT65 5BL
Tel 028-38341901
Very Rev Michael Maginn
The Presbytery, Tullygally Road,
Legahory, Craigavon BT65 5BL
Tel 028-38311872
Rev Colum Murphy CC
The Presbytery, Tullygally Road,
Legahory, Craigavon BT65 5BL
Email seagoeparish@dromorediocese.org

SEAPATRICK (BANBRIDGE)
Very Rev Andrew McMahon PP
6 Scarva Road, Banbridge,
Co Down BT32 3AR
Tel 028-40662136
Rev Michael Rooney, Permanent Deacon
Parish Office
Tel 028-40624950 Fax 028-40626547
Email
seapatrickparish@dromorediocese.org

SHANKILL, ST PAUL'S (LURGAN)
Very Rev Canon Liam Stevenson PP, VF
70 North Street, Lurgan,
Co Armagh BT67 9AH
Tel 028-38323161
Very Rev Colum Wright
Lisadell, 54 Francis Street,
Lurgan, Co Armagh BT66 6DL
Tel 028-38327173
Rev Josef Wozniak (SC) CC
68 North Street, Lurgan,
Co Armagh BT67 9AH
Tel 028-38323161 Fax 028-38347927
St Paul's Parish Office: Tel 028-38321289
Email
stpaulsparishlurgan@dromorediocese.org

SHANKILL, ST PETER'S (LURGAN)
Very Rev Canon Liam Stevenson PP, VF
70 North Street, Lurgan,
Co Armagh BT67 9AH
Tel 028-38323161
Very Rev Colum Wright
Lisadell, 54 Francis Street,
Lurgan, Co Armagh BT66 6DL
Tel 028-38327173
Rev Josef Wozniak (SC) CC
68 North Street, Lurgan,
Co Armagh BT67 9AH
Tel 028-38323161
Rev Kevin Devine, Permanent Deacon
c/o 70 North Street, Lurgan,
Co Armagh BT67 9AH
Email
stpetersparishlurgan@dromorediocese.org

TULLYLISH
Very Rev Desmond Loughran PP, VF
4 Holymount Road,
Gilford, Craigavon,
Co Armagh BT63 6AT
Tel 028-40624236 Fax 028-40625440
Email gpowellpp@aol.com
Parish Office: Tel 028-40624236
Email
tullylishparish@dromorediocese.org
Website www.tullylish.com

HOSPITALS AND THEIR CHAPLAINS

Craigavon Area Hospital
Co Armagh
Chaplain: Very Rev Michael Maginn PP

District Hospital
Lurgan and Portadown, Co Armagh
Chaplain: Very Rev Michael Maginn PP

Hospice
Southern Area Hospice Services,
St John's House,
Courtenay Hill, Newry,
Co Down BT34 2EB
Tel 028-30267711 Fax 028-30268492
Chaplain: Sr Fiona Galligan

PRIESTS OF THE DIOCESE ELSEWHERE
Very Rev Stephen Ferris
c/o Diocesan Office, Newry
Rev Matthew McConville
c/o Bishop's House
Rev Feidlimidh Magennis LSS
St Mary's University College, Belfast

RETIRED PRIESTS
Very Rev Canon Francis Boyle
Warrenpoint
Rt Rev Mgr Arthur Byrne
Castor's Bay Road, Lurgan
Very Rev John Joe Cunningham
Newcastle, Co Down

Rev Gerard Green
c/o Bishop's House, Newry, Co Down
Very Rev Canon Michael Hackett
Warrenpoint, Co Down
Rt Rev Mgr Aidan Hamill
c/o Bishop's House, Newry, Co Down
Very Rev Canon John Kearney
Warrenpoint, Co Down
Very Rev Canon Frank Kearney
Cabra, Hilltown, Co Down
Very Rev Oliver Mooney
Newry, Co Down
Very Rev Patrick Joe Murray
c/o Diocesan Office, Newry,
Co Down BT35 6PN
Very Rev Canon Gerald Parnell
c/o Bishop's House, Newry, Co Down
Rev Niall Sheehan
Portadown, Co Armagh

RELIGIOUS ORDERS AND CONGREGATIONS

PRIESTS

BENEDICTINES
Holy Cross Abbey, 119 Kilbroney Road,
Rostrevor, Co Down BT34 3BN
Tel 028-41739979
Abbot: Rt Rev Dom Mark-Ephrem M. Nolan (OSB)
Email benedictinemonks@btinternet.com
Website www.benedictinemonks.co.uk

DOMINICANS
St Catherine's,
Newry, Co Down BT35 8BN
Tel 028-30262178
Prior: Very Rev David Tohill (OP)

SOCIETY OF AFRICAN MISSIONS
African Missions, Dromantine, Newry,
Co Down BT34 1RH
Tel 028-30821224
Email sma.dromantine@sma.ie
Superior: Rev Damian Bresnahan (SMA)

Dromantine Retreat and Conference
Centre, Newry, Co Down BT34 1RH
Tel 028-30821964 Fax 028-30281704
Email
admin@dromantineconference.com
Website www.dromantineconference.com
Director: Rev Damian Bresnahan (SMA)

SISTERS

CONGREGATION OF THE SISTERS OF MERCY
Convent of Mercy, Catherine Street,
Newry, Co Down BT34 6JG
Tel 028-30262065/30264964
Community: 8

Convent of Mercy, 3 Glenashley,
Rostrevor, Co Down BT34 3FW
Tel 028-41738356
Community: 2

89 North Street, Lurgan,
Co Armagh BT67 9AH
Tel 028-38347858

Convent of Mercy, 9 Queen Street,
Warrenpoint, Co Down BT34 3HZ
Tel 028-41752221

12 Cloghogue Heights, Newry,
Co Down BT35 8BA
Tel 028-30261628

Sisters of Mercy, Edward Street,
Lurgan, Co Armagh BT66 6DB
Tel 028-38322635
Community: 7

No 4 Ummericam Road, Silverbridge,
Newry, Co Down BT35 9PB
Tel 028-30860441

8 The Woodlands,
Lower Dromore Road,
Warrenpoint, Co Down BT34 6WL
Tel 028-41752383

17 Oakleigh Grove, Lurgan,
Co Armagh BT67 9AY
Tel 028-38347984

204 Drumglass, Craigavon,
Co Armagh BT65 5BB
Tel 028-38343447

42 Antrim Road, Lurgan,
Co Armagh BT67 9BW
Tel 028-39328742

5A Catherine Street, Newry,
Co Down BT35 6JG
Tel 028-30264615

5B Catherine Street, Newry,
Co Down BT35 6JG
Tel 028-30265342

1 Kildarragh Close,
Old Warrenpoint Road, Newry,
Co Down BT34 2SU
Tel 028-30267141

Sisters of Mercy, 49 Ardfreelan,
Rathfriland Road, Newry,
Co Down BT34 1CD
Tel 028-30250951

7 Daly Park, Silverbridge,
Newry, Co Down BT35 9PJ

Allianz ⑪

ters of Mercy, 2 Carrickree,
dle Loanan, Co Down BT34 3FA
028-41752347

Catherine Street, Newry,
Down, BT35 6JG
028-30833641

Dominican Court,
wry, Co Down
028-30265184

t 4, Carlinn's Cove,
arrenpoint Road, Rostrevor,
Down BT34 3GJ
028-41737751

Bracken Close,
magh Road, Newry,
Down BT35 6RW
028-30250630

Planting Road, Cashel,
Jllaghbawn, Newry,
Down BT35 9YU
028-30888990

MISSIONARY SISTERS OF THE ASSUMPTION
Assumption Convent,
34 Crossgar Road, Ballynahinch,
Co Down BT24 8EN
Tel 028-97561765
Superior: Sr Maureen Carville
Email maureenc@msassumption.org
Community: 10
Assumption Grammar School
Tel 028-97562250
Pupils: 840

SISTERS OF OUR LADY OF APOSTLES
Rostrevor, Newry, Co Down
Tel 028-41737653 Fax 028-417377656
Community: 2
Email olagreendale@hotmail.com
1 Greendale Crescent, Greenpark Road,
Rostrevor, Newry, Co Down BT34 3HF

SISTERS OF ST CLARE
St Clare's Convent,
12 Ashgrove Avenue, Newry,
Co Down BT34 1PR
Tel 028-30252179
Contact: Sr Tarcisius Traynor
Community: 30

St Clare's Convent,
42 Glenvale Road, Newry,
Co Down BT34 2RD
Tel 028-30260116
Community: 3
Sacred Heart Grammar School,
10 Ashgrove Avenue,
Newry, Co Down BT34 1PR
Tel 028-30264632. Pupils: 875

EDUCATIONAL INSTITUTIONS

St Colman's College (Diocesan College)
Violet Hill,
Newry, Co Down
Tel 028-30262451
Principal: Mr Cormac McKinney
Vice Principal: Vacant

CHARITABLE AND OTHER SOCIETIES

ACCORD
Cana House,
Newry Parish Pastoral Centre, The Mall,
Newry, Co Down
Tel 028-30263577

Society of St Vincent de Paul
Conferences at:
Ballynahinch (St Patrick's)
Banbridge (St Patrick's)
Craigavon (St Anthony's)
Dromore (St Colman's)
Gilford (St John's)
Hilltown (St John's)
Laurencetown (St Patrick's)
Lurgan (St Peter's)
Newry (Cathedral)
Newry (St Brigid's)
Rathfriland (St Marys)
Rostrevor (St Bronach's)
Warrenpoint (St Patrick's)

DIOCESE OF ELPHIN

PATRONS OF THE DIOCESE
ST ASICUS, 27 APRIL; IMMACULATE CONCEPTION, 8 DECEMBER

INCLUDES PORTIONS OF COUNTIES ROSCOMMON, SLIGO AND GALWAY

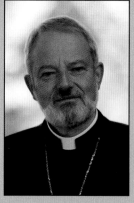

Most Rev Kevin Doran MA, PhD
Bishop of Elphin;
born 26 June 1953;
ordained priest 6 July 1977;
ordained Bishop of Elphin
13 July 2014

Residence: St Mary's,
Temple Street, Sligo
Tel 071-9150106
Email office@elphindiocese.ie

CATHEDRAL OF THE IMMACULATE CONCEPTION, SLIGO

The cathedral church dominates the skyline of Sligo town. It was erected during the episcopate of Bishop Laurence Gillooly (1858–1895), whose knowledge of ecclesiastical architecture is imprinted on every stone.

The foundation stone was laid on 6 October 1868. It was designed by a renowned English architect, George Goldie, and was modelled on Normano-Romano-Byzantine style. It was acclaimed by an eminent architect as a 'poem in stone'. It is 275 feet long, with transepts and nave, and can accommodate 1,000 people. A square tower incorporating the main entrance to the cathedral is surmounted by a four-sided pyramidal spire which reaches a height of 210 feet. The stained-glass windows and the original high altar are magnificent works of art.

Although the cathedral was open for public worship in 1874, it wasn't until 1882 that all construction work was completed. The cathedral was finally consecrated on 1 July 1897 and dedicated in honour of the Immaculate Conception of the Blessed Virgin Mary.

The cathedral has undergone extensive renovations on two occasions since it was erected, including the remodelling of the sanctuary to comply with liturgical norms in 1970.

Allianz ⑪

CHAPTER

Very Rev Canon Joseph Fitzgerald
Very Rev Canon Liam Devine
Very Rev Canon Eugene McLoughlin
Very Rev Canon Gerard Hanly VF
Very Rev Canon Niall Ahern
Very Rev Canon Ciaran Whitney
Very Rev Canon Thomas Hever VG

ADMINISTRATION

College of Consultors
Very Rev Canon Thomas Hever PP, VG
Very Rev John McManus PP, VG
Very Rev Canon Gerard Hanly PP, VF
Very Rev Raymond Milton PP, VF
Very Rev Michael Drumm PP
Very Rev Patrick Lombard PP, VF
Very Rev Eamonn O'Connor PP, VF

Vicars General
Very Rev Canon Tom Hever PP, VG
Very Rev John McManus PP, VG

Diocesan Education Commission
Chairperson: Very Rev Michael Drumm PP
St Mary's, Sligo
Tel 071-9150106

Vicars Forane
Very Rev Patrick Lombard (Sligo)
Very Rev Kevin Fallon (Roscommon)
Very Rev Canon Gerard Hanly (Boyle)
Very Rev Raymond Milton (Athlone)
Very Rev John McManus (Castlerea)
Very Rev Eamonn O'Connor
(Strokestown)

Council of Priests
Very Rev Declan Boyce (SPS) Adm
Very Rev Canon Liam Devine PE
Very Rev Pravin Dhason PP
Very Rev Michael Drumm PP
Very Rev Stephen Ezenwegbu PP
Very Rev Canon Gerard Hanly PP, VF
Very Rev Canon Thomas Hever PP, VG
Very Rev Patrick Lombard PP, VF
Very Rev Canon Eugene McLoughlin PE
Very Rev John McManus PP, VG
Very Rev Raymond Milton PP
Very Rev Eamonn O'Connor PP, VF

Data Protection Officer
Email dpo@elphindiocese.ie

Diocesan Finance Council
Secretary
Very Rev Raymond Milton PP, VF
St Mary's, Temple Street, Sligo
Tel 071-9150106
Email finance@elphindiocese.ie

Diocesan Secretary and Diocesan Communications Officer
Ms Sheena Darcy
St Mary's, Temple Street, Sligo
Tel 071-9150106
Email office@elphindiocese.ie

Finance and Asset Manager
Mr Conor Ward
St Mary's, Temple Street, Sligo
Tel 071-9151080
Email finance@elphindiocese.ie

Chancellor
Very Rev Thomas Hever PP, VG
St Mary's, Temple Street, Sligo
Tel 071-9150106
Email chancellor@elphindiocese.ie

Safeguarding
Director: Ms Mary Nicholson
St Mary's, Temple Street, Sligo
Tel 071-9151086/086-3750277

Secretary to the Bishop
Ms Sheena Darcy
St Mary's, Temple Street, Sligo
Tel 071-9150106
Email bishopsecretary@elphindiocese.ie

CATECHETICS EDUCATION

Religious Education (Primary Schools)
Diocesan Advisors
Ms Teresa Melia
Ms Kathleen O'Dowd
c/o St Mary's, Temple Street, Sligo

Education (Post-Primary)
Religious Education Advisor
Dr Justin Harkin

Education Commission
Chairperson
Rev Michael Drumm
St Mary's, Temple Street, Sligo
Tel 071-9150106

LITURGY

Liturgical Music
Adviser Church Organ Music:
Mr Charles O'Connor
Tel 071-9145722

Diocesan Magazine
The Angelus, St Mary's, Sligo
Tel 071-9150106
Email angeluspaper@gmail.com

PASTORAL

ACCORD
Director: Rev James Murray CC
Carraroe, Sligo
Tel 071-9162136

Diocesan Catechists (Partners in the Gospel)
Co-ordinator: Very Rev Michael Drumm
St Columba's Rosses Point, Co Sligo
Tel 071-9177133

Diocesan Pastoral Council
Chair: Mr Tomás Kenny
Secretary: Ms Bernie Flynn

Ecumenism
Very Rev Pat Lombard PP
St Anne's, Sligo
Tel 071-9145028

Marriage Tribunal
(See Marriage Tribunals section)

Pastoral Development
Director: Dr Justin Harkin
Pastoral Development Office,
Church Grounds, St Coman's Club,
Abbey Street, Roscommon
Tel 087-6171526
Email justin@elphindiocese.ie

Permanent Diaconate
Director: Most Rev Kevin Doran
Director of Formation
Very Rev Michael Drumm

Pilgrimage Director (Lourdes)
Very Rev Raymond Milton PP
Knockcroghery, Co Roscommon
Tel 090-6661127

Pioneer Total Abstinence Association
Diocesan Director
Vacant

Pontifical Mission Societies
Diocesan Director
Deacon Wando deAraujo
33 Ardsallagh Woods,
Roscommon, Co Roscommon
Tel 087-2600338

Retreat Centre
Star of the Sea Retreat Centre,
Mullaghmore, Co Sligo
Tel 071-9176722
www.statoftheseacentre.com

Social Services
Director: Ms Christine McTaggart
Sligo Social Services, Charles Street, Sligo
Tel 071-9145682

Travellers
Chaplain: Rev John Carroll (SPS)
Cregg House, Rosses Point, Co Sligo
Tel 071-9177241

Vocations
Director
Very Rev John Gannon PP
Tulsk, Co Roscommon
Tel 071-9639005
Email vocations@elphindiocese.ie

Youth Ministry
St Mary's, Sligo
Email youth@elphindiocese.ie

PARISHES

Mensal parishes are listed first. Other parishes follow alphabetically. Historical names are given in parentheses.

SLIGO, ST MARY'S
Very Rev Declan Boyce (SPS) Adm
Rev Willibrord Sakwe CC
Rev Victor Samugana (MSP) CC
St Mary's, Temple Street, Sligo
Tel 071-9162670/9162769

SLIGO, ST JOSEPH'S AND CALRY
Very Rev Noel Rooney PP
279 Sunset Drive, Cartron Point, Sligo
Tel 071-9142422
Rev Hugh McGonagle CC
7 Elm Park, Ballinode, Sligo
Tel 071-9143430

SLIGO, ST ANNE'S
Very Rev Patrick Lombard PP, VF
Tel 071-9145028
Rev Stephen Walsh (CSSp) CC
Tel 071-9145028
St Anne's, Sligo
Rev James Murray CC
Carraroe, Co Sligo
Tel 071-9162136
Rev Joseph Wenjeslaus CC
St Anne's, Sligo
Tel 071-9145028

AHAMLISH (GRANGE AND CLIFFONEY)
Very Rev Christopher McHugh PP
Grange, Co Sligo
Tel 071-9163100

AHASCRAGH (AHASCRAGH AND CALTRA)
Very Rev John Mahony PP
Ahascragh, Ballinasloe, Co Galway
Tel 090-9688617

ARDCARNE (COOTEHALL)
Very Rev Brendan McDonagh (SPS) PP
Cootehall, Boyle, Co Roscommon
Tel 071-9667004

ATHLEAGUE (ATHLEAGUE AND FUERTY)
Very Rev Christopher Edebianga (MSP) PP
Parochial House,
Athleague, Co Roscommon
Tel 090-6663338

ATHLONE, SS PETER AND PAUL'S
Very Rev John Deignan PP
10 Ashford, Monksland,
Athlone, Co Roscommon
Tel 090-6493262
Rev Innocent Sunu CC
Forthill House, The Batteries, Athlone,
Co Westmeath
Tel 090-6492171
Rev Michael Hickey (CSSp) CC
Drum, Athlone, Co Roscommon
Tel 090-6437125

AUGHRIM (AUGHRIM AND KILMORE)
Very Rev Stephen Ezenwegbu PP
The Presbytery, Elphin, Co Roscommon
Tel 071-9630486

AGHANAGH (BALLINAFAD)
Deacon Damien Kearns Adm
Ballinafad, Boyle, Co Roscommon
Tel 071-9666006

BALLINAMEEN (KILNAMANAGH AND ESTERSNOW)
Very Rev Lawrence Ebuk (MSP) PP
Ballinameen, Boyle, Co Roscommon
Tel 071-9668104

BALLINTUBBER (BALLINTOBER AND BALLYMOE)
Very Rev Julian Lupot PP
Tel 094-9655602
Rev Patrick O'Toole (CSSp) CC
Ballintubber, Castlerea,
Co Roscommon

BALLYFORAN (DYSART AND TISRARA)
Very Rev Francis Beirne PP
Tisrara, Four Roads, Co Roscommon
Tel 090-6623313

BALLYGAR (KILLIAN AND KILLERORAN)
Very Rev Douglas Zaggi PP
Ballygar, Co Galway
Tel 090-6624637
Rev Louis Lohan
Parish Chaplain

BOYLE
Very Rev Canon Gerard Hanly PP, VF
Tel 071-9662218
Rev Jonas Rebamontan CC
Tel 071-9662012
Boyle, Co Roscommon

CASTLEREA (KILKEEVAN)
Very Rev John McManus PP, VG
Parochial House,
Castlerea, Co Roscommon
Tel 094-9620040
Rev Kevin Reynolds (MHM) CC
Castlerea, Co Roscommon
Tel 094-9620039
Deacon Christopher Garrett

CROGHAN (KILLUKIN AND KILLUMMOD)
Very Rev Alan Conway PP
Drumlion, Carrick-on-Shannon,
Co Roscommon
Tel 071-9620415

DRUMCLIFF/MAUGHEROW
Very Rev Canon Thomas Hever PP, VG
Drumcliff, Sligo
Tel 071-9142779

ELPHIN (ELPHIN AND CREEVE)
Very Rev Stephen Ezenwegbu PP
Elphin, Co Roscommon
Tel 071-9630486
Very Rev John J Gannon PE
Elphin, Co Roscommon
Tel 071-9635058

FAIRYMOUNT (TIBOHINE)
Very Rev Micheál Donnelly PP
Parochial House, Ballingare,
Co Roscommon
Tel 094-9870039

FRENCHPARK (KILCORKEY AND FRENCHPARK)
Very Rev Micheál Donnelly PP
Parochial House, Ballinagare,
Co Roscommon
Tel 094-9870039

GEEVAGH
Very Rev Laurence Cullen PP
Geevagh, Boyle, Co Roscommon
Tel 071-9647107

KILBEGNET AND GLINSK
Very Rev Donal Morris PP
Parochial House, Garraun South,
Creggs, Co Roscommon
Tel 090-6621127

KILBRIDE (FOURMILEHOUSE)
Very Rev Pravin Dhason PP
Tel 087-1889885
Rev Eamon Conaty (SSC)
Parish Chaplain
Fourmilehouse, Roscommon
Tel 090-6629518

KILGEFIN (BALLAGH, CLOONTUSKERT, AND CURRAGHROE)
Very Rev Daniel Udofia (MSP) PP
Parochial House,
Ballyleague, Co Roscommon
Tel 043-3321171

KILGLASS (KILGLASS AND ROOSKEY)
Very Rev Evaristus Nkede PP
Rooskey, Carrick-on-Shannon,
Co Roscommon
Tel 071-9638014

KILTOOM (KILTOOM AND CAM)
Very Rev Michael McManus PP
Kiltoom, Athlone,
Co Roscommon
Tel 090-6489105

KNOCKCROGHERY/ST JOHN'S/RAHARA
Very Rev Raymond Milton PP, VF
Knockcroghery, Roscommon
Tel 090-6661115
Rev Joseph Ali CC
St John's Presbytery,
Lecarrow, Co Roscommon
Tel 090-6661115
Email knockcrogheyparish1@gmail.com

LOUGHGLYNN (LOUGHGLYNN AND LISACUL)
Very Rev Glenn Alipoyo PP
Loughglynn, Castlerea, Co Roscommon
Tel 094-9880007

ORAN (CLOVERHILL)
Very Rev Pravin Dhason PP
Cloverhill, Co Roscommon
Tel 090-6626275/087-1889885

RIVERSTOWN
Very Rev Yashin Jos PP
Parochial House,
Sooey, via Boyle, Co Sligo
Tel 071-9165144
Very Rev A.B. O'Shea PE
Rowantree Cottage, Church Grounds,
Riverstown, Co Sligo
Email aboshea@eircom.net

ROSCOMMON
Very Rev Kevin Fallon PP, VF
Parochial House, Roscommon
Tel 090-6626298
Rev Raul Cino CC
Curate's Residence, Abbey Street,
Roscommon
Tel 090-6626189
Rev Sean Beirne CC
Kilteevan, Roscommon
Tel 090-6626374
Very Rev Canon Joseph Fitzgerald
5 Hawthorn Park,
Ballygar, via Roscommon, Co Galway

ROSSES POINT
Very Rev Michael Drumm PP
St Columba's, Rosses Point, Co Sligo
Tel 071-9177133

STRANDHILL/RANSBORO
Very Rev Canon Niall Ahern PP
Strandhill, Co Sligo
Tel 071-9168147
Rev Christopher McCrann CC
Knocknahur, Sligo
Tel 071-9128470

STROKESTOWN (KILTRUSTAN, LISSONUFFY AND CLOONFINLOUGH)
Very Rev Eamonn O'Connor PP, VF
Strokestown, Co Roscommon
Tel 071-9633027

TARMONBARRY
Very Rev Jaroslaw (Jarek) Maszkiewicz PP
Carraun, Whitehall,
Tarmonbarry, Co Roscommon
Tel 085-2727279

TULSK (OGULLA AND BASLIC)
Very Rev John Gannon PP
Tulsk, Castlerea, Co Roscommon
Tel 071-9639005

CHAPLAINS

Chaplains to Overseas Communities
Deacon Wando de Araujo
Chaplain to Brazilian Community,
c/o Parish Office, Roscommon Town
Tel 090-6626298
Rev Bart Parys (SVD)
Chaplain to Polish Community,
Donamon Castle, Donamon,
Co Roscommon
Tel 086-3718883
Rev Julian Lupot
Chaplain to Filipino Community,
Presbytery, Ballintubber,
Castlerea, Co Roscommon
Tel 094-9655602

Ballinode Vocational School
Sligo
Tel 071-9147111
Very Rev Noel Rooney PP

Castlerea Prison
Tel 094-9625278
Deacon Seamus Talbot
Prison General Office: 094-9625213

Christian Brothers School
Roscommon
Tel 090-6626189
Very Rev Joe Fitzgerald

Coláiste Chiaráin
Summerhill, Athlone, Co Roscommon
Chaplain: Deacon Tony Larkin
Tel 090-6492383

College of the Immaculate Conception
Summerhill, Sligo
Ms Denise McCann
Tel 071-9160311

Coola Vocational School
Riverstown, Boyle, Co Roscommon
Tel 071-9165144
Very Rev Yashin Jos PP

Cregg House, Sligo
Tel 071-9177241
Rev John Carroll (SPS)

Custume Barracks
Athlone, Co Westmeath
Tel 090-6421277
Rev Declan Shannon CF

Grange Vocational School, Sligo
Tel 071-9163100
Very Rev Christopher McHugh PP

Nazareth House, Sligo
Rt Rev Mgr Gerard Dolan
Church Hill, Sligo
Tel 071-9162278

Plunkett Home
Boyle, Co Roscommon
Tel 071-9662218
Very Rev Canon Gerard Hanly PP, VF

Post-Primary School, Elphin,
Co Roscommon
Tel 071-9635058
Clergy of the Parish

Post-Primary School, Strokestown
Co Roscommon
Tel 071-9633041
Very Rev Eamonn O'Connor PP, VF

Roscommon Hospital
Tel 090-6620039
Sr Gabriel Mee

St Angela's College
Lough Gill, Co Sligo
Tel 071-9143580
Rev Joseph Ali

St Cuan's College
Castleblakeney, Ballinasloe, Co Galway
Tel 090-9678127
Mr Kevin McGeeney

St Mary's Post-Primary School
Ballygar, Co Galway
Tel 090-664637
Very Rev Douglas Zaggi PP

Sligo University Hospital
St Columba's, St John's
Tel 071-9171111
Chaplain: Rev Dr Brian Conlon

PRIESTS OF THE DIOCESE ELSEWHERE

Rev Anthony Conry
Brazil
Rev John Cullen
Chaplain, Nazareth House,
Hammersmith, London

RETIRED PRIESTS

Rev Liam Sharkey
Ballyweelin, Rosses Point, Co Sligo
Very Rev Dominick Gillooly
St Anne's, Sligo
Very Rev Ciarán Whitney
24 Kildallogue Heights,
Strokestown, Co Roscommon
Very Rev Francis Glennon
11 Convent Court, Roscommon
Very Rev Michael Donnelly
c/o St Mary's, Temple Street, Sligo
Very Rev Canon Eugene McLoughlin
1 Convent Court, Roscommon
Very Rev Canon Liam Devine PE
Presbytery, Kilmurray, Co Roscommon
Very Rev Michael Breslin PE
Presbytery, Castlecoote, Co Roscommon

PERMANENT DEACONS

Rev Wando de Araujo
Rev William Gacquin
Rev Damien Kearns
Rev Tony Larkin
Rev Frank McGuinness
Rev David Muldowney
Rev Martin Reidy
Rev Seamus Talbot

RELIGIOUS ORDERS AND CONGREGATIONS

PRIESTS

DIVINE WORD MISSIONARIES
Donamon Castle, Roscommon
Tel 090-6662222 Fax 090-6662511
Rector: Very Rev George Agger (SVD)

DOMINICANS

Holy Cross, Sligo
Tel 071-9142700 Fax 071-9146533
Superior
Rev Augustine Champion (OP)
Email sligofriary@eircom.net

SISTERS

CONGREGATION OF THE SISTERS OF MERCY

Sisters of Mercy,
3 Newtown Terrace,
Athlone, Co Westmeath N37 D266
Tel 090-6473944
Community: 3

Sisters of Mercy,
Dún Mhuire, Lyster Street,
Athlone, Co Westmeath N37 E3V5
Tel 090-6494166 Fax 090-6440079
Community: 19

Sisters of Mercy,
Cois Abhann, Lyster Street,
Athlone, Co Westmeath
Community: 26

St Cecilias, Coosan Road West,
Athlone, Co Westmeath N37 K4X5
Tel 090-6472987
Community: 1

Sisters of Mercy, Bethany,
Chapel Hill, Sligo F91 KCH9
Tel 071-9138498
Community: 6

Our Lady of Mercy,
3 St Patrick's Avenue, Sligo F91 R85D
Tel 071-9142731 Fax 071-9147090
Community: 11

Sisters of Mercy,
No 1 St Patrick's Avenue,
Sligo F91 RK6C
Tel 071-9142393
Community: 3

Sisters of Mercy,
No 2 St Patrick's Avenue,
Sligo F91 E9TY
Tel 071-9145755

Sisters of Mercy,
1 Racecourt Manor,
Tonaphubble, Sligo F91 T91X
Tel 071-9154656
Community: 2

McAuley House,
Roscommon F42 XV70
Tel 090-6627904 Fax 090-6627581
Community: 6

Convent of Mercy,
St Catherine's,
Roscommon F42 CA26
Tel 090-6626767
Community: 5

Galilee Community,
Sisters of Mercy, Tintagh,
Boyle, Co Roscommon F52 TX93
Tel 071-9664101 Fax 071-9664684
Community: 3

Sisters of Mercy, Crubyhill,
Croscomon F42 VC55
Tel 090-6625725
Community: 4

Sisters of Mercy,
76 Oldwood, Ardsallagh,
Roscommon F42 YX88
Community: 1

DAUGHTERS OF WISDOM

2 The Greenlands,
Rosses Point,
Sligo F91 A6XE
Tel 071-9177607
Contact: Sr Margaret Morris
Email srmegmorris@gmail.com
Community: 2

DISCIPLES OF THE DIVINE MASTER

8 Castle Street, Athlone,
Co Westmeath N37 W9H6
Tel 090-6498755 *(Community)*
090-6492278 *(Liturgical Centre)*
Email kathrynwilliams@pddm.org
Contact: Sr Kathryn Williams
Community: 5
Contemplative-apostolic Congregation.
Chapel of Adoration with daily
Adoration, open to public. Prayer,
support and intercession for priests.
Liturgical Centre-distributor and
producer of liturgical vestments/altar
linens, high-quality liturgical art,
religious gifts. Promotion of liturgical
formation. Bethany House available for
private retreats. Daily prayer and
support groups.
Websites www.ppdm.ie
www.liturgicalcentre.ie

MISSIONARIES OF CHARITY

Temple Street, Sligo
Tel 071-9154843
Superior: Sr Marie Noel (MC)
Community: 6
Contemplative

CONGREGATION OF THE SISTERS OF NAZARETH

Nazareth House, Sligo
Tel 071-9154446
Superior: Sr Mary Theresa Mallon
Email
superior.sligo@sistersofnazareth.com
Community: 7
Home for the elderly. Beds 70
Nursing Home operated by Nazareth
House Management
Director of Nursing: Mrs Linda Hallett
Tel 071-9180900

Ballymote Community Nursing Unit
Tel 071-9183195
Home for the Elderly: Beds 24
Owned by HSE
Operated by Nazareth House
Management
Director of Nursing: Mary Teresa Nolan

PRESENTATION OF MARY SISTERS

4 Lower John Street,
Sligo
Tel 071-9160740
Superior: Sr Emma Dublan (PM)
Community: 4

URSULINES

Ursuline Convent, Temple Street, Sligo
Tel 071-9161538
Community: 7
Primary School
Tel 071-9154573 Fax 071-9154573
Secondary School
Tel 071-9161653 Fax 071-9146141

Ursuline Sisters,
'Brescia', Ballytivnan, Sligo
Community: 5
Pastoral Ministry

EDUCATIONAL INSTITUTIONS OF CATHOLIC ETHOS (POST-PRIMARY)

College of the Immaculate Conception
Summerhill, Sligo
Tel 071-9160311
Principal
Mr Paul Keogh
Priest on Staff
Rev Gerard Cryan BA, HDE, STB, L Eccl His

Coláiste Chiaráin
Summerhill, Athlone, Co Roscommon
Tel 090-6492383
Principal: Mr Brendan Waldron

St Cuan's College
Castleblakeney,
Ballinasloe, Co Galway
Tel 090-9678127
Principal
Ms Colette Kennedy Walsh

CHARITABLE AND OTHER SOCIETIES

Legion of Mary
Assumpta House, John Street, Sligo

Social Services Centre
Charles Street, Sligo
Tel 071-9145682

Society of St Vincent de Paul
Conferences at Athlone, Boyle, Castlere
Roscommon, Sligo

PAPAL ENCYCLICALS

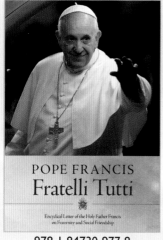

POPE FRANCIS
Fratelli Tutti

Encyclical Letter of the Holy Father Francis on Fraternity and Social Friendship

978 1 84730 977 8
€4.99/£4.50

LAUDATO SI'
ON CARE FOR OUR COMMON HOME

Encyclical Letter
POPE FRANCIS

978 1 84730 597 8
€5.99/£5.40

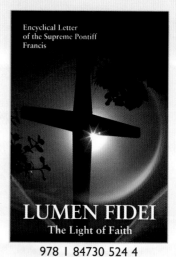

Encyclical Letter of the Supreme Pontiff Francis

LUMEN FIDEI
The Light of Faith

978 1 84730 524 4
€4.75/£4.30

ALSO AVAILABLE, THE FOLLOWING APOSTOLIC EXHORTATIONS

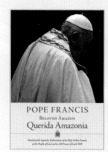

POPE FRANCIS
BELOVED AMAZON
Querida Amazonia

Post-Synodal Apostolic Exhortation of the Holy Father Francis to the People of God and to All Persons of Good Will

978 1 84730 964 8
€4.99/£4.50

POPE FRANCIS

CHRISTUS VIVIT
Christ is Alive

Apostolic Exhortation to Young People and to the Entire People of God

978 1 84730 903 7
€4.99/£4.50

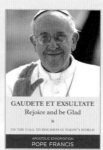

GAUDETE ET EXSULTATE
Rejoice and be Glad

ON THE CALL TO HOLINESS IN TODAY'S WORLD
APOSTOLIC EXHORTATION
POPE FRANCIS

978 1 84730 856 6
€4.99/£4.50

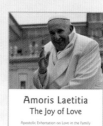

Amoris Laetitia
The Joy of Love

Apostolic Exhortation on Love in the Family
POPE FRANCIS

978 1 84730 735 4
€4.99/£4.50

EVANGELII GAUDIUM
The Joy of the Gospel

POPE FRANCIS
Apostolic Exhortation on the Proclamation of the Gospel in Today's World

978 1 84730 542 8
€4.99/£4.50

Available from Veritas stores
Abbey Street, Blanchardstown Centre, and Tallaght, Dublin
Cork • Derry • Letterkenny • Limerick • Newry
www.veritas.ie

✳ VERITAS

Educating, reflecting and making a difference since 1795

St Patrick's Pontifical University offers a range of Undergraduate, Postgraduate and Continuing Education programmes in Theology and Philosophy, attracting students from home and abroad and a wide variety of careers. If you are interested in developing your critical thinking, analysis, reasoning and communication skills, why not take a look at what we offer.

maynoothcollege.ie/courses

St Patrick's
Pontifical University

INTERCOM

A CATHOLIC PASTORAL AND LITURGICAL RESOURCE

15% DISCOUNT ON NEW SUBSCRIPTIONS

To avail of a twelve-month subscription to *Intercom* for
IRL €59.50 · UK£58.65 · AIRMAIL €73.95, a saving of 15%,
contact Intercom Subscriptions: 01-8788177 · intercomsubscriptions@veritas.ie

Intercom is published on behalf of the Irish Catholic Bishops' Conference by
Veritas Publications, 7–8 Lower Abbey Street, Dublin 1, Ireland

IRISH CATHOLIC
BISHOPS' CONFERENCE

DIOCESE OF FERNS

PATRON OF THE DIOCESE
ST AIDAN, 30 JANUARY

INCLUDES ALMOST ALL OF COUNTY WEXFORD
AND PART OF COUNTY WICKLOW

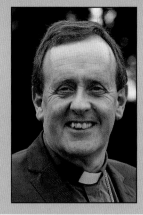

Most Rev Ger Nash DD
Bishop of Ferns
Ordained Bishop
5 September 2021

Residence: Bishop's House,
Summerhill, Wexford
Tel 053-9122177
Fax 053-9123436
Email adm@ferns.ie

ST AIDAN'S CATHEDRAL, ENNISCORTHY

The foundation stone for St Aidan's Cathedral, Enniscorthy, was laid in 1843. The cathedral was designed by the architect Augustus Welby Northmore Pugin and is the largest church Pugin built in Ireland. The recent renovations of 1996 have restored to a great extent the original beautiful building as visualised by Pugin. The external stonework was executed by Irish stonemasons who were praised by Pugin. The restored stencilling of the interior gives some idea of what Pugin visualised for his churches.

Pugin, a Londoner, was as important an influence on the history of nineteenth-century English architecture as Frank Lloyd Wright was to be on American architecture. He was an extraordinarily gifted artist and designed ceramics, stained glass, wallpapers, textiles, memorial brasses, church plate, etc. His connection with the Diocese of Ferns came through the patronage of John, 16th Earl of Shrewsbury, Waterford and Wexford. Shrewsbury's wife was a native of Blackwater, Co Wexford. Her uncle, John Hyacinth Talbot, was the first Catholic MP for Co Wexford after Catholic Emancipation in 1829. A rich man through his marriage into the Redmond family, John Hyacinth Talbot introduced Pugin to Wexford, where through the patronage of the Talbot and Redmond family connections, he was to gain most of his Irish commissions.

Pugin was to die through overwork at the age of forty in 1852, but he has left a unique diocesan heritage in Ferns in his churches. His son and son-in-law, E.W. Pugin and George Ashlin, were to continue the building of Gothic Revival churches and monuments in Ireland.

Most Rev Denis Brennan DD
Retired Bishop of Ferns
PO Box 40, Summerhill, Wexford

Most Rev Brendan Comiskey DD
Retired Bishop of Ferns
PO Box 40, Summerhill, Wexford

CHAPTER

Very Rev Seamus De Val
Very Rev Felix Byrne
Very Rev Lorenzo Cleary
Very Rev Seamus Larkin
Very Rev Richard Hayes
Rt Rev Mgr James Hammel
Very Rev Diarmuid Desmond
Rt Rev Mgr Denis Lennon
Very Rev Thomas McGrath

ADMINISTRATION

College of Consultors
Very Rev Brian Broaders
Rt Rev Joseph McGrath
Very Rev Matthew Boggan
Very Rev William Swan
Rev Patrick Stafford
Rev Gerald O'Leary

Vicar General
Rt Rev Mgr Joseph McGrath VG, VF
New Ross, Co Wexford
Tel 051-447080

Vicar for Clergy
Very Rev Brian Broaders PP, VF
Rathnure, Enniscorthy,
Co Wexford

Vicars Forane
Very Rev Brian Broaders PP, VF
Rt Rev Mgr Joseph McGrath VG, VF
Very Rev Aodhan Marken PP, VF
Very Rev Denis Browne PP, VF

Diocesan Finance Council
Rt Rev Mgr Joseph McGrath VG, VF
Very Rev Patrick Cushen PP
Very Rev James Fegan PP
Mr Liam Gaynor
Mr John Murphy
Ms Pauline O'Neill
Ms Annette McCarthy
Ms Martha Cooney
Very Rev Tom Dalton
Finance Officer and Chairman:
Mr Tom Brazil

Diocesan Archivist
Rt Rev Mgr James Hammel
Ballygarron, Kilmuckridge
Gorey, Co Wexford
Tel 086-1688295

Diocesan Chancellery
Rev James Murphy
PO Box 40, Bishop's House,
Summerhill, Wexford
Tel 053-9122177

Diocesan Secretary
Ms Patricia Murphy
PO Box 40, Bishop's House,
Summerhill, Wexford
Tel 053-9122177

Diocesan Pastoral Council
Co-ordinator: Sr Stephanie O'Brien
Ferns Diocesan Centre,
St Peter's College, Wexford
Tel 053-9122177
Email pastoral@ferns.ie

CATECHETICS EDUCATION

**Catholic Primary School Management
Association (CPSMA)**
Mr Colm O'Tiarnaigh
Tel 087-1841412
Email fernsed@gmail.com

**Diocesan Adviser for Primary School
Catechetics**
Ms Mairin Jackson
c/o Bishop's House, Summerhill, Wexford
Tel 087-2222522

Director of Religious Education
Ms Colette O'Doherty
Ferns Diocesan Centre,
St Peter's College, Wexford
Tel 053-9145511
Email fernsda@ferns.ie

PASTORAL

Apostolic Work Society
Diocesan Director
Very Rev Joseph Power PP
Kilrush, Bunclody, Enniscorthy,
Co Wexford
Tel 053-9377262

Chaplain to Special Needs Groups
Very Rev Tom Dalton Adm
St Aidan's Cathedral,
Enniscorthy, Co Wexford
Tel 053-9235777

CORI (Ferns Branch)
Secretary: To be confirmed

Ecumenism
Director: Rev James Murphy PP
St Brigid's, Rosslare,
Co Wexford
Tel 053-9132118

Fatima Pilgrimage
Director: Very Rev Denis Browne
Kilanerin, Gorey, Co Wexford

House of Mission
Rev Thaddeus Doyle
Shillelagh, Arklow, Co Wicklow
Tel 053-9429926

Knock Pilgrimage
Director
Very Rev Gerald O'Leary PP
Horeswood, Campile,
Co Wexford

Legion of Mary
Very Rev Seamus Canon De Val
1 Irish Street, Bunclody,
Co Wexford
Tel 053-9376140

Lourdes Pilgrimage
Director
Very Rev Matthew Boggan PP
Parochial house, Clongeen,
Foulksmill, Co Wexford

Marriage Tribunal
(See also Marriage Tribunals section)
*Ferns Diocesan Auditor for Dublin
Regional Marriage Tribunal*
Very Rev Kevin Cahill (DCL)
c/o Bishop's House,
Summerhill, Wexford

Our Lady's Island Pilgrimage
Director
Very Rev James Cogley PP
Our Lady's Island, Broadway,
Co Wexford
Tel 053-9131167

Pioneer Total Abstinence Association
Diocesan Director
Very Rev Robert McGuire Adm
Parochial House, Taghmon, Co Wexford
Tel 053-9134123

Pontifical Mission Societies
Diocesan Director
Very Rev Patrick Cushen PP
Parochial House, Ferns,
Enniscorthy, Co Wexford

St Aidan Retirement Fund
Chairman
Very Rev James Murphy PP
Parochial House, Rosslare, Co Wexford
Tel 053-9132118

St Joseph's Young Priests' Society
Diocesan Chaplain
Right Rev Mgr Joseph McGrath PP, VF,
New Ross, Co Wexford
Tel 051-447080

Travellers
Diocesan Co-ordinator
Rev Thomas Orr CC
Traveller Resource Centre,
Mary Street, New Ross, Co Wexford
Tel 051-422272

...cations
...rector
...ry Rev William Swan Adm
...e Presbytery,
...hool Street, Wexford
...l 053-9122055

PARISHES

...ensal parishes are listed first. Other
...rishes follow alphabetically.

NISCORTHY, CATHEDRAL OF ST AIDAN
...ry Rev Tom Dalton Adm
...v William Caulfield CC
...Aidan's, Enniscorthy, Co Wexford
...l 053-9235777 Fax 053-9237700

EXFORD
...ry Rev William Swan Adm
...v Michael O'Shea CC
...v James Cullen CC
...e Presbytery,
...School Street, Wexford
...053-9122055 Fax 053-9121724

AMSTOWN
...ry Rev Robert Nolan PP
...amstown, Enniscorthy, Co Wexford
...053-9240512

NACURRA
...ry Rev John-Paul Sheridan PP
...nacurra, Aughrim, Co Wicklow
...0402-36119

LLINDAGGIN
...ry Rev James Fegan PP
...lindaggin, Enniscorthy,
...Wexford
...053-9388559

LLYCULLANE
...ry Rev William Byrne PP
...lycullane, New Ross, Co Wexford
...051-562123
...ry Rev Sean Laffan CC
...sserane, Co Wexford
...051-562111

LLYGARRETT
...ry Rev James Butler PP
...lygarrett, Gorey, Co Wexford
...053-9427330

LLYMORE AND MAYGLASS
...v Aodhan Marken Adm
...rochial House,
...rcestown, Co Wexford
...053-9158000

NNOW
...ry Rev James Kehoe PP
...rrig-on-Bannow,
...llington Bridge, Co Wexford
...051-561192

BLACKWATER
Very Rev Brendan Nolan PP
Blackwater, Enniscorthy,
Co Wexford
Tel 053-9127118

BREE
Very Rev Michael Byrne PP
Bree, Enniscorthy, Co Wexford
Tel 053-9247843

BUNCLODY
(*Parish Office:* Tel/Fax 053-9376190)
Very Rev Laurence O'Connor PP
Bunclody, Enniscorthy, Co Wexford
Tel 053-9377319
Rev Patrick Duffy CC
Kilmyshall, Enniscorthy, Co Wexford
Tel 053-9377188

CAMOLIN
Very Rev Joseph Kavanagh PP
Camolin, Co Wexford
Tel 053-9383136
Rev Tomás Kehoe CC
Ballycanew, Gorey, Co Wexford
Tel 053-9427184

CARNEW
Very Rev Martin Casey PP
Woolgreen, Carnew, Co Wicklow
Tel 053-9426888

CASTLEBRIDGE AND CURRACLOE
Very Rev Denis Kelly PP
Ballymore, Screen,
Enniscorthy, Co Wexford
Tel 053-9137140

CLONARD
(*Parish Office:* Tel 053-9123672
Fax 053-9146699)
Very Rev Barry Larkin Adm
1 Clonard Park, Clonard, Co Wexford
Tel 053-9147686
Rt Rev Mgr Denis Lennon PE
39 Beechlawn, Wexford
Tel 053-9124417

CLONGEEN AND BALLYMITTY
Very Rev Matthew Boggan PP
Clongeen, Foulksmills, Co Wexford
Tel 051-565610

CLOUGHBAWN AND POULPEASTY
Very Rev Bernard Cushen PP
Clonroche, Enniscorthy,
Co Wexford
Tel 053-9244115

CRAANFORD
Rev Brian Whelan Adm
Craanford, Gorey, Co Wexford
Tel 053-9428163
Very Rev Felix Canon Byrne CC
Monaseed, Gorey, Co Wexford
Tel 053-9428207

CROSSABEG AND BALLYMURN
Very Rev James Finn PP
Crossabeg, Co Wexford
Tel 053-9159015

CUSHINSTOWN AND RATHGAROGUE
Very Rev Sean Devereux PP
Cushinstown, Newbawn,
Co Wexford
Tel 051-428347

DAVIDSTOWN AND COURTNACUDDY
Very Rev James Nolan PP
Davidstown, Enniscorthy,
Co Wexford
Tel 053-9238240

DUNCANNON
Very Rev John P. Nolan PP
Duncannon, New Ross,
Co Wexford
Tel 051-389118

FERNS
Very Rev Patrick Cushen PP
Ferns, Enniscorthy, Co Wexford
Tel 053-9366152

GLYNN
Very Rev John Carroll PP
Barntown, Co Wexford
Tel 053-9120853

GOREY
Very Rev William Flynn PP
St Michael's, Gorey, Co Wexford
Tel 053-9421112
Rev Roger O'Neill CC
St Michael's, Gorey, Co Wexford
Tel 053-9421117

HORESWOOD AND BALLYKELLY
Very Rev Gerald O'Leary PP
Horeswood, Campile, Co Wexford
Tel 051-388129

KILANERIN AND BALLYFAD
Very Rev Denis Browne PP
Kilanerin, Gorey,
Co Wexford
Tel/Fax 0402-37120

KILLAVENEY AND CROSSBRIDGE
Very Rev Raymond Gahan PP
Killaveney, Tinahely,
Co Wicklow
Tel 0402-38188

KILMORE AND KILMORE QUAY
Very Rev Pat Mernagh PP
Kilmore, Co Wexford
Tel 053-9135181

KILMUCKRIDGE (LITTER) AND MONAMOLIN
Very Rev Francis Murphy PP
Kilmuckridge, Gorey, Co Wexford
Tel 053-9130116
Very Rev Seamus Canon Larkin *(priest in residence)*
Monamolin, Gorey, Co Wexford

KILRANE AND ST PATRICK'S
Very Rev Diarmuid Desmond PP
Kilrane, Co Wexford
Tel 053-9133128

KILRUSH AND ASKAMORE
Very Rev Joseph Power PP
Kilrush, Bunclody, Enniscorthy,
Co Wexford
Tel 053-9377262

MARSHALLSTOWN AND CASTLEDOCKRELL
Very Rev Patrick Banville PP
Marshallstown, Enniscorthy,
Co Wexford
Tel 053-9388521

MONAGEER
Very Rev William Cosgrave PP
Monageer, Ferns, Enniscorthy,
Co Wexford
Tel 053-9233530
Rev Morgan White CC
Boolavogue, Ferns, Wexford
Tel 053-9366282

NEWBAWN AND RAHEEN
Very Rev James Moynihan PP
Newbawn, Co Wexford
Tel 051-428227

NEW ROSS
Rt Rev Mgr Joseph McGrath PP, VF, VG
New Ross, Co Wexford
Tel 051-447080
Rev Tom Orr CC
New Ross, Co Wexford

OULART AND BALLAGHKEENE
Very Rev Patrick Browne PP
Oulart, Gorey, Co Wexford
Tel 053-9136139

OUR LADY'S ISLAND AND TACUMSHANE
Very Rev James Cogley PP
Our Lady's Island, Broadway,
Co Wexford
Tel 053-9131167

OYLEGATE AND GLENBRIEN
Very Rev John Byrne PP
Oylegate, Co Wexford
Tel 053-9138163

PIERCESTOWN AND MURRINTOWN
Very Rev Aodhan Marken PP
Piercestown, Co Wexford
Tel 053-9158000

RAMSGRANGE
Very Rev Richard Redmond PP
Ramsgrange, New Ross,
Co Wexford
Tel 051-389148

RATHANGAN AND CLEARIESTOWN
Very Robert McGuire Adm
Parochial House,
Taghmon, Co Wexford
Tel 053-9134123

RATHNURE AND TEMPLEUDIGAN
Very Rev Brian Broaders PP
Rathnure, Co Wexford
Tel 053-9255122

RIVERCHAPEL, COURTOWN HARBOUR
Very Rev James Butler Adm
Parochial House,
Ballygarrett, Gorey, Co Wexford
Tel 053-9427330

ST SENAN'S, ENNISCORTHY
Parish Office: Tel 053-9237611
Very Rev Patrick Banville Adm
Marshallstown, Co Wexford
Tel 053-9388521

TAGHMON
Very Rev Robert McGuire Adm
Taghmon, Co Wexford
Tel 053-9134123

TAGOAT
Rev James Murphy PP
St Brigid's, Rosslare,
Co Wexford
Tel 053-9132118

TEMPLETOWN AND POULFUR
Very Rev Michael Doyle PP
Poulfur, Fethard-on-Sea,
New Ross, Co Wexford
Tel 051-397113

INSTITUTIONS AND THEIR CHAPLAINS
Community School
Gorey, Co Wexford
Tel 053-9421000

Vocational College Wexford
Rev James Cullen CC
The Presbytery, Wexford
Tel 053-9122753

Wexford General Hospital
Tel 053-9142233
Chaplain: Rev Odhran Furlong
General Hospital, Wexford
Tel 053-9142233

Community School
Ramsgrange
Tel 051-389211
Ms Maria McCabe

St John of God Convent
Newtown Road, Wexford
Chaplain: Vacant

St John's Hospital
Enniscorthy, Co Wexford
Chaplain: St Aidan's Parish
Tel 053-9233228

PRIESTS OF THE DIOCESE ELSEWHERE IN IRELAND
Rev David Murphy CF
Chaplain to Defence Forces
Rev Chris Hayden
c/o Bishop's House
Rev Richard Lawless
c/o Bishop's House
Rev James Doyle
Chaplain, Irish College, Paris

PRIESTS OF THE DIOCESE ABROAD
Rev Thomas Brennan, USA
Rev Dermot Gahan, USA

RETIRED PRIESTS
Most Rev Denis Brennan DD
PO Box 40, Wexford
Very Rev James Byrne
Ballylannon, Wellingtonbridge,
Co Wexford
Rev Michael Byrne
Serene Valley, Borris Road, Kiltealy,
Enniscorthy, Co Wexford
Very Rev Matthew L. Cleary
The Stables, Bridgetown, Co Wexford
Most Rev Brendan Comiskey (SSCC) DD
PO Box 40, Wexford
Very Rev James Curtis
3 Oldtown Court,
Clongreen, Foulkmills,
New Ross, Co Wexford
Very Rev Seamus Canon De Val
1 Irish Streeet, Bunclody, Co Wexford
Very Rev Denis Doyle
Starvehall, Coolballon, Co Wexford
Very Rev Thomas Eustace
The Cools, Barntown, Wexford
Very Rev James Furlong
Tomgarrow, Adamstown, Co Wexford
Very Rev Sean Gorman
Ballask, Kilmore,
Co Wexford
Very Rev James Hammel
Ballygarron, Kilmuckridge,
Gorey, Co Wexford

ry Rev William Howell
Bishop's House
ry Rev Richard Hayes
llinstown, Duncormick,
Wexford
ry Rev John Jordan
le, Oulart, Gorey, Co Wexford
Rev Mgr Don Kenny
is Cuan Arthurstown,
w Ross, Co Wexford
ry Rev Seamus Canon Larkin
namolin, Gorey, Co Wexford
053-9389223
ry Rev Danny McDonald
iterock South, Wexford,
Wexford
ry Rev Thomas McGrath
is Tra, Chapel Road,
ncannon, Co Wexford
ry Rev Colm Murphy
lla Maria', Kilrane,
sslare Harbour, Co Wexford
ry Rev Anthony O'Connell
arkside, Stoneybatter, Wexford
ry Rev John O'Reilly
sslare, Co Wexford
v Patrick Sinnott
rkannesley, Ballyarrett,
rey, Co Wexford
ry Rev Patrick Stafford
msollagh, Ferns,
niscorthy, Co Wexford
ry Rev Oliver Sweeney
The Willows, Wellingtonbridge,
Wexford

RELIGIOUS ORDERS AND CONGREGATIONS

PRIESTS

UGUSTINIANS
od Counsel College,
w Ross, Co Wexford
051-421363/421909
x 051-421909
or: Rev Michael Collender (OSA)
rsar: Rev David Crean (OSA)

NVENTUAL FRANCISCANS
e Friary,
rancis Street, Wexford
053-9122758
ardian
v Aquino Maliakkal (OFMConv)

BROTHERS

RISTIAN BROTHERS
ristian Brothers' House,
eph Street, Wexford
053-45659
mmunity Leader
Éamonn Mac Loughlainn
mmunity: 6

SISTERS

CARMELITES
Mount Carmel Monastery,
New Ross, Co Wexford
Tel 051-421076
Email nrcarmelites@gmail.com
Prioress: Sr Anne McGlynn
Community: 13
Contemplatives
Altar breads

CONGREGATION OF THE SISTERS OF MERCY
Convent of Mercy,
Clonard Road, Wexford
Tel 053-9123024

Sisters of Mercy, Lower South Knock,
New Ross, Co Wexford
Tel 051-425340

The Lodge, 38 Irishtown, New Ross,
Co Wexford

40 Willow Park, Mountgarret,
New Ross, Co Wexford

77 Pineridge, Summerhill, Wexford

21 Castle Gardens, St Helen's Village,
Kilrane, Co Wexford

FAMILY OF ADORATION
St Aidan's Monastery of Adoration,
Ferns, Co Wexford
Tel 053-9366634
Email staidansferns@eircom.net
Contemplative life with adoration of the
Eucharist. 8 hermitages for private
retreats. Icon reproduction workshop.

LORETO (IBVM)
Conabury, 11 Newtown Court, Wexford
Tel 053-43470
Community: 1
Secondary School

PERPETUAL ADORATION SISTERS
Perpetual Adoration Convent,
Newtown Road, Wexford Town,
Co Wexford
Tel 053-9124134
Email sisterpeterleech@gmail.com
Superior: Sr M. Peter Leech
Community: 5
Perpetual adoration of the Blessed
Sacrament

PRESENTATION SISTERS
Presentation Sisters,
Francis Street, Wexford Y35 P9CF
Tel 053-9122504
Community: 6

SISTERS OF ST JOHN OF GOD
St John of God Congregational Centre,
Newtown Road, Wexford
Tel 053-9142396
Email stjohnogoffice@ssjgcc.ie
Congregational Leader
Sr Geraldine Fitzpatrick

St John of God Convent,
Sallyville House,
Newtown Road, Wexford
Tel 053-9142276
Local Leader: Sr Mary Cahill
Community: 27

St John of God Convent,
Newtown Road, Wexford
Community: 8

St John of God Heritage Centre,
Sallyville, Newtown Road,
Wexford
Tel 053-9142293

Sisters of St John of God,
1 Summerhill Heights, Wexford
Tel 053-9171625

Sisters of St John of God,
'Granada', Ballyvaloo, Blackwater,
Enniscorthy, Co Wexford Y21 HX73
Tel 053-9137160
Retreat ministry

Sisters of St John of God,
Moorefield House, Loreto Village,
Enniscorthy, Co Wexford
Tel 053-9239734
Sheltered homes for the elderly

Sisters of St John of God,
6 Parkside, Stoneybatter,
Wexford
Tel 053-9146058

Sisters of St John of God,
Ard Coilm, 15 Millpark,
Castlebridge, Co Wexford
Tel 053-9159862
Community: 2

Sisters of St John of God,
1 Beechville, Clonard, Wexford
Tel 053-9142601
Community: 3

Sisters of St John of God,
26 Mansfield Drive,
Coolcots, Wexford
Tel 053-9144427

Sisters of St John of God, Caritas,
Glenbrook, Newtown Road,
Wexford
Tel 053-9143752
Community: 2

Sisters of St John of God,
3 Cluain Aoibhinn,
Clonard, Wexford
Community: 3

Sisters of St John of God,
Rectory Mews,
Spawell Road, Wexford
Community: 9

EDUCATIONAL INSTITUTIONS

St Peter's Diocesan College
Tel 053-9142071
Principal: Mr John Banville
Chaplain/Counsellor
Very Rev William Swan

CHARITABLE AND OTHER SOCIETIES

Aiseiri
Roxborough House,
Wexford
Tel 053-9141818

Christian Media Trust
Tel 053-9145176

FDYS Youth Work Ireland
Wexford
Tel 053-9123262/9123358

Society of St Vincent de Paul
17 Conferences in the Diocese of Ferns
South Ferns President
Ms Eileen Godkin
Barntown, Co Wexford
North Ferns President: Brian Keenan
SVDP, Market Square,
Enniscorthy, Co Wexford

Traveller Resource Centre
Tel 051-422272

Special Schools
Our Lady of Fatima, Wexford
Tel 053-9123376
St John of God, Enniscorthy
Tel 053-9233419
St Patrick's, Enniscorthy
Tel 053-9233657
Dawn House, Wexford
Tel 053-9145351
Community Workshop
Enniscorthy Ltd
Tel 053-9233069
Community Workshop
New Ross Ltd
Tel 051-421956

DIOCESE OF GALWAY, KILMACDUAGH AND KILFENORA

Most Rev Michael Duignan DD
Bishop of Galway
born 15 July 1970
ordained priest 17 July 1994
ordained Bishop of Clonfert
13 October 2019
installed Bishop of Galway
1 May 2022

Residence: Coorheen,
Loughrea, Co Galway H62 TD82
Tel 091-841560
Email info@galwaydiocese.ie
Website www.galwaydiocese.ie

PATRONS OF THE DIOCESE
GALWAY – OUR LADY ASSUMED INTO HEAVEN, 15 AUGUST
KILMACDUAGH – ST COLMAN, 29 OCTOBER
KILFENORA – ST FACHANAN, 20 DECEMBER

INCLUDES PORTIONS OF COUNTIES GALWAY, MAYO AND CLARE
KILFENORA IS IN THE PROVINCE OF CASHEL BUT THE BISHOP OF GALWAY AND
KILMACDUAGH IS ITS APOSTOLIC ADMINISTRATOR

CATHEDRAL OF OUR LADY ASSUMED INTO HEAVEN AND ST NICHOLAS, GALWAY

In 1484, the Church of St Nicholas in Galway became a collegiate church, with a warden and vicars. However, with the Reformation, after 1570, the Catholic people of Galway lost the right to practise their religion publicly. Mass was celebrated in private houses until the rigour of persecution moderated and a parish chapel was built in Middle Street about 1750. The Diocese of Galway was established in 1831, and the parish chapel became its pro-cathedral. A fund for the building of a more fitting

cathedral was inaugurated in 1876 and was built up by successive bishops. In 1883 the Diocese of Kilmacduagh was joined with Galway, and the Bishop of Galway was made Apostolic Administrator of Kilfenora.

In 1941, Galway County Council handed over Galway Jail to Bishop Michael Browne as a site for the proposed new cathedral. The jail was demolished, and in 1949 John J. Robinson of Dublin was appointed architect for the new cathedral. Planning continued until 1957, when Pope Pius XII approved the plans submitted to him by Dr Browne. Cardinal D'Alton, the Archbishop of

Armagh, blessed the site and the foundation stone on 27 October 1957. The construction, which began in February 1958, was undertaken by Messrs John Sisk Ltd of Dublin. The people of the diocese contributed to a weekly collection, and donations were received from home and abroad. The total cost, including furnishing, was almost one million pounds.

Pope Paul VI appointed Cardinal Richard Cushing, Archbishop of Boston, Pontifical Legate to dedicate the cathedral. The cathedral was dedicated on the Feast of the Assumption, 15 August 1965.

Most Rev Brendan Kelly DD
Born 20 May 1946;
ordained priest 20 June 1971;
ordained Bishop of Achonry
27 January 2008;
installed Bishop of Galway
11 February 2018;
retired 25 February 2022
Residence: Mount Saint Mary's,
Taylor's Hill, Galway

CHAPTER

Very Rev Dean Michael McLoughlin VF,
Moycullen, Galway
Very Rev Mgr Peter Rabbitte PP, VG
The Cathedral
Very Rev Canon Martin Downey,
St Joseph's, Galway
Very Rev Canon Derek Feeney,
Craughwell, Co Galway
Very Rev Michael Canon Reilly PP,
Castlegar, Galway
Very Rev Canon Thomas Marrinan VF,
Gort, Co Galway
Very Rev Canon Martin Glynn
Mervue, Galway
Very Rev Canon Ian O'Neill
Claregalway, Co Galway
Very Rev Canon Tadhg Quinn
Knocknacarra, Galway

ADMINISTRATION

Vicar General
Very Rev Mgr Peter Rabbitte
The Cathedral, Galway
Tel 091-563577

Vicars Forane
Very Rev Mgr Peter Rabbitte, Galway
West
Very Rev Dean Michael McLoughlin,
Galway Rural
Very Rev Canon Thomas Marrinan,
Kilmacduagh
Very Rev Canon Martin Glynn, Galway
East
Very Rev Richard Flanagan, Kilfenora

Chancellor
Very Rev Canon Ian O'Neill PP
Claregalway, Co Galway
Tel 091-798104

Diocesan Council of Priests
Pending appointment

Finance Committee
Mr Enda McGowan
Rev Martin Whelan
Mr Thomas Hansberry, Secretary
Mr Peter Casserly
Very Rev Michael Dean McLoughlin
Very Rev Mgr Peter Rabbitte

Financial Administrator
Mr Thomas Hansberry
Diocesan Office,
The Cathedral, Galway
Tel 091-563566

Diocesan Development (Meitheal)
Secretary: Mr Thomas Hansberry
Diocesan Office,
The Cathedral, Galway
Tel 091-563566

Diocesan Secretary
Rev Martin Whelan
Diocesan Office,
The Cathedral, Galway
Tel 091-563566
Email secretary@galwaydiocese.ie

Diocesan Archivist
Mr Thomas Hansberry
Tel 091-563566
Email info@archive.galwaydiocese.ie

CATECHETICS EDUCATION

Primary Education
Diocesan Adviser: Vacant

Post-primary Education
Diocesan Adviser: Rev Martin Whelan
Diocesan Office,
The Cathedral, Galway
Tel 091-563566

LITURGY

Liturgical Committee
Chairperson: Vacant
Members
Vacant

Sacred Music
Diocesan Director
Mr Raymond O'Donnell MA, HDE, LTCL
Tel 091-563577/087-2241365
Email music@galwaycathedral.ie

PASTORAL

ACCORD
Árus de Brún,
Newtownsmith, Galway
Tel 091-562331
Diocesan Director
Very Rev Michael Dean McLoughlin PP
Parochial House,
Moycullen, Co Galway
Tel 091-555106
Email galwayaccord@gmail.com

Brazilian Community
Chaplain: Rev Kevin Keenan (SVD)
Church of the Sacred Heart,
Seamus Quirke Road, Galway
Tel 091-524751

Safeguarding Office
Director: Mr Kevin Duffy
Administrator: Ms Ita O'Mahony
Diocesan Pastoral Outreach Centre,
Árus de Brún,
Newtownsmith, Galway
Tel 091-575051
Email
info@safeguarding.galwaydiocese.ie

Communications Committee
Diocesan Communications Officer (DCC
Very Rev Diarmuid Hogan PP
Parochial House,
Oranmore, Co Galway
Tel 087-1037452
Email info@comms.galwaydiocese.ie

Diocesan Education Office
Pastoral Centre, Árus de Brún,
Newtownsmith, Galway
Tel 091-565066
Co-ordinator: Mr Patrick Kelly
Email education@galwaydiocese.ie

Diocesan Pastoral Outreach Centre
Árus de Brún, Newtownsmith, Galway
Tel 091-565066
Director: Rev Gerard McCarthy (SVD)
Email pastoral@galwaydiocese.ie

Diocesan Pilgrimage Committee
Pilgrimage Director
Very Rev Dean Martin Moran PP
Rosscahill, Co Galway
Tel 091-550106

Ecumenism
Rev Thomas McCarthy OP
St Mary's Dominican Priory,
Claddagh, Galway
Tel 091-563566
Email info@galwaydiocese.ie

Emigrants Committee
Director
Very Rev Gearóid Ó Griofa PP
Lettermore, Co Galway
Tel 091-551169
Email gogriofa@gmail.com
Secretary
Very Rev Canon Michael Reilly PP
Castlegar, Galway
Tel 091-751548
Email
castlegar@parishes.galwaydiocese.ie

Legion of Mary
Annunciata House,
15 Fr Griffin Road, Galway
Tel 091-521871
Contact: Mr Bernard Finan

Marriage Tribunal
Officials: Rev Barry Horan
(see also Marriage Tribunals section)

Missions Committee
Chairman
Very Rev Canon Martin Downey PP
4 Presentation Road, Galway
Tel 091-562276
Email
stjosephs@parishes.galwaydiocese.ie

Pioneer Total Abstinence Association
Diocesan Director
Very Rev Patrick Dean Callanan
Kilbeacanty, Gort, Co Galway
Tel 091-631691

Polish Community
Chaplain: Rev Grzegorz Mazur (OP)
St Mary's Priory, Claddagh, Galway
Tel 091-582884
Email galway.dominikanie@gmail.com

Pontifical Mission Societies
Diocesan Director: Rev Declan Lohan
Renmore, Co Galway
Tel 091-751707
Email
renmore@parishes.galwaydiocese.ie

St Joseph's Young Priests' Society
Diocesan Chaplain: Rev Martin Whelan
Diocesan Office,
The Cathedral, Galway
Tel 091-563566

Trócaire
Diocesan Director: Rev Declan Lohan
St Oliver Plunkett Church,
Renmore, Galway
Tel 091-751707
Email
renmore@parishes.galwaydiocese.ie

Vocations
Director: Very Rev Ian Canon O'Neill PP
Parochial House,
Claregalway, Co Galway
Tel 091-798741
Email galwaypriesthood@gmail.com

PARISHES

Church titulars, if different from parish name, are in italics.

CATHEDRAL
Our Lady Assumed into Heaven and St Nicholas
Very Rev Mgr Peter Rabbitte PP, VG
Tel 091-563577
Rev John Gerard Acton CC
8 University Road, Galway
Tel 091-524875/563577
Email info@galwaycathedral.ie

City Parishes

BALLYBANE
St Brigid
Very Rev Canon Martin Glynn Adm
St Brigid's, Ballybane, Galway
Tel 091-755381
Email info@stbrigidsparishballybane.com

GOOD SHEPHERD
Very Rev Canon Martin Glynn PP
Parochial House, Mervue, Galway
Tel 091-751721/087-2527124
Rev Jose Thomas CC
Good Shepherd Church
Cumasú Centre, Doughiska, Galway
Tel 091-756823
Email goodshepherdgalway@gmail.com
Website www.goodshepherdgalway.com

MERVUE
Holy Family
Very Rev Canon Martin Glynn PP
Mervue, Galway
Tel 091-751721/087-2527124
Email mervuechurch@gmail.com

RENMORE
St Oliver Plunkett
Rev Declan Lohan CC
Parochial House, Renmore, Galway
Tel 091-751707
Email
renmore@parishes.galwaydiocese.ie

SACRED HEART CHURCH
Very Rev Kevin Keenan PP
Church of the Sacred Heart
Seamus Quirke Road, Galway
Tel 091-524751
Email
sacredheart@parishes.galwaydiocese.ie

ST AUGUSTINE'S
Rev Anthony Finn (OSA) PP
St Augustine's Priory,
St Augustine's Street, Galway
Tel 091-562524

ST JOHN THE APOSTLE
Very Rev Tadhg Canon Quinn PP
Rev James Clesham (SMA) CC
St John the Apostle,
Knocknacarra, Galway
Tel 091-590059
Email tadhgknocknacarra@gmail.com

ST JOSEPH'S
Very Rev Canon Martin Downey PP
24 Presentation Road, Galway
Tel 091-562276
Email
stjosephs@parishes.galwaydiocese.ie

ST MARY'S
Very Rev Matthew Farrell (OP) PP
Email claddaghweddings@hotmail.com
Rev Denis Murphy (OP) CC
Rev Jordan O'Brien (OP) CC
Rev Grzegorz Mazur (OP) CC
St Mary's Priory,
Claddagh, Galway
Tel 091-582884

ST PATRICK'S
Very Rev Patrick Whelan PP
St Patrick's Presbytery,
Forster Street, Galway
Tel 091-567994
Email pgcwhelan@gmail.com

SALTHILL
Christ the King
Very Rev Gerard Jennings PP
Tel 091-523413
Email salthill@parishes.galwaydiocese.ie
Monksfield, Salthill, Galway
Rev Charles Sweeney (MSC)
Cruí Nua, Rosary Lane,
Taylor's Hill, Galway
Email charles.sweeney4@gmail.com

TIRELLAN
Resurrection
Very Rev Tony Horgan (MSC) PP
Church of the Resurrection,
Headford Road, Galway, H91 W298
Tel 091-762883
Email ballinfoyleparish@gmail.com

Country Parishes

ARDRAHAN
St Teresa's
Very Rev Joseph Roche PP
Ardrahan, Co Galway
Tel 091-635164
Email kaparishes@gmail.com

BALLINDERREEN
St Colman's
Very Rev Hugh Clifford PP
Parochial House, Kinvara, Co Galway
Tel 091-637154
Email
bkoffice@parishes.galwaydiocese.ie

BALLYVAUGHAN
St John the Baptist
Rev Richard Flanagan PP, VF
Ballyvaughan, Co Clare
Tel 065-7077045
Email bvfanore@icloud.com

BEARNA
Mary Immaculate Queen
Very Rev Michael Brennan PP
Bearna, Galway
Tel 091-590956
Email bearna@parishes.galwaydiocese.ie

CARRON AND NEW QUAY
St Columba's, Carron,
St Patrick's, New Quay
Rev Colm Clinton (SPS) *(Administrator)*
New Quay, Co Clare
Tel 065-7078026
Email colmcc@gmail.com

CASTLEGAR
St Columba's
Rev Kevin Blade (MSC) Adm
Castlegar, Co Galway
Tel 091-751548
Email
castlegar@parishes.galwaydiocese.ie

CLAREGALWAY
Assumption and St James
Very Rev Ian Canon O'Neill PP
Claregalway, Co Galway
Tel 091-798104
Email
claregalway@parishes.galwaydiocese.ie

CLARINBRIDGE
Annunciation of the BVM
Very Rev Barry Horan PP
Main Street, Clarinbridge, Co Galway
Tel 091-776741
Email thebridgeparish@gmail.com

CRAUGHWELL
St Colman's
Very Rev Canon Derek Feeney PP
Parochial House,
Craughwell, Co Galway
Tel 091-846057
Email
craughwell@parishes.galwaydiocese.ie

ENNISTYMON
Our Lady and St Michael
Very Rev William Cummins PP
Ennistymon, Co Clare
Tel 065-7071063
Rev Des Forde CC
Curate's House, Sea Park,
Lahinch, Co Clare
Tel 065-7081307
Email
ennistymon@parishes.galwaydiocese.ie

GORT/BEAGH
St Colman's and St Ann
Very Rev Thomas Canon Marrinan PP, VF
Rev Patrick Madden, *Priest in Residence*
Gort, Co Galway
Tel 091-631220
Email
gort.beagh@parishes.galwaydiocese.ie

KILBEACANTY/PETERSWELL
St Columba and St Thomas Apostle
Very Rev Joseph Roche PP
Ardrahan, Co Galway
Tel 091-635164
Email
kilbeacantyparishoffice@gmail.com

KILCHREEST
Nativity and Church of St Teresa
Very Rev Joseph Roche *(priest in charge)*
Parochial House, Ardrahan, Co Galway
Tel 091-635164
Email kaparishes@gmail.com

KILFENORA
St Fachanan's
Very Rev Edward Crosby Adm
Kilfenora, Co Clare
Tel 065-7088006
Email crosby32000@yahoo.com

KINVARA
St Colman's
Very Rev Hugh Clifford PP
Parochial House, Kinvara, Co Galway
Tel 091-637154
Email
bkoffice@parishes.galwaydiocese.ie

LETTERMORE
Naomh Colmcille
Very Rev Gearóid Ó Griofa PP
Lettermore, Co Galway
Tel 091-551169
Email paroisteleitirmoir@gmail.com

LISCANNOR
St Brigid's
Very Rev Denis Crosby PP
Liscannor, Co Clare
Tel 065-7081248
Email denis.crosby@icloud.com

LISDOONVARNA AND KILSHANNY
Corpus Christi
Very Rev Robert McNamara PP
The Rectory, Lisdoonvarna, Co Clare
Tel 065-7074142
Email lisdoonpp@parish.galwaydiocese.ie

MOYCULLEN
Immaculate Conception
Very Rev Michael Dean McLoughlin PP
Parochial House, Moycullen, Co Galway
Email
moycullen@parishes.galwaydiocese.ie
Website www.moycullenparish.com

ORANMORE
Immaculate Conception
Very Rev Diarmuid Hogan PP
Oranmore, Co Galway
Tel 091-794634
Email oranmorepp@gmail.com
Rev Martin Whelan CC
Maree, Oranmore, Co Galway
Tel 091-794113
Email oranmorecc@gmail.com

OUGHTERARD
Immaculate Conception
Very Rev Michael Connolly PP
Oughterard, Co Galway
Tel 091-552290
Email oughterparish@gmail.com

ROSMUC
Séipéal an Ioncolnaithe
Very Rev Gearóid Ó Griofa *(priest in charge)*
Rosmuc, Co Galway
Tel 091-551169
Email paroistenaomhbriocan@gmail.com

ROSSCAHILL (KILLANNIN)
Immaculate Heart of Mary
Very Rev Martin Dean Moran PP
Rosscahill, Co Galway
Tel 091-550106
Email
killannin@parishes.galwaydiocese.ie

SHRULE
St Joseph's
Very Rev Vivian Loughrey PP
Shrule, Galway
Tel 093-31262
Email parishofshrule3@gmail.com

AN SPIDÉAL
Cill Éinne
Rev Daniel Gallagher Adm
Teach an Sagairt, An Spidéal,
Co na Gaillimhe
Tel 091-553155
Email ce@parishes.galwaydiocese.ie

INSTITUTIONS AND THEIR CHAPLAINS

Bon Secours Hospital
Renmore, Galway
Tel 091-751534/757711
Co-ordinator: Very Rev Martin Glynn

Coláiste Muire Máthair
Chaplain's Office
Rev Martin Whelan
Tel 091-563566

Dún Uí Mhaoilíosa
Renmore Barracks, Renmore, Galway
Rev Paul Murphy
Tel 091-751156

Extraordinary Form (Latin Mass)
Canon Wulfran Lebocq
Institute of Christ the King Sovereign Priest, 12-14 The Crescent, Limerick

Atlantic Technological University
Dublin Road, Galway
Tel 091-753161/757298
Chaplain: Br Ronan Sharpley
Email chaplain@gmit.ie

Galway Clinic
Doughiska, Galway
Chaplain's Office
Very Rev John D. Keane
Tel 091-785000

Allianz (ⁱⁱⁱ)

ort Community School
haplain's Office
el 091-632163
1s Orla Duggan

1erlin Park University Hospital
haplains Office
el 091-757631
ery Rev John D. Keane

niversity of Galway
niversity Road, Galway
haplain's Office
el 091-495055
ev Ben Hughes
mail ben.hughes@nuigalway.ie

t Enda's College
hreadneedle Road, Salthill, Galway
r Pauline Uhlemann (RJM)
el 091-522458

t Joseph's Secondary College
un's Island, Galway
riests of Augustinian Parish
el 091-562524

t Thomas Syro-Malabar Chaplaincy
oly Family Church, Mervue, Galway
ev Jose Thomas
el 091-756823
mail goodshepherdgalway@gmail.com

niversity Hospital
haplain's Office
el 091-524222
ev Seán McHugh
ev John O'Halloran
mail jmtohalloran@gmail.com

PRIESTS OF THE DIOCESE ELSEWHERE

ev Michael Conway
t Patrick's College, Maynooth, Co Kildare
el 01-6285222
ev Thomas Lyons
ork University Hospital, Wilton, Cork
el 021-4546109
ev Patrick O'Donohue (FSSP)
1 The Folly,
Jaterford City X91 KWD8
n tAth Dáithí Ó Murchú
iocese of Arundel & Brighton,
t Richard's Church, Cawley Road,
hichester PO19 1XB, UK
ery Rev Canon Michael Reilly
arochial House, Castlegar, Galway

RETIRED PRIESTS

ev Patrick Canon Callanan PE
ilbeacanty, Gort, Co Galway
el 091-631691
ev Patrick Connaughton
t Columban's, Dalgan Park,
avan, Co Meath
el 046-21525

Very Rev Dean Patrick Considine PE
No. 2 St Mary's Apartments,
Shantalla Road, Galway
Tel 091-563566
Very Rev Michael Crosby
Main Street, Ballinrobe, Co Mayo
Very Rev Canon Joseph Delaney
Castlelawn Heights, Headford Road,
Galway
Very Rev Canon Eamonn Dermody PE
Clarinbridge, Co Galway
Tel 091-796208
Very Rev Enda Glynn
13 Lios Na Mara, Station Road,
Lahinch, Co Clare
Rt Rev Mgr Malachy Hallinan
Church of the Sacred Heart,
Seamus Quirke Road, Galway
Tel 091-522713
Rev Barry Hogg
15 Parklands, Tubbercurry, Co Sligo
Very Rev Canon Francis Larkin
7 Presentation Road, Galway
Very Rev Canon Michael Mulkerrins PE
Curate's Residence,
Renmore, Galway
Tel 091-757859
Very Rev Dean Christopher O'Connor PE
Kilkerrin, Ballinasloe, Co Galway
Very Rev Canon John O'Dwyer PE
20 Cloonarkin Drive,
Oranmore, Co Galway
Tel 091-484501
Rt Rev Mgr Seán O'Flaherty PE
St Mary's Nursing Home,
Shantalla Road, Galway
Tel 091-540500

PERSONAL PRELATURE

Opus Dei
Gort Ard University Residence,
Rockbarton North, Salthill,
Galway H91 KH94
Tel 091-523846
Rev Charles Connolly

RELIGIOUS ORDERS AND CONGREGATIONS

PRIESTS

AUGUSTINIANS
St Augustine's Priory, Galway
Tel 091-562524
www.augustinians.ie/galway
Prior & PP: Rev Desmond Foley (OSA)
Bursar: Rev Sean MacGearailt (OSA)

DOMINICANS
St Mary's, The Claddagh, Co Galway
Tel 091-582884
Prior: Very Rev Matthew Farrell (OP) PP

FRANCISCANS
The Abbey, 8 Francis Street, Galway
Tel 091-562518 Fax 091-565663
Guardian: Rev David Collins (OFM)

JESUITS
St Ignatius Community & Church
27 Raleigh Row, Galway
Tel 091-523707
Email galway@jesuit.ie
Rector: Rev Dermot O'Connor (SJ)

Coláiste Iognáid,
24 Sea Road, Galway
Tel 091-501500 Fax 091-501551
Email admin@colaisteiognaid.ie
Secondary School Principal
Mr David O'Sullivan
Scoil Iognaid (National School) Principal
Ms Laoise Breathnach

MISSIONARIES OF THE SACRED HEART
Croí Nua, Rosary Lane,
Taylor's Hill, Galway, H91 WY2A
Tel 091-520960 Fax 091-521168
Co-Leaders: Rev Kevin Blade (MSC) and
Rev Thomas Plower (MSC)

SALVATORIANS
Parochial House,
Pairc Na Mara, Lahinch, Co Clare
Tel 065-7081307
Email henrynevinsds@hotmail.com
Superior: Rev Henry Nevin (SDS)

Ard Mhuire, Kilmoon,
Lisdoonvarna, Co Clare
Tel 086-1030261
Email seamusoduill@eircom.net
Rev Seamus O'Duill (SDS)

SOCIETY OF AFRICAN MISSIONS
Cloonbigeen, Claregalway,
Co Galway H91 YK64
Tel 091-798880 Fax 091-798879
Email sma.claregalway@sma.ie
Superior
Rev Billy Sheridan (SMA)
Bursar
Rev Colman Nilan (SMA)

BROTHERS

BROTHERS OF CHARITY
Regional Office,
Kilcornan Centre,
Clarinbridge, Co Galway
Tel 091-721517
Regional Leader: Br John O'Shea
Community: 4

CHRISTIAN BROTHERS
Christian Brothers' House,
Mount St Joseph,
Ennistymon, Co Clare
Tel 065-7071130
Community: 2

PATRICIAN BROTHERS
Manor Drive, Kingston, Galway
Tel 091-523267
Superior: Br Niall Coll (FSP)
Community: 3

SISTERS

BRIGIDINE SISTERS
27 Cimín Mór,
Cappagh Road, Bearna, Co Galway
Tel 091-592234
Contact: Sr Margaret Coyle
Community: 1
Retired

CONGREGATION OF THE SISTERS OF MERCY
Convent of Mercy,
St Vincent's, Newtownsmith,
Galway H91 N7PW
Tel 091-565519 Fax 091-564739
Community: 20

Aisling Court,
Ballyloughaun Road, Renmore, Galway
Community: 4

Sisters of Mercy,
3 Greenview Heights, Inishannagh Park,
Newcastle, Galway H91 T8FT
Tel 091-526126
Community: 1

146 Seacrest Road,
Knocknacarra, Galway H91 EEP0
Tel 091-591685
Community: 2

Sisters of Mercy, McAuley House,
7A Francis Street, Galway H91 W6X4
Community: 3

17 Newtownsmith,
Galway H91 W7X3
Apt 1 Tel 091-563297
Apt 2 Tel 091-563698
Community: 1

Sisters of Mercy, Teaghlach Mhuire,
Ballyloughane Road,
Renmore, Galway
Community: 40

St Anne's Lodge, Taylor's Hill Road,
Taylor's Hill, Galway H91 DCW9
Tel 091-527710
Community: 1

147 Seacrest Road,
Knocknacarra, Galway H91 DE0C
Tel 091-591598

Sisters of Mercy, Stella Maria,
Taylor's Hill, Galway H91 XY93
Community: 40

Sisters of Mercy,
Cnoc Mhuire, Ballyloughaun Road,
Renmore, Galway H91 TDY9
Community: 5

Sister of Mercy, 61 The Green,
College Road, Galway H91 R5FY
Community: 1

DAUGHTERS OF MARY MOTHER OF MERCY
Sr Magdalena Ohaja
Apt 10 Bridgewater Court, Fairhill Lower,
Claddagh, Galway

DOMINICAN SISTERS
Dominican Convent,
Taylor's Hill, Galway H91 Y1RT
Tel 091-522124
Email dominicancg@eircom.net
Community: 8
Varied ministries
Primary School. Tel 091-521517
Secondary School. Tel 091-523171
Congregation Archivist
Sr Mary O'Byrne (OP)
Tel 01-8386150

JESUS AND MARY, CONGREGATION OF
Convent of Jesus and Mary,
23 Lenaboy Gardens, Salthill, Galway
Tel 091-524277
Superior: Sr Maria O'Toole
Community: 7
Sisters in principalship and chaplaincy of
post-primary schools
Scoil Íde Primary School
Tel 091-522716. Pupils: 279
Salerno Post-Primary School
Tel 091-529500. Pupils: 720

LA RETRAITE SISTERS
No. 1 St Mary's Mews, Shantalla Road,
Galway H91 W86C
Tel 086-3505779
Contact: Sr Moira McDowall
Email moiramcdlr@gmail.com

LA SAINTE UNION DES SACRES COEURS
Sarsfield Road,
Ballinasloe, Co Galway
Community: 2
Pastoral

2 Boherbradagh House,
Coy's Boreen, Old Galway Road,
Loughrea, Co Galway
Community: 1
Healthcare

St Mary's Residential Care Centre,
Shantalla Road, Galway

10 Dún na Carraige,
Blackrock, Salthill, Galway
Community: 1
Pastoral

Milltown, Dysart,
Ballinasloe, Co Galway
Community: 1
Pastoral

LITTLE SISTERS OF THE ASSUMPTION
50 St Finbarr's Terrace,
Bohermore, Galway
Tel 091-568870

POOR CLARES
St Clare's Monastery,
Nuns' Island, Galway
www.poorclares.ie
www.clairinibochta.ie
Abbess: Sr M. Colette
Community: 10
Contemplatives. Adoration of the
Blessed Sacrament. Altar breads

PRESENTATION SISTERS
Presentation Convent,
Presentation Road, Galway H91 TFD4
Tel 091-561067
Community: 15

Shantalla Road, Galway H91 X44W
Tel 091-522598
Community: 7
School and pastoral ministry

160 Corrib Park,
Newcastle, Galway H91 RKK2
Tel 091-581715
Community: 2
Pastoral

Apt 103, Duirling, Roscam,
Galway H91 VY83
Community 1

Apt 100 Duirling, Roscam,
Galway H91 DH61
Community 1

ASSOCIATION OF THE FAITHFUL

FRATERNITY OF MARY IMMACULATE QUEEN
'Síiol Dóchas',
Ballard, Barna, Galway
Tel/Fax 091-592196
Email miq@eircom.net

Allianz (ili)

EDUCATIONAL INSTITUTIONS

oláiste Einde, Gaillimh
el 091-521407
rincipal: Ms Deirbhle Quinn
haplain's Office: Tel 091-522458/524904
* Pauline Uhlemann (RJM)

oláiste Muire Máthais, Galway
el 091-522369
rincipal: Mrs Betty Hernon
haplain: Fr Martin Whelan
mail info@cmmg.ie

ort Community School
rincipal: Mr Brian Crossan
haplain's Office
el 091-632163
Ms Orla Duggan

St Joseph's Patrician College
Nun's Island, Galway
Principal: Mr John Madden
Tel 091-565980
Chaplain: Priests of Augustinian Parish
Tel 091-562524 (Augustinian Priory)

Seamount College
Tel 091-637362
Principal: Mairéad Mhic Dhomhnaill
Email admin@seamountcollege.ie
Chaplain: Rev Hugh Clifford

CHARITABLE AND OTHER SOCIETIES

COPE Galway
(Crisis Housing, Caring Support) Ltd
3–5 Calbro House,
Tuam Road, Galway
Tel 091-778750
CEO: Michael Smyth
Cope provides emergency
accommodation for homeless persons
and families and women and children
experiencing domestic violence. It also
provides a community catering service in
Galway City and runs a day centre for
older people in Mervue.

Society of St Vincent de Paul
Ozanam House,
St Augustine Street, Galway
Tel 091-563233
Regional Coordinator: Deirdre Swords

DIOCESE OF KERRY

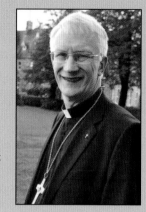

Most Rev Raymond Browne DD
Bishop of Kerry;
born 23 January 1957;
ordained priest 4 July 1982
ordained Bishop of Kerry
21 July 2013

Residence:
Bishop's House, Killarney,
Co Kerry
Tel 064-6631168
Fax 064-6631364
Email kdaadministration@
dioceseofkerry.org

PATRON OF THE DIOCESE
ST BRENDAN, 16 MAY

INCLUDES COUNTY KERRY, EXCEPT KILMURRILY, AND PART OF COUNTY CORK

ST MARY'S CATHEDRAL, KERRY

The Cathedral of Our Lady of the Assumption, better known as St Mary's, was designed by Augustus Welby Pugin. The main part of the cathedral was built between 1842 and 1855. Work was suspended between 1848 and 1853 because of the Famine and the building was used as a shelter for victims of the Famine.

Between 1908 and 1912 the nave and side aisles were extended and the spire, sacristy and mortuary chapel were added.

In 1972/3 the cathedral was extensively renovated. The interior was reordered to meet the demands of the liturgical renewal that followed the Second Vatican Council.

Most Rev William Murphy DD
Retired Bishop of Kerry; born 6 June
1936; ordained priest 18 June 1961;
ordained Bishop of Kerry 10 September
1995; retired 2 May 2013
Residence: No. 2 Cathedral Place,
Killarney, Co Kerry
Email bfmurphy13@gmail.com

CHAPTER

Rt Rev Mgr Tadhg Fitzgerald VG
Tralee, Dean of Kerry
Very Rev Maurice Canon Brick
Castleisland
Very Rev Declan Canon O'Connor
Listowel
Archdeacon: Venerable George Hayes
Kenmare
Very Rev Larry Canon Kelly, Cahirciveen
Very Rev Noel Canon Spring,
Castletownbere
Very Rev Kevin Canon Sullivan,
Killorglin
Very Rev Jack Canon Fitzgerald,
Millstreet
Very Rev Michael Canon Moynihan,
Dingle

Honorary Canons
Rt Rev Mgr Sean Hanafin,
Ballybunion
Very Rev Pat Canon O'Donnell, Rathmore
Very Rev Gearóid Canon Walsh,
Ballymacelligott
Very Rev Joseph Canon Begley, Killarney

Retired Members
Very Rev Seamus Linnane
Very Rev Eoin Mangan
Rt Rev Mgr Daniel O'Riordan
Very Rev Thomas Looney
Venerable Thomas Crean

ADMINISTRATION

College of Consultors
Rt Rev Mgr Tadhg Fitzgerald
Rev Gearóid Godley
Very Rev Nicholas Flynn
Very Rev Pat O'Donnell
Rev Niall Howard
Very Rev Padraig Walsh
Very Rev John Buckley

Vicar General
Rt Rev Mgr Tadhg Fitzgerald
c/o Diocesan Office, Cathedral Walk,
Killarney, Co Kerry

Vicars Forane
Very Rev Pat Canon O'Donnell
Venerable George Hayes
Very Rev Larry Canon Kelly
Very Rev Kevin Canon Sullivan
Very Rev Declan Canon O'Connor
Very Rev Denis O'Mahony
Very Rev Kieran O'Brien
Rt Rev Mgr Tadhg Fitzgerald
Very Rev John Buckley
Very Rev Michael Canon Moynihan
Very Rev Noel Canon Spring
Rt Rev Mgr Sean Hanafin

Finance Council
Chairman
Very Rev Gearóid Walsh

Foreign Missions Committee
Chairman
Rev Gearóid Godley
John Paul II Pastoral Centre,
Rock Road, Killarney, Co Kerry
Tel 064-6630535 Fax 064-6631170

Diocesan Archivist
Dr Shane Lehane
Diocesan Centre, Cathedral Walk,
Killarney, Co Kerry
Tel 064-6631168
Email dr.shanelehanearchivist@
dioceseofkerry.org

Diocesan Secretary
Very Rev Nicholas Flynn
Bishop's House, Killarney, Co Kerry
Tel 064-6631168
Email nicholasflynn@dioceseofkerry.org

Diocesan Communications Officer
Ms Mary Fagan
Tel 087-1301555/066-7123787
Email maryfagan@dioceseofkerry.ie

Property Committee
Property Administrator
Mr Shane O'Donoghue
Diocesan Centre, Cathedral Walk,
Killarney, Co Kerry
Tel 064-6631168
Email
shaneodonoghue@dioceseofkerry.org

CATECHETICS EDUCATION

Post-Primary Religious Education
Director
Mr Tomás Kenny
John Paul II Pastoral Centre,
Rock Road, Killarney, Co Kerry
Tel 064-6632644 Fax 064-6631170

Primary Religious Education
c/o John Paul II Pastoral Centre,
Rock Road, Killarney, Co Kerry
Tel 064-6632644

Primary School Management
St Senan's Education Office
Tel 061-347777

LITURGY

Liturgical Committee
Tomás Kenny
Tel 064-6632644

PASTORAL

ACCORD
Killarney Centre: John Paul II Pastoral
Centre, Killarney, Co Kerry
Tel 064-6632644
Email jp2centre@eircom.net
Director: Very Rev John Buckley
Tralee Centre: St John's Parish Centre,
Castle Street, Tralee, Co Kerry
Tel 066-7122280
Director
Very Rev Francis Nolan

Council of Priests
Chairman
Very Rev Pádraig Walsh PP
Secretary
Very Rev Joseph Begley PP

Diocesan Pastoral Centre
Director: Rev Gearóid Godley
John Paul II Pastoral Centre,
Rock Road, Killarney, Co Kerry
Tel 064-6632644

Diocesan Pastoral Council
Chairperson: Mr Shane O'Donoghue
Secretary: Mr Tomás Kenny
John Paul II Pastoral Centre,
Rock Road, Killarney, Co Kerry
Tel 064-6632644

**Diocesan Safeguarding Children
Committee**
Chairperson: Ms Rosarii O'Connor
c/o Diocesan Office, Cathedral Walk,
Killarney, Co Kerry
Director of Safeguarding:
Ms Jacklyn McCarthy,
c/o Diocesan Office, Cathedral Walk,
Killarney, Co Kerry
Tel 087-6362780

Ecumenism
Secretary: Very Rev Pat Crean-Lynch
The Presbytery, Ardfert, Co Kerry
Tel 066-7134131

Marriage Tribunal
(See Marriage Tribunals Section)

Pastoral Renewal Team
Director
Rev Gearóid Godley
John Paul II Pastoral Centre,
Killarney, Co Kerry
Tel 064-6632644

Pilgrimage Director
Very Rev Nicholas Flynn
Bishop's House, Killarney, Co Kerry
Tel 064-6631168

Pioneer Total Abstinence Association
Diocesan Director
Very Rev Noel Spring PP
The Presbytery, Castletownbere,
Co Cork
Tel 027-70849

Pontifical Mission Societies
Diocesan Director
Rev Gearóid Godley
John Paul II Pastoral Centre,
Killarney, Co Kerry
Tel 064-6632644 Fax 064-6631170

Vocations
Director
Rev Conor Bradley
Tel 027-63045

Youth Director
c/o John Paul II Pastoral Centre,
Rock Road, Killarney, Co Kerry
Tel 064-6632644

PARISHES

The mensal parish is listed first. Other parishes follow alphabetically Historical names are given in parentheses. Church titulars are in italics.

KILLARNEY
St Mary's Cathedral, Killarney
Holy Spirit, Muckross
Resurrection, Park Road
Very Rev Kieran O'Brien Adm, VF
Very Rev Canon Joseph Begley CC
Rev Sean Jones CC
Killarney, Co Kerry
Tel 064-6631014
Email killarney@dioceseofkerry.ie

ABBEYDORNEY
St Bernard's, Abbeydorney
St Mary's, Kilflynn
Very Rev Denis O'Mahony PP, VF
Abbeydorney, Co Kerry
Tel 066-7135146
Email abbeydorney@dioceseofkerry.ie

ADRIGOLE
St Fachtna's
Very Rev Martin Sheehan
Adrigole, Bantry, Co Cork
Tel 027-60006
Email adrigole@dioceseofkerry.ie

ALLIHIES
St Michael's, Allihies,
St Michael's, Cahermore
Rev Jerry Keane, Moderator
Allihies, Bantry, Co Cork
Tel 027-73012
Email allihies@dioceseofkerry.ie

ANNASCAUL
Sacred Heart, Annascaul
St Mary's, Camp
St Joseph's, Inch
Rev Michael Moynihan, Moderator
Annascaul, Co Kerry
Tel 066-9157103
Email annascaul@dioceseofkerry.ie

ARDFERT
St Brendan's, Ardfert
Sacred Heart, Kilmoyley
Very Rev Pat Crean-Lynch PP
Ardfert, Co Kerry
Tel 066-7134131
Email ardfert@dioceseofkerry.ie

BALLINSKELLIGS (PRIOR)
St Michael the Archangel, Ballinskelligs,
St Patrick's, Portmagee,
Sacred Heart and St Finan, The Glen
Rev Patsy Lynch (SMA)
St Michael's, Ballinskelligs, Co Kerry
Tel 066-9479108
Email ballinskelligs@dioceseofkerry.ie

BALLYBUNION
St John's
Rt Rev Mgr Sean Hanafin PP
Ballybunion, Co Kerry
Tel 068-27102
Email ballybunion@dioceseofkerry.ie

BALLYDESMOND
St Patrick's
Very Rev Joseph Tarrant PP
Ballydesmond, Mallow, Co Cork
Tel 064-7751104
Email ballydesmond@dioceseofkerry.ie

BALLYDONOGHUE
St Teresa's
Rev Sean Hanafin, Moderator
Ballydonoghue, Lisselton, Co Kerry
Tel 068-47103
Email ballydonoghue@dioceseofkerry.ie

BALLYFERRITER
Uinseann Naofa, Baile an Fheitearaigh
Naomh Gobnait, Dún Chaoin
Séipéal na Carraige
Very Rev Eugene Kiely PP
Tel 066-9156131
Email
baileanfheirtearaigh@dioceseofkerry.ie

BALLYHEIGUE
St Mary's
Rev Brendan Walsh, Moderator
Ballyheigue, Tralee, Co Kerry
Tel 066-7133110
Email ballyheigue@dioceseofkerry.ie

BALLYLONGFORD
St Michael the Archangel, Ballylongford
Very Rev Michael Hussey PP
Ballylongford, Co Kerry
Tel 068-43110
Email ballylongford@dioceseofkerry.ie
St Mary's, Asdee

BALLYMACELLIGOTT
Immaculate Conception, Ballymacelligott
St Brendan's, Clogher
Very Rev Gearóid Canon Walsh PP
Ballymacelligott, Co Kerry
Tel 066-7137118
Email ballymacelligott@dioceseofkerry.ie

BEAUFORT (TUOGH)
St Mary's, Beaufort
Our Lady of the Valley, The Valley
Very Rev Fergal Ryan PP
The Presbytery, Beaufort, Co Kerry
Tel 064-6644128
Email beaufort@dioceseofkerry.ie

BOHERBUE/KISKEAM
Immaculate Conception, Boherbue
Sacred Heart, Kiskeam
Very Rev Séamus Kennelly PP
Boherbue, Mallow, Co Cork
Tel 029-76151
Email boherbue@dioceseofkerry.ie

BROSNA
St Carthage, Brosna
Our Lady of the Assumption, Knockaclarig
Very Rev Martin Spillane PP
Brosna, Co Kerry
Tel 068-44112
Email brosna@dioceseofkerry.ie

CAHIRCIVEEN
Holy Cross, O'Connell Memorial,
Immaculate Conception, Filemore;
St Joseph's, Aghatubrid
Very Rev Larry Canon Kelly PP, VF
Cahirciveen, Co Kerry
Tel 066-9472210
Email cahersiveen@dioceseofkerry.ie

CAHERDANIEL
St Crohan's, Mary Immaculate, Lohar
Most Precious Blood, Castlecove
Rev Gerard Finucane, Moderator
Caherdaniel, Co Kerry
Tel 066-9475111
Email caherdaniel@dioceseofkerry.ie

CASTLEGREGORY
St Mary's, Castlegregory
St Brendan's, Cloghane
Very Rev Eamon Mulvihill PP
Castlegregory, Co Kerry
Tel 066-7139145
Email castlegregory@dioceseofkerry.ie

CASTLEISLAND
SS Stephen and John, Castleisland
Our Lady of Lourdes, Scartaglin
Immaculate Conception, Cordal
Very Rev Maurice Canon Brick PP
Castleisland, Co Kerry
Tel 066-7141241
Email castleisland@dioceseofkerry.ie

CASTLEMAINE
St Gobnait, Keel
St Carthage, Kiltallagh
Rev Danny Broderick, Moderator
Castlemaine, Co Kerry
Tel 066-9767322
Email castlemaine@dioceseofkerry.ie

CASTLETOWNBERE AND BERE ISLAND
Sacred Heart, Castletownbere
St Bartholomew, Rossmacowen
St Michael's, Bere Island
Very Rev Noel Canon Spring PP, VF
Castletownbere, Co Cork
Tel 027-70849
Email castletownbere@dioceseofkerry.ie

CAUSEWAY
St John the Baptist, Causeway
SS Peter and Paul, Ballyduff
Very Rev Brendan Walsh PP
Causeway, Co Kerry
Tel 066-7131148
Email causeway@dioceseofkerry.ie

DINGLE
St Mary's, Dingle
St John the Baptist, Lispole
Naomh Caitlin, Ceann Trá
Very Rev Michael Canon Moynihan PP
Dingle, Co Kerry
Tel 066-9151208
Email dingle@dioceseofkerry.ie

DROMTARIFFE
St John's, Dromagh
Presentation of the BVM, Derrinagree
Rev Jack Fitzgerald, Moderator
Dromagh, Mallow, Co Cork
Tel 029-78096
Email dromtariffe@dioceseofkerry.ie

DUAGH
St Brigid's, Duagh
Sacred Heart, Lyreacrompane
Rev Declan O'Connor, Moderator
Duagh, Listowel, Co Kerry
Tel 068-45102
Email duagh@dioceseofkerry.ie

EYERIES
St Kentigern, Eyeries
Resurrection, Ardgroom
Very Rev Jerry Keane PP
Eyeries, Co Cork
Tel 027-74008
Email eyeries@dioceseofkerry.ie

FIRIES
St Gertrude, Firies
Sacred Heart, Ballyhar
Very Rev Padraig Kennelly PP
Firies, Killarney, Co Kerry
Tel 066-9764122
Email firies@dioceseofkerry.ie

FOSSA
Christ, Prince of Peace
Very Rev Niall Geaney PP
Fossa, Killarney, Co Kerry
Tel 064-6631996
Email fossa@dioceseofkerry.ie

GLENBEIGH
St James's, Glenbeigh
St Stephen's, Glencar
Very Rev Kieran O'Sullivan PP
Glenbeigh, Co Kerry
Tel 066-9768209
Email glenbeigh@dioceseofkerry.ie

GLENFLESK
St Agatha, Glenflesk
Sacred Heart, Barraduff
Our Lady of the Wayside, Clonkeen
Very Rev Jim Lenihan PP
St Agatha's Parish Centre, Headford,
Killarney, Co Kerry
Tel 064-7754008
Email glenflesk@dioceseofkerry.ie

GLENGARRIFF (BONANE)
Sacred Heart, Glengarriff
St Fachtna's, Bonane
Very Rev Niall Howard PP
Glengarriff, Co Cork
Tel 027-63045
Email glengarriff@dioceseofkerry.ie

KENMARE
Holy Cross, Kenmare
Our Lady of Perpetual Help,
Derreenderagh
Our Lady of the Assumption,
Templemore
Venerable George Hayes PP, VF
Kenmare, Co Kerry
Tel 064-6641352
Email kenmare@dioceseofkerry.ie

KILCUMMIN
Our Lady of Lourdes
Rev Kieran O'Brien, Moderator
Kilcummin, Killarney, Co Kerry
Tel 064-6643176
Email kilcummin@dioceseofkerry.ie

KILGARVAN
St Patrick's
Rev Niall Howard, Moderator
Kilgarvan, Co Kerry
Tel 064-6685313
Email kilgarvan@dioceseofkerry.ie

KILLEENTIERNA
Immaculate Conception, Currow
SS Thérèse & Colmcille, Currans
Very Rev John Buckley PP
Killeentierna, Killarney, Co Kerry
Tel 066-9764141
Email killeentierna@dioceseofkerry.ie

KILLORGLIN
St James, Killorglin
Our Lady, Star of the Sea, Cromane
Very Rev Kevin Canon Sullivan PP, VF
Killorglin, Co Kerry
Tel 066-9761172
Email killorglin@dioceseofkerry.ie

KNOCKNAGOSHEL
St Mary's
Rev John Buckley, Moderator
Knocknagoshel, Co Kerry
Tel 068-46107
Email knocknagoshel@dioceseofkerry.ie

LISTOWEL
St Mary's
Very Rev Declan Canon O'Connor PP, VF
Listowel, Co Kerry
Tel 068-21188
Email listowel@dioceseofkerry.ie

LIXNAW
St Michael's, Lixnaw
Our Lady of the Assumption, Rathea
Our Lady of Fatima and St Senan,
Irremore
Very Rev Anthony O'Sullivan PP
The Presbytery, Lixnaw, Co Kerry
Tel 066-7132111 Fax 066-7132171
Email lixnaw@dioceseofkerry.ie

MILLSTREET
St Patrick's, Millstreet
Our Lady of Lourdes, Ballydaly
Blessed Virgin Mary, Cullen
Very Rev Jack Canon Fitzgerald PP
Millstreet, Co Cork
Tel 029-70043
Email millstreet@dioceseofkerry.ie

MILLTOWN
Sacred Heart, Milltown
Immaculate Conception, Listry
Very Rev Daniel Broderick PP
Milltown, Killarney, Co Kerry
Tel 066-9767312
Email milltown@dioceseofkerry.ie

MOYVANE
Assumption of the BVM, Moyvane
Corpus Christi, Knockanure
Very Rev Brendan Carmody (SJ) PP
Moyvane, Listowel, Co Kerry
Tel 068-49308
Email moyvane@dioceseofkerry.ie

RATHMORE
Christ the King, Knocknagree
St Joseph's, Rathmore
Our Lady of Perpetual Succour, Shrone
Holy Rosary, Gneeveguilla
Very Rev Pat Canon O'Donnell PP, VF
Rathmore, Co Kerry
Tel 064-7758026
Email rathmore@dioceseofkerry.ie

SNEEM
St Michael, Sneem; St Brendan,
Glenlough; St Patrick, Tahilla
Very Rev Liam O'Brien PP
Sneem, Co Kerry
Tel 064-6645141
Email sneem@dioceseofkerry.ie

SPA
Church of the Purification, Churchill
St Joseph's, Fenit
Very Rev Francis Nolan PP
Fenit, Tralee, Co Kerry
Tel 066-7136145
Emailspa@dioceseofkerry.ie

TARBERT
St Mary's
Rev Sean Hanafin, Moderator
The Presbytery, Tarbert, Co Kerry
Tel 068-36111
Email tarbert@dioceseofkerry.ie

TRALEE, ST BRENDAN'S
Our Lady and St Brendan, Rock Street
Very Rev Pádraig Walsh PP
Rev Amos Surungai Ruto
St Brendan's, Tralee, Co Kerry
Tel 066-7125932
Email stbrendans@dioceseofkerry.ie

TRALEE, ST JOHN'S
St John the Baptist, Castle Street, Tralee
Immaculate Conception, Rathass
St Brendan's, Curaheen
Rt Rev Mgr Tadhg Fitzgerald PP, VG
Rev Mark Moriarty
Rev Bernard Healy
Rev Vitalis Barasa
St John's Presbytery, Tralee, Co Kerry
Tel 066-7122522
Email stjohns@dioceseofkerry.ie
Email stjohnscastlestreet@eircom.net

TUOSIST
St Killian's, Lauragh
Dawros, Dawros
Very Rev John Kerin PP
St Joseph's, Lauragh, Killarney, Co Kerry
Tel 064-6683107
Email tuosist@dioceseofkerry.ie

VALENTIA
Immaculate Conception, Knightstown
SS Derarca and Teresa, Chapeltown
Rev Larry Kelly, Moderator
Valentia Island, Co Kerry
Tel 066-9476104
Email valentia@dioceseofkerry.ie

WATERVILLE (DROMOD)
St Finian's, Dromod
Our Lady of the Valley, Cillin Liath
Very Rev Gerard Finucane PP
The Presbytery, Waterville, Co Kerry
Tel 066-9474703
Email waterville@dioceseofkerry.ie

INSTITUTIONS AND THEIR CHAPLAINS

Boherbue Comprehensive School
Mallow, Co Cork
Ms Fiona O'Donoghue
Tel 029-76032

Castletownbere Community School,
Co Cork
Ms Marie Murphy
Tel 027-70177

Causeway Comprehensive School
Mr Paul Montgomery
Tel 066-7131197

Coláiste na Sceilge
Cahirciveen
Tel 066-9473335
Liam Egan

Kenmare Pobalscoil Inbhear Scéine
Ms Mairéad Hickey
Tel 064-6640846

Kerry General Hospital
Rev Teddy Linehan
Rev Gerard O'Leary
Tel 066-7126222

Killarney Community College
Rev Joe Begley
Tel 064-6632764

Killarney St Columbanus Home
Killarney Parish Clergy
Tel 064-6631014

Killorglin Post-Primary Schools
Parish Clergy
Tel 066-9761172

Millstreet Community School
Co Cork
Mr John Magee
Tel 029-70087/79028

Listowel Presentation Convent
Sr Eilis Daly
Tel 068-21452

Our Lady of Fatima Home
Oakpark, Tralee, Co Kerry
Tel 066-7125900
St John's Parish Clergy

Pobalscoil Chorca Dhuibhne
Dingle
Mr Antóin Ó Braoin
Tel 066-9150055

Rathmore Community School
Ms Agnes Riordan
Parish Clergy
Tel 064-7758135

St Brendan's College
Killarney, Co Kerry
Rev Sean Jones
Tel 064-6631021

St Michael's College
Listowel, Co Kerry
Parish Clergy
Tel 068-21049/21188

Tarbert, Comprehensive School
Listowel, Co Kerry
Ms Yvonne O'Connor
Tel 068-36105

Munster Technology University
Tralee, Co Kerry
Rev Donal O'Connor
Tel 066-7145639/7135236

Tralee Mercy Secondary Mounthawk
Tel 066-7102550
Our Lady and St Brendan's Parish Clergy
Tel 066-7125932

PRIESTS OF THE DIOCESE ELSEWHERE

Rev Liam Lovell
c/o Diocesan Office,
Killarney, Co Kerry
Rev Tomás O'Caoimh
c/o Diocesan Office,
Killarney, Co Kerry
Rev Seamus O'Connell
St Patrick's College,
Maynooth, Co Kildare
Tel 01-6285222
Rev Richard O'Connor
Villa Maria Assenta, Via Aurellia 284,
00-165 Roma, Italy
Rev Anthony O'Reilly
Newry, Co Armagh

RETIRED PRIESTS

Rev Pat Ahern
Rev Con Buckley
Rev Tom Crean
Rev Brendan Harrington
Rev Martin Hegarty
Rev Roger Kelleher
Rev Tom Leane
Rev Seamus Linnane
Rev Tom Looney
Rev Eoin Mangan
Rev Pat McCarthy
Rev Seamus McKenna
Rev Joseph Nolan
Rev Philip O'Connell
Rev Michael O'Dochartaigh
Rev Tadhg Ó Dochartaigh
Rev Dan O'Riordan
Rev John Quinlan
Rev Bill Radley
Rev Luke Roche
Rev John Shanahan
Rev Patrick Sugrue

RELIGIOUS ORDERS AND CONGREGATIONS

PRIESTS

DOMINICANS
Holy Cross, Tralee, Co Kerry
Tel 066-7121135
Superior: Gregory Carroll (OP)
Email domstralee@gmail.com

ANCISCANS
anciscan Friary,
llarney, Co Kerry
l 064-6631334/6631066
x 064-6637510
ail friary@eircom.net
ardian: Rev Pat Lynch (OFM)
car: Rev Rev Antony Jukes (OFM)

BLATES OF MARY IMMACULATE
epartment of Chaplaincy,
alee General Hospital, Co Kerry
v Edward Barrett
l 066-7126222

BROTHERS

HRISTIAN BROTHERS
ristian Brothers, 14 The Orchard,
llyrickard, Tralee, Co Kerry
l 066-713910
mmunity Leader: Br Daithi O'Connell
mmunity: 2

RESENTATION BROTHERS
rt Road,
llarney, Co Kerry
l 064-6631267
ntact: Br Richard English (FPM)
mmunity: 6

AINT JOHN OF GOD BROTHERS
llorglin, Co Kerry V93 EY96
mmunity Superior
Martin Taylor (OH)
mmunity: 2

AINT JOHN OF GOD KERRY SERVICES
oonanorig, Monavalley,
alee, Co Kerry J92 HK73
l 066-7124333 Fax 066-7126197
nail kerry@sjog.ie
egional Director: Ms Claire O'Dwyer
aining and supported employment
rvice with back-up residential and
mmunity services

Mary of the Angels,
eaufort, Co Kerry V92 K738
l 064-44133 Fax 064-44302
aining, residential and community
rvices for people with an intellectual
sability

Francis Special School,
eaufort, Co Kerry
l 064-44452 Fax 064-24884
hool Principal: Liam Twomey

SISTERS

ON SECOURS SISTERS (PARIS)
n Secours Convent,
rand Street, Tralee, Co Kerry
l 066-7149800 Fax 066-7129068
o-ordinator: Sr Teresita Hoare
mmunity: 3
astoral ministry

6 Strand Street,
Tralee, Co Kerry
Tel 066-7194647
Community: 1

CONGREGATION OF THE SISTERS OF MERCY
Sisters of Mercy, Convent of Mercy,
Rock Road, Killarney, Co Kerry
Tel 064-6671498

Apartment 1, Convent of Mercy,
Rock Road, Killarney, Co Kerry

21 The Grove, Mounthawk,
Tralee, Co Kerry
Tel 066-7189029

St Brigid's Convent,
Greenville, Listowel, Co Kerry
Tel 068-21557

14 Brandon Place, Basin Road,
Tralee, Co Kerry
Tel 066-7144997

9 Carraig Lí, Killerisk,
Tralee, Co Kerry

10 Carraig Lí, Killerisk,
Tralee, Co Kerry
Tel 066-7192364

Goodwin House, The Mall,
Dingle, Co Kerry
Tel 066-9151943

Mercy Sisters, Aoibhneas,
103 Gort na Sidhe, Mounthawk,
Tralee, Co Kerry
Tel 066-7128056

7 Woodview, Moyderwell, Tralee,
Co Kerry
Tel 066-7118027

2 Carrigeendaniel Court, Caherslee,
Tralee, Co Kerry
Tel 066-7127517

1 St Brendan's Park,
Tralee, Co Kerry

3 Siena Court, Oakpark,
Tralee, Co Kerry

7 Siena Court, Oakpark,
Tralee, Co Kerry

10 Siena Court, Oakpark,
Tralee, Co Kerry

Apartment 7, Riverville House,
Oakview Village, Tralee, Co Kerry

15 Castlemorris Orchard,
Ballymullen, Tralee, Co Kerry

Apartment 6, Closheen Lane,
Roscarbery, Co Cork
Tel 023-8851753

Apartment 16, Riverville House,
Oakview Village, Tralee, Co Kerry

DOMINICAN SISTERS (KING WILLIAM'S TOWN)
Oakpark, Tralee, Co Kerry
Tel 066-7125641
Community: 3
Our Lady of Fatima Retirement Home
Tel 066-7125900 Fax 066-7180834
Email dominicansisterstralee@gmail.com
Beds: 66
Siena Court for Active Retired:
Bungalows: 10 en suite
Contact Person: Sr Teresa McEvoy OP
Email teresamcevoy@fatimahome.com

Our Lady of Fatima Home,
Tralee, Co Kerry
Contact Person: Sr Rose Clarke (OP)

Bungalow 8, Siena Court,
Tralee, Co Kerry
Contact Person: Sr Agnes Murphy (OP)
Tel 087-4439102
Email amurphy44@icloud.com

FRANCISCAN MISSIONARIES OF THE DIVINE MOTHERHOOD
Sancta Chiara,
5 St Margaret's Road,
Killarney, Co Kerry W93 Y47P
Tel 064-6626866 Fax 064-6626414
Community: 4

INFANT JESUS SISTERS
12 West End,
Millstreet, Co Cork P51 YF76

13 West End, Millstreet,
Co Cork P51 YF76

No. 1 Cois Locha,
Coolea, Co Cork P12 VH67

7 Blackrock, St Brendan's Road,
Tralee, Co Kerry V92 KC0E
Tel 066-7124455
Teaching and pastoral ministry

LITTLE COMPANY OF MARY
Park Road,
Killarney, Co Kerry
Tel 064-6671220
Community: 4

PRESENTATION SISTERS
Teach na Toirbhirte,
Miltown, Co Kerry
Tel 066-9767387
Non-resident Leader: Sr Marie Wall
Community: 3
Primary School. Tel 066-9767626
Post-Primary School. Tel 066-9767168

Presentation Convent,
Castle Street, Tralee, Co Kerry
Tel 066-7122128
Email
presentationconvtralee@gmail.com
Local Leader: Sr Mary Hoare
Community: 11
Primary School. Tel 066-7123314
Secondary School. Tel 066-7122737

Apt. 1, Presentation Convent,
Castle Street, Tralee, Co Kerry
Tel 066-7181627

Apt. 2, Presentation Convent,
Castle Street, Tralee, Co Kerry
Tel 066-7118539
Community: 1

Apt. 3, Presentation Convent,
Castle Street, Tralee, Co Kerry
Tel 066-7122828
Email elizabethbehan2012@gmail.com
Community: 1

Apt. 4, Presentation Convent,
Castle Street, Tralee, Co Kerry
Tel 066-7102862
Email joanpbvm@yahoo.com
Community: 1

Apt. 5, Presentation Convent,
Castle Street, Tralee, Co Kerry
Tel 066-7121827
Community: 1

Presentation Convent,
Castleisland, Co Kerry
Tel 066-7141256
Email prescastle1@gmail.com
Non-resident Leader: Sr Miriam Pollard
Community: 4
Primary School. Tel 066-7141147
Secondary School. Tel 066-7141178

44 The Meadows,
Listowel, Co Kerry V31 WK11
Community: 1

Presentation Convent,
Lixnaw, Co Kerry
Tel 066-7132138
Email lixnawpbvm@gmail.com
Non-resident Leader
Sr Bríd Clifford
Community: 6
Primary School. Tel 066-7132600

Presentation Convent,
Rathmore, Co Kerry
Tel 064-7758027
Email rathmoreconvent@gmail.com
Non-resident Leader: Sr Margaret O'Brien
Community: 4
Primary School. Tel 064-7758499

48 Hawley Park,
Tralee, Co Kerry
Tel 066-7122111
Community: 2

'Tigh na Féile', Ballygologue Road,
Listowel, Co Kerry
Tel 068-21156
Community: 1
Primary School. Tel 068-22294
Secondary School. Tel 068-21452
Nano Nagle School. Tel 068-21942

9 Beech Grove, Cahirdown,
Listowel, Co Kerry
Tel 068-53951
Community: 1

Mail Road, Cahirdown,
Listowel, Co Kerry
Tel 068-22500
Community: 2

7 Tamhnach Lí,
Monavalley, Tralee, Co Kerry
Tel 066-7180800
Email careyrosalie77@gmail.com
Community: 1

8 Tamhnach Lí,
Monavalley, Tralee, Co Kerry
Tel 066-7194174
Community: 1

9 Tamhnach Lí,
Monavalley, Tralee, Co Kerry
Tel 066-7193544
Community: 2

9 Woodbrooke Manor,
Monavalley, Tralee, Co Kerry
Tel 066-7185454
Email pres9wbrooke@yahoo.ie
Community: 2

31 St Joseph's Gardens,
Millstreet, Co Cork
Tel 029-71627
Email kgivenmillstreet@gmail.com
Community: 1

SISTERS OF ST CLARE
St Clare's Convent,
Kenmare, Co Kerry
Tel 064-6641385
Email stclareskenmare@eircom.net
Community: 3
St Clare's Primary. Pupils: 151
Kenmare Community School
Tel 064-6640846/7

ST JOSEPH OF ANNECY SISTERS
St Joseph's Convent,
Killorglin, Co Kerry
Tel 066-9761809 Fax 066-9761127
Superior: Sr Helena Lyne
Email margaret.lyne@talk21.com
Community: 4

St Joseph's Home for the Aged,
Killorglin, Co Kerry
Tel 066-9761124 (H)
Tel 066-9761808 (Patients)
Beds: 40

ST JOSEPH OF THE SACRED HEART SISTERS
Sisters of St Joseph of Sacred Heart,
St Joseph's, Brosna Road,
Castleisland, Co Kerry
Tel 066-7141472
Sr Theresa Herlihy

Sisters of St Joseph of Sacred Heart,
St Joseph's, 5 Allman's Terrace,
Killarney, Co Kerry
Tel 064-6623528
Sr Ellen Lane
Email eireregion@gmail.com

Sisters of St Joseph of Sacred Heart,
Apt 2, Park Avenue, Oakdale,
Killarney, Co Kerry V93 W3KN
Tel 064-6671662
Sr Eily Deasy

DIOCESAN SECONDARY SCHOOLS

St Brendan's College (Diocesan College)
Killarney, Co Kerry
Tel 064-6631021
Principal: Mr Sean Coffey

St Michael's College
Listowel, Co Kerry
Tel 068-21049
Principal: Mr John Mulvihill

CHARITABLE AND OTHER SOCIETIES

Legion of Mary
Dingle, Firies, Fossa, Glenflesk,
Kilcummin, Killarney, Killeentierna,
Knocknagree, Millstreet, Milltown,
Scartaglin, Tralee

St Vincent de Paul
Conferences at: Abbeydorney,
Annascaul, Ardfert, Ballybunion,
Ballyduff, Ballyferiter, Ballyheigue,
Ballylongford, Boherbue, Cahirciveen,
Castlemaine, Castlegregory, Castleisland
Castletownbere, Dingle, Firies, Kenmare
Killarney (four conferences), Killorglin,
Knocknagoshel, Listowel, Lixnaw,
Millstreet, Milltown, Moyvane,
Rathmore, Tralee (five conferences)

COMPREHENSIVE SELECTION OF CHURCH FURNISHINGS & SUPPLIES

Church Candles | Altar Wine | Incense & Charcoal
Mass Kits | Priest's Sick Call Sets | Indoor & Outdoor Statuary
Vestments | Stations of the Cross | Lecterns | Priedieux
Tabernacles | Papal Blessings | Chalices | Ciboria

CBC
DISTRIBUTORS

Greenbank, Newry, Co. Down BT34 2JP
Tel: (028) 3026 5216 Fax: (028) 3026 3927
If dialling from the Irish Republic: **Tel: (042) 93 32321/2 Fax: (042) 93 37248**
www.cbcdistributors.co.uk E.Mail: sales@cbcdistributors.co.uk

STOP MALNUTRITION
SAVE CHILDREN'S LIVES

Children in Crossfire have supported St Luke's Hospital in Wolisso, Ethiopia since 2009. Through our partnership, the lives of more than 5,500 very sick children have been saved.

Here you see community health checks, where early signs of severe acute malnutrition are identified and vulnerable children are referred to St Luke's.

Please support this vital work.

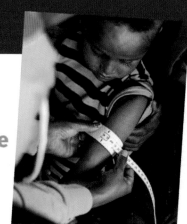

TO DONATE...

Go to:
www.childrenincrossfire.org/donate

Call us on:
028 / 048 7126 9898

Send a cheque to:
2 St Joseph's Avenue, Derry, BT48 6TH

FOR ALL YOUR PARISH NEEDS

We have the widest range of religious titles, missals, chalices, ciboria, thuribles, statues, holy water fonts, prayer cards, celebration cards and everything you need for Baptisms, Communions, Confirmations and more …

Mass Kit

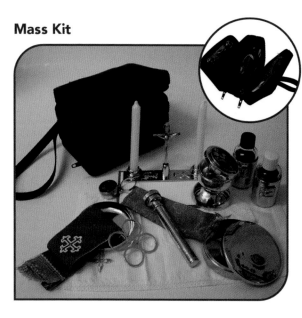

Gold- & Silver-Plated Chalice

Gold- & Silver-Plated Ciborium

Large HIS Pxy

Gold-Plated Chalice

Gold-Plated Thurible

Gold-Plated Incense Boat

20% Parish Discount Available!

Drop into one of our stores throughout Ireland
**Dublin City Centre · Blanchardstown · Cork · Derry
Letterkenny · Limerick · Newry · Tallaght**
Or order online at www.veritas.ie

DIOCESE OF KILDARE AND LEIGHLIN

PATRONS OF THE DIOCESE
ST BRIGID, 1 FEBRUARY; ST CONLETH (KILDARE), 4 MAY;
ST LAZERIAN (LEIGHLIN) 18 APRIL

INCLUDES COUNTY CARLOW AND PARTS OF COUNTIES KILDARE, LAOIS,
OFFALY, KILKENNY, WICKLOW AND WEXFORD

Most Rev Denis Nulty DD
Bishop of Kildare and Leighlin
Born 1963;
ordained priest 1988;
ordained Bishop of Kildare &
Leighlin 4 August 2013

Residence:
Bishop's House, Carlow
Tel 059-9176725/059-9142796
Email bishop@kandle.ie

CATHEDRAL OF THE ASSUMPTION, CARLOW

The ancient cathedrals of the Diocese of Kildare and Leighlin passed into Protestant usage in the period of the Reformation. Thus the cathedrals of Kildare and Old Leighlin stand on the sites of the ancient monasteries of St Brigid and St Laserian. Even before the Catholic Emancipation Act passed through the Westminster Parliament 1829), Bishop James Doyle OSA was working on the building of the Cathedral of the Assumption, Carlow. It is built on the site of and incorporates parts of the previous parish church of Carlow, which had been built in the 1780s by Dean Henry Staunton.

Carlow cathedral is not particularly large, having more the dimensions of a big parish church. The architectural work was begun by Joseph Lynch, but the final building is stamped with the design of Thomas Cobden, who replaced Lynch in 1829. Cobden gave the cathedral quite an elaborate exterior, with the obvious influence of the Bruges Town Hall tower. The cost of the building work was about £9,000. At its opening in November 1833, the interior decoration was incomplete. In fact, many elements were integrated over the following hundred years, sometimes adding to the mixture of styles.

The cathedral was consecrated on the occasion of its centenary, on 29 November 1933. A thorough reordering of the interior was completed in 1997, giving a very bright, welcoming, prayerful location for both diocesan and parish liturgical celebrations. The most notable elements are: the baptistry, the aumbry, the bishop's and president's chairs, the Hogan statue of James Doyle, former Bishop of Kildare and Leighlin popularly known as JKL, and the newly installed reliquary of St Willibrord, patron saint of Luxembourg who was educated in the Carlow area in the 7th century.

ADMINISTRATION

Diocesan Website
www.kandle.ie

Vicar General
Rt Rev Mgr John Byrne PP, VG
Dublin Road, Portlaoise, Co Laois
Tel 057-8621142

Vicars Forane
Very Rev Thomas Little PP, VF
(K&L South Deanery)
St Mary's Presbytery,
Brownshill Avenue, Carlow
Tel 059-9131559
Very Rev Mícheál Murphy PP, VF
(K&L West Deanery)
Mountmellick, Co Laois
Tel 057-8679302
Very Rev Liam Morgan PP, VF
(K&L North Deanery)
Sallins Road, Naas, Co Kildare
Tel 045-949576

Episcopal Vicar for the Pastoral Care of Priests
Very Rev Andy Leahy PP
The Presbytery, Kildare Town, Co Kildare
Tel 045-520347

Episcopal Vicar for Parish Renewal and Development
Very Rev Liam Morgan PP
Sallins Road, Naas, Co Kildare
Tel 045-949576

Consultors
Rt Rev Mgr Brendan Byrne, Chancellor
Rt Rev Mgr John Byrne PP, VG
Very Rev Andy Leahy PP
Very Rev Thomas Little PP, VF
Very Rev Mícheál Murphy PP, VF
Very Rev Liam Morgan PP, VF

Chancellor/Diocesan Secretary
Rt Rev Mgr Brendan Byrne
Email chancellor@kandle.ie
c/o Bishop's House, Carlow
Tel 059-9176725
Assistant Chancellor:
Very Rev Thomas O'Byrne Adm
c/o Bishop's House, Carlow
Tel 059-9176725
Email frthomas@kandle.ie

Diocesan Communications Liaison
Very Rev Mícheál Murphy PP, VF
Tel 057-8679302
Email mfmurphy59@gmail.com

Diocesan Communications
Very Rev Bill Kemmy PP
Tel 087-2308053
www.icatholic.ie
Rev David Vard CC
Te 057-8600121

Finance Committee
Chairperson: Mrs Anna-May McHugh
Fallaghmore, Ballylinan, Athy, Co Kildare
Recording Secretary: Rosie Boyd
Bishop's House, Carlow
Tel 059-9176725
Email rosie@kandle.ie

Diocesan Commission for Church, Art and Architecture
Chairman
Very Rev Francis MacNamara PE
Mountmellick, Co Laois
Tel 057-8624198
Secretary: Very Rev Denis Harrington PE
Clane, Co Kildare
Tel 045-868224

Director of Vocations
Very Rev Ruairí Ó Domhnaill PP
Chapel Lane, Newbridge, Co Kildare
Tel 045-431741
Email vocations@kandle.ie

Director of Diaconal Formation
Rt Rev Mgr John McEvoy PP
Rathvilly, Co Carlow
Tel 059-9161114
Email permanentdiaconate@kandle.ie

Diocesan Commission for Liturgical Formation
Chairperson: Ms Margarita Bedding
c/o Bishop's House, Carlow
Tel 059-9176725

Patron's Secretary for Primary Schools
Mr Bryan O'Reilly
c/o Bishop's House, Carlow
Tel 059-9176725/086-3400141
Email bryan@kandle.ie

Safeguarding Office
Director of Safeguarding & Diocesan Designated Liaison Person
Ms Kathleen Sherry
c/o Bishop's House, Carlow
Tel 085-8021633
Email safeguarding@kandle.ie
Deputy Designated Liaison Persons
Ms Michele Hughes
c/o Bishop's House, Carlow
Tel 086-1710643
Fr Mícheál Murphy PP
Mountmellick
Tel 057-8679302
Mr Mick Daly
c/o Bishop's House, Old Dublin Road
Carlow
Tel 059-9176725
Diocesan Garda Vetting Administrator
Rosie Boyd
c/o Bishop's House, Carlow
Tel 059-9176725
Email rosie@kandle.ie

Archivist
Diocesan Archivist: Bernie Deasy
Delany Archive, Carlow College,
St Patrick's, College Street, Carlow
Tel 059-9153200
Email bdeasy@carlowcollege.ie

FAITH DEVELOPMENT SERVICES

Faith Development Services
Cathedral Parish Centre, College Street,
Carlow Town
Tel 059-9164084 Fax 059-9164020
Email fds@kandle.ie
Primary Diocesan Advisor
Ms Maeve Mahon
Email maeve.mahon@kandle.ie
Post-Primary Diocesan Advisor
Ms Hilda Campbell
Email hilda.campbell@kandle.ie
Youth Ministry/Meitheal Co-ordinator
Mr Robert Norton
Email robert.norton@kandle.ie
Pastoral Resource Person
Ms Julie Kavanagh
Email julie.kavanagh@kandle.ie

Church Music
Rev Liam Lawton Adm
Edenderry, Co Offaly Tel 046-9732352
Email liamlawtonireland@gmail.com

Catholic Primary School Managers Association
Chairman
Very Rev Thomas O'Byrne Adm
The Presbytery, Old Dublin Road, Carlow
Tel 059-9131227
Secretary: Br Camillus Regan
c/o Bishop's House, Carlow
Tel 087-2244175
Email patbros@iol.ie

PASTORAL

ACCORD
Centre Directors
Carlow: Very Rev Patrick Hennessy PP
The Presbytery,
Leighlinbridge, Co Carlow
Tel 059-9721463
Ms Mary Merrigan
Tel 059-9138738
Portlaoise: Fr Paddy Byrne PP
Tel 087-9948505
Accord, Parish Office, Portlaoise, Co Laois
Newbridge: Very Rev Joseph McDermott
Accord Office, Parish Centre,
Station Road, Newbridge, Co Kildare
Tel 045-431695

ALPHA
Very Rev James O'Connell Adm
The Parochial House, Ballon, Co Carlow
Tel 059-9159329

Conciliators
Rt Rev Mgr John McDonald PE, CC
Curragh Camp, Co Kildare
Tel 045-441369
Very Rev William O'Byrne PP
Kill, Co Kildare
Tel 045-878008
Mr Brian O'Sullivan
Drumcooley, Edenderry, Co Offaly
Tel 046-9731522 (W) 046-31435 (H)

Diocesan Committee for Adoration
Chairperson: Br Matthew Hayes
Tel 057-8755964
Secretary: Elizabeth Murphy
Email murphylizls@gmail.com

Ecumenism
Director: Deacon Patrick Roche
Leighlinbridge, Co Carlow
Tel 083-1957783

Pioneer Total Abstinence Association
Diocesan Director
Very Rev Mark Townsend PP
Graignamanagh, Co Kilkenny
Tel 059-9724238

Pontifical Mission Societies
Diocesan Director
Very Rev George Augustine PP
Kilcock, Co Kildare
Tel 01-6103512

Polish Chaplaincy
Rev Piotr Jakubiak
The Presbytery, Ballymany,
Newbridge, Co Kildare
Tel 045-434069

Prisons
Contact Priest: Rev Eugene Drumm (SPS)
Portlaoise Prison, Portlaoise, Co Laois
Tel 057-8622549

Travellers
Chaplains
Very Rev Thomas Dooley PP
Portarlington, Co Laois
Tel 057-8643004
Very Rev John Brickley PP
Cooleragh, Coill Dubh, Naas, Co Kildare
Tel 045-860281

Youth Ministry Team
Meitheal Co-ordinator: Mr Robert Norton
Email robert.norton@kandle.ie
Faith Development Services,
Cathedral Parish Centre,
College Street, Carlow
Tel 059-9164084 Fax 059-9164020

PARISHES

Mensal parishes are listed first. Other parishes follow alphabetically. Historical names are given in parentheses. Church titulars are in italics.

CATHEDRAL, CARLOW
Cathedral of the Assumption
Email info@carlowcathedral.ie
Website www.carlowcathedral.ie
Very Rev Thomas O'Byrne Adm
The Presbytery, Carlow
Tel 059-9131227 Fax 059-9130805

Rev Teodor Tomasik (SVD) CC
The Presbytery, Carlow
Tel 059-9131227
Rev Yanbo Chen (SVD) CC
Rev Martin Smith (SPS) CC
1 Green Road, Carlow
Tel 059-9142632
Permanent Deacon: Rev David O'Flaherty
Tel 059-9164086
Cathedral Parish Shop & Office
Tel 059-9164087

ASKEA
Holy Family
Email office@askeaparish.ie
Very Rev Thomas Little PP, VF
Browneshill Avenue, Carlow
Tel 059-9131559
Email tomedwardlittle@gmail.com
Rev Tommy Dillon PE, CC
Parochial House, Askea, Carlow
Tel 059-9164882
Email dillontommy@gmail.com

ABBEYLEIX
Holy Rosary, Abbeyleix
St Patrick, Ballyroan
Very Rev Paddy Byrne PP
Abbeyleix, Co Laois
Tel 057-8731135
Rev Petru Medves CC
Abbeyleix Parish Office,
Abbeyleix, Co Laois
Tel 085-1853069

ALLEN
Holy Trinity, Allen
St Brigid's, Milltown
Immaculate Conception, Allenwood
Very Rev William Byrne PP
Allen, Kilmeague, Naas, Co Kildare
Tel 045-860135
Rev Brian Kavanagh CC
St Patrick's College, Maynooth, Co Kildare
Tel 045-890559

ARLES
Sacred Heart, Arles, St Anne's, Ballylinan
St Abban's, Maganey
Email arlesparish@gmail.com
Very Rev Padraig Shelley PP
The Presbytery, Arles, Co Carlow
Tel 059-9147637

BALLINAKILL
St Brigid's, Ballinakill
St Lazarian's, Knock
Very Rev Paddy Byrne PP
Abbeyleix, Co Laois
Tel 087-9948505
Rev Petru Medves CC
Tel 085-1853069
Very Rev Seán Conlon PE, CC
Ballinakill, Co Laois
Tel 057-8733336

BALLON
SS Peter and Paul, Ballon
St Patrick's, Rathoe
Very Rev James O'Connell Adm
Parochial House, Ballon, Co Carlow
Tel 059-9159329

BALLYADAMS
St Joseph's, Ballyadams
St Mary's, Wolfhill
Holy Rosary, Luggacurren
Very Rev Daniel Dunne PP
Tullamoy, Stradbally, Co Laois
Tel 059-8627123

BALLYFIN
St Fintan's
Very Rev Joseph Brophy PP
Ballyfin, Portlaoise, Co Laois
Tel 057-8755227
Rev P.J. Fitzgerald (SPS) CC
Mountrath, Co Laois
Tel 057-8732234

BALTINGLASS
St Joseph's, Baltinglass
St Oliver's, Grange Con
St Mary's, Stratford
Email admin@baltinglassparish.ie
Very Rev Gerard Ahern PP
Parkmore, Baltinglass, Co Wicklow
Tel 059-6482678
Email aherngerard22@gmail.com

BALYNA
St Mary's, Broadford,
St Patrick's Johnstownbridge,
St Brigid's, Clogherinchoe
Email balynaparish2020@gmail.com
Website www.balynaparish.ie
Very Rev Séan Maher PP
Broadford, Co Kildare
Tel 046-9551203

BENNEKERRY
St Mary's
Email office@askeaparish.ie
Very Rev Thomas Little PP, VF
St Mary's, Browneshill Avenue, Carlow
Tel 059-9131559
Email tomedwardlittle@gmail.com
Rev Tommy Dillon PE, CC
Parochial House, Askea, Carlow
Tel 059-9164882
Email dillontommy@gmail.com

BORRIS
Sacred Heart, Borris
St Patrick's, Ballymurphy
St Forchan's, Rathanna
Email borrisparish@gmail.com
Very Rev Rory Nolan PP
Borris, Co Carlow via Kilkenny
Tel 059-9773128

CARAGH
Our Lady and St Joseph, Caragh,
Email parishoffice@caragh.net
Very Rev Rúairí O'Domhnaill Adm
Chapel Lane, Newbridge, Co Kildare
Tel 045-431741
Very Rev Joseph McDermott PE, CC
Parochial House, Caragh, Naas, Co Kildare
Tel 045-903889

CARBURY
Holy Trinity, Carbury
Holy Family, Derrinturn
Email carburyparish@gmail.com
Very Rev John Fitzpatrick PP
Carbury, Co Kildare
Tel 046-9553355

CLANE
SS Patrick and Brigid, Clane
Sacred Heart, Rathcoffey
Email claneparish@eircom.net
Website www.claneparish.com
Very Rev Paul O'Boyle PP
Clane, Naas, Co Kildare
Tel 045-868249
Email oboylepaul@eircom.net
Permanent Deacon: Rev John Dunleavy
Tel 045-861393

CLONASLEE
St Manman's
Email clonaslee@eircom.net
Very Rev Thomas O'Reilly Adm
Clonaslee, Co Laois
Tel 057-8648030

CLONBULLOGUE
Sacred Heart, Clonbullogue
St Brochan's, Bracknagh,
Immaculate Conception, Walsh Island
Very Rev Gregory Corcoran PP
Rhode, Co Offaly
Tel 087-9402669
Rev Sean Hyland CC
29 Pine Villa, Portarlington, Co Laois
Tel 057-8645582/087-9486769
Permanent Deacon: Rev Gary Moore
Tel 046-9737579

CLONEGAL
St Brigid's, Clonegal
St Lasarian's, Kildavin
Very Rev Pat Hughes PP
Myshall, Co Carlow
Tel 059-9157635
Very Rev Joseph Fleming PE, CC
Clonegal, Enniscorthy, Co Wexford
Tel 053-9377298

CLONMORE
St Mary's, Ballyconnell
St Finian's, Kilquiggan
Our Lady of the Wayside, Clonmore
St Finian's Oratory, Killinure
Email clonmoreoffice.parish@gmail.com
Very Rev John O'Brien PP
Parochial House, Killinure,
Tullow, Co Carlow
Tel 059-9156344
Email frjohn51@gmail.com

COOLERAGH AND STAPLESTOWN
Christ the King, Cooleragh,
St Benignus, Staplestown
Email standco100@gmail.com
Very Rev John Brickley PP
Cooleragh, Coill Dubh, Naas, Co Kildare
Tel 045-860281

CURRAGH CAMP
St Brigid's
Very Rev P. J. Somers PP
Chaplain's House, Curragh Camp,
Co Kildare
Tel 045-441277
Email spj44@hotmail.com
Rt Rev Mgr John McDonald PE, CC
Chaplain's House, Curragh Camp,
Co Kildare
Tel 045-441369

DAINGEAN
Mary Mother of God, Daingean
SS Peter and Paul, Kilclonfert
St Francis of Assisi and St Brigid,
Ballycommon; Oratory of the
Immaculate Conception, Cappincur
Email daingeanparish@eircom.net
Very Rev Declan Thompson (SPS) PP
St Mary's Road, Daingean, Co Offaly
Tel 057-9362653
Very Rev Patrick O'Byrne PE, CC
St Mary's Road, Daingean, Co Offaly
Tel 057-9353064

DOONANE
St Abban's, Doonane
Blessed Virgin Mary, Mayo
Very Rev Denis Murphy Adm
Tolerton, Ballickmoyler, Carlow
Tel 056-4442126

DROICHEAD NUA/NEWBRIDGE
St Conleth's, Newbridge
Cill Mhuire, Ballymany
St Eustace's, Dominican Church
Parish Office: 045-431394
Email parishoffice@newbridgeparish.net
Very Rev Rúairí O'Domhnaill PP
Chapel Lane, Newbridge, Co Kildare
Tel 045-431741
Rev Michal Cudzilo
Curate's House, Chapel Lane,
Newbridge, Co Kildare
Very Rev Joseph McDermott PE, CC
Caragh, Naas, Co Kildare
Tel 045-903889
Email jmcder44@gmail.com
Rev Eugen Dragos Tamas CC
Curate's House, Chapel Lane,
Newbridge, Co Kildare
Tel 045-433979
Rev Piotr Jakubiak
The Presbytery, Ballymany,
Newbridge, Co Kildare
Tel 045-434069
Website www.newbridgeparish.ie
Permanent Deacon: Rev Jim Stowe
c/o Parish Office, Station Road,
Droichead Nua, Co Kildare
Tel 045-431394

EDENDERRY
St Mary's
Email edenderryparishcentre@gmail.com
Very Rev Liam Lawton Adm
Very Rev P.J. McEvoy PP
St Mary's, Edenderry, Co Offaly
Tel 046-9732352
Rev Larry Malone *(in residence)*
Edenderry, Co Offaly
Tel 046-9732352
Permanent Deacon: Rev Paul Wyer
Tel 046-9733311

EMO
St Paul's, Emo; Sacred Heart, Rath
Email
portarlingtonparishoffice@eircom.net
Very Rev Thomas Dooley Adm
Patrick Street, Portarlington, Co Laois
Tel 057-8643004
Email frtomdooley@eircom.net
Rev Joe O'Neill CC
Priest's House, Emo, Portlaoise, Co Laois
Tel 089-4535533

GRAIGNAMANAGH
Duiske Abbey, Graignamanagh
Our Lady of Lourdes,
Skeoughvosteen, Co Kilkenny
Email graigparish@kandle.ie
Very Rev Mark Townsend PP
Parochial House,
Graignamanagh, Co Kilkenny
Tel 059-9724238
Abbey Centre: 059-9724238

GRAIGUECULLEN
St Clare's, Graiguecullen
Holy Cross, Killeshin
Email gkparish@gmail.com
www.graiguecullenkilleshin.com
Very Rev John Dunphy PP
Graiguecullen, Carlow
Tel 059-9141833
Email dunphiej@gmail.com
Permanent Deacon: Rev Joe O'Rourke
c/o Parish Office, Graiguecullen, Carlow
Tel 059-9141833

HACKETSTOWN
St Brigid's, Hacketstown
Our Lady, Killamoate
Church of the Immaculate Conception,
Knockananna
Church of Our Lady, Askinagap
Email hacketstownparish@gmail.com
Very Rev Terence McGovern PP
Main Street, Hacketstown, Co Carlow
Tel 087-6754811

KILCOCK
St Coca, Kilcock
Nativity of the BVM, Newtown
Email info@kilcockandnewtownparish.i
Website www.kilcockandnewtownparish.
Very Rev George Augustine PP
Mill Lane, Kilcock, Co Kildare
Tel 01-6103512
Rev Adriano De Oliveira CC
Curate's House, Mill Lane,
Kilcock, Co Kildare
Tel 01-6757311

KILDARE

St Brigid's, Kildare
Our Lady of Victories, Kildangan
Sacred Heart, Nurney
Parish Office: 045-521352
Email kildareparish@gmail.com
Website www.kildareparish.ie
Very Rev Andy Leahy PP
The Presbytery, Kildare Town
Tel 045-520347
Very Rev Adrian Carbery PE, CC
6 Beech Grove, Kildare
Tel 045-521900

KILL

St Brigid's, Kill
St Anne's, Ardclough
Email admin@killparish.ie
Website www.killparish.ie
Very Rev William O'Byrne PP
Kill, Naas, Co Kildare
Tel 045-878008
Very Rev Matthew Kelly PE, CC
10 Hartwell Green, Kill, Naas, Co Kildare
Tel 045-877880

KILLEIGH

St Patrick's, Killeigh
St Joseph's, Ballinagar
St Mary's, Raheen
Email office@killeigh.com
Website www.killeigh.com
Very Rev John Stapleton PP
Killeigh, Co Offaly
Tel 057-9344161
Email john@killeigh.com
Rt Rev Mgr Thomas Coonan PE, CC
Geashill, Co Offaly
Tel 057-9343517

LEIGHLIN

St Laserian's, Leighlin
St Fintan's, Ballinabranna
Very Rev Patrick Hennessy PP
Leighlinbridge, Co Carlow
Tel 059-9721463
Permanent Deacon: Rev Pat Roche
Leighlinbridge, Co Carlow
Tel 059-9722607

MONASTEREVIN

SS Peter and Paul, Monasterevin
Email monasterevin.parish@gmail.com
Very Rev Liam Merrigan PP
Drogher Road, Monasterevin, Co Kildare
Tel 045-525346

MOUNTMELLICK

St Joseph's, Mountmellick
St Mary's, Clonaghadoo
Email stjosephs1878@gmail.com
Very Rev Mícheál Murphy PP, VF
1 Ashgrove, Mountmellick, Co Laois
Tel 057-8679302
Very Rev Noel Dunphy PE, CC
Mountmellick, Co Laois
Tel 057-8624141

MOUNTRATH

St Fintan's, Mountrath
Sacred Heart, Hollow
Very Rev Joseph Brophy PP
Ballyfin, Portlaoise, Co Laois
Tel 057-8755227
Rev P.J. Fitzgerald (SPS) CC
Mountrath, Co Laois
Tel 057-8732234

MUINEBHEAG/BAGENALSTOWN

St Andrew's, Bagenalstown
St Patrick's Newtown
St Laserian's, Ballinkillen
Email bagenalstownparish@gmail.com
Website www.bagenalstownparish.ie
Very Rev Declan Foley PP
The Presbytery, Muinebheag, Co Carlow
Tel 059-9721154
Email pdlfoley@gmail.com
Rev Shem Furlong CC
Muinebheag Parish Office,
Bagenalstown, Co Carlow
Tel 087-2400582

MYSHALL

Exaltation of the Cross, Myshall
St Laserian's, Drumphea
Very Rev Pat Hughes PP
Myshall, Co Carlow
Tel 059-9157635

NAAS

Our Lady and St David, Naas
Irish Martyrs, Ballycane
Very Rev Liam Morgan PP, VF
Sallins Road, Naas, Co Kildare
Tel 045-949576
Rev Robert Petrisor CC
Sallins Road, Naas, Co Kildare
Tel 045-897703
Rev Alex Kochatt CC
77 The Lakelands, Naas, Co Kildare
Tel 045-949576
Rev Michael Flattery (SMA) CC
364 Sundays Well, Naas, Co Kildare
Tel 045-876197
Permanent Deacon: Rev Fergal O'Neill
Tel 086-3816133

PAULSTOWN

The Assumption, Paulstown
Holy Trinity, Goresbridge
Email gbptparish@gmail.com
Very Rev James Kelly PP
Goresbridge, Co Kilkenny
Tel 059-9775180

PORTARLINGTON

St Michael's, Portarlington
St John the Evangelist, Killenard
Email
portarlingtonparishoffice@eircom.net
Very Rev Thomas Dooley PP
Patrick Street, Portarlington, Co Laois
Tel 057-8643004
Email frtomdooley@eircom.net
Rev Joe O'Neill CC
Emo, Portlaoise, Co Laois
Tel 057-8646517

PORTLAOISE

SS Peter and Paul, Portlaoise
The Assumption, The Heath
The Holy Cross, Ratheniska
Email info@portlaoiseparish.ie
Website www.portlaoiseparish.ie
Rt Rev Mgr John Byrne PP, VG
Parochial House,
Portlaoise, Co Laois
Tel 057-8692153
Email john@portlaoiseparish.ie
Rev David Vard CC
Annebrook, Stradbally Road,
Portlaoise, Co Laois
Tel 057-8688440
Rev Ciprian Matei CC
Tower Hill, Portlaoise, Co Laois
Tel 057-8621142
Permanent Deacon: Eugene Keyes
c/o Parish Office
Tel 057-8621142

PROSPEROUS

Our Lady and St Joseph, Prosperous
Email prosperousparishoffice@eircom.net
Rev Bernard Reyhart CC
c/o Parish Office,
Prosperous, Co Kildare
Tel 045-841806

RAHEEN

St Fintan's, Raheen
St Brigid's, Shanahoe
Very Rev Paddy Byrne PP
The Presbytery, Ballinakill Road,
Abbeyleix, Co Laois
Tel 057-8731135
Rev Petru Medves CC
Abbeyleix Parish Office,
Abbeyleix, Co Laois
Tel 087-1853069

RATHANGAN

Assumption and St Patrick
Very Rev Bill Kemmy PP
Rathangan, Co Kildare
Tel 087-2308053
Very Rev Gerard O'Byrne PE, CC
Rathangan, Co Kildare
Tel 045-524316
Email gerobyrne@eircom.net

RATHVILLY

St Patrick's, Rathvilly
St Brigid's, Talbotstown
Blessed Virgin Mary, Tynock
Email office@rathvillykilteganparish.ie
Rt Rev Mgr John McEvoy PP
Rathvilly, Co Carlow
Tel 059-9161114
Rev Pat O'Brien (SPS) CC
Kiltegan, Co Wicklow
Tel 059-6473211
Permanent Deacon Liam Dunne
c/o Parish Office
Tel 059-9161114

RHODE

St Peter's, Rhode
St Anne's, Croghan
Website www.rhodeparish.ie
Very Rev Gregory Corcoran PP
Rhode, Co Offaly
Tel 046-9737010
Rev Sean Hyland CC
29 Pine Villa, Portarlington, Co Laois
Tel 057-8645582/087-9486769
Permanent Deacon: Rev Gary Moore
Tel 046-9737579

ROSENALLIS

St Brigid's
Email rosenallisparish@eircom.net
Website www.rosenallis.com
Very Rev Thomas Walshe PP
Rosenallis, Portlaoise, Co Laois
Tel 057-8628513

ST MULLINS

St Moling's, Glynn
St Brendan's, Drummond
Very Rev Edward Aughney Adm
Glynn, St Mullins via Kilkenny
Tel 051-424563

SALLINS

Our Lady of the Rosary & Guardian Angels
Email office@naasparish.net
Very Rev Liam Morgan PP,VF
Sallins Road, Naas, Co Kildare
Tel 045-949576

STRADBALLY

Sacred Heart, Stradbally
Assumption, Vicarstown
St Michael, Timahoe
Email stradballychurch@gmail.com
Very Rev Gerard Breen PP
Parochial House, Stradbally, Co Laois
Tel 057-8625132
Very Rev Seán Kelly PE, CC
Stradbally, Co Laois
Tel 057-8625831

SUNCROFT

St Brigid's
Email suncroftparish@eircom.net
Very Rev Barry Larkin PP
Suncroft, Curragh, Co Kildare
Tel 045-441586

TINRYLAND

St Joseph's
Website www.tinryland.ie
Very Rev Thomas Little Adm, VF
Brownshill Avenue, Carlow
Tel 059-9131559
Email tomedwardlittle@gmail.com

TULLOW

Most Holy Rosary, Tullow
Immaculate Conception, Ardattin
St John the Baptist, Grange
Email tullowparish@outlook.com
Website www.tullowparish.com
Very Rev Brian Maguire (SPS) PP
The Shroughaun, Tullow, Co Carlow
Tel 059-9180377
Permanent Deacon: Vincent Crowley
c/o Parish Office
Tel 059-9151277

TWO-MILE-HOUSE

Very Rev Liam Morgan PP, VF
Sallins Road, Naas, Co Kildare
Tel 045-949576

INSTITUTIONS AND THEIR CHAPLAINS

Abbeyleix District Hospital
Very Rev Paddy Byrne PP
Tel 057-8731135

Baltinglass District Hospital
Very Rev Gerard Ahern PP
Tel 087-6298881

County Hospital, Portlaoise
Rt Rev Mgr John Byrne PP, VG
Portlaoise, Co Laois
Tel 057-8621142

Curragh Camp
Very Rev P.J. Somers PP
Tel 045-441369

Edenderry Hospital
Very Rev Liam Lawton Adm
Tel 046-9731296

Institute of Technology, Carlow
Rev Martin Smith (SPS)
Tel 059-9142632

Naas General Hospital, Co Kildare
Stiofan O'Murchadha
Tel 045-897221

Portlaoise Prison
Rev Eugene Drumm (SPS)
Tel 057-8622549

Sacred Heart Hospital, Carlow
Very Rev Thomas O'Byrne Adm
Tel 059-9131227

St Brigid's Hospital
Shaen, Portlaoise, Co Laois
Rt Rev Mgr John Byrne PP, VG
Tel 057-8621142

St Dympna's Hospital, Carlow
Very Rev Thomas O'Byrne Adm
Tel 059-9131227

St Fintan's Hospital, Portlaoise
Rt Rev Mgr John Byrne PP, VG
Dublin Road, Portlaoise, Co Laois
Tel 057-8621142

St Vincent's Hospital, Mountmellick
Very Rev Micheál Murphy PP, VF
Mountmellick, Co Laois
Tel 057-8679302

PRIESTS OF THE DIOCESE ELSEWHERE

Rev Kilian Byrne
Dublin Regional Marriage Tribunal
Very Rev Peter Cribbin
c/o Bishop's House, Dublin Road, Carlow
Very Rev Patrick Dunny
Wood Road, Graignamanagh, Co Kilkenny
Tel 059-9724518
Rev Paul McNamee
c/o Bishop's House, Dublin Road, Carlow

RETIRED PRIESTS

Rt Rev Mgr Brendan Byrne PE
c/o Bishop's House, Carlow
Tel 059-9176725
Very Rev Charles Byrne
c/o Bishop's House, Carlow
Very Rev Gerald Byrne PE
15 New Road, Leighlinbridge, Co Carlow
Very Rev Patrick Daly PE
Braganza, Athy Road, Carlow
Very Rev James Gahan PE
c/o Bishop's House, Carlow
Very Rev Denis Harrington PE
Clane, Co Kildare
Tel 045-868224
Very Rev Brendan Howard PE
Hillview Nursing Home,
Tullow Road, Carlow
Very Rev Edward Kavanagh PE
Rath, Emo, Co Laois
Very Rev Tom Lalor PE
The Presbytery, Tinryland, Co Carlow
Tel 087-2360355
Rev James McCormack
c/o Bishop's House, Carlow
Very Rev Francis McNamara PE
Parochial House, Davitt Road,
Mountmellick, Co Laois
Tel 057-8624198
Rev Michael Moloney PE
43 The Waterways, Sallins,
Naas, Co Kildare
Very Rev Edward Moore PE
Marian House, Sallins Road,
Naas, Co Kildare
Very Rev Alphonsus Murphy PE
Carbury, Co Kildare
Tel 046-9553020
Very Rev Michael Noonan PE
Portarlington, Co Laois
Tel 057-8623431
Very Rev John O'Connell PE
The Presbytery, Two-Mile-House,
Naas, Co Kildare
Tel 045-876160
Rt Rev Mgr Caomhín O'Neill PE
Emmaus, Abbeyleix, Co Laois

ery Rev Philip O'Shea PE
onagoose, Borris, Co Carlow
ery Rev Thomas O'Shea PE
owran Abbey Nursing Home,
owran, Co Kilkenny
ery Rev Denis O'Sullivan PE
o Bishop's House, Carlow

RELIGIOUS ORDERS AND CONGREGATIONS

PRIESTS

ARMELITES (OCARM)
armelite Priory, White Abbey,
o Kildare R51 X827
el 045-521391 Fax 045-522318
mail carmeliteskildare@gmail.com
rior: Rev Chacko Antony
nandiparahibil (OCarm)

OMINICANS
ominican College Newbridge,
roichead Nua, Co Kildare
el 045-487200
mail
ewbridge.community@dominicans.ie
rior: Very Rev Joseph Bulman
econdary School

SUITS
ongowes Wood College,
ane, Co Kildare
el 045-868663/868202 Fax 045-861042
mail (College) reception@clongowes.ie
ommunity) reception@clongowes.ie
ector: Rev Michael Sheil (SJ)
eadmaster: Mr Chris Lumb
ce-Rector: Rev Bernard McGuckian (SJ)
inister: Br Tom Phelan (SJ)
oarding School for Secondary Pupils

T PATRICK'S MISSIONARY SOCIETY
Patrick's, Kiltegan, Co Wicklow
el 059-6473600 Fax 059-6473622
mail spsoff@iol.ie (office)
ciety Leader: Rev Richard Filima (SPS)
ssistant Society Leader
ev Sean Cremin (SPS)

BROTHERS

ATRICIAN BROTHERS
Hawthorn Drive,
llow, Co Carlow
l 059-9181727 Fax 059-9181728
ovince Leader: Br Camillus Regan (FSP)
ommunity: 1

ewbridge, Co Kildare
l 045-431475 Fax 045-431505
perior: Br James O'Rourke (FSP)
ommunity: 2

trician Brothers,
vansheath, Mountrath, Co Laois
l 057-8755964
perior: Br Gerard Reburn (FSP)
ommunity: 3

The Irish Province has seven houses
in Kenya
Regional Superior
Br Placido Kaburu (FSP)
Patrician Formation House,
PO Box 5064, via Eldoret, Kenya
Tel/Fax 0321-61134
Email pbroskam@africaonline.co.ke
Community: 9

SISTERS

BRIGIDINE SISTERS
16 Mount Clare,
Graguecullen, Co Carlow
Tel 059-9135869
Contact: Sr Maureen O'Leary
Community: 1
Retired

Brigidine Convent, Tullow, Co Carlow
Tel 059-9151308
Community Co-ordinator
Sr Thomasina Murphy
Community: 7
Education, Parish Work, Pastoral Care
and Retired

Brigidine Sisters,
Delany Court, New Chapel Lane,
Tullow, Co Carlow
Contact: Sr Elizabeth Mary McDonald
Community: 5
Parish Work, Education, Retired

Teach Bhríde, Tullow, Co Carlow
Tel/Fax 059-9152465
Email teachbhride@eircom.net
Contact: Sr Carmel McEvoy
Community: 1
Holistic education centre

11 The Rise,
Ballymurphy Road, Tullow, Co Carlow
Tel 059-9152498
Contact: Sr Betty McDonald
Community: 1

1 Salem House,
Chantiere Gate, Portlaoise, Co Laois
Tel 057-8665516
Contact: Sr Angela Phelan
Community: 1

Sue Ryder Centre
Kilminchy, Portlaoise, Co Laois
Community: 1

Carlow Road, Abbeyleix, Co Laois
Tel 057-8731467
Community: 2
Contact: Sr Mary Hiney
Parish, Adult education

Brigidine Sisters,
Castletown Road, Mountrath, Co Laois
Tel 057-8732799
Contact: Sr Mary Sheedy
Community: 4
Parish and Pastoral Work

Solas Bhríde, 14 Dara Park, Kildare
Tel 045-522890 Fax 045-522212
Contact: Sr Rita Minehan
Community: 1
Education, spirituality centre

Solas Bhride Centre & Hermitages
Tully Road, Kildare Town, Co Kildare
Tel 045-522890
Contact: Sr Mary Minehan
Community: 2
Spirituality Centre

Brigidine Sisters, 22 Marble Court,
Paulstown, Co Kilkenny
Tel 059-9726156
Contact: Sr Margaret Walsh
Community: 2
Parish Ministry

**CHARITY OF JESUS AND MARY,
SISTERS OF**
Ros Glas, Moore Abbey,
Monasterevan, Co Kildare
Tel 045-525478
Matron: Majella Keefe
Email maryannal@eircom.net
Community: 5
Assisted Living Community

Grove House Community, Moore Abbey,
Monasterevin, Co Kildare
Contact: Sr Philomena Enright
Tel 087-2480738
Email philomena194@hotmail.com
Community: 1

Suaimhneas, Cappakeel, Emo, Co Laois
Tel 057-8626541
Community: 3

**CONGREGATION OF THE SISTERS OF
MERCY**
*The Sisters of Mercy minister throughout
the diocese in pastoral and social work,
community development, counselling,
spirituality, education and health care,
answering current needs.*

St Leo's Convent of Mercy,
Carlow R93 CX81
Tel 059-9131158 Fax 059-9142226
Community: 7

4 Pinewood Avenue,
Rathnapish, Carlow R93 X242
Tel 059-9140408
Community: 1

Convent of Mercy,
Monasterevin, Co Kildare W34 HH79
Tel/Fax 045-525372
Community: 2

St Helen's Convent of Mercy,
Naas, Co Kildare W91 H9TC
Tel 045-897673
Community: 4

Convent of Mercy,
Leighlinbridge, Co Carlow R93 CP80
Tel 059-9721350 Fax 059-9721350
Community: 3

4 Lacken View, Naas,
Co Kildare W91 R8AF
Tel 045-874168
Community: 1

37 Lakelands, Naas,
Co Kildare W91 XR9Y
Tel 045-875496
Community: 1

9 Spring Gardens, Naas,
Co Kildare W91 A5DF
Tel 045-876013
Community: 3

DAUGHTERS OF MARY AND JOSEPH
3/4 Sycamore Road, Connell Drive,
Newbridge, Co Kildare
Tel 045-431842
Community: 2
Pastoral

SISTERS OF THE HOLY FAMILY OF BORDEAUX
Holy Family Convent,
Droichead Nua, Co Kildare
Tel 045-431268
Contact: Sr Colette Keegan
Community: 23
Retired sisters, parish work, teaching
English to non-nationals, counselling

'Sonas Chríost', Moorfield Park,
Droichead Nua, Co Kildare
Tel 045-431939
Contact: Sr Eileen Murphy
Community: 3
Sisters involved in community, parish
work, chaplaincy to secondary school

LA SAINTE UNION DES SACRES COEURS
Mountpleasant Lodge
Nursing Care Home,
Kilcock, Co Kildare
Community: 4

POOR CLARES
Poor Clare Colettine Monastery,
Graiguecullen, Carlow
Email poorclarescarlow@gmail.com
Abbess: Mother Rosario Byrne
Community: 9
Perpetual adoration, contemplatives

PRESENTATION SISTERS
Generalate, Monasterevin,
Co Kildare W34 PV32
Tel 045-525335/525503 Fax 045-525209
Email admin@pbvm.org
www.pbvm.org
Congregational Leader
Sr Julie Watson
Community: 5

Presentation Sisters,
127 Brocanwood House,
Monasterevin, Co Kildare
Community: 2

Mount St Anne's
Retreat and Conference Centre,
Killenard, Portarlington, Co Laois
Tel 057-8626153 Fax 057-8626700
Director: Dr Oonagh O'Brien
Email ceo.mountstannes@gmail.com
Facilities available for seminars, retreats,
conferences and meetings on request
Community: 2 (Intercongregational)
Tel 057 9647057

Presentation Convent, Ashbrook Gardens,
Mountrath Road, Portlaoise,
Co Laois R32 HD43
Tel 057-8670877
School, counselling and pastoral
Community: 9
School and pastoral work

Apr 6, 53 Beechfield,
Portlaoise, Co Laois R32 A891
Community: 1

56 Oakley Park,
Tullow Road, Carlow R93 A2W2
Tel 059-9143103
Community: 2
School ministry and pastoral

Presentation Convent,
Bridge Street, Mountmellick,
Co Laois R32 HH77
Tel 057-8624129
Community: 11
Parish and pastoral ministry

Shalom, Kilcock,
Co Kildare W23 FH30
Tel 01-6287018 Fax 01-6287316
Community: 15
Care of sick and elderly sisters

Cul na Cille, Kilcock,
Co Kildare W23 HC95
and
No. 2 Dean's Court, Kilcock,
Co Kildare W23 P086
Tel 01-6284502
Community: 6

Presentation Sisters,
27 Abbeyfield, Kilcock,
Co Kildare W23 HV22
and No. 1 Dean's Court, Kilcock,
Co Kildare W23 XE84
Tel 01-6284579
Community: 4
Spirituality, pastoral ministry

SISTERS OF ST JOHN OF GOD
49 Blundell Wood,
Edenderry, Co Offaly
Tel 046-9731582

EDUCATIONAL INSTITUTIONS

Carlow College (founded 1782)
College Street, Carlow
Tel 059-9153200
Email infocc@carlowcollege.ie
Website www.carlowcollege.ie
President
Rev Conn Ó Maoldhomhnaigh MA
Vice-President and Bursar
Rt Rev Mgr John McEvoy
Chaplain: Rev Liam Dunne, Deacon
Priests on Staff
Rev Dr Fergus Ó Fearghaill DSS
Rev Dr Dermot Ryan DD

Holy Family Secondary School
Newbridge, Co Kildare
Principal: Ms Sarah Allen
Chaplain: Sr Kate Cuskelly

St Mary's, Knockbeg College
Knockbeg, Carlow
Tel 059-9142127 Fax 059-9134437
Email info@knockbegcollege.ie
Headmaster: Mr Michael Carew
Chaplain: Fr John Dunphy
www.knockbegcollege.ie

St Mary's Secondary School
Edenderry
Principal: Emmett McDonnell
Chaplain: Fr Liam Lawton

St Paul's Secondary School
Monasterevin
Principal: Brian Bergin
Chaplain: Fr Liam Merrigan

CHARITABLE AND OTHER SOCIETIES

Community Services
St Catherine's
Community Services Centre,
St Joseph's Road, Carlow
Tel 059-9138700

DIOCESE OF KILLALA

PATRON OF THE DIOCESE
ST MUREDACH, 12 AUGUST

INCLUDES PORTIONS OF COUNTIES MAYO AND SLIGO

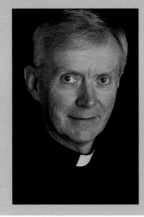

Most Rev John Fleming DD, DCL
Bishop of Killala;
born 16 February 1948;
ordained priest 18 June 1972;
ordained Bishop of Killala
7 April 2002

Residence: Bishop's House,
Ballina, Co Mayo
Tel 096-21518
Fax 096-70344
Email bishop@killaladiocese.org

ST MUREDACH'S CATHEDRAL, BALLINA

ilt between 1827 and 1831, St uredach's Cathedral is the fourth dest Roman Catholic Cathedral in land. It follows a building tradition gun by Waterford and Lismore in 1796 d followed by Dublin in 1825 and omore in 1829. While Bishop Peter aldron (1814-1835) put forward the ea of building a cathedral, Bishop John Hale was the force which saw the

Cathedral open its doors for the celebration of the Eucharist in 1831.

Ten years later the ornate ceiling, which is a distinguishing mark of the cathedral, was put in place. Work on the cathedral was suspended during the Famine and only resumed in 1853, when the construction of the Spire began. The entire work was completed in 1892.

Marcus Murray, the architect of the cathedral, gave the work of creating the

very ornate ceiling to Arthur Canning. This work was interrupted by the Famine and only completed in 1855. In 2014 marks on the ceiling indicated some deterioration. Following examination, all the timbers supporting the entire ceiling were replaced and the ceiling itself repaired by George O'Malley. During 2015 and 2016 a major program of restoration has taken place and the work continues.

Photo: David Farrell, The Western People, Ballina

CHAPTER

Dean: Vacant
Chancellor
Rt Rev Mgr Seán Killeen PP, VG
Archdeacon: Vacant
Members
Very Rev John George Canon MacHale
PP, VF

ADMINISTRATION

Vicar General
Rt Rev Mgr Seán Killeen VG
Cloghans, Ballina, Co Mayo

Vicars Forane
Very Rev Dr Aidan O'Boyle VF
Very Rev Gerard O'Hora PP, VF
Very Rev Edward Rogan PP, VF
Very Rev John Loftus PP, VF

College of Consultors
Most Rev John Fleming DD, DCL
Very Rev Michael Flynn PP
Very Rev Michael O'Horo PP
Very Rev Edward Rogan PP
Very Rev Dr Michael Gilroy PP
Rev Liam Reilly CC

Finance Secretary
Very Rev Dr Michael Gilroy DD, PP
Skreen, Co Sligo
Tel 071-9166629

Diocesan Secretary
Mrs Anne Forbes
Bishop's House, Ballina, Co Mayo
Tel 096-21518 Fax 096-70344
Email secretary@killaladiocese.org

CATECHETICS EDUCATION

Diocesan Advisers for Religious Education
Primary: Sr Patricia Lynott
Post-Primary: Vacant
Newman Institute, Cathedral Close,
Ballina, Co Mayo
Tel 096-72066

Diocesan Education Council
Chairman: Mr John Cummins

LITURGY

Church Music
Director: Ms Regina Deacy
c/o The Pastoral Centre, Ballina, Co Mayo
Tel 096-70555

Diocesan Liturgy and Music Commission
Chairman: Very Rev Michael Flynn PP
Parochial House, Knockmore,
Ballina, Co Mayo
Tel 094-58108

PASTORAL

ACCORD
Director: Very Rev Gerard O'Hora
The Pastoral Centre, Ballina, Co Mayo
Tel 096-70555

Building Committee
Chairperson
Rt Rev Mgr Seán Killeen VG

Child Safeguarding Committee
Chairperson: Dr Mairín Glynn

Communications
Director: Vacant

Council of the Laity
Chairperson: Peter McLoughlin

Council of Priests
Chairperson: Very Rev Francis Judge PP
Parochial House, Mullenmore Road,
Crossmolina, Co Mayo
Tel 096-31677
Secretary
Very Rev Michael Reilly, Co-pastor
Rathduff, Ballina, Co Mayo
Tel 096-21596

Diocesan Finance Committee
Chairman
Most Rev John Fleming DD, DCL
Secretary: Ms Anne Forbes

Ecumenism
Director
Very Rev Anthony Gillespie PP

Emigrants
Advisor: Very Rev Michael Harrison PP
Killala, Co Mayo
Tel 096-32176

Immigrants
Diocesan Representative
Vacant

Legion of Mary
Director
Very Rev John Loftus PP
Ballycastle

Marriage Tribunal
(See Marriage Tribunals section)

Pilgrimages
Director: Rev Tom Doherty CC

Pioneer Total Abstinence Association
Diocesan Director
Very Rev Patrick Munnelly PP
Ardagh, Ballina, Co Mayo
Tel 096-31144

Pontifical Mission Societies
Diocesan Director
Very Rev Edward Rogan PP

Travellers
Chaplain: Very Rev Michael Reilly PP

Trócaire
Secretary: Rev Michael Nallen
Aughoose, Ballina, Co Mayo
Tel 097-87990

Vocations
Director: Rev Tom Doherty CC

Youth Ministry
Co-ordinator: Rev Francis Judge

PARISHES

BALLINA (KILMOREMOY)
St Muredach's Cathedral, St Patrick's
Parish Team
Very Rev Dr Aidan O'Boyle PP
Cathedral Presbytery, Ballina, Co Mayo
Tel 096-71365
Very Rev Anthony Gillespie
Cathedral Presbytery, Ballina, Co Mayo
Tel 096-71355
Very Rev Kieran Holmes
St Patrick's Presbytery, Ballina, Co Mayo
Tel 096-71360

BACKS
Christ the King
Very Rev Michael Flynn PP
Knockmore, Ballina, Co Mayo
Tel 094-9258108
St Teresa's
Very Rev Michael Reilly, Co-pastor
Rathduff, Ballina, Co Mayo
Tel 096-21596

ARDAGH
Very Rev Patrick Munnelly PP
Ardagh, Ballina, Co Mayo
Tel 096-31144

BALLYCASTLE (KILBRIDE AND DOONFEENY)
St Bridget's, St Teresa's
Very Rev John Loftus PP
Ballycastle, Co Mayo
Tel 096-43010

BALLYCROY
Holy Family
Very Rev Christopher Ginnelly PP
Parochial House, Ballycroy,
Westport, Co Mayo
Tel 098-49134

BALLYSOKEARY
Very Rev James Corcoran PP
Cooneal, Ballina, Co Mayo
Tel 096-32242

[BE]LMULLET
[Sa]cred Heart, Our Lady of Lourdes
[Ve]ry Rev Edward Rogan PP
[Re]v Tom Doherty
[Re]v Tony Cavanagh
[Be]lmullet, Co Mayo
[Tel] 097-81426

[CA]STLECONNOR
[St] Joseph's
[Ve]ry Rev Desmond Kelly PP
[Co]rballa, Ballina, Co Mayo
[Tel] 096-36266

[CR]OSSMOLINA
[St] Tiernan's, Holy Souls,
[Ou]r Lady of Mercy, St Mary's
[Ve]ry Rev Francis Judge PP
[Cr]ossmolina, Co Mayo
[Tel] 096-31677
[Re]v Gabriel Rosbotham CC
[Ch]apel Road, Crossmolina, Co Mayo
[Tel] 096-31344

[DR]OMORE-WEST (KILMACSHALGAN)
[Ve]ry Rev Joseph Hogan PP
[Dr]omore West, Co Sligo
[Tel] 096-47012

[EA]SKEY
[St] James's
[Ve]ry Rev Joseph Hogan PP
[Ea]skey, Co Sligo
[Tel] 096-49011

[KIL]COMMON-ERRIS
[Ve]ry Rev Michael Nallen PP
[Ag]hoose, Ballina, Co Mayo
[Tel] 097-87990
[Re]v Tom Doherty CC
[Ch]urch Road, Belmullet, Co Mayo

[KIL]FIAN
[Sa]cred Heart
[Ve]ry Rev Gerard O'Donnell PP
[Kil]fian, Killala, Co Mayo
[Tel] 096-32420

[KIL]GLASS
[Ho]ly Family, Christ the King
[Ve]ry Rev Gerard O'Hora PP
[En]niscrone, Ballina, Co Mayo
[Tel] 096-36164
[Ve]ry Rev Canon John George MacHale
[(pr]iest in residence)
[Kil]glass, Enniscrone, Ballina, Co Mayo
[Tel] 096-36191

[KIL]LALA
[St] Patrick's
[Ve]ry Rev Michael Harrison PP
[Kil]ala, Co Mayo
[Tel] 096-32176

[KIL]MORE-ERRIS
[St] Joseph's, Holy Family, Seven Dolours
[Ve]ry Rev Kevin Hegarty PP
[Ki]rne, Belmullet, Co Mayo
[Tel] 097-81011
[Re]v Tony Cavanagh CC
[Bin]ghamstown Ballina, Co Mayo
[Tel] 097-82350

KILTANE
Sacred Heart
St Pius X
Very Rev James Cribbin, PP
Geesala, Bangor, Ballina, Co Mayo
Tel 097-86740

LACKEN
St Patrick's
Very Rev Michael Harrison PP
Carrowmore, Ballina, Co Mayo
Tel 096-34014

LAHARDANE (ADDERGOOLE)
St Patrick's
Very Rev John Reilly PP
Lahardane, Ballina, Co Mayo
Tel 096-51007

MOYGOWNAGH
St Cormac's
Very Rev Matthew McGrath (SPS) PP
(protem)
Moygownagh,
Ballina, Co Mayo
Tel 096-31288

SKREEN AND DROMARD
St Adamnan's
Very Rev Dr Michael Gilroy DD, PP
Skreen, Co Sligo
Tel 071-9166629

TEMPLEBOY
Very Rev Dr Michael Gilroy DD, PP
Skreen, Co Sligo
Tel 071-9166629

INSTITUTIONS AND THEIR CHAPLAINS

An Coláiste
Rossport, Ballina, Co Mayo
Tel 097-88940

Convent of Mercy
Belmullet, Co Mayo
Tel 097-81044
Rev Kevin Hegarty

Convent of Jesus and Mary
Enniscrone, Ballina, Co Mayo
Tel 096-36151
Rev Gerard O'Hora

Convent of Jesus and Mary
Crossmolina, Co Mayo
Tel 096-30876/30877
Very Rev Francis Judge PP

Distrist Hospital
Ballina, Co Mayo
Tel 096-21166
Very Rev Dr Aidan O'Boyle

District Hospital
Belmullet, Co Mayo
Tel 097-81301
Very Rev John Loftus

St Mary's Secondary School
Ballina, Co Mayo
Tel 096-70333

Vocational School
Easkey, Co Sligo
Tel 096-49021
Very Rev Kieran Holmes

Vocational School
Ballina, Co Mayo
Tel 096-21472
Rev Tom Doherty

Vocational School
Crossmolina, Co Mayo
Tel 096-31236
Rev Gabriel Rosbotham CC

Vocational School
Belmullet, Co Mayo
Tel 097-81437
Rev Michael Nallen

Vocational School
Lacken Cross, Co Mayo
Tel 096-32177
Very Rev Michael Harrison

PRIESTS OF THE DIOCESE ELSEWHERE

Rev Liam Reilly
On loan to Diocese of Reno, Nevada

RETIRED PRIESTS

Very Rev Michael Conway
Barr Trá, Enniscrone, Co Sligo
Very Rev Gerard Gillespie
Rathball, Ballina, Co Mayo
Very Rev Martin Keveny
Cathedral Place, Ballina, Co Mayo
Very Rev Brendan Hoban
Sliabh Rua, Breaffy, Ballina, Co Mayo
Very Rev Patrick Hoban
St Jude's Avenue,
Crossmolina, Co Mayo
Rev John Judge
Killaser, Swinford, Co Mayo
Rt Rev Mgr Sean Killeen
Cloghans, Ballina, Co Mayo
Rt Rev Mgr Kevin Loftus
Enniscrone, Co Sligo
Very Rev Peter O'Brien
Ballina, Co Mayo
Very Rev Michael O'Horo
Templeboy, Co Sligo

Retired Priests (Other Dioceses)
Very Rev Joseph Cahill (SSC)
Bohernasup, Ballina, Co Mayo
Very Rev Leonard Taylor
Rathlee, Easkey, Co Sligo

RELIGIOUS ORDERS AND CONGREGATIONS

PRIESTS

SPIRITUAL LIFE INSTITUTE
Holy Hill Hermitage, Skreen, Co Sligo
Tel 071-66021
Superior: Sr Patricia McGowan
Community: 2

SISTERS

CONGREGATION OF THE SISTERS OF MERCY
Sisters of Mercy, 'Bethany',
8/9 Rockwell Estate, Killala Road,
Ballina, Co Mayo F26 H7D5
Tel 096-23066
Community: 5

Sisters of Mercy,
28 Moy Heights, Ballina,
Co Mayo F26 D8P6
Community: 1

35 Amana Estate,
Ballina, Co Mayo F26 H9N6
Community: 2

96 Knocknalyre, Sligo Road,
Ballina, Co Mayo F26 T6X9
Community: 1

JESUS AND MARY, CONGREGATION OF
Convent of Jesus and Mary,
Mullinmore Road,
Crossmolina, Co Mayo
Tel 096-30877
Contact person: Sr Anne Dyar
Headmistress: Tel 096-31194/096-31597
Community: 4
Post-Primary Coeducational Day School
Tel 096-31131
Principal: Mr John Mangan
Pupils: 520

'St Claudines',
Convent of Jesus and Mary,
Church Road, Enniscrone, Co Sligo
Tel 096-36151
Animator: Sr Mary Kelly
Community: 4
Post-Primary, Coeducational School
Tel 096-36496
Principal: Sr Mary Kelly
Pupils: 370

EDUCATIONAL INSTITUTIONS

St Muredach's College
Ballina, Co Mayo
Tel 096-21298
Principal: Mr Leo Golden
Chaplain: Rt Rev Mgr Sean Killeen

Newman Institute Ireland
Centre for Pastoral Care,
Cathedral Place, Ballina, Co Mayo
Tel 096-72066
Chancellor
Most Rev John Fleming, DD, DCL
Director: Very Rev Dr Michael Gilroy DC

CHARITABLE AND OTHER SOCIETIES

Society of St Vincent de Paul
Ozanam House, Teeling Street,
Ballina, Co Mayo
Tel 096-72905

St Joseph's Young Priests Society
c/o Pastoral Centre, Ballina, Co Mayo
Tel 096-70555

Legion of Mary
c/o Pastoral Centre, Ballina, Co Mayo
Tel 096-70555

ACCORD
CMAC Centre
c/o Pastoral Centre, Ballina, Co Mayo
Tel 096-70555

DIOCESE OF KILLALOE

PATRON OF THE DIOCESE
ST FLANNAN, 18 DECEMBER

INCLUDES PORTIONS OF COUNTIES CLARE, LAOIS, LIMERICK,
OFFALY AND TIPPERARY

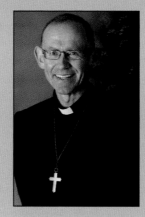

Most Rev Fintan Monahan DD
Bishop of Killaloe;
born 23 January 1967,
ordained priest 16 June 1991,
ordained Bishop of Killaloe
25 September 2016

Residence:
Westbourne, Ennis, Co Clare
Tel 065-6828638
Fax 065-6842538
Email office@killaloediocese.ie
Website www.killaloediocese.ie

CATHEDRAL OF SS PETER AND PAUL, ENNIS

e church that now serves as the hedral of the Diocese of Killaloe was ginally built to serve as the parish urch of Ennis. The diocese had not had ermanent cathedral since the formation. In 1828, Francis Gore, a otestant landowner, donated the site the new Catholic church. Dominick dden, who also designed the hedrals in Ballina and Tuam, was osen as the architect.

The construction of the new church s a protracted affair. Shortly after the rk began, the project ran into ancial difficulties and was suspended three years. Aided by generous nations from local Protestants, luding Sir Edward O'Brien of omoland and Vesey Fitzgerald, the rk began again in 1831. Progress was w throughout the 1830s and there re many problems. In September 1837 ere was a serious accident on the site en the scaffolding collapsed, killing o and seriously injuring two more. ally, in 1842, the roof was on and the rish priest, Dean O'Shaughnessy, was le to say the first Mass inside the still-finished building.

On 26 February 1843, the new church s blessed and placed under the tronage of Saints Peter and Paul, by hop Patrick Kennedy. Fr Matthew, e Apostle of Temperance', preached sermon.

Much still remained to be done on project, but the Great Famine ught the work to a halt. After the nine, the work recommenced. J. J. Carthy, one of the leading church hitects in nineteenth-century Ireland, s commissioned to oversee the erior decoration of the building. ch of this is still visible, including the ernal pillars and arches and the organ lery.

A local committee decided in 1871 to mplete the tower and spire, but owing financial difficulties, it was not until October 1874 that the final stone was t in place.

In 1889 Dr Thomas McRedmond was pointed coadjutor bishop and he was

consecrated in 1890. He had full charge of the diocese, owing to the illness of Bishop Flannery. Though he was already Parish Priest of Killaloe, the new bishop chose to make Ennis his home, remaining there after he succeeded to the office of diocesan bishop, on the death of Dr Flannery. The Parish Church of Ss Peter and Paul was thus designated the pro-cathedral of the diocese.

Major renovations were carried out in 1894. The present main entrance under the tower was constructed, a task that necessitated breaking through a six-foot-thick wall. The building was also redecorated. The improvements were under the direction of Joshua Clarke, father of the stained-glass artist Harry Clarke. The large painting of the Ascension, which dominates the sanctuary, the work of the firm Nagle and Potts, was also installed at this time. The building remained largely unchanged for the next eighty years. A new sacristy and chapter room were added in the 1930s, as were the pipe organ and chapter stalls for the canons.

Another major renovation was carried out in 1973 to bring the building into line with the requirements of the Second Vatican Council. The architect for the work was Andrew Devane and the main contractors were Ryan Brothers, Ennis. The artistic adviser was Enda King. The building was reopened after six months in December 1973. The Clare

Champion reported: 'The main features of the renovation included new altar, ambo, new tabernacle on granite pillar, baptismal font located near sanctuary, new flooring. New heating system, new amplification system and complete reconstruction of the sanctuary.'

In 1990, 163 years after work on the building began, Bishop Harty named it The Cathedral of the Diocese. The solemn dedication of the cathedral and the altar took place on 18 November 1990. A fire at a shrine in the cathedral in October 1995 caused serious internal damage. The sanctuary had to be rebuilt and the building redecorated. The restoration was celebrated with Solemn Evening Prayer in November 1996.

In 2006 major repair and refurbishment was completed on the Cathedral spire.

Most Rev William Walsh DD
Retired Bishop of Killaloe;
born 1935; ordained priest 21 February
1959; ordained Bishop of Killaloe
2 October 1994
Residence: 'Camblin', College View,
Clare Road, Ennis, Co Clare
Tel 087-2618960

CHAPTER

Dean: Vacant
Archdeacon: Vacant
Chancellor: Very Rev Brendan Canon
O'Donoghue AP, Shannon
Precentor: Vacant
Treasurer: Vacant
Members
Very Rev Seamus Canon Mullin AP,
Miltown Malbay

COLLEGE OF CONSULTORS

Rev Des Hillery VG
Rev Pat Malone
Rev Albert McDonnell, Chancellor
Rev Tom Ryan
Rev Ger Jones
Rev John Molloy

ADMINISTRATION

Killaloe Diocesan Office
Diocesan Chancellor
Rev Albert McDonnell
Email a.mcdonnell@killaloediocese.ie
Diocesan Secretary: Rev Ger Jones
Email g.jones@killaloediocese.ie
Diocesan Finance Manager
Ms Cathy Sheehan
Email c.sheehan@killaloediocese.ie
Diocesan Office Administrator
Ms Claire Thynne
Secretarial: Ms Mary Brohan
Westbourne, Ennis, Co Clare
Tel 065-6828638 Fax 065-6842538
Email office@killaloediocese.ie
Education Secretary: Rev Gerry Kenny
Westbourne, Ennis, Co Clare
Tel 085-7858344

Vicar General
Rev Des Hillery VG
c/o Diocesan Office

Safeguarding
Ms Cleo Yates
Westbourne, Ennis, Co Clare
Tel 086-8096027
Email c.yates@killaloediocese.ie

Finance Committee
Chairman: Mr Aidan Spooner
Recording Secretary: Ms Cathy Sheehan
Mr David Williams
Mr Owen Smyth
Mr Des Leahy
Rev Albert McDonnell Co-PP, VF
Bishop Fintan Monahan
Rev Des Hillery VG
Rev Ger Jones Co-PP

Killaloe Priests' Benevolent Fund
Secretary: Ms Cathy Sheehan
c/o Westbourne, Ennis, Co Clare
Tel 065-6828638 Fax 065-6842538

Killaloe Priests' Subsidy Fund
Secretary: Ms Cathy Sheehan
c/o Westbourne, Ennis, Co Clare
Tel 065-6828638 Fax 065-6842538

Killaloe Priests' Hospital Fund
Secretary: Ms Cathy Sheehan
c/o Westbourne, Ennis, Co Clare
Tel 065-6828638 Fax 065-6842538

Diocesan Archivist
c/o Diocesan Chancellor
Westbourne, Ennis, Co Clare
Tel 065-6828638 Fax 065-6842538

Diocesan Secretary
Rev Ger Jones
c/o Westbourne, Ennis, Co Clare
Tel 065-6828638

Episcopal Vicars for Retired Priests
Rev Tony Casey Co-PP, VF
Cooraclare, Co Clare
Tel 065-9059008
Rev Pat Larkin Co-PP, VF
Kilmaley, Co Clare
Tel 065-6839735
Rev Michael Cooney Co-PP
Terryglass, Co Tipperary
Tel 067-22017

CATECHETICS EDUCATION

Boards of Management
Primary Schools
St Senan's Education Office,
Diocesan Pastoral Centre,
St Munchin's College, Limerick
Tel 061-347777
Director: Fiona Shanley
Email sseo@ldo.ie
Acting Director: Aoife Foley

Religious Education in Primary Schools
Directors: Sr Essie Hayes
Ashe Road, Nenagh, Co Tipperary
Tel 067-33835
Mr Joe Searson
Mullagh, Co Clare
Tel 065-7087875/087-6762023

Religious Education in Post-Primary Schools
c/o Diocesan Office
Westbourne, Ennis, Co Clare
Tel 065-6828638

PASTORAL

Diocesan Pastoral Development
Pastoral Worker: Ms Maureen Kelly
Secretary: Ms Jean Gaynor
45 Garden View, Greggaun na Hilla,
Clarecastle, Co Clare
Tel 065-6847096

Biblical Ministry
Sr Marie McNamara
c/o Killaloe Diocesan Office,
Westbourne, Ennis, Co Clare
Tel 065-6842235

Diocesan Pastoral Council
Chair: Don O'Sullivan
Secretary: Jean Gaynor
45 Garden View, Creggaun na Hilla,
Clarecastle, Co Clare
Tel 065-6847096

ACCORD
Director: Rev Damien Nolan Co-PP, VF
Ennis ACCORD Centre,
7 Carmody Street Business Park,
Ennis, Co Clare
Tel 1850-585000

Communications
Director
Rev Brendan Quinlivan Co-PP, VF
c/o Bishop's House, Westbourne,
Ennis, Co Clare
Tel 065-6828638

Child Protection Committee
Chairperson: Tracey Murray
Delegates:
Ms Cleo Yates, Director of Safeguardin
Tel 086-8096027
Mr Joe Searson
Tel 085-2535326

Ecumenism
Director: Dr Susan O'Brien
Westbourne, Ennis, Co Clare
Tel 065-6724721
Email se.obrien@me.com

Lourdes Pilgrimage
Director: Very Rev Tom Ryan Co-PP, VF
Cathedral House, Ennis, Co Clare
Te 065-6824043

Marriage Tribunal
(See Marriage Tribunals section)

Pastoral Care of Immigrants
c/o Bishop's House,
Westbourne, Ennis, Co Clare
Tel 065-6828638

ntifical Mission Societies
ocesan Director*
v Tom O'Halloran Co-PP, VF
rrisokane, Co Tipperary
067-27105

cial Services
ver Arch Family Resource Centre
Silver Street,
nagh, Co Tipperary E45 P624
067-31800
recare
rmony Row, Ennis, Co Clare
065-6828178

vellers
aplain
Bishops House, Westbourne,
nis, Co Clare
065-6828638

cations
ector: Rev Ignatius McCormack
Flannan's College,
nis, Co Clare
065-6828019/086-2777139

PARISHES

e Diocese of Killaloe was divided into Pastoral Areas in July 2018. Historical mes are given in parentheses. Church lars are in italics.

ASTORAL AREA 1 – COIS FHARRAIGE

RISHES: CARRIGAHOLT, CROSS, ONBEG & KILKEE
r Lady of Lourdes, Cross; St John the ptist, Kilbaha; Blessed Virgin Mary, rigaholt; The Holy Spirit, Doonaha; dy Assumed into Heaven, Doonbeg; St nan, Belaha; The Immaculate nception and St Senan, Kilkee; St nnan, Lisdeen

-PPs
v Gerard Kenny Co-PP
ircular Road, Kilkee, Co Clare
065-9056580
v Michael Casey Co-PP, VF
ochial House, Cross,
rush, Co Clare
065-9058008

toral Offices
KEE: Parish Office, Circular Road,
kee, Co Clare
065-9056580
ish email office@kilkeeparish.com
ish Website www.doonbeginfo.com
OSS: Parish Office, Cross,
rush, Co Clare
065-9058008
ish email kilballyowen@eircom.net
ish Website www.loopheadclare.com

PASTORAL AREA 2 – INIS CATHAIGH

PARISHES: COORACLARE, KILMIHIL, KILLIMER & KILRUSH
St Senan, Cooraclare; St Mary, Cree; St Michael, Kilmihil; St Senan, Knockerra; St Imy, Killimer; St Senan, Kilrush; Little Senan Church, Monmore

Co-PPs
Rev Anthony Casey Co-PP, VF
Kilmacduane, Cooraclare, Co Clare
Tel 065-9059008
Rev Pat Larkin Co-PP
47 Woodfield Crescent, Kilrush, Co Clare
Tel 065-9262729

Priest in Residence
Rev Peter O'Loughlin AP
Kilmihil, Co Clare
Tel 065-9050016

Pastoral Offices
KILRUSH: Toler Street, Kilrush, Co Clare
Tel 065-9051093
Parish email kilrushparishoffice@gmail.com
COORACLARE: Kilmacduane, Cooraclare, Co Clare
Tel 065-9059008
Parish email cooraclareandcreeparish@gmail.com
KILMIHIL: Parish Office, Kilmihil, Co Clare
Tel 065-9050824
Parish email kilmihilparishoffice@gmail.com

PASTORAL AREA 3 – RADHARC NA NOILEÁN

PARISHES: BALLYNACALLY/LISSYCASEY, COOLMEEN, KILDYSART & KILMURRY MCMAHON
Our Lady of the Wayside, Lissycasey; Christ the King, Ballynacally; St Benedict, Coolmeen; St Mary, Cranny; St Michael, Kildysart; St Mary, Kilmurry McMahon; St Kieran, Labasheeda

Co-PPs
Rev Albert McDonnell Co-PP, VF
The Presbytery, Kings Road, Kildysart, Co Clare
Tel 085-7811823
Rev Brendan Kyne Co-PP
The Presbytery, Ballycorick, Co Clare

Priests in Residence
Rev Joseph Hourigan
Parochial House, Lissycasey, Co Clare
Tel 065-6834145
Rev Tom McGrath (MHM)
Mountshannon, Labasheeda, Co Clare
Rev Paddy McMahon
The Presbytery, Labasheeda, Co Clare
Tel 065-6830932

Pastoral Office
RADHARC NA NOILEAN: Community Centre, Kildysart, Co Clare V95 XKP3
Tel 065-6832838
Email radharcpastoralarea@gmail.com

PASTORAL AREA 4 – CRÍOCHA CALLAN

PARISHES: INAGH/KILNAMONA, KILMALEY, MILTOWN MALBAY & MULLAGH
St Mary, Mullagh; Our Lady, Star of the Sea, Quilty; The Most Holy Redeemer, Coore; St Joseph, Milltown Malbay; St Mary, Moy; Immaculate Conception, Inagh; The Blessed Virgin Mary, Cloonanaha; St Joseph, Kilnamona; St John the Baptist, Kilmaley; Our Lady of the Wayside, Inch; St Michael the Archangel, Connolly

Co-PPs
Rev John McGovern Co-PP
Parochial House, Kilmaley,
Ennis, Co Clare V95 ENK6
Tel 065-6839735
Rev Donagh O'Meara Co-PP, VF
Parochial House, Carhuligane,
Mullagh, Co Clare
Tel 065-7087012
Rev Martin Shanahan Co-PP
Parochial House, Inagh, Co Clare
Tel 087-7486935

Priests in Residence
Rev Seán Murphy AP
The Presbytery,
Miltown Malbay, Co Clare
Tel 065-7084129
Canon Seamus Mullin AP
The Presbytery,
Miltown Malbay, Co Clare
Tel 065-7084003
Rev Sean Sexton AP
Kilnamona, Ennis, Co Clare
Tel 065-6829507
Canon Michael McLaughlin
Airfield, Inch, Co Clare
Tel 065-6839332

Pastoral Offices
INAGH-KILNAMONA: Parish office, Inagh, Ennis, Co Clare
Tel 085-2315709
Parish email parishofficeik@gmail.com
KILMALEY: Parish Office, Parochial House, Kilmaley, Ennis, Co Clare
Tel 065-6839735
Parish email kilmaleyparish@gmail.com
MILLTOWN MALBAY: Parish Office, The Presbytery, Miltown Malbay, Co Clare
Tel 065-7079829
Parish email malbayparish@eircom.net
MULLAGH: Parish Office, Carhuligane, Mullagh, Co Clare
Tel 065-7087161
Parish email:office@kibparish.ie

PASTORAL AREA 5 – ABBEY

PARISHES: ENNIS, CLARECASTLE, DOORA-BAREFIELD & QUIN

Cathedral of St Peter and Paul, Ennis; St Joseph's Lifford; Christ the King, Cloughleigh; St Breckan, Doora; The Immaculate Conception, Barefield; Church of Our Lady, Roslevan; St Mary's, Quin; St Stephen's, Maghera; St John XXIII, Clooney

Co-PPs
Rev Tom Ryan Co-PP, VF
Cathedral Presbytery, O'Connell Street,
Ennis, Co Clare
Tel 065-6824043
Rev Ger Jones Co-PP
The Presbytery, 1 Shallee Drive,
Cloughleigh, Ennis, Co Clare
Tel 065-6840715
Rev David Carroll Co-PP
St Joseph's Presbytery, 52 Kincora Park,
Lifford, Ennis, Co Clare
Tel 065-6822166
Rev Tom O'Gorman Co-PP
The Presbytery, Quin, Co Clare
Tel 065-6824043
Rev Patrick Malone Co-PP
Parochial House, Church Drive,
Clarecastle, Co Clare
Tel 065-6823011
Rev Tom Fitzpatrick Co-PP
3 The Woods, Cappahard, Tulla Road,
Ennis, Co Clare
Tel 065-6822225
Rev Martin Blake Co-PP
Cathedral Presbytery,
O'Connell Street, Ennis, Co Clare
Tel 065-6824043

Curate
Rev Joy Njarakattuvely CC
Catherdral Presbytery,
O'Connell Street, E
nnis, Co Clare
Tel 065-6824043

Priests in Residence
Rev Harry Brady AP
10 Beechwood, Lissane,
Clarecastle, Co Clare
Tel 065-6797256
Rev Ignatius McCormack
St Flannan's College, Ennis

Pastoral Sisters
Sr Betty Curtin, Ennis
Tel 065-6868542

Pastoral Offices
CLARECASTLE: Parish Office, Church
Drive, Clarecastle, Co Clare
Tel 065-6823011
Parish email
clarecastleballyea@eircom.net
Parish website
www.clarecastleballyeaparish.ie
DOORA-BAREFIELD: 3 The Woods,
Cappahard, Tulla Road, Ennis, Co Clare
Tel 065-6822225
Parish email
doorabarefieldparish@eircom.net

ENNIS: Cathedral House, O'Connell
Street, Ennis, Co Clare
Tel 065-6824043 Fax 065-6842541
Parish email info@ennisparish.com
Parish website www.ennisparish.com
QUIN: Parish Office, Parochial House,
Quin, Co Clare
Tel 065-6825612
Parish email qcm@gmail.com
Parish website
quinclooneymagheraparish.ie

PASTORAL AREA 6 – TRADAREE

PARISHES: NEWMARKET-ON-FERGUS, SHANNON, SIXMILEBRIDGE

BVM of the Rosary, Newmarket on Fergus; Our Lady of the Wells, Clonmoney; St Conaire, Carrigerry; The Immaculate Mother of God, Shannon; SS John & Paul, Shannon; St Finaghta, Sixmilebridge; St Mary's Kilmurry

Co-PPs
Rev Arnold Rosney Co-PP, VF
SS John & Paul Presbytery, 4 Dún na Rí,
Shannon, Co Clare
Tel 061-364133
Rev Michael Collins Co-PP
Parochial House, 19 Goodwood Estate,
Newmarket-on-Fergus, Co Clare
Tel 061-700883

Curate
Rev James Michael CC
The Presbytery, 5 Drumgeely Avenue,
Shannon, Co Clare
Tel 061-471513

Priests in Residence
Rev Harry Bohan AP
172 Drumgeely Hill, Shannon, Co Clare
Canon Brendan O'Donoghue AP
12 Tullyglass Square, Shannon, Co Clare
Tel 061-361257

Pastoral Offices
NEWMARKET ON FERGUS:
19 Goodwood,
Newmarket-on-Fergus, Co Clare
Tel 061-368127
Parish email
office@newmarketonfergusparish.ie
Parish website
www.newmarketonfergusparish.ie
SHANNON: Parish Office, 4 Dún na Rí,
Shannon, Co Clare
Tel 061-363243 Fax 061-364516
Parish email office@shannonparish.ie
Parish website www.shannonparish.ie
SIXMILEBRIDGE: Parish Office, The
Green, Sixmilebridge, Co Clare
Tel 061-713682
Parish email
office@sixmilebridgeparish.ie
Parish website
www.sixmilebridgeparish.ie

PASTORAL AREA 7 – CEANNTAR NA LOCHANNA

PARISHES: BROADFORD, O'CALLAGHAN'S MILLS, TULLA

St Peter, Broadford; St Mary, Kilbane; S Joseph, Kilmore; St Patrick, O'Callagha Mills; St Senan, Kilkishen; St Vincent de Paul, Oatfield; SS Peter & Paul, Tulla; Th Immaculate Conception, Tulla; St Jame Knockjames

Co-PPs
Rev Brendan Quinlivan Co-PP, VF
Parochial House,
Newline, Tulla, Co Clare
Tel 065-6835117
Rev Donal Dwyer Co-PP
Parochial House,
O'Callaghan's Mills, Co Clare
Tel 065-6835148

Pastoral Offices
BROADFORD: Parochial House,
Gortnaglough, Broadford, Co Clare
Tel 061-473123
Parish email broadfordclare@gmail.cor
O'CALLAGHAN'S MILLS:
Parochial House,
O'Callaghan's Mills, Co Clare
Tel 065-6835148
Parish email
ocallaghansmillskot@gmail.com
TULLA: Parish Office, Newline,
Tulla, Co Clare
Tel 065-6835117

PASTORAL AREA 8 – IMEALL BOIRNE

PARISHES: COROFIN, CRUSHEEN, RUAN TUBBER

St Brigid, Corofin; St Joseph, Kilnaboy; Mary, Rath; St Cronan, Crusheen; The Immaculate Conception, Ballinruan; St Mary, Ruan; St Tola, Dysart; St Michael, Tubber; All Saints, Boston

Co-PPs
Rev Damien Nolan Co-PP, VF
1A Laghtagoona, Corofin, Co Clare
Tel 065-6837178

Priests in Residence
Rev Patrick O'Neill Co-PP
Ruan, Co Clare
Tel 065-6827799

Pastoral Offices
IMEALL BOIRNE PASTORAL OFFICE:
Parish Centre, Crusheen, Co Clare
Tel 065-6890865
Email imeallboirne@outlook.com
CRUSHEEN (INCHICRONAN): Parish
Centre, Crusheen, Co Clare
Parish email
inchicronanparish@gmail.com
COROFIN: Parish Office, 1A
Laghtagoona, Corofin, Co Clare
Tel 065-6837178
Parish email corofinparish@yahoo.co.u

JAN/DYSART: Parish Office,
uan, Co Clare
l 065-6827799
rish email ruandysartparish@gmail.com

PASTORAL AREA 9 – INIS CEALTRA

RISHES: BODYKE, FEAKLE,
LLANENA, MOUNTSHANNON,
GONNELLOE, SCARIFF
ur Lady, Assumed into Heaven, Bodyke;
Joseph, Tuamgraney; St Mary, Feakle;
Joseph, Kilclarin; St Mary, Killanena;
Mary, Flagmount; St Caimin,
ountshannon; St Flannan, Whitegate;
Molua, Ogonnelloe; St Mary,
allybrohan; The Sacred Heart, Scariff;
Mary, Clonusker

-PPs
ev Darius Plasek Co PP
rochial House, Bodyke, Co Clare
l 061-921060
ev Joe McMahon Co-PP, VF
rochial House, Scariff, Co Clare
l 061-921051

iests in Residence
ev John Jones AP
Caimin's, Mountshannon, Co Clare
l 061-927213
ev James O'Brien AP
rochial House, Feakle, Co Clare
l 061-924035
ev Jackie Sharpe
gonnelloe, Co Clare
l 086-8940556

storal Offices
ODYKE-TUAMGRANEY: Parochial
ouse, Bodyke, Co Clare
l 061-921060
rish email
odykeparishnewsletter@gmail.com
rish website
ww.bodyketuamgraneyparish.ie
AKLE: Parochial House, Fossabeg,
ariff, Co Clare
l 061-921051
rish email feakleparish@gmail.com
LLANENA-FLAGMOUNT: Parochial
ffice, Fossabeg, Scariff, Co Clare
l 061-921051
rish email killanenaparish@gmail.com
OUNTSHANNON: St Caimin's,
ountshannon, Co Clare
l 061-927213
GONNELLOE: Ballybrohan,
llaloe, Co Clare
rish email newsletter@ogonnelloe.ie
rish website www.ogonnelloeparish.ie
ARIFF: Parochial House, Fossabeg,
ariff, Co Clare
l 061-921051
rish email scariffparish@gmail.com

PASTORAL AREA 10 – SCÁTH NA SIONNAINE

PARISHES: CASTLECONNELL, CLONLARA, KILLALOE
St Joseph, Castleconnell; St Patrick, Ahane; St Senan, Clonlara; Mary, Mother of God, Truagh; St Flannan's Killaloe; St Thomas, Bridgetown; The Sacred Heart & St Lua, Garraunboy

Co-PPs
Rev William Teehan Co-PP, VF
The Spa, Castleconnell, Co Limerick
Tel 061-377170
Rev James Grace Co-PP
Parochial House, Killaloe, Co Clare
Tel 061-376137
Rev Pat Mulcahy Co-PP
Parochial House, 18 Churchfield, Clonlara, Co Clare
Tel 061-354334
Rev Tom Whelan Co-PP
The Spa, Castleconnell, Co Limerick
Tel 061-219482

Priests in Residence
Rev Jerry O'Brien AP
Bridgetown, Co Clare
Tel 061-376137

Pastoral Offices
CASTLECONNELL: Parochial House, Castleconnell, Co Limerick
Tel 061-377170
Parish email castleconnellrcchurch@gmail.com
CLONLARA: Parish Office, Clonlara Community Sports Centre, Clonlara, Co Clare
Tel 061-354977
Parish email senanclon@gmail.com
KILLALOE: Parochial House, Killaloe, Co Clare
Tel 061-376137
Parish email killaloeparish@gmail.com

PASTORAL AREA 11 – ODHRAN

PARISHES: NENAGH, PORTROE, PUCKANE, SILVERMINES, TEMPLEDERRY, YOUGHALARRA
St Mary of the Rosary, Nenagh; St John the Baptist, Tyone; Blessed Virgin Mary, Portroe; Our Lady & St Patrick, Puckane; St Mary's, Carrig; Our Lady of Lourdes, Silvermines; Our Lady of the Wayside, Ballinclough; The Immaculate Conception, Templederry; Our Lady of the Wayside, Killeen; Our Lady of the Wayside, Curreeney; The Holy Spirit, Youghalarra; The Immaculate Conception, Ballywilliam

Co-PPs
Rev Pat Gilbert Co-PP, VF
Maryville, Church Road, Nenagh, Co Tipperary
Tel 067-31272
Rev Michael Geraghty Co-PP
The Presbytery, Church Road, Nenagh, Co Tipperary
Tel 067-37134

Rev Rexon Chullickal Co-PP
The Presbytery, Church Road, Nenagh, Co Tipperary
Tel 067-37130

Priests in Residence
Rev Timothy O'Brien AP
Carrigatogher, Nenagh, Co Tipperary
Tel 067-31231
Rev Brendan Moloney AP
Silvermines, Nenagh, Co. Tipperary
Tel 067-25864
Rev William McCormack
Puckane, Nenagh, Co Tipperary
Tel 067-24105

Pastoral Offices
NENAGH: Parish Office, Church Road, Nenagh, Co Tipperary
Tel 067-31272/37136
Parish email parishoffice@nenaghparish.com
Parish website www.nenaghparish.ie
Nenagh Pastoral Centre
Church Road, Nenagh, Co Tipperary
Tel 067-37590
Email nenaghpastoralcentre@gmail.com
SILVERMINES: Silvermines, Nenagh, Co Tipperary
Tel 067-25864
Parish email silverminesparish@gmail.com
TEMPLEDERRY: Parochial House, Templederry, Co Tipperary
Tel 0504-52988
Parish email templederryparish@gmail.com
PORTROE: Teach a t'Sagairt, Portroe, Nenagh, Co Tipperary
Tel 067-23105
Parish email portroeparish@gmail.com
PUCKANE: Parochial House, Puckane, Nenagh, Co Tipperary
Tel 067-24105
YOUGHLARRA: Carrigatogher, Nenagh, Co Tipperary
Tel 067-31231
Parish email burgess.youghal@gmail.com

PASTORAL AREA 12 – OLLATRIM

PARISHES: CLOUGHJORDAN, DUNKERRIN, TOOMEVARA
St Michael & St John, Cloughjordan; St Flannan, Ardcroney; St Ruadhán, Kilruane; St Mary, Dunkerrin; St Joseph, Moneygall; Sacred Heart, Barna; St Joseph, Toomevara; St Joseph, Ballinree; St Joseph, Gortagarry; St Joseph, Grennanstown

Co-PPs
Rev Patrick Greed Co-PP, VF
Parochial House, Templemore Road, Cloughjordan, Co Tippeary
Tel 0505-42266
Rev Francis Xavier Kochuveettil Co-PP
Parochial House, Toomevara, Co Tipperary
Tel 067-26023

Priests in Residence
Rev Joseph Kennedy AP
Parochial House, Moneygall, Birr, Co Offaly
Tel 0505-45110

Pastoral Offices
CLOUGHJORDAN: Parish Office,
Templemore Road,
Cloughjordan, Co Tipperary
Tel 0505-42266
Parish email
cloughjordanrcparish@gmail.com
DUNKERRIN: Moneygall, Birr, Co Offaly
Tel 0505-45110
Parish email:dunkerrinparish@eircom.net
TOOMEVARA: Toomevara, Co Tipperary
Tel 067-26023
Parish email toomevaraparish@gmail.com

PASTORAL AREA 13 – COIS DEIRGE

PARISHES: BORRISOKANE, LORRHA, TERRYGLASS
*SS Peter & Paul, Borrisokane; St Michael
the Archangel, Aglish; St Ruadhan,
Lorrha; Our Lady Queen of Ireland,
Rathcabban; Holy Redeemer, Redwood;
The Immaculate Conception, Terryglass;
St Barron, Kilbarron*

Co-PPs
Rev Tom O'Halloran Co-PP, VF
Parochial House,
Borrisokane, Co Tipperary
Tel 067-27105
Rev Michael Cooney Co-PP
Parochial House, Terryglass, Co Tipperary
Tel 067-22017

Priests in Residence
Rev Pat Deely AP
Lorrha, Co Tipperary
Tel 086-8330225

Pastoral Offices
BORRISOKANE: Parochial House,
Borrisokane, Co Tipperary
Tel 067-27105
Parish email
borrisokaneparish@gmail.com
LORRHA: Parochial House, Lorrha,
Nenagh, Co Tipperary
Parish email
lorrhaparishoffice@gmail.com
TERRYGLASS: Parochial House,
Terryglass, Co Tipperary
Tel 067-22017
Parish email terryglasskilbarron@gmail.com

PASTORAL AREA 14 – BRENDAN

PARISHES: BIRR, KILCOLMAN, KINNITTY, SHINRONE
*St Brendan, Birr; Our Lady of the
Annunciation, Carrig; St Colman,
Kilcolman; St Ita, Coolderry; St John,
Ballybritt; St Flannan, Kinnitty; St Luna,
Cadamstown; St Finan Cam, Longford; St
Molua, Roscomroe; St Mary, Shinrone; St
Patrick, The Pike*

Co-PPs
Rev Tom Hogan Co-PP, VF
The Presbytery, John's Mall,
Birr, Co Offaly
Tel 057-9121757

Rev Kieran Blake Co-PP
Kilcolman, Sharavogue, Birr, Co Offaly
Tel 057 9120812
Rev Michael O'Meara Co-PP
Kinnitty, Birr, Co Offaly
Tel 057-9137021

Priests in Residence
Rev Antony Puthiyaveettil CC
The Presbytery, John's Mall,
Birr, Co Offaly
Tel 057-9120098

Pastoral Offices
BIRR: Parish Office, St Brendan's Church,
Birr, Co Offaly
Tel 057-9122028
Parish email info@stbrendansbirr.ie
KILCOLMAN: Parish Office Kilcolman,
Sharavogue, Birr, Co Offaly
Tel 057-9120812 Fax 057-9120812
Parish email
kilcolmanparishoffaly@gmail.com
KINNITTY: Parochial House, Kinnitty,
Birr, Co Offaly
Tel 057-9137021

PASTORAL AREA 15 – CRONAN

PARISHES: BOURNEA, KYLE & KNOCK, ROSCREA
*St Patrick, Bournea; St Brigid,
Clonakenny; St Molua, Ballaghmore; St
Patrick, Knock; St Cronan, Roscrea; St
John the Baptist, Camblin*

Co-PP
Rev John Molloy Co-PP, VF
Templemore Road,
Roscrea, Co Tipperary
Tel 0505-21218

Curate
Rev Antun Pasalic CC
The Presbytery, Convent Hill,
Roscrea, Co Tipperary
Tel 0505-21370

Priests in Residence
Dr Thomas Corbett AP
Convent Hill, Roscrea, Co Tipperary
Tel 0505-21108
Rev Noel Kennedy AP
Bournea, Roscrea, Co Tipperary
Tel 0505-43211
Rev Lorcan Kenny (Chaplain)
Curates' Residence, Convent Hill,
Roscrea, Co Tipperary
Tel 0505-23637

Pastoral Offices
ROSCREA: Parish Office, Abbey Street,
Roscrea, Co Tipperary
Tel 0505-31835
Parish email rosrc@eircom.net
Parish website stcronanscluster.ie
BOURNEA: Parish email
bourneaparish@eircom.net
KYLE & KNOCK: Parish Office
Tel 0505-31835
Parish email rosrc@eircom.net

INSTITUTIONS AND THEIR CHAPLAINS

Carrigoran House
Newmarket-on-Fergus, Co Clare
Tel 061-368100
Priests of Tradaree Pastoral Area
Tel 061-700883

Community Hospital
Kilrush, Co Clare
Tel 065-9051966
Priests of Inis Cathaigh Pastoral Area
Tel 065-9051093

General Hospital, Ennis
Tel 065-6824464
Acute Psychiatric Unit
Tel 065-6863218
Priests of Abbey Pastoral Area
Tel 065-6824043

Cahercalla Community Hospital and Hospice
Cahercalla, Ennis, Co Clare
Tel 065-6824388
Priests of Abbey Pastoral Area
Tel 065-6824043

Community Nursing Unit, Birr
Co Offaly
Tel 057-9123200
Priests of Brendan Pastoral Area

County Hospital, Nenagh
Co Tipperary
Tel 067-31491
Priests of Odhran Pastoral Area
Tel 067-37130

District Hospital, Raheen
Tuamgraney, Co Clare
Tel 061-923007
Priests of Inis Cealtra Pastoral Area
Tel 061-921060

St Joseph's Hospital
Ennis, Co Clare
Tel 065-6840666
Priests of Abbey Pastoral Area
Tel 065-6824043

Welfare Home, Nenagh
Co Tipperary
Tel 067-31893
Priests of Odhran Pastoral Area

Welfare Home, Roscrea
Co Tipperary
Tel 0505-21389
Priests of Cronan Pastoral Area
Tel 0505-21108

Regina House
Kilrush, Co Clare
Tel 065-9051209
Priests of Inis Cathaigh Pastoral Area
Tel 065-9051209

Allianz (ll)

mmunity School, Roscrea
Tipperary
l 0505-21454
v Lorcan Kenny
l 0505-23637

Anne's Community College
llaloe, Co Clare
l 061-376257
ronica Molloy

Brendan's Community School
rr, Co Offaly
l 0509-20510
s Kate Liffey
l 057-9120098

Caimin's Community School
annon, Co Clare
l 061-364211
ra Guinnane

lrush Community School
l 065-9051359
r Karol Torpey

Joseph's Community College
lkee, Co Clare
l 065-9056138
rs Ann Healy

Patrick's Comprehensive School
annon, Co Clare
l 061-361428
uala Murray

ladysart Community College
Clare
l 065-6832300
anne O'Brien

PRIESTS OF THE DIOCESE ELSEWHERE

v Pascal Hanrahan HCF
ffice of the Head Chaplain,
cKee Barracks, Dublin D07 A065
l 01-8042637
gr Seamus Horgan
ostolic Nunciature,
39 Massachusetts Avenue,
ashington DC 20008-3610, USA
chbishop Eugene M. Nugent
ostolic Nunciature, Yarmouk Block 1,
reet 2, Villa NI, Kuwait City, Kuwait
l +965-25337767
n Sabbatical
v Des Hillery
Diocesan Office
v Michael Harding
Diocesan Office
v Pat Treacy
Diocesan Office

RETIRED PRIESTS

v John Bane
Garden View, Clarecastle, Co Clare
l 086-8246555

Rev Enda Burke
Cloughjordan, Co Tipperary
Tel 0505-42120
Rev Paschal Flannery
Ballinderry, Nenagh, Co Tipperary
Tel 067-22916/086-2225099
Rev Seamus Gardiner
Portroe, Co Tipperary
Tel 067-23101/086-8392741
Rev Brian Geoghegan
Carrigoran Nursing Home,
Newmarket on Fergus, Co Clare
Tel 087-2387067
Rev Tom Hannon
The Bungalow, Moynure,
Brosna, Birr, Co Offaly
Tel 086-8768116
Rev Martin O'Brien
2 Powerscourt, Tulla, Co Clare
Tel 065-6835284
Rev Pat Sexton
5 Cottage Gardens, Station Road,
Ennis, Co Clare
Tel 065-6840828/087-2477814

RELIGIOUS ORDERS AND CONGREGATIONS

PRIESTS

CISTERCIANS
Mount Saint Joseph Abbey
Roscrea, Co Tipperary E53 D6S1
Tel 0505-25600 Fax 0505-25610
Email info@msjroscrea.ie
Website www.msjroscrea.ie
Superior ad nutum
Rev Dom Malachy Thompson (OCSO)
Prior: Rev Aodhán McDunphy (OCSO)

FRANCISCANS
Franciscan Friary, Ennis, Co Clare
Tel 065-6828751 Fax 065-6822008
Email friars.ennis@eircom.net
Guardian: Rev Brendan McGrath (OFM)

BROTHERS

CHRISTIAN BROTHERS
Christian Brothers' House,
New Road, Ennis, Co Clare
Tel 065-6821471/6828469 (office)
Community Leader: Br Dan V. Healy
Community: 5

Christian Brothers' House,
Nenagh, Co Tipperary
Tel 067-31557
Community Leader: Br Seamus C. Whelan
Community: 3

PRESENTATION BROTHERS
Presentation Brothers, Birr, Co Offaly
Tel 0509-20247
Contact: Br Walter Hurley (FPM)
Community: 4

SISTERS

BRIGIDINE SISTERS
Sue Ryder House, The Streame,
Limerick Road, Nenagh, Co Tipperary
Contact: Sr Mary Slattery
Community: 1

SISTERS OF CHARITY OF THE INCARNATE WORD
St Michael Convent, Carrigoran,
Newmarket-on-Fergus, Co Clare
Tel 061-368381
Contact person: Sr Maureen Costello
Email smaureencostello@gmail.com
Community: 5

CONGREGATION OF THE SISTERS OF MERCY
The Sisters of Mercy minister throughout the diocese in pastoral and social work, community development, counselling, spirituality, education and health care, answering current needs.

Mercy Sisters,
Garinis Clonroadmore,
Ennis, Co Clare V95 RF3A
Tel 065-6820768
Community: 2

St Xavier's, Ennis, Co Clare V95 P9KT
Tel 065-6828024 Fax 065-6828776
Community: 20

1 Corovorrin Crescent,
Ennis, Co Clare V95 N15P
Tel 065-6841375
Community: 4

7 Shallee Drive,
Cloughleigh, Ennis, Co Clare V95 F3CN
Tel 065-6828894 Fax 065-6828892
Community: 2

8 Greendale, Clonroad,
Ennis, Co Clare V95 R3KH
Tel 065-6840385
Community: 4

5 & 6 Rosanore, Gort Road,
Ennis, Co Clare V95 Y7DY
Tel 065-6821554
Community: 4

Milltown Road, Kilkee,
Co Clare V15 HD92
Tel 065-9056116
Community: 4

Convent of Mercy,
Kilkee Road, Kilrush, Co Clare V15 NC58
Tel 065-9051068
Community: 6

Ashe Road, Nenagh,
Co Tipperary E45 X773
Tel 067-33835
Community: 6

5 Dromin Court, Nenagh,
Co Tipperary E45 WV38
Tel/Fax 067-31591
Community: 2

Church Road, Tulla,
Co Clare V95 P1H3
Tel 065-6835118
Community: 2

2 Fergus Drive, Shannon,
Co Clare V14 F825
Tel 061-471637
Community: 4

St Mary's, Nenagh,
Co Tipperary E45 D283
Tel 067-31357 Fax 067-31151
Community: 11

33 Yewston Estate,
Nenagh, Co Tipperary E45 Y290
Tel 067-32830
Community: 4

St John's, Riverside, Birr,
Co Offaly R42 XP40
Tel 057-9120891
Community: 9

10/11 Ardlea Close,
Clare Road, Ennis, Co Clare V95 K2K0
Tel 065-6842399
Community: 4

LA SAINTE UNION DES SACRES COEURS
LSU Sisters, 40 Cregaun,
Tobartaoscáin, Ennis, Co Clare
Community: 2
Education, pastoral, therapy

POOR CLARES
Poor Clare Monastery,
Francis Street, Ennis, Co Clare V95 VNP5
Email bernardinemeskell@live.ie
Abbess: Sr Bernardine Meskell
Community: 9
Contemplative

SISTERS OF ST JOHN OF GOD
Sisters of St John of God,
9 Cuan an Chlair, Ennis Co Clare
Tel 065-6843579

ST JOSEPH OF THE SACRED HEART SISTERS
57 Woodlands, Kilrush Road,
Ennis, Co Clare
Tel 065-6891178
Sr Betty Curtin

ST MARY MADELEINE POSTEL SISTERS
Mount Carmel Nursing Home,
Abbey Street, Roscrea, Co Tipperary
Tel 0505-21146
Apply Provider: Sr Majella Larkin
Community: 5

Ard Mhuire Convent, Parkmore,
New Line, Roscrea, Co Tipperary
Regional Superior: Sr M. Luke Minogue
Community: 4

EDUCATIONAL INSTITUTIONS

St Flannan's College (Diocesan College)
Ennis, Co Clare
Tel 065-6828019 Fax 065-6840644
Principal: Rev Ignatius McCormack
Tel 086-2777139

CHARITABLE AND OTHER SOCIETIES

Apostolic Work Society
Diocesan Headquarters at Maria
Assumpta Hall, Station Road, Ennis,
Co Clare

Birr Social Service Council
c/o 47 New Road, Birr, Co Offaly

Clarecare
Clarecare, Harmony Row,
Ennis, Co Clare
Tel 065-6828178

Clare Youth Service
Carmody Street, Ennis, Co Clare
Tel 065-6845350

Geriatric Centre
Carrigoran House,
Newmarket-on-Fergus, Co Clare
Tel 061-368100

Legion of Mary
Headquarters at Maria Assumpta Hall,
Station Road, Ennis, Co Clare

Mount Carmel Nursing home
Parkmore, Abbey Street, Roscrea,
Co Tipperary
Tel 0505-21146

North Tipperary Community Services
52 Silver Street, Nenagh, Co Tipperary
Tel 067-31800

Roscrea Community Service Centre
Rosemary Street, Roscrea, Co Tipperary
Tel 0505-21498

Schools for children with Special Needs
St Vincent's, Woodstown House,
Lisnagry, Co Limerick
(Daughters of Charity)
Tel 061-501400

St Anne's, residential and day school,
Sean Ross Abbey, Roscrea, Co Tipperary
Tel 0505-21187

St Clare's, day school,
Gort Road, Ennis, Co Clare
Tel 065-6821899

St Anne's, day school,
Ennis, Co Clare
Tel 065-6829072

Society of St Vincent de Paul
Conferences at: Birr, Castleconnell,
Clarecastle, Cloughjordan, Ennis, Kilrush
Kilkee, Nenagh, Newmarket-on-Fergus,
Roscrea, Scariff/Tuamgraney and
Shannon

DIOCESE OF KILMORE

PATRONS OF THE DIOCESE
ST PATRICK, 17 MARCH; ST FELIM, 9 AUGUST

INCLUDES ALMOST ALL OF COUNTY CAVAN,
AND A PORTION OF COUNTIES LEITRIM, FERMANAGH, MEATH AND SLIGO

Most Rev Martin Hayes DD
Bishop of Kilmore;
born 24 October 1959;
ordained priest 10 June 1989;
ordained Bishop of Kilmore
20 September 2020

Residence:
Bishop's House,
Cullies, Co Cavan
Tel 049-4331496
Email admin@kilmorediocese.ie
Website www.kilmorediocese.ie

CATHEDRAL OF ST PATRICK AND ST FELIM, CAVAN

he original cathedral of the diocese as situated about four miles south of avan in the present parish of Kilmore. ome time in the sixth century, St Felim ad established a church there. Bishop ndrew MacBrady (1445–1455) rebuilt e ancient church of St Felim and ceived permission from Pope Nicholas to raise it to the status of a cathedral. fter the confiscation of the Cathedral f St Felim at Kilmore, the diocese had cathedral for three hundred years. shop James Browne extended Cavan arish church and erected it into a thedral in 1862. It was replaced by the ew Cathedral of St Patrick and St Felim, uilt by Bishop Patrick Lyons in the years 938–1942. The architects were W. H. rne & Son and the contractors John sk & Son. The cathedral cost £209,000 d was opened and dedicated in 1942. was consecrated in 1947.

he cathedral is neo-classical in style ith a single spire rising to 230 feet. e portico consists of a tympanum pported by four massive columns of ortland stone with Corinthian caps. e tympanum figures of Christ, Patrick and St Felim were executed a Dublin sculptor, George Smith. The venty-eight columns in the cathedral, e pulpit on the south side and all the atues are of Pavinazetto marble and me from the firm of Dinelli Figli of etrasanta in Italy.

e fine work of George Collie can be en in the Stations of the Cross and in e mural of the Risen Christ on the all of the apse. Directly above the ural are twelve small windows, owing the heads of the twelve ostles. The High Altar is of green nnemara marble and pink Middleton arble, while the altar rails are of hite Carrara marble. The apse has two de-chapels on the north and two on e south. The Blessed Sacrament is ow reserved in the south chapel osest to the altar. The six splendid ained-glass windows in the nave and e in the south transept came from e studios of Harry Clarke.

Most Rev Leo O'Reilly DD
Retired Bishop of Kilmore
born 1944; ordained priest 15 June 1969;
ordained bishop 2 February 1997;
installed as Bishop of Kilmore 15
November 1998; retired 31 December
2018
Residence: 4 Carraig Beag,
Cootehill Road, Cavan

ADMINISTRATION

College of Consultors
Rt Rev Mgr Liam Kelly PP
Very Rev John Gilhooly PP
Very Rev Sean Mawn PP, VF
Very Rev John McTiernan Adm
Very Rev Kevin Fay Adm, VF
Very Rev Donal Kilduff PP
Very Rev Brian Flynn
Very Rev Andrew Tully
Very Rev Ultan McGoohan

Vicar General
Rt Rev Mgr Liam Kelly

Council of Priests
Chairman: Very Rev John Gilhooly
Secretary: Very Rev Donal Kilduff

Deanery Vicars
Very Rev John Gilhooly VF
Very Rev Sean Mawn PP, VF
Very Rev Ultan McGoohan PP, VF
Very Rev John McTiernan Adm

Diocesan Finance Officer
Ms Jennifer O'Reilly
Bishop's House, Cullies, Cavan
Tel 049-4331496
Email accounts@kilmorediocese.ie

Finance Committee
Bishop Martin Hayes
Rt Rev Mgr Liam Kelly PP
Very Rev Gerard Alwill PP
Mrs Joan Quinn
Ms Carmel Denning
Mr Paul Kelly
Ms Lauren Tierney
Secretary: Very Rev Donal Kilduff

Chancellor/Diocesan Secretary
Very Rev Donal Kilduff
Bishop's House, Cullies, Co Cavan
Tel 049-4331496 Fax 049-4361796
Email
diocesansecretary@kilmorediocese.ie

Bishop's Secretary
Ms Ann-Marie Kilduff
Bishop's House, Cullies, Co Cavan
Tel 049-4331496
Email admin@kilmorediocese.ie

Diocesan Archivist
Rev Thomas McKiernan
Bishop's House, Cullies, Co Cavan
Tel 049-4331496
Email admin@kilmorediocese.ie

CATECHETICS EDUCATION

Catholic Primary School Managers' Association
Secretary: Kathy McGoldrick
Kilmore Diocesan Pastoral Centre,
Cullies, Cavan
Tel 049-4375004 (ext 4) Fax 049-4327497
Email edsec@kilmorediocese.ie

Diocesan Catechetical Advisers
Primary: Sr Anna Smith
Sisters of Mercy, 2 Dún na Bó,
Willowfield Road, Ballinamore,
Co Leitrim
Tel 071-9645973
Mr Terence Leddy
Drumsilla, Butlersbridge, Co Cavan
Second level: Mrs Patricia Sheridan
Kells Road, Bailieborough,
Co Cavan

LITURGY

Pastoral Team: Kilmore Diocesan Pastoral
Centre, Cullies, Cavan
Tel 049-4375004
Advisor: Vacant

Church Music
Director: Rev Thomas Hanley
The Presbytery, Farnham Street, Cavan
Tel 049-4375004

Art, Architecture and Buildings
Chairman: Vacant

PASTORAL

Kilmore Diocesan Pastoral Centre
Cullies, Cavan
Director: Mr Sean Coll
Tel 049-4375004 Ext 102 Fax 049-4327497
Email directorkdpc@kilmorediocese.ie

ACCORD
Kilmore Diocesan Pastoral Centre
Tel 049-4375004
Diocesan Director: Angela Flynn
Email cavanaccord@eircom.net

Apostolic Society
Diocesan President
Ms Suzanna Tinnenny
Quivvy, Belturbet, Co Cavan
Tel 049-9522928
Spiritual Director
Rev John McMahon
Carrigallen
Tel 049-4339610

Communications
Diocesan Director: Very Rev Donal Kilduff
Bishop's House, Cullies, Co Cavan
Tel 049-4331496
Email
diocesansecretary@kilmorediocese.ie

Diocesan Pastoral Council
Chairperson: Mr Christy Dooley
c/o Pastoral Centre, Cavan

Ecumenism
Director: Rev Gerry Comiskey PP
Staghall, Belturbet, Co Cavan
Tel 049-9522140

Eucharistic Adoration
Chairperson: Rev John Cooney
Parochial House, Cootehill, Co Cavan
Tel 049-5552120

Knock Pilgrimage
Director: Very Rev Sean Maguire
Parochial House, Bawnboy
Tel 049-9523103

Legion of Mary
Spiritual Director: Rev Tom McKiernan

Lourdes Pilgrimage
Director: Very Rev Tom Mannion PP
Ballinglera, Carrick-on-Shannon,
Co Leitrim
Tel 071-9643014

Marriage Tribunal
*Kilmore Office of Armagh Regional
Marriage Tribunal:* Sr Kathleen Gormley
Kilmore Diocesan Pastoral Centre,
Cullies, Cavan
Tel 049-4375004
Email tribunal@kilmorediocese.ie

Safeguarding Children & Vulnerable Adults Diocesan Committee
Chairperson: Ms Rita Martin
Director: Sr Suzie Duffy
Kilmore Diocesan Pastoral Centre
Tel 049-4375004 Ext 105
Designated Persons
Sr Suzie Duffy, Mr Paul Cullen
Kilmore Diocesan Pastoral Centre
Tel 049-437500 4 Ext 105
Email safeguarding@kilmorediocese.ie

Pastoral Services
Director: Ms Martina Gilmartin
Kilmore Diocesan Pastoral Centre,
Cullies, Cavan
Tel 049-4375004 Ext 108
Email pastoralservices@kilmorediocese.ie

Permanent Diaconate
Director: Vacant

Pioneer Total Abstinence Association
Diocesan Director: Rev John Cusack CC
Ballinamore, Co Leitrim
Tel 071-9644050

Pontifical Mission Societies
Diocesan Director
Very Rev John McMahon PP
Parochial House, Carrigallen, Co Leitrim
Tel 049-4339610

Joseph's Young Priests' Society
ocesan President: Mr Pat Denning
umcave, Cavan
l 049-4331362

avellers
aplain: Very Rev Sean McDermott PP, VF
cken, Ballinagh, Co Cavan
l 049-4337106

migrants
ocesan Representative: Vacant

cations
rector: Very Rev Ultan McGoohan
Anne's, Bailieborough, Co Cavan

uth Ministry
rector: Mr Francis Keaney
more Diocesan Pastoral Centre,
ullies, Cavan
l 049-4375004 Ext 103
nail youthministry@kilmorediocese.ie

PARISHES

ensal parishes are listed first. Other
rishes follow alphabetically. Historical
mes are given in parentheses. Church
ulars appear in italics

VAN (URNEY AND ANNAGELLIFF)
thedral of SS Patrick and Felim, Cavan
Clare's, Cavan
Brigid's, Killygarry
Aidan's, Butlersbridge
v Kevin Fay Adm, VF
v Peter Okpetu CC
v Thomas Small
e Presbytery, Cavan
l 049-4331404/4332269 Fax 049-4332000
formation line 049-4371787
nail cavan@kilmorediocese.ie
v Brian McElhinney CC
tlersbridge, Co Cavan
l 049-4365266
acon Andrew Brady

AILIEBORO (KILLANN)
Anne's, Bailieboro; St Anne's, Killann
Patrick's, Shercock
ry Rev Ultan McGoohan PP, VF
Anne's, Bailieboro, Co Cavan
l 042-9665117
nail bailieboro@kilmorediocese.ie
v Antony Kidarathil CC
rochial House, Shercock, Co Cavan
l 042-9669127
nail shercock@kilmorediocese.ie

ALLAGHAMEEHAN
Aidan's, Ballaghameehan
Mary's, Rossinver
Aidan's, Glenaniff
Patrick's, Kiltyclogher
ry Rev John Sexton Adm
rochial House, Rossinver, Co Leitrim
l 071-9854022
nail rossinver@kilmorediocese.ie

BALLINAGLERA
St Hugh's, Ballinaglera
St Columcill, Newbridge
Immaculate Conception, Doobally
Very Rev Tom Mannion PP
Ballinaglera, Carrick-on-Shannon,
Co Leitrim
Tel 071-9643014
Email ballinaglera@kilmorediocese.ie

BALLINAMORE/DRUMREILLY LOWER
St Patrick's Ballinamore,
St Mary's Aughnasheelin
St Bridgid's, Coraleehan
St Patrick's Aughawillan
Very Rev Sean Mawn PP, VF
Ballinamore, Co Leitrim
Tel 071-9644039
Email ballinamore@kilmorediocese.ie
Rev John Cusack CC
Ballinamore, Co Leitrim
Tel 071-9644050

BALLINTEMPLE
St Michael's, Potahee
St Mary's, Bruskey
St Patrick's, Aghaloora
Very Rev Sean McDermott PP, VF
Lacken, Ballinagh, Co Cavan
Tel 049-4337106
Email potahee@kilmorediocese.ie

BELTURBET (ANNAGH)
Immaculate Conception, Belturbet
St Patrick's, Drumalee
St Brigid's, Redhills
Very Rev John McTiernan Adm
Bridge Street, Belturbet, Co Cavan
Tel 049-9522109
Email belturbet2@kilmorediocese.ie
Rev Joseph Long CC
Curate's House, Fairgreen,
Belturbet, Co Cavan
Tel 049-9522151
Rev Jason Murphy (priest in residence)
Killoughter, Redhills, Co Cavan
Tel 047-55021

CARRIGALLEN
St Mary's, Carrigallen
St Mary's, Drumeela
St Mary's, Drumreilly
Very Rev John McMahon PP
Carrigallen, Co Leitrim, via Cavan
Tel 049-4339610
Email carrigallen@kilmorediocese.ie

CASTLERAHAN AND MUNTERCONNAUGHT
St Bartholomew's, Munterconnaught
St Mary's, Castlerahan
St Joseph's, Ballyjamesduff
Very Rev Kevin Donohoe PP, VF
Ballyjamesduff, Co Cavan
Tel 049-8544410
Email ballyjamesduff@kilmorediocese.ie
Rev Brian Flynn CC
Knocktemple, Virginia, Co Cavan
Tel 049-8547435

CASTLETARA
St Mary's Ballyhaise,
St Patrick's, Castletara
Very Rev Gerard Cassidy PP
Ballyhaise, Co Cavan
Tel 049-4338121
Email ballyhaise@kilmorediocese.ie

CLOONCLARE AND KILLASNETT
St Clare's, Manorhamilton
Annunciation, Mullies
St Osnat's, Glencar
Very Rev John Gilhooly PP, VF
Manorhamilton, Co Leitrim
Tel 071-9855042
Email manorhamilton@kilmorediocese.ie
Rev Rodney Tanko CC
Glencar, Manorhamilton, Co Leitrim
Tel 071-9855433
Email glencar@kilmorediocese.ie
Deacon Padraig Kelly

COOTEHILL (DRUMGOON)
St Michael's, Cootehill
St Mary's, Middle Chapel
St Patrick's, Maudabawn
Very Rev John Cooney PP, VF
Cootehill, Co Cavan
Tel 049-5552120
Email cootehill@kilmorediocese.ie
Rev Michael Gilsenan (SSCC) CC
Gallonreagh, Maudabawn,
Cootehill, Co Cavan

CORLOUGH/TEMPLEPORT
St Patrick's, Corlough,
St Patrick's, Kilnavart,
St Mogue's, Bawnboy
Very Rev Sean Maguire PP
Bawnboy, Co Cavan
Tel 049-9523103
Email bawnboy@kilmorediocese.ie

CROSSERLOUGH
St Patrick's, Kilnaleck
St Mary's, Crosserlough
St Joseph's, Drumkilly
Very Rev Peter McKiernan PP
Crosserlough, Co Cavan
Tel 049-4336122
Email crosserlough@kilmorediocese.ie

DENN
St Matthew's, Crosskeys
St Matthew's, Drumavaddy
Very Rev Donal Kilduff PP
Crosskeys, Co Cavan
Tel 049-4336102
Email crosskeys@kilmorediocese.ie

DERRYLIN (KNOCKNINNY)
St Ninnidh's, Derrylin
St Mary's, Teemore
Very Rev Gerard Alwill PP
56 Main Street, Derrylin,
Co Fermanagh BT92 9PD
Tel 028-67748315
Email derrylin@kilmorediocese.ie

DRUMAHAIRE AND KILLARGUE
St Patrick's, Drumahaire
St Mary's, Newtownmanor
St Brigid's, Killargue
Very Rev Paul Casey PP
Drumahaire, Co Leitrim
Tel 071-9164143
Email drumahaire@kilmorediocese.ie

DRUMKEERIN (INISHMAGRATH)
St Brigid's, Drumkeerin
St Patrick's, Tarmon
St Brigid's, Creevalea
Very Rev Tom McManus PP, VF
Drumkeerin, Co Leitrim
Tel 071-9648025
Email drumkeerin@kilmorediocese.ie

DRUMLANE
St Mary's, Staghall
St Patrick's, Milltown
Very Rev Gerard Comiskey PP
Staghall, Belturbet,
Co Cavan
Tel 049-9522140
Email staghall@kilmorediocese.ie

GLENFARNE
St Michael's, Glenfarne
St Mary's, Brockagh
Very Rev Oliver Kelly Adm
West Barrs, Glenfarne,
Co Leitrim
Tel 071-9855134
Email glenfarne@kilmorediocese.ie

KILDALLAN AND TOMREGAN
Our Lady of Lourdes, Ballyconnell
St Dallan's, Kildallan
Rt Rev Mgr Liam Kelly PP
Ballyconnell, Co Cavan
Tel 049-9526291
Email ballyconnell@kilmorediocese.ie

KILLESHANDRA
St Brigid's, Killeshandra
Sacred Heart, Arva
Immaculate Conception, Coronea
Very Rev Charles O'Gorman PP
Killeshandra, Co Cavan
Tel 049-4334179
Email killeshandra@kilmorediocese.ie
Rev Oliver O'Reilly CC
Arva, Co Cavan
Tel 049-4335246
Email arva@kilmorediocese.ie

KILLINAGH AND GLANGEVLIN
St Patrick's, Killinagh
St Patrick's, Glangevlin
St Felim's, Gowlan
Very Rev Loughlain Carolan PP
Blacklion, Co Cavan
Tel 071-9853012
Email blacklion@kilmorediocese.ie

KILLINKERE
St Ultan's, Killinkere
St Mary's, Clanaphilip
Very Rev Darragh Connolly PP
Killinkere, Virginia, Co Cavan
Tel 049-8547307
Email killinkere@kilmorediocese.ie

KILMAINHAMWOOD AND MOYBOLOGUE
Sacred Heart
St Patrick's
Very Rev Addison Okpeh PP
Kilmainhamwood, Kells, Co Meath
Tel 046-9052129
Email kilmainhamwood@kilmorediocese.ie

KILMORE
St Felim's, Ballinagh
St Patrick's, Drumcor
Very Rev Sean McDermott Adm
Lacken Ballinagh, Co Cavan
Tel 049-4337106
Very Rev Peter Casey CC
Ballinagh, Co Cavan
Tel 049-4337232
Email ballinagh@kilmorediocese.ie

KINAWLEY/KILLESHER
St Mary's, Swanlinbar
St Naile's, Kinawley
St Patick's, Killesher
St Lasir's, Wheathill
Very Rev Maurice McMorrow PP, VF
Kinawley, Enniskillen,
Co Fermanagh BT92 4FH
Tel 028-66348250
Email kinawley@kilmorediocese.ie

KILSHERDANY AND DRUNG
Immaculate Conception, Drung
St Patrick's, Corick
St Patrick's, Bunnoe
St Brigid's, Kill
Very Rev Yusuf Bamai PP
Parochial House, Bunnoe,
Cootehill, Co Cavan
Tel 049-5553035
Email drung@kilmorediocese.ie

KINLOUGH AND GLENADE
St Aidan's, Kinlough
St Patrick's, Tullaghan
St Michael's, Glenade
St Brigid's, Ballintrillick
Very Rev John Phair PP
Kinlough, Co Leitrim
Tel 071-9841428
Email kinlough@kilmorediocese.ie

KNOCKBRIDE
St Brigid's, Tunnyduff
St Brigid's, East Knockbride
Very Rev Anthony Fagan PP
Knockbride, Bailieboro, Co Cavan
Tel 042-9660112
Email tunnyduff@kilmorediocese.ie

LARAGH
St Brigid's, Laragh
St Brigid's, Carrickallen
St Michael's, Clifferna
Very Rev Martin Gilcreest PP
Laragh, Stradone, Co Cavan
Tel 049-4330142
Email laragh@kilmorediocese.ie

LAVEY
St Dympna's, Upper Lavey
St Dympna's, Lower Lavey
Very Rev Andrew Tully PP
Lavey, Stradone, Co Cavan
Tel 049-4330125
Email lavey@kilmorediocese.ie

MULLAGH
St Kilian's, Mullagh
St Mary's, Cross
Very Rev Paul Prior PP
Mullagh, via Kells, Co Meath
Tel 046-42208
Email mullagh@kilmorediocese.ie

VIRGINIA (LURGAN)
Mary Immaculate, Virginia
St Patrick's, Lurgan
St Matthew's, Maghera
Very Rev Dermot Prior PP, VF
Virginia, Co Cavan
Tel 049-8547063
Email virginia@kilmorediocese.ie
Parish Office: 049-8548727

INSTITUTIONS AND THEIR CHAPLAINS

Bailieboro Community School
Chaplain: Ms Alison Holton
Tel 042-9665295

Ballinamore Community School
Ballinamore, Co Leitrim
Chaplain: Mr Micheál Kane
Email office@ballinamorecs.ie
Website www.ballinamorecs.ie

reifne College
ootehill Road, Cavan
atechist: Rev Jason Murphy
el 049-4331735

arrigallen Vocational School
Visiting Chaplain
ev John McMahon PP
el 049-4339640

avan General Hospital
el 049-4361399
ev Gerard Kearns
ev Gabriel Kelly
avan General Hospital,
isdaran, Cavan

avan Institute
athedral Road, Cavan
haplaincy and Pastoral Care
ev Gerard Kearns
el 049-4332334

oreto College, Cavan
el 049-4331354
Visiting Chaplain: Rev Gabriel Kelly

ough Allen College
rumkeerin, Co Leitrim
Visiting Chaplain: Rev Tom McManus
el 071-9648025

oughan House
lacklion, Co Cavan
Visiting Chaplain
ery Rev Loughlain Carolan
eneral Office: 071-9853059

t Aidan's Comprehensive School
ootehill, Co Cavan
el 049-5552161
haplain: Mr Gabriel McQuillan

t Aidan's High School
errylin, Co Fermanagh
Visiting Chaplain: Rev Gerard Alwill
el 028-67748337

t Bricin's Vocational School
elturbet, Co Cavan
el 049-9522170

t Clare's College
allyjamesduff, Co Cavan
Visiting Chaplain
ev Brian Flynn
el 049-8547435

St Clare's Comprehensive School, Manorhamilton
Chaplain: Rev John Sexton
Tel 071-9855060

St Mogue's College
Bawnboy, Co Cavan
Visiting Chaplain: Rev Sean Maguire PP
Tel 049-9523112

St Patrick's College, Cavan
Chaplain: Rev Andrew Tully
Tel 049-4330125

Virginia College
Virginia, Co Cavan
Visiting Chaplain: Rev Dermot Prior
Tel 049-8547063

PRIESTS OF THE DIOCESE ELSEWHERE

Rev Enda Murphy
Rome

RETIRED PRIESTS

Rev Patrick Bannon
15 Lisdarn Heights, Cavan
Rev Philip Brady
Creighan, Cavan
Rev Owen Collins
22 River Crescent,
Virginia, Co Cavan
Rt Rev Mgr Michael Cooke
15 Meadow Park,
Dublin Road, Cavan
Very Rev Patrick Farrelly
Knocknagilla, New Inn,
Ballyjamesduff, Co Cavan
Rev Frank Kelleher
15 The Drumlins,
Virginia, Co Cavan
Very Rev Thomas Keogan
7 Quary Park, Mullaghmore, Co Sligo
Rev Eamonn Lynch
Bailieborough Road, Virgina, Co Cavan
Rev Patrick McHugh
Derrylester,
Enniskillen, Co Fermanagh
Tel 048-66349984
Rev Thomas McKiernan
Rosskeeragh, Belturbet, Co Cavan
Very Rev Denis Murray
Parochial House,
Derrylin, Co Fermanagh
Rev Thomas Woods
Edenville, Kinlough, Co Leitrim
Rev Patrick V. Brady
Rev Eamonn Bredin
Rev Bernard Doyle
Rev Donald Hannon
Rev Colm Hurley
Rev John Murphy

RELIGIOUS ORDERS AND CONGREGATIONS

PRIESTS

NORBERTINE CANONS
Holy Trinity House
Lismacanican, Mountnugent, Co Cavan
Email kilnacrottabbeytrust@gmail.com
Prior: Rt Rev James J. Madden (OPraem)

SISTERS

CONGREGATION OF THE SISTERS OF MERCY
Church Street,
Belturbet, Co Cavan H14 Y300
Tel 049-9522110

No. 4 Oriel Lodge, Church Sreet,
Belturbet, Co Cavan H14 V188
Tel 049-9524657

No. 2 Dún na Bó,
Willowfield Road, Ballinamore,
Co Leitrim N41 EH94
Tel 071-9645973
Community: 2

3 Drumalee, Co Cavan

55 Cavan Road, Cootehill, Co Cavan
Tel 049-5552904

No. 16 Dún na Bó, Willowfield Road,
Ballinamore, Co Leitrim N41 TY38
Tel 071-9644006
Community: 2

LORETO (IBVM)
Loreto Post-Primary School
Tel 049-4331354

MISSIONARY SISTERS OF THE HOLY ROSARY
Cavan Town
House 1
Tel 049-4332735
Superior: Sr Benen Mullen
Community: 7

House 2
Tel 049-4332733
Superior: Sr Kathleen O'Brien
Community 8

27 Cherrymount,
Keadue, Cavan Town
Tel 049-4372936
Pastoral, healthcare
Community: 2

SISTERS OF ST CLARE
St Clare's, Keadue Lane, Cavan
Tel 049-4331134
Primary School. Pupils: 550
Tel 049-4332671

Allianz (ⁱⁱ)

EDUCATIONAL INSTITUTIONS

St Clare's College
Ballyjamesduff, Co Cavan
Tel 049-8544551
Fax 049-8544081
Principal: Ms Teresa Donnellan
Visiting Chaplain: Rev Brian Flynn
Tel 049-8547435

Bailieborough Community School
Virginia Road, Bailieborough, Co Cavan
Tel 042-966295
Principal: Ms Martha Lievens
Chaplain: Ms Alison Holton
Email info@bailieborocs.ie
Website www.bailieborocs.ie

Ballinamore Community School
Ballinamore, Co Leitrim
Tel 071-9644049
Principal: Mr Diarmuid McCaffrey
Chaplain: Mr Micheál Kane
Email office@ballinamorecs.ie
Website www.ballinamorecs.ie

St Aidan's Comprehensive School
Cootehill, Co Cavan
Tel 049-5552161
Principal: Ms Mary Ann Smith
Chaplain: Mr Gabriel McQuillan
Email office@staidans.ie

St Aidan's High School
Derrylin,
Tel 048-67748337
Principal: Mr Pat McTeggart
Visiting Chaplain: Rev Gerard Alwill

St Clare's Comprehensive School
Manorhamilton, Co Leitrim
Tel 071-9855087
Principal: Mr John Irwin
Chaplain: Rev John Sexton
Email stclares@iol.ie
Website www.stclarescomprehensive.ie

St Patrick's College
Cullies, Co Cavan
Tel 049-4361888
Email stpats@kilmorediocese.ie
Website www.stpatscavan.com
Principal: Mr Christopher Rowley
Chaplain: Rev Andrew Tully

TIMEW⌀RKS

Provider of Time Management & Security Solutions

Experience

The Timeworks team have been involved in implementing time & attendance & access control solutions within Ireland for the past 20 years.

High end software and hardware

Our systems offer high end software and hardware solutions in the areas of time recording, flexi time, absence management, rostering, complete work force management, human resources, access control and biometric fingerprint or facial recognition clocking terminals.

Remote working applications

Online cloud hosted solutions for staff working from home with our remote working applications that can be used from your laptop, pc, tablet or mobile phone.

Our aim is to continue to provide companies with products and solutions that are important for their business in the areas of our expertise.

Tel: +353 (01) 215 0030
Email: info@timeworks.ie
Web: www.timeworks.ie

Address: Unit 11 Keypoint Business Park, Rosemount Business Park, Dublin 11, D11W2YC

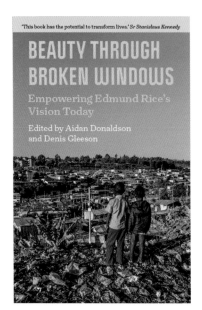

Beauty Through Broken Windows

Empowering Edmund
Rice's Vision Today

Edited by Aidan Donaldson and Denis Gleeson

ISBN 978 1 80097 016 8
PRICE €12.99/£11.70

More than two centuries ago, Edmund Rice looked out a window in Waterford and saw people in dire poverty. Looking into his own heart, he trusted in the Spirit for guidance and was moved to action as he answered God's call to serve the excluded and marginalised. Thus, the foundations of what has become the Edmund Rice Network throughout the world today were laid.

In *Beauty Through Broken Windows: Empowering Edmund Rice's Vision Today*, editors Aidan Donaldson and Denis Gleeson bring together a diverse range of international contributors who, inspired by the gospel call to service, looked out onto a world in need and responded. This timely and valuable work places Edmund Rice's vision and the gospel message in a wide range of contemporary settings, inspiring us to find the courage, passion and commitment to serve others.

'This book has the potential to transform lives. A most engaging and inspiring book, it challenges us to stop and reflect and look at the world with new eyes and a new heart opened to be transformed in the deepest Christian sense.' **Sr Stanislaus Kennedy, social campaigner and founder of Focus Ireland**

TOM SMYTH & ASSOCIATES
HR & EMPLOYMENT LAW SERVICES
SUPPORTING YOUR HUMAN RESOURCES REQUIREMENTS

Since 1991, Tom Smyth & Associates has assisted employers in Ireland meet their Human Resources objectives. Both Irish and International employers across the country trust us to support their HR and Employment Law requirements.

Any organisation classed as an employer is obliged to have correct paperwork and policies in place and all employees have certain legal rights which must be upheld. Our HR Consultancy Practice provides expert advice and guidance to help you manage the HR demands of your organisation, manage employee performance and build a positive and collaborative culture, while ensuring you operate within the boundaries of Irish employment law.

We provide various support options to meet the particular needs of any organisation and we are happy to prepare a tailored proposal on request.

HR Consultancy

Employment Law

Contracts & Policies

On-Site Services

Training and Development

Conflict Resolution

Mediation Services

Unit 6, Euro House,
Euro Business Park,
Little Island, Cork.

021-4634154
info@tsaconsultants.ie
www.tsaconsultants

HIS HOMEWARD JOURNEY

The Life and Works of Pope Benedict XVI

BISHOP FINTAN MONAHAN

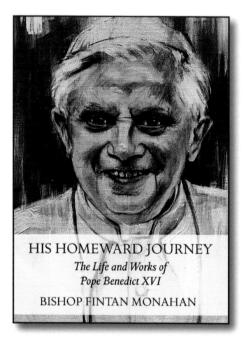

In *His Homeward Journey: The Life and Works of Pope Benedict XVI* Bishop Fintan Monahan takes a fresh look at the life and impact of Pope Benedict XVI, from his early life through his career as a respected theologian, his papacy (2005–13) and time as pope emeritus. Written in an accessible style, this book provides an introduction to Pope Benedict's writings, highlighting the most important texts from his prolific career as a theologian, spiritual writer, teacher and man of God.

Bishop Monahan explores Pope Benedict's relationship with his family, friends and his former students to give a rare glimpse into the private side of this scholar-pope. Pope Benedict was sometimes regarded as a divisive figure, and his career and papacy were not without controversy, but he contributed greatly to the Catholic Church and, above all, he was deeply committed to the Church and its founder, Jesus Christ.

978 1 80097 014 4 • €9.99/£8.99

 VERITAS

Veritas Publications, Veritas House, 7–8 Lower Abbey Street, Dublin D01W2C2
publications@veritas.ie · 01 8788177

DIOCESE OF LIMERICK

Most Rev Brendan Leahy DD
Bishop of Limerick;
born 28 March 1960;
ordained priest 5 June 1986;
ordained Bishop of Limerick
14 April 2013

Diocesan Office:
Limerick Diocesan Centre,
St Munchin's, Corbally, Limerick
Tel 061-350000
Email
bishop@limerickdiocese.org
Website
www.limerickdiocese.org

ST JOHN'S CATHEDRAL, LIMERICK

Since the twelfth century, a church dedicated to St John has stood in the area of Limerick city known as Garryowen. The earliest reference to the first church comes from the year 1205 when the Cathedral Chapter of the Diocese of Limerick was founded by Bishop Donatus O'Brien, Bishop of Limerick from 1195 to 1207. In the document of foundation, the revenues from the Church of St John were given to the Archdeacon of Limerick. This medieval church was replaced by a penal church, which in turn was supplanted by the parish church of St John in the middle of the eighteenth century. With an increase in population in the area around Garryowen, it was decided to build a new church to accommodate the estimated 15,000 parishioners of St John's. An appeal for funds was so well received that the decision was made to abandon the plans for a parish church and build a cathedral for the diocese instead.

Designed by Philip Charles Hardwick, a contemporary and associate of Pugin, St John's Cathedral is revival Gothic in the early English style. It was opened for worship in 1861 and consecrated in 1894 by Cardinal Logue. The spire, standing at 265 feet, 9 inches, was built between 1878 and 1883.

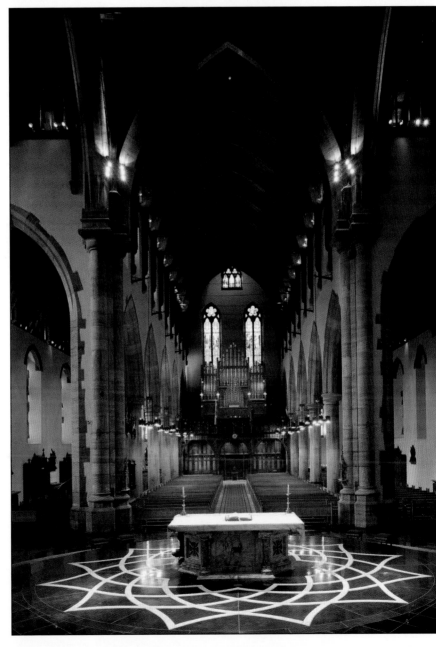

Most Rev Donal Murray DD
Bishop Emeritus
born 29 May 1940; ordained priest 22 May 1966; ordained bishop 18 April 1982; installed as Bishop of Limerick 24 March 1996; retired December 2009

CHAPTER
Dean: Canon Anthony Mullins VG
Archdeacon
Rt Rev Mgr Michael Lane
Theologian: Canon Donough O'Malley
Penitentiary
Canon Gerard Garrett
Chancellor: Canon Frank Duhig
Precentor: Canon James Ambrose
Prebendaries and Canons
Ardcanny: Canon John Daly
Croagh: Canon Joseph Shire
Dysart: Canon John O'Shea
Tullybrackey: Canon Anthony O'Keeffe
Donoghmore
Rt Rev Mgr Daniel Neenan
Ballycahane
Canon William Fitzmaurice
Killeedy: Canon Donal McNamara

Honorary Canons (Pastores Emeriti)
Canon James Ambrose *(Precentor)*
Canon Gary Bluett
Canon Micheál Liston
Canon James Costello
Canon Patrick Kelly

COLLEGE OF CONSULTORS
Most Rev Brendan Leahy
Very Rev Anthony Canon Mullins VG
Very Rev Éamonn Fitzgibbon EV
Very Rev Timothy Curtin
Very Rev John Daly
Very Rev Gerard Garrett
Very Rev Joseph Hayes (SJ)
Rev Seán Harmon
Very Rev Michael Noonan
Rev Frank O'Connor
Rev Chris O'Donnell

ADMINISTRATION
Vicars General
Very Rev Anthony Canon Mullins VG
Very Rev Eamon Fitzgibbon VG

Episcopal Vicars
Episcopal Vicar for Pastoral Care of Priests
Very Rev Frank Canon Duhig

Vicar for Religious
Sr Phyllis Moynihan (RSM)

Episcopal Vicar for Evangelisation
Rev Chris O'Donnell EV

Vicar for Vocations
Sr Mara Rose McDonnell (OP)

Episcopal Vicar for Pastoral Ministry
Very Rev Canon Anthony Mullins VG

Episcopal Vicar for Promotion of Synodality
Very Rev Éamonn Fitzgibbon VG

Diocesan Chancellor
Very Rev Donough Canon O'Malley
Tel 086-2586908
Email donough@ldo.ie

Council of Priests
Most Rev Brendan Leahy
Very Rev Canon Anthony Mullins VG, ex officio
Very Rev Éamonn Fitzgibbon VG, ex officio
Rev Chris O'Donnell EV, ex officio
Rev Joe Hayes (SJ), religious congregation
Rev Krzysztof Tyburowski, bishop's nominee
Very Rev Canon O'Malley, retired priests representative
Rev Eugene Boyce, Curraghchase Area
Rev Frank O' Connor, Cathedral Area
Rev David Casey, Pobal Mocheallog Area
Canon John Daly, Maigue Area
Very Rev Michael Noonan, Our Lady's Area
Rev Gerard O'Leary, Thomond Area
Rev Tim Curtin, Tuath Phadraig Naofa
Rev Denis Mullane, Íde Naofa Area
Rev Seán Harmon, Pobal Neasain
Very Rev Canon Gerard Garrett, bishop's nominee

General Manager/Diocesan Secretary
Catherine Kelly
Limerick Diocesan Centre,
St Munchin's, Corbally, Limerick
Tel 061-350000
Email catherine.kelly@limerickdiocese.org
Website www.limerickdiocese.org
Finance Manager: Patricia Quirke
Secretarial Staff: Stephanie Cleary
Diocesan Spokesperson and Communications: Catherine Kelly
Finance Administrator: Karen Kiely

Diocesan Archivist
David Bracken
Limerick Diocesan Centre, St Munchin's, Corbally, Limerick
Tel 061-350000
Email david.bracken@limerickdiocese.org

DIOCESAN PASTORAL COUNCIL
Bishop Brendan Leahy
Very Rev Éamonn Fitzgibbon VG
Ms Rose O'Connor
Very Rev Mike Cussen
Ms Veronica Garvey
Very Rev Tony Mullins
Ms Siobhán Barrett
Very Rev Michael O'Shea
Mr Pat Condon
Sr Caitríona Kavanagh OP
Ms Ann Breen

CATECHETICS EDUCATION
Primary Level Religious Education
Veronica Behan
Email veronica.behan@limerickdiocese.org
Sr Mary Magdalene Soileau (OP)
Email SisterMaryMagdalene@limerickdiocese.org
Limerick Diocesan Centre,
St Munchin's, Corbally, Limerick
Tel 061-350000

Second Level Religious Education
Dermot Cowhey
Limerick Diocesan Centre,
St Munchin's, Corbally, Limerick
Tel 061-350000
Email dermot.cowhey@limerickdiocese.org

Primary Education Secretary
Acting Director: Ms Aoife Foley
Email aoife.foley@limerickdiocese.org
Assistant Director: Mr Kevin Kelly
Email kevin.kelly@limerickdiocese.org

St Senan's Education Office,
Limerick Diocesan Centre,
St Munchin's, Corbally, Limerick
Tel 061-347777
Administration Staff
Linda Fleming
Email linda.fleming@limerickdiocese.org
Gwen O'Sullivan
Email gwen.osullivan@limerickdiocese.org

LITURGY
Liturgy Advisory Committee
Chair: Rev Frank O'Connor
Very Rev Gerard Garrett, Paudie Hurley,
Bernadette Kiely, Sarah Murphy,
Josie Sweeney
Cathedral House,
Cathedral Place, Limerick
Tel 061-414624
Email oconfrank@eircom.net

PASTORAL
ACCORD
Limerick City Centre:
Social Service Centre,
Henry Street, Limerick
Contact: Ms Jacinta Tierney
Email accordlimerick@eircom.net
www.accord.ie
Spiritual Director: Rev Joseph Hayes (SJ)
Enquiries: Tel 061-343000 Fax 061-35000
Newcastle West Centre:
Parish Centre, Newcastle West,
Co Limerick
Contact: Helen Ahern
Tel 069-61000
Spiritual Director: Rev Frank Canon Duhig
Parochial House, Castlemahon,
Co Limerick
Tel 087-6380299

Allianz (ⅱ)

Apostleship of the Sea, Foynes
Director and Port Chaplain
Rev Anthony Canon O'Keeffe
Shanagolden, Co Limerick
Tel 069-60112

Charismatic Renewal Groups
Liaison Priest: Rev Damian Ryan
Manister, Co Limerick
Tel 061-397335/087-2274412

Neocatechumenal Way
Contacts: Rev Nikola Mladineo
Tel 083-4578388
Emanuele and Bernadetta Cuinaglia
Tel 086-2198186

Ecumenism
Director: Vacant

Emigrant Apostolate
Director: Rev John McCarthy
Tel 085-8066468

Marriage Tribunal
Contact: Rev Richard Keane
Judicial Vicar of the Cork Regional
Marriage Tribunal
Tel 021-4963653

Military Chaplain
Rev Piotr Delimat
Sarsfield Barracks, Limerick
Tel 061-314233

Pioneer Total Abstinence Association
Spiritual Director: Rev Eamon Purcell

Pilgrimage
(Lourdes) Director: Rev Frank O'Dea
Tel 087-2443106
Email frankodea@eircom.net

Pontifical Mission Societies
Diocesan Director: Rev Derek Leonard
Tel 087-6261287

Safeguarding Children
*Director of Safeguarding and
Designated Person:* Ger Crowley
Email ger.crowley@limerickdiocese.org

Social Service Council
General Manager: Brian Ryan
Henry Street, Limerick
Tel 061-314111/314213

Travelling Community
Diocesan Chaplain: Rev Pat Hogan
Tel 087-6522746

Trócaire
Director: Rev Derek Leonard
Parochial House, Knockaderry, Limerick
Tel 087-6261287
Email derekleonard0007@gmail.com

Vocations
Sr Mara Rose McDonnell (OP)
Limerick Diocesan Centre, St Munchin's,
Corbally, Limerick
Tel 061-350000

Youth Apostolate
Contact: Pending
Limerick Diocesan Centre,
St Munchin's, Corbally, Limerick
Tel 061-350000/085-2527465

PARISHES

*The Diocese of Limerick has been divided
into 16 Pastoral Units. Church titulars are
in italics.*

PASTORAL UNIT 1

**PARISHES: ST JOHN'S, MONALEEN, ST
PATRICK'S, ST MICHAEL'S, OUR LADY
HELP OF CHRISTIANS (associated parish)**
*St John's Cathedral, St Mary Magdalene,
St Patrick's, St Brigid's, St Michael's.
Associated Parish: Our Lady Help of
Christians*

Co Parish Priests
Rev Frank O'Connor
Cathedral House,
Cathedral Place, Limerick
Tel 061-414624/087-2642393
Email oconfrank@eircom.net
Rev Leo McDonnell
Cathedral House,
Cathedral Place, Limerick
Tel 061-414624/087-2200366
Email revleomcdonnell@yahoo.co.uk
Rev Gerard Garrett *(Moderator)*
1 Trinity Court, Monaleen Road,
Monaleen, Limerick
Tel 061-330974/086-3233268
Email gergarrett54@gmail.com
Rev Canon Joseph Shire
St Patrick's Presbytery, Dublin Road,
Limerick
Tel 087-6924563
Email canonjshire@gmail.com
Rev Seamus Madigan
1A Trinity Court, Monaleen, Limerick
Tel 086-8441609
Email
seamus.madigan@limerickdiocese.org

Assistant Priest
Rev Krzysztof Tyburowski
134 Cosgrove Park, Moyross, Limerick
Tel 087-4110997
Email vincensleo@hotmail.com
Rev John Daly
Cathedral House,
Cathedral Place, Limerick
Tel 061-414624

*Associated Parish: Our Lady Help of
Christians*
Rev Koenraad Van Gucht (SDB)
Salesian House, Milford,
Castletroy, Limerick
Tel 061-330268/086-3814353
Email koenraad@sdb.ie

Rev Robbie Swinburne (SDB)
Salesian House, Milford,
Castletroy, Limerick
Tel 061-330268
Email robei2iq@eircom.net

PASTORAL UNIT 2

**PARISHES: ST JOSEPH'S, ST SAVIOUR'S,
OUR LADY OF LOURDES**
*St Joseph's, St Saviour's, Our Lady of
Lourdes*

Co Parish Priests
Rev John Walsh *(Moderator)*
Mount David, North Circular Road,
Limerick
Tel 087-4493228
Email frjohnwalsh1963@gmail.com
Rev Liam Enright
5 Lifford Avenue, Ballinacurra, Limerick
Tel 087-7415603
Sr Catríona Kavanagh (OP)
Administrator St Saviour's and team
member of pastoral unit

Assistant Priest
Rev Donough Canon O'Malley
19 School House Lane,
rear of Barrington Street, Limerick
Tel 086-2586908

PASTORAL UNIT 3

**PARISHES: DONOUGHMORE/KNOCKEA/
ROXBORO, OUR LADY QUEEN OF PEACE,
HOLY FAMILY**
*St Patrick, Our Lady Queen of Peace,
Holy Family*

Co Parish Priests
Rev Tom Mangan *(Moderator)*
Donoghmore, Co Limerick
Tel 087-2348226
Email tjmangan86@gmail.com
Rev Daniel Tomasik
Elm View, Roxboro Road, Limerick
Tel 061-410846/087-6092086
Email dantomasik@gmail.com
Rev Joseph Hayes (SJ)
Della Strada, Dooradoyle, Co Limerick
Tel 061-480929/087-4647634
Email jhayessj@gmail.com

PASTORAL UNIT 4

**SUB UNIT A – PARISHES: ST
MUNCHIN'S/ST LELIA'S, CORPUS CHRISTI,
PARTEEN/MEELICK**
*St Munchin's/St Lelia's, Corpus Christi, St
Patrick's, St John the Baptist*

Co Parish Priests
Rev Canon Donal McNamara *(Moderator)*
St Munchin's, Clancy Strand, Limerick
Tel 061-455635/087-2402518
Email
donal.mcnamara@limerickdiocese.org

Rev Pat Hogan
Sruth Lan, South Circular Road, Limerick
Tel 087-6522746
Email pkfhogan@gmail.com
Rev Pat Seaver
4 Glenview Terrace, Farranshone,
Limerick
Tel 061-328838/086-0870297
Email patseaver@gmail.com
Rev Eamonn Purcell
Parteen, Co Clare
Tel 087-7635617
Email eamon.purcell@hse.ie

Assistant Priest
Rev Oliver Plunkett
13 Castle Court, Clancy Strand, Limerick]
Tel 087-6593176
Email bohereenop@gmail.com

**SUB UNIT B – PARISHES: ST NICHOLAS,
ST MARY'S**
St Nicholas, St Mary's

Co Parish Priests
Rev Richard Davern *(Moderator)*
St Mary's, Authlunkard Street, Limerick
Tel 087-9577500
Email frrichie@hotmail.com
Rev John O'Byrne
St Mary's, Athlunkard Street, Limerick
Tel 085-7491268
Email johnbyrne.beda@yahoo.co.uk
Rev Gerard O'Leary
The Curate's House,
Athlunkard Street, Limerick
Tel 087-9378685
Email gerardoleary58@gmail.com

Assistant Priest
Rev Liam Enright
St Nicholas Presbytery, Westbury, Limerick
Tel 087-2546335

PASTORAL UNIT 5

**PARISHES: CHRIST THE KING, CRATLOE/
SIXMILEBRIDGE, OUR LADY OF THE
ROSARY**
*Christ the King, St John's, Little Church,
Our Lady of the Rosary*

Co Parish Priests
Rev Richard Keane *(Moderator)*
Parochial House, Cratloe, Co Clare
Tel 087-9552729
Email richardkeane2002@yahoo.co.uk
Rev Patrick O'Sullivan
17 Alderwood Avenue,
Caherdavin, Limerick
Tel 087-2376032
Rev Des McAuliffe
'Sheen Lodge', Ennis Road, Limerick
Tel 061-324825/087-2336476
Email desmondmcauliffe@gmail.com

Assistant Priest
Rev Tom Ryan
Gleneden, North Circular Road, Limerick
Tel 087-2997733

PASTORAL UNIT 6

**PARISHES: PATRICKSWELL/
BALLYBROWN, MUNGRET/RAHEEN/
CRECORA, ST PAUL'S**
*Blessed Virgin Mary, St Joseph's, St
Nessan's, St Oliver Plunkett, Ss Peter &
Paul's, St Paul's*

Co Parish Priests
Rev Michael Cussen *(Moderator)*
The Presbytery, Ballybrown, Co Limerick
Tel 061-353711/087-1279015
Email mikecussen@outlook.com
Rev Canon John O'Shea
St Nessan's Presbytery,
Raheen, Co Limerick
Tel 061-210869/087-9708282
Email frjohnoshea@gmail.com
Rev Noel Murphy (CSSp)
14 Springfield, Dooradoyle, Limerick
Tel 061-304508/087-2228971

Assistant Priests
Rev Éamonn Fitzgibbon
The Presbytery, Patrickswell, Co Limerick
Tel 087-6921191
Email
eamonn.fitzgibbon@limerickdiocese.org
Mgr Michael Lane
2 Meadowvale, Raheen, Limerick
Tel 087-2544450
Email michaellane@outlook.ie
Rev Shoji Varghese
42 Nessan Court, Lower Church Road,
Raheen, Limerick
Tel 089-4431922
Email shojiputhenpurackal@gmail.com
Rev Seán Harmon
37 Gouldavoher, Dooradoyle, Limerick
Tel 087-9870284
Rev Tim Wrenn (SDB)
Salesian House Don Bosco Road,
Pallaskenry, Co Limerick
Tel 089-2507825
Prince Zacharia Maliyil
42 Nessan Court, Raheen, Limerick
Tel 089-2070570
Email princezmaliyil@gmail.com

PASTORAL UNIT 7

**SUB UNIT A – PARISHES: MANISTER,
FEDAMORE, BRUFF/MEANUS/GRANGE/
CROOM, BANOGUE, DROMIN/ATHLACCA**
*St Michael's, St John the Baptist, Ss Peter
& Paul's, St Mary's, Ss Patrick & Brigid,
St Mary's, Ss Peter & Paul's, Holy Trinity,
St John the Baptist*

Co Parish Priests
Rev William Canon Fitzmaurice
(Moderator)
Croom, Co Limerick
Tel 061-397231/0862423728
Email croomchurch@eircom.net
Rev Noel Kirwan
The Presbytery, Bruff, Co Limerick
Tel 087-2589279
Email nkirwan62@gmail.com

Rev Damian Ryan
Manister, Croom, Co Limerick
Tel 061-523954/087-2274412
Email 4dlord@eircom.net

Assistant Priests
Rev Michael Hanley
Parochial House, Fedamore, Co Limerick
Tel 086-8595733
Email hanleymichaelangelo@gmail.com
Rev James Canon Costello
Bruff, Co Limerick
Tel 061-382555
Rev Francesco Okonkwo
San Michel, Mill Road, Corbally, Limerick
Tel 087-7151260

PASTORAL UNIT 8

**PARISHES: ROCKHILLL/BRUREE,
BALLYAGRAN/COLMANSWELL**
*St Munchin's, Immaculate Conception,
St Michael's, St Colman's*

Co Parish Priests
Rev David Gibson *(Moderator)*
Ballyagran, Kilmallock, Co Limerick
Tel 087-2528738
Email brookhaven.gibson@gmail.com
Rev Tim O'Connor CC
St Munchin's Church,
Rockhill, Co Limerick
Tel 087-7859028
Email timoconnor@rcdow.org.uk

PASTORAL UNIT 9

**PARISHES: BULGADEN/
MARTINSTOWN, EFFIN/GARRIENDERK,
KILMALLOCK, ARDPATRICK,
GLENROE/BALLYORGAN, KILFINANE**
*Our Lady of the Assumption (Bulgaden),
Our Lady of the Assumption
(Martinstown), Our Lady Queen of
Peace, St Patrick's (Garrienderk),
Ss Peter & Paul's, St Mary's, St Patrick's
(Ardpatrick), Our Lady of Ransom,
St Joseph's, St Andrew*

Co Parish Priest
Rev Michael O'Shea *(Moderator)*
Glenduff Cottage, Kilfinane, Co Limerick
Tel 087-9791432
Email mjtoshea@gmail.com

Assistant Priests
Rev Chris O'Donnell
Jerpoint, Sheares Street,
Kilmallock, Co Limerick
Tel 087-6323309
Email chris.odonnell@limerickdiocese.or
Rev Tom Coughlan
Effin, Kilmallock, Co Limerick
Tel 063-71314/087-2229223
Email frtomcoughlan@hotmail.com
Rev Anthony Bluett
Parochial House,
Ardpatrick, Co Limerick
Tel 087-1848833
Email frtonybluett@gmail.com

PASTORAL UNIT 10

PARISHES: RATHKEALE, BALLINGARRY/ GRANAGH, KNOCKADERRY/CLONCAGH
St Mary's, Our Lady of the Immaculate Conception, St Joseph's, St Munchin's, St Mary's

Co Parish Priests
Rev Thomas Carroll (Moderator)
Burrett Street, Ballingarry, Co Limerick
Tel 087-2036229
Email carrollgtom@gmail.com
Rev Robert Coffey
5 Orchard Avenue, Rathkeale, Co Limerick
Tel 087-6540908
Email coffeyrobert@gmail.com
Rev Derek Leonard
Parochial House, Knockaderry, Co Limerick
Tel 087-6261287
Email derekleonard0007@gmail.com

PASTORAL UNIT 11

PARISHES: CROAGH/KILFINNY, ADARE, APPAGH
St John the Baptist, St Kieran, Holy Trinity, St James

Co Parish Priests
Rev Mgr Daniel Neenan (Moderator pro-tem)
Holy Trinity Abbey Church,
Adare, Co Limerick
Tel 061-396172/ 087-2208547
Email danneenan@outlook.com
Rev Eugene Boyce
Croagh, Rathkeale, Co Limerick
Tel 069-64185/086-2542517
Email croaghkilfinny@eircom.net

Assistant Priests
Canon Anthony O'Keeffe
Parochial House, Shanagolden, Limerick
Tel 087-4163401
Rev Raphael Okanumeh
Holy Trinity Church, Adare, Co Limerick
Tel 087-9490083

PASTORAL UNIT 12

PARISHES: KILDIMO/PALLASKENRY, KILCORNAN, ASKEATON/BALLYSTEEN
St Joseph, St Mary, St John the Baptist, St Mary, St Patrick

Co Parish Priests
Rev John Donworth (Moderator)
Parochial House, Kildimo, Co Limerick
Tel 061-394134/087-2237501
Email johndonworth@hotmail.com
Rev Seán O'Longaigh
Askeaton, Co Limerick
Tel 061-392249
Email seanolongaigh@eircom.net

Assistant Priest
Rev Muiris O'Connor
Askeaton, Co Limerick
Tel 086-6075628
Email muiris.oconnor@limerickdiocese.org

PASTORAL UNIT 13

PARISHES: SHANAGOLDEN/FOYNES/ ROBERTSTOWN, LOUGHILL/ BALLYHAHILL, GLIN, COOLCAPPA/ KILCOLMAN
St Senan (Shanagolden), St Senan (Foynes), St Senan (Robertstown), Church of the Assumption, Ballyhahill, Immaculate Conception, St Kyran, St Colman

Co Parish Priests
Rev Tim Curtin (Moderator)
The Presbytery, Carrons,
Kilcolman, Co Limerick
Tel 069-60126 /086-3697735
Email frtcurtin@gmail.com
Rev Austin McNamara
Parochial House, Ballyhahill, Co Limerick
Tel 069-82103/087-2615471
Email austinmcnamara1896@yahoo.com

PASTORAL UNIT 14

PARISHES: ABBEYFEALE, ATHEA, TEMPLEGLANTINE, TOURNAFULLA/ MOUNTCOLLINS
Our Lady of the Assumption, St Bartholomew's, Most Holy Trinity, St Patrick's, Our Lady of the Assumption

Co Parish Priests
Rev Denis Mullane (Moderator)
The Presbytery, Templeglantine,
Co Limerick
Tel 069-84021/087-2621911
Email 3parishesttm@gmail.com
Very Rev Canon Anthony Mullins VG
The Presbytery, Abbeyfeale, Co Limerick
Tel 068-31157
Email mullinstrev@gmail.com
Rev William Russell
Convent Street, Abbeyfeale, Limerick
Tel 087-2272825
Email wfruss@gmail.com

Assistant Priest
Rev Daniel Lane
1 Cedarville, Abbeyfeale, Co Limerick
Tel 087-2533030
Email danfl44@outlook.com

PASTORAL UNIT 15

PARISHES: NEWCASTLEWEST, MAHOONAGH, MONAGEA, ARDAGH/ CARRICKERRY
Immaculate Conception of the Blessed Virgin Mary, St John the Baptist & St Nicholas, St Mary's, Church of Visitation of BVM, St Molua, St Mary's

Co Parish Priests
Rev Frank O'Dea (Moderator)
St Ita's Presbytery, Newcastlewest,
Co Limerick
Tel 087-2443106
Email frank.odea@limerickdiocese.org

Rev John Mockler
Gortboy, Newcastlewest, Co Limerick
Tel 086-2342242
Email jmmockler@gmail.com
Rev Joseph Cussen, Lisieux, Gortboy,
Newcastlewest, Co Limerick
Tel 069-77090
Email cussenjos@gmail.com
Rev Michael Noonan
Parochial House, Ardagh, Co Limerick
Tel 069-76121/087-6796217
Email manoonan2@eircom.net

Assistant Priest
Rev Tom Crawford
Gortboy, Newcastlewest, Co Limerick
Tel 087-2218078
Email frtdec@gmail.com

PASTORAL UNIT 16

PARISHES: DROMCOLLOGHER/ BROADFORD, KILEEDY/ASHFORD, FEENAGH/KILMEEDY
St Bartholomew, Our Lady of the Snows, St Ita (Kileedy), St Ita (Ashford), St Ita (Feenagh), St Ita (Kilmeedy)

Co Parish Priests
Rev David Casey (Moderator)
Parochial House, The Square,
Dromcollogher, Co Limerick
Tel 087-2272791
Email Daibhidhc@hotmail.com
Rev John Keating
Parochial House, Raheenagh,
Ballagh, Co Limerick
Tel 069-85014/087-6322212

SYRO MALABAR CHAPLAIN
Chaplain: Prince Zacharia Maliyil
42 Nessan Court, Raheen, Limerick
Tel 089-2070570
Email princezmaliyil@gmail.com

INSTITUTIONS, COLLEGES AND THEIR CHAPLAINS

Askeaton Community College
Coláiste Mhuire, Askeaton, Co Limerick
Diane Brown
Tel 061-392368

Castletroy Community College
Castletroy, Limerick
Tel 061-330785
Ms Brenda Cribben

Coláiste Iósaef
Kilmallock, Co Limerick
Theresa Mulcaire
Tel 063-98275

Coláiste Na Trócaire
Rathkeale, Co Limerick
Olivia Giltenane
Tel 069-64094

Coláiste Ide & Iosef
Abbeyfeale, Co Limerick
Ms Noírín McCarthy
Tel 068-30631

Thomond Community College
Dooneen Road, Woodview Park, Limerick
Tel 061-452422
Suzanne O'Connor

Brothers of Charity Services
Bawnmore, Clonlong Road, Limerick
Rev Joseph Young
The House of Bernadette, Dooneen,
Crecora, Co Limerick
Tel 061-405835

Prison, Limerick
Mulgrave Street, Limerick
Prison General Office: Tel 061-415111
Ms Christine Hoctor
Rev Michael Kelleher (CSsR)

Croom County Hospital
Croom, Co Limerick
Rev Garrett Canon Bluett
Tel 061-397335

St Camillus's Hospital
Shelbourne Road, Limerick
Clergy, St Munchin's Parish

St Ita's Hospital
Newcastle West, Co Limerick
Tel 069-62311
Rev Frank O'Dea
Tel 069-62141

St John's Hospital, Limerick
Pastoral Care Department
Tel 061-462111
Clergy, St John's Parish
Tel 061-414624

Sarsfield Barracks, Limerick
Rev Piotr Delimat
Tel 061-314233

University Maternity Hospital
Ennis Road, Limerick
Parish clergy, Our Lady of the Rosary
087-2997733

University Hospital
Dooradoyle, Limerick
Tel 061-301111
Chaplains: Rev Shoji Varghese
42 Nessan Court, Lower Church Road,
Raheen, Limerick
Tel 089-4431922
Rev Seán Harmon
37 Gouldavoher Estate,
Dooradoyle, Limerick
Tel 087-9870284

University of Limerick
Chaplains: Rev John Campion (SDB)
Salesian House, Milford,
Castletroy, Limerick
Tel 061-330268/202180
Email johncampion@ul.ie
Sr Sarah O'Rourke (FMA)

PRIESTS OF THE DIOCESE ELSEWHERE

Rev David Costello
c/o The Missionary Society of St James
the Apostle, 24 Clark Street,
Boston, MA 02109, USA
Email perudavid@gmail.com
Rev Paul Finnerty, Rector
Pontificio Collegio Irlandese,
Via dei Santi Quattro 1,
00184 Roma, Italy
Tel +39-06-772631
Email paulfinnerty@irishcollege.org
Rev John McCarthy
Chaplain
Irish Pastoral Center, Boston

RETIRED PRIESTS

Very Rev James Canon Ambrose
Very Rev Garrett Canon Bluett
Very Rev Patrick Bluett
Very Rev Patrick Bowen
Rev Jeremiah Brouder
Rev James Costello
Rev Maurice Costello
Very Rev Thomas Coughlan
Rev Sean Condon
Very Rev Tom Crawford
Very Rev Frank Canon Duhig
Very Rev John Duggan
Very Rev Liam Enright
Very Rev Thomas Hurley
Rev Ed Irwin
Very Rev Patrick Canon Kelly
Very Rev Joseph Kennedy
Very Rev Daniel Lane
Venerable Archdeacon Michael Lane
Very Rev John Leonard
Very Rev Micheál Canon Liston
Very Rev Laurence Madden
Very Rev Martin Madigan
Very Rev Anthony Mulvihill
Most Rev Donal Murray, Bishop Emeritus
Rev Terence O'Connell
Very Rev Anthony Canon O'Keeffe
Very Rev Timothy O'Leary
Very Donough Canon O'Malley
Very Rev Oliver Plunkett
Very Rev Tom A. Ryan
Rev Willie Walsh

PERSONAL PRELATURE

OPUS DEI
Rev Brian McCarthy
Castleville Study Centre, Golf Links Road
Castletroy, Limerick V94 YC95
Tel 061-331223 Fax 061-331204
Email castleville@eircom.net

RELIGIOUS ORDERS AND CONGREGATIONS

PRIESTS

AUGUSTINIANS
St Augustine's Priory,
O'Connell Street, Limerick
Tel 061-415374
Prior: Rev Noel Hession (OSA)
Bursar: Rev Flor O'Callaghan (OSA)

FRANCISCAN FRIARS OF THE RENEWAL (CFR)
St Patrick Friary, 64 Delmege Park,
Moyross, Limerick V94 859Y
Tel 061-458071 Fax 061-457626
Email limerickfranciscans@gmail.com
Local Servant (Superior)
Rev Joseph Mary Deane

INSTITUTE OF CHRIST THE KING SOVEREIGN PRIEST
Sacred Heart Church, The Crescent,
Limerick V94 HK29
Tel 061-315812
Email limerick@icrsp.org
Prior: Canon Lebocq
1st Vicar: Canon Arrasate
2nd Vicar: Canon O'Connor

JESUITS
Crescent College Comprehensive SJ,
Dooradoyle, Limerick
Tel 061-229655 Fax 061-229013
Email jhayessj@eircom.net
Superior: Rev Joseph Hayes (SJ)
Principal: Ms Karin Fleming

REDEMPTORISTS
Mount St Alphonsus Mission House,
South Circular Road, Limerick
Tel 061-315099 Fax 061-315303
Superior: Rev Seamus Enright (CSsR)

St Clement's College, Laurel Hill Avenue
South Circular Road, Limerick
Tel 061-315878 Fax 061-316640
Email cssrlimerick@eircom.net
Secondary school for boys
Principal: Mr Pat Talty

SALESIANS
Salesian College, Don Bosco Road,
Pallaskenry,
Co Limerick, V94 WP86
Tel 061-393105 Fax 061-393298
Rector: Rev John Horan (SDB)
Email salesian@indigo.ie
Secondary and agricultural schools

alesian House, Milford,
astletroy, Limerick, V94 DK44
el 061-330268/330194
ector: Very Rev John Campion (SDB)
ice-Rector: Rev Martin Loftus
arish Priest
ery Rev Koenraad Van Guch (SDB) PP
tudent hostel and parish

BROTHERS

ROTHERS OF CHARITY
awnmore, Clonlong Road, Limerick
el 061-308149
esidential & Day Care for persons with
arning disabilities
haplain: Rev Joe Young

HRISTIAN BROTHERS
hristian Brothers, St Teresa's,
orth Circular Road, Limerick
el 061-451811
ommunity Leader: Br Senan Ryan
ommunity: 5

SISTERS

STERS OF BON SECOURS DE TROYES
Paul's Nursing Home, Dooradoyle,
merick
el 061-304690
mail bonsecours792@gmail.com
ontact: Sr Margaret Costello
ommunity: 2

HARITY OF ST PAUL THE APOSTLE
STERS
Paul's Convent,
lfinane, Co Limerick
el 063-91025 Fax 063-91639
mail stpaulsfin@gmail.com
ontact: Sr Eileen Kelly
ommunity: 2
ducation and parish work

Paul's, Glenfield Road,
lmallock, Co Limerick
el 063-98086
mail sisterskilm@eircom.net
ontact: Sr Mary Hannigan
ommunity: 2
arish work

ONGREGATION OF THE SISTERS OF
ERCY
he Sisters of Mercy minister throughout
e diocese in pastoral and social work,
mmunity development, counselling,
irituality, education and health care,
aswering current needs.

ount St Vincent,
Connell Avenue, Limerick V94 K6EH
l 061-314965 Fax 061-404175
mmunity: 18

Sisters of Mercy, St Mary's Convent,
Bishop Street, Limerick V94 CT9X
Tel 061-317356 Fax 061-317361
Community: 7

16 Portland Estate,
St Clare's, Newcastlewest,
Co Limerick V42 V302
Tel 069-62373
Community: 2

33 Danesfort, Corbally,
Limerick V94 YE2X
Tel 061-341214
Community: 2

34 Danesfort, Corbally,
Limerick V94 H66E
Tel 061-349131
Community: 2

7 Fitzhaven Square,
Ashbourne Avenue,
Limerick V94 H2HW
Tel 061-304614
Community: 2

1 Greenfields, Rosbrien,
Limerick V94 X7WE
Tel 061-229773
Community: 3

Catherine McAuley House Nursing Home,
Old Dominic Street,
Limerick V94 DX58
Tel 061-315313/315384 Fax 061-315455
Community: numbers vary

136 Fortview Drive,
Ballinacurra Gardens,
Limerick V94 HHN4
Tel 061-304798
Community: 2

1 Mount Vincent Place,
O'Connell Avenue, Limerick V94 KN29
Tel 061-468448
Community: 3

22 Galtee Drive,
O'Malley Park, Southill,
Limerick V94 N5TF
Tel 061-416706
Community: 2

Sisters of Mercy,
St Ita's Voluntary Housing,
Convent Street,
Abbeyfeale, Co Limerick V94 R283
Tel 068-310203
Community: 2

DOMINICAN SISTERS OF ST CECILIA
St Saviours, Glentworth Street, Limerick
Tel 085-2255796
Parish mail
stsavioursdominican@gmail.com
Convent email limerick@op-tn.org
Superior: Sr Caitríona Kavanagh (OP)
Community: 4

FRANCISCAN MISSIONARIES OF MARY
Castle View Gardens,
Clancy Strand, Limerick
Tel 061-455320
Email jomcglynnfmm@yahoo.co.uk
Superior: Sr Mary Shanahan
Email mary.e.shanahan@gmail.com
Community: 6
Pastoral work

**SISTERS OF ST FRANCIS OF
PHILADELPHIA**
Delamarie, Hassett's Cross, Limerick
Email bajosf@gmail.com
Contact: Sr Barbara Jackson

Cuan Mhuire, Bruree, Co Limerick
Email moman@osfphila.com
Contact: Sr Marie Oman

**CONGREGATION OF OUR LADY OF
CHARITY OF THE GOOD SHEPHERD**
Good Shepherd Avenue,
12 Pennywell Road,
Limerick V94 AFP3
Tel 061-415178
Leader: Sr Noreen O'Shea
Community: 13

Omega B, Roxboro Road,
Janesboro, Limerick V94 K2N7
Tel 061-416676
Email rgsroxboro@hotmail.com
Community: 4

LA SAINTE UNION DES SACRES COEURS
Apartment 14, Sylvan House,
Park Village, Castletroy, Limerick
Tel 061-332598
Community: 1
Pastoral

LITTLE COMPANY OF MARY
Milford Convent
Plassey Park Road,
Castletroy, Limerick
Tel 061-485800 Fax 061-330351
Email lcm.milfordc@gmail.com
Community: 11
Milford Care Centre Nursing Home: 4

St Joseph's Convent,
Plassey Park Road,
Castletroy, Limerick
Tel 061-331144
Email stjoslcm@gmail.com
Community: 3

1 Mary Potter Court,
Plassey Park Road,
Castletroy, Limerick
Tel/Fax 061-332798
Community: 1

2 Mary Potter Court,
Plassey Park Road,
Castletroy, Limerick
Tel 061-332777
Community: 1

3 Mary Potter Court,
Plassey Park Road,
Castletroy, Limerick
Tel 061-332755
Community: 1

SISTERS OF MARIE REPARATRICE
Laurel Hill Avenue,
South Circular Road, Limerick V94 XN29
Tel 061-315045
Contact: Sr Eileen Carroll
Email eileencarrollsmr@gmail.com
Community: 10
Spiritual direction/retreats
Regional Animator: Sr Eileen Carroll

POOR SERVANTS OF THE MOTHER OF GOD
43 Liosan, Sheehan Road,
Newcastle West, Co Limerick
Tel 069-20936
Community: 2
Daycare Centre

Dún Íosa, Main Street,
Drumcollogher, Co Limerick
Tel 063-83844
Community: 3
Pastoral

PRESENTATION SISTERS
8-9 Oakvale Drive,
Dooradoyle, Limerick
Tel 061-302011
Community: 1

Roxboro Road, Limerick
Tel 061-417204
Email presconvent@gmail.com
Team Leadership
Community: 15

34 McDonagh Avenue,
Janesboro, Limerick
Tel 061-594777
Email amsheehy1@gmail.com
Community: 2

Apartment A,
6 Sexton Street, Limerick
Tel 061-467866
Email colettemhourigan@gmail.com
Community: 1

Apartment B,
6 Sexton Street, Limerick
Tel 061-467983
Community: 1

Apt 1 Presentation House,
Parnell Place, Parnell Street, Limerick
Tel 061-481674
Community: 1

Apt 3 Presentation House,
Parnell Place, Parnell Street, Limerick
Tel 061-419370
Community: 1

Apt 4 Presentation House,
Parnell Place, Parnell Street, Limerick
Tel 061-467867
Community: 1

Apt 8 Presentation House,
Parnell Place, Parnell Street, Limerick
Tel 061-310036
Community: 1

SALESIAN SISTERS OF ST JOHN BOSCO
'Bethel',
Caherdavin Heights, Limerick
Contact person: Sr Anne Collins

33/34 Bracken Crescent,
North Circular Road, Limerick
Tel 061-455132
Email brken@gofree.indigo.ie
Superior: Sr Mary McInerney
Community: 4
Teaching, related activities

Salesian Convent, Dun Ide,
Lower Shelbourne Road, Limerick
Tel 061-454511
Superior: Sr Sarah O'Rourke
Community: 9
Parish work, spiritual accompaniment,
pioneers, clubs

Salesian Convent, Ard Mhuire,
Caherdavin Heights, Limerick
Tel 061-451322
Email caherdavinhouse@gmail.com
Superior: Sr Catherine Sweeney
Community: 11
Ministry to the elderly, Parish ministry

Salesian Sisters, Cill Leala,
New Road, Thomondgate,
Limerick
Tel 061-453099
Email cillleala@gmail.com
Contact person: Sr Noelle Costello
Community: 4
Involvement in parish and Blue Box,
Mission promotion

Salesian Sisters, 'Sonas',
3 Oakton Road, Westbury,
Corbally, Limerick
Email 3oaktonroad@eircom.net
Superior: Sr Patricia Murtagh
Community: 3
Parish and youth work

ST JOSEPH OF THE SACRED HEART SISTERS
Coolcranogue, Upper Dunganville,
Ardagh, Co Limerick
Tel 069-76668
Regional Leader: Sr Margaret O'Sullivan
Email margaretosullivan1@outlook.ie

7 Plassey Grove, Castletroy, Limerick
Tel 061-335794
Sr Cecilia Keating

Mackillop House, Dromcollogher,
Co Limerick
Tel 063-83911
Sr Maureen Cahill

No. 2 St Ita's Centre, Convent Street,
Abbeyfeale, Co Limerick
Tel 068-51984
Sr Elizabeth Kirby

4 Clover Field, Glin, Co Limerick
Tel 068-26015
Sr Mary Doody

St Catherine's, Bungalow 1, Bothar Buí,
Newcastle West, Co Limerick
Tel 069-62584
Sr Anne Keaty

St Catherine's, Bungalow 2, Bothar Buí,
Newcastle West, Co Limerick
Tel 069-62584
Sr Mary Keating

St Catherine's, Bungalow 3, Bothar Buí,
Newcastle West, Co Limerick
Tel 069-62579
Sr Margaret Hanrahan

St Catherine's, Bungalow 5, Bothar Buí,
Newcastle West, Co Limerick
Tel 069-62607
Sr Kathleen Murphy

Apt 15, Liosan Court, Gort Boy,
Newcastle West, Co Limerick
Tel 069-69603
Sr Catherine Duggan

'St Joseph's' Banogue Cross,
Croom, Co Limerick
Tel 061-600932
Sr Eileen Lenihan
Email eileen.lenihan@sosj.org.au

Allianz (ⅰⅰ)

t. 39, Halcyon Place,
e Park Village,
stletroy, Co Limerick 94N CC7
l:061-332725
Sarah Hogan

t. 20, Sylvan House,
e Park Village,
stletroy, Co Limerick
061-276545
Bridget Moloney

se Cottage, Ballyloughane,
wcastle West, Co Limerick
069-76655
Bridie O'Sullivan
ail bridie06os@eircom.net

echwood House,
wcastle West, Co Limerick
Dymphna O'Brien
ail dymphna.obrien@sosj.org.au

EDUCATIONAL INSTITUTIONS

ary Immaculate College of Education
061-204300
aplain: Rev Michael Wall
061-204331
ail michael.wall@mic.ul.ie
ad of Department of Theology &
rector of Institute for Pastoral Studies
v Eamonn Fitzgibbon
Patrick's Campus, Thurles, Co Tipperary
ail eamonn.fitzgibbon@mic.ul.ie

Munchin's College (Diocesan College)
rbally, Limerick
061-348922 Fax 061-340465
ail stmunchins@eircom.net
ncipal: David Quilter
ail davequilter@hotmail.com
aplain: Tom Conneely

elscoileanna
aplain: Rev Micheál Canon Liston
Sullane Crescent, Raheen Heights,
erick
087-2314804

CHARITABLE AND OTHER SOCIETIES

Apostolic Work Society
Contact: Brid Shine
Glenbrohane, Garryspillane,
Kilmallock, Co Limerick
Tel 062-46612
Email dirb@iol.ie

Catholic Institute Athletic Club
Rosbrien, Limerick
President: Tel 061-455635
Secretary: Tel 061-452023

**Doras Luimní
(Development organisation for Refugees
and Asylum Seekers)**
Central Buildings,
51A O'Connell Street, Limerick
Tel 061-609960
Email dorasluimni@eircom.net

Knights of St Columbanus
Contact: Mr William Ryan
Tel 061-414173 (work)/061-227530
(home)

Legion of Mary
Assumpta House, Windmill Street,
Limerick
Tel 061-314071

Limerick Youth Service
5 Lower Glentworth Street, Limerick
Tel 061-412444/412545 Fax 061-412795
CEO: Fiona O'Grady
Email lys@limerickyouthservice.net

Order of Malta
7A Davis Street, Limerick
Tel/Fax 061-314250

St Joseph's Young Priests' Society
Contact: Una Nunan
10 Garravogue Road, Raheen, Limerick
Tel 061-227852

St Vincent de Paul Society
Ozanam House, Hartstonge Street,
Limerick
Tel 061-317327 Fax 061-310320
Email info@svpmw.com
Administrator: Mary Leahy
Drop-In Centre
The Lane, Hartstonge Street, Limerick
Manager: Tom Flynn
Tel 061-313557

DIOCESE OF MEATH

PATRON OF THE DIOCESE
ST FINIAN, 12 DECEMBER

INCLUDES THE GREATER PART OF COUNTIES MEATH, WESTMEATH AND OFFALY,
AND A PORTION OF COUNTIES LONGFORD, LOUTH, DUBLIN AND CAVAN

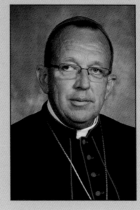

Most Rev Tom Deenihan DD, Ed.D
Bishop of Meath;
born 1967;
ordained priest 1 June 1991;
ordained Bishop of Meath
2 September 2018

Residence: Bishop's House,
Dublin Road, Mullingar,
Co Westmeath N91 DW32
Tel 044-9348841 Fax 044-934302
Email
secretary@dioceseofmeath.ie
Website www.dioceseofmeath.

CATHEDRAL OF CHRIST THE KING, MULLINGAR

As the Penal Laws began to be relaxed, Bishop Patrick Plunkett was appointed Bishop of Meath in 1778. He was to spend the next forty-nine years of his life restoring and rebuilding the diocese. He had no cathedral, but providing one was not his immediate priority. Towards the end of his time as bishop, work began on the magnificent new Church of St Mary in Navan. This was opened in 1830 and was considered the Cathedral Church of the Diocese. In 1870 Bishop Thomas Nulty decided to locate the

bishop's residence in Mullingar, and the parish church there was designated Cathedral Church of the Diocese. It had been built in 1828 but was quite small.

On his appointment as bishop in 1900, Matthew Gaffney called a public meeting to discuss the building of a cathedral for the Diocese of Meath. This meeting adopted the following resolution: 'The Diocese of Meath not having a cathedral nor the parish of Mullingar a suitable church, be it resolved that a church be built in Mullingar which will fulfil this double purpose.' A building fund was established, and £15,000 was subscribed

at this first meeting – a very sizeable su at that time. It was not until the day of his consecration as bishop in 1929 that Thomas Mulvany was able to announce the decision to proceed with the projec Ralph A. Byrne, chief architect with William H. Byrne & Son, Dublin, prepared plans, which were accepted. Work began in 1932, and the Cathedra of Christ the King was opened for worship in September 1936. It was consecrated on 30 August 1939, the del having been cleared. In recent years, a major renovation, including the replacement of the roof, has been completed.

Most Rev Michael Smith DCL, DD
Bishop Emeritus of Meath
Born 1940; ordained priest 1963;
Consecrated Bishop 29 January 1984;
Co-adjutor Bishop of Meath 10 October
1988; succeeded 16 May 1990;
Retired 18 June 2018.
Residence: St Oliver's, Beechfield,
Dublin Road, Mullingar, Co Westmeath
Tel 044-9340636
Email msmith@dioceseofmeath.ie

ADMINISTRATION
Diocesan website
www.dioceseofmeath.ie

Vicars General
Very Rev Declan Hurley Adm, VG
St Mary's, Navan, Co Meath
Tel 046-9027518
Very Rev Joseph Gallagher PP, VG
Parochial House, Tullamore, Co Offaly
Tel 057-9321587

Chancellor
Very Rev Paul Connell Phd
Meath Diocesan Office, Dublin Road,
Mullingar, Co Westmeath
Tel 044-9348841
Email chancellor@dioceseofmeath.ie

Vicars Forane
Very Rev John Byrne PA, VF
Parochial House, Kells, Co Meath
Tel 046-9240213
Very Rev Gerry Stuart PP, VF
Parochial House, Ratoath, Co Meath
Tel 01-8256207
Very Rev Tom Gilroy PP, VF
Parochial House,
Kinnegad, Co Westmeath
Tel 044-9375117
Very Rev Joseph Gallagher PP, VF
Parochial House, Tullamore, Co Offaly
Tel 057-9321587
Very Rev Patrick Moore PP, VF
Parochial House,
Castlepollard, Co Westmeath
Tel 044-9661126 Fax 044-9661881
Very Rev Andrew Doyle PP, VF
Parochial House, Durhamstown,
Bohermeen, Navan, Co Meath
Tel 046-9073805
Very Rev Denis McNelis PP, VF
Parochial House, Laytown, Co Meath
Tel 041-9827258
Very Rev Padraig McMahon PP, VF
Parochial House, Athboy, Co Meath
Tel 046-9432184 Fax 046-9430021

College of Consultors
Most Rev Tom Deenihan DD, Ed.D
Very Rev Declan Hurley Adm, VG
Very Rev John Byrne PA, VF
Very Rev Phil Gaffney Adm
Very Rev Joseph Gallagher PP, VG
Very Rev Derek Darby EV
Very Rev Sean Henry PP
Very Rev Denis McNelis PP, VF
Very Rev Patrick Moore PP, VF
Very Rev Paul Connell Phd

**Episcopal Vicar for Pastoral
Development**
Very Rev Derek Darby
Meath Diocesan Office, Dublin Road,
Mullingar, Co Weatmeath
Tel 044-9348841
Email pastoral@dioceseofmeath.ie

Secretary
Ms Irene Carton
Bishop's House, Dublin Road, Mullingar,
Co Westmeath
Tel 044-9348841 Fax 044-9343020
Email secretary@dioceseofmeath.ie

EDUCATION
Diocesan Office for Education
Very Rev Paul Connell Phd
Mr Matt Melvin
Meath Diocesan Office, Dublin Road,
Mullingar, Co Westmeath
Tel 044-9348841
Email education@dioceseofmeath.ie

Post-Primary Religious Education
Diocesan Director: Vacant

Primary Religious Education
Diocesan Advisers
Eileen Burns
Kathleen Duffy
Mairin Fanning
Shirley Finn
Anne Fitzpatrick
Fergal Fitzpatrick
Meath Diocesan Office, Dublin Road,
Mullingar, Co Westmeath
Tel 044-9348841

LITURGY
Liturgical Commission
Chairman: Vacant
Secretary: Mr James Walsh
18 Beechgrove,
Laytown, Co Meath

PASTORAL
ACCORD
Secretary, Mullingar Centre
Ms Angie Daly
Tel 044-9348707
Secretary, Navan Centre
Ms Mary McCabe
Tel 046-9023146
Secretary, Tullamore Centre
Ms Michelle Cleary
Tel 057-9341831

Apostolic Work Society
Mullingar Branch
Cathedral House,
Mullingar, Co Westmeath

Navan Branch
Chaplain: Vacant
St Mary's, Navan, Co Meath
Tel 046-9027518

Chaplain to Polish Community
Rev Janusz Lugowski
Parochial House, Moynalvey, Co Meath
Tel 087-9908922

Council of Priests
Chairman: Very Rev Denis McNelis PP, VF
Parochial House, Laytown, Co Meath
Tel 041-9827258
Secretary: Rev Brendan Ludlow
c/o Diocesan Office, Dublin Road,
Mullingar, Co Westmeath

**Diocesan Eucharistic Adoration
Committee**
St Anne's Centre,
Fairgreen, Navan, Co Meath
John Howard 087-2478519
Bartle Ó Curraoin 086-3020848
Email info@eucharisticadoration.ie

Ecumenism
Secretary: Very Rev William Coleman PP
Parochial House, Rochfortbridge,
Co Westmeath
Tel 044-9222107

Fr Matthew Union
Secretary: Very Rev Séamus Houlihan PP
Parochial House, Ballycumber Road,
Moate, Co Westmeath
Tel 090-6481951

Knock Pilgrimage
Director: Very Rev Martin Halpin PP
Parochial House, Ballinabrackey,
Kinnegad, Co Westmeath
Tel 046-9739015

Lourdes Pilgrimage
Director
Very Rev Joseph Gallagher PP, VG
Parochial House, Tullamore, Co Offaly
Tel 057-9321587

Marriage Tribunal
(See Marriage Tribunals section)

Pioneer Total Abstinence Association
Very Rev Seamus Houlihan PP
Parochial House, Ballycumber Road,
Moate, Co Westmeath
Tel 090-6481951

Pontifical Mission Societies
Diocesan Director
Rev Tony Gavin

Vocations

Directors: Rev Tony Gonoude
Parochial House, Ballynacargy,
Co Westmeath
Tel 044-9373923
Email vocations@dioceseofmeath.ie

PARISHES

Mensal parishes are listed first. Other parishes follow alphabetically.

MULLINGAR

Cathedral of Christ the King
St Paul's, Mullingar
Assumption, Walshestown
Immaculate Conception, Gainstown
Little Flower and Our Lady of Good Counsel, Brotenstown
Very Rev Phil Gaffney Adm
Rev Vincent Daka CC
Rev Andrei Stolnicu CC
Rev Norman Allred CC
Rev Barry White CC
Cathedral House, Mullingar,
Co Westmeath
Tel 044-9348338/9340126
Fax 044-9340780
Email office@mullingarparish.ie
Website www.mullingarparish.ie

NAVAN

St Mary's; St Oliver's
Very Rev Declan Hurley Adm, VG
Rev Robert McCabe CC
Rev Noel Weir CC
Rev Eusebius Tulbure CC
St Mary's, The Fairgreen,
Navan, Co Meath C15 X0A3
Tel 046-9027518
Email office@navanparish.ie
Website www.navanparish.ie

ARDCATH

St Mary's, Ardcath
St John the Baptist, Clonalvy
Very Rev Gerry Stuart Adm (see Ratoath Parish)
Rev Kevin Heery CC
Parochial House, Curraha, Co Meath
Tel 01-8350136
Email accparish@gmail.com
www.ardcath.com

ASHBOURNE-DONAGHMORE

Immaculate Conception, Ashbourne
St Patrick, Donaghmore
Parish Office: Frederick Street,
Ashbourne, Co Meath A84 P582
Tel/Fax 01-8353149
Email
ashbournedonaghmoreparish@gmail.com
Website www.ashbourneparish.ie
Very Rev Michael Kilmartin PP
54 Brookville, Ashbourne, Co Meath
Rev Ciaran Clarke CC
Parochial House, Ashbourne, Co Meath

ATHBOY

St James', Athboy
St Lawrence, Rathmore
Naomh Pádraig, Rathcairn
Very Rev Padraig McMahon PP, VF
Parochial House, Athboy, Co Meath
Tel 046-9432184 Fax 046-9430021
Email athboyensis@gmail.com
Website www.athboyparish.ie

BALLINABRACKEY

Assumption, Ballinabrackey
Trinity, Castlejordan
Very Rev Martin Halpin PP
Parochial House, Ballinabrackey,
Kinnegad, Co Westmeath
Tel/Fax 046-9739015
Email martinhalpin@gmail.com
Parish ballinabrackeyparish@gmail.com
Website
www.ballinabrackeyandcastlejordan.com

BALLYNACARGY

The Nativity, Ballynacargy
St Michael, Sonna
Very Rev Tony Gonoude PP
Parochial House, Ballynacargy,
Co Westmeath
Tel 044-9373923

BALLIVOR

St Columbanus
Very Rev Mark Mohan PP
Parochial House, Ballivor, Co Meath
Tel/Fax 046-9546488
Parish email bkparishoffice@gmail.com
Website www.ballivorkildalkey.ie

BALLYMORE

The Holy Redeemer, Ballymore
St Brigid's, Boher
Very Rev Oliver Devine PP
Parochial House, Drumraney,
Athlone, Co Westmeath
Tel 044-9356207
Email oliver_devine@eircom.net
Website
www.ballymoreanddrumraneyparishes.ie

BEAUPARC

The Assumption, Beauparc
The Assumption, Kentstown
Very Rev David Brennan PP
Parochial House,
Kentstown, Navan, Co Meath
Tel 041-9825276 Fax 041-9825252
Email bkyfparish@gmail.com
Website www.beauparcparish.ie
Very Rev Peter Farrelly AP
Parochial House, Beauparc,
Navan, Co Meath
Tel 046-9024114
Email peterfarrelly9@gmail.com

BOHERMEEN

St Ultan's, Bohermeen
St Cuthbert's, Boyerstown
Christ the King, Cortown
Very Rev Andrew Doyle PP, VF
Durhamstown, Bohermeen,
Navan, Co Meath
Tel 046-9073805
Email bohermeenparish1@gmail.com

CARNAROSS

St Ciaran, Carnaross
Sacred Heart, Mullaghea
Very Rev Michael Walsh PP
Parochial House, Carnaross,
Kells, Co Meath
Tel 046-9245904

CASTLEPOLLARD

St Michael's, Castlepollard
St Michael's, Castletown
St Mary's, Finea
Very Rev Patrick A. Moore PP, VF
Parochial House, Castlepollard,
Co Westmeath
Tel 044-9661126/087-2510855
Fax 044-9661881
Email fr.patrick.moore@gmail.com

CASTLETOWN-GEOGHEGAN

St Michael, Castletown-Geoghegan
St Stephen, Tyrrellspass
St Peter, Raheenmore
Very Rev Barry Condron PP
Tyrrellspass, Co Westmeath
Tel 044-9223115
Email info@ourlittleparish.ie

CASTLETOWN-KILPATRICK

St Patrick's, Castletown-Kilpatrick
St Colmcille's, Fletcherstown
Very Rev Maurice Henry Adm
Parochial House,
Castletown-Kilpatrick,
Navan, Co Meath
Office: Tel 046-9054142
Email castletownkpparish@gmail.com

CLARA

St Brigid's, Clara
Sts Peter & Paul, Horseleap
Very Rev Joseph Deegan PP
Rev Luke Ohiemi CC
St Brigid's Parish Office, Church Street,
Clara, Co Offaly R35 PW97
Tel 057-9331170
Email claraparish7@gmail.com

CLONMELLON

Sts Peter & Paul, Clonmellon
St Bartholomew, Killallon
Very Rev Sean Garland PP
Parochial House, Clonmellon
Navan, Co Meath
Tel 046-9433124
Email clonmellonparish@gmail.com

COLLINSTOWN
St Mary's, Collinstown
St Feichin's, Fore
Very Rev Martin Carley PP
Parochial House, Collinstown,
Co Westmeath
Tel 044-9666326
Email collinstownforeparish@gmail.com

COOLE (MAYNE)
Immaculate Conception, Coole
St John the Baptist, Whitehall
Very Rev Oliver Skelly PP
Parochial House, Coole, Co Westmeath
Tel 044-9661191
Email cooleparish@gmail.com
Website coolemayneparish.ie

CURRAHA
St Andrew's
Very Rev Gerry Stuart Adm (see Ratoath Parish)
Rev Kevin Heery CC
Parochial House, Curraha, Co Meath
Tel 01-8350136
Email accparish@gmail.com
Website www.currahaparish.ie

DELVIN
Assumption, Delvin
St Livinus, Killulagh
Very Rev Seamus Heaney PP
Parochial House, Delvin, Co Westmeath
Tel 044-9664127
Email info@delvinparish.ie
Website www.delvinparish.ie

DONORE
The Nativity of Our Lady, Donore
The Nativity of Our Lady, Rosnaree
Very Rev Mark English Adm
Parochial House, Duleek, Co Meath
Tel 041-9823205
Email donorerossnareeparish@gmail.com
Website www.donorerossnareeparish.com

DROGHEDA, HOLY FAMILY
Rev Stepen Kennedy
Rev Brendan O'Rourke
The Presbytery, Ballsgrove,
Drogheda, Co Louth
Tel 041-9831991
Email holyfamilyballsgrove@outlook.ie
Website www.holyfamilydrogheda.ie

DROGHEDA, ST MARY'S
Very Rev John Conlon PP
Rev Ciprian Solomon CC
St Mary's, Drogheda, Co Louth
Tel 041-9834958 Fax 041-9845144
Parish Office: Tel 041-9834587
Email stmarysdrogheda@gmail.com
Website www.stmarysdrogheda.ie

DRUMCONRATH
Sts Peter & Paul, Drumconrath
Sts Brigid & Patrick, Meath Hill
Very Rev Finian Connaughton PP
Parochial House, Drumconrath,
Navan, Co Meath
Tel 041-6854146
Email drumconrathparish@topmail.ie
Website www.drumconrathparish.ie

DRUMRANEY
Immaculate Conception, Drumraney
Immaculate Conception, Tang
Immaculate Conception, Forgney
Very Rev Oliver Devine PP
Drumraney, Athlone,
Co Westmeath
Tel 044-9356207
Email drumraneyparish@gmail.com
Website www.ballymoreanddrumraneyparishes.ie
Rev Godwin Atede CC
St Mary's, Tang,
Ballymahon, Co Longford
Tel 0906-432214
Email atedegodwin@hotmail.com

DULEEK
St Cianan, Duleek
St Thérèse, Bellewstown
Very Rev Mark English PP
Rev Anthony Ayoola
Parochial House, Duleek, Co Meath
Tel 041-9823205
Email duleekparish@gmail.com
Rev David Jones
The Hemitage, Duleek, Co Meath
Website www.duleekbellewstownparish.com

DUNBOYNE
SS Peter & Paul, Dunboyne
St Brigid & Sacred Heart, Kilbride
Very Rev Patrick O'Connor PP
Parochial House,
Dunboyne, Co Meath
Tel 01-8255342 Fax 01-8252321
Email dunboynekilbride.parish@gmail.com
Rev Declan Kelly CC
2 Orchard Court, Dunboyne, Co Meath
Website www.dunboynekilbrideparish.org

DUNDERRY
Assumption, Dunderry
Assumption, Robinstown
Assumption, Kilbride
Very Rev Noel Horneck PP
Parochial House, Dunderry,
Navan, Co Meath
Tel 046-9431433
Email dunderryparish@gmail.com

DUNSHAUGHLIN
Sts Patrick & Seachnall, Dunshaughlin
St Martin of Tours, Culmullen
Very Rev Sean Henry PP
Parochial House, Dunshaughlin,
Co Meath
Tel 01-8259114
Rev Joseph Clavin AP
St Martin's, Culmullen, Drumree,
Co Meath
Tel 01-8241976
Email office@dcparish.ie
Website www.dunshaughlin-culmullenparish.ie

DYSART
St Patrick's, Dysart
Assumption, Loughanavalley
Very Rev David O'Hanlon PP
Parochial House, Dysart, Mullingar,
Co Westmeath
Tel 044-9226122
Email ppdysartwestmeath@gmail.com

EGLISH
St James, Eglish
St John the Baptist, Rath
Very Rev John Moorhead PP
Parochial House, Eglish,
Birr, Co Offaly
Tel 057-9133010
Website www.eglishdrumcullen.com

ENFIELD
St Michael, Rathmolyon
Assumption, Jordanstown
Very Rev Patrick Donnelly PP
The Presbytery, Enfield, Co Meath
Tel 046-9541282
Email enfieldrathmolyonparish@gmail.com
Rev John Kennedy
Parochial House,
Rathmolyon, Co Meath
Tel 046-9555212
Website www.enfieldparish.ie

GLASSON–TUBBERCLAIRE
Immaculate Conception, Tubberclaire
Very Rev Seamus Mulvany PP
Parochial House, Tubberclaire-Glasson,
Athlone, Co Westmeath
Tel 090-6485103
Email tubberclairchurch@gmail.com
Website www.tubberclairchurch.com

JOHNSTOWN
Nativity of Our Lady, Johnstown
Assumption, Walterstown
Very Rev Michael Cahill PP
Parochial House, Johnstown,
Navan, Co Meath
Tel 046-9021731
Email johnsnavan@eircom.net

KELLS
St Columcille, Kells
Immaculate Conception, Girley
Very Rev David Bradley PP
Email jplowebyrne@gmail.com
Rev John Byrne AP
Parochial House, Kells, Co Meath
Tel 046-9240213
Email info@kellsparish.ie
Website www.kellsparish.ie

KILBEG
Nativity of Our Lady, Kilbeg
St Michael, Staholmog
Very Rev Liam Malone Adm
Parochial House, Kilbeg, Kells, Co Meath
Tel 046-9246604
Email kilbegparish@gmail.com

KILBEGGAN
St James, Kilbeggan
St Hugh, Rahugh
Very Rev Brendan Corrigan PP
Parochial House, Harbour Road,
Kilbeggan, Co Westmeath
Tel 057-9332155
Email info@kilbegganparish.ie
Website www.kilbegganparish.ie

KILCLOON
St Oliver Plunkett, Kilcloon
The Assumption, Batterstown
Little Chapel of the Assumption, Kilcock
Very Rev Declan Kelly PP
Parochial House, Batterstown,
Dunboyne, Co Meath
Tel 01-8259267
Email secretary@kilcloonparish.ie
Website www.kilcloonparish.com

KILCORMAC
Nativity of the Blessed Virgin Mary,
Kilcormac
St Brigid, Mountbolus
Very Rev Michael Meade PP
Parochial House, Kilcormac, Co Offaly
Tel 057-9135989
Email kilcormacparish@outlook.ie
Website
www.kilcormackilougheyparish.com

KILDALKEY
St Dympna's
Very Rev Mark Mohan PP
Parochial House, Ballivor, Co Meath
Tel 046-9546488
Parish email bkparishoffice@gmailcom
Website www.ballivorkildalkey.ie

KILLUCAN
St Joseph's, Rathwire
St Brigid's, Raharney
Very Rev Stan Deegan PP
St Joseph's Parochial House,
Killucan, Co Westmeath N91 F292
Tel 044-9374127
Email parishofkillucan@gmail.com

KILMESSAN
Nativity of Our Lady, Kilmessan
Assumption, Dunsany
Very Rev Terence Toner PP
Parochial House, Kilmessan, Co Meath
Tel 046-9025172
Email kilmessanparish@gmail.com

KILSKYRE
St Alphonsus Liguori, Kilskyre
Assumption, Ballinlough
Very Rev Patrick Kearney PP
Parochial House, Kilskyre,
Kells, Co Meath
Tel 046-9243623
Email kilskyreparish@gmail.com
Website www.kilskyreballinlough.ie

KINGSCOURT
Immaculate Conception, Kingscourt
St Joseph's, Corlea
Our Lady of Mount Carmel, Muff
Very Rev Gerard MacCormack PP
Parochial House, Kingscourt, Co Cavan
Tel 042-9667314
Email info@kingscourtparish.ie
Website www.kingscourtparish.ie

KINNEGAD
Assumption, Kinnegad
St Agnes, Coralstown
St Finian, Clonard
Very Rev Thomas Gilroy PP
Parochial House, Kinnegad, Co Meath
Tel 044-9375117
Email info@kinnegadparish.ie
Website www.kinnegadparish.ie
Parish Office: 044-9391030
Fridays 10.00 am-4.00 pm

LAYTOWN-MORNINGTON
Sacred Heart, Laytown
Star of the Sea, Mornington
Very Rev Denis McNelis PP, VF
Parochial House, Laytown, Co Meath
Tel 041-9827258
Email
parishoffice@sacredheartlaytown.com
Website www.sacredheartlaytown.com
Rev Joseph Apust CC
Parochial House,
Mornington, Co Meath
Tel 041-9827384
Email mgtparish@gmail.com
Website www.morningtonchurch.com

LOBINSTOWN
Holy Cross
Very Rev Gerry Boyle Adm
Rev Timothy Mejida
Parochial House, Lobinstown,
Navan, Co Meath
Tel 046-9053155

LONGWOOD
Church of the Holy Family, Longwood
Our Lady & St Dominic, Killyon
Very Rev Tom Gilroy Adm (see Kinnegac
Parish)
Rev Louis Illah CC
52 Edgeworth Court,
Longwood, Co Meath
Parish mobile 087-1723903
Email longwoodparish@gmail.com

MILLTOWN
St Matthew, Milltown
St Matthew, Empor
St Patrick, Moyvore
Very Rev William Fitzsimons PP
Parochial House, Milltown,
Rathconrath, Co Westmeath
Tel 044-9355106

MOUNTNUGENT
St Brigid, Mountnugent
Sts Brigid & Fiach, Ballinacree
Very Rev Philip O'Connor PP
Parochial House,
Mountnugent, Co Cavan
Tel 049-8540123
Email stbrigids.parish@outlook.com

MOYNALTY
Assumption, Moynalty
Assumption, Newcastle
Very Rev Joseph McEvoy PP
Parochial House, Moynalty,
Kells, Co Meath
Tel 046-9244305
Email moynaltyparish@gmail.com

MOYNALVEY
Nativity, Moynalvey
Assumption, Kiltale
Very Rev Declan Kelly Adm (see Kilcloon
Parish)
Rev Janusz Lugowski CC
Parochial House, Moynalvey,
Summerhill, Co Meath
Tel 046-9557031
Email mknotices@gmail.com
Website www.moynalveykiltaleparish.co

MULTYFARNHAM
St Nicholas, Multyfarnham
St Patrick's, Leney
Very Rev Paul Connell Adm
Rev Conor McGee CC
Parochial House, Rathganny,
Multyfarnham, Co Westmeath N91 E18
Tel 044-9371124
Email
stnicholasmultyfarnham@gmail.com

NOBBER
St John the Baptist
Very Rev Liam Malone PP
Parochial House, Nobber, Co Meath
Tel 046-9052197
Email nobberparish@gmail.com
Tel (office) 046-9089688

LDCASTLE

Brigid, Oldcastle
Mary, Moylough
ery Rev Ray Kelly PP
arochial House, Oldcastle, Co Meath
l 049-8541142
nail oldcastleparish@gmail.com
ebsite
ww.oldcastleandmoylaghparish.com

RISTOWN

Catherine, Oristown
John the Baptist, Kilberry
ry Rev John O'Brien PP
arochial House, Oristown,
lls, Co Meath
l 046-9054124
nail oristownparish@gmail.com
ebsite www.oristownparish.com

AHAN

Carthage, Killina
Patrick, The Island
Colman, Mucklagh
ery Rev Michael Whittaker PP
arochial House, Killina, Rahan,
llamore, Co Offaly
l 057-9355917
v Frank Guinan
e Presbytery, Mucklagh,
llamore, Co Offaly
l 057-9321892
nail rahanparish@gmail.com
ebsite www.rahanparish.ie

ATHKENNY

Louis & Mary, Rathkenny
Patrick, Rushwee
Brigid, Grangegeeth
ry Rev Gerry Boyle PP
rochial House, Rathkenny, Co Meath
l 046-9054138
ebsite www.rathkennyparish.ie

ATOATH

ly Trinity
ry Rev Gerard Stuart PP
v Yohanna Jacob CC
rochial House, Ratoath, Co Meath
l 01-8256207 Fax 01-8256662
nail ratoathparish@gmail.com
ebsite www.ratoathparish.ie

CHFORTBRIDGE

maculate Conception, Rochfortbridge
cred Heart, Meedin
Joseph, Milltownpass
ry Rev William Coleman PP
rochial House, Rochfortbridge,
Westmeath
l 044-9222107
nail rochfortbridgeparish@gmail.com

SKRYNE

St Colmcille, Skryne
Immaculate Conception, Rathfeigh
Very Rev Thomas O'Mahony PP
Parochial House, Skryne, Tara, Co Meath
Tel 046-9025152
Email office@skryneandrathfeighparish.ie
Website
www.skryneandrathfeighparish.ie

SLANE

St Patrick, Slane
Assumption, Monknewtown
Very Rev Richard Matthews PP
Parochial House, Slane, Co Meath
Tel 041-9824249 Office 041-9884429
Email slaneparish@gmail.com
Website www.slaneparish.com

STAMULLEN

St Patrick, Stamullen
St Mary's, Julianstown
Very Rev Brendan Ferris PP
Preston Hill, Stamullen, Co Meath
Tel/Fax 01-8412647
Parish Email secretary@sjparish.ie

SUMMERHILL

Our Lady of Lourdes, Dangan
Assumption, Coole
Very Rev Paul Crosbie Adm (see Trim
Parish)
Rev Vincent McKay (CSSp)
Parochial House, Summerhill, Co Meath
Tel 046-9557021
Email coolsummerhillparish@gmail.com
Website www.summerhillparish.ie

TAGHMON

Assumption, Taghmon
St Joseph, Turin
Very Rev Declan Smith PP
Parochial House, Taghmon,
Mullingar, Co Westmeath
Tel 044-9372140

TRIM

St Patrick, Trim
St Brigid, Boardsmill
Very Rev Paul Crosbie PP
Rev Warren Collier CC
Parochial House, Trim, Co Meath
Tel 046-9431251
Parish email spcctrim@gmail.com

TUBBER

Holy Family, Tubber
St Thomas the Apostle, Rosemount
Rev Seamus Houlihan PP
Parochial House, Ballycumber Road,
Moate, Co Westmeath
Tel 090-6481951
Email
tubberrosemountparish@gmail.com

TULLAMORE

Assumption, Tullamore
St Colmcille, Durrow
Very Rev Joseph Gallagher PP, VG
Rt Rev Mgr Seán Heaney AP
Email heaneysean56@gmail.com
Rev Fergal Cummins CC
Email fergalcummins100@yahoo.ie
Rev Damian Budau CC
Rev Joe Campbell CC
Parochial House, Tullamore, Co Offaly
Tel 057-9321587
Email
tullamoreparishsecretary@gmail.com
Website www.tullamoreparish.ie

INSTITUTIONS AND THEIR CHAPLAINS

St Loman's Hospital
Mullingar, Co Westmeath
Tel 044-9340191
Priests of the parish

Longford & Westmeath General Hospital
Mullingar, Co Westmeath
Tel 044-9340221
Priests of the parish

Our Lady's Hospital
Navan, Co Meath
Tel 046-9021210
Priests of the parish

Tullamore General Hospital
Tullamore, Co Offaly
Tel 057-9321501
Priests of the parish

PRIESTS OF THE DIOCESE ELSEWHERE

Rev Shane Crombie
c/o Meath Diocesan Office, Mullingar
Rev Gabriel Flynn
DCU, Dublin
Rev Tony Gavin
c/o Meath Diocesan Office, Mullingar
Rev David Hanratty
Tierhogar, Portarlington, Co Laois
Tel 057-8645719
Rev Michael Hinds
Chaplain to the Defence Forces
Rev John Hogan (OCDS)
Mount Rivers, Navan, Co Meath
Rev Stephen Kelly
Apostolic Nunciature, Uruguay
Rev Brendan Ludlow
Chaplain UCD
Rev Martin McErlean
c/o Meath Diocesan Office, Mullingar
Rev John Nally
Waterford & Lismore
Rev Thomas O'Connor DD
St Patrick's College,
Maynooth, Co Kildare

RETIRED PRIESTS

Very Rev Ray Brady
c/o Bishop's House, Mullingar
Rev Anthony Draper DD
Millbury Nursing Home,
Navan, Co Meath
Rev Jim Lynch
1 Orchard Court,
Dunboyne, Co Meath
Rt Rev Mgr Eamonn Marron PE
The Presbytery,
Raharney, Co Westmeath
Tel 044-9374271
Very Rev Frank McNamara PE
Cluan Lir, Mullingar, Co Westmeath
Very Rev Matthew Mollin PE
Elm Hall, Loughlinstown Road,
Celbridge, Co Kildare
Very Rev Eamonn O'Brien PE
Newbrook Nursing Home,
Mullingar, Co Westmeath
Very Rev Michael Sheerin PE
Woodlands Nursing Home,
Navan, Co Meath
Rev Philip Smith PE
Tir-ee, Harbourstown,
Stamullen, Co Meath
Tel 01-8020708

PERSONAL PRELATURE

OPUS DEI
Lismullin Conference Centre
Navan, Co Meath C15 XW40
Tel 046-9026936
Rev Philip Griffin, Chaplain

RELIGIOUS ORDERS AND CONGREGATIONS

PRIESTS

BENEDICTINE MONKS OF PERPETUAL ADORATION
Silverstream Priory
Stamullen, Co Meath K32 T189
Tel 01-8417142
Email info@cenacleosb.org
Prior
Very Rev Dom Basil Mary MacCabe (OSB)
Monastery Website http://cenacleosb.org/
Vocations Website
http://cenacleosb.org/vocations/
Vultus Christi Weblog
http://vultus.stblogs.org/

CAMILLIANS
St Camillus Community,
Killucan, Co Westmeath
Tel 044-74115
Superior: Br John O'Brien (OSCam)
Nursing Centre
Tel 044-74196

CARMELITES (OCARM)
Carmelite Priory,
Moate, Co Westmeath
Tel 090-6481160/6481398
Fax 090-6481879
Email carmelitemoate@eircom.net
Prior: Rev Jaison Kuthanapillil (OCarm)

FRANCISCANS
Franciscan Abbey,
Multyfarnham, Co Westmeath
Tel 044-9371114/9371137
Fax 044-9371387
Email theabbeymulty@gmail.com
Provincial Delegate
Rev Kieran Cronin (OFM)

HOLY SPIRIT CONGREGATION
Spiritan Missionaries,
Ardbraccan, Navan, Co Meath
Tel 046-9021441
Community Leader
Rev Peter Conaty (CSSp)

ST COLUMBAN'S MISSIONARY SOCIETY
St Columban's, Dalgan Park,
Navan, Co Meath
Tel 046-9021525
Regional Director
Rev Raymond Husband (SSC)
Regional Vice-Director
Rev Padraig O'Donovan (SSC)
Email padraigssc@gmail.com

St Columban's Retirement Home,
Dalgan Park, Navan, Co Meath
Tel 046-9021525
Person in Charge: Ms Anna Brozek

BROTHERS

FRANCISCAN BROTHERS
The Monastery, Clara, Co Offaly
Tel 057-9331130
Local Minister: Br Charles Conway
Community: 3

SISTERS

BLESSED SACRAMENT SISTERS
Denene, New Road,
Tullamore, Co Offaly R35 N528
Tel 057-9351371
Email imelda.doorley@gmail.com
Community: 2

CHARITY OF JESUS AND MARY SISTERS
Residential centre transferred to
Muiriosa Foundation

Aisling, Mitchelstown,
Delvin, Co Westmeath
Tel 044-64379
Contact: Sr Kathleen O'Connor
Community: 2

CONGREGATION OF THE SISTERS OF MERCY
St Mary's Convent of Mercy,
Athlumney, Navan,
Co Meath C15 PK72
Tel 046-9021271
Facilitator: Sr Consilio Rock
Community: 6

Sisters of Mercy,
3 St Brigid's Court, Connaught Street,
Athboy, Co Meath C15 E433
Tel 046-9400032

Sisters of Mercy, Charlestown,
Clara, Co Offaly
Tel 057-9331184

202 Ballsgrove,
Drogheda, Co Louth A92 NY5E
Tel 041-9830160

Convent of Mercy, Kells,
Co Meath A82 C7P3
Tel 046-9240159
Community: 15

Cill na Gréine, Convent of Mercy,
Kells, Co Meath
Tel 046-9252536

Sisters of Mercy,
13 Grand Priory, Kells,
Co Meath A82 H1F2
Tel 046-9249027

Convent of Mercy, Tullamore Road,
Kilbeggan, Co Westmeath
Tel 057-9332161
Community: 6

Sisters of Mercy, Loughcrew,
Laytown, Co Meath
Tel 041-9827432
Community: 2

29 Green Road,
Mullingar, Co Westmeath N91 E6D6
Tel 044-9341680

10 College Court, College Street,
Mullingar, Co Westmeath N91 E276
Tel 044-9330768

Allianz (ⅰⅰ)

Joseph's,
ighsbrook, Navan,
Meath C15 HW32
l 046-9071760
mmunity: 5

ters of Mercy,
ount Carmel, 15 Aylesbury Lodge,
avan, Co Meath C15 P9P9
l 046-9071757
mmunity: 3

ters of Mercy, 4 Ferndale,
avan, Co Meath C15 T2W7
l 046-9023844

ters of Mercy, Sacre Coeur,
e Commons, Navan, Co Meath
l 046-9021970

ters of Mercy,
Mornington Way, Trim,
Meath C15 V064
046-9437025 Fax 046-9437025
mmunity: 3

nvent of Mercy,
Joseph's, Tullamore,
Offaly R35 PC80
057-9321221
mmunity: 25
aders: Srs Cecilia Cadogan &
aeve Hyland & Ann O'Neill

ters of Mercy,
0 Arden Vale, Tullamore,
Offaly R35 ED66
057-9352733

ters of Mercy,
Tara Crescent, Clonminch,
lamore, Co Offaly R35 Y526
057-9322150

Carne Hill, Johnstown,
van, Co Meath C15 RRN2
046-9091772

ters of Mercy,
ckfriary, Trim, Co Meath C15 R276
046-9437759

ters of Mercy, 5 Headfort Road,
lls, Co Meath A82 T6T8
046-9249775
mmunity: 3

riars Park, Trim,
Meath C15 Y861
046-9437037
mmunity: 3

nem, Laytown,
Meath A92 T6R0

Sisters of Mercy, 133 College Hill,
Irishtown, Mullingar,
Co Westmeath N91 X6H0
Tel 044-9335303

135 Droim Liath, Collins Lane,
Tullamore, Co Offaly R35 C3W7
Tel 057-9361133

Apartment 6, Knightsbridge Village,
Longwood Road, Trim,
Co Meath C15 AX22
Tel 046-9486028

1 Summerhill Road,
Trim, Co Meath

1 Oakfield, Church Road,
Tullamore, Co Offaly R35 YC83

Harbour Road,
Kilbeggan, Co Westmeath
Tel 057-9332147

3 Roselawn, High Street,
Tullamore, Co Offaly R35 CV04
Tel 057-9352077

Apt B6, Friar's Court,
McCurtain Street,
Mullingar, Co Westmeath

'Solanus',
St Joseph's Convent of Mercy,
Tullamore, Co Offaly

Santa Maria Apartment,
Convent Road, Athlumney,
Navan, Co Meath C15 PK72
Tel 046-9071298

9 Derravagh Mews,
Castlepollard,
Co Westmeath N91 N4A4

DAUGHTERS OF MARY AND JOSEPH
22 Northlands, Eastham Road,
Bettystown, Co Meath
Community: 1

FRANCISCAN MISSIONARIES OF OUR LADY
La Verna Centre,
Franciscan House of Spirituality &
Hospitality, Franciscan Convent,
Ballinderry, Mullingar,
Co Westmeath N91 K680
Tel 044-9352000/087-3935613
Email lavernacentre@gmail.com
Website www.fmolireland.ie
lavernacentre on Facebook
Superior: Sr Clare Brady
Email info@fmolireland.ie
Commmunity: 3
House of solitude for those wishing to
spend time in solitude and quiet space

FRANCISCAN SISTERS OF THE RENEWAL
St Anthony Convent, Dublin Road,
Drogheda, Co Louth A92 X044
Tel 041-9830441 Fax 041-9842321
Website www.franciscansisterscfr.com
Superior: Sr Agnes Holtz
Community: 4

LORETO (IBVM)
Loreto Community,
St Michael's, Navan, Co Meath
Tel 046-9021740
Leader: Sr Siobhan Quill
Community: 10
Loreto Secondary School
Tel 046-9023830
Day Care Centre

Loreto Sisters, Athlumney Road,
Navan, Co Meath
Tel 046-9073423
Community: 1
Education

Anam Aras, Laytown,
Drogheda, Co Louth
Tel 041-9828952
Retreat centre

MEDICAL MISSIONARIES OF MARY
Bruach na Mara, Golf Links Road,
Bettystown, Co Meath A92 X2N1
Tel 041-9888541
Email btown.mmm@gmail.com
Community: 3

MISSIONARY SISTERS OF THE HOLY ROSARY
Holy Rosary Convent,
Dublin Road, Bettystown, Co Louth
Tel 041-9827362
Community: 8
Pastoral

EDUCATIONAL INSTITUTIONS

St Finian's College
Mullingar, Co Westmeath
Tel 044-9348313 Fax 044-9345275
President: Very Rev Paul Connell PhD
Tel 044-9348672
Principal: Mr John McHale
Chaplain: Barry White

St Mary's Diocesan School
Beamore Road,
Drogheda, Co Louth
Tel Office: 041-9837581
Staff: 041-9838001 Fax 041-9841151
Principal: Mr Ciaran O'Hare
Chaplain: Priests of Parish

St Patrick's Classical School
Mount Rivers, Moatlands,
Navan, Co Meath
Tel 046-9021847
Principal: Mr Harry McGarry
Chaplain: Mr Mark Donnelly

Coláiste Choilm
Tullamore, Co Offaly
Tel 057-9351756
Headmaster: Mr Tadhg O'Sullivan
Chaplain: Fr Fergal Cummins

Boyne Community School
Trim, Co Meath
Tel 046-9431358
Principal: Ms Elizabeth Cahill
Chaplain: Ms Aoife Daly

Ashbourne Community School
Ashbourne, Co Meath
Tel 01-8353066
Principal: Mr Ciarán Stewart
Chaplain: Mr James McAuley

St Peter's College
Dunboyne, Co Meath
Tel 01-8252552
Principal: Ms Deirdre Maye
Chaplain: Mr John Tighe

St Ciaran's Community School
Kells, Co Meath
Tel 046-9241551
Principal: Ms Cora McLoughlin
Chaplain: Mr Sean Wright

Athboy Community School
Athboy, Co Meath
Tel 046-9487894
Principal: Mr Anthony Leavy
Chaplain: Mr Joe Tynan

Ratoath College
Jamestown, Ratoath, Co Meath
Tel 01-8254102
Principal: Mr Seamus Meehan
Chaplain: Vacant

CHARITABLE AND OTHERSOCIETIES

Society of St Vincent de Paul
Ozanam Holiday Home, Mornington,
Co Meath
Tel 041-9827924

Partner With An Expert IT Company

IT should be responsive, adaptive and smart.
Now more than ever, you need a business that runs effeciently
and can adapt to today's challenges.
We can help with custom IT solutions designed to meet your needs.

Outsourcing and Managed IT Services
Expert support, consulting and implementation

Managed IT Security Services
Protect your data and your brand

Cloud
*Increase business agility
and improve productivity*

ERP, CRM, eCommerce
Unify your business on one platform

☎ Shannon: (061) 708 820
☎ Dublin: (01) 531 3777

https://newtecservices.ie

VERITAS STORES

Dublin City Centre
7–8 Lower Abbey Street, Dublin D01 W2C2
T: 01-878 8177 • E: sales@veritas.ie

Blanchardstown
Unit 309, Blanchardstown Centre, Dublin D15 N447
T: 01-886 4030 • E: blanchardstownshop@veritas.ie

Cork
Carey's Lane, Cork T12 AW26
T: 021-425 1255 • E: corkshop@veritas.ie

Derry
20 Shipquay Street, Derry BT48 6DW
T: 028-7126 6888 • E: derryshop@veritas.ie

Letterkenny
12–14 Upper Main Street,
Letterkenny, Co. Donegal F92 HR9W
T: 074-912 4814 • E: letterkennyshop@veritas.ie

Limerick
122 O'Connell Street, Limerick V94 TF79
T: 061-511075 • E: limerickshop@veritas.ie

Newry
The Mall, Newry, Co. Down BT34 1AN
T: 028-3025 0321 • E: newryshop@veritas.ie

Tallaght
Unit 127, The Square, Tallaght, Dublin D24 XV52
T: 01-885 3737 • E: tallaghtshop@veritas.ie

www.veritas.ie

DIOCESE OF OSSORY

PATRON OF THE DIOCESE
ST KIERAN, 5 MARCH

INCLUDES MOST OF COUNTY KILKENNY
AND PORTIONS OF COUNTIES LAOIS AND OFFALY

Most Rev Niall Coll
Bishop of Ossory
born 25 August 1963;
ordained priest 3 July 1988;
ordained bishop 22 January
2023

Residence:
Blessed Felix House,
Tilbury Place,
Kilkenny R95 DXC9
Tel 056-7762448
Email bishop@ossory.ie
Website www.ossory.ie

ST MARY'S CATHEDRAL, KILKENNY – RESTORATION – RENOVATION – RECONNECTION

Mary's Cathedral, Kilkenny, dates from 857 and is one of the finest cathedrals of pure Gothic design in Ireland. Along with being the Mother Church of the ocese of Ossory and a prayerful sacred ace for the faithful, it is of special terest in a number of architectural, storical, archaeological, artistic, ltural and social categories. It forms e centrepiece of St Mary's rchitectural Conservation Area within lkenny City. It is in this context also at the essential restoration works to e building fabric commenced on site in nuary 2015, with the replacement of e roof over the Sanctuary and the ppropriate cleaning and repainting of e highly ornate ceiling below. The pair works were undertaken by a ecialist team of restoration painters ver a period of many months and nged through plaster repair, paint atching, gold leaf work, and paint

stencilling, all done by hand by local specialist craftsmen and women. Painted features adorning the window surround, and supporting columns were also revealed and reinstated with particular attention paid to investigating and recording the underlining history as evidenced throughout the works.

Beneath the ceiling the hand-cut mosaics which decorate all the Sanctuary walls were also in need of cleaning and restoration. This was undertaken through the application of non-abrasive pumice to the entire area and removal after drying, which lifted the build-up of carbonation, dirt and smoke gathered over the decades, all carried out without damage to the mosaics themselves. In tandem, the magnificent and original stained glass windows running to over five metres tall were fully removed, repaired, re-leaded, and replaced by a local stained glass expert, securing their integrity for future generations.

Work was completed in time for the first ordination to priesthood in our diocese in fourteen years, celebrated in

our beautiful cathedral by Bishop Séamus Freeman on 28 June 2015.

At floor level a number of statues were cleaned and reinstated to their positions, bespoke furniture was designed and installed within the alcoves, the altar was repaired, and the floor mosaics cleaned. Appropriate modern lighting systems were added in concealed locations to highlight the complete works, and the dramatic impact of the restoration works is now evident for the citizens of Kilkenny, the faithful of the forty-two parishes in the Diocese of Ossory and the many visitors who come to view, to be uplifted and to appreciate its beauty and craftsmanship.

> They devoted themselves to the apostles' teaching and to fellowship, to the breaking of bread and to prayer. (Acts 2:42)

We welcome you to come to our diocese, to come see and pray, and experience our newly restored Sanctuary, the most sacred space of St Mary's Cathedral, the Mother Church of the Diocese of Ossory.

Allianz (ⅱ)

CHAPTER

Dean: Very Rev Seamus McEvoy
Archdeacon
Very Rev Sean Canon O'Doherty
Members
Very Rev James Canon Crotty
Very Rev Patrick Canon Dalton
Very Rev Patrick Canon Duggan
Very Rev Laurence Canon Dunphy
Very Rev Frank Canon Maher
Very Rev Noel Canon Maher

ADMINISTRATION

Vicar General
Vacant

Chancellor
Very Rev William Dalton
c/o Diocesan Office, James's Street,
Kilkenny
Tel/Fax 056-7725287

College of Consultors
Rev Patrick Carey
Very Rev Daniel Carroll
Rt Rev Mgr Daniel Cavanagh
Very Rev Patrick Dalton
Very Rev Martin Delaney
Very Rev Frank Purcell
Rev Dermot Ryan

Financial Administrator
Mr Tom Keating
Diocesan Office, James's Street, Kilkenny
Tel 056-7762448

Diocesan Secretary
Mrs Frances Lennon
Diocesan Office, James's Street, Kilkenny
Tel 056-7762448 Fax 056-7763753
Email admin@ossory.ie

Finance Secretary
Mrs Sheila Walshe
Diocesan Office, James's Street, Kilkenny
Tel 056-7762448 Fax 056-7763753
Email sheilawalshe@ossory.ie

Diocesan Accountant
Mr Michael Dundon
Diocesen Office, James's Street, Kilkenny
Tel 056-7762448
Email accounts@ossory.ie

Data Protection Officer
Mr David O'Brien
Diocesan Office, James's Street, Kilkenny
Tel 056-7775414
Email dpo@ossory.ie

Communications Officer
Rev Dr Dermot Ryan
St Kieran's College, Kilkenny
Tel 056-7721086
Email communication@ossory.ie

Finance Committee
Chairperson: Mr Geoff Meagher
Diocesan Office, James's Street, Kilkenny
Tel 056-7762448

Council of Priests
Pending election

Episcopal Vicars
Family and Social Affairs
Rt Rev Mgr Kieron Kennedy PP
Freshford, Co Kilkenny
Retired Priests
Very Rev Thomas O'Toole PP
Glenmore, Co Kilkenny
Care of Clergy
Very Rev Roderick Whearty TL
St Patrick's Parish Centre,
Loughbay, Kilkenny
Primary Education
Rev Dr Dermot Ryan
St Kieran's College, Kilkenny

Director of Youth Ministry
Very Rev Brian Griffin
Parochial House, Camross, Co Laois
Tel 087-0644158
Email griffinmilepost@yahoo.ie

Diocesan Forum Co-ordinator
Sr Helen Maher
St Kieran's College, Kilkenny
Tel 056-7789714
Email diocesanforum@ossory.ie

Diocesan Pastoral Plan Co-ordinator
Ms Gemma Mulligan
St Kieran's College, Kilkenny
Tel 087-7571250
Email gemmamulligan@ossory.ie

CATECHETICS EDUCATION

Diocesan Advisers for Religious Education
Primary Education: Sr Maria Comerford
Convent of Mercy, Callan, Co Kilkenny
Tel 087-2350719
Email mgcomerford@hotmail.com
Post Primary: Ms Olivia Maher
Email office@cbskilkenny.ie

Catholic Primary School Managers Association
Secretary
Rev Dr Dermot Ryan
St Kieran's College, Kilkenny
Tel 086-6097483
Email education@ossory.ie

LITURGY

Liturgy Chairperson
Very Rev Richard Scriven Adm
St Mary's Cathedral, Kilkenny
Tel 056-7721253/087-2420033
Email rscriven2009@gmail.com

PASTORAL

Adult Faith Formation
Director: Rev Dr Dermot Ryan
St Kieran's College, Kilkenny
Tel 056-7721086/086-6097483
Email afd@ossory.ie

Vocations
Director: Very Rev Kieran O'Shea PP
Ferrybank, Waterford
Tel 086-8272828
Email vocations@ossory.ie

Safeguarding Children
Director of Safeguarding and Diocesan Liaison Person: Ms Kathleen Sherry
Safeguarding Office, Waterford Road,
Kilkenny
Tel 056-7721685/085-8021633
Email safeguarding@ossory.ie
Safeguardinfg Vetting Authorised Signatories
Sr Ena Kennedy
Tel 087-1953850
Email vetting@ossory.ie
Ms Frances Lennon
Tel 056-7762448
Email admin@ossory.ie

Chaplain to the Travelling Community
Very Rev Sean O'Connor PP
Ballyhale, Co Kilkenny
Tel 086-3895911
Email seanoconnor@ossory.ie

ACCORD
Seville Lodge, Callan Road, Kilkenny
Tel 056-7722674
Chaplain: Very Rev Daniel Bollard

Emigrant Commission
Very Rev Laurence Wallace PP
Muckalee, Ballyfoyle, Co Kilkenny
Tel 056-4441271/087-2326807
Fax 056-4440007
Email muckalee@ossory.ie

Trócaire
Very Rev Raymond Dempsey
St John's Presbytery, Kilkenny
Tel 087-2859682
Email 1dempseyr@gmail.com

Lourdes Pilgrimage
Director: Very Rev Anthony O'Connor
Molassy, Freshford Road, Kilkenny
Tel 087-2517766

Marriage Tribunal
(See Marriage Tribunals section)

Ossory Adoption and Referral Services
Information and Guidance in all matter
in relation to adoption
Tel 056-7721685
Ms Mary Curtin, Social Service Centre,
Waterford Road, Kilkenny
Tel 056-7721685

Allianz ⓘ

ssory Priests Fraternal Fund
dministrator: Mr Donal Cadogan
*coesan Office, James's Street, Kilkenny
l 056-7762448
nail kilfera2008@live.com

ssory Priests Society
dministrator: Mrs Maura Joyce
coesan Office, James's Street, Kilkenny
l 056-7762448

ssory Youth
EO: Ms Mary Mescal
esart Hall, New Street, Kilkenny
l 056-7761200 Fax 056-7752385
hairperson:* Padraig Fleming

ntifical Mission Societies
ocesan Director
ery Rev Sean O'Connor PP
llyhale, Co Kilkenny
l 086-3895911
nail rsoc1973@gmail.com

PARISHES

lkenny city parishes are listed first.
ther parishes follow alphabetically.
hurch titulars are in italics.

MARY'S
Mary's Cathedral
ery Rev Richard Scriven Adm
Mary's Cathedral, Kilkenny R95 CP46
l 056-7721253/087-2420033
nail rscriven2009@gmail.com
rish sister: Sr Maria Comerford
l 056-7721253
nail mgcomerfordrsm@gmail.com
nail stmaryscathedral@ossory.ie
ebsite www.stmaryscathedral.ie

JOHN'S
John the Evangelist, Holy Trinity,
John the Baptist
John's Presbytery, Kilkenny R95 ND2W
nail stjohns@ossory.ie
ebsite www.stjohnskilkenny.com
ery Rev Daniel Carroll
l 056-7721072/087-9077769
nail dancarroll@ossory.ie
ery Rev Raymond Dempsey
l 087-2859682
nail ldempseyr@gmail.com

CANICE'S
Canice's
ery Rev James Murphy PP
Canice's Presbytery, Dean Street,
lkenny R95 K6PH
l 056-7752991/087-2609545
x 056-7721533
nail jimmurphy@ossory.ie
v Thomas Norris CC
Canice's Presbytery,
lkenny R95 VY0T
l 056-7752994/083-3241438

ST PATRICK'S
St Patrick's, St Fiacre's, St Joseph's
St Fiacre's Gardens,
Bohernatownish Road, Loughboy,
Kilkenny R95 RF97
Tel 056-7764400 Fax 056-7770173
Email stpatricksparish@ossory.ie
Website www.patricksparish.com
Very Rev Roderick Whearty
Tel 056-7764400/086-8133661
Email roderick1@eircom.net
Very Rev Peter Muldowney
Tel 086-8265955
Email peter.muldowney@hotmail.com

AGHABOE
Immaculate Conception, St Canice
Very Rev Noel Canon Maher PP
Clough, Ballacolla, Portlaoise, Co Laois
Tel 057-8738513/087-2326200 Fax 057-8738909
Email nmaher@outlook.ie

AGHAVILLER
St Brendan's, Stoneyford,
St Brendan's, Newmarket
Holy Trinity
Very Rev Liam Cassin PP
Hugginstown, Co Kilkenny
Tel/Fax 056-7768693/087-2312354
Email liamcassin@ossory.ie

BALLYCALLAN
Queen of Peace, St Molua, St Brigid
Parish email ballycallan@ossory.ie
Very Rev Liam Taylor PP
Ballycallan, Co Kilkenny R95 E8N0
Tel 056-7769564/086-8180954
Email frliamtaylor@gmail.com

BALLYHALE
St Martin of Tours, Our Lady of the
Assumption, All Saints
Very Rev Sean O'Connor PP
Ballyhale, Co Kilkenny R95 Y9F4
Tel 086-3895911
Email rsoc1973@gmail.com

BALLYRAGGET
St Patrick's, Assumption of BVM
Very Rev Eamonn O'Gorman PP
Ballyragget, Co Kilkenny
Tel 087-2236145
Email eamonnogorman123@gmail.com

BORRIS-IN-OSSORY
St Canice, Assumption, St Kieran
Very Rev John Robinson PP
Borris-in-Ossory, Portlaoise, Co Laois
Tel 0505-41148/087-2431412
Fax 0505-41148
Email binoparish@gmail.com

CALLAN
Assumption, All Saints, Nativity of BVM
Very Rev William Dalton PP
Callan, Co Kilkenny
Tel 056-7725287/086-8506215
Fax 056-7725287
Email williamdalton@ossory.ie
Website www.callanparish@irishchurch.net

CAMROSS
St Fergal
Very Rev Brian Griffin Adm
Camross, Co Laois
Tel 087-0644158
Email griffinmilepost@yahoo.ie

CASTLECOMER
Immaculate Conception
Rt Rev Mgr Michael Ryan PP
Castlecomer, Co Kilkenny
Tel 056-4441262/086-3693863
Fax 056-4441969
Parish email castlecomer@ossory.ie

CASTLETOWN
St Edmund
Very Rev Brian Griffin Adm
Camross, Co Laois
Tel 087-0644158
Email griffinmilepost@yahoo.ie

CLARA
St Coleman
Very Rev William Purcell PP
Clifden Villa, Clifden, Co Kilkenny
Tel 056-7726560/087-6286858
Fax 056-7726558
Email wpurcell@eircom.net
Parish email clara@ossory.ie

CLOGH
St Patrick's, Sacred Heart
Pastoral Area Co-ordinator
Clogh Parish Office,
Clogh, Co Kilkenny
Tel 056-4441942
Email clogh@ossory.ie

CONAHY
St Coleman, Our Lady of Perpetual Help
Very Rev William Hennessy Adm
Conahy, Jenkinstown, Co Kilkenny
Tel 087-8736155
Email williehennessy@ossory.ie

DANESFORT
St Michael the Archangel, Holy Cross, Kells
Holy Cross, Cuffesgrange
Very Rev Mark Condon PP
Danesfort, Co Kilkenny
Tel 056-7727137/086-6005402
Email markcondon@ossory.ie

DUNAMAGGAN
St Leonard, St Eoghan
Very Rev Fergus Farrell PP
Windgap, Co Kilkenny
Tel 086-0782066/051-648111

DURROW

Holy Trinity, St Tighearnach
Very Rev Martin Delaney Adm
Rathdowney, Co Laois
Tel 0505-46282/086-2444594
Email delaneymartindl@gmail.com
Rev Thomas McGree CC
Durrow, Cullohill, Co Laois
Tel 087-7619235 Fax 057-8736226
Email frtommcgree@gmail.com

FERRYBANK

Sacred Heart
Very Rev Kieran O'Shea PP
Ferrybank, Waterford
Tel 086-8272828
Email kieranoshea@ossory.ie
Website www.ferrybankparish.com

FRESHFORD

St Lachtain, St Nicholas
Rt Rev Mgr Kieron Kennedy PP
Freshford, Co Kilkenny R95 X2E0
Tel 056-8832426/087-2523521
Email kieronkennedy@ossory.ie
Email freshford@ossory.ie
Website parishoffreshford.com

GALMOY

Immaculate Conception
Very Rev Oliver Maher PP
Urlingford, Co Kilkenny
Tel 086-8323010
Email olivermaher@ossory.ie

GLENMORE

St James
Very Rev Thomas O'Toole PP
Glenmore, via New Ross, Co Kilkenny
Tel 051-880080/087-2240787
Email tm5-tle@hotmail.com

GOWRAN

Assumption
Very Rev Patrick Canon Dalton PP
Gowran, Co Kilkenny R95 E2Y4
Tel 056-7726128/086-8283478
Fax 056-7726134
Email daltonpadraig@gmail.com

INISTIOGE

St Columcille, Assumption, St Brendan
Very Rev Frank Purcell PP
Inistioge, Co Kilkenny
Tel 051-423619/086-6010001
Email sevillelawns@gmail.com

JOHNSTOWN

St Kieran, St Michael
Very Rev Oliver Maher PP
Urlingford, Co Kilkenny
Tel 056-883112/086-8323010
Email olivermaher@ossory.ie
Very Rev Frank Canon Maher CC
Johnstown via Thurles, Co Kilkenny
Tel 056-8831219/087-2402487
Fax 056-8831219
Email frankmaher@ossory.ie

KILMACOW

St Senan
Rev James O'Reilly (SPS) Adm
Kilmacow, via Waterford, Co Kilkenny
Tel 087-6802201
Email oreillyjimmy@gmail.com
Email kilmacowparish@ossory.ie

LISDOWNEY

St Brigid, St Munchin, St Fiacre
Very Rev Eamonn O'Gorman PP
Ballyragget, Co Kilkenny
Tel 087-2236145
Email eamonnogorman@gmail.com
Parish email lisdowney@ossory.ie

MOONCOIN

Assumption, St Kevin, St Kilgoue
Very Rev Martin Tobin Adm
Mooncoin, Co Kilkenny
Tel 086-2401278
Email frmartintobin@ossory.ie
Parish Office
Tel 051-895123
Email mooncoin@ossory.ie

MUCKALEE

St Brendan, St Brigid, St Joseph
Very Rev Laurence Wallace PP
Muckalee, Ballyfoyle, Co Kilkenny
Tel 056-4441271/087-2326807
Fax 056-4440007
Email lwallace@gmail.com
Parish email muckalee@ossory.ie

MULLINAVAT

St Beacon, St Paul
Very Rev Liam Barron PP
Tel 051-898108/087-2722824
Fax 051-898108
Mullinavat, via Waterford, Co Kilkenny
Email mullinavat@ossory.ie

RATHDOWNEY

Holy Trinity, Our Lady, Queen of the Universe
Very Rev Martin Delaney PP
Rathdowney, Portlaoise, Co Laois
Tel 0505-46282/086-2444594
Email delaneymartindl@gmail.com
Email rathdowney@ossory.ie

ROSBERCON

Assumption, St David, St Aidan
Rt Rev Mgr Daniel Cavanagh PP
Rosbercon, New Ross, Co Wexford
Tel 051-421515/087-2335432
Fax 051-425093
Email danieljcavanagh49@gmail.com

SEIR KIERAN

St Kieran
Very Rev Michael Reddan (SVD) Adm
Seir Kieran, Clareen, Birr, Co Offaly
Tel 057-9131080/087-4345898
Email mjreddan2016@gmail.com
Parish email seirkierparish35@gmail.com

SLIEVERUE

Assumption
Very Rev Kieran O'Shea PP
Ferrybank, Waterford
Tel 086-8272828
Parish email slieverue@ossory.ie
Website www.slieverue.com

TEMPLEORUM

Assumption
Very Rev Paschal Moore PP
Piltown, Co Kilkenny
Tel 051-643112/087-2408078
Fax 051-644911
Email templeorum@ossory.ie
Website www.templeorum.ie

THOMASTOWN

Assumption
Very Rev Daniel Bollard PP
Tel/Fax 056-7724279/087-6644858
Email bollard.dan@gmail.com
Parish email thomastown@ossory.ie

TULLAHERIN

St Bennet, St Kieran
Very Rev Patrick Canon Dalton PP
Tel 056-7726128/086-8283478
Email daltonpadraig@gmail.com
Very Rev Patrick Canon Duggan PE
Tel 056-7727140/086-2557471
Fax 056-7727755
Bennetsbridge, Co Kilkenny
Email patduggan@ossory.ie

TULLAROAN

Assumption
Very Rev Liam Taylor Adm
Ballycallan, Co Kilkenny
Tel 056-7769564/086-8180954
Email frliamtaylor@gmail.com
Very Rev Patrick Guilfoyle CC
Tullaroan, Co Kilkenny
Tel 056-7769141/087-9932117
Fax 056-7769141
Email guilfoylepat@eircom.net

URLINGFORD

Assumption, St Patrick
Very Rev Oliver Maher PP
Urlingford, Co Kilkenny
Tel 056-8831121/086-8323010
Email olivermaher@ossory.ie

WINDGAP
t Nicholas, Windgap
t Nicholas, Tullahought
ery Rev Fergus Farrell PP
Windgap, Co Kilkenny
el 051-648111/086-0782066
mail fearghus.ofearghail@dcu.ie

INSTITUTIONS AND THEIR CHAPLAINS

Aut Even Hospital
Aut Even, Kilkenny
riests of St Canice's Parish
el 056-7721523/087-9335663

City Vocational School, Kilkenny
Very Rev William Purcell
el 087-6286858
mail wpurcell@eircom.net

Community School
Castlecomer, Co Kilkenny
Ms Edel O'Connor
el 056-4441447

Abbey Community College
errybank, Waterford
Ms Claire Bolger
el 051-832930

District Hospital
Castlecomer, Co Kilkenny
t Rev Mgr Michael Ryan
el 056-4441262/086-3034155

Orthopaedic Hospital
Kilcreene, Kilkenny
Very Rev Richard Scriven Adm
t Mary's Parish
el 056-7721253/087-2420033

St Canice's Hospital, Kilkenny
riests of St John's Parish
el 056-7721072

St Columba's Hospital
homastown, Co Kilkenny
Very Rev Daniel Bollard
el 056-7724279/087-6644858

St Luke's Hospital, Kilkenny
Rev Patrick Carey
el 056-7785000/7771815/087-2599087
mail patrick.carey@hse.ie

Stephen Barracks, Kilkenny
Rev Daniel McCarthy
el 056-7761852

PRIESTS OF THE DIOCESE ELSEWHERE

Rt Rev Mgr Liam Bergin
St Brigid's Parish, 841 East Broadway,
Boston, MA 02127, USA
Tel 001-617-4477770
Email lbergin@ossory.ie
Very Rev Thomas Corcoran
Clogh, Castlecomer, Co Kilkenny
Email tomjcorcoran@gmail.com
Very Rev Laurence O'Keeffe
The Presbytery,
Slieverue, Co Kilkenny
Tel 051-832773

RETIRED PRIESTS

Very Rev Thomas Coyle
Friary Street, Kilkenny
Tel 087-7668969
Very Rev James Canon Crotty
Ferrybank, Waterford
Tel 086-8317711
Email jimcrotty@ossory.ie
Very Rev Liam Dunne
The Forge, Martin's Lane,
Upper Main Street,
Arklow, Co Wicklow
Tel 0402-32779
Very Rev Laurence Canon Dunphy
Urlingford, Co Kilkenny
Tel 087-2300849
Very Rev Eamon Foley
6 Woodlawn, Archers Avenue,
Kilkenny
Tel 087-7828784
Very Rev Peter Hoyne
Newmarket,
Hugginstown, Co Kilkenny
Tel 056-7768678
Very Rev Dean Seamus McEvoy
Drakelands Nursing Home,
Ballycallan Road, Kilkenny
Tel 086-2634093
Very Rev Archdeacon Sean O'Doherty
Durrow, Co Laois
Tel 057-8736156

RELIGIOUS ORDERS AND CONGREGATIONS

PRIESTS

CAPUCHINS
Capuchin Friary, Friary Street,
Kilkenny R95 NX60
Tel 056-7721439 Fax 056-7722025
Guardian: Rev Adrian Curran (OFMCap)
Vicar: Br Joseph Gallagher (OFMCap)

DOMINICANS
Black Abbey, Kilkenny, Co Kilkenny
Tel 056-7721279
Superior: Rev Thomas Monahan (OP)
Email blackabbey@dominicans.ie

BROTHERS

BROTHERS OF CHARITY
St Vincent's Brothers' Community,
9 Arbourmount, Rockshire Road,
Ferrybank, Waterford
Tel 051-832180
Community Leader: Br Joseph Killoran
Email joseph.killoran@bocsi.ie
Community: 3

CHRISTIAN BROTHERS
Christian Brothers,
Edmund Rice House,
Westcourt, Callan, Co Kilkenny
Tel 056-7725141
Community Leader
Br Chrisy O'Carroll
Community: 6

Edmund Rice Centre,
Callan, Co Kilkenny
Tel 056-7725993

DE LA SALLE BROTHERS
De La Salle Monastery,
Castletown, Portlaoise, Co Laois
Tel 057-8732359 (residence)
Fax 057-8732925
Superior: Br Stephen Deignan
Community: 3

Miguel House, Castletown,
Portlaoise, Co Laois
Tel 057-8732136 Fax 057-8756648
Superior: Br Martin Curran
Community: 16
House for retired brothers

La Salle Pastoral Centre,
Castletown, Portlaoise, Co Laois
Tel 057-8732442 Fax 057-872925
Director: Mr Derek Doherty
Retreat centre

SISTERS

CONGREGATION OF THE SISTERS OF MERCY
Convent of Mercy, Ballyragget,
Co Kilkenny
Tel 056-8833114

Convent of Mercy,
Callan, Co Kilkenny
Tel 056-7725223

1 Mountain View, Borris-in-Ossory,
Portlaoise, Co Laois
Tel/Fax 0505-41964

Villa Maria, Talbot's Inch, Kilkenny
Tel 056-7765774

20 Archer's Court, Loughboy,
Kilkenny
Tel 056-7780437

DAUGHTERS OF MARY AND JOSEPH
10 Parcnagowan, Waterford Road,
Kilkenny
Community: 2

10 Hazelwood,
Parcnagowan, Kilkenny

LITTLE COMPANY OF MARY
Troy's Court, Kilkenny
Tel 056-7763117
Community: 3

LITTLE SISTERS OF THE POOR
St Joseph's, Abbey Road,
Ferrybank, Waterford
Tel 051-833006
Superior: Sr Roseline
Email ms.waterford@lspireland.com
Community: 13
Care for the elderly

LORETO (IBVM)
Loreto Community,
Freshford Road, Kilkenny
Tel 056-7721187
Leader
Sr Louvenagh Heffernan
Community: 10
Loreto Secondary School
Tel 056-7765131
Education and pastoral work

PRESENTATION SISTERS
Presentation Sisters,
Kilkenny R95 T6XW
Tel 056-7721351
Community: 16

Presentation Sisters,
33 Newpark Close,
Newpark Drive, Kilkenny R95 E6V2
Tel 056-7708544
Community: 1

RELIGIOUS OF SACRED HEART OF MARY
Ferrybank, Waterford
Tel 051-832592
Community: 14
Primary School. Pupils: 200+
Secondary School. Pupils: 630

22 Castle Oaks, Rockshire Road,
Ferrybank, Waterford
Tel 051-851606
Community: 1
Education, pastoral work

An Grianán, Ferrybank, Waterford
Community: 8

Naomh Bríd, Ferrybank, Waterford
Community: 8

SISTERS OF ST JOHN OF GOD
Regional Centre,
College Road, Kilkenny
Tel 056-7722870 Fax 056-7751411
Email regionaloffice@ssjg.ie
Regional Leader
Sr Geraldine Fitzpatrick

Sisters of St John of God,
Galtrim, Waterford Road, Kilkenny
Tel 056-7775510

Sisters of St John of God,
7 Maudlin Court,
Thomastown, Co Kilkenny
Tel 056-7724046

Sisters of St John of God,
11 Dean's Court,
Waterford Road, Kilkenny
Tel 056-7764576

St John of God House,
College Road, Kilkenny
Tel 056-7756790

Sisters of St John of God,
'Fermoyle', Greenshill, Kilkenny
Tel 056-7751259

Sisters of St John of God,
Aut Even Convent, Kilkenny
Tel 056-7761451

EDUCATIONAL INSTITUTIONS

St Kieran's College
Kilkenny
Tel 056-7721086 Fax 056-7770001
Email school@stkieranscollege.ie
President: Rev Dr Dermot Ryan
Principal: Mr Adrian Finan
Tel 056-7721086 Ext 223/7761707
Chaplain: Mr Ken Maher
Tel 056-7761707

Our Lady of Lourdes Secondary School
Rosbercon, via New Ross, Co Kilkenny
Principal: Ms Toni Ormond
Tel 051-422177

Adult Educational Institute
Seville Lodge, Callan Road, Kilkenny
Tel/Fax 056-7721453
Business Manager: Mr Richard Curtin

CHARITABLE AND OTHER SOCIETIES

Cathedral Bookshop
St Mary's Cathedral,
James's Street, Kilkenny
Contact: Very Rev Richard Scriven
Tel 056-7721253
Email rscriven2009@gmail.com

Cathedral Cafe
St Mary's Cathedral,
James's Street, Kilkenny
Contact: Very Rev Richard Scriven
Tel 056-7721253
Email rscriven2009@gmail.com

Good Shepherd Centre
Administrator: Mr Seamus Roche
Hostel for transient homeless men
Tel 056-7722566

Homes for Elderly People
Kilkenny: Troy's Court
Tel 056-7763117
St Patrick's Parish: Tel 056-7764400
St Johns' Parish: Tel 056-7721072
Ballyragget: O'Gorman House
Tel 056-8833377
St Mary's: Tel 056-7721253
Callan: Mount Carmel
Tel 056-7725301
Freshford: Prague House
Tel 056-8832281
Kilmacow: Rosedale
Tel 051-885125
Kilmoganny: St Joseph's
Tel 051-648091
Owning, Piltown: Lady Sue Ryder Home
Tel 051-643136
Rathdowney: Cuan Bhríde
Tel 0505-46521

L'Arche, Workshops and Accommodation for People with Learning Difficulties
Moorefield House, Kilmoganny,
Co Kilkenny
Tel 051-64809
An Siol: 42 West Street, Callan,
Co Kilkenny
Tel 056-7725230
Cluain Aoibhin: Fairgreen, Callan,
Co Kilkenny
Tel 056-7725628

Ossory Social Services
Social Service Centre,
Waterford Road, Kilkenny
Tel 056-7721685 Fax 056-7763636
Email kilkennysocialservices@gmail.com
Director: Rt Rev Mgr Kieron Kennedy

Local Social Services Centres:
Callan: Sr Cecilia Dowley
Tel 056-7725223
Castlecomer: Ms Bridget McLean
Tel 056-4441679
Ferrybank: Sr Constance O'Sullivan
Tel 051-832592
Freshford: Sr Brigid Lonergan
Tel 056-8832281
Rathdowney Cuan Bhride
Sr Catherine O'Brien
Tel 0505-46521

SOS (Kilkenny) Ltd,
Sheltered Workshop and
Accommodation for People with
Learning Difficulties
SOS (Kilkenny) Ltd,
Callan Road, Kilkenny
Tel 056-7764000 Fax 056-7761212

Apostolic Work Society
Secretary: Mrs Nora Ryan
Ross, Rathdowney, Co Laois
Tel 0505-46524

St Joseph's Young Priests' Society
Chairperson: Mr Paul Clarke
Clonkil, Callan, Co Kilkenny
Tel 056-7725108/086-2523534
Email paulfclarke@eircom.net
Chaplain: Rev William Purcell
St Kieran's College, Kilkenny
Tel 056-7721086/087-6286858
Email wpurcell@eircom.net

DIOCESE OF RAPHOE

PATRON OF THE DIOCESE
ST EUNAN, 23 SEPTEMBER

INCLUDES THE GREATER PART OF COUNTY DONEGAL

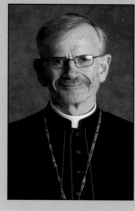

Most Rev Alan McGuckian (SJ) DD
Bishop of Raphoe;
born 26 Ferbruary 1953;
ordained priest 22 June 1984;
ordained Bishop of Raphoe
6 August 2017

Residence: Ard Adhamhnáin,
Cathedral Road, Letterkenny,
Co Donegal F92 W2W9
Tel 074-9121208
Fax 074-9124872
Email
diocesanoffice@raphoediocese.ie
Website www.raphoediocese.ie

ST EUNAN'S CATHEDRAL, LETTERKENNY

The old cathedral of Raphoe passed into Protestant hands at the Reformation. In the eighteenth century the Catholic bishops came to live in Letterkenny. A church was built circa 1820 and, having been extended by Bishop Patrick McGettigan, was used as a pro-cathedral. Bishop McDevitt (1871–1879) thought of building a new cathedral, and Lord Southwell promised a site, but it was not until 1891, when Bishop O'Donnell was in office, that actual building began. The cathedral was completed in 1901. Besides overseeing the cathedral project, Bishop O'Donnell had the task of providing a house for the bishop and priests of the cathedral parish.

The main benefactors were Fr J.D. McGarvey PP, Killygarvan, and Mr Neil Gillen of Airdrie. Various priests of the diocese spent considerable time fund-raising in Britain, the US and Canada. The style is Gothic, with some Hiberno-Romanesque features, and the building is of white Mountcharles sandstone. The cathedral dominates the Letterkenny skyline. Among the artistic features to be noted are the 'Drumceat' window, by Michael Healy (North Transept); the pulpit, by Messrs Pearse (Patrick Pearse's family); the Great Arch, with its St Columba and St Eunan columns; and, outside, the fine statue of Bishop O'Donnell, by Doyle of Chelsea.

Remodelling of the cathedral took place in 1985, with the addition of an altar table and chairs; great care was taken to preserve the style and materials of the original altar. Bishop Hegarty promoted this tasteful restoration work, which left intact the architectural character of the building.

Allianz (iii)

Most Rev Philip Boyce (OCD)
Bishop Emeritas of Raphoe;
born 25 January 1940;
ordained priest 17 April 1966;
ordained Bishop of Raphoe 1 October
1995; Retired 6 August 2017
Residence: 'Columba House', Windyhall,
Letterkenny, Co Donegal F92 EK4W
Tel 074-9122729

CHAPTER

Dean
Very Rev Canon Austin Laverty PE,
Ardara
Archdeacon
Ven Archdeacon William McMenamin PE
Raphoe
Members
Very Rev Canon Denis McGettigan PE
Raphoe
Very Rev Canon John Gallagher PE
Ardara
Very Rev Canon Francis McAteer AP
Glencolmcille
Very Rev Canon James Friel PE
Rathmullan
Very Rev Canon Michael Herrity AP
Cnoc Fola

ADMINISTRATION

Vicars General
Very Rev Francis McLoone PP, VG
Parochial House, Killymard,
Donegal Town, Co Donegal F94 C6T7
Very Rev Michael McKeever PP, VG
Parochial House, Church Hill,
Letterkenny, Co Donegal F92 H2V6

Diocesan Secretary
Very Rev Michael McKeever
Diocesan Office, Ard Adhamhnáin,
Letterkenny, Co Donegal F92 W2W9
Tel 074-9121208 Fax 074-9124872
Email diocesanoffice@raphoediocese.ie

Administration Secretary
Ms Marie McGill
Diocesan Office, Ard Adhamhnáin,
Letterkenny, Co Donegal R92 W2W9
Tel 074-9121208 Fax 074-9124872
Email diocesanoffice@raphoediocese.ie

Diocesan Chancellor
Rt Rev Mgr Kevin Gillespie Adm, VF
Ard Choluim, Cathedral Road,
Letterkenny, Co Donegal F92 CF88
Email chancellor@raphoediocese.ie

College of Consultors
Very Rev Francis McLoone PP, VG
Killymard
Very Rev Michael McKeever PP, VG
Church Hill
Rt Rev Mgr Kevin Gillespie Adm, VF
Letterkenny
Very Rev Michael Carney PP, Ramelton
Very Rev Paddy Dunne PP, Kilmacrennan
Very Rev Ciaran Harkin PP
Aughaninshin
Rev Danny McBrearty
Very Rev Brian O'Fearraigh PP, Gaoth
Dobhair

Vicars Forane
Rt Rev Mgr Kevin Gillespie Adm, VF
Letterkenny
Very Rev Cathal O'Fearrai PP, VF
Ballyshannon
Very Rev Gerard Cunningham PP, VF
Glenties
Very Rev Pat Ward PP, VF
Burtonport
Very Rev Kieran McAteer PP, VF
Stranorlar
Very Rev Charlie Byrne PP, VF
Carrigart

Financial Administrator
Mrs Carmel Doherty
Ard Adhamhnáin,
Letterkenny, Co Donegal

Finance Committee
Bishop Alan McGuckian (SJ)
Very Rev Michael McKeever
Rev Stephan Gorman *(Secretary)*

Building Committee
Very Rev Canon Austin Laverty PE
Very Rev Canon John Gallagher PE

Diocesan Archives
Faíche Ó Dónaill Building
Ard Adhamhnáin, Letterkenny,
Co Donegal
Tel 074-9161109
Email archives@raphoediocese.ie

CATECHETICS EDUCATION

Religious Education in Primary Schools
Co-ordinator
Very Rev Aodhan Cannon PP
Ardara, Co Donegal
Tel 074-9541135

**Religious Education in Secondary
Schools**
Vacant

LITURGY

Perpetual Eucharistic Adoration
Diocesan Director: Vacant

PASTORAL

ACCORD
Pastoral Centre,
Monastery Ave, Letterkenny
Tel 074-9122218
LoCall 1850-201878

Child Safeguarding Office
Pastoral Centre, Monastery Avenue,
Letterkenny, Co Donegal
Tel 074-9125669
Email safeguarding@raphoediocese.ie

Ecumenism
Diocesan Director
Very Rev Canon Francis McAteer AP
Glencolmcille, Co Donegal
Tel 074-9730888

Fatima Pilgrimage
Director: Very Rev James Sweeney PP
Frosses, Co Donegal
Tel 074-9736006

Knock Pilgrimage
Director
Very Rev Michael McKeever PP, VG
Church Hill, Co Donegal
Tel 074-9137057

Lourdes Pilgrimage
Director: Rev Stephen Gorman CC
Parochial House, Milford,
Co Donegal
Tel 074-9153236/074-9125090 *(Lourdes office)*

Marriage Tribunal
(See also Marriage Tribunals section)
Secretary: Rhona Healy
Judicial Vicar/Instructor
Mgr Kevin Gillespie
Assistant: Rev Brendan Ward
The Pastoral Centre, Letterkenny,
Co Donegal
Tel 074-9121853
Email
marriagetribunal@raphoediocese.ie

Pioneer Total Abstinence Association
Diocesan Director
Very Rev Canon James Friel PE
Rathmullan, Co Donegal
Very Rev James Sweeney PP
Frosses, Co Donegal
Tel 074-9736006

Religious Broadcasting
Diocesan Director
Very Rev Patrick Dunne PP
Parochial House, Kilmacrennan,
Letterkenny
Tel 074-9139018

Vocations
Director
Very Rev Rory Brady PP
Parochial House,
Bruckless, Co Donegal
Tel 074-9737015

Missio Ireland
Diocesan Director
Rev Damien Nejad CC
Parochial House,
Letterkenny, Co Donegal F92 CF88
Tel 074-9121021

PARISHES

The mensal parish is listed first. Other parishes follow alphabetically. Historical names are given in parentheses.

LETTERKENNY (CONWAL AND LECK)
Cathedral of St Eunan and St Columba
Mgr Kevin Gillespie Adm, VF
Rev Damien Nejad CC
Rev Kizito Kalemeera
Parochial House, Letterkenny,
Co Donegal F92 CF88
Tel 074-9121021
Email office@steunanscathedral.ie
Website www.steunanscathedral.ie
Letterkenny General Hospital
Rev Martin Chambers
2 Chaplain's House, Knocknamona,
Letterkenny, Co Donegal
Tel 074-9125090
Rev Shane Gallagher
1 Chaplain's House, Knocknamona,
Letterkenny, Co Donegal
Tel (Hospital) 074-9125888

ANNAGRY
Very Rev Nigel Ó Gallachóir PP
Annagry, Co Donegal
Tel 074-9548902

ARDARA
Very Rev Aodhan Cannon PP
Tel 074-9541135
Very Rev Canon Austin Laverty PE
Tel 074-9537033
Ardara, Co Donegal
Rev Philip Daly CC
Kilclooney, Co Donegal
Tel 074-9545114

AUGHANINSHIN
Website www.irishmartyrs.com
Very Rev Ciaran Harkin PP
Ballyraine, Letterkenny, Co Donegal
Tel 074-9127600
Rev Dominic Thoomkuzhy CC
Carnamuggagh Lower,
Letterkenny, Co Donegal
Tel 074-9122608

BALLINTRA (DRUMHOLM)
Very Rev Adrian Gavigan PP
Parochial House, Lisminton,
Ballintra, Co Donegal
Tel 074-9734642

BALLYSHANNON (KILBARRON)
Website www.kilbarron.org
Very Rev Cathal Ó Fearraí PP, VF
Kilbarron House, College Street,
Ballyshannon, Co Donegal
Tel 071-9851295

BRUCKLESS (KILLAGHTEE)
Very Rev Rory Brady PP
Bruckless, Co Donegal
Tel 074-9737015

BURTONPORT (KINCASSLAGH)
Very Rev Pat Ward PP, VF
Burtonport, Co Donegal
Tel 074-9542006
Rev John Boyce CC
Arranmore Island, Co Donegal
Tel 074-9520504
www.kincasslagh.ie

CARRICK (GLENCOLMCILLE)
Very Rev Denis Quinn PP
Carrick, Co Donegal
Tel 074-9739008
Very Rev Canon Francis McAteer AP
Glencolmcille, Co Donegal
Tel 074-9730888

CARRIGART (MEEVAGH)
Very Rev Charles Byrne PP
Carrigart, Co Donegal
Tel 074-9155154

CLOGHAN (KILTEEVOGUE)
Very Rev Lorcan Sharkey PP
Cloghan, Lifford, Co Donegal
Tel 074-9133007

DONEGAL TOWN (TAWNAWILLY)/CLAR
PP Vacant
Donegal Town, Co Donegal
Tel 074-9721026

DRUMOGHILL (RAYMOCHY)
Very Rev Martin Cunningham PP
Drumoghill, Co Donegal
Tel 074-9157169

DUNFANAGHY (CLONDAHORKEY)
Very Rev Martin Doohan PP
Dunfanaghy, Co Donegal
Tel 074-9136163
Rev John Joe Duffy CC
Creeslough, Co Donegal
Tel 074-9138011

DUNGLOE (TEMPLECRONE AND LETTERMACAWARD)
Very Rev Johnny Moore PP
Dungloe, Co Donegal
Tel 074-9521008
Very Rev Eddie Gallagher AP
Leitirmacaward, Co Donegal
Tel 074-9544102

FALCARRAGH
Very Rev James Gillespie PP
Falcarragh, Co Donegal
Tel 074-9135196

GLENSWILLY (GLENSWILLY AND TEMPLEDOUGLAS)
Rev Liam Boyle CC
Glenswilly, New Mills, Letterkenny,
Co Donegal
Tel 074-9137456

GLENTIES (INISKEEL)
Very Rev Gerard Cunningham PP, VF
Glenties, Co Donegal
Tel 074-9551117

GORTAHORK/TORY ISLAND
Very Rev Donnchadh Ó Baoill SP
Gortahork, Co Donegal
Tel 074-9135214

GWEEDORE
Very Rev Brian O'Fearraigh PP
Tel 087-9935544
Rev Brendan Ward CC
Tel 074-9531310
Derrybeg, Letterkenny
Very Rev Canon Michael Herrity AP
Bun-a-leaca, Letterkenny, Co Donegal
Tel 074-9531155

INVER
Very Rev James Sweeney PP
Frosses, Co Donegal
Tel 074-9736006
Rev Francis Ferry CC
Mountcharles, Co Donegal
Tel 074-9735009
Rev Morty O'Shea (SOLT) CC
Ardaghey, Co Donegal
Tel 074-9736007

KILCAR
Very Rev William Peoples PP
Kilcar, Co Donegal
Tel 074-9738007

KILLYBEGS
www.killybegsparish.com
Very Rev Colm O'Gallchoir PP
Killybegs, Co Donegal
Tel 074-9731030

KILLYMARD
Very Rev Francis McLoone PP, VG
Killymard, Co Donegal
Tel 074-9721929

KILMACRENNAN
Very Rev Patrick Dunne PP
Kilmacrennan, Co Donegal
Tel 074-9139018

NEWTOWNCUNNINGHAM & KILLEA
Very Rev Philip Kemmy PP
Parochial House, Newtowncunningham,
Lifford, Co Donegal
Tel 074-9156138

RAMELTON (AUGHNISH)
Very Rev Michael Carney PP
Ramelton, Co Donegal
Tel 074-9151304

RAPHOE

www.parishofraphoe.com
Very Rev Eamonn Kelly PP
Convoy, Lifford, Co Donegal
Tel 087-9077985

RATHMULLAN (KILLYGARVAN AND TULLYFERN)

www.mrparishes.ie
Very Rev Martin Collum PP
Rathmullan, Co Donegal
Tel 074-9158156
Rev Stephen Gorman CC
Milford, Co Donegal
Tel 074-9153236

ST JOHNSTON (TAUGHBOYNE)

Rt Rev Mgr Daniel Carr PP
St Johnston, Lifford, Co Donegal
Tel 074-9148203

STRANORLAR

www.stranorlarparish.com
Very Rev Kieran McAteer PP, VF
Parochial House, Ballybofey,
Co Donegal
Tel 074-9131135
Rev Anthony Briody CC
Parochial House, Stranorlar,
Co Donegal
Tel 074-9131157

TAMNEY (CLONDAVADDOG)

Very Rev Patrick McGarvey PP
Tanavolty, Kindrum,
Letterkenny, Co Donegal
Tel 074-9159007

TERMON (GARTAN AND TERMON)

Very Rev Michael McKeever PP, VG
Church Hill, Letterkenny,
Co Donegal
Tel 074-9137057
www.gartantermonparish.ie

INSTITUTIONS AND THEIR CHAPLAINS

General Hospital
Letterkenny, Co Donegal
Tel 074-9125888
Rev Martin Chambers
c/o General Hospital, Letterkenny
or 2 Chaplain's House,
Knocknamona, Letterkenny
Rev Shane Gallagher
Chaplain's House,
Knocknamona, Letterkenny
St Joseph's Hospital
Stranorlar, Co Donegal
Tel 074-9131038
Parochial clergy Stranorlar

PRIESTS OF THE DIOCESE ELSEWHERE

Rev Patrick Bonner
c/o Diocesan Office,
Letterkenny, Co Donegal
Rev Joseph Briody
St John's Seminary, 127 Lake Street,
Brighton, MA 02135, USA
Rev Jonathan Flood
c/o Diocesan Office,
Letterkenny, Co Donegal
Rev Brendan McBride
St Philip's Church,
725 Diamond Street, San Francisco,
California, 94114
Rev Eamonn McLaughlin
Congregation for the Clergy, Rome

RETIRED PRIESTS

Rev Anthony Griffith
Rushbrook, Laghey, Co Donegal
Tel 074-9734021
Very Rev Daniel O'Doherty PE
St Eunan's Nursing Home,
Letterkenny, Co Donegal
Very Rev Desmond Sweeney PE
17 Meadowvale, Ramelton
Tel 074-9151085
Very Rev Michael Connaghan PE
c/o Hillcrest Nursing Home, Letterkenny,
Co Donegal
Very Rev Canon James Friel PE
Massreagh, Rathmullen, Co Donegal
Tel 074-9158306
Archdeacon William McMenamin PE
'St Columba's',
Meeting House Street,
Raphoe, Co Donegal
Tel 074-9144834
Very Rev Dermot McShane PE
c/o Community Hospital, Killybegs,
Co Donegal
Very Rev Seamus Meehan PE
Main Street, Dungloe, Co Donegal
Tel 074-9521895
Very Rev Canon John Gallagher PE
Ardara, Co Donegal
Tel 087-6636434
Very Rev Seamus Dagens PE
Drimarone, Co Donegal
Tel 085-8590936
Very Rev Michael Sweeney PE
Ballynabrockey, Fanad, Co Donegal
Very Rev Canon Dinny McGettigan PE
Meetinghouse Street,
Raphoe, Co Donegal
Rev Daniel McBrearty
Gortnavern, Coolboy,
Letterkenny, Co Donegal
Rev Paul McGeehan
79 The Maples, Lismonaghan,
Letterkenny, Co Donegal
Very Rev Patrick McHugh PE
6 the Croft, Glencar,
Letterkenny, Co Donegal

Very Rev Seán Ó Gallchoir PE
Coitin na Doirí Beaga,
Leitir Ceanainn, Co hDún na nGall
Very Rev Padraig Ó Baoighill PE
58 Tara Court, Ramelton Road,
Letterkenny, Co Donegal

RELIGIOUS ORDERS AND CONGREGATIONS

PRIESTS

CAPUCHINS (OFMCAP)
Capuchin Friary, Ard Mhuire,
Creeslough, Letterkenny,
Co Donegal F92 Y23R
Tel 074-9138005 Fax 074-9138371
Guardian: Rev Philip Baxter (OFMCap)
Vicar: Rev Kieran Shorten (OFMCap)

FRANCISCANS (OFM)
Franciscan Friary, Rossnowlagh,
Co Donegal
Tel 072-9851342 Fax 072-9852206
Email info.rossnowlagh@franciscans.ie
Guardian: Rev Eugene Barrett (OFM)
Vicar: Rev Vincent Finnegan (OFM)

SISTERS

CONGREGATION OF THE SISTERS OF MERCY
Convent of Mercy, Donegal Town,
Co Donegal F94 D8Y8
Tel 074-9721175
Shared leadership
Community: 5

17 Blackrock Drive, Ballybofey,
Co Donegal F93 VW1X
Tel 074-9132721

St Catherine's,
Ballyshannon, Co Donegal F94 D309
Tel 071-9851268
Community: 9

Sisters of Mercy,
Ceoil na Coille, Stranorlar,
Lifford, Co Donegal F93 ET28
Tel 074-9131711

35 Brookfield Manor,
Donegal Town, Co Donegal F94 K2N5
Tel 074-9725996

No 7 Slí Na mBroc,
Arkeskin, Donegal Town F94 H2K4
Tel 074-9742652

St Anne's, Ballyshannon,
Co Donegal F94 FD85

18 Westpoint, Mount Charles Road,
Donegal Town, Co Donegal F94 RHP0

Allianz (ili)

EDUCATIONAL INSTITUTIONS

Coláiste Cholmcille
Ballyshannon, Co Donegal
Tel 071-9858288/9851369/9852459
Principal: Ms Cora Fagan
Chaplain: Vacant

Rosses Community School
Dungloe, Co Donegal
Tel 074-9521122
Principal: Mr John Gorman

Comprehensive School
Glenties, Lifford, Co Donegal
Tel 074-9551172
Fax 074-9551664
Principal: Mr Brendan O'Mahoney
Chaplain: Mr Hugh Doyle

Atlantic Technological University
Director: Mr Paul Hannigan
Tel 074-9124888
Chaplain: Rev Liam Boyle

Loreto Convent Secondary School
Letterkenny, Co Donegal
Tel 074-9121850
Principal: Ms Geraldine Mullin
Chaplain: Parish Clergy

Loreto Community School
Milford, Co Donegal
Tel 074-9153253 Fax 074-9153518
Principal: Ms Margaret O'Connor
Tel 074-9153399
Chaplain: Mr John Lynch

Pobalscoil Chloich Cheannfhaola
Falcarragh,
Letterkenny, Co Donegal
Tel 074-9135424/9135231
Fax 074-9135019
Príomh-Oide: Ms Maeve Sweeney
Séiplineach: Mr Oliver Gallagher

Pobalscoil Ghaoth Dobhair
Derrybeg,
Letterkenny, Co Donegal
Tel 074-9531040
Príomh-Oide: Seoirse Ó Dochartaigh
Séiplineach: Rev Brendan Ward CC

St Columba's College
Stranorlar, Co Donegal
Tel 074-9131246
Principal: Mr Tom Rowan
Chaplain: Parish Clergy

St Eunan's College
Letterkenny, Co Donegal
Tel 074-9121143
Principal: Mr Damien McCroary
Chaplaincy: Rev Brendan Ward and Rev Damien Nejad

CHARITABLE AND OTHER SOCIETIES

Ards Friary Retreat Centre
Manager: Mr Joe Conroy
Tel 074-9138909
Email info@ardsfriary.ie
Website www.ardsfriary.ie

Trócaire
Very Rev Aodhan Cannon PP
Parochial House,
Ardara, Co Donegal
Tel 074-9541135

DIOCESE OF WATERFORD AND LISMORE

PATRONS OF THE DIOCESE
ST OTTERAN, 27 OCTOBER; ST CARTHAGE, 15 MAY;
ST DECLAN, 24 JULY

INCLUDES COUNTY WATERFORD
AND PART OF COUNTIES TIPPERARY AND CORK

Most Rev Alphonsus Cullinan DD
Bishop of Waterford and Lismore
born 7 May 1959;
ordained priest 12 June 1994;
ordained Bishop of Waterford and Lismore 12 April 2015

Residence: Bishop's House, John's Hill, Waterford
Tel 051-874463
Email info@waterfordlismore.ie

CATHEDRAL OF THE MOST HOLY TRINITY, WATERFORD

The Cathedral of the Most Holy Trinity, Barronstrand Street, Waterford is the oldest Roman Catholic cathedral in Ireland. The work began in 1793 with the Protestant Waterford man, John Roberts, as architect. Roberts also designed the Church of Ireland cathedral.

Over the years, additions and alterations have been made. Most of the present sanctuary was added in the 1830s; the apse and a main altar in 1854. The beautiful baldachin, which is supported by five Corinthian columns, was erected in 1881.

The carved oak Baroque pulpit, the chapter stalls and bishop's chair, designed by Goldie and Sons of London and carved by Buisine and Sons of Lille, were installed in 1883.

The stained-glass windows, mainly by Meyer of Munich, were installed between 1883 and 1888.

The Stations of the Cross, which are attached to the columns in the cathedral, are nineteenth-century paintings by Alcan of Paris. The cut-stone front was built in 1892–1893 for the centenary of the cathedral.

In 1977, a new wooden altar was placed in the redesigned sanctuary. The Belgian walnut panels of the base of the altar were originally part of the altar rails at St Carthage's Church, Lismore.

There are many plaques in the cathedral. One of them commemorates fourteen famous Waterford men: Luke

Wadding OFM; Peter Lombard; Patrick Comerford OSA; James White; Michael Wadding SJ: Peter Wadding SJ; Thomas White; Paul Sherlock SJ; Ambrose Wadding SJ; Geoffrey Keating; Luke Wadding SJ; Stephen White SJ; Thomas White SJ and Bonaventure Barron OFM.

Ten Waterford Crystal chandeliers were presented by Waterford Crystal in 1979.

In 1993 the Bicentenary of the Cathedral was celebrated.

Most Rev William Lee DD
Retired Bishop of Waterford and Lismore
born 1941;
ordained priest 19 June 1966;
ordained Bishop of Waterford and
Lismore 25 July 1993;
retired 1 October 2013
Residence: 5 The Brambles,
Ballinakill Downs, Waterford
Tel 051-821485

CHAPTER

Right Rev Mgr Nicholas O'Mahony PP, VG
Tramore
Very Rev Canon William Ryan PP, VG
Dungarvan
Very Rev Canon Daniel O'Connor PE
Dungarvan
Very Rev Canon Brendan Crowley PP, VF
SS Peter & Paul's, Clonmel
Very Rev Canon Edmond Cullinan Adm,
VF
Holy Trinity Cathedral
Very Rev William Meehan PP
St Mary's, Clonmel

College of Consultors
Right Rev Mgr Nicholas O'Mahony PP
Very Rev Patrick Fitzgerald PP
Very Rev Canon William Ryan
Very Rev Robert Power PP
Very Rev Michael Toomey Adm
Very Rev Paul Waldron PP

ADMINISTRATION

Diocesan Development Committee
Right Rev Mgr Nicholas O'Mahony PP
Very Rev Michael Cullinan PP
Very Rev Milo Guiry PP
Very Rev Richard O'Halloran PP

Diocesan Finance Committee
Most Rev Alphonsus Cullinan
Right Rev Mgr Nicholas O'Mahony
Mr Jim Kennedy
Mr Lee Walsh
Mr David O'Brien
Mr Patrick Slevin
Mr Paul L'Estrange
Very Rev John Harris

Diocesan Secretary and Director of Finance
Mr Lee Walsh
Bishop's House, John's Hill, Waterford
Tel 051-874463

Episcopal Vicar for Retired Priests
Very Rev John Kiely PP
Cappoquin, Co Waterford
Tel 058-54216

Vicars for Clergy
Very Rev Brian Power PP
Parochial House, Killea,
Dunmore East, Co Waterford
Tel 051-383127
Very Rev Patrick Butler
Parochial House, Youghal Road,
Tallow, Co Waterford

CATECHETICS EDUCATION

Catechetics
Primary Schools Religious Education:
Sr Antoinette Dilworth
St John's Pastoral Centre, John's Hill,
Waterford
Tel 051-874199
Sr De Lourdes Breen
Presentation Sisters, Youghal Road,
Dungarvan, Co Waterford
Tel 058-41359
Very Rev Conor Kelly Adm
11 The Orchard, Dungarvan,
Co Waterford
Tel 086-8231807
Director Post-Primary Schools Religious Education: Vacant
St John's Pastoral Centre, John's Hill,
Waterford
Tel 051-874199

Catholic Primary School Managers' Association
Secretary: Very Rev Paul Waldron PP
Parochial House, Chapel Street,
Carrick-on-Suir, Co Tipperary
Tel 051-640168

LITURGY

Assistant to Parishes
Ms Mary Dee
St John's Pastoral Centre,
John's Hill, Waterford
Tel 051-874199

Diocesan Liturgy and Sacred Music Committee
Assistant to Parishes: Mary Dee
St John's Pastoral Centre
Very Rev Canon William Ryan PP
Very Rev Paul Waldron PP
Very Rev William Meehan PP
Mr Noel Casey
Ms Mary Dunphy
Ms Anna Fennessey
Ms Fidelma Nugent
Mr Donal Kenefick
Mr Nicholas de Paor

PASTORAL

ACCORD
Director: Very Rev Liam Power PP
St John's Pastoral Centre, John's Hill
Waterford
Tel 051-874199

Bereavement Counselling
Director: Ms Ann O'Farrell
Family Ministry Office,
St John's Pastoral Centre,
John's Hill, Waterford
Tel 051-874199/858772

Communications Office
Email media@waterfordlismore.ie

Charismatic Groups
Very Rev Patrick Gear PP
14 Heathervue Road, Riverview,
Knockboy, Waterford
Tel 051-820452

Diocesan Archivist
Bishop's House,
John's Hill, Waterford
Tel 051-874463

Emigrant Bureau
Director: Very Rev Michael Enright PE
Dunabrattin, Annestown,
Co Waterford
Tel 087-2371546

Historic Churches Advisory Committee
Mr Eamonn McEneaney
Very Rev Canon William Ryan PP, VF
Very Rev Michael Walsh PE
Tel 051-874463

Marriage Tribunal
Diocesan Official
Cork Marriage Tribunal
(See also Marriage Tribunals section)

Ministry to Polish Community
Rev Marek Kowalkowski
The Presbytery, Kill, Co Waterford

Ministry to the Latin Mass Chaplaincy
Rev Patrick O'Donohue (FSSP)
St John's Parish, Waterford
Email office@fssp.ie

Pilgrimage
Director: Very Rev Martin Keogh
Parochial House, Cappoquin,
Co Waterford
Te 058-54216

Allianz (ⅼ)

Pontifical Mission Societies
Bishop's House
John's Hill, Waterford

Travellers
Chaplain
Very Rev Robert Grant PP

Trócaire
Diocesan Director
Very Rev Conor Kelly Adm
The Orchard, Dungarvan, Co Waterford
Tel 058-64284

Youth Ministry Officer
Ms Nodlaig Lilis
St John's Pastoral Centre,
John's Hill, Waterford
Tel 051-874199

PARISHES

City parishes are listed first. Other parishes follow alphabetically. Italics denote church titulars where they differ from parish names.

TRINITY WITHIN AND ST PATRICK'S
Holy Trinity Cathedral
Very Rev John Harris Adm
Holy Family Presbytery,
Luke Wadding Street, Waterford
Tel 051-350023
Sacristy: Tel 051-875166

ST JOHN'S
Very Rev Thomas Rogers PP
Carmel, Priest's Road,
Tramore, Co Waterford
Tel 051-511275
Sacristy: Tel 051-875849

SS JOSEPH AND BENILDUS
SS Joseph & Benildus, Newtown
St Mary, Ballygunner
Very Rev Liam Power PP
Parish Office, SS Joseph and Benildus,
Newtown, Waterford
Tel 051-873073
Very Rev Raymond Liddane AP
Newtown, Waterford
Tel 051-874284
Very Rev Pat Gear Co-PP
4 Heathervue Road, Riverview,
Knockboy, Waterford
Tel 051-820452
Sacristy: Tel 051-878977

BALLYBRICKEN
Holy Trinity Without
Very Rev Thomas Rogers Adm
Very Rev Michael Mullins PE
St Anne's Presbytery, Convent Hill,
Waterford
Tel 051-855819
Sacristy: Tel 051-874519

HOLY FAMILY
Very Rev Gerard Langford PP
Holy Family Presbytery,
Luke Wadding Street, Waterford
Tel 051-375274

ST PAUL'S
Very Rev Patrick Fitzgerald PP
Parochial House,
Lisduggan, Waterford
Tel 051-372257
Sacristy: Tel 051-378073

SACRED HEART
Very Rev Gerard Chestnutt PP
The Presbytery, The Folly, Waterford
Tel 051-878429
Sacristy: Tel 051-873792
Rev Jamon Varkey Kakkanattu CC
Sacred Heart Presbytery,
21 The Folly, Waterford
Tel 051-873759

ST SAVIOUR'S
Very Rev Robert Grant PP
Parochial House, Fenor, Co Waterford
Tel 051-376032

ABBEYSIDE
St Augustine, Abbeyside
St Laurence, Ballinroad
St Vincent de Paul, Garranbane
Very Rev Edmond Hassett PP
Strandside South, Abbeyside,
Dungarvan, Co Waterford
Tel 058-42036

AGLISH
Our Lady of the Assumption, Aglish
St James, Ballinameela
St Patrick, Mount Stuart
Very Rev Conor Kelly Adm
The Orchard, Dungarvan,
Co Waterford
Tel 058-64284
Very Rev Philip Amooti Balikuddembe CC
Parochial House, Aglish,
Co Waterford
Tel 024-96287

ARDFINNAN
Holy Family, Ardfinnan
St Nicholas, Grange, Ballybacon Church
Very Rev Michael Toomey Adm
Ardfinnan, Clonmel, Co Tipperary
Tel 052-7466216

ARDMORE
St Declan, Ardmore
Our Lady of the Assumption, Grange
Very Rev Michael Guiry PP
Ardmore, Youghal, Co Waterford
Tel 024-94275

BALLYDUFF
St Michael
Very Rev Gerard McNamara PP
Ballyduff, Co Waterford
Tel 058-60227

BALLYLOOBY
Our Lady & St Kieran, Ballylooby
St John the Baptist, Duhill
Rev John Nally PP
Ballylooby, Cahir, Co Tipperary
Tel 052-7441489

BALLYNEALE AND GRANGEMOCKLER
St Mary, Ballyneale
St Mary, Grangemockler
Very Rev Paul Waldron PP *(priest in charge)*
Rev James Browne (IC) CC
Ballyneale, Carrick-on-Suir, Co Tipperary
Tel 051-640148

BALLYPOREEN
Our Lady of the Assumption
Very Rev Bobby Power Adm
Very Rev Joseph Flynn AP
Ballyporeen, Cahir, Co Tipperary
Tel 052-7467105

BUTLERSTOWN
St Mary
Very Rev Patrick Fitzgerald PP *(priest in charge)*
Parochial House, Lisduggan,
Waterford
Tel 051-372257

CAHIR
St Mary
Rev Peter Cullen Adm
20 Bengurragh, Cahir, Co Tipperary
Tel 052-7441585

CAPPOQUIN
St Mary's
Very Rev Martin Keogh PP
Cappoquin, Co Waterford
Tel 058-54216

CARRICKBEG
St Molleran, Carrickbeg
St Bartholomew, Windgap
Very Rev Thomas Flynn PP
Carrickbeg, Carrick-on-Suir, Co Tipperary
Tel 051-640340

CARRICK-ON-SUIR
St Nicholas, Carrick-on-Suir
St Patrick, Faugheen
Very Rev Paul Waldron PP
Parochial House, Carrick-on-Suir,
Co Tipperary
Tel 051-640168

CLASHMORE
St Cronan, Clashmore
St Bartholomew, Piltown
Very Rev Michael Guiry *(Moderator)*
Ardmore, Co Waterford
Tel 024-94275

CLOGHEEN
St Mary, Clogheen
Our Lady of the Assumption, Burncourt
Very Rev Robert Power PP
Parochial House, Clogheen, Cahir,
Co Tipperary
Tel 052-7465268

CLONMEL, ST MARY'S
St Mary
Very Rev. William Meehan PP
St Mary's, Clonmel, Co Tipperary
Tel 052-6122954

CLONMEL, ST OLIVER PLUNKETT
St Oliver Plunkett
Very Rev Michael Hegarty (IC) PP
Rev Deacon Lazarus Gidolf
Cooleens, Glenconnor, Clonmel,
Co Tipperary, E91 N578
Tel 052-6125679

CLONMEL, SS PETER AND PAUL'S
SS Peter and Paul's,
Church of the Resurrection
Very Rev John Treacy PP
Very Rev Canon Brendan Crowley PE
SS Peter and Paul's, Clonmel, Co Tipperary
Tel 052-6126292

DUNGARVAN
St Mary
Very Rev Canon William Ryan PP, VF
Parochial House, Dungarvan,
Co Waterford
Tel 058-42374
Rev John McEneaney
The Presbytery, Mitchell Street,
Dungarvan, Co Waterford
Rev Matthew Cooney (OSA)
The Presbytery, Dungarvan,
Co Waterford

DUNHILL
Sacred Heart, Dunhill
Immaculate Conception, Fenor
Very Rev Richard O'Halloran PP (priest in charge)
Priest's Road, Tramore, Co Waterford
Tel 051-356336

KILGOBINET
St Gobnait, Kilgobinet
St Anne, Colligan
St Patrick, Kilbrian
Very Rev Canon William Ryan PP
Kilgobinet

KILLEA (DUNMORE EAST)
Holy Cross, Killea
St John the Baptist, Crooke
St Nicholas, Faithlegg
Very Rev P.J. Breen PP
Dunmore East, Co Waterford
Tel 051-383127

KILROSSANTY
St Brigid, Kilrossanty
St Anne, Fews
Very Rev John Delaney PP
Parochial House, Kilrossanty,
Kilmacthomas, Co Waterford
Tel 051-291985

KILSHEELAN
St Mary, Gambonsfield
St John the Baptist, Kilcash
Very Rev Brian Power PP
Kilsheelan, Clonmel, Co Tipperary
Tel 052-6133118

KNOCKANORE
Very Rev Patrick T. Condon PP
Knockanore, Tallow, Co Waterford
Tel 024-97140

LISMORE
St Carthage
Very Rev Michael Cullinan PP, VF
Parochial House,
Lismore, Co Waterford
Tel 058-54246

MODELIGO
Our Lady of the Assumption, Modeligo
St John the Baptist, Affane
Priest in charge:
Very Rev Martin Keogh
Cappoquin, Co Waterford
Tel 058-54216

NEWCASTLE AND FOURMILEWATER
Our Lady of the Assumption, Newcastle
Our Lady & St Laurence, Fourmilewater
Very Rev Michael Toomey Adm
Newcastle, Clonmel, Co Tipperary
Tel 052-6136387

NEWTOWN
All Saints, Newtown
St Mary, Saleen, Kill Church
Very Rev Garrett Desmond PP
Lemybrien, Co Waterford
Tel 087-1735178

PORTLAW
St Patrick, Portlaw
St Nicholas, Ballyduff
Very Rev Francis Xavier (HGN) PP
Portlaw, Co Waterford
Tel 051-387227
Very Rev Michael O'Byrne AP
Kilmeaden, Co Waterford
Tel 051-384117

POWERSTOWN
St John the Baptist, Powerstown
St John the Baptist, Lisronagh
Very Rev Peter Ahearne PP
Rathronan, Clonmel, Co Tipperary
Tel 052-6121891

RATHGORMACK
SS Quan & Broghan, Clonea
Sacred Heart, Rathgormack
Rev P. J. Fegan (IC) (priest in charge)
Rathgormack, Carrick-on-Suir,
Co Waterford
Tel 051-646006

RING AND OLD PARISH
Nativity of the BVM
St Nicholas
Very Rev William Canon Ryan Adm
The Orchard, Dungarvan,
Co Waterford
Tel 058-64284

STRADBALLY
Exaltation of the Holy Cross, Stradbally
St Anne, Ballylaneen, Faha Church
Very Rev Jeremiah Condon PP
Stradbally, Kilmacthomas,
Co Waterford
Tel 051-293133

TALLOW
Immaculate Conception
Priest in Charge
Very Rev Gerard McNamara PP
Ballyduff Upper, Co Waterford
Tel 058-60227

TOURANEENA
St Mary, Touraneena, Nire Church
Very Rev Jim Denmead AP
Ardfinnan, Clonmel, Co Tipperary

TRAMORE
Holy Cross, Tramore
Our Lady, Carbally
Very Rev Richard O'Halloran PP
Parochial House, Tramore,
Co Waterford
Tel 051-356336
Rev Paul Yang
Rev Tadeusz Durajczyk (SVD)
Tel 051-338291
Priest's Road, Tramore, Co Waterford

INSTITUTIONS AND CHAPLAINS

Bon Sauveur Services
Carriglea, Dungarvan, Co Waterford
Tel 058-41322 Fax 058-41432
Email bonsav@eircom.net

niversity Hospital, Waterford
el 051-873321
haplains
ev John Philip Kakkarakunel
ev Russell Jacob (OSCam)
Vaterford University Hospital,
unmore Road, Waterford
el 051-848000

outh Tipperary General Hospital
haplains: Rev Deogratias Mayanja
ev Godfrey Lubega
el 052-6177000

outh East Technological University
haplain: Rev David Keating
) Claremont, Cork Road, Waterford
el 051-378878

Military Chaplaincy
ery Rev Paul F. Murphy (CF)
haplain's House, Dún Uí Mhaoilíosa,
enmore, Galway
el 091-751156

PRIESTS OF THE DIOCESE ELSEWHERE

ery Rev Edmond Cullinan
ice-Rector, Irish College, Rome
ery Rev Michael O'Connor
o St John's Pastoral Centre,
ohn's Hill, Waterford
mail mnoc@iol.ie
ev Shane O'Neill
irector of Formation,
 Patrick's College, Maynooth,
o Kildare

RETIRED PRIESTS

ev Thomas Burns
 Anne's Presbtery, Convent Hill,
aterford
ery Rev William Carey PE
onmel, Co Tipperary
ery Rev Eanna Condon PE
 Mary's, Clonmel, Co Tipperary
el 052-6127870
ery Rev Joseph Condon PP
partment 2, St John's College,
ne Folly, Waterford
l 051-876843
ery Rev Canon Brendan Crowley PE
 Peter and Paul's, Clonmel,
o Tipperary
ev James Curran
l Tournane Court, Dungarvan,
o Waterford
l 058-45177
ery Rev Michael Enright PE
unabrattin,
nnestown, Co Waterford
l 087-2371546

Rev Pat Hayes
Dunabbey House,
Dungarvan, Co Waterford
Very Rev Michael Kennedy PE
Parochial House, Colligan, Dungarvan,
Co Waterford
Tel 058-41629
Very Rev John Kiely PE
'The Cottage', Ballinaparka,
Aglish, Co Waterford
Very Rev Francis Lloyd PE
The Presbytery, Dungarvan,
Co Waterford
Very Rev Finbarr Lucey PE
Ardmore, Youghal, Co Cork
Tel 024-94177
Very Rev Michael Mullins PE
St Anne's Presbytery, Convent Hill,
Waterford
Very Rev Paul Murphy PE
St Joseph's, Ferrybank, Co Waterford
Rev Michael O'Brien
St Anne's Presbytery, Convent Hill,
Waterford
Very Rev Canon Daniel O'Connor PE
Dunabbey House, Dungarvan,
Co Waterford
Tel 058-42381
Very Rev Gerard O'Connor PE
23 Beechwood Grove,
Portlaw, Co Waterford
Very Rev Sean O'Dwyer PE
Clonmel Road, Cahir, Co Tipperary
Tel 087-4184213
Very Rev Nicholas O'Mahony PE, VG
'Woodleigh', Summerville Avenue,
Waterford
Rev Charles Scanlan
Ballinwillin, Lismore, Co Waterford
Very Rev Michael F. Walsh PE
Ballinarrid, Bonmahon, Co Waterford
Tel 051-292992

RELIGIOUS ORDERS AND CONGREGATIONS

PRIESTS

AUGUSTINIANS
St Augustine's Priory, Dungarvan,
Co Waterford
Tel 058-41136 Fax 058-44534
Prior & Bursar: Rev Tony Egan (OSA)

St Augustine's College,
Dungarvan, Co Waterford
Tel 058-41140/41152 Fax 058-41152

Duckspool House (Retirement
Community)
Abbeyside, Dungarvan, Co Waterford
Tel 058-23784
Prior: Rev Ben O'Brien (OSA)

CISTERCIANS
Mount Melleray Abbey,
Cappoquin, Co Waterford P51 R8XW
Tel 058-54404 Fax 058-52140
Email info@mtmelleray.ie
Abbot
Rt Rev Dom Richard Purcell (OCSO)
Prior: Rev Patrick Ryan (OCSO)

DOMINICANS
Bridge Street, Waterford
Tel 051-875061 Fax 051-858093
Superior
Rev Krzsztof Kupczakiewiczy (OP)

FRANCISCANS
Franciscan Friary,
Clonmel, Co Tipperary
Tel 052-6121378 Fax 052-6125806
Email franciscans.clonmel@outlook.com
Guardian: Rev Jim Hasson (OFM)
Vicar: Rev Liam McCarthy (OFM)

Franciscan Friary,
Lady Lane, Waterford
No longer resident community. Church
served from Clonmel

ROSMINIANS
St Joseph's Doire na hAbhann
Tickincor, Clonmel,
Co Tipperary, E91 XY71
Tel 052-26914 Fax 052-26915
Residential centre for children in care.

(See also under parishes – St Oliver
Plunkett)

BROTHERS

CHRISTIAN BROTHERS
Mount Sion, Barrack Street, Waterford
Tel 051-879580 Fax 051-841578
Community Leader: Br Peadar Gleeson
Community: 3

International Heritage Centre & Chapel
Mount Sion, Barrack Street, Waterford
Tel 051-874390 Fax 051-841578

DE LA SALLE BROTHERS
De La Salle College, Newtown,
Waterford
Tel 051-875294 Fax 051-841321
Email delasall@iol.ie
Superior: Br Benedict Hanlon
Community: 5
Secondary School
Principal: Mr Michael Walsh

De La Salle Brothers
25 Patrick Street, Waterford
Tel 051-874623
Community: 3
Superior: Br Francis McCallig
St Stephen's Primary School
Principal: Ms Sinead Lowe
Tel 051-871716

PRESENTATION BROTHERS

Glór na hAbhann,
Ballinamona Lower, Old Parish,
Dungarvan, Co Waterford
Tel 058-46904
Contact: Br John Hunt (FPM)
Community: 2

SISTERS

CARMELITES

St Joseph's Carmelite Monastery, Tallow,
Co Waterford
Tel 058-56205
Email carmelprint1@gmail.com
Superior: Sr Patrice Buckley
Community: 12
Contemplatives

CISTERCIANS

St Mary's Abbey,
Glencairn, Lismore,
Co Waterford P51 X725
Tel 058-56168
Email info@glencairnabbey.org
Abbess: Sr Marie Fahy
Tel 058-56197
Email mariebfahy@gmail.com
Community: 26
Monastic

CONGREGATION OF THE SISTERS OF MERCY

Teach Bride, Convent Road,
Townspark, Cahir, Co Tipperary
Tel 052-7443809

Greenhill, Carrick-on-Suir,
Co Tipperary
Tel 051-640059

Springwell, Pill Road,
Carrick-on-Suir, Co Tipperary
Tel 051-642870

12 Comeragh View,
Carrick-on-Suir, Co Tipperary
Tel 051-645012

10 Ash Park, Carrick-on-Suir,
Co Tipperary
Tel 051-640814

31 Willow Park,
Clonmel, Co Tipperary
Tel 052-6128903

Convent of Mercy, Church Street,
Dungarvan, Co Waterford
Tel 058-41293/41337

1 Park Lane Drive, Abbeyside,
Dungarvan, Co Waterford
Tel 058-48795

22 Blackrock Court,
Youghal Road, Dungarvan,
Co Waterford
Tel 058-48286

16 Blackrock Court,
Youghal Road, Dungarvan,
Co Waterford
Tel 058-45713

17 Blackrock Court,
Youghal Road, Dungarvan,
Co Waterford
Tel 058-44865

11 Blackrock Court,
Youghal Road, Dungarvan,
Co Waterford
Tel 058-24656

Convent of Mercy,
Military Road, Waterford
Tel 051-374161/377909

104 Glenville,
Dunmore Road, Waterford

2 Chestnut Grove,
Waterford
Tel 051-373542

93 Clonard Park,
Ballybeg, Waterford
Tel 051-379110

7 Aisling Court,
Hennessy's Road, Waterford

Apartment 57, College House,
St John's College,
John's Hill, Waterford

CONGREGATION OF OUR LADY OF CHARITY OF THE GOOD SHEPHERD

Virginia Crescent, Hennessy's Road,
Waterford X91 N267
Tel 051-874294
Email rgswat33@hotmail.co.uk
Community: 9

Good Shepherd Sisters,
37 Clonard Park, Ballybeg,
Waterford X91 CH02
Email rgsanna18@gmail.com
Community: 1

LITTLE COMPANY OF MARY

36 Willowbrook,
Tallow, Co Waterford
Tel 058-55962
Community: 1

LORETO (IBVM)

Loreto Secondary School,
Clonmel, Co Tipperary
Tel 052-21402
Community: 2

MISSIONARY SISTERS OF THE GOSPEL

Carriglea,
Dungarvan, Co Waterford
Tel 058-45884 (office line)
Email mary.fitzgeraldmsg20@gmail.com
Superior: Sr Mary Fitzgerald (MSG)
Community: 5
Pastoral Ministry to Carriglea Cairde
Service – Residential and day care
services for persons with an intellectual
disability

PRESENTATION SISTERS

Presentation Sisters,
Clonmel, Co Tipperary E91 E329
Tel 052-6121538
Community: 16
Community and pastoral

Presentation Sisters,
Youghal Road, Dungarvan,
Co Waterford X35 YR89
Tel 058-41359
Community: 7

Presentation Play School Ltd.
Tel 087-6204077
Email presplayschool@eircom.net

Presentation Sisters,
81 Treacy Park, Carrick-on-Suir,
Co Tipperary E32 W225
Tel 051-641733
Community: 1

11 Convent Lodge,
Mitchell Street, Dungarvan,
Co Waterford X35 D683
Community: 1

SISTERS OF ST JOHN OF GOD

9 The Cloisters, John's Hill, Waterford
Tel 051-874370

Sisters of St John of God,
41 Grange Cove, Waterford
Tel 051-855585

URSULINES

Ursuline Convent, Waterford
Tel 051-874068
Email stangurs@yahoo.com
Community: 7
Primary School
Tel 051-873788/852855
Fax 051-852855
Secondary School
Tel 051-8766510 Fax 051-879022

Allianz (ⁱⁱⁱ)

Shannon Drive,
vondale, Waterford
el 051-854680
mail bolandmaureen88@gmail.com
ommunity: 2

St Anne's,
rsuline Court, Waterford
l 051-857015
nail brettelizabeth9@gmail.com
ommunity: 2

ST JOHN'S PASTORAL CENTRE

St John's Pastoral Centre
John's Hill, Waterford
Tel 051-874199 Fax 051-843107
Email
pastoralcentre@waterfordlismore.ie
Administrator: Ms Mary Dee

CHARITABLE AND OTHER SOCIETIES

Holy Family Mission
Glencomeragh House,
Kilsheelan, Co Waterford
Tel 052-6133636
House of Formation for Young People
Retreat House
Rev Patrick Cahill

Home of the Mother
St Saviour's Priory, Bridge Street,
Waterford
Tel 051-875061
Rev Kevin Deakin
Rev Dominic Feehan

Hostels
Men's Hostel, Ozanam House,
Lady Lane, Waterford
(St Vincent de Paul)

Neo-Catechumenal Way/Missio Ad Gentes
Rev Ireneusz Drewniak
7 Newtown Woods,
Newtown, Waterford

PERSONAL PRELATURES

Prelature of the Holy Cross and Opus Dei

Founded by Saint Josemaría Escrivá in 1928, it was erected as a Personal Prelature (cf CIC 294-297) in 1982, and is constituted by the Prelate (Mgr Fernando Ocáriz), incardinated clergy, and lay people, married and celibate. The faithful of the Prelature try to promote a deep consciousness of the universal call to holiness and apostolate in all sectors of society and, more specifically, an awareness of the sanctifying value of ordinary work.

Information Office:
10 Hume Street, Dublin D02 VY39
Tel 087-7690049

Website www.opusdei.ie
Email info.ie@opusdei.org

Vicar for North West Europe
(Ireland, UK, Sweden, The Netherlands)
Rt Rev Mgr Christian Van De Ploeg
Harvieston,
22 Cunningham Road, Dalkey,
Co Dublin A96 CX59
Tel 00-31-85-8901190

Archdiocese of Dublin
Harvieston, 22 Cunningham Road,
Dalkey, Co Dublin A96 CX59
Tel 01-2859877
Rev Patrick Gorevan
Rev Donncha Ó hAodha
Rev Francis Planell

30 Knapton Road,
Dun Laoghaire, Co Dublin A96 XA46
Tel 01-2804353
Rev Daniel Cummings
Rev Thomas McGovern

Cleraun Study Centre,
90 Fosters Avenue, Mount Merrion,
Co Dublin A94 VX73
Tel 01-2881734
Rev Brendan O'Connor
Rev Philip Griffin
Rev Walter Macken

Ely University Centre
10 Hume Street, Dublin D02 VY39
Tel 01-6767420
Rev Gavan Jennings
Rev Thomas Dowd

Diocese of Cork & Ross
Dunmahon Study Centre
Model Farm Road, Cork T12 KHC1
Tel 021-2029112
www.dunmahon.ie
Rev Brian McCarthy

Diocese of Down & Connor
Dunraven
104 Malone Road, Belfast BT9 5HP
Tel 028-90506947
Email dunraven104bt9@gmail.com
Rev Brendan O'Connor

Diocese of Galway
Gort Ard University Residence,
Rockbarton North, Galway H91 KH94
Tel 091-523846
Rev Charles Connolly

Diocese of Limerick
Castleville Study Centre,
Golf Links Road, Castletroy,
Limerick V94 YC95
Tel 061-331223
Rev Brian McCarthy

Diocese of Meath
Lismullin Conference Centre
Navan, Co Meath C15 XW40
Tel 046-9026936
Rev Philip Griffin, Chaplain

RELIGIOUS ORDERS AND CONGREGATIONS

MALE RELIGIOUS

AUGUSTINIANS (OSA)

Irish Province
www.augustinians.ie

Archdiocese of Dublin

**Dublin South Community
St Augustine's**
Taylor's Lane,
Ballyboden, Dublin 16
Tel 01-4241000
Fax 01-4939915

Provincial: Rev John Hennebry
Tel 01-4241030
Fax 01-4932457
Email osaprov@eircom.net
Secretary: Tel 01-4241040
Email
osaprovsec@irishbroadband.net
Prior: Rev Francis Aherne
*Sub-prior & Provincial
Secretary:* Rev Dick Lyng (CC
Ballyboden)

Rev John Byrne
Rev Gabriel Daly
Rev Senan Doran
Rev Patrick Farrell
Rev Michael Fitzgerald
Rev John Hughes (PP
Ballyboden)
Rev Richard Hughes
Rev Giles O'Halloran
Rev Aidan O'Leary
Rev Liam Ryan
Rev David Slater
Rev John Williams

St John's Priory
Thomas Street, Dublin 8
Tel 01-6770393/0415/0601
Fax 01-6713102 (Mission Office)
Fax 01-6770423 (House)

Prior: Rev Padraig A. Daly
Sub-Prior: Rev Niall Coghlan
(PP Meath St)
Bursar: Rev Bernard Twomey

Rev Pat Gayer
Rev Richard Goode
Rev Nicholas Kearney
Rev Michael Mernagh
Rev John Joe O'Connor
Bishop Louis O'Donnell
Rev Kieran O'Mahony
Rev Brian O'Sullivan

Meath Street Parish
St Catherine's Presbytery,
Dublin 8
Tel 01-4543356
Fax 01-4738303

No Resident Community

Rivermount Parish
Parochial House,
5 St Helena's Drive, Dublin 11
Tel 01-8343444/8343722
Fax 01-8642192

Prior: Rev Paddy O'Reilly

Very Rev Seamus Ahearne PP
Rev Paul O'Connor

Archdiocese of Armagh

St Augustine's Priory
Shop Street,
Drogheda, Co Louth
Tel 041-9838409
Fax 041-9831847

*Prior and Master of Pre-
Novices:* Rev Colm O'Mahony
Bursar: Rev Declan Brennan

Rev Lazarus Barkindo
(Hospital Chaplain)
Rev Malachy Loughran

*Archdiocese of Cashel and
Diocese of Emly*

The Abbey
Fethard, Co Tipperary
Tel 052-31273

Prior
Rev Ignatius O'Donovan
Bursar: Rev Gerard Horan

Rev David Fitzgerald
Rev Henry MacNamara
Rev Paul O'Brien

Diocese of Cork & Ross

St Augustine's Priory
Washington Street, Cork
Tel 021-4275398/4270410
Fax 021-4275381

Prior: Rev John Lyng
Bursar: Rev Tom Sexton

Rev Michael Boyle
Rev Martin Crean
Rev Michael Leahy
Rev James Maguire
Rev Tommy McManus
Rev Pat Twohig

Diocese of Ferns

Good Counsel College
New Ross, Co Wexford
Tel 051-421182
Fax 051-421909

Prior
Rev Michael Collender
Bursar
Rev David Crean

Diocese of Galway

St Augustine's Priory
St Augustine's Street,
Galway
Tel 091-562524
www.augustinians.ie/galway

Prior & PP
Rev Desmond Foley
Bursar
Rev Sean MacGearailt

Rev Declan Deasy
Rev Anthony Finn
Rev John Whelan

Diocese of Limerick

St Augustine's Priory
O'Connell Street,
Limerick
Tel 061-415374

Prior
Rev Noel Hession
Bursar & Rector Ecclesiae
Rev Flor O'Callaghan

Rev Michael Danaher
Rev Paul Flynn
Rev David Kelly (Provincial
Archivist)

*Diocese of Waterford &
Lismore*

St Augustine's College
Dungarvan, Co Waterford
Tel 058-41140/41152
Fax 058-41152

No Resident Community

St Augustine's Priory
Dungarvan,
Co Waterford
Tel 058-41136
Fax 058-44534

Prior & Bursar
Rev Tony Egan
Sub-prior
Rev Seamus Humphreys

Rev Michael Brennock
Rev Matthew Cooney
Rev Finbarr Spring

Duckspool House
(Retirement Community)
Abbeyside, Dungarvan,
Co Waterford
Tel 058-23784

Prior
Rev Ben O'Brien
Bursar
Rev Patrick Lennon

Rev Ailbe Brennan
Rev Vincent McCarthy
Rev John O'Connor

The Irish Province of the
Augustinians also has missions
in Ecuador and Nigeria.

*Irish Augustinian Personnel on
Other Assignments*

USA
Rev John Grace

BENEDICTINES (OSB)

*Archdiocese of Cashel and
Diocese of Emly*

Attached to the Benedictine
Congregation of the
Annunciation, Belgium.

Glenstal Abbey
Murroe,
Co Limerick V94 A725
Tel 061-621000 Fax 061-386328
Email monks@glenstal.org

Abbot
Rt Rev Dom Brendan Coffey
Prior
Very Rev Senan Furlong
Sub-Prior
Rev Christopher Dillon

Novice Masters
Rev Columba McCann
Br Pádraig McIntyre

Rev Anselm Barry
Rev Cuthbert Brennan
Rev Martin Browne
Rev Alan Crawford
Rev William Fennelly
Rev Mark Patrick Hederman
Rev Denis Hooper
Br Anselm Hurt
Rev Anthony Keane
Rev Jaroslaw Kurek
Br Cyprian Love
Rev Fintan Lyons
Br Timothy McGrath
Br Oscar McDermott
Rev Luke Macnamara
Rev Lino Moreira
Rev Placid Murray
Rev John O'Callaghan
Br Colmán Ó Clabaigh
Br Emmaus O'Herlihy
Br Cillian Ó Sé
Rev Henry O'Shea
Rev Simon Sleeman
Br Justin Robinson
Rev Philip Tierney

Diocese of Dromore

Attached to the Benedictine
Congregation of St Mary of
Monte Oliveto.

Benedictine Monks
Holy Cross Abbey,
119 Kilbroney Road,
Rostrevor,
Co Down BT34 3BN
Tel 028-41739979
Email benedictinemonks@
btinternet.com
Website
www.benedictinemonks.co.uk

Abbot: Rt Rev Dom Mark-
Ephrem M. Nolan

Rev D. Eric M. Loisel
Rev D. Thierry M. Marteaux
D. Gregory M. Foret
D. Benoît M. Charlet
D. Joshua M. Domenzain Canul
D. David Joseph M. Mayer
D. Laurent M. Salud Abila

Dependent House
Monastery of Christ our
Saviour
Turvey,
Bedfordshire, England

**BENEDICTINE MONKS OF
PERPETUAL ADORATION
OF THE MOST HOLY
SACRAMENT (OSB)**

Diocese of Meath

Silverstream Priory
Stamullen, Co Meath K32 T189
Tel 01-8417142
Email info@cenacleosb.org

Prior: Very Rev Dom Basil
Mary MacCabe

Very Rev Dom Mark Daniel
Kirby
Rev Dom Benedict Andersen
Dom Finnian King
Dom Elijah Carroll
Dom Cassian Aylward
Rev Dom Hildebrand Houser
Dom John Baptist DeCant
Dom Chrysostom Gryniewicz
Dom Thomas Aquinas Borders
Dom Placid McKee
Dom Isaias Kwasniewski
Dom Isaac Conard
Dom Theodore Lee
Dom Aelred Tillotson
Dom David Watters

**BLESSED SACRAMENT
CONGREGATION (SSS)**

Provincial
Rev Peter Dowling
St Columba's Church,
74 Hopehill Road,
Glasgow G20 7HH

Archdiocese of Dublin

Blessed Sacrament Chapel
20 Bachelors Walk,
Dublin D01 NW14
Tel 01-8724597 Fax 01-8724724
Email sssdublin@eircom.net
Web
www.blessedsacramentuki.org

Superior
Rev James Campbell

Rev Renato Esoy
Br Andrew McTeigue
Rev Raphael O'Halloran
Rev Martin Peter Raja

**CAMILLIANS (OSCam)
Order of St Camillus**

Anglo-Irish Province

Archdiocese of Dublin

St Camillus
South Hill Avenue,
Blackrock, Co Dublin
Tel 01-2882873/2833380

Superior: Rev Denis Sandham

Rev Suresh Babu
Rev Jayan Joseph *(Chaplain to
St James' Hospital)*
Rev Tom O'Connor

St Camillus
11 St Vincent Street North,
Dublin 7
Tel 01-8300365 (residence)
Tel 01-8301122 (Mater Hospital)

Superior & Provincial
Rev Stephen Forster
Tel 01-8304635

Rev Bobit Augusthy
Rev Russel Jacob
Rev Prince Mathew *(Chaplain
to Mater Hospital)*
Rev Tomy Paradiyil
Rev John Philip *(Chaplain to
Waterford Hospital)*
Rev Vincent Xavier *(Chaplain
to Mater Hospital)*
4 St Vincent Street North,
Dublin 7

Diocese of Meath

St Camillus
Killucan, Co Westmeath
Tel 044-74196 (nursing centre)
Tel 044-74115 (community)
Fax 044-74309

Superior: Br John O'Brien

Rev Martin Geraghty
Rev Suneesh Mathew
(Chaplain to Mater Hospital)
Rev Frank Monks

CAPUCHINS (OFM Cap)

Province of Ireland

Includes six friaries in Ireland,
plus one *pro tem* house,
Provincial Custodies in South
Africa, Zambia, and South
Korea and the delegation of
Great Britain.

Archdiocese of Dublin

Provincial Office
12 Halston Street,
Dublin D07 Y2T5
Tel 01-8733205 Fax 01-8730294
Email capcurirl@eircom.net

Provincial Minister
Very Rev Seán Kelly
Guardian: Rev Bryan Shortall
*Vicar, Secretary of the
Province:* Rev Paul Murphy

Capuchin Friary
137-142 Church Street,
Dublin D07 HA22
Tel 01-8730599 Fax 01-873025●

Guardian: Rev Kevin Kiernan
Email frklkiernan@gmail.com
Vicar: Rev Severino Pinheiro
da Silva Neto

Br Phlip Tobin
Rev Paul Tapley
Rev Owen O'Sullivan
Rev James Connolly
Rev Peter Rodgers
Rev Christopher Twomey
Rev Richard Henrick PP
Br Anthony Kurian

Capuchin Friary
Station Road,
Raheny, Dublin D05 T9E4
Tel 01-8313886 Fax 01-851149●

Guardian: Rev Seán Donohoe
Email
seandonohoe25@gmail.com
Vicar: Rev Desmond McNoboe

Rev Tom Bennett
Rev Alexius Healy
Rev Eustace McSweeney
Rev Anthony Boran
Rev Pádraig Ó Cuill
Rev Jude McKenna
Br Patrick Mulligan
Rev Michael Duffy
Rev Dan Joe O'Mahony
Br Bernard McAllister
Rev Bill Ryan
Rev Martin Bennett

Dicoese of Tuam

Capuchin Presence
Knock Shrine

Guardian
Br John Wright
Vicar
Rev Maitiú Ó Clerichin

Rev Patrick Flynn
Rev Dermot Lynch
Rev Terance Harrington

Diocese of Cork & Ross

Capuchin Friary
Holy Trinity, Fr Mathew Quay,
Cork T12 PK24
Tel 021-4270827
Fax 021-4270829

Guardian
Br Declan O'Callaghan
Vicar
Rev Eddie Dowley

Rev Kenneth Reynolds
Rev Silvester O'Flynn
Rr Kevin Crowley
Rr John Hickey
Rev Daian Loughrey
Rev Aidan Vaughan
Rev John Manley
Rr Albert Cooney
Rev Tony O'Keeffe
Rr Ignatius Galvin
Rev Jack Twomey
Rev Joe Nagle

t Francis Capuchin Franciscan
ollege
ochestown,
o Cork T12 TK82
el 021-4891417
ax 021-4361254

rincipal: Mrs Marie Ring

iocese of Ossory

apuchin Friary
riary Street,
ilkenny R95 NX60
el 056-7721439
ax 056-7722025

uardian
ev Adrian Curran
icar
r Joseph Gallagher

ev Benignus Buckley
ev Pius Higgins
ev Michael Murphy
ev Leo McAuliffe
ev Mike Burgess
ev Jerzy Stopa

iocese of Raphoe

apuchin Friary
rd Mhuire, Creeslough,
etterkenny,
o Donegal F92 Y23R

uardian
ev Philip Baxter
icar
ev Kieran Shorten

ev Pat Lynch
r Vianney Holmes
ev Flan Lynch
r Alphonsus Ryan
r Charles Stewart
ev Thomas Forde
ev Jeremy Heneghan
r Ade Green

ustody of Zambia

apuchin Franciscans
ost Net Box 147, P/Bag E891,
saka, Zambia
l 00260-211-250969
ax 00260-211-252828
nail capzam@iconnect.zm

Custody of South Africa

Capuchin Franciscans
PO Box 118,
Howard Place 7450,
South Africa
Tel 00272-16370026
Fax 00272-16370014
Email capadmin@iafrica.com

Custody of South Korea

Capuchin Franciscans
Hyochang Won Ro 70 Gil 13,
Yong San-Gu, Seoul,
South Korea 140-896
Tel 0082-2-7015727
Fax 0082-2-7176128
Email
capuchin@capuchin.or.kr

Great Britain

Delegate
Franciscan Friary,
Carlton Drive, Erith,
Kent KA8 1DN, UK

For further details concerning
the Missions contact:

Capuchin Mission Office
138-142 Church Street,
Dublin D07 HA22
Tel 01-8731022/8740478
Email missoffdub@gmail.com

CARMELITES (OCarm)

Irish Province

Archdiocese of Dublin

Provincial Office and
Carmelite Community
Gort Muire, Ballinteer,
Dublin D16 EI67
Tel 01-2984014
Fax 01-2987221

Provincial
Very Rev Michael Troy
Email
provincial@gortmuire.com

Assistant Provincial
Rev David Twohig
Prior & Bursar
Rev Fintan Burke
Sub-Prior
Rev David Twohig

Rev Fintan Burke
Rev Ambrose Costello
Rev Genildo De Querioz
Rev Gerard Galvin

Rev Robert Kelly
Rev Fred Lally
Rev Anthony McKinney
Rev Michael Morrissey
Rev Bernard Murphy
Rev Francis O'Gara
Rev Bernard O'Reilly
Rev Patrick Mullins
Rev Martin Ryan
Rev Michael Troy
Rev David Weakliam

Whitefriar Street Church
56 Aungier Street,
Dublin D02 R598
Tel 01-4758821
Fax 01-4758825
Email whitefriars@eircom.net

Prior
Rev Simon Nolan
Parish Priest
Rev Seán MacGiollarnáth
Bursar
Rev Martin Baxter

Rev Donal Byrne
Rev Christopher Conroy
Rev Patrick Graham
Rev Thomas Higgins
Rev Desmond Kelly
Rev Frank McAleese
Rev Anthony McDonald
Rev Joseph Mothersill
Rev Patrick Smyth

Terenure College
Terenure,
Dublin D6W DK72
Tel 01-4904621
Fax 01-4902403
Email
admin@terenurecollege.ie

Prior/Bursar
Rev Éanna Ó hÓbain
Principal Senior School
Rev Éanna Ó hÓbáin

Rev John Keating
Rev Peter Kehoe
Rev Martin Kilmurray
Rev Daniel O'Callaghan
Rev Martin Parokkaran

Diocese of Cork & Ross

Carmelite Friary
Kinsale,
Co Cork P17 WR88
Tel 021-4772138
Email
kinsale@irishcarmelites.com

Prior: Rev James Eivers
Bursar
Rev Benedict O'Callaghan

Rev Stan Hession
Rev Laurence Lynch
Rev Eoin Moore

Diocese of Kildare & Leighlin

Carmelite Priory
White Abbey,
Co Kildare R51 X827
Tel 045-521391
Fax 045-522318
Email
carmeliteskildare@gmail.com

Prior
Rev Chacko Anthony
Thandiparahbil
Bursar
Rev Rojan Peter Pazhampilly

Rev Yesudas Asariparambil
Abraham

Diocese of Meath

Carmelite Priory
Moate,
Co Westmeath N37 AW34
Tel 090-6481160/6481398
Fax 090-6481879
Email
carmelitemoate@eircom.net

Prior/Bursar
Rev Jaison Kuthanapillil

Rev Brian Mckay
Rev James Murray

CARMELITES (OCD)

Anglo-Irish Province

The Province has five
communities in Ireland and
thirteen overseas including
five in Nigeria.

Provincial
Rev John Grennan
Avila Carmelite Centre,
Bloomfield Avenue,
Morehampton Road,
Dublin 4
Tel 01-6430200
Fax 01-6430281
Email jtgrennan@hotmail.com
Website www.ocd.ie

Allianz (ii)

Archdiocese of Dublin

St Teresa's
Clarendon Street,
Dublin 2
Tel 01-6718466/6718127
Fax 01-6718462

Prior
Very Rev Jim Noonan
Email stteresa@ocd.ie

Rev Michael Brown
Rev Sean Conlon
Rev David Donnellan
Rev Patrick Keenan
Rev Nicholas Madden
Rev Vincent O'Hara
Rev Edmond Smyth

Avila
Bloomfield Avenue,
Morehampton Road,
Dublin 4
Tel 01-6430200
Fax 01-6430281
Email avila@ocd.ie

Prior
Rev Liam Finnerty

Rev Joseph Birmingham
Rev Willie Moran
Br Noel O'Connor
Rev Felix Okolo
Rev Tom Stone

Diocese of Clonfert

The Abbey
Loughrea, Co Galway
Tel 091-841209
Fax 091-842343

Prior
Rev Mícheál MacLaifeartaigh

Rev Patrick Beecher
Rev Christopher Clarke
Rev Cronan Glynn
Rev Ambrose McNamee
Rev Tom Shanahan

Diocese of Derry

St Joseph's Carmelite
Retreat Centre
Termonbacca,
Derry BT48 9XE
Tel 028-71262512
Fax 028-71373589

Prior: Rev Stephen Quinn

Rev Michael McGoldrick
Rev Michael Spain

CISTERCIAN ORDER (OCSO)

The mother house of the
Cistercian Order is the Arch-
abbey of Cîteaux, Côte d'Or,
France.

Archdiocese of Armagh

Mellifont Abbey
Collon, Co Louth
Tel 041-9826103
Fax 041-9826713
Email info@mellifontabbey.ie

Superior
Rt Rev Brendan Freeman
Email
frbrendan@newmelleray.org

Br Brian Berkeley
Rev Michael Burleigh
Br Denis Bernard Cazes
Br Andrew Considine
Rev William Cullinan
Br William Foster
Br Brendan Garry
Br Thomas Maher
Rev Rufus Pound

Archdiocese of Dublin

Bolton Abbey
Moone, Co Kildare
Tel 059-8624102
Mobile 087-9366723
Email
boltonabbeymoone@gmail.com
Website www.boltonabbey.ie

Abbot
Rt Rev Dom Michael Ryan
Prior
Br Anthony Jones
Guestmaster
Br Francis McLean
Novice Director

Rev Eoin de Bhaldraithe

Diocese of Down & Connor

Our Lady of Bethlehem Abbey
11 Ballymena Road,
Portglenone, Ballymena,
Co Antrim BT44 8BL
Tel 028-25821211
Email info@bethabbey.com
www.bethlehemabbey.com

Abbot/Superior
Rt Rev Dom Celsus Kelly

Prior
Rev Martin Dowley
Sub-Prior
Rt Rev Dom Charles Kaweesi

Br Simon Cassidy
Br Robert Folian
Br Michael McCourt
Br Finbar McLoughlin
Rev Aelred Magee
Rev Francis Morgan
Br Vianney O'Donnell
Rev Finnian Owens
Rev Philip Scott

Diocese of Killaloe

Mount Saint Joseph Abbey
Roscrea,
Co Tipperary E53 D6S1
Tel 0505-25600
Fax 0505-25610
Email info@msjroscrea.ie
www.msjroscrea.ie

Superior ad nutum
Dom Malachy Thompson
Email malachy@msjroscrea.ie
Prior
Rev Aodhán McDunphy
Sub-prior
Rev Laurence Walsh

Rev Laurence Walsh
Br Laurence Molloy
Rev Anthony O'Brien (at
Tautra, Norway)
Rev Liam O'Connor
Rev Bavo Samosir
Br Vladimir Tkachenko

Diocese of Waterford & Lismore

Mount Melleray Abbey
Cappoquin,
Co Waterford P51 R8XW
Tel 058-54404 Fax 058-52140
Email info@mtmelleray.ie

Abbot
Rt Rev Dom Richard Purcell
Prior
Rev Patrick Ryan

Br Seamus Corrigan
Br Edmund Costin
Rev Donal Davis
Rev John Dineen
Rt Rev Dom Eamon Fitzgerald
(Abbot General)
Rev Ignatius Hahessy
Rt Rev Augustine McGregor
Rev Denis Luke O'Hanlon

COMBONI MISSIONARIE (MCCJ)

Verona Fathers

Provincial
Rev Alberto Pelucchi
Comboni Missionaries,
London Road, Sunningdale,
Berks SL5 0JY, UK

Archdiocese of Dublin

8 Clontarf Road
Clontarf, Dublin 3
Tel/Fax 01-8330051
Email
combonimission@eircom.net

Superior
Rev Ruben Padilla Rocha

Rev Sean Dempsey
Rev Jose Manuel Casillas
Hernandez

Congregation of the Sacred Hearts of Jesus and Mary (SSCC)

Sacred Hearts Communit

Archdiocese of Dublin

Coudrin House,
27 Northbrook Road,
Dublin 6 D06 W294
Tel 01-6604898
Email
ssccdublin@sacredhearts.ie
Website
www.sacred-hearts.net

Delegation Superior
Very Rev Michael Ruddy
Tel 01-6604898
Secretary
Sheila O'Dowd

Rev Eamon Aylward
Tel 01-6473756
Email eamonmoz@yahoo.cor
Most Rev Brendan Comiskey D
Rev Michael F. Foley
Tel 01-6473759
Email
michaelffoley@gmail.com
Rev Ultan Naughton
Email
ultan.naughton@hotmail.cor

Sacred Heart Presbytery
St John's Drive,
Clondalkin,
Dublin D22 W1W6
Tel 01-4570032

Rev Vincent Fallon
Email renovin@aol.com

Allianz ⑪

Diocese of Clogher

Cootehill
Co Cavan H16 CA22
Tel 049-5552188

Rev Jerry White
Email jerrysscc@gmail.com
Rev Pearse Mullen
Email
pearsepmullen@gmail.com
Rev Kieran Murtha

Rockcorry
Co Monaghan

Rev Jerry White CC
Email jerrysscc@gmail.com

Diocese of Kilmore

Ballonreagh
Maudabawn, Cootehill,
Co Cavan H16 K576

Rev Michael Gilsenan CC
Email gilsenbawn@gmail.com

DIVINE WORD MISSIONARIES (SVD)

Irish & British Province

Each Province of the Society is independent. When members are assigned to work in the missions, they automatically become members of the territory to which they are assigned and are no longer members of the Irish British Province.

Archdiocese of Dublin

2 & 3 Pembroke Road,
Ballsbridge, Dublin 4
Rector: Rev Liam Dunne
Email
pembroke@svdireland.com

Provincial
Rev Timothy Lehane
Email
provincial@svdireland.com

Rev Pat Byrne
Rev Binoy Mathew
Rev John McAteer

133 North Circular Road,
Dublin 7
Tel 01-8386743

Praeses
Rev Anthony O'Riordan

Rev Michael Egan
Rev John Feighery
Rev Alan Geoghegan
Rev Paul St John

Church of St Philip the Apostle,
Mountview, Dublin 15
Tel 01-8249695

Parish Priest
Rev George Adzato

Rev John Owen
Rev Justin Purba

Maynooth
Co Kildare
Tel 01-6286391/2
Fax 01-6289184
Email secretary@svdireland.com

Rector
Rev Finbarr Tracey
Provincial Treasurer
Rev Gerhard Osthues

Rev Gaspar Habara
Rev Gerard McCarthy
Rev George Millar
Rev Pat Moroney
Rev Sean Moynihan
Rev Jim Perry
Rev Garrett Roche
Rev Jega Susai

Diocese of Elphin

Donamon Castle
Roscommon
Tel 090-6662222
Fax 090-6662511
accounts@dwmcards.ie

Rector: Rev George Agger

Rev Tony Coote
Rev Charles Guthrie
Rev Pat Hogan
Rev Michael Joyce
Rev Tom Kearney
Rev Jerry Lanigan
Rev Peter McHugh
Rev Bert Parys
Rev Michael Reddan
Rev Krzysztof Sikora
Rev Vincent Twomey

Elsewhere in Ireland

Carlow Cathedral
Rev Chen Yanbo
Rev Teodor Tomasik
Tramore, Co Waterford
Rev Tadeusz Durajczyk
Rev Yang Yongde

British District

London
8 Teignmouth Road,
London, NW2 4HN
Tel 020-84528430

Praeses: Rev Albert Escoto

Rev John Bettison
Rev Eamonn Donnelly
Rev Krzyskow Krsysztof
Rev Vinsensius Mbu'i
Rev John McCarthy
Rev Martin McPake
Rev Kevin O'Toole
Rev Paul Zhao

Bristol
St Mary-on-the-Quay
Presbytery, 20 Colston Street,
Bristol BS1 5AE
Tel 0117-9264702

Parish Priest: Rev Sanjeeb Xaxa

Rev Joseph Mensah

Isleworth, London
Our Lady of Sorrows &
St Bridget of Sweden,
112 Twickenham Road,
Isleworth TW7 6DL

Parish Priest
Rev Nico Lobo Ratu

Rev Kieran Fitzharris
Rev Clement K. Narcher

DOMINICAN ORDER (OP)
Order of Preachers

Irish Province

Archdiocese of Dublin

Provincial Office
St Mary's,
Tallaght, Dublin D24 X585
Tel 01-4048118
Email provincial@dominicans.ie

Provincial
Very Rev John Harris

Secretary of the Province
Very Rev Joseph Bulman
Email provincialsecretary@
dominicans.ie
Provincial Bursar
Rev David Walker
Email provincialbursar@
dominicans.ie
Children Protection Officer
Ms Mary Tallon
Email safeguardingoffice@
dominicans.ie

Dominican Community
St Mary's Priory
Tallaght, Dublin 24
Tel 01-4048100
Parish 01-4048188
Email
parish@stmarys-tallaght.ie
Retreat House
Tel 01-4048123/8191
Email
dominicanretreats@gmail.com

Prior
Very Rev Donal Roche Adm

Rev Wilfrid Harrington
Rev Patrick Brennan
Rev Vincent Travers
Rev Philip Gleeson
Rev Donagh O'Shea
Rev Thomas O'Flynn
Rev Donal Sweeney
Rev Philip McShane
Br Martin Cogan
Rev Eamonn Moran
Rev Gerard Norton
Rev Séamus Touhy
Rev Michael Dunleavy
Rev Robert Regula CC
Rev Atanasio Flores
Rev Albert Leonard
Rev Leo Donavan
Rev Columba Mary Toman
Rev Bernard Treacy

St Saviour's
Upper Dorset Street,
Dublin 1
Tel 01-8897610 Fax 01-8734003
Email stsaviours@eircom.net

Prior
Very Rev Joseph Dineen PP

Rev Liam Walsh
Rev Diarmuid Clifford
Rev Noel Molloy
Rev Martin Boyle
Rev Stephen Hutchinson
Rev Bernard McCay-Morrissey
Rev Terence Crotty
Rev Joseph O'Brien
Rev Alan O'Sullivan
Rev John H. Walsh
Rev Patryk Zaczrzewski
Rev Conor McDonough
Br Ruaidhi Crieve
Br Darran McGlinchey
Br Christopher Gault
Br Blazej Bialek
Br Bruno Kelleher
Br Mark Murphy
Br Nathan Peer
Br Sean Blackwell
Br Desmond Conway
Br Ivan Maher
Br Sean Hurley
Br Joseph McGinty
Br Michael Donohue
Rev Krzysztof Kupczakiewicz

St Aengus's
Tymon North, Balrothery,
Tallaght, Dublin 24
Tel 01-4513757 Fax 01-4624038

Superior
Very Rev Benedict Moran PP
Email
ben.moran25@gmail.com

Rev Pat Lucey CC

St Dominic's
St Dominic's Road,
Tallaght, Dublin 24
Tel 01-4510620 Fax 01-4623223

Superior
Very Rev Laurence Collins Adm
Email collinsl11@eircom.net

Rev Timothy Mulcahy CC
Rev Richard Walsh

Archdiocese of Armagh

St Malachy's
Dundalk, Co Louth
Tel 042-9334179/9333714
Fax 042-9329751

Superior: Rev David Barrins

Rev Bede McGregor
Rev Ronan Cusack
Rev Anthony McMullan
Rev Patrick Desmond

Diocese of Cork & Ross

St Mary's
Pope Quay, Cork
Tel 021-4502267

Prior: Very Rev Maurice Colgan

Rev Finian Lynch
Rev Benedict Hegarty
Br Thomas Casey
Rev Brendan Clifford
Rev Pawel Zybura
Rev Philip Mulryne
Rev Eoin Casey
Rev Gerard Dunne
Rev Brian McKevitt

Diocese of Dromore

St Catherine's
Newry, Co Down BT35 8BN
Tel 028-30262178

Prior: Very Rev David Tohill

Rev Stephen Tumilty
Rev Noel McKeown
Rev Adrian Farrelly
Rev Cesare Decio
Rev Joseph Ralph
Rev Donal Mehigan

Diocese of Elphin

Holy Cross
Sligo, Co Sligo
Tel 071-9142700
Fax 071-9146533

Superior
Rev Augustine Champion
Email sligofriary@eircom.net

Rev Anthony Morris
Rev Luuk Jansen

Diocese of Galway

St Mary's
The Claddagh, Co Galway
Tel 091-582884

Prior
Very Rev Matthew Farrell PP

Rev Denis Murphy
Rev Ambrose O'Farrell
Rev Jordan O'Brien
Rev Thomas McCarthy
Br James Ryan
Rev Gregory Mazur
Rev Frank Downes

Diocese of Kerry

Holy Cross
Tralee, Co Kerry
Tel 066-7121135

Superior: Rev Gregory Carroll
Email
domstralee@gmail.com

Rev James Duggan
Rev John O'Rourke
Rev Declan Corish
Rev David McGovern

Diocese of Kildare & Leighlin

Dominican College Newbridge
Droichead Nua, Co Kildare
Tel 045-487200
Email newbridgecommunity
@dominicans.ie
Secondary School

Prior: Very Rev Joseph Bulman

Rev Archie Byrne
Rev Edmund Murphy
Rev Benedict MacKenna
Rev Michael Commane
Rev Laurence Kelly
Rev Carlyle Fortune
Rev Damian Polly
Rev Anthony Kavanagh

Diocese of Ossory

Black Abbey
Kilkenny, Co Kilkenny
Tel 056-7721279

Superior:
Rev Thomas Monahan
Email
blackabbey@dominicans.ie

Rev Thomas Jordan
Rev Joseph Kavanagh
Rev Brian Doyle
Rev Stephen Cummins

Rome

Convent of SS Xystus and Clement
Collegio San Clemente,
Via Labicana 95,
00184 Roma,
Italy
Tel 0039-06-7740021

Prior: Very Rev Paul Lawlor

Rev Paul Murray
Rev Michael Carragher
Rev Vivian Boland
Rev Fergus Ryan
Rev Kevin O'Reilly
Rev Ronan Connolly
Rev Matthew Martinez
Rev Kellan Scott
Rev Jesse Maingot

Tehran

St Abraham's Church
PO Box 14185-868
Jamalzadeh Shomali 252,
Tehran, Iran
Tel 98-21-66926535

PP Vacant

Trinidad

St Finbar's
Morne Coco Road,
Four Roads, Diego Martin,
Republic of Trinidad and
Tobago, West Indies
Tel 001-868-6328119

Superior: Rev Thomas Lawson

Very Rev Urban Hudlin PP
Rev Alan Mohammed
Rev Dwight Black

Holy Cross
Arina, Republic of Trinidad
and Tobago, West Indies
Tel 001-868-6673208

Superior
Rev Ferdinand Warner

Rev Matthew Ahye

FRANCISCAN ORDER (OFM)

Province of Ireland

Provincial Office,
Franciscan Friary,
4 Merchant's Quay,
Dublin D08 XY19
Tel 01-6742500
Fax 01-6742549
Email info@franciscans.ie

Provincial
Rev Aidan McGrath
Email
provincial@franciscans.ie

Vicar Provincial and Secretary of the Province
Rev Joseph Condren
4 Merchants' Quay,
Dublin D08 XY19
Email sec.prov@franciscans.ie

Archdiocese of Dublin

Adam & Eve's
4 Merchants' Quay,
Dublin D08 XY19
Tel 01-6771128
Fax 01-6771000

Guardian
Br Niall O'Connell
Vicar
Rev Joseph Condren

Rev Brian Allen
Br Laurence Brady
Rev Damien Casey
Rev Richard Kelly
Rev Aidan McGrath
Br Seán Murphy
Rev Ulic Troy

Franciscan House of Studies
Dún Mhuire, Seafield Road,
Killiney, Co Dublin
Tel 01-2826760
Fax 01-2826993
Email franciscans.killiney@
franciscans.ie

Guardian
Br Stephen O'Kane
Vicar
Rev Micheál Mac Craith

ev Michael Bailey
r Ronald Bennett
ev Patrick Conlan
ev Francis Cotter
ev John Dalton
ev Ignatius Fennessy
ev John Harty
ev Hugh O'Donnell
ev Maelisa Ó Huallacháin
ev Declan Timmons
r Bonaventure Ward

iocese of Cork & Ross

anciscan Friary
berty Street, Cork
l 021-4275481
x 021-4271841

uardian
ev Patrick Younge
car
ev Hilary Steblecki

 Denis Aherne
ev Louis Brennan
ev Colin Garvey
ev Tony Hardiman
ev Jim Hasson
ev Michael Holland
ev Larry Mulligan
ev Peter O'Grady
ev Oscar O'Leary
ev Jude Ronayne-Forde
ev Brendan Scully
 Nicholas Shanahan

ocese of Galway

e Abbey
Francis Street, Galway
 091-562518
x 091-565663
ail
lwayabbey@franciscans.ie

ardian
v David Collins
car
v Frank McGrath

v Liam Kelly
ev Ralph Lawless
v Adrian Peelo
v Jacopo Pozzerle
 Ronan Sharpley

ocese of Kerry

anciscan Friary
larney, Co Kerry
 064-6631334/6631066
x 064-6637510
ail friary@eircom.net

ardian
 Pat Lynch
car
v Antony Jukes

Rev PJ Brady
Rev Walter Gallahue
Rev William Hoyne
Rev Caoimhín Ó Laoide

Diocese of Killaloe

Franciscan Friary
Ennis, Co Clare
Tel 065-6828751
Fax 065-6822008
Email
ennis.friary@franciscans.ie

Guardian
Rev Brendan McGrath
Vicar
Rev Joseph MacMahon

Rev Seamus Donohoe
Br Philip Lane
Rev Liam McCarthy
Rev Paschal McDonnell
Rev Cletus Noone
Br Elzear O'Brien
Rev Ailbe Ó Murchú

Diocese of Meath

Franciscan Abbey
Multyfarnham,
Co Westmeath
Tel 044-9371114/9371137
Fax 044-9371387
Email
theabbeymulty@gmail.com

Provincial Delegate
Rev Kieran Cronin

Rev Seán Cassin
Rev John Kealy
Br Salvador Kenny
Rev Lomán Mac Aodha
Rev John O'Brien
Rev Diarmaid Ó Riain
Rev Malcolm Timothy
Rev Joseph Walsh

Diocese of Raphoe

Franciscan Friary
Rossnowlagh, Co Donegal
Tel 071-9851342
Fax 071-9852206
Email info.rossnowlagh@
franciscans.ie

Guardian
Rev Eugent Barrett
Vicar: Rev Vincent Finnegan

Rev Vincent Gallogley
Rev Feargus McEveney
Rev Pius McLaughlin
Rev Eamon O'Driscoll

Other Individual Addresses

Rev Jim Hynes
Chaussee de Vleurgat 189
B10,
1050 Brussels, Belgium

*Franciscan Communities
Abroad*

St Anthony's Parish
(English-Speaking Chaplaincy)
23/25 Oudstrijderslaan,
1950 Kraainem, Belgium
Tel 0032-2-7201970
Fax 0032-2-7255810
Email
stanthonyparish@telnet.be

Rev Michael Nicholas
*(Provincial Delegate/Parish
Priest)*
Rev Patrick Power *(Associate
Pastor)*

Collegio S. Isidoro
Via degli Artisti 41,
00187 Roma, Italy
Tel 0039-06-4885359
Fax 0039-06-4884459
Email
collegio_s_isidoro@libero.it

Guardian
Rev Hugh McKenna

Rev Padraig Breheny
Br Ian Cunningham
Br Philip McMahon

**Franciscan Custody in
Zimbabwe**
Custos: Rev Naison Manjovha

CONVENTUAL
FRANCISCANS (OFMConv)

Provincial Custodial Office
St Patrick's Friary
26 Cornwall Road, Waterloo,
London SE1 8TW, England
Tel +44-2079288897

Provincial Custos
Very Rev Ciprian Budau

Archdiocese of Dublin

**Friary of the Visitation of the
BVM**
Fairview Strand, Dublin 3
Tel 01-8376000 (office)
Tel 01-4825821 (priest)

Rev Maximilian McKeown PP
Rev Joseph Connick CC
Rev Aidan Walsh CC *(Guardian)*
Rev Marius Tomulesei
Br Joseph Fenton

Diocese of Ferns

The Friary
St Francis Street, Wexford
Tel 053-9122758

Rev Aquino Maliakkal
(Guardian)
Rev Robert Cojoc
Rev Kazimierz Trzcinski
Br Solanus Mary

FRANCISCAN FRIARS OF
THE RENEWAL (CFR)

Community of the Franciscan
Friars of Renewal
Community Servant
Rev John-Paul Ouellette
Our Lady of the Angels,
427 East 155th Street,
Bronx, NY 10455
Tel 001-718-4028255

Vocation Contact
Br Angelo Lefever
St Pio Friary,
Sedgefield Terrace, Westgate,
Bradford BD1 2RU, UK
Tel 01274-721989
Fax 01274-740038
Email
cfrfriar@cfrfranciscan.co.uk

Diocese of Derry

St Columba Friary
Fairview Road,
Derry BT48 8NU
Tel 028-71419980
Fax 028-71417652
Email
derryfranciscans@gmail.com

Local Servant (Superior)
Rev Francesco Gavazzi

Rev Isaac Spinharney
Rev Thomas Cacciola
Br Benedict Joseph Deiarmi
Rev Charles-Benoit Reche

Diocese of Limerick

St Patrick Friary
64 Delmege Park,
Moyross, Limerick V94 859Y
Tel 061-458071
Fax 061-457626
Email
limerickfranciscans@gmail.com

Local Servant (Superior)
Rev Joseph Mary Deane

Rev Oisin Martin
Rev Gabriel Joseph Kyte
Br Seraphim Roycourt
Rev Bernardino Maria Soukup

HOLY SPIRIT CONGREGATION (CSSp)

Province of Ireland

Archdiocese of Dublin

Holy Spirit Provincialate
Temple Park, Richmond
Avenue South,
Dublin D06 AW02
Tel 01-4975127/4977230
Fax 01-4975399
Website www.spiritan.ie

Provincial Leadership Team
Rev Martin Kelly *(Provincial)*
Rev Peter Conaty
Rev Patrick Moran
Rev Colm Reidy
Rev David Conway *(Provincial Bursar)*
Rev Michael Kilkenny
(Provincial Secretary)

Rev Brendan Carr *(in residence)*
Rev Erasmus Manwa (c/o Holy
Spirit Provincialate)

Communications Manager
Mr Peter O'Mahony
Email communications@
spiritanplt.ie

Safeguarding Office
Mr Liam Lally *(Safeguarding
Coordinator/Designated
liaison person)*
Tel 087-6709461
Email liam.lally@spiritanplt.ie

Spiritan Education Trust
Kimmage Manor, Dublin 12
Tel 01-4997610
www.spiritaneducation.ie
Mr Patrick Kitterick *(Chair)*

Heritage and Archives Centre
Kimmage Manor,
Dublin 12
Manager
Rev Brendan Cogavin
Email heritage@spiritan.ie

Holy Spirit Missionary College
Kimmage Manor,
Whitehall Road,
Dublin D12 P5YP
Tel 01-4064300
Email
kimmagereception@spiritan.ie

Community Leader
Rev Eddie O'Farrell

Rev Desmond Arigho
Rev Joseph Beere
Rev Michael Begley
Rev William Bradley
Rev John Brown
Rev Vincent Browne
Br Albert Buckley
Rev Tony Byrne

Rev James Byrnes
Rev Patrick Carroll
Rev Michael Casey
Rev Brendan Cogavin
Rev David Conway
Rev Brian Cronin
Rev Patrick Cully
Rev Roderick Curran
Rev Hugh de Blacam
Rev Seán de Léis
Rev Patrick Doody
Rev Dermot Doran
Rev Patrick Doran
Rev James Duncan
Most Rev Robert Ellison
Rev John Flavin
Rev Michael Fillie
Rev John Flavin
Rev Michael Foody
Rev Denis Gavin
Rev Reginald Gillooly
Rev Brian Gogan
Rev Ronan Grimshaw
Rev Brendan Hally
Rev Austin Healy
Rev James Heneghan
Rev Gregory Iwuozor
Rev Michael Kane
Rev Martin Keane
Rev Paschal Kearney
Rev Daithí Kenneally
Rev John Laizer
Rev Owen Lambert
Rev Patrick Leonard
Rev Anthony Little
Rev Jude Lynch
Rev Naos Mac Cumhaill
Rev John Mahon
Rev Liam Martin
Rev Vincent McDevitt
Rev Martin McDonagh
Rev Peter J. McEntire
Rev Patrick McGlynn
Rev Brian McLaughlin
Rev Michael McMahon
Rev Walter McNamara
Rev Michael Moore
Rev Noel Moynihan
Rev Brian Murtagh
Rev John O'Brien
Rev James O'Connell
Rev Vincent O'Grady
Rev Michael O'Looney
Rev Noel O'Meara
Rev Sean O'Shaughnessy
Rev Joseph Poole
Rev Thomas Raftery
Rev Noel Redmond
Rev Desmond Reid
Rev Colm Reidy
Rev Patrick Roe
Rev Patrick J. Ryan
Rev Patrick M. Ryen
Rev Larry Shine
Rev Maurice Shortall
Rev Terence Smith
Rev Jim Stapleton
Br Conleth Tyrrell
Rev Paul Walsh
Rev Tom Whelan

Church of the Holy Spirit
Kimmage,
Dublin 12
Tel 01-4064377
www.kimmagemanorparish.com

Church of the Holy Spirit
Greenhills,
Dublin 12
Tel 01-4504040
www.holyspiritparishgreenhills.ie
Team Leader
Rev Michael Kilkenny

Rev Isaac Antwi-Boasiako CC
Rev John Mahon

Blackrock College
Blackrock, Co Dublin
Tel 01-2888681
Fax 01-2834267
www.blackrockcollege.com
Email
info@blackrockcollege.com

Community Leader
Rev Cormac Ó Brolcháin
Principal: Alan MacGinty

Rev Patrick Dundon
Rev Myles Healy
Rev Liam Kehoe
Rev Denis Kennedy
Rev John Kevin
Rev Thomas McDonald
Rev Tom Nash
Rev Richard Quinn

Willow Park
Tel 01-2881651
Fax 01-2783353
Email
admin@willowparkschool.ie

Principal Senior School
Mr Alan Rogan
Principal Junior School
Mr James Docherty

St Mary's College
Rathmines, Dublin 6
Community Tel 01-4995760
Fax 01-4972621
www.stmarys.ie
Junior School Tel 01-4995721
Email junsec@stmarys.ie
Senior School Tel 01-4995700
Fax 01-4972574
Email sensec@stmarys.ie

Community Leader
Rev Patrick Moran
Principal Secondary School
Mr Denis Murphy
Principal Junior School
Ms Judith Keane

Rev Martin Andama *(Studies)*
Rev Augustine Bangalie
Br Ignatius Curry
Rev Richard Olin
Wilfred Otubo *(Student)*

St Michael's College
Ailesbury Road,
Dublin 4
Tel 01-2189400
www.stmc.com
Email admin@stmc.ie

Principal: Mr Tim Kelleher
Principal Junior School
Ms Lorna Heslin

Duquesne University
Duquesne in Dublin,
St Michael's College,
1 Ailesbury Road,
Ballsbridge, Dublin 4
Tel/Fax 01-2080940
www.duq.edu/ireland
Resident Director:
Ms Nora McBurney
Email
nora.mcburney@gmail.com

Spiritan House
**Spiritan Asylum Services
Initiative (SPIRASI)**
213 North Circular Road,
Dublin 7
Tel 01-8389664
Fax 01-8823547
www.spirasi.ie
Mr Rory Halpin *(Executive
Director, SPIRASI)*
Commmunity Leader
Rev Edward Flynn

Rev Edward Flynn
Br Michael Liston
Rev Samson Mann
Br Liam Sheridan

Templeogue College
Templeville Road,
Dublin 6W
Tel 01-4905788
www.templeoguecollege.ie
Email
info@templeoguecollege.ie

Principal: Ms Niamh Quinn

Church of the Transfiguratic
Presbytery, Bawnogue,
Clondalkin, Dublin 22
Tel 01-4519810
www.facebook.com/
bawnogueparishclondalkin

arish of St Ronan's
eansrath, Clondalkin,
ublin 22
l 01-4570380
mail stronansdeansrath@
otmail.com

am Leader
ev Brian Starken

ev Patrick Coughlan
ev Edvaldo Rodrigues da Silva

rchdiocese of Cashel and
ocese of Emly

ockwell College
ashel, Co Tipperary
l 062-61444 Fax 062-61661
ww.rockwell-college.ie
nail info@rockwellcollege.ie

condary Residential and
ay School

incipal: Ms Audrey O'Byrne

 Gerard Cummins
ev Patrick Downes
ev Brendan Duggan
ev Bernard M. Frawley
ev Gerard Griffin
ev Thomas Hogan
ev William Kingston
ev Matthew Knight
ev Patrick McGeever
ev John Meade
ev Noel Murphy

ocese of Meath

iritan Missionaries
dbraccan, Navan,
 Meath C15 T884
l 046-9021441

ommunity Leader
ev Peter Conaty

ev Niall Greene
ev Jeremiah Kirwin
wis Kapchanga *(Student)*
mund Chipulu *(Student)*

JESUITS (SJ)
SOCIETY OF JESUS

sh Province

rchdiocese of Dublin

sh Jesuit Provincialate
illtown Park,
illtown Road, Dublin 6
l 01-4987333
x 01-4987334
nail curia@jesuit.ie

ovincial
ev Leonard Moloney
ssistant Provincial
ev Shane Daly

Jesuit Centre for Faith and Justice
54/57 Upper Gardiner Street,
Dublin 1
Tel 01-8556814
Email info@jcfj.ie
www.jcfj.ie
Director: Mr Kevin Hargaden

Jesuit Communication Centre
Irish Jesuit Provincialate,
Milltown Park,
Milltown Road, Dublin 6
Tel 01-4987347/4987348
Director: Ms Pat Coyle
Email coylep@jesuit.ie
Irish Jesuit News
amdg@jesuit.ie
Sacred Space
Website www.sacredspace.ie

Jesuit Curia Community
Loyola House,
Milltown Park,
Milltown Road, Dublin 6
Tel 01-2180276
Email loyola@jesuit.ie

Superior: Rev Terry Howard

Rev Shane Daly
Rev Leonard Moloney
Rev Leon Ó Giolláin
Rev Peter Sexton

Applications for *retreats* to
Rev Ashley Evans
Manresa House, Dollymount,
Dublin 3
Tel 01-8331352
or online at www.manresa.ie

Enquiries in respect of *foreign missions* to Rev Director, Irish Jesuits International,
20 Upper Gardiner Street,
Dublin 1
Tel 01-8366509
Fax 01-8366510
Email info@iji.ie
Website www.iji.ie

St Francis Xavier's
Upper Gardiner Street,
Dublin 1
Tel 01-8363411 Fax 01-8555624
Email sfxcommunity@jesuit.ie
Parish church and residence

Superior
Rev Richard O'Dwyer
Vice-Superior
Rev Dermot Mansfield
Parish Priest
Very Rev Niall S. Leahy PP

Rev Patrick Carberry
Rev Brendan Comerford
Br Eamonn Davis

Rev Paul Farquharson
Rev Edmond Grace
Rev Timothy Healy
Rev Micheál MacGréil
Rev Krzysztof Madel
Rev Caoimhin O'Ruairc
Rev Brendan Staunton
Eamon Walls *(Scholastic)*

Residing Elsewhere
Rev Brian Lennon
Rev Peter McVerry
Rev Kevin O'Higgins
Rev Fergus O'Keefe
Rev James Smyth

Belvedere College SJ
Great Denmark Street, Dublin 1
Jesuits reside in SFX Gardiner Street

Secondary day school
Tel 01-8586600 (College)
Fax 01-8744374
Rector: Rev Patrick Greene
Headmaster: Mr Gerard Foley

Gardiner Street Primary School,
Belvedere Court, Dublin 1
Tel 01-8722894
Principal: Ms Eileen O'Doherty

St Ignatius House of Writers
35 Lower Leeson Street
Dublin 2
Tel 01-6761248 Fax 01-7758598
Residence

Superior: Rev Jim Culliton
Vice-Superior
Rev Michael Kirwan (Bri)

Rev Juan Diego Galaz Carvajal
Rev Nemo Castelli (Chl)
Rev Emmanuel Malekani
Chisanga (Zam)
Rev David Coughlan
Rev Patrick Davis
Rev Michael O. Gallagher
Rev Brian Grogan
Rev John Looby
Rev Donal Neary
Rev Myles O'Reilly
Rev Michael O'Sullivan
Rev Elil Rajendram
Rev Arunmozhi Ramesh (Del)
Theodar Auram *(Scholastic)*

Residing Elsewhere
Rev Ronan Geary
Br Gerard Marks

Sacred Heart Messenger – a Jesuit Publication
37 Lower Leeson Street,
Dublin 2
Tel 01-6767491
Editor: Rev Donal Neary
Commissioning Editor
Rev Paddy Carberry
Manager: Ms Cecilia West
Email manager@messenger.ie
Website www.messenger.ie

Manresa House
426 Clontarf Road,
Dollymount, Dublin 3
Tel 01-8331352
Retreat House

Rector: Rev William Reynolds
Director of Retreat House
Rev Ashley Evans

Rev Michael Drennan
Rev Patrick Greene
Rev Peter Hannan

Milltown Park
Milltown Road,
Dublin D06 V9K7
Tel 01-2698411/2180230
Email milltown@jesuit.ie

Rector
Rev Tom Casey
Vice-Rector
Rev Bruce Bradley

Br John Adams
Rev Noel Barber
Rev Fergal Brennan
Rev William Callanan
Rev Brendan Duddy
Br George Fallon
Rev John K. Guiney
Rev Niall Leahy
Rev William Mathews
Rev Thomas Morrissey
Rev Laurence Murphy
Rev Brian O'Leary
Rev Frank Sammon
Rev Patrick Sheary

Residing Elsewhere
Rev John Dooley
Rev Finbarr Lynch
Rev Henry Grant
Rev Conor Harper
Br James McCabe
Rev Alan Mowbray

Administrator
Ms Barbara Dempsey
Tel 01-2180243

Gonzaga College SJ
Sandford Road, Dublin 6
Tel 01-4972943 (community)
Tel 01-4972931 (college)
Fax 01-4967769
Email
(Community) gonzaga@jesuit.ie
(College) office@gonzaga.ie

Rector: Rev John O'Keeffe
Headmaster
Mr Damon McCaul

Rev John Callanan
Rev Edward O'Donnell
Rev Fergus O'Donoghue

Residing Elsewhere
Rev Desmond O'Grady
Rev Colin Warrack

25 Croftwood Park
Cherry Orchard, Dublin 10
Tel 01-6267413

Rev Gerard O'Hanlon
Rev William Toner

Archdiocese of Armagh

Iona
211 Churchill Park
Portadown, BT62 1EU
Tel 028-38330366
Fax 028-38338334
Email iona@jesuit.ie

Superior
Rev Brendan MacPartlin
Rev Prionsias Mac Brádaigh

Diocese of Down & Connor

Peter Faber House
28 Brookvale Avenue
Belfast BT14 6BW
Tel 028-90757615
Fax 028-90747615
Email
peter_faber@lineone.net

Superior: Rev Tom Layden

Rev Gerry Clarke
Rev Piaras Jackson
Rev Brendan McManus

Diocese of Galway

St Ignatius Community & Church
27 Raleigh Row, Galway
Tel 091-523707
Email galway@jesuit.ie

Rector: Rev Dermot O'Connor

Rev Martin Curry
Rev Sunny Jacob (JAM)

Rev Liam O'Connell
Rev Enda O'Callaghan
Rev Ciaran Quirke
Rev Patrick Tyrrell

Residing Elsewhere
Rev Paul Brassil *(Zambia)*

Coláiste Iognáid SJ
24 Sea Road, Galway
College Tel 091-501550
Fax 091-501551
Email
admin@colaisteiognaid.ie

Secondary School Principal
Mr David O'Sullivan
Scoil Iognaid (National School)
Principal
Ms Laoise Breathnach
Tel 091-584491

Diocese of Kildare & Leighlin

Clongowes Wood College SJ
Clane, Co Kildare W91 DN40
Tel 045-868663/868202
Fax 045-861042
Email *(College)*
reception@clongowes.net
(Community)
reception@clongowes.net
Secondary Boarding School

Rector
Rev Michael Sheil
Headmaster: Mr Chris Lumb
Email hm@clongowes.net
Vice-Rector
Rev Bernard McGuckian
Minister: Br Tom Phelan
Sub-Minister
Br Charles Connor

Rev Kevin Casey

Residing Elsewhere
Rev Dermot Murray

Diocese of Limerick

Crescent College Comprehensive SJ
Dooradoyle, Limerick
(Community)
Tel 061-229655 Fax 061-229013
Email jhayessj@eircom.net
(College)
Email info@crescentsj.com
Comprehensive Day School for Boys and Girls

Superior: Rev Joseph Hayes
Minister: Rev James Maher
Principal: Mr Diarmuid Mullins

Rev Brendan Carmody
Rev Declan Murray

Jesuits temporarily outside Ireland

Correspondence to
Irish Jesuit Provincialate
Milltown Park,
Milltown Road, Dublin 6
Tel 01-4987333
Email curia@jesuit.ie

Rev James Corkery
Rev John Dardis
Rev Cathal Doherty
Rev Brian Mac Cuarta
Rev Michael McGuckian
Rev James Murphy
Rev Anthony O'Riordan
Rev Patrick Riordan
Rev Gerard Whelan

Diocese of Raphoe

Most Rev Alan McGuckian
Bishop of Raphoe

LEGIONARIES OF CHRIST (LC)

Archdiocese of Dublin

Community
Leopardstown Road,
Foxrock, Dublin 18
Tel 01-2955902
Email ireland@legionaries.org

Superior: Rev Joseph Fazio
Vocations Director
Rev Timothy Moran
Email tmoran@legionaries.org
Regnum Christi
Rev Aaron Vinduska
Email
avinduska@legionaries.org
Community Secretary
Rev Timothy Moran
Email tmoran@legionaries.org

Creidim Centre
Leopardstown Road,
Dublin D18 FF64
Tel 01-2955902
Email
faithandfamilycentre@arcol.org
School Retreats
Email team@clonlost.ie
School retreats, Communion and Confirmation retreats, Children and Adult Catechesis Programmes, Marriage Enrichment days, Spiritual retreats, Courses on the Faith, Spiritual Direction

Director: Rev Aaron Vinduska
Email
avinduska@legionaries.org

Dublin Oak Academy
Kilcroney, Bray, Co Wicklow
Tel 01-2863290
Fax 01-2865315
Email secretary@
dublinoakacademy.com

Director: Rev Oscar Sanchez
Chaplain: Rev Joseph Fazio

Woodlands Academy
Wingfield House, Bray
Co Wicklow
Tel 01-2866323
Fax 01-2864918

Chaplain
Rev Vincent McMahon

MARIANISTS (SM)
Society of Mary

Provincial Headquarters
4425 West Pine Boulevard,
St Louis, MO 63108-2301, US
Tel 314-533-1207

Provincial
Rev Oscar Vasquez

Archdiocese of Dublin

Marianist Community
13 Coundon Court, Killiney,
Co Dublin A96 K0T9
Tel 01-2858301
Residence for Religious

Director: Br Gerard McAuley
Email
gerardmcauley001@gmail.co

Rev Michael Reaume
Br Fred Rech
Br James Contadino

St Laurence College
Loughlinstown, Dublin 18
Tel 01-2826930
Coeducational Secondary Da
School

Principal: Mr Shane Fitzgeral

MARIST FATHERS (SM)
Society of Mary

Archdiocese of Dublin

Marist Fathers Chanel
Finance & Administrative
Office, Coolock Village,
Dublin D05 KU62
Tel 01-8505022/086-2597905

Administrator
Rev Declan Marmion
Email
dmarmion50@gmail.com

Allianz ⑪

: Brendan's Parish
polock Village, Dublin 5
l 01-8484799

rish Priest
ev Edwin McCallion PP

ev Frank Corry (Parish
haplain)
ev John Harrington CC
ev Paddy Stanley CC

anel Community
polock, Dublin 5
l 01-8477133

perior
ev Edwin McCallion PP

ev Tom Dooley
ev Edmund Duffy
ev Joe Rooney,
azareth House,
alahide Road, Dublin 9
rchbishop Adrian Smith,
azareth House,
alahide Road, Dublin 9
ev Ray Staunton

anel College
polock, Dublin 5
l 01-8480655/8480896

eadmaster: Mr Dara Gill

Teresa's
onore Avenue, Dublin 8
l 01-4542425/4531613

arish Priest
ev David Corrigan PP
perior
ev John O'Gara
ev John Hannan (Parish
aaplain)

atholic University School
Lower Leeson Street,
ublin 2
l 01-6762586

eadmaster
r Clive Martin

rchdiocese of Armagh

rdon
arist Fathers,
Mary's Road,
indalk, Co Louth
l 042-9334019

perior
ev James O'Connell

ev Bernard (Barney) King
ev Michael Maher
ev Sean McArdle

St Mary's College
Dundalk, Co Louth
Tel 042-9339984

Principal: Mr Alan Craven

Marist Fathers elsewhere in Ireland

Dublin
Rev Kieran Butler
Little Sisters of the Poor,
Sybill Hill Road, Raheny
Rev P. G. Byrne
Little Sisters of the Poor,
Sybill Hill Road, Raheny

Marist Fathers outside Ireland

Rev Aidan Carvill, Australia
Rev Larry Duffy, Italy
Rev Patrick Muckian,
Philippines
Rev Paddy O'Hare, Italy
Rev Martin McAnaney,
London
Rev James McElroy, France
Rev Seamus McMahon,
Australia
Rev Cormac McNamara, Spain
Rev Rory Mulligan, Norway
Rev Jim Ross, Fiji
Rev Paul Walsh
Communaté Mariste
22 Rue Victor Clappier,
83000 Toulon, France

MILL HILL MISSIONARIES (MHM)

Archdiocese of Dublin

St Joseph's House
50 Orwell Park,
Rathgar,
Dublin D06 C535
Tel 01-4127700
Email josephmhm@eircom.net

Regional Superior
Rev Philip O'Halloran
Tel 01-4127773/4127735/
089-4385320
Email
millhillregional.irl@gmail.com

Rector
Rev Philip O'Halloran
Vice Rector
Rev Patrick Molloy
Bursar
Rev Maurice McGill
Email millhill@iol.ie

Rev John Ambrose
Rev Matt Carpenter
Rev Tom Connors
Rev Donal Harney
Rev Maurice McGill
(Organising Secretary)
Email
organisingmhm@gmail.com
Rev Sean O'Brien
Rev Jim O'Connell
(Editor, St Joseph's Advocate)
Email jimocmhm@eircom.net
Rev John Nevin
Rev Philip Shube Bawe
Rev Patrick O'Connell
Rev Matthew Grier
Rev Tom Keane
Rev Anthony Murphy
Rev Patrick Molloy
Rev Desmond McGillicuddy
Rev Damien Afuti Fuh
Rev Philip Odhiambo Obaso
Rev Hugh O'Donnell

Archdiocese of Tuam

St James Apartments
Knock Shrine,
Knock, Co Mayo

Rev Denis Hartnett
Rev Gerald Doyle

Elsewhere in Ireland

Rev Tom McGrath, Diocese of
Killaloe
Rev Kevin Reynolds, Diocese
of Elphin
Care of St Joseph's House:
Rev Christopher O'Connor
Rev Kevin O'Rourke
Rev Thomas Sinnott
Rev James A. Boyle
Rev Patrick Ryan
Rev Daniel O'Connor,
St Laurence O'Toole,
Kilmacud Parish

Generalate

Mill Hill Missionaries
1 Colby Gardens,
Cookham Road,
Maidenhead SL6 7GZ,
England
Tel 0044-1628-789752

Superior General
Very Rev Michael Corcoran

MISSIONARIES OF AFRICA (White Fathers)

Province of Europe
Irish Community

Archdiocese of Dublin

Community House
Cypress Grove Road,
Templeogue,
Dublin D6W, YV12
Tel 01-4055263 (House)
Tel 01-4063966
Email pep.irl.del@mafr.org

Community Superior
Rev Michael P. O'Sullivan
Bursar
Rev Diarmuid Sheehan

Cypress Grove
Templeogue,
Dublin D6W YV12
Tel 01-4055263
Tel 01-4055526 (Promotion)
Email m.africaprom@yahoo.com
House of promotion/retired
priests and brothers/studies

Superior
Rev Michael P. O'Sullivan
Promotion Director
Rev Neil Loughrey
Mite Boxes
Rev Neil Loughrey

Rev Ian Buckmaster
Rev Eugene Lewis
Rev Neil Loughrey
Rev Jim McTiernan
Rev Sean O'Leary
Rev Michael P. O'Sullivan
Rev Diarmuid Sheehan
Rev Charles Timoney

Members of the Irish sector outside Ireland

Rev P. J. Cassidy (South Africa)
Rev James Greene (South
Sudan)
Br Raymond Leggett
(Scotland)
Rev Ciaran McGuinness
(England)
Rev Joseph McMenamin
(Zambia)
Rev Raymond McQuarrie
(South Africa)
Rev Gerard Murphy (Ethiopia)
Rev John O'Donoghue
(Malawi)
Rev Brendan O'Shea (Malawi)
Rev Peter Reilly (Uganda)
Rev David Sullivan
(Jerusalem)

MISSIONARIES OF THE SACRED HEART (MSC)

The Missionaries of the Sacred Heart is a congregation of 16 provinces. Members of the Irish Province work in Ireland, England, USA, South Africa and Venezuela.

Archdiocese of Dublin

Provincialate
65 Terenure Road West,
Dublin 6W, D6W P295
Tel 01-4906622
Email office@mscmissions.ie

Provincial Leader
Rev Carl Tranter

Woodview House
Mount Merrion Avenue,
Blackrock,
Co Dublin A94 DW95
Tel 01-2881644 (community)

Leader: Rev Manus Ferry

Rev John Bennett
Rev Frank Bray
Rev Eugene Clarkson
Rev Joseph Falloon
Rev Frank Gallagher
Rev Patrick McGlanaghy
Rev Martin McNamara
Rev John O'Sullivan
Rev Mike Serrage
Rev Michael Screene
Rev Vincent Screene
Rev David Smith
Rev Carl Tranter

Sacred Heart Parish
Killinarden,
Tallaght, Dublin D24 R521
Tel 01-4522251

Rev Fintan O'Dricsoll PP
Rev Con O'Connell

Formation House
Rev Joseph McGee
Rev Con O'Connell
Rev Diarmuid Ó Murchú
56 Mulvey Park, Dundrum,
Dublin D14 K223
Tel 01-2951856

Diocese of Cork & Ross

MSC Mission Support Centre
PO Box 23, Western Road,
Cork, T12 WT72
Tel 021-4545704/4543988
Fax 021-4343587
info@mscmissions.ie
www.mscmissions.ie

Rev John Fitzgerald

Western Road
Cork T12 TN80
Tel 021-4804120
Fax 021-4543823

Leader: Rev John Finn

Parish Priest
Rev Con Doherty

Rev Christopher Coleman
Rev Charles Conroy
Rev Jeremiah Daly
Rev Desmond Farren
Rev Michael Fitzgibbon
Rev John Fitzgerald
Br Donal Hallissey
Rev Seamus Kelly
Rev Donncha Mac Cárthaigh
Rev Thomas Mulcahy
Rev Alan Neville
Rev Michael O'Connell

Carrignavar
Co Cork
Tel 021-4884044

Rev Gerard Thornton
Rev Seán Horgan
Rev Jimmy Stubbs

Leap-Glandore Parish
Parish House, Leap,
Skibbereen, Co Cork,
P81 NN52
Tel 028-33177

Parish Priest
Rev Terence O'Brien PP

Rev Michael Curran

Diocese of Galway

'Croí Nua'
Rosary Lane,
Taylor's Hill,
Galway H91 WY2A
Tel 091-520960
Fax 091-521168

Co-Leaders
Rev Kevin Blade and
Rev Thomas Power

Rev Eamon Donohoe
Rev Hugh Hanlon
Rev Patrick Kelly
Rev Martin Morrissey
Rev Michael Smyth
Rev Charles Sweeney
Rev Augustine O'Brien

Parish of the Resurrection
Ballinfoyle, Headford Road,
Galway, H91 W298
Tel 091-762883

Parish Priest
Rev Anthony Horgan PP

NORBERTINE CANONS (OPraem)

Diocese of Kilmore

Holy Trinity House
Lismacanican,
Mountnugent, Co Cavan
Email kilnacrottabbeytrust@gmail.com

Prior
Rt Rev James J. Madden
Email kilnacrottabbeytrust@gmail.com

Rev Kilian Mitchell
Br Kevin O'Brien
Rev Joseph O'Donohoe
Rev Terry Smyth

Priests working elsewhere in Ireland
Rt Rev James J. Madden
Rev Pat Reilly

Priests working outside Ireland
Rt Rev William M. Fitzgerald

OBLATES OF MARY IMMACULATE (OMI)

Archdiocese of Dublin

Provincial Residence
Oblates of Mary Immaculate
House of Retreat,
Tyrconnell Road, Inchicore,
Dublin 8
Tel 01-4541160/4541161
Fax 01-4541138
Email
provincialoffice@oblates.ie

Provincial
Very Rev Oliver Barry
Provincial Treasurer
Rev Liam Griffin
Provincial Secretary
Angela Malone

Oblate House of Retreat
Inchicore, Dublin 8
Tel 01-4534408/4541805
Fax 01-4543466

Superior
Rev William Fitzpatrick

Very Rev Anthony Clancy (Co-PP Bluebell)
Rev Peter Clucas
Rev Peter Daly
Very Rev Dominik Domagala (Co-PP Inchicore, St Michael's)
Br Francis Flanagan
Br Patrick Flanagan
Rev Liam Griffin
Very Rev Paul Horrocks (Co-PP Inchicore, Mary Immaculate)

Rev Michael Hughes
Rev Gerard Kenny
Rev Patrick McGrath
Rev Vincent Mulligan
Rev Conor Murphy
Rev Kevin O'Connor
Rev Desmond O'Donnell
Rev Martin O'Keeffe
Rev Joseph O'Melia
Rev Thomas O'Shea
Rev Noel Ormonde
Rev John Poole

170 Merrion Road
Ballsbridge, Dublin 4
Tel 01-2693658
Fax 01-2600597
Rev Brian de Burca

Oblate Scholasticate
St Anne's, Goldenbridge Wa
Inchicore, Dublin 8
Tel 01-4540841/4542955
Fax 01-4731903

Rev Oliver Barry
Rev Thomas McCabe

Inchicore
St Michael's Parish
52a Bulfin Road,
Inchicore, Dublin 8
Tel 01-4531660 Fax 01-454819
Rev Michael Brady
Rev Dermot Mills

Bluebell Parish
Our Lady of the Wayside
118 Naas Road,
Bluebell, Dublin 12
Tel 01-4501040
Email
olowbluebell@oceanfree.net

Moderator of Bluebell/Inchicore Pastoral Area
Very Rev Martin Moran

Darndale Parish
The Presbytery,
Darndale, Dublin 17
Tel 01-8474547
Fax 01-8479295
Email omiddale@eircom.net

Superior
Very Rev Michael O'Connor (

Rev Eduardo Nunez Yepez C
PP
Rev Edward Quinn

Diocese of Kerry

Department of Chaplaincy
Tralee General Hospital,
Tralee, Co Kerry
Tel 066-7126222

Rev Edward Barrett

Allianz ⓘ

PALLOTTINES (SAC)
Society of the Catholic Apostolate

he Pallottine houses in
eland and England are
nited in the Mother of
ivine Love Province as are
ne houses in Argentina,
ome and the USA.

rchdiocese of Dublin

ovincial House
Homestead',
andyford Road,
undrum, Dublin 16
el 01-2956180/2954170
mail
otherofdivinelove@gmail.com

ovincial
ery Rev Liam McClarey
ector
ev Michael Irwin
mail
irwinyawl99@gmail.com
ovincial Bursar/Secretary
r Missions
ev John Kelly
mail pallbursar@gmail.com

* Tony Doherty

ttached to Provincial House
ev Gerard Fleming CC
pringfield/Jobstown/
ookfield parishes)
ev Liam Sweeney
acred Heart Residence,
bil Hill Road, Raheny,
ublin 5

: Anne's
ankill, Co Dublin
ev Jeremiah Murphy PP
Benin's, Dublin Road,
ankill, Co Dublin
l 01-2824425

ev Michael O'Dwyer CC
ev Jaimie Twohig CC
Benin's, Dublin Road,
ankill, Co Dublin
l 01-2824381

Patrick's
rduff, Blanchardstown,
ublin 15
l 01-8213596/8215930

ev John O'Connor PP
ev John Regan CC

Archdiocese of Cashel and Diocese of Emly

Pallottine College
Thurles, Co Tipperary
Tel 0504-21202

Rector
Very Rev George Ranahan
Vice-Rector
Br Stephen Buckley

Rev John Casey
Rev John Coen
Rev Michael Coen
Rev Patrick Dwyer
Rev John Bergin
Rev Philip Barry
Rev Martin Mareja *(Director, Mission Promotion Office)*
Rev Brendan Walsh
Rev Kevin Ward
Rev Michael Barry
Rev Donal McCarthy

Attached to Pallottine College
Rev Vincent Kelly
18 Silvercourt,
Silversprings, Cork

PASSIONISTS (CP)
Congregation of the Passion

Province of St Patrick: houses
in Ireland, Scotland and Paris.

Archdiocese of Dublin

St Paul's Retreat
Mount Argus, Dublin 6W
Tel 01-4992000 Fax 01-4992001
Email
passionistsmtargus@eircom.net
Provincial Office
Tel 01-4992050
passionistprov@eircom.net

Provincial: Rev James Sweeney
Superior: Rev Bernard Lowe

Rev Kenneth Brady
Rev Kieran Creagh
Rev Ralph Egan
Rev James Feehan
Rev Patrick Fitzgerald
Rev Dermot Gallagher
Rev Augustine Hourigan
Rev Joseph Kennedy
Rev Eugene McCarthy
Rev Brendan McKeever
Rev Brian Mulcahy
Rev Patrick Rogers
Rev James Sheridan
Rev Patrick Sheridan
Rev Paul Francis Spencer PP
Bro Joesph Ward
Rev Ignatius Waters

Applications for missions and
retreats to Rev Superior of
any of our local Communities

Diocese of Clogher

St Gabriel's Retreat
The Graan, Enniskillen,
Co Fermanagh BT7 45PB
Tel 028-66322272
Fax 028-66325201

Superior
Rev Charles Cross
Email
charlescrosscp@gmail.com

Rev Brian D'Arcy
Rev Victor Donnelly
Br Brendan Gallagher
Rev Arthur McCann
Rev Anthony O'Leary

Diocese of Down & Connor

Passionist Retreat Centre
16 A Downpatrick Road,
Crossgar, Downpatrick,
Co Down BT30 9EQ
Tel 028-44830242
Fax 028-44831382

Superior
Rev Thomas Scanlon

Rev Ephrem Blake
Rev Mel Byrne
Rev Aidan O'Kane

Holy Cross Retreat
Ardoyne,
Crumlin Road,
Belfast BT14 7GE
Tel 028-90748231
Fax 028-90740340

Parish Priest
Rev John Craven
Superior
Rev John Friel

Rev Gary Donegan
Rev Patrick Duffy
Rev Myles Kavanagh
Rev Terence McGuckin
Rev Francis Trias

Scotland

Passionist Community
26 Plantation Parkway,
Bishopbriggs,
Glasgow G64 2FD, Scotland
Tel 141-7729697

France

St Joseph's Church
50 Avenue Hoche,
75008 Paris
Tel 33-1-42272856
Fax 33-1-42278649

REDEMPTORISTS (CSSR)
Congregation of the Most Holy Redeemer

The Irish Province of the
Redemptorists is a complete
province, with one
dependent.
Vice-Province in Brazil, ten
other members assigned to
the Province of CEBU/
Philippines, one member
assigned to the Province of
Bangalore, India, and two
members in Mozambique.

Office of the Provincial
St Joseph's Monastery,
St Alphonsus Road,
Dundalk,
Co Louth A91 F3FC
Email provincial@cssr.ie
Provincial Secretary
Email secretary@cssr.ie

Provincial
Rev Dan Baragry
Provincial Vicar
Rev Ciarán O'Callaghan
2nd Provincial Consultor
Rev Gerry O'Connor

Archdiocese of Dublin

Dún Mhuire
461/463 Griffith Avenue,
Dublin D09 X651
Tel 01-5180196
Fax 01-8369655

Rev Thomas Hogan *(Hospital Chaplain, Our Lady of Lourdes)*
Rev Patrick Kelly
Rev Denis O'Connor *(parish)*
Rev Brendan O'Rourke

Most Holy Sacrament Parish
Cherry Orchard, Dublin 10
Tel 01-6267930

Rev Michael Murtagh PP

Ballyfermot Assumption Parish
197 Kylemore Road,
Ballyfermot, Dublin 10
Parish Tel 01-6264691
Community Tel 01-5356977

Rev Adrian Egan PP &
Coordinator
Rev Séamus Devitt
Rev Cornelius J. Casey

Archdiocese of Armagh

St Joseph's
St Alphonsus Road,
Dundalk, Co Louth A91 F3FC
Tel 042-9334042/9334762
Fax 042-9330893
Provincial administration,
parish and Redemptorist
Communications

Superior
Rev Noel Kehoe PP
Vicar-Superior
Rev Richard Delahunty

Rev Dan Baragry *(Provincial)*
Rev John Bermingham
Rev Brendan Callanan
Rev Sean Cannon
Rev John Corbett
Rev Cathal Cumiskey
Br Patrick Doherty
Rev Philip Hearty
Rev Ryan Holovlasky
Rev Patrick Horgan
Rev Eamon Kavanagh
Rev Stan Mellett
Rev Anthony Mulvey
Rev Richard Rooney
Rev Derek Ryan
Rev Richard Tobin

Diocese of Cork & Ross

Scala
Castlemahon House,
Castle Road, Blackrock, Cork
Tel 021-4358800
Fax 021-4359696

Co-ordinator: Rev Brian Nolan

Rev Michael Forde
Rev Gerard O'Connor
Rev Pat Sugrue

Diocese of Down & Connor

Clonard Monastery
1 Clonard Gardens,
Belfast, BT13 2RL
Tel 028-90445950
Fax 028-90445988

Superior
Rev Peter Burns
Vicar
Rev Ciaran O'Callaghan

Rev Anthony Branagan
Rev Gerry Cassidy
Rev Edmond Creamer
Rev Michael Dempsey
Rev Johnny Doherty
Rev Alphonsus Doran
Rev John Hanna
Rev Brendan Keane
Rev Sean Keeney

Rev Clement MacMánus
Rev Barney McCahery
Rev Brendan McConvery
Rev Anthony McCrave
Rev William McGettrick
Rev Sean Moore
Rev Patrick O'Keeffe
Rev Paul Turley

St Gerard's Parish
722 Antrim Road,
Newtownabbey,
Co Antrim BT36 7PG
Tel 028-90774833
Fax 028-90770923
PP: Rev Kevin Browne

Rev Denis Luddy

Diocese of Limerick

Mount Saint Alphonsus
South Circular Road,
Limerick
Tel 061-315099
Fax 061-315303
Mission House

Superior
Rev Seamus Enright
Vicar-Superior
Rev Gerard Moloney

Rev James Buckley
Rev Tony Flannery
Rev Laurence Gallagher
Rev Raphael Gallagher
Rev John Goode
Br Nicholas Healy
Rev Michael Kelleher
Rev Cornelius Kenneally
Rev John Lucey
Br Dermot McDonagh
Rev Aidan McMahon
Rev Richard McMahon
Rev Derek Meskell
Rev Michael G. O'Connor
Rev Pat O'Connor
Rev Michael O'Flynn
Rev John J. Ó Ríordáin
Rev John P. O'Riordan
Rev Sean Purcell

St Clement's College
Laurel Hill Avenue,
South Circular Road,
Limerick
Tel 061-315878/318749 (staff)
Tel 061-310294 (students)
Fax 061-316640
Secondary school for boys

Principal: Mr Pat Talty

Province of Cebu (Philippines)

PO Box 280
6000 Cebu City,
Philippine Islands
Tel +63-32-2536341/2536315

Provincial
Rev Bert Cepe

Province of Bangalore (India)

Redemptorist Community
R.C. Church,
Morrispet PO, Tenali, Guntur
DT 522 202,
Andhra Pradesh,
India
Tel +91-8644-223382

Rev Martin Cushnan

*Vice-Province of Fortaleza
(Brazil)*

Missionarios Redentoristas
Caixa Postal 85
60,001-970 Fortaleza
Est. do Ceara, Brazil
Tel +55-8532232016

Mission in Rome

Via Merulana 31
CP 2458,
00185 Roma-PT158, Italy
Tel 0039-06-494901

Rev Brendan Kelly
(Administration)
Rev Martin McKeever
(Alphonsian Academy)

Mission in Mozambique

**Santa Maria dei Monti
Mission**
Furancungo,
Mozambique, Africa

Rev Eridian Goncalves
de Lima
Rev Brian Holmes
Contact: c/o Provincial,
Dublin

ROSMINIANS (IC)
Institute of Charity

Irish Province

Archdiocese of Dublin

Clonturk House
Ormond Road, Drumcondra,
Dublin 9, D09 F821
Tel 01-6877014

*Provincial & Vocations
Director:* Rev Joseph O'Reilly
Rector: Rev Matt Gaffney

Rev John Mullen
Rev William Stuart
Rev Michael O'Neill
Rev Michael O'Shea
Rev Christanand Varghese
Kuttikkatt
Br Eamon Fitzpatrick

**Rosminian Mission
Development Office**
Clonturk House,
Ormond Road,
Drumcondra,
Dublin D09 F821
Tel 01-6877023

Rev Wilhad Shayo

Archdiocese of Armagh

Faughart Parish
St Brigid's, Kilcurry,
Dundalk,
Co Louth A91 E8N8
Tel 042-9334410

Parish Priest
Rev Vinod Thennattil Kurian
Rev Oliver Stansfield

Parochial House,
Knocknagoran,
Omeath,
Co Louth A91 HK76

Rev Christopher McElwee

Diocese of Cork & Ross

Rosmini House
Dunkereen, Innishannon,
Co Cork, T12 N9DH
Tel 021-4776268/4776923
Fax 021-4776268

Rector
Rev Polachan Thettayil

Rev Joyel John Michael

*Diocese of Waterford &
Lismore*

St Joseph's
Doire na hAbhann,
Tickincar, Clonmel,
Co Tipperary, E91 XY71
Tel 052-6126914
Fax 052-6126915

Rev James Browne
Rev Tom Coffey
Rev P. J. Fegan
Rev Michael Melican
Rev Patrick Pierce

t Oliver Plunkett's Parish
:ooleens, Glenconnor,
Ionmel,
o Tipperary E91 N578
el 052-6125679

ev Michael Hegarty PP

nquiries concerning the
issions to:
ev Joseph O'Reilly
Ionturk House,
rmond Road,
rumcondra, Dublin 9

ACRED HEART FATHERS
(SCJ) Congregation of
he Priests of the Sacred
Heart of Jesus

ritish-Irish Province

rchdiocese of Dublin

acred Heart Fathers
airfield,
5 Inchicore Road,
ublin 8
el 01-4538655
mail scjdublin@eircom.net

rovincial
ev John Kelly

ev Thomas Stanley
r Daniel Yentsa

rdlea Parish
. John Vianney
rdlea Road,
ublin 5
el 01-8474123/8474173
mail jvianney@indigo.ie

ev Hugh Hanley
ev Marian Szalwa CC
ev Michel Simo Temgo PP

ST COLUMBAN'S
MISSIONARY SOCIETY
(SSC)

aynooth Mission to China –
eland

uperior General
ev Tim Mulroy
o 3 and 4, Ma Yau Tong
illage,
o Lam Road, Tseung Kwan O,
ong Kong, SAR
mail
olumban@columban.org.hk
icar General: Rev Brian Vale
mail
ocietyvicar@columban.org.hk

Councillors
Kang Seung-Won Joseph
Email
jkswing@columban.org.hk
Rev Alvaro Martinez Ibánez
Email
amartinezgc@columban.org.hk

Procurator General
Rev Robert McCulloch
Collegio San Colombano,
Corso Trieste 57, 00198 Roma
Email procol.roma@gmail.com
Bursar General
Rev Jovito Dales
Hong Kong
Email
jovitodales@columban.org.hk
Columban Intercom Editor
Rev Peter Woodruff
PO Box 752, Vic 3042,
Australia
Email
intercom@columban.org.au

Research on Mission and
Culture: Rev Sean Dwan
Columban Fathers,
c/o St Columban's,
Dalgan Park,
Navan, Co Meath
Tel 046-9021525
Email seandwan@gmail.com

Research on JPIC Priorities
Rev Sean McDonagh
St Columban's, Dalgan Park,
Navan, Co Meath
Tel 046-9021525
Email
seanmcdonagh10@gmail.com

Society Archivist and
Columban History
Coordinator
Rev Patrick O'Donoghue
St Columban's, Dalgan Park,
Navan, Co Meath
Tel 046-9021525
Email neilcollins93@gmail.com
Assistant Archivist
Barbara Scally
Email
barbara.scally@columban.ie

Archdiocese of Dublin

St Columban's
67-68 Castle Dawson,
Rathcoffey Road, Maynooth,
Co Kildare
Tel 01-6286036
Rev Hugh MacMahon
(Priest in charge)
Email hugh.macmahonssc@
columban.ie

Columban Centre
13 Store Street,
Dublin 1
Tel 01-8942078
Contact person
Michael O'Sullivan
Email michael.osullivan@
columban.ie

Diocese of Meath

St Columban's
Dalgan Park, Navan,
Co Meath
Tel 046-9021525

Regional Director
Rev Raymond Husband
Tel 046-9021525
Email
ray.husbandssc@columban.ie
Regional Vice-Director
Rev Padraig O'Donovan
Email padraigssc@gmail.com
Regional Secretary
Evelyn Honan
Email
evelynhonan@columban.ie

Regional Council
Rev Gerry Neylon
Email
mgneylon@gmail.com
Rev Tom O'Reilly
Email
tomoreilly60@hotmail.com
Rev David Kenneally
Email
kenneallyd@gmail.com

Regional Offices
Fax 046-9071297
Email
missionoffice@columban.com
Regional Bursar
Evelyn Maguire *(Head of*
Finance/Regional Board)
Email
regionalbursar@columban.ie

Mission Outreach Co-ordinator
Vacant
Email missionoutreach@
columban.com

Communications Co-ordinator
Rev Cyril Lovett
Email
cyrillovet39@gmail.com

Ongoing Education
Rev Cyril Lovett
Email
cyril.lovett@columban.ie

JPIC Outreach
Michael O'Sullivan
Email michael.osullivan@
columban.ie
Rev Frank Nally
Email
frank.nallyssc@columban.ie

Lay Missionary Contact Person
Angie Escarsca
Email clm.ireland@columban.ie

Vocations Contact Person
Rev Padraig O'Donovan
Email padraigssc@gmail.com

Inter-faith Dialogue
Michael O'Sullivan
Email michael.osullivan@
columban.ie
Sean Dwan
Email
sean.dwanssc@columban.ie

Regional Newsletter
Rev Hugh MacMahon
Office Manager
Ada Coughlan
Email irishfareast@gmail.com

Focus on China
Rev Hugh MacMahon

Far East Editor
Sarah MacDonald
Email
sarah.mcdonald@columban.ie
www.columbans.ie

Board of Reconciliation
Rev Gerald French
Rev Joseph Hargaden
Rev Conal O'Connell

Alcoholic Advisory Board
Rev Brendan Hoban
Email brendan.hobanssc@
columban.ie
John Norris *(Lay Advisor)*

Safeguarding Officer and
Designated Liaison Person
Sandra Neville
Tel 087-9844779
Email
sandra.neville@columban.ie
Deputy Safeguarding Officer
Rev Donal Hogan
Email
doniehogan@gmail.com

HR Manager
Denis Kelly
Email
hrmanager@columban.ie

St Columban's

Dalgan Park,
Navan, Co Meath
Tel 046-9021525
Fax 046-9022799
House Superior
Rev Padraig O'Donovan
Email padraig.odonovanssc@
columban.ie

Bursar & Vice-Superior
Rev Joseph McDonnell
Email
joe.mcdonnell@columban.ie

Residents
Rev John Colgan (Ret)
Rev Neil Collins
Rev Sean Coyle
Email scoylumban@gmail.com
Rev Noel Daly
Email
noel.dalyssc@columban.ie
Rev Michael Dodd
Rev Sean Dwan
Rev Patrick Egan (Ret)
Rev Gerald French
Rev John Gilmore
Rev Malachy Hanratty (Ret)
Rev Jeremiah Healy
Rev Brendan Hoban
Rev Donal Hogan
Rev John Hogan
Rev Maurice Hogan
Rev Raymond Husband
Rev Norman Jennings
Rev David Kenneally
Rev Cyril Lovett
Rev Barry Maguire
Rev Bernard Martin (Ret)
Rev Brendan MacHale
Rev Oliver McCrossan
Rev Sean McDonagh
Rev Joseph McDonnell
Rev Austin McGuinness
Rev Kevin McHugh
Rev John McLaughlin (Ret)
Rev Patrick McManus
Rev Charles Meagher
Rev John Molloy (Ret)
Rev Michael Molloy (Ret)
Rev Bernard Mulkerins
Rev Cornelius Murphy (Ret)
Rev Brendan Murray (Ret)
Rev Frank Nally
Rev Gerry Neylon
Rev Kevin O'Boyle

Rev Anthony O'Brien (Ret)
Rev Conal O'Connell
Rev Padraig O'Donovan
Rev Donal O'Hanlon
Rev Peter O'Neill
Rev Thomas O'Reilly
Rev Brian Oxley (Ret)
Rev Patrick Raleigh
Email praleighssc@gmail.com
Rev Patrick Smyth
Rev Bernard Steed

St Columban's Retirement Home

Dalgan Park,
Navan, Co Meath
Tel 046-9021525

Person in Charge
Ms Anna Brozek

Pastoral Care Team
Rev Sean Coyle
Rev Brendan Hoban
Rev John Hogan
Rev Bernard Mulkerins
Rev Brendan Murray

Residents
Rev Donal N. Bennett
Rev William Byrne
Rev John Chute
Rev Sean Connaughton
Rev Padraig Digan
Rev Michael Doohan
Rev Derek Harris
Rev Michael Irwin
Rev Gerard McNicholas
Rev Cyril Murphy
Rev Jeremiah Murphy
Rev Michael O'Farrell
Rev Francis O'Kelly

Columbans living outside Dalgan (Retired)
Rev Dan Ahern, Tralee
Rev Jody Cahill, Ballina,
Co Mayo
Rev Timothy Collins, Cork
Rev Patrick Conway, Ennis
Rev Joseph Hargaden,
Wexford
Rev Sean McNulty, Galway
Rev Eamonn O'Brien, Kerry
Rev Michael O'Loughlin, Ennis
Rev Myles Roban, Enniscorthy
Rev James Sheehy, Dungarvan,
Co Waterford

Promotion Work/Mission Awareness
Rev Barry Maguire
Rev Oliver McCrossan
Rev Donal O'Hanlon
Rev Bernard Steed
Angie Escarsa LM

Priests on Special Work
Rev P. Aloysius Connaughton
(Thailand)

Rev John Hickey (Columban
Sisters, Magheramore,
Co Wicklow)

Rev John Gilmore
(Immigration Apostolate)
Rev Donal Hogan (Deputy
Safeguarding Office)
Rev Sean McDonagh
(Research JPIC)

Priests on diocesan work in Ireland
Rev Eamon Conaty (Elphin)
Rev Kevin Fleming (Meath)
Rev Seamus O'Neill (Derry)

Columban Lay Missionaries from the Philippians working in Ireland
Angie Escarsa (Co-ordinator)

ST PATRICK'S MISSIONARY SOCIETY (SPS)

Diocese of Kildare & Leighlin

St Patrick's

Kiltegan,
Co Wicklow W91 YO22
Tel 059-6473600
Fax 059-6473622
Society Leader
Rev Richard Filima
Assistant Society Leader
Rev Sean Cremin
Councillors
Rev Patrick Esekon
Rev Raphael Mwenda
Email ccullen@spms.ie
Bursar General
Rev Seamus O'Neill

District Leader for Ireland
Rev Thomas O'Connor
Email
districtleaderireland@spms.ie
Assistant District Leader
Rev Pat Murphy
Tel 059-6473600
Email pmurphysps@gmail.com
District Secretary
Ms Carly Cullen
Tel 059-6473615
Kiltegan House Leader
Rev Enda Kelly
Assistant House Leader
Rev John Roche
Director of Promotion
Rev David Walsh
Office Manager
Ms Joanne Fortune
Kiltegan House Manager
Ms Fiona Hawkins
Editor, Africa
Rev Sean Deegan
Email africa@spms.ie

Director of Slí an Chroí
Rev Pat Murphy
Tel 059-6473488

Rev Anthony Barrett
Rev Bernard Bohan
Rev Jim Brady
Rev Richie Brennan
Rev Joe Cantwell
Rev John P. Carroll
Rev Noel Connolly
Rev Colm Cooke
Rev Michael Conroy
Rev Patrick Corcoran
Rev Jim Crowe
Rev Sean Cullen
Rev Steve Donohue
Rev Paddy Feeney
Rev Peter Finegan
Rev Padraig Flanagan
Rev Dermot Foley
Rev William Fulton
Rev John Garry
Rev Ned Grace
Rev Thomas Greenan
Rev Thomas Grenham
Rev Patrick Hagan
Rev Eamonn Hayden
Rev Andy Keating
Rev Michael Kelly
Rev Liam Kelly
Rev Maurice Kelly
Rev Michael Kelly
Rev Edward Lalor
Rev Oliver Leavy
Rev Michael Long
Rev James McAuliffe
Rev Patrick McCallion
Rev Fintan McDonald
Rev James McDonnell
Rev Thomas McDonnell
Rev Patrick McGivern
Rev Noel McHenry
Rev Oliver McHugh
Rev Gregory McManus
Rev Frank Minogue
Rev Frank Morgan
Rev Nicholas Motherway
Rev Dermot Nolan
Rev Patrick O'Brien
Rev Rory O'Brien
Rev Gerard O'Carroll
Rev Thomas O'Connor
Rev Bartie O'Doherty
Rev Ciaran O'Flynn
Rev Seamus O'Reilly
Rev Brendan Payne
Rev Joseph Rabbitt
Rev Norbert Reid
Rev Edmond Ryan
Rev Tom Ryan
Rev Sean Rynn
Rev Liam V. Scanlan
Rev Thomas Scott
Rev Tony Sheerin
Rev Joe Taylor
Rev Donal Twomey
Rev David Walsh

Allianz (ⁱ)

ev Edward Walsh
ev William Walshe
ev Seamus Whelan
ev Seamus Whitney

Archdiocese of Dublin

t Patrick's
1 Leeson Park,
ublin D06 DE76
el 01-4977897
ax 01-4962812

House Leader
ev David Larkin

ev Michael Browne
ev Brendan Cooney
ev Peter Coyle
ev Dermot Connolly
ev Donal Dorr
ev Danny Gibbons
ev David Larkin
ev George O'Brien
ev Brendan McCarron
ev Con Ryan

rchdiocese of Tuam

t Patrick's
Main Street, Knock, Co Mayo
el 094-9388661

House Leader
ev Gary Howley

iocese of Cork & Ross

iltegan House
1 Douglas Road, Cork
el 021-4969371

House Leader
ev James Kelleher

ev Martin Barry
ev William Greene
ev John O'Brien

riests on special ministries
ev Michael Rodgers,
earmann Spirituality Centre,
rockagh, Glendalough,
o Wicklow
el 0404-45208
ev Martin Smith

riests on temporary diocesan
ork

ev Liam Blayney
ev Declan Boyce
ev John Carroll
ev Colm Clinton
ev Frank Conlisk (Tuam –
illtown, Co Galway)
ev Bernard Conway
ev Eugene Drumm
ev PJ Fitzgerald (Kildare &
eighlin)
ev Niall Geaney (Kerry)

Rev John Heinhold
Rev Joseph Long (Kilmore)
Rev Brian Maguire (Kildare &
Leighlin)
Rev Brendan McDonagh
Rev Martin McGrath,
Parochial House,
Moygownagh,
Co Mayo (Killala Diocese)
Rev Michael Morris (Ardagh &
Clonmacnois)
Rev Sean O'Dowd
Rev Martin Spillane
Rev Declan Thompson

SALESIANS (SDB)

Archdiocese of Dublin

Provincialate
Salesian House,
45 St Teresa's Road,
Crumlin, Dublin D12 XK52
Tel 01-4555787
Email (secretary)
office@salesians.ie
www.salesiansireland.ie

Provincial
Very Rev Eunan McDonnell
Email
provincial@salesiansireland.ie
Provincial Secretary
Rev Lukasz Nawrat

Salesian House
45 St Teresa's Road,
Crumlin, Dublin D12 XK52
Tel 01-4555605
House of residence

Rector
Rev Martin McCormack
Vice-Rector
Rev Daniel Carroll
Bursar
Rev Raymond McIntyre

Rev Patrick Brewster
Rev Michael Browne
Rev Thomas Clowe CC
Rev Charles Cunningham
Rev John Finnegan
Br Colum Maguire
Rev James Somers

Rinaldi House
40-41 Sean McDermott Street,
Dublin D01 H7P6

Rector
Rev Michael Casey Adm
Vice-Rector
Rev Hugh O'Donnell
Bursar
Rev Selvaraj Mallavarappu

Rev Val Collier
Rev John Quinn

Our Lady of Lourdes Parish
Seán McDermott Street,
Dublin D01 AD73
Tel 01-8363554

Rev Michael Casey Adm

Salesian College
Maynooth Road, Celbridge,
Co Kildare, W23 W0XK
Tel 01-6275058/60
Fax 01-6272208
Secondary School
Tel 01-6272166/6272200

Rector: Rev Patrick Hennessy
Vice-Rector
Rev Apap Jesmond
Bursar
Rev Tran Xuan Binh Paul

Rev Lukasz Nawrat
Rev A. McEvoy
Br James O'Hare

Diocese of Limerick

Salesian College
Don Bosco Road, Pallaskenry,
Co Limerick V94 WP86
Tel 061-393105 Fax 061-393298
Secondary and agricultural
schools

Rector
Rev John Horan
Vice-Rector
Rev Daniel Devitt
Bursar
Rev Nguyen Viet Binh Dominic

Rev Timothy Wrenn

Salesian House
Milford, Castletroy,
Limerick, V94 DK44
Tel 061-330268/330914
Student hostel and parish

Rector and Chaplain,
University of Limerick
Rev John Campion
Vice-Rector
Rev Mrtin Loftus
Economer
Rev Koenraad Van Gucht PP

Rev John Fagan
Rev Martin Loftus
Rev Michael Smyth
Rev Bob Swinburne

Elsewhere in Ireland
Rev Desmond Campion
(Chaplain Naval Service,
Haulbowline, Cobh, Cork)
Rev G. Dowd
(c/o Provincialate,
Salesian House, Crumlin)

Rev James O'Halloran
(St Catherine's Centre, North
Campus, Maynooth, Co
Kildare)
Rev P.J. Healy
(Chaplain, Mount Carmel
Nursing Home,
Roscrea, Co Tipperary)

SALVATORIANS (SDS)

Diocese of Derry

Rev Malachy McBride
'Naomh Mhuire',
Upper Slavery, Buncrana,
Co Donegal
Tel 074-9322264

Diocese of Galway

Rev Seamus O'Duill
Ard Mhuire, Kilmoon,
Lisdoonvarna, Co Clare
Tel 086-1030261
Email seamusoduill@eircom.net

SERVITES (OSM)
Order of Friar Servants
of Mary

Prior Provincial
Rev Colm M. McGlynn
Servite Priory
36 Grangewood Estate,
Rathfarnham,
Dublin D16 V263
Tel 01-4936755/086-4060124
Email
colmmcglynn154@hotmail.com

Province of the Isles

Archdiocese of Dublin

Servite Priory
St Peregrine,
36 Grangewood Estate,
Rathfarnham, Dublin 16
Tel 01-4936755

Prior: Rev Jimmy M. Kelly
(Chaplain,
Cloverhill Prison,
Clondalkin, Dublin 24

Rev Timothy M. Flynn
(Director, St Peregrine
Ministry)
Rev Raymond O'Connell
(assigned to Grangewood –
living in Youghal & District
Nursing Home, Cork)

Church of the Divine Word

Marley Grange,
25–27 Hermitage Downs,
Rathfarnham, Dublin 16
Tel 01-4944295/4941064
Fax 01-4941069

Prior
Rev Liam Tracey PP

Rev Jim Mulherin CC

*Monthly St Peregrine Mass on
first Saturday of every month
at 10.00 a.m. – also on
webcam.*

Archdiocese of Armagh

Servite Priory

Benburb, Dungannon,
Co Tyrone, BT71 7JZ
Northern Ireland
Tel 028-37548241
Tel 01861-548241/548533
Retreat, Conference Centre
and youth centre

Prior
Rev Bernard Thorne

Rev Gabriel Bannon
Br Patrick Gethins
Rev Sean Lennon
Rev Dermot MacNeice

SOCIETY OF AFRICAN MISSIONS (SMA)
Societas Missionum Ad Afros

Diocese of Cork & Ross

African Missions

Provincial House, Feltrim,
Blackrock Road,
Cork T12 N6C8
Tel 021-4292871
Fax 021-4292873
www.sma.ie
Email provincial@sma.ie

Provincial
Rev Malachy Flanagan
Vice Provincial
Rev Eamonn Finnegan
Provincial Councillor
Rev Anthony Kelly
Provincial Secretary
Rev Martin Kavanagh
*Safeguarding and Data
Protection*
Ms Elizabeth Murphy
Compiance Officer
Ms Thora McMahon

African Missions

Blackrock Road,
Cork T12 TD54
Tel 021-4292871
Email sma.blackrock@sma.ie

Superior
Rev Patrick O'Rourke
Provincial Bursar
Rev Jarlath Walsh
Assistant Bursar
Mr Paul Murphy
Provincial Archivist
Rev Edmund M. Hogan

Rev Jerome S. Anoumou
Rev John Bowe
Rev Lee Cahill
Most Rev Timothy Carroll
(Retired Bishop)
Rev Denis Collins
Rev Francis Coltsmann
Rev Patrick Connolly
Rev Bernard Cotter
Rev Timothy Cullinane
Br Patrick Dowd
Rev Christopher Emokhare
Rev Thomas Fenlon
Rev Alphonsus Flatley
Rev Joseph Foley
Rev Francis Geoghegan
Rev William Ghent
Rev Hugh Harkin
Rev Edmund Hogan
Rev Valentine Hynes
Rev Michael Igoe
Rev Martin Kavanagh
Rev Michael Kidney
Rev Angelo Lafferty
Rev Sean Lynch
Rev Michael McCabe
Rev Aidan McCrystal
Rev Michael McGrath
Rev Gerard Murray
Rev Michael Nohilly
Rev Matthew O'Connell
Rev Edward O'Connor
Rev Fionnbarra O'Cuilleanáin
Rev Martin O'Hare
Rev John O'Hea
Rev James O'Kane
Rev John O'Keeffe
Rev Michael O'Shea
Rev Andrew O'Sullivan
Rev Denis J. Ryan
Rev Thomas Wade
Rev Jarlath Walsh
Rev Michael Waters
Rev Oscar Welsh

SMA House

Wilton, Cork T12 KR23
Tel 021-4541069/4541884
Email sma.wilton@sma.ie

Superior
Rev Noel O'Leary
Vice-Superior
Rev Colum O'Shea
Local Bursar
Mr Pat Coughlan

Rev Cormac Breathnach
Rev Daniel Cashman
Rev John Dunne
Rev Thomas Harlow
Most Rev Patrick Harrington
(Retired Bishop)
Rev John Horgan
Rev Cornelius Murphy
Rev Seamus Nohilly
Rev Augustine O'Driscoll
Rev Kevin O'Gorman

Most Rev Noel O'Regan
(Retired Bishop)
Rev Denis O'Sullivan
Rev Richard Wall

St Joseph's SMA Parish

Blackrock Road, Cork T12 X281
Tel 021-4293325
Email parish.blackrock@sma.ie

Rev Augustine O'Driscoll
(protem)
Rev Jerome Sassou CC

St Joseph's SMA Parish

Wilton, Cork T12 E436
Tel 021-4341362
Fax 021-4343940
Email stjosephschurchwilton@
yahoo.com

Rev Michael O'Leary PP

Justice Office

SMA House, Wilton,
Cork T12 KR23
Email justice@sma.ie
Mr Gerry Forde

Archdiocese of Dublin

SMA House

81 Ranelagh Road,
Dublin D06 WT10
Tel 01-4968162 Fax 01-4968164
Email sma.dublin@sma.ie

Superior
Rev Joseph Egan
Vice-Superior
Rev John O'Brien
Bursar
Rev Thomas Curran

Rev Noel Gillespie
Rev Patrick Kelly
Rev Paul Monahan
Rev Alphonse Sekongo

Also in Dublin
Rev Sean Healy
Social Justice Ireland,
Arena House, Arena Road,
Sandyford, Dublin 18
Tel 01-2130724
www.socialjustice.ie

Diocese of Galway

SMA House

Cloonbigeen
Claregalway,
Co Galway H91 YK64
Tel 091-798880
Fax 091-798879
Email
sma.claregalway@sma.ie

Superior
Rev Billy Sheridan
Bursar
Rev Colman Nilan

Rev Martin Costello
Rev Fintan Daly
Rev John Dunleavy
Rev Alphonsus Kelly
Rev Paraic Kelly
Rev Francis McGrath
Rev Eugene McLoughlin
Rev Kieran Morahan
Rev Desmond Smith
Rev Gerard Sweeney

Diocese of Dromore

African Missions

Dromantine,
Newry,
Co Down BT34 1RH
Tel 028-30821224
Fax 028-30821704
Email
sma.dromantine@sma.ie

Superior
Rev Damian Bresnahan
Bursar
Mrs Paula Murtagh

Rev Desmond Corrigan
Rev Edward Deeney
Rev Thomas Faherty
Rev John Gallagher
Rev Hugh Lagan
Rev Daniel McCauley
Rev Cathal McKenna
Rev Hugh O'Kane
Rev Peter Thompson

Dromantine Retreat and Conference Centre
Newry,
Co Down BT34 1RH
Tel 028-30821964
Fax 028-30821704
Email admin@
dromantineconference.com
www.dromantineconference.com

Accommodation:
42 single en suite rooms,
30 double en suite rooms,
3 conference rooms

Director
Rev Damian Bresnahan

Temporary diocesan work in Ireland
Rev Chris Brennan
Rev John Brown
Rev Michael Flattery
Rev Anthony Gill
Rev Maurice Henry
Rev Patrick Lynch
Rev Thomas McNamara
Rev Kevin Mulhern
Rev Patrick O'Mahony
Rev Donal Toal
Rev Fergus Tuohy
Rev Thomas Walsh

Church of Our Lady of the Rosary and St Patrick
1 Blackhorse Road,
Walthamstow,
London E17 7AS,
England
Tel +44-208-5203647

Rev Kevin Conway
Rev Freddy Warner

Rome
Generalate
Missioni Africane,
Via della Nocetta 111,
00164 Roma, Italy
Tel +39-06-6616841
Fax +39-06-66168490
Email
secgen@smainternational.org

Superior General
Rev Antonio Porcellato
Email
supgen@smainternational.org

SOCIETY OF ST PAUL (SSP)

The Society of St Paul in Ireland operates exclusively through the mass media.

Archdiocese of Dublin

Society of St Paul
Moyglare Road,
Maynooth,
Co Kildare W23 NX34
Tel 01-6285933
Fax 01-6289330
Email sspireland@gmail.com

Rev Sebastian Kanayammakunnel
Rev Alexander Anandam
Rev Thomas Devasia Perumparambil
Rev Bangcaya Jose Jereus

St Paul Book Centre
Moyglare Road,
Maynooth,
Co Kildare W23 NX34
Email sspireland@gmail.com
www.stpauls.ie

St Paul's Books and Mass Leaflets
Moyglare Road,
Maynooth,
Co Kildare W23 NX34
Email sales@stpauls.ie

SONS OF DIVINE PROVIDENCE (FDP)

The Irish Foundation is part of the Missionary English-speaking Delegation of 'Mary Mother of the Church'.

Regional Superior
Rev Marcelo Boschi
c/o Via Etruria 6,
00183 Rome, Italy
Local Co-ordinator
Rev Philip Kehoe
25 Lower Teddington Road,
Kingston-on-Thames,
Surrey
Tel 208-9775130

Archdiocese of Dublin

Sarsfield House
Sarsfield Road,
Ballyfermot,
Dublin 10
Tel 01-6266193/6266233
Fax 01-6260303
Email don-orion@clubi.ie

Rev John Perrotta
Email jperrotta16@yahoo.ie

VINCENTIANS (CM)

Vincentian communities of the Irish Province are established in Ireland and England.

Archdiocese of Dublin

Provincial Office
Sybil Hill, Raheny,
Dublin D05 AE38
Tel 01-8510842 Fax 01-8510846
Email cmdublin@vincentians.ie
www.vincentians.ie

Provincial
Very Rev Paschal Scallon
Secretary to the Provincial
Ms Avril Gibson
Email cmdublin@vincentians.ie

St Paul's
Raheny, Dublin D05 AE38
Tel 01-8318113 (community)
Fax 01-8316387
Community Residence

Superior
Very Rev Stephen Monaghan

Rev Roderic Crowley
Rev Michael Dunne
Rev John Gallagher
Rev Joseph McCann
Rev Michael McCullagh
Rev Bernard Meade
Rev Harry Slowey
Rev Philip Walshe

Phibsborough
St Peter's, Dublin D07 FW29
Tel 01-8389708/8389841
Email
info@stpetersphibsboro.ie

Superior
Very Rev Eamon Devlin PP
Email
pp@stpetersphibsboro.ie

Rev John Concannon
Rev Sean Farrell
Rev Eamon Flanagan
Rev Kieran MaGovern
Rev Mark Noonan
Rev Padraig Regan

St Joseph's
44 Stillorgan Park, Blackrock,
Co Dublin A94 PC62
Tel 01-2886961

Superior
Very Rev Patrick Collins

Rev Aidan Galvin
Rev Jack Harris
Rev Colm McAdam

St Vincent's Castleknock College
Castleknock,
Dublin D15 PD95
Tel 01-8213051
Secondary Day School for Boys

Superior
Very Rev Paschal Scallon

Rev Joseph Loftus
Rev Cornelius Nwaogwugwu

Diocese of Down & Connor

99 Cliftonville Road
Belfast BT14 6JQ
Tel 028-90751771
Fax 028-90740547

Superior
Very Rev Adrian Eastwood

Rev Peter Gildea
Rev James Rafferty

COMMUNITIES OF RELIGIOUS BROTHERS

In this section, details of each community's main house are given, followed by a list of the dioceses in which the community is present. For more information on houses in particular dioceses, please see the entry for the appropriate diocese.

ALEXIAN BROTHERS (CFA)

Anglo-Irish Province

Regional Residence
Churchfield, Knock,
Co Mayo
Tel 094-9376996
Email cellerbruders@gmail.com

Regional Leader
Br Barry Butler

Tuam

BROTHERS OF CHARITY

St Joseph's Region

Regional Office
Regional Administration
Kilcornan Centre,
Clarinbridge, Co Galway
Tel 091-721517
Email john.oshea@bocsi.ie

Regional Leader
Br John O'Shea

Cork & Ross, Galway,
Limerick, Ossory

CHRISTIAN BROTHERS (CFC)

European Province

Province Centre
Marino, Griffith Avenue,
Dublin 9

Leadership Team
Province Leader
Br David Gibson
Deputy Leader
Br Jim Donovan
Councillor: Br Phil Ryan
Councillor: Br Chris Glavey
Councillor: Br Tom Costello

Dublin, Cork, Down & Connor,
Ferns, Kerry, Killaloe, Limerick,
Ossory, Waterford & Lismore

DE LA SALLE BROTHERS (FSC)

Provincialate
121 Howth Road,
Dublin D03 XN15
Tel 01-8331815 Fax 01-8339130
Email province@iol.ie

Assistant Provincial
Br Ben Hanlon

Armagh, Dublin, Tuam,
Down & Connor, Ossory,
Waterford & Lismore

FRANCISCAN BROTHERS (OSF)

Franciscan Brothers of the
Third Order Regular

A branch of the Regular Third
Order of Penance of St Francis
of Asissi, with communities in
East Africa and the USA as
well as Ireland.

Generalate
Mountbellew, Co Galway
Tel 090-9679295
Fax 090-9679687
Email franciscanbrs@eircom.net

Minister General
Br Tony Dolan
Assistant General
Br Sean Conway
Councillors
Br Hilarion O'Connor
Br Charles Lagu
Br Boniface Kyalo
Procurator General
Br Boniface Kyalo
Bursar General
Br Hilarion O'Connor
Secretary General
Br Bernard Kariuki

Dublin, Tuam, Meath

MARIST BROTHERS (FMS)

The Marist Brothers in Ireland
are part of the province of
West Central Europe principally
involved in education.

Provincialate
Frères Maristes,
Rue de Linthout 91,
1030 Bruxelles, Belgium
Tel +32-27342641
Fax +31-27341599
Email provincial@maristen.org

Provincial Superior
Frère Robert Thunus

Dublin, Ardagh & Clonmacnois

PATRICIAN BROTHERS (FSP)

Brothers of St Patrick

Patrician Brothers
Fairfield, PO Box 980,
NSW 1860, Australia

Congregation Leader
Br Peter D. Ryan *(Australia)*
Email bropryan@gmail.com
*Deputy Congregation Leader
& First Councillo*
Br George Xavier Thlaikat
(India)
Second Councillor
Br George Mangara (India
Prov)
Third Councillor
Br Stephen Sweetman
(Australia–PNG)
Fourth Councillor
Br Nicholas Harsan
(Australia–PNG)

Irish Province Leader
Br Camillus Regan
Tullow, Co Carlow

Dublin, Kildare & Leighlin,
Galway

PRESENTATION BROTHERS (FPM)

Generalate
Mount St Joseph,
Blarney Street, Cork
Tel 021-4392160
Fax 021-4398200
Email generalate@
presentationbrothers.org

Congregation Leader
Br Francis Agoah

Provincial Office
Mardyke House,
Mardyke, Cork
Tel 021-4251819
Email aiprovince@
presentationbrothers.org

Province Leader
Br Raymond Dwyer

Dublin, Cork & Ross, Kerry,
Killaloe, Waterford & Lismore

SAINT JOHN OF GOD BROTHERS (OH)

Hospitaller Order of
Saint John of God

West European Province of
Saint John of God (Great
Britain, Ireland, Malawi)

Saint John of God Brothers
Provincial Curia,
Granada, Stillorgan,
Co Dublin A94 D9N1
Tel 01-5333313
Email provincial@sjog.ie

Provincial
Br Donatus Forkan (OH)

Saint John of God Hospitaller Ministries
Hospitaller House,
Stillorgan,
Co Dublin A94 X5K8
Tel 01-5333300
Fax 01-2831257
Group Chief Executive
Mr Conor McCarthy
Email groupchiefexecutive@sjog.ie

Saint John of God Hospitaller Services
Suite 1-3 Yarn,
Lingfield House,
Lingfield Point,
Darlington DL1 1RW,
Co Durham, England
Tel +44-1325-373700
Fax +44-1325-373707
Chief Executive
Mr Paul Bott

Saint John of God Communty Services CLG
Crinken House, Crinken Lane,
Shankill, Co Dublin C18 K2Y8
Website www.sjog.ie
Chief Executive
Ms Clare Dempsey
Tel 01-5333395
Email clare.dempsey@sjog.ie

Armagh, Dublin, Kerry

Allianz (i)

COMMUNITIES OF RELIGIOUS SISTERS

In this section, details of each community's main house are given, followed by a list of the dioceses in which the community is present. For more information on houses in particular dioceses, please see the entry for the appropriate diocese.

ADORERS OF THE SACRED HEART OF JESUS OF MONTMARTRE (OSB)

St Benedict's Priory
The Mount, Cobh, Co Cork
Tel 021-4811354

Prioress
Mother M. Catherine

Cloyne

BENEDICTINE NUNS (OSB)

Kylemore Abbey
Kylemore, Connemara,
Co Galway H91 VR90
Tel 095-52011
Email info@kylemoreabbey.ie

Abbess: Sr Máire Hickey

Tuam

BLESSED SACRAMENT SISTERS

Blessed Sacrament Convent
Tenene, New Road,
Tullamore,
Co Offaly R35 N528
Email
nelda.doorley@gmail.com

Dublin, Meath

BON SECOURS SISTERS (Paris)

Leadership Office
College Road, Cork
Tel 021-4543310
Fax 021-4542533

Country Leader
Sr Eileen O'Connor
Email leadership@
congregation.bonsecours.ie

Dublin, Cloyne, Cork & Ross, Kerry

SISTERS OF BON SECOURS DE TROYES

St Paul's Nursing Home,
Dooradoyle, Limerick
Tel 061-304690
Email
bonsecours792@gmail.com

Contact: Sr Margaret Costello

Limerick

BRIGIDINE SISTERS
Sisters of St Brigid

106 The Edges 1,
Beacon South Quarter,
Sandyford, Dublin D18 WY00

Congregational Leadership Team
Sr Catherine O'Connor
Email
coconnorcsb07@gmail.com

Dublin, Galway, Kildare & Leighlin, Killaloe

CARMELITE MONASTERIES

Archdiocese of Dublin

Carmelite Monastery of the Immaculate Conception
Roebuck, Dublin D14 T1H9
Tel 01-2884732
Altar Breads
Email altarbreads@
roebuckcarmel.com
Email
carmel@roebuckcarmel.com

Prioress: Sr Teresa Whelan

Star of the Sea Carmelite Monastery
Seapark, Malahide,
Dublin K36 P586
Tel 01-8454259
Tel 087-9643953
Email rmebodc@gmail.com
www.malahidecarmelites.ie
Contemplative Community

Prioress: Sr Rosalie Burke

Carmelite Monastery of St Joseph
Upper Kilmacud Road,
Stillorgan, Blackrock,
Co Dublin A94 YY33
Tel 01-2886089
Email
contact@kilmacudcarmel.ie
www.kilmacudcarmel.ie

Prioress
Sr Mary Brigeen Wilson

Archdiocese of Tuam

Carmelite Monastery
Tranquilla, Knock,
Claremorris,
Co Mayo F12 AH64
Email
tranquilla.knock@gmail.com

Prioress: Sr Claire

Diocese of Ferns

Mount Carmel Monastery
New Ross,
Co Wexford

Prioress: Sr Anne McGlynn

Diocese of Waterford & Lismore

St Joseph's Carmelite Monastery
Tallow, Co Waterford
Tel 058-56205
Email
carmelprint1@gmail.com

Prioress: Sr Patrice Buckley

CARMELITE SISTERS FOR THE AGED AND INFIRM

Our Lady's Manor
Bulloch Castle,
Dalkey, Co Dublin
Tel 01-2806993 Fax 01-2844802
Email
ourladysmanor1@eircom.net

Superior
Sr Mary Therese Healy
Email smtjhealy57@gmail.com
Administrator
Sr Bernadette Murphy

Dublin

SISTERS OF CHARITY OF THE INCARNATE WORD

Carrigoran House
Newmarket-on-Fergus,
Co Clare
Tel 061-368100
Fax 061-368170
Email info@carrigoranhouse.ie

Contact person
Sr Maureen Costello
Email
smaureencostello@gmail.com

Administrator
Ms Marie O'Malley

Killaloe

CHARITY OF JESUS AND MARY SISTERS

Anglo-Irish Province
Moore Abbey
Monasterevin, Co Kildare
Tel 045-525478

Contact
Sr Mary-Anna Lonergan
Email maryannal@eircom.net
Provincial Superior
Sr Elizabeth Roche
108 Spring Road, Letchworth,
Hertfordshire SG6 3B
Tel 0462-675694

Our residential centres have been transferred to Muiriosa Foundation since 1 January 2012

Kildare & Leighlin, Meath

CHARITY OF NEVERS SISTERS

76 Cherrywood
Loughlinstown Drive,
Dun Laoghaire, Co Dublin

Contact person
Sr Rosaleen Cullen
Tel 01-4585654/086-8411466
Email
rosaleencullen@upcmail.ie

Dublin

CHARITY OF ST PAUL THE APOSTLE SISTERS

St Paul's Convent
Selly Park,
Birmingham B29 7LL
Tel 0044-121-4156100

Superior: Sr Ann Sullivan
Email
annsullivan@sellypark.org

Dublin, Limerick

CHRISTIAN RETREAT SISTERS

'The Demesne'
Mountbellew, Ballinasloe,
Co Galway H53 RH61
Tel 090-9679311

Contact: Sr Assumpta Collins
Email assumptahrc@gmail.com

Superior General
Sr Rose Marie Prongue
17 Rue Du Couvent,
25210 Les Fontenelles,
France

Tuam

Allianz ⑪

CISTERCIANS

St Mary's Abbey
Glencairn, Lismore,
Co Waterford P51 X725
Tel 058-56168
Email
info@glencairnabbey.org

Abbess: Sr Marie Fahy

Waterford & Lismore

CLARISSAN MISSIONARY SISTERS OF THE BLESSED SACRAMENT

Our Lady of Guadalupe Residence for Students
28 Waltersland Road,
Stillorgan, Co Dublin
Tel 01-2886600
Email info@ourladyof
guadaluperesidence.com
www.ourladyof
guadaluperesidence.com

Superior: Sr Elisa Padilla
Tel 087-0510783

Dublin

CONGREGATION OF THE SISTERS OF MERCY

The Congregation of the Sisters of Mercy is an International Congregation. It has 1,467 members currently serving in Ireland, Brazil, South Africa, Peru, US and Kenya.

Congregational Leadership Team
Sr Marie Louise White
(Congregational Leader)
Sr Anna Burke
Sr Cait O'Dwyer
Sr Bernie Ryan
Sr Helena O'Donoghue

Congregational Offices
'Rachamim', 13/14 Moyle Park,
Convent Road, Clondalkin,
Dublin D22 HR94
Tel 01-4673737
Email mercy@csm.ie
Website www.sistersofmercy.ie

The Northern Province
comprising the dioceses of
Raphoe, Derry, Down &
Connor, Armagh, Dromore,
Clogher, Kilmore and Meath.

Provincial
Sr Rose Marie Conlan

Sr Áine Campbell
Sr Mary De Largy
Sr Mabel Marron
Sr Perpetua McNulty

Provincial Office
74 Main Street, Clogher,
Co Tyrone BT76 0AA
Tel 028-85548127
Fax 028-85549459
Email mercy@mercynth.org

The Western Province
Comprising the dioceses of
Killala, Achonry, Elphin,
Galway, Tuam, Clonfert,
Ardagh & Clonmacnois.

Provincial: Sr Breege O'Neill

Sr Áine Barrins
Sr Maura Bane
Sr Margaret Casey
Sr Una Purcell

Provincial Office
Caoineas, Society Street,
Ballinasloe, Co Galway
Tel 090-9645202
Fax 090-9645203
Email caoineas@smwestprov.ie

The South Central Province
Comprising the dioceses of
Dublin, Cashel & Emly,
Kildare & Leighlin, Killaloe,
Limerick.

Provincial: Sr Brenda Dolphin

Sr Patricia O'Meara
Sr Margaret Prendergast
Sr Ailish O'Brien

Provincial Office,
Oldtown, Sallins Road,
Naas, Co Kildare W91 A5RK
Tel 045-876784
Fax 045-871509
Email
provoffice@mercyscp.ie

The Southern Province
Comprising the dioceses of
Cork & Ross, Cloyne, Kerry,
Ferns, Ossory, Waterford &
Lismore.

Provincial: Sr Eileen O'Flynn

Sr Nora Anne Lombard
Sr Julianne Sullivan
Sr Anna Mai Middleton
Sr Bríd Biggane

Provincial Office
Bishop Street, Cork
Tel 021-4975380
Fax 021-4915220
Email
provincialoffice@mercysouth.ie

CROSS AND PASSION CONGREGATION

Province Office,
299 Boarshaw Road,
Middleton,
Manchester M24 2PF
Tel 0044-161-6553184
Fax 0044-161-6533666

Province Leader
Sr Savio Steed

Dublin, Down & Connor

DAUGHTERS OF CHARITY OF ST VINCENT DE PAUL

St Catherine's Provincial House
Dunardagh, Blackrock,
Co Dublin
Tel 01-2882669/2882896/
2882660 Fax 01-2834485
Email
provincialsecretary@daughters
ofcharity.ie

Local Superior: Sr Marie Fox
Provincial Superior
Sr Áine O'Brien
Email aineobrien@
daughtersofcharity.ie

Dublin, Tuam, Cork & Ross,
Down & Connor

DAUGHTERS OF THE CROSS OF LIÈGE

Daughters of the Cross
Beech Park Convent,
Beechwood Court, Stillorgan,
Co Dublin
Tel 01-2887401/2887315
Fax 01-2881499
Email
beechpark1833@gmail.com

Superior
Sr Kathleen McKenna

Dublin

DAUGHTERS OF THE HEART OF MARY

St Joseph's
1 Crosthwaite Grove,
Crosthwaite Park South,
Dun Laoghaire, Co Dublin
Tel 01-2801204

Dublin

DAUGHTERS OF THE HOLY SPIRIT

9 Walnut Park
Drumcondra, Dublin 9
Tel 01-8371825

Contact person: Sr Ita Durnin
Email itadhs@yahoo.co.uk

Provincial Superior
Sr Anne Morris
22 Holyrood Road,
Northhampton, NN5 7AH,
England

Dublin

DAUGHTERS OF MARY AND JOSEPH

Leadership Team
Email dmjireland@gmail.com

Dublin, Kildare & Leighlin,
Meath, Ossory

DAUGHTERS OF OUR LADY OF THE SACRED HEART

Provincial House
14 Rossmore Avenue,
Templeogue, Dublin 6W
Tel 01-4903200
Tel/Fax 01-4903113
Email olshprov@eircom.net

Provincial: Sr Mairéad Kellehe

Dublin, Clogher

DAUGHTERS OF WISDOM (LA SAGESSE)

2 The Greenlands
Rosses Point, Sligo F91 A6XE
Tel 071-9177607

Contact: Sr Margaret Morris
Email srmegmorris@gmail.cor

Dublin, Elphin

DISCIPLES OF THE DIVINE MASTER

Newtownpark Avenue,
White's Cross, Blackrock,
Co Dublin A94 V2N8
Tel 01-2114949/2886414

Delegation Superior
Sr M. Kathryn Williams
Email
kathrynwilliams@pddm.org
www.pddm.ie

Dublin, Elphin

DOMINICAN CONTEMPLATIVE NUNS

Monastery of St Catherine of Siena
The Twenties, Drogheda,
Co Louth A92 KR84
Tel 041-9838524
Email
sienamonastery@gmail.com

Prioress
Sr M. Breda Carroll OP

Armagh

DOMINICAN SISTERS (King William's Town)

Our Lady of Fatima Convent
Oakpark, Tralee, Co Kerry
Tel 066-7125641/066-7125900
Fax 066-7180834
Email teresamcevoy@
fatimahome.com

Contact: Sr Teresa McEvoy OP

Kerry

DOMINICAN SISTERS

Congregation of Dominican
Sisters
Mary Bellew House,
Dominican Campus, Cabra,
Dublin D07 Y2E7
Tel 01-8299700 Fax 01-8299799
Email
omgen@dominicansisters.com
www.dominicansisters.com

Congregation Prioress
Sr Martina Phelan OP

Dublin, Down & Connor,
Galway

DOMINICAN SISTERS OF ST CECILIA

St Saviour's
Glentworth Street, Limerick
Tel 085-2255796

Superior
Sr Caitríona Kavanagh OP
Email limerick@op-tn.org

Limerick

FAMILY OF ADORATION SISTERS

St Aidan's Monastery
Ferns, Co Wexford
Tel 053-9366634
Email
staidansferns@eircom.net

Ferns, Down & Connor

FRANCISCAN MISSIONARIES OF THE DIVINE MOTHERHOOD

Franciscan Convent
Corbally Drive, Ballinasloe,
Co Galway H53 RF84

Country Leader
Sr Kathleen Murphy
Tel 090-9643642
Email admin@fmdm.ie

Dublin, Clonfert, and Kerry

FRANCISCAN MISSIONARIES OF MARY

Provincial House
5 Vaughan Avenue,
London W6 0XS
Tel 020-87484077

Provincial Superior
Sr Lillian Hunt
Email provincial@fmmuk.org

Provincial Secretary
Email provsec@fmmuk.org

Dublin, Limerick

FRANCISCAN MISSIONARIES OF OUR LADY

La Verna Centre
Franciscan House of
Spirituality & Hospitality,
Ballinderry, Mullingar,
Co Westmeath N91 K680
Tel 044-9352000/087-3935613
Email
lavernacentre@gmail.com
www.fmolireland.ie
lavernacentre on Facebook

Regional Superior
Sr Clare Brady
Email info@fmolireland.ie

Meath

FRANCISCAN MISSIONARIES OF ST JOSEPH

St Joseph's
16 Innismore,
Crumlin Village, Dublin 12
Tel 01-4563445

Regional Leader
Sr Mary Butler

Dublin, Cork & Ross

FRANCISCAN MISSIONARY SISTERS FOR AFRICA

Central Team
34a Gilford Road,
Sandymount, Dublin 4
Tel 01-2838376
Fax 01-2602049
Email generalate@fmsa.net

Leader: Sr Jeanette Watters

Armagh, Dublin

FRANCISCAN SISTERS OF THE IMMACULATE CONCEPTION

Franciscan Sisters,
97/99 Riverside Park,
Clonshaugh, Dublin 17
Tel 087-6703715

Contact person
Sr Immaculata Owhotemu
99 Riverside Park, Clonshaugh,
Dublin 17
Tel 01-8771778
Email immachwo@hotmail.com

Dublin

FRANCISCAN SISTERS OF THE RENEWAL

St Anthony Convent
Dublin Road, Drogheda,
Co Louth A92 X044
Tel 041-9830441
Fax 041-9842321
Website
www.franciscansisterscfr.com

Superior: Sr Agnes Holtz

Meath

FRANCISCAN SISTERS OF LITTLEHAMPTON

Eden
Knock, Claremorris,
Co Mayo FT12 YC83
Tel 094-9388302
Registered charity 232931

Leader
Sr Anastasia McGonagle

Tuam

SISTERS OF ST FRANCIS OF PHILADELPHIA

Our Lady of Angels Convent
609 S. Convent Road,
Aston, PA 19014
Tel 6105587733
Fax 6104500195

Congregational Minister
Sr Mary Kathryn Dougherty

Dublin, Cloyne, Limerick

CONGREGATION OF OUR LADY OF CHARITY OF THE GOOD SHEPHERD

Province Administration
63 Lower Sean McDermott
Street, Dublin D01 NX93
Tel 01-8711109
Email
province.office@rgs.ie
www.goodshepherdsisters.ie

Province Leader
Sr Cait O'Leary

Dublin, Cork & Ross, Derry,
Down & Connor, Limerick,
Waterford & Lismore

HANDMAIDS OF THE SACRED HEART OF JESUS

St Raphaela's
Upper Kilmacud Road,
Stillorgan,
Co Dublin A94 TP38
Tel 01-2889963
Fax 01-2889536

Superior: Sr Irene Guia
Email iguiaci@gmail.com

Dublin

HOLY CHILD JESUS, SOCIETY OF THE

European Province
Sr Angela O'Connor
14 Norham Gardens,
Oxford OX2 6QB, England

Provincial Representative
Sr Eileen Crowley
21 Grange Park Avenue,
Raheny, Dublin D05 AY65
Email
crowley.eileen@gmail.com

Dublin

HOLY FAITH SISTERS

Generalate
Aylward House,
Glasnevin, Dublin D11 YEF1
Tel 01-8520306
Email
congregationalleader@hfaith.ie

Congregational Leader
Sr Rosaleen Cunniffe

Dublin

SISTERS OF THE HOLY FAMILY OF BORDEAUX

65 Griffith Downs
Drumcondra, Dublin 9
Tel 01-5477709

Councillor for Ireland
Sr Claire McGrath
Email
clairemcgrath.hfb@gmail.com

Dublin, Kildare & Leighlin

INFANT JESUS SISTERS

Provincial House
56 St Lawrence Road,
Clontarf,
Dublin D03 Y5F2
Tel 01-8338930

Provincial: Sr Marie Pitcher
Email
mariepitcher1@gmail.com

Dublin, Cloyne, Cork & Ross,
Kerry

JESUS AND MARY, CONGREGATION OF

The sisters from the Irish
Province work in Haiti,
Cameroon, Ekpoma, Lagos
and Pakistan. The sisters are
involved in education,
working with the
handicapped and in
formation, including a house
of formation in Nigeria.

Provincialate, 'Errew House'
110 Goatstown Road,
Dublin 14
Tel 01-2966059

Provincial Superior
Sr Marie O'Halloran
Tel 01-2969150/087-7203649
Email
marieohalloran68@gmail.com

Dublin, Galway, Killala

SISTERS OF LA RETRAITE

77 Grove Park
Rathmines, Dublin 6
Tel 01-491171

Congregational Leader
Sr Avril O'Regan
Email avriloregan@
congregationlaretraite.org

Dublin, Galway

LA SAINTE UNION DES SACRES COEURS

Provincial Office
53 Croftdown Road,
London NW5 1EL
Tel 020-74827225
Email lsuahtprovince@gmail.com

Province leadership Team
Sr Annemarie Egan
Sr Michele Totman

Dublin, Ardagh & Clonmacnois,
Galway, Kildare & Leighlin,
Killaloe, Limerick, Tuam

LITTLE COMPANY OF MARY

Provincialate
Cnoc Mhuire, 29 Woodpark,
Ballinteer Avenue,
Dublin 16
Tel 01-2987040
Email lcom@lcm.ie

Province Leader
Sr Mary Flanagan

Dublin, Cloyne, Kerry,
Limerick, Ossory, Waterford &
Lismore

LITTLE SISTERS OF THE ASSUMPTION

Administration Office
42 Rathfarnham Road,
Terenure, Dublin 6W
Tel 01-4909850 Fax 01-4925740
Email pernet42r@gmail.com

Sr Mary O'Sullivan, Sr Maria
Flynn, Sr Mary Malone

Dublin, Cork & Ross, Galway

LITTLE SISTERS OF THE POOR

Mother Provincial
St Peter's Residence,
2A Meadow Road,
South Lambeth,
London SW8 1QH
Tel 0044-020-73350788
Email mp.lond@lsplondon.co.uk

Provincial: Sr Anthony Francis

Dublin, Ossory

LORETO (IBVM)

Provincialate
Loreto House, Beaufort,
Rathfarnham,
Dublin D14 H3V2
Tel 01-4933827
Email provadmin@loreto.ie

Provincial: Sr Carmel Swords

Dublin, Derry, Ferns, Kilmore,
Meath, Ossory, Waterford &
Lismore

MARIE AUXILIATRICE SISTERS

7 Florence Street,
Portobello, Dublin 8
Tel/Fax 01-4537622

Dublin

SISTERS OF MARIE REPARATRICE

Laurel Hill Avenue,
South Circular Road,
Limerick V94 XN29
Tel 061-315045

Contact
Sr Eileen Carroll
Email
eileencarrollsmr@gmail.com

Cork & Ross, Limerick

MARIST SISTERS

Provincialate
51 Kenilworth Square,
Dublin 6
Tel 01-4972196
Email secirlmarists@gmail.com

Leader – Ireland
Sr Miriam McManus

Dublin, Achonry, Ardagh &
Clonmacnois

MEDICAL MISSIONARIES OF MARY

Rosemount,
Rosemount Terrace,
Booterstown, Blackrock,
Co Dublin A94 AH63
Tel 01-2882722
Email rcsmmm@mmm37.org

Armagh, Dublin, Meath

MISSIONARIES OF CHARITY

Gift of Love
223 South Circular Road,
Dublin 8

Regional Superior
Sr M. Chantal
177 Bravington Road
London W9 3AR
Tel 0208-9602644

Armagh, Dublin, Cloyne,
Elphin

MISSIONARY FRANCISCAN SISTERS OF THE IMMACULATE CONCEPTION

Franciscan Convent
Assisi House, Navan Road,
Dublin 7
Tel 01-8682216

Dublin

MISSIONARY SISTERS OF THE ASSUMPTION

Assumption Convent
34 Crossgar Road,
Ballynahinch,
Co Down BT24 8EN
Tel 028-97561765

Superior
Sr Maureen Carville
Email
maureenc@msassumption.org

Dromore

MISSIONARY SISTERS OF THE GOSPEL

Carriglea
Dungarvan, Co Waterford
Tel 058-45884
Email
mary.fitzgeraldmsg20@gmail.com

Superior: Sr Mary Fitzgerald

Waterford & Lismore

MISSIONARY SISTERS OF THE HOLY CROSS

86 Glen Road,
Belfast BT11 8BH
Tel 028-90614631
Email
holycrossbelfast@gmail.com

Superior
Sr Patricia Kelly

Down & Connor

MISSIONARY SISTERS OF THE HOLY ROSARY

Regional Administration
11 Westpark,
Artane, Dublin 5
Tel 01-8510010
Email mshrreg@eircom.net

Regional Superior for Ireland and England: Sr Paula Molloy

Dublin, Cork & Ross, Kilmore, Meath

MISSIONARY SISTERS OF ST COLUMBAN

+ Columban's Convent
Magheramore,
Wicklow A67 HY02
Tel 0404-67348

Community Leaders
Sr Anne Ryan (Main House)
Sr Margaret Murphy (Nursing Home)

Dublin

MISSIONARY SISTERS OF ST PETER CLAVER

31 Bushy Park Road,
Terenure, Dublin D06 V6Y9
Tel 01-4909360

Contact Person
Sr Juli Thottungal
Email
missiondublin@stpeterclaver.ie

Dublin

MISSIONARY SISTERS SERVANTS OF THE HOLY SPIRIT

43 Philipsburgh Avenue,
Fairview, Dublin D03 HF80
Tel 01-8369383
Email
spsfairview1@gmail.com

Community Leader
Sr Joan Quirke

Dublin

CONGREGATION OF OUR LADY OF THE MISSIONS

Notre Dame Convent,
Upper Churchtown Road,
leading to Sweetmount
Avenue, Dublin D14 N8E8
Tel 01-2983306

Dublin, Ardagh &
Clonmacnois

OUR LADY OF THE CENACLE

19 St Francis' Gardens,
Blackpool, Cork
Tel 087-2891545

Contact: Sr Peggy Cronin
Email
peggycronin.8@gmail.com

Dublin, Cork & Ross

PERPETUAL ADORATION SISTERS

Perpetual Adoration Convent
Wexford
Tel 053-9124134
Email adoration44@eircom.net

Superior: Sr M. Peter Leech

Ferns

POOR CLARES

Archdiocese of Dublin

St Damian's
3A Simmonscourt Road,
Ballsbridge,
Dublin D04 P8A0
Fax 01-6685464
Email pccdamians@mac.com

Abbess/Contact
Sr Mary Brigid Haran

Diocese of Ardagh & Clonmacnois

Poor Clare Monastery of Perpetual Adoration
Drumshanbo,
Co Leitrim

Abbess
Mother Jemma Hayag

Diocese of Cork & Ross

Poor Clare Colettine Monastery
College Road, Cork

Abbess: Sr Miriam Buckley

Diocese of Galway

St Clare's Monastery
Nuns' Island, Galway

Abbess
Sr M. Colette

Diocese Kildare & Leighlin

Poor Clare Colettine Monastery
Graiguecullen, Carlow

Abbess
Mother Rosario Byrne

Diocese of Killaloe

Poor Clare Monastery
Francis Street, Ennis,
Co Clare V95 VNP5
Email
bernardinemeskell@live.ie

Abbess
Sr Bernardine Meskell

POOR SERVANTS OF THE MOTHER OF GOD

Generalate
Maryfield Convent,
Mount Angelus Road,
Roehampton SW15 4JA,
England
Tel 0208-7884351

General
Sr Margaret Cashman

Local Leader (Dublin region North): Sr Mary Beecher
Email
mary.beecher@psmgs.org
Local Leader (Dublin region West): Sr Ann Coughlan
Email
acoughlan1942@gmail.com
Local Leader (outside Dublin)
Sr Nora Daly
Email nora.daly@psmgs.org

Dublin, Tuam, Down & Connor, Limerick

CONGREGATION OF THE SISTERS OF NAZARETH

Nazareth House
Malahide Road, Dublin 3
Tel 01-8338205
Email
regional.ie@nazarethcare.com

Regional Superior
Sr Patricia Enright

Dublin, Cloyne, Derry, Down & Connor, Elphin

PRESENTATION SISTERS

Generalate
Monasterevin,
Co Kildare W34 PV32
Tel 045-525335/525503
Fax 045-525209
Email admin@pbvm.org
Website www.pbvm.org

Congregational Leader
Sr Julie Watson

Armagh, Dublin, Cashel & Emly, Tuam, Clogher, Cloyne, Cork & Ross, Ferns, Galway, Kerry, Kildare & Leighlin, Limerick, Ossory, Waterford & Lismore

PRESENTATION OF MARY SISTERS

4 Lower John Street,
Sligo
Tel 071-9160740

Superior: Sr Emma Dublan

Elphin

REDEMPTORISTINES

Monastery of St Alphonsus
St Alphonsus Road Upper,
Dublin D09 HN53

Superior: Sr Gabrielle
Email
gabrielle.fox@redemptorists.ie

Dublin

RELIGIOUS OF CHRISTIAN EDUCATION

Generalate Office
3 Bushy Park House,
Templeogue Road,
Dublin D6W E128

Congregational Leader
Sr Cara Nagle
Tel 01-4909912
Email cara.nagle@gmail.com

Dublin

RELIGIOUS OF SACRED HEART OF MARY

13/14 Huntstown Wood,
Dublin D15 XT9X
Tel 01-8223566/086-0876154

Contact person
Sr Catherine Gough
Email catherinegoughshm@
yahoo.co.uk

Dublin, Down & Connor, Ossory

RELIGIOUS SISTERS OF CHARITY

Generalate
Caritas, 15 Gilford Road,
Sandymount, Dublin 4
Tel 01-2697833/2697935

Provincialate, Provincial House,
Our Lady's Mount, Harold's
Cross, Dublin D6W W934
Tel 01-4973177

Dublin, Cork & Ross

SACRED HEART SOCIETY

Provincial Administration Office
76 Home Farm Road,
Drumcondra, Dublin D09 R903
Tel 01-8375412

Provincial Secretary
Email provsec@rscjirs.org
Canonical Leader
Sr Dairne McHenry
Executive Officer
Email executive@rscjirs.org

Armagh, Dublin

SACRED HEARTS OF JESUS AND MARY (PICPUS)

Delegation House
11 Northbrook Road
Ranelagh,
Dublin D06 Y962
Tel 01-4974831 (Community)

Contact
Sr Aileen Kennedy (SSCC)

Dublin

SACRED HEARTS OF JESUS AND MARY

Sacred Heart Convent
Blackrock, Cork T12 W200
Tel 021-4936200

Community Leader
Sr Annie Mary Nally

Tuam, Cork & Ross

SALESIAN SISTERS OF ST JOHN BOSCO

Provincialate
203 Lower Kilmacud Road,
Stillorgan, Co Dublin
Tel 01-2985188
Email
provincial@salesiansisters.net

Provincial Superior
Sr Bridget O'Connell

Dublin, Limerick

SERVANT SISTERS OF THE HOME OF THE MOTHER

Knockaire, Galway Road,
Roscommon Town

Superior: Sr Ruth O'Callaghan

Elphin

SISTERS OF OUR LADY OF APOSTLES

Provincialate
Ardfoyle Convent,
Ballintemple, Cork T12 Y304
Tel 021-4294076
Fax 021-4291019
Email prov@ardfoyle.com

Provincial
Sr Kathleen McGarvey

Dublin, Tuam, Cork & Ross,
Dromore

SISTERS OF ST CLARE

St Clare's Generalate
63 Harold's Cross Road,
Dublin 6W
Tel 01-4966880/4995135
Fax 01-4966388
Email annedkelly@yahoo.com

Abbess General
Sr Anne Kelly

Dublin, Down & Connor,
Dromore, Kerry, Kilmore

Regional Superior
Sr Zita Daly
St Clare's Convent,
12 Ashgrove Avenue, Newry,
Co Down BT34 1PR
Tel 028-30253877
Email zitadaly@gmail.com

SISTERS OF ST JOHN OF GOD

St John of God Congregational Centre
Newtown Road,
Wexford
Tel 053-9142396
Email stjohnogoffice@ssjgcc.ie

Congregational Leader
Sr Geraldine Fitzpatrick

Dublin, Ferns, Kildare &
Leighlin, Killaloe, Ossory,
Waterford & Lismore

ST JOSEPH OF ANNECY SISTERS

St Joseph's Convent
Killorglin, Co Kerry
Tel 066-9761809
Fax 066-9761127
Email
margaret.lyne@talk21.com

Superior: Sr Helena Lyne

Kerry

ST JOSEPH OF THE APPARITION SISTERS

St Joseph's Convent
Dun Bríd, Ballymote, Co Sligo
Tel 071-9183973
Email stjsligo@eircom.net

Achonry

SISTERS OF ST JOSEPH OF CHAMBERY

St Joseph's Convent
Springdale Road, Raheny,
Dublin 5
Tel 01-8774985

Superior: Sr Marian Connor
Email
marianconnor91@gmail.com
Regional Superior
Sr Joan Margaret Kelly
Email joanmkelly1@yahoo.fr

Dublin

ST JOSEPH OF CLUNY SISTERS

Mt Sackville Convent
Chapelizod, Dublin 20
Tel 01-8213134
Fax 01-8224002
Email provirlgb@sjc.ie
Website www.sjc.ie

Provincial Superior
Sr Maeve Guinan

Dublin, Ardagh & Clonmacnois

ST JOSEPH OF THE SACRED HEART SISTERS

Coolcranogue
Dunganville Upper, Ardagh,
Co Limerick
Tel 069-76794

Regional Leader
Sr Margaret O'Sullivan
margaretosullivan1@outlook.ie

Dublin, Tuam, Achonry,
Cloyne, Kerry, Killaloe,
Limerick

ST LOUIS SISTERS

131 Beaufort Downs
Rathfarnham, Dublin 14
Tel 01-4934194
Email regionalate@stlouisirl.ie

Regional Leader
Sr Uainín Clarke

Armagh, Dublin, Tuam,
Clogher, Down & Connor

ST MARY MADELEINE POSTEL SISTERS

Ard Mhuire Convent
Parkmore, New Line,
Roscrea, Co Tipperary

Regional Superior
Sr M. Luke Minogue

Killaloe

ST PAUL DE CHARTRES SISTERS

6-8 Garville Avenue,
Rathgar, Dublin 6
Tel 01-4975381/4972366
Email fabiolapak@gmail.com

Regional Superior
Sr Fabiola Pak

Dublin

URSULINES

Ursuline Provincialate
17 Trimleston Drive,
Booterstown, Co Dublin
Tel 01-2693503
Email
angemeriwk@gmail.com
Website www.ursulines.ie

Provincial
Sr Anne Harte Barry

Dublin, Cashel & Emly, Cork &
Ross, Elphin, Waterford &
Lismore

URSULINES OF JESUS

26 The Drive
Seatown Park,
Swords, Co Dublin
Tel 01-8404323

Delegated Councillor
Sr Hilary Brown
Ursulines of Jesus,
Flat 14 Kimpton Court,
2 Murrain Road,
London N4 2BN
Email hiliaryuj@gmail.com

Dublin

INSTITUTES

LAY SECULAR INSTITUTES

Lay secular institutes come under the jurisdiction of the Sacred Congregation for Religious Secular Institutes as laid down by the Apostolic Constitution, *Provida Mater Ecclesia*.

Caritas Christi

Secular institute of pontifical right founded in 1937 for laywomen.

Priest Assistant
Rev Jordan O'Brien (OP)
St Mary's, The Claddagh,
Galway H91 CD36
Tel 091-582884
Email pjobpjob@gmail.com

Priest Assistant for Dublin
Rev Gregory Carroll (OP)
St Mary's Priory,
Tallaght, Dublin 24
Tel 01-4048118
Fax 01-4515584
Email gregcop@eircom.net

Contacts: www.ccinfo.org
Veronica Doolan
Tel 086-8660384
Kathleen Tel 087-9005767

Columba Community

Private association of the faithful involved in prayer, Christian teaching, counsel, reconciliation and healing and rehabilitation from drugs and alcohol.

Columba House,
11 Queen Street,
Derry BT48 7EG
Tel 028-71262407
Email columbacommunity@hotmail.com
Website www.columbacommunity.com

Treasurer: Ms Kathleen Devlin
Contact: Tommy McCay

Servitium Christi

A Secular Institute of Pontifical right for women in the Eucharistic Family of St Peter Julian Eymard (also includes the Congregation of the Blessed Sacrament).

Enquiries: Mary Keane
58 Moyne Road,
Ranelagh, Dublin 6

CATHOLIC EDUCATION

COMMISSION FOR CATHOLIC EDUCATION AND FORMATION

Executive Secretary to the Episcopal Commission/Department
Rev Paul Connell PhD
Tel 01-5053014
Email education@iecon.ie

COUNCIL FOR CATECHETICS OF THE IRISH EPISCOPAL CONFERENCE

Members of the Council
Most Rev Brendan Leahy DD *(Chair)*
Most Rev William Crean DD, Mr Eoin Walshe, Dr Gerry O'Connell, Dr Cora O'Farrell, Mrs Hilda Campbell, Rev Dr Edward McGee, Sr Antoinette Dilworth (RSJ), Dr Aiveen Mullaly, Mrs Kate Liffey, Dr Daniel O'Connell, Dr Amalee Meehan, Rev Dr Billy Swan and Rev Paul Connell PhD *(Council for Education of the IEC)* and Dr Alexander O'Hara KM *(Executive Secretary and National Director for Catechetics)*
Contact details: Dr Alexander O'Hara KM
Columba Centre, Maynooth, Co Kildare
Tel 086-0588786
Email alex.ohara@iecon.ie

COUNCIL FOR EDUCATION OF THE IRISH EPISCOPAL CONFERENCE [WITH NORTHERN IRELAND COUNCIL FOR CATHOLIC EDUCATION (NICCE)]

The Council for Education articulates policy and vision for Catholic Education in Ireland, north and south, on behalf of the Episcopal Conference. It has responsibility for the forward planning necessary to ensure the best provision for Catholic Education in the country. It liaises with other Catholic Education Offices, the Department of Education and Skills and the Department of Education, Northern Ireland. The Council advises the Conference on all government legislation as applied to education. It responds to and acts as spokesperson for the Episcopal Conference on issues related to the work of education. It seeks also to develop long-term strategies in education for the Episcopal Conference

Members of the Council for Education
Most Rev Thomas Deenihan DD *(Chair)*
Most Rev Donal McKeown DD
Most Rev Francis Duffy DD
Rt Rev Mgr Dan O'Connor, Sr Evelyn Byrne, Mr Seamus Mulconry, Mr John Curtis, Dr Marie Griffin, Mr Fintan Murphy

Executive Secretary
Rev Paul Connell PhD
Council for Education of the IEC,
Columba Centre, Maynooth, Co Kildare
Tel +353-1-5053014
Email education@iecon.ie
Administrative Assistant
Ms Cora Hennelly
Tel +353-1-5053027
Email chennelly@iecon.ie

Northern Ireland Commission for Catholic Education (NICCE)
Until 2005, there was no central body seeking to offer leadership across the Catholic education sector in NI. The 'Maintained' schools (nursery, primary and non-selective post-primary) were managed by CCMS (a statutory body) while the Voluntary Grammar schools had a considerable degree of independence. The Northern Ireland Commission for Catholic Education (NICCE) was set up in 2005 by the Trustees in order to provide co-ordination of the Catholic sector in a time of rapid change. Today, there are 460 Maintained Schools and 29 Voluntary Grammar Schools.

Current Directors of the Northern Ireland Commission for Catholic Education (NICCE)
Most Rev Donal McKeown DD (Chair), Most Rev Eamon Martin DD, Sr Eithne Woulfe (SSL) (Vice-Chair), Mr Dermot McGovern (ERST NI), Monsignor Peter O'Reilly, Dean Kevin Donaghy, Sr Maureen O'Dee (Sister of St Clare), Rev Feidhlimidh Magennis, Rev Timothy Bartlett, Rev Gerard Fox and Sr Brighde Vallely
In attendance
Rev Paul Connell

Secretary
Mr Fintan Murphy
Northern Ireland Commission for Catholic Education (NICCE)
St Mary's College, Belfast BT12 6FE
Tel 028-90268368
Email f.murphy@csts.stmarys-belfast.ac.uk
Website info@catholiceducation-ni.org

The Catholic Education Services Committee (CESC)

The CESC is an education committee established by the Irish Episcopal Conference (IEC) and the Association of Leaders of Missionaries and Religious of Ireland (AMRI). Formally consisting of six Bishops and six Religious nominated by AMRI, it was reconstituted in 2019.

The membership now consists of six Bishops, four Religious nominated by AMRI, two representatives of the six educational Trusts that have Public Juridic Person status (PJPs), and a representative of third level Catholic Education. As such, it is now representative of the entire Catholic Education sector.

CESC aims to support a vibrant Catholic education sector in response to changing social, economic and political conditions in Ireland. It promotes the Catholic education sector nationally and assists providers and practitioners in encouraging people to choose Catholic education at all stages of lifelong learning. The development of a co-ordinated and strategic approach to education across the entire Catholic sector in Ireland is a priority for CESC.

Members of the Catholic Education Services Committee (CESC)
Most Rev Thomas Deenihan DD (Chair), Most Rev Francis Duffy DD, Most Rev Donal McKeown DD, Most Rev Dermot Farrell DD, Most Rev Kieran O'Reilly DD, Fr Leonard Moloney (SJ), Fr John Hennebry (OSA), Sr Ella McGuinness (RSM), Mr T.J. Coakley, Mr Noel Merrick. *In attendance* Dr Marie Griffin (Chair CEP).

Executive Secretary: Rev Paul Connell
Catholic Education Service
Columba Centre, Maynooth, Co Kildare
Tel +353-1-5053014
Email education@iecon.ie

Catholic Education Service Trust (CEST)
The Catholic Education Service is a charity created by Deed of Trust. The Trustees of CEST are four Catholic Bishops who are Ordinaries of Catholic dioceses in Ireland and each representing one of the four ecclesiastical provinces of Ireland (Most Rev Thomas Deenihan DD, Most Rev Dermot Farrell DD, Most Rev Kieran O'Reilly DD, Most Rev Francis Duffy DD) and two Religious appointed by AMRI, Rev Leonard Moloney (SJ) and Rev John Hennebry (OSA). The Trustees of the CEST are *ex officio* members of Catholic Education Service Committee (CESC).

Catholic Education Partnership (CEP)

In November 2020, a new structure for the management and trusteeship of Catholic Post-Primary Education came into being. As part of this new structure, two new companies have been established: the Association of Patrons and Trustees of Catholic Schools (APTCS) (see below), and the Catholic Education Partnership (CEP). The CEP replaces the Catholic Schools Partnership (CSP) and will continue its work of providing support for all the partners in Catholic education at first, second and third level in the Republic of Ireland. The CEP going forward will be closely aligned with the Secretariat of Secondary Schools (SSS) which provides support for Boards of Management and Principals in Catholic Post Primary Schools. In addition, it will also be closely aligned with the APTCS which provides support and advice for Patrons and Trustees of Catholic Schools. The activities of the CEP will be supported and funded by CEST.

The Directors of the CEP Company are: Most Rev Leo O'Reilly DD, Dr Marie Griffin *(Chair)*, Fr Gareth Byrne, Ms Mary Fergin, Dr John McCafferty, Dr Andrew McGrady, Ms Deirdre Matthews, Dr Amalie Meehan, Mr Jonathan Tiernan, Mr Paul Meany, Ms Cathy Burke, Ms Angela Mitchell and Sr Eithne Woulfe SSL).

Chair: Dr Marie Griffin
CEO: Mr Alan Hynes
Company Secretary: Fr Paul Connell
Columba Centre,
Maynooth, Co Kildare
Tel 01-5053100
Email ceo@catholiceducation.ie
Website www.catholiceducation.ie

Association of Patrons and Trustees of Catholic Schools (APTCS)

The Association of Patrons and Trustees of Catholic Schools (APTCS) came into being in November 2020. The APTCS is the representative body for the 'Catholic Trustee Voice' in Irish education at primary and post-primary level. Its membership includes members of the Irish Episcopal Conference, representatives of various religious congregations, representatives of the PJP trusts, as well as the trustees of a number of other Catholic schools.

The Directors of APTCS are:
Mr Paul Meany (Chair), Mr Michael Sexton, Ms Sheila McManamly (Company Secretary), Sr Ann O'Donoghue, Ms Maeve Mahon, Ms Deirdre Matthews, Mr John Barry, Mr Declan Lawlor, Fr Paul Connell, Mr Gerry Bennett, Mr Edmund Corrigan.

Contact details:
Association of Patrons and Trustees of Catholic Schools (APTCS)
Chairperson: Mr Paul Meany
CEO: Dr Eilis Humphreys
New House, St Patrick's College,
Maynooth, Co Kildare
Tel 01-5053164
Email ceo@aptcs.ie

Secretariat of Secondary Schools (SSS)

General Secretary: Ms Deirdre Matthews
Secretariat of Secondary Schools,
Emmet House, Dundrum Road,
Milltown, Dublin 14
Tel +353-1-2838255 Fax +353-1-2695461
Email info@jmb.ie
Website www.jmb.ie

The Secretariat of Secondary Schools is the company which governs the Association of Management of Catholic Secondary Schools (AMCSS). The AMCSS promotes, advises and supports Catholic Voluntary Secondary Schools in Ireland. Founded in the 1960s, it adopted its present structure in 1987. Its membership includes a principal and chairperson of a Board of Management from each of its ten constituent regions. It also includes a representative of the Irish Episcopal Conference and a representative of AMRI (Association of Leaders of Missionaries and Religious of Ireland). The Council cooperates and maintains links with other national and international groups interested in Catholic education. Its Secretariat provides a wide range of educational services and advice to its members. When the Council joins with representatives of the Protestant Voluntary Secondary Schools the Irish School Heads (ISA) it forms the Council of the Joint Managerial Body ((JMB). The JMB is recognised by the Department of Education & Skills as the negotiating body for Voluntary Secondary Schools.

Catholic Primary School Management Association (CPSMA)

Chair: Ms Anne Fay
General Secretary: Mr Seamus Mulconry
New House, St Patrick's College,
Maynooth, Co Kildare
Tel +353-1-6292462/1850-407200
Fax +353-1-6292654
Email info@cpsma.ie
Website www.cpsma.ie

CPSMA represents the boards of management of all Catholic primary schools. Its standing committee has close links with the Episcopal Commission for Education.

* * *

CEIST

Chairperson, Board of Directors
Ms Maeve Mahon
CEO: Mr Gerry McGuill
CEIST Ltd, Summit House,
Embassy Office Park, Kill, Co Kildare
Tel 01-6510350 Fax 01-6510180
Email info@ceist.ie
www.ceist.ie

CEIST: Catholic Education – An Irish
Schools Trust is a collaborative trustee
body for the voluntary secondary schools
of the following congregations:
• Presentation Sisters
• Sisters of the Christian Retreat
• Congregation of the Sisters of Mercy
• Missionaries of the Sacred Heart
• Daughters of Charity

CEIST CLG was incorporated in May 2007

Vision: A compassionate and just society
inspired by the life and teachings of
Jesus Christ.

Mission Statement: To provide a holistic
education in the Catholic tradition

Values: Promoting spiritual and human
development, achieving quality in
teaching and learning, showing respect
for every person, creating community
and being just and responsible.

ERST – Edmund Rice School Trust

Chairperson: Mr Brendan McAuley
Chief Executive: Mr Gerry Bennett
Co-ordinator of Ethos: Mr Eddie Bourke
Co-ordinator of Governance Services
Ms Helen O'Brien
Finance/Property Officer
Ms Louise Callaghan
Meadow Vale, Clonkeen Road
Blackrock, Co Dublin A94 YN96
Tel 01-2897511 Fax 01-2897540
Email reception@erst.ie
www.erst.ie

The Edmund Rice Schools Trust, an
independent lay company based in
Dublin, ensures that the schools in the
former Christian Brothers Network
(currently 96) will continue to provide a
Catholic education into the future, in the
spirit and tradition of Blessed Edmund
Rice, for the people of Ireland.

ERST was incorporated in May 2008.

Vision: Promoting full personal and
social development in caring Christian
communities of learning and teaching.

Mission Statement: To provide Catholic
Education in the Edmund Rice tradition.

The five keys elements of an Edmund
Rice Schools Trust School are:
• nurturing faith, Christian spirituality
  and Gospel-based values;
• promoting partnership in the school
  community;
• excelling in teaching and learning;
• creating a caring school community;
• inspiring transformational leadership.

ERST – Edmund Rice School Trust (NI)

Chairperson, Board of Directors
Mr Dermot McGovern
Chief Executive: Mr Kevin Burke
Office Administrator
Ms Andrea Irwin
Edmund Rice Schools Trust,
Westcourt Centre, 8-30 Barrack Street,
Belfast. BT12 4AH
Tel 028-90333205
Email erstni1@live.com

Edmund Rice Schools Trust (NI) is a body
of lay people and an autonomous Public
Juridical Person in canon law. It is also a
limited company in civil law. The Trust
has eight schools which were formerly
under the Trusteeship of the Christian
Brothers.

The Trust was incorporated in February
2009.

Vision: Promoting full personal and
social development in caring Christian
communities of learning and teaching.

Mission Statement: To provide Catholic
Education in the Edmund Rice tradition.

The five keys elements of an Edmund
Rice Schools Trust School are:
• Nurturing faith, Christian spirituality
  and Gospel-based values
• Promoting partnership in the school
  community
• Excelling in teaching and learning
• Creating a caring school community
• Inspiring transformational leadership.

PBST – Presentation Brothers Schools Trust

Chairperson, Board of Directors:
Ms Carmel Murphy
CEO: Mr Michael Sexton
Presentation Brothers Schools Trust,
10 Deerpark Court,
Friars Walk, Cork T12 D8H3
Tel 021-2417144
Email michaelsexton@pbst.ie
www.pbst.ie

PBST is the trustee body for five
voluntary secondary schools and three
primary schools formerly in the
trusteeship of the Presentation Brothers.

Presentation Brothers Schools Trust CLG
was incorporated in January 2009.

Vision: to ensure that the 'characteristic
spirit' of each school is in keeping with
Christ's teaching as exemplified by
Blessed Edmund Rice and, as legal
owner, to take overall responsibility for
the properties and finances of the
schools and to ensure compliance with
statutory requirements.

Mission Statement: 'to make Christ's
Gospel of love known and relevant to
each succeeding generation' … ' seeing
education as the key to growth and
transformation in the context of the
search for meaning, happiness and the
common good'.

Values: The four core elements of a PBS
education (as outlined in our Charter)
are:
• a genuine and tangible spirit of
  respect and caring for each member
  the school community
• a comprehensive and holistic
  education
• a vibrant experience of community
  and partnership
• a deep commitment to Gospel values
  as lived in the Edmund Rice tradition

Le Chéile Schools Trust

Chairperson: Mr Ciaran Flynn
Executive Director
Ms Marie-Therese Kilmartin
Le Chéile Schools Trust, Moibhi Block B,
Alexandra College,
96 Rathmines Road Upper, Rathmines,
Dublin D06 W9N4
Tel 01-5380104
Email admin@lecheiletrust.ie

The Le Chéile Schools Trust is a
collaborative Trust set up by twelve
religious congregations (now fifteen) to
affirm their commitment to the future o
Catholic Education in Ireland and to
work in partnership with the
government in the education system.

Le Chéile schools provide an education
that acknowledges and affirms the
dignity and uniqueness of every human
being as a child of God. Our main
motivation is the holistic flourishing of
every student – 'the glory of God is
humanity fully alive' (St Irenaeus) and
embraces the physical, mental,
emotional, social, moral and spiritual
growth of each student. It seeks to buil
a learning community that welcomes
and witnesses through the Gospel
values. We use the three words
Welcome, Wisdom and Witness to draw
together the core elements of what we
call a Le Chéile spirituality. This vision
reflects the rich heritage of the foundin
congregations in providing for the nee
of the students and communities in its
schools.

The Trust was incorporated in October
2008 and is now patron of 63 post
primary schools and will welcome
primary schools into the Trust in 2019-
2020. Together with its sister company,
Síol Schools Trust, Le Cheile Education
Trust is a recognised Catholic body, with
juridic person status granted by the Irish
Episcopal Commission in 2012.

ducena

hairperson, Board of Directors
Ir James Corbett
EO: Mr John D'Arcy
he Educena Foundation, Summit House,
mbassy Office Park, Kill, Co Kildare
el 01-6510434
mail info@educena.ie

he Educena Foundation is responsible
r the ownership and management of
EIST school properties, licensing these
 providing finance to CEIST in fulfilling
s responsibility as trustees.

he Company was incorporated in May
007

ision: A thriving community of faith-
ased schools

Mission Statement: Our mission is to
ecure faith-based education in the
atholic tradition for second- level
udents.

alues: Collaboration, Faith-based
ducation, Integrity, Commitment and
ompassion.

National Association of Primary Diocesan Advisors (NAPDA)

Chairperson: Mr John McDonagh
Secretary: Sr Maria Comerford

The National Association of Primary
Diocesan Advisors in Religious Education
is a national organisation whose
members support, educate and resource
the partners in religious education at a
primary school level in Ireland.

Membership of the Association is open to
all full-time or part-time primary
Diocesan Advisers. Associate membership
is open to others who work in the area of
Religious Education in primary schools.

The association aims to:
- support individual members in their work.
- provide a forum for discussion and debate.
- offer further formation and education for the members.
- review nationally the work of religious education in the Primary School and to actively encourage continual evaluation of progress.
- liaise with other agencies involved in the field of Religious Education.
- articulate nationally the needs of Religious Education at primary level.
- foster co-operation between the three partners involved in Religious Education – home, school and parish.

The association holds an Annual
Conference and a minimum of two other
meetings during the year. It is
represented and organised by an
executive, which is elected by the
membership and holds office for three
years. Members of the Executive
represent the Association at the Catholic
Primary School Management
Association, the Episcopal Commission
on Catechetics, and the Consultation
Group for the National Primary School
Programme.

National Association of Post-Primary Diocesan Advisors (NAPPDA)

Chairperson
Ms Anna Maloney
Secretary
Mr Tomás Kenny, Diocese of Kerry

The National Association of Post-Primary
Diocesan Advisers provides support,
resources, in-service and pastoral care for
Religious Education teachers and
chaplains working in Post-Primary
schools. Membership of the association is
open to all full-time and part-time Post-
Primary DAs.

The association:
- provides continuous support for all members of the association – full-time and part-time.
- provides faith and professional development opportunities for all members.
- participates in ongoing review of the current situation of Post-Primary RE.
- collaborates with the Council for Catechetics of the Irish Bishops' Conference.
- liaises with the National Director for Catechetics.
- collaborates with the National Association of Post-Primary Chaplains.
- collaborates with all parties involved in Post-Primary RE.

The association holds four meetings a
year, including the AGM. These meetings
are organised by the executive
committee. The NAPPDA currently has
representatives on the National Council
for Catechetics and on Consultation
Group for Post-Primary education.

SEMINARIES AND HOUSES OF STUDY

SEMINARIES

PONTIFICAL IRISH COLLEGE, ROME
Founded in 1628 the Irish National College in Rome provides formation to seminarians and priests for the diocesan priesthood in Ireland and beyond.
Via dei SS Quattro 1, 00184 Roma, Italy
Tel 003906-772631 Fax 003906-77263323
Email ufficio@irishcollege.org
www.irishcollege.org
Rector
Rev Paul Finnerty BA, BD, STL
Email paul.finnerty@irishcollege.org
Vice-Rector
Very Rev Canon Edmond Cunninan BA, BD, DD
Email edmond.cullinan@irishcollege.org

ST PATRICK'S COLLEGE, MAYNOOTH
Founded in 1795, the National Seminary for Ireland and Pontifical University, Maynooth, Co Kildare W23 TW77

President
Rev Professor Michael Mullaney BA, BD, JCD
Tel 01-7083958
Email president@spcm.ie

Seminary
Seminary Rector
Rev Tomás Surlis B.Rel.Sc, BD, STL, SThD
Tel 01-7083727
Email rector@spcm.ie
Director of Formation (Stage of Discipleship)
Rev Shane O'Neill MA, BPhil, BD
Email shane.oneill@spcm.ie
Director of Formation (Stage of Configuration)
Rev Sean Corkery
Email sean.corkery@spcm.ie
Coordinator of Intellectual Formation
Rev Michael Shortall
Email michael.shortall@spcm.ie
Spiritual Director
Rev Chris Hayden
Email chris.hayden@spcm.ie
Vocational Growth Counsellor
Rev Leon Ó Giolláin SJ
Email leon.ogiollain@spcm.ie
Human Formation Advisor
Rev Hugh Lagan (SMA)
Email hugh.lagan@spcm.ie
Director of Sacred Music
John O'Keeffe KSG, PhD, HDE, LTCL
Email john.okeeffe@spcm.ie

College Officers
Financial Officer
Ms Fidelma Madden ACA, AITI
Registrar and Supervisor of Examinations
Maurice Garde BATh, MSocSci
Email registrar@spcm.ie
Librarian: Cathal McCauley
Archivist: archives@spcm.ie

Pontifical University Officers
Dean, Faculty of Theology
Dr Jessie Rogers
Dean, Faculty of Philosophy
Rev Dr Simon Nolan (OCarm)
Dean, Postgraduate Studies
Rev Dr Michael Shortall
Academic Registrar
Maurice Garde
Marketing Director
Paul Hurley

Pontifical University Courses –
Professors/Department Heads
Systematic Theology
Rev Professor Declan Marmion (SM) MtF STD, HDE, Dip Pastoral Theology
Sacred Scripture
Rev Professor Seamus O'Connell BSc, LSS
Moral Theology
Professor Tobias Winright PhD
Faith and Culture
Rev Professor Michael A. Conway MSC, D.Theol
Canon Law
Rev Professor Michael Mullaney BA, BD, JCD
Liturgy
Rev Professor Liam Tracey (OSM) STB, SLD, DipMar, DipPastoral Theology
Rev Neil Xavier O'Donoghue PhD
Ecclesiastical History
Professor Salvador Ryan BA, PhD
Director of Pastoral Theology
Dr Aoife McGrath PhD, MACSPW

Allianz (ili)

HOUSES OF STUDY

*or details see Religious Orders and
ongregations Section

amillians (OSCam)
Camillus, South Hill Avenue,
lackrock, Co Dublin
el 01-2882873/2833380

armelites (OCarm)
rior: Rev Fintan Burke
ort Muire, Ballinteer, Dublin D16 E167
el 01-2984014 Fax 01-2987221
mail gortmuire@gortmuire.com

ominicans (OP)
Saviour's Priory, Upper Dorset Street,
ublin 1
el 01-8897610 Fax 01-8734003
mail dominican.studium@dominicans.ie
egent: Rev Terence Crotty (OP)

Mary's Priory, Tallaght, Dublin 24
el 01-4048100
he Priory Institute
el 01-4048124 Fax 01-4626084
mail enquiries@prioryinstitute.com

anciscans (OFM)
ún Mhuire, Seafield Road,
illiney, Co Dublin A96 R590
el 01-2826760 Fax 01-2826993
mail franciscans.killiney@franciscans.ie
uardian: Br Stephen O'Kane
icar: Rev Micheál Mac Craith

Missionaries of Africa (White Fathers)
Cypress Grove, Templeogue,
Dublin 6W YV12
Tel 01-4055263
Contact Person: Rev Sean O'Leary
Email pep.irl.del@mafr.org

Oblates (OMI)
St Anne's, Goldenbridge Walk, Inchicore,
Dublin 8
Tel 01-4540841

Mona,
12 Tyrconnell Road, Inchicore, Dublin 8
Rev Patrick Carolan (OMI)
Rev Paul Horrocks

Salesians (SDB)
St Catherine's Centre, North Campus,
Maynooth, Co Kildare W23 TN90
Tel 01-6286111
Email sdbmaynooth@iol.ie
Rector: Rev Cyril Odia
Vice-Rector: Rev Michael Connell
Bursar: Rev Miroslaw Niechwiej
Rev Michael Scott
Students
Br Vincent Tran Hien Vinh
Br António Paulo Cristovao
Br Mulugeta Woldemeskel
Br Leopoldo Pinto
Br Gbertyo Peter Sesugh
Br Johan Bugeja
Br Clint Rizzo

SPECIAL INSTITUTES OF EDUCATION

Irish School of Ecumenics
Trinity College Dublin
School of Religion
ISE-LI Building,
Trinity College, Dublin 2
Contact: Prof. Andrew Pierce, Head of
Discipline, Religious Studies
Tel 01-8964778 Fax 01-6725024
Email isedir@tcd.ie
www.tcd.ie/ise

Irish School of Ecumenics
Trinity College Dublin
School of Religion
9 Lennoxvale, Belfast BT9 5BY
Tel 028-90775010 Fax 028-90373986
Email isedir@tcd.ie
www.tcd.ie/ise

Redemptoris Mater Archdiocesan
Missionary Seminary
(Archdiocese of Armagh)
Founded in 2012 to form priests for the
New Evangelisation who are both
diocesan and missionary.

De La Salle Terrace,
Dundalk, Co Louth A91 C5D6
Tel 042-9336584
Email seminary@redmatarmagh.org
Web www.redmatarmagh.org
Rector: Rev Giuseppe Pollio
Director of Studies
Rev Maciej Zacharek
Spiritual Director
His Eminence Cardinal Seán Brady
Spiritual Director
Rev Bede McGregor (OP)

Mater Dei Centre for Catholic Education
DCU Institute of Education,
DCU St. Patrick's Campus,
Upper Drumcondra Road,
Dublin D09 DY00
Tel 01-8842003
Email materdei.cce@dcu.ie
www.dcu.ie/materdei.cce
Director: Dr Cora O'Farrell
Tel 01-7009154
Email cora.ofarrell@dcu.ie

RETREAT AND PASTORAL CENTRES

RETREAT HOUSES

ANTRIM

Drumalis Retreat & Conference Centre,
Glenarm Road, Larne,
Co Antrim BT40 1DT
Tel 028-28272196/28276455
Email drumalis@btconnect.com
www.drumalis.co.uk
Offering an organised programme of
events as well as catering for groups,
conferences, retreats and chapters, on a
residential or non-residential basis.
Facilities include:
• Chapel, Oratory and Prayer Spaces.
• 2 large conference tooms (1 of which
can also be used as a chapel),variety of
smaller meeting rooms and breakout
rooms, craft room, library, spacious
dining room and 2 lounges with
tea/coffee-making facilities.
• Accommodation in custom built retreat
building (39 double/twin en-suite rooms
– 4 of which are disabled friendly) and
15 additional bedrooms in Heritage
House. Lift access and free wifi available
throughout centre.
Set in spacious grounds overlooking
Larne Lough and the sea, Drumalis offers
space for contemplation and prayer – 'an
oasis on the journey of life'.

CORK

St Benedict's Priory Retreat House,
The Mount, Cobh, Co Cork
Tel 021-4811354
Acc: 6 single rooms, 2 double rooms
available for private individual or group
retreats, private day retreats,
opportunity to share in the liturgical life
of the Sisters – Holy Mass, Liturgy of the
Hours and Eucharistic Adoration. Quiet
peaceful setting, Bible Garden, all meals
supplied.
Contact for private retreats
Guest Mistress
Email cobhtyburnconvent@gmail.com

Ennismore Retreat & Conference Centre,
Ennismore, Montenotte, Cork
Tel 021-4502520 Fax 021-4502712
Email info@ennismore.ie
www.ennismore.ie
Contact person: The Secretary
Acc: singles 31, doubles 2
Dominicans

DERRY

Carmelite Retreat Centre,
Termonbacca, Derry BT48 9XE
Tel 028-71262512
Email ocdderry@hotmail.co.uk
www.termonbacca.org
Contact person: The Secretary
Acc: singles 15, twin 20, ensuite rooms 12
Carmelites (OCD)

DONEGAL

St Anthony's Retreat Centre,
Dundrean, Burnfoot, Co Donegal
Tel 074-9368370
Email stanthonysretreat7@gmail.com
Acc: 5 hermitages, 1 double (all en suite)
Director: Ms Marguerite Hamilton
Spiritual direction available
Full board: €60 per day

DOWN

Dromantine Retreat and Conference,
Centre, Newry, Co Down BT34 1RH
Tel 028-30821964 (048 from ROI)
Email admin@dromantineconference.com
www.dromantineconference.com
Contact: Rev Damian Bresnahan (SMA)
Accommodation: 47 single en suite
rooms, 25 double en suite rooms, 8
conference rooms

An Cuan, Youth with a Mission,
44 Shore Road, Rostrevor, Newry,
Co Down BT34 3ET
Tel 028-41738492
Email info@ywamrostrevor.com
Acc: singles 3, double/family 1, twin 5
Contact: Scott Sotomayor (Director)
www.ywamrostrevor.com

Passionist Retreat Centre,
16 A Downpatrick Road, Crossgar,
Downpatrick, Co Down BT30 9EQ
Tel 028-44830242
Email managertobarmhuire@gmail.com
Accommodation: 18 bedrooms
Superior: Rev Thomas Scanlon

DUBLIN

Avila Carmelite Centre
Bloomfield Avenue
Morehampton Road, Dublin 4
Tel 01-6430200 Fax 01-6430281
Email info@avilacentre.ie
Prior: Fr Vincent O'Hara (OCD)
Carmelites (OCD)

Dominican Retreat Centre
Tallaght Village, Dublin D24 KA40
Tel 01-4048123/4048189
Email dominicanretreats@gmail.com
www.goodnews.ie or
www.retreats.dominicans.ie
Secretary/Contact: Anita Kenny
Acc: singles 26, doubles 2; 1 large, 5
medium conference rooms; oratory.
Free wifi and parking. Extensive garden
Dominicans

The Emmaus Centre, Ennis Lane,
Lissenhall, Swords, Co Dublin K67 Y274
Tel 01-8700050
Email emmauscentre@emmauscentre.ie
www.emmauscentre.ie
Acc: 63 ensuite bedrooms, 3 prayer
rooms, 13 meeting rooms
Director: Julie Cosden
Assistant Director: Nora Meenaghan
Christian Brothers

Tallaght Rehabilitation Project
Kiltalown House, Jobstown,
Tallaght, Dublin 24
Tel 01-4597705 Fax 01-4148123
Email info@tallaghtrehabproject.ie
Co-ordinator: Marie Hayden

Manresa Jesuit Centre of Spirituality
426 Clontarf Road,
Dollymount, Dublin D03 FP52
Tel 01-8331352
Email reception@manresa.ie
www.manresa.ie
Located on Dublin Bay, Manresa offers
the Spiritual Exercises of Saint Ignatius
a variety of forms. The retreat house ha
forty ensuite rooms and a number of
prayer and meeting spaces to facilitate
quiet retreats, reflection and prayer.
Interim Director: Ashley Evans (SJ)

GALWAY

Emmanuel House of Providence,
Clonfert, Ballinasloe,
Co Galway H53 E5N6
Tel 057-9151552
Email contact@emmanuelhouse.ie
www.emmanuelhouse.ie
No Accommodation
Eddie and Lucy Stones
Catholic centre for prayer and
evangelisation. It is a new community of
Christ's faithful, a spiritual hospital where
people can experience the healing power
of God in spirit, mind and body.

Esker Retreat House and Youth Village,
Athenry, Co Galway
Tel 091-844549 Fax 091-845698
Email eskerret@indigo.ie
www.eskercommunity.net
Acc: singles 17, doubles 26 in retreat
house, 70 in 2 dorms in youth village
Retreat House Co-ordinator
Fr Fonsie Doran CSsR
Email rev_dorancssr@yahoo.com
Youth Village Co-ordinator
Fr Michael Cusack CSsR
Contact: The Secretary

LAOIS

La Salle Pastoral Centre, Castletown,
Portlaoise, Co Laois R32 N6D8
Tel 057-8732442
Email castletownretreats@gmail.com
Contact: Derek Doherty
Administrator: Br Kevin McEvoy (FSC)
Email kevinmcevoy@lasalleigbm.org
Tel 087-1763729
Acc: 40. De La Salle Brothers

Mount St Anne's Retreat and Conference
Centre, Killenard,
Portarlington, Co Laois
Tel 057-8626153
Email secretary@mountstannes.com
http://www.mountstannes.com
Acc: 36 rooms (incl. 3 individual
apartments)
CEO: Dr Oonagh O'Brien
Email ceo@mountstannes.com
Contact Person: Catherine Gorey
(Secretary)
Email secretary@mountstannes.com

LOUTH

Dominican Nuns
Monastery of St Catherine of Siena,
The Twenties, Drogheda,
Co Louth A92 KR84
Tel 041-9838524
Email sienasilence@gmail.com
www.dominicannuns.ie
In a quiet country setting – self-catering
Retreat House
Acc: 4 en suite rooms. Oratory with
reserved Blessed Sacrament; fully
equipped kitchen; private garden.
Conference room suitable for day groups.
Eucharistic Adoration; opportunity to
attend the monastic liturgy
Contact: Sister in Charge (Retreat Rooms)

TYRONE

Servite Priory, Benburb, Dungannon,
Co Tyrone BT71 7JZ
Tel 028-37548241
Residential groups and conferences
Email hello@benburbpriory.com

WEXFORD

Sisters of St John of God,
Ballyvaloo Retreat & Conference Centre,
Ballyvaloo, Blackwater, Enniscorthy,
Co Wexford Y21 X392
Tel 053-9137160
Email operations@ballyvaloo.ie
www.ballyvaloo.ie
Director: Michael Dillon
Acc: 32 ensuite rooms

PASTORAL CENTRES

CORK

Dominican Pastoral Centre,
Popes Quay, Cork
Tel 021-4502067/021-4502267
Email dompastoralcentre@gmail.com
Contact: Director of the Pastoral Centre

Nano Nagle Birthplace,
Ballygriffin, Mallow, Co Cork
Tel 022-26411
Email secretary@nanonaglebirthplace.ie
www.nanonaglebirthplace.ie
Presentation Sisters
Heritage, Spirituality and Ecology
Centre.
Retreats, workshops and courses.
Conference Centre for Hire.
Self-catering accommodation:
2 bungalows and 3 apartments.

DONEGAL

Whiteoaks Rehabilitation Centre
Derryvane, Muff, Co Donegal
Tel 07493-84400 Fax 07493-84883
Email info@whiteoakscentre.com
www.whiteoaksrehabcentre.com
The purpose of White Oaks is to aid the
recovery of people suffering from
addictions. We offer a 30-day residential
treatment programme, for people
addicted to drugs, alcohol and gambling,
based on the 12-step model. There is a
two year aftercare programme.
The Centre has full international
accreditation with CHKS Ltd for the
quality of its services. It is approved by
the main Healthcare Insurances.

KERRY

St John Paul II Pastoral Centre
Rock Road, Killarney, Co Kerry
Tel 064-6632644
Email pastoralcentre@dioceseofkerry.ie
Non-residential
Director: Rev Gearóid Godley
Kerry Diocese

MEATH

Dowdstown Counselling Services,
Cyws Hall, Fairgreen, Navan, Co Meath
Tel 046-9031196
Email
dowdstowncounsellingservices1@gmail.com
www.dowdstowncounsellingservices.com
Administrator: Mary Mahon
Dowdstown Counselling Services offers
affordable counselling to all in the
Meath and surrounding areas.
Meath Diocese

WATERFORD

St John's Pastoral Centre
John's Hill, Waterford
Tel 051-874199
Administrator: Ms Mary Dee
Email
pastoralcentre@waterfordlismore.ie

PRIVATE RETREATS

ANTRIM

Adoration Sisters
63 Falls Road, Belfast BT12 4PD
Tel 02890-325668
www.adorationsisters.info
Altar Bread Suppliers
'Saint Joseph's House of Bread'
Tel 02890 247175
Email stjosephsltd@gmail.com
Superior General
Mother Mary Josephine Caldwell
Email info@adorationsisters.info

Our Lady of Bethlehem Abbey
11 Ballymena Road, Portglenone,
Co Antrim BT44 8BL
Tel 028-25821211
Email info@bethabbey.com
www.bethlehemabbey.com
Contact: Rev Guestmaster
9.30am-5.00 pm, Monday-Saturday
Acc: 10 rooms: 8 singles/doubles, 2 singles
Cistercians

DERRY

Columba Community,
Columba House of Prayer and
Reconciliation
11 Queen Street, Derry BT48 7EG
Tel 028-71262407
Email columbacommunity@hotmail.com
www.columbacommunity.com
Contact: Tommy McCay
Email columbacommunity@hotmail.com
A basic Christian community with 20
members offering opportunities for
private reflection and group worship.
Prayer and pastoral counselling available
on a one-to-one and group basis.
Blessed Sacrament Chapel open daily
9.30am-5.00pm
Monday to Friday: all welcome
Thursday 7.30pm Mass and Prayer for
Healing

DOWN

Holy Cross Abbey
119 Kilbroney Road, Rostrevor,
Co Down BT34 3BN
Tel 028-41739979
Email benedictinemonks@btinternet.com
www.benedictinemonks.co.uk
Contact: The Guestmaster
Accommodation: 8 singles
Benedictines

GALWAY

Spiritual Direction – La Retraite
3 St Mary's Mews, Shantalla Road,
Galway H91 WF6N
Tel 091-524548
Contact: Sr Moira McDowall
Tel 086-3505779
Email moira.mcdowall@outlook,com
La Retraite Sisters

LEITRIM

La Verna, Convent Avenue,
Drumshanbo, Co Leitrim
Tel 071-9641308
Contact: Sr Helen Keegan
Self-catering: 3 bedroom retreat house
Poor Clare Monastery of Perpetual
Adoration

LIMERICK

Glenstal Abbey, Monastic Guest House,
Murroe, Co Limerick
Tel 061-621000
Contact: The Guestmaster
Email guestmaster@glenstal.org
Acc: 12
Benedictines

MEATH

Silverstream Priory,
Stamullen, Co Meath K32 T189
Tel 01-8417142
Contact: Dom Cassian Aylward (OSB)
Email guestmaster@cenacleosb.org
Acc: 3 rooms, clergy and seminarians
only (en suite)
Benedictines Monks of Perpetual
Adoration

WEXFORD

St Aidan's Monastery of Adoration
Ferns, Enniscorthy, Co Wexford
Tel 053-9366634
Email staidansferns@eircom.net
Web www.adorationsisters.info
Acc: 8 hermitages, 1 wheelchair-friendly

PERMANENT DEACONS

The Church teaches that there are three degrees within the Sacrament of Holy Orders: bishops, priests and deacons.

In recent centuries the Order of Deacon within the Roman Rite, tended to be seen as a step towards becoming a priest. This was revisited during the Second Vatican Ecumenical Council in the 1960s. At this Council a decision was taken to restore the diaconate as a distinct ministry of service within the Church to help renew and enrich the Church's missionary endeavours.

In recent years, many of the Irish dioceses have ordained permanent deacons and they are listed as follows:

ARMAGH
Rev Martin Barlow
Rev Martin Brennan
Rev Patrick Butterly
Rev Philip Carder
Rev Paul Casey
Rev Dermot Clarke
Rev Martin Cunningham
Rev Kevin Duffy
Rev David Durrigan
Rev Andrew Hegarty
Rev Tony Hughes
Rev George Kingsnorth
Rev Paul Mallon
Rev Eunan McCreash
Rev Malachy McElmeel
Rev Eamon Quinn
Rev John Taaffe

DUBLIN
Rev Jim Adams
Rev Declan Barry
Rev Frank Browne
Rev Declan Colgan
Rev Eric Cooney
Rev Gabriel Corcoran
Rev Don Devaney
Rev James Fennell
Rev Paul Ferris
Rev Victor Garvin
Rev Michael Giblin
Rev John Graham
Rev Thomas Groves
Rev Paul Kelly
Rev Gerard Larkin
Rev Derek Leonard
Rev Gerard Malone
Rev Dermot McCarthy
Rev Noel McHugh
Rev Damien Murphy
Rev Matthew Murphy
Rev Tim Murphy
Rev Eamonn Murray
Rev Michael O'Connor
Rev Victor Okafor
Rev John O'Neill
Rev Padraic O'Sullivan
Rev Greg Pepper
Rev Gerard Reilly
Rev Noel Ryan
Rev Jeremy Seligman

ACHONRY
Rev Kevin Flynn
Rev Martin Lynch

CLOGHER
Rev Martin Donnelly
Rev Paul Flynn

CLOYNE
Rev Paul Alapini
Rev Leonard Cleary
Rev Garrett Cody
Rev Damian McCabe
Rev John McCarthy
Rev Edward Mulhare
Rev John Nestor
Rev Gerard Rooney
Rev James Sheahan
Rev Brian Williams

CORK & ROSS
Rev David Lane
Rev John Guirey
Rev Frank McKevitt

DOWN & CONNOR
Rev Joseph Baxter
Rev Jackie Breen
Rev Terence Butcher
Rev Brendan Dowd
Rev John Downey
Rev Kieran Hunt
Rev Patrick Keown
Rev Mark Lenaghan
Rev Brett Lockhart
Rev Ricky Looney
Rev James McAllister
Rev Gregory McGuigan
Rev Patrick McNeill
Rev Kevin Webb
Rev Martin Whyte

DROMORE
Rev Kevin Devine
Rev Gerry Heaney
Rev Brendan McAllister
Rev Gerard McBrien
Rev John McClelland
Rev Frank Rice
Rev Michael Rooney

ELPHIN
Rev Wando de Araujo
Rev William Gacquin
Rev Damien Kearns
Rev Tony Larkin
Rev Frank McGuinness
Rev David Muldowney
Rev Martin Reidy
Rev Seamus Talbot

KERRY
Rev Conor Bradley
Rev Jean Yves Letanneur
Rev Denis Kelleher
Rev Thady O'Connor
Rev Pat Coffey
Rev Francis White

KILDARE & LEIGHLIN
Rev Vincent Crowley
Rev John Dunleavy
Rev Liam Dunne
Rev Eugene Keyes
Rev Gary Moore
Rev David O'Flaherty
Rev Fergal O'Neill
Rev Joe O'Rourke
Rev Patrick Roche
Rev Jim Stowe
Rev Paul Wyer

KILMORE
Rev Andrew Brady
Rev Padraig Kelly

WATERFORD & LISMORE
Rev Lazarus Gidolf
Rev Brendan Gallagher
Rev Hugh Nugent

MARRIAGE TRIBUNALS

By Decree dated 24 March 1975, the Irish Episcopal Conference decided to establish four Regional Marriage Tribunals of first instance to be located at Armagh, Dublin, Cork and Galway. This decree was formally approved by the Supreme Tribunal of the Apostolic Signatur on 6 May 1975. In accordance with the terms of the Roman rescript, the Episcopal Conference, in a decision of 30 September 1975, determined the Regional Tribunals would come into effect on 1 January 1976. From that date they replaced all previous diocesan marriage tribunals.

By the same process which established in Ireland Regional Marriage Tribunals of first instance, the Episcopal Conference set up a sole Appeal Tribunal, located in Dublin, to hear cases on appeal from each of the four Regional Tribunals. It also came into effect on 1 January 1976. Its personnel and administration are wholly distinct from the Dublin Regional Marriage Tribunal.

NATIONAL MARRIAGE APPEAL TRIBUNAL

Columba Centre, Maynooth, Co Kildare
Tel 01 5053119 Fax 01-5053122
Judicial Vicar: Very Rev Peter O'Kane JCL
Administrator: Mrs Stephanie Walpole
Associate Judges
Very Rev Canon Eugene Mangan PP, Very Rev Gerard McNamara PP, Very Rev Patrick Gill AP, Very Rev John Canon O'Boyle BA, Very Rev Patrick Williams AP, Very Rev S.J. Clyne PP, VF, Rev Patrick Connolly DCL, Rev Brendan Kilcoyne LCL, Rev Michael Mullaney DCL, Rev Brian Flynn PP,Rev John Whelan (OSA), Mr Michael V. O'Mahony, Rev Seán O'Neill, Very Rev Francis Maher PP, Rev Lorcan Moran PP, Rt Rev Mgr Gerard Dolan PP, LCL, Very Rev Patrick Canon Twomey PE, Most Rev William Walsh DD, Sr Máirín McDonagh (RJH), Very Rev Patrick McCarthy BL, PP

Defenders of the Bond
Rev Brian Kavanagh LCL,
Rev Michael Bannon
Rev Gabriel Kelly, Rev Kevin O'Gorman
Correspondence to: Administrator

REGIONAL MARRIAGE TRIBUNALS

ARMAGH INTER-DIOCESAN MARRIAGE TRIBUNAL

Regional Office: 15 College Street, Armagh BT61 9BT
Tel 028-37524537 Fax 028-37528763
Email armagh@marriagetribunal.org
Judicial Vicar
Very Rev Joseph Rooney JCL
Administrator
Very Rev John McKeever LLB, STL
Presiding Judges
Very Rev Joseph Rooney JCL;
Rev Vincent Cushnahan JCL
Contact Person for Constituent Dioceses
Armagh
Very Rev John McKeever LLB, STL;
Rev Colm Hagan LLB, STB;
Rev Paul Murphy JCL
Tel 028-37524537
Clogher: Mr Kevin Slowey
Tel 028-66327222
Derry: Rev Micheál McGavigan JCL
Tel 028-71362475
Down & Connor
Very Rev Joseph Rooney SCL;
Rev Vincent Cushnahan JCL
Tel 028-90491990
Dromore: Rev Mr Michael Rooney
Tel 028-37524537
Kilmore: Sr Kathleen Gormley (RSM)
Tel 049-4375004
Raphoe: Rt Rev Mgr Kevin Gillespie;
Rev Brendan Ward
Tel 074-9121853

DUBLIN INTER-DIOCESAN MARRIAGE TRIBUNAL

Tribunal Offices, 14A Berkeley Street, Phibsboro, Dublin D07 XRT1
Tel 01-9123939
Email dublinrmt3@gmail.com
Judicial Vicar: Rev Paul Churchill
Tribunal Staff Members
Rev Kilian Byrne LCL (Kildare and Leighlin)
Sr Mary Grennan LCL (PBVM)
Rev William Richardson PhD, JCD (Dublin)
Mgr Alex Stenson DCL (Dublin)
Very Rev Laurence Collins (OP)
Maeve Cotter, Rev Tom Dowd,
Anne Giblin (RSC), Jane O'Donoghue,
Mrs Pamela van de Poll
Correspondence to: The Rev Judicial Vicar
Constituent Dioceses: Dublin, Ferns, Kildare and Leighlin, Meath, Ossory

CORK INTER-DIOCESAN MARRIAGE TRIBUNAL

Tribunal Offices, The Lough, Cork T12 C654
Tel 021-4963653 Fax 021-4314149
Judicial Vicar
Very Rev Richard Keane BA, BD, MTh, JC
Email frrichard.tribunal@gmail.com
Associate Judicial Vicar: Vacant
Judge: Very Rev Seamus McKenna BA, HDE, LCL
Constituent Dioceses
Cashel, Cloyne, Cork and Ross, Kerry, Limerick, Waterford and Lismore
Correspondence to: Aileen Coleman (Tribunal Secretary)
Email aileen@tribunal.ie

GALWAY INTER-DIOCESAN MARRIAGE TRIBUNAL

7 Waterside, Woodquay, Galway H91 PF61
Tel 091-565179
Email tribunal@galwaydiocese.ie
Website
www.galwayregionalmarriagetribunal.or
Moderator
Most Rev Michael Duignan, Bishop of Galway, Kilmacduagh & Kilfenora
Judicial Vicar
Very Rev Barry Horan JCL
Associate Judicial Vicar: Vacant
Judge Instructor
Mairéad Uí Mhurchadha
Correspondence to the Administrator: Nicola Burke
Constituent Dioceses: Tuam, Achonry, Ardagh and Clonmacnois, Clonfert, Elphin, Galway, Killala, Killaloe

CHAPLAINS

THE DEFENCE FORCES CHAPLAINCY SERVICE

Head Chaplain
Rev Pascal Hanrahan HCF
Email pascalh@icloud.com
Defence Forces Headquarters,
McKee Barracks, Blackhorse Avenue,
Dublin 7
Tel 01-8042637/087-3128209
Email pascal.hanrahan@defenceforces.ie

Administration Secretary
Sgt Declan Mooney
Defence Forces Headquarters,
McKee Barracks, Blackhorse Avenue,
Dublin 7
Tel 01-8042638
Email declan.mooney@defenceforces.ie

Aiken Barracks
Dundalk, Co Louth
Rev Michael Hinds CF
Tel 087-3940186
Email: Michaelhinds1@hotmail.com

Casement Aerodrome
Baldonnel, Co Dublin
Tel 01-4037536
Rev Bernard McCay-Morrissey CF
Email bernardmccaymorrissey@gmail.com

Cathal Brugha Barracks
Rathmines, Dublin 6
Tel 01-8046484
Vacant

Collins Barracks (Cork)
Tel 021-4502734
Rev Edward Sheehan CF
Email tedsheehan64@gmail.com

Curragh Camp
Co Kildare
Rt Rev Mgr John McDonald CF
Tel 045-441369
Email frjohnmcdonald@gmail.com
Rev P.J. Somers CF
Tel 045-445071
Email somerspj@gmail.com

Custume Barracks
Athlone, Co Westmeath
Tel 090-6421277
Rev Declan Shannon
Email declanjjshannon@gmail.com

Finner Camp
Ballyshannon, Co Donegal
Tel 071-9842294
Rev Jeremiah Carroll CF
Email jerryzulu@gmail.com

Gormanston Camp
Co Meath
Rev Michael Hinds CF
Tel 087-3940186
Email: Michaelhinds1@hotmail.com

McKee Barracks
Dublin 7
Tel 086-2256794
Rev Damian Farnon
Email damian.farnon@defenceforces.ie

The Naval Base
Haulbowline, Co Cork
Tel 021-4378046
Rev Desmond Campion (SDB) CF
Email campiond@eircom.net

Renmore Barracks
Galway
Tel 091-751156
Rev Paul Murphy CF
Email papamurfi@gmail.com
Tel 086-2326851

Saint Bricin's Hospital
Infirmary Road, Dublin 7
Tel 01-8042637
Rev Seamus Madigan HCF

Sarsfield Barracks
Limerick
Tel 087-6381489
Rev Piotr Delimat CF
Email pieetro@wp.pl

James Stephens Barracks
Kilkenny
Tel 056-7772015
Rev Dan McCarthy CF
Tel 086-8575155
Email danielmaccarthy@icloud.com

International Military Pilgrimage to Lourdes (Pèlerinage Militaire International)
Director: Rev Pascal Hanrahan HCF
Email pascalh@icloud.com
Defence Forces Headquarters,
McKee Barracks, Blackhorse Avenue,
Dublin 7
Tel 01-8042637/087-3128209

Substitute Chaplain
Tel 087-2511488
Rev David Murphy CF
Email revcorporal@gmail.com

BRITAIN

Irish Chaplaincy
52 Camden Square
London NW1 9XB
Tel 0044-2074825528
Fax 0044-2074824815
Email info@irishchaplaincy.org.uk
Trustees: Mr John Walsh (Chair),
Mgr Canon Tom Egan (Hon. Treasurer)

EUROPE

Brussels
Rev Michael Nicholas (OFM)
23/25 Oudstrijderslaan,
1950 Kraainem, Belgium
Tel 0032-2-7201970
Fax 0032-2-7255810

Copenhagen
Skt Annae Kirke, Hans Bogbinders Alle 2,
2300 Copenhagen S, Denmark
Tel 0045-31-582102

Lisbon
Rev Gus Champion
St Mary's, Rua do Murtal 368
San Pedro do Estoril
2765 Estoril, Portugal
Tel 00-351-1-4673771 *(Residence)*
Tel 00-351-1-4681676 *(Parish)*

Luxembourg
Rev Michael Cusack (CSsR)
European Parish, 34 Rue des Capucins,
Luxembourg BP 175
Tel 00352-470039 Fax 00352-220859

Munich
Rev Chetus Cohace
Landsberger Strasse 39,
80399 Munich, Germany
Email englischsprachige-
mission.muenchen@erzbistum-
muenchen.de
Tel 0049-89-5003580
Fax 0049-89-50035826
Website
www.englishspeking-mission-munic.de

Paris
Rev Tom Scanlon (CP)
Rev Anthony Behan (CP)
St Joseph's Church,
50 Avenue Hoche, 75008 Paris, France
Tel 0033-1-42272856
Fax 0033-1-42278649
Rev Sean Maher
Irish College, Paris, 5 Rue des Irlandais,
75005 Paris, France
Tel 0033-1-58521030 *(College)*
Email dechurley@eircom.net

Rome
Redentoristi, Via Merulana 31,
CP2458, Rome, Italy Tel 0039-6-494932
Email rgallagher@alfonsiana.edu

AUSTRALIA

Sydney
Rev Tom Devereux OMI
Parish of St Patrick's,
2 Wellington St, Bondi, NSW 2026
Tel 0061-02-93651195
Fax 0061-02-93654002
Mobile 0061-04-07347301
Email stpatbon@bigpond.net.au

UNITED STATES OF AMERICA

USA Episcopal liaison
ost Rev Richard Higgins
*82 Van Carol Drive,
s Vegas, NV 89147
l 001-719-3319551
nail irlbiker@aol.com

ston
sh Pastoral Centre
ecutive Director: Mary Swanton
haplain: Rev Dan Finn
0 Gallivan Blvd Ground Floor,
orchester, MA 02124
l 001-617-4121331
nail danfinn@ipcboston.org
haplain: Rev John McCarthy
0 Gallivan Blvd Ground Floor,
orchester, MA 02124

Chicago
Chicago Irish Community Services
Executive Director: Paul Dowling
Chalpain: Rev Michael Madigan
St Patrick's Missionary Society,
8422 W Windsor Avenue,
Chicago, IL 60656-4252
Tel 001-773-5012973
Email Mgmadigan87@gmail.com

New York
Chaplain: Sr Christine Hennessey (RSM)
152 Ridge Road, Hartsdale, NY 10530
Tel 001-718-6444309
Email Sr.Christine.Hennessy@archny.org

San Diego
Irish Outreach San Diego Inc.
Executive Director: Cathy Ward
2725 Congress Street 2G,
San Diego, CA 92110
Tel 001-619-2911630
Email irishsd@sbcglobal.net
Website www.irishoutreachsd.org
Chaplain: Rev Nick Clavin
St Gregory the Great, 11451 Blue Cypress
Drive, San Diego, CA 92131
Tel 001-619-8236312
Email svdpc3@aol.com

San Francisco
Irish Immigration Pastoral Centre
Executive Director: Celine Kennelly
5340 Geary Boulevard #206,
San Francisco, CA 94121
Tel 001-415-7526006
Fax 001-415-7526910
Email iipc@pacbell.net
Website www.sfiipc.org
Cellphone 001-415-7605762
Chaplain: Rev Brendan McBride
5340 Geary Boulevard #206,
San Francisco, CA 94121
Tel 001-415-7609818
Email bmcbride3@yahoo.com

Seattle
Irish Heritage Club, Settle, WA
Board Member/Chair: Caron McMahon
Chaplain: Rev John Madigan
Sacred Heart Parish, 9460 NE 14th Street,
Clyde Hill, WA 98004
Tel 001-206-3064362
Email atsean47@gmail.com

GENERAL INFORMATION

OBITUARY LIST

Beata mortui qui in Domino moriuntur
Rv 14:13

PRIESTS AND BROTHERS

Arthure, Robert (Waterford & L.) 27 April 2021
Bellew, Gerry (SSC) 24 September 2021
Bermingham, James (SPS) 26 July 2022
Binham, Michael (SJ) 12 January 2022
Boyle, Huge (SDB) 31 December 2021
Boyle, Liam (Limerick) 2 December 2021
Bracken, P. J. (Clonfert) 20 January 2022
Brazil, Sean (SSC) 8 October 2021
Brennan, Loughlin (Cashel & E.) 11 June 2022
Breslin, Eamonn (CSsR) 3 April 2022
Browne, Tom (SPS) 14 October 2021
Burke, Colm (Tuam) 4 November 2022
Butler (Duggan), John (SDB) 1 October 2021
Byrne, Patrick (SPS) 23 January 2022
Cargan, John (Seán) (Derry) 14 April 2022
Carlin, Neal (Derry) 6 August 2021
Carney, Michael (Galway) 27 August 2022
Carolan, Edward (OMI) 29 May 2022
Carr, Frank (SSC) 28 July 2021
Carrigan, Bill (SSC) 21 May 2022
Carroll, Andrew William (OSCam) 3 June 2021
Carroll, Patrick (Dublin) 18 February 2022
Casey, Gerard (Cloyne) 21 November 2022
Casey, James (CSsR) 19 March 2022
Clarke, Paddy (SSC) 26 April 2022
Coffey, Oliver Valerian (CFC) 9 November 2021
Comerford, Patrick (Ossory) 13 November 2022
Condon, John (Ossory) 29 January 2022
Conlon, Brian (Killala) 16 August 2022
Connolly, Bosco (OFM Cap) 22 June 2022
Corcoran, Philip (Dublin) 9 February 2022
Corr, Sean (SSC) 8 June 2022
Corrigan, Kevin (CSSp) 7 April 2022
Costelloe, Patrick (Limerick) 16 August 2022
Cronin, Isidore (OFM) 3 July 2022

Cronin, Peter (SSC) 10 July 2021
Curtis, James B. (Ferns) 4 February 2022
Daly, Bartholomew (MHM) 6 August 2022
Daly, Kevin (OCSO) 16 April 2022
Davitt, Norman (SVD) 16 October 2021
Delaney, John (Ossory) 3 March 2022
Dennehy, Philip (Dublin) 31 January 2022
Donovan, Jeremiah (OMI) 26 April 2022
Dooher, Patrick (SSC) 25 March 2022
Doran, Joseph (Dublin) 7 May 2022
Dowley, Martin (OCSO) 10 August 2022
Doyle, Noel (SSC) 15 April 2022
Doyle, Owen (SSC) 10 April 2022
Doyle, Thomas (Ferns) 25 January 2022
✠ Drennan, Martin (Galway) 26 November 2022
Egan, James Januarius (CFC) 20 November 2021
Egan, Seamus (SSC) 21 October 2021
Ennis, Laurence Finian (CFC) 16 December 2021
Fagan, Hugh (CSSp) 8 June 2022
Farrelly, Florian (OFM) 7 September 2022
Flynn, Brian (Ossory) 21 May 2022
Flynn, Edwin (OFM Cap) 27 August 2022
Flynn, James (IC) 20 November 2021
Flynn, John (SMA) 22 June 2022
Flynn, Leo (SPS) 7 January 2022
Foley, Edward (OP) 12 July 2021
Forbes, Ciarán (OSB) 1 January 2022
Fox, Christopher (MHM) 14 March 2022
✠ Freeman, Seámus (SAC) (Ossory) 20 August 2022
Freeney, Paul (Dublin) 10 December 2022
French, John (Ferns) 16 November 2022
Frost, Laurence (OCarm) 24 February 2022
Fullerton, Robert (Down & C.) 3 May 2022
Furlong, Thomas Luke (CFC) 16 June 2022
Gavigan, James (Prelature of Opus Dei) 27 February 2022
Gillooly, Thomas (SPS) 19 July 2022
Gleeson, Michael Canice (CFC) 20 November 2021
Glover, Joseph M. (Down & C.) 29 October 2022
Glynn, Michael (Elphin) 18 November 2022

Gray, Francis (Ardagh & Cl.) 25 May 2022
Hannon, Martin (Prelature of Opus Dei 21 May 2022
Hastings, Micheal (Dublin) 25 November 2022
Hoey, Eamon (CSsR) 5 May 2022
Houston, Joe (SSC) 14 May 2022
Howard, Paddy (Patrick) (Limerick) 12 August 2022
Hurley, Denis Conleth (CFC) 27 January 2022
Imholte, Otto (SSC) 25 July 2022
Johnston, Cecil (Dublin) 25 October 2022
Kavanagh, Robert (SPS) 6 March 2022
Kearney, Thomas (SMA) 22 November 2021
Kearns, John (SPS) 20 December 2021
Kelleher, Maurice (SMA) 10 August 2022
Kelly, Patrick James (CSSp) 5 April 2022
Kennedy, Colm (SDB) 31 March 2022
Kennedy, David (Limerick) 5 April 2022
Kenny, Paul (SSC) 29 June 2021
Kilkell, Christopher (Tuam) 5 July 2022
Lalor, John (SPS) 24 September 2021
Larkin, Patrick (Armagh) 9 February 2022
Lavery, Pat (CSsR) 8 January 2022
Lawlor, Brendan (Killaloe) 7 June 2022
Lawlor, John (Kerry) 1 March 2022
Lee, Angelus (OFM) 18 February 2022
Lindsay, Augustine (CSSp) 18 August 2022
Loftus, Gerald Majella (CFC) 19 June 2022
Long, Leo (Michael) (Killaloe) 19 October 2022
Madden, James (O Pream) 13 July 2022
Maloney, Peter (SVD) 22 January 2022
McAteer, John (Brothers of Charity) 1 September 2021
McCaffrey, Ultan (OFM) 13 June 2022
McCarthy, John (Tuam) 19 April 2022
McCarthy, Thomas (Dublin) 5 August 2022
McCaughey, George (SDB) 27 October 2021
McCormack, James (CM) 25 March 202
McCormick, Paul (Down & C.) 6 Januar 2022
McCreave, Eamon (OSM) 13 June 2022
McCrory, Gerard (Dromore) 19 December 2021

McDermott, Louis (OMI) 18 October 2022

McDonagh, Donald (SPS) 1 June 2022

McDonnell, Patrick (Armagh) 12 October 2022

McGettrick, Bernard Alphonsus (CFC) 29 May 2022

McGinley, Seamus (Armagh) 10 February 2022

McGrane, Camilus (OSM) 27 February 2022

McGrath, Sean (SPS) 28 March 2022

McGreevy, Mark (OP) 10 April 2022

McHugh, James Camillus (OSCam) 31 May 2021

McHugh, Patrick (Clogher) 27 April 2022

McKenna, Owen (SMA) 2 May 2022

McKenna, Robert (Armagh) 1 September 2022

McQuillan, Ignatius (Derry) 20 August 2021

Moloughney, William Columba (CFC) 19 August 2022

Moore, Angelus (FSP) 24 July 2022

Moran, Bill (SSC) 8 July 2022

Moran, John (SSC) 11 June 2021

Moran, Lorcan (Ossory) 6 August 2022

Moriarty, Frank (Limerick) 2 May 2022

Moriarty, James (Jim) (Kildare & L.) 26 March 2022

Mowles, Alan (SDB) 12 April 2022

Mullan, Aidan (Derry) 9 September 2021

Mullan, Patrick J. (Derry) 2 September 2021

Murray, Brendan (Down & C.) 31 October 2022

Murphy, Brendan (SVD) 4 July 2022

Murphy, Brian (OSB) 16 May 2022

Murphy, Canice (OP) 22 December 2021

Murphy, Pat (Kerry) 19 July 2022

Murphy, Thomas (Ossory) 14 November 2022

Murtagh, Colm (Meath) 8 November 2022

Murtagh, Raymond (SPS) 28 August 2022

Noonan, Joseph (Limerick) 8 October 2022

Nyland, P.J. (Patrick Joseph) (SDB) 11 August 2021

O'Brien, Michael (MHM) 27 April 2022

O'Brien, Patrick (Ferns) 17 June 2022

O'Brien, Patrick (Tuam) 25 November 2021

O'Connell, John (Dublin) 28 February 2022

O'Connor, Patrick (MSC) 22 July 2022

O'Conor, Joseph (Derry) 24 October 2022

Ó Dálaigh, Tadhg (MSC) 27 October 2021

O'Doherty, Donal (Dublin) 14 February 2022

O'Doherty, Micheál (Kerry) 16 January 2022

O'Donoghue, Hugh (CSsR) 11 December 2021

O'Farrell, Patrick (Ossory) 17 October 2022

O'Gorman, Dan (SSC) 3 April 2022

O'Halpin, Aodh (SSC) 2 April 2022

O'Kane, Patrick (Derry) 28 March 2022

O'Neill, Charles (Limerick) 29 May 2022

O'Neill, Daniel (MSC) 22 October 2021

O'Rourke, Denis M. (SPS) 15 November 2021

O'Shea Fintan (OFM) 1 November 2021

O'Sullivan, Brendan (OMI) 23 September 2021

O'Sullivan, Richard (SSC) 26 March 2022

Olden, Michael (Waterford & Lismore) 30 August 2021

Osborne, Fergus (FSP) 23 March 2022

Patton, Gerard (Down & C.) 4 November 2022

Peyton, Martin (Down & C.) 5 November 2022

Poland, James (Dromore) 21 March 2022

Power, Oliver (Prelature of Opus Dei) 2 October 2021

Power, Seamus (Limerick) 15 November 2022

Prior, John (SVD) 2 July 2022

Quinn, Brian (Raphoe) 26 June 2022

Quinn, Seán F (Armagh) 7 September 2022

Raftery, Gregory (Galway) 3 March 2022

Regan, James (SPS) 4 May 2022

Reihill, Seamus (SPS) 17 April 2022

Reynolds, Michael (CSSp) 11 February 2022

Rock, Andrew Denis (CFC) 29 April 2022

Russell, Thomas (OFM) 14 July 2022

Ryan, James (Ferns) 21 January 2022

Ryder, John (Derry) 12 December 2021

Sheehan, Patsy (Kerry) 26 August 2022

Staples, Leo (SPS) 22 August 2022

Swan, Colum (Kildare &Leighlin) 26 November 2021

Travers, Charles (Elphin) 15 January 2022

Treacy, Thomas (SMA) 11 December 2021

Walsh, Thomas (SSC) 17 March 2021

Wilmsen, Jerry (SSC) 6 April 2021

Woods, Thomas (Meath) 26 June 2022

SISTERS

Beashel, Gerard (Ann Mary) (Little Sisters of the Poor) 5 May 2022

Boden, Rosaire (Dominican) 25 February 2022

Brosnan, Frances (Sisters of Mercy, Western Province) 28 May 2022

Browne, Elizabeth (Infant Jesus Sisters) 3 June 2022

Buckley, Angela Mary (Presentation Sisters) 12 March 2022

Buckley, Kathleen (Sacred Hearts of Jesus and Mary) 21 January 2022

Burkart, Mary (IBVM) 9 July 2022

Burke, Brigitte (St Louis Sisters) 14 May 2022

Byrne, Carmel (Sisters of Mercy, South Central Province) 15 May 2022

Byrne, Clare (RNDn) 15 October 2021

Campion, Mary Patricia (Presentation Sisters) 2 March 2022

Carty, Mary (Sisters of Mercy, Western Province) 18 November 2021

Casey, Maura (Presentation Sisters) 26 February 2022

Cashman, Mary (Sisters of Mercy, Southern Province) 13 March 2022

Chambers, Marie Therese (Franciscan Missionaries of Mary) 6 November 2021

Chambers, Rita (Sisters of Mercy, South Central Province) 10 October 2021

Collins, Greta (St Joseph of Cluny Sisters) 15 January 2022

Collins, Maria Goretti (OLCGS) 9 January 2022

Coman, Breda (Sisters of Mercy, South Central Province) 15 May 2022

Corbally, Mary (Philomena) (Daughters of Charity of St Vincent de Paul) 17 June 2022

Corkery, Nora (Hanora) (Daughters of Charity of St Vincent de Paul) 1 May 2022

Corvin, Colette (St Louis Sisters) 2 December 2021

Costello, Sheila (Sisters of Mercy, Western Province) 1 May 2022

Costigan, Nora (Sisters of Mercy, Southern Province) 10 April 2022

Coughlan, Teresa (OLCGS) 16 May 2021

Crowley, Ann (Infant Jesus Sisters) 26 May 2022

Cullen, Cosmas (Franciscan Missionary Sisters for Africa) 2 June 2022

Curtin, De Lourdes (Bon Secours Sisters) 28 May 2022

Cusack, Helena (OLCGS) 14 July 2022

Daly, Monica (St Mary Madeleine Postel Sisters) 5 December 2021

Deady, Mary (Sisters of Mercy, Southern Province) 16 December 2021

Derwin, Elizabeth (Sisters of St Joseph of Chambery) 23 June 2022

Doherty, Ursula (Sisters of Mercy, Western Province) 16 September 2021

Donaghy, Philomena (Sisters of Mercy, Northern Province) 9 July 2022

Donavan Catherine (Sisters of Mercy, Northern Province) 28 February 2022

Donohue, Margaret (Sisters of Mercy, Western Province) 27 February 2022

Drea, Maura (IBVM) 26 January 2022

Drury, Dympna (St Louis Sisters) 11 December 2021

Duffy, Catherine (Sisters of Mercy, Northern Province) 26 October 2021

Duggan, Breege (Sisters of Mercy, Western Province) 3 January 2022

Durkan, Sarah (DMJ) 26 December 2021

Egan, Gerard (Sisters of Mercy, South Central Province) 24 June 2022

Eivers, Mai (Sisters of Mercy, Western Province) 25 March 2021

Fahy, Evelyn (Sisters of Mercy, Western Province) 9 March 2022

Farragher, Mary (Sisters of Mercy, Western Province) 13 May 2021

Farrell, Helena (OLCGS) 16 November 2021

Farrell, Ignatius (Sisters of Mercy, Northern Province) 9 May 2022

Feely, Pauline (Sisters of Mercy, Western Province) 15 March 2022

Fennessy, Sheila (LSA) 8 May 2022

Field, Monica (Franciscan Missionaries of Mary) 12 April 2022

Fitzgerald, Dolores (Sisters of Mercy, South Central Province) 11 May 2022

Fitzharris, Josephine (Sisters of Mercy, South Central Province) 1 January 2022

Flannery, Pius (Perpetual Adoration) 27 November 2021

Fleming, Victoire (Sisters of Mercy, South Central Province) 16 December 2021

Flemming, Marie (LSA) 5 November 2021

Foley, Breda (FMDM) 10 April 2022

Foley, Rose (LSA) 19 March 2022

Folliard, Attracta (SMG) 11 April 2022

Fox, Mary (Sisters of Mercy, Western Province) 21 December 2021

Fraher, Eugene (Bon Secours Sisters) 20 January 2022

Galvin, Mary (Sisters of Mercy, South Central Province) 9 December 2021

Galvin, Patricia (Sisters of Mercy, South Central Province) 24 November 2021

Gavigan, Camilus (Sisters of Mercy, Western Province) 2 August 2022

Gibbons, Catherine (Sisters of Mercy, Northern Province) 21 October 2021

Gill, Imelda (Sisters of Mercy, Western Province) 30 June 2022

Griffin, Cyril (Sisters of Mercy, Southern Province) 22 June 2022

Hanly, Maura (Sisters of Mercy, South Central Province) 10 December 2021

Hawkins, Marie Christine (Sacred Hearts of Jesus and Mary) 25 July 2022

Hayes, Maria (Sisters of Mercy, Southern Province) 25 August 2022

Hegarty, Finian (Sisters of Mercy, Northern Province) 18 November 2021

Hegarty, Immaculate (Sisters of Mercy, Southern Province) 14 July 2022

Hennebry, Eileen (Sacred Hearts of Jesus and Mary) 10 May 2022

Hickey, Eucharia (Sisters of Mercy, Northern Province) 7 January 2022

Hogan, Teresa (Sisters of Mercy, South Central Province) 25 August 2022

Horan, Peter (Presentation Sisters) 28 January 2022

Howard, Mary (Sisters of Mercy, South Central Province) 6 April 2022

Hughes, Lucia (Bon Secours Sisters) 18 January 2022

Hyndman, Myrtle (IBVM) 13 February 2022

Inglis, Mary (Franciscan Missionary sisters for Africa) 29 December 2021

Ireland, Mary (LSA) 23 March 2022

Joanes, Tryphonia (Sisters of Mercy, South Central Province) 20 July 2022

Jordan, Sheila (St Louis Sisters) 8 June 2022

Kealy, Dorothy (Sisters of Mercy, South Central Province) 4 March 2022

Keane, Assumpta (Sisters of Mercy, Western Province) 13 January 2022

Keane, Ita (Bon Secours Sisters) 17 February 2022

Keating, Celestine (Sisters of Mercy, Southern Province) 20 October 2021

Keegan, Teresa (SMG) 5 March 2022

Kelleher, Margaret (Little Sisters of the Poor) 30 May 2022

Kelly, Catherine (Presentation Sisters) 3 April 2022

Kelly, Maria (Sisters of Mercy, South Central Province) 5 May 2022

Kelly, Marie Josephine (St Louis Sisters) 27 April 2022

Kelly, Pauline (Presentation Sisters) 8 September 2022

Kennedy, Elizabeth (Congregation of the Sisters of Nazareth) 31 January 2022

Kennedy, Helen (Sisters of Mercy, South Central Province) 11 July 2022

Kennedy, M.Veronica (Christian Retreat Sisters) 6 October 2021

Kierans, Ann Louise (Presentation Sisters) 11 April 2022

Leen, Baptist (Sisters of Mercy, Southern Province) 10 August 2022

Loye, Mary (Sisters of Mercy, Northern Province) 26 October 2021

Lyons, Maire (Salesian Sisters of St John Bosco) 3 October 2021

Madden, Christina (Sisters of Mercy, Western Province) 12 June 2022

Maguire, Dolores (St Louis Sisters) 25 March 2022

Maguire, Margaret (DMJ) 30 July 2022

Maguire, Maura (Presentation Sisters) 14 April 2022

Maher, Margaret (St Mary Madeleine Postel Sisters) 25 July 2022

McCarthy, Carmel (Sisters of Mercy, South Central Province) 10 July 202

McCarthy, Kathleen (Presentation Sisters) 21 August 2021

McCarthy, Margaret (Sisters of Mercy, South Central Province) 22 March 2022

McConville, Hoysius (Sisters of Mercy, Northern Province) 5 December 202

McGilloway, Teresa (Sisters of Mercy, Northern Province) 29 January 202

McGinty, Triona (St Louis Sisters) 6 June 2022

McGrath, Eileen (St Joseph of Cluny Sisters) 7 December 2021

McMeel, Paschal (Ita) (Poor Clares) 8 May 2022

McMullan, Mary Ann (FMDM) 11 September 2022

McNally, Bernadette (OLCGS) 23 April 2022

McSweeney, Agnes (Daughters of Charity of St Vincent de Paul) 6 September 2022

Meade, Sacred Heart (Sisters of Mercy, Western Province) 2 February 2022

Molloy, Sheila (Sisters of Mercy, Western Province) 11 June 2022

Moloney, Angela (Sisters of Mercy, Southern Province) 10 October 202

Mooney, Declan (Sisters of Mercy, Northern Province) 8 June 2022

Moran, Elizabeth (Franciscan Missiona sisters for Africa) 12 June 2022

Moran, Elizabeth (Sisters of Mercy, Northern Province) 19 July 2022

Moran, Evelyn (Sisters of Mercy, Western Province) 12 October 2021

Morley, Anita (St Louis Sisters) 15 Mar 2022

Mullins, Catherine (SMG) 28 March 2022

Murphy, Andre (Joanne) (Daughters o Charity of St Vincent de Paul) 26 March 2022

Murphy, Antonia (Presentation Sisters 13 July 2022

Murphy, de Chantal (Sisters of Mercy, Southern Province) 20 December 2021

Allianz (Ⅱ)

Murphy, Eileen (Religious of Christian Education) 12 September 2021

Murphy, Martha (Sisters of Mercy, Western Province) 7 January 2022

Murphy, Mary (Sisters of Mercy, Southern Province) 5 July 2022

Murphy, Mary Catherine (Sacred Hearts of Jesus and Mary) 26 May 2022

Murphy, Stephanie (Sisters of Mercy, South Central Province) 6 August 2022

Myers, Alexis (FMDM) 17 April 2022

Newport, Vera (Sisters of Mercy, South Central Province) 3 May 2022

Nolan, Eithne (Sisters of Mercy, Western Province) 21 April 2022

O'Brien, Alphonsus (Presentation Sisters) 23 December 2021

O'Carroll, Dolores (Sisters of Mercy, Southern Province) 10 November 2021

O'Connor, Dominic (IBVM) 28 March 2022

O'Connor, Norah (Dominican) 10 July 2022

O'Dea, Brid (St Louis Sisters) 5 March 2022

O'Dea, Eileen (Sisters of Mercy, Western Province) 9 March 2022

O'Doherty Bridget (Presentation Sisters) 16 December 2021

O'Hara, Caitriona (Sisters of Mercy, South Central Province) 14 January 2022

O'Higgins, Kevin Maeve (Dublin OCD) 28 March 2022

O'Keefe, Eileen (Dominican) 30 June 2022

O'Keefe, Perpetua (Sisters of Mercy, Southern Province) 17 March 2022

O'Keeffe, Dolores (IBVM) 7 February 2022

O'Keeffe, Teresita (IBVM) 12 October 2021

O'Leary, Carmel (Sisters of Mercy, Southern Province) 2 November 2021

O'Leary, Deirdre (Sisters of Mercy, Northern Province) 2 February 2022

O'Mahoney, Berchmans (IBVM) 28 March 2022

O'Neill, Angela (Sisters of Mercy, South Central Province) 15 October 2021

O'Neill, Sheila (Franciscan Missionaries of Mary) 5 July 2022

O'Reilly, Bernadette (Infant Jesus Sisters) 15 January 2022

O'Reilly, Grainne (Sisters of Mercy, Northern Province) 4 June 2022

O'Rourke, Elizabeth (Sisters of Mercy, Western Province) 21 November 2021

O'Shea, Ciaran (FMDM) 16 October 2021

O'Sullivan, Angela (St Joseph of Cluny Sisters) 28 June 2022

O'Sullivan, Maeve (Presentation Sisters) 10 March 2022

O'Sullivan, Moira (Salesian Sisters of St John Bosco) 25 January 2021

Phelan, Philomena (Sisters of Mercy, Southern Province) 17 February 2022

Pillion, James (St Joseph of Cluny Sisters) 10 November 2021

Power, Mary Joseph (St Mary Madeleine Postel Sisters) 11 November 2021

Quinlan, Mary Margaret (Redemptoristines) 19 August 2022

Quirke, Columbanus (Presentation Sisters) 21 August 2022

Raleigh, Margaret (Sisters of St Joseph of Chambery) 30 June 2022

Ring, Loyola (IBVM) 15 November 2021

Ronayne, Paula (Mary) (Daughters of Charity of St Vincent de Paul) 19 May 2022

Ryan, Kathleen (Presentation Sisters) 2 May 2022

Ryan, Mary (Sisters of Mercy, South Central Province) 4 July 2022

Shanahan, Borgia (Presentation Sisters) 13 June 2022

Shannon, Mary (LSA) 10 July 2022

Shiels, Kathleen (Sisters of Mercy, Western Province) 23 October 2021

Smith, Bríd (IBVM) 23 February 2022

Spain, Mary (Sacred Hearts of Jesus and Mary) 25 October 2021

Stafford, Colette (Sisters of Mercy, Southern Province) 17 December 2021

Sweetnam, Philomena (Sisters of Mercy, Southern Province) 14 June 2022

Taylor, Cecilia (GSS) 4 October 2022

Terry, May (Presentation Sisters) 12 August 2022

Thompson, Agnes (IBVM) 26 November 2021

Trant, Una (Presentation Sisters) 22 February 2022

Wall, Nora (Sisters of Mercy, South Central Province) 13 November 2021

Walshe, de Lourdes (Sisters of Mercy, Southern Province) 31 August 2022

Wrafter, Ita Brigid (Presentation Sisters) 19 April 2022

ORDINATIONS

Breen, Jackie (Down & Connor) 4 December 2021 (Deacon)

Butterly, Patrick (Armagh) 30 January 2022 (Deacon)

Olleluori, Stefano (Armagh) 12 June 2022

Downey, John (Down & Connor) 4 December 2021 (Deacon)

Grapiewski, Julian (Tuam) 21 November 2021 (Deacon)

Flynn, Paul (Clogher) 2 February 2022 (Deacon)

Galligan, Cathal (Tuam) 21 November 2021 (Deacon)

Hagan, Colm (Armagh) 26 June 2022

Huang, Liwei (SVD) 29 January 2022

Hunt, Kieran (Down & Connor) 4 December 2021 (Deacon)

Kavanagh, Anthony (OP) 5 September 2022

Keegan, Joseph (Dublin) 20 February 2022

Keown, Patrick (Down & Connor) 4 December 2021 (Deacon)

Kingsnorth, George (Armagh) 30 January 2022 (Deacon)

Kurek, Jaroslaw (OSB) 23 April 2022

Lenaghan, Mark (Down & Connor) 4 December 2021 (Deacon)

Looney, Richs (Down & Connor) 4 December 2021 (Deacon)

McCormick, Paul (Down & Connor) 4 December 2021 (Deacon)

McCreesh, Eunan (Armagh) 30 January 2022 (Deacon)

McEneaney, John (Waterford & Lismore) 24 October 2021

McLoughlin, James (Tuam) 21 November 2021 (Deacon)

Mensah, Joseph (SVD) 29 January 2022

Narcher, Clement (SVD) 29 January 2022

O'Laverty, John (Down & Connor) 31 July 2022

Pasalic, Antun (Killaloe) 24 April 2022

Scott, Kellan (OP) 5 September 2022

White, Barry (Meath) 17 July 2022

Wilson, Stephen (Armagh) 26 June 2022

IRISH COUNCIL OF CHURCHES

Irish Council of Churches
President: Very Rev Dr Ivan Patterson
Vice-President: Rt Rev Andrew Forster

Inter-Church Centre
48 Elmwood Avenue, Belfast BT9 6AZ
Tel 028-90663145
Email info@irishchurches.org
Website www.irishchurches.org
General Secretary: Dr N. Brady

Member Churches of Council
Antiochian Orthodox Church in Ireland;
Church of Ireland; Greek Orthodox
Church in Ireland; Lutheran Church in
Ireland; Methodist Church in Ireland;
Moravian Church, Irish District; Non-
Subscribing Presbyterian Church in
Ireland; Presbyterian Church in Ireland;
Religious Society of Friends; Cherubim
and Seraphim Church; Romanian
Orthodox Church in Ireland; Salvation
Army (Ireland Division); Redeemed
Christian Church of God; Indian
Orthodox Church; Syrian Orthodox
Church

Leaders of Member Churches
Antiochian Orthodox Church in Ireland
Mr William Hunter (Sec to St Ignatius the
God-bearer of Antioch Parish, Belfast)
Antiochian Orthodox Church,
8 Wheatfield Gardens, Belfast BT14 7HU
Tel 028-90712523

Church of Ireland
Most Rev John McDowell
Archbishop of Armagh, Primate of All
Ireland, Church House, 46 Abbey Street,
Armagh BT61 7DZ
Tel 028-37527144
Email archbishop@armagh.anglican.org

Greek Orthodox Church
Church of the Annunciation
46 Arbour Hill, Dublin 7
Rev Fr Tom Carroll PP
Moneygall, Roscrea, Co Tipperary
Tel 0505-45849/086-2394539
Email fr.tomcarroll@gmail.com
Contact Person
Rev Fr Tom Carroll PP

Lutheran Church in Ireland
Lutherhaus,
24 Adelaide Road, Dublin D02 XP21
Tel 01-6766548
Pastors: Anja and Florian von Issendorff
Email info@lutheran-ireland.org
Website www.lutheran-ireland.org

Methodist Church in Ireland
President: Rev David H. Nixon
23 Burford Drive, Honeypark,
Dun Laoghaire, Co Dublin A96 EE05
Email president@irishmethodist.org
Secretary: Rev Dr Heather M. E. Morris
Edge Hill House, 9 Lennoxvale,
Belfast BT9 5BY
Tel 028-90767969

Moravian Church, Irish District
Right Rev Sarah Groves, Bishop
Moravian Church, Irish District,
25 Church Road, Gracehill,
Ballymena BT42 2NL
Email sarah.groves@moravian.org.uk

Non-Subscribing Presbyterian Church
Moderator: Right Rev Lena Cockroft
51 Lakeview Manor,
Newtownards BT23 4US
Tel 028-91800690
Email revsemeriti@gmail.com
Clerk: Very Rev Robert A. McKee
10 Dalways Bawn Road, Carrickfergus,
Co Antrim BT38 9BY
Tel 028-93372257/078-77631737
Email clerkofnspci@gmail.com
Rev Dr Heather Catherine Walker *(Editor,
Non-Subscribing Presbyterian Magazine)*
6 Love Lane, Carrickfergus BT38 8SL
Tel 079-03803391/028-93365482
Email hwalker.research@gmail.com
Clerk of the Presbytery of Antrim
Rev Dr J. W. Nelson
102 Carrickfergus Road,
Larne, Co Antrim BT40 3JX
Tel 028-28272600
Clerk of the Presbytery of Bangor
Rev Brian Moodie
33 Beechgrove, Dromore,
Co Down BT25 1BS
Tel 074-27662828
Email dromorensp@gmail.com
Clerk of the Synod of Munster
Rev Simon Henning
61 Beechfield Crescent, Bangor BT19 7ZJ
Tel 077-40362093
Email simon.henning@hotmail.co.uk

Presbyterian Church in Ireland
Right Rev Dr David Bruce
Moderator, c/o Assembly Buildings,
Fisherwick Place, Belfast BT1 6DW
Tel 028-90322284 Fax 028-90417301
Email moderator@presbyterianireland.org
Rev Trevor D. Gribben, Clerk
Assembly Buildings, Belfast BT1 6DW
Tel 028-90417208 Fax 028-90417301
Email clerk@presbyterianireland.org

Religious Society of Friends
Denise C. Gabuzda
Clerk of Yearly Meeting
For information contact
Mary F. McNeilly
National Administrative Office,
Quaker House Dublin,
Stocking Lane, Dublin D16 V3F8
Tel 01-4998003
Email office@quakers.ie

**Rock of Ages Cherubim & Seraphim
Church in Ireland**
Mother Cherub Prophetess Agnes
Oluyinka Olushoo-Aderanti
Rock of Ages Cherubim & Seraphim
Church, 46 Priory Gate, Athboy, Co Meath
Tel 086-8134747/087-9727699
Email rockofagescs@hotmail.com
Website rockofagescs@hotmail.com

Romanian Orthodox Church in Ireland
Romanian Orthodox Parish of the
Exaltation of the Holy Cross,
Christ Church, Leeson Park, Dublin 6
Dean: Fr Calin Florea
St John the Baptist Missionary & Cultural
Centre, Drimnagh Castle, Dublin 12
Tel 087-6148140
Email revcalin.florea@gmail. com

Salvation Army
Colonel Neil Webb
Divisional Commander,
Divisional Headquarters, 12 Station Mews
Sydenham, Belfast BT4 1TL
Tel 028-90675000
Email neil.webb@salvationarmy.org.uk
Major Eleanor Haddick
Dublin Chaplain
Tel 01-8476415
Email eleanor.haddick@salvationarmy.ie

Allianz ⑪

ANTIOCHIAN ORTHODOX CHURCH IN IRELAND

Dublin
Rev Fr John Hickey PP
Tel 086-7913689
Email hickeyjohnp@gmail.com
Parish of the Three Patrons
(Ss Patrick, Columba and Bridget)
Worshipping @ 7 Grange Terrace,
Deansgrange, Blackrock, Co Dublin

Tralee
Parish of the 'Pantanassa'
Worshipping @ Collis Sandes House,
Tralee, Co Kerry

Belfast
Fr John Hickey and Fr Gregory Hoban
Parish of St Ignatius the God-bearer of
Antioch
Worshipping at Belfast Central Mission,
3rd Floor, Grosvenor House,
Belfast BT12 5AD
Mr William Hunter (Secretary to Parish of
St Ignatius, Belfast)
7 Wheatfield Gardens, Belfast BT14 7HU
Tel 028-90712523

CHURCH OF IRELAND ARCHBISHOPS AND BISHOPS

Armagh
Most Rev John McDowell
Archbishop of Armagh, Primate of All
Ireland and Metropolitan,
Church House, 46 Abbey Street,
Armagh BT61 7DZ
Tel 028-37527144
Email archbishop@armagh.anglican.org
Diocesan Secretary: Mrs J. Leighton
Church House, 46 Abbey Street,
Armagh BT61 7DZ
Tel 028-37522858
Email secretary@armagh.anglican.org

Dublin and Glendalough
Most Rev Dr M.G. St A. Jackson MA, PhD,
DPhil
Archbishop of Dublin, Bishop of
Glendalough, Primate of Ireland and
Metropolitan, Church of Ireland House,
Church Avenue, Rathmines, Dublin 6
Tel 01-4125663
Email archbishop@dublin.anglican.org
Diocesan Secretary: Mrs S. Heggie
Diocesan Office, Church of Ireland House,
Church Avenue, Rathmines, Dublin 6
Tel 01-4966981
Email secretary@dublin.anglican.org

Meath and Kildare
Most Rev P.L. Storey MA(Hons), BTh
Bishop of Meath and Kildare,
Bishop's House, Moyglare,
Maynooth, Co Kildare
Tel 01-6289825
Email bishop@meath.anglican.org

Diocesan Secretary: Mrs K. Seaman
Meath & Kildare Diocesan Centre
Moyglare, Maynooth, Co Kildare
Tel 01-6292163
office@meath.anglican.org

Clogher
Rt Rev Dr Ian W. Ellis BTh, BSc, PGCE, EdD
Bishop of Clogher, The See House,
152A Ballagh Road,
Co Tyrone BT75 0QP
Tel 028-89522461
Email bishop@clogher.org
Diocesan Secretary: Mr G. M. T. Moore
Clogher Diocesan Office,
St Macartin's Cathedral Hall, Hall's Lane,
Enniskillen, Co Fermanagh BT74 7DR
Tel 028-66347879
Email secretary@clogher.org

Derry and Raphoe
Rt Rev A.J. Forster BA (Hons), BTh
Bishop of Derry and Raphoe,
The See House, 112 Culmore Road,
Londonderry BT48 8JF
Tel 028-71377013
Email bishopsoffice@derryandraphoe.org
Diocesan Secretary
Mr G. Harkin
Diocesan Office, 24 London Street,
Londonderry BT48 6RQ
Tel 028-71262440
Email gavin@derryandraphoe.org

Down and Dromore
Rt Rev David McClay BTh, MA
Bishop of Down and Dromore,
Church of Ireland House,
61-67 Donegall Street, Belfast BT1 2QH
Tel: 028-90828850
Email bishop@downdromorediocese.org
Diocesan Secretary: Mr R. Lawther
Diocesan Office, Church of Ireland House,
61-67 Donegall Street, Belfast BT1 2QH
Tel 028-90828830
Email
rlawther@downdromorediocese.org

Connor
Rt Rev G.T.W. Davison BTh, BD
Bishop of Connor, Bishop's House,
27 Grange Road, Doagh,
Ballyclare BT39 0RQ
Tel 028-90828870 (office)
Email bishop@connor.anglican.org
Finance and Administration Manager
Mr R. Cotter
The Diocesan Office,
Church of Ireland House,
61-67 Donegall Street, Belfast BT1 2QH
Tel 028-90828830
Email richardcotter@connordiocese.org

Kilmore, Elphin and Ardagh
Rt Rev Dr S.F. Glenfield MA, MTh, PhD
Bishop of Kilmore, Elphin and Ardagh,
The See House, Kilmore Upper,
Co Cavan
Tel 049-5559954

Diocesan Administrator: Mrs Sarah Taylor
Email dkeatreasurer@gmail.com
Diocesan Office, 20A Market Street,
Cootehill, Co Cavan
Tel 049-5559954
(From NI) 00353-49-5559954
Email office@kilmore.anglican.org

Cashel, Ferns and Ossory
Rt Rev A.M. Wilkinson BA, HDipEd, Bth,
Post Grad Dip
Bishop of Cashel, Ferns and Ossory,
Bishop's House, Troysgate, Kilkenny
Tel 056-7786633
Email bishopadrianwilkinson@gmail.com
Diocesan Secretary: Ms Elizabeth Keyes
The Diocesan Office,
The Palace Coach House, Church Lane,
Kilkenny R95 A032
Tel 056-7761910
Mon-Fri 10.00 a.m.-2.00 p.m.
Email palacecoachhouse@gmail.com
Assistant Diocesan Secretary: Vacant
Email cfo.asec@gmail.com

Cork
Rt Rev W.P. Colton BCL (Hons), DipTh,
MPhil (Ecum), LL.M, PhD
Bishop of Cork, Cloyne and Ross,
St Nicholas' House, 14 Cove Street,
Cork T12 RP40
Tel 021-5005080
Email bishop@corkchurchofireland.com
Diocesan Secretary: Mr Billy Skuse
St Nicholas House, 14 Cove Street,
Cork T12 RP40
Tel 021-5005080 Fax 021-4320960
Email
secretary@corkchurchofireland.com

Tuam, Limerick and Killaloe
Rt Rev M.A.J. Burrows, MA, MLitt,
Prof.Dip.Th
Bishop of Tuam, Limerick & Killaloe,
Kilbane House, Golf Links Road,
Castletroy, Limerick
Email tlkbishop22@gmail.com
Tuam Diocesan Administrator
Mrs Heather Pope
11 Ros Ard, Cappagh Road, Barna,
Galway
Tel 086-8336666
Email secretary@tuam.anglican.org
Limerick & Killaloe Diocesan Secretary
Ms Lorna Sharpe
Kellysgrove, Ballinasloe, Galway
Tel 087-6130063
Email
diocesansecretary@limerick.anglican.org

GREEK ORTHODOX CHURCH IN IRELAND

Greek Orthodox Church of the
Annunciation,
46 Arbour Hill, Dublin 7
Rev Tom Carroll PP
Monegall, Roscrea, Co Tipperary
Tel 0505-45849/086-2394539
Email fr.tomcarroll@gmail.com
Contact Person: Rev Tom Carroll PP

METHODIST CHURCH IN IRELAND

District Superintendents
Southern District
Rev Andrew J. Dougherty
Mayo House,
16 Meadowfield, Sandyford,
Dublin D18 HF80
North Eastern District
Rev W. Philip Agnew
1 Royal Lodge Road,
Belfast BT8 7UL
Tel 028-90402202
North Western District
Rev Dr Stephen F. Skuce
19 Derry Road, Strabane
Co Tyrone BT82 8DU

PRESBYTERIES OF THE PRESBYTERIAN CHURCH

Ards
Rev J.H. Flaherty
The Manse, 17 Ballywalter Road,
Millisle BT22 2HS
Email jflaherty@presbyterianireland.org

Armagh
Rev E.P. Gamble
'Greenfield Manse',
72 Newry Road, Armagh BT60 1ER
Tel 028-37525522
Email pgamble@presbyterianireland.org

Ballymena
Rev J.J. Andrews
1 Forthill Park, Ballymena BT42 2HL
Tel 028-25645544
Email jandrews@presbyterianireland.org

East Belfast
Rev Stephen Moore
234 Lower Braniel Road, Belfast BT5 7NJ
Tel 028-90795136
Email smoore@presbyterianireland.org

North Belfast
Mr T. Long OBE
12 Shinningdale Park North,
Belfast BT14 6RZ
Tel 028-90710012
Email taslong@hotmail.com

South Belfast
Rev M.S. Gault
15 Park Road, Belfast BT7 2FW
Tel 028-90642981
Email mgault@presbyterianireland.org

Carrickfergus
Rev Dr C.D. McClure
5 Whitla's Brae, Larne BT40 3BY
Tel 028-28272441
Email cmcclure@presbyterianireland.org

Coleraine and Limavady
Rev Dr T.J. McCormick
6 Garvagh Road, Kilrea,
Coleraine BT51 5QP
Tel 028-29540256
Email
tmccormick@presbyterianireland.org

Derry and Donegal
Rev Paul Linkens
19 Clearwater, Caw,
Londonderry BT47 6BE
Tel 028-71311425
Email plinkens@presbyterianireland.org

Down
Rev D.M. Spratt
17 Downpatrick Road, Crossgar,
Downpatrick BT30 1EQ
Tel 028-44830041
Email iabraham@presbyterianireland.org

Dromore
Rt Rev Dr William J. Henry
47 Kesh Road, Maze,
Lisburn BT27 5RR
Tel 028-92621269
Email whenry@presbyterianireland.org

Dublin and Munster
Mr Stuart Ferguson
'Brianna', Ballyclough, Camolin,
Enniscorthy, Co Wexford
Tel 053-9383854
Email stuartfer@gmail.com

Iveagh
Rev G.E Best
28 Manse Road, Portadown,
Craigavon BT63 5NW
Tel 028-38831265
Email gbest@presbyterianireland.org

Monaghan
Rev D.T.R. Edwards
The Manse, Old Bridge Road,
Cootehill, Co Cavan
Tel 049-5555456
Email dedwards@presbyterianireland.org

Newry
Rev S.A. Finlay
156 Glassdrumman Road, Annalong,
Newry BT34 4QL
Tel 028-43768232
Email sfinlay@presbyterianireland.org

Omagh
Rev Robert Herron
10 Mullaghmenagh Avenue,
Omagh BT78 5QH
Tel 028-82243776
Email rherron@presbyterianireland.org

Route
Rev Noel McClean
Kilraughts Manse, 24 Topp Road,
Ballymoney BT53 8LT
Tel 074-69719000
Email nmcclean@presbyterianireland.org

Templepatrick
Rev D.J. Paul
50 Killead Road, Aldergrove,
Crumlin BT29 4EN
Tel 028-94422436
Email jmurdock@presbyterianireland.org

Tyrone
Rev T.J. Conway
29 Belvedere Park, Castlerock,
BT51 4XW
Tel 077-84105843
Email tconway@presbyterianireland.org

ROMANIAN ORTHODOX CHURCH IN IRELAND

www.mitropolia.eu

Parish of the Exaltation of the Holy Cross
Christ Church, Leeson Park, Dublin 6
www.romanianorthodox.ie

St Colman of Oughaval's Church
Stradbally Hall, Abbeyleix Road,
Stradbally, Co Laois
Fr Calin Florea
St John the Baptist Missionary & Cultural
Centre, Drimnagh Castle, Longmile Road,
Dublin 12
Tel 087-6148140
Email revcalin.florea@gmail.com
Fr Constantin Uncu
2 Charnwood Gardens,
Clonsilla, Dublin 15
Tel 087-2512101
Email uncu_expres@yahoo.com

Parish of St Columba
Hartstown Community Centre,
Hartstown Road, Dublin 15
www.bisericaortodoxadublin.com
Fr Raul Simion
Hartstown Community Centre,
Hartstown, Dublin 15
Tel 01-8131969/087-6394530
Email pr_simion@yahoo.com
Deacon Dragos Blanaru
24 Littlepace Close, Clonee, Dublin 11
Tel 086-6087652
Email dragosblanaru85@yahoo.com

Parish of the Annunciation & All Saints
of Romania
52B Western Way, Broadstone, Dublin 7
www.bisericasfintiiromani.com
Rev Dr Irineu Craciun
38 Ardmore Crescent, Artane, Dublin 5
Tel 01-8474956
Email i.craciun@iolfree.ie
Fr Petru Vlaic
Tel 086-3940784
Email petruioanvlaic@yahoo.com

Allianz ⓘ

Romanian Orthodox Community (2nd &
4th Sunday)
Sacred Heart Church, Arles, Co Laois
Fr Petru Vlaic
32 Paddocks Square, Adamstown,
Lucan, Co Dublin
Tel 086-3940784
Email petruioanvlaic@yahoo.com

St John the Baptist Missionary & Cultural
Centre, Drimnagh Castle, Longmile Road,
Dublin 12
Fr Calin Florea
Tel 087-6148140

Parish of St Nicholas & St Brigid of
Kildare, Collegiate Church of St Nicholas
(COI), Lombard Street, Galway

Romanian Orthodox Community (3rd
Sunday of Month)
Sisters of Mercy Chapel,
Westbourne Convent,
Courtbrack Avenue, Limerick
Fr Tudor Ghita
102 Friar Hill, Rahoon, Galway
Tel 086-2282690
Email tuxghita@yahoo.com

Parish of St Calinic of Cernica & St Patrick
Fr Collins Community Centre,
Cork Road, Passage West, Cork
Fr Viorel Hurjui
6 Marriner's Quay, Passage West, Co Cork
Tel 089-4423580
Email viohur@yahoo.com

Parish of St John the Evangelist Parish
Centre, All Saints RC Church, 4
Broughshane Road,
Ballymena BT43 7DX, Co Antrim
www.romanianparish.com
Fr Cornel Clepea
4 Broughshane Road,
Ballymena BT43 7DX,
Co Antrim, Northern Ireland
Email clepiai@yahoo.com

St Paul's RC Church
Falls Road, Belfast BT12 6AB
Fr Toma Romeo Puiu
Tel +44-7598845950
Email puiu_romeotoma@oo.com

Romanian Orthodox Parish
Edmund Rice Heritage Centre,
Mount Sion, Barrack Street, Waterford
Fr Calin Florea
Tel 087-6148140
email revcalin.florea@gmail.com

Romanian Missionary Parish, Mullingar
Contact: Fr Calin Florea
Tel 087-6148140

Romanian Missionary Parish, Sligo
Contact: Fr Tudor Ghitá
Tel 086-2282690
Email tuxghita@yahoo.com

IRELAND'S CARDINALS

Since 1866, when Ireland received its first residential cardinal, to the present, eleven Irish bishops have been elected to the Sacred College. By 'Irish bishops' is meant those who, while exercising actual pastoral government, were cardinals; not included are those Irish prelates who were made cardinals but whose ministry was spent overseas (e.g. Cardinal Glennon), or in the service of the Roman Curia (e.g. Cardinal Browne), or those who, having been territorial bishops in Ireland, were elevated to the Sacred College while exercising pastoral government in a diocese overseas (e.g. Cardinal Moran).

Paul Cullen (1803-78)
Ordained Archbishop of Armagh (1850); translated to Dublin (1852); created Cardinal (22 June 1866) by Pius IX.

Edward McCabe (1816-85)
Ordained Bishop of Gadara and appointed auxiliary to the Archbishop of Dublin, Cardinal Cullen (1877); appointed Archbishop of Dublin, following Cardinal Cullen's death (1879); created Cardinal (27 March 1882) by Leo XIII.

Michael Logue (1840-1924)
Ordained Bishop of Raphoe (1879); translated to be Co-adjutor to Archbishop Daniel McGettigan of Armagh (March 1887), whom he succeeded (December 1887); created Cardinal (16 January 1893) by Leo XIII.

Patrick O'Donnell (1856-1927)
Ordained Bishop of Raphoe (1888); translated to be Co-adjutor to Cardinal Logue (1922), whom he succeeded as Archbishop of Armagh (1924); created Cardinal (14 December 1925) by Pius XI.

Joseph MacRory (1861-1945)
Ordained Bishop of Down and Connor (1915); translated to Armagh as Archbishop in succession to Cardinal O'Donnell (1928); created Cardinal (12 December 1929) by Pius XI.

John D'Alton (1882-1963)
Ordained Bishop of Binda and appointed Co-adjutor to the Bishop of Meath (1942), whom he succeeded (1943); translated to Armagh in succession to Cardinal MacRory (1946); created Cardinal (12 January 1953) by Pius XII.

William Conway (1913-77)
Ordained Bishop of Neve and appointed auxiliary to the Archbishop of Armagh, Cardinal D'Alton (1958), whom he succeeded (1963); created Cardinal (22 February 1965) by Paul VI.

Tomás Ó Fiaich (1923-90)
Ordained Archbishop of Armagh (1977) and created Cardinal (30 June 1979) by John Paul II.

Cahal Brendan Daly (1917-2009)
ordained priest 22 June 1941; ordained Bishop of Ardagh and Clonmacnois 16 July 1967; installed Bishop of Down and Connor 17 October 1982; installed Archbishop of Armagh 16 December 1990; created Cardinal 28 June 1991 by John Paul II; retired 1 October 1996.

Cardinal Desmond Connell (1926-2017)
Ordained Archbishop of Dublin 6 March 1988; created Cardinal 21 February 2001; retired 26 April 2004.

Cardinal Seán Brady is the eleventh Irish Cardinal. He is the Emeritus Archbishop of Armagh *(see Diocese of Armagh)*.

STATISTICS

TABLE 1: NULLITY OF MARRIAGE

Year	Applications Nationwde	Decrees of Nullity
2012	224	259
2013	231	188
2014	215	191
2015	188	215
2016	395	216
2017	321	231
2018	23	18
2019	33	30
2020	14	16
2021	258	106

XPLANATORY NOTES:

. The above figures relate to application received and decrees of nullity issued by the four first instant tribunals and the National Marriage Appeal Tribunal.

. Only a minority of applications persist beyond the preliminary stages. About 40% are found to have no *prima facie* case for nullity and do not reach the stage of formal investigation; a further third are withdrawn by the applicants.

. In about 75–80% of cases ending with a nullity decree, a veto – technically called a *vetitum* – on marriage in the Church is imposed on one or both parties. This is because the defect which caused the nullity is judged to be still present, putting at risk the validity of a future marriage. The *vetitum* may be lifted by the local bishop only if he is satisfied, after investigation, of the person's fitness for marriage in all essential respects. The purpose of the *vetitum* is to prevent the sacrament of marriage being brought into disrepute and to protect the genuine interests of any future spouse.

. Before a decree is granted it must be judged by a Religional Tribunal. It must be established with moral certainty – probability alone is not enough – that nullity exists in a particular case; that is, that, because of fundamental defect of capacity for, or consent to, that marriage, established to have been present at the time of marriage, there was in fact, no valid marriage. The tribunal starts with the presumption that the marriage is valid; the onus is on the applicants to provide convincing evidence that it is not. The decision of the First Instance Tribunal, whether it is in favour of the nullity of marriage or not, can be appealed to the National Marriage Appeal Tribunal, located in the Columba Centre, Maynooth, Co Kildare. Futher evidence may be presented in the Appeal Process before the Judgement is made and a Decree is issued.

. COST OF THE PROCEDURE: The costs involved for the applicant are kept as low as possible and are, in fact, very modest. Applicants are expected to pay if they can afford it. However, each applicant is formally told that the progress of the case or its outcome does not in any way depend on the ability or willingness to pay any or all of these expenses. If they genuinely cannot pay, the Church will come to their aid. In practice, only a minority pay the full case fee. Over half pay nothing.

Allianz ⓘ

TABLE 2: CATHOLICS

TABLE 3: CATHOLIC SCHOOLS

	Parishes	Catholic Population	Churches	Schools (no)		School Population	
				Primary	Secondary[1]	Primary	Secondary
Armagh	61	239,229	146	151	27	29,577	21,854
Dublin	197	1,093,095	246	452	181	134,668	127,304
Cashel	46	78,878	84	115	20	12,143	11,143
Tuam	56	145,312	31	195	20	14,900	5,899
Achonry	23	42,200	47	49	9	3,780	3,969
Ardagh[2]	41	74,000	80	76	6	11,256	7,857
Clogher	37	83,882	85	89	15	12,345	6,993
Clonfert[2]	24	36,000	47	49	7	6,800	3,200
Cloyne	46	159,246	107	121	29	22,187	15,919
Cork & Ross[2]	68	220,000	124	173	35	n/a	n/a
Derry	51	253,747	104	111	21	20,566	15,892
Down & Connor	86	357,089	146	123	33	32,109	24,593
Dromore[2]	22	63,400	48	51	14	10,270	11,524
Elphin	38	90,559	90	107	13	10,385	4,116
Ferns[2]	49	116,001	101	96	20	16,598	16,276
Galway[2]	39	116,752	71	84	14	14,030	7,607
Kerry[2]	53	139,650	111	150	30	17,077	12,973
Kildare & Leighlin	56	261,887	117	162	41	35,619	24,721
Killala	22	36,051	48	63	10	4,050	4,217
Killaloe	58	125,453	133	144	21	17,895	11,374
Kilmore[2]	34	69,794	95	81	14	10,674	6,046
Limerick[2]	60	154,836	94	102	25	16,512	14,186
Meath	69	270,000	149	186	36	37,820	25,338
Ossory	42	82,540	88	83	16	11,546	9,012
Raphoe[2]	33	82,505	71	100	20	10,662	13,151
Waterford & Lismore	45	155,643	85	95	23	16,439	12,527
Totals[3]	1,356	4,547,749	2,548	3,208	701	529,908	417,691

Notes:
1. Includes voluntary secondary schools and state schools.
Source: Diocesan returns

2. Data unchanged from 2021.
3. Total estimates only.

Allianz ⑪

TABLE 4: NUMBER OF PRIESTS, RELIGIOUS AND PERMANENT DEACONS

	Active in Ministry			Others[3]	Members of Religious Congregations		
	Incardinated Priests[1]	Other priests[2]	Permanent Deacons		Clerical[4]	Brothers	Sisters
Armagh	79	16	17	31	39	10	230
Dublin	312	155	31	76	513	206	1,665
Cashel[5]	72	4	0	-	56	12	92
Tuam	83	11	3	35	0	11	220
Achonry	22	1	2	10	1	0	30
Ardagh[5]	46	5	0	16	11	6	94
Clogher	59	-	2	5	3	0	100
Clonfert[5]	25	6	0	6	22	0	92
Cloyne	62	3	10	37	0	2	133
Cork & Ross	90	-	3	22	40	29	195
Derry[5]	64	5	0	30	6	2	64
Down & Connor	95	34	15	11	43	7	120
Dromore	25	-	7	18	7	1	134
Elphin	33	29	8	11	7	0	143
Ferns[5]	75	2	1	28	9	6	131
Galway[5]	38	8	0	23	43	11	180
Kerry[5]	47	4	6	26	9	12	85
Kildare & Leighlin	66	15	11	23	0	22	168
Killala	30	3	0	13	0	0	35
Killaloe	58	7	0	23	10	12	124
Kilmore[5]	43	6	2	17	0	0	44
Limerick[5]	58	18	-	45	42	9	233
Meath	81	15	-	20	75	3	78
Ossory	41	2	0	13	8	21	102
Raphoe	49	4	0	22	7	3	19
Waterford & Lismore[5]	61	-	3	19	46	34	266
Totals[6]	1,714	353	121	586	997	419	4,777

Notes:
1. Priests incardinated in the Diocese are in active ministry in the Dioceses.
2. Priests who are in active ministry in the Diocese but who are incardinated elsewhere.
3. Priests incardinated in the Diocese who are either retired or working outside the Diocese
4. Priests of religious orders who are not in active ministry in the Diocese.
5. Data unchanged from 2021.
6. Totals estimates only.
Source: Diocesan returns

CATHOLIC ARCHBISHOPS AND BISHOPS OF BRITAIN

APOSTOLIC NUNCIO

Most Rev Claudio Gugerotti
54 Parkside, London SW19 5NF
Tel 020-89447189
Fax 020-89472494

ENGLAND AND WALES

PROVINCE OF WESTMINSTER

H.E. Cardinal Vincent Nichols
Archbishop of Westminister

Auxiliaries
Rt Rev John Sherrington
Rt Rev Nicholas Hudson
Rt Rev Paul McAleenan

Suffragans
Right Rev Alan Williams
Bishop of Brentwood
Right Rev Patrick McKinney
Bishop of Nottingham
Right Rev Alan Hopes
Bishop of East Anglia
Right Rev David Oakley
Bishop of Northhampton

PROVINCE OF BIRMINGHAM

Most Rev Bernard Longley
Archbishop of Birmingham

Auxilary
Rt Rev David Evans
Rt Rev Stepen Wright

Suffragans
Right Rev Mark Davies
Bishop of Shrewsbury
Right Rev Declan Lang
Bishop of Clifton

PROVINCE OF LIVERPOOL

Most Rev Malcolm McMahon
Archbishop of Liverpool

Auxilary
Right Rev Thomas Williams
Right Rev Thomas Neylon

Suffragans
Right Rev John Arnold
Bishop of Salford
Right Rev Marcus Stock
Bishop of Leeds
Right Rev Ralph Heskett
Bishop of Hallam
Right Rev Terence Drainey
Bishop of Middlesbrough
Right Rev Robert Byrne
Bishop of Hexham and Newcastle
Right Rev Paul Swarbrick
Bishop of Lancaster

PROVINCE OF CARDIFF

Most Rev Mark O'Toole
Archbishop of Cardiff and Bishop of Menevia

Suffragans
Right Rev Peter Brignall
Bishop of Wrexham

PROVINCE OF SOUTHWARK

Most Rev John Wilson
Archbishop of Southwark

Auxiliaries
Rt Rev Paul Hendricks

Suffragans
Vacant See Plymouth
Right Rev Richard Moth
Bishop of Arundel and Brighton
Right Rev Philip Egan
Bishop of Portsmouth

Bishop of the Forces
Right Rev Paul Mason

BISHOPS' CONFERENCE OF ENGLAND AND WALES

Bishops' Conference
39 Eccleston Square, London SW1V 1BX
Tel 020-76308220 Fax 020-79014821
Email secretariat@cbcew.org.uk

H.E. Cardinal Vincent Nichols
Archbishop's House, Ambrosden Avenue,
London SW1P 1QJ
Tel 020-77989033 Fax 020-77989077

Right Rev Declan Lang
Bishop of Clifton, St Ambrose,
North Road, Leigh Woods,
Bristol BS8 3PW
Tel 0117-9733027 Fax 0117-9735913

Most Rev John Wilson
Archbishop of Southwark,
Archbishop's House, St George's Road,
Southwark, London SE1 6HX
Tel 020-79282495 Fax 020-79287833

Right Rev Paul Swarbrick
Bishop of Lancaster,
Bishop's Office, Balmoral Road,
Lancaster LA1 3BT
Tel 01524-596050

Apostolic Administrator of Plymouth,
45 Cecil Street, Plymouth,
Devon PL1 5HW
Tel 01752-224414 Fax 01752-223750

Right Rev Alan Hopes
The White House, 21 Upgate,
Poringland, Norwich, Norfolk NR14 7SH
Tel 01586-2202/3956 Fax 01586-5358

Most Rev Bernard Longley
Archbishop of Birmingham,
8 Shadwell Street, Birmingham B4 6EY
Tel 0121-2369090 Fax 0121-2120171

Right Rev Mark Davies
Bishop of Shrewsbury,
Curial Offices, 2 Park Road South,
Prenton, Wirral CH43 4UX
Tel 0151-6529855

Right Rev Peter Brignall
Bishop of Wrexham, Bishop's House,
Sontley Road, Wrexham,
Clwyd LL13 7EW
Tel 01978-262726 Fax 01978-354257

Right Rev Terence Drainey
Bishop of Middlesbrough,
Bishop's House, 16 Cambridge Road,
Middlesbrough, Cleveland TS5 5NN
Tel 01642-818253 Fax 01642-850548

Right Rev Philip Egan
Bishop of Portsmouth, Bishop's House,
Bishop Crispian Way, Portsmouth PO1 3H(
Tel 01705-820894 Fax 01705-863086

Right Rev John Arnold
Bishop of Salford, Wardley Hall, Worsley
Manchester M28 5ND
Tel 0161-7942825 Fax 0161-7278592

Right Rev Marcus Stock
Bishop's House,
13 North Grange Road, Headingley,
Leeds LS6 2BR
Tel 01532-304533 Fax 01532-789890

Right Rev Robert Byrne
Bishop of Hexham and Newcastle,
Bishop's House,
26 West Avenue, Gosforth,
Newcastle Upon Tyne NE3 4ES
Tel 0191-2280003 Fax 0191-2740432

Right Rev David Oakley
Bishop of Northampton,
Bishop's House, Marriott Street,
Northhampton NN2 6AW
Tel 01604-715635 Fax 01604-792186

Right Rev Patrick McKinney
Bishop of Nottingham, Bishop's House,
17 Cavendish Road East, The Park,
Nottingham NG7 1BB
Tel 0115-9474786 Fax 0115-9475235

Right Rev Alan Williams
Bishop of Brentwood,
Cathedral House, Ingrave Road,
Brentwood, Essex CM15 8AT
Tel 01277-232266 Fax 01277-214060

Right Rev John Sherrington
Auxiliary Bishop of Westminster
Archbishop's House,
Ambrosden Avenue, London SWIP IQJ
Tel 020-7798 9033 Fax 020-7798 9077

Right Rev Ralph Heskett
Bishop of Hallam, Bishop's House
5 Norfolk Road, Sheffield 52 2SZ
Tel 0114 278 7988 Fax 0114 278 7988

Right Rev Richard Moth
Bishop of Arundel and Brighton
Highoaks, Old Brighton Road North,
Pease Pottage, West Sussex RH11 9AJ
Tel 01293-526428 Fax 01293-385276

Right Rev Paul Mason
Bishop of the Forces, Bishop's Oak,
6 The Crescent, Farnborough Park,
Farnborough, Hants GU14 7AS
Tel 01252-543649 Fax 01252-373748

Most Rev Mark O'Toole
Archbishop of Cardiff,
Archbishop's House,
42-43 Cathedral Road, Cardiff CF1 9HD
Tel 01222-20411 Fax 01222-345950

Most Rev Malcolm McMahon
Archbishop of Liverpool,
Archbishop's House, 19 Salisbury Road,
Cressington Park, Liverpool L10 0PH
Tel 0151-4940686

Right Rev Thomas Williams
34 Hope Place, Liverpool L1 9BG
Tel 0151-7030109 Fax 0151-7030267

Right Rev Paul Hendricks
Auxiliary Bishop of Southwark,
5 Carshalton Road, Sutton,
Surrey SMI 4LL
Tel 020-86438007

Right Rev Nicholas Hudson
Auxiliary Bishop of Westminster
Archbishop's House, Ambrosden Avenue,
London SW1P 1QJ
Tel 020-77989033 Fax 020-77989077

Right Rev Paul McAleenan
Auxiliary Bishop of Westminster
Archbishop's House, Ambrosden Avenue,
London SW1P 1QJ
Tel 020-77989033 Fax 020-77989077

Right Rev Tom Neylon
Auxiliary Bishop of Liverpool
The Priory, 5 Lancaster Lane,
Parbold, Wigan WN8 7HS

UKRAINIAN APOSTOLIC EPARCHY

Right Rev Kenneth Nowlakowski
Eparch of the Ukrainians
90 Binney Street, London W1Y 1YN
Tel 0171-6291534

SYRO-MALABAR EPARCHY

Right Rev Joseph Srampickal
Eparch of the Syro-Malabar Church of
Great Britain, Bishop's Office,
St Alphonsa of Immaculate Conception,
St Ignatius Square, Preston PR1 1TT
Tel 01772-396065

RETIRED BISHOPS IN ENGLAND AND WALES

Right Rev Howard Tripp
Former Auxiliary in Southwark
Little Sisters of the Poor,
2A Meadow Road,
London SW8 1QH

Right Rev Philip Pargeter
Auxiliary in Birmingham,
Grove House, 90 College Road,
Sutton Coldfield,
West Midlands B73 5AH

Right Rev Mark Jabalé
Emeritus Bishop of Menevia,
Belmont Abbey,
Ruckhall Lane,
Hereford HR2 9RZ

Most Rev Kevin McDonald
Emeritus Archbishop of Southwark,
c/o Archbishop's House,
St George's Road, Southwark,
London SE1 6HX

Most Rev Patrick Kelly
Emeritus Archbishop of Liverpool,
c/o Archbishop's House, Lowood,
Carnatic Road, Liverpool L18 8BY

Right Rev Edwin Regan
Emeritus Bishop of Wrexham,
c/o Bishop's House, Sontley Road,
Wrexham, Clwyd LL13 7EW

Right Rev Crispian Hollis
Emeritus Bishop of Portsmouth,
c/o Bishop's House,
Bishop Crispian Way,
Portsmouth PO1 3HG

Right Rev Christopher Budd
Emeritus Bishop of Plymouth
The Presbytery, Silver Street,
Lyme Regis DT7 3HS

Right Rev John Hine
Former Auxiliary in Southwark
St Andrews, 47 Ashford Road,
Tenterden, Kent TN30 6LL

Right Rev John Rawsthorne
Emeritus Bishop of Hallam
Bishop's House, 75 Norfolk Road,
Sheffield S2 2SZ

Right Rev Thomas McMahon
Bishop's House, Stock,
Ingatestone, Essex CM4 9BU

Right Rev Terence Brain
c/o Diocese of Salford Cathedral Centre,
3 Ford Street, Salford M3 6DP

Right Rev Michael Campbell
St Augustine's Priory,
55 Fulham Palace Road, Hammersmith,
London W6 8AU

Right Rev Thomas Burns
St Anne's Presbytery, Oliphant Circle,
Malpas, Newport NP20 6PF

Right Rev Seamus Cunningham
9 Clifton Road, Sunderland SR6 9DW

Right Rev David McGough
Former Auxiliary Bishop of Birmingham,
160 Draycott Road, Tean,
Stoke on Trent ST10 4JT

Right Rev Patrick Lynch
Former Auxiliary in Southwark,
Park House, 6a Cresswell Park,
Blackheath, London SE3 9RD

Right Rev William Kenney
Former Auxiliary in Birmingham,
St Hugh's House, 27 Hensington Road,
Woodstock, Oxfordshire OX20 1JH

Most Rev George Stack
c/o Archbishop's House,
42-43 Cathedral Road,
Cardiff CF1 9HD

THE HIERARCHY OF SCOTLAND

PROVINCE OF
ST ANDREWS AND EDINBURGH

Most Rev Archbishop Leo Cushley
Archbishop of St Andrews and
Edinburgh, 42 Greenhill Gardens,
Edinburgh EH10 4BJ
Tel 0131-4473337 Fax 0131-4470816
Email Abp.Cushley@staned.org.uk

Suffragans
Right Rev Hugh Gilbert
Bishop of Aberdeen,
Bishop's House, St Mary's House,
14 Chanonry, Old Aberdeen AB24 1RP
Tel 01224-319154 Fax 01224-325570
Email bishop.hugh@gmx.com

Right Rev Stephen Robson
Bishop of Dunkeld, Diocese of Dunkeld,
24028 Lawside Road, Dundee DD3 6XY
Tel 01382-225453 Fax 01382-204585
Email bishop@dunkelddiocese.org.uk

Right Rev Brian McGee
Bishop of Argyll and The Isles
Bishop's House, Esplanade, Oban,
Argyll PA34 5AB
Tel 01631-571395 Fax 01631-564930
Email Brian-Mcgee@btconnect.com

Right Rev William Nolan
Bishop of Galloway, Candida Casa,
8 Corsehill Road, Ayr KA7 2ST
Tel 01292-266750 Fax 01292-289888
Email bishop@gallowaydiocese.org.uk

PROVINCE OF GLASGOW

Suffragans
Right Rev Joseph A. Toal
Bishop of Motherwell,
Diocesan Centre, Coursington Road,
Motherwell ML1 1PP
Tel 01698-269114
Email bishop@rcdom.org.uk

Right Rev John Keenan
Bishop of Paisley, Diocesan Centre,
Cathedral Precincts, Incle Street,
Paisley PA1 1HR
Tel 0141-8476130
Email bishopjohn@rcdop.org.uk

BISHOPS' CONFERENCE OF SCOTLAND

General Secretary
Rev Dr Gerard Maguiness
General Secretariat,
64 Aitken Street, Airdrie,
Lanarkshire ML6 6LT
Tel 01236-764061 Fax 01236-762489
Email gensec@bcos.org.uk
www.bcos.org.uk

Assistant General Secretary
Mr Michael McGrath
64 Aitken Street,
Airdrie ML6 6LT

RETIRED BISHOPS IN SCOTLAND

Right Rev Maurice Taylor
Bishop Emeritus (Galloway Diocese)
41 Overmills Road, Ayr KA7 3LH
Email mauricetaylor1926@sky.com

Right Rev Peter A. Moran
Bishop Emeritus of Aberdeen,
10 Cathedral Square, Fortrose IV10 8TB
email pmoran@bcos.org.uk

Most Rev Mario Joseph Conti
Archbishop Emeritus of Glasgow,
40 Newlands Road, Glasgow G43 2JD
Email Mario.Conti@rcag.org.uk

Right Rev John Cunningham
Bishop Emeritus (Galloway)
29 Johnstone Terrace,
Greenock PA16 8BD

FORMS OF ECCLESIASTICAL ADDRESS

These notes should be understood as a guide to present-day practice in Ireland, rather than as 'prescriptive' rules. Forms of address – for example, whether someone is 'Very Rev', 'Right Rev', or 'Most Rev' – vary from country to country and language to language. The aim here has been to reflect Irish usage. These conventions are not static but are subject to gradual change. Some of the more involved forms of address have disappeared, and a dual standard of formality has emerged. For instance, 'Canon John Nonnullus' has in recent years tended to replace 'John Canon Nonnullus'. Where the older form is still found, the norm of normal address is given with the older form in parentheses ( ) as the more formal form of address. Since the form used is often a matter of preference of the person addressed, or the customary usage of a particular diocese or religious order, where this is known it should be followed. This directory uses what is considered to be the normal Irish form.

THE HIERARCHY

The Apostolic Nuncio
Written address: His Excellency Most Rev Dr John Nonnullus
Spoken address: same
In conversation: Your Excellency.
Reference to: 'The Nuncio said...'
('His Excellency said...')

Cardinals
Written address: His Eminence Cardinal John Nonnullus (H.E. John Cardinal Nonnullus)
Spoken address: Cardinal John Nonnullus (the more formal address is either of the written forms)
In conversation: Cardinal (Your Eminence)
Reference to: 'The Cardinal said...'
('His Eminence said...')

Note: The majority of cardinals are bishops, and they are divided into three groups, a small number known as the cardinal bishops, another small group who are the 'cardinal deacons', and the majority, who are called 'cardinal priests'. From this has arisen the form 'Cardinal-Archbishop of ...' or 'the cardinal-archbishop said', sometimes used in the media for emphasis. There is no category of 'cardinal-archbishops'; rather there are bishops and archbishops who are also cardinals. If one wishes to refer to a cardinal and also to draw attention to the see of which he is bishop, the following form should be used: 'Cardinal John Nunnullus, the Archbishop of Nusquam'.

Archbishops
Written address: The Most Rev John Nonnullus
Spoken address: Archbishop Nonnullus (His Grace the Archbishop of Nusquam)
In conversation: Your Grace
Reference to: 'The Archbishop said...'
('His Grace said...')

Bishops
Written address: The Most Rev John Nonnullus
Spoken address: Dr John Nonnullus, Bishop of Nusquam (His Lordship Dr...)
In conversation: Doctor (My Lord)
Reference to: 'The Bishop said...'

Note: The practice of using the word 'Bishop' in spoken address (e.g. Bishop John Nonnullus of Nusquam) and in conversation (e.g. 'Bishop, I am pleased to meet you') is becoming increasingly common.

CLERGY

Secular:
Monsignor
Written: Right Rev Mgr
Spoken: Monsignor

Capitular Dignitaries:
Archdeacon
Written: The Venerable John Nonnullus, Archdeacon of Nusquam
Spoken: Archdeacon

Dean
Written: The Very Rev Dean Nonnullus
Spoken: Dean

Canon
Written: The Very Rev Canon John Nonnullus (John Canon Nonnullus)
Spoken: Canon

Others
Those holding other capitular offices (e.g. precentor) are addressed as canons.

Parish Priest
Written: The Very Rev John Nonnullus PP
Spoken: Father

Curates
Written: The Very Rev John Nonnullus CC
Spoken: Father

Other Priests
Secular priests not included above:
Written: Rev John Nonnullus
Spoken: Father
Priests using academic titles are referred to by these titles, and in writing these are prefixed by 'Rev', e.g. Rev Prof John Nonnullus

Deacons
Written: Rev John Nonnullus
Spoken: Mister (Rev Mister)

Regular
The conventional protocol varies with religious orders, many of whom preserve forms of address peculiar to themselves. A general rule is that priests are addressed as found under Other priests above, and superiors (of houses or provinces) are addressed in writing as 'The Very Rev'.

Abbots
Written: 'The Right Rev' is placed before the conventional form of address of a member of that community.

NON-CLERICAL RELIGIOUS

Men
Non-clerical religious orders of men and non-clerical members of clerical religious orders are referred to as 'Br John Nonnullus' in writing, and `Brother' in speech.

Note 1. The use of Christian name or surname (e.g. 'Br John' or 'Br Nonnullus') depends on the usage of the order.

Note 2. Some orders have traditional ways of referring to their non-clerical members other than 'Brother'.

Women
Members of religious orders of women are referred to as 'Sr' in writing and 'Sister' in speech, irrespective of the position they hold in their institute.
Note 1. The form 'Reverend Mother' is obsolete and its use does not arise.
Note 2. The use of Christian name, name in religion, or surname, or the prefixing of the forename with 'M' (Mary) depends on the usage of the order.
Note 3. Some orders, in particular monastic and enclosed orders, use titles derived from their own traditions (e.g. abbess and prioress). There is no consistent usage with regard to these titles (e.g. it may be `Mother Abbess' or 'Sr Mary, the Abbess') and the usage depends on the order or the house.

THE ROMAN PONTIFFS

Information includes the name of the Pope, in many cases his name before becoming Pope, his birth-place or country of origin, the date of accession to the Papacy, and the date of the end of reign which, in all but a few cases, was the date of death. Double dates record the day of election and coronation.
Source: *Annuario Pontificio*

St Peter (Simon Bar-Jona) of Bethsaida, in Galilee, Prince of the Apostles, who received from Jesus Christ supreme pontifical power to be transmitted to his successors, resided first at Antioch, then at Rome, where he was martyred in the year 64 or 67, having governed the Church from that city for twenty-five years.
St Linus, Tuscany, 67-76
St Anacletus (Cletus), Rome 76-88
St Clement, Rome 88-97
St Evaristus, Greece, 97-105
St Alexander I, Rome, 105-25
St Sixtus I, Rome, 115-25
St Telesphorus, Greece, 125-36
St Hyginus, Greece, 136-40
St Pius I, Aquilea, 140-55
St Anictus, Syria, 155-66
St Soter, Campania, 166-75
St Eleutheius, Nicopolis in Epirus, 175-89

Up to the time of St Eleutherius, the years indicated for the beginning and end of pontificates are not certain. Also, up to the middle of the eleventh century, there are some doubts about the exact days and months given in chronological tables.

St Victor I, Africa, 189-99
St Zephyrinus, Rome, 199-217
St Callistus I, Rome, 217-22
St Urban I, Rome, 222-30
St Pontian, Rome, 21 July 230 to 28 Sept 235
St Anterus, Greece, 21 Nov 235 to 3 Jan 236
St Fabian, Rome, 10 Jan 236 to 20 Jan 250
St Cornelius, Rome, Mar 251 to June 253
St Lucius I, Rome, 12 May 254 to 2 Aug 254
St Stephen I, Rome, 12 May 254 to 2 Aug 257
St Sixtus II, Greece, 30 Aug 257 to 6 Aug 258
St Dionysius, birthplace unknown, 22 July 259 to 26 Dec 268
St Felix I, Rome, 5 Jan 269 to 30 Dec 274
St Eutychian, Luni, 4 Jan 275 to 7 Dec 283
St Caius, Dalmatia, 17 Dec 283 to 22 Apr 296
St Marcellinus, Rome, 30 June 296 to 25 Oct 304
St Marcellus I, Rome, 27 May 308 or 26 June 308 to 16 Jan 309

St Eusebius, Greece, 18 Apr 309 or 310 to 17 Aug 309 or 310
St Melchiades (Miltiades), Africa, 2 July 311 to 11 Jan 314
St Sylvester I, Rome, 31 Jan 314 to 31 Dec 335

Most of the popes before St Sylvester I were martyrs.

St Marcus, Rome, 18 Jan 336 to 7 Oct 336
St Julius I, Rome, 6 Feb 337 to 12 Apr 352
Liberius, Rome, 17 May 352 to 24 Sept 366
St Damasus I, Spain, 1 Oct 366 to 11 Dec 384
St Siricius, Rome, 15 or 22 or 29 Dec 384 to 26 Nov 399
St Anastasius I, Rome, 27 Nov 399 to 19 Dec 401
St Innocent I, Albano, 22 Dec 401 to 12 Mar 417
St Zozimus, Greece, 18 Mar 417 to 26 Dec 418
St Bonifice I, Rome, 28 or 29 Dec 418 to 4 Sept 422
St Celestine I, Campania, 10 Sept 422 to 27 July 432
St Sixtus III, Rome, 31 July 432 to 19 Aug 440
St Leo I (the Grant), Tuscany, 29 Sept 440 to 10 Nov 461
St Hilary, Sardinia, 19 Nov 461 to 29 Feb 468
St Simplicius, Tivoli, 3 Mar 468 to 10 Mar 483
St Felix III (II), Rome, 13 Mar 483 to 1 Mar 492

He should be called Felix II, and his successors of the same name should be numbered accordingly. The discrepancy in the numerical designation of popes named Felix was caused by the erroneous insertion in some lists of the name of St Felix of Rome, a martyr.

St Gelasius I, Africa, 1 Mar 492 to 21 Nov 496
Anastasius II, Rome, 24 Nov 496 to 19 Nov 498
St Symmachus, Sardinia, 22 Nov 498 to 19 July 514
St Hormisdas, Frosinone, 20 July 514 to 6 Aug 523
St John I, Martyr, Tuscany, 13 Aug 523 to 18 May 526
St Felix IV (III), Samnium, 12 July 526 to 22 Sept 530

Boniface II, Rome, 22 Sept 530 to 17 Oct 532
John II, Rome, 2 Jan 533 to 8 May 535

John II was the first pope to change his name. His given name was Mercury.

St Agapitus I, Rome, 13 May 535 to 22 Apr 536
St Silverius, Martyr, Campania, 1 or 8 June 536 to 11 Nov 537 (d. 2 Dec 537)

St Silverius was violently deposed in March 537 and abdicated on 11 Nov 537. His successor, Vigilius, was not recognised as pope by all the Roman clergy until his abdication.

Vigilius, Rome, 29 Mar 537 to 7 June 555
Pelagius I, Rome, 16 Apr 556 to 4 Mar 561
John III, Rome, 17 July 561 to 13 July 574
Benedict I, Rome, 2 June 575 to 30 July 579
Pelagius II, Rome, 26 Nov 579 to 7 Feb 590
St Gregory I (the Great), Rome, 3 Sept 590 to 12 Mar 604
Sabinian, Blera in Tuscany, 13 Sept 604 to 22 Feb 606
Bonifcace III, Rome, 19 Feb 607 to 12 Nov 607
St Boniface IV, Abruzzi, 25 Aug 608 to 8 May 615
St Deusdedit (Adeodatus I), Rome, 19 Oct 615 to 8 Nov 618
Boniface V, Naples, 23 Dec 619 to 25 Oct 625
Honorius I, Campania, 27 Oct 625 to 12 Oct 638
Severinus, Rome, 28 May 640 to 2 Aug 640
John IV, Dalmatia, 24 Dec 640 to 12 Oct 642
Theodore I, Greece, 24 Nov 642 to 14 May 649
St Martin I, Martyr, Todi, July 649 to 16 Sept 655 (in exile from 17 June 653)
St Eugene I, Rome, 10 Aug 654 to 2 June 657

St Eugene I was elected during the exile of St Martin I, who is believed to have endorsed him as pope.

St Vitalian, Segni, 30 July 657 to 27 Jan 672

Adeodatus II, Rome, 11 Apr 672 to 17 June 676

Donus, Rome, 2 Nov 676 to 11 Apr 678

St Agatho, Sicily, 27 June 678 to 10 Jan 681

St Leo II, Sicily, 17 Aug 682 to 3 July 683

St Benedict II, Rome, 26 June 684 to 8 May 685

John V, Syria, 23 July 685 to 2 Aug 686

Conon, birthplace unkown, 21 Oct 686 to 21 Sept 687

St Sergius I, Syria, 15 Dec 687 to 8 Sept 701

John VI, Greece, 30 Oct 701 to 11 Jan 705

John VII, Greece, 1 Mar 705 to 18 Oct 707

Sisinnius, Syria, 15 Jan 708 to 4 Feb 708

Constantine, Syria, 25 Mar 708 to 9 Apr 715

St Gregory II, Rome, 19 May 715 to 11 Feb 731

St Gregory III, Syria, 18 May 731 to Nov 741

St Zachary, Greece, 10 Dec 741 to 22 Mar 752

Stephen II (III), Rome, 26 Mar 752 to 26 Apr 757

After the death of St Zachary, a Roman priest named Stephen was elected but died (four days later) before his consecration as Bishop of Rome, which would have marked the beginning of his pontificate. Another Stephen was elected to succeed Zachary as Stephen II. The first pope with this name was St Stephen 254-7). The ordinal III appears in parentheses after the name of Stephen II because the name of the earlier elected but deceased priest was included in some lists. Other Stephens have double numbers.

St Paul I, Rome, Apr (29 May) 757 to 28 June 767

Stephen III (IV), Sicily, 1 (7) Aug 768 to 24 Jan 772

Adrian I, Rome, 1 (9) Feb 772 to 25 Dec 795

St Leo III, Rome, 26 (27) Dec 795 to 12 June 816

Stephen IV (V), Rome, 22 June 816 to 24 Jan 817

St Paschal I, Rome, 25 Jan 817 to 11 Feb 824

Eugene II, Rome, Feb (May) 824 to Aug 827

Valentine, Rome, Aug 827 to Sept 827

Gregory IV, Rome, 827 to Jan 844

Sergius II, Rome, Jan 844 to 27 Jan 847

St Leo IV, Rome, Jan (10 Apr) 847 to 17 Jan 855

Benedict III, Rome, July (29 Sept) 855 to 17 Apr 858

St Nicholas I (the Great), Rome, 24 Apr 858 to 13 Nov 867

Adrian II, Rome, 14 Dec 867 to 14 Dec 872

John VIII, Rome, 14 Dec 872 to 16 Dec 882

Marinus I, Gallese, 16 Dec 882 to 15 May 884

St Adrian III, Rome, 17 May 884 to Sept 885

Stephen V (VI), Rome, Sept 885 to 14 Sept 891

Formosus, Portus, 6 Oct 891 to 4 Apr 896

Boniface VI, Rome, Apr 896 to Apr 896

Stephen VI (VII), Rome, May 896 to Aug 897

Romanus, Gallese, Aug 897 to Nov 897

Theodore II, Rome, Dec 897 to Dec 897

John IX, Tivoli, Jan 898 to Jan 900

Benedict IV, Rome, Jan (Feb) 900 to July 903

Leo V, Ardea, July 903 to Sept 903

Sergius III, Rome, 29 Jan 904 to 14 Apr 911

Anastasius III, Rome, Apr 911 to June 913

Landus, Sabina, July 913 to Feb 914

John X, Tossignano (Imola), Mar 914 to May 928

Leo VI, Rome, May 928 to Dec 928

Stephen VII (VIII), Rome, Dec 928 to Feb 931

John XI, Rome, Feb (Mar) 931 to Dec 935

Leo VII, Rome, 3 Jan 936 to 13 July 939

Stephen VIII (IX), Rome, 14 July 939 to Oct 942

Marinus II, Rome, 30 Oct 942 to May 946

Agapitus II, Rome, 10 May 946 to Dec 955

John XII (Octavius), Tusculum, 16 Dec 955 to 14 May 964 (date of his death)

Leo VIII, Rome, 4 (6) Dec 963 to 1 Mar 965

Benedict V, Rome, 22 May 964 to 4 July 966

Confusion exists concerning the legitamcy of claims to the pontificate by Leo VII and Benedict V. John XII was deposed on 4 Dec 963 by a Roman council. If this deposition was invalid, Leo was an antipope. If the deposition of John was valid, Leo was the legitimate pope and Benedict was an antipope.

John XIII, Rome, 1 Oct 965 to 6 Sept 972

Benedict VI, Rome, 19 Jan 973 to June 974

Benedict VIII, Rome, Oct 974 to 10 July 983

John XIV (Peter Campenora), Pavia, Dec 983 to 20 Aug 984

John XV, Rome, Aug 985 to Mar 996

Gregory V (Bruno of Carinthia), Saxony, 3 May 996 to 18 Feb 999

Sylvester II (Gerbert), Auvergne, 2 Apr 999 to 12 May 1003

John XVII (Siccone), Rome, June 1003 to Dec 1003

John XVIII (Phasianus), Rome, Jan 1004 to July 1009

Sergius IV (Peter), Rome, 31 July 1009 to 12 May 1012

The custom of changing one's name on election to the papacy is generally considered to date from the time of Sergius IV. Before his time, several popes had changed their names. After his time, this became a regular practice, with few exceptions, e.g. Adrian VI and Marcellus II.

Benedict VIII (Theophylactus), Tusculum, 18 May 1012 to 9 Apr 1024

John XIX (Rosmanus), Tusculum, Apr (May) 1024 to 1032

Benedict IX (Theophylactus), Tusculum, 1032-44

Sylvester III (John), Rome, 20 Jan 1045 to 10 Feb 1045

Sylvester III was an antipope if the forcible removal of Benedict IX in 1044 was not legitimate.

Benedict IX (second time), 10 Apr 1045 to 1 May 1045

Gregory VI (John Gratian), Rome, 5 May 1045 to 20 Dec 1046

Clement II (Suitger, Lord of Morsleben and Homburg), Saxony, 24 (25) Dec 1046 to 9 Oct 1047

If the resignation of Benedict IX in 1045 and his removal at the December 1046 synod were not legitimate, Gregory VI and Clement II were antipopes.

Benedict IX (third time), 8 Nov 1047 to 17 July 1048 (d. c.1055)

Damasus II (Poppo), Bavaria, 17 July 1048 to 9 Aug 1048

St Leo IX (Bruno), Alsace 12 Feb 1049 to 19 Apr 1054

Victor II (Gebhard), Swabia, 16 Apr 1055 to 28 July 1057

Stephen IX (X) (Frederick), Lorraine, 3 Aug 1057 to 29 Mar 1058

Nicholas II (Gerard), Burgundy, 24 Jan 1059 to 27 July 1061

Alexander II (Anselmo da Baggio), Milan, 1 Oct 1061 to 21 Apr 1073

St Gregory VII (Hildebrand), Tuscany, 22 Apr (30 June) 1073 to 25 May 1085

Bl Victor III (Dauferius; Desiderius), Benevento, 24 May 1086 to 15 Sept 1087

Bl Urban II (Otto di Lagery), France, 12 Mar 1088 to 29 July 1099

Paschall II (Raniero), Ravenna, 13 (14) Aug 1099 to 21 Jan 1118

Gelasius II (Giovanni Caetani), Gaeta, 24 Jan (10 Mar) 1118 to 28 Jan 1119

Callistus II (Guido of Burgundy), Burgundy, 2 (9) Feb 1119 to 13 Dec 1124

Honorius II (Lamberto), Fiagnano (Imola), 15 (21) Dec 1124 to 13 Feb 1130
Innocent II (Gregorio Paperschi), Rome, 14 (23) Feb 1130 to 24 Sept 1143
Celestine II (Guido), Città di Castello, 26 Sept (3 Oct) 1143 to 8 Mar 1144
Lucius II (Gerardo Caccianemici), Bologna, 12 Mar 1144 to 15 Feb 1145
Bl Eugene III (Bernardo Paganelli di Montemagno), Pisa, 15 (18) Feb 1145 to 8 July 1153
Anastasius IV (Corrado), Rome, 12 July 1153 to 3 Dec 1154
Adrian IV (Nicholas Breakspear), England, 4 (5) Dec 1154 to 1 Sept 1159
Alexander III (Rolando Bandinelli), Siena, 7 (20) Sept 1159 to 30 Aug 1181
Lucius III (Ubaldo Allucingoli), Lucca, 1 (6) Sept 1181 to 25 Sept 1185
Urban III (Uberto Crivelli), Millan, 25 Nov (1 Dec) 1185 to 20 Oct 1187
Gregory VIII (Alberto de Morra), Benevento, 21 (25) Oct 1187 to 17 Dec 1187
Clement III (Paolo Scolari), Rome, 19 (20) Dec 1187 to Mar 1191
Celestine III (Giacinto Bobone), Rome, 30 Mar (14 Apr) 1191 to 8 Jan 1198
Innocent III (Lotario dei Conti di Segni), Anagni, 8 Jan (22 Feb) 1198 to 16 July 1216
Honorius III (Cencio Savelli), Rome, 18 (24) July 1216 to 18 Mar 1227
Gregory IX (Ugolino, Count of Segni), Anagni, 19 (21) Mar 1227 to 22 Aug 1241
Celestine IV (Goffredo Castiglioni), Milan, 25 (28) Oct 1241 to 10 Nov 1241
Innocent IV (Sinibaldo Fieschi), Genoa, 25 (28) June 1243 to 7 Dec 1254
Alexander IV (Rinaldo, Count of Segni) Anagni, 12 (20) Dec 1254 to 25 May 1261
Urban IV (Jacques Pantaléon), Troyes, 29 Aug (4 Sept) 1261 to 2 Oct 1264
Clement IV (Guy Foulques or Guido le Gros), France, 5 (15) Feb 1265 to 29 Nov 1268
Bl Gregory X (Teobaldo Visconti), Piacenza, 1 Sept 1271 (27 Mar 1272) to 10 Jan 1276
Bl Innocent V (Peter of Tarentaise), Savoy, 21 Jan (22 Feb) 1276 to 22 June 1276
Adrian V (Ottobono Fieschi), Genoa, 11 July 1276 to 18 Aug 1276
John XXI (Petrus Juliani or Petrus Hispanus), Portugal, 8 (20) Sept 1276 to 20 May 1277

Elimination was made of the name of John XX in an effort to rectify the numerical designation of popes named John. The error dates back to the time of John XV.

Nicholas III (Giovanni Gaetano Orsini), Rome, 25 Nov (26 Dec) 1277 to 22 Aug 1280

Martin IV (Simon de Brie), France, 22 Feb (23 Mar) 1281 to 28 Mar 1285

The names of Marinus I (882-4) and Marinus II (942-6) were construed as Martin. In view of these two pontificates and the earlier reign of St Martin I (649-55), this pope was called Martin IV.

Honorius IV (Giacomo Savelli), Rome, 2 Apr (20 May) 1285 to 3 Apr 1287
Nicholas IV (Girolamo Masci), Ascoli, 22 Feb 1288 to 4 Apr 1292
St Celestine V (Pietro del Murrone), Isernia, 5 July (29 Aug) 1294 to 13 Dec 1294; d. 1296. Canonised 5 May 1313
Boniface VIII (Benedetto Caetani), Anagni, 24 Dec 1294 (23 Jan 1295) to 11 Oct 1303
Bl Benedict XI (Niccolo Boccasini), Treviso, 22 (27) Oct 1303 to 7 July 1304
Clement V (Bertrand de Got), France, 5 June (14 Nov) 1305 to 20 Apr 1314 (first of Avignon popes)

From 1309 to 1377 Avignon was the residence of a series of French popes during a period of power struggles between the rulers of France, Bavaria and England and the Church. Despite some positive achievments it was the prologue to the Western Schism which began in 1378.

John XXII (Jacques d'Euse), Cahors, 7 Aug (5 Sept) 1316 to 4 Dec 1334
Benedict XII (Jacques Fournier), France, 20 Dec 1334 (8 Jan 1335) to 25 Apr 1342
Clement VI (Pierre Roger), France, 7 (19) May 1342 to 6 Dec 1352
Innocent VI (Etienne Aubert), France, 18 (30) Dec 1352 to 12 Sept 1362
Bl Urban V (Guillaume de Grimoard), France, 28 Sept (6 Nov) 1362 to 19 Dec 1370
Gregory XI (Pierre Roger de Beaufort), France, 30 Dec 1370 (5 Jan 1371) to 26 Mar 1378 (last of Avignon popes)
Urban VI (Bartolomeo Prignano), Naples, 8 (18) Apr 1378 to 15 Oct 1389
Boniface IX (Pietro Tomacelli), Naples, 2 (9) Nov 1389 to 1 Oct 1404
Innocent VII (Cosma Migliorati), Sulmona, 17 Oct (11 Nov) 1404 to 6 Nov 1406
Gregory XII (Angelo Correr), Venice, 30 Nov (19 Dec)1406 to 4 July 1415 when he voluntarily resigned from the papacy to permit the election of his successor.

This brought to an end in the Council of Constance the Western Schism which had divided Christendom into two and then three papal obediences from 1370 to 1417. Gregory XII died on 18 Oct 1417.

Martin V (Oddone Colonna), Rome, 11 (21) Nov 1417 to 20 Feb 1431

Eugene IV (Gabriel Condulmer), Venice, (11) Mar 1431 to 23 Feb 1447
Nicholas V (Tommaso Parentucelli), Sarzana, 6 (19) Mar 1447 to 24 Mar 1455
Callistus III (Alfonso Borgia), Jativa (Valencia), 8 (20) Apr 1455 to 6 Aug 1458
Pius II (Enea Silvio Piccolomini), Siena, 19 Aug (3 Sept) 1458 to 14 Aug 1464
Paul II (Pietro Barbo), Venice, 30 Aug (16 Sept) 1464 to 26 July 1471
Sixtus IV (Francesco della Rovere), Savona, 9 (25) Aug 1471 to 12 Aug 1484
Innocent VIII (Giovanni Battista Cibo), Genoa, 29 Aug (12 Sept) 1484 to 25 July 1492
Alexander VI (Rodrigo Borgia), Jativa (Valencia), 11 (26) Aug 1492 to 18 Aug 1503
Pius III (Francesco Todeschini-Piccolomini), Siena, 22 Sept (1, 8 Oct) 1503 to 18 Oct 1503
Julius II (Guiliano della Rovere), Savona, 31 Oct (26 Nov) 1503 to 21 Feb 1513
Leo X (Giovanni de' Medici), Florence, 9 (19) Mar 1513 to 1 Dec 1521
Adrian VI (Adrian Florensz), Utrecht, 9 Jan (31 Aug) 1522 to 14 Sept 1523
Clement VII (Giulio de' Medici), Florence 19 (26) Nov 1523 to 25 Sept 1534
Paul III (Alessandro Farnese), Rome, 13 Oct (3 Nov) 1534 to 10 Nov 1549
Julius III (Giovanni Maria Ciocchi del Monte), Rome, 7 (22) Feb 1550 to 23 Ma 1555
Marcellus II (Marcello Cervini), Montepulciano, 9 (10) Apr 1555 to 1 Ma 1555
Paul IV (Gian Pietro Carafa), Naples, 23 (26) May 1555 to 18 Aug 1559
Pius IV (Giovan Angelo de' Medici), Milan, 25 Dec 1559 (6 Jan 1560) to 9 Dec 1565
St Pius V (Antonio-Michele Ghislieri), Bosco (Alexandria), 7 (17) Jan 1566 to 1 May 1572. Canonised 22 May 1712
Gregory XIII (Ugo Buoncompagni), Bologna, 13 (25) May 1572 to 10 Apr 1585
Sixtus V (Felice Peretti), Grottammare (Ripatransone), 24 Apr (1 May) 1585 to 27 Aug 1590
Urban VII (Giovanni Battista Castagna) Rome, 15 Sept 1590 to 27 Sept 1590
Gregoryy XIV (Niccolo Sfondrati), Cremona, 5 (8) Dec 1590 to 16 Oct 1591
Innocent IX (Giovanni Antonio Facchinetti), Bologna, 19 Oct (3 Nov) 1591 to 30 Dec 1591
Clement VIII (Ippolito Aldobrandini), Florence, 30 Jan (9 Feb) 1592 to 3 Mar 1605
Leo XI (Alessandro de' Medici), Florence 1 (10) Apr 1605 to 27 Apr 1605
Paul V (Camillo Borghese), Rome, 16 (29 May 1605 to 28 Jan 1621
Gregory XV (Alessandro Ludovisi), Bologna, 9 (14) Feb 1621 to 8 July 1623

Allianz ⓘ

Urban VIII (Maffeo Barberini), Florence, 6 Aug (29 Sept) 1623 to 29 July 1644

Innocent X (Giovanni Battista Pamfili), Rome, 15 Sept (4 Oct) 1644 to 7 Jan 1655

Alexander VII (Fabio Chigi), Siena, 7 (18) Apr 1655 to 22 May 1667

Clement IX (Giulio Rospigliosi), Pistoia, 20 (26) June 1667 to 9 Dec 1669

Clement X (Emilio Altieri), Rome, 29 Apr (11 May) 1670 to 22 July 1676

Innocent XI (Benedetto Odescalchi), Como, 21 Sept (4 Oct) 1676 to 12 Aug 1689. Beatified 7 Oct 1956

Alexander VIII (Pietro Ottoboni), Venice, 6 (16) Oct 1689 to 1 Feb 1691

Innocent XII (Antonio Pignatelli), Spinazzola, 12 (15) July 1691 to 27 Sept 1700

Clement XI (Giovanni Francesco Albani), Urbino, 23, 30 Nov (8 Dec) 1700 to 19 Mar 1721

Innocent XIII (Michelangelo dei Conti), Rome, 8 (18) May 1721 to 7 Mar 1724

Benedict XIII (Pietro Francesco [in religion Vincenzo Maria] Orsini), Gravina (Bari), 29 May (4 June) 1724 to 21 Feb 1730

Clement XII (Lorenzo Corsini), Florence, 12 (16) July 1730 to 6 Feb 1740

Benedict XIV (Prospero Lambertini), Bologna, 17 (22) Aug 1740 to 3 May 1758

Clement XIII (Carlo Rezzonico), Venice, 6 (16) July 1758 to 2 Feb 1769

Clement XIV (Giovanni Vincenzo Antonio [in religion Lorenzo] Gaganelli), Rimini, 19, 28 May (4 June) 1769 to 22 Sept 1774

Pius VI (Giovanni Angelo Braschi), Cesena, 15 (22 Feb) 1775 to 29 Aug 1799

Pius VII (Barnabà [in religion Gregirio] Chiaramonti, Cesena, 14 (21) Mar 1800 to 20 Aug 1823

Leo XII (Annibale della Genga), Genga (Fabriano), 28 Sept (5 Oct) 1823 to 10 Feb 1829

Pius VIII (Francesco Saverio Castiglioni), Cingoli, 31 Mar (5 Apr) 1829 to 30 Nov 1830

Gregory XVI (Bartolomeo Alberto [in relgion Mauro] Cappellari), Belluno, 2 (6) Feb 1831 to 1 June 1846

Pius IX (Giovanni M. Mastai-Ferretti), Senigallia, 16 (21) June 1846 to Feb 1878

Leo XIII (Gioacchino Pecci), Carpineto (Anagni), 20 Feb (3 Mar) 1878 to 20 July 1903

St Pius X (Giuseppe Sarto), Riese (Treviso), 4 (9) Aug 1903 to 20 Aug 1914. Canonised 29 May 1954

Benedict XV (Giacomo della Chiesa), Genoa, 3 (6) Sept 1914 to 22 Jan 1922

Pius XI (Achille Ratti), Desio (Milan), 6 (12) Feb 1922 to 10 Feb 1939

Pius XII (Eugenio Pacelli), Rome, 2 (12) Mar 1939 to 9 Oct 1958

John XXIII (Angelo Giuseppe Roncalli), Sotto il Monte (Bergamo), 28 Oct (4 Nov) 1958 to 3 June 1963

Paul VI (Giovanni Battista Montini), Concessio (Brescia, 21 (30) June 1963 to 6 Aug 1978

John Paul I (Albino Luciani), Forno di Canale (Belluno), 26 Aug (3 Sept) 1978 to 28 Sept 1978

John Paul II (Karol Wojtyla), Wadowice, Poland, 16 (22) Oct 1978 to 2 April 2005

Benedict XVI (Joseph Ratzinger), Germany, 19 April 2005 to 28 Feb 2013 (retired), died 31 Dec 2022

Francis (Jorge Mario Bergoglio) 13 March 2013A

Index of Advertisers

ALPHABETICAL LIST OF CLERGY IN IRELAND

DIOCESAN, RELIGIOUS AND MISSIONARY

Irish Diocesan clergy working or studying abroad are also listed.

Telephone numbers are included in this list.

For all other forms of telephonic or electrical communications, including mobiles, faxes, email addresses and websites, please refer to the main entries in this directory.

All STD numbers in this Directory are listed with both the number and the local area code.
Callers from the Irish Republic to Northern Ireland simply need to dial 048 followed by the 8-digit local number.

A

braham, Yesudas
Asariparambil (OCarm)
Carmelite Priory,
White Abbey,
Co Kildare R51 X827
Tel 045-521391

cton, John Gerard, CC
18 University Road,
Galway
Tel 091-524875/563577
(*Cathedral*, Galway)

dzato, George (SVD), Very Rev, Co-PP
c/o St Philip the Apostle Church,
No. 2 Presbtery,
Mountview Road,
Clonsilla, Dublin 15
Tel 01-8249695
(*Blakestown/Huntstown/Mountview*, Dublin)

gger, George (SVD)
Rector,
Donamon Castle,
Roscommon
Tel 090-6662222

guilar, Arturo (SSC), VG
No 3 and 4,
Ma Yau Tong Village,
Po Lam Road,
Tseung Kwan O,
Hong Kong, SAR

guilar-Díez, Juan José (SJ)
John Sullivan House,
56/56A Mulvey Park,
Dundrum, Dublin 14
Tel 01-2983978

hearne, Peter, Very Rev, PE
(Waterford & L., retired)

hearne, Seamus (OSA), Very Rev, TA
The Presbytery,
50 Glenties Park,
Finglas South, Dublin 11
Tel 01-8343722/
087-6782746
(*Finglas, Finglas West, Rivermount*, Dublin)

Ahern, Dan (SSC)
c/o St John's Parish Centre,
Castle Street, Tralee,
Co Kerry

Ahern, Gerard, Very Rev, PP
Parkmore,
Baltinglass, Co Wicklow
Tel 087-6482678
(Kildare & L.)

Ahern, Niall, Very Rev
Canon, PP
Strandhill, Co Sligo
Tel 071-9168147
(*Strandhill/Ransboro*, Elphin)

Ahern, Pat
(Kerry, retired)

Aherne, Francis (OSA),
Prior,
St Augustine's,
Taylor's Lane,
Balyboden, Dublin 16
Tel 01-4241000

Akaolisa, John Damascene,
PC
St Catherine's, Meath
Street, Dublin 8
Tel 01-4543356
(*James's Street, Meath Street*, Dublin)

Akongwale, Victor, CC
Curate's House,
Carrowbeg,
Swinford,
Co Mayo F12 FK81
Tel 094-9252895
(*Swinford (Kilconduff and Meelick)*, Achonry)

Akubuenyi, Samuel, PC
32 Earlsfort Road, Lucan,
Co Dublin K78 AP11
Tel 01-4572900
(*Lucan South*, Dublin)

Alexander, Anthony, Very
Rev, PP
46 Blackstaff Road,
Ballycranbeg, Kircubbin,
Newtownards,
Co Down BT22 1AG
Tel 028-42738294
(*Kircubbin (Ardkeen)*,
Down & C.)

Alexander, Paul, Very Rev,
PP
10 St Patrick's Road, Saul,
Downpatrick,
Co Down BT30 7JE
Tel 028-44612525
(*Saul and Ballee*, Down & C.)

Ali, Joseph, CC
St John's Presbytery,
Lecarrow, Co Roscommon
Tel 090-6661115
(*Knockcroghery*, Elphin)

Alipoyo, Glenn, Very Rev, PP
Parochial House,
Loughglynn, Castlerea,
Co Roscommon
Tel 090-9880007
(*Loughglynn*, Elphin)

Allen, Brian (OFM)
Adam & Eve's
4 Merchants' Quay
Dublin D08 XY19
Tel 01-6771128

Allman, Colm, Very Rev, BA,
HDE
President,
St Joseph's College,
Garbally Park, Ballinasloe,
Co Galway
Tel 090-9642504/9642254
(*Ballinasloe, Creagh And Kilclooney*, Clonfert)

Allred, Norman, CC,
Cathedral House,
Mullingar,
Co Westmeath
Tel 044-9348338/9340126
(*Mullingar*, Meath)

Alwill, Gerard, Very Rev, PP
56 Main Street, Derrylin
Co Fermanagh BT92 9PD
Tel 028-67748315
(*Derrylin (Knockninny)*,
Kilmore)

Ambrose, James, Very Rev
Canon
Dromcollogher,
Charleville, Co Limerick
Tel 087-7740753
(Limerick, retired)

Ambrose, John Rev (MHM)
St Joseph's House,
50 Orwell Park,
Rathgar, Dublin D06 C535
Tel 01-4127700

Ameh, Christian, PC
c/o The Sacristy, St Vincent
de Paul Church,
Griffith Avenue, Dublin 9
Tel 01-8339756
(*Marino*, Dublin)

Anandam, Alexander (SSP)
Society of Saint Paul,
Moyglare Road,
Maynooth,
Co Kildare W23 NX34
Tel 01-6285933

Andama, Martin (CSSp)
St Mary's College,
Rathmines, Dublin 6
Tel 01-4995760

Andersen, Dom Benedict
Maria (OSB)
Silverstream Priory,
Stamullen,
Co Meath K32 T189

Anoumou, Jerome S. (SMA)
African Missions,
Blackrock Road,
Cork T12 TD54
Tel 021-4292871

Antwi-Boasiako, Isaac (CSSp)
55 Fernhill Road,
Greenhills, Dublin 12
Tell 01-4504040
(*Greenhills, Kimmage Manor*, Dublin)

Apap, Jesmond (SDB)
Vice-Rector,
Salesian College,
Maynooth Road,
Celbridge,
Co Kildare W23 W0XK

Apust, Joseph, CC
Parochial House,
Mornington, Co Meath
Tel 01-9827384
(*Laytown-Mornington*,
Meath)

Arigho, Desmond (CSSp)
Holy Spirit Missionary
College
Kimmage Manor,
Whitehall Road,
Dublin D12 P5YP
Tel 01-4064300

Arkinson, Patrick, PP
Sessiaghoneill, Ballybofey,
Co Donegal
Tel 074-9131149
(Killygordon
(Donaghmore), Derry)

Armstrong, Paul, Very Rev,
PE
5 Balmoral Mews,
Belfast BT9 6NM
(Down & C., retired)

Arnasius, Egidijus
Chaplain to Lithuainian
Community,
48 Westland Row,
Dublin 2
Tel 01-6761030/
087-7477554
(Westland Row, Dublin)

Atede, Godwin, CC
St Mary's, Tang,
Ballymahon, Co Longford
Tel 090-6432214
(Drumraney, Meath)

Audley, Pádraig, Very Rev,
PE
Leitir Mealláin,
Co na Gaillimhe
(Tuam, retired)

Aughney, Edward, Very Rev,
Adm
Glynn, St Mullins via
Kilkenny
Tel 051-424563
(St Mullins, Kildare & L.)

Augusthy, Bobit (OSCam)
St Camillus,
11 St Vincent Street North,
Dublin 7
Tel 01-8300365

Augustine, George, Very
Rev, PP
Mill Lane, Kilcock,
Co Kildare
Tel 01-6103512
(Kilcock, Kildare & L.)

Aylward, Cassian (OSB)
Silverstream Priory,
Stamullen,
Co Meath K32 T189
Tel 01-8417142

Aylward, Eamon (SSCC)
27 Northbrook Road,
Ranelagh, Dublin 6
Tel 01-6473756

Ayoola, Anthony, CC
Parochial House, Duleek,
Co Meath
Tel 041-9823205
(Duleek, Meath)

B

Babu, Suresh (OSCam)
St Camillus,
South Hill Avenue,
Blackrock, Co Dublin
Tel 01-2882873/2833380

Bachara, Kamil, CC
64 Westcourt,
Ballincollig, Co Cork
Tel 021-4871206
(Ballinora, Ballincollig and
Ovens, Cork & R.)

Bailey, Michael (OFM)
Dún Mhuire,
Seafield Road,
Killiney, Co Dublin
Tel 01-2826760

Baker, Eugene, Very Rev, PP
The Presbytery,
Richmond Street,
Buttevant, Co Cork
Adm, Churchtown
Tel 086-8031876
(Buttevant, Churchtown
(Liscarroll), Cloyne)

Baker, Patrick, CC
Parochial House, Fahan,
Lifford, Co Donegal
Tel 074-9360151
(Fahan (Burt, Inch and
Fahan), Derry)

Balikuddembe, Philip
Amooti, CC
Parochial House,
Aglish, Co Waterford
Tel 024-96287
(Aglish, Waterford and L.)

Bamai, Yusuf, Very Rev, PP
Kill, Cootehill, Co Cavan
Tel 049-5553035
(Kilsherdany and Drung,
Kilmore)

Bane, John
46 Garden View,
Clarecastle, Co Clare
Tel 086-8246555
(Killaloe, retired)

Bangalie, Augustine (CSSp)
St Mary's College,
Rathmines, Dublin 6
Tel 01-4995760

Bannon, Gabriel (OSM),
Very Rev
Servite Priory, Benburb,
Dungannon,
Co Tyrone BT71 7JZ
Northern Ireland
Tel 028-37548241

Bannon, Michael, PP
Gowna, Co Cavan
Tel 043-6683120
(Lough Gowna and
Mullinalaghta, Ardagh &
Cl.)

Bannon, Patrick
15 Lisdarn Heights, Cavan
(Kilmore, retired)

Banville, Patrick, Very Rev,
PP
Marshallstown,
Co Wexford
Tel 0539388521
Adm, St Senan's,
Enniscorthy
(Marshallstown and
Castledockrell,
St Senans, Enniscorthy,
Ferns)

Baragry, Dan (CSsR)
Provincial, St Joseph's,
St Alphonsus Road,
Dundalk,
Co Louth A71 F3FC
Tel 042-9334042/9334762

Barasa, Vitalis
St John's Presbytery,
Tralee, Co Kerry
Tel 066-7122522
(Tralee, St John's, Kerry)

Barber, Noel (SJ)
Milltown Park,
Miltown Road,
Dublin D04 NX39
Tel 01-269898411

Barden, Thomas, PP
Kenagh, Co Longford
Tel 043-3322127
(Kilcommoc, Ardagh & Cl.)

Barkindo, Lazarus (OSA)
St Augustine's Priory,
Shop Street, Drogheda,
Co Louth

Barrett, Anthony (SPS)
St Patrick's, Kiltegan,
Co Wicklow W91 Y022
Tel 059-6473600

Barrett, Edward (OMI)
Department of Chaplaincy,
Tralee General Hospital,
Tralee, Co Kerry
Tel 066-7126222

Barrett, Eugene (OFM)
Guardian,
Franciscan Friary,
Rossnowlagh,
Co Donegal F94 PH21
Tel 071-9851342

Barrins, David (OP),
Superior,
Dundalk, Co Louth
Tel 042-9334179/9333714
(Droichead
Nua/Newbridge, Kildare &
L.)

Barron, Liam, Very Rev, PP
Mullinavat, via Waterford,
Co Kilkenny
Tel 051-898108/
087-2722824
(Mullinavat, Ossory)

Barry, Anselm (OSB)
Glenstal Abbey, Murroe,
Co Limerick
Tel 061-621000

Barry, Eamonn
Gortacrue
Midleton, Co Cork
Tel 086-8157952
(Cloyne, retired)

Barry, Martin (SPS)
Kiltegan House,
11 Douglas Road, Cork
Tel 021-4969371

Barry, Maurice (OCarm)
Carmelite Friary, Kinsale,
Co Cork
Tel 021-772138

Barry, Michael (SAC)
Pallottine College,
Thurles, Co Tipperary
Tel 0504-21202

Barry, Oliver (OMI), Very
Rev
Provincial,
Oblates of Mary
Immaculate House of
Retreat,
Tyreconell Road,
Inchicore, Dublin 8
Tel 01-4541160/4541160

Barry, Philip (SAC)
Pallottine College,
Thurles, Co Tipperary
Tel 0504-21202

Bartlett, Timothy, Very Rev
PP, EV
St Mary's, Marquis Street,
Belfast BT1 1JJ
Tel 028-90320482
(St Mary's, Down & C.)

Bartley, Kevin, Very Rev,
Adm
The Presbytery,
Chapel Green, Rush,
Co Dublin
Tel 01-8437208
(Rush, Dublin)

Bawe, Philip Shube (MHM)
St Joseph's House,
50 Orwell Park,
Rathgar, Dublin D06 C53!
Tel 01-4127700

Baxter, Martin (OCarm)
Bursar, Carmelite Priory,
Whitefriar Street Church,
56 Aungier Street,
Dublin 2 D02 R598
Tel 01-4758821

Baxter, Philip (OFMCap)
Guardian, Capuchin Friar
Ard Mhuire,
Creeslough, Letterkenny,
Co Donegal
Tel 074-9138005

Baxter, Turlough, Adm
Parochial House, Killashe
Co Longford
Tel 043-3345546
PP, Lanesborough
(Rathcline)
Lanesboro, Co Longford
Tel 043-3321166
(Killashee, Lanesboro,
Ardagh & Cl.)

ayaca, Darwin (SSC)
No 3 and 4,
Ma Yau Tong Village,
Po Lam Road,
Tseung Kwan O,
Kow Loon, Hong Kong,
SAR

eagon, Brendan, Very Rev,
CC
1 Christine Road,
Newtownabbey,
Co Antrim BT36 6TG
Tel 028-90841507
(*St Mary's on the Hill*,
Down & C.)

eatty, John, Very Rev, AP
St Michael's Street,
Tipperary Town,
Co Tipperary
Tel 062-80475
(*Tipperary*, Cashel & E.)

eecher, Patrick (OCD)
The Abbey, Loughrea,
Co Galway
Tel 091-841209

eere, Joseph (CSSp)
Holy Spirit Missionary
College,
Kimmage Manor,
Whitehall Road, Dublin 12
Tel 01-4064300

eggan, Nguekam Tiernach,
Very Rev, PP
6 Boa Island, Belleek,
Enniskillen,
Co Fermanagh BT93 3AE
Tel 028-68658229
(*Belleek-Garrison*, Clogher)

eglan, Peter, PE
The Presbytery,
Edgeworthstown,
Co Longford
(Ardagh & Cl., retired)

egley, George P., Adm
Parochial House,
Chapel Road,
Lusk, Co Dublin
Tel 01-8949229
(*Lusk*, Dublin)

egley, Joseph, Very Rev
Canon, CC
Killarney, Co Kerry
Tel 064-6631014
(*Killarney*, Kerry)

egley, Michael (CSSp)
Holy Spirit Missionary
College,
Whitehall Road, Dublin
D12 P5YP
Tel 01-4064300

ehan, Laurence, Very Rev
On Leave
(Dublin)

Behan, Richard, Very Rev,
PP
The Presbytery,
Main Street,
Blessington, Co Wicklow
Tel 045-865442
(*Blessington, Valleymount*,
Dublin)

Beirne, Francis, Very Rev, PP
Tisrara, Four Roads,
Co Roscommon
Tel 090-6623313
(*Ballyforan (Dysart and
Tisrara)*, Elphin)

Beirne, Seán, CC
Kilteevan, Roscommon
Tel 090-6626374
(*Roscommon*, Elphin)

Belton, Liam, Very Rev
Canon,
Moderator
Presbytery No 1,
Ballinteer Avenue,
Dublin D16 PY54
Tel 01-4944448
(*Ballinteer, Dundrum,
Meadowbrook*, Dublin)

Bennett, Donal N. (SSC)
St Columban's Retirement
Home,
Dalgan Park, Navan,
Co Meath
Tel 046-9021525

Bennett, John (MSC)
Woodview House,
Mount Merrion Avenue,
Blackrock, Co Dublin
Tel 01-2881644

Bennett, Mark, CC
St Mary's,
Carrick-on-Shannon,
Co Leitrim
Tel 071-9620347
(*Carrick-on-Shannon
(Kiltoghert)*, Ardagh & Cl.)

Bennett, Martin (OFMCap),
PP
Clonshaugh Drive,
Priorswood,
Dublin 17 D17 RP20
Tel 01-8474469/8474358
(*Priorswood*, Dublin)

Bennett, Paul, CC
2 Cathedral Terrace,
Cobh, Co Cork
Tel 021-4908317
(*Cobh*, Cloyne)

Bennett, Roch (OFMCap)
Capuchin Friary,
Ard Mhuire, Creeslough,
Letterkenny,
Co Donegal F92 Y23R
Tel 074-9138005

Bennett, Terence (SSC)
St Columban's Retirement
Home,
Dalgan Park,
Navan, Co Meath
Tel 046-9021525

Bergin, John (SAC)
Pallottine College,
Thurles, Co Tipperary
Tel 0504-21202

Bergin, Liam, Rt Rev Mgr
St Brigid's Parish,
841 East Broadway,
Boston, MA 02127, USA
Tel 001-617-4477770
(Ossory)

Bermingham, John (CSsR)
St Joseph's,
St Alphonsus Road,
Dundalk,
Co Louth A71 F3FC
Tel 042-9334042

Bermingham, William, Very
Rev Canon, PP
Youghal, Co Cork
Tel 083-8687196
(*Youghal*, Cloyne)

Berney, Donal, PP
Kilanerin, Gorey,
Co Wexford
Tel 0402-37120
(*Kilanerin and Ballyfad*,
Ferns)

Bettison, John (SVD)
8 Teignmouth Road,
London, NW2 4HN
Tel 020-84528430

Binh, Dominic Nguyen Viet
(SDB)
Salesian College, Don
Bosco Road
Pallaskenry,
Co Limerick V94 WP86
Tel 061-393105

Binh, Paul Tran Xuan Rev
(SDB)
Salesian College,
Maynooth Road,
Celbridge,
Co Kildare W23 W0XK

Birmingham, Joseph (OCD)
Avila Carmelite Centre,
Bloomfield Avenue,
Morehampton Road,
Dublin 4
Tel 01-6430200

Black, Andrew
Canadian Pontifical
College,
Via Crecenzio, 75,
00193 Rome
(Down & C.)

Blade, Kevin (MSC), Adm
Castlegar, Galway
Tel 091-751548
(*Castlegar*, Galway)

Blake, Ciarán, Very Rev, PP
Cummer, Tuam,
Co Galway
(*Cummer (Kilmoylan and
Cummer)*, Tuam)

Blake, Declan, Very Rev
Presbytery 2,
Shangan Road, Dublin 9
Tel 01-8421486
(*St Pappin's, Ballymun*,
Dublin)

Blake, Ephrem (CP)
Passionist Retreat Centre,
Downpatrick Road,
Crossgar,
Co Down BT30 9EQ
Tel 028-44830242

Blake, Kieran, Very Rev,
Co-PP
Kilcolman, Sharavogue,
Birr, Co Offaly
Tel 057-9120812/
087-9302214
(*Brendan Pastoral Area*,
Killaloe)

Blake, Martin, Co-PP
Cathedral Presbytery,
O'Connell Street,
Ennis, Co Clare
Tel 065-6824043
(*Abbey Pastoral Area*,
Killaloe)

Blayney, Liam (SPS), Very
Rev
12 Bellaghy Road,
Dunloy, Ballymena
Co Antrim BT44 9AE

Bluett, Anthony
Parochial House,
Ardpatrick, Co Limerick
Tel 087-1934525
(*Pastoral Unit 9*, Limerick)

Bluett, Garrett, Very Rev
Canon
Croom, Co Limerick
Tel 061-397335
(Limerick, retired)

Bluett, Patrick
Glenfield,
Kilmallock,
Co Limerick
(Limerick, retired)

Bluitt, Tobias, Very Rev
Canon, PP, VF
Kanturk, Co Cork
Tel 029-50192
(*Kanturk/Castlemanger*,
Cloyne)

Boggan, Matthew, PP
Clongeen, Foulksmills,
Co Wexford
Tel 051-565610
(*Clongeen and Ballymitty*,
Ferns)

Bohan, Bernard (SPS)
St Patrick's, Kiltegan,
Co Wicklow
Tel 059-6473600

Bohan, Harry, Very Rev, AP
172 Drumgeely Hill,
Shannon, Co Clare
Tel 061-713682/086-
8223362
(*Tradaree Pastoral Area*,
Killaloe)

Bohan, Seamus, Very Rev, PP
Tynagh, Loughrea,
Co Galway H62 DH32
Tel 090-9745113
Moderator, Duniry and Abbey
(Duniry and Kilnelehan)
(*Duniry and Abbey*
(*Duniry and Kilnelehan*),
Tynagh and Killeen,
Clonfert)

Boland, Declan, PP
44 Barrack Street,
Strabane,
Co Tyrone BT82 8HD
Tel 028-71883293
(*Strabane*, Derry)

Boland, Eugene
c/o Diocesan Offices,
St Eugene's Cathedral,
Francis Street,
Derry BT48 9AP
(Derry, retired)

Boland, Vivian (OP)
Convent of SS Xystus and Clement
Collegio San Clemente,
Via Labicana 95,
00184 Roma
Tel 0039-06-7740021

Bollard, Daniel, Very Rev, PP
Thomastown, Co Kilkenny
Tel 056-7724279/
087-6644858
(*Thomastown*, Ossory)

Bonner, Patrick
c/o Diocesan Office,
Letterkenny, Co Donegal
(Raphoe)

Boran, Anthony (OFMCap)
Capuchin Friary,
Station Road, Raheny,
Dublin D05 T9E4
Tel 01-8313886

Borders, Thomas Aquinas (OSB)
Silverstream Priory,
Stamullen,
Co Meath K32 T189
Tel 01-8417142

Boschi, Marcelo (FDP)
Regional Superior,
c/o Via Etruria 6, 00183
Rome, Italy

Bourke, Eamonn, Very Rev
Head Chaplain, UCD,
Belfield, Dublin 4
Tel 01-7161971
(Dublin)

Bourke, George, Very Rev, AP
Moycarkey, Thurles,
Co Tipperary
Tel 0504-44227
(*Moycarkey*, Cashel & E.)

Bowe, John (SMA)
African Missions,
Blackrock Road,
Cork T12 TD54
Tel 021-4292871

Bowen, Patrick, Very Rev, PP
Glenmore Avenue
Tel 0876532482
(Limerick, retired)

Boyce, Eugene, Co-PP
Croagh, Rathkeale,
Co Limerick
Tel 069-64185/087-
2542517
(*Pastoral Unit 11*, Limerick)

Boyce, Declan (SPS), Adm,
St Mary's, Temple Street,
Co Sligo
Tel 071-9162670
(*St Mary's, Sligo*, Elphin)

Boyce, John, CC
Arranmore Island,
Co Donegal
Tel 074-9520504
(*Burtonport (Kincasslagh)*,
Raphoe)

Boyce, Philip (OCD), Most
Rev, DD
Bishop Emeritus of
Raphoe,
'Columba House',
Windyhall, Letterkenny,
Co Donegal F92 EK4W
Tel 074-9122729
(Raphoe)

Boyers, John
16 'Wilfield',
Sandymount Avenue,
Ballsbridge, Dublin 4
Tel 087-1557887
(*Donnybrook*, Dublin)

Boyle, Brian, Very Rev, Adm
The Presbytery,
Ravenswood,
Fermoy, Co Cork
Tel 085-2553787
Administrator, Kilworth
(*Fermoy, Kilworth*, Cloyne)

Boyle, Con, Very Rev, PP
87 Cushendall Road,
Ballyvoy, Ballycastle,
Co Antrim BT54 6QY
Tel 028-20762248
(*Culfeightrin*, Down & C.)

Boyle, Francis, PE
(Dromore, retired)

Boyle, Gerry, Very Rev, PP
Parochial House,
Rathkenny, Co Meath
Tel 046-9054138
Administrator, Lobinstown
(*Lobinstown, Rathkenny*,
Meath)

Boyle, James A. (MHM)
c/o St Joseph's House,
50 Orwell Park,
Rathgar, Dublin D06 C535
Tel 01-4127700

Boyle, Laurence, Very Rev, PP
Parochial House,
1 Convert Road,
Cookstown,
Co Tyrone BT80 8QA
Tel 028-86763370
(*Cough, Cookstown*
(*Desertcreight
& Derryloran*), Armagh)

Boyle, Liam
Parochial House,
Newmills, Glenswilly,
Co Donegal
Tel 074-9137456
Chaplain,
Letterkenny Institute of
Technology,
(*Glenswilly*, Raphoe)

Boyle, Liam, Rt Rev
Knockaderry, Co Limerick
(Limerick, retired)

Boyle, Martin (OP)
St Saviour's,
Upper Dorset Street,
Dublin 1
Tel 01-8897610

Boyle, Michael (OSA)
St Augustine's Priory,
Washington Street, Cork
Tel 021-2753982

Boyle, Patrick, Very Rev,
Adm
8 Slademore Close,
Ard Na Greine,
Ayrfield, Dublin 13
Tel 086-1011415
(*Edenmore, Grange Park*,
Dublin)

Boyle, Ronnie, Very Rev, PP
Parochial House,
Chapel Field,
Abbeyknockmoy, Tuam,
Co Galway H54 DR02
Tel 093-43510
(*Abbeyknockmoy*, Tuam)

Bracken, John, Co-PP
Emmaus, Main Street,
Dundrum, Dublin 14
Tel 01-2983494
(*Dundrum*, Dublin)

Bradley, Bruce (SJ)
Vice-Rector, Milltown
Park,
Miltown Road, Dublin 6
Tel 01-2698411/2698113

Bradley, David, Very Rev, PP
Parochial House,
Kells, Co Meath
Tel 046-9240213
(*Kells*, Meath)

Bradley, Francis, Very Rev,
PP, Chancellor
Cockhill, Buncrana,
Co Donegal
Tel 074-9363455
(*Buncrana, Fahan (Burt,
Inch and Fahan)*, Derry)

Bradley, John, Very Rev, PE
8 Killymeal Road,
Dungannon,
Co Tyrone BT71 6DP
Tel 028-87722183
(Armagh, retired)

Bradley, Manus
3690 Croissant Oscar,
Brossard,
Quebec J4Y 2JB
Tel 001-1450-8127858
(Derry)

Bradley, Philip, Very Rev,
Adm, VF
Parochial House,
83 Terenure Road East,
Dublin 6
Tel 01-4905520
(*Terenure*, Dublin)

Bradley, William (CSSp)
Holy Spirit Missionary
College,
Whitehall Road, Dublin
D12 P5YP
Tel 01-4064300

Brady, Brian, Very Rev, PP,
VF
Parochial House,
Ardnascanlon, Co Donegal
Tel 074-9376264
(Derry)

Brady, Enda, Very Rev, PP
Bohereenglas, Cashel,
Co Tipperary
Tel 062-61127
(*Cashel*, Cashel & E.)

Brady, Frank, (SJ), PC
The Presbytery,
Shangan Road, Ballymun,
Dublin 9
Tel 01-8421551
(*Ballymun*, Dublin)

Brady, Frank Rev
Hydebank Wood,
Hospital Road,
Belfast BT8 8NA
(Down & C.)

Brady, Gerard, PP
Carrick, Finea,
Mullingar,
Co Westmeath
Tel 043-6681129
(*Carrick-Finea*, Ardagh &
Cl.)

Brady, Harry, Very Rev, AP
10 Beechwood, Lissane,
Clarecastle, Co Clare
Tel 086-2349798
(*Abbey Pastoral Area*,
Killaloe)

Brady, Jim (SPS)
St Patrick's, Kiltegan,
Co Wicklow W91 Y022
Tel 059-6473600

Brady, Kenneth (CP)
St Paul's Retreat,
Mount Argus, Dublin 6W
Tel 01-4992000

Allianz ⑪

ady, Michael (OMI)
2a Bulfin Road,
Dublin 8
Tel 01-4531660
ady, P.J. (OFM)
Franciscan Friary,
Killarney, Co Kerry
Tel 064-6631334/6631066
ady, Patrick V.
(Kilmore, retired)
ady, Peter, PE
Lenamore, Co Longford
Tel 044-9357404
Ardagh & Cl., retired)
ady, Philip, Very Rev
Creighan, Co Cavan
Kilmore, retired)
ady, Ray, Very Rev
c/o Bishop's House,
Mullingar, Co Westmeath
Meath, retired)
ady, Rory, Very Rev, PP
Bruckless, Co Donegal
Tel 074-9737015
Bruckless (Killaghtee),
Raphoe)
ady, Seán, His Eminence
Cardinal, DCL, DD
Archbishop Emeritus of
Armagh,
Parochial House,
36 Maydown Road
Tullysaran, Benburb,
Co Tyrone BT71 7LN
Armagh)
anagan, Anthony (CSsR)
Clonard Monastery,
1 Clonard Gardens,
Belfast BT13 2RL
Tel 028-90445950
anigan, Desmond, CC
Our Lady of Lourdes
Presbytery,
Hardman's Gardens,
Drogheda,
Co Louth A92 PXF3
Tel 041-9831899
(Drogheda, Armagh)
ankin, Aidan, Very Rev, PP
27 Glenveagh Drive,
Belfast BT11 9HX
Tel 028-90618180
(St Oliver Plunkett, Down
& C.)
annigan, David, Very Rev,
Co-PP
89 Sperrin Road,
Drimnagh, Dublin 12
Tel 01-4652418
(Mourne Road, Dublin)
assil, Paul (SJ) (Zambia)
c/o St Ignatius Community
& Church,
27 Raleigh Row,
Salthill, Galway
Tel 091-523707

Bray, Frank (MSC)
Woodview House,
Mount Merrion Avenue,
Blackrock, Co Dublin
Tel 01-2881644
Breathnach, Cormac (SMA)
SMA House, Wilton,
Cork T12 KR23
Tel 021-4541069/4541884
Bredin, Eamonn
(Kilmore, retired)
Breen, Gerard, Very Rev, PP
Parochial House,
Stradbally, Co Laois
Tel 057-8625132
(Stradbally, Kildare & L.)
Breen, P.J., Very Rev, PP
Parochial House,
Killea, Dunmore East,
Co Waterford
Tel 051-383127
(Killea (Dunmore East),
Waterford & L.)
Breen, Thomas O., Very Rev,
PP
Ballylanders, Kilmallock,
Co Limerick
Tel 062-46705
(Ballylanders, Cashel & E.)
Breheny, Pádraig (OFM)
Collegio S. Isidoro
Via degli Artisti 41
00187 Roma, Italy
Tel 0039-06-4885359
Brennan, Ailbe (OSA)
Duckspool House
(Retirement Community),
Abbeyside, Dungarvan,
Co Waterford
Tel 058-23784
Brennan, Brian, PE
Hollybrook, Drumanure,
Abbeyshrule, Co Longford
(Ardagh & Cl., retired)
Brennan, Christopher Very
Rev (SMA), Adm,
Islandeady, Castlebar,
Co Mayo
Tel 094-9024125
(Islandeady, Tuam)
Brennan, Darren, PP
Parochial House,
14 Presbytery Lane,
Dunloy,
Co Antrim BT44 9DZ
Tel 028-27657223
(Dunloy and Cloughmills,
Down & C.)
Brennan, David, Very Rev,
PP
Parochial House,
Kentstown,
Navan, Co Meath
Tel 041-9825276
(Beauparc, Meath)

Brennan, Declan (OSA)
Hospital Chaplain
St Augustine's Priory,
Shop Street,
Drogheda, Co Louth
Tel 041-9838409
Brennan, Denis, Most Rev,
DD
Retired Bishop of Ferns,
PO Box 40, Summerhill,
Wexford
(Ferns)
Brennan, Fergal (SJ)
Milltown Park,
Miltown Road, Dublin 6
Tel 01-2698411/2698113
Brennan, Kilian
Apartment 3, Seascape,
366 Clontarf Road,
Dublin 3
(Dublin, retired)
Brennan, Louis (OFM)
Franciscan Friary,
Liberty Street,
Cork T12 D376
Tel 021-4275481
Brennan, Michael, Very Rev,
PP
Bearna, Co Galway
Tel 091-590956
(Bearna, Galway)
Brennan, Oliver, Very Rev,
PE
Parochial House,
Dillonstown, Dunleer
Co Louth A92 HH24
(Armagh, retired)
Brennan, Patrick (OP)
Dominican Community,
St Mary's Priory, Tallaght,
Dublin 24
Tel 01-4048100
Brennan, Peter, Very Rev, PP
The Parochial House,
Clerihan, Clonmel,
Co Tipperary
Tel 087-2362603
(Clerihan, Cashel & E.)
Brennan, Richard (SPS)
St Patrick's, Kiltegan,
Co Wicklow W91 YO22
Tel 0596473600
Brennan, Thomas
USA
(Ferns)
Brennock, Michael (OSA)
St Augustine's Priory,
Dungarvan, Co Waterford
Tel 058-41136
Breslan, Fergus, PE
Parochial House,
17 Carnmore Drive,
Newry, Co Down
Tel 028-30269047
(Armagh, retired)

Breslan, Patrick, Very Rev,
PE, AP
Parochial House,
55 Dermanaught Road,
Galbally, Dungannon,
Co Tyrone BT70 2NR
Tel 028-87758277
(Donaghmore, Armagh)
Breslin, Michael, Very Rev,
PE
Priest in residence,
Presbytery, Castlecoote,
Co Roscommon
(Elphin, retired)
Bresnahan, Damian (SMA)
Superior,
African Missions,
Dromantine, Newry,
Co Down BT34 1RH
Tel 028-30821224
Brewster, Patrick (SDB)
Salesian House,
45 St Teresa's Road,
Crumlin, Dublin 12
Tel 01-4555605
Brick, Maurice, Very Rev
Canon, PP
The Presbytery,
Castleisland, Co Kerry
Tel 066-7141241
(Castleisland, Kerry)
Brickley, John, Very Rev, PP
Cooleragh, Coill Dubh,
Naas, Co Kildare
Tel 045-860281
(Kilcock, Kildare & L.)
Briody, Anthony, CC
Parochial House,
Stranorlar,
Co Donegal
Tel 074-9131157
(Stranorlar, Raphoe)
Briody, Joseph
St John's Seminary,
127 Lake Street,
Brighton, MA 01235, USA
(Raphoe)
Briscoe, Peter, Rt Rev Mgr,
Adm
67 Ramleh Park, Milltown,
Dublin 6
Tel 01-2196600
(Milltown, Dublin)
Broaders, Brian, Very Rev,
PP, VF
Rathnure, Enniscorthy,
Co Wexford
Tel 053-9255122
(Rathnure and
Templeudigan, Ferns)
Broderick, Daniel, Very Rev,
PP
Milltown,
Killarney, Co Kerry
Tel 066-9767312
Moderator, Castlemaine
Parish
(Milltown, Castlemaine,
Kerry)

Broderick, Donal, Very Rev, PE
Ballyhooly, Co Cork
Tel 025-39148
(Cloyne, retired)

Brodie, Thomas (OP)
St Saviour's,
Glentworth Street,
Limerick
Tel 061-412333

Brophy, Joseph, Very Rev, CC
Ballyfin, Portlaoise,
Co Laois
Tel 057-8755227
(Mountrath, Kildare & L.)

Brophy, Robert, Very Rev Canon, PP
The Presbytery,
Curraheen Road, Cork
Tel 021-4343535
(Curraheen Road, Cork & R.)

Brouder, Jeremiah
49 Halcyon Place,
Park Village,
Castletroy, Limerick
(Limerick, retired)

Brough, David, Very Rev, Co-PP
2, St Mary's Terrace,
Arklow, Co Wicklow
Tel 0402-3296
(Arklow, Dublin)

Brown, Brian, Very Rev, PP
Church Street,
Ballynahinch,
Co Down BT24 8LP
Tel 028-97562410
(Magheradroll (Ballynahinch), Dromore)

Brown, Francis, Very Rev Canon, Adm
Cathedral Presbytery,
38 Hill Street,
Newry BT34 1AT
Tel 028-30262586/
028-30256372
(Newry, Saval, Dromore)

Brown, John (SMA)
African Missions,
Dromantine, Newry,
Co Down BT34 1RH
Tel 028-30821224

Brown, John (CSSp)
Holy Spirit Missionary College
Kimmage Manor,
Whitehall Road,
Dublin D12 P5YP
Tel 01-4064300

Brown, Michael (OCD)
St Teresa's,
Clarendon Street, Dublin 2
Tel 01-6718466/6718127

Browne, Colm
c/o Bishop's House,
Dublin Road,
Mullingar, Co Westmeath
(Meath)

Browne, Denis, Very Rev, PP
Kilanerin, Gorey
Co Wexford
Tel 0402-37120
(Kilanerin & Ballyfad, Ferns)

Browne, James (IC)
Doire na hAbhann,
Tickincor, Clonmel,
Co Tipperary
Tel 052-6126914

Browne, Martin (OSB)
Glenstal Abbey, Murroe,
Co Limerick
Tel 061-621000

Browne, Michael (SPS)
St Patrick's,
21 Leeson Park,
Dublin D06 DE76
Tel 01-4977897

Browne, Michael (SBD)
Vice-Rector,
Salesian House,
45 St Teresa's Road,
Crumlin, Dublin 12
Tel 01-4555605

Browne, Patrick, Very Rev, PP
Oulart, Gorey, Co Wexford
Tel 053-9136139
(Oulart and Ballaghkeene, Ferns)

Browne, Raymond, Most Rev, DD
Bishop of Kerry,
Bishop's House, Killarney,
Co Kerry
Tel 064-6631168
(Kerry)

Browne, Richard, Very Rev, PP
Cappamore, Co Limerick
Tel 061-381288
(Cappamore, Cashel & E.)

Browne, Richard, Very Rev, PE
Nadrid, Coachford,
Co Cork
(Cloyne, retired)

Browne, Thomas, Very Rev, PE
Southabbey,
Youghal, Co Cork
Tel 024-93199
(Cloyne, retired)

Browne, Vincent (CSSp)
Holy Spirit Missionary College,
Whitehall Road,
Dublin D12 P5YP
Tel 01-4064300

Bucciarelli, Robert, Rt Rev, DD
Vicar for Ireland,
Harvieston,
Cunningham Road,
Dalkey, Co Dublin
Tel 01-2859877
(Opus Dei)

Buckley, Benignus (OFMCap)
Capuchin Friary,
Friary Street,
Kilkenny R95 NX60
Tel 056-7721439

Buckley, Con
(Kerry, retired)

Buckley, James (CSsR)
Mount St Alphonsus,
South Circular Road,
Limerick
Tel 061-315099

Buckley, John, Most Rev, DD
Bishop Emeritus of Cork and Ross,
Cork and Ross Offices,
Redemption Road, Cork
Tel 021-4301717
(Cork & R., retired)

Buckley, John, Very Rev, PP
Killeentierna, Killarney,
Co Kerry
Tel 066-974141
Moderator,
Knocknagoshel
Tel 068-46107
(Killeentierna, Knocknagoshel, Kerry)

Buckley, Michael Anthony, CC
The Presbytery, Goleen,
Co Cork
Tel 028-35188
(Bantry, Caheragh, Goleen, Muintir Bháire and Schull, Cork & R.)

Buckley, Patrick, Very Rev, PP
4 Upper Woodlands,
Cloghroe, Co Cork
Tel 021-4385311
(Inniscarra, Cloyne)

Buckmaster, Ian (White Fathers)
Cypress Grove Road,
Templeogue, Dublin 6W
Tel 01-4055263

Budau, Ciprian (OFMConv), Very Rev
Custodial Office,
St Patrick's Friary,
26 Cornwall Road,
Waterloo,
London SE1 8TW, England
Tel 020-79288897/
0044-2079288897

Budau, Damian, CC
Parochial House,
Tullamore, Co Offaly
Tel 057-9321587
(Tullamore, Meath)

Buggy, James
Castlebar, Co Mayo
(Tuam retired)

Bulman, Joseph (OP), Very Rev
Secretary of the Province,
Provincial Office,
St Mary's, Tallaght,
Dublin D24 X585
Tel 01-4048118
Prior, Dominican College,
Newbridge
Droichead Nua, Co Kildare
Tel 045-487200

Burger, John (SSC)
Knock, Mayo
(retired)

Burgess, Mike (OFMCap)
Capuchin Friary,
Friary Street,
Kilkenny R95 NX60

Burke, Colm, PE
Queen of Peace Nursing Home, Knock, Co Mayo
(Tuam, retired)

Burke, Enda, Very Rev
Cloughjordan,
Co Tipperary
Tel 0505-42120
(Killaloe, retired)

Burke, Fintan (OCarm)
Carmelite Community,
Gort Muire, Ballinteer,
Dublin D16 EI67
Tel 01-2984014

Burke, Gabriel,
5 Lavallin Drive,
Whitechurch, Co Cork
Tel 021-4200184
(Blarney, Cloyne)

Burke, Kieran, Very Rev, CC
Parochial House,
Letterbrickaun, Leenane,
Co Galway, H91 EC5R
Tel 095-42251
(Ballyhaunis (Annagh), Tuam)

Burke, Peter, PP
Ferbane, Co Offaly
Tel 090-6454380
(Ferbane High Street and Boora, Ardagh & Cl.)

Burke, Sean, CC
Mohill, Co Leitrim
Tel 071-9631097
(Mohill (Mohill-Manachain), Ardagh & Cl.

Burleigh, Michael (OCSO)
Mellifont Abbey,
Collon, Co Louth
Tel 041-9826103

Burns, Gerard, Very Rev, PP
The Parochial House,
Clonbur, via Claremorris,
Co Galway
Tel 094-9546030
(Clonbur (Ross), Tuam)

Burns, John
On sick leave
(Down & C.)

...urns, Karl, Very Rev, PP
Mount Bellew, Ballinasloe,
Co Galway
Tel 090-9679235
(*Moylough and
Mountbellew/Menlough
(Killascobe)*, Tuam)

...urns, Pat, PP
Bohermore, Cashel,
Co Tipperary
Tel 087-2036763
(*Cashel*, Cashel & E.)

...urns, Peter (CSsR)
Superior,
Clonard Monastery,
1 Clonard Gardens,
Belfast BT13 2RL
Tel 028-90445950

...urns, Thomas
St Anne's Presbytery,
Convent Hill, Waterford
(Waterford & L., retired)

...utler, James, PP
Ballygarrett, Gorey,
Co Wexford
Tel 053-9427330
Adm, Riverchapel,
Courtown Harbour
(*Riverchapel, Courtown
Harbour, Ballygarrett*,
Ferns)

...utler, Kieran (SM),
Little Sisters of the Poor,
Sybil Hill Road,
Raheny, Dublin 5
(Retired)

...utler, Patrick, Very Rev
Vicar for Clergy,
Chaplaincy for Religious
Houses
Parochial House,
Youghal Road,
Tallow, Co Waterford
Tel 086-1737499
(Waterford & L.)

...utler, Robert, Very Rev,
Adm (Pro-tem)
Parochial House,
Armoy, Ballymoney,
Co Antrim BT53 8RL
(*Armoy*, Down & C.)

...yrne, Archie (OP)
Dominican College,
Newbridge
Droichead Nua, Co Kildare
Tel 045-487200

...yrne, Arthur, Rt Rev Mgr
Castor's Bay Road, Lurgan
(Dromore, retired)

...yrne, Brendan, Rt Rev Mgr,
Chancellor
c/o Bishop's House, Carlow
Tel 059-9176725
(Kildare & L., retired)

...yrne, Charles, Very Rev
c/o Bishop's House, Carlow
(Kildare & L., retired)

Byrne, Charles, Very Rev, PP
91 Newry Road,
Rathfriland,
Co Down BT34 5AP
Tel 028-40630306
(*Clonduff (Hilltown),
Drumgath (Rathfriland)*,
Dromore)

Byrne, Charles, Very Rev, PP,
VF
Carrigart, Co Donegal
Tel 074-9155154
(*Carrigart*, Raphoe)

Byrne, Desmond (CSSp), TA
45 Woodford Drive,
Monastery Road,
Clondalkin, Dublin 22
Tel 01-4592323
(*Clondalkin/Rowlagh/
Neilstown/Deansrath/
Bawnogue*, Dublin)

Byrne, Diarmuid, Very Rev,
Co-PP
Parochial House,
Arklow, Co Wicklow
Tel 0402-32294
(*Aughrim*, Dublin)

Byrne, Donal (OCarm),
Whitefriar Street Church,
56 Aungier Street,
Dublin 2 D02 R598
Tel 01-4758821

Byrne, Felix, Very Rev
Canon, CC
Monaseed, Gorey,
Co Wexford
Tel 053-9428207
(*Craanford*, Ferns)

Byrne, Gareth, Very Rev, VG
Moderator of the Curia,
Office of the Moderator,
Dublin Diocesan Offices,
20–23 Arran Quay,
Dublin 7, D07 XK85
Tel 01-8087500
Team Assistant, Ballygall,
Ballymun Road,
Drumcondra, Glasnevin,
Iona Road parishes
(Dublin)

Byrne, Gerald, Very Rev, PP
15 New Road,
Leighlinbridge, Co Carlow
(Kildare & L., retired)

Byrne, James, Very Rev
Ballylannon,
Wellingtonbridge,
Co Wexford
(Ferns, retired)

Byrne, John (OSA)
St Augustine's,
Taylor's Lane,
Balyboden, Dublin 16
Tel 01-4241000

Byrne, John, Very Rev, PA
Oylegate, Co Wexford
Tel 053-9138163
(*Oylegate and Glenbrien*,
Ferns)

Byrne, John, Rt Rev Mgr, PP,
VG
Parochial House,
Dublin Road, Portlaoise,
Co Laois
Tel 057-8621142/
057-8692153
(*Portlaoise*, Kildare & L.)

Byrne, John, Very Rev, AP,
VF
Parochial House, Kells,
Co Meath
Tel 046-9240213
(*Kells*, Meath)

Byrne, Kilian
Archbishop's House,
Dromcondra, Dublin 9

Byrne, Martin, Very Rev, PP
Ballymore, Killinick,
Co Wexford
Tel 053-9158966
(*Ballymore and Mayglass*,
Ferns)

Byrne, Mel (CP)
Passionist Retreat Centre,
Downpatrick Road,
Crossgar,
Co Down BT30 9EQ
Tel 028-44830242

Byrne, Michael
Serene Valley, Borris Road,
Kiltealy, Enniscorthy,
Co Wexford
(Ferns, retired)

Byrne, Michael, Very Rev, PP
Bree, Enniscorthy,
Co Wexford
Tel 053-9247843
(*Bree*, Ferns)

Byrne, Paddy, PP
The Presbytery,
Ballinakill Road,
Abbeyleix, Co Laois
Tel 0578731135/
087-9948505
(*Abbeyleix, Ballinakill,
Raheen*, Kildare & L.)

Byrne, Patrick (SVD)
1 & 3 Pembroke Road,
Ballsbridge, Dublin 4

Byrne, Paul, Very Rev
3 Fortwilliam Demesne,
Belfast BT15 4FD
(Down & C.)

Byrne, Paul, Very Rev, PP
Parochial House,
Termonfeckin,
Drogheda,
Co Louth A92 W403
Tel 041-9822121
(*Techmonfechin*, Armagh)

Byrne, Peter F., TA
68 Clontarf Road
Clontarf
Dublin 3
(*Clontarf, St Anthony's,
Clontarf, St John's,
Dollymount*, Dublin)

Byrne, Tony (CSSp)
Holy Spirit Missionary
College
Kimmage Manor,
Whitehall Road,
Dublin D12 P5YP
Tel 01-4064300

Byrne, William Rev (SSC)
St Columban's Retirement
Home, Dalgan Park,
Navan, Co Meath
Tel 046-9021525

Byrne, William, PP
Ballycullane, New Ross,
Co Wexford
Tel 051-562123
(*Ballycullane*, Ferns)

Byrne, William, Very Rev, PP
Allen, Kilmeague, Naas,
Co Kildare
Tel 045-860135
(*Allen*, Kildare & L.)

Byrnes, James (CSSp)
Holy Spirit Missionary
College
Kimmage Manor,
Whitehall Road,
Dublin D12 P5YP
Tel 01-4064300

Byrnes, Michael, Very Rev,
PP, JV
Dunkellin Terrace,
Portumna,
Co Galway H53 F584
Tel 090-9741092
Moderator, Fahy and
Quansborough
(*Fahy and Quansborough
(Fahy and Kilquain)*,
Portumna, Clonfert)

C

Cacciola, Thomas (CFR)
St Columba Friary,
Fairview Road,
Derry BT48 8NU
Tel 028-71419980

Cadam, Simon, PP
St Mary's, Granard,
Co Longford
Tel 043-6686550
(*Granard*, Ardagh & Cl.)

Caffrey, Jim, Very Rev, Co-
PP
The Presbytery,
Hawthorns Road,
Dublin 18
(*Balally*, Dublin)

Cahill, Donal,
Lisheen, Skibbereen,
Co Cork
(Cork & R., retired)

Cahill, Éamonn, Very Rev,
TA
c/o parishes as listed
(*Finglas, Finglas West,
Rivermount*, Dublin)

Cahill, Joseph (SSC)
Bohernasup, Ballina,
Co Mayo
Tel 096-22984
(retired)

Cahill, Kevin, Very Rev, DCL,
c/o Bishop's House,
Summerhill, Wexford
(Ferns)

Cahill, Lee (SMA)
African Missions,
Blackrock Road,
Cork T12 TD54
Tel 021-4292871

Cahill, Michael, Very Rev, PP
Parochial House,
Johnstown, Navan,
Co Meath
Tel 046-9021731
(Johnstown, Meath)

Cahill, Patrick
Holy Family Mission,
Glencomeragh House,
Kilsheelin, Co Waterford
(Waterford & L.)

Cahill, Sean, Very Rev, PE
Curates' Residence,
Massforth,
152 Newry Road,
Kilkeel, Co Down BT34 4ET
Tel 028-41762257
(Kilkeel (Upper Mourne),
Down & C.)

Callan, Paul, Very Rev Mgr,
TA
c/o parishes as listed
(Ayrfield, Donaghmede-
Clongriffin-Balgriffin,
Edenmore, Grange Park,
Dublin)

Callanan, Brendan (CSsR),
St Joseph's,
St Alphonsus Road,
Dundalk,
Co Louth A71 F3FC
Tel 042-9334042/9334762

Callanan, John (SJ)
Parish Office
St. John's Church
Clontarf Road
Dublin 3
Tel 01-8334606
(Clontarf, St Anthony's,
Clontarf, St John's,
Dollymount, Dublin)

Callanan, Patrick, Very Rev
Canon, PE
Kilbeacanty, Gort,
Co Galway
Tel 091-631691
(Galway, retired)

Callanan, William (SJ)
Milltown Park,
Miltown Road,
Dublin D06 V9K7
Tel 01-2698411/2698113

Campbell, Garrett, PP
Parochial House,
17 Eagralougher Road,
Loughgall,
Co Armagh BT61 8LA
Tel 028-38891231
(Loughgall, Armagh)

Campbell, Gerard, Very Rev,
PP, EV, Adm
Parochial House,
Knockbridge, Dundalk,
Co Louth A91 NA03
Tel 042-9374125/042-
6827418
(Darver and Dromiskin,
Knockbridge, Armagh)

Campbell, James (SSS)
Superior,
Blessed Sacrament Chapel,
20 Bachelors Walk,
Dublin D01 NW14
Tel 01-8724597

Campbell, Joseph, CC
Parochial House,
Tullamore, Co Offaly
Tel 057-9321587
(Tullamore, Meath)

Campbell, Noel
Ballysmutton, Manor
Kilbride, Blessington,
Co Wicklow
(Dublin, retired)

Campion, Desmond (SDB)
Chaplain Naval Service,
Haulbowline, Cobh, Cork

Campion, John (SDB), Very
Rev
Rector, Salesian House,
Milford, Castletroy,
Limerick
Tel 061-330268

Canning, Thomas
143 Melmount Road,
Sion Mills, Strabane,
Co Tyrone BT82 9EX
Tel 028 81658264
(Derry)

Cannon, Aodhan, Very Rev,
PP
Ardara, Co Donegal
Tel 074-9541135
(Ardara, Raphoe)

Cannon, Seán (CSsR)
St Joseph's,
St Alphonsus Road,
Dundalk,
Co Louth A71 F3FC
Tel 042-9334042/9334762

Canny, Michael, Very Rev,
PP, VG
Parochial House,
32 Chapel Road,
Derry BT47 2BB
Tel 028-71342303
(Waterside (Glendermott),
Derry)

Cantwell, Joe (SPS)
St Patrick's, Kiltegan,
Co Wicklow
Tel 059-6473600

Caraher, Laurence, Very
Rev, PE, AP
The Ravel, School Lane,
Tullyallen, Drogheda,
Co Louth
Tel 041-9834293
(Armagh, retired)

Carbery, Patrick (SJ)
St Francis Xavier's,
Upper Gardiner Street,
Dublin 1
Tel 01-8363411

Carbery, Adrian, Very Rev,
PE, CC
26 Beech Grove, Kildare
Tel 045-521900
(Kildare, Kildare & L.)

Carey, John
Sacred Heart Residence,
Sybil Hill Road, Raheny,
Dublin 5
(Dublin, retired)

Carey, Michael, Very Rev, PP
Parochial House,
Blanchardstown, Dublin 15
Tel 01-8213660
Adm, Porterstown-
Clonsilla
(Blanchardstown,
Porterstown-Clonsilla,
Dublin)

Carey, Patrick
Chaplain,
St Luke's Hospital,
Kilkenny
Tel 056-7785000
(Ossory)

Carey, William, Very Rev, PE
Clonmel, Co Tipperary
(Waterford & L., retired)

Carley, Martin, Very Rev, PP
Parochial House,
Collinstown,
Co Westmeath
Tel 044-9666326
(Collinstown, Meath)

Carlin, Peter
St Matthew's Presbytery,
Bryson Street,
Newtownards Road,
Belfast BT5 4E5
Tel 028-90457626
(St Matthew's, Down & C.)

Carmody, Brendan (SJ), Very
Rev, PP
Moyvane, Listowel,
Co Kerry
Tel 068-49308
(Moyvane, Kerry)

Carney, Denis, Very Rev, PP
Balla, Co Mayo F23 ED65
Tel 094-9365025
Administration Mayo
Abbey (Mayo and Rosslea)
(Balla and Manulla,
Mayo Abbey (Mayo and
Rosslea), Tuam)

Carney, Michael, Very Rev,
PP
Ramelton, Co Donegal
Tel 074-9151304
(Ramelton, Raphoe)

Carolan, Loughlain, Very
Rev, PP
Blacklion, Co Cavan
Tel 071-9853012
(Killinagh and Glangevlin
Kilmore)

Carolan, Patrick (OMI)
12 Tyreconnell Road,
Inchicore, Dublin 8
Tel 01-4541117

Carpenter, Matt (MHM)
St Joseph's House,
50 Orwell Park,
Rathgar, Dublin D06 C53!
Tel 01-4127700

Carr, Brendan (CSSp)
Holy Spirit Provincialate,
Temple Park, Richmond
Avenue South,
Dublin 6 D06 AW02
Tel 01-4975127/01-
4977230

Carr, Daniel, Rt Rev Mgr, P▶
St Johnston, Lifford,
Co Donegal
Tel 074-9148203
(St Johnston
(Taughboyne), Raphoe)

Carragher, Michael (OP)
Convent of SS Xystus and
Clement,
Collegio San Clemente,
Via Labicana 95,
00184 Roma
Tel 039-06-7740021

Carrigy, Colman
Clonee, Killoe,
Co Longford
(Ardagh & Cl.)

Carroll, Aidan
9 Hillcrest Manor,
Templeogue, Dublin 6W
(Dublin, retired)

Carroll, Daniel (SDB), Very
Rev
Vice-Rector,
Salesian House,
45 St Teresa's Road,
Crumlin, Dublin 12
Tel 01-4555605

Carroll, Daniel, Very Rev
St John's Presbytery,
Kilkenny
Tel 056-7721072/
087-9077769
(St John's, Ossory)

Carroll, David, Very Rev, Cc
PP
St Joseph's Presbytery,
52 Kincora Park, Lifford,
Ennis, Co Clare
Tel 065-6822166/086-
3467909
(Abbey Pastoral Area,
Killaloe)

arroll, Declan, Very Rev, PP
Cong, Co Mayo
Tel 094-9546030
(Cong, Cross and The
Neale, Tuam)
arroll, Denis
Marymount Care Centre,
Westmanstown,
Lucan, Co Dublin
(Dublin, retired)
arroll, Dom Elijah (OSB),
Prior
Silverstream Priory,
Stamullen,
Co Meath K32 T189
Tel 01-8417142
arroll, Gregory (OP), Very
Rev
Superior, Holy Cross,
Tralee, Co Kerry
Tel 066-7121135
arroll, John (SPS)
Cregg House,
Rosses Point, Sligo
(Elphin, retired)
arroll, James, Rt Rev Mgr,
PP, EV
Parochial House,
Big Strand Road,
Clogherhead,
Drogheda, Co Louth
(Togher, Armagh)
arroll, Jeremiah (Jerry), CF
Finner Camp,
Ballyshannon,
Co Donegal F94 C985
Tel 071-9842294
(Clogher)
arroll, John, PP
Barntown, Co Wexford
Tel 053-9120853
Diocesan Secretary and
Chancellery,
PO Box 40, Bishop's House,
Summerhill, Wexford
Tel 053-9122177
(Glynn, Ferns)
arroll, John P. (SPS)
St Patrick's, Kiltegan,
Co Wicklow
Tel 059-6473600
arroll, Patrick (CSSp)
Holy Spirit Missionary
College,
Whitehall Road, Dublin
D12 P5YP
Tel 01-4064300
arroll, Thomas, Moderator
Turrett Street
Ballingarry, Co Clare
Tel 087-2036229
(Pastoral Unit 10, Limerick)
arroll, Timothy (SMA) Most
Rev
(Retired Bishop)
African Missions,
Blackrock Road,
Cork T12 TD54
Tel 021-4292871

Carvill, Aidan (SM)
Australia
Carvill, Andrew, CC
Mallow, Co Cork
Tel 022-51606
(Mallow, Cloyne)
Carvill, Gregory, Very Rev,
PP
Parochial House,
194 Newton Hamilton
Road, Ballymacnab,
Armagh, BT60 2QS
Tel 028-37531641
(Killcluney, Armagh)
Casey, Anthony, Co-PP, VF
Cooraclare, Co Clare
Tel 065-9059008/
087-9936950
(Inis Cathaigh Pastoral
Area, Killaloe)
Casey, Aquin, Very Rev, CC
Cobh, Co Cork
Tel 021-4908657
(Cobh, St Colman's
Cathedral, Cloyne)
Casey, Cornelius J. (CSsR)
97 Kylemore Road,
Ballyfermot, Dublin 10
Tel 01-6264691/5356977
Casey, Damian (OFM)
Chaplain,
Mater Misericordiae
University Hospital,
Eccles Street, Dublin 7
Tel 01-8301122
St Camillus, Adam & Eve's
4 Merchants' Quay
Dublin D08 XY19
Tel 01-6771128
Casey, David, Moderator
Parochial House,
The Square,
Dromcollogher,
Co Limerick
Tel 087-2272791
(Pastoral Unit 16, Limerick)
Casey, Eoin (OP)
St Mary's, Pope's Quay,
Cork
Tel 021-4502267
Casey, John (SAC)
Pallottine College,
Thurles, Co Tipperary
Tel 0504-21202
Casey, Kevin (SJ)
Clongowes Wood College,
Clane,
Co Kildare W91 DN40
Tel 045-868663/868202
Casey, Martin, Very Rev, PP
Woolgreen, Carnew,
Co Wicklow
Tel 053-9426888
(Carnew, Ferns)

Casey, Michael (CSSp)
Holy Spirit Missionary
College
Kimmage Manor,
Whitehall Road,
Dublin D12 P5YP
Tel 01-4064300
Casey, Michael, Co-PP, VF
Cross, Kilrush, Co Clare
Tel 065-9058008/
086-0842216
(Cois Fharraige Pastoral
Area, Killaloe)
Casey, Michael (SDB), Very
Rev, Adm
Rector, Rinaldi House,
40/41 Sean McDermott
Street,
Dublin D01 H7P6
Casey, Paul, PP
Drumahaire, Co Leitrim
Co Cavan
Tel 071-9164143
(Drumahaire and
Killargue, Kilmore)
Casey, Peter, Very Rev, CC
Ballinagh, Co Cavan
Tel 049-4337232
(Kilmore, Kilmore)
Casey, Seamus
11 Auburn Heights,
Athlone, Co Westmeath
Tel 090-6478318
(Ardagh & Cl.)
Casey, Sean, PP
Ennybegs, Longford
Tel 043-3323119
(Killoe, Ardagh & Cl.)
Casey, Thomas (SJ)
Rector, Milltown Park,
Miltown Road, Dublin 6
Tel 01-2698411/2698113
Cashman, Daniel (SMA)
SMA House, Wilton,
Cork, T12 KR23
Tel 021-4541069/4541884
Cashman, Denis, Very Rev
Ballincollig, Co Cork
(Cork & R., retired)
Cassidy, Gerard, Very Rev,
PP
Ballyhaise, Co Cavan
Tel 049-4338121
(Castletara, Kilmore)
Cassidy, Gerry, Very Rev
(CSsR)
Clonard Monastery,
1 Clonard Gardens,
Belfast BT13 2RL
Tel 028-90445950
Cassidy, Seamus, Very Rev
Tavis, Kilmainham Wood,
Kells, Co Meath
(Dublin, retired)
Cassin, Liam, Very Rev, PP
Hugginstown, Co Kilkenny
Tel 087-2312354/
056-7768693
(Aghaviller, Ossory)

Cassin, Seán (OFM)
Franciscan Abbey,
Multyfarnham,
Co Westmeath N91 X279
Tel 044-9371114/9371137
Castelli, Nemo S. (SJ)
35 Lower Leeson Street,
Dublin 2
Tel 01-6761248
Caulfield, William, CC
St Aidan's, Enniscorthy,
Co Wexford
Tel 053-9235777
(Enniscorthy, Cathedral of
St Aidan, Ferns)
Cavanagh, Daniel, Rt Rev
Mgr, PP
Rosbercon, New Ross,
Co Wexford
Tel 051-421515/
087-2335432
(Rosbercon, Ossory)
Cavanagh, Tony
Belmullet, Co Mayo
Tel 097-81426
CC, Kilmore-Erris
Binghamstown,
Ballina, Co Mayo
Tel 097-82350
(Belmullet, Kilmore-Erris,
Killala)
Cawley, Farrell, Very Rev, PE
Ballinacarrow,
Co Sligo
Tel 086-0864347
(Achonry, retired)
Cawley, Michael, Very Rev
River View Nursing Home,
Ballina, Co Mayo
(Killala, retired)
Chamakalayil, Jayan Joseph
(MI)
Chaplain,
St James's Hospital
St Camillus,
South Hill Avenue,
Blackrock, Co Dublin
Chamberlain, Gary (CSC)
c/o Parish Office,
Our Lady, Seat of Wisdom,
St Stephen's Green,
Dublin 2
(University Church, Dublin)
Chambers, Martin, PP
2 Chaplain's House,
Knocknamona,
Letterkenny, Co Donegal
Tel 074-9125090
(Letterkenny, Raphoe)
Champion, Augustine (OP)
Holy Cross, Sligo
Co Sligo
Tel 071-9142700
Charles, Nigel, Adm
Parochial House, Mohill,
Co Leitrim
Tel 071-9631024
(Mohill (Mohill-
Manachain), Ardagh & Cl.)

Charlet, Benoît M. (OSB)
Benedictine Monks,
Holy Cross Abbey,
119 Kilbroney Road,
Rostrevor,
Co Down BT34 3BN
Tel 028-41739979

Chen, Yanbo (SVD), CC
The Presbytery,
Old Dublin Road, Carlow,
Tel 059-9131227
(*Cathedral, Carlow*,
Kildare & L.)

Chester, John, PP
4a Monaghan Road,
Roslea. Co Fermanagh,
Tel 028-67751227
(*Roslea*, Clogher)

Chestnutt, Gerard, Very Rev,
PP
Sacred Heart Presbytery,
The Folly, Waterford
Tel 051-878429
(*Sacred Heart*, Waterford
& L.)

Chimalenji, Michel, PC
Presbytery 2, 6 Old Hill,
Leixlip, Co Kildare
Tel 01-6243673
(*Leixlip*, Dublin)

Chisanga, Emmanuel
Malekani
35 Lower Leeson Street,
Dublin 2
Tel 01-6761248

Chukwunenye, Alphonsus
(MSP)
Cathedral Presbytery,
38 Hill Street,
Newry BT34 1AT
Tel 028-30262586
(*Newry Pastoral Area*,
Dromore)

Chullickal, Rexon, Co-PP
The Presbytery,
Church Road,
Nenagh, Co Tipperary
Tel 067-37130
(*Odhran Pastoral Area*,
Killaloe)

Churchill, Paul, Very Rev, PP
St Joseph's, Berkeley Road,
Dublin 7
Tel 01-8306336
(*Berkeley Road*, Dublin)

Chute, John (SSC), Very Rev
St Columban's Retirement
Home, Dalgan Park,
Navan, Co Meath
Tel 046-9021525

Cino, Raul, CC
Curate's Residence,
Roscommon
Tel 090-6626189
(*Roscommon*, Elphin)

Cirhakarhula, Jean Paul
(White Fathers)
Promotion Director,
Cypress Grove,
Templeogue, Dublin 6W
Tel 01-4055263

Claffey, Pat (SVD), CC
The Presbytery,
Haddington Road,
Dublin 4
Tel 085-7123675
(*Haddington Road*,
Dublin)

Clancy, Anthony (OMI), Very
Rev, Co-PP
Oblate Fathers House of
Retreat,
Inchicore, Dublin 8
Tel 01-4541117
(*Bluebell*, Dublin)

Clancy, Peter, CC
75 Newtown Park, Leixlip,
Co Kildare
Tel 01-6243533
(*Confey*, Dublin)

Clancy, Tom, Very Rev, AP
Woodlawn,
Model Farm Road,
Ballineaspaig, Cork
(Cork & R., retired)

Clarke, Christopher (OCD)
The Abbey, Loughrea,
Co Galway
Tel 091-841209

Clarke, Ciaran, CC
Parochial House,
Ashbourne, Co Meath
Tel 01-8353149
(*Ashbourne-Donaghmore*,
Meath)

Clarke, Eamonn, CC
The Presbytery,
Beechwood Park,
Kilcoole, Co Wicklow
Tel 01-2876207
(*Kilquade*, Dublin)

Clarke, Gerard (SJ)
Belfast Jesuit Centre,
193-195 Donegall Street,
Belfast

Clarke, Joseph, Very Rev,
Foxhall, Gurlymadden,
Loughrea, Co Galway
(Clonfert, retired)

Clarke, Peter, Very Rev
Parochial House,
11 Moy Road, Portadown,
Co Armagh BT62 1QL
Tel 028-38332218
(*Portadown (Drumcree)*,
Armagh)

Clarkson, Eugene (MSC)
Woodview House,
Mount Merrion Avenue,
Blackrock, Co Dublin
Tel 01-2881644

Clavin, Joseph, Very Rev, AP
St Martin's,
Culmullen, Drumree,
Co Meath
Tel 01-8241976
(*Dunshaughlin*, Meath)

Clayton-Lea, Paul, Very Rev,
PE
Woodside, Strand Road,
Termonfeckin,
Drogheda,
Co Louth A92 W7W6
Tel 041-9822631
(Armagh, retired)

Cleary, Edward, Very Rev,
PP
Knockainey, Hospital,
Co Limerick,
Tel 061-584873
(*Knockainey*, Cashel & E.)

Cleary, Lorenzo, Very Rev
The Stables, Hayestown,
Wexford
Tel 053-9144346
(Ferns)

Cleary, Matthew L., Very
Rev
The Stables, Bridgetown,
Co Wexford
(Ferns, retired)

Clerkin, Colum, PEm
23 Thornhill Park,
Culmore, Derry BT48 4PB
Tel 028-71358519
(Derry, retired)

Clesham, James (SMA), CC
St John the Apostle,
Knocknacarra, Galway
Tel 091-590059
(*St John the Apostle*,
Galway)

Clifford, Brendan (OP)
St Mary's, Pope's Quay,
Cork
Tel 021-4502267

Clifford, Dermot, Most Rev,
PhD, DD
Archbishop Emeritus of
Cashel and Emly,
The Green, Holycross,
Thurles, Co Tipperary
(Cashel & E.)

Clifford, Diarmuid (OP)
St Saviour's,
Upper Dorset Street,
Dublin 1
Tel 01-8897610

Clifford, Hugh, Very Rev PP
Parochial House,
Kinvara, Co Galway
Tel 091 637154
(*Ballinderreen*, Galway)

Clinton, Colm (SPS), Adm
New Quay, Co Clare
Tel 065-7078026
(*Carron and New Quay*,
Galway)

Clowe, Thomas (SDB), TA
45 St Teresa's Road,
Crumlin, Dublin 12
Tel 01-4555383
(*Crumlin*, Dublin)

Clucas, Peter (OMI)
Oblate House of Retreat,
Inchicore, Dublin 8
Tel 01-4534408/4541805

Clyne, S. James, Very Rev
Canon, PE, AP
Parochial House,
24 Chapel Road, Killeavy,
Newry, Co Down BT35 8J
Tel 028-30848222
(*Cloghogue (Killeavy
Upper)*, Armagh)

Coady, Michael, Very Rev,
PP
St Mary's Presbytery,
Willbrook Road,
Rathfarnham, Dublin 14
Tel 01-4932390/
087-2401441
(*Rathfarnham*, Dublin)

Coakley, Donal, Very Rev,
PE
Buttevant, Co Cork
(Cloyne, retired)

Coen, John (SAC)
Pallottine College,
Thurles, Co Tipperary
086-3103934

Coen, Michael (SAC)
Pallottine College, Thurle
Co Tipperary
Tel 0504-21202

Coffey, Brendan (OSB)
Glenstal Abbey, Murroe,
Co Limerick
Tel 061-621000

Coffey, Patrick, Rev, PP
Golden, Co Tipperary
Tel 062-72146
(*Golden*, Cashel & E.)

Coffey, Robert
35 Orchard Avenue,
Rathkeale, Co Limerick
Tel 087-6540908
(*Pastoral Unit 10*, Limeric

Coffey, Thomas, Very Rev
Parochial House,
Corcaghan,
Monaghan H18 H673
Tel 042-9744806
(*Corcaghan (Kilmore and
Drumsnatt)*, Clogher)

Coffey, Tom (IC)
Doire na hAbhann,
Tickincor, Clonmel,
Co Tipperary
Tel 052-6126914

Cogan, John, Very Rev, PE
Killeen, Vicarstown,
Tel 021-4385535
(Cloyne, retired)

Allianz ⑪

ogan, Patrick (OFM)
15 Orchard Drive,
Ursuline Court, Waterford
Tel 087-2360239
Respond! Office
Tel 051-876865

ogavin, Brendan (CSSp)
Holy Spirit Missionary
College
Kimmage Manor,
Whitehall Road,
Dublin D12 P5YP
Tel 01-4064300

oghlan, David (SJ)
Vice-Superior,
Dominic Collins' House
Residence,
129 Morehampton Road,
Dublin 4 D04 NX39
Tel 01-2693075

oghlan, Kieran, Very Rev,
Moderator, VF
St Cecilia's, New Road,
Clondalkin, Dublin 22
Tel 01-4592665
(Bawnogue, Clondalkin,
Deansrath, Neilstown,
Rowlagh and Quarryvale,
Dublin)

oghlan, Niall (OSA)
Sub-Prior, St John's Priory,
Thomas Street, Dublin 8
Tel 01-6770393/0415/0601

ogley, James, Very Rev, PP
Our Lady's Island,
Broadway,
Co Wexford
Tel 053-9131167
(Our Lady's Island and
Tacumshane, Ferns)

ojoc, Robert (OFMConv)
The Friary,
St Francis' Street,
Wexford
Tel 053-9122758

olclough, Robert, Very Rev,
Adm
Parochial House,
49 Seville Place, Dublin 1
Tel 01-2865457
(North Wall-Seville Place,
Dublin)

oleman, Christopher (MSC)
Western Road,
Cork T12 TN80
Tel 021-4804120

oleman, Gerard, Very Rev,
PP
Castlelyons, Co Cork
Tel 025-36372
(Castlelyons, Cloyne)

oleman, Gerard, Very Rev,
PP
Dromahane, Mallow,
Co Cork
Tel 087-9580420
(Glantane, Cloyne)

Coleman, William, Very Rev,
PP
Parochial House,
Rochfortbridge,
Co Westmeath
Tel 044-9222107
(Rochfortbridge, Meath)

Colgan, John (SSC),
St Columban's, Dalgan
Park, Navan, Co Meath
Tel 046-9021525

Colgan, Maurice (OP), Very
Rev
St Mary's, Pope's Quay,
Cork
Tel 021-4502267

Colgan, Pat (SSC)
No 3 and 4,
Ma Yau Tong Village,
Po Lam Road,
Tseung Kwan O,
Kow Loon, Hong Kong,
SAR

Colhoun, Roland, CC
41 Moyle Road,
Newtownstewart,
Co Tyrone BT78 4AP
Tel 028-81661445
(Gortin (Badoney Lower),
Greencastle,
Newtownstewart and
Plumbridge, Derry)

Coll, Francis, CC
Parochial House,
Hanover Square,
Coagh, Cookstown,
Co Tyrone BT80 0EF
Tel 028-86737212
(Coagh, Armagh)

Coll, Niall, Most Rev, DD
Bishop of Ossory,
Blessed Felix House,
Tilbury Place,
Kilkenny R95 DXC9
Tel 056-7762448
(Ossory)

Colleluori, Stefano, CC
Parochial House,
Ardee Street, Collon,
Co Louth A92 F2P7
(Ardee and Collon,
Armagh)

Collender, Michael (OSA)
Good Counsel College,
New Ross, Co Wexford
Tel 051-421182

Collery, Seamus
St Attracta's Community
School,
Tubbercurry, Co Sligo
Tel 071-9120184
(Achonry)

Collier, Warren
Parochial House,
Trim, Co Meath
Tel 046-9431251
(Trim, Meath)

Collier, Val (SDB)
Rinaldi House,
40/41 Sean McDermott
Street,
Dublin D01 H7P6

Collins, Brendan, CC
c/o Bishop's House,
St Eugene's Cathedral,
Francis Street,
Derry BT48 6AP
(Derry)

Collins, David (OFM)
The Abbey,
8 Francis Street,
Galway H91 C53K
Tel 091-562518

Collins, Denis (SMA)
African Missions,
Blackrock Road,
Cork T12 TD54
Tel 021-4292871

Collins, Gregory (OSB)
Dormition Abbey,
Mount Sion, PO Box 22,
IL-91000, Jerusalem, Israel

Collins, John, Very Rev, Co-
PP
18 Aspen Road,
Kinseely Court,
Swords, Co Dublin
Tel 01-4531143
(Swords, Dublin)

Collins, John, AP
Parochial House,
Ballinora, Waterfall,
near Cork
Tel 021-4872792
(Ballinora, Ballincollig and
Ovens, Cork & R.)

Collins, Laurence (OP), Very
Rev, Adm
The Presbytery,
St Dominic's,
St Dominic's Road,
Tallaght, Dublin 24
Tel 01-4510620
(Tallaght, Dodder, Dublin)

Collins, Michael
2 Traverslea Woods,
Glenageary Road Lower,
Dun Laoghaire, Co Dublin,
(Dublin, retired)

Collins, Michael, PEm
119 Irish Green Street,
Limavady,
Co Derry BT49 9AB
Tel 028-77765649
(Derry, retired)

Collins, Michael, Co-PP
Parochial House, 19
Goodwood Estate,
Newmarket-on-Fergus
Tel 061-700883
(Tradaree Pastoral Area,
Killaloe)

Collins, Neil (SSC)
St Columban's,
Dalgan Park,
Navan, Co Meath
Tel 046-9021525

Collins, Owen,
22 River Crescent,
Virginia, Co Cavan
(Kilmore, retired)

Collins, P. Gerard, Very Rev
The Presbytery,
Passage West,
Co Cork
(Cork & R., retired)

Collins, Patrick (CM)
St Joseph's,
44 Stillorgan Park,
Blackrock,
Co Dublin A94 PC62
Tel 01-2886961

Collins, Timothy (SSC)
Cork

Collins, Timothy, Very Rev,
PP
The Presbytery,
O'Rahilly Street
Clonakilty, Co Cork
Tel 023-8834441
(Ardfield/Rathbarry,
Barryroe, Clonakilty,
Kilmeen/Castleventry,
Rosscarbery and
Timoleague, Cork & R.)

Collum, Martin, Very Rev,
PP
Rathmullan, Co Donegal
Tel 074-9158156
(Rathmullan, Raphoe)

Coltsmann, Francis (SMA)
African Missions,
Blackrock Road,
Cork T12 TD54
Tel 021-4292871

Comer, Micheál, Very Rev,
Adm
The Presbytery,
Eadestown, Naas,
Co Kildare
Tel 045-862187
(Eadestown, Dublin)

Comerford, Brendan (SJ)
St Francis Xavier's,
Upper Gardiner Street,
Dublin 1
Tel 01-8363411

Comiskey, Brendan, Most
Rev, DD
Retired Bishop of Ferns,
PO Box 40, Summerhill,
Wexford
(Ferns, retired)

Comiskey, Gerard, Very Rev,
PP
Staghall, Belturbet,
Co Cavan
Tel 049-9522140
(Drumlane, Kilmore)

Commane, Michael (OP)
Chaplain,
St Luke's Hospital,
Highfield Road,
Rathgar, Dublin 6
Tel 01-4065000

Commins, Thomas, PP
Kilkerrin, Ballinasloe,
Co Galway H53 Y326
Tel 094-9659212
(*Kilkerrin and Clonberne,*
Tuam)

Conaghan, Michael, Very
Rev, PE
6 Fields Court,
Kilmacrennan, Co Donegal
Tel 074-91198711
(*Raphoe, retired*)

Conard, Isaac (OSB)
Silverstream Priory,
Stamullen,
Co Meath K32 T189
Tel 01-8417142

Conaty, Eamonn (SSC), Very
Rev, PP
4 Cuan Mhuire,
Fourmilehouse,
Roscommon
Tel 090-6629518
(*Kilbride (Fourmilehouse),*
Elphin)

Conaty, Peter (CSSp)
Community Leader,
Spiritan Missionaries,
Ardbraccan, Navan,
Co Meath C15 T884
Tel 046-9021441

Concannon, Eamonn, Very
Rev Canon, PE
Ballyhowley, Knock,
Co Mayo F12 C920
(*Tuam, retired*)

Concannon, John (CM)
St Peter's, Phibsboro,
Dublin 7
Tel 01-8389708/8389841

Condon, Eanna, Very Rev,
PE
St Mary's, Clonmel,
Co Tipperary
Tel 052-6127870
(*Waterford & L., retired*)

Condon, Gerard, Very Rev,
PP
Ballygriffin, Killavullen,
Co Cork
Tel 022-46578
(*Killavullen, Cloyne*)

Condon, Jeremiah, Very
Rev, PP
Stradbally, Kilmacthomas,
Co Waterford
Tel 051-293133
(*Stradbally, Waterford &*
L.)

Condon, Joseph, Very Rev,
PP
Apartment 2,
St John's College,
The Folly, Waterford
Tel 051-876843
(*Waterford & L., retired*)

Condon, Mark, CC
Danesfort, Co Kilkenny
Tel 086-6005402
(*Danesfort, Ossory*)

Condon, Patrick T., Very
Rev, PP
Knockanore, Tallow,
Co Waterford
Tel 024-97140
(*Knockanore, Waterford &*
L.)

Condon, Sean
Cathedral House,
Cathedral Place, Limerick
Tel 061-414624
(*Limerick, retired*)

Condren, Joseph (OFM)
Vicar Provincial,
Secretary of the Province,
4 Merchants' Quay
Dublin, D08 XY19
Tel 01-6771128

Condron, Barry, Very Rev,
PP
Tyrrellspass,
Co Westmeath
Tel 044-9223115
(*Castletown-Geoghegan,*
Meath)

Conlan, Anthony
Chaplain,
St Vincent's University
Hospital, Elm Park,
Dublin 4
Tel 01-2694533
(*Dublin*)

Conlan, Patrick (OFM)
Dún Mhuire,
Seafield Road,
Killliney, Co Dublin
Tel 01-2826760

Conlisk, Frank (SPS), Adm
Parochial House
Milltown, Co Galway
Tel 089-2064773
(*Kilconly and Kilbannon,*
Milltown (Addergole and
Liskeevey), Tuam)

Conlon, Alex, Very Rev, PP
213B Harold's Cross,
Dublin 6W
Tel 01-4972816
(*Harold's Cross, Dublin*)

Conlon, Brian, Rev Dr
Chaplain,
Sligo University Hospital
The Mall, Co Sligo
Tel 071-9171111
(*Elphin*)

Conlon, John, Very Rev, PP
St Mary's, Drogheda,
Co Louth
Tel 041-9834958
(*Drogheda, St Mary's,*
Meath)

Conlon, Malachy, Very Rev,
PP, VF, EV, Adm
Top Rath, Carlingford,
Co Louth A91 XW24
Tel 042-9376105
(*Cooley, Armagh*)

Conlon, Noel,
(priest in residence)
Inniskeen, Dundalk,
Co Louth
Tel 042-9378678
(*Inniskeen, Clogher*)

Conlon, Sean (OCD)
St Teresa's
Claredon Street, Dublin 2
Tel 01-6718466/6718127

Conlon, Seán, Very Rev, PE,
CC
Ballinakill, Co Laois
Tel 057-8733336
(*Ballinakill, Kildare & L.*)

Connaughton, Finian, Very
Rev, PP
Parochial House,
Drumconrath, Navan,
Co Meath
Tel 041-6854146
(*Drumconrath, Meath*)

Connaughton, P. Aloysius
(SSC)
Thailand

Connaughton, Patrick
St Columban's,
Dalgan Park,
Navan, Co Meath
Tel 046-9021525
(*Galway, retired*)

Connaughton, Sean (SSC)
St Columban's,
Dalgan Park, Navan,
Co Meath
Tel 046-9021525

Connaughton, Vincent, PP
Ardagh, Co Longford
Tel 043-6675006
(*Ardagh and Moydow,*
Ardagh & Cl.)

Connell, Michael (SDB)
Vice-Rector,
St Catherine's Centre,
North Campus, Maynooth

Connell, Paul, Very Rev,
PhD, Adm
Parochial House,
Rathganny,
Multyfarnham,
Co Westmeath N91 E186
Tel 044-9371124
Chancellor, Meath
Diocesan Office,
Dublin Road, Mullingar,
Co Westmeath
Tel 044-9348841
(*Multyfarnharm, Meath*)

Connell, Seamus, Very Rev,
Adm
56 Foxfield St John,
Kilbarrack, Dublin 5
(*Dublin, retired*)

Connell, Seamus (SSC)
Padres de San Columbano,
Apartado 073/074,
Lima 39, Peru

Connelly, Christopher (OFM
Franciscan Friary,
Killarney, Co Kerry
Tel 064-6631334/6631066

Connick, Joseph (OFMConv
Friary of the Visitation,
Fairview Strand, Dublin 3
Tel 01-8376000

Connolly, Charles, (Opus
Dei)
Gort Ard University
Residence
Rockbarton North, Galwa
Tel 091-523846

Connolly, Darragh
Killinkere, Virginia,
Co Cavan
Tel 049-8547307
(*Killinkere, Kilmore*)

Connolly, David (OFM)
4 Merchants' Quay
Dublin D08 XY19
Tel 01-6711228

Connolly, Dermot (SPS)
St Patrick's,
21 Leeson Park,
Dublin 6 D06 DE76
Tel 01-4977897

Connolly, Hugh, Rt Rev Mg
PP
15 Chapel Hill,
Mayobridge, Newry,
Co Down BT34 2EX
Tel 028-30850089
(*Clonallon, St Patrick's*
(Mayobridge), Dromore)

Connolly, John, Very Rev
c/o Ara Coeli,
Armagh BT61 7QY
(*Armagh*)

Connolly, Joseph, Very Rev,
PP
Parochial House,
Ballymore Eustace, Naas
Co Kildare
Tel 045-864114
(*Ballymore Eustace,*
Dublin)

Connolly, Kevin, CC
St Joseph's,
Carrickmacross,
Co Monaghan A81 WP68
Tel 083-0025311/042-
9661231
(*Carrickmacross (Machaire*
Rois), Clogher)

Connolly, Michael, Very Rev
PP
Oughterard, Co Galway
Tel 091-456527
(*Oughterard, Galway*)

Connolly, Noel (SPS)
St Patrick's, Kiltegan,
Co Wicklow W91 Y022
Tel 059-6473600

onnolly, Patrick, Dr
Theology Department,
Mary Immaculate College,
South Circular Road,
Limerick V94 VN26
Tel 061-204575
(Clogher)

onnolly, Patrick (SMA)
African Missions,
Blackrock Road,
Cork T12 TD54
Tel 021-4292871

onnolly, Philip, Very Rev
Canon, PE
Doohamlet, Castleblayney,
Co Monaghan A75 PX09
Tel 042-9741239
(Clontibret, Clogher)

onnolly, Ronan (OP)
Convent of Ss Xystus and
Clement,
Collegio San Clemente
Via Labicana 95,
00184 Roma, Italy
Tel 0039-067740021

onnolly, Sean, Rt Rev Mgr
7 Tullyview, Loughguile,
Co Antrim BT44 9JY
(Down & C., retired)

onnolly, Terence, Very Rev,
PE
178 Newtownsaville Road,
Omagh,
Co Tyrone BT78 2RJ
Tel 028-82841306
(Eskra, Clogher)

onnolly, Vincent, Rt Rev
Mgr, PE
Magherarney,
Smithborough,
Co Monaghan H18 H297
Tel 047-57011
(Roslea, Clogher)

onnors, Tom Rev (MHM)
St Joseph's House,
50 Orwell Park,
Rathgar,
Dublin D06 C535
Tel 01-4127700

onroy, Charles (MSC)
Western Road,
Cork T12 TN80
Tel 021-4804120

onroy, Christopher
(OCarm)
Whitefriar Street Church,
56 Aungier Street,
Dublin D02 R598
Tel 01-4758821

onroy, Michael (SPS)
St Patrick's, Kiltegan,
Co Wicklow
Tel 059-6473600

onroy, Patrick, Very Rev,
PP
Ballinakill, Loughrea,
Co Galway H62 AW68
Tel 090-9745021
(Ballinakill and Derrybrien,
Clonfert)

Conry, Anthony
Brazil
(Elphin)

Considine, Patrick, Very Rev
Dean, PE
2 St Mary's Apartments,
Shantalla Road, Galway
(Galway, retired)

Convey, Martin, Very Rev,
BSc, MLitt, PhD, PP
Collooney, Co Mayo
Tel 094-9167235
(Collooney (Kilvarnet),
Achonry)

Conway, Alan, Very Rev, PP
Parochial House, Drumlion
Carrick-on-Shannon,
Co Roscommon
Tel 071-9620415
(Croghan, Elphin)

Conway, Brian (SPS)
18 Cartron Court,
Catron, Sligo
(Elphin, retired)

Conway, Bernard (SPS)
On temporary diocesan
work

Conway, David (CSSp)
Provincial Bursar,
Holy Spirit Missionary
College
Kimmage Manor,
Whitehall Road,
Dublin D12 P5YP
Tel 01-4064300

Conway, Éamon
University of Notre Dame,
Australia
(Limerick)

Conway, Edward, Very Rev,
PC
1 Maretimo Gardens West,
Blackrock, Co Dublin
Tel 01-2882248
(Blackrock, Dublin)

Conway, Kevin (SMA)
Church of Our Lady of the
Rosary and St Patrick,
61 Blackhorse Road,
Walthamstow,
London E17 7AS, UK

Conway, Michael
St Patrick's College,
Maynooth, Co Kildare
Tel 01-6285222
(Galway)

Conway, Michael, Very Rev
Barr Trá, Enniscrone,
Co Sligo
(Killala, retired)

Conway, Noel, Very Rev
(priest in residence)
23 Rathkeltair Road,
Downpatrick,
Co Down BT30 6NL
Tel 024-4461477
(Downpatrick, Down & C.)

Conway, Paddy,
(Killaloe, retired)

Conway, Patrick (SSC)
c/o Bishop's Residence,
Westbourne,
Ennis, Co Clare
Tel 065-6828638

Cooke, Colm (SPS)
St Patrick's, Kiltegan,
Co Wicklow W91 Y022
Tel 059-6473600

Cooke, Michael, Rt Rev Mgr
15 Meadow Park,
Dublin Road, Cavan,
Co Cavan
(Kilmore, retired)

Coonan, Thomas, Rt Rev
Mgr, PE, CC
Geashill, Co Offaly
Tel 057-9343517
(Killeigh, Kildare & L.)

Cooney, Brendan (SPS)
St Patrick's,
21 Leeson Park,
Dublin 6 D06 DE76
Tel 01-4977897

Cooney, John, Very Rev, PP
Parochial House,
Station Road,
Cootehill, Co Cavan
Tel 049-5552120
(Cootehill (Drumgoon),
Kilmore)

Cooney, Matthew (OSA)
The Presbytery,
Dungarvan, Co Waterford
(Dungarvan, Waterford &
L.)

Cooney, Michael, CC
Presbytery 1,
Thormanby Road, Howth,
Co Dublin
Tel 01-8323193
(Howth, Dublin)

Cooney, Michael, Very Rev,
Co-PP
Parochial House,
Terryglass,
Nenagh, Co Tipperary
Tel 067-22017/087-
6548331
(Cois Deirge Pastoral Area,
Killaloe)

Coote, Tony (SVD)
Donamon Castle,
Roscommon
Tel 090-6662222

Corbett, John (CSsR)
St Joseph's,
St Alphonsus Road,
Dundalk,
Co Louth A71 F3FC
Tel 042-9334042/9334762

Corbett, Padraig
Castleiney, Co Tipperary
(Cashel & E., retired)

Corbett, Thomas, Very Rev
Dr, AP
Convent Hill, Roscrea,
Co Tipperary
Tel 0505-21108/086-
8418570
(Cronan Pastoral Area,
Killaloe)

Corcoran, Gerard, Very Rev,
Moderator,
12 Grangemore Grove
Donaghmede,
Dublin D13 A264
Tel 01-8474652
(Ayrfield, Donaghmede-
Clongriffin-Balgriffin,
Dublin)

Corcoran, Gregory, Very
Rev, PP
Rhode, Co Offaly
Tel 087-9402669/
046-9737010
(Clonbullogue, Rhode,
Kildare & L.)

Corcoran, James, Very Rev,
PP
Cooneal, Ballina, Co Mayo
Tel 096-32242
(Ballysokeary, Killala)

Corcoran, Michael (MHM)
Superior General,
1 Colby Gardens,
Cookham Road,
Maidenhead SL6 7GZ,
England
Tel 0044-1628-789752

Corcorcan, Patrick (SM)
Chanel Community,
Coolock, Dublin 5
Tel 01-8477133

Corcoran, Patrick (SPS)
St Patrick's, Kiltegan,
Co Wicklow
Tel 059-6473600

Corcoran, Thomas, Very Rev
Clogh, Castlecomer,
Co Kilkenny
(Ossory)

Corish, Declan (OP), PP
Holy Cross,
Tralee, Co Kerry
Tel 066-7121135

Corkery, Eamonn, PE
Aughnacliffe,
Co Longford N39 T2P1
(Ardagh & Cl., retired)

Corkery, James (SJ)
c/o Irish Jesuit
Provincialate,
Milltown Park,
Miltown Road, Dublin 6
Tel 01-4987333

Corkery, Michael, Very Rev,
PP
Glanworth, Co Cork
Tel 025-38123
(Glanworth, Cloyne)

Corkery, Pádraig, Dr
St Patrick's College,
Maynooth, Co Kildare
Tel 01-7083639
(Cork & R.)

Corkery, Patrick, CC
Parochial House,
The Square,
Kilworth, Co Cork
Tel 087-9601558
(Fermoy, Cloyne)

Corkery, Seán
Director of Formation
St Patrick's College,
Maynooth, Co Kildare
Tel 086-2420240
(Mallow, Cloyne)

Cormac, Pierce
Chaplain,
Mercy University Hospital,
Grenville Place,
Cork
Tel 021-4271971
(Cork & R.)

Corrigan, Brendan, Very
Rev, PP
Parochial House,
Harbour Road,
Kilbeggan,
Co Westmeath
Tel 057-9332155
(Kilbeggan, Meath)

Corrigan, David (SM), PP
St Teresa's,
Donore Avenue, Dublin 8
Tel 01-4542425/4531613

Corrigan, Desmond
17 Chapel Street,
Poyntzpass, Newry
Co Down BT35 6SY
Tel 028-38318217
(Armagh, retired)

Corrigan, Desmond (SMA)
African Missions,
Dromantine, Newry,
Co Down BT34 1RH
Tel 028-30821224

Corrigan, Peter, Very Rev,
PE
Shanco, Newbliss,
Co Monaghan H18 K303
Tel 047-54011
(Killeevan, Clogher)

Corry, Edward
Presbytery 2,
Treepark Road,
Kilnamanagh, Dublin 24
(Dublin, retired)

Corry, Francis (SM), PC
The Presbytery,
Coolock Village, Dublin 5
Tel 01-8477133
(Coolock, Dublin)

Cosgrave, William, Very Rev,
PP
Monageer, Ferns,
Enniscorthy, Co Wexford
Tel 053-9233530
(Monageer, Ferns)

Cosgrove, John, Very Rev
Canon, PE
Claremorris, Co Mayo
(Tuam, retired)

Cosgrove, Martin, Very Rev
Canon, Moderator, VF
St Mary's Presbytery,
Willbrook,
Rathfarnham, Dublin 14
Tel 01-4954554
(Churchtown,
Rathfarnham, Dublin)

Costello, Aidan, CC
The Presbytery, Loughrea,
Co Galway H62 YE09
Tel 091-841212
(Loughrea, St Brendan's
Cathedral, Clonfert)

Costello, Ambrose (OCarm)
Carmelite Community,
Gort Muire, Ballinteer,
Dublin D16 EI67
Tel 01-2984014

Costello, Bernard
13 Garbally Oaks,
Ballinasloe,
Co Galway H53 KW27
Tel 087-2396208
(Lawrencetown and
Kiltormer, Clonfert)

Costello, David
c/o The Missionary Society
of St James the Apostle,
24 Clark Street, Boston,
MA 02109, USA
(Limerick)

Costello, James, Very Rev
Canon
Bruff, Kilmallock,
Co Limerick
Tel 061-382555
(Limerick, retired)

Costello, Martin (SMA)
SMA House, Cloonbigeen,
Claregalway,
Co Galway H91 YK64
Tel 091-798880

Costello, Maurice
Main Street, Rathkeale,
Co Limerick
Tel 069-63452
(Limerick, retired)

Costello, Padraig, Very Rev,
PP, VF
Chaplain, St Joseph's
Secondary School,
Foxford, Co Mayo
Tel 094-9860010
Parish: Foxford, Co Mayo
Tel 094-9256131
(Foxford, Achonry)

Costello, Shane, CC
Castlebar, Co Mayo
Tel 094-9021844
(Castlebar, Tuam)

Costelloe, Patrick,
Mount Sarto, Lower Park,
Corbally, Limerick
Tel 061-342276/
086-2444528
(Limerick, retired)

Costigan, Jim, Mgr, CC
Richmond Road
Templemore, Co Tipperary
Tel 0504 35772
(Templemore, Cashel & E.)

Cotter, Bernard (SMA)
African Missions,
Blackrock Road,
Cork T12 TD54
Tel 021-4292871

Cotter, Bernard, Very Rev,
Co-PP
Parish House, Union Hall,
Skibbereen,
Co Cork P81 C433
Tel 028-34940
(Aughadown, Castlehaven,
Kilmacabea,
Rath and the Islands and
Skibbereen, Cork & R.)

Cotter, Donal, Very Rev,
Adm
Ballineaspaig, Co Cork
Tel 021-4346818
(Ballineaspaig, Cork & R.)

Cotter, Francis (OFM)
Franciscan House of
Studies, Dún Mhuire,
Seafield Road,
Killiney, Co Dublin
Tel 01-2826760

Cotter, Seán, Very Rev
Canon, PE
Love Lane,
Charleville, Co Cork
(Cloyne, retired)

Coughlan, David Rev (SJ)
35 Lower Leeson Street,
Dublin 2
Tel 01-6761248

Coughlan, Patrick (CSSp)
The Presbytery,
Bawnogue, Clondalkin,
Dublin 22
Tel 01-4519810

Coughlan, Thomas, PC
Our Lady's Manor,
Bulloch Castle,
Dalkey, Co Dublin
(Dublin, retired)

Coughlan, Thomas, Very Rev
Effin, Limerick
Tel 0872229223
(Limerick, retired)

Coveney, Patrick, Most Rev,
AP
Crosshaven, Co Cork
Tel 021-4831218
(Crosshaven, Cork & R.)

Cox, Tom, Adm
Shannonbridge,
Athlone, Co Offaly
Tel 090-9674125
(Shannonbridge
(Clonmacnois), Ardagh &
Cl.)

Coyle, Mark (OFMCap)
Ard Mhuire, Creeslough,
Letterkenny,
Co Donegal F92 Y23R
Tel 074-9138005

Coyle, Patrick
c/o Ara Coeli,
Armagh BT61 7QY
(Armagh)

Coyle, Paul, Co-PP
159 Botanic Road,
Glasnevin, Dublin 9
Tel 01-83773455
Acting Chancellor,
The Chancellery,
Archbishop's House,
Dublin 9
Tel 01-8379253
(Glasnevin, Dublin)

Coyle, Peter (SPS)
St Patrick's,
21 Leeson Park,
Dublin D06 DE76
Tel 01-4977897

Coyle, Rory
c/o Ara Coeli,
Armagh, BT61 7QY
Tel 028-37522045
(Armagh, Armagh)

Coyle, Séan (SSC)
St Columban's,
Dalgan Park, Navan Road
Co Meath
Tel 046-9021525

Coyle, Thomas, Very Rev, PP
Galmoy, Crosspatrick,
via Thurles, Co Kilkenny
Tel 056-8831227/
087-7668969
(Galmoy, Ossory)

Coyne, Joseph, Very Rev,
Moderator
36 Ashfield Lawn,
Huntstown, Dublin 15
Tel 01-8216447
(Blakestown, Hartstown,
Huntstown, Mountview,
Dublin)

Coyne, Vincent (OSM)
Acting Provincial,
The Servite Priory,
500 Bury New Road,
Salford,
Manchester M7 4ND
Tel 01-617922152

Craemer, Eddie (CSsR)
Clonard Monastery,
Clonard Gardens
Belfast BT13 2RL

raven, John, PP
Holy Cross Retreat,
Crumlin Road, Ardoyne,
Belfast BT14 7GE
Tel 028-90748231
(*Holy Cross*, Down & C.)

rawford, Alan (OSB)
Glenstal Abbey, Murroe,
Co Limerick
Tel 061-386103

rawford, Thomas, AP
9 Chestnut Gardens,
Newcastlewest,
Co Limerick
Tel 087-2218078
(*Pastoral Unit 15*, Limerick)

rawley, Michael, Very Rev
Canon, PE,
Parochial House,
89 Derrynoose Road,
Keady,
Co Armagh BT60 3EZ
Tel 028-3751222
(Armagh, retired)

reagh, Kieran (CP), Adm
St Paul's Retreat,
Mount Argus, Dublin 6W
Tel 01-4992000

reamer, Edmond (CSsR)
Clonard Monastery,
1 Clonard Gardens,
Belfast BT13 2RL
Tel 028-90445950

rean, David (OSA)
Good Counsel College
New Ross, Co Wexford

rean, Jack (OSA)
Duckspool House
(Retirement Community),
Abbeyside, Dungarvan,
Co Waterford
Tel 058-23784

rean, Martin (OSA)
St Augustine's Priory,
Washington Street,
Cork

rean, Thomas, Venerable
(Kerry, retired)

rean, William, Most Rev,
DD
Bishop of Cloyne,
Cloyne Diocesan Centre,
Cobh, Co Cork
Tel 021-4811430
(Cloyne)

rean-Lynch, Pat, Very Rev,
PP
Ardfert, Co Kerry
Tel 066-7134131
(*Ardfert*, Kerry)

reelman, Leo, CC
St Joseph's Presbytery,
Park Street
Co Monaghan H18 C588
Tel 047-81220
(*Monaghan*, Clogher)

Cremin, Aidan, CC
Cork Road,
Carrigaline, Co Cork
Tel 021-4372229/4371109
(*Carrigaline, Crosshaven,
Harbour Parishes
and Tracton Abbey*, Cork
& R.)

Cremin, Gerard, CC
Upper strand, Youghal,
Co Cork
Tel 024-90296
(*Youghal*, Cloyne)

Cremin, Jerry, Very Rev, Co-
PP,
Parochial House,
Kilbrittain, Co Cork
Tel 023-8849637
(*Bandon, Enniskeane,
Innishannon, Killbrittain,
Kilmurry and
Murragh/Templemartin*,
Cork & R.)

Cremin, Sean (SPS)
St Patrick's,
Kiltegan,
Co Wicklow W91 YO22
Tel 059-6473600

Cribbin, James, Very Rev, PP
Geesala, Bangor,
Ballina, Co Mayo
Tel 097-86740
(*Kiltane*, Killala)

Cribbin, Peter, Very Rev
c/o Bishop's House,
Dublin Road, Carlow
(Kildare & L.)

Crilly, Oliver
(priest in residence)
Parochial House, Castlefin,
Lifford, Co Donegal
Tel 074-9146251
(*Doneyloop (Urney and
Castlefinn)*, Derry)

Crilly, Patrick, PEm
35 Rocktown Lane,
Knockloughrim,
Magerafelt,
Co Derry BT45 8QF
(Derry, retired)

Cristóbal, Jimenez A. (SJ)
Jesuit Community,
27 Leinster Road,
Rathmines, Dublin 6
Tel 01-4970250

Crombie, Shane, CC
c/o Bishop's House,
Dublin Road, Mullingar,
Co Westmeath N91 DW32
(Meath)

Cronin, Brian (CSSp)
Holy Spirit Missionary
College
Kimmage Manor,
Whitehall Road,
Dublin D12 P5YP
Tel 01-4064300

Cronin, Kieran (OFM)
Provincial Delegate,
Franciscan Abbey,
Multyfarnham,
Co Westmeath N91 X279
Tel 044-9371114/9371137

Crosbie, Paul, PP
Parochial House, Trim,
Co Meath
Tel 046-9431251
Adm, Summerhill
(*Summerhill, Trim*, Meath)

Crosby, Denis, Very Rev, PP
Liscannor, Co Clare
Tel 065-7081248
(*Liscannor*, Galway)

Crosby, Edward, Adm
Parochial House,
Kilfenora, Co Clare
Tel 065-7088006
(*Kilfenora*, Galway)

Crosby, Michael, Very Rev
Main Street, Ballinrobe,
Co Mayo
(Galway, retired)

Cross, Charles (CP), CC
St Gabriel's Retreat, The
Graan, Enniskillen
Co Fermanagh
Tel 028-66322272
(Down & C.)

Crossey, Colin, CC
81 Lagmore Grove,
Dunmurry,
Belfast, BT17 0TD
Tel 028-90309011
(*Christ the Redeemer,
Lagmore*, Down & C.)

Crosson, Eamonn, Very Rev,
Adm
Parochial House, Ashford,
Co Wicklow
Tel 0404-40540
(*Ashford*, Dublin)

Crotty, James, Very Rev
Canon, PP
Ferrybank, Waterford
Tel 051-832787/
086-8317711
(Ossory, retired)

Crotty, Terence (OP)
St Saviour's,
Upper Dorset Street,
Dublin 1
Tel 01-8897610

Crowe, Jim (SPS)
St Patrick's, Kiltegan,
Co Wicklow
Tel 059-6473600

Crowe, Philip (CSSp), CC
Drumgossatt,
Carrickmacross,
Co Monaghan
Tel 042-9661388
(*Magheracloone*, Clogher)

Crowley, Adrian, CC
4 Summerfield Lawn,
Clonsilla Road,
Blanchardstown, Dublin 15
(*Mulhuddart*, Dublin)

Crowley, Aidan, Very Rev,
PP
Doneraile, Co Cork
Tel 086-0434911
(*Doneraile*, Cloyne)

Crowley, Brendan, PP
78 Ballerin Road, Garvagh,
Co Derry BT51 5EQ
Tel 028-29558251
(*Garvagh (Errigal),
Kilrea (Kilrea and
Desertoghill)*, Derry)

Crowley, Brendan, Very Rev
Canon, PE, VF
SS Peter and Paul's,
Clonmel, Co Tipperary
Tel 052-6126292
(*Clonmel, SS Peter and
Paul's*, Waterford & L.)

Crowley, Dan, Very Rev
Canon, PE
Woodlawn,
Model Farm Road,
Co Cork.
(Cork & R, retired)

Crowley, Finbarr, Co-PP
Innishannon, Co Cork
Tel 021-4775348
(*Bandon, Enniskeane,
Innishannon, Killbrittain,
Kilmurry and
Murragh/Templemartin*,
Cork & R.)

Crowley, Kevin (OFMCap)
Capuchin Friary,
Holy Trinity,
Fr Mathew Quay,
Cork T12 PK24
Tel 021-4270827

Crowley, Liam, Co-PP
Drimoleague, Co Cork
Tel 028-31133
(*Drimoleague,
Dunmanway,
Kilmichael and Uibh
Laoire*, Cork & R.)

Crowley, Roderic (CM)
St Paul's, Sybil Hill,
Raheny, Dublin D05 AE38
Tel 01-8318113

Crowley, Seán, CC
Cathedral Presbytery,
Roman Street, Co Cork
Tel 021-4304325
(*Cathedral of St Mary &
St Anne, Blackpool/The
Glen*, Cork & R.)

Crudden, James, Very Rev,
PP
24 Downs Road,
Newcastle,
Co Down BT33 0AG
Tel 028-43722401
(*Newcastle (Maghera)*,
Down & C.)

Cryan, Gerard, BA, HDE,
STB, L Eccl Hist
(priest in residence)
St Mary's, Sligo
Tel 071-9162670/9162769
College of the Immaculate
Conception, Summerhill,
Sligo
Tel 071-9160311
(Elphin)
Cudzilo, Michal
Curate's House,
Chapel Lane,
Newbridge, Co Kildare
Tel 045-434069
(Droichead
Nua/Newbridge, Kildare &
L.)
Cuffe, Liam
Chaplain,
St Vincent's University
Hospital,
Elm Park, Dublin 4
Tel 01-2094325
(Ardagh & Cl.)
Cullen, James, CC
The Presbytery,
12 School Street, Wexford
Tel 053-9122055
(Wexford, Ferns)
Cullen, John, Very Rev
Chaplain, Nazareth House,
Hammersmith, London
(Elphin)
Cullen, Kevin, Very Rev, PP
Parochial House,
9A Newry Road
Crossmaglen, Newry,
Co Down BT35 9HH
Tel 028-30868698
(Armagh, retired)
Cullen, Laurence, Very Rev,
PP
Geevagh, Boyle,
Co Roscommon
Tel 071-9647107
(Geevagh, Elphin)
Cullen, Michael, Very Rev,
Adm
5 St Assam's Road West,
Raheny, Dublin 5
Tel 01-8313806
(Raheny, Dublin)
Cullen, Peter, Adm
20 Bengurragh, Cahir
Co Tipperary
Tel 052 7441585
(Cahir, Waterford & L.)
Cullen, Sean
St Patrick's, Kiltegan,
Co Wicklow
Tel 059-6473600
Cullinan, Alphonsus, Most
Rev, DD
Bishop of Waterford and
Lismore
Bishop's House, John's Hill,
Waterford
Tel 051-874463
(Waterford & L.)

Cullinan, Edmond, Very Rev
Canon, VF
Vice-Rector,
Pontifical Irish College,
Via Dei SS Quattro 1,
00184 Roma, Italy
(Waterford & L.)
Cullinan, William (OCSO)
Mellifont Abbey,
Collon, Co Louth
Tel 041-9826103
Cullinane, Michael, Very
Rev, PP, VF
Parochial House, Lismore,
Co Waterford
Tel 058-54246
(Lismore, Waterford & L.)
Cullinane, Timothy (SMA)
African Missions,
Blackrock Road,
Cork T12 TD54
Tel 021-4292871
Culliton, Jim (SJ)
Superior, St Ignatius
House of Writers,
35 Lower Leeson Street,
Dublin 2
Tel 01-6761248
Cully, Patrick (CSSp)
Cherry Orchard Hospital,
Ballyfermot, Dublin 10
Tel 01-6264702
Holy Spirit Missionary
College
Kimmage Manor,
Whitehall Road,
Dublin D12 P5YP
Tel 01-4064000
Cumiskey, Cathal (CSsR)
St Joseph's,
St Alphonsus Road,
Dundalk,
Co Louth A71 F3FC
Tel 042-9334042/9334762
Cummings, Daniel
30 Knapton Road,
Dun Laoghaire, Co Dublin
Tel 01-2804353
(Opus Dei)
Cummins, Fergal
Parochial House,
Tullamore, Co Offaly
Tel 057-9321587
(Tullamore, Meath)
Cummins, Stephen (OP)
Black Abbey
Kilkenny, Co Kilkenny
Tel 056-7721279
Cummins, William, Very Rev,
PP
Parochial House,
Ennistymon, Co Clare
Tel 065-7071063
(Ennistymon, Galway)

Cunnane, Fergal, Very Rev,
PP, VF
The Parochial House,
Dunmore,
Co Galway H54 E893
Tel 093-38124
(Dunmore, Tuam)
Cunnane, Seamus, Very Rev
Canon,
Grove House,
Vicar street, Tuam,
Co Galway H54 KW02
(Tuam, retired)
Cunningham, Charles (SDB)
Salesian House,
45 St Teresa's Road,
Crumlin, Dublin D12 XK52
Tel 01-4555605
Cunningham, Donal, AP
Upperchurch, Thurles,
Co Tipperary
Tel 0504-54181
(Upperchurch, Cashel & E.)
Cunningham, Enda, Very
Rev
47 Westland Row,
Dublin 2
Tel 01-6765517
(Westland Row/University
Church, Dublin)
Cunningham, Gerard, Very
Rev, PP, VF
Glenties, Co Donegal
Tel 074-9551117
(Glenties, Raphoe)
Cunningham, John Joe, Very
Rev
Newcastle, Co Down
(Dromore, retired)
Cunningham, Martin, Very
Rev, PP
Drumoghill, Co Donegal
Tel 074-9157169
(Drumoghill (Raymochy),
Raphoe)
Cunningham, Seán, Very
Rev, CC
Parochial House,
Corrandulla, Co Galway
Tel 091-791125
(Corrandulla
(Annaghdown), Tuam)
Curran, Adrian (OFMCap),
Very Rev
Guardian,
Capuchin Friary,
Friary Street,
Kilkenny R95 NX60
Tel 056-7721439
Curran, Anthony, Very Rev,
PP,
St Mary's Presbytery,
12 Ballymena Road,
Portglenone,
Co Antrim BT44 8BL
Tel 028-25821218
(Portglenone, Down & C.)

Curran, Colum, Very Rev
Parochial House,
22 Ballymartin Village,
Kilkeel,
Co Down BT34 4PA
Tel 028-43768208
(Lower Mourne, Down &
C.)
Curran, James
61 Tournane Court,
Dungarvan, Co Waterford
Tel 058-45177
(Waterford & L., retired)
Curran, Michael (MSC)
Parish House, Union Hall,
Skibbereen, Co Cork
Tel 028-34940
(Castlehaven, Cork & R.)
Curran, Michael, Very Rev,
PE
c/o Bishop's House,
John's Hill, Waterford
(Waterford & L., retired)
Curran, Philip, Very Rev, PP
231 Beech Park, Lucan,
Co Dublin
Tel 01-2533804
(Esker-Doddboro-
Adamstown,
Lucan, Dublin)
Curran, Roderick (CSSp)
Holy Spirit Missionary
College
Kimmage Manor,
Whitehall Road,
Dublin D12 P5YP
Tel 01-4064300
Curran, Thomas (SMA)
Bursar, SMA House,
81 Ranelagh Road,
Ranelagh, Dublin 6
Tel 01-4968162/3
Currivan, Patrick, Very Rev,
AP
Caherconlish, Co Limerick
Tel 061-351248
(Caherconlish, Cashel & E.
Curry, Colum, Rt Rev Mgr,
PE, AP, VG
Parochial House,
2 Tullynure Road,
Cookstown,
Co Tyrone BT8 09XH
Tel 028-86769921
(Lissan, Armagh)
Curry, Martin (SJ)
St Ignatius Community &
Church,
27 Raleigh Row, Galway
Tel 091-523707
Curtin, Timothy,
The Presbytery,
Carrons, Kilcolman,
Co Limerick
Tel 069-60126/086-
3697735
(Patoral Unit 13, Limerick)

urtis, James, Very Rev
3 Oldtown Court,
Clongreen, Foulksmills,
New Ross, Co Wexford
(Ferns, retired)

usack, John, CC
Ballinamore, Co Leitrim
Tel 071-9644050
(*Ballinamore
(Oughteragh),* Kilmore)

usack, Ronan (OP), Very
Rev
St Malachy's, Dundalk,
Co Louth
Tel 042-9334179

ushen, Bernard, Very Rev,
PP
Clonroche, Enniscorthy,
Co Wexford
Tel 053-9244115
(*Cloughbawn and
Poulpeasty,* Ferns)

ushen, Patrick, Very Rev,
PP
Ferns, Enniscorthy,
Co Wexford
Tel 053-9366152
(*Ferns,* Ferns)

ushnahan, Vincent, Very
Rev, PP
St Vincent de Paul
Presbytery,
169 Ligoniel Road,
Belfast BT14 8DP
Tel 028-90713401
(*St Vincent de Paul,* Down
& C.)

ushnan, Martin (CSsR)
Redemptorist Community,
R.C. Church,
Morrispet P.O., Tenali,
Guntur DT 522 202,
Andhra Pradesh, India
Tel 0091-8644-223-382

ussen, Joseph,
Lisieux, Gortboy,
Newcastlewest,
Co Limerick
Tel 069-77090
(*Pastoral Unit 15,* Limerick)

ussen, Michael,
The Presbytery,
Ballybrown, Clarina,
Co Limerick
Tel 061-353711/
087-1279015
(*Pastoral Unit 6,* Limerick)

D

'Arcy, Brian (CP)
St Gabriel's Retreat,
The Graan, Enniskillen,
Co Fermanagh
Tel 028-66322272

D'Souza, Darryl (SDB)
c/o Salesian House,
45 St Teresa's Road,
Crumlin, Dublin 12
Tel 01-4555605
(India)

Dagens, Seamus, PE
Drimarone, Co Donegal
(Raphoe, retired)

Daka, Vincent, CC
Cathedral House,
Mullingar, Co Westmeath
Tel 044-9348338/9340126
(*Mullingar,* Meath)

Dales, Jovito Rev (SSC)
Bursar General,
No 3 and 4,
Ma Yau Tong Village,
Po Lam Road,
Tseung Kwan O, Kow
Loon, Hong Kong, SA

Dallat, Ciaran, Very Rev, PP
Parochial House,
Loughinisland,
Downpatrick,
Co Down BT30 8QH
Tel 028-44811661
(*Loughinisland,* Down &
C.)

Dalton, John (OFM)
4 McSweeney House,
Berkeley Road, Dublin 7
Tel 01-2826760

Dalton, Patrick, Very Rev
Canon, PP, VF
Gowran,
Co Kilkenny R95 E2Y4
Tel 056-7726128/
086-8283478
(*Gowran, Tullaherin,*
Ossory)

Dalton, Tom, Very Rev, Adm
St Aidan's, Enniscorthy,
Co Wexford
Tel 053-9235777
(*Enniscorthy, Cathedral of
St Aidan,* Ferns)

Dalton, William, Very Rev,
PP
Callan, Co Kilkenny
Tel 056-7725287/
086-8506215
(*Callan,* Ossory)

Daly, Brian, Very Rev, PP
Parochial House,
15 Moyle Road,
Ballycastle,
Co Antrim BT54 6LB
Tel 028-20762223
Administration Ballintoy
(*Ballintoy, Ballycastle
(Ramoan),* Down & C.)

Daly, Fintan (SMA)
SMA House,
Cloonbigeen, Claregalway,
Co Galway H91 YK64
Tel 091-798880

Daly, Gabriel (OSA)
St Augustine's,
Taylor's Lane,
Ballyboden, Dublin 16
Tel 01-4241000

Daly, James, Very Rev, PP
Parochial House, St Anne's
Church,
Bohernabreena, Tallaght,
Dublin 24
Tel 01-4626893
(*Bohernabreena, Tallaght,
Oldbawn,* Dublin)

Daly, Jeremiah (MSC)
Western Road,
Cork T12 TN80
Tel 021-4804120

Daly, John, Very Rev, PP
Parochial House,
La Touche Road,
Greystones, Co Wicklow
Tel 01-2874278
(*Greystones, Kilquade,*
Dublin)

Daly, John, AP
Cathedral House,
Cathedral Place, Limerick
Tel 061-414624
(*Pastoral Unit 7,* Limerick)

Daly, Martin (SM)
2 Beresford House,
Custom House Square,
Mayor Street Lower,
IFSC, Dublin 1
(retired)

Daly, Martin, CC
'Renvyle', Corrig Avenue,
Dun Laoghaire, Co Dublin
Tel 01-2802100
(*Dun Laoghaire,* Dublin)

Daly, Michael, Very Rev
Canon, PP
Broomfield, Castleblayney,
Co Monaghan
A75 A344
Tel 042-9743617
(*Donaghmoyne,* Clogher)

Daly, Noel (SSC)
St Columban's,
Dalgan Park, Navan,
Co Meath
Tel 046-9021525

Daly, Pádraig A. (OSA)
Prior, St John's Priory,
Thomas Street, Dublin 8
Tel 01-6770393/0415/0601

Daly, Patrick, Very Rev, PE
Braganza, Athy Road,
Carlow
(Kildare & L., retired)

Daly, Peter (OMI)
Oblate House of Retreat,
Inchicore, Dublin 8
Tel 01-4534408/4541805

Daly, Philip, CC
Kilclooney, Co Donegal
Tel 074-9545114
(*Ardara,* Raphoe)

Daly, Shane (SJ)
Assistant Provincial,
Milltown Park
Miltown Road, Dublin 6
Tel 01-4987333

Daly, Thomas, Very Rev, PE,
AP
Parochial House,
Boicetown, Togher,
Drogheda,
Co Louth A92 C597
Tel 041-6852110
(*Togher,* Armagh)

Dalzell, Tom, Moderator,
Parochial House,
Church Avenue
Killiney, Co Dublin
Tel 01-2826404
(*Ballybrack-Killiney,
Loughlinstown,* Dublin)

Danaher, Michael (OSA)
St Augustine's Priory,
O'Connell Street, Limerick
Tel 061-415374

Danfulani, Kieran
Parochial House,
St Patrick's,
Ballybay,
Co Monaghan A75 K299
Tel 042-9741032
(*Ballybay (Tullycorbet),*
Clogher)

Daniels, Iomar, Very Rev, PP
Parochial House,
Leitrim, Loughrea,
Co Galway H62 RP4O
(*Leitrim and Ballyduggan
(Kilcooley and Leitrim),*
Clonfert)
Killoran, Ballinasloe,
Co Galway
Tel 091-841758 for both
parishes
(*Kilmeen,* Tuam)

Darby, Derek, EV
Meath Diocesan Office,
Dublin Road, Mullingar
Tel 044-9348841
(Meath)

Darby, Gary, Very Rev, PP
Parochial House,
Kilcullen, Co Kildare
Tel 045-481230
(*Kilcullen,* Dublin)

Dardis, John (SJ)
c/o Irish Jesuit
Provincialate,
Milltown Park,
Miltown Road, Dublin 6
Tel 01-4987333

Davern, Richard, Moderator
St Mary's,
Athlunkard Street,
Limerick
Tel 087-2977500
(*Pastoral Unit 4,* Limerick)

Davey, Gerard, Very Rev,
Adm
Carracastle,
Ballghaderreen,
Co Mayo F45 W822
Tel 094-9254301
(*Ballghaderreen*, Achonry)

David, Jerald, Adm, CC
Parochial House,
Aghamore, Ballyhaunis,
Co Mayo F35 WF51
Tel 094-9367024
(*Aghamore*, Tuam)

Davis, Donal (OCSO)
Mount Melleray Abbey,
Cappoquin,
Co Waterford P51 R8XW
Tel 058-54404

Davis, Patrick (SJ)
St Ignatius House of
Writers,
35 Lower Leeson Street,
Dublin 2
Tel 01-6761248

Davis, Joe, CC
4 Broughshane Road,
Ballymena BT43 7DX
Tel 028-25643828
(*Ballymena (Kirkinriola)*,
Down & C.)

Dawson, Laurence, Very Rev
Canon, PE
25 Teiges Hill,
Brookeborough,
Co Fermanagh BT94 4EZ
Tel 028-89531770
(*Brookeboro (Aghavea-
Aghintaine), Clogher*,
Clogher)

De Bhaldraithe, Eoin (OCSO)
Bolton Abbey, Moone,
Co Kildare
Tel 059-8624102

De Blacam, Hugh (CSSp)
Holy Spirit Missionary
College
Kimmage Manor,
Whitehall Road,
Dublin D12 P5YP
Tel 01-4064300

De Burca, Brian (OMI), Very
Rev
170 Merrion Road,
Ballsbridge, Dublin 4
Tel 01-2693658

De Léis, Seán (CSSp)
Holy Spirit Missionary
College
Kimmage Manor,
Whitehall Road,
Dublin D12 P5YP
Tel 01-4064300

De Oliveira, CC
Curate's House, Milll Lane,
Kilcock, Co Kildare
Tel 01-6757311
(*Kilcock*, Kildare & L.)

De Querioz, Genildo
(OCarm)
Gort Muire, Ballinteer,
Dublin D16 EI67
Tel 01-2984014

De Val, Seamus, Very Rev
Canon
1 Irish Street, Bunclody,
Co Wexford
Tel 053-9376140
(*Ferns*, retired)

Deakin, Kevin,
Home of the Mother,
St Savior's Priory,
Bridge Street, Waterford
Tel 051-875061
(*Waterford & L.*)

Deane, Joseph Mary (CFR)
Local Servant (Superior),
St Patrick Friary,
64 Delmege Park,
Moyross,
Limerick V94 859Y
Tel 061-458071

Deasy, Declan (OSA)
St Augustine's Priory,
St Augustine's Street,
Galway
Tel 091-562524

Deasy, John F., Very Rev
Mgr,
(Team Assistant)
55 St Agnes' Road,
Crumlin, Dublin 12
Tel 01-4550955
(*Crumlin*, Dublin)

DeCant, John Baptist (OSB)
Silverstream Priory,
Stamullen,
Co Meath K32 T189
Tel 01-8417142

Decio, Cesare (OP)
St Catherine's, Newry,
Co Down BT35 8BN
Tel 028-30262178

Deegan, Gerard, Very Rev,
Co-PP
28 Glentworth Park,
Ayrefield, Dublin 13
Tel 01-8674007
(*Ayrefield*, Dublin)

Deegan, Joseph, Very Rev,
PP
St Brigid's Parish Office,
Church Street, Clara,
Co Offaly R35 PW97
Tel 057-9331170
(*Clara*, Meath)

Deegan, Stan, Very Rev, PP
St Joseph's Parochial
House, Killucan,
Co Westmeath N91 F292
Tel 044-9374127
(*Killucan*, Meath)

Deely, Patrick, AP
Lorrha, Co Tipperary
Tel 086-8330225
(*Cronan Pastoral Area*,
Killaloe)

Deeney, Edward (SMA)
African Missions,
Dromantine, Newry,
Co Down BT34 1RH
Tel 028-30821224

Deenihan, Thomas, Most
Rev, DD, EdD
Bishop of Meath,
Bishop's House
Dublin Road, Mullingar
Co Meath
Tel 044-9348841
(*Meath*)

Deery, Cathal, Very Rev, CC
15 Knockmore Road,
Drumary, Derrygonnelly,
Co Fermanagh BT93 6GA
Tel 028-68641207
(*Derrygonnelly (Botha)*,
Clogher)

Deighan, Gerard, Very Rev,
Adm
Parochial House,
Harrington Street,
Dublin 8
Tel 01-4751506
(*Harrington Street*, Dublin)

Deignan, John, PP
10 Ashford, Monksland,
Athlone, Co Roscommon
Tel 090-6493262
(*Athlone, SS Peter and
Paul's*, Elphin)

Delahunty, Richard (CSsR),
CC
Holy Family Parish,
Hoey's Lane,
Muirhevnamor,
Dundalk,
Co Louth A91 K761
Tel 042-9336301
(*Dundalk, Holy Family*,
Armagh)

Delaney, Joseph, Very Rev
Canon
Castlelawn Heights,
Headford Road, Galway
(Galway, retired)

Delaney, John, Very Rev
Canon, Moderator
Parochial House, St Mary's,
Sandyford, Dublin 18
Tel 01-2956317
(*Balally*, Dublin)

Delaney, John, Very Rev, PP
Parochial House,
Kilrossanty, Kilmacthomas,
Co Waterford
Tel 051-291985
(*Kilrossanty*, Waterford &
L.)

Delaney, Joseph, Very Rev,
AP
Clonbealy, Newport,
Co Tipperary
Tel 061-378126
(*Newport*, Cashel & E.)

Delaney, Martin, Very Rev,
PP
Rathdowney, Co Laois
Tel 0505-46282/
086-2444594
Adm, Durrow
(*Durrow, Rathdowney*,
Ossory)

Delany, John, Very Rev
Canon, Moderator, VF
Parochial House, St Mary's
Sandyford Village,
Dublin 18
Tel 01-2956317
Chaplain,
Leopardstown Park
Hospital
Tel 01-2955055
(*Balally, Sandyford*,
Dublin)

Delargy, David, Very Rev, PP
824 Shore Road,
Newtownabbey,
Co Antrim BT36 7 DG
Tel 028-90370845
(*Greencastle, Whiteabbey
(St James), Whitehouse*,
Down & C.)

Delargy, Patrick, Rev Mgr
Priest in residence,
Parochial House,
111 Causeway Street,
Portrush, BT56 8JE
(*Portrush*, Down & C.)

Delimat, Piotr
Sarsfield Barracks,
Limerick
Tel 061-314233
(Limerick)

Dempsey, Michael (CSsR)
Clonard Monastery,
1 Clonard Gardens,
Belfast BT13 2RL
Tel 028-90445950

Dempsey, Michael Vincent
The Presbytery,
Kilmeade, Narraghmore,
Co Wicklow
(Dublin, retired)

Dempsey, Paul, Most Rev,
DD
Bishop of Achonry
Bishop's House,
Convent Road,
Ballaghaderreen,
Co Roscommon F45 H004
Tel 094-9860034
(Achonry)

Dempsey, Raymond
St John's Presbytery,
Kilkenny
Tel 087-2859682
(*St John's*, Ossory)

Dempsey, Sean (MCCJ)
8 Clontarf Road, Clontarf,
Dublin 3
Tel 01-8330051

enmead, Jim, AP
Ardfinnan, Clonmel,
Co Tipperary
(*Tournaneena*, Waterford
& L.)

ermody, Eamonn, Very Rev
Canon, PE
Clarinbridge, Co Galway
Tel 091-796208
(Galway, retired)

esmond, Diarmuid, Very
Rev, PP
Kilrane, Co Wexford
Tel 053-9133128
(*Kilrane and St Patrick's*,
Ferns)

esmond, Garrett, Very Rev,
PP
Lemybrien, Co Waterford
Tel 087-1735178
(*Newtown*, Waterford &
L.)

esmond, Patrick
The Lodge, Mount
Sackville, Chapelizod,
Dublin 20
Tel 01-8214004
(Dublin)

esmond, Patrick (OP)
St Malachy's, Dundalk,
Co Louth
Tel 042-9334179/9333714

evaney, Owen, PE
Treanlawn, Killoe,
Co Longford, N39 79F3
(Ardagh & Cl., retired)

eveney, Cathal, PP, VF
Parochial House,
19 Caledon Road,
Aughnacloy,
Co Tyrone BT69 6HX
Tel 028-85557212
(*Aughnacloy (Aghaloo)*,
Armagh)

evereux, Sean, Very Rev,
PP
Cushinstown, Newbawn,
Co Wexford
Tel 051-428347
(*Cushingtown and
Rathgarogue*, Ferns)

evine, James
On Sabbatical,
c/o Diocesan Offices
St Eugene's Cathedral,
Francis Street,
Derry BT48 9AP
(Derry)

evine, Liam, Very Rev
Canon, PE
Priests in residence,
Presbytery, Kilmurray,
Co Roscommon
(Elphin, retired)

evine, Oliver Very Rev, PP
Parochial House,
Drumraney, Athlone,
Co Westmeath
Tel 044-9356207

Devitt, Patrick, Adm
17 Prospect Lawn,
The Park, Cabinteely,
Dublin 18
(Dublin, retired)

Devitt, Séamus (CSsR), CC
The Presbytery,
197 Kylemore Road,
Ballyfermot, Dublin 10
Tel 01-6264789
(*Ballyfermot*, Dublin)

Devlin, Anthony, Very Rev,
PP
St Paul's Presbytery,
125 Falls Road,
Belfast BT12 6AB
Tel 028-90325034
(*St Paul's*, Down & C.)

Devlin, Brendan, Rt Rev
Mgr, MA, DD
St Patrick's College,
Maynooth, Co Kildare
Tel 01-6285222
(Derry)

Devlin, Eamon (CM), Very
Rev, PP
Superior,
St Peter's, Phibsboro,
Dublin 7
Tel 01-8389708/8389841
(*Phibsborough*, Dublin)

Devlin, Patrick, PP
23 Hannahstown Hill,
Belfast BT17 0LT
Tel 028-90614567
(*Hannahstown*, Down &
C.)

Devlin, Peter, PP
Parochial House,
Malin, Co Donegal
Tel 074-9370615
(*Malin (Clonca)*, Derry)

Digan, Padraig (SSC)
St Columban's Retirement
Home, Dalgan Park,
Navan, Co Meath
Tel 046-9021525

Diggin, Fintan, CC
Parochial House, Burt,
Lifford, Co Donegal
Tel 074-9368155
(*Fahan (Burt, Inch and
Fahan)*, Derry)

Dillon, Christopher (OSB)
Glenstal Abbey, Murroe,
Co Limerick
Tel 061-621000

Dillon, Sean, Very Rev, PP
Parochial House,
Greencastle Road, Kilkeel,
Co Down BT34 4DE
Tel 028-41762242
(*Kilkeel (Upper Mourne)*,
Down and C.)

Dillon, Thomas, Very Rev,
PE, CC
Parochial House,
Askea, Carlow
Tel 059-9164882
(*Bennekerry*, Kildare & L.)

Dineen, John (OCSO)
Mount Melleray Abbey,
Cappoquin,
Co Waterford P51 R8XW
Tel 058-54404

Dineen, Joseph (OP), PP
Prior, St Saviour's,
Upper Dorset Street,
Dublin 1
Tel 01-8897610
(*Dominick Street*, Dublin)

Dhason, Pravin, Very Rev, PP
Parochial House,
Cloverhill, Co Roscommon
Tel 090-6626275/087-
1889885
(*Kilbride, Oran*, Elphin)

Dobbin, Séamus, CC
c/o Ara Coeli,
Armagh BT61 7QY
(Armagh)

Dodd, Michael (SSC)
St Columban's,
Dalgan Park,
Navan, Co Meath
Tel 046-9021525

Doherty, Brendan, PEm,
4 Garvagh Road, Kilrea,
Co Derry BT51 5QP
Tel 028-29540343
(Derry, retired)

Doherty, Cathal (SJ)
Irish Jesuit Provincialate,
Milltown Park,
Miltown Road, Dublin 6
Tel 01-4987333

Doherty, Con (MSC), Very
Rev, PP
Sacred Heart Parish,
Western Road, Cork
Tel 021-4804120
(*Sacred Heart*, Cork & R.)

Doherty, John (CSsR)
Clonard Monastery,
1 Clonard Gardens,
Belfast BT13 2RL
Tel 028-90445950

Doherty, John, PEm
Parochial House,
447 Victoria Road,
Ballymagorry, Strabane,
Co Tyrone BT82 0AT
Tel 028-718802274
(Derry, retired)

Doherty, John, Rt Rev Mgr,
PE
(priest in residence),
Charlestown, Co Mayo
Tel 094-9255793
(Achonry, retired)

Doherty, Kevin, Co-PP
Apartment No. 1,
St Sylvester's Church,
Malahide, Co Dublin
Tel 01-8451244
(*Malahide*, Dublin)

Doherty, Michael, PP
39 Melmount Road,
Strabane,
Co Tyrone BT82 9EF
Tel 028-71882648
(*Melmount, Sion Mills*,
Derry)

Doherty, Patrick, Very Rev,
PP
159 Glen Road, Maghera,
Co Derry BT46 5JN
Tel 028-79642496
(*Maghera*, Derry)

Doherty, Tom
Church Road, Belmullet,
Co Mayo
Tel 097-81426
(*Belmullet, Kilmore-Erris*,
Killala)

Dolan, Andrew, Rt Rev Mgr,
Pem
53b Brisland Road,
Eglington,
Co Derry BT47 3EA
(Derry, retired)

Dolan, Denis, Very Rev, PE
Shanmullagh, Dromore
Co Tyrone BT78 3DZ
Tel 028-82898641
(*Dromore*, Clogher)

Dolan, Gerard, Rt Rev Mgr,
St Mary's, Temple Street,
Co Sligo
Tel 071-9162670
Nazareth House,
Churchill, Sligo
Tel 071-9162278
(Elphin, retired)

Dolan, John, Rt Rev Mgr,
LCL
The Chancellery,
Archbishop's House
Drumcondra,
Dublin D09 H4C2
Tel 01-8087500
(Dublin)

Dolan, Martin, Very Rev,
Adm
The Presbytery,
Francis Street, Dublin 8
Tel 01-4544861/
086-4035318
(*Francis Street*, Dublin)

Domagala, Dominick (OMI),
Co-PP
Oblate House of Retreat,
Inchicore, Dublin 8
Tel 01-4534408/4541805
(*Inchicore, St Michael's*,
Dublin)

Domenzain Canul, Joshua
M. (OSB)
Benedictine Monks,
Holy Cross Abbey,
119 Kilbroney Road,
Rostrevor,
Co Down BT34 3BN
Tel 028-41739979

Donaghy, Kevin, Very Rev, PP, Adm, VG, VF
4 Circular Road,
Dungannon,
Co Tyrone BT71 6BE
Tel 028-87722775
(*Dungannon (Drumglas, Killyman and Tullyniskin)*, Armagh)

Donegan, Gary, Very Rev (CP)
Holy Cross Retreat,
Crumlin Road, Ardoyne,
Belfast BT14 7GE
Tel 028-90748231

Donlon, Chris, Very Rev, PP
Ladysbridge, Co Cork
Tel 021-4667173
(*Ballymacoda & Ladysbridge*, Cloyne)

Donnellan, David (OCD)
St Teresa's,
Clarendon Street, Dublin 2
Tel 01-6718466/6718127

Donnellan, Patrick, Very Rev, PE
25 Drisín, Knocknacarra, Galway
(Tuam, retired)

Donnelly, Brian, Very Rev, PP
Parochial House,
Plumbridge, Omagh,
Co Tyrone, BT79 8EF
Tel 028-81648283
(*Gortin (Badoney Lower)*, *Greencastle*, *Newtownstewart and Plumbridge*, Derry)

Donnelly, Eamonn (SVD), Adm
Presbytery, Idrone Avenue,
Knocklyon, Dublin 16
Tel 01-4941204
(*Knocklyon*, Dublin)

Donnelly, James, Very Rev, PP,
Doon, Co Limerick
Tel 061-380165
(*Doon*, Cashel & E.)

Donnelly, Joseph, Rt Rev Mgr PEm
52 Brook Street, Omagh,
Co Tyrone BT78 5HE
Tel 028-82243011
(Derry, retired)

Donnelly, Liam, PEm
20 Loughermore Road,
Ogill, Ballykelly,
Co Derry BT49 9PD
Tel 028-77762721
(Derry, retired)

Donnelly, Michael, Very Rev,
c/o St Mary's, Temple
Street, Sligo
(Elphin, retired)

Donnelly, Micheál, Very Rev, PP,
Parochial House,
Ballinagare,
Co Roscommon
Administration
Fairymount Parish
Tel 094-9870039
(*Fairymount, Frenchpark*, Elphin)

Donnelly, Patrick, Very Rev, PP
The Presbytery, Enfield,
Co Meath
Tel 046-9541282
(*Enfield*, Meath)

Donnelly, Peter, Very Rev, VF
c/o Diocesan Office,
Lisbreen,
73 Somerton Road,
Belfast,
Co Antrim BT15 4DE
(Down & C.)

Donnelly, Peter, Very Rev, PP, VF
Parochial House,
130 Ballinderry Bridge
Road, Coagh, Cookstown,
Co Tyrone BT80 0AY
Tel 028-79418244
(*Ballinderry*, Armagh)

Donnelly, Raymond CC
4 Darling Street,
Enniskillen,
Co Fermanagh BT74 7DP
Tel 028-66322075
(*Enniskillen*, Clogher)

Donnelly, Victor (CP)
St Gabriel's Retreat,
The Graan, Enniskillen,
Co Fermanagh
Tel 028-66322272

Donohoe, Eamon (MSC)
'Croí Nua', Rosary Lane,
Taylor's Hill, Galway
Tel 091-520960

Donohoe, Kevin, PP, VF
Ballyjamesduff, Co Cavan
Tel 049-8544410
(*Castlerahan & Munterconnaught*, Kilmore)

Donohoe, Séamus (OFM)
Franciscan Friary,
Ennis, Co Clare
Tel 065-6828751

Donohoe, Sean (OFMCap)
Guardian, Capuchin Friary,
Station Road, Raheny,
Dublin 5 D05 T9E4
Tel 01-8313886

Donohue, Steve (SPS)
St Patrick's, Kiltegan,
Co Wicklow W91 Y022
Tel 059-6473600

Donovan, Bernard, Very Rev Canon, Co-PP
Cloughdubh, Crookstown,
Co Cork
Tel 021-7336054
(*Bandon, Enniskeane, Innishannon, Killbrittain, Kilmurry and Murragh/Templemartin*, Cork & R.)

Donovan, Leo (OP)
Dominican Community,
St Mary's Priory,
Tallaght, Dublin 24
Tel 01-4048100

Donovan, Roy, PP
Caherconlish,
Co Limerick
Tel 061-450730
(*Caherconlish*, Cashel & E.)

Donworth, John,
Parochial House,
Kildimo, Co Limerick
Tel 061-394134/
087-2237501
(*Pastoral Unit 12*, Limerick)

Doocey, Colin, Very Rev, PP, Adm
1 The Presbytery,
Holy Cross Church,
Mahon, Cork
Tel 021-2414624
(*Blackrock, Mahon*, Cork & R.)

Doody, Patrick (CSSp)
Holy Spirit Missionary College
Kimmage Manor,
Whitehall Road,
Dublin D12 P5YP
Tel 01-4064300

Doohan, Martin, Very Rev, PP
Dunfanaghy,
Co Donegal
Tel 074-9136163
(*Dunfanaghy*, Raphoe)

Doohan, Michael (SSC)
St Columban's Retirement
Home, Dalgan Park,
Navan, Co Meath
Tel 046-9021525

Dooley, Francis, Very Rev
Our Lady's Manor,
Bulloch Castle,
Dalkey, Co Dublin
(Dublin, retired)

Dooley, John (SJ)
c/o Milltown Park,
Miltown Road, Dublin 6
Tel 01-2698411/2698113

Dooley, Maurice, Rt Rev Mgr, AP
Loughmore, Templemore,
Co Tipperary
Tel 0504-31375
(*Loughmore*, Cashel & E.)

Dooley, Seán, Very Rev, PP
Parochial House,
Tullyallen, Drogheda,
Co Louth
Tel 041-9838520
(*Mellifont*, Armagh)

Dooley, Thomas, Very Rev, PP, Adm
Patrick Street,
Portarlington,
Co Laois A92 H243
Tel 057-8643004
Administration Emo
(*Emo, Portarlington*, Kildare & L.)

Dooley, Tom (SM),
Chanel Community,
Coolock Village, Dublin 5
Tel 01-8484799

Doran, Dermot (CSSp)
Holy Spirit Missionary College
Kimmage Manor,
Whitehall Road,
Dublin D12 P5YP
Tel 01-4064300

Doran, Alphonsus (CSsR)
Clonard Monastery,
Clonard Gardens
Belfast BT13 2RL
Tel 028-90445950

Doran, Joseph, Very Rev, Adm
Parochial House,
Kilbride, Co Wicklow
Tel 087-2288579
(*Kilbride and Barndarrig*, Dublin)

Doran, Kevin, Most Rev, MA, PhD
Bishop of Elphin
St Mary's, Temple Street, Sligo
Tel 071-9150106
(Elphin)

Doran, Patrick (CSSp)
Holy Spirit Missionary College,
Kimmage Manor,
Whitehall Road, Dublin 12
Tel 01-4064300

Doran, Senan (OSA)
St Augustine's,
Taylor's Lane,
Ballyboden, Dublin 16
Tel 01-4241000

Dorgan, Michael, Very Rev, PE
Curate's House,
Ballycotton, Co Cork
Tel 083-8230854
(*Cloyne*, Cloyne)

Dorr, Donal (SPS)
St Patrick's,
21 Leeson Park,
Dublin D06 DE76
Tel 01-4977897

Dowd, Gerard (SDB)
c/o Salesian House,
45 St Teresa's Road,
Crumlin, Dublin D12 XK52

Dowd, Thomas
Ely University Centre,
10 Hume Street, Dublin 2
Tel 01-6767420
(Opus Dei)

Dowley, Eddie (OFMCap)
Vicar,
Capuchin Friary,
Holy Trinity,
Fr Mathew Quay,
Cork T12 PK24
Tel 021-4270827

Dowley, Martin (OCSO)
Prior,
Our Lady of Bethlehem
Abbey,
11 Ballymena Road,
Portglenone, Ballymena,
Co Antrim BT44 8BL
Tel 028-25821211

Dowling, Cornelius
Our Lady's Manor,
Bullock Harbour, Dalkey,
Co Dublin
(Dublin, retired)

Downes, Edward, CC
Sacred Heart Residence,
Sybil Hill Road, Raheny,
Dublin 5
(Dublin, retired)

Downes, Frank (OP)
St Mary's Priory,
The Claddagh,
Galway
Tel 091-582884

Downes, Patrick (CSSp)
Rockwell College,
Cashel, Co Tipperary
Tel 062-61444

Downey, John, PEm
(Derry, retired)

Downey, Martin, Very Rev
Canon, PP
24 Presentation Road,
Galway
Tel 091-562276
(St Joseph's, Galway)

Downing, Mortimer, Very
Rev, PE
Stuake, Donoughmore,
Co Cork
(Cloyne, retired)

Doyle, Andrew, Very Rev, PP
Durhamstown,
Bohermeen, Navan,
Co Meath
Tel 046-9073805
(Bohermeen, Meath)

Doyle, Bernard
(Kilmore, retired)

Doyle, Brian (OP)
Black Abbey
Kilkenny, Co Kilkenny
Tel 056-7721279

Doyle, Derek, Very Rev,
Moderator
Parochial House,
Rathdrum, Co Wicklow,
Tel 0404-46229
(Glendalough, Rathdrum,
Roundwood, Dublin)

Doyle, Denis, Very Rev,
Starvehall,
Coolballon, Co Wexford
(Ferns, retired)

Doyle, Desmond G., Very
Rev, Moderator
Chaplain's Residence,
Dublin Airport, Co Dublin
Tel 01-8405948/8447283
(Brackenstown, River
Valley, Swords, Dublin)

Doyle, Gerald (MHM)
St James Apartments,
Our Lady of Knock Shrine,
Knock,
Co Mayo F12 R982

Doyle, James
Chaplain,
Irish College, Paris
(Ferns)

Doyle, Michael A.,
Poulfur, Fethard-on-Sea,
New Ross, Co Wexford
Tel 051-397048
(Templetown and Poulfur,
Ferns)

Doyle, Rory (OFMConv)
Fairview Strand, Dublin3
Tel 01-8376000

Doyle, Thaddeus
Shillelagh, Arklow,
Co Wicklow
Tel 053-9429926
(Ferns)

Draper, Anthony, Rev DD
Millbury Nursing Home,
Navan, Co Meath
(Meath, retired)

Drennan, Martin, Most Rev,
DD
Retired Bishop of Galway,
17 Doughiska Road,
Galway
(Galway)

Drennan, Michael (SJ)
Manresa House,
Dollymount, Dublin 3
Tel 01-8331352

Drescher, Frank, Very Rev,
Adm
Presbytery No 1,
Treepark Road,
Kilnamanagh, Dublin 24
Tel 01-4523805
(Kilnamanagh-Castleview,
Dublin)

Drewniak, Ireneusz
Neo-Catechumenal
Way/Missio Ad Gentes
7 Newtown Woods,
Newtown, Waterford
(Waterford & L.)

Drumm, Eugene (SPS)
On temporary diocesan
work

Drumm, Michael PP
St Columba's,
Rosses Point, Co Sligo
Tel 071-9177133
(Rosses Point, Elphin)

Duddy, Brendan (SJ)
Milltown Park,
Miltown Road, Dublin 6
Tel 01-2698411/2698113

Duffy, Aquinas T., Very Rev,
Acting Moderator,
19 Woodlands Road,
Johnstown
Glenageary, Co Dublin
Tel 01-5672374
(Cabinteely, Dublin)

Duffy, Eddie (SM)
Chanel Community,
Coolock, Dublin 5
Tel 01-8477133

Duffy, Eugene, DD
Convent Road,
Balaghaderreen,
Co Roscommon
Tel 087-9621410
(Achonry)

Duffy, Francis, Most Rev, DD
Archbishop of Tuam,
Archbishop's House,
Tuam,
Co Galway H54 HP57
Tel 093-24166
(Tuam)

Duffy, John Joe, CC
Creeslough,
Co Donegal
Tel 074-9138011
(Dunfanaghy
(Clondahorkey), Raphoe)

Duffy, Joseph, Most Rev, DD
Bishop Emeritus,
Doire na gCraobh,
Monaghan
Tel 047-62725
(Clogher)

Duffy, Kevin, Very Rev, PP
42 Church Street,
Burfits Hill, Irvinestown,
Co Fermanagh BT94 1EN
Tel 028-68621856
(Irvinestown, Clogher)

Duffy, Larry (SM)
Italy

Duffy, Lawrence, Most Rev
DD
Bishop of Clogher,
Bishop's House,
Monaghan H18 PN35
Tel 047-81019
(Clogher)

Duffy, Michael (OFMCap)
Capuchin Friary,
Station Road, Raheny,
Dublin D05 T9E4
Tel 01-8313886

Duffy, Patrick (CP)
Holy Cross Retreat,
Crumlin Road, Ardoyne,
Belfast BT14 7GE
Tel 028-90748231

Duffy, Patrick, CC
Kilmyshall, Enniscorthy,
Co Wexford
Tel 053-9377188
(Bunclody, Ferns)

Duffy, Stephen, CC
Parochial House,
Beech Corner,
Castleblaney,
Co Monaghan A75 PF98
Tel 042-9740637
(Castleblaney, Clogher)

Duffy, Stephen, Very Rev,
Adm
Parochial House,
Ravensdale, Dundalk,
Co Louth A91 V523
Tel 042-9371327
(Lordship (and
Ballymascanlon), Armagh)

Duggan, Brendan (CSSp),
Rockwell College,
Cashel, Co Tipperary
Tel 062-61444

Duggan, Frank
(Dublin, retired)

Duggan, James (OP)
Holy Cross, Tralee,
Co Kerry
Tel 066-7121135

Duggan, John, Very Rev, PE
44 An Cuirt,
Monard, Co Tipperary
(Limerick, retired)

Duggan, Patrick, Very Rev
Canon, PE
Bennetsbridge,
Co Kilkenny
Tel 056-7727140/
086-2557471
(Tullaherin, Ossory)

Duhig, Frank, Very Rev
Canon,
Parochial House,
Castlemahon, Co Limerick
Tel 087-6380299
(Limerick, retired)

Duignan, Michael, Most
Rev, SThD, DD
Bishop of Galway,
Kilmacduagh and
Kilfenora
Bishop of Clonfert,
Coorheen, Loughrea
Co Galway H62 TD82
Tel 091-841560
(Galway, Kilmacduagh and
Kilfenora, Clonfert)

Dullea, Gearóid, Rt Rev
Mgr, PP
The Presbytery,
Ballinlough, Cork
Tel 021-4292296
(Ballinlough, Cork & R.)

Duncan, James (CSSp)
Holy Spirit Missionary College
Kimmage Manor,
Whitehall Road,
Dublin D12 P5YP
Tel 01-4064300

Dundon, Patrick (CSSp)
Blackrock College,
Blackrock, Co Dublin
Tel 01-2888681

Dunleavy, John (SMA)
SMA House, Cloonbigeen,
Claregalway,
Co Galway H91 YK64
Tel 091-798880

Dunleavy, Michael, Very Rev (OP)
Dominican Community,
St Mary's Priory, Tallaght,
Dublin 24
Tel 01-4048100

Dunne, Aidan, Very Rev, PP
Parochial House,
11 Chapel Road,
Bessbrook, Newry,
Co Down BT35 7AU
Tel 028-30830206
(Bessbrook (Killeavy Lower), Armagh)

Dunne, Daniel, Very Rev, PP
Tullamoy, Stradbally,
Co Laois
Tel 059-8627123
(Ballyadams, Kildare & L.)

Dunne, Gerard (OP)
Univeristy College, Cork
Chaplaincy Office, Iona,
College Road
Tel 021-4902704
St Mary's, Pope's Quay, Cork
Tel 021-4502267

Dunne, John (SMA)
SMA House, Wilton,
Cork, T12 KR23
Tel 021-4541069/4541884

Dunne, Kieran, CC
50 Cremore Road,
Glasnevin, Dublin 9
Tel 01-8373455
(Glasnevin, Dublin)

Dunne, Liam (SVD), Rector,
1 & 3 Pembroke Road,
Ballsbridge, Dublin 4

Dunne, Liam, Very Rev
The Forge, Martin's Lane,
Upper Main Street,
Arklow, Co Wicklow
Tel 0402-32779
(Ossory, retired)

Dunne, Michael (CM)
St Paul's College, Raheny,
Dublin 5
Tel 01-8318113

Dunne, Patrick, Very Rev, PP
Parochial House,
Kilmacrennan,
Letterkenny
Co Donegal
Tel 074-9139018
(Kilmacrennan, Raphoe)

Dunne, Paul, CC
24 Watermill Road,
Raheny, Dublin 5
Tel 01-8313232
(Raheny, Dublin)

Dunne, Ronald
(priest in residence)
60 Grange Park Grove,
Raheny, Dublin 5
Tel 086-4513904
(Edenmore, Grange Park, Dublin)

Dunne, Thomas (SDB)
Salesian House,
45 St Teresa's Road,
Crumlin, Dublin 12
Tel 01-4555605

Dunne, Thomas, Very Rev, PP
Parochial House,
Liscreagh, Murroe,
Co Limerick
Tel 083-4854776
(Murroe and Boher, Cashel & E.)

Dunny, Patrick, Very Rev
Wood Road,
Graignamanagh,
Co Kilkenny
Tel 059-9724518
(Kildare & L.)

Dunphy, John
On sabbatical
(Dublin)

Dunphy, John, Very Rev, Adm
Graiguecullen, Co Carlow
Tel 059-9141833
(Graiguecullen, Kildare & L.)

Dunphy, Laurence, Very Rev Canon
Urlingford, Co Kilkenny
Tel 087-2300849
(Ossory, retired)

Dunphy, Noel, Very Rev, PE, CC
Mountmellick, Co Laois
Tel 057-8624141
(Mountmellick, Kildare & L.)

Dunphy, Paul
Two-Mile-House,
Naas, Co Kildare
Tel 045-876160
(Naas, Kildare & L.)

Durajczyk, Tadeusz (SVD)
Priest's Road,
Tramore, Co Tipperary
(Tramore, Waterford & L.)

Durkan, John, Very Rev, PP
Killasser, Swinford,
Co Mayo
Tel 094-9024761
(Killasser, Achonry)

Durnin, Brian, CC
12 Brookwood Grove,
Artane, Dublin 5
Tel 01-8187996
(Artane, Dublin)

Dwan, Sean (SSC)
St Columban's,
Dalgan Park,
Navan, Co Meath
Tel 046-9021525

Dwyer, Donal, Very Rev, Co-PP
Parochial House,
O'Callaghan's Mills,
Co Clare
Tel 065-6835148/
086-1050090
(Ceanntar na Lochanna Pastoral Area, Killaloe)

Dwyer, Patrick (SAC)
Pallottine College, Thurles,
Co Tipperary
Tel 0504-21202

Dziduch, Włodzimierz (SCHR)
Chaplain to Polish Community,
201 Donegall Street,
Belfast BT1 2FL
Tel 075-87101979
(Down & C.)

Dziedzic, Bartolomiej, CC
The Presbytery,
Bandon, Co Cork
Tel 023-8865067
(Bandon, Enniskeane, Innishannon, Killbrittain, Kilmurry and Murragh/Templemartin, Cork & R.)

E

Earley, Patrick, Mgr, PE
Parochial House,
Rathowen, Co Westmeath
Tel 043-6676044
(Ardagh & Cl., retired)

Early, Brian, Very Rev, PE
St Dympna's, Tydavnet,
Co Monaghan H18 Y190
Tel 047-79434
(Tydavnet, Clogher)

Eastwood, Adrian (CM)
Superior,
99 Cliftonville Road,
Belfast BT14 6JQ
Tel 028-90751771

Ebuk, Lawrence (MSP), PP
Ballinameen, Boyle,
Co Roscommon
Tel 071-9668104
(Ballinameen (Kilnamanagh and Esternsnow), Elphin)

Ebuka, Martins, TA
75 Ludford Road,
Ballinteer, Dublin 16
(Meadowbrook, Dublin)

Echavarria, John (SSP)
c/o Society of St Paul,
Moyglare Road,
Maynooth, Co Kildare
Tel 01-6285933

Edebianga, Christopher (MSP), Very Rev, PP
Parochial House,
Roscommon
Tel 090-6663338
(Athleague, Elphin)

Edwards, Brian
c/o Archbishop's House,
Drumcondra,
Dublin D09 H4C2
(Dublin)

Egan, Adrian (CSsR), Very Rev, PP
The Presbytery,
197 Kylemore Road,
Ballyfermot, Dublin 10
Tel 01-6264789
(Ballyfermot, Dublin)

Egan, James, Very Rev, PP
Knockavilla, Dundrum,
Co Tipperary
Tel 062-71157
(Knockavilla, Cashel & E.)

Egan, John, Very Rev, AP
Lattin, Co Tipperary
Tel 062-55240
(Lattin and Cullen, Cashel & E.)

Egan, Joseph (SMA)
Superior,
SMA House,
81 Ranelagh Road,
Ranelagh, Dublin 6
Tel 01-4968162/3

Egan, Joseph, Very Rev, PP
Boherlahan, Cashel,
Co Tipperary
Tel 0504-41114
(Boherlahan and Dualla, Cashel & E.)

Egan, Michael (SVD)
133 North Circular Road,
Dublin 7
Tel 01-8386743

Egan, Patrick (SDB)
c/o Salesian House,
45 St Teresa's Road,
Crumlin, Dublin D12 XK52

Egan, Patrick (SSC)
St Columban's,
Dalgan Park, Navan
Co Meath
Tel 046-9021525

gan, Ralph (CP), CC
St Paul's Retreat,
Mount Argus, Dublin 6W
Tel 01-4992000

gan, Seamus (SSC)
St Columban's Retirement
Home, Dalgan Park,
Navan, Co Meath
Tel 046-9021525

gan, Sean
Kilrickle, Loughrea,
Co Galway H62 PO27
(Clonfert, retired)

gan, Thomas F., Very Rev
Clonoulty, Cashel,
Co Tipperary
Tel 086-8199678
(Clonoulty & Rossmore,
Cashel & E.)

gan, Tony (OSA)
Prior,
St Augustine's Priory,
Dungarvan, Co Waterford
Tel 058-41136

ivers, James (OCarm)
Prior, Carmelite Priory,
Kinsale,
Co Cork P17 WR88
Tel 021-4772138

llison, Robert (CSSp), Most
Rev
Holy Spirit Missionary
College
Kimmage Manor,
Whitehall Road,
Dublin D12 P5YP
Tel 01-4064300

mechebe, Anselm (MSP),
CC
Parochial House,
Kilsaran,
Castlebellingham,
Dundalk,
Co Louth A91 A256
Tel 042-9372255
(Kilsaran, Armagh)

merson, Sean, Very Rev,
Adm, VF
Parochial House,
3 Oriel Road,
Antrim BT41 4HP
Tel 028-94428016
(Antrim, St Comgall's and
St Joseph's, Down & C.)

mokhare, Christopher
(SMA)
African Missions,
Blackrock Road,
Cork T12 TD54
Tel 021-4292871

nglish, Mark, Very Rev, PP
Parochial House, Duleek,
Co Meath
Tel 041-9823205
Adm, Donore Parish
(Donore, Duleek, Meath)

Ennis, John Very Rev, PP
Parochial House,
78 St Mary's Road,
East Wall, Dublin 3
Tel 01-8742320
(East Wall-North Strand,
Dublin)

Enright, Ciarán, CC
(Dun Laoghaire, Glasthule,
Dublin)

Enright, Liam
5 Lifford Avenue,
Ballinacurra, Co Limerick
Tel 087-7415603
(Pastoral Unit 2, Limerick)

Enright, Liam, Very Rev, PP
St Nicholas Presbytery,
Westbury, Limerick
(Limerick, retired)

Enright, Michael, Very Rev,
PE
Dunabratlin, Annestown,
Co Waterford
(Waterford & L., retired)

Enright, Séamus (CSsR)
Superior, Mount Saint
Alphonsus, Limerick
Tel 061-315099

Escoto, Albert (SVD)
Praeses,
8 Teignmouth Road,
London, NW2 4HN
Tel 020-84528430

Esekon, Patrick (SPS)
Councillor, St Patrick's,
Kiltegan,
Co Wicklow W91 YO22
Tel 059-6473600

Esoy, Renato (SSS)
Blessed Sacrament Chapel,
20 Bachelors Walk,
Dublin 1
Tel 01-8724597

Etomike, Hilary, CC
The Presbytery,
St Martin de Porres Parish,
Firhouse Road West
Dublin 24 D24 K198
Tel 01-4510160
(Bohernabreena, Tallaght,
Oldbawn, Dublin)

Eustace, Conal, Very Rev
Canon, PP, VF
The Parochial House
Castlebar,
Co Mayo F31 YA29
Tel 094-9541784/9021844
(Castlebar, Tuam)

Eustace, Thomas, Very Rev
The Cools, Barntown,
Wexford
(Ferns, retired)

Evans, Ashley (SJ)
Director of Retreat House,
Manresa House,
426 Clontarf Road,
Dollymount, Dublin 3
Tel 01-8331352
Director, Sacred Space

Evans, Ian
c/o Archbishop's House,
Dublin 9
(Dublin)

Everard, Eugene, Venerable
Archdeacon, PP, VG
St Michael's Street,
Tipperary Town,
Co Tipperary
Tel 062-51536
(Templemore, Cashel & E.)

Everard, Liam, Very Rev, PP
The Parochial House,
Fethard, Clonmel,
Co Tipperary
Tel 052 6131178
(Fethard, Cashel & E.)

Eze, John (MSP), CC
St Mary's Athlone,
Co Westmeath
Tel 090-6472088
(Athlone, Ardagh & Cl.)

Ezenwata, Anastasius, PC
Parochail House,
Parish of the Assumption,
Booterstown, Co Dublin
(Booterstown, Dublin)

Ezenwegbu, Stephen, Very
Rev, PP
The Presbytery,
Elphin, Co Roscommon
Tel 071-9630486
(Aughrim, Elphin, Elphin)

F

Faber, Dixy, Very Rev, Adm
Parochial House, Kilcoona
Headford, Co Galway
Tel 089-9428637
(Caherlistrane
(Donaghpatrick and
Kilcoona), Tuam)

Fagan, Anthony, Very Rev,
PP
Knockbride, Bailieboro,
Co Cavan
Tel 042-9660112
(Knockbride, Kilmore)

Fagan, John (SDB)
Salesian House, Milford,
Castletroy, Limerick
Tel 061-330268/330914

Fagan, Patrick, Very Rev
Canon
Our Lady's Manor,
Bulloch Harbour,
Dalkey, Co Dublin
(Dublin, retired)

Faherty, Thomas (SMA)
African Missions,
Dromantine, Newry,
Co Down BT34 1RH
Tel 028-30821224

Fahey, Francis, CC
Ballintubber,
Claremorris, Co Mayo
(Tuam, retired)

Fallon, Kevin, Very Rev, PP,
VF
Parochial House,
Roscommon
Tel 090-662698
(Roscommon, Elphin)

Fallon, Vincent, (SSCC), Very
Rev, PP
Sacred Heart,
St John's Drive,
Clondalkin,
Dublin D22 W1W6
Tel 01-4570032
(Sruleen, Dublin)

Falloon, Joseph (MSC)
Woodview House,
Mount Merrion Avenue,
Blackrock, Co Dublin

Farnon, Damian CF
McKee Barracks, Dublin 7
Tel 086-2256794
(Dublin)

Farquhar, Anthony, Most
Rev, DD
Titular Bishop of Ermiana
and Former Auxiliary
Bishop of Down & Connor,
24 Fruithill Park,
Belfast BT11 8GE
Tel 028-90624252
(Down & C.)

Farquharson, Paul (SJ)
Vice-Superior,
St Francis Xavier's,
Upper Gardiner Street,
Dublin 1
Tel 01-8363411

Farragher, Michael, Very
Rev, PP
The Parochial House,
Carnacon, Claremorris,
Co Mayo
Tel 094-9360205
(Burriscarra and
Ballintubber, Tuam)

Farragher, Patrick, Very Rev,
Adm
The Presbytery, Tuam,
Co Galway H54 HR58
Tel 093-24250
(Tuam (Cathedral of the
Assumption), Tuam)

Farragher, Stephen, Very
Rev Canon, PP, VG
Parochial House,
Ballyhaunis,
Co Mayo F35 YY65
Tel 094-9630006
(Ballinlough (Kiltullagh),
Ballyhaunis (Annagh),
Tuam)

Farrell, Derek Very Rev
Canon, Moderator
Parochial House,
Main Street, Garristown,
Co Dublin A42 PF64
Tel 01-8412932
(Garristown, Naul,
Rolestown-Oldtown,
Dublin)

Farrell, Dermot, Most Rev, DD
Archbishop of Dublin,
Archbishop's House,
Drumcondra,
Dublin D09 H4C2
(Dublin)

Farrell, Fergus, Very Rev, PP
Windgap, Co Kilkenny
Tel 051-648111/
086-0782066
(Dunamaggan, Windgap, Ossory)

Farrell, Fergus, PC
St Laurence O'Toole's
Presbytery,
49 Seville Place, Dublin 1
Tel 01-8740796
(North Wall-Seville Place, Dublin)

Farrell, John, PEm
5 Ballyreagh Road,
Portrush, Co Antrim
(Derry, retired)

Farrell, Liam, CC
Moate, Co Westmeath
Tel 090-6481189
(Moate and Mount Temple, Ardagh & Cl.)

Farrell, Matthew (OP), PP
St Mary's Priory,
The Claddagh,
Galway
Tel 091-582884
(St Mary's, Galway)

Farrell, Patrick (OSA)
St Augustine's,
Taylor's Lane,
Ballyboden, Dublin 16
Tel 01-4241000

Farrell, Sean (CM)
Phibsboro, St Peter's,
Dublin 7
Tel 01-8389708/8389841

Farrell, William, Very Rev, CC
Parochial House,
St Joseph's, Glasthule,
Co Dublin
Tel 01-2801226
(Glasthule, Dublin)

Farrelly, Adrian (OP) Very Rev
St Catherine's,
Newry,
Co Down BT35 8BN
Tel 028-30262178

Farrelly, Pat, Very Rev, PP
Knocknagilla, New Inn,
Ballyjamesduff, Co Cavan
(Kilmore, retired)

Farrelly, Peter, Very Rev, AP
Parochial House,
Beauparc, Navan,
Co Meath
Tel 046-9024114
(Beauparc, Meath)

Farren, Desmond (MSC), CC
Sacred Heart Parish,
Western Road, Cork
Tel 021-4804120
(Sacred Heart, Cork & R.)

Farren, John, PP
Muff, Co Donegal
Tel 074-9384037
(Iskaheen (Iskaheen & Upper Moville), Derry)

Farren, Neil, PP
Chapelfield,
59 Laurel Hill,
Coleraine,
Co Derry BT51 3AY
Tel 028-70343130
(Coleraine (Dunboa, Macosquin and Aghadowney), Derry)

Farren, Paul, Adm
Parochial House,
St Eugene's Cathedral,
Derry BT48 9AP
Tel 028-71262894/
028-71365712
(Derry City, Derry)

Faruna, Pius, PC
c/o Parish Office,
Balgaddy Road, Lucan,
Co Dublin, K78 NH05
Tel 01-4572900
(Lucan South, Dublin)

Fasakin, Emmanuel (MSP), CC
Parochial House,
42 Abbey Street,
Armagh BT61 7D2
Tel 028-37522802
(Armagh, Armagh)

Faughnan, Cathal, PP
Keadue, Boyle,
Co Roscommon
Tel 071-9647212
(Keadue, Arigna & Ballyfarnon (Kilronan), Ardagh & Cl.)

Fay, Kevin, Adm, VF
(priest in residence)
The Presbytery,
Cavan Town, Co Cavan
Tel 049-4331404
(Cavan (Urney & Annagelliff), Kilmore)

Fazio, Joseph (LC)
Chaplain, Dublin Oak
Academy,
Kilcroney, Bray,
Co Wicklow
Tel 01-2863290

Fee, Benedict, Very Rev
Canon, PP, EV, VF
Teac na h'Ard Croise,
3 Cloghog Road,
Clonoe, Coalisland,
Co Tyrone, BT71 5EH
Tel 028-87749184
(Clonoe, Armagh)

Fee, Ian, Rev, CC
The Rock, Ballyshannon,
Co Donegal
Tel 071-9851221
(Magh Ene, Clogher)

Feehan, Dominic
Home of the Mother,
St Savior's Priory,
Bridge Street, Waterford
Tel 051-875061
(Waterford & L.)

Feehan, James (CP)
St Paul's Retreat,
Mount Argus, Dublin 6W
Tel 01-4992000

Feeney, Ciaran, Very Rev, Adm
200 Finaghy Road North,
Belfast BT11 9EG
Tel 028-90617519
(St Michael's, Down & C.)

Feeney, Derek, Very Rev
Canon, PP
Parochial House,
Craughwell, Co Galway
Tel 091-846057
(Craughwell, Galway)

Feeney, Joseph, Very Rev
Canon, AP
The Prochial House,
Ballinlough,
Co Roscommon F45 R208
Tel 094-9640155
(Ballinlough (Kiltullagh), Tuam)

Feeney, Paddy (SPS)
St Patrick's, Kiltegan,
Co Wicklow
Tel 059-6473600

Fegan, James, Very Rev, PP
Ballindaggin, Enniscorthy,
Co Wexford
Tel 053-9388559
(Ballindaggin, Ferns)

Fegan, P.J. (IC) (Priest in Charge)
Rathgormack,
Carrick-on-suir,
Co Waterford
Tel 051-646006
(Rathgormack, Waterford & L.)

Fehily, G. Thomas, Rt Rev
Mgr, PE
Hampstead Hospital,
Glasnevin, Dublin 11
(Dublin, retired)

Feighery, John (SVD)
133 North Circular Road,
Dublin 7
Tel 01-8386743

Fenlon, Thomas (SMA)
African Missions,
Blackrock Road,
Cork T12 TD54
Tel 021-4292871

Fennelly, Sean, Very Rev, PP
Chaplain, St John the
Baptist Community School
Barrysfarm, Hospital,
Co Limerick V35 YF53
Tel 061-383565
(Hospital, Cashel & E.)

Fennelly, William (OSB)
Glenstal Abbey, Murroe,
Co Limerick
Tel 061-386103

Fennessy, Ignatius (OFM)
Franciscan House of
Studies, Dún Mhuire,
Seafield Road,
Killiney, Co Dublin
Tel 01-2826760

Fergus, Austin, Very Rev
Canon, AP
The Parochial House,
Mayo Abbey, Claremorris,
Co Mayo F12 D6P9
Tel 094-9365086
(Mayo Abbey (Mayo and Rosslea), Tuam)

Ferguson, Christopher,
c/o Diocesan Offices,
St Eugene's Cathedral,
Francis Street,
Derry BT48 9AP
(Derry)

Ferris, Brendan, Very Rev, PP
Preston Hill,
Stamullen, Co Meath
Tel 01-8412647
(Meath)

Ferris, John, Co-PP
14 The Coral, The Grange,
Stillgorgan, Co Dublin
(Dublin, retired)

Ferris, Stephen, Very Rev, P
c/o Diocesan Office, Newr
(Dromore)

Ferry, Francis, CC
Mountcharles, Co Donega
Tel 074-9735009
(Inver, Raphoe)

Ferry, Manus (MSC)
Leader, Woodview House
Mount Merrion Avenue,
Blackrock, Co Dublin
Tel 01-2881644
Tallaght Hospital Pastoral
Care Team
Tel 01-4142485

Field, Raymond, Most Rev, DD
Auxiliary Bishop Emeritus
of Dublin,
Marymount Care Centre,
Westmanstown,
Lucan, Co Dublin
(Dublin)

Filima, Richard (SPS)
Society Leader,
St Patrick's,
Kiltegan,
Co Wicklow W91 YO22
Tel 059-6473600

illie, Michael (CSSp)
Holy Spirit Missionary
College
Kimmage Manor,
Whitehall Road,
Dublin D12 P5YP
Tel 01-4064300

inan, James, Very Rev
Canon, CC
Colloney, Co Sligo
Tel 071-9167109
(Collooney (Kilvarnet),
Achonry)

inegan, Peter (SPS)
St Patrick's, Kiltegan,
Co Wicklow W91 Y022
Tel 059-6473600

ingleton, James, Very Rev
Canon
279 Howth Road, Raheny,
Dublin 5
(Dublin, retired)

inn, Anthony (OSA), PP
St Augustine's Priory,
St Augustine's Street,
Galway
Tel 091-562524
(St Augustine's, Galway)

inn, John (MSC)
Leader,
Western Road,
Cork T12 TN80
Tel 021-4804120

inn, Tony (OSA)
St Augustine's Priory
St Augustine's Street
Co Galway
Rector Ecclesiae,
St Patrick's College and
Church,
Via Piemonte 60,
00187 Rome, Italy
Tel 00396-4203121

inn, William (OCD)
St Teresa's,
Clarendon Street, Dublin 2
Tel 01-6718466/6718127

nnegan, Eamonn (SMA)
Vice Provincial, African
Missions,
Provincial House, Feltrim,
Blackrock Road,
Cork T12 N6C8
Tel 021-4292871

nnegan, John (SDB)
Salesian House,
45 St Teresa's Road,
Crumlin, Dublin 12
Tel 01-4555605

nnegan, John, Very Rev
Canon, PE
51 Arney Road,
Mullymesker, Enniskillen,
Co Fermanagh BT92 2AB
Tel 028-66348217
(Arney (Cleenish), Clogher)

Finnegan, Vincent F. (OFM)
Vicar, Franciscan Friary,
Rossnowlagh, Co Donegal
F94 PH21
Tel 071-9851342

Finneran, Michael, Very Rev,
PP
Clontuskert, Ballinasloe,
Co Galway H53 CV99
Tel 090-9642256
(Clontuskert, Clonfert)

Finnerty, Liam (OCD)
Prior,
Avila Carmelite Centre,
Bloomfield Avenue,
Morehampton Road,
Dublin 4
Tel 01-6430200

Finnerty, Paul
Rector,
Pontifico Collegio
Irlandese,
Via dei Santi Quattro 1,
00184 Roma, Italy
Tel 0039-06-772631
(Limerick)

Finnerty, Peter, Very Rev, PP
Parochial House, Bayside
Square North,
Sutton, Dublin 13
Tel 01-8323150
(Bayside, Kilbarrack-
Foxfield, Dublin)

Finucane, Gerard, Very Rev,
PP
Our Lady of the Valley,
Cillin Liath
Tel 066-9474703
Moderator, Caherdaniel
Caherdaniel, Co Kerry
Tel 066-9475111
(Caherdaniel, Waterville
(Dromod), Kerry)

Fitzgerald, Brendan
St Barnabas Church,
409 East 241 Street,
Bronx, New York 10470,
USA

Fitzgerald, Christopher,
Very Rev, Co-PP
Moderator,
Parochial House,
Watergrasshill, Co Cork
Tel 021-4889103
(Carrignavar, Glanmire,
Glounthaune and
Watergrasshill, Cork & R.)

Fitzgerald, David (OSA)
The Abbey, Fethard,
Co Tipperary
Tel 052-31273

Fitzgerald, Eamon (OCSO),
Rt Rev Dom,
Abbot General,
Mount Melleray Abbey,
Cappoquin,
Co Waterford P51 R8XW
Tel 058-54404

Fitzgerald, Jack, Very Rev
Canon, PP
Millstreet, Co Cork
Tel 029-70043
Moderator, Dromtariffe
Dromagh, Mallow,
Co Cork
Tel 029-78096
(Dromtariffe, Millstreet,
Kerry)

Fitzgerald, John (MSC)
Western Road,
Cork T12 TN80
Tel 021-4804120

Fitzgerald, John, Very Rev,
PP
Abbeydorney, Co Kerry
Tel 066-7135146
(Abbeydorney, Kerry)

Fitzgerald, John, Very Rev,
PP
Parish Administrator
Rockhill, Bruree,
Co Limerick
087-6522746
(Limerick)

Fitzgerald, Joseph,
5 Hawthorn Park, Ballygar,
via Roscommon,
Co Galway
(Roscommon, Elphin)

Fitzgerald, Michael, Very
Rev, PP
Blarney, Co Cork
Tel 021-4385105
(Blarney, Cloyne)

Fitzgerald, Michael, Very
Rev Canon, PE
Garrycahera, Ballynoe,
Mallow, Co Cork
(Cloyne, retired)

Fitzgerald, Michael (OSA),
St Augustine's,
Taylor's Lane,
Ballyboden, Dublin 16
Tel 01-4241000

Fitzgerald, P.J. (SPS), CC
Mountrath, Co Laois
Tel 057-8732234
(Ballyfin/Mountrath,
Kildare & L.)

Fitzgerald, Patrick (CP), CC
St Paul's Retreat,
Mount Argus, Dublin 6W
Tel 01-4992000
(Mount Argus, Dublin)

Fitzgerald, Patrick, Very Rev,
PP
Parochial House,
Lisduggan, Waterford
Tel 051-372257
Priest in Charge,
Butlerstown Parish
(St Paul's, Waterford & L.)

Fitzgerald, Tadhg, Rt Rev
Mgr, VG
St John's Presbytery
Ballybunion, Co Kerry
Tel 066-7122522
Ardfert, Co Kerry
Tel 066-7134131
Ardfert Retreat Centre
Tel 066-7134276
(Kerry)

Fitzgibbon, John, Very Rev
Canon, PE
Parochial House,
Chapel Road, Lusk,
Co Dublin
Tel 01-8438023
(Dublin, retired)

Fitzgibbon, Michael (MSC)
Western Road,
Cork T12 TN80
Tel 021-4804120

Fitzharris, Kieran (SVD)
Our Lady of Sorrows & St
Bridget of Sweden
112 Twickenham Road
Ilseworth, TW7 6DL

Fitzmaurice, William,
Canon, Co-PP
Moderator,
Croom, Co Limerick
Tel 061-397231/
086-2423728
(Pastoral Unit 7, Limerick)

Fitzpatrick, Brian, Very Rev,
PP
The Presbytery,
11 Tullygally Road,
Legahory,
Craigavon BT65 5BL
Tel 028-38341901
(Moyraverty (Craigavon),
Seagoe (Derrymacash),
Shankill, St Paul's & St
Peter's (Lurgan), Dromore)

Fitzpatrick, Jeremiah (OCD)
Prior, St Joseph's
Carmelite Retreat Centre,
Termonbacca,
Derry BT48 9XE
Tel 028-71262512

Fitzpatrick, John, Very Rev,
PP
Carbury, Co Kildare
Tel 046-9553355
(Carbury, Kildare & L.)

Fitzpatrick, P.J., CC
6 St Ciaran Park,
Tullamore Road,
Shannonbridge,
Co Offaly
(Ardagh & Cl., retired)

Fitzpatrick, Tom, Co-PP
3 The Woods, Cappahard,
Tulla Road, Ennis, Co Clare
Tel 065-6822225/
087-2720187
(Abbey Pastoral Area,
Killaloe)

Fitzpatrick, William (OMI), Co-PP
Superior, Oblate Fathers, House of Retreat, Inchicore, Dublin 8
Tel 01-4541117
(*Inchicore, Mary Immaculate*, Dublin)

Fitzsimons, Anthony, Very Rev, PP
51 Bay Road, Carnlough, Ballymena,
Co Antrim BT44 0HJ
Tel 028-28885220
(*Carnlough, Glenarm (Tickmacreevan)*, Down & C.)

Fitzsimons, Patrick, Very Rev Canon
Holy Family Residence, Roebuck, Dundrum, Dublin 14
(Dublin, retired)

Fitzsimons, William, Very Rev, PP
Parochial House, Milltown, Rathconrath, Co Westmeath
Tel 044-9355106
(*Milltown*, Meath)

Flaherty, John, Very Rev Canon, VF, Co-PP
St Anne's, Strand Road, Portmarnock, Co Dublin
Tel 01-8461081
(*Portmarnock*, Dublin)

Flaherty, Raymond, Very Rev, PP
The Parochial House, Headford,
Co Galway H91 PXH5
Tel 093-35448
(*Headford (Killursa and Killower)*, Tuam)

Flanagan, Benny, PE
14 Kilgarve Gardens, Creagh, Ballinasloe, Co Galway
(Clonfert, retired)

Flanagan, Eamon (CM)
Phibsboro, St Peter's, Dublin 7
Tel 01-8389708/8389841

Flanagan, John, Very Rev, PP
Ballyoisin, Emyvale, Co Monaghan H18 F207
Tel 047-87152
(*Errigal Truagh*, Clogher)

Flanagan, Malachy (SMA)
Provincial, African Missions,
Provincial House, Feltrim, Blackrock Road,
Cork T12 N6C8
Tel 021-4292871

Flanagan, Padraig Rev (SPS)
St Patrick's, Kiltegan, Co Wicklow W91 Y022

Flanagan, Richard, PP, VF
Ballyvaughan, Co Clare
Tel 065-7077045
(*Ballyvaughan*, Galway)

Flannery, Anthony (CSsR)
Mount St Alphonsus, South Circular Road, Limerick
Tel 061-315099

Flannery, John D., Very Rev Canon, PE
Cartron, Milltown, Co Galway H54 YD54
(Tuam, retired)

Flannery, Paschal, Very Rev
Ballinderry, Nenagh, Co Tipperary
Tel 067-22916/
086-2225099
(Killaloe, retired)

Flatley, Alphonsus (SMA)
African Missions, Blackrock Road, Cork T12 TD54
Tel 021-4292871

Flattery, Michael (SMA), CC
364 Sundays Well, Naas, Co Kildare
Tel 045-876197
(*Naas*, Kilare & L.)

Flavin, John P. (CSSp)
Holy Spirit Missionary College
Kimmage Manor, Whitehall Road, Dublin D12 P5YP
Tel 01-4064300

Fleck, Robert, Very Rev, PP
Parochial House, Dundrum, Newcastle, Co Down BT33 0LU
Tel 028-43751212
(*Dundrum and Tyrella*, Down & C.)

Fleming, David, CC
87 Beechwood Lawns, Rathcoole, Co Dublin
Tel 01-4587187
(*Newcastle, Saggart/ Rathcoole/Brittas*, Dublin)

Fleming, Gerard (SAC)
Parochial House, Sperrin Road, Drimnagh, Dublin 12
Tel 01-4556103
(*Mourne Road*, Dublin)

Fleming, John Kevin (MSC)
(Resident elsewhere)

Fleming, John, Most Rev, DD, DCL
Bishop of Killala, Bishop's House, Ballina, Co Mayo
Tel 096-21518
(Killala)

Fleming, Joseph, Very Rev, CC
Clonegal, Enniscorthy, Co Wexford
Tel 053-9377298
(*Clonegal*, Kildare & L.)

Fleming, Kevin (SSC)
St Columban's, Dalgan Park, Navan, Co Meath
Tel 046-9021525
(Meath)

Fleming, Paul, BA, BD, STL, PhD
St Mary's University College, 191 Falls Road, Belfast 12 6FE
Tel 028-90327678
(Down & C.)

Fletcher, Robert, CC,
New Inn, Cashel, Co Tipperary
Tel 086-1927455
(*New Inn*, Cashel & E.)

Flood, Jonathan, CC
c/o Diocesan Office, Letterkenny, Co Donegal
(Raphoe)

Flores, Atanasio (OP)
Dominican Community, St Mary's Priory, Tallaght, Dublin 24
Tel 01-4048100

Flynn, Brian, CC
Knocktemple, Virginia, Co Cavan
Tel 049-8547435
(*Castlerahan and Munterconnaught*, Kilmore)

Flynn, Edward (CSSp)
Community Leader, Spiritan House, 213 North Circular Road, Dublin 7
01-8389664

Flynn, Gabriel, TA
1 The Presbytery, Greenfield Road, Sutton, Dublin 13
(*Sutton*, Dublin)
(Meath)

Flynn, Joseph, Very Rev, PP
Ballyporeen, Cahir, AP Co Tipperary
Tel 052-7467105
(*Ballyporeen*, Waterford & L.)

Flynn, Laurence, Rt Rev Mgr, Adm
Priest's House, Main Street, Pettigo, Co Donegal F94 FYN7
Tel 071-9861666
(*Pettigo*, Clogher)

Flynn, Michael, Very Rev, PP
Christ the King Church, Knockmore, Ballina, Co Mayo
Tel 094-9258108
(*Backs*, Killala)

Flynn, Nicholas, Very Rev
Diocesan Secretary, Bishop's House, Killarney, Co Kerry
Tel 064-6631168
(Kerry)

Flynn, Patrick (OFMCap)
Capuchin Presence
Our Lady of Knock Shrine, Knock, Co Mayo

Flynn, Paul (OSA)
St Augustine's Priory
O'Connell Street, Co Limerick

Flynn, Seán, CC
The Presbytery, Dublin Road, Tuam, Co Galway H54 HR58
Tel 093-24250
(*Tuam (Cathedral of the Assumption)*, Tuam)

Flynn, Thomas, Very Rev, PP
Carrickbeg, Carrick-on-Suir, Co Tipperary
Tel 051-640340
(*Carrickbeg*, Waterford & L.)

Flynn, Timothy (OSM)
Director, St Peregrine Ministry
Servite Priory, St Peregrine, 36 Grangewood Estate, Rathfarnham, Dublin 16
Tel 01-4936755

Flynn, Tomás, PP
Drumcong, Carrick-on-Shannon, Co Leitrim
Tel 071-9642021
(*Kiltubrid*, Ardagh & Cl.)

Flynn, William, PP
St Patrick's, Gorey, Co Wexford
Tel 053-9421117
(*Gorey*, Ferns)

Fogarty, Pat, Very Rev, Co-PP
Glanmire, Co Cork
Tel 021-4866307
(*Carrignavar, Glanmire, Glounthaune and Watergrasshill*, Cork & R.)

Fogarty, Thomas, Very Rev, PP
Ballydavid, Littleton, Thurles, Co Tipperary
Tel 0504-44317
(*Moycarkey*, Cashel & E.)

Fokchet, Augustine, PC
St Mary's, Donabate, Co Dublin
Tel 01-8434604
(*Donabate*, Dublin)

Foley, Declan, Very Rev, PP
Bagenalstown, Co Carlow
Tel 059-9721154
(*Muinebheag/
Bagenalstown*, Kildare &
L.)

Foley, Denis, Very Rev, PE
c/o Archbishop's House,
Dromcondra, Dublin 9
(Dublin, retired)

Foley, Dermot (SPS)
St Patrick's, Kiltegan,
Co Wicklow W91 Y022
Tel 059-6473600

Foley, Desmond (OSA)
Prior & Bursar,
St Augustine's Priory,
St Augustine's Street,
Galway
Tel 091-562524

Foley, Eamon, Very Rev, PE
6 Woodlawn, Archers
Avenue, Kilkenny
Tel 087-7828784
(Ossory, retired)

Foley, Joseph (SMA)
African Missions,
Blackrock Road,
Cork T12 TD54
Tel 021-4292871

Foley, Michael F. (SSCC)
Coudrin House,
27 Northbrook Road,
Dublin 6
Tel 01-6473759

Foley, Niall, BSc, BD, HDE
Vice-President,
St Joseph's College,
Garbally Park, Ballinasloe,
Co Galway H62 AR27
Tel 090-9642504/9642254
(Clonfert)

Foody, Michael (CSSp)
Holy Spirit Missionary
College
Kimmage Manor,
Whitehall Road,
Dublin D12 P5YP
Tel 01-4064300

Forbes, John Pem
19 Rathmore Crescent,
Derry BT48 9RL
(Derry, retired)

Ford, Seán (OCarm), Very
Rev, PP, VF
Our Lady of Mount Carmel
Parish,
Whitefriar Street Church,
56 Aungier Street,
Dublin 2
(*Whitefriar Street*, Dublin)

Forde, Denis, Very Rev
Tigh an tSagairt,
Clogheen, Cork
(Cork & R.)

Forde, Des, CC
Curate's House, Sea Park,
Lahinch, Co Clare
Tel 065-7081307
(*Ennistymon*, Galway)

Forde, Michael (CSsR)
Scala, Castlemahon House,
Castle Road,
Blackrock, Cork
Tel 021-4358800

Forde, Tom (OFMCap)
Capuchin Friary,
Ard Mhuire,
Creeslough, Letterkenny,
Co Donegal
Tel 074-9138005

Foret, Gregory M. (OSB)
119 Kilbroney Road,
Rostrevor,
Co Down BT34 3BN
Tel 028-41739979

Forster, Stephen (MI)
Superior and Provincial,
St Camillus,
4 St Vincent Street North,
Dublin 7
Tel 01-8300365

Forsythe, John, Very Rev, PP
Parochial House,
1 Craigstown Road,
Randalstown,
Co Antrim BT41 2AF
Tel 028-94472640
(*Randalstown*, Down & C.)

Fortune, Carlyle (OP)
Dominican College,
Newbridge
Droichead Nua, Co Kildare
Tel 045-487200

Fortune, William, PC
32 Newtownpark Avenue,
Blackrock, Co Dublin
Tel 01-2100337
(*Newtownpark*, Dublin)

Fox, Gerard, Very Rev
Lisbreen,
75 Somerton Road,
Belfast BT15 4DE
Tel 028-90776185
(Down & C.)

Fox, John, Very Rev, PP
Parochial House,
153 Aughrim Road,
Toomebridge,
Antrim BT41 3SH
Tel 028-79468277
(*Newbridge*, Armagh)

Francis, Britus Kadavunkal,
Very Rev, Adm
Aughagower, Westport,
Co Mayo F28 PH61
Tel 098-25057
(*Aughagower*, Tuam)

Fraser, Paul, PP
16 Castlefin Road,
Castlederg
Co Tyrone BT81 7BT
Tel 028-81670728
(*Castlederg (Ardstraw
West and Castlederg)*,
Aghyaran
(*Termonamongan*), Derry)

Frawley, Bernard M. (CSSp)
Rockwell College,
Cashel, Co Tipperary
Tel 062-61444

Freeman, Brendan (OCSO),
Rt Rev, Dom, Superior
Mellifont Abbey,
Collon, Co Louth
Tel 041-9826103

French, Gerry (SSC)
St Columban's,
Dalgan Park,
Navan, Co Meath
Tel 046-9021525
(Dublin)

Friel, James, Very Rev
Canon, PE
Massreagh, Rathmullan,
Co Donegal
Tel 074-9158306
(Raphoe, retired)

Friel, John (CP)
Superior,
Holy Cross Retreat,
432 Crumlin Road,
Ardoyne,
Belfast BT14 7GE
Tel 028-90748231
(*Holy Cross*, Down & C.)

Fuentes, Alejandro (LC)
Chaplain,
Woodlands Academy,
Wingfield House, Bray,
Co Wicklow
Tel 01-2866323

Fuh, Damien Afuti (MHM)
St Joseph's House,
50 Orwell Park, Rathgar,
Dublin 6
Tel 01-4127700

Fulton, Raymond, Very Rev,
PP
4 Gortanclochair Park,
Ballycastle BT54 6NV
(Down & C., retired)

Fulton, William (SSC)
St Patrick's, Kiltegan,
Co Wicklow
Tel 059-6473600

Furlong, James, Very Rev
Tomgarrowm,
Adamstown,
Co Wexford
(Ferns, retired)

Furlong, Odhrán
Chaplain to Wexford
General Hospital,
Newton Road, Wexford
Tel 053-9142233
(Ferns)

Furlong, Senan (OSB), Very
Rev
Prior, Glenstal Abbey,
Murroe, Co Limerick
Tel 061-621000

Furlong, Shem
Muinebheag Parish Office,
Bagenalstown, Co Carlow
Tel 087-2400582
(*Muinebheag/
Bagenalstown*, Kildare &
L.)

Furlong, Tadhg, Very Rev,
PP
Cappawhite, Co Tipperary
Tel 062-75427
(*Cappawhite*, Cashel & E.)

G

Gaffney, Matthew (IC)
Rector, Clonturk House,
Ormond Road,
Drumcondra, Dublin 9
Tel 01-6877014

Gaffney, Philip, Very Rev,
Adm
Cathedral House,
Mullingar, Co Westmeath
Tel 044-9348338/9340126
(*Mullingar*, Meath)

Gahan, Dermot
c/o PO Box 40, Bishop's
House, Wexford
(Ferns)

Gahan, James, Very Rev, PE
c/o Bishop's House, Carlow
(Kildare & L., retired)

Gahan, Raymond, Very Rev,
PP
Killaveney, Tinahely,
Co Wicklow
Tel 0402-38188
(*Killaveney and
Crossbridge*, Ferns)

Galaz Carvajal, Juan Diego
(SJ)
35 Lower Leeson Street,
Dublin 2
Tel 01-6761248

Gallagher, Brendan, PP
146 Ballagh Road,
Fivemiletown,
Co Tyrone BT75 0QP
Tel 028-89521291
(*Brookeboro (Aghavea-
Aghintaine)*, Clogher)

Gallagher, Daniel, Adm
Teach an Sagairt,
An Spidéal,
Co na Gaillimhe
Tel 091-553155
(*An Spidéal*, Galway)

Gallagher, Declan, CC
No. 3 Prebytery,
Castle Street, Dalkey,
Co Dublin
Tel 01-2859212
(*Dalkey*, Dublin)

Gallagher, Denis
c/o Archbishop's House,
Tuam
(Tuam)

Gallagher, Dermot (CP)
St Paul's Retreat,
Mount Argus, Dublin 6W
Tel 01-4992000

Gallagher, Edward, PP
Parochial House, Moville,
Co Donegal
Tel 074-9382057
(Moville (Moville Lower),
Derry)

Gallagher, Edward, Very
Rev, AP
Leitrimacaward,
Co Donegal
Tel 074-9544102
(Dungloe (Templecrone
and Lettermacaward)
Raphoe)

Gallahger, Frank (MSC)
Woodview House,
Mount Merrion Avenue,
Blackrock, Co Dublin
Tel 01-2881644

Gallagher, John (CM)
St Paul's, Raheny,
Dublin 5
Tel 01-8318113

Gallagher, John, (SMA), CC
African Missions,
Dromantine, Newry,
Co Down BT34 1RH
Tel 028-30821224

Gallagher, John, Very Rev
Canon, PE,
Ardara, Co Donegal
Tel 087-6636434
(Raphoe, retired)

Gallagher, Joseph, Very Rev,
PP, VG
Parochial House,
Tullamore, Co Offaly
Tel 057-9321587
(Tullamore, Meath)

Gallagher, Laurence (CSsR)
Mount Saint Alphonsus,
South Circular Road,
Limerick
Tel 061-315099

Gallagher, Malachy, CC
44 Barrack Street,
Strabane
Co Tyrone BT82 8HD
(Melmount (Mourne),
Sion Hills, Derry)

Gallagher, Michael O. (SJ)
35 Lower Leeson Street,
Dublin 2
Tel 01-6761248

Gallagher, Peter, Very Rev,
PP
Lavagh, Ballymote,
Co Sligo
Tel 071-9184002
(Achonry, Achonry)

Gallagher, Raphael (CSsR)
Mount Saint Alphonsus,
South Circular Road,
Limerick
Tel 061-315099

Gallagher, Shane, CC
1 Chaplain's House,
Knocknamona,
Letterkenny, Co Donegal
Tel 074-9125888 (Hospital)
(Letterkenny (Conwal and
Leck), Raphoe)

Gallagher, Thomas
Cloughmore,
Achill, Co Mayo
(Tuam)

Gallahue, Walter (OFM)
Franciscan Friary,
Killarney, Co Kerry
Tel 064-6631334/6631066

Gallinagh, Padraic, Very Rev
'Polperro',
8 Beverley Close,
Newtownards BT23 7FN
(Down & C., retired)

Gallogley, Vincent (OFM)
Franciscan Friary,
Rossnowlagh, Co Donegal
Tel 071-9851342

Galvin, Aidan (CM)
St Joseph's,
44 Stillorgan Park,
Blackrock,
Co Dublin A94 PC62
Tel 01-2886961

Galvin, Gerald (OCarm)
Carmelite Community,
Gort Muire, Ballinteer,
Dublin D16 EI67
Tel 01-2984014

Galvin, Ignatius (OFMCap)
Capuchin Friary,
Holy Trinity,
Fr Mathew Quay,
Cork T12 PK24
Tel 021-4270827

Galvin, John, PE
Passage West, Co Cork
Tel 021-4841267
(Monkstown, Passage
West, Cork & R.)

Galvin, John
60 Lower Mount Pleasant
Avenue,
Rathmines, Dublin 6
(Dublin, retired)

Gannan, John
St James' Apts,
Knock, Co Mayo F12 HE19
(Knock, Tuam)

Gannon, John, Very Rev, PP
Parochial House, Tulsk,
Co Roscommon
Tel 071-9639005
(Tulsk, Elphin)

Gannon, John J., Very Rev,
PE
Parochial House
Elphin, Co Rosscommon
Tel 071-9635058
(Elphin, Elphin)

Gannon, Peter, Very Rev, PP
Dalton Street, The
Presbytery, Claremorris,
Co Mayo F12 X8C2
Tel 094-9362477
(Claremorris (Kilcolman),
Tuam)

Gardiner, Seamus, Very Rev
Portroe, Nenagh,
Co Tipperary
Tel 067-23101/
086-8392741
(Killaloe, retired)

Garland, Sean, Very Rev, PP
Parochial House,
Clonmellon, Navan,
Co Meath
Tel 046-9433124
(Clonmellon, Meath)

Garrett, Gerard, Very Rev
Canon, Moderator
1 Trinity Court,
Monaleen Road,
Monaleen, Limerick,
Tel 061-330974/
086-3233268
(Pastoral Unit 1, Limerick)

Garry, John (SPS)
St Patrick's, Kiltegan,
Co Wicklow
Tel 059-6473600

Garvey, Colin (OFM)
Franciscan Friary,
Liberty Street,
Cork T12 D376
Tel 021-4270302/4275481

Garvey, Francis, PP
Carrick-on-Shannon,
Co Leitrim
Tel 071-9620118
(Carrick-on-Shannon,
Ardagh & Cl.)

Garvey, John, Very Rev, PP
St Michael's Presbytery,
Ballinasloe,
Co Galway H53 EC98
Tel 090-9643916
(Ballinasloe, Creagh and
Kilclooney, Clonfert)

Garvey, John, Very Rev, PE
Clonbur Road,
Ballinrobe,
Co Mayo F31 WF70
(Tuam, retired)

Gates, John, Very Rev, PP,
VF
Parochial House,
30 King Street,
Magherafelt,
Co Derry BT45 6AS
Tel 028-79632439
(Magherafelt and Ardtrea
North, Armagh)

Gaughan, J. Anthony, Very
Rev Canon, PE
56 Newtownpark Avenue,
Blackrock, Co Dublin
(Dublin, retired)

Gavazzi, Francesco (CFR)
Local Servant (Superior),
St Columba Friary,
Fairview Road,
Derry, BT48 8NU
Tel 028-71419980

Gavigan, Adrian, PP
Parochial House,
Lisminton, Ballintra,
Co Donegal
Tel 074-9734642
(Ballintra, Raphoe)

Gavigan, James
30 Knapton Road,
Dun Laoghaire, Co Dublin
Tel 01-2804353
(Opus Dei)

Gavigan, Joseph, Very Rev,
PP
Parochial House,
Kilmovee,
Ballaghadereen, Co Mayo
Tel 094-9649137
(Kilmovee, Achonry)

Gavin, Aiden (CM)
St Paul's, Sybil Hill,
Raheny, Dublin D05 AE38
Tel 01-8318113

Gavin, Denis J. (CSSp)
Holy Spirit Missionary
College,
Kimmage Manor,
Whitehall Road, Dublin 12
Tel 01-4064300

Gavin, Fintan, Most Rev, DD
Bishop of Cork and Ross,
Cork and Ross Offices,
Redemption Road, Cork
Tel 021-4301717
(Cork & R.)

Gavin, Tony, Very Rev, PP
c/o Bishop's House,
Dublin Road, Mullingar,
Co Westmeath N91 DW32
(Meath)

Gayer, Pat (OSA)
St John's Priory,
Thomas Street, Dublin 8
Tel 01-6770393

Gaynor, Harry, Very Rev,
Co-PP
112 Ballygall Road East,
Glasnevin, Dublin 11
Tel 01-8342248
(Ballygall, Dublin)

Geaney, Niall, PP
Fossa, Killinary, Co Kerry
Tel 064-6631996
(Fossa, Kerry)

Gear, Patrick, Very Rev, CC
14 Heathervue Road,
Riverview,
Knockboy, Co Waterford
Tel 051-820452
(Ss Joseph and Benildus,
Waterford and L.)

Geary, Ronan (SJ)
c/o 35 Lower Leeson
Street, Dublin 2
Tel 01-6761248

Geelan, John, Very Rev, PP
Parochial House,
Bonniconlon,
Ballina, Co Mayo
Tel 096-45016
(*Bonniconlon*, Achonry)

Geoghegan, Alan (SVD)
133 North Circular Road,
Dublin 7
Tel 01-8386743

Geoghegan, Brian, Very Rev
Carrigoran Nursing Home
Newmarket On Fergus,
Co Clare
Tel 087-2387067
(Killaloe, retired)

Geoghegan, Francis (SMA)
African Missions,
Blackrock Road,
Cork T12 TD54
Tel 021-4292871

George, Roy, PC
500 South Circular Road,
Rialto, Dublin 8
(*Rialto/Dolphin's Barn*,
Dublin)

Geraghty, Cathal, Rt Rev
Mgr, PP, VG
Chancellor,
The Presbytery, Loughrea,
Co Galway H62 YE09
Tel 091-841212
Moderator, Kilnadeema
and Aille,
Administrator, Kiltullagh,
Killimordaly and
Clooncagh
(*Loughrea, St Brendan's
Cathedral,
Kilnadeema and Aille
(Kilnadeema and
Kilteskill),
Kiltullagh, Killimordaly
and Clooncagh*, Clonfert)

Geraghty, Gerard, Very Rev,
PP
Aughrim, Ballinasloe,
Co Galway H53 PY13
Tel 090-9673724
(*Aughrim and Kilconnell*,
Clonfert)

Geraghty, Martin (MI)
St Camillus, Killucan,
Co Westmeath
Tel 044-74196/044-74115

Geraghty, Michael, Co-PP
The Presbytery,
Church Road,
Nenagh, Co Tipperary
Tel 067-37134/0879926519
(*Odhran Pastoral Area*,
Killaloe)

Gesla, Marceli (OFM)
Chaplain to Polish
Community,
Franciscan Friary,
Killarney, Co Kerry
Tel 064-6631334/6631066

Ghent, William (SMA)
African Missions,
Blackrock Road,
Cork T12 TD54
Tel 021-4292871

Gibbons, Danny (SPS)
St Patrick's,
21 Leeson Park,
Dublin D06 DE76
Tel 01-4977897

Gibbons, Richard, Very Rev,
PP
The Presbytery,
Knock Shrine,
Knock, Co Mayo
Tel 094-9388100
(*Knock*, Tuam)

Gibson, David, Moderator
Parochial House,
Ballyagran,
Kilmallock, Co Limerick
Tel 087-2528738
(*Pastoral Unit 8*, Limerick)

Gibson, Steve (CSC)
Fr Patrick Peyton Centre,
Attymass,
Co Mayo
Tel 096-45374

Gilbert, Patrick, Co-PP, VF
Maryville, Church Road,
Nenagh, Co Tipperary
Tel 067-31272
(*Odhran Pastoral Area*,
Killaloe)

Gilcreest, Martin
Laragh, Stradone,
Co Cavan
Tel 049-4330142
(*Laragh*, Kilmore)

Gildea, Peter (CM), Very Rev
99 Cliftonville Road,
Belfast BT14 6JQ
Tel 028-90751771

Gildea, Seán (OFM)
Drumderrig House Nursing
Home,
Abbeytown, Boyle,
Co Rosscommon F52 RC95

Gilhooly, Anthony, CC
The Presbytery, Longford
Tel 043-3346465
(*Longford
(Templemichael,
Ballymacormack)*, Ardagh
& Cl.)

Gilhooly, John, Very Rev, PP
Manorhamilton,
Co Leitrim
Tel 071-9855042
(*Cloonclare and Killasnet*,
Kilmore)

Gill, Patrick, Very Rev
Louisburgh, Co Mayo
(Tuam, retired)

Gill, Anthony (SMA)
Apt 1, Parochial House,
Balbriggan, Co Dublin
Tel 087-3695332
(*Balbriggan*, Dublin)

Gillan, Hugh (OH)
St John of God Hospital,
Stillorgan, Co Dublin
Tel 01-2771400
(Dublin)

Gillespie, Anthony, Very Rev
Cathedral Presbytery,
Ballina, Co Mayo
Tel 096-71365
(*Ballina (Kilmoremoy)*,
Killala)

Gillespie, Gerard, Very Rev,
PE
Rathball, Ballina,
Co Mayo
(Killala, retired)

Gillespie, James, Very Rev,
PP
Falcarragh, Co Donegal
Tel 074-9135196
(*Falcarragh*, Raphoe)

Gillespie, Kevin, Mgr, Adm,
VF
Parochial House,
Letterkenny,
Co Donegal
Tel 074-9121021
(*Letterkenny*, Raphoe)

Gillespie, Noel (SMA)
SMA House,
81 Ranelagh Road,
Ranelagh, Dublin 6
Tel 01-4968162/3

Gilligan, John, Very Rev,
Moderator, VF
St Mary's Parochial House,
Saggart, Co Dublin
Tel 087-4103239
(*Newcastle*, Dublin)

Gillooly, Dominick, Very
Rev, PE
St Anne's, Sligo
(Elphin, retired)

Gillooly, Reginald (CSSp)
Holy Spirit Missionary
College
Kimmage Manor,
Whitehall Road,
Dublin D12 P5YP
Tel 01-4064300

Gilmore, John (SSC)
St Columban's, Dalgan
Park, Navan, Co Meath
Tel 046-9021525

Gilmore, John, PE
(Derry, retired)

Gilmore, Sean, Very Rev, PP
Parochial House,
284 Glassdrumman Road,
Annalong, Newry,
Co Down BT34 4QN
Tel 028-43768208
(*Lower Mourne*, Down &
C.)

Gilroy, Michael, Very Rev
Dr, DD, PP
Skreen, Co Sligo
Tel 071-9166629
(*Skreen and Dromard,
Templeboy*, Killala)

Gilroy, Thomas, Very Rev,
PP, VF
Parochial House,
Kinnegad, Co Westmeath
Tel 044-9375117
Adm, Longwood
Tel 087-1723903
(*Kinnegad, Longwood*,
Meath)

Gilsenan, Michael (SSCC), CC
Gallonreagh,
Maudabawn, Cootehill,
Co Cavan H16 K576
(*Cootehill (Drumgoon)*,
Kilmore)

Gilton, Michael, CC
48 Aughrim Street,
Dublin 7
Tel 01-8386176
(*Aughrim Street*, Dublin)

Ginnelly, Christopher, Very
Rev, PP
Parochial House, Ballycroy,
Westport, Co Mayo
Tel 098-49134
(*Ballycroy*, Killala)

Gleeson, Martin, Very Rev
Canon, PE
Tuam, Co Galway
(Tuam, retired)

Gleeson, Padraig, Adm
St Kevin's Presbytery,
Pearse Street, Sallynoggin,
Co Dublin
Tel 01-2854667
(*Sallynoggin*, Dublin)

Gleeson, Patrick
14 Deerpark Road,
Mount Merrion,
Dublin A94 Y0C1
(Dublin, retired)

Gleeson, Philip (OP)
St Mary's Priory, Tallaght,
Dublin 24
Tel 01-4048100

Glennon, Francis, Very Rev
11 Convent Court,
Roscommon
(Elphin, retired)

Glennon, Paul, PP
162 Walkinstown Road,
Dublin 12 D12 YOF1
Tel 01-4501372
(*Walkinstown*, Dublin)

Glynn, Cronan (OCD)
The Abbey, Loughrea,
Co Galway
Tel 091-841209

Glynn, Enda, Very Rev
c/o 13 Lios Na Mara,
Station Road, Lahinch,
Co Clare
(Galway, retired)

Glynn, John, Very Rev, PP
Parochial House,
Tourlestrane, Ballymote,
Co Sligo
Tel 071-9181105
(*Tourlestrane
(Kilmactigue)*, Achonry)

Glynn, Martin, Very Rev
Canon, PP
Parochial House, Mervue,
Galway
Tel 091-751721/
087-2527124
Administrator, Ballybane
(Ballybane, Good
Shepherd, Mervue,
Galway)

Goaley, Michael, Very Rev
Canon, PE,
Corrandulla, Co Galway
(Tuam, retired)

Godley, Gearóid
John Paul II Pastoral
Centre, Rock Road,
Killarney, Co Kerry
Tel 064-6632644
(Kerry)

Gogan, Brian M. (CSSp)
Holy Spirit Missionary
College
Kimmage Manor,
Whitehall Road,
Dublin D12 P5YP
Tel 01-4064300

Goncalves de Lima, Eridian
(CSsR)
Santa Maria dei Monti
Mission,
Furancungo,
Mozambique, Africa
c/o Marianella,
75 Orwell Road,
Rathgar, Dublin 6
Tel 01-4067100

Gonoude, Anthony, Very
Rev, PP
Parochial House,
Ballynacargy,
Co Westmeath
Tel 044-9373923
(Ballynacargy, Meath)

Gonzalez-Borrallo, Juan
Jesus, CC
Parochial House,
12 Aughrim Road,
Magherafelt,
Co Derry BT45 6AY
Tel 077-36955013
(Magherafelt and Ardtrea
North, Armagh)

Goode, John (CSsR)
Mount Saint Alphonsus,
Limerick
Tel 061-315099

Goode, Richard (OSA)
St John's Priory,
Thomas Street, Dublin 8
Tel 01-6770393

Goold, Eamonn, Rt Rev Mgr,
PE,
Midleton, Co Cork
Tel 021-4633659
(Cloyne, retired)

Gorevan, Patrick
Harvieston,
Cunningham Road,
Dalkey, Co Dublin
Tel 01-2859877
(Opus Dei)

Gormally, Michael, Very
Rev, PP
Parochial House,
Ballinrobe, Co Mayo
Tel 094-9541085/541784
Administration for
Kilmaine
(Ballinrobe, Kilmaine,
Tuam)

Gorman, Owen, (OCDS), CC
(Priest in Residence)
Priest's House,
Shantonagh,
Castleblayney,
Co Monaghan A75 NN12
Tel 042-9745015
(Aughnamullen East,
Clogher)

Gorman, Seán, Very Rev,
Ballask, Kilmore,
Co Wexford
(Ferns, retired)

Gorman, Stephen, CC
Parochial House,
Milford, Co Donegal
Tel 074-9153236
(Rathmullan (Killygarvan
and Tullyfern), Raphoe)

Gormey, Frank (OMI)
Oblate House of Retreat,
Inchicore, Dublin 8
Tel 01-4534408/4541805

Gormley, Joseph, PP
1 Aileach Road,
Ballymagroarty,
Derry BT48 0AZ
Tel 028-71267070
(Holy Family,
Ballymagroarty, Derry)

Gough, Brian
Chaplain,
St James's Hospital,
James's Street, Dublin 8
Tel 01-4103659/4162023
(Dublin)

Gould, Daniel, Very Rev, PE
Ballindangan,
Mitchelstown, Co Cork
(Cloyne, retired)

Grace, Edmond (SJ)
St Francis Xavier's,
Upper Gardiner Street,
Dublin 1
Tel 01-8363411

Grace, James, Very Rev, Co-
PP
Parochial House, Killaloe,
Co Clare
Tel 061-376137/
087-6843315
(Scáth na Sionnaine
Pastoral Area, Killaloe)

Grace, John (OSA)
On assignment in USA

Grace, Ned (SPS)
St Patrick's, Kiltegan,
Co Wicklow
Tel 059-6473600

Graham, Eamon, PP
65 Mayogall Road,
Knockloughrim,
Magherafelt,
Co Derry BT45 8PG
Tel 028-7964248
(Lavey (Termoneeny and
part of Maghera), Derry)

Graham, Martin, Very Rev,
PP, Adm
81 Lagmore Grove,
Dunmurry,
Belfast BT17 0TD
Tel 028-90309011
Cathedral Presbytery,
St Peter's Square,
Belfast BT12 4BU
Tel 028-90327573
(Down & C.)

Graham, Patrick (OCarm)
Whitefriar Street Church,
56 Aungier Street,
Dublin 2 D02 R598
Tel 01-4758821

Grant, Colin, MA, STL, PGCE
Diocesan Ecumenical
Commission,
Aquinas Grammar School,
518 Ravenhill Road,
Belfast BT6 0BY
Tel 028-90643939
(Down & C.)

Grant, Henry (SJ)
c/o Milltown Park,
Miltown Road, Dublin 6
Tel 01-2698411/2698113

Grant, Robert, Very Rev, PP
Parochial House,
Fenor, Co Waterford
Tel 051-376032
(St Saviour's, Waterford &
L.)

Greed, Patrick, Very Rev,
Co-PP, VF
Parochial House,
Templemore Road,
Cloughjordan, Co Clare
Tel 0505-42266/
086-6067003
(Ollatrim Pastoral Area,
Killaloe)

Green, Gerard
c/o Bishop's House, Newry,
Co Down
(Dromore, retired)

Greenan, Thomas (SPS)
St Patrick's
Kiltegan, Co Wicklow
Tel 059-6473600

Greene, James (White
Fathers)
c/o Cypress Grove Road,
Templeogue, Dublin 6W
Tel 01-4055263

Greene, James, Adm
Clondrohid, Macroom,
Co Cork
Tel 085-8471249
(Clondrohid, Cloyne)

Greene, John, CC
Parochial House,
St Kevin's Parish,
Laragh, Glendalough,
Co Wicklow
Tel 044-45140
(Glendalough, Rathdrum,
Roundwood, Dublin)

Greene, Niall (CSSp)
Holy Spirit Missionaries,
Ardbraccan, Navan,
Co Meath C15 T884
Tel 046-9021441

Greene, Patrick (SJ)
Manresa House,
426 Clontarf Road,
Dollymount, Dublin 3
Tel 01-8331352

Greene, William (SPS)
House Leader,
Kiltegan House,
11 Douglas Road, Cork
Tel 021-4969371

Grenham, Thomas (SPS)
St Patrick's, Kiltegan,
Co Wicklow W91 Y022
Tel 059-6473600

Grennan, John (OCD)
Provincial
Avila Carmelite Centre
Bloomfield Avenue
Morehampton Road,
Dublin 4
Tel 01-643 0200

Grier, Matthew (MHM)
St Joseph's House,
50 Orwell Park,
Rathgar, Dublin D06 C535
Tel 01-4127700

Griffin, Brian, Very Rev,
Adm
Camross, Co Laois,
Tel 087-0644158
(Camross, Castletown,
Ossory)

Griffin, Edward, Very Rev
10 Connawood, Bray,
Co Wicklow
(Dublin, retired)

Griffin, Gerard (CSSp)
Rockwell College,
Cashel, Co Tipperary
Tel 062-61444

Griffin, Liam (OMI)
Oblates of Mary
Immaculate House of
Retreat, Tyrconnell Road,
Inchicore, Dublin 8
Tel 01-4541160/4541161
Oblate House of Retreat,
Inchicore, Dublin 8
Tel 01-4534408/4541805

Griffin, Pat
Ashborough Lodge, Lyre,
Milltown, Co Kerry
(Kerry, retired)

Griffin, Philip
Nullamore, Richmond
Avenue South, Dublin 6
Tel 01-4971239
(Opus Dei)

Griffin, Thomas (IC),
Parochial House,
Kilcurry,
Dundalk, Co Louth
Tel 042-9334410

Griffith, Anthony
Rushbrook, Laghey,
Co Donegal
Tel 074-9734021
(Raphoe, retired)

Grimshaw, Ronan (CSSp)
Holy Spirit Missionary
College,
Whitehall Road,
Dublin D12 P5YP
Tel 01-4064300

Grogan, Brian (SJ)
35 Lower Leeson Street,
Dublin 2
Tel 01-6761248

Grogan, Desmond, Very Rev
Canon, PE
Partry, Claremorris,
Co Mayo
Tel 094-9543013
(Tuam, retired)

Gryniewicz, Chrysostom
(OSB)
Silverstream Priory,
Stamullen,
Co Meath K32 T189
Tel 01-8417142

Guilfoyle, Patrick, Very Rev,
CC
Tullaroan, Co Kilkenny
Tel 056-7769141/
087-9932117
(Tullaroan, Ossory)

Guinan, Frank
The Presbytery, Mucklagh,
Tullamore, Co Offaly
Tel 057-9321892
(Rahan, Meath)

Guiney, John K. (SJ)
Milltown Park,
Milltown Road,
Dublin 6 D06 V9K7
Tel 01-2698411/2698113

Guiry, Michael, Very Rev, PP
Ardmore, Youghal,
Co Waterford
Tel 024-94275
Moderator, Clashmore
(Ardmore, Clashmore,
Waterford & L.)

Gunn, Joseph, Very Rev, PP,
VF
St Comgall's Presbytery,
27 Brunswick Road,
Bangor,
Co Down BT20 3DS
Tel 028-91465522
(Bangor, Down & C.)

Guthrie, Charles (SVD)
Donamon Castle,
Roscommon
Tel 090-6662222

Gutu, Lovemore (OCarm)
Provincial Office and
Carmelite Community,
Gort Muire, Ballinteer,
Dublin 16
Tel 01-2984014

H

Haan, Karl, CC
Parochial House, Culdaff,
Co Donegal
Tel 074-9379107
(Culdaff, Derry)

Habara, Gaspar (SVD)
Maynooth,
Co Kildare
Tel 01-6286391/2

Hackett, Michael, Very Rev
Canon, PE
Warrenpoint, Co Down
(Dromore, retired)

Hagan, Patrick (SPS)
St Patrick's, Kiltegan,
Co Wicklow
Tel 059-6473600

Hahessy, Ignatius (OCSO)
Mount Melleray Abbey,
Cappoquin,
Co Waterford P51 R8XW
Tel 058-54404

Hallinan, Malachy, Rt Rev
Mgr, PP, VG, VF
Church of the Sacred
Heart,
Seamus Quirke Road,
Galway
Tel 091-522713
(Sacred Heart Church,
Galway)

Hally, Brendan (CSSp)
Holy Spirit Missionary
College,
Whitehall Road,
Dublin D12 P5YP
Tel 01-4064300

Halpin, Martin, Very Rev, PP
Parochial House,
Ballinabrackey,
Kinnegad, Co Westmeath
Tel 046-9739015
(Ballinabrackey, Meath)

Halton, John, Very Rev, PE
26 Cullion Road,
Tempo, Enniskillen,
Co Fermanagh BT94 3LY
Tel 028-89541344
(Tempo, Clogher)

Hamill, Aidan, Rt Rev Mgr
c/o Bishop's House, Newry
(Dromore, retired)

Hammel, James, Rt Rev
MgrDiocesan Archivist,
Ballygarron, Kilmuckridge
Gorey, Co Wexford
Tel 086 1688295
(Ferns, retired)

Hampson, Paul
St Patricks Campus,
Drumcondra Road Upper,
Dublin 9
Tel 01-8842000
(Dublin)

Hanafin, Sean, Rt Rev Mgr,
PP
Ballybunion, Co Kerry
Tel 068-27102
Moderator,
Ballydonoghue, Tarbert
(Ballybunion,
Ballydonoghue, Tarbert,
Kerry)

Hanley, Hugh, Very Rev
(SCJ)
St John Vianney,
Ardlea Road, Dublin 5
Tel 01-8474173

Hanlon, Hugh, (MSC)
'Croí Nua', Rosary Lane,
Taylor's Hill Road,
Galway H91 WY2A
Tel 091-520960

Hanlon, Joseph, Very Rev
(Assistant Priest)
St Mary's Presbytery,
Willbrook Road,
Rathfarnham, Dublin 14
Tel 01-4932390
(Rathfarnham, Dublin)

Hanly, Gerard, Very Rev
Canon, PP, VF
Boyle, Co Roscommon
Tel 071-9662218
(Boyle, Elphin)

Hanna, John (CSsR)
Clonard Monastery,
1 Clonard Gardens,
Belfast BT13 2RL
Tel 028-90445950

Hannan, John (SM) PC
The Presbyerty,
78A Donore Avenue,
Dublin 8
Tel 01-4542425
(Donore Avenue, Dublin)

Hannan, Peter (SJ)
Manresa House,
426 Clontarf Road,
Dollymount, Dublin 3
Tel 01-8331352

Hannigan, Patrick, Very Rev,
PP,
Parochial House,
65 Tullyallen Road,
Dungannon,
Co Tyrone BT70 3AF
Tel 028-87769111/
028-87769211
(Killeeshil, Armagh)

Hannon, Donal
(Kilmore, retired)

Hannon, Martin
30 Knapton Road,
Dun Laoghaire, Co Dublin
Tel 01-2804353
(Opus Dei)

Hannon, Patrick, Dr
Emeritus Professor of
Theology,
St Patrick's College,
Maynooth, Co Kildare
Tel 01-6285222
(Cloyne, retired)

Hannon, Timothy, CC
3 Stanhope Place, Athy
Tel 059-8631698
(Athy, Dublin)

Hannon, Tom, Very Rev
The Bungalow, Moynure,
Bosna, Birr,
Co Offaly
(Killaloe, retired)

Hanrahan, Paschal, HCF
Head Chaplain,
Defence Forces
Headquarters,
McKee Barracks,
Blackhorse Avenue
Dublin 7
Tel 01-8042637/
087-3128209
(Killaloe)

Hanratty, David
Tierhogar, Portarlington,
Co Laois
Tel 057-8645719
(Meath)

Hanratty, Malachy (SSC)
St Columban's,
Dalgan Park,
Navan, Co Meath
Tel 046-9021525

Hanratty, Oliver
The Bungalow,
Crescent Road,
Rogerstown, Rush,
Co Dublin
(Dublin, retired)

Hao, Joseph, PC
Parochial House,
Brackenstown Road,
Swords, Co Dublin
Tel 01-8408926
(Brackenstown, Dublin)

Hardiman, Tony (OFM)
Franciscan Friary,
Liberty Street, Cork
Tel 021-4270302/4275481

Harding, Michael
c/o Diocesan Office,
Westbourne,
Ennis, Co Clare
(Killaloe)

Hargaden, Joseph (SCC)
Wexford, retired

Harkin, Ciarán, Very Rev, PP
Ballyraine, Letterkenny,
Co Donegal
Tel 074-9127600
(Aughaninshin, Raphoe)

Harkin, Dermott, CC
20 Loughermore Road,
Ballykelly,
Co Derry BT49 9PD
(Limavady, Derry)

Harkin, Hugh (SMA)
African Missions,
Blackrock Road,
Cork T12 TD54
Tel 021-4292871

Harlow, Thomas (SMA)
SMA House, Wilton, Cork
Tel 021-4541069/4541884

Harmon, Sean,
37 Gouldavoher,
Dooradoyle, Limerick
Tel 087-9870284
(Pastoral Unit 4, Limerick)

Harnan, Nick (MSC)
c/o Formation House,
56 Mulvey Park, Dundrum,
Dublin 16
Tel 01-2951856

Harney, Donal (MHM)
St Joseph's House,
50 Orwell Park,
Rathgar, Dublin D06 C535
Tel 01-4127700

Harper, Conor (SJ), PC
Jesuit House,
Milltown Park,
Miltown Road, Dublin 6
Tel 01-2698411
(Donnybrook, Dublin)

Harrington, Brendan
(Kerry, retired)

Harrington, Denis, Very Rev,
PE
Clane, Naas, Co Kildare
Tel 045-868224
(Kildare & L., retired)

Harrington, John (SM), TA
The Presbytery,
Coolock Village, Dublin 5
Tel 01-8477133

Harrington, Patrick (SMA)
Retired Bishop,
SMA House, Wilton,
Cork T12 KR23
Tel 021-4541069/4541884

Harrington, Terence
(OFMCap)
Capuchin Presence
Our Lady of Knock Shrine,
Knock, Co Mayo

Harrington, Wilfred (OP)
St Mary's Priory, Tallaght,
Dublin 24
Tel 01-4048100

Harris, Derek (SSC)
St Columban's Retirement
Home,
Dalgan Park,
Navan,
Co Meath
Tel 046-9021525

Harris, Jack (CM)
St Joseph's,
44 Stillorgan Park,
Blackrock,
Co Dublin A94 PC62
Tel 01-2886961

Harris, John (OP), Very Rev
Provincial, St Mary's,
Tallaght,
Dublin 24 D24 X585
Tel 01-4048118

Harris, John, CC
Holy Family Presbytery,
Luke Wadding Street,
Waterford
Tel 051-323947
(Cathedral, Waterford &
L.)

Harris, Walter, Very Rev
Canon
The Four Ferns, Brighton
Road
Foxrock, Co Dublin
(Dublin, retired)

Harrison, Michael, Very Rev,
PP
Killala, Co Mayo
Tel 096-32176
Carrowmore, Ballina,
Co Mayo
Tel 096-34014
(Killala/Lacken, Killala)

Harte, Martin, CC
Presbytery,
Kilcullen, Co Kildare
Tel 045-481222
(Kilcullen, Dublin)

Hartnett, Denis (MHM)
St James Apartments,
Our Lady of Knock Shrine,
Knock,
Co Mayo F12 R982

Harty, John (OFM)
Dún Mhuire,
Seafield Road,
Killliney, Co Dublin
Tel 01-2826760

Hassan, Peter, CC
St Patrick's Presbytery,
Roden Place, Dundalk,
Co Louth A91 K2P4
Tel 042-9334648
(Dundalk, St Patrick's,
Dundalk, Holy Redeemer,
Armagh)

Hassett, Edmond, Very Rev,
PP
Strandside South,
Abbeyside, Dungarvan,
Co Waterford
Tel 058-42036
(Abbeyside, Waterford &
L.)

Hassett, John, CC
127 Castlegate Way,
Adamstown, Co Dublin
Tel 01-62812088
(Esker-Doddsboro-
Adamstown, Dublin)

Hasson, Eugene, PP
52 Brook Street, Omagh,
Co Tyrone BT78 5HE
Tel 028-82243011
Adm, Drumquin
(Langfield)
(Drumquin (Langfield),
Omagh (Drumragh),
Derry)

Hasson, Gerald, CC
33 Cullycapple Road,
Aghadowney,
Co Derry BT51 4AR
Tel 048-70869019
(Coleraine, Derry)

Hasson, James (OFM)
Franciscan Friary,
Liberty Street,
Cork T12 D376
Tel 021-4275481

Hastings, Mícheál, Very Rev
Sacred Heart Hospital,
Pontoon Road,
Carrowncurry,
Castlebar,
Co Mayo F23 XV38
(Dublin, retired)

Hayden, Chris
c/o Bishop's House,
Summerhill, Wexford
(Ferns)

Hayden, Desmond
Ampleforth Abbey,
York YO62 4EN, UK
(Dublin)

Hayden, Eamonn Rev (SPS)
St Patrick's Kiltegan,
Co Wicklow W91 Y022

Hayes, Conor, Very Rev, PP
Templemore, Co Limerick
Tel 0504-31684
(Templemoore, Cashel &
E.)

Hayes, George, Venerable
Archdeacon, PP, VF
Kenmare, Co Kerry
Tel 064-6641352
(Kenmare, Kerry)

Hayes, Joseph (SJ)
Superior, Della Strada,
Dooradoyle, Limerick
Tel 061-480929/
087-4647634
(Pastoral Unit 3, Limerick)

Hayes, Patrick,
Dunabbey House,
Dungarvan,
Co Waterford
(Waterdord & L., retired)

Hayes, Richard, Very Rev
Collinstown, Duncormack,
Co Wexford
(Ferns, retired)

Hayes, Tom, Very Rev, Co-
PP, VG
Moderator,
The Presbytery,
Clonakilty, Co Cork
Tel 023-8833165
(Ardfield/Rathbarry,
Barryroe, Clonakilty,
Kilmeen/Castleventry,
Rosscarbery and
Timoleague, Cork & R.)

Hazelwood, Timothy, Very
Rev, PP
Killeagh, Co Cork
Tel 024-95133
(Killeagh, Cloyne)

Heagney, John, Very Rev,
PP, VF
124 Eglish Road,
Dungannon,
Co Tyrone BT70 1LB
Tel 028-37549661
(Eglish, Armagh)

Healy, Alexius (OFMCap)
Capuchin Friary,
Station Road, Raheny,
Dublin D05 T9E4
Tel 01-8313886

Healy, Austin (CSSp)
Holy Spirit Missionary
College
Kimmage Manor,
Whitehall Road,
Dublin D12 P5YP
Tel 01-4064300

Healy, Bernard,
St John's Presbytery,
Tralee, Co Kerry
Tel 066-7122522
(Tralee, St John's, Kerry)

Healy, Charles, PP
Carrickedmond, Colehill
Co Longford
Tel 044-9357442
(Carrickedmond And
Abbeyshrule,
Legan and Ballycloghan,
Ardagh & Cl.)

Healy, Jeremiah (SSC)
St Columban's,
Dalgan Park,
Navan, Co Meath
Tel 046-9021525

Healy, Myles (CSSp)
Blackrock College,
Blackrock, Co Dublin
Tel 01-2888681

...aly, Patrick J. (SDB)
...haplain,
...Mount Carmel Nursing
...ome, Roscrea,
...o Tipperary
...aly, Peter, Rev, Co-PP
...arochial House,
...oundwood, Co Wicklow
...el 01-2818149/087-
...463876
...Roundwood, Dublin)
...aly, Sean (SMA)
...ocial Justice Ireland,
...rena House
...rena Road, Sandyford,
...ublin 18
...el 01-2130724
...aly, Thomas,
...iocesan Administrator
...t Michael's,
...allinalee Road,
...o Longford N39 Y4X5
...el 043-3346432
...Ardagh & Cl.)
...aly, Timothy (SJ)
...t Francis Xavier's,
...pper Gardiner Street,
...ublin 1
...el 01-8363411
...aney, Seamus, Very Rev,
...P
...arochial House, Delvin,
...o Westmeath
...el 044-9664127
...Delvin, Meath)
...aney, Seán, Rt Rev Mgr,
...P
...arochial House,
...ullamore, Co Offaly
...el 057-9321587/
...57-9351510
...Tullamore, Meath)
...arne, Thomas, PP
...ohermore, Cashel,
...o Tipperary
...el 052-7462810
...Clonoulty, Cashel & E.)
...arty, Philip (CSsR)
...t Joseph's,
...t Alphonsus Road,
...undalk,
...o Louth A71 F3FC
...el 042-9334042/9334762
...derman, Mark Patrick
...OSB)
...bbot, Glenstal Abbey,
...Murroe, Co Limerick
...el 061-621000
...ery, Kevin, CC
...arochial House, Curraha,
...o Meath
...el 01-8350136
...Ardcath, Curraha, Meath)
...effernan, Martin, Very
...Rev, PE, PhD
...kahardgannon,
...Doneraile, Co Cork
...el 022-24570
...Cloyne, retired)

Hegarty, Benedict (OP), Very Rev,
St Mary's, Pope's Quay, Cork
Tel 021-4502267
Hegarty, Ciarán, Adm
(Down & Connor Diocese)
Doneyloop, Castlefin, Lifford, Co Donegal
Tel 074-9146183
(Doneyloop (Urney and Castlefinn), Derry)
Hegarty, John Paul, Very Rev Canon, Co-PP
The Lough Presbytery, St Finbarr's West, Cork
Tel 021-4322633
(Ballyphehane, The Lough and Togher, Cork & R.)
Hegarty, Kevin, Very Rev, PP
Carne, Belmullet, Co Mayo
Tel 097-81011
(Kilmore-Erris, Killala)
Hegarty, Martin
(Kerry, retired)
Hegarty, Michael (IC), Very Rev, PP
St Oliver Plunkett's Parish, Cooleens, Clonmel, Co Tipperary
Tel 052-6125679
(Clonmel, St Oliver Plunkett, Waterford & L.)
Hegarty, Richard, Very Rev, PE,
Killavullen, Co Cork
Tel 022-26125
(Cloyne, retired)
Hehir, Mark, CC
Midleton, Co Cork
Tel 021-4621670
(Midleton, Cloyne)
Heinhold, John (SPS), Co-PP Moderator,
The Presbytery, Skibbereen, Co Cork
Tel 028-22878/22877
(Aughadown, Castlehaven, Kilmacabea, Rath and the Islands and Skibbereen, Cork & R.)
Hendrick, Richard (OFMCap), Very Rev, PP
Capuchin Friary, Church Street, Dublin 7
Tel 01-8730599
(Halston Street and Arran Quay, Dublin)
Heneghan, James (CSSp)
Holy Spirit Missionary College
Kimmage Manor, Whitehall Road, Dublin D12 P5YP
Tel 01-4064300

Heneghan, Jeremy (OFMCap)
Ard Mhuire, Creeslough, Letterkenny, Co Donegal F92 Y23R
Tel 074-9138005
Hennebry, John (OSA)
Provincial, St Augustine's Taylor's Lane, Ballyboden, Dublin 16
Tel 01-4241000
Hennessy, Gerard, PP
The Parochial House, Borrisoleigh, Thurles, Co Tipperary
Tel 0504-51935
(Borrisoleigh, Cashel & E.)
Hennessy, Patrick (SDB)
Salesian College, Maynooth Road, Celbridge, Co Kildare W23 W0XK
Tel 01-62755058/60
Hennessy, Patrick, Very Rev, PP
Leighlinbridge, Co Carlow
Tel 059-9722607
(Leighlin, Kildare & L.)
Hennessy, William, Very Rev, Adm
Conahy, Jenkinstown, Co Kilkenny
Tel 087-8736155
(Conahy, Ossory)
Hennigan, Frank (SM)
181 South Circular Road, Dublin 8
Henry, Denis, Co-PP
1A Ballydowd Grove, Lucan, Co Dublin
Tel 01-2955541
(Lucan, Dublin)
Henry, Leo, Very Rev, BA, HDE, PP
Curry, Ballymote, Co Sligo
Tel 087-6306938
(Curry, Achonry)
Henry, Martin
St Patrick's College, Maynooth, Co Kildare
Tel 01-6285222
(Down & C.)
Henry, Martin
St Nathy's College, Ballaghaderreen, Co Roscommon
Tel 094-9861728
(Achonry)
Henry, Maurice, Very Rev, PE
54 St Patrick's Avenue, Downpatrick, Co Down BT30 6DN
Tel 028-44851221
(Downpatrick, Down & C.)

Henry, Maurice, Very Rev, Adm
Parochial House, Castletown-Kilpatrick, Navan, Co Meath
(Castletown-Kilpatrick, Meath)
Henry, Seán, Very Rev, PP
Parochial House, Dunshaughlin, Co Meath
Tel 01-8259114
(Dunshaughlin, Meath)
Heraty, Jarlath, PP
Killererin, Barnderg, Tuam, Co Galway
Tel 093-49222
(Killererin, Tuam)
Herlihy, David, Very Rev Canon, PE
Freemount, Charleville, Co Cork
(Cloyne, retired)
Hernandez, Jose Manuel Casillas (MCCJ)
8 Clontarf Road, Clontarf, Dublin 3
Tel 01-8330051
Herrity, Michael, Very Rev Canon, AP
Bun-a-leaca, Letterkenny, Co Donegal
Tel 074-9531155
(Gweedore, Raphoe)
Herron, Frank, Very Rev, PP
Parochial House, Foxrock, Dublin 18
Tel 01-2893229
(Dublin)
Hession, Noel (OSA)
Prior and Bursar, St Augustine's Priory, O'Connell Street, Limerick
Tel 061-415374
Hession, Stan (OCarm)
Carmelite Friary, Kinsale, Co Cork P17 WR88
Tel 021-4772138
Hever, Thomas, Very Rev, PP, VG
Parochial House Rathcormac, Co Sligo
Tel 071-9635058
(Drumcliff-Maugherow, Elphin)
Hickey, John (SSC)
Columban Sisters, Magheramore, Co Wicklow
Hickey, Michael (CSSp)
Drum, Athlone, Co Roscommon
Tel 090-6437125
(Athlone, SS Peter and Paul, Elphin)

Hickey, Michael, Very Rev,
PP
Bansha, Co Tipperary
Tel 062-54132
(*Bansha and Kilmoyler*,
Cashel & E.)
Hickey, Patrick, Very Rev, PE
The Presbytery,
Newcestown
Bandon, Co Cork
(Cork & R., retired)
Hickland, Brendan, Very
Rev, PP
503 Ormeau Road,
Belfast BT7 3GR
Tel 028-90642446
Administrator,
St Bernadette's Parish
(*Holy Rosary, St
Bernadette's*, Down & C.)
Higgans, Pius (OFMCap)
Capuchin Friary,
Friary Street,
Kilkenny R95 NX60
Tel 056-7721439
Higgins, Thomas (OCarm)
Whitefriar Street Church,
56 Aungier Street,
Dublin 2 D02 R598
Tel 01-4758821
Hillery, Desmond, VG
c/o Diocesan Office,
Westbourne,
Ennis, Co Clare
(Killaloe)
Hilliard, Alan
On Sabbatical
(Dublin)
Hinds, Michael, CF
Aiken Barracks,
Dundalk, Co Louth
Tel 042-9331759
Gormanston Army Camp,
Stamullen, Co Meath
Tel 087-3940186
(Meath)
Hoban, Brendan (SSC)
Alcoholic Advisory Board,
St Columban's,
Dalgan Park,
Navan, Co Meath
Tel 046-9021525
Hoban, Brendan, Very Rev,
PP
Sliabh Rua, Breaffy,
Ballina, Co Mayo
Tel 096-31288
(Killala, retired)
Hoban, Patrick, Very Rev
St Jude's Avenue,
Crossmolina, Co Mayo
(Killala, retired)
Hodnett, Ben, CC
The Presbytery,
Togher, Cork
Tel 027-50193
(*Bantry, Caheragh,
Goleen,
Muintir Bháire and Schull*,
Cork & R.)

Hogan, Bernard, PP
Drumlish, Co Longford
Tel 043-3324132
(*Drumlish*, Ardagh & Cl.)
Hogan, Diarmuid, Very Rev,
PP
Parochial House,
Oranmore, Co Galway
Tel 091-794634/
087-1037452
(*Oranmore*, Galway)
Hogan, Donal (SSC)
Deputy Safeguarding
Office, St Columban's,
Dalgan Park,
Navan, Co Meath
Tel 046-9021525
Hogan, Edmund M. (SMA)
African Missions,
Blackrock Road,
Cork T12 TD54
Tel 021-4292871
Hogan, John Rev (SSC)
St Columban's,
Dalgan Park,
Navan, Co Meath
Hogan, John Very Rev
(OCD)
Mount Rivers,
Navan, Co Meath
(Meath)
Hogan, Joseph, PP
Dromore West, Co Sligo
Tel 096-47012
PP, Easkey, Co Sligo
Tel 096-49011
(*Dromore-West
(Kilmacshalgan), Easkey*,
Killala)
Hogan, Martin, Very Rev
Canon, CC
Parochial House,
4 The Lawn, Finglas,
Dublin 11
Tel 01-8341000
(*Finglas, Rivermount*,
Dublin)
Hogan, Maurice (SSC),
St Columban's,
Dalgan Park, Navan,
Co Meath
Tel 046-9021525
Hogan, Patrick (SVD)
Donamon Castle,
Roscommon
Tel 090-6662222
Hogan, Patrick,
Sruth Lan,
South Circular Road,
Limerick
Tel 087-6522746
(*Pastoral Unit 4*, Limerick)
Hogan, Thomas (CSSp)
Rockwell College,
Cashel, Co Tipperary
Tel 062-61444

Hogan, Thomas (CSsR)
Dún Mhuire,
461/463 Griffith Avenue,
Dublin D09 X651
Tel 01-5180196
Hogan, Tom, Very Rev, Co-
PP, VF
The Presbytery,
John's Mall,
Birr, Co Offaly
Tel 055-9121757/
087-6446410
(*Brendan Pastoral Area*,
Killaloe)
Hogg, Barry, Very Rev
15 Parkelands
Tubbercurry
Co Sligo
Tel 091-522458/524904
(Galway)
Holland, Michael (OFM)
Franciscan Abbey,
Liberty Street, Cork
Tel 021-4270302/4275481
Holleran, Patrick, Very Rev,
PP
Coolaney, Co Sligo
Tel 071-9167745
(*Coolaney (Killoran)*,
Achonry)
Holmes, Brian (CSsR)
c/o Provincial Office,
St Joseph's,
St Alphonsus Road,
Dundalk,
Co Louth A71 F3FC
Holmes, Kieran
St Patrick's Presbytery,
Ballina, Co Mayo
Tel 096-71360
(*Ballina (Kilmoremoy)*,
Killala)
Holovlasky, Ryan (CSsR), CC
St Joseph's,
St Alphonsus Road,
Dundalk,
Co Louth A71 F3FC
Tel 042-9334042/9334762
(*Dundalk, St Joseph's*,
Armagh)
Horan, Barry PP
Main Street,
Clarinbridge, Co Galway
Tel 091-776741
(*Clarinbridge*, Galway)
Horan, Gerard (OSA)
Bursar, The Abbey,
Fethard, Co Tipperary
Tel 052-31273
Horan, John (SDB), Very Rev
Rector, Salesian College,
Don Bosco Road,
Pallaskenry,
Co Limerick V94 WP86
Tel 061-393105
Horgan, John (SMA),
SMA House, Wilton,
Cork T12 KR23
Tel 021-4541069/4541884

Horgan, Patrick (CSsR)
St Joseph's,
St Alphonsus Road,
Dundalk,
Co Louth A71 F3FC
Tel 042-9334042/9334762
Horgan, Seamus, Mgr
Apostolic Nunciature,
3339 Massachusetts Ave.
Washington DC,
20008-3610
USA
(Killaloe)
Horgan, Seán (MSC), CC
(pro tem)
Carrignavar, Co Cork
Tel 021-4884044
Horgan, Tony (MSC) PP
Church of the
Resurrection,
Headford Road,
Galway H91 W298
Tel 091-762883
(*Tirellan*, Galway)
Horneck, Noel, Very Rev, P
Parochial House,
Dunderry, Navan,
Co Meath
Tel 046-9431433
(*Dunderry*, Meath)
Horrocks, Paul (OMI)
Oblates Fathers, House o
Retreat,
Inchicore, Dublin 8
Tel 01-4541117
Hou, Anthony
Chaplain to Chinese
Community,
Westland Row, Dublin 2
Tel 01-6761270
(*Westland Row*, Dublin)
Houlihan, Séamus, Very Re
PP,
Parochial House,
Ballycumber Road
Moate, Co Westmeath,
Tel 090-6481951
(*Tubber*, Meath)
Hourigan, Augustine (CP)
St Paul's Retreat,
Mount Argus, Dublin 6W
Tel 01-4992000
Hourigan, Joseph, Very Re
AP
Parochial House,
Lissycasey, Ennis,
Co Clare
Tel 065-6834145
(*Radharc na nOileán
Pastoral Area*, Killaloe)
Houser, Dom Hildebrand
(OSB)
Silverstream Priory,
Stamullen,
Co Meath K32 T189
Tel 01-8417142

Allianz (lii)

oward, Brendan, Very Rev, PE
Hillview Nursing Home,
Tullow Road, Carlow
(Kildare & L. retired)
oward, Greg, Co-PP,
Moderator,
The Prebytery,
Ballyphehane, Cork
Tel 021-4965560
(Ballyphehane, The Lough and Togher, Cork & R.)
oward, Niall, Very Rev, PP
Glengarriff, Co Cork
Tel 027-63045
Moderator, Kilgarvin
Kilgarvan, Co Kerry
Tel 064-6685313
(Glengarriff (Bonane), Kilgarvan, Kerry)
oward, Terence (SJ)
Superior,
Loyola House,
Milltown Park,
Miltown Road, Dublin 6
Tel 01-2180276
owell, William, Very Rev
c/o Bishop's House,
Summerhill, Wexford
(Ferns, retired)
owley, Enda, Very Rev
Canon, PE
College Road, Galway
(Tuam, retired)
owley, Gary (SPS)
St Patrick's Missionary
Society,
Main Street, Knock,
Co Mayo F12 KX34
Tel 094-9388661
oyne, Peter, Very Rev, PE
Newmarket,
Hugginstown,
Co Kilkenny
Tel 056-7768678
(Ossory, retired)
oyne, William (OFM)
Franciscan Friary,
Killarney, Co Kerry
Tel 064-6631334/6631066
ughes, Augustine (OFM)
Franciscan Friary,
Clonmel, Co Tipperary
Tel 052-6121378
ughes, Benedict
(On study leave)
Chaplaincy Centre,
NUI Galway,
University Road,
Galway H91 TK 33
Tel 086-3864907
(Clogher)
ughes, Eoin
Chaplain,
Beaumont Hospital,
Beaumont Road, Dublin 9
Tel 01-8477573
(Dublin)

Hughes, John (OSA), PP
St Augustine's,
Taylor's Lane,
Ballyboden, Dublin 16
(Ballyboden, Dublin)
Hughes, John, Very Rev, PE, CC
30 Jockey Lane, Moy,
Dungannon,
Co Tyrone BT71 7SR
Tel 028-87784240
(Armagh, retired)
Hughes, Martin,
Team Assistant,
447 The Oaks,
Belgard Heights
Tallaght, Dublin 24
Tel 01-4519399
(Brookfield, Springfield, Dublin)
Hughes, Michael (OMI)
Oblate House of Retreat,
Inchicore, Dublin 8
Tel 01-4534408/4541805
Hughes, Michael (SCJ)
Sacred Heart Fathers,
Fairfield,
66 Inchicore Road,
Dublin 8
Tel 01-4538655
Hughes, Pat, CC
Parochial House, Myshall,
Co Carlow
Tel 059-9157635
(Clonegal, Myshall, Kildare & L.)
Hughes, Patrick, Very Rev, PP, Adm
Parochial House,
10 Cloughfin Road,
Kildress, Cookstown,
Co Tyrone BT80 9JB
Administration Kildress
Tel 028-86751206
(Kildress, Lissan, Armagh)
Hughes, P.J., PP
Mullahoran,
Kilcogy via Longford,
Co Cavan
Tel 043-6683141
(Mullahoran and Loughduff, Ardagh & Cl.)
Hughes, Richard (OSA),
St Augustine's,
Taylor's Lane,
Ballyboden, Dublin 16
Humphries, Seamus (OSA)
St Augustine's Priory,
Dungarvan, Co Waterford
Tel 058-41136
Hunt, Anselm (OSB)
Abbot, Glenstal Abbey,
Murroe, Co Limerick
Tel 061-386103
Hurley, Colm
(Kilmore, retired)

Hurley, Declan, Very Rev, Adm, VG
St Mary's Presbytery,
The Fairgreen, Navan,
Co Meath C15 X0A3
Tel 046-9027518
(Navan, Meath)
Hurley, James (Opus Dei), CC
31 Herbert Avenue,
Merrion Road, Dublin 4
Tel 01-2692001
(Merrion Road, Dublin)
Hurley, Michael C., Very Rev
Canon, PP, VF
Killeshandra, Co Cavan
Tel 049-4334155
(Killeshandra, Kilmore)
Hurley, Michael, Very Rev
Canon, PC
85 Tymon Crescent,
Oldbawn, D24 FK0W,
Tel 01-4627080
(Bohernabreena, Tallaght, Oldbawn, Dublin)
Hurley, Richard, Very Rev
Canon
c/o Cork & Ross Offices
Redemption Road,
Co Cork
(Cork & R., retired)
Hurley, Thomas, Very Rev
Templeglantine,
Co Limerick
Tel 068-84021
(Limerick, retired)
Husband, Raymond (SSC)
Regional Director,
St Columban's,
Dalgan Park,
Navan, Co Meath
Tel 046-9021525
Hussey, Michael, Very Rev, PP
Ballylongford, Co Kerry
Tel 06843110
(Ballylongford, Kerry)
Hutchinson, Stephen (OP)
St Saviour's,
Upper Dorset Street,
Dublin 1
Tel 01-8897610
Hutton, John, Very Rev
Nazareth House Care Village
516 Ravenhill Road,
Belfast BT6 OBW
(Down & C., retired)
Hyland, Richard, Very Rev, PP
5 The Lawn, Finglas
Dublin 1,
Tel 01-8341894
(Finglas, Finglas West, Rivermount, Dublin)

Hyland, Sean, CC
29 Pine Villa,
Portarlington, Co Laois
Tel 057-8645582/
087-9486769
(Clonbollogue and Rhode, Kildare & L.)
Hynes, James (OFM)
Chauseee de Vleurgat 189 B10,
1050 Brussels,
Belgium
Hynes, Valentine (SMA)
African Missions,
Blackrock Road,
Cork T12 TD54
Tel 021-4292871

I

Ifiora, Michael, CC
The Presbytery, Loughrea,
Co Galway H62 YE09
Tel 091-841212
(Loughrea, St Brendan's Cathedral, Clonfert)
Ifunanya, Onwe (OCSO)
Our Lady of Bethlehem Abbey,
11 Ballymena Road,
Portglenone, Ballymena,
Co Antrim, BT44 8BL
Tel 028-25822795
Igoe, Michael (SMA)
African Missions,
Blackrock Road,
Cork T12 TD54
Tel 021-4292871
Illah, Louis, CC
52 Edgeworth Court,
Longwood, Co Meath
Tel 087-1723903
(Longwood, Meath)
Irwin, Charles,
Kevin Villa,
O'Connell Avenue,
Limerick
Tel 061-348922
(Limerick)
Irwin, Edwin
(Limerick, retired)
Irwin, John
c/o Diocesan Offices,
St Eugene's Cathedral,
Francis Street,
Derry BT48 9AP
(Derry)
Irwin, Michael (SAC)
St Columban's Retirement Home,
Dalgan Park, Navan,
Co Meath
Tel 046-9021525
Irwin, Michael (SSC)
36 Clonmore, Kilteragh,
Dooradoyle,
Co Limerick
Tel 069-83972

Irwin, Nicholas J., Very Rev, PP
Diocesan Secretary/Chancellor,
Archbishop's House,
Thurles, Co Tipperary
Tel 0504-21512
PP, Gortnahoe
The Parochial House,
Gortnahoe, Thurles,
Co Tipperary
Tel 056-8834855
(*Gortnahoe*, Cashel & E.)

Issac, Sunil (SCJ)
Sacred Heart Fathers,
Fairfield,
66 Inchicore Road,
Dublin 8
Tel 01-4538655

Iwuozor, Gregory (CSSp)
Holy Spirit Missionary College
Kimmage Manor,
Whitehall Road,
Dublin D12 P5YP
Tel 01-4064300

Iyans, Cosmas, PC
Holy Redeemer Parish,
Main Street, Bray,
Co Wicklow
Tel 2868413
(*Bray (Holy Redeemer)*, Dublin)

Izidor, George, CC
Ballyconneely,
Clifden, Co Galway
Tel 095-21251
(*Clifden (Omey and Ballindoon)*, Tuam)

J

Jackson, Piaras (SJ)
Peter Faber House,
28 Brookvale Avenue,
Belfast BT14 6BW
Tel 028-90757615

Jacob, John, CC
12 Walkinstown Road,
Dublin 12
Tel 01-4502541
(*Walkinstown*, Dublin)

Jacob, Russel (OSCam)
Chaplain, Waterford University Hospital,
Dunmore Road, Waterford
Tel 051-848000
(Waterford & L.)

Jacob, Sunny (SJ)
St Ignatius Community & Church,
27 Raleigh Row, Galway
Tel 091-523707

Jacob, Yohanna, CC
Parochial House,
Ratoath, Co Meath
Tel 01-8256207
(*Ratoath*, Meath)

Jakubiak, Piotr
Polish Chaplaincy
The Presbytery, Ballymany,
Newbridge, Co Kildare
Tel 045-434069
(*Droichead Nua/Newbridge*, Kildare & L.)

James, Jibin, CC
Parochial House,
6 Circular Road,
Dungannon,
Co Tyrone BT71 6BE
Tel 028-87722631
(*Dungannon (Drumglass, Killyman and Tullyniskin)*, Armagh)

Jansen, Luuk (OP)
Holy Cross, Sligo
Co Sligo
Tel 071-9142700

Jennings, Gavan
Harvieston,
Cunningham Road,
Dalkey, Co Dublin
Tel 01-2859877
(Opus Dei)

Jennings, Gerard, Very Rev, PP
Monksfield, Salthill,
Galway
Tel 091-523413
(*Salthill*, Galway)

Jennings, Martin, Very Rev, PE
4 St Mary's House
Shantalla, Galway
Tel 087-9476115
(Achonry, retired)

Jennings, Norman (SSC)
St Columban's,
Dalgan Park,
Navan, Co Meath
Tel 046-9021525

Jereus, Bangcaya Jose (SSP)
Society of Saint Paul,
Moyglare Road,
Maynooth Co Kildare,
W23 NX34
Tel 01-6285933

Jjooga, Matthias, CC
1 Grangemore Avenue,
Donaghmede, Dublin 13
01-5556232
(*Donaghmede-Clongriffin-Balgriffin*, Dublin)

John, Sijo, CC
Parochial House,
Louth Village, Dundalk,
Co Louth A91 XE42
Tel 042-9374285
(*Louth*, Armagh)

Johnston, Anthony
8 Corrig Park,
Dun Laoghaire, Co Dublin
Tel 01-2805594
(Dublin, retired)

Johnston, Cecil
Sacred Heart Residence,
Sybil Hill Road,
Raheny, Dublin 5
(Dublin, retired)

Johnston, Thomas, Rt Rev Mgr, Adm
Charlestown, Co Mayo
Tel 094-9254315
(*Charlestown (Kilbeagh)*, Achonry)

Jones, Bernard (OFM)
Franciscan Friary,
Rossnowlagh,
Co Donegal F94 PH21
Tel 071-9851342

Jones, David
The Hermitage
Duleek, Co Meath
Tel 041-9823205
(*Duleek*, Meath)

Jones, Gerard, Co-PP
The Presbytery,
1 Shallee Drive,
Cloughleigh,
Ennis, Co Clare
Tel 065-6840715
Diocesan Office,
Westbourne,
Ennis, Co Clare
Tel 065-6828638
(*Abbey Pastoral Area*, Killaloe)

Jones, John (SPS)
Dysart, Mullingar,
Co Westmeath

Jones, John, Very Rev, PC
151 Swords Road,
Whitehall, Dublin 9
Tel 01-8374887
(*Larkhill-Whitehall-Santry*, Dublin)

Jones, John, Very Rev, AP
St Caimin's,
Mountshannon, Co Clare
Tel 061-927213/086-1933479
(*Inis Cealtra Pastoral Area*, Killaloe)

Jones, Joseph, Very Rev, Moderator,
122 Greencastle Road,
Dublin 17
Tel 01-8487657
Moderator, Bonnybrook and Kilmore Road West
(*Bonnybrook*, *Kilmore Road West*, Dublin)

Jones, Patrick, Very Rev, Team Assistant
87 Iona Road,
Dublin 9
Tel 01-8308257
(*Iona Road*, Dublin)

Jones, Sean, CC
Killarney, Co Kerry
Tel 064-6631014
Chaplain,
St Brendan's College,
Killarney, Co Kerry
Tel 064-6631021
(*Killarney*, Kerry)

Jordan, John, Very Rev, PP
Kyle, Oulart,
Gorey, Co Wexford
(Ferns, retired)

Jordan, Michael, CC
(Priest in Residence)
Parochial House, Killanny
Carrickmacross,
Co Monaghan
A81 PX31
Tel 042-9661452
(*Killanny*, Clogher)

Jordan, Thomas (OP), Very Rev
Black Abbey, Kilkenny,
Co Kilkenny
Tel 056-7721279

Jos, Yashin, Very Rev, PP
Parochial House
Sooey, Coola,
Via Boyle, Co SLigo
Tel 071-9165144
(*Riverstown*, Elphin)

Joseph, Nelson, CC
Achill Sound, Achill,
Co Mayo
Tel 098-45109
(*Achill*, Tuam)

Joseph, Rajesh, CC
Presbytery No. 2
Shangan Road,
Ballymun, Dublin 9
Tel 01-8421551
(*Ballymun, St Pappin's*, Dublin)

Joseph, Renson, CC
St Paul's Presbytery,
125 Falls Road
Belfast BT12 6AB
Tel 028-90325034

Joyce, Michael (SVD)
Donamon Castle,
Roscommon
Tel 090-6662222

Joyce, Stephen, Very Rev, P
Parochial House,
Stracrunnion,
Scotstown,
Co Monaghan H18 X620
Tel 047-89204
(*Tydavnet*, Clogher)

Joyel John Michael (IC),
Rosmini House,
Dunkereen,
Innishannon,
Co Cork T12 N9DH
Tel 021-4776268/4776923
Chaplain, Cork University Hospital,
Tel 021-4546400
(Cork & R.)

Allianz (ili)

...dge, Francis, Very Rev, PP
Parochial House,
Mullenmore Road
Crossmolina, Ballina
Co Mayo
Tel 096-31677
(Crossmolina, Killala)

...dge, John
Killaser,
Swinford, Co Mayo
(Killala, retired)

...kes, Antony (OFM)
Franciscan Friary
Killarney, Co Kerry
Tel 064-6631334/6631066

K

...aboré, Julien, Very Rev
Mgr
Chargé d'Affaires,
Apostolic Nunciature in
Ireland
183 Navan Road
Dublin D07 CT98
Tel 01-8380577

...akkadampallil, Vincent
Xavier (OSCam)
Chaplain,
Mater Misericordiae
University Hospital,
Eccles Street, Dublin 7
Tel 01-8301122
(Dublin)

...ev Jamon Varkey
Kakkanattu CC
Sacred Heart Presbytery,
21 The Folly, Waterford
Tel 051-873759
(Sacred Heart, Waterford
& L.)

...akkarakunel, John Philip
Chaplain, Waterford
University Hospital,
Dunmore Road,
Co Waterford
Tel 051-848000
(Waterford & L.)

...alema, Godfrey
Team Assistant, Holy
Redeemer Parish,
Herbert Road, Bray,
Co Dublin
Tel 01-2868413
(Bray, Holy Redeemer,
Dublin)

...alemeera, Kizito, CC
Parochial House,
Letterkenny,
Co Donegal
Tel 074-9121021
(Letterkenny (Conwal and
Leck), Raphoe)

Kanayammakunnel,
Sebastian (SSP)
Society of Saint Paul,
Moyglare Road,
Maynooth,
Co Kildare W23 NX34
Tel 01-6285933

Kane, Gerry, Very Rev, PP
Parochial House,
Foxrock, Co Dublin
Tel 01-2784860
(Foxrock, Newtownpark,
Dublin)

Kane, Michael (CSSp)
Holy Spirit Missionary
College
Kimmage Manor,
Whitehall Road,
Dublin D12 P5YP
Tel 01-4064300

Kavanagh, Anthony (OP)
Dominican College,
Newbridge
Droichead Nua, Co Kildare
Tel 045-487200

Kavanagh, Brian, Very Rev,
CC
St Patricks College,
Maynooth, Co Kildare
Tel 045-890559
(Allen, Kildare & L.)

Kavanagh, Eamon (CSsR)
St Joseph's,
St Alphonsus Road,
Dundalk,
Co Louth A71 F3FC
Tel 042-9334042/9334762

Kavanagh, Edward, Very
Rev, PE
Rath, Emo, Co Laois
(Kildare & L., retired)

Kavanagh, Hugh, Very Rev,
Co-PP
The Prebytery, Neilstown
Clondalkin, Dublin 22,
Tel 01-6263920
(Neilstown, Rowlagh and
Quarryvale, Dublin)

Kavanagh, Joseph (OP)
St Dominic's Retreat
House,
Montenotte, Co Cork
Tel 021-4502520

Kavanagh, Joseph, Very Rev,
PP
Camolin, Co Wexford
Tel 053-9383136
(Camolin, Ferns)

Kavanagh, Martin (SMA)
Provincial Secretary,
African Missions,
Blackrock Road,
Cork T12 TD54
Tel 021-4292871

Kavanagh, Myles (CP), CC
Holy Cross Retreat,
432 Crumlin Road,
Ardoyne, Belfast BT14 7GE
Tel 028-90748231/2
(Holy Cross, Down & C.)

Kaweesi, Charles (OCSO), Rt
Rev Dom
Sub-Prior, Our Lady of
Bethlehem Abbey,
11 Ballymena Road,
Portglenone, Ballymena,
Co Antrim BT44 8BL
Tel 028-25821211

Kealy, Brendan, Very Rev,
Adm
Parochial House,
46 North William Street,
Dublin1
Tel 01-8556474
(North William Street,
Dublin)

Kealy, John (OFM)
Franciscan Abbey,
Multyfarnham,
Co Westmeath
Tel 044-9371114/9371137

Keane, Anthony (OSB)
Glenstal Abbey, Murroe,
Co Limerick
Tel 061-621000

Keane, Brendan (CSsR)
Clonard Monastery,
1 Clonard Gardens,
Belfast, BT13 2RL
Tel 028-90445950

Keane, Jerry, Very Rev, PP
Eyeries, Co Cork
Tel 027-74008
Moderator, Allihies Parish,
Tel 027-73012
(Eyeries, Kerry)

Keane, John, CC
Ballyvongane,
Coachford, Co Cork
Tel 089-7078770
(Macroom, Cloyne)

Keane, John D., Very Rev
Chaplain's Office,
Galway Clinic,
Doughiska, Galway
Tel 091-785000
Chaplain's Office,
Merlin Park University
Hospital, Galway
(Galway)

Keane, Martin
No. 3 St Mary's College
House,
Shantalla Road, Galway
(Galway, retired)

Keane, Martin (CSSp)
Holy Spirit Missionary
College
Kimmage Manor,
Whitehall Road,
Dublin D12 P5YP
Tel 01-4064300

Keane, Richard,
Cratloe, Co Clare
Tel 087-9552729
(Pastoral Unit 5, Limerick)

Keane, Tom (MHM)
St Joseph's House,
50 Orwell Park,
Rathgar,
Dublin D06 C535
Tel 01-4127700

Keaney, Charles, PP
34 Moneysharvin Road,
Swatragh, Maghera,
Co Derry BT46 5PY
Tel 028-79401236
(Swatragh, Derry)

Kearney, Francis, Very Rev
Canon
Cabra, Hilltown,
Co Down
(Dromore, retired)

Kearney, John, Very Rev
Canon
Warrenpoint, Co Down
(Dromore, retired)

Kearney, Paschal (CSSp)
Holy Spirit Missionary
College,
Whitehall Road, Dublin
D12 P5YP
Tel 01-4064300

Kearney, Patrick, Very Rev,
PP
Parochial House, Kilskyre,
Kells, Co Meath
Tel 046-9243623
(Kilskyre, Meath)

Kearney, Thomas (SVD)
Donamon Castle,
Roscommon
Tel 090-6662222

Kearney, Thomas, PC
137 Shantalla Road,
Whitehall, Dublin 9
Tel 01-8420260
(Larkhill-Whitehall-Santry,
Dublin)

Kearney, Tom (SVD)
St Mary-on-the-Quay
Presbytrey,
20 Colston Street,
Bristol BS1 5AE
Tel 0117-9264702

Kearns, Brendan, PP
Parochial House,
Great George's Street,
Warrenpoint,
Co Down, BT34 3NF
Tel 028-41754684
(St Peter's (Warrenpoint),
St Mary's (Burren),
Dromore)

Kearns, Gerard
Cavan General Hospital
Tel 049-4361399
(Kilmore)

Kearney, Nicholas (OSA)
St John's Priory,
Thomas Street, Dublin 8
Tel 01-6770393/0415/0601

Keating, Andy (SPS)
St Patrick's, Kiltegan,
Co Wicklow
Tel 059-6473600

Keating, David
Chaplain, South East
Technological University,
10 Claremont, Cork Road,
Waterford
Tel 051-378878
(Waterford & L.)

Keating, John,
Raheenagh, Ballagh,
Co Limerick
Tel 069-85014/087-6322212
(Pastoral Unit 16, Limerick)

Keating, John (OCarm)
Terenure College,
Terenure,
Dublin D6W DK72
Tel 01-4904621

Keaveny, Michael, PEm
53 Brisland Road,
Eglinton,
Co Derry BT47 3EA
Tel 028-71810234
(Derry, retired)

Keegan, Joe, CC
The Presbytery,
1 Dunmanus Court,
Kilkiernan Road,
Cabra West
Dublin D07 C8K1
Tel 01-8680804
(Cabra, Cabra West,
Dublin)

Keegan, John F., Very Rev,
Co-PP
Rolestown, Swords,
Co Dublin
Tel 01-8401514
(Rolestown-Oldtown,
Dublin)

Keenan, Aidan, Very Rev
c/o Diocesan Office,
Lisbreen,
75 Somerton Road,
Belfast BT15 4DE
(Down & C., retired)

Keenan, Brian (SM)
CUS Community,
89 Lower Leeson Street,
Dublin 2
Tel 01-6762586

Keenan, Kevin, Very Rev, PP
Church of the Sacred
Heart,
Seamus Quirke Road,
Galway
Tel 091-524751
(Sacred Heart Church,
Galway)

Keenan, Pádraig, Very Rev,
PP
Parochial House,
Chapel Road,
Haggardstown,
Dundalk,
Co Louth A91 XOPR
Tel 042-9321621
(Haggardstown and
Blackrock, Armagh)

Keenan, Patrick (OCD)
St Teresa's,
Clarendon Street, Dublin 2
Tel 01-6718466/6718127

Keeney, Sean (CSsR)
Clonard Monastery,
1 Clonard Gardens,
Belfast, BT13 2RL
Tel 028-90445950

Kehoe, James, Very Rev, PP
Carrig-on-Bannow,
Wellington Bridge,
Co Wexford
Tel 051-561192
(Bannow, Ferns)

Kehoe, Liam (CSSp)
Blackrock College,
Blackrock, Co Dublin
Tel 01-2888681

Kehoe, Noel (CSsR) PP
Superior, St Joseph's,
Alphonsus Road, Dundalk,
Co Louth A71 F3FC
Tel 042-9334042
(Dundalk, St Joseph's,
Armagh)

Kehoe, Peter, (OCarm)
Terenure College,
Terenure,
Dublin D6W DK72
Tel 01-4904621

Kehoe, Philip (FDP)
25 Lower Teddington
Road,
Kingston-on-Thames,
Surrey
Tel 208-9775130

Kehoe, Tomás, CC
Ballycanew, Gorey,
Co Wexford
Tel 053-9427184
(Camolin, Ferns)

Kelleher, Anthony, CC
Priest's House,
Kilcornan, Co Limerick
Tel 0862666822
(Limerick)

Kelleher, Denis, Very Rev
Canon, PE
Inegrega,
Middleton, Co Cork
(Cloyne, retired)

Kelleher, Eamonn, Very Rev
PP
Kildorrery, Co Cork
Tel 022-40703
(Kildorrery, Cloyne)

Kelleher, Francis, Very Rev,
PP
The Drumlins, Virginia,
Co Cavan
(Kilmore, retired)

Kelleher, James (SPS)
Kiltegan House,
11 Douglas Road, Cork
Tel 021-4969371

Kelleher, Liam, Very Rev, PE
Cobh, Co Cork
Tel 087-8516984
(Cloyne, retired)

Kelleher, Michael, Very Rev,
Co-PP
Parochial House,
Enniskeane, Co Cork
Tel 023-8847769
(Bandon, Enniskeane,
Innishannon, Killbrittain,
Kilmurry and
Murragh/Templemartin,
Cork & R.)

Kelleher, Michael G. (CSsR)
Mount Saint Alphonsus,
South Circular Road,
Limerick
Tel 061-315099

Kelleher, Roger
(Kerry, retired)

Kelleher, Thomas, Very Rev
Canon, PE
Kinsale, Co Cork
(Cork & R., retired)

Kelliher, Padraig, CC
St Mary's, Athlone,
Co Westmeath
Tel 090-6472088
(Athlone, Ardagh & Cl.)

Kelly, Anthony (SMA)
Provincial Councillor,
African Missions,
Provincial House, Feltrim,
Blackrock Road,
Cork T12 N6C8
Tel 021-4292871

Kelly, Alphonsus Rev (SMA)
SMA House Cloonbigeen,
Claregalway,
Co Galway H91 YK64
Tel 091-798880

Kelly, Brendan (CSsR), Adm
Via Merulana 31, CP 2458,
00185 Roma-PT158, Italy
Tel 0039-06-494901

Kelly, Brendan, Most Rev,
DD
Bishop Emeritus of
Galway,
Mount Saint Mary's,
Taylor's Hill, Galway
Tel 091-563566
(Galway, retired)

Kelly, Celsus (OCSO), Rt Rev
Dom
Abbot and Superior, Our
Lady of Bethlehem Abbey,
11 Ballymena Road,
Portglenone, Ballymena,
Co Antrim BT44 8BL
Tel 028-25821211

Kelly, Conor, Very Rev, Adm
1 The Orchard,
Dungarvan,
Co Waterford
Tel 058-64284/086-8231807
(Aglish, Waterford & L.)

Kelly, David (OSA)
St Augustine's Priory,
O'Connell Street,
Limerick

Kelly, Declan, CC
2 Orchard Court,
Dunboyne, Co Meath
(Dunboyne, Meath)

Kelly, Declan, Very Rev, PP
Parochial House,
Batterstown,
Dunboyne, Co Westmeath
Tel 01-8259267
Adm, Moynalvey
(Kilcloon, Stamullen,
Meath)

Kelly, Denis, Very Rev, PP
Ballymore, Screen,
Enniscorthy, Co Wexford
Tel 053-9137140
(Castlebridge and
Curracloe, Ferns)

Kelly, Dermot (OCarm)
Director of Vocations,
Gort Muire Centre,
Ballinteer, Dublin 16
Tel 01-2984014

Kelly, Desmond (OCarm)
Whitefriar Street Church,
56 Aungier Street,
Dublin 2 D02 R598
Tel 01-4758821

Kelly, Desmond, Very Rev,
PP
Corballa, Ballina,
Co Mayo
Tel 096-36266
(Castleconnor, Killala)

Kelly, Eamonn, PP, VF
Raphoe, Convoy,
Co Donegal
Tel 087-9077985
(Raphoe, Raphoe)

Kelly, Enda, (SPS)
Kiltegan House Leader,
St Patrick's, Kiltegan,
Co Wicklow
Tel 059-6473600

Kelly, Fergus, Very Rev (CM)
Sacred Heart Presbytery
2 Flower Lane, Mill Hill,
London NW7 2JB
Tel 0044-2089591021

Kelly, Gabriel, Very Rev
Chaplain,
Cavan General Hospital,
Lisdaran, Co Cavan
Tel 049-4361399
(Kilmore)

Kelly, James, PP
Goresbridge, Co Kilkenny
Tel 059-9775180
(Paulstown, Kildare & L.)

Kelly, Jimmy (OSM)
Chaplain, Cloverhill Prison
Clondalking, Dublin 24
c/o Prior, Servite Priory,
St Peregrine,
36 Grangewood Estate,
Rathfarnham, Dublin 16
Tel 01-4517115

Allianz (ⅲ)

elly, Jimmy, Very Rev, PP
Raheen, Abbeyleix,
Co Laois
Tel 057-8731182
(*Raheen*, Kildare & L.)
elly, Joe, CC
5 Bayside Square East,
Sutton, Dublin 13
Tel 01-8322305
(*Bayside*, Dublin)
elly, John
Director of Pastoral Care,
Tallaght Hospital,
22 Nugent Road,
Churchtown, Dublin 14
Tel 01-4142482
(Dublin)
elly, John (SAC)
Bursar/Secretary for
Missions,
Provincial House,
'Homestead',
Sandyford Road,
Dundrum, Dublin 16
Tel 01-2956180/2954170
elly, John (SCJ)
Provincial,
Sacred Heart Fathers,
Fairfield,
66 Inchicore Road,
Dublin 8
Tel 01-4538655
elly, Larry, Rev Canon,
Modereator,
Cahirciveen, Co Kerry
Tel 066-9472210
Valentia Island, Co Kerry
Tel 066-9476104
(*Cahirciveen, Valentia
Island*, Kerry)
elly, Laurence (OP)
Dominican College,
Newbridge
Droichead Nua, Co Kildare
Tel 045-487200
elly, Liam (OFM)
The Abbey,
8 Francis Street,
Galway H91 C53K
Tel 091-562518
elly, Liam, Rt Rev Mgr, PP
Ballyconnell, Co Cavan
Tel 049-9526291
(*Kildallan and Tomregan*,
Kilmore)
elly, Liam (SPS)
St Patrick's, Kiltegan,
Co Wicklow W91 Y022
elly, Martin (CSSp)
Provincial,
Holy Spirit Provincialate,
Temple Park,
Richmond Avenue South,
Dublin D06 AW02
Tel 01-4975127/01-
4977230
elly, Martin, Very Rev
93 Ballyenaghan Park,
Belfast BT8 6WR
Down & C., retired)

Kelly, Matthew, Very Rev,
PE, CC
60 Hartwell Green, Kill,
Naas, Co Kildare
Tel 045-877880
(*Kill*, Kildare & L.)
Kelly, Maurice (SPS)
St Patrick's, Kiltegan,
Co Wicklow
Tel 059-6473600
Kelly, Michael
Crumlin, Dublin 12
Tel 01-4542308
(Dublin)
Kelly, Michael (SPS)
St Patrick's, Kiltegan,
Co Wicklow
Tel 059-6473600
Kelly, Michael (SPS)
St Patrick's, Kiltegan,
Co Wicklow
Tel 059-6473600
Kelly, Oliver, Very Rev, PP,
VF
West Barrs, Glenfarne,
Co Leitrim
Tel 071-9855134
(*Glenfarne*, Kilmore)
Kelly, Paddy (CSsR)
Dún Mhuire,
461/463 Griffith Avenue,
Dublin D09 X651
Tel 01-5180196
Kelly, Paraic (SMA)
SMA House, Cloonbigeen,
Claregalway,
Co Galway H91 YK64
Tel 091-798880
Kelly Jnr, Patrick (CSsR)
Dún Mhuire
461/463 Griffith Avenue,
Dublin D09 X651
Tel 01-5180196
Kelly Snr, Patrick (CSsR)
St Joseph's, Dundalk,
Co Louth
Kelly, Patrick (MSC)
'Croí Nua', Rosary Lane,
Taylor's Hill,
Co Galway
Tel 091-520960
Kelly, Patrick
(Limerick, retired)
Kelly, Paul, Very Rev, CC
The Presbytery,
18 Straffan Way,
Maynooth, Co Kildare
Tel 087-2463876
(*Maynooth*, Dublin)
Kelly, Ray, Very Rev, PP
Parochial House,
Oldcastle, Co Meath
Tel 049-8541142
(*Oldcastle*, Meath)
Kelly, Richard (OFM)
Adam & Eve's,
4 Merchants' Quay
Dublin, D08 XY19
Tel 01-6771128

Kelly, Richard, Very Rev, PP
Kilbehenny, Mitchelstown,
Co Cork
Tel 025-24040
(*Kilbehenny*, Cashel & E.)
Kelly, Robert (OCarm)
Gort Muire, Ballinteer,
Dublin D16 EI67
Tel 01-2984014
Kelly, Seamus, PP
19 Chapel Road,
Dungiven,
Co Derry BT47 4RT
Tel 028-77741219
(*Dungiven*, Derry)
Kelly, Seamus (MSC)
Western Road,
Cork T12 TN80
Tel 021-4804120
Kelly, Seán (OFMCap)
Provincial Minister,
Provincial Office,
12 Halston Street,
Dublin D07 Y2T5
Tel 01-8733205
Kelly, Seán, Very Rev, PE, CC
Stradbally, Co Laois
Tel 057-8625831
(*Stradbally*, Kildare & L.)
Kelly, Stephen
Apostolic Nunciature
Uraguay
(Meath)
Kelly, Vincent (SAC)
(attached to Pallottine
College, Thurles)
18 Silvercourt,
Silversprings, Cork
Kemmy, Bill, PP
Diocesan Communications,
c/o Bishops House, Carlow
Tel 087-2308053
Rathangan, Co Kildare
Tel 045-524316
(*Rathangan*, Kildare & L.)
Kemmy, Philip, Very Rev, PP
Parochial House,
Newtowncunningham,
Lifford, Co Donegal
Tel 074-9156138
(*Newtowncunningham &
Killea*, Raphoe)
Kenneally, Cornelius (CSsR)
Mount St Alphonsus,
South Circular Road,
Limerick
Tel 061-315099
Kenneally, Daithí (CSSp)
Kimmage Manor,
Whitehall Road, Dublin 12
Tel 01-4064300
Kennedy, Bernard, MA,
MSc, Adm
Parochial House,
Enniskerry, Co Wicklow
Tel 01-2863506
(*Enniskerry/Kilmacnogue
(Bray Grouping)*, Dublin)

Kennedy, Denis, (CSSp)
c/o St Joseph's Pastoral
Centre,
Glasthule, Co Dublin
Blackrock College,
Blackrock, Co Dublin
Tel 01-2888681
(*Glasthule*, Dublin)
Kennedy, Hugh, Very Rev
More House,
53 Cromwell Road,
London SW7 2EH
(Down & C.)
Kennedy, James, Very Rev,
PP
Anacarty,
Co Tipperary
Tel 062-71104
(*Anacarty*, Cashel & E.)
Kennedy, John
Parochial House,
Rathmolyon, Co Meath
Tel 046-9555212
(*Enfield*, Meath)
Kennedy, John, Rt Rev Mgr
(Dicastery for the Doctrine
of the Faith)
Via del Mascherino 12,
00193 Roma, Italy
(Dublin)
Kennedy, Joseph (CP), PC
St Paul's Retreat,
Mount Argus, Dublin 6W
Tel 01-4992000
(*Mount Argus*, Dublin)
Kennedy, Joseph, Very Rev,
AP
Parochial House,
Moneygall, Birr, Co Offaly
Tel 0505-45110/
086-4072488
(*Ollatrim Pastoral Area*,
Killaloe)
Kennedy, Joseph, Very Rev
(Limerick, retired)
Kennedy, Kieron, Rt Rev
Mgr, PP
Freshford,
Co Kilkenny R95 X2EO
Tel 056-8832426/
087-2523521
(*Freshford*, Ossory)
Kennedy, Michael (CSSp)
Chaplain, NRH,
Rochestown Avenue,
Dun Laoghaire, Co Dublin
Tel 01-2355272
Kennedy, Michael, Very Rev
Ballylaneen,
Kilmacthomas,
Co Waterford
(Waterford & L.)
Kennedy, Michael, Very Rev,
PP
Lusmagh, Banagher,
Co Offaly R42 WP40
Tel 0509-51358
(*Lusmagh*, Clonfert)

Kennedy, Michael, Very Rev, PP
Lattin, Co Tipperary
Tel 087-4147229
(*Lattin and Cullen*, Cashel & E.)

Kennedy, Michael, Very Rev, PE
Parochial House, Colligan,
Dungarvan, Co Waterford
Tel 058-41629
(*Kilgobinet*, Waterford & L.)

Kennedy, Noel, Very Rev, PP
Bournea, Roscrea,
Co Tipperary
Tel 0505-43211/
086-3576775
(*Cronan Pastoral Area*,
Killaloe)

Kennedy, Stephen
The Presbytery, Ballsgrove,
Drogheda, Co Louth
Tel 041-9831991
(*Drogheda, Holy Family*,
Meath)

Kennedy, Tom, Very Rev, PP
Parochial House,
Castledermot, Co Kildare
Tel 059-9144164
(*Castledermot*, Dublin)

Kennelly, Pádraig, PP
Firies, Killarney, Co Kerry
Tel 066-9764122
(*Firies*, Kerry)

Kennelly, Séamus, Very Rev, PP
Boherbue, Mallow,
Co Cork
Tel 029-76151
(*Boherbue/Kiskeam*, Kerry)

Kenny, Donald, Rt Rev Mgr
Cois Cuan, Arthurstown,
New Ross, Co Wexford
(Ferns, retired)

Kenny, Gerard, Co-PP
Circular Road, Kilkee,
Co Clare
Tel 065-9056580
(*Cois Fharraige Pastoral
Area*, Killaloe)

Kenny, Gerard (OMI)
Oblate House of Retreat,
Inchicore, Dublin 8
Tel 01-4534408/4541805

Kenny, John, Very Rev, PP, VF
Partry, Claremorris,
Co Mayo
Tel 094-9543013
(*Partry (Ballyovey)*, Tuam)

Kenny, Lorcan
Curates House,
Convent Hill,
Roscrea, Co Tipperary
Tel 0505-21454
Chaplain, The Valley,
Roscrea, Co Tipperary
Tel 0505-23637/
087-6553402
(*Cronan Pastoral Area
(Roscrea)*, Killaloe)

Kenny, Merlyn, PP
Newtowncashel,
Co Longford
Tel 043-3325112
PP, Lanesborough
(Rathcline)
Lanesboro, Co Longford
Tel 043-3321166
(*Newtowncashel (Cashel)*,
Lanesboro, Ardagh & Cl.)

Kenny, Pat, Very Rev, PP
St Killian Church, Newinn,
Ballinasloe,
Co Galway H53 P6C0
Tel 090-9675819
(*New Inn and Bullaun*,
Clonfert)

Kenny, Paul, Moderator
149 Swords Road,
Whitehall, Dublin 9
Tel 01-8375274
(*Larkhill-Whitehall-Santry*,
Dublin)

Kenny, Paul (SSC)
St Columban's Retirement
Home,
Dalgan Park, Navan,
Co Meath
Tel 046-9021525

Keogan, Thomas M., Adm
7 Quary Park,
Mullaghmore, Co Sligo
(Kilmore, retired)

Keogh, Martin, Very Rev, PP
Cappoquin, Co Waterford
Tel 058-54216
Priest in charge, Modeligo
(*Cappoquin, Modeligo*,
Waterford & L.)

Keohane, Martin, Very Rev
Canon, Co-PP
Parish House,
Carraig na bhFear,
Co Cork
Tel 021-4884119
(*Carrignavar, Glanmire,
Glounthaune and
Watergrasshill*, Cork & R.)

Keohane, Michael, Very Rev, AP
Diocesan Secretary,
1 The Presbytery,
Blackrock,
Tel 021-4301717
(*Blackrock*, Cork & R.)

Kerin, John, Very Rev, PP
St Joseph's, Lauragh,
Killarney, Co Kerry
Tel 064-6683107
(*Tuosist*, Kerry)

Kerr, Aidan, Very Rev, PE
142 Carnmoney Road,
Newtownabbey,
Co Antrim BT36 6JU
Tel 028-90832488
(*St Mary's on the Hill*,
Down & C.)

Kerr, Peter, Very Rev, PE, AP
42 Innishatieve Road,
Carrickmore, Omagh,
Co Tyrone BT79 9HS
Tel 028-80761837
(Armagh, retired)

Kett, Patrick J., Very Rev
27 Huntsgrove,
Ashbourne,
Co Meath
(Dublin, retired)

Keveny, Martin, Very Rev
Cathedral Place,
Ballina, Co Mayo
(Killala, retired)

Kevin, John (CSSp)
Blackrock College,
Blackrock, Co Dublin
Tel 01-2888681

Kidarathil, Antony, CC
Parochial House,
Shercock, Co Cavan
Tel 042-9669127
(*Bailieboro (Killann)*,
Kilmore)

Kidney, Michael (SMA)
African Missions,
Blackrock Road,
Cork T12 TD54
Tel 021-4292871

Kiely, Charles, Dr, PP
The Presbytery,
Our Lady Crowned,
Upper Mayfield, Cork
Tel 021-4503116
(*Upper Mayfield*, Cork & R.)

Kiely, Eugene, Very Rev, PP
Ballyferriter West,
Tralee, Co Kerry
Tel 066-9156131
(*Ballyferriter*, Kerry)

Kiely, John, Very Rev, PE
'The Cottage',
Ballinaparka,
Aglish, Co Waterford
(Waterford & L., retired)

Kieran, Aidan, PP
Parochial House,
Foxdene Avenue,
Balgaddy,
Lucan South
Co Dublin K78 DD89
Tel 01 4572900
(*Lucan South*, Dublin)

Kiernan, Brian (OCarm)
Gort Muire, Ballinteer,
Dublin 16
Tel 01-2984014

Kiernan, Kevin (OFMCap)
Vicar, Capuchin Friary,
Church Street,
Dublin D07 HA22
Tel 01-8730599

Kiernan, Patrick, PP
Banagher, Co Offaly
Tel 057-9151338
(*Cloghan and Banagher
(Gallen and Reynagh)*,
Ardagh & Cl.)

Kilcoyne, Brendan, Very Re
Canon, PP, VF
The Parochial House,
St Mary's Presbytery,
Athenry,
Co Galway H65 VX67
Tel 091-844076
(*Athenry*, Tuam)

Kilduff, Donal, Very Rev, P
Crosskeys, Co Cavan
Tel 049-4336102
(*Denn*, Kilmore)

Kilkenny, Michael (CSSp)
Very Rev, Moderator
Team Leader
Church of the Holy Spirit
Greenhills, Dublin 12
Tell 01-4504040
Moderator, Greenhills,
Kimmage Manor
(*Greenhills, Kimmage
Manor*, Dublin)

Killeen, Jim, Rt Rev Mgr, P
VG
Midleton, Co Cork
Tel 021-4631750
(*Midleton*, Cloyne)

Killeen, John, Very Rev
Canon, CC
20 Abbey Court,
Abbey Road, Monkstown
Co Dublin
Tel 01-2802533
(*Kill-O'-The-Grange*,
Dublin)

Killeen, Seán, Rt Rev Mgr,
VG
Cloghans, Ballina,
Co Mayo
(Killala, retired)

Killenga, Malasi S. (AOR)
John Sullivan House of
Formation,
27 Leinster Road,
Rathmines, Dublin 6
Tel 01-5242134

Kilmartin, Michael, Very
Rev, PP
54 Brookville, Ashbourne
Co Meath
Tel 01-8353149
(*Ashbourne-Donaghmore*
Meath)

ilmurray, Martin (OCarm),
Terenure College,
Terenure,
Dublin D6W DK72
Tel 01-4904621
ilpatrick, Edward, PE
(Derry, retired)
ilroy, Peter
64 Cherbury Court,
Booterstown, Co Dublin
(Dublin, retired)
inahan, Gabriel (OFM)
Franciscan Abbey,
Multyfarnham,
Co Westmeath
Tel 044-9371114/9371137
ng, Anthony, Very Rev
Canon, PE
Parklands, New Road,
Westport,
Co Mayo F28 K236
(Tuam, retired)
ng, Bernard (SM), CC
Marist Fathers,
St Mary's Road,
Dundalk, Co Louth
Tel 0429334019
ng, Finnian (OSB)
Silverstream Priory,
Stamullen,
Co Meath K32 T189
Tel 01-8417142
ng, Michael, Very Rev, PE
21 Wattlebridge Road,
Drumquilla,
Newtownbutler,
Co Fermanagh BT92 8JP
Tel 028-67738229
(Newtownbutler
(Galloon), Clogher)
ng, William, Very Rev
156b Rathgar Road,
Dublin 6
Parish Chaplain (pro tem),
Harold's Cross
(Dublin, retired)
ngston, John, Very Rev
Canon, Co-PP
Parochial House,
Timoleague, Co Cork
Tel 023-8839114
(Ardfield/Rathbarry,
Barryroe, Clonakilty,
Kilmeen/Castleventry,
Rosscarbery and
Timoleague, Cork & R.)
ngston, William (CSSp)
Rockwell College,
Cashel, Co Tipperary
Tel 062-61444
rby, John, Most Rev, DD,
P
Retired Bishop of Clonfert,
Cappatagle, Balinasloe,
Co Galway, H53 X206
Tel 091-843017
(Cappataggle and
Killrickle
(Killalaghtan and Kilickle),
Clonfert)

Kirby, Dom Mark Daniel
(OSB), Very Rev
Silverstream Priory,
Stamullen,
Co Meath K32 T189
Tel 01-8417142
Kirwan, Michael Rev (SJ)
Vice Superior,
35 Lower Leeson Street,
Dublin 2
Tel 01-6761248
Kirwan, Noel, Co-PP
The Presbytery,
Bruff, Co Limerick
Tel 087-2589279
(Pastoral Unit 7, Limerick)
Kirwin, Jeremiah (CSSp)
Spiritan Retreat &
Sprituality Centre,
Ardbraccan, Navan,
Co Meath C15 T884
Tel 046-9021441
Kitching, Ciarán, Very Rev,
PP
St Joseph's,
Killimor, Ballinasloe,
Co Galway H53 R8C4
Tel 090-9676151
(Killimor & Tiranascragh,
Clonfert)
Kivlehan, Paul, Very Rev,
Adm
The Presbytery,
Ballaghdereen,
Co Roscommon
Tel 094-9860011
(Ballaghaderreen
(Castlemore and
Kilcolman), Achonry)
Knight, Matthew J. (CSSp)
Rockwell College,
Cashel, Co Tipperary
Tel 062-61444
Kochatt, Alex CC
77 The Lakelands,
Naas, Co Kildare
Tel 045-949576
(Naas, Kildare & L.)
Kochuveettil, Francis Xavier,
Co-PP
Parochial House,
Toomevara, Co Tipperary
Tel 067-26023
(Ollatrim Pastoral Area,
Killaloe)
Kokkandathil, Jilson, CC
South Presbytery,
Dunbar Street, Cork
(South Parish, St Patrick's
and Ss Peter and Paul's,
Cork & R.)
Kornitsky, Vasil
Chaplain to Ukranian
Community,
3 Maypark,
Malahide Road, Dublin 5
Tel 01-5164752
(Donnycarney, Dublin)

Kowalkowski, Marek
Ministry to Polish
Community,
The Presbytery
Kill, Co Waterford
(Waterford & L.)
Kowalski, Wojciech (SJ)
Jesuit Community,
27 Leinster Road,
Rathmines, Dublin 6
Tel 01-4970250
Krawiec, Jaroslaw (OP)
St Saviour's,
Upper Dorset Street,
Dublin 1
Tel 01-8897610
Krzystof, Krzysków (SVD)
8 Teignmouth Road,
London, NW2 4HN
Tel 020-84528430
Kupczakiewicz, Krzysztof
(OP)
St Saviour's,
Upper Dorset Street,
Dublin 1
Tel 01-8897610
Kurek, Jaroslaw (OSB)
Glenstal Abbey, Murroe,
Co Limerick
Tel 061-621000
Kuthanapillil, Jaison
(OCarm)
Prior, Bursar,
Carmelite Priory, Moate,
Co Westmeath N37 AW34
Tel 090-6481160/6481398
Kuttikkatt, Christanand
Varghese (IC)
Clonturk House,
Ormond Road,
Drumcondra,
Dublin D09 F821
Tel 01-6877014
Kwasniewski, Isaias (OSB)
Silverstream Priory,
Stamullen,
Co Meath K32 T189
Tel 01-8417142
Kwikirza, Dominic, CC
Presbytery 1,
Montrose Park,
Beaumont, Dublin 5
Tel 01-8477740
(Beaumont, Dublin)
Kyne, Brendan, Very Rev,
Co-PP
The Prebytery,
Ballycoricick, Co Clare
(Radharc na nOileán
Pastoral Area, Killaloe)
Kyte, Gabriel Joseph (CFR)
St Patrick Friary,
64 Delmege Park,
Moyross,
Limerick V94 859Y
Tel 061-458071

L

Lacey, Liam, Very Rev, PP
No. 1 Prebytery,
Castle Street, Dalkey,
Co Dublin
Tel 01-2857773
(Dalkey, Dublin)
Laffan, Sean, Very Rev, CC
Gusserane, Co Wexford
Tel 051-562111
(Ballycullane, Ferns)
Lafferty, Angelo (SMA)
African Missions,
Blackrock Road,
Cork T12 TD54
Tel 021-4292871
Lagan, Hugh (SMA)
African Missions,
Dromantine, Newry,
Co Down BT34 1RH
Tel 028-30821224
Lagan, Patrick, CC
Parochial House,
32 Chapel Road,
Derry BT47 2BB
Tel 028-71342303
(Waterside (Glendermott),
Derry)
Laizer, John (CSSp)
Holy Spirit Missionary
College
Kimmage Manor,
Whitehall Road,
Dublin D12 P5YP
Tel 01-4064300
Lally, Fredrick (OCarm)
Gort Muire, Ballinteer,
Dublin 16 D16 EI67
Tel 01-2984014
Lalor, Eddie (SPS)
St Patrick's, Kiltegan,
Co Wicklow W91 YO22
Tel 0596473600
Lalor, Thomas, Very Rev, PE
The Presbytery,
Tinryland, Co Carlow
Tel 087-2360355
(Kildare & L., retired)
Lambe, Anthony, Very Rev,
PP
Drangan, Thurles,
Co Tipperary
Tel 052-9152103
(Drangan, Cashel & E.)
Lambert, Owen (CSSp)
Holy Spirit Missionary
College
Kimmage Manor,
Whitehall Road,
Dublin D12 P5YP
Tel 01-4064300
Lane, Daniel, AP
1 Cedarville,
Abbeyfeale, Co Limerick
Tel 087-2533030
(Pastoral Unit 14, Limerick)

Lane, Dermot A., Rt Rev
Mgr, PC
162 Sandyford Road,
Dublin 16
Tel 01-2956165
(*Balally*, Dublin)

Lane, Michael, Venerable
Archdeacon, PE,
2 Meadowvale, Raheen,
Limerick
Tel 061-228761/
087-2544450
(Limerick, retired)

Lane, Thomas, CC
2 Bellevue Circle,
Mallow, Co Cork
Tel 087-0660615
(*Mallow*, Cloyne)

Langford, Gerard, Very Rev,
PP
Holy Family Presbytery,
Luke Wadding Street,
Waterford
Tel 051-323213
(*Holy Family*, Waterford &
L.)

Lanigan-Ryan, Thomas, PP
Ballina, Killaloe,
Co Clare
Tel 061-376178
(*Ballina*, Cashel & E.)

Lanigan, Jerry (SVD)
Donamon Castle,
Roscommon
Tel 090-6662222

Larkin, Barry, Very Rev,
Adm
1 Clonard Park,
Clonard, Co Wexford
Tel 053-9147686
(*Clonard*, Ferns)

Larkin, Barry, Very Rev, PP
Suncroft, Curragh,
Co Kildare
Tel 045-441586
(*Suncroft*, Kildare & L.)

Larkin, David (SPS)
House Leader,
St Patrick's,
21 Leeson Park,
Dublin 6 D06 DE76
Tel 01-4977897

Larkin, Francis, Very Rev
Canon, AP
7 Presentation Road,
Co Galway
Tel 091-449727
(Galway, retired)

Larkin, James,
Chaplain to Loreto Sisters,
Rathfarnham/
Chaplain to Coiste
Treadach, 72 Bird Avenue,
Clonskeagh, Dublin 14
Tel 01-2196869
(Dublin)

Larkin, Pat, Very Rev, Co-PP,
VF
47 Woodfield Crescent,
kilrush, Co Clare
Tel 065-9262729
(*Inis Cathaigh Pastoral
Area*, Killaloe)

Larkin, Seamus, Very Rev
Canon
(priest in residence)
Monamolin,
Gorey, Co Wexford
(Ferns, retired)

Larkin, Seán, PE, AP
Parochial House,
9 Chapel Road,
Bessbrook, Newry,
Co Down BT35 7AU
Tel 028-30830272
(*Bessbrook (Killeavy
Lower)*, Armagh)

Lavelle, Paul, Very Rev
123 Foxfield Grove,
Kilbarrack, Dublin 5
(Dublin, retired)

Laverty, Austin, Very Rev
Canon, PE
Ardara, Co Donegal
Tel 074-9537033
(*Ardara*, Raphoe)

Laverty, Denis
47 Silken Vale,
Maynooth, Co Kildare
(Dublin, retired)

Lawless, Brendan, Very Rev,
PP
Carrabane, Athenry,
Co Galway H65 EP04
Tel 091-841103
(*Clostoken and
Kilconieran*, Clonfert)

Lawless, Brian, Very Rev,
Adm
54 Clogher Road
Dublin 12
Tel 01-4536988
(*Clogher Road*, Dublin)

Lawless, Ralph (OFM)
The Abbey,
8 Francis Street, Galway
H91 C53K
Tel 091-562518

Lawless, Richard, Very Rev
c/o Bishop's House,
Summerhill, Wexford
(Ferns)

Paul Lawlor (OP), Prior
Convent of SS Xystus and
Clement
Collegio San Clemente,
Via Labicana 95,
00184 Roma
Tel 0039-06-7740021

Lawton, Liam, Adm
St Mary's,
Edenderry, Co Offaly
Tel 046-9732352
(*Edenderry*, Kildare & L.)

Layden, Thomas (SJ)
Superior,
Peter Faber House,
28 Brookvale Avenue,
Belfast BT14 6BW
Tel 028-90757615

Leader, Mícheál, Very Rev,
PP
Ballyclough, Mallow,
Co Cork
Tel 022-27650
(*Ballyclough*, Cloyne)

Lehane, Timothy (SVD)
Provincial,
1 & 3 Pembroke Road,
Ballsbridge, Dublin 4

Leahy, Andy, Very Rev, PP
Episcopal Vicar for the
Pastoral Care of Priests,
The Presbytery,
Kildare Town, Kildare
Tel 045-520347
(*Kildare*, Kildare & L)

Leahy, Brendan, Most Rev,
DD
Bishop of Limerick,
Limerick Diocesan Centre,
St Munchin's,
Corbally, Limerick
Tel 061-350000
(Limerick)

Leahy, Donal, Very Rev
Canon, PE
Jamesbrook,
Midleton, Co Cork
(Cloyne, retired)

Leahy, Michael (OSA)
St Augustine's Priory,
Washington Street, Cork
Tel 021-2753982

Leahy, Niall (SJ)
Milltown Park,
Miltown Road, Dublin 6
Tel 01-4987333

Leahy, Niall S. (SJ), Very Rev,
PP
The Presbytery,
Upper Gardiner Street,
Dublin 1
Tel 01-8363411
(*Gardiner Street*, Dublin)

Leamy, Michael, Very Rev
Canon, PP, VF
Mitchelstown, Co Cork
Tel 025-41765
(*Mitchelstown*, Cloyne)

Leane, Thomas,
(Kerry, retired)

Leavy, Oliver (SPS)
St Patrick's, Kiltegan,
Co Wicklow W91 Y022
Tel 059-6473600

Lebocq, Wulfran, Canon
Institute of Christ the King
Sovereign Priest
12–14 The Crescent,
Limerick
(Galway)

Lee, Theodore (OSB)
Silverstream Priory,
Stamullen,
Co Meath K32 T189
Tel 01-8417142

Lee, William, Most Rev, DD
Retired Bishop of
Waterford and Lismore,
5 The Brambles,
Ballinakill Downs,
Waterford
Tel 051-821485
(Waterford & L.)

Lenihan, Jim, Very Rev, PP
St Agatha's Parish Centre
Headford, Killarney,
Co Kerry
Tel 064-7754008
(*Glenflesk*, Kerry)

Lennon, Brian (SJ)
St Francis Xavier's,
Upper Gardiner Street,
Dublin 1
Tel 01-8363411
(Zam-Mal)

Lennon, Denis, Rt Rev Mgr
CC
39 Beechlawn, Clonard,
Wexford
Tel 053-9124417
(*Clonard*, Ferns)

Lennon, James, CC
(Hexham & Newcastle)
Castledockrell,
Ballycarney, Enniscorthy,
Co Wexford
Tel 053-9388569
(*Marshallstown*, Ferns)

Lennon, Patrick, PP
Dromard, Moyne,
Co Longford
Tel 049-4335248
(*Dromard*, Ardagh & Cl.)

Lennon, Patrick (OSA)
Duckspool House
(Retirement Community)
Abbeyside, Dungarvan,
Co Waterford
Tel 058-23784

Lennon, Sean (OSM)
Servite Priory,
Benburb, Dungannon,
Co Tyrone, BT71 7JZ
Tel 028-37548241

Leonard, Albert (OP), Very
Rev
St Mary's Priory,
Tallaght, Dublin 24
Tel 01-4048100

Leonard, Derek, Very Rev,
Parochial House,
Knockaderry, Co Limerick
Tel 087-6261287
(*Pastoral Unit 10*, Limerick)

Leonard, John
(Limerick, retired)

Allianz ⑪

eonard, Patrick (CSSp)
Holy Spirit Missionary
College
Kimmage Manor,
Whitehall Road,
Dublin D12 P5YP
Tel 01-4064300

evakovic, Josip, CC
(Chaplain to the Croatian
Community)
The Presbytery,
Haddington Road,
Dublin 4
Tel 01-660075

ewis, Eugene (White
Fathers)
Cypress Grove,
Templeogue, Dublin 6W
Tel 01-4055263/4055264

eycock, Dermot, Very Rev
64 Newtownpark Avenue,
Blackrock, Co Dublin
(Dublin, retired)

iddane, Raymond, Very
Rev, AP
Newtown, Waterford
Tel 051-874284
(SS Joseph and Benildus,
Waterford & L.)

inehan, Patrick, Very Rev,
PP
Cloyne, Midleton,
Co Cork
Tel 021-4652597
(Cloyne, Cloyne)

inehan, Terry,
Kerry General Hospital,
Tralee, Co Kerry
Tel 066-7126222
(Kerry)

innane, Seámus, Very Rev,
(Kerry, retired)

iston, Micheál, Very Rev
Canon
Chaplain to
Gaelscoileanna,
21 Sullane Crescent,
Raheen Heights, Limerick
Tel 087-2314804
(Limerick, retired)

ittle, Anthony G. (CSSp)
Holy Spirit Missionary
College
Kimmage Manor,
Whitehall Road,
Dublin D12 P5YP
Tel 01-4064300

ittle, Thomas, Very Rev,
Adm, PP, VF,
Brownshill Avenue,
Carlow
Tel 059-9131559
(Askea, Tinryland, Kildare
& L.)

ittleton, John
The Priory Institute,
Tallaght Village,
Dublin 24
Tel 01-4048100
(Cashel & E.)

Littleton, Patrick
2 May Park, Donnycarney,
Dublin 5
(Dublin, retired)

Lloyd, Enda, Rt Rev Mgr, EV,
Co-PP
10 The Oaks,
Loughlinstown Drive,
Dun Laoghaire
Tel 01-2826895
(Loughlinstown,
Ballybrack-Killiney, Dublin)

Lloyd, Francis, Very Rev, PE
The Presbytery,
Dungarvan, Co Waterford
(Waterford & L., retired)

Loftus, Hughie, Very Rev, PP
Carraroe, Co Galway
Tel 091-595452
(Carraroe (Kileen),
Spiddal/Knock, Tuam)

Loftus, John, Very Rev, PP,
VF
Ballycastle, Co Mayo
Tel 096-43010
(Ballycastle (Kilbride and
Doonfeeny), Killala)

Loftus, Joseph (CM)
St Vincent's Castleknock
College,
Castleknock,
Dublin D15 PD95
Tel 01-8213051
Chaplain,
Room RD-117,
Rathdown House,
TU Dublin, Grangegorman
Dublin D07 H6K8
Tel 01-2207079
(Dublin)

Loftus, Kevin, Rt Rev Mgr,
VG
St James's,
Enniscrone, Co Sligo
Tel 096-49011
(Killala, retired)

Loftus, Martin (SDB)
Vice-Rector, Salesian
House, Milford,
Castletroy, Limerick
Tel 061-330268

Logue, Charles, CC
Malin Head, Co Donegal
Tel 074-9370134
(Malin (Clonca), Derry)

Lohan, Declan, CC
Parochial House,
Renmore, Galway
Tel 091 751707
(Renmore, Galway)

Lohan, Louis
Parish Chaplain,
Ballygar, Co Galway
(Ballygar (Kilian and
Killeroran), Elphin)

Loisel, D. Eric M. (OSB)
Benedictine Monks,
Holy Cross Abbey,
119 Kilbroney Road,
Rostrevor,
Co Down BT34 3BN
Tel 028-41739979

Lombard, Patrick, Very Rev,
PP, VF
St Anne's, Sligo
Tel 071-9145028
(Sligo, St Anne's, Elphin)

Long, Joseph (SPS), CC
Curate's House, Fairgreen,
Belturbet, Co Cavan
Tel 049-9522151
(Belturbet (Annagh),
Kilmore)

Long, Leo
Carrigoran Nursing Home,
Newmarket-on-Fergus,
Co Clare
Tel 086-8353388
(Killaloe, retired)

Long, Martin, Very Rev, PP
The Parochial House,
Westport Road,
Louisburgh,
Co Mayo F28 PH00
Tel 098-66198
(Louisburgh (Kilgeever),
Tuam)

Long, Michael (SPS)
St Patrick's, Kiltegan,
Co Wicklow W91 Y022
Tel 059-6473600

Looby, John (SJ)
35 Lower Leeson Street,
Dublin 2
Tel 01-6761248

Looney, Thomas, Very Rev,
(Kerry, retired)

Loughran, Alfred (OFM)
Franciscan Friary,
Killarney, Co Kerry
Tel 064-6631334/6631066

Loughran, Desmond, Very
Rev, PP, VF
4 Holymount Road,
Gilford, Craigavon,
Co Armagh BT63 6AT
Tel 028-40624236
(Tullylish, Dromore)

Loughran, Malachy (OSA)
St Augustine's Priory,
Shop Street,
Drogheda, Co Louth
Tel 041-9838409

Loughrey, Damien
(OFMCap)
Capuchin Friary,
Holy Trinity,
Fr Mathew Quay,
Cork T12 PK24
Tel 021-4270827

Loughrey, Neil (White
Fathers)
Promotion Director/Mite
Boxes
Cypress Grove,
Templeogue, Dublin 6W
Tel 01-4055263/4055264

Loughrey, Vivian, Very Rev,
PP
Shrule, Galway
Tel 093-31262
(Shrule, Galway)

Lovell, Liam
c/o Diocesan Office,
Killarney, Co Kerry
(Kerry)

Lovett, Cyril (SSC)
(Editor, Far East
Magazine),
St Columban's,
Dalgan Park, Navan,
Co Meath
Tel 046-9021525

Lowe, Bernard (CP)
Superior, St Paul's Retreat,
Mount Argus, Dublin 6W
Tel 01-4992000

Lubega, Godfrey
22 Gladstone Street,
Clonmel, Co Tipperary
Chaplain,
South Tipperary General
Hospital
Tel 052-6177000
(Waterford & L.)

Lucey, Finbarr, Very Rev, PP
Ardmore, Youghal,
Co Cork
Tel 024-94177
(Waterford & L., retired)

Lucey, John (CSsR)
Mount Saint Alphonsus,
Limerick
Tel 061-315099

Lucey, Pat (OP), CC
St Mary's, Tallaght,
Dublin D24 X585
Tel 01-4048100

Ludden, Paul, Very Rev, Co-
PP
c/o St Mary's, Sandyford,
Dublin 18
(Sandyford, Dublin)

Luddy, Denis (CSsR), CC
722 Antrim Road,
Newtownabbey,
Co Antrim BT36 7PG
Tel 028-90774833
(St Gerard's, Down & C.)

Ludlow, Brendan,
Chaplain, UCD
Chaplains' Room, UCD
Belfield, Dublin 4
Tel 01-7168317
(Meath)

Allianz (ⁱⁱⁱ)

Lugowski, Janusz
Chaplain to Polish
Community,
Parochial House,
Moynalvey, Summerhill,
Co Meath
Tel 046-9557031/
087-9908922
(*Moynalvey*, Meath)

Lumsden, David, Very Rev,
PP
Director, Knock Diocesan
Pilgrimage,
83 Tonlegee Drive,
Raheny, Dublin 5
Tel 01-8480917/
087-2569873
(*Edenmore, Grange Park*,
Dublin)

Lupot, Julian, PP
The Presbytery,
Ballintubber
Castlerea, Co Roscommon
Tel 094-9655602
(*Ballintubber (Ballintubber
and Ballymoe)*, Elphin)

Lynch, Damien, CC
4 Bellevue Circle,
Mallow, Co Cork
Tel 022-53909
(*Mallow*, Cloyne)

Lynch, Dermot (OFMCap)
Capuchin Presence
Our Lady of Knock Shrine,
Knock, Co Mayo

Lynch, Eamonn
Bailieborough Road,
Virginia,
Co Cavan
(Kilmore, retired)

Lynch, Finbarr (SJ)
c/o Milltown Park,
Miltown Road, Dublin 6
Tel 01-4987333

Lynch, Finian (OP)
St Mary's,
Pope's Quay, Cork
Tel 021-4502267

Lynch, Flannan (OFMCap),
CC
Capuchin Friary,
Ard Mhuire,
Creeslough, Letterkenny,
Co Donegal
Tel 074-9138005

Lynch, Jim,
1 Orchard Court,
Dunboyne, Co Meath
(Meath, retired)

Lynch, Jude (CSSp)
Holy Spirit Missionary
College
Kimmage Manor,
Whitehall Road,
Dublin D12 P5YP
Tel 01-4064300
Clonskeagh Hospital,
Vergemount, Dublin 6

Lynch, Laurence (OCarm)
Carmelite Friary,
Kinsale,
Co Cork P17 WR88
Tel 021-4772138

Lynch, Lorcan, Very Rev
St Anne's Nursing Home,
Clones Road, Ballybay,
Co Monaghan A75 K193
(Clogher, retired)

Lynch, Owen, TA
Chapel Lane,
St Peter's Road, Little Bray
Co Wicklow A98 C5V9
(*Bray (Ballywaltrim)*,
Bray (Holy Redeemer),
Bray, Putland Road,
Dublin)

Lynch, Patrick (OFM)
Guardian,
Franciscan Friary,
Killarney, Co Kerry
Tel 064-6631334/6631066

Lynch, Patrick (OFMCap)
Capuchin Friary,
Ard Mhuire,
Creeslough, Letterkenny,
Co Donegal
F92 Y23R

Lynch, Patrick, Very Rev, PE
(priest in residence)
Kiltimagh, Co Mayo
(Achonry, retired)

Lynch, Patsy (SMA), PP
St Michael's, Ballinskelligs,
Co Kerry
Tel 066-9479108
(*Ballinskelligs (Prior)*,
Kerry)

Lynch, Sean (SMA)
African Missions,
Blackrock Road,
Cork T12 TD54
Tel 021-4292871

Lyng, Dick (OSA), CC
Provincial Secretary,
St Augustine's,
Taylor's Lane,
Ballyboden, Dublin 16
Tel 01-4241000
(*Ballyboden*, Dublin)

Lyng, John (OSA)
Prior,
St Augustine's Priory,
Washington Street, Cork
Tel 021-4275398/4270410

Lyon, Kevin, Archdeacon, CC
Archdeacon of
Glendalough,
Parochial House,
Crosschapel, Blessington,
Co Wicklow
Tel 045-865215
(*Blessington*, Dublin)

Lyons, Fintan (OSB)
Glenstal Abbey, Murroe,
Co Limerick
Tel 061-386103

Lyons, Gabriel, Very Rev, PP
St Teresa's Presbytery,
Glen Road,
Belfast BT11 8BL
(*St Teresa's*, Down & C.)

Lyon, Kevin, Rev
Archdeacon, CC,
Parochial House,
Crosschapel,
Blessington, Co Wicklow
Tel 01-865215
(*Blessington*, Dublin)

Lyons, Thomas
Chaplain,
Cork University Hospital,
Wilton, Cork
Tel 021-4546400/4922391/
4546109
(Galway)

M

Ma Ming, Cyril (SVD), CC
Presbytery, Idrone Avenue,
Knocklyon, Dublin 16
Tel 01-4941204
(*Knocklyon*, Dublin)

MacAodh, Lomán (OFM)
Franciscan Abbey,
Multyfarnham,
Co Westmeath
Tel 044-9371114/9371137

MacBradaigh, Proinsias (SJ)
Superior,
Arrupe Community,
127 Shangan Road,
Ballymun, Dublin 9
Tel 01-8625345

MacCabe, Basil Mary (OSB),
Very Rev Dom
Silverstream Priory,
Stamullen,
Co Meath K32 T189
Tel 01-8417142

MacCárthaigh, Donncha
(MSC)
Western Road,
Cork T12 TN80
Tel 021-4804120

MacCarthaigh, Pádraig
Irremore, Listowel,
Co Kerry
(Kerry, retired)

MacCormack, Gerard, Very
Rev, PP
c/o Bishop's House,
Dublin Road,
Mullingar, Co Westmeath
(Meath)

MacCraith, Micheál (OFM)
Dún Mhuire,
Seafield Road,
Killiney, Co Dublin
Tel 01-2826760

Mac Cuarta, Briain (SJ)
c/o Irish Jesuit
Provincialate,
Milltown Park,
Miltown Road, Dublin 6
Tel 01-4987333

Mac Cumhaill, Naos (CSSp)
Holy Spirit Missionary
College
Kimmage Manor,
Whitehall Road,
Dublin D12 P5YP
Tel 01-4064300

MacDaid, Liam S., Most Rev
DD
Retired Bishop of Clogher,
Drumhirk, Dublin Road,
Co Monaghan H18 YE30
Tel 047-82208
(Clogher)

MacDonagh, Fergal, Very
Rev, PP
18 St Anthony's Road,
Rialto, Dublin 8
Tel 01-4534469
(*Rialto/Dolphin's Barn*,
Dublin)

MacDonald, Criostóir, Very
Rev, PP
Murmont Lawn,
Mayfield, Cork
Tel 021-4501861
(*St Joseph's (Mayfield)*,
Cork & R.)

MacEntee, Patrick, Very Rev
Canon, PP
35A Esker Road, Dromore,
Co Tyrone BT78 3LE
Tel 028-82898641
(*Dromore, Fintona
(Donacavey)*, Clogher)

MacGearailt, Sean (OSA)
St Augustine's Priory,
St Augustine's Street,
Galway

MacGiolla Catháin, Darach
Chaplain, Royal Victoria
Hospital,
111 Queensway, Lambeg,
Lisburn, BT27 4QS
Tel 028-90606980
(Down & C)

MacGiollarnáth, Seán,
(OCarm)
Carmelite Priory,
56 Aungier Street,
Dublin 2 D02 R598
Tel 01-4758821

MacGréil, Mícheál (SJ)
St Francis Xavier's,
Upper Gardiner Street,
Dublin 1
Tel 01-8363411

MacHale, Brendan (SSC)
St Columban's,
Dalgan Park, Navan,
Co Meath
Tel 046-9021525

MacHale, John George, Very
Rev Canon
(Priest in Residence)
Kilglass, Enniscrone,
Ballina, Co Mayo
Tel 096-36191
(*Kilglass*, Killala)

Macken, Walter
Ely University Centre,
10 Hume Street, Dublin 2
Tel 01-6767420
(Opus Dei)

MacKenna, Benedict (OP)
Dominican College,
Newbridge
Droichead Nua, Co Kildare
Tel 045-487200

Mackey, Niall, TA
The Presbytery
Vevay Road, Bray
Co Wicklow A98 F90
(*Bray (Ballywaltrim)*,
Bray (Holy Redeemer),
Bray, Putland Road,
Dublin)

MacKiernan, James, Adm
The Presbytery, Longford,
Co Offaly
Tel 043-3346465
(*Longford
(Templemichael,
Ballymacormack)*, Ardagh
& Cl.)

MacLaifeartaigh, Mícheál
(OCD)
Prior, The Abbey,
Loughrea, Co Galway
Tel 091-841209

MacLochlainn, Piaras, Very
Rev, Adm
No. 2 Presbytery,
148D Presbytery,
Blackditch Road
Dublin 10
Tel 01-6265119
(*Ballyfermot Upper*,
Dublin)

MacMahon, Hugh (SSC)
Priest in Charge,
St Columban's,
67-68 Castle Dawson,
Rathcoffey Road,
Maynooth, Co Kildare
Tel 01-8286036

MacMahon, Joseph (OFM)
Vicar, Franciscan Friary,
Ennis, Co Clare
Tel 065-6828751

MacMánuis, Clement (CSsR)
St Patrick's, Esker,
Athenry, Co Galway
Tel 091-844007

MacNamara, Francis, Very
Rev, PE, CC
Mountmellick,
Co Laois
Tel 057-8624198
(Kildare & L., retired)

MacNamara, Henry (OSA)
The Abbey, Fethard,
Co Tipperary
Tel 052-31273

MacNamara, Luke (OSB)
Glenstal Abbey, Murroe,
Co Limerick
Tel 061-386103

MacNeice, Dermot (OSM)
Servite Priory,
Benburb, Dungannon,
Co Tyrone, BT71 7JZ
Tel 028-37548241

MacPartlin, Brendan (SJ)
Superior,
Iona, 211 Churchill Park,
Portadown BT62 1EU
Tel 028-38330366

MacRaois, Brian, Very Rev,
PP, AP
The Holly Tree, Grange
Knockbridge, Dundalk,
Co Louth A91 VK18
Tel 042-6827409
(*Kilkerley*, Armagh)

Madden, Brendan, Very Rev,
PP
2 Rossmore Road
Dublin 6W
Tel 01-4508432
(*Willington*, Dublin)

Madden, Laurence, Very Rev
Doonmore, Doonbeg,
Co Clare
(Limerick, retired)

Madden, Michael, Very Rev,
PE
c/o Cloyne Diocesan
Centre,
Cobh, Co Cork
(Cloyne, retired)

Madden, Nicholas (OCD)
St Teresa's,
Clarendon Street, Dublin 2
Tel 01-6718466/6718127

Madden, Patrick, Very Rev,
Adm
Parochial House,
34 Aughrim Street,
Dublin 7
Tel 01-8386571
(*Aughrim Street*, Dublin)

Madden, Patrick
Priest in Residence,
Gort, Co Galway
Tel 091-631220
(*Gort/Beagh*, Galway)

Madden, Peter, Very Rev,
PP, VF
40 Derrynoid Road,
Draperstown,
Magherafelt,
Co Derry BT45 7DN
Tel 028-79628376
(*Ballinascreen
(Draperstown) and
Desertmartin*, Derry)

Madel, Krzysztof (SJ)
St Francis Xavier's,
Upper Gardiner Street,
Dublin 1
Tel 01-8363411

Madigan, Martin, Very Rev
Suaimhneas Church,
Foynes, Co Limerick,
(Limerick, retired)

Madigan, Seamus
1A Trinity Court,
Monaleen, Limerick
Tel 086-8441609
(*Pastoral Unit 1*, Limerick)

Magee, Aelred (OCSO)
Our Lady of Bethlehem
Abbey,
11 Ballymena Road,
Portglenone, Ballymena,
Co Antrim BT44 8BL
Tel 028-25821211

Magee, Gerard
The Chaplaincy,
28 Elmwood Avenue,
Belfast BT9 6AY
Tel 028-90669737
(Down & C.)

Magee, John, Most Rev, DD
Retired Bishop of Cloyne,
'Carnmeen', Convent Hill,
Mitchelstown, Co Cork
Tel 025-41887
(Cloyne)

Magennis, Feidlimidh, Very
Rev, PP, Adm
Maypole Hill, Dromore
Co Down BT35 1BQ
(*Dromore, Magheralin*,
Dromore)

Magill, Martin, Very Rev,
Adm
470 Falls Road,
Belfast BT12 6EN
Tel 028-90321511
(*St John*, Down & C.)

Maginn, Michael, Very Rev
The Presbytery,
Tullygally Road, Legahory,
Craigavon BT65 5BL
Tel 028-38311872
(*Moyraverty (Craigavon)*,
Seagoe (Derrymacash),
Dromore)

Magner, John, CC
Church Street, Kanturk,
Co Cork
Tel 029-50061
(*Kanturk*, Cloyne)

Magorrian, Eamon, CC
Parochial House,
27 Chapel Hill, Lisburn,
Co Antrim BT28 1EP
Tel 028-92660206
(*Lisburn (Blaris)*, Down &
C.)

Maguire, Barry (SSC)
St Columban's,
Dalgan Park,
Navan, Co Meath
Tel 046-9021525

Maguire, Brian (SPS) CC
The Shroughaun, Tullow
Co Carlow
Tel 059-9180377
(*Tullow*, Kildare & L.)

Maguire, James (OSA)
St Augustine's Priory,
Washington Street, Cork
Tel 021-2753982

Maguire, Sean, Very Rev, PP
Parochial House,
Bawnboy, Co Cavan
Tel 049-9523103
(*Courlough/Templeport*,
Kilmore)

Maguire, Vincent, Very Rev
26 Rodney Street,
Portrush,
Co Antrim BT56 8LB
(Down and C., retired)

Maher, Frank, Very Rev
Canon, CC
Johnstown via Thurles,
Co Kilkenny
Tel 056-8831219/
087-2402487
(*Johnstown*, Ossory)

Maher, James (SJ) Minister,
Crescent College
Comprehensive,
Dooradoyle, Limerick
Tel 061-480920

Maher, Jerry, Very Rev, PP,
Presbytery, Idrone Avenue
Knocklyon, Dublin 16
(*Knocklyon*, Dublin)

Maher, Michael (SM)
Cerdon, Marist Fathers,
St Mary's Road, Dundalk,
Co Louth
Tel 042-9334019

Maher, Noel, Very Rev
Canon, PP
Clough, Ballacolla,
Portlaoise, Co Laois
Tel 057-8738513/
087-2326200
(*Aghaboe*, Ossory)

Maher, Oliver, Very Rev, PP
Urlingford, Co Kilkenny
Tel 056-883112/
086-8323010
(*Urlingford*, Ossory)

Maher, Sean, PP
The Presbytery,
Broadford, Co Kildare
Tel 046-9551203
(*Balyna*, Kildare & L.)

Mahon, John (CSSp)
Holy Spirit Missionary
College
Kimmage Manor,
Whitehall Road,
Dublin D12 P5YP
Tel 01-4064300

Allianz (Ⅲ)

Mahony, John, Very Rev, PP
Ahascragh, Ballinasloe,
Co Galway
Tel 090-9688617
(*Ahascragh (Ahascragh and Caltra*), Elphin)

Mailey, Anthony, CC
Parochial House,
Quigley's Point,
Co Donegal
Tel 074-9383008
(*Iskaheen (Iskaheen & Upper Moville*), Derry)

Maingot, Jesse (OP)
Convent of SS Xystus and Clement
Collegio San Clemente,
Via Labicana 95,
00184 Roma
Tel 0039-06-7740021

Malcolmson, Kevin, CC
3 Landbrook Road,
Drumquilla,
Newtownbutler,
Co Fermanagh BT92 8JJ
Tel 028-67738244
(*Newtownbutler (Galloon*), Clogher)

Maliakkal, Aquino (OFMConv)
Guardian, The Friary,
St Francis' Street,
Wexford
Tel 053-9122758

Maliyil, Prince Zacharia, AP
Syro Malabar Chaplain
42 Nessan Court,
Raheen, Limerick
Tel 089-2070570
(*Pastoral Unit 6*, Limerick)

Mallavarappu, Selvaraj (SDB)
Rinaldi House,
40/41 Sean McDermott Street,
Dublin D01 H7P6

Mallon, Brendan, CC
Youghal, Co Cork
Tel 024-92456
(*Youghal*, Cloyne)

Mallon, Dominic
13 Richview Heights,
Keady,
Co Armagh BT60 3SW
(Armagh)

Mallon, Thomas, Very Rev, PE, AP
Parochial House,
170 Loughmacrory Road,
Loughmacrory, Omagh,
Co Tyrone BT79 9LG
Tel 028-80761230
(*Termonmaguirc (Carrickmore, Loughmacrory & Creggan*), Armagh)

Malone, Douglas, Adm
The Presbytery, Dunlavin,
Co Wicklow
Tel 045-401227
(*Dunlavin*, Dublin)

Malone, Larry
(priest in residence)
Edenderry, Co Offaly
Tel 046-9732352
(*Edenderry*, Kildare & L.)

Malone, Liam, Very Rev, PP, Adm
Administrator
Parochial House, Kilbeg,
Kells, Co Meath
Tel 046-9246604
Parish Priest
Parochial House,
Nobber, Co Meath
Tel 046-9089688
(*Kilbeg/Nobber*, Meath)

Maloney, Dermot, Very Rev, PP
Parochial House,
9 Newry Road,
Crossmaglen, Newry,
Co Down BT35 9HH
(*Crossmaglen (Cregan Upper) Armagh*)

Maloney, John, Very Rev, Adm
Attymass, Ballina,
Co Mayo
Tel 096-29990
(*Ballina*, Achonry)

Malone, Patrick, Co-PP,
Parochial House,
Church Drive,
Clarecastle, Co Clare
Tel 065-6823011
(*Abbey Pastoral Area*, Killaloe)

Mandi, Josephat
Parish Chaplain,
287 South Circular Road,
Dublin 8
Tel 01-4533490
(*Dolphin's Barn*, Dublin)

Mangan, Cyril, Very Rev,
Moderator
8 Greenfield Road, Sutton,
Dublin 13
Tel 01-8322396
(*Baldoyle, Howth, Sutton*, Dublin)

Mangan, Eoin, Very Rev
Canon, PP
(Kerry, retired)

Mangan, Patrick J., Very Rev,
Dún Mhuire,
44 Beechwood Avenue
Upper, Dublin 6
Tel 01-4975180/
087-9857264
(Dublin, retired)

Mangan, Thomas,
Donaghmore,
Co Limerick
Tel 087-2348226-313898
(*Pastoral Unit 3*, Limerick)

Manik, Robert (OCarm)
Gort Muire, Ballinteer,
Dublin 16
Tel 01-2984014

Manley, John (OFMCap)
Capuchin Friary,
Holy Trinity,
Fr Mathew Quay,
Cork T12 PK24
Tel 021-4270827

Mann, Robert (SCJ), Very Rev
On sabbatical
(Dublin)

Mann, Samson (CSSp)
Spiritan House,
213 North Circular Road,
Dublin 7
01-8389664
Chaplain,
St Mary's Hospital,
Pheonix Park, Dublin 20
Tel 01-6250300
Chaplain,
Stewart's Hospital,
Palmerstown
Tel 01-6264444
(Dublin)

Mannathukara, Jain Matthew, CC
5 Oriel Road,
Antrim BT41 4HP
Tel 028-94428086
(*Antrim*, Down & C.)

Manning, Francis, Very Rev, PP
Newmarket, Co Cork
Tel 029-60999
(*Newmarket*, Cloyne)

Mannion, Colm (OP)
Dominican College,
Newbridge
Droichead Nua, Co Kildare
Tel 045-487200

Mannion, Tom, Very Rev PP
Ballinaglera,
Carrick-on-Shannon,
Co Leitrim
Tel 071-9643014
(*Ballinaglera*, Kilmore)

Mansfield, Declan,
Chaplain,
Mary Mount Hospice
Curraheen, Co Cork
(Cork & R.)

Mansfield, Dermot (SJ)
Vice-Superior,
St Francis Xavier's,
Upper Gardiner Street,
Dublin 1
Tel 01-8363411

Manwa, Erasmus (CSSp)
c/o Holy Spirit
Provincialate,
Temple Park,
Richmond Avenue South,
Dublin D06 AW02
Tel 01-4975127/01-4977230

Mareja, Martin (SAC)
Pallottine College,
Thurles, Co Tipperary
Tel 0504-21202

Marken, Aodhan, Very Rev, PP, VF
Piercestown, Co Wexford
Tel 053-9158000
Adm, Ballymore and Mayglass
(*Ballymore and Mayglass, Piercestown and Murrintown*, Ferns)

Marmion, Declan (SM)
Administrator, Marist
Fathers Chanel,
Finance & Administrative Office,
Coolock Village,
Dublin D05 KU62
Tel 01-8505022/086-2597905

Marrinan, Thomas, Very Rev
Canon, PP, VF
Gort, Co Galway
Tel 091-631220
(*Gort/Beagh*, Galway)

Marrion, Declan (SM)
181 South Circular Road,
Dublin 8

Marron, Eamonn, Rt Rev
Mgr, PE
The Presbytery, Raharney,
Co Westmeath
Tel 044-9374271
(Meath, retired)

Marron, Patrick, Very Rev
Canon, PE
St Anne's Nursing Home,
Clones Road, Ballybay,
Co Monaghan A75 K193
(Clogher, retired)

Marteaux, D. Thierry (OSB)
Benedictine Monks,
Holy Cross Abbey,
119 Kilbroney Road,
Rostrevor,
Co Down BT34 3BN
Tel 028-41739979

Martin, Bernard (SSC)
St Columban's,
Dalgan Park, Navan,
Co Meath
Tel 046-9021525

Allianz (!)

Martin, Diarmuid, Most Rev,
DD
Archbishop Emeritus of
Dublin
c/o Archbishop's House,
Drumcondra,
Dublin D09 H4C2
Tel 01-8373732
(Dublin)

Martin, Eamon, Most Rev,
DD
Archbishop of Armagh,
Primate of All Ireland,
Ara Coeli, Cathedral Road,
Armagh BT61 7QY
Tel 028-37522045
Apostlic Administrator of
Dromore
Bishop's House,
44 Armagh Road, Newry,
Co Down
Tel 028-300262444
(Armagh)

Martin, Hubert, Very Rev,
PP
Parochial House, Glennan,
Glaslough, Monaghan
H18 FV10
Tel 047-88120
(Donagh, Clogher)

Martin, Liam (CSSp)
Holy Spirit Missionary
College
Kimmage Manor,
Whitehall Road,
Dublin D12 P5YP
Tel 01-4064300

Martin, Oisin (CFR)
St Patrick Friary,
64 Delmege Park,
Moyross,
Limerick V94 859Y
Tel 061-458071

Martin, Valentine, Very Rev,
PP
Logatryna, Dunlavin,
Co Wicklow
(Dublin, retired)

Martinez, Matthew (OP)
Convent of SS Xystus and
Clement
Collegio San Clemente,
Via Labicana 95,
00184 Roma
Tel 0039-06-7740021

Maszkiewicz, Jaroslaw
(Jarek), PP
Carraun, Whitehall,
Tarmonbarry,
Co Roscommon
Tel 043-3326020/
085-2727279
(Tarmonbarry, Elphin)

Matei, Ciprian, CC
Tower Hill,
Portlaoise, Co Laois
Tel 057-8621142
(Portlaoise, Kildare & L.)

Mathew, Joseph
St Thomas Pastoral Centre,
19 Saint Anthony's Road
Rialto,
Dublin D08 E8P3
(Rialto/Dolphin's Barn,
Dublin)

Mathew, Prince (OSCam)
St Camillus,
11 St Vincent Street North,
Dublin 7
Tel 01-8300365
Chaplain,
Mater Misericordiae
University Hospital,
Eccles Street, Dublin 7
Tel 01-8301122

Mathew, Suneesh (OSCam)
Chaplain,
Mater Misericordiae
University Hospital,
Eccles Street, Dublin 7
Tel 01-8301122
St Camillus,
(Dublin)

Mathews, William (SJ)
Milltown Park,
Miltown Road, Dublin 6
Tel 01-2698411/2698113

Matthew, Binoy (SVD),
1 & 3 Pembroke Road,
Dublin 4

Matthews, Barry, CC
Parochial House,
42 Abbey Street,
Armagh BT61 7DZ
Tel 028-37522802
(Armagh, Armagh)

Matthews, Richard, Very
Rev, PP
Parochial House,
Slane, Co Meath
Tel 041-9824249/
041-9884429
(Slane, Meath)

Mawn, Sean, Very Rev, PP,
VF
Ballinamore, Co Leitrim
Tel 071-9644039
(Ballinamore/Drumreilly
Lower, Kilmore)

Mayanja, Deogratias,
22 Gladstone Street,
Clonmel, Co Tipperary
Chaplain,
South Tipperary General
Hospital
Tel 052-6177000
(Waterford & L.)

Mayer, David Joseph (OSB)
Benedictine Monks,
Holy Cross Abbey,
119 Kilbroney Road,
Rostrevor,
Co Down BT34 3BN
Tel 028-41739979

Mazur, Grzegorz (OP), CC
St Mary's Priory,
The Claddagh,
Galway
Tel 091-582884
(St Mary's, Galway)

McAdam, Colm (CM), Very
Rev
St Joseph's,
44 Stillorgan Park,
Blackrock,
Co Dublin A94 PC62
Tel 01-2886961

McAleer, Brendan, Very Rev,
PP
Parochial House,
Garristown, Co Dublin
Tel 01-8354138
(Garristown, Dublin)

McAleer, Gerard, Very Rev,
PP, VF
Parochial House,
63 Castlecaulfield Road,
Donaghmore,
Dungannon,
Co Tyrone BT70 3HF
Tel 028-87761327
(Donaghmore, Armagh)

McAleer, Ryan
Sint-Michielsstraat 4/3101,
3000 Leuven, Belgium
(Armagh)

McAleese, Anthony CC
St Patrick's Presbytery,
199 Donegall Street,
Belfast BT1 2FL
Tel 028-90324597
(St Patrick's, Down & C.)

McAleese, Frank (OCarm)
Whitefriar Street Church,
56 Aungier Street,
Dublin 2 D02 R598
Tel 01-4758821

McAlinden, John, PP
Parochial House,
Slane Road, Mell,
Drogheda,
Co Louth A92 WAC4
Tel 041-983 8278
(Mell, Armagh)

McAnaney, Martin (SM)
London

McAnelly, Peter, Very Rev,
Adm
Parochial House,
42 Abbey Street,
Armagh BT61 7D2
Tel 028-37522802
(Armagh, Armagh)

McAnerney, Arthur, Very
Rev, PE, AP
Parochial House,
10 Aughrim Road,
Magherafelt,
Co Derry BT45 6AY
Tel 028-79632351
(Magherafelt and Ardtrea
North, Armagh)

McArdle, Martin, Very Rev,
PP, VF
Parochial House,
10 Springhill Road,
Moneymore, Magherafelt,
Co Derry BT45 7NG
Tel 028-86748242
(Moneymore (Ardtrea),
Armagh)

McArdle, Sean (SM)
Cerdon, Marist Fathers,
St Mary's Road,
Dundalk, Co Louth
Tel 042-9334019

McAreavey, John, Most Rev,
DD
Bishop Emeritus of
Dromore,
Bishop's House,
44 Armagh Road, Newry,
Co Down BT35 6PN
Tel 028-30262444
(Dromore)

McAteer, Francis, Very Rev
Canon, AP
Glencolmcille, Co Donegal
Tel 074-9730888
(Carrick (Glencolmcille),
Raphoe)

McAteer, John (SVD)
1 & 3 Pembroke Road,
Dublin 4

McAteer, Kieran, Very Rev,
PP, VF
Parochial House,
Ballybofey, Co Donegal
Tel 074-9131135
(Stranorlar, Raphoe)

McAuliffe, David, Dr
Chaplaincy Base, Cork
Institute of Technology,
3 Elton Lawn,
Rossa Avenue,
Bishopstown, Cork
Tel 021-4346244
(Cork & R.)

McAuliffe, Desmond,
Sheen Lodge,
Ennis Road,
Co Limerick
Tel 063-324825/
087-2336476
(Pastoral Unit 5, Limerick)

McAuliffe, James (SPS)
St Patrick's, Kiltegan,
Co Wicklow
Tel 059-6473600

McAuliffe, Leo (OFMCap)
Capuchin Friary,
Friary Street,
Kilkenny R95 NX60
Tel 056-7721439

McBrearty, Danny,
Gortnavern, Coolboy,
Letterkenny, Co Donegal
(Raphoe, retired)

McBrearty, Stephen, Very
Rev, PP
2A My Lady's Mile,
Holywood,
Co Down BT18 9EW
Tel 028-90422167
(*Holywood*, Down & C.)

McBride, Brendan
St Philip's Church,
725 Diamond Street,
San Francisco,
California 94114
(Raphoe)

McBride, Colm, Very Rev, PP
Parochial House,
59 Chapel Road,
Glenavy, Crumlin,
Co Antrim, BT29 4LY
Tel 028-94422262
(*Glenavy and Killead*,
Down & C.)

McBride, Malachy (SDS)
'Naomh Mhuire',
Upper Slavery,
Buncrana, Co Donegal
Tel 074-9322264

McCabe, Michael (SMA)
African Missions,
Feltrim, Blackrock Road,
Cork T12 N6C8
Tel 021-4292871

McCabe, Robert, CC
St Mary's Presbytery,
The Fairgreen, Navan,
Co Meath C15 X0A3
Tel 046-9027518
(*Navan*, Meath)

McCabe, Thomas (OMI)
Oblate Scholasticate,
St Anne's,
Goldenbridge Walk,
Inchicore, Dublin 8
Tel 01-4540841/4542955

McCafferty, Patrick, PP
Corpus Christi Presbytery,
4-6 Springhill Grove,
Belfast BT12 7SL
Tel 028-90246857
(*St Luke's*, Down & C.)

McCafferty, Paul
Derry Diocesan Office,
St Eugene's Cathedral,
Francis Street,
Derry BT48 9AP
Tel 028-71262302
(Derry)

McCague, Brendan, CC
Castleross Retirement
Home,
Castleross Village,
Carrickmacross,
Co Monaghan A81 X242
(Clogher, retired)

McCahery, Barney (CSsR), CC
74a Moyle Road,
Ballycastle BT54 6LG
Tel 028-20762202
(*Ballycastle (Ramoan)*,
Down & C.)

McCallion, Edwin (SM), Very
Rev, PP
Superior, The Presbytery,
Coolock Village,
Dublin 5
Tel 01-8477133
(*Coolock*, Dublin)

McCallion, John, CC
Parochial House,
140 Mountjoy Road,
Brocagh, Dungannon,
Co Tyrone BT71 5DY
Tel 028-87738381
(*Clonoe*, Armagh)

McCallion, Patrick (SPS)
St Patrick's, Kiltegan,
Co Wicklow W91 Y022
Tel 059-6473600

McCamley, Eamonn, Very
Rev, PP, VF
Parochial House,
6 Circular Road,
Dungannon,
Co Tyrone BT71 6BE
Tel 028-87722631
(*Dungannon (Drumglass,
Killyman and Tullyniskin)*,
Armagh)

McCann, Aidan, CC
Parochial House,
34 Madden Row,
Keady,
Co Armagh BT60 3RW
Tel 028-3751242
(*Keady (Derrynoose)*,
Armagh)

McCann, Arthur (CP)
St Gabriel's Retreat,
The Graan,
Enniskillen, Co Fermanagh
Tel 028-66322272
(Clogher)

McCann, Brian, Very Rev,
PP, VF
St Luke's Presbytery,
Twinbrook Road,
Dunmurry,
Co Antrim BT17 0RP
Tel 028-90619459
Administrator, *The
Nativity*, Derriaghy Parish
(*The Nativity, St Luke's,
Derriaghy*, Down & C.)

McCann, Columba (OSB)
Glenstal Abbey, Murroe,
Co Limerick
Tel 061-621000

McCann, Henry, Very Rev,
PP
St Anthony's Presbytery,
4 Willowfield Crescent,
Belfast BT6 8HP
Tel 028-90458158
(*St Anthony's*, Down & C.)

McCann, Joseph (CM)
St Paul's, Sybil Hill,
Raheny,
Dublin D05 AE38
Tel 01-8318113

McCanny, Bryan, Rt Rev
Mgr, PP
119 Irish Green Street,
Limavady,
Co Derry BT49 9AB
Tel 028-77729759
(*Limavady*, Derry)

McCarney, Eugene, Very
Rev, PE
Middletown House
Nursing Home,
Middletown, Courtown,
Co Wexford
Y25 P6H7
(Dublin, retired)

McCarron, Brendan (SPS)
St Patrick's,
21 Leeson Park,
Dublin D06 DE76
Tel 01-4977897

McCarron, Peter,
(Dublin, retired)

McCartan, Seán, Very Rev,
PP
Parochial House,
Beragh, Omagh,
Co Tyrone BT79 OSY
(*Beragh*, Armagh)

McCarthy, Brian
Castleville Study Centre,
Golf Links Road,
Castletroy, Limerick
Tel 061-331223
(Opus Dei)

McCarthy, Daniel, CF
(Cloyne)
Chaplain,
James Stephens Barracks,
Kilkenny
Tel 056-7761852
(Ossory)

McCarthy, Dermod
26 Brackenbush Road,
Killiney, Co Dublin
(Dublin, retired)

McCarthy, Donal (SAC)
Pallottine College,
Thurles, Co Tipperary
Tel 0504-21202

McCarthy, Eamonn, CC
Radio Maria Ireland,
Unit 8,
St Anthony's Business
Park, Ballymount Road,
Dublin 22
Tel 085-8585308
(Cloyne)

McCarthy, Eamonn, CC
The Presbytery, Donard,
Co Wicklow
Tel 045-404614
(*Dunlavin*, Dublin)

McCarthy, Eugene (CP)
St Paul's Retreat,
Mount Argus, Dublin 6W
Tel 01-4992000

McCarthy, Fachtna, Very
Rev, Adm,
Parochial House,
St Mary's,
Haddington Road,
Dublin 4
Tel 01-6600075/
087-3936327
(*Haddington Road*,
Dublin)

McCarthy, Francis
Parochial House,
Crookstown, Co Kildare
Tel 087-6978143
(*Athy*, Dublin)

McCarthy, John, Very Rev,
Adm
Ballyvourney, Co Cork
Tel 085-8783823
(*Cill na Martra*, Cloyne)

McCarthy, John, Very Rev,
Co-PP
Rosscarbery, Co Cork
Tel 023-8848168
(*Ardfield/Rathbarry,
Barryroe, Clonakilty,
Kilmeen/Castleventry,
Rosscarbery and
Timoleague*, Cork & R.)

McCarthy, John,
Chaplain, Irish Pastoral
Centre,
(Limerick)

McCarthy, John (SVD)
8 Teignmouth Road,
London, NW2 4HN
Tel 020-84528430

McCarthy, Liam (OFM)
Franciscan Friary,
Ennis, Co Clare
Tel 065-6828751

McCarthy, Pat
(Kerry, retired)

McCarthy, Pat,
Chaplain,
Mercy University Hospital,
Grenville Place, Cork
Tel 021-4271971
(Cork & R.)

McCarthy, Patrick J., Very
Rev, PE
The Presbytery,
O'Rahilly Street,
Clonakilty, Co Cork
(Cork & R., retired)

McCarthy, Patrick, CC
Callas, Berrings,
Co Cork
Tel 086-3831621
(*Inniscarra*, Cloyne)

McCarthy, Thomas (OP),
Very Rev
St Mary's, The Claddagh,
Co Galway
Tel 091-582884

McCarthy, Vincent (OSA)
Duckspool House
(Retirement Community),
Abbeyside, Dungarvan,
Co Waterford
Tel 058-23784

McCartney, Sean, Very Rev,
PP
25 Alt-Min Avenue,
Belfast BT8 6NJ
(Down & C., retired)

McCaughan, Aidan
(priest in residence)
St Peter's Catherdral
Presbytery,
St Peter's Square,
Belfast BT12 4BU
(Cathedral (St Peter's),
Down & C.)

McCaughan, Damian, CC
81 Castle Street,
Ballymoney,
Co Antrim BT53 6JT
Tel 028-27662003
(Ballymoney and
Derrykeighan, Down & C.)

McCaughan, Dermot, Very
Rev, PP
St Patrick's Presbytery,
29 Chapel Hill, Lisburn,
Co Antrim BT28 1EP
Tel 028-92662341
(Lisburn (Blaris), Down &
C.)

McCaughey, Michael M., PP
St Patrick's,
Buncrana Road,
Pennyburn,
Derry BT48 7QL
Tel 028-71262360
(The Three Patrons, Derry)

McCaughey, Shane, Rt Rev
Mgr Canon, PP, VG,
St Joseph's,
Carrickmacross,
Co Monaghan A81 F688
Tel 047-81019
(Carrickmacross (Machaire
Rois)/Magheracloone,
Clogher)

McCaul, Dermot (SMA)
(Priest in residence)
Parochial House,
56 Minterburn Road,
Lairakean, Caledon
Co Tyrone BT68 4XH
Tel 028-37568288
(Aughnacloy (Aghaloo),
Armagh)

McCauley, Daniel (SMA)
African Missions,
Dromantine, Newry,
Co Down BT34 1RH
Tel 028-30821224

McCay-Morrissey, Bernard
(OP)
Casement Aerodome,
Baldonnel, Co Dublin
Tel 01-4037536

McClarey, Liam Very Rev,
(SAC)
Provincial, 'Homestead',
Sandyford Road,
Dundrum, Dublin 16
Tel 01-2956180/2954170

McCloskey, Gerard, Very
Rev, PP
Parochial House, Ardglass,
Co Down BT30 7TU
(Dunsford and Ardglass,
Down & C.)

McCluskey, Brian, Very Rev
Canon, PE
Apt 2,
2 Danesfort Park North,
Stranmillis Road,
Belfast BT9 5RB
Tel 028-90683544
(Clogher, retired)

McConvery, Brendan (CSsR)
Clonard Monastery,
1 Clonard Gardens,
Belfast BT13 2RL
Tel 028-90445950

McConville, Conor, Very
Rev, PP
17 Monteith Road,
Annaclone, Banbridge,
Co Down BT32 5AQ
Tel 028-40671201
(Aghaderg, Annaclone,
Dromore)

McConville, Matthew
c/o Bishop's House,
44 Armagh Road,
Newry, Co Down
(Dromore)

McConville, Michael,
Nazareth House Care
Village
516 Ravenhill Road,
Belfast BT15 OBW
(Down & C., retired)

McCormack, Christy
Fohenagh, Ahascragh,
Ballinasloe,
Co Galway H53 K037
Tel 090-9688623
(Fohenagh and Killure,
Clonfert)

McCormack, Gerard, Very
Rev, PP
Parochial House,
Kingscourt, Co Cavan
Tel 042-966734
(Kingscourt, Meath)

McCormack, Ignatius,
St Flannan's College,
Ennis, Co Clare
Tel 065-68280/086-
2777139
(Abbey Pastoral Area,
Killaloe)

McCormack, James, PE,
c/o Bishop's House, Carlow
(Kildare & L., retired)

McCormack, Martin (SDB),
Rector, Salesian House,
45 St Teresa's Road,
Crumlin,
Dublin D12 XK52
Tel 01-4555605

McCormack, William
Puckane, Nenagh,
Co Tipperary
Tel 067-24105/087-
4168855
(Odhran Pastoral Area,
Killaloe)

McCrann, Christopher, CC
Knocknahur, Sligo
Tel 071-9128470
(Strandhill/Ransboro,
Elphin)

McCrory, Patrick, J., Very
Rev, PE
Parochial House,
Sixemilecross, Omagh,
Co Tyrone BT79 9NF
Tel 028-80758344
(Armagh, retired)

McCrossan, Oliver (SSC)
St Columban's,
Dalgan Park, Navan,
Co Meath
Tel 046-9021525

McCrystal, Aidan (SMA)
African Missions,
Blackrock Road,
Cork T12 TD54
Tel 021-4292871

McCullagh, Michael (CM)
St Paul's, Sybil Hill,
Raheny,
Dublin D05 AE38
Tel 01-8318113

McCullagh, Raymond
143 Andersonstown Road,
Belfast BT11 9BW
Tel 028-90615702/
028-90603951
(St Agnes', Down & C.)

McCulloch, Robert (SSC)
Collegio San Colombano,
Corso Trieste 57,
00198 Roma

McDermott, Christopher, CC
4 Garvagh Road, Kilrea,
Co Derry BT51 5QP,
Tel 028-29540343
(Garvagh (Errigal),
Kilrea (Kilrea and
Desertoghill), Derry)

McDermott, Joseph, Very
Rev, PE, CC
Parochial House, Caragh,
Naas, Co Kildare
Tel 045-903889
(Caragh, Droichead Nual
Newbridge, Kildare & L.)

McDermott, Kieran, Very
Rev, Adm
Pro-Cathedral House,
83 Marlborough Street,
Dublin 1
Tel 01-8745441
(Pro-Cathedral, Dublin)

McDermott, L. (OMI)
Oblate House of Retreat,
Inchicore, Dublin 8
Tel 01-4534408/4541805

McDermott, Niall, Very Rev
The Presbytery,
91 Grange Road,
Baldoyle, Dublin 13
(Dublin, retired)

McDermott, Noel, PP
91 Ervey Road, Eglinton,
Co Derry BT47 3AU
Tel 028-71810235
(Faughanvale, Derry)

McDermott, Padraic, (CSSp),
CC
The Presbytery,
Manor Kilbride,
Blessington, Co Wicklow
Tel 01-4582154
(Blessington, Dublin)

McDermott, Patsy, PP
Killenummery, Dromahair,
via Sligo,
Co Leitrim
Tel 071-9164125
(Killenummery and
Ballintogher
(Killenummery and
Killery), Ardagh & Cl.)

McDermott, Sean, Very Rev,
PP, VF
Lacken, Ballinagh,
Co Cavan
Tel 049-4337106
Adm, Kilmore
(Ballintemple, Kilmore,
Kilmore)

McDermott, Thomas, Very
Rev, Adm
1 Cathedral Terrace, Cobh,
Co Cork
Tel 021-4815934
(Cobh, Cloyne)

McDevitt, Eamon, PP
78 Lisnaragh Road,
Dunamanagh, Strabane,
Co Tyrone BT82 0QN
Tel 028-71398212
(Dunamanagh
(Donagheady), Derry)

McDevitt, John, PP
The Presbytery,
11 Steelstown Road,
Derry BT48 8EU
Tel 028-71351718
Adm, Culmore Parish
(Culmore, Our Lady of
Lourdes, Steelstown,
Derry)

McDevitt, Vincent (CSSp)
Holy Spirit Missionary
College
Kimmage Manor,
Whitehall Road,
Dublin D12 P5YP
Tel 01-4064300

McDonagh, Brendan (SPS),
Very Rev, PP
Cootehall, Boyle,
Co Roscommon
Tel 071-9667004
(Ardcarne (Cootehall),
Elphin)

McDonagh, James, Very
Rev, PP, VF
Ballymote, Co Sligo
Tel 071-9191770
(Ballymote (Emlefad and
Kilmorgan), Achonry)

McDonagh, John, Very Rev,
PP
'Stella Maris',
15 Oswald Road,
Sandymount, Dublin 4
Tel 01-6684265
(Sandymount, Dublin)

McDonagh, Martin, (CSSp)
Holy Spirit Missionary
College
Kimmage Manor,
Whitehall Road,
Dublin D12 P5YP
Tel 01-4064300

McDonagh, Sean (SSC)
(Research JPIC)
St Columban's,
Dalgan Park,
Navan, Co Meath
Tel 046-9021525

McDonald, Anthony
(OCarm)
Carmelite Priory,
Whitefriar Street Church,
56 Aungier Street,
Dublin 2 D02 R598
Tel 01-4758821

McDonald, Daniel,
Whiterock South,
Wexford, Co Wexford
(Ferns, retired)

McDonald, Fintan (SPS)
St Patrick's, Kiltegan,
Co Wicklow W91 YO22

McDonald, John, CC
3 Stanhope Place, Athy,
Co Kildare
Tel 059-8631698
(Athy, Dublin)

McDonald, John, Rt Rev
Mgr, PE, CC
Chaplains House,
Curragh Camp,
Co Kildare
Tel 045-441369
(Curragh Camp, Kildare &
L.)

McDonald, Joe, PP, VF
Parochial House,
Celbridge, Co Kildare
Tel 01-6275874
(Celbridge, Dublin)

McDonald, Thomas (CSSp)
Blackrock College,
Blackrock, Co Dublin
Tel 01-2888681

McDonnell, Albert, Rev, Co-
PP, VF
The Presbytery,
King's Road,
Kildysart, Co Clare
Tel 085-7811823
(Radharc na nOileán
Pastoral Area, Killaloe)

McDonnell, Charles, Very
Rev, Adm, VF
The Presbytery,
Westport,
Co Mayo F28 TN28
Administration, Kilmeena
(Westport (Aughaval),
Tuam)

McDonnell, Eunan (SDB)
Pronvicial, Salesian House,
45 St Teresa's Road,
Crumlin,
Dublin D12 XK52

McDonnell, Joseph (SSC)
Bursar, St Columban's,
Dalgan Park,
Navan, Co Meath
Tel 046-9021525

McDonnell, Leo, Very Rev,
Cathedral House,
Cathedral Place, Limerick
Tel 061-414624/
087-2200366
(Pastoral Unit 1, Limerick)

McDonnell, Paschal (OFM)
Franciscan Friary,
Ennis, Co Clare
Tel 065-6828751

McDonnell, Paudge, Very
Rev, PE
Parochial House,
Annyalla, Castleblayney,
Co Monaghan
A75 PX20
Tel 042-9740121
(Clontibret, Clogher)

McDonnell, Thomas (SPS)
St Patrick's, Kiltegan,
Co Wicklow
Tel 059-6473600

McDonough, Conor (OP)
St Saviour's,
Upper Dorset Street,
Dublin 1
Tel 01-8897610

McDunphy, Aodhán (OCSO)
Prior,
Mount Saint Joseph
Abbey, Roscrea,
Co Tipperary E53 D651
Tel 0505-25600

McElhennon, Kevin, Very
Rev, PP, VF
14 Killyclogher Road,
Omagh,
Co Tyrone BT79 0AX
Tel 028-82243375
(Killyclogher (Cappagh),
Derry)

McElhill, Laurence, Very
Rev, PE
(priest in residence),
43B Glen Road,
Belfast BT11 8BB
Tel 028-90613949
(St Teresa's, Down & C.)

McElhinney, Brian, Very Rev,
PP
Butlersbridge, Co Cavan
Tel 049-4365266
(Cavan (Urney &
Annagelliff), Kilmore)

McElroy, James (SM)
France

McElwee, Christopher (IC),
CC,
Knocknagoran, Omeath,
Co Louth A91 HK76
Tel 042-9375198
(Carlingford and
Clogherny, Armagh)

McEneaney, John
The Presbytery,
Mitchell Street,
Dungarvan,
Co Waterford
(Dungarvan, Waterford &
L.)

McEneaney, Owen J., Very
Rev Canon, PP
Parochial House,
St Patrick's,
Ballybay,
Co Monaghan A75 K299
Tel 042-9741032
(Ballybay (Tullycorbet),
Latton (Aughnamullen
West), Rockcorry (Ematris),
Clogher)

McEnroe, Patrick, Very Rev,
PE, AP
Darver, Readypenny,
Dundalk,
Co Louth A91 YC60
Tel 042-9379147
(Darver and Dromiskin,
Armagh)

McEntee, Patrick, Very Rev,
PP
8 Abbey Court, Dromore,
Co Tyrone BT78 3JB
(Dromore, Clogher)

McEntee, Seamus
Chaplain Dublin City
University, St Mary's,
New Road, Clondalkin,
Dublin 22
(Clondalkin, Dublin)

McEntire, Peter J. (CSSp)
Holy Spirit Missionary
College
Kimmage Manor,
Whitehall Road,
Dublin D12 P5YP
Tel 01-4064300

McErlean, Martin
c/o Bishop's House,
Mullingar
Co Westmeath
(Meath)

McEveney, Feargus (OFM)
Franciscan Friary,
Rossnowlagh,
Co Donegal
Tel 071-9851342

McEvoy, A. (SDB)
Salesian College,
Maynooth Road,
Celbridge, Co Kildare
Tel 01-6275058/60

McEvoy, Francis, Very Rev
Canon, Adm
Parochial House,
Moyglare Road,
Maynooth
Tel 01-6286220
(Maynooth, Dublin)

McEvoy, John, Rt Rev Mgr,
PP
Rathvily, Co Carlow
Tel 059-961114
(Paulstown, Kildare & L.)

McEvoy, Joseph, Very Rev,
PP
Parochial House,
Moynalty, Kells, Co Meath
Tel 046-9244305
(Moynalty, Meath)

McEvoy, P.J., Very Rev, PP
Francis Street, Edenderry,
Co Offaly
Tel 046-9732352
(Edenderry, Kildare & L.)

McEvoy, Seamus, Very Rev
Dean
Drakelands Nursing Home,
Ballycallan Road, Kilkenny
Tel 086-2634093
(Ossory, retired)

McEvoy, Seán, Very Rev, PP
St Moninna's Hermitage,
207 Dublin Road,
Newry, Co Down BT35 8RL
Tel 028-30849424
(Armagh)

McFaul, Daniel, PP
Parochial House,
St Mary's, Creggan
Derry BT48 9QE
Tel 028-71263152
(St Mary's, Creggan, Derry)

McFlynn, Gerard
18 Maresfield Gardens,
London NW3 5SX
(Down & C.)

Allianz (Ⅲ)

McGahan, Noel, Very Rev Canon, PP
25 Augher Road, Clogher,
Co Tyrone BT76 0AD
Tel 028-85549604
Priest in charge Eskra
(*Clogher, Eskra*, Clogher)

McGarvey, Patrick, Very Rev, PP
Fanavolty, Kindrum,
Letterkenny, Co Donegal
Tel 074-9159007
(*Tamney (Clondavaddog)*,
Raphoe)

McGavigan, Micheál, Adm
42 Glenedra Road,
Feeny,
Co Derry BT47 4TW
Tel 028-77781223
(*Banagher*, Derry)

McGee, Conor, CC,
Parochial House,
Rathganny,
Multyfarnham,
Co Westmeath N91 E186
Tel 044-9371124
(*Multyfarnharm*, Meath)

McGee, Edward, Very Rev,
BSc, MA, DD
120 Cliftonville Road,
Belfast BT14 4DE
Tel 078-11144268
(Down & C.)

McGee, Joseph (MSC)
Formation House,
56 Mulvey Park, Dundrum,
Dublin 16
Tel 01-2951856

McGeehan, Declan, CC
5 Strathroy Road,
Omagh,
Co Tyrone, BT79 7DW
Tel 028-82251055
(*Killyclogher (Cappagh)*,
Derry)

McGeehan, Paul,
79 The Maples,
Lismonaghan,
Letterkenny, Co Donegal
(Raphoe, retired)

McGeever, Patrick (CSSp)
Rockwell College,
Cashel, Co Tipperary
Tel 062-61444

McGettigan, Denis, Very Rev
Canon, PE
Meetinghouse Street,
Raphoe
Co Donegal
(Raphoe, retired)

McGettrick, William (CSsR)
Clonard Monastery,
1 Clonard Gardens,
Belfast BT13 2RL
Tel 028-90445950

McGill, Maurice (MHM)
Bursar,
St Joseph's House,
50 Orwell Park,
Rathgar, Dublin D06 C535
Tel 01-4127700

McGillicuddy, Desmond
(MHM)
St Joseph's House,
50 Orwell Park,
Rathgar, Dublin D06 C535
Tel 01-4127700

McGinn, Emlyn, PP, VF
Parochial House,
9a Forkhill Road,
Mullaghbawn, Newry,
Co Down BT35 9RA
Tel 028-30888286
(*Mullaghbawn (Forkhill)*,
Armagh)

McGinn, Patrick, Very Rev
Canon, PP
St Joseph's Presbytery,
Park Street,
Co Monaghan H18 C588
Tel 047-81220
Adm, Monaghan,
Tyholland
(*Corcaghan, Monaghan,
Tyholland*, Clogher)

McGinnity, Gerard, Very
Rev, PE
Rowan Road,
Co Armagh BT60 3DR
(Armagh, retired)

McGinnity, Michael, Very
Rev, PP, VF
4 Broughshane Road,
Ballymena BT43 7DX
Tel 028-25643828
(*Ballymena (Kirkinriola)*,
Down & C.)

McGirr, Austin, Very Rev,
Ranamona, Annagry,
Co Donegal, F94 CY99
(Down & C., retired)

McGirr, Dermot, CC
50 Tobermore Road,
Desertmartin,
Magherafelt,
Co Derry BT45 5LE
Tel 028-79632196
48 Brook Street, Omagh
Co Tyrone, BT78 5HE
Tel 028-82242092
(*Omagh (Drumragh)*,
Derry)

McGivern, Patrick (SPS)
Assistant House Leader,
St Patrick's, Kiltegan,
Co Wicklow
Tel 059-6473600

McGlanaghy, Patrick (MSC)
Woodview House,
Mount Merrion Avenue,
Blackrock, Co Dublin
Tel 01-2881644

McGlynn, Colm (OSM)
Prior Provincial
Servite Priory,
St Peregrine,
36 Grangewood Estate,
Rathfarnham,
Dublin D16 V263
Tel 01-4517115/
086-4060124

McGlynn, Fergus
43 Chestnut Grove,
Ballymount Road,
Dublin 24
Tel 01-4515570
(Dublin, retired)

McGlynn, Patrick (CSSp)
Holy Spirit Missionary
College
Kimmage Manor,
Whitehall Road,
Dublin D12 P5YP
Tel 01-4064300

McGlynn, Thomas, Very Rev,
PP
St Malachy's Presbytery,
24 Alfred Street,
Belfast BT2 8EN
Tel 028-90321713
(*St Malachy's*, Down & C.)

McGoldrick, Brian, PEm
St Orans Road,
Buncrana, Co Donegal
(Derry, retired)

McGoldrick, John, Very Rev
St Richard's,
3010 S 18th Street,
Philidelphia, PA 19145,
USA
Tel 001-215-9291362
(Armagh)

McGoldrick, Michael (OCD)
St Joseph's Carmelite
Retreat Centre
Termonbacca
Derry BT48 9XE
Tel 028-71262512

McGoldrick, Neil, PE
(Derry, retired)

McGonagle, Hugh, CC
7 Elm Park, Ballinode,
Sligo
Tel 071-9143430
(*Sligo, St Joseph's-Calry*,
Elphin)

McGonagle, James, Very
Rev, PEm
Radharc an Lochan,
New Road, Stroove,
Greencastle, Co Donegal
Tel 074-9325736
(Derry, retired)

McGoohan, Ultan, Very Rev,
PP, VF
St Anne's, Bailieborough
Co Cavan
Tel 042-9665117
(*Bailieboro (Killann)*,
Kilmore)

McGourty, Michael, Very
Rev Canon, PE
Lisnarick Road,
Irvinestown,
Co Fermanagh
Tel 071-9871221
(*Bundoran (Magh Ene)*,
Clogher)

McGovern, Ciarán, PP
Newtownforbes,
Co Longford
Tel 043-3346805
(*Newtownforbes*, Ardagh
& Cl.)

McGovern, David (OP)
Holy Cross, Tralee,
Co Kerry
Tel 066-7121135

McGovern, John, Very Rev,
Co-PP
Parochial House, Kilmaley,
Co Clare V95 ENK6
Tel 065-6839735/086-
3221210
(*Críocha Callan Pastoral
Area*, Killaloe)

McGovern, Kieran (CM)
St Peter's, Phibsboro,
Dublin 7
Tel 01-8389708/8389841

McGovern, Terence, Very
Rev, PP
Main Street, Hacketstown,
Co Carlow
Tel 087-6754811
(*Hacktstown*, Kildare & L.)

McGovern, Thomas
30 Knapton Road,
Dun Laoghaire,
Co Dublin
Tel 01-2804353
(Opus Dei)

McGowan, Michael, PC
7 St Patrick's Crescent,
Rathcoole, Co Dublin
Tel 01-4589210
(*Saggart*, Dublin)

McGowan, Thomas
Beechtree Nursing Home,
Murragh,
Oldtown, Co Dublin
(Dublin, retired)

McGrady, Feargal, Very Rev,
PP
Parochial House,
60 Windmill Hill,
Portaferry,
Co Down BT22 1RH
Tel 028-42728234
(*Ballygalget, Portaferry*,
Down & C.)

McGrath, Aidan (OFM)
Provincial Office,
Franciscan Friary
4 Merchants' Quay
Dublin, D08 XY19
Tel 01-67425000

McGrath, Brendan (OFM)
Gaurdian, Franciscan Friary,
Ennis, Co Clare V95 A4N2
Tel 065-6828751

McGrath, Conor, Adm,
191 Upper Newtownards Road,
Belfast BT4 3JB
Tel 028-90654157
(*St Colmcille's*, Down & C.)

McGrath, Frank (OFM)
Vicar, The Abbey,
8 Francis Street,
Galway H91 C53K
Tel 091-562518

McGrath, Francis (SMA)
SMA House,
Cloonbigeen, Claregalway,
Co Galway H91 YK64
Tel 091-798880

McGrath, Joseph, CC
Mount Temple, Moate
Co Westmeath
Tel 090-6481239
(*Moate and Mount Temple*, Ardagh & Cl.)

McGrath, Joseph, Rt Rev, PP, VG, VF
New Ross, Co Wexford
Tel 051-447080
(*New Ross,* Ferns)

McGrath, Martin (SPS), PP (pro tem)
Moygownagh,
Ballina, Co Mayo
Tel 096-31288
(*Moygownagh*, Killala)

McGrath, Matthew, Very Rev, AE, AP
Cashel, Co Tipperary
Tel 0504-42494
(*Clonoulty*, Cashel & E.)

McGrath, Michael
The Presbytery, Longford
Tel 043-3346465
(*Longford (Templemichael, Ballymacormack)*, Ardagh & Cl.)

McGrath, Michael (SMA)
African Missions,
Blackrock Road,
Cork T12 TD54
Tel 021-4292871

McGrath, Patrick (OMI)
Oblate House of Retreat,
Inchicore, Dublin 8
Tel 01-4534408/4541805

McGrath, Thomas, Very Rev
Cois Tra, Chapel Road,
Duncannon,
Co Wexford
(Ferns, retired)

McGrath, Tom (MHM),
Mountshannon,
Labasheeda, Co Clare
Tel 065-6830932
(*Radharc na nOileán Pastoral Area*, Killaloe)

McGrattan, Dominic
Cliftonville Road,
Belfast BT14 6LA
028-90690920
(Down and C.)

McGree, Thomas
Durrow, Cullohill,
Co Laois
Tel 087-7619235
(*Durrow*, Ossory)

McGregor, Augustine (OCSO), Rt Rev
Retired Abbot,
Mount Melleray Abbey,
Cappoquin,
Co Waterford P51 R8XW
Tel 058-54404

McGregor, Bede (OP)
St Malachy's, Dundalk,
Co Louth
Tel 042-9334179/9333714

McGrory, James, CC
Parochial House,
49 Ardmore Road,
Derry BT47 3QP
Tel 028-71349490
(*Ardmore*, Derry)

McGuckian, Alan, Most Rev (SJ)
Bishop of Raphoe,
Ard Adhamháin,
Cathedral Road,
Letterkenny,
Co Donegal F92 W2W9
(Raphoe)

McGuckian, Bernard (SJ)
Vice-Rector and Minister,
Clongowes Wood College,
Clane,
Co Kildare W91 DN40
Tel 045-868663/868202

McGuckian, Michael (SJ)
c/o Milltown Park,
Miltown Road,
Dublin D06 V9K7
Tel 01-4987333

McGuckien, Kevin, Very Rev, PP, VF
Parochial House,
4 The Crescent,
Portstewart,
Co Derry BT55 7LH
Tel 028-709832534
Adm, Colraine, Portrush
(*Coleraine*, *Portrush*, *Portstewart*, Down & C.)

McGuckin, Terence (CP)
Holy Cross Retreat,
Ardoyne, Crumlin Road,
Belfast BT14 7GE
Tel 028-90748231

McGuckin, Patrick, Very Rev, PE
79 Reclain Road, Galbally,
Dungannon,
Co Tyrone BT70 2PG
Tel 028-87759692
(Armagh, retired)

McGuigan, Seán, Very Rev, PE
65 Iniscarn Road,
Desertmartin,
Magherafelt, Co Derry
BT45 5NG
(Armagh, retired)

McGuinness, Austin (SSC)
St Columban's,
Dalgan Park,
Navan, Co Meath
Tel 046-9021525

McGuinness, Brendan, Very Rev, PP
The Parochial House,
Bekan, Claremorris,
Co Mayo F12 HC79
Tel 094-9380203
(*Bekan*, Tuam)

McGuinness, David
St Joseph's Catholic Church,
134 Prince Avenue,
Athens, Georgia 30601,
USA
(Waterford & L.)

McGuinness, Joseph, Rt Rev Mgr,
Executive Secretary to the Irish Episcopal Conference,
Columba Centre,
Maynooth,
Co Kildare W23 P6D3
Tel 01-5053000
(Clogher)

McGuire, Robert, Adm
Parochial House,
Taghmon,
Mullingar,
Co Westmeath
Tel 053-9134123
(*Rathangan and Cleariestown, Taghmon*, Ferns)

McHale, Benny, CC
The Parochial House,
New Line, Athenry,
Co Galway H65 DW20
Tel 091-844227
(*Athenry*, Tuam)

McHenry, Noel (SPS)
St Patrick's, Kiltegan,
Co Wicklow
Tel 059-6473600

McHugh, Anthony, Very Rev, PP
Parochial House,
33 Crossgar Road,
Saintfield, Ballynahinch,
Co Down BT24 7JE
Tel 028-97510237
(*Saintfield and Carrickmannon*, Down & C.)

McHugh, Christopher, Very Rev, PP,
Grange, Co Sligo
Tel 071-9163100
(*Ahamlish (Grange and Cliffoney)*, Elphin)

McHugh, Kevin (SSC)
St Columban's,
Dalgan Park,
Navan, Co Meath
Tel 046-9021525

McHugh, Oliver (SPS)
St Patrick's, Kiltegan,
Co Wicklow
Tel 059-6473600

McHugh, Patrick
Derrylester, Enniskillen,
Co Fermanagh
Tel 048-66349984
(Kilmore, retired)

McHugh, Patrick, Very Rev, PE
6 The Craft, Glencar,
Letterkenny, Co Donegal
(Raphoe, retired)

McHugh, Peter (SVD)
Donamon Castle,
Roscommon
Tel 090-6662222

McHugh, Seán
Chaplain,
University Hospial,
Galway
Tel 091-524222
(Galway)

McHugh, Thomas, Very Rev, Adm
75 Clonfeacle Road,
Blackwatertown,
Dungannon,
Co Tyrone BT71 7HP
Tel 028-87511215
(*Eglish, Moy (Clonfeacle)*, Armagh)

McIlraith, Cormac, Adm
10 Cranfield Place,
Sandymount,
Dublin 4
Tel 01-6686845
(*Sandymount*, Dublin)

McInerney, Declan, Very Rev, PP
Eyrecourt, Ballinasloe
Co Galway H53 KX85
Tel 090-9675113
(*Eyrecourt, Clonfert and Meelick)*, Clonfert)

McIntyre, Raymond (SDB)
Bursar,
Salesian House,
45 St Teresa's Road,
Crumlin, Dublin 12
Tel 01-4555605

McKay, Brian (OCarm)
Carmelite Priory, Moate,
Co Westmeath N37 AW34
Tel 090-6481160/6481398

McKay, Dermott, Very Rev, PP
53 Ballinlea Road,
Ballycastle
(Down & C., retired)

McKay, Vincent (CSSp)
Parochial House,
Summerhill, Co Meath
Tel 046-9557021
(*Summerhill*, Meath)
McKee, Placid (OSB)
Silverstream Priory,
Stamullen,
Co Meath K32 T189
Tel 01-8417142
McKeever, Brendan (CP)
St Paul's Retreat,
Mount Argus, Dublin 6W
Tel 01-4992000
McKeever, John, Very Rev,
PP, VF
Assistant Chancellor of the
Diocese
Parochial House,
35 St Patrick Street, Keady,
Co Armagh BT60 3TQ
Tel 028-37531246
(*Keady (Derrynoose)*,
Armagh)
McKeever, Martin (CSsR)
Alphonsian Academy,
Via Merulana 31, CP 2458,
00185 Roma-PT158, Italy
Tel 0039-06494901
McKeever, Michael, Very
Rev, PP, VG
Church Hill, Letterkenny,
Co Donegal
Tel 074-9137057
(*Termon*, Raphoe)
McKenna, Cathal (SMA)
African Missions,
Dromantine, Newry,
Co Down BT34 1RH
Tel 028-30821224
McKenna, Hugh (OFM)
Collegio S. Isidoro,
Via degli Artisti 41,
00187 Roma, Italy
Tel 0039-06-4885359
McKenna, John F., CC
Scotshouse, Clones,
Co Monaghan H23 YTI0
Tel 047-56016
(*Killeevan (Currin,
Killeevan and Aghabog)*,
Clogher)
McKenna, John, Very Rev
Canon, PP
Trillick, Omagh,
Co Tyrone BT78 3RD
Tel 028-89561350
(*Trillick*, Clogher)
McKenna, Joseph
(Birmingham Diocese)
Shannagh Nursing Home,
Belleek, Co Fermanagh
(Clogher, retired)
McKenna, Jude (OFMCap)
Capuchin Friary,
Station Road,
Raheny,
Dublin D05 T9E4
Tel 01-8313886

McKenna, Pádraig, Very
Rev, PP
Parochial House, Millbank,
Trillick, Co Tyrone
Tel 028-89561982k
(*Trillick (Kilskeery)*,
Clogher)
McKenna, Patrick, Very Rev,
PE
19 Broughshane Road,
Ballymena BT43 7DX
Tel 028-25643828
(*Ballymena (Kirkinriola)*,
Down & C.)
McKenna, Seamus, BA, HDE
(Kerry, retired)
McKeon, Seamus, PP
Aughnacliffe, Co Longford
Tel 043-6684118
(*Colmcille*, Ardagh & Cl.)
McKeown, Donal, Most Rev,
DD
Bishop of Derry,
Diocesan Offices,
St Eugene's Cathedral,
Francis Street,
Derry BT48 9AP
Tel 028-71262302
(Derry)
McKeown, Noel (OP)
St Catherine's, Newry,
Co Down BT35 8BN
Tel 028-30262178
McKeown, Maximilian
(OFMConv), Very Rev
Friary of the Visitation of
the BVM,
Fairview Strand, Dublin 3
Tel 01-8376000
(*Fairview*, Dublin)
McKevitt, Brian (OP)
St Mary's, Pope's Quay,
Cork
Tel 021-4502267
McKiernan, Peter, Very Rev,
PP
Crosserlough, Co Cavan
Tel 049-4336122
(*Crosserlough*, Kilmore)
McKiernan, Thomas
Rosskeeragh, Belturbet,
Co Cavan
(Kilmore, retired)
McKinlay, Denis, Very Rev,
PP
Parochial House,
41 Lower Square,
Castlewellan,
Co Down BT31 9DN
Tel 028-43770377
Administrator, Kilcoo
(*Castlewellan (Kilmegan)*,
Kilcoo, Down & C.)
McKinley, Patrick, Very Rev
On Sabbatical
(Dublin)

McKinney, Anthony
(OCarm)
Gort Muire, Ballinteer,
Dublin 16 D16 EI67
Tel 01-2984014
McKinney, Liam, Very Rev,
Adm
'Glenshee',
9 Dublin Road, Newry,
Co Down BT35 8DA
Tel 028-30262376
(*Middle Killeavy (Newry)*,
Armagh)
McKinstry, Gordon
12 The Meadows,
Randalstown,
Co Antrim BT41 2JB
(Down & C., retired)
McKittrick, Brian, Co-PP
St Columba Parish House,
New Road, Clondalkin,
Dublin 22
Tel 01-4640441
(*Bawnogue, Clondalkin,
Deansrath,
Neilstown, Rowlagh and
Quarryvale*, Dublin)
McLaughlin, Brian (CSSp)
Holy Spirit Missionary
College
Kimmage Manor,
Whitehall Road,
Dublin D12 P5YP
Tel 01-4064300
McLaughlin, Con, PP
Barrack Hill, Carndonagh,
Lifford, Co Donegal
Tel 074-9374104
Director,
Inishowen Pastoral Centre,
Carndonagh, Co Donegal
Tel 074-9374103
(*Carndonagh (Donagh)*,
Derry)
McLaughlin, Eamonn, CC
Congregation for the
Clergy, Rome
(Raphoe)
McLaughlin, George, PEm
Chez Nous, Drumawier,
Greencastle, Co Donegal
(Derry, retired)
McLaughlin, John (SSC)
St Columban's,
Dalgan Park,
Navan, Co Meath
Tel 046-9021525
McLaughlin, Kevin (OMI)
An Tobar, Ardbraccan,
Navan, Co Meath
McLaughlin, Michael, Very
Rev Canon,
Airfield, Inch, Ennis,
Co Clare
Tel 065-6839332
(*Críocha Callan Pastoral
Area*, Killaloe)

McLaughlin, Peter, PEm
c/o Bishop's Office,
St Eugene's Cathedral,
Francis Street,
Derry BT48 9AP
Tel 028-71262302
(Derry, retired)
McLaughlin, Pius (OFM)
Franciscan Friary,
Rossnowlagh,
Co Donegal
Tel 071-9851342
McLaverty, Anthony, Very
Rev, CC
518 Donegall Road,
Belfast BT12 6DY
Tel 028-90314112
(*St John's*, Down & C.)
McLoone, Francis, Very Rev,
PP
Parochial House,
Killymard, Donegal Town,
Co Donegal F94 C6T7
Tel 074-9721929
(*Killymard*, Raphoe)
McLoughlin, Eamonn, CC
Parochial House,
Letterkenny, Co Donegal
Tel 074-9121021
(*Letterkenny (Conwal and
Leck)*, Raphoe)
McLoughlin, Eugene Rev
(SMA)
SMA House Cloonbigeen,
Claregalway,
Co Galway H91 YK64
Tel 091-798880
McLoughlin, Eugene, Very
Rev Canon, PE
1 Convent Court,
Roscommon
(Elphin, retired)
McLoughlin, Michael, Very
Rev Dean, PP, VF
Parochial House,
Moycullen, Co Galway
Tel 091-555106
(*Moycullen*, Galway)
McMahon, Aidan (CSsR)
Mount Saint Alphonsus,
South Circular Road,
Limerick
Tel 061-315099
McMahon, Andrew, Very
Rev PP
6 Scarva Road, Banbridge,
Co Down BT32 3AR
Tel 028-40662136
(*Annaclone*, Dromore)
McMahon, John, Very Rev,
PP
Carrigallen, Co Leitrim,
via Cavan
Tel 049-4339610
(*Carrigallen*, Kilmore)
McMahon, Joseph (OFM)
Vicar, Franciscan Friary,
Ennis, Co Clare
Tel 065-6828751

McMahon, Joseph, Very Rev, Co-PP, VF
Parochial House,
Scariff, Co Clare
Tel 061-921051/087-2665793
(*Inis Cealtra Pastoral Area*, Killaloe)

McMahon, Michael (CSSp)
Holy Spirit Missionary College
Kimmage Manor,
Whitehall Road,
Dublin D12 P5YP
Tel 01-4064300

McMahon, Padraig, Very Rev, PP, VF
Parochial House, Athboy,
Co Meath
Tel 046-9432184
(*Athboy*, Meath)

McMahon, Patrick,
The Presbytery,
Labasheeda, Co Clare
Tel 065-6830126
(*Radharc na nÓilean Pastoral Area*, Killaloe)

McMahon, Paul (SSC)
Belfast (on compassionate leave)

McMahon, Richard (CSsR)
Mount St Alphonsus,
South Circular Road,
Limerick
Tel 061-315099

McMahon, Seamus (SM)
Australia

McMahon, Vincent (LC)
Woodlands Academy,
Wingfield House, Bray,
Co Wicklow
Tel 01-2866323

MacMánus, Clement (CSsR)
St Joseph's, Dundalk,
Co Louth
Tel 042-9334042/9334762

McManus, Brendan (SJ)
Peter Faber House,
28 Brookvale Avenue,
Belfast BT14 6BW
Tel 028-90757615

McManus, Frank, Very Rev, PP,
19 Ardvarney Road,
Ederney, Enniskillen,
Co Fermanagh BT93 0EG
Tel 028-68631315
(*Ederney (Cúl Máine)*, Clogher)

McManus, Gregory (SPS)
St Patrick's,
21 Leeson Street,
Kiltegan,
Co Wicklow W91 YO22

McManus, John, Very Rev, PP, VG
Parochial House, Castlerea,
Co Roscommon
Tel 094-9620040
(*Castlerea (Kilkeevan)*, Elphin)

McManus, John
Parochial House,
Strangford,
Co Down BT30 7NL
Tel 028-44881206
(*Kilclief and Strangford*, Down & C.)

McManus, Kevin (OSA), PP
St John's Priory,
Thomas Street, Dublin 8
Tel 01-6770393

McManus, Michael, PP
Kiltoom, Athlone
(*Kiltoom*, Elphin)

McManus, Patrick (SSC)
St Columban's,
Dalgan Park, Navan,
Co Meath
Tel 046-9021525

McManus, Patrick, Very Rev, CC
34 Dollymount Grove,
Clontarf, Dublin 3
Tel 01-8057692/087-2371089
(*Dollymount*, Dublin)

McManus, Thomas, VF
Drumkeerin, Co Leitrim
Tel 071-9648025
(*Drumkeerin (Inisgmagrath)*, Kilmore)

McManus, Tommy (OSA)
St Augustine's Priory,
Washington Street, Cork
Tel 021-4275398/4270410

McMenamin, Joseph (White Fathers)
Promotion Director,
Cypress Grove,
Templeogue, Dublin 6W
Tel 01-4055526

McMenamin, William, Very Rev Archdeacon, PE
'St Columba's'
Meeting House Street,
Raphoe, Co Donegal
Tel 074-9144834
(*Raphoe*, retired)

McMorrow, Maurice, Very Rev, PP, VF
Kinawley, Enniskillen
Co Fermangh BT92 4FH
Tel 028-6638250
(*Kinawley/Killesher*, Kilmore)

McMullan, Anthony (OP)
St Malachy's, Dundalk,
Co Louth
Tel 042-9334179/9333714

McMullan, Brendan, Very Rev
26 Willowbank Park,
Belfast BT6 0LL
Tel 028-90794440
(Down & C., retired)

McMullan, Kevin, Very Rev
Nazareth House Care Village
516 Ravenhill Road,
Belfast BT6 0BW
(Down & C., retired)

McNaboe, Desmond (OFMCap),
Vicar, Capuchin Friary,
Station Road,
Raheny,
Dublin D05 T9E4
Tel 01-8313886
Chaplain,
St Francis Hospice, Raheny
Tel 01-8327535

McNally, Albert, Very Rev, PP, VF
6 Hillside Avenue,
Dunloy BT44 9DQ
(Down and C., retired)

McNamara, Austin, Very Rev, PP
Parochial House,
Ballyhahill, Co Limerick
Tel 069-82103/087-2615471
(*Pastoral Unit 13*, Limerick)

McNamara, Cormac (SM),
Sahagun, Spain

McNamara, Donal, Very Rev Canon,
St Munchin's,
Clancy Strand, Limerick
Tel 061-455635/087-2402518
(*Pastoral Unit 4*, Limerick)

McNamara, Henry (OSA)
The Abbey, Fethard,
Co Tipperary
Tel 052-31273

McNamara, Francis, Very Rev, PE
Parochial House,
Davitt Road,
Mountmellick, Co Laois
057-8624194
(Kildare & L., retired)

McNamara, Frank, Very Rev, PE
Cluan Lir,
Mullingar, Co Westmeath
(Meath, retired)

McNamara, Gerard, Very Rev, PP
Ballyduff Upper,
Co Waterford
Tel 058-60227
(*Ballyduff*, Waterford & L.)

McNamara, John, Very Rev Canon, PP, VF
Apt 2, The Presbytery,
Dublin Road, Balbriggan,
Co Dublin
Tel 01-8020185
(*Balbriggan*, Dublin)

McNamara, Liam, Very Rev Canon, AP
Tipperary Town
Co Tipperary
Tel 062-82664
(*Tipperary*, Cashel & E.)

McNamara, Martin (MSC)
Woodview House,
Mount Merrion Avenue,
Blackrock, Co Dublin
Tel 01-2881644

McNamara, Martin
Kiltulla, Athenry,
Co Galway H65 DYM0
(Clonfert, retired)

McNamara, Oliver, CC
Annaghdown, Co Galway
Tel 091-791142
(*Corrandulla (Annaghdown)*, Tuam)

McNamara, Robert, CC
The Rectory,
Lisdoonvarna, Co Clare
Tel 065-7074142
(*Lisdoonvarna and Kilshanny*, Galway)

McNamara, Thomas (SMA)
SMA House,
81 Ranelagh Road,
Ranelagh, Dublin 6
Tel 01-4968162/3

McNamara, Walter (CSSp)
Holy Spirit Missionary College
Kimmage Manor,
Whitehall Road,
Dublin D12 P5YP
Tel 01-4064300

McNamee, Ambrose (OCD)
The Abbey, Loughrea,
Co Galway
Tel 091-841209

McNamee, Paul
c/o Bishop's House,
Dublin Road, Carlow
(Kildare & L.)

McNeice, Damian, PP, VF
6 Beechpark Lawn,
Castleknock, Dublin 15
Tel 01-6408595
(*Castleknock, Laurel Lodge-Carpenterstown*, Dublin)

McNeice, Dermot (OSM)
Servite Priory, Benburb,
Dungannon,
Co Tyrone, BT71 7JZ

Allianz (ill)

McNeill, Peter, Very Rev, PP
58 Ballydrumman Road,
Ballyward, Castlewellan,
Co Down BT31 9UG
Tel 028-40650207
(*Drumgooland, Dromara*,
Dromore)

McNelis, Denis, Very Rev,
PP, VF
Parochial House, Laytown,
Co Meath
Tel 041-9827258
(*Laytown-Mornington*,
Meath)

McNerney, John
Chaplains' Residence,
St Stephen's, UCD,
Belfield, Dublin 4
Tel 01-7164789
(Dublin)

McNicholas, Gerard (SSC)
St Columban's Retirement
Home,
Dalgan Park,
Navan, Co Meath
Tel 046-9021525

McNulty, Sean (SSC)
Gortnalea, Dunmore,
Tuam,
Co Galway H54 ET02

McNulty, Thomas
Goretti Cottage,
Acre Road, Carlingford,
Co Louth, A91 PW95
Tel 042-9376577
(Armagh, retired)

McPartland, Jimmy, Very
Rev, Co-PP
St Fergal's, Killarney Road,
Bray, Co Wicklow
(*Bray (Ballywaltrim)*,
Dublin)

McPhillips, James, Very Rev,
PP, VG
10 Knocks Road,
Lisnaskea,
Co Fermanagh BT92 0GA
Tel 028-67721324
(*Linaskea (Aghalurcher)*,
Clogher)

McQuaid, Macartan, Very
Rev Canon
Mullanarockan, Tydavnet,
Co Monaghan H18 YV20
Tel 087-2454705
(*Corcaghan (Kilmore and
Drumsnatt)*, Clogher)

McShane, Dermot, Very Rev,
PE
c/o Community Hospital,
Killybegs, Co Donegal
(Raphoe, retired)

McShane, Philip (OP)
St Mary's Priory,
Tallaght, Dublin 24
Tel 01-4048100

McSorley, Gerard, Rt Rev
Mgr
St Anne's Nursing Home,
Clones Road, Ballybay,
Co Monaghan A75 K193
(Clogher, retired)

McSweeney, Eustace
(OFMCap)
Capuchin Friary,
Station Road, Raheny,
Dublin D05 T9E4
Tel 01-8313886

McSweeney, James, Very
Rev, Co-PP
Cork Road,
Carrigaline, Co Cork
Tel 021-4371860
(*Carrigaline, Crosshaven,
Harbour Parishes
and Tracton Abbey*, Cork
& R.)

McSweeney, Myles, Very
Rev, Co-PP,
Moderator,
Meenvane, Schull,
Co Cork
Tel 028-28171
(*Bantry, Caheragh,
Goleen,
Muintir Bháire and Schull*,
Cork & R.)

McTiernan, Jim (White
Fathers)
Cypress Grove,
Templeogue, Dublin 6W
Tel 01-4055263/4055264

McTiernan, John, Very Rev,
Adm
Bridge Street, Belturbet,
Co Cavan
Tel 049-9522109
(*Belturbet (Annagh)*,
Kilmore)

McVeigh, Joseph, PE
Tattygar House,
4 Tattygar, Lisbellaw,
Co Fermanagh BT94 5GQ
(Clogher, retired)

McVeigh, Martin, Very Rev,
PP
Parochial House,
Clogherhead,
Drogheda,
Co Louth A92 K970
Tel 041-9822224
(*Clogherhead*, Armagh)

McVerry, Peter (SJ)
Arrupe Community,
217 Silloge Road,
Ballymun, Dublin 11
Tel 01-8420886
(Zam-Mal)

McWilliams, Luke, Very Rev,
PP
Parochial House,
9 Gortahor Road,
Rasharkin, Ballymena,
Co Antrim BT44 8SB
Tel 028-29571212
(*Rasharkin*, Down & C.)

McWilliams, Patrick, Very
Rev, PP
103 Roguery Road,
Moneyglass, Toomebridge,
Co Antrim BT41 3PT
Tel 028-79650225
(*Duneane*, Down & C.)

Meade, Bernard (CM)
St Paul's, Sybil Hill,
Raheny, Dublin D05 AE38
Tel 01-8318113

Meade, John (CSSp)
Rockwell College,
Cashel, Co Tipperary
Tel 062-61444

Meade, Michael, Very Rev
PP
Parochial House,
Kilcormac, Co Offaly
Tel 057-9135989
(*Kilcormac*, Meath)

Meagher, Charles (SSC)
St Columban's,
Dalgan Park,
Navan, Co Meath
Tel 046-9021525

Medina, Nelson (OP)
St Saviour's,
Upper Dorset Street,
Dublin 1
Tel 01-8897610

Medves, Petru, CC
Abbeyleix Parish Office
Abbeyleix, Co Laois
Tel 085-1853069
(*Abbeyleix, Ballinakill,
Raheen*, Kildare & L.)

Meehan, Conleth, Co-PP
21 Wheatfield Grove,
Portmarnock,
Co Dublin
Tel 01-8461561
(*Kinsealy*, Dublin)

Meehan, Dermot, Very Rev,
PP, VG
Swinford, Co Mayo
Tel 094-9251790
(*Swinford (Kilconduff and
Meelick)*, Achonry)

Meehan, Dominic, Very Rev,
PP
Church Avenue,
Templemore,
Co Tipperary
Tel 0504-31492
(*Loughmore*, Cashel & E.)

Meehan, Séamus, Very Rev,
PE
Main Street, Dungloe,
Co Donegal
Tel 074-9521895
(Raphoe, retired)

Meehan, William, Very Rev,
PP
St Mary's, Clonmel,
Co Tipperary
Tel 052-6122954
(*Clonmel, St Mary's*,
Waterford & L.)

Mehigan, Donal (OP)
St Catherine's, Newry,
Co Down BT35 8BN
Tel 028-30262178

Mejida, Timothy
Parochial House,
Lobinstown, Navan,
Co Meath
Tel 046-9053155
(*Lobinstown*, Meath)

Melican, Michael (IC)
Doire na hAbhann,
Tickincor, Clonmel,
Co Tipperary
Tel 052-6126914

Mellett, Stan (CSsR),
St Joseph's,
St Alphonsus Road,
Dundalk,
Co Louth A71 F3FC
Tel 042-9334042/9334762

Mernagh, Michael (OSA)
St John's Priory,
Thomas Street, Dublin 8
Tel 01-6770393/0415/0601

Mernagh, Patrick, Very Rev,
PP
Kilmore, Co Wexford
Tel 053-9135181
(*Kilmore and Kimore
Quay*, Ferns)

Merrigan, Liam, Very Rev,
PP
Drogheda Road,
Monasterevin,
Co Kildare
Tel 045-525346
(*Monasterevin*, Kildare &
L.)

Meskell, Derek (CSsR)
Mount Saint Alphonsus,
Limerick
Tel 061-315099

Mhamwa, Thaddeus, PC
128 Roselawn Road,
Blanchardstown, Dublin 15
Tel 01-8219014
(*Blanchardstown*, Dublin)

Michael, James, CC
The Presbytery,
5 Drumgeely Avenue,
Shannon, Co Clare
Tel 061-471513
(*Tradaree Pastoral Area*,
Killaloe)

Millar, George (SVD)
Maynooth, Co Kildare
Tel 01-6286391/2

Mills, Dermot (OMI)
St Michael's Parish,
52a Bulfin Road,
Dublin 8
Tel 01-4531660

Allianz (ⅱ)

Milo, Manuelito,
(Chaplain, Belfast City
Hospital)
Sacred Heart Presbytery,
1 Glenview Street
Belfast BT14 7DP
Tel 028-90351851
(*St Paul's*, Down & C.)
Milton, Raymond, Very Rev,
PP, VF
Knockcroghery,
Co Roscommon
Tel 090-666115
(*Knockcroghery/
St John's/Rahara*, Elphin)
Minogue, Frank (SPS)
St Patrick's, Kiltegan,
Co Wicklow W91 Y022
Mitchell, Francis, Rev,
Archbishop's House,
Tuam,
Co Galway H54 HP57
Tel 093-24166
(Tuam)
Mitchell, Kilian (OPraem)
Holy Trinity House,
Lismacanican,
Mountnugent,
Co Cavan
Mockler, John,
Gortboy, Newcastlewest,
Co Limerick
Tel 086-2342242
(*Pastoral Unit 15*, Limerick)
Mohan, Mark, Very Rev, PP
Parochial House,
Ballivor, Co Meath
Tel 046-9546488
(*Ballivor/kildalkey*, Meath)
Mohan, Richard, Rt Rev
Mgr, PE
34 Lacky Road,
Drumswords, Roslea,
Co Fermanagh BT92 YNQ
Tel 048 67751374
(*Clones*, Clogher)
Moley, John, Very Rev
24 Mallard Road,
Downpatrick,
Co Down BT30 6DY
(Down & C., retired)
Mollin, Matthew, Very Rev,
PE
Elm Hall,
Loughlinstown Road,
Celbridge, Co Kildare
(Meath, retired)
Molloy, John, Co-PP, VF
Templemore Road,
Roscrea, Co Tipperary
Tel 0505-21218
(*Cronan Pastoral Area*,
Killaloe)
Molloy, John (SSC)
St Columban's,
Dalgan Park, Navan,
Co Meath
Tel 046-9021525

Molloy, Michael (SSC)
St Columban's,
Dalgan Park,
Navan, Co Meath
Tel 046-9021525
Molloy, Michael, Very Rev,
PP, VF
The Presbytery, Moore
Ballydangan, Athlone,
Co Roscommon
Tel 090-9673539
(*Moore*, Tuam)
Molloy, Noel (OP)
St Saviour's,
Upper Dorset Street,
Dublin 1
Tel 01-8897610
Molloy, Patrick (MHM)
Vice Rector, St Joseph's
House,
50 Orwell Park,
Rathgar,
Dublin D06 C535
Tel 01-4127700
Moloney, Bernie, Very Rev,
PP
Emly, Co Tipperary
Tel 062-57111
(*Emly*, Cashel & E.)
Moloney, Brendan, Very
Rev, AP, VF
Silvermines, Nenagh,
Co Tipperary
Tel 067-25864
(*Odhran Pastoral Area*,
Killaloe)
Moloney, Dermot, Rt Rev
Mgr, PE
5 Gold Cave Crescent,
Tuam, Co Galway
(Tuam, retired)
Moloney, Gerard (CSsR)
Vicar-Superior,
Mount Saint Alphonsus,
South Circular Road,
Limerick
Tel 061-315099
Moloney, Joseph, Very Rev,
PE
Grove House, Vicar Street,
Tuam, Co Galway
(Tuam, retired)
Moloney, Leonard (SJ)
Provincial, Milltown Park
Milltown Road, Dublin 6
Tel 01-4987333
Moloney, Michael, PE
43 The Waterways,
Sallins, Naas,
Co Kildare
(Kildare & L., retired)
Molovlasky, Ryan (CSsR)
Clonard Monastery,
1 Clonard Gardens,
Belfast BT13 2RL
Tel 028-90445950

Monaghan, Stephen (CM),
Superior,
St Paul's, Sybil Hill,
Raheny, Dublin D05 AE38
Tel 01-8318113
Monahan, Fintan, Most Rev,
DD
Bishop of Killaloe,
Westbourne, Ennis,
Co Clare V95 W63H
Tel 065-6828638
(Killaloe)
Monahan, Patrick
Earlsfort,
291A Old Greenfield,
Maynooth,
Co Kildare
(Dublin, retired)
Monahan, Paul (SMA)
SMA House,
81 Ranelagh Road,
Ranelagh, Dublin 6
Tel 01-4968162/3
Monahan, Thomas (OP)
Black Abbey, Kilkenny,
Co Kilkenny
Tel 056-7721279
Mongan, Gerard, Adm
St Columba's Presbytery,
6 Victoria Place,
Derry BT48 6TJ
Tel 028-71262301
(*Derry City*, Derry)
Monks, Frank (MI)
St Camillus, Killucan,
Co Westmeath
Tel 044-74115
Montades, Rudy (SVD), CC
The Presbytery, City Quay,
Dublin 2
Tel 01-6773706
(*City Quay*, Dublin)
Montague, Paul, Very Rev,
PP
Parochial House,
Reaghstown, Ardee,
Co Louth A92 KW68
Tel 041-6855117
(*Tallanstown*, Armagh)
Mooney, Desmond, Very
Rev, PP
44 Church Street,
Rostrevor,
Co Down BT34 3BB
Tel 028-41738277
(*Kilbroney (Rostrevor)*,
Dromore)
Mooney, Oliver, Very Rev
Newry, Co Down
(Dromore, retired)
Mooney, Patrick, Very Rev
Canon
Glenamaddy, Co Galway
(Tuam, retired)

Moore, David, Very Rev,
Adm
c/o Parochial House,
9 Cavanakeeran Road,
Pomeroy, Dungannon,
Co Tyrone, BT70 2RD
Tel 028-87757867
(*Pomeroy*, Armagh)
Moore, Edward, Very Rev,
PE
Marian House, Sallins,
Naas, Co Kildare
(Kildare & L., retired)
Moore, Eóin (OCarm)
Carmelite Friary,
Kinsale,
Co Cork P17 WR88
Tel 021-4772138
Moore, Gerard, PP
23 Wainsfort Park
Terenure, Dublin 6W
Tel 01-4900218
(*Templeogue*, Dublin)
Moore, James,
Rushbrooke, Cobh,
Co Cork
Tel 086-8694744
(*Cobh, St Colman's
Cathedral*, Cloyne)
Moore, James, Very Rev, PP
Clonkeencole, Clones,
Co Monaghan H23 V895
Tel 047-51048
(*Clones, Killeevan*,
Clogher)
Moore, Johnny, Very Rev,
PP
Parochial House, Dungloe
Co Donegal
Tel 074-9521008
(*Dungloe (Templecrone
and Lettermacaward)*,
Raphoe)
Moore, Kevin, Very Rev, CC
30 Willow Park Crescent,
Dublin 11
Tel 01-8423865
(*Ballymun, St Pappin's*,
Dublin)
Moore, Michael (CSSp)
Holy Spirit Missionary
College
Kimmage Manor,
Whitehall Road,
Dublin D12 P5YP
Tel 01-4064300
Moore, Paschal, Very Rev,
PP
Piltown, Co Kilkenny
Tel 051-643112/
087-2408078
(*Templeorum*, Ossory)
Moore, Patrick, Very Rev,
PP, VF
Parochial House,
Castlepollard,
Co Westmeath
Tel 044-9661126/
087-2510855
(*Castlepollard*, Meath)

Allianz (ili)

Moore, Sean (CSsR)
Clonard Monastery,
1 Clonard Gardens,
Belfast, BT13 2RL
Tel 028-90445950

Moore, Seán, Very Rev, PP
Parochial House,
290 Monaghan Road,
Middletown,
Co Armagh BT60 4HS
Tel 028-37568406
(*Middletown (Tynan)*,
Armagh)

Moorhead, John, Very Rev,
PP
Parochial House, Eglish,
Birr, Co Offaly
Tel 057-9133010
(*Eglish*, Meath)

Morahan, Kieran (SMA)
SMA House, Cloonbigeen,
Claregalway,
Co Galway H91 YK64
Tel 091-798880

Moran, Benedict (OP), Very
Rev, PP
Dominican Community,
St Aengus's, Balrothery,
Tallaght, Dublin 24
Tel 01-4624038
(*Tallaght, Tymon North*,
Dublin)

Moran, John F., CC
192 Navan Road,
Dublin 7
Tel 01-8387902
(Dublin, retired)

Moran, Martin, Very Rev
Dean, PP
Rosscahill, Co Galway
Tel 091-550106
(*Rosscahill (Killannin)*,
Galway)

Moran, Martin (OMI), Very
Rev, Moderator
Oblate Fathers House of
Retreat,
Inchicore, Dublin 8
Tel 01-4541117
(*Bluebell, Inchicore, Mary
Immaculate, Inchicore, St
Michael's*, Dublin)

Moran, Patrick (CSSp)
Community Leader,
St Mary's College,
Rathmines, Dublin 6
Tel 01-4995760

Moran, Patrick
1 Seapark,
Mount Prospect Avenue
Dublin 3
(Dublin, retired)

Moran, Timothy (LC)
Vocations Director,
Leopardstown Road,
Foxrock, Dublin 18
Tel 01-2955902

Moran, Willie (OCD)
Avila Carmelite Centre,
Bloomfield Avenue,
Morehampton Road,
Dublin 4
Tel 01-6430200

Moreira, Lino (OSB)
Glenstal Abbey,
Murroe, Co Limerick
Tel 061-621000

Morely, Paul, Very Rev, PP
28 Willowbank Park,
Belfast BT6 0LL
Tel 028-90793023
(*St Bernadette's*, Down &
C.)

Morgan, Francis (OCSO)
Our Lady of Bethlehem
Abbey,
11 Ballymena Road,
Portglenone, Ballymena,
Co Antrim BT44 8BL
Tel 028-25821211

Morgan, Frank (SPS)
St Patrick's, Kiltegan,
Co Wicklow
Tel 059-6473600

Morgan, Liam, Very Rev, PP,
VF
Sallins Road, Naas,
Co Kildare
Tel 045-949576
(*Two-Mile-House*, Kildare
& L.)

Moriarty, Declan
Sacred Heart Residence,
Sybil Hill Road, Raheny,
Dublin 5
(Dublin, retired)

Moriarty, Mark
St John's Presbytery,
Tralee, Co Kerry
Tel 066-7122522
(*Tralee, St John's*, Kerry)

Moroney, Pat (SVD)
Maynooth, Co Kildare
Tel 01-6286391/2

Morris, Anthony (OP)
Holy Cross, Sligo,
Co Sligo
Tel 071-9142700

Morris, Dónal, Very Rev, PP
Parochial House,
Garraun South,
Creggs, Co Roscommon
Tel 090-6621127
(*Kilbegnet and Glisnk*,
Elphin)

Morris, John, Very Rev, PP
Solohead, Co Limerick
Tel 062-47614
(*Solohead*, Cashel & E.)

Morris, Michael, (SPS), CC
Curate, The Presbytery,
Ferbane, Co Offaly.
Tel 090-6454309
(*Ferbane High Street and
Boora*, Ardagh & Cl.)

Morrissey, Martin (MSC)
'Croí Nua', Rosary Lane,
Taylor's Hill Road,
Galway H91 WY2A
Tel 091-520960

Morrissey, Michael (OCarm)
Carmelite Community,
Gort Muire, Ballinteer,
Dublin 16 D16 EI67
Tel 01-2984014

Morrissey, Robin, Very Rev,
PP
Castletownroche, Co Cork
Tel 087-6727925
(*Castletownroche*, Cloyne)

Morrissey, Thomas (SJ)
Milltown Park,
Miltown Road,
Dublin D06 V9K7
Tel 01-2698411/2698113

Mortell, Anthony (SSC)
St Columban's Retirement
Home, Dalgan Park,
Navan, Co Meath
Tel 046-9021525

Mothersill, Joseph (OCarm),
CC
Carmelite Priory,
Whitefriar Street Church,
56 Aungier Street,
Dublin 2 D02 R598
Tel 01-4758821

Motherway, Nicholas (SPS)
St Patrick's, Kiltegan,
Co Wicklow
Tel 059-6473600

Mowbray, Alan (SJ),
c/o Milltown Park,
Miltown Road,
Dublin 6 D06 V9K7
Tel 01-2698411/2698113

Moynihan, James, Very Rev,
PP
Newbawn, Co Wexford
Tel 051-428227
(*Newbawn and Raheen*,
Ferns)

Moynihan, Michael, Very
Rev Canon, PP, VF
Dingle, Co Kerry
Tel 066-9151208
Moderator, Annascaul
Tel 066-9157103
(*Annascaul, Dingle*, Kerry)

Moynihan, Noel (CSSp)
Holy Spirit Missionary
College
Kimmage Manor,
Whitehall Road,
Dublin D12 P5YP
Tel 01-4064300

Moynihan, Seán (SVD)
Maynooth, Co Kildare
Tel 01-6286391/2

Muckian, Patrick (SM)
Philippines

Mudungwe, Francis, CC
Church Avenue,
Templemore, Co Tipperary
Tel 0504-35772
(*Templemore*, Cashel & E.)

Muhindo, Ubaldo, CC
14 Roselawn, Lucan,
Co Dublin
Tel 01-5037528
(*Lucan South*, Dublin)

Mulcahy, Brian (CP)
St Paul's Retreat,
Mount Argus, Dublin 6W
Tel 01-4992000

Mulcahy, Kevin
Ballymacoda, Co Cork
Tel 024-98110
(Cloyne, retired)

Mulcahy, Pat, Very Rev, Co-
PP
Parochial House,
18 Churchfield
Clonlara, Co Clare
Tel 061-354334/
087-6329913
(*Scáth na Sionnaine
Pastoral Area*, Killaloe)

Mulcahy, Richard, Rt Rev
30 Knapton Road,
Dun Laoghaire,
Co Dublin
Tel 01-2804353
(Opus Dei)

Mulcahy, Thomas (MSC)
Western Road,
Cork T12 TN80
Tel 021-4804120

Mulcahy, Timothy (OP), CC
St Dominic's,
St Dominic's Road,
Tallaght, Dublin 24
Tel 01-4510620
(*Tallaght, Dodder*, Dublin)

Muldowney, Peter, Very Rev
St Fiacre's Gardens,
Bohernatownish Road,
Loughboy,
Kilkenny R95 RF97
Tel 056-77701730/
086-8265955
(*St Patrick's*, Ossory)

Mulhall, Brendan (CSsR)
Clonard Monastery,
1 Clonard Gardens,
Belfast BT13 2RL
Tel 028-90445950

Mulhall, Brendan, Very Rev,
Adm
Holy Trinity Presbytery,
26 Norglen Gardens,
Belfast BT11 8EL
Tel 028-90590985/6
(*Coleraine*, Down & C.)

Mulherin, Jim (OSM), CC
Church of the Divine
Word,
Marley Grange,
25–27 Hermitage Downs,
Rathfarnham, Dublin 16
Tel 01-4944295/4941064
(*Marley Grange*, Dublin)

Mulhern, Kevin (SMA), CC
1 Aileach Road,
Ballymagroarty,
Derry BT48 0AZ
Tel 028-71267070
(*Holy Family,
Ballymagroarty*, Derry)

Mulholland, Patrick, Very
Rev, PP
Parochial House,
44 Lough Road,
Loughguile, Ballymena,
Co Antrim BT44 9JN
Tel 028-27641206
(*Loughguile*, Down & C.)

Mulkerins, Bernard (SSC)
St Columban's,
Dalgan Park,
Navan, Co Meath
Tel 046-9021525

Mulkerrins, Michael, Very
Rev Canon, PE
Curate's Residence,
Renmore, Galway
Tel 091-757859
(Galway, retired)

Mullaly, Kevin
8 Finglaswood Road,
Finglas West, Dublin 11
Tel 01-8238354
(*Blanchardstown*, Dublin)

Mullan, Joseph, Very Rev,
Adm
79 The Rise,
Mount Merrion,
Co Dublin
Tel 01-2889879
Moderator, Kilmacud-
Stillorgan and Mount
Merrion.
(*Clonskeagh, Kilmacud-
Stillorgan,
Mount Merrion*, Dublin)

Mullan, Kevin, PE
(Derry, retired)

Mullane, Denis,
The Presbytery,
Templeglantine,
Co Limerick
Tel 069-84021/
087-2621911
(*Pastoral Unit 14*, Limerick)

Mullaney, Michael Very Rev
DD
St Patrick's College,
Maynooth, Co Kildare
Tel 01-7084700
(Dublin)

Mullan, Joseph, PP
49 Rathgar Road,
Dublin 6
Tel 01-4970039/
087-2326254
(*Rathgar*, Dublin)

Mullen, John (IC)
Clonturk House,
Ormond Road,
Drumcondra, Dublin 9
Tel 01-6877014

Mullen, Pearse (SSCC)
Sacred Hearts Community,
Tanagh, Cootehill,
Co Cavan H16 CA22
Tel 049-5552188

Mulligan, Ben, Very Rev, PE
The Fern Dean,
Grange Terrace,
Deansgrange,
Co Dublin A94 TN25
(Dublin, retired)

Mulligan, Declan, Very Rev,
PP
Parochial House,
5 Aghalee Road,
Aghagallon,
Craigavon,
Co Armagh BT67 0AR
Tel 028-92651214
(*Aghagallon and
Ballinderry*, Down & C.)

Mulligan, Larry (OFM)
Franciscan Friary,
Liberty Street,
Cork T12 D376
Tel 021-4275481

Mulligan, Rory (SM)
Norway

Mulligan, Seán, CC
Parochial House,
25 Lisdergan Road,
Fintona,
Co Tyrone BT78 2NR
Tel 028-82841907
(*Fintona (Donacavey)*,
Clogher)

Mulligan, Thomas, Very Rev,
PE
Árd Aoibhinn,
Madogue, Swinford,
Co Mayo
Tel 083 8997039
(Achonry, retired)

Mulligan, Vincent (OMI)
Oblate House of Retreat,
Inchicore, Dublin 8
Tel 01-4534408/4541805

Mullin, Joseph, Very Rev
Canon, PE
c/o 10 Knock's Road,
Lisnaskea,
Co Fermanagh BT92 OJA
(Clogher, retired)

Mullin, Seamus, Very Rev
Canon, AP
Miltown Malbay,
Co Clare
Tel 065-7084003
(*Críocha Callan Pastoral
Area*, Killaloe)

Mullins, Anthony, Canon,
VG
The Presbytery,
Abbeyfeale, Co Limerick
Tel 068-31157
(*Pastoral Unit 14*, Limerick)

Mullins, Melvyn, Very Rev,
PP
42 Strand Street,
Skerries, Co Dublin
Tel 01-8491250
(*Skerries*, Dublin)

Mullins, Michael, Very Rev,
PE
St Anne's Presbytery,
Convent Hill, Waterford
(*Ballybricken*, Waterford &
L.)

Mullins, Patrick (OCarm)
Carmelite Community,
Gort Muire, Ballinteer,
Dublin D16 EI67
Tel 01-2984014

Mullins, Patrick, Very Rev
Canon, PE
Tuam, Co Galway
(Tuam, retired)

Mulroy, Tim (SSC)
No 3 and 4,
Ma Yau Tong Village,
Po Lam Road,
Tseung Kwan O,
Kowloon, Hong Kong, SAR

Mulryne, Philip Rev (OP)
St Mary's, Pope's Quay,
Cork
Tel 021-4502267

Mulvany, Seamus, Very Rev
PP
Parochial House,
Tubberclaire-Glasson,
Athlone, Co Westmeath
Tel 090-6485103
(*Glasson*, Meath)

Mulvey, Anthony (CSsR)
St Joseph's,
St Alphonsus Road,
Dundalk,
Co Louth A71 F3FC
Tel 042-9334042/9334762

Mulvihill, Anthony, Very Rev
Ballymarkham, Quin,
Co Clare
(Limerick)

Mulvihill, Eamonn, Very
Rev, PP
Castlegregory, Co Kerry
Tel 066-7139145
(*Castlegregory*, Kerry)

Mundisye, Simon, PC
Presbytery,
Blackditch Road
Ballyfermot, Dublin 10
Tel 01-6265695
(*Ballyfermot Upper*,
Dublin)

Mundow, Sean, Very Rev,
Adm
Parochial House,
Chapelizod, Dublin 20
Tel 01-6264645/087-
8195073
(*Chapelizod*, Dublin)

Munnelly, Patrick, Very Rev
PP
Ardagh, Ballina,
Co Mayo
Tel 096-31144
(*Ardagh*, Killala)

Munster, Ramon, Very Rev
Canon, PP
Parochial House,
Church Road,
Bundoran,
Co Donegal F94 AK80
Tel 071-9841290
(*Bundoran*, Clogher)

Muresan, Coriolan, CC
Presbytery No 2,
St Joseph's Road, Dublin
Tel 01-8386571
(*Aughrim Street*, Dublin)

Murney, Peadar, Very Rev
Archdeacon,
25 Thomastown Road,
Dun Laoghaire, Co Dublin
Tel 01-2856660
(Dublin, retired)

Murphy Amos, Patrick, CC
No. 1 The Glebe,
Peamount Road
Newcastle Lyons,
Co Dublin
Tel 086-0108420
(*Newcastle,
Saggart/Ratcool/Brittas*,
Dublin)

Murphy O'Connor, Kerry,
Venerable Archdeacon, P
The Bungalow,
Turner's Cross, Cork
(Cork & R., retired)

Murphy, Aidan, Very Rev,
PP
St Peter's Presbytery,
10 Fair Street,
Drogheda,
Co Louth A92 NX3T
Tel 041-9838239
(*Drogheda*, Armagh)

Murphy, Alphonsus, Very
Rev, PE
Carbury, Co Kildare
Tel 046-9553020
(Kildare & L., retired)

Murphy, Anthony (MHM)
St Joseph's House,
50 Orwell Park,
Rathgar,
Dublin D06 C535
Tel 01-4127700

Murphy, Bernard (OCarm)
Gort Muire, Ballinteer,
Dublin 16 D16 EI67
Tel 01-2984014

Murphy, Colm, Very Rev,
Clongeen,
Foulksmills,
Co Wexford
Tel 051-565610
(Ferns, retired)

Murphy, Colum, CC
The Presbytery,
Tullygally Road,
Legahory,
Craigavon BT65 5BL
(Moyraverty (Craigavon),
Seagoe (Derrymacash),
Dromore)

Murphy, Conor (OMI)
Oblates House of Retreat
Inchicore, Dublin 8
Tel 01-4534408/4541805

Murphy, Cornelius (SMA)
SMA House,
Wilton,
Cork T12 KR23
Tel 021-4541069/4541884

Murphy, Cornelius (SSC)
St Columban's,
Dalgan Park, Navan,
Co Meath
Tel 046-9021525

Murphy, Cyril (SSC)
St Columban's Retirement
Home,
Dalgan Park,
Navan, Co Meath
Tel 046-9021525

Murphy, Daniel, Very Rev,
PP
Church Road, Aghada,
Co Cork
Tel 086-0224682
(Aghada, Cloyne)

Murphy, David, CC, CF
Chaplain to Defence
Forces
c/o Bishop's House,
Summerhill,
Wexford
(Ferns)

Murphy, Denis (OP)
(leave of absence)
St Catherine's, Newry,
Co Down BT35 8BN
Tel 028-30262178

Murphy, Denis, Very Rev,
Adm
Tolerton, Ballickmoyler,
Carlow
Tel 056-4442126
(Doonane, Kildare & L.)

Murphy, Derry (SAC), Very
Rev, PP
St Benin's Parish,
Dublin Road,
Shankill, Co Dublin
Tel 01-2824425
(Shankill, Dublin)

Murphy, Edmund (OP)
Dominican College,
Newbridge
Droichead Nua, Co Kildare
Tel 045-487200

Murphy, Enda
Rome
(Kilmore)

Murphy, Eoin,
25 The Haven, Glasnevin,
Dublin 9
(Dublin, retired)

Murphy, Francis, Very Rev,
PP
Kilmuckridge, Gorey,
Co Wexford
Tel 053-9130116
(Kilmuckridge (Litter) and
Monamolin, Ferns)

Murphy, Gabriel, Very Rev,
PP
Keash, Ballymote,
Co Sligo
Tel 086-3249686
(Keash (Drumrat),
Achonry)

Murphy, George, Very Rev
Canon, PE
Minane Bridge, Co Cork
(Cork & R., retired)

Murphy, James (SJ)
Irish Jesuit Provincialate,
Milltown Park,
Miltown Road, Dublin 6
Tel 01-4987333

Murphy, James, Very Rev,
PP
St Brigid's, Rosslare,
Co Wexford
Tel 053-9132118
(Tagoat, Ferns)

Murphy, James, Very Rev,
PP
St Canice's Presbytery,
Dean Street,
Kilkenny R95 K6PH
Tel 056-7752991/
087-2609545
(St Canice's, Ossory)

Murphy, Jason
(priest in residence)
Killoughter, Redhills,
Co Cavan
Tel 047-55021
(Belturbet (Annagh),
Kilmore)

Murphy, Jeremiah (SAC), PP
St Benin's, Dublin Road,
Shankill, Co Dublin
Tel 01-2824425

Murphy, Jerry (SSC)
St Columban's,
Dalgan Park, Navan,
Co Meath
Tel 046-9021525

Murphy, John
(Kilmore, retired)

Murphy, Joseph, Very Rev
Mgr
Head of Protocol, Office
of Secretariat of State,
(Section for Relations with
States),
00120 Vatican City
Tel 0039-0669883193
(Cloyne)

Murphy, Laurence (SJ)
Milltown Park,
Miltown Road,
Dublin D06 V9K7
Tel 01-2698411/2698113

Murphy, Malachy, PP
Parochial House,
25 Priestbush Road,
Whitecross,
Co Armagh BT60 2TP
Tel 028-37507214
(Whitecross (Loughilly),
Armagh)

Murphy, Martin, Very Rev,
PP
Drom, Thurles,
Co Tipperary
Tel 0504-51196
(Drom and Inch, Cashel &
E.)

Murphy, Michael, Very Rev,
Co-PP
Parochial House,
Avoca, Co Wicklow
(Avoca, Dublin)

Murphy, Michael (OFMCap)
Capuchin Frary,
Friary Street,
Kilkenny R95 NX60
Tel 056-7721439

Murphy, Michael, CC
The Parochial House,
Roundfort,
Hollymount,
Co Mayo F12 A3Y8
Tel 094-9540026
(Robeen, Tuam)

Murphy, Michael, Very Rev
Canon, PP
Willow Lawn, Ballinlough,
Cork
(Ballinlough, Cork & R.)

Murphy, Mícheál, Very Rev,
PP, VF
11 Ashgrove,
Mountmellick, Co Laois
Tel 057-8679302
(Mountmellick, Kildare &
L.)

Murphy, Noel (CSSp)
Rockwell College,
Cashel, Co Tipperary
Tel 062-61444

Murphy, Noel, (CSSp)
14 Springfield Drive,
Dooradoyle, Limerick
Tel 061-304508/
087-2228971
(Pastroal Unit 6, Limerick)

Murphy, Pádraig, Very Rev,
PE
Parochial House,
Jenkinstown, Dundalk,
Co Louth A91 CC79
Tel 042-9371328
(Armagh, retired)

Murphy, Patrick (SPS)
Assistant District Leader,
Director of Slí an Chroí,
St Patrick's, Kiltegan,
Co Wicklow W91 Y022

Murphy, Patrick, Adm
St Mary's, Athlone,
Co Westmeath
Tel 090-6472088
(Athlone, Ardagh & Cl.)

Murphy, Patrick, Very Rev,
PP
Templetuohy, Thurles,
Co Tipperary
Tel 0504-53114
(Templetuohy, Cashel & E.)

Murphy, Paul, CC
Parochial House,
114 Battlehill Road,
Richhill,
Co Armagh BT61 8QJ
Tel 028-38871661
(Kilmore, Armagh)

Murphy, Paul (OFMCap)
Vicar, Secretary of the
Province,
Provincial Office,
12 Halston Street,
Dublin D07 Y2T5
Tel 01-8733205

Murphy, Paul F., Very Rev,
CF
Chaplain's House,
Dún Uí Mhaoilíosa
Renmore, Galway
Tel 091-751156
(Waterford & L.)

Murphy, Paul, Very Rev, PE
St Joseph's, Ferrybank,
Co Waterford
(Waterford & L., retired)

Murphy, Peadar, Very Rev,
PP
Aghabullogue, Co Cork
Tel 021-7334035
(Aghabullogue, Cloyne)

Murphy, Peter
Chaplain,
Mater Private Hospital,
Dublin 7
Tel 01-8858888
(Dublin)

Murphy, Peter, Very Rev
Canon, PP, VF
Parochial House,
Hale Street,
Ardee,
Co Louth A92 PXF3
Tel 041-6850920
(*Ardee & Collon*, Armagh)

Murphy, Seán, Very Rev, PP
Miltown Malbay,
Co Clare
Tel 065-7084129
(*Críocha Callan Pastoral
Area*, Killaloe)

Murphy Timothy, PC
St Mary's, Barndarrig
Co Wicklow
(*Kilbride and Barndarrig*,
Dublin)

Murphy, William, Most Rev,
DD
Retired Bishop of Kerry
No. 2 Cathedral Place,
Killarney,
Co Kerry
(Kerry)

Murray, Brendan (SSC)
St Columban's,
Dalgan Park,
Navan, Co Meath
Tel 046-9021525

Murray, Declan (SJ)
Crescent College
Comprehensive,
Dooradoyle, Limerick
Tel 061-480920

Murray, Denis, Very Rev
Parochial House,
Derrylin, Co Fermanagh
(Kilmore, retired)

Murray, Dermot (SJ)
Cherryfield Lodge,
Milltown Park,
Ranelagh,
Dublin D06 V9K7
Tel 01-4985800

Murray, Donal, Most Rev,
DD
Bishop Emeritus, Former
Bishop of Limerick,
Limerick Diocesan Centre,
St Munchin's,
Corbally, Limerick
Tel 061-350000
(Limerick, retired)

Murray, Francis, PP
Drumshanbo,
Co Leitrim
Tel 071-9641010
(*Drumshanbo (Murhaun)*,
Ardagh & Cl.)

Murray, Gerard, (SMA)
African Missions,
Blackrock Road,
Cork T12 TD54
Tel 021-4292871

Murray, James (OCarm)
Carmelite Priory, Moate,
Co Westmeath N37 AW34
Tel 090-6481160/6481398

Murray, James, CC
Director of ACCORD,
Carraroe, Sligo,
Co Sligo
Tel 071-9162136
(*Sligo, St Anne's*, Elphin)

Murray, John, Very Rev, PP
Achill Sound, Achill,
Co Mayo
Tel 098-45288
(*Achill*, Tuam)

Murray, John, Very Rev
c/o 75 Somerton Road
Belfast BT15 4DE
(Down & C., retired)

Murray, Liam, PP
Ballymahon,
Co Longford
Tel 090-6432253
Diocesan Secretary,
Diocesan Office, St
Michael's,
Longford
Tel 043-3346432
(*Ballymahon (Shrule)*,
Ardagh & Cl.)

Murray, Michael, CC
Belcarra, Castlebar,
Co Mayo
Tel 094-9032006
(*Balla and Manulla*, Tuam)

Murray, Michael, Very Rev
c/o 73 Somerton Road,
Belfast, BT15 4DE
(Down & C., retired)

Murray, Patrick J., Very Rev,
PP
c/o Diocesan Office,
Newry
(Dromore, retired)

Murray, Patrick (MHM)
St Joseph's House,
50 Orwell Park,
Rathgar,
Dublin D06 C535
Tel 01-4127700

Murray, Paul (OP)
Convent of SS Xystus and
Clement
Collegio San Clemente,
Via Labicana 95,
00184 Roma
Tel 0039-06-7740021

Murray, Placid (OSB)
Glenstal Abbey, Murroe,
Co Limerick
Tel 061-386103

Murray, Raymond, Rt Rev
Mgr, PE
60 Glen Mhacha,
Cathedral Road,
Armagh BT61 8AF
Tel 028-37510821
(Armagh, retired)

Murray, Tom PP
Ballinalee, Co Longford
Tel 043-3323110
(*Clonbroney*, Ardagh &
Cl.)

Murtagh, Brian (CSSp)
Holy Spirit Missionary
College,
Kimmage Manor,
Whitehall Road,
Dublin 12
Tel 01-4064300

Murtagh, Michael (CSsR), PP
103 Cherry Orchard
Avenue,
Cherry Orchard,
Dublin 10
Tel 01-6267930
(*Cherry Orchard*, Dublin)

Murtagh, Michael, Co-PP
69 Anne Devlin,
Ballyroan, Dublin 14
Tel 01-4950444
(*Ballyroan*, Dublin)

Murtagh, G. Michael, Very
Rev, PP
Parochial House,
Old Chapel Lane,
Dunleer,
Co Louth A92 W29X
Tel 041-6851278
(*Dunleer*, Armagh)

Murtagh, Liam, Very Rev
33 Grace Park Road,
Drumcondra,
Dublin 9
(Dublin, retired)

Murtagh, Michael (CSsR)
Superior,
Clonard Monastery,
1 Clonard Gardens,
Belfast, BT13 2RL
Tel 028-90445950

Murtagh, Michael, CC
5 St Mary's Terrace,
Arklow,
Co Wicklow
Tel 0402-41505
(*Arklow*, Dublin)

Murtala, Moses Daniel, TA
75 Ludford Road,
Ballinteer, Dublin 16
(*Meadowbrook*, Dublin)

Murtha, Kieran (SSCC)
Cootehill, Co Cavan
Tel 049-5552188

Mushawasha, Martin, PC
80 St Mary's Road,
East Wall, Dublin 3
Tel 01-8560980
(*East Wall-North Strand*,
Dublin)

Mwale, Hector, PC
The Presbytery,
St Martin de Porres Parish,
Firhouse Road West
Dublin 24 D24 K198
Tel 01-4510160
(*Bohernabreena, Tallaght,
Oldbawn*, Dublin)

Mwenda, Raphael (SPS
Councillor, St Patrick's,
Kiltegan,
Co Wicklow W91 YO22
Tel 059-6473600

Myers, David (IC)
Provincial, Clonturk House,
Ormond Road,
Drumcondra, Dublin 9
Tel 01-6877014

N

Nagle, Cathal
(Galway, retired)

Nagle, Joseph (OFMCap)
Capuchin Friary,
Holy Trinity,
Fr Mathew Quay,
Cork T12 PK24
Tel 021-4270827

Nallen, Michael, Very Rev
PP
Aughoose, Ballina,
Co Mayo
Tel 097-87990
(*Kilcommon-Erris*, Killala)

Nallukunnel, Antony
(OFMConv)
Friary of the Visitation,
Fairview Strand, Dublin 3
Tel 01-8376000

Nally, Frank Rev (SSC)
St Columban's,
Dalgan Park,
Navan, Co Meath
Tel 046-9021525

Nally, John, Very Rev
Ballylooby, Cahir,
Co Tipperary
Tel 052-7441489
(*Ballylooby*, Waterford &
L.)

Nash, Ger, Most Rev, DD
Bishop's House
Summerhill, Wexford
Tel 053-9122177
(Ferns)

Nash, Tom (CSSp)
Blackrock College,
Blackrock, Co Dublin
Tel 01-2888681

Naughton, John, Very Rev
Clonfert Avenue,
Portumna,
Co Galway H53 WC82
(Clonfert, retired)

Naughton, Richard, Very
Rev, PP, VF
Mountain Lodge,
132 Dublin Road, Newry,
Co Down BT35 8QT
Tel 028-30262174
(*Cloghogue (Killeavy
Upper)*, Armagh)

Allianz ⓘ

Naughton, Ultan (SSCC)
Coudrin House,
27 Northbrook Road,
Dublin 6
Tel 01-6686590
Chaplain, TU Dublin,
Grangegorman
Room RD-117,
Rathdown House,
Dublin D07 H6K8
Tel 01-2207078

Nawrat, Lukasz (SDB)
Provicial Secretary,
Salesian College,
Maynooth Road,
Celbridge,
Co Kildare W23 W0XK

Neary, Donal (SJ)
35 Lower Leeson Street,
Dublin 2
Tel 01-6761248
(Editor, *Sacred Heart
Messenger*)
Tel 01-6767491

Neary, Michael, Most Rev,
DD
Retired Archbishop of
Tuam,
Blackfort, Castlebar,
Co Mayo
(Tuam)

Nechikattil, Pius (SSP)
c/o Society of St Paul,
Moyglare Road,
Maynooth, Co Kildare
Tel 01-6285933

Ndugwa, Severinus, PC
No. 2 Presbytery,
St Canice's Parish,
Finglas, Dublin 11
Tel 087-8180097
(*Finglas*, Dublin)

Needham, Gerard, Very Rev
The Presbytery,
Bunowen Road,
Louisburgh,
Co Mayo F28 P635
(Tuam)

Neenan, Daniel, Rt Rev Mgr
Moderator (pro tem),
Holy Trinity Abbey Church,
Adare, Co Limerick
Tel 061-396172/
087-2208547
(*Pastoral Unit 11*, Limerick)

Neeson, Patrick, Very Rev,
Parochial House,
Drumardan Road,
Ballygalget BT22 1NE
(Down & C., retired)

Nejad, Damian, CC
Parochial House,
Letterkenny,
Co Donegal F92 CF88
Tel 074-9121021
(*Letterkenny*, Raphoe)

Nestor, Dermot, Very Rev,
Co-PP
Parochial House,
Nutgrove Avenue,
Dublin 14
Tel 01-2985916
(*Churchtown*, Dublin)

Neville, Alan (MSC)
Western Road,
Cork T12 TN80
Tel 021-4804120

Neville, Anthony
Moycullen, Co Galway
Tel 095-44668
(Tuam, retired)

Nevin, John (MHM)
St Joseph's House,
50 Orwell Park,
Rathgar,
Dublin D06 C535
Tel 01-4127700

Nevin, Michael G.
(priest in residence)
The Presbytery,
Harrington Street,
Dublin 8
Tel 01-4789093
(*Harrington Street*, Dublin)

Newell, Martin, Very Rev
Canon, PE
Claran, Ower P.O.,
Co Galway H91 YR6A
Tel 093-35436
(Tuam, retired)

Newman, John, Very Rev,
Co-PP
Moderator,
The Presbytery,
Bandon, Co Cork
Tel 023-8854666
(*Bandon, Enniskeane,
Innishannon, Killbrittain,
Kilmurry and
Murragh/Templemartin*,
Cork & R.)

Neylon, Gerry (SSC)
St Columban's,
Dalgan Park,
Navan, Co Meath
Tel 046-9021525

Neylon, Finbarr
On Sabbatical
(Dublin)

Neylon, Sean, Very Rev, PP
Taghmaconnell,
Ballinasloe,
Co Galway H53 RT28
Tel 090-9683929
(*Taghmaconnell*, Clonfert)

Nguyen, Dan An, Very Rev,
Co-PP
Parochial House,
Sperrin Road, Dublin 12
Tel 01-4550133
(*Mourne Road*, Dublin)

Nicholas, Michael (OFM)
23/25 Oudstrijderslaan,
1950 Kraainem, Belgium
Tel 0032-2-720-1970

Niyoyita, Kizito (SJ)
Jesuit Community,
27 Leinster Road,
Rathmines, Dublin 6
Tel 01-4970250

Njarakattuvely, Joy, CC
Cathedral Presbytery,
O'Connell Street,
Ennis, Co Clare
Tel 065-6824043
(*Abbey Pastoral Area*,
Killaloe)

Nkede, Evaristus, Very Rev,
PP
Parochial House, Rooskey,
Carrick-on-Shannon,
Co Roscommon
(*Kilglass*, Elphin)

Nkem, Clinton, CC
2 Ceol Na Mara,
Rush, Co Dublin
Tel 01-8949464
(*Rush*, Dublin)

Nohilly, Michael (SMA)
African Missions,
Blackrock Road,
Cork T12 TD54
Tel 021-4292871

Nohilly, Seamus (SMA)
SMA House, Wilton,
Cork T12 KR23
Tel 021-4541069/4541884

Nolan, Anthony (MSC)
Woodview House,
Mount Merrion Avenue,
Blackrock, Co Dublin
Tel 01-2881644

Nolan, Brendan, Very Rev,
PP
Blackwater, Enniscorthy,
Co Wexford
Tel 053-9127118
(*Blackwater*, Ferns)

Nolan, Brian (CM)
41 Park View,
Dunard Road, Dublin 7

Nolan, Brian (CSsR)
Coordinator, Scala,
Castlemahon Road,
Castle Road, Blackrock,
Cork
Tel 021-4358800

Nolan, Damien, Co-PP
Director,
Ennis ACCORD Centre,
7 Carmody Street
Business Park,
Ennis, Co Clare
Tel 1850-585000
Parish: 1a Laghtagoona,
Corofin, Co Clare
Tel 065-6837178/
086-8396636
(*Imeall Boirne Pastoral
Area*, Killaloe)

Nolan, Dermot (SPS)
St Patrick's,
Kiltegan,
Co Wicklow W91 YO22
Tel 059-6473600

Nolan, Francis, Very Rev, PP
The Presbytery, Fenit,
Tralee, Co Kerry
Tel 066-7136145
Director, Accord,
St John's Pastoral Centre,
Castle Street, Tralee,
Co Kerry
Tel 066-7122280
(*Spa*, Kerry)

Nolan, J. Michael, Rt Rev
Mgr
26 Harmony Avenue,
Donnybrook, Dublin 4
(Dublin, retired)

Nolan, James, Very Rev, PP
Davidstown, Enniscorthy,
Co Wexford
Tel 053-9238240
(*Davidstown and
Courtnacuddy*, Ferns)

Nolan, John P., Very Rev, PP
Duncannon, New Ross,
Co Wexford
Tel 051-389118
(*Duncannon*, Ferns)

Nolan, Joseph
(Kerry, retired)

Nolan, Mark-Ephrem M.
(OSB), Rt Rev Dom
Abbot,
Benedictine Monks,
Holy Cross Abbey,
119 Kilbroney Road,
Rostrevor,
Co Down BT34 3BN
Tel 028-41739979

Nolan, Martin (OSA)
St John's Priory,
Thomas Street, Dublin 8
Tel 01-6770393

Nolan, Robert, Very Rev, PP
Adamstown, Enniscorthy,
Co Wexford
Tel 053-9240512
(*Adamstown*, Ferns)

Nolan, Rory, Very Rev, PP
Borris, Co Carlow via
Kilkenny
Tel 059-9773128
(*Borris*, Kildare & L.)

Nolan, Seán, Very Rev, PE
Gate Lodge,
St Macartan's Cathedral,
Dublin Road,
Monaghan H18 TR79
Tel 042-9661586
(Clogher, retired)

Nolan, Simon (OCarm)
Prior, Carmelite Priory,
Whitefriar Street Church,
56 Aungier Street,
Dublin D02 R598
Tel 01-4758821

Nolan, Tod, Very Rev, PP,
VG
Newport, Co Mayo
Tel 098-41123
(*Newport (Burrishoole),*
Tuam)
Noonan, Bernard, Mgr, PP
Moate, Co Westmeath
Tel 090-6481180
(*Moate and Mount*
Temple, Ardagh & Cl.)
Noonan, James (OCD)
St Teresa's,
Clarendon Street
Dublin 2
Tel 01-6718466/6718127
Noonan, Mark (CM), Very
Rev
Phibsboro,
St Peter's, Dublin 7
Tel 01-8389708/8389841
Noonan, Michael, Very Rev,
PE
Portarlington, Co Laois
Tel 057-8623431
(Kildare & L., retired)
Noonan, Michael, Very Rev,
PP
Parochial House, Ardagh,
Co Limerick
Tel 087-6796217
(*Pastoral Unit 15,* Limerick)
Noone, Cletus (OFM)
Franciscan Friary,
Ennis, Co Clare
Tel 065-6828751
Noone, Martin, Very Rev,
Moderator, VF
7 Seabury Drive,
Malahide,
Co Dublin K36 YN67
Tel 01-8451902
Moderator, Portmarnock
(*Kinsealy, Malahide,*
Portmarnock,
Yellow Walls, Malahide,
Dublin)
Noone, Sean
The Presbytery,
Pollathomas,
Co Mayo
(Dublin, retired)
Noone, Thomas, Very Rev,
PP
69 Griffith Avenue,
Dublin 9
Tel 01-8332864
(*Marino,* Dublin)
Norman, James, PC
Dun Bhríd,
64 Orwell Park Rise,
Dublin 6W
Tel 01-8376027
(*Willington,* Dublin)
Norris, Thomas, Dr, CC
St Canice's Presbytery,
Kilkenny R95 VYOT
Tel 056-7752994/
083-3241438
(*St Canice's,* Ossory)

Norton, Gerard (OP)
Prior, St Mary's Priory,
Tallaght, Dublin 24
Tel 01-4048100
Ntambang, Roland, PC
St Luke the Evangelist
Parish,
Kilbarron Road,
Kilmore West, Dublin 5
Tel 01-8488149
(*Kilmore Road West,*
Dublin)
Nugent, Eugene M., Most
Rev, DCL
Apostolic Nunciature,
Yarmouk,
Block 1, Street 2, Villa NI,
Kuwait City, Kuwait
Tel +965-25337767
(Killaloe)
Nugent, Pat, CC
Springhill,
Glanmire, Co Cork
Tel 021-4866306/
086-1689292
(*Carrignavar, Glanmire,*
Glounthaune and
Watergrasshill, Cork & R.)
Nulty, Denis, Most Rev, DD
Bishop of Kildare and
Leighlin,
Bishop's House, Carlow
Tel 059-9142796/
059-9176725
Apostolic Administrator,
Diocese of Ossory
Ossory Diocesan Office,
James Street,
Kilkenny R95 NH60
Tel 056-7762448
(Kildare & L.)
Nunez Yepez, Eduardo
(OMI), PP
The Presbytery, Darndale,
Dublin 17
Tel 086-7954706
(*Darndale-Belcamp,*
Dublin)
Nwanko, Jonathan, PC
c/o 12 Coarsemoor Park,
Straffan, Co Kildare
Tel 01-6288827
(*Celbridge,* Dublin)
Nwaogwugwu, Cornelius
(CM)
St Vincent's Castleknock
College,
Castleknock,
Dublin D15 PD95
Tel 01-8213051
Nwakuna, Hyacinth (CSSp),
CC
The Presbytery,
Kilmacanogue,
Co Wicklow
Tel 01-2760030
(*Enniskerry/Kilmacanogue,*
Dublin)

Nwigwe, Peter, PC
12 Coarsemoor Park,
Straffan, Co Kildare
Tel 01-6012303
(*Celbridge,* Dublin)
Nyameh, Charles, CC
St Michael's Presbytery,
Ballinasloe,
Co Galway H53 EC98
Tel 090-9643916
(*Ballinasloe, Creagh and*
Kilclooney, Clonfert)
Nyhan, Charles
c/o Diocesan Office,
Redemption Road, Cork
(Cork & R., retired)
Nzinang, Anthony, CC
The Presbytery, Loughrea,
Co Galway H62 YE09
Tel 091-841212
(*Loughrea, St Brendan's*
Cathedral, Clonfert)

O

Ó Baoighill, Padraig, Very
Rev PE
58 Tara Court,
Ramelton Road,
Letterkenny, Co Donegal
(Raphoe, retired)
Ó Baoill, Donnchadh, Very
Rev, SP
Tory Island, Co Donegal
Tel 074-9135214
(*Gortahork/Tory Island,*
Raphoe)
Ó Bréartúin, Liam S. (OCD)
53/55 Marlborough Road,
Dublin 4
Tel 01-6601832
Ó Brolcháin, Cormac (CSSp)
Community Leader,
Blackrock College,
Blackrock, Co Dublin
Tel 01-2888681
Ó Clerichin, Matiú
(OFMCap)
Capuchin Presence
Our Lady of Knock Shrine,
Knock, Co Mayo
Ó Cochlain, Padraig, Very
Rev Canon, Moderator
Parochial House,
Arklow, Co Wicklow
Tel 0402-32294
(*Arklow, Avoca,*
Castletown, Dublin)
Ó Cochláin, Seosamh
c/o Diocesan Office,
Redemption Road, Cork
(Cork & R., retired)
Ó Conaire, Máirtín, PP
Teach an tSagairt
Kilronan, Aran Islands,
Co Galway H91 H7YW
Tel 099-61221
(*Aran Islands,* Tuam)

Ó Conghaile, Eamon
Árd Thiar, Carna, Co na
Gaillimhe
(Tuam, retired)
Ó Cuill, Pádraig (OFMCap)
Capuchin Friary,
Station Road,
Raheny, Dublin D05 T9E4
Tel 01-8313886
Ó Cuív, Liam, Very Rev, PP
Parochial House,
211 Navan Road, Dublin 7
Tel 01-8681436
(*Navan Road,* Dublin)
Ó Dochartaigh, Michael
(Kerry, retired)
Ó Dochartaigh, Tadhg, Very
Rev
(Kerry, retired)
Ó Domhnaill, Ruairí, Very
Rev, PP
Chapel Lane,
Newbridge, Co Kildare
Tel 045-431741
(*Caragh, Droichead*
Nua/Newbridge, Kildare &
L.)
Ó Dúill, Séamus (SDS)
Ard Mhuire, Kilmoon,
Lisdoonvarna, Co Clare
Tel 086-1030261
(retired)
Ó Fatharta, Pádraig (SPS)
St Patrick's, Kiltegan,
Co Wicklow
Tel 059-6473600
Ó Fearghaill, Fergus, DSS
Carlow College,
College Street, Carlow
Tel 059-9153200
(Kildare & L.)
Ó Fearraí, Cathal, Very Rev,
PP, VF
Kilbarron House,
College Street
Ballyshannon, Raphoe
Tel 071-9851295
(*Ballyshannon (Kilbarron),*
Ballintra (Drumholm),
Raphoe)
Ó Galláchóir, Nigel, PP
Annagry, Co Donegal
Tel 074-9548902
(*Annagry,* Raphoe)
Ó Gallchóir, Colm, Very Rev,
PP
Killybegs, Co Donegal
Tel 074-9731030
(*Killybegs,* Raphoe)
Ó Gallchóir, Seán, Very Rev,
PE
Coitín Na Doirí Beaga,
Leitir Ceanainn, Co Dhún
na nGall
(Raphoe, retired)
Ó Giolláin, Leon (SJ)
Loyola House,
Milltown Park,
Miltown Road, Dublin 6
Tel 01-2180276

Griofa, Gearóid, Very Rev, PP
Lettermore, Co Galway
Tel 091-551169
(*Lettermore*, Galway)

hÍcí, Liam, Co-PP
Ovens, Co Cork
Tel 021-4871180
(*Ballinora, Ballincollig and Ovens*, Cork & R.)

hAodha, Donncha
Nullamore,
Richmond Avenue South,
Dublin 6
Tel 01-4971239
(Opus Dei)

hÓbáin, Éanna (OCarm)
Prior and Bursar,
Principal Senior School,
Terenure College,
Terenure,
Dublin D6W DK72
Tel 01-4904621

Huallacháin, Maelísa (OFM)
Franciscan House of Studies, Dún Mhuire,
Seafield Road, Killiney,
Co Dublin
Tel 01-2826760

kereke, Christopher
St Mary's,
Lucan, Co Dublin
Tel 01-6217041
(*Lucan*, Dublin)

kolo, Felix (OCD)
Avila, Bloomfield Avenue,
Morehampton Road,
Dublin 4
Tel 01-6430200

Laoide, Caoimhín (OFM)
Franciscan Friary,
Killarney, Co Kerry
Tel 064-6631334/6631066

Loingsigh, Micheál, Very Rev, PP
Grenagh, Co Cork
Tel 021-4886128
(*Grenagh*, Cloyne)

Longaigh, Seán,
Askeaton, Co Limerick
Tel 061-392249
(*Pastoral Unit 12*, Limerick)

Maoldhomhnaigh, Conn, MA
Vice-President and Chaplain,
Carlow College,
College Street, Carlow
Tel 059-9153200
(Kildare & L.)

Mathúna, Tadhg, Very Rev Canon, PE
2 The Presbytery,
Blackrock, Cork

Murchú, Ailbe (OFM)
Franciscan Friary,
Ennis, Co Clare V95 A4N2
Tel 065-6828751

Ó Murchú, Daithí
Diocese of Arundel and Brighton,
St Richard's Church,
Cawley Road,
Chichester PO19 1XB, UK
(Galway)

Ó Murchú, Tomás, SP
Riverstick, Kinsale, Co Cork
Tel 021-4771332
(*Clontead*, Cork & R.)

Ó Murchú, Diarmuid (MSC)
Formation House,
56 Mulvey Park,
Dundrum, Dublin 16
Tel 01-2951856

Ó Riain, Diarmaid (OFM)
Franciscan Friary,
Multyfarnham,
Co Westmeath
Tel 044-9371114/9371137

Ó Ríordáin, John J. (CSsR)
Mount Saint Alphonsus,
Limerick
Tel 061-315099

Ó Ruairc, Caoimhín (SJ)
St Francis Xavier's,
Upper Gardiner Street,
Dublin 1
Tel 01-8363411

Ó Siochrú, Colm R.
Our Lady's Manor,
Bulloch Castle, Dalkey,
Co Dublin
(Dublin, retired)

Ó Tuathaigh, Antoin
c/o Diocesan Office,
Social Service Centre,
Henry Street, Limerick
(Limerick, retired)

O'Boyle, Aidan, Very Rev, VF
Cathedral Presbytery,
Ballina, Co Mayo
Tel 096-71365
(*Ballina*, Killala)

O'Boyle, Eugene
Parochial House,
Glenamaddy,
Co Galway F45 YD27
Tel 094-9659962
Administrator,
Williamstown
(Templetoher)
Parochial House,
Williamstown,
Co Galway
(*Glenamaddy
(Boyounagh)*,
*Williamstown
(Templetoher)*, Tuam)

O'Boyle, John, Rt Rev Mgr
Dalysfort Road,
Salthill, Co Galway
(Tuam, retired)

O'Boyle, Kevin, (SSC)
St Columban's,
Dalgan Park,
Navan, Co Meath
Tel 046-9021525

O'Boyle, Paul, Very Rev, PP
Clane, Naas, Co Kildare
Tel 045-868249
(*Clane*, Kildare & L.)

O'Brien, Anthony, Rt Rev Mgr, PP, VG, Adm
Mallow, Co Cork
Tel 022-20391
(*Mallow/Mourne Abbey*, Cloyne)

O'Brien, Anthony (OCSO)
Mount Saint Joseph
Abbey, Roscrea,
Co Tipperary E53 D651
Tel 0505-25600

O'Brien, Anthony (SSC)
St Columban's,
Dalgan Park
Navan, Co Meath
Tel 046-9021525

O'Brien, Augustine (MSC)
'Croí Nua', Rosary Lane,
Taylor's Hill, Galway
Tel 091-520960

O'Brien, Ben (OSA)
Duckspool House
(Retirement Community),
Abbeyside, Dungarvan,
Co Waterford
Tel 058-23784

O'Brien, Daniel (MSC)
Parish House,
Leap, Skibbereen,
Co Cork P81 NN52
Tel 028-33177

O'Brien, Eamon, Very Rev
No. 5 Hopecroft,
Main Street,
Glenavy BT29 4LN
(Down & C., retired)

O'Brien, Eamonn
Church Road, Croom,
Co Limerick
Tel 061-397213/
087-0767521
(Limerick)

O'Brien, Eamonn, Very Rev, PE
Newbrook Nursing Home,
Mullingar, Co Westmeath
(Meath, retired)

O'Brien, Evin, CC
The Presbytery,
Skibbereen, Co Cork
Tel 028-22878/22877
(*St Patrick's Cathedral,
Skibbereen, Rath and the
Islands*, Cork & R.)

O'Brien, Francis, Very Rev, PP
Parochial House,
51 Victoria Road, Larne,
Co Antrim BT40 1LY
Tel 028-28273230/
28273053
(*Larne*, Down & C.)

O'Brien, George (SPS)
St Patrick's,
21 Leeson Park,
Dublin D06 DE76
Tel 01-4977897

O'Brien, Gerard, PP
Bornacoola,
Carrick-on-Shannon,
Co Leitrim
Tel 071-9638229
(*Bornacoola*, Ardagh & Cl.)

O'Brien, Gregory, Very Rev, PP
Parochial House,
Old Hill, Leixlip,
Co Kildare
Tel 01-6245597
(*Confey, Leixlip*, Dublin)

O'Brien, James, Rt Rev Mgr, PP
Ballyea, Co Cork
Tel 063-81470
(*Ballyhea*, Cloyne)

O'Brien, James, Very Rev, AP
Parochial House,
Feakle, Co Clare
Tel 061-924035/
087-2665793
(*Inis Cealtra Pastoral Area*, Killaloe)

O'Brien, Jerry, AP
Bridgetown, Co Clare
Tel 061-376137
(*Scáth na Sionnaine*, Killaloe)

O'Brien, John (CSSp)
Holy Spirit Missionary
College
Kimmage Manor,
Whitehall Road,
Dublin D12 P5YP
Tel 01-4064300

O'Brien, John (OFM)
Franciscan Abbey,
Multyfarnham,
Co Westmeath
Tel 044-9371114/9371137

O'Brien, John (SMA)
Vice-Superior, SMA House,
81 Ranelagh Road,
Ranelagh, Dublin 6
Tel 01-4968162/3

O'Brien, John, Very Rev, PP
Parochial House, Killinure,
Tullow, Co Carlow
Tel 059-9156344
(*Clonmore*, Kildare & L.)

O'Brien, John, Very Rev, PP
Parochial House, Oristown,
Kells, Co Meath
Tel 046-9054124
(*Oristown*, Meath)

O'Brien, John (SPS)
Kiltegan House,
11 Douglas Road, Cork
Tel 021-4969371

O'Brien, John, Very Rev, Adm
186 Clontarf Road,
Dublin 3
Tel 01-8338575
(*Clontarf, St Anthony's, Clontarf, St John's, Dollymount*, Dublin)

O'Brien, Jordan (OP), CC
St Mary's Priory,
The Claddagh, Galway
Tel 091-582884
(*St Mary's*, Galway)

O'Brien, Joseph (OP)
Prior, Holy Cross,
Tralee, Co Kerry
Tel 066-7121135

O'Brien, Joseph, Very Rev Canon, PP
Lackaghmore,
Turloughmore, Co Galway
(Tuam, retired)

O'Brien, Kieran, Very Rev, Adm, VF
Killarney, Co Kerry
Tel 064-6631014
Moderator,
Kilcummin Parish
(*Killarney, Kilcummin*, Kerry)

O'Brien, Liam, Very Rev, PP
Sneem, Co Kerry
Tel 064-6645141
(*Sneem*, Kerry)

O'Brien, Lorcan, Rt Rev Mgr, Adm
Pro-Cathedral House,
83 Marlborough Street,
Dublin 1
Tel 01-8745441
(*Pro-Cathedral*, Dublin)

O'Brien, Martin
2 Powerscourt,
Tulla, Co Clare
Tel 065-6835284
(Killaloe, retired)

O'Brien, Michael
St Anne's Presbytery,
Convent Hill, Waterford
Tel 051-855819
(Waterford & L., retired)

O'Brien, Rory (SPS)
St Patrick's, Kiltegan,
Co Wicklow
Tel 059-6473600

O'Brien, Ned (SAC)
(Residing elsewhere)

O'Brien, Pat (SPS), CC
Kiltegan, Co Wicklow
Tel 059-6473211
(*Rathvilly*, Kildare & L.)

O'Brien, Pat, Very Rev, PP
The Parochial House,
Cahreenard
Caherlistrane,
Co Galway H91 Y06D
Tel 093-55428
(*Caherlistrane (Donaghpatrick and Kilcoona)*, Tuam)

O'Brien, Paul (OSA)
The Abbey, Fethard,
Co Tipperary
Tel 052-31273

O'Brien, Peter, Very Rev, PP
Kilfian, Killala, Co Mayo
Tel 096-32420
(Killala, retired)

O'Brien, Sean (MHM)
St Joseph's House,
50 Orwell Park, Rathgar,
Dublin 6
Tel 01-4127700

O'Brien, Terence (MSC), Co-PP
Parochial House,
Leap, Co Cork
Tel 028-33177
(*Aughadown, Castlehaven, Kilmacabea, Rath and the Islands and Skibbereen*, Cork & R.)

O'Brien, Timothy, Very Rev, AP
Carrigatoher, Nenagh,
Co Tipperary
Tel 067-31231/
087-6548331/087-2623922
(*Odhran Pastoral Area*, Killaloe)

O'Byrne, Christopher, Rt Rev Mgr, PE
3 Grange Court,
Magherafelt,
Co Derry BT45 5RU
Tel 028-79631791
(Armagh, retired)

O'Byrne, Gerard, Very Rev, PE, CC
Rathangan, Co Kildare
Tel 045-524316
(*Rathangan*, Kildare & L.)

O'Byrne, John,
St Mary's,
Athlunkard Street,
Limerick
Tel 085-7491268
(*Pastoral Unit 4*, Limerick)

O'Byrne, Michael, Very Rev, AP
Kilmeaden, Co Waterford
Tel 051-384117
(*Portlaw*, Waterford & L.)

O'Byrne, Paddy, CC
Presbytery No 2,
Church Grounds
Tel 01-2882257
(*Kilmacud-Stillorgan*, Dublin)

O'Byrne, Patrick, Very Rev, PE, CC
St Mary's, Daingean,
Co Offaly
Tel 057-9353064
(*Daingean*, Kildare & L.)

O'Byrne, Patrick, Co-PP
No. 2 The Presbytery,
Mountview,
Blanchardstown, Dublin 15
Tel 01-8216380
(*Mountview*, Dublin)

O'Byrne, Patrick J., CC
194 Navan Road,
Dublin 7
Tel 01-8383313
(*Navan Road*, Dublin)

O'Byrne, Thomas, Very Rev, Adm
The Presbytery,
Old Dublin Road, Carlow,
Tel 059-9131227
(*Cathedral, Carlow*, Kildare & L.)

O'Byrne, William, Very Rev, PP
Kill, Naas, Co Kildare
Tel 045-878008
(*Kill*, Kildare & L.)

O'Callaghan, Flor (OSA)
St Augustine's Priory,
Dungarvan, Co Waterford
Tel 058-41136

O'Callaghan, Benedict (OCarm),
Prior, Carmelite Priory,
Kinsale,
Co Cork P17 WR88
Tel 021-4772138

O'Callaghan, Ciarán (CSsR)
Vicar, Clonard Monastery,
1 Clonard Gardens,
Belfast BT13 2RL
Tel 028-90445950

O'Callaghan, Daniel (OCarm)
Terenure College,
Terenure,
Dublin D6W DK72
Tel 01-4904621

O'Callaghan, Denis, Very Rev, PE
Teach an tSagairt,
Main Street,
Carrigtwohill, Co Cork
Tel 086-8054040
(Cloyne, retired)

O'Callaghan, Enda (SJ)
St Ignatius Community & Church,
27 Raleigh Row, Galway
Tel 091-523707

O'Callaghan, Flor (OSA)
St Augstine's Priory
O'Connell Street,
Co Limerick

O'Callaghan, John (OSB)
Glenstal Abbey, Murroe,
Co Limerick
Tel 061-386103

O'Callaghan, Kevin, Rt Rev Mgr, AP,
The Presbytery, Lissarda,
Co Cork
(Cork & R., retired)

O'Callaghan, Peadar, Very Rev, PE
Suimhneas, Charleville,
Co Cork
Tel 086-8054040
(Cloyne, retired)

O'Caoimh, Tomás
c/o Diocesan Office,
Killarney, Co Kerry
(Kerry)

O'Carroll, Ciaran, Rt Rev Mgr, PP, VG
Presbytery No. 1,
Sacred Heart Parish,
Stillorgan Road,
Donnybrook,
Dublin 4 D04 E8C7
Tel 01-2693926
PP, Booterstown
(*Booterstown, Donnybrook*, Dublin)

O'Carroll, Gerard (SPS)
St Patrick's, Kiltegan,
Co Wicklow W91 Y022
Tel 059-6473600

O'Ciarain, Peadar
Sons of Divine Providence
Orione House,
13 Lower Teddington
Road, Hampton, Wick,
Kinston-upon-Thames,
KT1 4EU
(Dublin, retired)

O'Connell, Anthony, Very Rev
5 Parkside, Stoneybatter,
Wexford
(Ferns, retired)

O'Connell, Con (MSC)
Formation House,
56 Mulvey Park, Dundrum
Dublin 16
Tel 01-2951856

O'Connell, Conal (SSC)
St Columban's,
Dalgan Park,
Navan, Co Meath
Tel 046-9021525

O'Connell, David, Very Rev, Co-PP
Lislevane, Bandon,
Co Cork
Tel 023-8846171
(*Ardfield/Rathbarry, Barryroe, Clonakilty, Kilmeen/Castleventry, Rosscarbery and Timoleague*, Cork & R.)

O'Connell, James (SM), Very Rev, Adm
Cerdon, Marist Fathers,
St Mary's Road,
Dundalk, Co Louth
(*Dundalk*, Armagh)

O'Connell, James, Very Rev, Adm
Parochial House,
Ballon, Co Carlow
Tel 059-9159329
(*Ballon*, Kildare & L.)

'Connell, James (CSSp)
Holy Spirit Missionary
College
Kimmage Manor,
Whitehall Road,
Dublin D12 P5YP
Tel 01-4064300

'Connell, Jim (MHM)
Editor of St Joseph's
Advocate,
St Joseph's House,
50 Orwell Park,
Rathgar, Dublin D06 C535
Tel 01-4127700

'Connell, Jimmy (SM), Adm
Superior,
Holy Family Parish,
Parochial House, Dundalk,
Co Louth
Tel 042-9336301
(Holy Family, Armagh)

'Connell, John, Very Rev,
PE
The Presbytery,
Two-Mile-House,
Naas, Co Kildare
Tel 045-876160
(Kildare & L., retired)

'Connell, Liam (SJ)
St Ignatius (Residence),
27 Raleigh Row,
Galway H91 FTX8
Tel 091-523707

'Connell, Matthew (SMA)
African Missions,
Blackrock Road,
Cork T12 TD54
Tel 021-4292871

'Connell, Michael (MSC)
Western Road,
Cork T12 TN80
Tel 021-4804120

'Connell, Patrick (MHM)
St Joseph's House,
50 Orwell Park,
Rathgar, Dublin D06 C535
Tel 01-4127700

'Connell, Philip, Very Rev,
PE
(Kerry, retired)

'Connell, Raymond (OSM),
Very Rev
Servite Priory,
St Peregrine,
36 Grangewood Estate,
Rathfarnham, Dublin 16
Tel 01-4936755

'Connell, Seamus, PEm
St Patrick's College,
Maynooth, Co Kildare
Tel 01-6285222
(Derry, retired)

'Connell, Terence
142 Mayorstone Park,
Limerick
(Limerick, retired)

O'Connell, Tomás Very Rev,
PP
Pallasgreen, Co Limerick
Tel 061-384114
(Pallasgreen, Cashel & E.)

O'Connor, Anthony, Very
Rev
Molassy, Freshford Road,
Kilkenny
Tel 087-2517766
(Ossory)

O'Connor, Benjamin
c/o Cloyne Diocesan
Centre, Cobh, Co Cork
Tel 021-4811430
(Cloyne)

O'Connor, Brendan
Ely University Centre,
10 Hume Street, Dublin 2
Tel 01-6767420
(Opus Dei)

O'Connor, Charles (OMI)
170 Merrion Road,
Ballsbridge, Dublin 4
Tel 01-2693658

O'Connor, Christopher
(MHM)
St Mary's Parish,
25 Marquis Street,
Belfast BT1 1JJ
Tel 028-90320482

O'Connor, Christopher, Very
Rev Dean, PE
Kilkerrin, Ballinasloe,
Co Galway
(Galway, retired)

O'Connor, Columba (OSA)
Duckspool House
(Retirement Community),
Abbeyside, Dungarvan,
Co Waterford
Tel 058-23784

O'Connor, Daniel J., Very
Rev Mgr, PC
St Mary's, Irishtown Road,
Dublin 4
Tel 01-6697429
(Ringsend, Dublin)

O'Connor, Daniel, Very Rev
Canon, PE
Dunabbey House,
Dungarvan, Co Waterford
(Waterford & L., retired)

O'Connor, Donie (Daniel)
(MHM)
6 Allen Park Road,
Stillorgan,
Co Dublin A94 X261
Tel 089-9796447
(Clonskeagh, Kilmacud-
Stillorgan,
Mount Merrion, Dublin)

O'Connor, Declan,
Moderator,
Duagh, Listowel, Co Kerry
Tel 068-45102
(Duagh, Kerry)

O'Connor, Denis, (CSsR) CC
Dún Mhuire,
461/463 Griffith Avenue,
Dublin D09 X651
Tel 01-5180196
(Dún Mhuire, Dublin)

O'Connor, Dermot (SJ)
Rector, St Ignatius
Community & Church,
27 Raleigh Row, Galway
Tel 091-523707

O'Connor, Donal
Chaplain, Munster
Technological University,
Tralee, Co Kerry
Tel 066-7145639/7135236
(Kerry)

O'Connor, Eamonn, Very
Rev, PP, VF
Strokestown,
Co Roscommon
Tel 071-9633027
(Strokestown (Kiltrustan,
Lissonuffy and
Cloonfinlough), Elphin)

O'Connor, Edward (SMA)
African Missions,
Blackrock Road,
Cork T12 TD54
Tel 021-4292871

O'Connor, Fergus (Opus
Dei), Very Rev, PP, VF
31 Herbert Avenue,
Dublin 4
Tel 01-2692001
(Merrion Road, Dublin)

O'Connor, Frank,
Cathedral House,
Cathedral Place, Limerick
Tel 061-414624/
087-2642393
(Pastoral Unit 1, Limerick)

O'Connor, Gerard, Very Rev,
PE
23 Beechwood Grove,
Portlaw, Co Waterford
(Waterford & L., retired)

O'Connor, Gerard (CSsR)
Scala, Castlemahon House,
Castle Road,
Blackrock, Cork
Tel 021-4358800

O'Connor, John (SAC), Very
Rev,
St Patrick's, Corduff,
Blanchardstown, Dublin 15
Tel 01-8213596/8215930
(Corduff, Dublin)

O'Connor, John C., Very Rev
c/o Lisbreen,
73 Somerton Road,
Belfast BT15 4DE
(Down & C., retired)

O'Connor, John (OSA)
Duckspool House
(Retirement Community),
Abbeyside, Dungarvan,
Co Waterford
Tel 058-23784

O'Connor, John, J. (OSA)
St John's Priory,
Thomas Street, Dublin 8
Tel 01-6770393

O'Connor, Kevin (OMI)
Oblate House of Retreat,
Inchicore, Dublin 8
Tel 01-4534408/4541805

O'Connor, Laurence, Very
Rev, PP
Bunclody, Enniscorthy,
Co Wexford
Tel 053-9377319
(Bunclody, Ferns)

O'Connor, Liam (OCSO)
Mount Saint Joseph
Abbey, Roscrea,
Co Tipperary
Tel 0505-25600

O'Connor, Martin, Very Rev
Canon, PP, VF
The Parochial House,
Ballindine, Claremorris,
Co Mayo F12 EO96
Tel 094-9364423
Administration for
Crossboyne and Taugheen
(Ballindine (Kilvine),
Tuam)

O'Connor, Michael Very
Rev, Adm
Presbytery No. 2,
Church Grounds,
Kill Avenue, Dun
Laoghaire, Co Dublin
Tel 01-2140863
(Kill-O'-The-Grange,
Dublin)

O'Connor, Michael, Very
Rev
c/o St John's Pastoral
Centre, John's Hill,
Waterford
(Waterford & L.)

O'Connor, Michael (OMI),
CC
Superior, The Presbytery,
Darndale, Dublin 17
Tel 01-8474547
(Darndale-Belcamp,
Dublin)

O'Connor, Michael G. (CSsR)
Mount Saint Alphonsus,
Limerick
Tel 061-315099

O'Connor, Muiris, Very Rev,
Pastoral Area Assignment,
Askeaton,
Co Limerick
(Limerick)

O'Connor, Pat (CSsR)
Mount Saint Alphonsus,
South Circular Road,
Limerick
Tel 061-315099

O'Connor, Patrick, Very Rev, PP, VF
Parochial House,
Dunboyne, Co Meath
Tel 01-8255342
(*Dunboyne*, Meath)

O'Connor, Peter, Very Rev, Adm
24 Barclay Court,
Blackrock, Co Dublin
Tel 01-2832302
(*Blackrock*, Dublin)

O'Connor, Philip, Very Rev, PP
Parochial House,
Mountnugent, Co Cavan
Tel 049-8540123
(*Mountnugent*, Meath)

O'Connor, Richard
Villa Maria Assunta, Via Aurelia Antica 284,
00-165, Roma, Italia
(Kerry)

O'Connor, Sean, Very Rev, PP
Ballyhale,
Kilkenny R95 Y9F4
Tel 056-7756889/
086 3895911
(*St John's*, Ossory)

O'Connor, Thomas, DD
St Patrick's College,
Maynooth, Co Kildare
Tel 01-6285222
(Meath)

O'Connor, Tim
Abbeyville, Manister,
Croom, Co Limerick
Tel 087-7859028
(*Pastoral Unit 8*, Limerick)

O'Connor, Tom, CC
Dublin Road, Portlaoise,
Co Laois
Tel 057-8692153
(*Portlaoise*, Kildare & L.)

O'Connor, Tom (OSCam)
St Camillus,
South Hill Avenue,
Blackrock, Co Dublin

O'Connor, Tom (SPS)
District Leader for Ireland,
St Patrick's, Kiltegan,
Co Wicklow
Tel 059-6473600

O'Cuilleanáin, Fionnbarra (SMA)
African Missions,
Blackrock Road,
Cork T12 TD54
Tel 021-4292871

O'Cuiv, Shan
Team Assistant, c/o The Presbytery, Clonburris,
Clondalkin, Dublin 22
Tel 01-4573440
(*Clondalkin/Rowlagh/
Neilstown/Deansrath/
Bawnogue*, Dublin)

O'Dea, Francis, Moderator
St Ita's Presbytery,
Newcastlewest,
Co Limerick
Tel 087-2443106
(*Pastoral Unit 15*, Limerick)

O'Doherty, Bartie (SPS)
St Patrick's, Kiltegan,
Co Wicklow
Tel 059-6473600

O'Doherty, Colm, PP
6 Orchard Park,
Murlog, Lifford,
Co Donegal
Tel 074-9142022
(*Lifford (Clonleigh)*, Derry)

O'Doherty, Daniel, Very Rev, PE
St Eunan's Nursing Home,
Letterkenny,
Co Donegal
(Raphoe, retired)

O'Doherty, Kieran, Very Rev,
159 Glen Road,
Maghera,
Co Derry BT46 5JN
Tel 028-79642496
(*Maghera*, Derry)

O'Doherty, Seán, Very Rev
Archdeacon
Durrow, Co Laois
Tel 057-8736156
(Ossory, retired)

O'Donnell, Chris, AP, EV
Jerpoint, Sheares Street,
Kilmallock,
Co Limerick
Tel 087 6323309
(*Pastoral Unit 9*, Limerick)

O'Donnell, Cornelius, Very Rev, PE
Rathcormac, Fermoy,
Co Cork
Tel 025-36286
(Cloyne, retired)

O'Donnell, Desmond (OMI)
Oblate House of Retreat,
Inchicore, Dublin 8
Tel 01-4534408/4541805

O'Donnell, Edward (SJ)
Gonzaga College,
Sandford Road, Dublin 6
Tel 01-4972943

O'Donnell, Edward, Very Rev, PP
42 Derryvolgie Avenue,
Belfast BT9 6FP
Tel 028-90665409
(*St Brigid's*, Down & C.)

O'Donnell, Gerard, Very Rev, PP
Kilfian, Killala
Co Mayo
Tel 096-32420
(*Kilfian*, Killala)

O'Donnell, Hugh (MHM)
St Joseph's House,
50 Orwell Park, Rathgar,
Dublin 6
Tel 01-4127700

O'Donnell, Hugh (OFM)
Dún Mhuire,
Seafield Road,
Killiney, Co Dublin
Tel 01-2826760

O'Donnell, Hugh (SDB), CC
Vice-Rector, Rinaldi House,
40/41 Sean McDermott Street,
Dublin D01 H7P6
Tel 01-8363358
(*Sean McDermott Street*, Dublin)

O'Donnell, James, Very Rev, PP
Killenaule, Co Tipperary
Tel 052-9156244
(*Killenaule*, Cashel & E.)

O'Donnell, James, Rt Rev Mgr, AP
Macroom, Co Cork
Tel 026-41042
(*Macroom*, Cloyne)

O'Donnell, Louis (OSA), Most Rev
St John's Priory,
Thomas Street, Dublin 8
Tel 01-6770393

O'Donnell, Owen, Very Rev, PE
Parochial House,
Dunamore, Cookstown,
Co Tyrone
Tel 028-86751216
(Armagh, retired)

O'Donnell, Pat, Very Rev Canon, PP, VF
Rathmore, Co Kerry
Tel 064-7758026
(*Rathmore*, Kerry)

O'Donnell, Sean, CC
St Brigid's,
Carnhill, Co Derry
BT48 9QE
Tel 028-71263152
(*The Three Patrons*, Derry)

O'Donnell, Terence (IC)
Clonturk House,
Ormond Road,
Drumcondra, Dublin 9
Tel 01-6877014

O'Donoghue, Brendan, Very Rev Canon, AP
12 Tullyglass Square,
Shannon, Co Clare
Tel 061-361257/
086-8308153
(*Tradaree Pastoral Area*, Killaloe)

O'Donoghue, Fergus (SJ), PC
Gonzaga College,
Sandford Road, Dublin 6
Tel 01-4972943
(*Clonskeagh*, Dublin)

O'Donoghue, James
Ballinahinch, Birdhill,
Limerick
Tel 061-781510
(*Ballinahinch*, Cashel & E.)

O'Donoghue, Neil Xavier
Theology Faculty,
St Patrick's College,
Maynooth, Co Kildare
Tel 087-7708819
(Newark, NJ, USA)

O'Donoghue, Neville (SM)
St Columba's,
Church Avenue,
Ballybrack, Co Dublin
Tel 01-2858301

O'Donoghue, Patrick
119 Grace Park Manor,
Drumcondra, Dublin 9
(Dublin)

O'Donoghue, Patrick, CC
Mitchelstown, Co Cork
Tel 025-84077
(*Mitchelstown*, Cloyne)

O'Donoghue, Patrick (SSC)
St Columban's,
Dalgan Park,
Navan, Co Meath
Tel 046-9021525

O'Donoghue, Paul, CC
c/o Cork and Ross Diocesan Office,
(Cork & R., retired)

O'Donohoe, Joseph (OPraem)
Holy Trinity House,
Lismacanican,
Mountnugent, Co Cavan

O'Donohoe, Seán (OFMCap)
Guardian, Capuchin Friary
Station Road,
Raheny,
Dublin D05 T9E4
Tel 01-8313886

O'Donohue, Patrick (FSSP)
21 The Folly,
Waterford City X91 KWD8
Ministry to the Latin Mass
Chaplaincy, St John's Parish, Waterford & L.
(Galway)

O'Donovan, Chris, Very Rev Co-PP
New Parochial House,
Monkstown, Cork
Tel 021-4863267
(*Carrigaline, Crosshaven, Harbour Parishes
and Tracton Abbey*, Cork & R.)

O'Donovan, Colman, Very Rev Canon, PE
1 Youghal Road,
Midleton, Co Cork
Tel 021-4621617
(Cloyne, retired)

O'Donovan, Ignatius (OSA)
The Abbey,
Fethard, Co Tipperary

Allianz (il)

'Donovan, Jim, Very Rev Canon, AP
St Finbarr's West,
The Lough, Co Cork
Tel 087-2553021
(Ballyphehane, The Lough, Cork & R.)

'Donovan, John, Very Rev Canon, PP, Adm
Cathedral Presbytery,
Roman Street, Cork
Tel 021-4501022
(Cathedral of St Mary & St Anne, Blackpool/ The Glen/Ballyvolane, Cork & R.)

'Donovan, John C., AP
The Presbytery, Dromore
Bantry, Co Cork
Tel 028-31126
(Bantry, Caheragh, Goleen, Muintir Bháire and Schull, Cork & R.)

'Donovan, Padraig (SSC)
Regional Vice-Director,
House Superior,
St Columban's,
Dalgan Park,
Navan, Co Meath
Tel 046-9021525

'Donovan, Pat, Co-PP
Moderator,
The Presbytery,
Dunmanway, Co Cork
Tel 023-8845000
(Drimoleague, Dunmanway, Kilmichael and Uibh Laoire, Cork & R.)

'Donovan, William, Very Rev, PP
Conna, Mallow, Co Cork
Tel 058-59138
(Conna, Cloyne)

'Dowd, Sean (SPS), CC
Disciples of Divine Master,
3 Castle Streer, Athlone,
Co Westmeath
Tel 090 6490575
Chaplain to Sisters of Mercy
(Athlone, Elphin)

'Driscoll, Aidan, Rt Rev Mgr, Co-PP, VG
Moderator,
Cork Road,
Carrigaline, Co Cork
Tel 021-4371684
(Carrigaline, Crosshaven, Harbour Parishes and Tracton Abbey, Cork & R.)

Driscoll, Eamonn (OFM)
Franciscan Friary,
Rossnowlagh,
Co Donegal
Tel 071-9851342

O'Driscoll, Fintan (MSC), PP
Sacred Heart Parish,
Killinarden, Tallaght,
Dublin D24 R521
Tel 01-4522251
(Killinarden, Dublin)

O'Driscoll, Gus (SMA), AP
Father in charge,
St Joseph's,
Blackrock Road,
Cork T12 X281
Tel 021-4292871
(St Joseph's (Blackrock Road), Cork & R.)

O'Driscoll, Kieron, PP
The Presbytery,
Togher, Co Cork
Tel 021-4964986
(Ballinhassig, Cork & R.)

O'Driscoll, Martin, Very Rev Canon, Co-PP
The Presbytery,
Bantry, Co Cork
Tel 027-50096
(Bantry, Caheragh, Goleen, Muintir Bháire and Schull, Cork & R.)

O'Driscoll, Michael
Bushmount,
Clonakilty, Co Cork
Tel 023-33991
(Cork & R., retired)

O'Driscoll, P.J., CF
29th Commando Regiment, RA
The Royal Citadel,
Lamabhay Hill,
Plymouth PL1 2PD
Tel 0044-7816135137
(Cloyne)

O'Driscoll, Paul, Very Rev Canon, PP
6 New Cabra Road,
Phibsboro, Dublin 7
Tel 01-8388874/
087-2573857
(Travelling People, Dublin)

O'Duill, Seamus (SDS)
Ard Mhuire, Kilmoon,
Lisdoonvarna, Co Clare
Tel 086-1030261

O'Dúill, Fergal (LC)
Vocations Director,
Leopardstown Road,
Foxrock, Dublin 18
Tel 01-2955902
Chaplain, Clonlost Retreat and Youth Centre,
Killiney Road, Killiney,
Co Dublin
Tel 01-2350064

O'Dwyer, Christy, Rt Rev Mgr, AP, VG
Diocesan Archivist,
Moyne, Thurles,
Co Tipperary
Tel 0504 45129
(Templetuohy, Cashel & E.)

O'Dwyer, John, Very Rev Dean, PE
20 Cloonarkin Drive,
Oranmore, Co Galway
Tel 091-484501
(Galway, retired)

O'Dwyer, Michael (SAC), CC
9 Seaview Lawn, Shankill,
Co Dublin
Tel 01-2822277
(Shankill, Dublin)

O'Dwyer, Michael, Very Rev, PP
Parochial House,
31 Church Street,
Ballygawley,
Co Tyrone BT70 2HA
Tel 028-85567096
(Ballygawley (Errigal Kieran), Armagh)

O'Dwyer, Richard (SJ)
Superior,
St Francis Xavier's,
Upper Gardiner Street,
Dublin 1
Tel 01-8363411

O'Dwyer, Sean, Very Rev, PE
Clonmel Road, Cahir,
Co Tipperary
Tel 087-4184213
(Waterford & L., retired)

O'Farrell, Ambrose (OP)
St Mary's,
The Claddagh, Galway
Tel 091-582884

O'Farrell, Edward (CSSp)
Community Leader,
Holy Spirit Missionary College,
Whitehall Road,
Dublin D12 P5YP
Tel 01-4064300

O'Farrell, Martin, Very Rev
Acorn Nursing Home,
Cashel, Co Tipperary
(Dublin, retired)

O'Farrell, Michael (SSC)
St Columban's Retirement Home
Dalgan Park,
Navan, Co Meath
Tel 046-9021525

O'Farrell, Peter, PP
Milford, Charleville,
Co Cork
Tel 063-80038
(Milford, Cloyne)

O'Fearraigh, Brian, Very Rev, PP
Derrybeg, Letterkenny
Tel 087-9935544
(Gweedore, Raphoe)

O'Flaherty, Séan, Rt Rev Mgr, PE
St Mary's Nursing Home,
Shantalla, Galway
Tel 091-540500
(Galway, retired)

O'Flynn, Ciaran (SPS)
St Patrick's,
Kiltegan,
Co Wicklow W91 YO22
Tel 059-6473600

O'Flynn, Finbarr, CC
Dungourney, Co Cork
Tel 021-4668406
(Imogeela (Castlemartyr), Cloyne)

O'Flynn, Michael (CSsR)
Mount St Alphonsus,
South Circular Road,
Limerick
Tel 061-315099

O'Flynn, Silvester (OFMCap)
Capuchin Friary,
Holy Trinity,
Fr Mathew Quay,
Cork T12 PK24
Tel 021-4270827

O'Flynn, Thomas (OP)
St Mary's Priory, Tallaght,
Dublin 24
Tel 01-4048100

O'Gara, Francis (OCarm)
Carmelite Community,
Gort Muire, Ballinteer,
Dublin D16 EI67
Tel 01-2984014

O'Gara, John (SM), PC
The Presbyerty,
78A Donore Avenue,
Dublin 8
Tel 01-4542425
(Donore Avenue, Dublin)

O'Gorman, Charles, CC
Killeshandra, Co Cavan
Tel 049-4334179
(Killeshandra, Kilmore)

O'Gorman, Daniel, Very Rev, PP
The Parochial House,
Mullinahone,
Co Tipperary
Tel 052-9153152
(Mullinahone, Cashel & E.)

O'Gorman, Eamonn, Very Rev, PP
Ballyragget, Co Kilkenny
Tel 087-2236145
(Ballyragget, Lisdowney, Ossory)

O'Gorman, John, Very Rev, PP
Turloughmore, Co Galway
Tel 091-797114
(Lackagh, Tuam)

O'Gorman, Maurice, Very Rev, PP
Clashmore, Co Waterford
Tel 024-96110
(Clashmore, Waterford & L.)

O'Gorman, Patrick, Very Rev, AP
Golden, Co Tipperary
Tel 087-6347773
(Kilcommon, Cashel & E.)

O'Gorman, Tom, Co-PP,
The Presbytery, Quin,
Co Clare
(*Abbey Pastoral Area*,
Killaloe)

O'Grady, Desmond (SJ)
Gonzaga College,
Sandford Road, Dublin 6
Tel 01-4972943

O'Grady, James, Very Rev
120, Eallaigh Estate,
Galway Road, Headford,
Co Galway H91 R9F5
Tel 093-35448
(Tuam)

O'Grady, Michael, Very Rev,
PP, VF
1 Maypark,
Malahide Road, Dublin 5
Tel 01-8313033
(*Donnycarney*, Dublin)

O'Grady, Peter (OFM)
Franciscan Friary,
Liberty Street,
Cork T12 D376
Tel 021-4270302/4275481

O'Grady, Vincent (CSSp)
Holy Spirit Missionary
College
Kimmage Manor,
Whitehall Road,
Dublin D12 P5YP
Tel 01-4064300

O'Hagan, Eugene, Very Rev,
75 Somerton Road,
Belfast BT15 4DE
Tel 028-90776185
(Down & C.)

O'Hagan, Francis, PP
71 Duncrun Road,
Bellarena, Limavady,
Co Derry BT49 0JD
Tel 028-77750226
(*Magilligan*, Derry)

O'Hagan, Hugh J., Very Rev,
PP
Parochial House,
31 Ballynafie Road,
Ahoghill BT42 1LF
Tel 028-25871351
(*Ahoghill*, Down & C.)

O'Hagan, Mark, Very Rev,
PP, Adm, VF
St Patrick's Presbytery,
Roden Place, Dundalk,
Co Louth, A91 K2P4
Tel 042-9334648
(*Dundalk, St Patrick's*,
Dundalk, Holy Redeemer,
Armagh)

O'Hagan, Martin, Very Rev,
PP
71 North Street,
Newtownards,
Co Down BT23 4JD
Tel 028-91812137
(*Newtownards*, Down &
C.)

O'Hagan, Patrick, PP
25 Ballynease Road,
Bellaghy, Magherafelt,
Co Derry BT45 8JS
Tel 028-79386259
Adm, Greenlough
(*Bellaghy (Ballyscullion)*,
*Greenlough (Tamlaght
O'Crilly)*, Derry)

O'Halloran, Giles (OSA)
Bursar and Sub-Prior,
St John's Priory,
Thomas Street, Dublin 8
Tel 01-6770393

O'Halloran, James (SDB)
St Catherine's Centre,
North Campus, Maynooth
Co Kildare

O'Halloran, John
Chaplain's Office,
University Hospital
Galway,
Galway
Tel 091-524222
(Galway)

O'Halloran, Philip (MHM)
Regional Superior, Rector,
St Joseph's House,
50 Orwell Park,
Rathgar, Dublin D06 C535
Tel 01-4127773/4127735/
089-4385320

O'Halloran, Raphael (SSS)
Blessed Sacrament Chapel,
20 Bachelors Walk,
Dublin 1 D01 NW14
Tel 01-8724597

O'Halloran, Richard, PP
Parochial House,
Tramore, Co Waterford
Tel 051-356336
Priest in charge, Dunhill
(*Dunhill*, *Tramore*,
Waterford & L.)

O'Halloran, Tom, Very Rev,
Co-PP, VF
Parochial House,
Borrisokane, Co Tipperary
Tel 067-27105
(*Cois Deirge Pastoral Area*,
Killaloe)

O'Hanlon, David, PP
Parochial House, Dysart,
Mullingar, Co Westmeath
Tel 044-9226122
(*Dysart*, Meath)

O'Hanlon, Denis, Very Rev,
PP
Lisgoold
Tel 021-4642363
(*Lisgoold*, Cloyne)

O'Hanlon, Denis Luke
(OCSO)
Mount Melleray Abbey,
Cappoquin,
Co Waterford P51 R8XW
Tel 058-54404

O'Hanlon, Donal (SSC)
St Columban's,
Dalgan Park,
Navan, Co Meath
Tel 046-9021525

O'Hanlon, Francis, PE
c/o Diocesan Office,
St Michael's, Longford
Tel 043-6672319
(Ardagh & Cl., retired)

O'Hanlon, Gerard (SJ)
25 Croftwood Park,
Cherry Orchard, Dublin 10
Tel 01-6267413

O'Hara, Jarlath (OCarm)
Gort Muire, Ballinteer,
Dublin 16
Tel 01-2984014

O'Hara, Vincent (OCD)
St Teresa's,
Clarendon Street, Dublin 2
Tel 01-6718466/6718127

O'Hare, Martin (SMA)
African Missions,
Blackrock Road,
Cork T12 TD54
Tel 021-4292871

O'Hare, Paddy (SM)
Italy

O'Hare, Peter, Very Rev, PP
St Anne's Parochial House,
Kingsway, Finaghy,
Belfast BT10 0NE
Tel 028-90610112
(*St Anne's*, Down & C.)

O'Hea, John (SMA)
African Missions,
Blackrock Road,
Cork T12 TD54
Tel 021-4292871

O'Higgins, Kevin (SJ)
c/o St Francis Xavier's,
Upper Gardiner Street,
Dublin 1

O'Hora, Gerard, Very Rev,
PP, VF
Enniscrone, Ballina,
Co Mayo
Tel 096-36164
(*Kilglass*, Killala)

O'Horo, Michael, Very Rev
Templeboy,
Co Sligo
(Killala, retired)

O'Kane, Aidan (CP)
Passionist Retreat Centre
Downpatrick Road,
Crossgar, Downpatrick
Co Down BT30 9EQ
Tel 028-44830242

O'Kane, David, Very Rev, PP,
VF
9 Church Street, Claudy,
Co Derry BT47 4AA
Tel 028-71337727
(*Claudy (Cumber Upper &
Learmount)*, Derry)

O'Kane, Hugh (SMA)
African Missions,
Dromantine, Newry,
Co Down BT34 1RH
Tel 028-30821224

O'Kane, James (SMA)
African Missions,
Blackrock Road,
Cork T12 TD54
Tel 021-4292871

O'Kane, James, Very Rev,
PE, CC
21 Knocknacarry Avenue,
Cushenden,
Co Antrim BT44 0NX
Tel 028-21761269
(*Cushendun*, Down and C

O'Kane, Peter, CC,
48 Brook Street, Omagh,
Co Tyrone, BT78 5HD
Tel 028-82242092
(*Drumquin (Langfield)*,
Omagh (Drumagh), Derry

O'Kane, Peter (OP)
St Mary's Dominican
Priory,
Pope's Quay, Cork
Tel 021-4502267
(Cork)

O'Kane, Peter, Very Rev, PF
16 Rossglas Road,
Killough,
Co Down BT30 7QQ
Tel 028-44841221
(*Killough (Bright)*, Down
C.)

O'Kane, Peter (OP)
St Mary's Priory,
Tallaght, Dublin 24
Tel 01-4048189

O'Keeffe, Anthony
(OFMCap)
Capuchin Friary,
Holy Trinity,
Fr Mathew Quay,
Cork T12 PK24
Tel 021-4270827
(Cork & R.)

O'Keeffe, Anthony, AP
Parochial House,
Shanagolden, Limerick
Tel 087-4163401
(*Pastoral Unit 11*, Limeric

O'Keefe, Fergus (SJ)
c/o St Francis Xavier's,
Upper Gardiner Street,
Dublin 1
Tel 01-8363411

O'Keeffe, John, Very Rev, F
Birdhill, Killaloe,
Co Tipperary
Tel 061-379172/
087-2421678
(*Newport*, Cashel & E.)

O'Keeffe, John (SJ)
Gonzaga Community,
Sandford Road,
Ranelagh,
Dublin D06 KF95
Tel 01-4972943

'Keeffe, John (SMA)
African Missions,
Blackrock Road,
Cork T12 TD54
Tel 021-4292871
'Keeffe, Joseph
42 Nessan Court,
Church Road, Raheen,
Limerick
Tel 061-309151/
086-3333539
(Limerick)
'Keeffe, Joseph, Very Rev,
PP
Main Street, Rathcormac,
Co Cork
Tel 025-37371
(Rathcormac, Cloyne)
'Keeffe, Laurence, Very
Rev,
The Presbytery,
Slieverue, Co Kilkenny
Tel 051-832773
(Ossory)
'Keeffe, Martin (OMI)
Oblate House of Retreat,
Inchicore, Dublin 8
Tel 01-4534408/4541805
'Keeffe, Patrick (CSsR) PP,
Rector
722 Antrim Road,
Newtownabbey,
Co Antrim BT36 7PG
Tel 028-90774833/4
(St Gerard's, Down & C.)
'Keeffe, Thomas, Very Rev
Assistant,
20 Glen Avenue,
The Park, Cabinteely,
Dublin 18
Tel 01-2853643/
086-2646270
(Dublin, retired)
'Keeffe, Martin (OMI)
Mazenod House,
Churchfield,
Knock, Co Mayo
'Kelly, Francis (SSC)
St Columban's Retirement
Home
Dalgan Park,
Navan, Co Meath
Tel 046-9021525
'Kelly, Michael, Very Rev,
Moderator
Cluain Mhuire,
Killarney Road,
Bray, Co Wicklow
Tel 01-2116639
(Bray Grouping, Dublin)
'Laverty, John
Venerable English College,
Via di Monserrato, 45
Roma 00186, Italy
(Down & C.)
'Leary, Aidan (OSA)
St Augustine's,
Taylor's Lane,
Ballyboden, Dublin 16
Tel 01-4241000

O'Leary, Alan, Very Rev, Co-
PP
Moderator,
Parochial House,
Ballincollig, Co Cork
Tel 021-4871206
(Ballinora, Ballincollig and
Ovens, Cork & R.)
O'Leary, Anthony (CP)
St Gabriel's Retreat,
The Graan, Enniskillen,
Co Fermanagh
Tel 028-66322272
O'Leary, Brian (SJ)
Milltown Park,
Miltown Road, Dublin 6
Tel 01-2698411
O'Leary, Finbarr, Rt Rev Mgr
The Presbystery, Clogagh
Co Cork
Tel 023-8869682
(Timoleague and Clogagh,
Cork & R.)
O'Leary, Gerald, Very Rev,
PP
Horeswood, Campile,
Co Wexford
Tel 051-388129
(Horeswood and
Ballykelly, Ferns)
O'Leary, Gerard
Kerry General Hospital,
Tralee, Co Kerry
Tel 066-7126222
(Kerry)
O'Leary, Gerard
Curates House,
Athlunkard, Limerick
Tel 087-9378685
(Pastoral Unit 4, Limerick)
O'Leary, John, Very Rev, PE,
AP
4 Moorehall Retirement
Village,
Hale Street, Ardee,
Co Louth A92 K6R9
Tel 041-9826106
(Ardee & Collon, Armagh)
O'Leary, Joseph
1-38-16 Ekoda, Nakanoku,
Tokyo, 16J0022 Japan
(Cork & R.)
O'Leary, Michael (SMA),
Very Rev, PP
St Joseph's SMA Parish,
Wilton, Cork T12 E436
Tel 021-4341362
(Wilton, St Joseph's, Cork
& R.)
O'Leary, Noel (SMA),
Superior, SMA House,
Wilton, Cork
Tel 021-4541069/4541884
O'Leary, Oscar (OFM)
Franciscan Friary,
Liberty Street, Cork
Tel 021-4270302/4275481

O'Leary, Sean (White
Fathers)
Cypress Grove,
Templeogue, Dublin 6W
Tel 01-4055263/4055264
O'Leary, Timothy, Very Rev
Mount Oliver,
Martinstown,
Kilmallock, Co Limerick
(Limerick, retired)
O'Leary, Oscar (OFM)
Franciscan Friary,
Liberty Street, Cork
Tel 021-4270302/4275481
O'Leary, Seán (White
Fathers)
Provincial Delegate
Cypress Grove Road,
Templeogue,
Dublin D6W YV12
Tel 01-4063965
O'Loan, Fergus (OCarm)
Gort Muire, Ballinteer,
Dublin 16
Tel 01-2984014
O'Looney, Michael (CSSp)
Holy Spirit Missionary
College
Kimmage Manor,
Whitehall Road,
Dublin D12 P5YP
Tel 01-4064300
O'Loughlin, Declan
Diocesan Advisor for
Religious Education (Post-
Primary),
Parochial House,
30 Newline, Killeavy,
Newry, Co Down BT35 8TA
Tel 028-30889609
(Armagh)
O'Loughlin, Michael (SSC)
43 Moyland, Shanballa,
Loughville, Lahinch Road,
Ennis, Co Clare
Tel 065-6845321
O'Loughlin, Peter, AP
Kilmihil, Co Clare
Tel 065-9050016/
086-8250016
(Inis Cathaigh Pastoral
Area, Killaloe)
O'Mahony, Anthony, Co-PP
Parochial House
Inchigeela, Macroom,
Co Cork
Tel 026-49838/087-
2691432
(Drimoleague,
Dunmanway,
Kilmichael and Uibh
Laoire, Cork & R.)

O'Mahony, Bertie, Very Rev
Canon, AP
The Presbytery,
Bandon, Co Cork
Tel 023-8841666
(Bandon, Enniskeane,
Innishannon, Killbrittain,
Kilmurry and
Murragh/Templemartin,
Cork & R.)
O'Mahony, Colm (OSA)
Prior and Master of Pre-
Novices,
St Augustine's Priory,
Shop Street,
Drogheda, Co Louth
Tel 041-9838409
O'Mahony, Damien, Very
Rev, Co-PP
Glounthaune, Co Cork
Tel 021-4232881
(Carrignavar, Glanmire,
Glounthaune and
Watergrasshill, Cork & R.)
O'Mahony, Dan, Very Rev,
PE
Magheraboy, Kilmovee,
Ballaghaderreen,
Co Mayo
Tel 087-2401625
(Achonry, retired)
O'Mahony, Dan Joe
(OFMCap)
Capuchin Friary,
Station Road,
Raheny,
Dublin D05 T9E4
Tel 01-8313886
O'Mahony, Denis, Very Rev,
PP, VF
Abbeydorney, Co Kerry
Tel 066-7135146
(Abbeydorney, Kerry)
O'Mahony, Donal, Very Rev
Canon, PP
Charleville, Co Cork
Tel 063-81319
(Charleville, Cloyne)
O'Mahony, John K., Very
Rev Canon, PE
Mount Desert, Lee Road,
Cork
(Cork & R., retired)
O'Mahony, Joseph, Adm
Sandyhill,
Macroom, Co Cork
Tel 026-41092
(Aghinagh, Cloyne)
O'Mahony, Kieran (OSA), PC
Presbytery No. 2,
Stillorgan Road,
Dublin 4
(Donnybrook, Dublin)
O'Mahony, Michael, Co-PP
Ballinspittle, Co Cork
Tel 021-4778055
(Ballinhassig, Clontead,
Courceys and Kinsale, Cork
& R.)

O'Mahony, Nicholas, Very
Rev, PE
'Woodleigh',
Summerville Avenue,
Waterford
(Waterford & L., retired)
O'Mahony, Pat (SMA), CC
St Patrick's Presbytery,
Rochestown Road, Cork
Tel 021-4892363
(Douglas, Cork & R.)
O'Mahony, Stephen, Very
Rev, PP
Bohola, Claremorris,
Co Mayo
Tel 094-9384115
Administrator, Straid
(Templemore)
Straide, Foxford, Co Mayo
Tel 094 9031029
(Bohola, Straide, Achonry)
O'Mahony, Stephen, Very
Rev, PE
Liscarroll, Mallow, Co Cork
Tel 022-48128
(Cloyne, retired)
O'Mahony, Thomas, Very
Rev, PP
Parochial House, Skryne,
Tara, Co Meath
Tel 046-9025152
(Skryne, Meath)
O'Malley, Donough, Very
Rev Canon,
19 School House Lane,
Rear of Barrington Street,
Limerick
Tel 086-2586908
(Limerick, retired)
O'Malley, Michael
c/o Archbishop's House,
Tuam
(Tuam, retired)
O'Meara, Donagh, Co-PP, VF
Parochial House,
Carhuligane,
Mullagh, Co Clare
Tel 065-7087012
(Críocha Callan Pastoral
Area, Killaloe)
O'Meara, Michael, Very Rev,
Co-PP
Kinnity, Birr, Co Offaly
Tel 057-9137021/
087-7735977
(Brendan Pastoral Area,
Killaloe)
O'Meara, Noel (CSSp)
Holy Spirit Missionary
College
Kimmage Manor,
Whitehall Road,
Dublin D12 P5YP
Tel 01-4064300
O'Melia, Joseph (OMI)
Oblate House of Retreat,
Inchicore, Dublin 8
Tel 01-4534408/4541805

O'Neill, Arthur, TA
1B Willow Court,
Druid Valley, Cabinteely,
Dublin 18
Tel 087-2597520
(Cabinteely, Dublin)
O'Neill, Eugene, Very Rev,
PP
Parochial House,
31 Brackaville Road,
Coalisland,
Co Tyrone BT71 4NH
Tel 028-87740221
(Coalisland, Armagh)
O'Neill, Eugene, Very Rev,
PP, VF
St Patrick's Presbytery,
199 Donegal Street,
Belfast BT1 2FL
Tel 028-90324597
(St Patrick's, Down & C.)
O'Neill, Francis, Very Rev, PP
Castlemartyr, Co Cork
Tel 021-4667133
(Imogeela (Castlemartyr),
Cloyne)
O'Neill, Ian, Very Rev
Canon, PP
Parochial House,
Claregalway, Co Galway
Tel 091-798104
(Claregalway, Galway)
O'Neill, Joe, CC
Priest's House, Emo,
Portlaoise, Co Laois
Tel 089-4535533
(Emo, Portarlington,
Kildare & L.)
O'Neill, John, Very Rev
Canon, PP, VF
Lisvernane, Aherlow
Co Tipperary
Tel 062-56155
(Galbally, Cashel & E.)
O'Neill, Kevin, Rt Rev Mgr,
BA, MSc Ed
President, Carlow College,
College Street, Carlow
Tel 059-9153200
(Kildare & L.)
O'Neill, Kevin (SSC)
No 3 and 4,
Ma Yau Tong Village,
Po Lam Road,
Tseung Kwan O,
Kowloon, Hong Kong, SAR
O'Neill, Larry (SPS)
St Patrick's, Kiltegan,
Co Wicklow
Tel 059-6473600
O'Neill, Míceál (OCarm)
Centro Internazionale S.
Alberto,
Via Sforza Pallavicini 10,
00193 Roma, Italia
O'Neill, Michael (IC)
Clonturk House,
Ormond Road,
Drumcondra, Dublin 9
Tel 01-6877014

O'Neill, Niall (SJ)
Crescent College
Comprehensive,
Dooradoyle, Limerick
Tel 061-480920
O'Neill, Patrick, Co-PP
Ruan, Co Clare
Tel 065-6827799/
086-2612124
(Imeall Boirne Pastoral
Area, Killaloe)
O'Neill, Peter (SSC)
House Superior,
St Columban's,
Dalgan Park,
Navan, Co Meath
Tel 046-9021525
O'Neill, Roger, CC
St Michael's, Gorey,
Co Wexford
Tel 053-9421117
(Gorey, Ferns)
O'Neill, Seamus (SPS)
Bursar General,
St Patrick's, Kiltegan,
Co Wicklow
Tel 059-6473600
O'Neill, Seamus (SSC)
20 Tobermore Road,
Moykeenan, Draperstown,
Co Derry BT45 7HG
Tel 048-79627206
O'Neill, Sean, PP
Parochial House,
1 Rockstown Road,
Carrickmore, Omagh,
Co Tyrone BT79 9BE
Tel 028-80761207
(Termonmaguirc
(Carrickmore,
Loughmacrory & Creggan),
Armagh)
O'Neill, Shane
Director of Formation
St Patrick's College,
Maynooth
Co Kildare
(Waterford & L.)
O'Rahelly, Edmond V., Very
Rev, AP
Main Street,
Ballina, Co Tipperary
Tel 087-2262636
(Ballina, Cashel & E.)
O'Regan, Kevin, Very Rev,
PP
The Presbytery,
Frankfield, Cork
Tel 021-43061711
(Frankfield-Grange, Cork &
R.)
O'Regan, Liam, Very Rev
Canon, PE
Cramer's Court Nursing
Home,
Ballindeenisk,
Kinsale, Co Cork
(Cork & R., retired)

O'Regan, Noel (SMA), Mos
Rev
(Retired Bishop)
SMA House, Wilton,
Cork, T12 KR23
Tel 021-4541069/4541884
O'Reilly, Anthony
Newry, Co Armagh
(Kerry)
O'Reilly, Arthur P.
(Derry, retired)
O'Reilly, Bernard (OCarm)
Gort Muire, Ballinteer,
Dublin D16 EI67
Tel 01-2984014
O'Reilly, Brian, Team
Assistant,
83 The Rise,
Mount Merrion,
Co Dublin
Tel 01-2881271/
01-2783804
Team Assistant, Kilmacuc
Stillorgan
Tel 087-7414857
(Mount Merrion,
Kilmacud-Stillorgan,
Dublin)
O'Reilly, Colm, Most Rev,
DD
Retired Bishop of Ardagh
and Clonmacnois,
Deanscurragh, Longford
Tel 043-3347831
(Ardagh & Cl.)
O'Reilly, Damian, Very Rev
Canon,
83 Marlborough Street,
Dublin 1
Tel 01-8745441
Chaplain, St Vincent's
University Hospital,
Elm Park, Dublin 4
Tel 01-2094325
(Pro-Cathedral, Dublin)
O'Reilly, Desmond
Our Lady of Lourdes, 195
North Avenue,
Sacramento, CA 95838
USA
(Dublin)
O'Reilly, James (SPS)
Kilmacow, via Waterford
Co Kilkenny
Tel 087-6802201
(Kilmacow, Ossory)
O'Reilly, James, Very Rev,
CC
St Joseph's Presbytery,
56 Greystone Road,
Antrim BT41 1JZ
Tel 028-9429103
(Antrim, Down & C.)
O'Reilly, John
Drinagh, Rosslare,
Co Wexford
(Ferns, retired)

'Reilly, Joseph (IC)
Provincial, Vocations Director,
Clonturk House,
Drumcondra,
Dublin D09 F821
Tel 01-6877014

'Reilly, Kevin (OP)
Dominican College,
Newbridge
Droichead Nua, Co Kildare
Tel 045-487200

'Reilly, Kieran (SMA), Most Rev, DD
Archbishop of Cashel and Emly,
Archbishop's House,
Thurles,
Co Tipperary E41 NY92
Tel 0504-21512
(Cashel & E.)

'Reilly, Leo, Most Rev, DD
Retired Bishop of Kilmore,
4 Carraig Beag,
Cootehill Road, Co Cavan
(Kilmore, retired)

'Reilly, Marius
35 Paul Street, Cork
Tel 021-4276573
(South Parish, St Patrick's and Ss Peter and Paul's, Cork & R.)

'Reilly, Myles (SJ)
35 Lower Leeson Street,
Dublin 2
Tel 01-6761248

'Reilly, Oliver, CC
Arva, Co Cavan
Tel 049-4335246
(Killeshandra, Kilmore)

'Reilly, Paddy (OSA), CC
Parochial House,
St Helena's Drive,
Dublin 11
Tel 01-8343444/
086-8279504
(Rivermount, Dublin)

'Reilly, Peter, Rt Rev Mgr, PP, VG
1 Darling Street,
Enniskillen,
Co Fermanagh BT74 7DP
Tel 028-66322075
(Enniskillen, Tempo (Pobal), Clogher)

'Reilly, Peter, Very Rev, Adm
16 Brookwood Grove,
Artane, Dublin 5
(Artane, Dublin)

'Reilly, Seamus, (SPS)
St Patrick's, Kiltegan,
Co Wicklow W91 YO22
Tel 0596473600

'Reilly, Thomas, Very Rev, Adm
Clonaslee, Co Laois
Tel 057-8648030
(Clonaslee, Kildare & L.)

O'Reilly, Thomas (SSC)
St Columban's,
Dalgan Park,
Navan, Co Meath
Tel 046-9021525

O'Riordan, Anthony (SJ)
Irish Jesuit Provincialate,
Milltown Park,
Miltown Road,
Dublin 6
Tel 01-4987333

O'Riordan, Anthony (SVD)
Chaplain, Connolly Hospital,
Blanchardstown, Dublin15
Tel 01-8213844
Praeses,
133 North Circular Road,
Dublin 7
Tel 01-8386743

O'Riordan, Daniel, Rt Rev Mgr, PP
(Kerry, retired)

O'Riordan, David, Very Rev, PE
2 Connolly Street,
Midleton, Co Cork
Tel 086-3590047
(Cloyne, retired)

O'Riordan, Jeremiah, Very Rev, PP
Donoughmore, Co Cork
Tel 021-7337023
(Donoughmore, Cloyne)

O'Riordan, John P. (CSsR), CC
Mount Saint Alphonsus,
South Circular Road,
Limerick
Tel 061-315099

O'Riordáin, John J. (CSsR)
Mount St Alphonsus,
South Circular Road,
Limerick
Tel 061-315099

O'Rourke, Brendan
The Presbytery, Ballsgrove,
Drogheda, Co Louth
Tel 041-9831991
(Drogheda, Holy Family, Meath)

O'Rourke, Brendan (CSsR)
Dún Mhuire,
461/463 Griffith Avenue,
Dublin D09 X651
Tel 01-5180196

O'Rourke, John (OP)
Holy Cross,
Tralee, Co Kerry
Tel 066-7121135

O'Rourke, Kieran, Very Rev, PP
Looscaun, Woodford,
Co Galway H62 AK18
Tel 090-9749100
(Woodford and looscaun, Clonfert)

O'Rourke, Patrick (SMA)
Superior,
African Missions,
Blackrock Road,
Cork T12 TD54
Tel 021-4292871

O'Rourke, Patrick, CC
The Prebytery,
St Patrick's Road,
Wicklow Town,
Co Wicklow
(Wicklow, Dublin)

O'Rourke, Sean
15 Seaview Park, Shankill,
Co Dublin
(Dublin, retired)

O'Rourke, Seamus, CC
Curate's Residence,
Dublin Road,
Carrick-on-Shannon,
Co Leitrim
Tel 071-9620054
(Carrick-on-Shannon (Kiltoghert), Ardagh & Cl.)

O'Ruairc, Caoimhin (SJ)
St Francis Xavier's,
Upper Gardiner Street,
Dublin 1
Tel 01-8363411

O'Shaughnessy, Anthony, Very Rev, Moderator
41 St Agnes' Road,
Crumlin, Dublin 12
Tel 01-5611500
(Clogher Road, Crumlin, Mourne Road, Dublin)

O'Shaughnessy, Sean (CSSp)
Holy Spirit Missionary College
Kimmage Manor,
Whitehall Road,
Dublin D12 P5YP
Tel 01-4064300

O'Shaughnessy, Thomas F.,
73 Annamoe Road,
Dublin 7
Tel 01-8385626
(Cabra, Dublin)

O'Shaughnessy, William, Very Rev, Moderator, VF
70 Maplewood Road
Tallaght, Dublin 24
Tel 01-4590746
(Brookfield, Jobstown, Springfield, Dublin)

O'Shea, A. B., Very Rev, PE
Rowantree Cottage,
Church Grounds,
Riverstown, Co Sligo
(Riverstown, Elphin)

O'Shea, Colum (SMA)
Vice-Superior, SMA House,
Wilton,
Cork, T12 KR23
Tel 021-4541069/4541884

O'Shea, Donagh (OP)
St Mary's Priory, Tallaght,
Dublin 24
Tel 01-4048100

O'Shea, Henry (OSB)
Glenstal Abbey, Murroe,
Co Limerick
Tel 061-386103

O'Shea, John, Canon
St Nessan's Presbytery,
Raheen, Co Limerick
Tel 061-301112/
087-9708282
(Pastoral Unit 6, Limerick)

O'Shea, Kieran, Very Rev PP
Ferrybank, Waterford
Tel 086-8272828
(Slieverue, Ossory)

O'Shea, Martin, Rt Rev Mgr, Co-PP
23 Clare Road,
Drumcondra, Dublin 9
Tel 01-8378552
(Drumcondra, Dublin)

O'Shea, Maurice, Very Rev, PE
64 White Oaks,
Clonskeagh, Dublin 14
(Dublin, retired)

O'Shea, Michael (IC)
Clonturk House,
Ormond Road,
Drumcondra,
Dublin D09 F821
Tel 01-6877014

O'Shea, Michael, Moderator
Glenduff Cottage,
Kilfinane, Co Limerick
Tel 087-9791432
(Pastoral Unit 9, Limerick)

O'Shea, Michael, Very Rev, PP
The Presbytery,
12 School Street, Wexford
Tel 053-9122055
(Wexford, Ferns)

O'Shea, Michael (SMA)
African Missions,
Blackrock Road,
Cork T12 TD54
Tel 021-4292871

O'Shea, Morty (SOLT), CC
Ardaghey, Co Donegal
Tel 074-9736007
(Inver, Raphoe)

O'Shea, Philip, Very Rev, PE
Clonagoose,
Borris, Co Carlow
(Kildare & L., retired)

O'Shea, Thomas, Very Rev, PE
Gowran Abbey Nursing Home,
Gowran, Co Kilkenny
(Kildare & L., retired)

O'Shea, Thomas (OMI)
Oblate House of Retreat,
Inchicore, Dublin 8
Tel 01-4534408/4541805

O'Siochru, Colm
Our Lady's Manor,
Bulloch Castle,
Dalkey, Co Dublin
(Dublin, retired)

Osthues, Gerhard (SVD), PC
c/o Parish Office,
Maynooth, Co Kildare
Tel 01-6286220
(*Maynooth*, Dublin)

O'Sullivan, Alan (OP)
St Saviour's,
Upper Dorset Street,
Dublin 1
Tel 01-8897610

O'Sullivan, Andrew, PP
52 Lower Rathmines Road,
Dublin 6 D06 AK19
Tel 01-4969049
(*Rathgar, Rathmines*,
Dublin)

O'Sullivan, Andrew (SMA)
African Missions,
Blackrock Road,
Cork T12 TD54
Tel 021-4292871

O'Sullivan, Anthony, Very
Rev, PP
Irremore, Listowel,
Co Kerry
Tel 066-7132111
(*Lixnaw*, Kerry)

O'Sullivan, Billy, PE
The Presbytery,
The Lough, Cork (Cork &
R., retired)

O'Sullivan, Brendan, PP
Ballinahown, Athlone,
Co Westmeath
Tel 090-6430124
(*Ballinahown, Boher &
Pullough
(Lemanaghan)*, Ardagh &
Cl.)

O'Sullivan, Brian, PE
The Cottage,
Glengara Park,
Glenageary, Co Dublin
Tel 01-2360681
(Dublin, retired)

O'Sullivan, Brian (OSA)
St John's Priory,
Thomas Steet,
Dublin 8

O'Sullivan, Cian, Very Rev,
Co-PP
The Presbytery,
Knocknaheeny, Co Cork
Tel 021-4392459
(*Clogheen/Kerry Pike,
Farranree,
Gurranabraher and
Knocknaheeny*, Cork & R.)

O'Sullivan, Denis (SMA)
SMA House, Wilton,
Cork T12 KR23
Tel 021-4541069/4541884

O'Sullivan, Denis, Very Rev,
PE
c/o Bishop's House, Carlow
(Kildare & L., retired)

O'Sullivan, John (MSC)
Woodview House,
Mount Merrion Avenue,
Blackrock, Co Dublin
Tel 01-2881644

O'Sullivan, Kieran, Very Rev,
PP
Glenbeigh, Co Kerry
Tel 066-9768209
(*Glenbeigh*, Kerry)

O'Sullivan, Louis
Our Lady's Manor,
Bullock Castle, Dalkey,
Co Dublin
(Dublin, retired)

O'Sullivan, Michael (SJ)
35 Lower Leeson Street,
Dublin 2
Tel 01-6761248

O'Sullivan, Michael P.
(White Fathers)
Community Superior,
Cypress Grove,
Templeogue, Dublin 6W
Tel 01-4055263/4055264

O'Sullivan, Noel, Very Rev
Dr, Adm
The Presbytery,
Turner's Cross, Cork
(*Turner's Cross*, Cork & R.)

O'Sullivan, Owen (OFMCap)
Chaplain,
St Francis Hospice,
Blanchardstown
Tel 01-8294000
Capuchin Friary,
137-142 Church Street,
Dublin D07 HA22
Tel 01-8730599

O'Sullivan, Padraig, Very
Rev, Co-PP
St Lukes, Kilbarron Road
Kilmore West, Dublin 5
Tel 01-8488149
(*Kilmore Road West*,
Dublin)

O'Sullivan, Patrick, Very Rev
(MSC), Adm
Leap, Co Cork
Tel 028-33177
(*Kilmacabea*, Cork & R.)

O'Sullivan, Patrick
17 Alderwood Avenue,
Caherdavin Heights,
Limerick
Tel 061-421050/
087-2376032
(*Pastoral Unit 5*, Limerick)

O'Sullivan, Séan, Very Rev,
Co-PP
Moderator,
The Presbytery,
Farrantree, Co Cork
021-4393815/4210111
(*Clogheen/Kerry Pike,
Farranree,
Gurranabraher and
Knocknaheeny*, Cork & R.)

O'Sullivan, Ted, Very Rev
Canon, PP
Parochial House, Douglas
Co Cork
Tel 021-4891265
(*Douglas*, Cork & R.)

O'Sullivan, Timothy, Very
Rev
Mount Desert,
Lee Road, Cork
(Cork & R., retired)

O'Toole, Patrick (CSSp)
The Presbytery,
Ballintubber, Castlerea,
Co Roscommon
Tel 094-9655226

O'Toole, Sean
Our Lady's Manor,
Bullock Harbour,
Dalkey, Co Dublin
(Dublin, retired)

O'Toole, Thomas, Very Rev,
PP
Glenmore,
Via New Ross,
Co Kilkenny
Tel 051-880080/
087-2240787
(*Glenmore*, Ossory)

Obaso, Philip Odhiambo
(MHM)
St Joseph's House,
50 Orwell Park, Rathgar,
Dublin 6
Tel 01-4127700

Ogbonna, Magnus (MSP), PP
Parochial House,
Chapel Hill,
Carlingford,
Co Louth A91 FX76
Tel 042-9373111
(*Carlingford and
Clogherny*, Armagh)

Ohiemi, Luke, CC
St Brigid's Parish Office,
Church Street, Clara,
Co Offaly R35 PW97
Tel 057-9331170
(*Clara*, Meath)

Okanumeh, Raphael, AP
Holy Trinity Church,
Adare, Co Limerick
Tel 087-9490083
(*Pastoral Unit 11*, Limerick)

Okonkwo, Francesco, AP
San Michel, Mill Road,
Corbally, Limerick
Tel 0877151260
(*Pastoral Unit 7*, Limerick)

Okpeh, Addison, PP
Kilmainhamwood,
Kells, Co Meath
Tel 046-9052129
(*Kilmainhamwood and
Moybologue*, Kilmore)

Okpetu, Peter, CC
The Presbytery,
Cavan
Tel 049-4331404/4332269
(*Cavan (Urney and
Annagelliff)*, Kilmore)

Olin, Richard (CSSp)
St Mary's College,
Rathmines, Dublin 6
Tel 01-4995760

Ormonde, Noel (OMI)
Oblate House of Retreat,
Inchicore, Dublin 8
Tel 01-4534408/4541805

Orr, Thomas, CC,
New Ross, Co Wexford
(*New Ross*, Ferns)

Orzechowski, Arkadiusz
(SDB)
St Catherine's Centre,
North Campus, Maynooth

Owen, John (SVD)
Church of St Phillip the
Apostle,
Mountview, Dublin 15
Tel 018249695

Owens, Finnian (OCSO)
Our Lady of Bethlehem
Abbey,
11 Ballymena Road,
Portglenone, Ballymena,
Co Antrim BT44 8BL
Tel 028-25821211

Owens, John (SVD)
The Presbytery,
Blakestown,
Clonsilla, Dublin 15
Tel 01-8210874
(*Blakestown/Mountview*,
Dublin)

Owens, Peter, Very Rev, PP
Parochial House,
8 Minorca Place,
Carrickfergus,
Co Antrim, BT38 8AU
Tel 028-93363269
(*Carrickfergus*, Down & C

Oxley, Brian (SSC)
St Columban's,
Dalgan Park, Navan,
Co Meath
Tel 046-9021525

Pace, Paul (SJ)
Manresa House,
426 Clontarf Road,
Dollymount, Dublin 3
Tel 01-8331352

Padathiparambil, Clement,
CC
St Thomas Pastoral Centr
19 Saint Anthony's Road
Rialto, Dublin 8, D08 E8P
(*Rialto/Dolphin's Barn*,
Dublin)

Allianz (ⅲ)

dilla Rocha, Rubén (MCCJ)
3 Clontarf Road, Clontarf,
Dublin 3
Tel 01-8330051

radiyil, Tomy (OSCam)
St Camillus,
11 St Vincent Street North,
Dublin 7
Tel 01-8300365

rokkaran, Joshi, CC
Parochial House,
32 Chapel Road,
Derry BT47 2BB
Tel 028-71342303
(Waterside (Glendermott),
Derry)

rokkaran, Martin (OCarm)
Terenure College,
Terenure,
Dublin D6W DK72
Tel 01-4904621

rys, Bart (SVD)
Donamon Castle,
Roscommon
Tel 090-
5662222/0863718883

salic, Antun, CC
The Presbytery,
Convent Hill,
Roscrea, Co Tipperary
Tel 0505-21370
(Cronan Pastoral Area,
Killaloe)

tton, Gerard, Very Rev
13 Head Road, Kilkeel,
Co Down BT34 4HX
Down & C., retired)

yne, Brendan (SPS)
t Patrick's, Kiltegan,
Co Wicklow
Tel 059-6473600

zhampilly, Rojan Peter
OCarm)
Bursar,
Carmelite Priory,
White Abbey,
Co Kildare R51 X827
Tel 045-521391

cak Marek
priest in residence)
Castlelyons, Fermoy,
Co Cork
Tel 087-1410470
(Castlelyons, Cloyne)

elo, Adrian (OFM)
he Abbey,
Francis Street,
Galway H91 C53K
Tel 091-562518

uchi, Alberto (MCCJ)
rovincial, Comboni
Missionaries,
ondon Road, Sunningdal,
Berks SI5 OJY, UK

oples, William, Very Rev,
P
ilcar, Co Donegal
el 074-9738007
Kilcar, Raphoe)

Pepper, Pierre, CC
Parochial House,
Boherquill,
Lismacaffrey, Mullingar,
Co Westmeath
Tel 043-6685847
(Rathowen (Rathaspic,
Russagh & Streete),
Ardagh & Cl.)

Perrotta, John (FDP)
Sarsfield House,
Sarsfield Road,
Ballyfermot, Dublin 10
Tel 01-6266193/6266233

Perry, Jim (SVD)
Maynooth, Co Kildare
Tel 01-6286391/2

Perumparambil, Thomas
Devesia
Society of Saint Paul,
Moyglare Road,
Maynooth,
Co Kildare W23 NX34
Tel 01-6285933

Petrisor, Robert, CC
Sallins Road,
Naas, Co Kildare
Tel 045-897703
(Naas, Kildare & L.)

Peyton, Patrick, Very Rev
Canon, PE
Carrownanty, Ballymote,
Co Sligo
Tel 071-9328537
(Achonry, retired)

Phair, John, Very Rev, PP
Kinlough, Co Leitrim
Tel 071-9841428
(Kinlough and Glenade,
Kilmore)

Philip, John (OSCam)
Chaplain to Waterford
Hospital,
St Camillus,
11 St Vincent St North,
Dublin 7
Tel 01-8300365

Pierce, Patrick (IC)
Doire na hAbhann,
Tickincar, Clonmel,
Co Tipperary E91 XY71
Tel 052-6126914

Piert, John, Very Rev Canon,
Team Assistant,
Our Lady's Manor,
Bulloch Harbour,
Glenageary,
Dalkey, Co Dublin
(Dublin)

Pinheiro da Salva Neto,
Severino (OFMCap)
Capuchin Friary,
137-142 Church Street,
Dublin D07 HA22
Tel 01-8730599

Plasek, Dariusz, Co-PP
Parochial House,
Bodyke, Co Clare
Tel 061-921060
(Inis Cealtra Pastoral Area,
Killaloe)

Planell, Francis
Harvieston,
Cunningham Road,
Dalkey, Co Dublin
Tel 01-2859877
(Opus Dei)

Plower, Thomas (MSC)
'Croí Nua', Rosary Lane,
Taylor's Hill,
Galway H91 WY2A
Tel 091-520960

Plunkett, Oliver, AP
13 Castle Court,
Clancy Strand,
Limerick
Tel 087-6593176
(Pastoral Unit 4, Limerick)

Polly, Damian (OP)
Dominican College,
Newbridge
Droichead Nua, Co Kildare
Tel 045-487200

Poole, John (OMI)
Oblate House of Retreat,
Inchicore,
Dublin 8
Tel 01-4534408/4541805

Poole, Joseph (CSSp),
Holy Spirit Missionary
College
Kimmage Manor,
Whitehall Road,
Dublin D12 P5YP
Tel 01-4064300

Porcellato, Antonio (SMA)
Superior General,
Missioni Africane,
Via della Nocetta 11
00164 Rome, Italy
Tel 06-6616841

Porter, Michael, PE
(Derry, retired)

Pound, Rufus (OSCO)
Mellifont Abbey,
Collon, Co Louth
Tel 041-9826103

Powell, Gerald, Very Rev
Cannon, VF
c/o Bishop's House,
44 Armagh Road, Newry
Co Down BT35 6PN
(Dromore, retired)

Powell, Oliver
Gort Ard University
Residence,
Rockbarton North, Galway
Tel 091-523846
(Opus Dei)

Power, Anthony, CC
35 Grange Park Avenue,
Raheny, Dublin 5
Tel 01-8480244/
086-3905205
(Grange Park, Dublin)

Power, Brian, Very Rev, PP
Kilsheelan, Clonmel,
Co Tipperary
Tel 052-6133118
(Kilsheelan, Waterford &
L.)

Power, Jackie (OSA)
St Augustine's,
Taylor's Lane,
Ballyboden, Dublin 16
Tel 01-4241000

Power, Joseph, Very Rev, PP
Kilrush, Bunclody,
Enniscorthy, Co Wexford
Tel 053-9377262
(Kilrush and Askamore,
Ferns)

Power, Liam, Very Rev, PP
Parish Office, SS Joseph
and Benildus,
Newtown, Waterford
Tel 051-873073
(St Joseph and Benildus,
Waterford & L.)

Power, Patrick (OFM), PP
Provincial Delegate,
St Anthony's Parish
(English-Speaking
Chaplaincy),
23/25 Oudstrijderslaan,
1950 Kraainem, Belgium
Tel 0032-2-7201970

Power, Robert, Very Rev,
Adm
Parochial House,
Clogheen, Cahir,
Co Tipperary
Tel 052-7465268
Administrator,
Ballyporeen
(Ballyporeen, Clogheen,
Waterford & L.)

Power, Thomas J., (MSC) PP
The Presbytery,
Killinarden, Tallaght,
Dublin 24
Tel 01-4522251
(Killinarden, Dublin)

Pozzerle, Iaccopo (OFM)
The Abbey,
8 Francis Street, Galway
H91 C53K
Tel 091-562518

Prendiville, James, CC
The Presbytery, Hollywood
(via Naas), Co Wicklow
Tel 045-864206
(Ballymore Eustace,
Dublin)

Price, Cathal
54 Foxfield St John,
Dublin 5
Tel 01-8323683
(Dublin, retired)

Prior, Dermot, Very Rev, PP,
VF
Virginia, Co Cavan
Tel 049-8547063
(Virginia (Lurgan),
Kilmore)

Prior, Paul
Mullagh, via Kells,
Co Meath
Tel 046-42208
(*Mullagh*, Kilmore)

Pudota, Anthaiah, Very Rev,
Adm
Parochial House,
Letterfrack,
Connemara, Co Galway
Tel 095-41053
(*Inishbofin, Letterfrack
(Ballinakill),* Tuam)

Purba, Justin (SVD), PC
St Philip the Apostle
Church,
No. 2 Presbtery,
Mountview Road,
Clonsilla, Dublin 15
Tel 01-8249695
(*Blakestown/Huntstown/M
ountview*, Dublin)

Purcell, Brendan
St Mary's Cathedral House,
St Mary's Road,
Sydney NSW 2000,
Australia
(Dublin)

Purcell, Denis
Mount Carmel, Callan,
Co Kilkenny
(Ossory)

Purcell, Eamon, Co-PP
Parteen, Co Clare
Tel 087-7635617
(*Pastoral Unit 4*, Limerick)

Purcell, Frank, Very Rev, VF
Inistioge, Co Kilkenny
Tel 051-423619/
086-6010001
(*Inistioge*, Ossory)

Purcell, James, Very Rev, PP
Cathedral Presbytery,
Thurles, Co Tipperary
Tel 0504 22229/22779/
087-8211045
(*Thurles, Cathedral,* Cashel
& E.)

Purcell, Richard (OCSO) Rt
Rev Dom, Abbot,
Mount Melleray Abbey,
Cappoquin, Co Waterford
Tel 058-54404

Purcell, Sean (CSsR)
Mount Saint Alphonsus,
South Circular Road,
Limerick
Tel 061-315099

Purcell, William Very Rev
Director of Vocations,
St Kieran's College,
Kilkenny
Tel 056-7721086
St Mary's Cathedral,
Kilkenny
Tel 056-7721253/
087-6286858
(*St Mary's,* Ossory)

Puthiyaveettil, Antony, CC
The Presbytery,
John's Mall,
Birr, Co Offaly
Tel 057-9120098
(*Brendan Pastoral Area,*
Killaloe)

Pyburn, Daniel, Very Rev Dr,
Co-PP
Barrett's Hill,
Ballinhassig, Co Cork
Tel 021-4885104
(*Ballinhassig, Clontead,
Courceys and Kinsale,* Cork
& R.)

Q

Quigley, Damien. Rev, CC
27 Woodhill,
Monaghan Row,
Newry,
Co Down BT35 8DP
(*Middle Killeavy (Newry),*
Armagh)

Quigley, Sean
Tara Wintrop Nursing
Home,
Nevinstown Lane,
Pinnockhill, Swords,
Co Dublin
(Dublin, retired)

Quigley, Thomas, Very Rev,
PE
Parochial House,
Latton, Castleblayney,
Co Monaghan
A75 E953
Tel 042-9742212
(*Latton (Aughnamullen
West),* Clogher)

Quinlan, Brendan, CC
Presbytery, Church
Grounds,
Laurel Lodge, Castleknock,
Dublin 15
Tel 01-8208144
(*Castleknock, Laurel
Lodge-Carpenterstown,*
Dublin)

Quinlan, John
(Kerry, retired)

Quinlan, Leo, Very Rev
The Fern Dean Nursing
Home,
Grange Terrace,
Deansgrange, Co Dublin
A94 TN25
(Dublin, retired)

Quinlivan, Brendan, Very
Rev, Co-PP, VF
Parochial House,
Newline, Tulla, Co Clare
Tel 065-6835117
(*Ceanntar na Lochanna
Pastoral Area,* Killaloe)

Quinn, Denis, CC
The Presbytery,
Kimberley Road,
Greystones, Co Wicklow
Tel 01-2877025
(*Greystones,* Dublin)

Quinn, Denis, Very Rev, PP
Carrick, Co Donegal
Tel 074-9739008
(*Carrick (Glencolmcille),*
Raphoe)

Quinn, Edward (OMI)
The Presbytery,
Darndale, Dublin 17
Tel 01-8474547

Quinn, James, Very Rev
Canon, AP, Adm
Taugheen, Claremorris,
Co Mayo
Administration Taugheen
Tel 094-9362500
(*Crossboyne and
Taugheen,* Tuam)

Quinn, John (SDB)
Rinaldi House,
40/41 Sean McDermott
Street,
Dublin D01 H7P6

Quinn, John, PP
Gortletteragh,
Carrick-on-Shannon,
Co Leitrim
Tel 071-9631074
(*Gortletteragh,* Ardagh &
Cl.)

Quinn, Michael, Very Rev,
PP
Kiltimagh (Killedan),
Co Mayo
Tel 094-9381198
(*Kiltimagh (Killedan),*
Achonry)

Quinn, Richard (CSSp)
Blackrock College,
Blackrock, Co Dublin
Tel 01-2888681

Quinn, Séamus, Very Rev, PP
Parochial House,
Belcoo East, Belcoo
Co Fermanagh BT93 5FL
Tel 028-66386225
(*Arney (Cleenish),* Clogher)

Quinn, Sean J., Very Rev, PE
c/o The Diamond,
Pomeroy
Dungannon, Co Tyrone
BT70 2QX
(Armagh, retired)

Quinn, Stephen (OCD)
Prior,
St Joseph's Carmelite
Retreat Centre
Termonbacca
Derry BT48 9XE
Tel 028-71262512

Quinn, Tadhg, Very Rev
Canon, PP
St John the Apostle,
Knocknacarra, Galway
Tel 091-590059
(*St John the Apostle,*
Galway)

Quirke, Ciaran (SJ)
St Ignatius Community &
Church,
27 Raleigh Row, Galway
Tel 091-523707

Quirke, Gerard
Priestly Society of St Peter
(Tuam, retired)

Quirke, Gerard, Very Rev,
Ballingarry, Thurles,
Co Tipperary
Tel 052-9154115
(*Ballingarry,* Cashel & E.)

R

Rabbitt, Joseph (SPS)
St Patrick's, Kiltegan,
Co Wicklow
Tel 059-6473600

Rabbitte, Peter, Very Rev
Mgr, PP, VG
The Cathedral, Galway
Tel 091-563577
(*Cathedral,* Galway)

Radley, William, Very Rev,
PP
(Kerry, retired)

Rafferty, James (CM)
99 Cliftonville Road,
Belfast BT14 6JQ
Tel 028-90751771

Rafferty, Terence, Very Rev
c/o Bishop's House
(Dromore)

Raftery, Eamon (SMA)
St Vincent's College,
Castleknock,
Dublin D15 PD95
Tel 01-8213051

Raftery, Thomas (CSSp)
Holy Spirit Missionary
College,
Whitehall Road, Dublin
D12 P5YP
Tel 01-4064300

Raja, Martin Peter (SSS)
Blessed Sacrament Chapel
20 Bachelors Walk,
Dublin 1 D01 NW14
Tel 01-8724597

Rajendram, Elil (SJ)
St Ignatious House of
Writers,
35 Lower Leeson Street,
Dublin 2
Tel 01-6761248

Allianz (ⅲ)

aju, Jose, CC
Castlebar, Co Mayo
Tel 094-9021844
(*Castlebar (Aglish,
Ballyheane and
Breaghwy*), Tuam)

aleigh, Patrick (SSC)
St Columban's,
Dalgan Park,
Navan, Co Meath
Tel 046-9021525

alph, Joseph (OP)
St Catherine's,
Newry,
Co Down BT35 8BN
Tel 028-30262178

amesh, Arunmozhi (SJ)
St Ignatious House of
Writers,
35 Lower Leeson Street,
Dublin 2
Tel 01-6761248

anahan, George Very Rev
(SAC)
Pallottine College, Thurles,
Co Tipperary
Tel 0504-21202

atu, Nicodemus Lobo (SVD)
Our Lady of Sorrows &
St Bridget of Sweden
112 Twickenham Road,
Islworth TW7 6DL, UK

eaume, Michael (SM)
Marianist Community,
13 Coundon Court,
Killiney,
Co Dublin A96 K0T9
Tel 01-2858301

ebamontan, Jonas, CC
Parichial House, Boyle,
Co Roscommon
Tel 071-9662012
(*Boyle*, Elphin)

.eburn, Frank, Co-PP, VF
137 Ballymun Road,
Dublin 11
Tel 01-8376341
(*Ballymun Road*, Dublin)

.eche, Charles-Benoit (CFR)
St Columba Friary,
Fairview Road,
Derry BT48 8NU
Tel 028-71419980

.eddan, Michael (SVD),
Seir Kieran,
Clareen, Birr, Co Offaly
Tel 0509-31080/
087-4345898
(*Seir Kieran*, Ossory)

.edmond, Noel (CSSp)
Holy Spirit Missionary
College
Kimmage Manor,
Whitehall Road,
Dublin D12 P5YP
Tel 01-4064300

Redmond, Richard, PP
Ramsgrange, New Ross
Co Wexford
Tel 051-389148
(*Ramsgrange*, Ferns)

Redmond, Tim (SPS)
Editor, Africa,
St Patrick's, Kiltegan,
Co Wicklow
Tel 059-6473600

Regan, Harry
Presbytery 1,
Church Grounds,
Kill Avenue, Dun
Laoghaire, Co Dublin
Tel 01-2800901
(Dublin, retired)

Regan, John (SAC), CC
The Presbytery, Corduff,
Blanchardstown,
Dublin 15
Tel 01-8215930
(*Corduff*, Dublin)

Regan, Michael, Very Rev,
Co-PP
Unit 1B, Riverside Grove,
Riverstick, Co Cork
(*Ballinhassig, Clontead,
Courceys and Kinsale*, Cork
& R.)

Regan, Padraig (CM)
St Peter's, Phibsboro,
Dublin 7
Tel 01-8389708/8389841

Regula, Robert (OP), CC
St Mary's Priory, Tallaght,
Dublin 24
Tel 01-4048100
(*Tallaght, St Mary's*,
Dublin)

Reid, Desmond (CSSp)
Holy Spirit Missionary
College
Kimmage Manor,
Whitehall Road,
Dublin D12 P5YP
Tel 01-4064300

Reid, Norbert (SPS)
St Patrick's, Kiltegan,
Co Wicklow
Tel 059-6473600

Reidy, Colm (CSSp)
Holy Spirit Missionary
College
Kimmage Manor,
Whitehall Road,
Dublin D12 P5YP
Tel 01-4064300

Reidy, Denis, Very Rev Mgr,
PE
4 Carrigdowns,
Carrigtwohill, Co Cork
(Cloyne, retired)

Reilly, Anthony, Very Rev
Canon, PP
Parochial House,
Palmerstown, Dublin 20
Tel 01-6266254
(*Palmerstown*, Dublin)

Reilly, John, Very Rev, PP
Lahardane, Ballina,
Co Mayo
Tel 096-51007
(*Lahardane*, Killala)

Reilly, Liam
On Loan to Diocese of
Reno, Nevada, USA
(Killala)

Reilly, Michael,
Park Place, Colehill,
Co Longford
(Ardagh & Cl., retired)

Reilly, Michael, Very Rev, PP
Parochial House,
Bunninadden, Ballymote,
Co Sligo
Tel 071-9183232
(*Bunninadden (Kilshalvey,
Kilturra and Cloonoghill)*,
Achonry)

Reilly, Michael, Very Rev,
Co-pastor
Rathduff,
Ballina, Co Mayo
Tel 096-21596
(*Backs*, Killala)

Reilly, Michael, Very Rev
Canon
Castlegar, Galway
(Galway)

Reilly, Patrick (OPraem),
Very Rev, PP
13 Seaview Park, Portrane,
Co Dublin
Tel 01-8436099
Chaplain, St Ita's, Portrane
Tel 01-8436337
(*Donabate*, Dublin)

Reilly, Peter J., Very Rev,
Adm
Presbytery 1,
Ballycullen Avenue,
Firhouse, Dublin 24
Tel 01-4599855
(*Firhouse*, Dublin)

Reilly, William
Casilla 09-01-5825,
Guayaquil, Ecuador
(Killala)

Reji, Kurian
Boher, Ballycumber,
Co Offaly
Tel 057-9336119
(*Ballinahown, Boher and
Pullough (Lemanaghan)*,
Ardagh & Cl.)

Reyhart, Bernard, CC
c/o Parish Office,
Prosperous, Co Kildare
Tel 045-841806
(*Prosperous*, Kildare & L.)

Reynolds, Daniel (LC)
Community Secretary,
Leopardstown Road,
Dublin 18
Tel 01-2955902
Chaplain, Woodlands
Academy,
Wingfield House, Bray,
Co Wicklow
Tel 01-2866323

Reynolds, Kenneth
(OFMCap)
Capuchin Friary,
Holy Trinity,
Fr Mathew Quay,
Cork T12 PK24
Tel 021-4270827
(Cork & R.)

Reynolds, Kevin (MHM), CC
Presbytery, Patrick Street,
Castlerea, Co Roscommon
Tel 094-9620039
(*Castlerea (Kilkeevan)*,
Elphin)

Reynolds, William (SJ)
Rector, Manresa House,
426 Clontarf Road,
Dollymount, Dublin 3
Tel 01-8331352

Rice, Patrick, Very Rev
Canon, PE
Little Sisters of the Poor,
Holy Family Residence,
Roebuck Road, Dundrum,
Dublin 14
(Dublin, retired)

Rice, Séamus, Very Rev, PE
4 Ballymacnab Road,
Armagh BT60 2QS
Tel 028-37531620
(Armagh, retired)

Rice, Tony (CSsR)
St Joseph's, Dundalk,
Co Louth
Tel 042-9334042/9334762

Richardson, William
c/o The Presbytery,
Harrington Street,
Dublin 8
Tel 01-4789093
(*Harrington Street*, Dublin)

Rigney, Liam, Very Rev
Canon, PP, PhD
Parochial House,
1 Stanhope Place, Athy,
Co Kildare
Tel 059-8631781
PP Moone Parish
Tel 059-8624109
Chaplain, St Vincent's
Hospital,
Athy, Co Kildare
Tel 059-8646022
(*Athy, Moone,
Narraghmore*, Dublin)

Riordan, Michael, Very Rev
Canon
Mount Desert,
Lee Road, Cork
(Cork & R., retired)

Riordan, Patrick (SJ)
Irish Jesuit Provincialate,
Milltown Park,
Miltown Road, Dublin 6
Tel 01-4987333

Riordan, Raymond CC
(Chaplain to Cork Prison)
1 The Presbytery,
Farranree, Co Cork
Tel 021-2388000/
086-1689292
(Cork & R.)

Riordan, Tom, Very Rev
Willow Lawn,
Ballinlough, Cork
(Cork & R., retired)

Roban, Myles (SSC)
10 Belfield Springs,
Enniscorthy, Co Wexford
Tel 053-9237770

Roberts, Donal, Very Rev
Canon, PP, VF
Macroom, Co Cork
Tel 026-21068
Administrator,
Aghinagh Parish, Co Cork
(Cloyne)

Robinson, Denis, CC
The Presbytery,
Mourne Road, Dublin 12
Tel 01-4556199
(Mourne Road, Dublin)

Robinson, John, Very Rev,
PP
Borris-in-Ossory,
Portlaoise, Co Laois
Tel 0505-41148/
087-2431412
(Borris-in-Ossory, Ossory)

Roche, Donal (OP), PP
Prior, St Mary's Priory,
Tallaght, Dublin 24
Tel 01-4048100
(Tallaght, St Mary's,
Dublin)

Roche, Donal, Very Rev, PP,
VG
The Abbey,
Wicklow, Co Wicklow
Tel 0404-67196
(Kilbride and Barndarrig,
Wicklow, Dublin)

Roche, Eamon, CC
Monument Hil,
Fermoy, Co Cork
Tel 086-9978539
(Fermoy, Cloyne)

Roche, Garrett (SVD)
Maynooth, Co Kildare
Tel 01-6286391/2

Roche, John (SPS)
Assistant House Leader,
St Patrick's, Kiltegan,
Co Wicklow W91 Y022
Tel 059-6473600

Roche, Joseph, Very Rev, PP
Parochial House, Labane,
Ardrahan, Co Galway
Tel 091-635164
Priest in charge, Kilchreest
(Ardrahan, Kilchreest,
Galway)

Roche, Luke, Very Rev
(Kerry, retired)

Rochford, Seamus, Very Rev,
AP
Emly, Co Tipperary
Tel 062-57103
(Emly, Cashel & E.)

Rodgers, Michael (SPS)
Tearmann Spirituality
Centre, Brockagh,
Glendalough,
Co Wicklow
Tel 0404-45208

Rodgers, Peter (OFMCap)
Capuchin Friary,
137-142 Church Street,
Dublin D07 HA22
Tel 01-8730599

Rodrigues Da Silva, Edvaldo
(CSSp), Very Rev, Co-PP
Parish of St Ronan's,
Deansrath,
Clondalkin, Dublin 22
Tel 01-4570380
(Deansrath, Dublin)

Rodriguez, Paulino (MSC)
(Peru) c/o Parish Office,
Herbert Road, Bray,
Co Wicklow
Tel 01-2868413
(Bray, Holy Redeemer,
Dublin)

Rogan, Edward, Very Rev,
PP, VF
Belmullet, Co Mayo
Tel 097-81426
(Belmullet, Killala)

Rogan, Sean, Very Rev, PE
546 Saintfeild Road,
Carryduff,
Belfast BT8 8EU
Tel 028-90812238
(Drumbo & Carryduff,
Down & C.)

Rogers, Patrick (CP)
St Paul's Retreat,
Mount Argus, Dublin 6W
Tel 01-4992000

Rogers, Thomas, Very Rev,
PP
2 Carmel, Priest's Road,
Tramore, Co Tipperary
Tel 051-511275
Administrator,
Ballybricken
(St John's, Ballybricken,
Waterford & L.)

Ronayne, James, Very Rev,
PP, VF
The Parochial House,
Clifden,
Co Galway H71 WF44
Tel 095-21251
(Clifden (Omey and
Ballindoon), Tuam)

Ronayne-Forde, Jude, (OFM)
Franciscan Friary,
Liberty Street,
Cork T12 D376
Tel 021-4275481

Rooney, Joe (SM)
Nazareth House,
Malahide Road, Dublin 9

Rooney, Joseph, Very Rev
(priest in residence)
45 Ballyholme Esplanade,
Bangor,
Co Down BT20 5NJ
Tel 028-91465425
(Bangor, Down & C.)

Rooney, Joseph, Very Rev,
JCL
Parochial House,
69 Doagh Road,
Ballyclare,
Co Antrim BT39 9BG
Tel 028-93342226
(Ballyclare & Ballygowan,
Down & C.)

Rooney, Noel, Very Rev, PP
279 Sunset Drive,
Cartron Point, Sligo
Tel 071-9142422
Chaplain,
Ballinode Vocational
School, Sligo
Tel 071-9147111
(Sligo, Calry St Joseph's,
Elphin)

Ronney, Richard (CSsR)
St Joseph's,
St Alphonsus Road,
Dundalk,
Co Louth A71 F3FC
Tel 042-9334042/9334762

Rosario, Ripon (SJ)
John Sullivan House
56/56A Mulvey Park,
Dundrum, Dublin 14
Tel 01-298397

Rosbotham, Gabriel, CC
Crossmolina, Chapel Road,
Co Mayo
Tel 096-31344
(Crossmolina, Killala)

Rosney, Arnold, Co-PP, VF
Ss John and Paul
Presbytery,
4 Dún na Rí, Shannon,
Co Clare
Tel 061-471513/
087-8598710
(Tradaree Pastoral Area,
Killaloe)

Ross, Jim (SM)
Fiji

Rothery, Colin, CC
68 Maplewood Road
Springfield, Tallaght
Dublin 24
Tel 01-4513109
(Brookfield, Jobstown,
Springfield, Dublin)

Router, Michael, Most Rev,
DD
Titular Bishop of Lugmad
and Auxiliary Bishop of
Armagh
Annaskeagh, Ravensdale,
Dundalk,
Co Louth A91 KP64
(Armagh)

Rowan, Kevin, Co-PP
Parochial House,
Carrickbrennan Road,
Monkstown, Co Dublin
Tel 01-2802130
(Monkstown, Dublin)

Ruddy, Michael (SSCC), Very
Rev
Delegation Superior,
Coudrin House,
27 Northbrook Road,
Dublin 6
Tel 01-6604898
PC, Sruleen
Sacred Heart,
St John's Drive,
Clondalkin,
Dublin D22 W1W6
Tel 01-4570032
(Sruleen, Dublin)

Rushe, Patrick, Very Rev, PP,
VF
Parochial House,
Monasterboice,
Drogheda,
Co Louth A92 RT66
Tel 086-8807470
(Monasterboice, Armagh)

Russell, William,
Convent Street,
Abbeyfeale, Limerick
Tel 087-2272825
(Pastoral Unit 14, Limerick

Ryan, Aidan
Lake Road, Moate,
Co Westmeath
(Ardagh & Cl.)

Ryan, Anthony, Rev, PP
Upperchurch, Thurles,
Co Tipperary
Tel 054-54492
(Upperchurch, Cashel & E.)

Ryan, Con (SPS)
St Patrick's,
21 Leeson Park,
Dublin 6 D06 DE76
Tel 01-4977897

Ryan, Conor, Very Rev
Canon, AP, VF
Castlefarm, Hospital,
Co Limerick V35 X257
Tel 061-383108
(Hospital, Cashel & E.)

Allianz (ⓘ)

.yan, Damian,
Manister, Croom,
Co Limerick
Tel 061-397335/
087-2274412
(*Pastoral Unit 7*, Limerick)

.yan, Daniel J.
c/o Archbishop's House,
Thurles, Co Tipperary
(Cashel & E., retired)

.yan, Denis J. (SMA)
African Missions,
Blackrock Road,
Cork T12 TD54
Tel 021-4292871

.yan, Derek (CSsR), Very
Rev Adm
Holy Family Parish,
Hoey's Lane,
Muirhevnamor,
Dundalk,
Co Louth A91 K761
Tel 042-9336301
(*Dundalk, Holy Family*,
Armagh)

.yan, Dermot, Rt Rev Dr
President,
St Kieran's College,
Kilkenny
Tel 056-7721086
Priest Secretary to Apostlic
Administrator,
Diocesan Office,
James's Street, Kilkenny
Tel 056-7762448
(Ossory)

.yan, Edmond (SPS)
St Patrick's, Kiltegan,
Co Wicklow
Tel 059-6473600

.yan, Fergal, Very Rev, PP
The Presbytery,
Beaufort, Co Kerry
Tel 064-6644128
(*Beaufort (Tuogh)*, Kerry)

.yan, Fergus (OP)
Convent of SS Xystus and
Clement
Collegio San Clemente,
Via Labicana 95,
00184 Roma
Tel 0039-06-7740021

.yan, James, Rt Rev Mgr, AP
Bohermore, Cashel,
Co Tipperary
Tel 062-61353
(*Cashel*, Cashel & E.)

.yan, John, Very Rev, PE, CC
Midleton, Co Cork
Tel 086-2697503
(*Midleton*, Cloyne)

Ryan, Joseph, Very Rev,
Moderator
41 Cremore Heights,
St Canice's Road,
Glasnevin, Dublin 11
Tel 01-8573776
(*Ballygall, Ballymun Road,
Drumcondra,
Glasnevin, Iona Road*,
Dublin)

Ryan, Liam (OSA)
St Augustine's,
Taylor's Lane,
Balyboden, Dublin 16
Tel 01-4241000

Ryan, Martin (OCarm)
Gort Muire, Ballinteer,
Dublin 16 D16 EI67
Tel 01-2984014

Ryan, Michael
c/o Archbishop's House,
Thurles, Co Tipperary
Tel 0504-21512
(Cashel and E.)

Ryan, Michael (SSC)
112 The Sycamores,
Freshford Road, Kilkenny
Tel 086-8977569

Ryan, Michael, Rt Rev Dom
(OCSO)
Abbot, Bolton Abbey,
Moone, Co Kildare
Tel 059-8624102

Ryan, Michael, Rt Rev Mgr,
PP, VG
Castlecomer, Co Kilkenny
Tel 056-4441262/
086-3693863
(*Castlecomer*, Ossory)

Ryan, Patrick (OCSO)
Prior,
Mount Melleray Abbey,
Cappoquin,
Co Waterford P51 R8XW
Tel 058-54404

Ryan, Patrick J. (CSSp)
Holy Spirit Missionary
College
Kimmage Manor,
Whitehall Road,
Dublin D12 P5YP
Tel 01-4064300

Ryan, Patrick, M. (CSSp)
Holy Spirit Missionary
College
Kimmage Manor,
Whitehall Road,
Dublin D12 P5YP
Tel 01-4064300

Ryan, Seamus, Very Rev
Milbrea Nursing Home,
Newport, Co Tipperary
(Dublin, retired)

Ryan, Thomas, Very Rev, CC
Gleneden,
North Circular Road,
Limerick
Tel 087-2997733
(*Pastoral Unit 5*, Limerick)

Ryan, Thomas A.,
8 Merval Crescent,
Clareview, Limerick
Tel 085-1387001
(Limerick, retired)

Ryan, Thomas J., Very Rev
Canon, AP, VF
Bohergar, Brittas,
Co Limerick
Tel 061-352223
(*Murroe and Boher*, Cashel
& E.)

Ryan, Tom, Very Rev, Co-PP,
VF
Director, Lourdes
Pilgrimage,
Cathedral Presbytery,
O'Connell Street,
Ennis, Co Clare
Tel 065-6869097
(*Abbey Pastoral Area*,
Killaloe)

Ryan, Tom (SPS)
St Patrick's, Kiltegan,
Co Wicklow W91 Y022
Tel 059-6473600

Ryan, William (OFMCap) PC
Capuchin Friary,
Clonshaugh Drive,
Priorswood,
Dublin D17 RP20
Tel 01-8474469
(*Priorswood*, Dublin)

Ryan, William, Very Rev
Canon, PP, VF
Parochial House,
Dungarvan, Co Waterford
Tel 058-42374
Adm, Ring and Old Parish
(*Dungarvan, Kilgobnet,
Ring and Old Parish*,
Waterford & L.)

Ryder, Andrew (SCI)
Sacred Heart Fathers,
Fairfield,
66 Inchicore Road,
Dublin 8
Tel 01-4538655

Rynn, Sean (SPS)
St Patrick's, Kiltegan,
Co Wicklow W91 Y022

S

Sakwe, Willibrord, CC
St Mary's Temple Street,
Sligo
Tel 071-9162670
(*Sligo, St Mary's*, Elphin)

Salud Abila, Laurent M.
(OSB)
119 Kilbroney Road,
Rostrevor,
Co Down BT34 3BN
Tel 028-41739979

Samugana, Victor (MSP), CC
St Mary's,
Temple Street, Sligo
071-9162670
(*Sligo, St Mary's*, Elphin)

Sammon, Frank (SJ)
Milltown Park,
Miltown Road,
Dublin D04 NX39

Samosir, Bavo (OCSO)
Mount Saint Joseph
Abbey, Roscrea,
Co Tipperary E53 D651
Tel 0505-25600

Sanchez, Oscar (LC)
Director, Dublin Oak
Academy,
Kilcroney, Bray,
Co Wicklow
Tel 01-2863290

Sandham, Denis (OSCam)
Superior, St Camillus,
South Hill Avenue,
Blackrock, Co Dublin
Tel 01-2882873

Saniuta, Ignacy, CC
Parochial House,
St Mary's, Creggan
Derry BT48 9QE
Tel 028-71263152
(*St Mary's, Creggan*, Derry)

Sassou, Jerome (SMA), CC
St Joseph's,
Blackrock Road,
Cork T12 X281
Tel 021-4292871
(*St Joseph's (Blackrock
Road)*, Cork & R.)

Savio, Dominic,
10 Castletroy Heights,
Castletroy, Co Limerick
Tel 089-2322418
(Limerick)

Scallon, Paschal (CM), Very
Rev
Provincial,
Provincial Office,
St Paul's, Sybil Hill,
Raheny, Dublin D05 AE38
Tel 01-8510842
Superior,
St Vincent's College,
Castleknock,
Dublin D15 PD95
Tel 01-8213051

Scanlan, Charles
Ballinwillin, Lismore,
Co Waterford
Tel 058-54282
(Waterford & L., retired)

Scanlan, Liam V. (SPS)
St Patrick's, Kiltegan,
Co Wicklow
Tel 059-6473600

Scanlan, Patrick, Very Rev,
PE
Castlemagner,
Mallow, Co Cork
(Cloyne, retired)

Scanlon, Michael, PE
Parochial House, Cloghan,
Co Offaly
(Ardagh & Cl., retired)

Scanlon, Thomas (CP)
Superior,
Passionist Retreat Centre
Downpatrick Road,
Crossgar, Downpatrick
Co Down BT30 9EQ

Scheifele, Claus (OFM)
Franciscan Friary,
Killarney, Co Kerry
Tel 064-6631334/6631066

Scott, Kellan (OP)
Convent of SS Xystus and
Clement
Collegio San Clemente,
Via Labicana 95,
00184 Roma
Tel 0039-06-7740021

Scott, Michael (SDB)
Salesian House,
45 St Teresa's Road,
Crumlin, Dublin 12
Tel 01-4555605

Scott, Philip (OCSO)
Our Lady of Bethlehem
Abbey,
11 Ballymena Road,
Portglenone, Ballymena,
Co Antrim BT44 8BL
Tel 028-25821211

Scott, Thomas (SPS)
St Patrick's, Kiltegan,
Co Wicklow W91 Y022
Tel 059-6473600

Screene, Michael (MSC)
Woodview House,
Mount Merrion Avenue,
Blackrock, Co Dublin
Tel 01-2881644

Screene, Vincent (MSC)
Woodview House,
Mount Merrion Avenue,
Blackrock, Co Dublin
Tel 01-2881644

Scriven, Richard, Very Rev,
Adm,
St Mary's Cathedral,
Kilkenny R95 CP46
Tel 056-7721253/
087-2420033
(St Mary's, Ossory)

Scully, Anthony
Dunmanus Road,
Cabra, Dublin 7
(Dublin, retired)

Scully, Brendan (OFM)
Franciscan Friary,
Liberty Street,
Cork T12 D376
Tel 021-4270302/4275481

Seaver, Patrick, CC
4 Glenview Terrace,
Farranshone, Limerick
Tel 061-328838/
086-0870297
(Pastoral Unit 4, Limerick)

Sebastian, Ceban
St Thomas Pastoral Centre,
19 Saint Anthony's Road
Rialto, Dublin 8, D08 E8P3
(Rialto/Dolphin's Barn,
Dublin)

Sekongo, Alphonse (SMA)
SMA House,
81 Ranelagh Road,
Ranelagh, Dublin 6
Tel 01-4968162/3

Serrage, Michael (MSC)
Woodview House,
Mount Merrion Avenue
Blackrock,
Co Dublin A94 DW95
Tel 01-2881644

Sexton, Frank (OSA)
St Augustine's,
Taylor's Lane,
Ballyboden, Dublin 16
Tel 01-4241000

Sexton, John
Rossinver, Co Leitrim
Tel 071-9854022
(Ballaghameehan,
Kilmore)

Sexton, Pat, Very Rev
5 Cottage Gardens,
Station Road, Ennis,
Co Clare
Tel 065-6840828/
087-2477814
(Killaloe, retired)

Sexton, Peter (SJ)
Loyola House,
Milltown Park,
Miltown Road, Dublin 6
Tel 01-2180276
House 27, Trinity College,
Dublin 2
Tel 01-8961260
(Dublin)

Sexton, Sean, Very Rev, AP
Kilnamona, Ennis,
Co Clare
Tel 065-6829507/
087-2621884
(Críocha Callan Pastoral
Area, Killaloe)

Sexton, Tom (OSA)
St Augustine's Priory
Washington Street, Cork
Tel 021-4275398/4270410

Shanahan, John,
(Kerry, retired)

Shanahan, Martin, Co-PP
Parochial House,
Inagh, Co Clare
Tel 087-7486935
(Críocha Callan Pastoral
Area, Killaloe)

Shanahan, Tom (OCD)
The Abbey, Loughrea,
Co Galway
Tel 091-841209

Shanet, Jacob
Parish Chaplain,
c/o 12 Coarsemoor Park,
Straffan, Co Kildare
Tel 01-6288827
(Celbridge, Dublin)

Shannon, Declan CF
Chaplain, Custume
Barracks, Athlone,
Co Westmeath
Tel 090-6421277
(Ardagh & Cl.)

Shannon, Richard, TA
107 Mount Prospect
Avenue,
Dollymount,
Dublin 3
(Dollymount, Dublin)

Sharkey, Liam (SPS)
St Patrick's, Kiltegan,
Co Wicklow
Tel 059-6473600

Sharkey, Liam
Ballyweelin, Rosses Point,
Co Sligo
(Elphin, retired)

Sharkey, Lorcan, Very Rev,
PP
Cloghan, Lifford,
Co Donegal
Tel 074-9133007
(Cloghan, Raphoe)

Sharpe, Jackie
Ogonnelloe, Co Clare
Tel 086-8940556
(Inis Cealtra Pastoral Area,
Killaloe)

Sharpe, John M. (CSSp)
Parish House,
Ballybrohan, Ogonnelloe
Co Clare

Shaughnessy, Bernard
The Parochial House,
Coolarne, Athenry,
Co Galway
(Tuam)

Shayo, Wilhad (IC)
Clonturk House,
Ormond Road,
Drumcondra, Dublin 9
Tel 01-6877014

Sheary, Patrick (SJ), CC
Milltown Park,
Miltown Road,
Dublin D06 V9K7
Tel 01-2693903
(Donnybrook, Dublin)

Sheehan, Anthony, AP
Love Lane,
Charleville, Co Cork
Tel 063-32320
(Charleville, Cloyne)

Sheehan, Diarmuid, (White
Fathers)
Bursar,
Cypress Grove,
Templeogue, Dublin 6W
Tel 01-4055263/4055264

Sheehan, Edward CF
Chapain, Collin's Barracks,
Cork
Tel 021-4502734
(Cork & R.)

Sheehan, Martin, Very Rev,
Adm
Adrigole, Bantry,
Co Cork
Tel 027-60006
(Adrigole, Kerry)

Sheehan, Michael, Very Rev
PP, Adm
Parochial House,
15 Moy Road, Portadown,
Co Armagh BT62 1QL
Tel 028-38350610
(Kilmore, Portadown
(Drumcree), Armagh)

Sheehan, Michael, Very Rev
PP
546 Saintfeild Road,
Carryduff,
Belfast BT8 8EU
Tel 028-90812238
(Drumbo & Carryduff,
Down & C.)

Sheehan, Niall
Portadown, Co Armagh
(Dromore, retired)

Sheehan, Patrick, Very Rev,
PP
Elmfield,
165 Antrim Road,
Glengormley
Newtownabbey,
Co Antrim BT36 7QR
Tel 028-90832979
(St Mary's on the Hill,
Down & C.)

Sheehan, Ronan, CC
The Bungalow, St Mary &
St John,
Ballincollig, Co Cork
Tel 021-4877161
(Ballinora, Ballincollig and
Ovens, Cork & R.)

Sheehan, Rory, Very Rev, PP
Netherley Lodge,
130 Upper Dunmurry
Lane,
Belfast BT17 0EW
Tel 028-90616300
(Our Lady Queen of Peace
Kilwee, Down & C.)

Sheehy, James (SSC)
Dungarvan, Co Waterford
(retired)

Sheehy, Richard, Very Rev,
Co-PP, EV
Parochial House,
Brackenstown Road,
Swords, Co Dublin
Tel 01-8401661
(Brackenstown, Dublin)

Sheerin, Michael, Very Rev
Woodlands Nursing Home
Navan, Co Meath
Tel 046-9053155
(Meath, retired)

heerin, Tony (SPS)
St Patrick's, Kiltegan,
Co Wicklow
Tel 059-6473600

heil, Michael (SJ)
Rector,
Clongowes Wood College,
Clane,
Co Kildare W91 DN40
Tel 045-868663/868202

helley, Padraig, Very Rev,
PP
The Presbytery, Arles
Tel 059-9147637
(*Arles*, Kildare & L.)

hen-yi Hssii, Matthew (SJ)
John Sullivan House,
56/56A Mulvey Park,
Dundrum, Dublin 14
Tel 01-2983978

heppard, Jim, Very Rev
c/o 32 Dromlin Drive,
Lurgan, BT66 8PG
(Down & C., retired)

heridan, Billy (SMA)
Superior, SMA House,
Cloonbigeen, Claregalway,
Co Galway H91 YK64
Tel 091-798880

heridan, Christopher CC
7 Bayside Square East,
Sutton, Dublin 13
Tel 01-8322964
(*Bayside*, Dublin)

heridan, James (CP)
St Paul's Retreat,
Mount Argus, Dublin 6W
Tel 01-4992000

heridan, John-Paul
Annacurra, Aughrim,
Co Wicklow
Tel 0402-36119
(Ferns)

heridan, Paddy, CC
Robeen, Hollymount,
Co Mayo
Tel 094-9540026
(*Robeen*, Tuam)

heridan, Patrick (CP)
St Paul's Retreat,
Mount Argus, Dublin 6W
Tel 01-4992000

herlock, Vincent, Very Rev,
PP
Diocesan Communications
Officer,
Parochial House,
Emmet Street,
Tubbercurry,
Co Sligo F91 NH34
Tel 071-9185049
(*Tubbercurry (Cloonacool)*,
Achonry)

hibanada, Julius
Church of the Sacred
Heart, Donnybrook,
Dublin 4
(*Donnybrook*, Dublin)

Shiel, Patrick, Very Rev
Canon
74 Mount Drinan Avenue,
Kinsealy Downs,
Swords, Co Dublin
(Dublin, retired)

Shiels, Michael, CC
Presbytery 1,
St Canice's Parish,
Finglas, Dublin 11
Tel 01-8341051
(*Finglas*, Dublin)

Shine, Larry (CSSp)
Holy Spirit Missionary
College, Kimmage Manor,
Whitehall Road,
Dublin D12 P5YP
Tel 01-4064300

Shire, Joseph, Canon,
St Patrick's Presbytery,
Dublin Road, Limerick
Tel 087-6924563
(*Pastoral Unit 1*, Limerick)

Shortall, Bryan (OFMCap),
Guardian,
12 Halston Street,
Dublin D07 Y2T5
Tel 01-8733205

Shortall, Maurice (CSSp)
Holy Spirit Missionary
College
Kimmage Manor,
Whitehall Road,
Dublin D12 P5YP
Tel 01-4064300

Shortall, Michael, TA
28 Greenfield Park,
Ballycullen
Firhouse, Dublin 24
Tel 01-4610971
(*Brookfield, Jobstown,
Springfield*, Dublin)

Shorten, Kieran (OFMCap)
Vicar, Capuchin Friary,
Ard Mhuire,
Creeslough, Letterkenny,
Co Donegal
Tel 074-9138005

Sikora, Krzysztof (SVD), PP
Polish Chaplain,
Roundstone, Co Galway
Tel 095-37123
(*Roundstone*, Tuam)

Simpson, Michael, CC
St Kevin's Presbytery,
Pearse Street,
Sallynoggin, Co Dublin
Tel 01-2854667
(*Sallynoggin*, Dublin)

Sinnott, John, Very Rev, Co-
PP
56 Auburn Road, Killiney,
Co Dublin
Tel 01-2856660
(*Johnstown-Killiney*,
Dublin)

Sinnott, Patrick
Parkannesley,
Ballygarrett,
Gorey, Co Wexford
(Ferns, retired)

Sinnott, Peter J., CC
No. 3 Presbytery,
Castle Street, Dalkey,
Co Dublin
Tel 01-2859212
(*Dalkey*, Dublin)

Skelly, Oliver, Very Rev, PP
Parochial House, Coole,
Co Westmeath
Tel 044-9661191
(*Coole*, Meath)

Slater, Brian, CC, VF
Parochial House,
3 Convent Road,
Cookstown,
Co Tyrone BT80 8QA
Tel 028-86763490
(*Cookstown (Desertcreight
and Derryloran)*, Armagh)

Slater, David (OSA)
St Augustine's,
Taylor's Lane,
Ballyboden, Dublin 16
Tel 01-4241000

Slattery, Sean, Very Rev
18 The Orchard,
Limerick V94 F97N
(Clonfert, retired)

Sleeman, Simon (OSB)
Glenstal Abbey, Murroe,
Co Limerick
Tel 061-621000

Sloan, Robert, CC
Holy Family Presbytery
Newington Avenue,
Belfast BT15 2HP
Tel 028-90743119
(*Holy Famly*, Down and C.)

Slowey, Harry (CM)
St Paul's, Sybil Hill,
Raheny,
Dublin D05 AE38
Tel 01-8318113

Small, Thomas
Okpetu, Peter, CC
The Presbytery,
Cavan
Tel 049-4331404/4332269
(*Cavan (Urney and
Annagelliff)*, Kilmore)

Smith, Adrian (SM), Most
Rev Archbishop
Nazareth House,
Malahide Road,
Dublin 9

Smith, David (MSC)
Woodview House,
Mount Merrion Avenue,
Blackrock, Co Dublin
Tel 01-2881644

Smith, Declan, Very Rev, PP
Parochial House,
Taghmon,
Mullingar, Co Westmeath
Tel 044-9372140
(*Taghmon*, Meath)

Smith, Desmond (SMA)
SMA House,
Cloonbigeen, Claregalway,
Co Galway H91 YK64
Tel 091-798880

Smith, Martin (SPS), CC
1 Green Road, Carlow
Tel 059-9142632
(*Cathedral, Carlow*,
Kildare & L.)

Smith, Michael, Most Rev,
DCL, DD
Bishop Emeritus of Meath,
St Oliver's, Beechfield
Dublin Road, Mullingar,
Co Westmeath
Tel 044-9340636
(Meath)

Smith, Philip, Very Rev, PP
Tir-ee, Harbourstown,
Stamullen, Co Meath
Tel 01-8020708
(Meath, retired)

Smith, Sean, Very Rev
Canon, CC
The Presbytery,
Newtownmountkennedy,
Co Wicklow
Tel 01-2819253
(*Kilquade*, Dublin)

Smith, Terence (CSSp)
Holy Spirit Missionary
College
Kimmage Manor,
Whitehall Road,
Dublin D12 P5YP
Tel 01-4064300

Smyth, Brendan, Very Rev,
PP
Parochial House,
10 Downpatrick Street,
Crossgar, Downpatrick,
Co Down BT30 9EA
Tel 028-44830229
(*Crossgar (Kilmore)*, Down
& C.)

Smyth, Derek
No. 2 Kill Lane,
Foxrock, Dublin 18
Tel 01-2894734
(Dublin, retired)

Smyth, Edmund (OCD)
St Teresa's
Claredon Street, Dublin 2
Tel 01-6718466/6718127

Smyth, James (SJ)
Cherryfield Lodge,
Milltown Park,
Ranelagh,
Dublin D06 V9K7
Tel 01-4985800

Smyth, Michael (MSC)
'Croí Nua', Rosary Lane,
Taylor's Hill, Galway
Tel 091-520960

Smyth, Michael (SDB)
Vice-Rector,
Salesian House,
Milford, Castletroy,
Limerick
Tel 061-330268

Smyth, Patrick (OCarm)
Carmelite Priory,
Whitefriar Street Church,
56 Aungier Street,
Dublin D02 R598
Tel 01-4758821

Smyth, Patrick (SSC)
St Columban's,
Dalgan Park,
Navan, Co Meath
Tel 046-9021525

Smyth, Robert, Very Rev,
Adm
Presbytery, Montrose Park,
Beaumont, Dublin 5
Tel 01-8710013
(Beaumont, Dublin)

Smyth, Terry (OPraem)
Holy Trinity House,
Lismacanican,
Mountnugent, Co Cavan

Solomon, Ciprian
St Mary's Drogheda,
Co Louth
Tel 041-9834958
(Drogheda, St Mary's,
Meath)

Somers, James (SDB)
Salesian House,
45 St Teresa's Road,
Crumlin, Dublin 12
Tel 01-4555605

Somers, P.J., Very Rev, PP
Chaplains House, Curragh
Camp, Co Kildare
Tel 045-441277
(Curragh Camp, Kildare &
L.)

Soukup, Bernardino Maria
Rev (CFR)
St Patrick Friary
64 Delmege Park,
Moyross,
Limerick V94 859Y
Tel 061-458071

Spain, Michael (OCD)
St Joseph's Carmelite
Retreat Centre
Termonbacca
Derry BT48 9XE
Tel 028-71262512

Spence, Michael, Very Rev,
PP
Holy Family Presbytery
Newington Avenue,
Belfast BT15 2HP
Tel 028-90743119
(Holy Famly, Down and C.)

Spencer, Paul Francis (CP),
Very Rev, PP
St Paul's Retreat,
Mount Argus, Dublin 6W
Tel 01-4992000
(Mount Argus, Dublin)

Spillane, David (LC)
Dublin Oak Academy
Kilcroney, Bray,
Co Wicklow
Tel 01-2863290

Spillane, Martin, Very Rev,
PP
Brosna, Co Kerry
Tel 068-44112
(Brosna, Kerry)

Spillane, Martin (SPS)
On temporary diocesan
work

Spinharney, Isaac (CFR)
St Columba Friary,
Fairview Road,
Derry BT48 8NU
Tel 028-71419980

Spring, Finbarr (OSA)
St Augustine's Priory,
Dungarvan,
Co Waterford
Tel 058-41136

Spring, John Joe, PC
Presbytery No. 2,
2 Dunmanus Road,
Cabra West, D07 Y6TI
Tel 01-8384418
(Cabra West, Dublin)

Spring, Noel, Very Rev
Canon, PP
Castletownbere, Co Cork
Tel 027 70849
(Castletownbere and Bere
Island, Kerry)

St John, Paul (SVD), Adm
4 Claremont Drive,
Ballygall, Dublin 11
Tel 01-8087553
(Ballygall, Dublin)

Stachyra, Wojciech (SCHr)
Cathedral Presbytery,
38 Hill Street,
Newry BT34 1AT
Tel 028-30262586
(Newry, Dromore)

Stafford, Patrick, Very Rev,
Tomsollagh, Ferns,
Enniscorthy, Co Wexford
(Ferns, retired)

Standún, Padraic, Very Rev
Canon, PE
Cill Chiaráin, Co Galway
(Tuam, retired)

Stanley, Cathal
Dominic Street, Portumna,
Co Galway H53 EC66
Tel 090-9759182
(Clonfert, retired)

Stanley, Gerard, Very Rev,
PP
Parochial House,
Rathkenny, Co Meath
Tel 046-9054138
(Rathkenny, Meath)

Stanley, Paddy (SM), PC
The Presbytery,
Coolock Village, Dublin 5
Tel 01-8477133
(Coolock, Dublin)

Stanley, Thomas (SCJ)
Sacred Heart Fathers,
Fairfield,
66 Inchicore Road,
Dublin 8
Tel 01-4538655

Stansfield, Oliver, (IC), CC
Parochial House,
Kilcurry, Dundalk,
Co Louth A91 E8N8
Tel 042-9334410
(Faughart, Armagh)

Stapleton, Christy
St Michael's, Longford
(Ardagh & Cl.)

Stapleton, Jim (CSSp)
Holy Spirit Missionary
College
Kimmage Manor,
Whitehall Road,
Dublin D12 P5YP
Tel 01-4064300

Stapleton, John, Very Rev,
PP
Killeigh, Co Offaly
Tel 057-9344161
(Killeigh, Kildare & L.)

Stapor, Tomasz (SJ) (PME)
Jesuit Community,
27 Leinster Road,
Rathmines, Dublin 6
Tel 01-4970250

Starken, Brian (CSSp), Co-PP
The Prebystery,
Bawnogue,
Clondalkin, Dublin 22
Tel 01-4519810/4570380
(Bawnogue, Deansrath,
Dublin)

Staunton, Brendan (SJ), PC
Pro-Cathedral House,
83 Marlborough Street,
Dublin 1
Tel 01-8745441
(Pro-Cathedral, Dublin)

Staunton, Ray (SM)
Chanel College, Coolock,
Dublin 5
Tel 01-8480655/8480896

Steblecki, Hilary (OFM)
Vicar,
Franciscan Friary,
Liberty Street, Cork
Tel 021-4270302/4275481

Steed, Bernard (SSC)
St Columban's,
Dalgan Park, Navan,
Co Meath
Tel 046-9021525

Stenson, Alex, Rt Rev
5 Calderwood Avenue,
Drumcondra,
Dublin 9
(Dublin, retired)

Stevenson, Liam, Very Rev
Canon, PP,
70 North Street, Lurgan,
Co Armagh BT67 9AH
Tel 028-38323161
(Shankill, St Paul's
(Lurgan), Dromore)

Stevenson, Patrick, Very
Rev, PP
The Presbytery,
Crosshaven, Co Cork
Tel 021-4831218
(Carrigaline, Crosshaven,
Harbour Parishes
and Tracton Abbey, Cork
& R.)

Stokes, John, Very Rev
Sacred Heart Residence,
Sybil Hill Road,
Raheny, Dublin 5
(Dublin, retired)

Stolnicu, Andrei
Cathedral House,
Mullingar,
Co Westmeath
Tel 044-9348338/9340126
(Mullingar, Meath)

Stone, Tom (OCD)
Avila, Bloomfield Avenue,
Morehampton Road,
Dublin 4
Tel 01-6430200

Stopa, Jerzy (OFMCap)
Capuchin Friary,
Friary Street,
Kilkenny R95 NX60
Tel 056-7721439

Strain, Paul, Very Rev, PP
119A Glenravel Road,
Martinstown, Ballymena,
Co Antrim BT43 6QL
Tel 028-21758217
(Glenravel and The Braid
(Skerry), Down & C.)

Stritch, Denis, Very Rev, PP
Meelin, Newmarket,
Co Cork
Tel 029-68007
(Rockchapel and Meelin,
Cloyne)

Stuart, Gerard, Very Rev, PP
VF
Parochial House, Ratoath,
Co Meath
Tel 01-8256207
Adm, Ardcath and Curaha
(Ardcath, Curraha,
Ratoath, Meath)

Stuart, William (IC)
Clonturk House,
Ormond Road,
Drumcondra, Dublin 9
Tel 01-6877014

Allianz ⑪

tubbs, Jimmy (MSC)
Carrignavar, Co Cork
Tel 021-4884044

ugrue, Patrick (CSsR)
2 The Presbytery,
Mahon, Cork
(*Mahon*, Cork & R.)

ullivan, Kevin, Very Rev
Canon, PP
The Presbytery, Killorglin,
Co Kerry
Tel 066-9761172
(*Killorglin*, Kerry)

ullivan, Paul (OCD)
St Teresa's,
Clarendon Street,
Dublin 2
Tel 01-6718466/6718127

ullivan, Shane, CC
Carna, Co Galway
Tel 095-32232
(*Carna (Moyrus)*, Tuam)

unu, Innocent, CC
Forthill House,
The Batteries,
Athlone, Co Westmeath
Tel 0906-492171
(*Athlone, Ss Peter and
Paul's*, Elphin)

urlis, Tómas Very Rev, DD
St Patrick's College,
Maynooth, Co Kildare
Tel 01-784700
(Achonry)

urungai Ruto, Amos, CC
St Brendan's,
Tralee, Co Kerry
Tel 066-7125932
(*Tralee, St Brendan's*,
Kerry)

usai, Jega (SVD)
Maynooth, Co Kildare
Tel 01-6286391/2

uttle, Peter (CSSp), Very
Rev, Adm,
Parochial House, Parke,
Castlebar, Co Mayo
Tel 094-9031314
(*Keelogues/Parke
(Turlough)*, Tuam)

wan, William, Very Rev,
Adm
The Presbytery,
12 School Street, Wexford
Tel 053-9122055
(*Wexford*, Ferns)

weeney, Charles (MSC)
'Croí Nua', Rosary Lane,
Taylor's Hill, Galway
Tel 095-520960

weeney, Dennis (IC)
Clonturk House,
Ormond Road,
Drumcondra, Dublin 9
Tel 01-8374840

Sweeney, Desmond, Very
Rev, PE
17 Meadowvale,
Ramelton
Tel 074-9151085
(Raphoe, retired)

Sweeney, Donal, (OP)
St Mary's Priory, Tallaght,
Dublin 24
Tel 01-4048100

Sweeney, Eugene, Very Rev,
PP, VG
Parochial House,
9 Fair Street, Drogheda,
Co Louth
Tel 041-9838537
(*Drogheda*, Armagh)

Sweeney, Gerard (SMA)
SMA House, Cloonbigeen,
Claregalway,
Co Galway H91 YK64
Tel 091-798880

Sweeney, Gerard, PP
Parochial House, 447
Victoria Road,
Ballymagorry, Strabane,
Co Tyrone BT82 0AT
Tel 028-718802274
(*Leckpatrick (Leckpatrick
and part of Donagheady)*,
Derry)

Sweeney, James, Very Rev,
PP
Director of Fatima
Pilgrimage,
Frosses, Co Donegal
Tel 074-9736006
(*Inver*, Raphoe)

Sweeney, James (CP)
Provincial,
St Paul's Retreat,
Mount Argus,
Dublin 6W
Tel 01-4992000/4992050

Sweeney, John (SAC)
Pallottine College, Thurles,
Co Tipperary
Tel 0504-21202

Sweeney, Liam (SAC)
Sacred Heart Residence,
Sybil Hill Road,
Raheny, Dublin 5

Sweeney, Michael, Very Rev,
PE
Ballynabrockey, Fanad
Co Donegal
(Raphoe, retired)

Sweeney, Oliver, Very Rev,
24 The Willows,
Wellingtonbridge,
Co Wexford
(Ferns, retired)

Sweeney, Patrick,
Team Assistant,
13 Home Farm Road,
Drumcondra, Dublin 9
Tel 01-8377402
(*Ballymun Road*, Dublin)

Sweeney, Raymond, Very
Rev, PP
Ballymacward,
Ballinasloe,
Co Galway H53 P2W0
Tel 090-9687614
(*Ballymacward & Gurteen
(Ballymacward &
Clonkeenkerril)*, Clonfert)

Swinburne, Robbie (SDB),
Salesian House,
Milford, Castletroy,
Limerick
Tel 061-330268
(*Pastoral Unit 1*, Limerick)

Symonds, Paul
c/o Lisbreen,
73 Somerton Road,
Belfast BT15 4DE
(Down & C.)

Szalwa, Marian (SCJ), PC
Parochial House,
St John Vianney,
Ardlea Road, Dublin 5
Tel 01-8474123
(*Ardlea*, Dublin)

T

Taaffe, Eugene, Very Rev,
PP
The Presbytery,
James Street, Dublin 8
Tel 01-4531143
(*James's Street, Meath
Street*, Dublin)

Talbot, Denis, Very Rev
Canon, AP
Millbrae Lodge,
Newport, Co Tipperary
(*Galbally*, Cashel & E.)

Talty, Robert (OP)
St Mary's, Pope's Quay,
Cork
Tel 021-4502267

Tamas, Eugen Dragos, CC
Curate's House,
Chapel Lane,
Newbridge, Co Kildare
Tel 045-433979
(*Droichead
Nua/Newbridge*, Kildare &
L.)

Tanham, Gerard, Very Rev,
PC,
Presbytery No 1,
Thormanby Road,
Howth, Co Dublin
Tel 01-8232193/8167599
(*Baldoyle, Howth, Sutton*,
Dublin)

Tanko, Rodney, CC
Glencar, Manorhamilton,
Co Leitrim
Tel 071-9855433
(*Cloonclare and Killasnett*,
Kilmore)

Tapley, Paul (OFMCap)
Capuchin Friary,
137-142 Church Street,
Dublin D07 HA22
Tel 01-8730599

Tarrant, Joseph, Very Rev,
PP
Ballydesmond,
Mallow, Co Cork
Tel 064-7751104
(*Ballydesmond*, Kerry)

Taylor, Joe (SPS)
St Patrick's, Kiltegan,
Co Wicklow W91 Y022

Taylor, Leonard, Very Rev
Rathlee, Easkey, Co Sligo
(Killala, retired)

Taylor, Liam, Very Rev, PP
Ballycallan,
Co Kilkenny R95 E8N0
Tel 056-7769564/
086-8180954
Administrator, Tullaroan
Parish
(*Ballycallan, Tullaroan*,
Ossory)

Taylor, Paul, Adm, VF
43 Upper Beechwood
Avenue,
Ranelagh,
Dublin D06 X3F4
Tel 01-4967449
(*Beechwood Avenue*,
Dublin)

Teehan, William, Very Rev,
Co-PP, VF
The Spa, Castleconnell,
Co Limerick
Tel 061-377170/
087-2347927
(*Scáth na Sionnaine
Pastoral Area*, Killaloe)

Temgo, Michel Simo (SCJ),
Very Rev, PP
Parochial House,
St John Vianney,
Ardlea Road, Dublin 5
Tel 01-8474173
(*Ardlea*, Dublin)

Terry, John, Very Rev
Canon, PE
Terriville, Ballylanders,
Cloyne, Co Cork
Tel 087-2584091
(Cloyne, retired)

Thandiparambil Chacko,
Antony (OCarm)
Prior,
Carmelite Priory,
White Abbey,
Co Kildare R51 X827
Tel 045-521391

Thankachan Njaliath, Paul
Chaplain for Pastoral Care
of the Syro-Malabar
Community in the Dublin
Diocese, based in Tallaght
Tel 01-4510166
(Dublin)

Allianz (ⅱ)

Thazamhon, Cherian, CC
Chaplain to Syro
Malankara Community
30 Wheatfield Close,
Clondalkin, Dublin 22
(*Neilstown, Rowlagh and
Quarryvale*, Dublin)
Thennattil, Vinod Kurian
(IC), Very Rev, PP
Parochial House, Kilcurry,
Dundalk, Co Louth
Tel 042-9334410/9333235
(*Faughart*, Armagh)
Thettayil, Polachan (IC)
Rector, Rosmini House,
Dunkereen,
Innishannon,
Co Cork T12 N9DH
Tel 021-4776268/4776923
Thomas, Jose, CC
Good Shepherd Church,
Comasú Centre,
Doughiska, Galway
Tel 091-756823
St Thomas Syro-Malabar
Chaplaincy
(*Good Shepherd*, Galway)
Thompson, Declan (SPS), PP
St Mary's, Daingean,
Co Offaly
Tel 057-9362653
(*Daingean*, Kildare & L.)
Thoomkuzhy, Dominic, CC
Carnamuggagh Lower,
Letterkenny, Co Donegal
(*Aughaninshin*, Raphoe)
Thorne, Bernard (OSM)
Prior, Servite Priory,
Benburb, Dungannon,
Co Tyrone, BT71 7JZ
Tel 028-37548241
Thornton, Gerry (MSC)
Carrignavar, Co Cork
Tel 021-4884044
Chaplain,
St Stephen's Hospital,
Glanmire, Co Cork
Tel 021-4821411
Thornton, Paul, PP, EV
124 New Cabra Road,
Dublin 7
Tel 01-8385244
(*Cabra, Cabra West*,
Dublin)
Thynne, Eoin, Rt Rev Mgr,
Adm
24 The Court,
Mulhuddart Wood,
Mulhuddart, Dublin 15
Tel 087-2401432
(*Mulhuddart*, Dublin)
Tiernan, Peter, PP
Cloone, Co Leitrim
Tel 071-9636016
(*Aughavas and Cloone*,
Ardagh & Cl.)

Tierney, Celsus, PP
The Parchioal House,
Holy Cross, Thurles,
Co Tipperary
Tel 0504-43124
(*Holy Cross*, Cashel & E.)
Tierney, Philip (OSB)
Glenstal Abbey, Murroe,
Co Limerick
Tel 061-386103
Tighe, Paul, Rt Rev Mgr
Secretary of the Pontifical
Council for Social
Communications,
Vatican City
(Dublin)
Tillotson, Aelred (OSB)
Silverstream Priory,
Stamullen,
Co Meath K32 T189
Tel 01-8417142
Timmons, Declan (OFM)
Dún Mhuire,
Seafield Road,
Killiney, Co Dublin
Tel 01-2826760
Timoney, Charles (White
Fathers)
Cypress Grove,
Templeogue, Dublin 6W
Tel 01-4055263/4055264
Timothy, Malcolm (OFM)
Franciscan Abbey,
Multyfarnham,
Co Westmeath
Tel 044-9371114/9371137
Timpu, Eugene
Sean McDermott Street,
Dublin 1
Tel 086-3266467
(*Sean McDermott Street*,
Dublin)
Toal, Donal (SMA)
Apt 1, Parochial House,
Balbriggan, Co Dublin
Tel 01-8412116
(*Balbriggan*, Dublin)
Tobin, James
St Patrick's Presbytery,
Lower Road, Cork
(Cork & R., retired)
Tobin, Martin, Very Rev, PP
Mooncoin, Co Kilkenny
051-895123/086-2401278
(*Clogh*, Ossory)
Tobin, Richard (CSsR)
St Joseph's,
St Alphonsus Road,
Dundalk,
Co Louth A71 F3FC
Tel 042-9334042/9334762
Tohill, David (OP)
Prior,
St Catherine's, Newry,
Co Down BT35 8BN
Tel 028-30262178

Toland, Liam, Very Rev, CC
29 Killough Road,
Downpatrick,
Co Down BT30 6PX
Tel 028-44612443
(*Downpatrick*, Down & C.)
Toman, Columba Mary (OP)
St Mary's Priory, Tallaght,
Dublin 24
Tel 01-4048100
Tomasik, Daniel
'Elm View', Roxboro Road,
Limerick
Tel 061-410846/087-
6092086
(*Pastoral Unit 3*, Limerick)
Tomasik, Teodor (SVD), CC
The Presbytery, Carlow,
Tel 059-9131227
(*Catheral*, Kildare & L.)
Tomulesei, Marius
(OFMConv)
Friary of the Visitation of
the BVM,
Fairview Strand, Dublin 3
Tel 01-8376000
(*Fairview*, Dublin)
Toner, Michael C., Very Rev
Canon, PP
Parochial House,
Tullynaval Road,
Cullyhanna, Newry,
Co Down BT35 0PZ
Tel 028-30861235
(*Cullyhanna (Creggan
Lower)* Armagh)
Toner, Terence, Very Rev, PP
Parochial House,
Kilmessan, Co Meath
Tel 046-9025172
(*Kilmessan*, Meath)
Toner, William (SJ)
25 Croftwood Park,
Cherry Orchard, Dublin 10
Tel 01-6267413
Tonge, Ivan, Very Rev, PP
St Patrick's,
2 Cambridge Road,
Dublin 4
Tel 087-2726868
(*Ringsend*, Dublin)
Toomey, Michael, Very Rev
Adm
Newcastle, Clonmel,
Co Tipperary
Tel 052-6136387
(*Newcastle and
Fourmilewater/Ardfinnan*,
Waterford & L.)
Touhy, Fergus (SMA), CC
The Presbytery,
Clonakilty, Co Cork
Tel 023-8834441
(*Ardfield/Rathbarry,
Barryroe, Clonakilty,
Kilmeen/Castleventry,
Rosscarbery and
Timoleague*, Cork & R.)

Touhy, Séamus (OP)
St Mary's Priory, Tallaght,
Dublin 24
Tel 01-4048100
Towey, Thomas, Very Rev,
PP
Ballisodare, Co Sligo
Tel 071-9167467
(*Ballisodare*, Achonry)
Townsend, Mark, Very Rev,
PP
Parochial House,
Graignamanagh,
Co Kilkenny
Tel 059-9724238
(*Graignamanagh*, Kildare
& L.)
Tracey, Finbarr (SVD)
Rector, Maynooth,
Co Kildare
Tel 01-6286391/2
Tracey, Liam (OSM), Very
Rev, PP
Prior,
Church of the Divine
Word,
Marley Grange,
25-27 Hermitage Downs,
Rathfarnham, Dublin 16
Tel 01-4944295/4941064
(*Marley Grange*, Dublin)
Tranter, Carl (MSC)
Provincial Leader,
65 Terenure Road West,
Dublin 6W
Tel 01-4906622
Travers, Vincent (OP)
St Mary's Priory,
Tallaght, Dublin 24
Tel 01-4048100
Treacy, Bernard (OP), Prior,
St Mary's Priory,
Tallaght, Dublin 24
Tel 01-4048100
Treacy, John, PP
SS Peter and Paul's,
Clonmel, Co Tipperary
Tel 052-6126292
(*Clonmel, SS Peter and
Paul's*, Waterford & L.)
Treacy, Patrick
c/o Diocesan Office,
Westbourne,
Ennis, Co Clare
(Killaloe)
Treanor, Martin, Very Rev,
PP
Inniskeen, Dundalk,
Co Louth A91 WN32
Tel 042-9378105
(*Inniskeen/Killanny*,
Clogher)
Treanor, Oliver
St Patrick's College,
Maynooth, Co Kildare
Tel 01-6285222
(Down & C.)

remer, Gerard, Very Rev,
PP
Parochial House,
19 Ardoe Road,
Moortown, Cookstown
Co Tyrone BT80 0HT
Tel 028-86737236
(*Ardboe*, Armagh)

rias, Francis (CP)
Holy Cross Retreat,
432 Crumlin Road,
Ardoyne, Belfast BT14 7GE
Tel 028-90748231

roy, Michael (OCarm)
Provincial,
Gort Muire, Ballinteer,
Dublin 16 D16 EI67
Tel 01-2984014

roy, Ulic (OFM)
Franciscan Friary,
Friary Lane,
Athlone, Co Westmeath
Tel 090-6472095

rzcinski, Kazimierz
(OFMConv)
The Friary,
St Francis' Street, Wexford
Tel 053-922758

ulbure, Eusebius, CC
St Mary's Presbytery,
The Fairgreen, Navan,
Co Meath C15 X0A3
Tel 046-9027518
(*Navan*, Meath)

ully, Andrew, Very Rev, PP
Lavey, Stradone,
Co Cavan
Tel 049-4330125
(*Lavey*, Kilmore)

umilty, Stephen (OP)
St Catherine's, Newry,
Co Down BT35 8BN
Tel 028-30262178

uohy, Fergus (SMA), CC
The Presbytery, Clonakilty,
Co Cork
Tel 023-8834441
(*Clonakilty and Darrara*,
Cork & R.)

uohy, Thomas (SM)
Mount St Mary's,
Milltown, Dundrum Road,
Dublin 14
Tel 01-2697322

urbitt, Hugh,
St Michael's, Longford
(Ardagh & Cl.)

urley, Paul (CSsR)
Clonard Monastery,
1 Clonard Gardens,
Belfast BT13 2RL
Tel 028-90445950

wohig, David (OCarm)
Assistant Provincial,
Gort Muire, Ballinteer,
Dublin D16 EI67
Tel 01-2984014

Twohig, Jamie (SAC) CC
St Benin's, Dublin Road,
Shankill, Co Dublin
Tel 01-2824425
(*Shankill*, Dublin)

Twohig, Pat (OSA)
St Augustine's Priory
Washington Street, Cork

Twomey, Bernard (OSA)
St Catherine's,
Meath Street, Dublin 8
Tel 01-4543356
(*Meath Street and
Merchants' Quay*, Dublin)

Twomey, Christopher
(OFMCap)
Capuchin Friary,
137-142 Church Street,
Dublin D07 HA22
Tel 01-8730599
Chaplain,
Bon Secours Hospital,
Glasnevin, Dublin 9
Tel 01-8065300

Twomey, Donal (SPS)
St Patrick's, Kiltegan,
Co Wicklow
Tel 059-6473600

Twomey, John (Jack)
(OFMCap)
Capuchin Friary,
Holy Trinity,
Fr Mathew Quay,
Cork T12 PK24
Tel 021-4270827
(Cork & R.)

Twomey, Patrick, Very Rev
Canon, PE
Bellevue,
Mallow, Co Cork
Tel 022-55632
(Cloyne, retired)

Twomey, Vincent (SVD)
Donamon Castle,
Roscommon
Tel 090-6662222

Tyburowski, Krzysztof,
134 Cosgrove Park,
Moyross, Limerick
Tel 087-4110997
(*Pastoral Unit 1*, Limerick)

Tynan, Joseph, PP, Adm
The Parochial House.
Kilteely, Co Limerick
Tel 061-384213
(*Kilteely, Knocklong*,
Cashel & E.)

Tyndall, David
c/o Archbishop's House,
Dublin 9
(Dublin)

Tyrrell, Gerard, CC
Presbytery, Blacklion,
Greystones, Co Wicklow
Tel 012860704
(*Greystones*, Dublin)

Tyrrell, Patrick (SJ)
27 Raleigh Row, Galway
Tel 091-523707

Tyrrell, Paul, Very Rev PP, VF
St Michael's Parochial
House,
4 Eblana Avenue,
Dun Laoghaire, Co Dublin
Tel 01-28012100
(*Crumlin*, Dublin)

U

Udofia, Daniel (MSP), PP
Parochial House,
Ballyleague,
Co Roscommon
Tel 043-3321171
(*Kilgefin (Ballagh,
Cloontuskert and
Curraghroe)*, Elphin)

Ugwu, Stephen (OCD)
Avila, Bloomfield Avenue,
Morehampton Road,
Dublin 4
Tel 01-6430200

Ukut, Joseph (MSP), CC
The Presbytery,
Longford
Tel 043-3346465
(*Longford
(Templemichael,
Ballymacormack)*, Ardagh
& Cl.)

Uwah, Innocent
The Presbytery,
12 Coarse Moor Park,
Straffan, Co Kildare
Tel 01-6012197/
085-1404355
(*Celbridge*, Dublin)

V

Van Gucht, Koenraad (SDB),
Salesian House, Milford,
Castletroy,
Co Limerick V94 DK44
Tel 061-330268/
086-3814353
(*Pastoral Unit 1*, Limerick)

Vard, David, CC,
Annebrook,
Stradbally Road,
Portlaoise, Co Laois
Tel 057-8688440
(*Portlaoise*, Kildare & L.)

Varghese, Joseph, CC,
2 Station Road,
Dungiven,
Derry BT47 4LN
Tel 028-77741256
(*Dungiven*, Derry)

Varghese, Nideesh, CC
72 Nursery Avenue,
Coleraine,
Co Derry BT52 1LR
Tel 028-70343156
(*Coleraine*, Derry)

Varghese, Shoji, AP
42 Nessan Court
Lower Church Road,
Raheen, Co Limerick
Tel 089-4431922
(*Pastoral Unit 6*, Limerick)

Vasquez, Oscar (SM)
Provincial, Provincial
Headquaters,
4425 West Pine Boulevard,
St Louis, MO 6308-2301,
USA
Tel 001-314-533-1207

Vaughan, Aidan (OFMCap),
CC
Ascension Presbytery,
Gurranabraher, Cork
Tel 021-4303655
(*Clogheen/Kerry Pike,
Farranree,
Gurranabraher and
Knocknaheeny*, Cork & R.)

Vaughan, Denis
45 The Oaks,
Maryborough Ridge,
Douglas, Cork
(Cloyne, retired)

Villarreal, Andres (LC)
Chaplain,
Dublin Oak Academy,
Kilcroney, Bray,
Co Wicklow
Tel 01-2863290

Vinduska, Aaron (LC) PC
The Presbytery, St Mary's
Sandyford, Dublin 18
Tel 01-2958933
(*Sandyford*, Dublin)

W

Wadding, George (CSsR)
Vicar-Superior,
Dún Mhuire,
461/463 Griffith Avenue,
Dublin D09 X651
Tel 01-5180196

Wade, Thomas (SMA)
African Missions,
Blackrock Road,
Cork T12 TD54
Tel 021-4292871

Waldron, Kieran, Very Rev
Canon, PE
Devlis, Ballyhaunis,
Co Mayo F35 AP62
Tel 094-9630246
(Tuam, retired)

Waldron, Paul, Very Rev, PP
Parochial House,
Chapel Street,
Carrick-on-suir,
Co Tipperary
Tel 051-640168
(*Carrick-on-Suir*,
Waterford & L.)

Walker, David (OP)
Provincial Bursar
Provincial Office,
St Mary's, Tallaght,
Dublin D24 X585
Tel 01-4048118

Wall, John, PP
Annaduff,
Carrick-on-Shannon,
Co Leitrim
Tel 071-9624093
(*Annaduff*, Ardagh & Cl.)

Wall, Michael
Chaplain,
Mary Immaculate College
of Education
Tel 061-204331
(*Limerick*)

Wall, Richard (SMA)
SMA House, Wilton,
Cork, T12 KR23
Tel 021-4541069/4541884

Wallace, Laurence, Very
Rev, PP, VF
Muckalee, Ballyfoyle,
Co Kilkenny
Tel 056-4441271/
087-2326807
(*Muckalee*, Ossory)

Walls, Eamonn (SJ)
St Francis Xavier's,
Upper Gardiner Street,
Dublin 1
Tel 01-8363411

Walsh, Aidan (OFMConv)
Friary of the Visitation of
the BVM,
Fairview Strand,
Dublin 3
Tel 01-8376000
(*Fairview*, Dublin)

Walsh, Brendan, Very Rev,
PP
Causeway, Co Kerry
Tel 066-7131148
Moderator, Ballyheigue
Tel 0667133110
(*Ballyheigue, Causeway*,
Kerry)

Walsh Brendan (SAC)
Pallottine College,
Thurles, Co Tipperary
Tel 0504-21202

Walsh, David (SPS)
Director of Promotion,
St Patrick's, Kiltegan,
Co Wicklow
Tel 059-6473600

Walsh, Des, Very Rev Canon,
PE
Claremorris, Co Mayo
(Tuam, retired)

Walsh, Donal, Very Rev
Tinnahinch,
Graiguenamanagh,
Co Kilkenny
Tel 059-9725550
(Ossory, retired)

Walsh, Eamonn, Most Rev,
DD
Titular Bishop of Elmham
and Auxiliary Bishop
Emeritus of Dublin,
Head of the Office for
Clergy,
Naomh Brid,
Blessington Road,
Tallaght, Dublin 24
Tel 01-4598032
Chaplain, Blackrock Clinic
Blackrock, Co Dublin
Tel 01-2832222
(Dublin)

Walsh, Edward (SPS)
St Patrick's, Kiltegan,
Co Wicklow
Tel 059-6473600

Walsh, Gearóid, Very Rev
Canon, PP, VF
Ballymacellicyott,
Co Kerry,
Tel 066-7137118
(*Ballymacellicyott*, Kerry)

Walsh, James, Very Rev
Canon, AP
Parochial House,
Kilmeena, Westport,
Co Mayo F28 T628
Tel 098-41270
(*Kilmeena*, Tuam)

Walsh, Jarlath (SMA)
Provincial Bursar
African Missions, Feltrim,
Blackrock Road,
Cork T12 N6C8
Tel 021-4292871

Walsh, John H. (OP), Very
Rev,
St Saviour's Priory,
Upper Dorset Street,
Dublin 1
Tel 01-8897610

Walsh, John,
Mount David,
North Circular Road,
Limerick
Tel 087-4493228
(*Pastoral Unit 2*, Limerick)

Walsh, John, Very Rev, Co-
PP
The Presbytery,
Togher, Cork
Tel 021-4316700
(*Ballyphehane, The Lough
and Togher*, Cork & R.)

Walsh, John, Very Rev
Canon
Knock, Co Mayo
(Tuam, retired)

Walsh, John R., CC
Parochial House,
Buncrana, Co Donegal
Tel 074-9361393
(*Buncrana*, Derry)

Walsh, Joseph, CC
Cathedral Presbytery,
Thurles, Co Tipperary
Tel 0504-22229
(*Thurles, Cathedral*, Cashel
& E.)

Walsh, Joseph (OFM)
Franciscan Abbey,
Multyfarnham,
Co Westmeath
Tel 044-9371114/9371137

Walsh, Kevin, CC
c/o Bishop's House,
Dublin Road, Carlow
(Kildare & L.)

Walsh, Laurence (OCSO)
Mount Saint Joseph
Abbey,
Roscrea, Co Tipperary
E53 D651
Tel 0505-25600

Walsh, Liam (OP)
St Saviour's Priory,
Upper Dorset Street,
Dublin 1
Tel 01-8897610

Walsh, Michael, Very Rev,
PP
Parochial House,
Carnaross, Kells, Co Meath
Tel 046-9245904
(*Carnaross*, Meath)

Walsh, Michael F., Very Rev,
PE
Ballinarrid, Bonmahon,
Co Waterford
Tel 051-292992
(Waterford & L., retired)

Walsh, Pádraig, Very Rev, PP
St Brendan's, Tralee,
Co Kerry
Tel 066-7125932
(*Tralee, St Brendan's*,
Kerry)

Walsh, Pat
Priests House, Ahiohill,
Enniskeane, Co Cork
(Cork & R., retired)

Walsh, Patrick J., Most Rev,
DD
Retired Bishop Emeritus of
Down and Connor,
Nazareth House Care
Village
516 Ravenhill Road,
Belfast BT6 OBW
Tel 0044-7732104366
(Down & C.)

Walsh, Paul (CSSp)
Holy Spirit Missionary
College
Kimmage Manor,
Whitehall Road,
Dublin D12 P5YP
Tel 01-4064300

Walsh, Paul (SM)
Communaté Mariste,
22 Rue Victor Clappier,
83000 Toulon, France

Walsh, Pearse, Very Rev,
Adm
The Presbytery,
City Quay, Dublin 2
Tel 01-6773073
(*City Quay*, Dublin)

Walsh, Richard (OP)
St Dominic's,
St Dominic's Road,
Tallaght, Dublin 24
Tel 01-4510620

Walsh, Stephen (CSSp), CC
St Anne's, Sligo
Tel 071-9145028
(*Sligo, St Anne's*, Elphin)

Walsh, Tomás (SMA), Co-PP
Ascension Presbytery,
Gurranabraher, Cork
Tel 021-4303655
(*Clogheen/Kerry Pike,
Farranree,
Gurranabraher and
Knocknaheeny*, Cork & R.)

Walsh, William, Most Rev,
DD
Retired Bishop of Killaloe,
'Camblin',
College View,
Clare Road, Ennis,
Co Clare
Tel 087-2618960
(Killaloe, retired)

Walsh, William,
Cathedral House,
Cathedral Place, Limerick
Tel 061-414624/
086-8564673
(*Pastoral Unit 1*, Limerick)

Walshe, Adrian, Very Rev,
PP
Teach na Sagart,
Beech Corner
Castleblayney,
Co Monaghan A75 KR96
Tel 042-9740027
(*Castleblaney (Muckno),
Aughnamullen East,
Clontibret*, Clogher)

Walshe, Philip Rev (CM)
St Paul's, Sybil Hill,
Raheny, Dublin D05 AE38
Tel 01-8318113

Walshe, Thomas, Very Rev,
PP
Rosenallis, Portlaoise,
Co Laois
Tel 057-8628513
(*Rosenallis*, Kildare & L.)

Walshe, William (SPS)
St Patrick's, Kiltegan,
Co Wicklow
Tel 059-6473600

Walton, James, Very Rev, PP
Ballybricken,
Grange, Killmallock,
Co Limerick
Tel 061-351158
(*Ballybricken*, Cashel & E.)

Vard, Alan,
(On sabbatical)
18 Drumlin Heights,
Enniskillen,
Co Fermanagh BT74 7NR
(Clogher)
Vard, Brendan, CC
Derrybeg, Letterkenny,
Co Donegal
Tel 074-9531310
(Gweedore, Raphoe)
Vard, John M.
1 Chestnut Grove,
Ballymount Road,
Dublin 24
(Dublin, retired)
Vard, Kevin (SAC)
Pallottine College,
Thurles, Co Tipperary
086-3103934
Vard, Pat, Very Rev, PP, VF
Burtonport, Co Donegal
Tel 074-9542006
(Burtonport, Raphoe)
Vard, Paul, TA
St Mochta's, Porterstown,
Dublin 15
Tel 01-8213218
(Porterstown-Clonsilla,
Dublin)
Varner, Freddy (SMA)
Church of Our Lady of the
Rosary and St Patrick,
61 Blackhorse Road,
Walthamstow,
London E17 7AS, UK
Varrack, Colin (SJ)
Gonzaga College,
Sandford Road, Dublin 6
Tel 01-4972943
Vaters, Ignatius (CP)
St Paul's Retreat,
Mount Argus,
Dublin 6W
Tel 01-4992000
Vaters, Michael (SMA)
African Missions,
Blackrock Road,
Cork T12 TD54
Tel 021-4292871
Vatters, Brian, CC
St Peter's Cathedral
Presbytery,
St Peter's Square,
Belfast BT12 4BU
Tel 028-90327573
Assistant Priest,
St Mary's Parish
(The Cathedral (St Peter's),
St Mary's, Down & C.)
Vatters, David (OSB)
Silverstream Priory,
Stamullen,
Co Meath K32 T189
Tel 01-8417142
Veakliam, David (OCarm),
Gort Muire, Ballinteer,
Dublin D16 EI67
Tel 01-2984014

Weir, Noel, CC
St Mary's Presbytery,
The Fairgreen, Navan,
Co Meath C15 X0A3
Tel 046-9027518
(Navan, Meath)
Wenjeslaus, Joseph, CC
St Anne's, Sligo
Tel 0871-9145028
(Sligo, St Anne's, Elphin)
Welsh, Oscar (SMA)
African Missions,
Blackrock Road,
Cork T12 TD54
Tel 021-4292871
Whearty, Roderick, Very
Rev,
St Fiacre's Gardens,
Bohernatownish Road,
Loughboy,
Kilkenny R95 RF97
Tel 056-77701730/
086-8133661
(St Patrick's, Ossory)
Whelan, Brian, Adm
Craanford, Gorey,
Co Wexford
Tel 053-9428163
(Craanford, Ferns)
Whelan, Gerard (SJ)
c/o Irish Jesuit
Provincialate,
Milltown Park,
Miltown Road, Dublin 6
Tel 01-4987333
Whelan, John (OSA)
St Augustine's Priory,
St Augustine's Street,
Galway
Tel 091-562524
Whelan, Joe, Very Rev, Adm
126 Furry Park Road,
Dublin 5
Tel 01-8333793
(Killester, Dublin)
Whelan, Martin CC,
Parochial House,
Maree, Oranmore,
Co Galway
Tel 091-794113
(Galway)
Whelan, Michael
c/o Archbishop's House,
Tuam
(Tuam)
Whelan, Patrick, Very Rev,
PP
St Patrick's Presbytery,
Forster Street, Galway
Tel 091-567994
(St Patrick's, Galway)
Whelan, Seamus (SPS)
St Patrick's, Kiltegan,
Co Wicklow
Tel 059-6473600

Whelan, Tom (CSSp)
Holy Spirit Missionary
College
Kimmage Manor,
Whitehall Road,
Dublin D12 P5YP
Tel 01-4064300
Whelan, Tom, Co-PP
The Spa, Castleconnell,
Co Limerick
Tel 061-377126
/087-2730299
(Scáth na Sionnaine,
Killaloe)
White, Barry, CC
Cathedral House,
Mullingar,
Co Westmeath
Tel 044-9348338/9340126
(Mullingar, Meath)
White, Brian, CC
Parochial House,
6 Circular Road,
Dungannon,
Co Tyrone BT71 6BE
Tel 028-87722631
(Dungannon (Drumglass,
Killyman and Tullyniskin),
Armagh)
White, David, Very Rev, PP
Parochial House,
182 Garron Road,
Glenariffe,
Co Antrim BT44 0RA
Tel 028-21771249
(Glenariffe, Down & C.)
White, Jerry (SSCC), CC
Sacred Hearts Community,
Tanagh, Cootehill,
Co Cavan H16 CA22
Tel 049-5552188
(Rockcorry (Ematris),
Clogher)
White, Laurence, Very Rev,
Co-PP
119 Stiles Road,
Clontarf, Dublin 3
Tel 01-8333394/
086-4143888
(Clontarf, St Anthony's,
Dublin)
White, Morgan
Boolavogue, Ferns,
Wexford
Tel 053-9366282
(Monageer, Ferns)
White, Patrick
Training and Development
Officer,
Youth Link Training
Offices,
Farset Enterprise Park,
683 Springfield Road,
Belfast BT12 7DY
Tel 028-90323217
(Down & C.)

White, Séamus, Very Rev,
PP, VF
Parochial House,
40 The Village,
Jonesboro, Newry,
Co Down BT35 8HP
Tel 028-30849345
(Dromintee, Armagh)
Whiteford, Kieran, Very
Rev, PP
Parochial House,
28 Chapel Road,
Ballymena BT44 0RS
Tel 028-21771240
(Cushendall, Cushendun,
Down and C.)
Whitney, Ciarán, Very Rev
Canon
24 Kildallogue Heights,
Strokestown,
Co Roscommon
(Elphin, retired)
Whitney, Seamus (SPS)
St Patrick's, Kiltegan,
Co Wicklow
Tel 059-6476488
Whittaker, Michael, Very
Rev, PP
Parochial House,
Killina, Rahan,
Tullamore, Co Offaly
Tel 057-9355917
(Rahan, Meath)
Whooley, Eoin, Very Rev, PP
Moderator,
South Presbytery,
Dunbar Street, Cork
Tel 085-1471147
(South Parish, St Patrick's
and Ss Peter and Paul's,
Cork & R.)
Whyte, Daniel, Very Rev
53 Marlo Park, Bangor,
Co Down BT19 6NL
Tel 078-12184624
(Down & C., retired)
Wickham, Anthony, Very
Rev, PP
Newtownshandrum,
Charleville, Co Cork
Tel 063-70836
(Newtownshandrum,
Cloyne)
Williams, John (OSA)
St Augustine's,
Taylor's Lane,
Balyboden, Dublin 16
Tel 01-4241000
Wilson, John Rt Rev Mgr
St Mary's,
97 Ballymun Road,
Dublin 9
Tel 01-8375440
(Dublin, retired)

Wilson, Stephen, CC
St Patrick's Presbytery,
Roden Place, Dundalk,
Co Louth A91 K2P4
Tel 042-9334648
(*Dundalk, St Patrick's,
Dundalk, Holy Redeemer,*
Armagh)
Winkle, Patrick, Very Rev,
PP
Carrigtwohill, Co Cork
Tel 021-4882439
(*Carrigtwohill*, Cloyne)
Winter, William, Very Rev
PP
Banteer, Co Cork
Tel 029-56010
(*Banteer (Clonmeen),*
Cloyne)
Wojtala, Piotr, CC
Our Lady of Lourdes
Presbytery,
Hardman's Gardens,
Drogheda,
Co Louth A92 PXF3
Tel 041-9831899
(*Drogheda*, Armagh)
Woodruff, Peter (SSC)
PO Box 752, Niddrie,
VIC 3042 Australia
Woods, Daniel, Very Rev, PP
Kilcommon,
Co Tipperary
Tel 062-78103
(*Kilcommon*, Cashel & E.)

Woods, Michael, Very Rev,
PP, VF
Parochial House,
10 Acton Road,
Poyntzpass, Newry,
Co Down BT35 6TB
Tel 028-38318471
(*Tandragee (Ballymore
and Mullaghbrack),*
Armagh)
Woods, Thomas
Edenville, Kinlough,
Co Leitrim
(Kilmore, retired)
Wozniak, Josef (SC), CC
68 North Street,
Lurgan,
Co Armagh BT67 9AH
Tel 028-38323161
(*Shankill, St Paul's & St
Peter's (Lurgan),* Dromore)
Wrenn, Timothy (SDB), AP
Salesian House,
Don Bosco Road
Pallaskenry, Co Limerick
Tel 089-2507825
(*Pastoral Unit 6,* Limerick)
Wright, Colum, Very Rev
Lisadell, 54 Francis Street,
Lurgan,
Co Armagh BT66 6DL
Tel 028-38327173
(*Shankill, St Paul's & St
Peter's (Lurgan),* Dromore)

X

Xavier, Francis (HGN), PP
The Presbytery, Priest's
Lane,
Portlaw, Co Waterford
Tel 051-387227
(*Portlaw*, Waterford & L.)
Xianbin, Anthony Xiao
Chaplain to the Chinese
Community,
The Presbytery,
51 Home Farm Road,
Dublin 9
Tel 085-7417168
(*Drumcondra*, Dublin)

Y

Yang, Paul
Priest's Road,
Tramore, Co Tipperary
(*Tramore*, Waterford & L.)
Yaqoob, Amer
Parochial House,
Ballivor, Co Meath
Tel 046-9546488
(*Ballivor/Kildalkey*, Meath)
Young, Callum,
Cathedral Presbytery,
38 Hill Street,
Newry BT34 1AT
Tel 028-30262586
(*Newry*, Dromore)
Young, Joseph
21 Marian Avenue,
Janesboro, Limerick
Tel 061-405835
(Limerick)
Young, Robert, Very Rev,
Co-PP
Moderator,
The Presbytery, Kinsale,
Co Cork
Tel 021-4774019
(*Ballinhassig, Clontead,
Courceys and Kinsale,* Cor
& R.)
Younge, Patrick (OFM)
Franciscan Friary,
Liberty Street,
Cork T12 D376
Tel 021-4270302/4275481

Z

acharek, Maciej, CC
St Patrick's Presbytery,
Roden Place, Dundalk,
Co Louth, A91 K2P4
Tel 042-9334648
(*Dundalk, St Patrick's,*
Dundalk, Holy Redeemer,
Armagh)

acharias, Roni, CC
Parochial House,
St Eugene's Cathedral,
Derry BT48 9AP
Tel 028-
71262894/71365712
(*Cathedral, St Eugene's,*
Derry)

acrzewski, Patryk (OP)
St Saviour's,
Upper Dorset Street,
Dublin 1
Tel 01-8897610

aggi, Douglas, Very Rev, PP
Ballygar, Co Galway
Tel 090-6624637
(*Ballygar (Killian and*
Killeroran), Elphin)

Zielonka, Rafal, CC
The Presbytery,
Dunmanway, Co Cork
Tel 023-8845000
(*Drimoleague,*
Dunmanway,
Kilmichael and Uibh
Laoire, Cork & R.)

Zong, Bernard, PC
Churh of the Assumption,
Howth, Dublin 13
Tel 01-8397398
(*Howth,* Dublin)

Zuribo, Aloysius, CC
Presbytery No. 1,
4 Old Hill, Leixlip,
Co Kildare
Tel 01-6243718
(*Leixlip,* Dublin)

Zybura, Pawel (OP)
St Mary's, Pope's Quay,
Cork
Tel 021-4502267

PARISH INDEX

*Where a parish has an alternative or historical name, both names are given e.g. Arney/Cleenish.
In such cases the parish appears in the list in each form,
i.e. Arney/Cleenish and Cleenish/Arney.*

Allianz (ili)

Allianz (ⅲ)

Allianz (Ⓜ)

Allianz ⏺

L

Allianz Ⓐ

Allianz ⑪

0

GENERAL INDEX

Allianz (ⁱⁱ)

Wherever the Church is, Missio is there

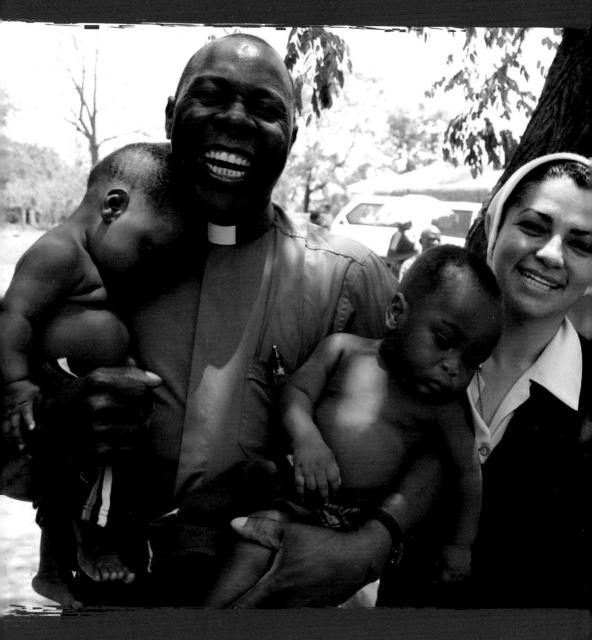

Please send any excess Mass
All Mass Stipends received s

Missio Ireland, 64 Lower Rathmines Road, Dublin D06